The Blackwell Companion to Natural Theology

Blackwell Companions to Philosophy

This outstanding student reference series offers a comprehensive and authoritative survey of philosophy as a whole. Written by today's leading philosophers, each volume provides lucid and engaging coverage of the key figures, terms, topics, and problems of the field. Taken together, the volumes provide the ideal basis for course use, representing an unparalleled work of reference for students and specialists alike.

Recent books in the series:

Forthcoming:

THE BLACKWELL COMPANION TO NATURAL THEOLOGY

Edited by

William Lane Craig
and
J. P. Moreland

WILEY-BLACKWELL

A John Wiley & Sons, Ltd., Publication

This edition first published 2012
© 2012 Blackwell Publishing Ltd

Edition history: Blackwell Publishing Ltd (hardback, 2009)

Blackwell Publishing was acquired by John Wiley & Sons in February 2007. Blackwell's publishing program has been merged with Wiley's global Scientific, Technical, and Medical business to form Wiley-Blackwell.

Registered Office
John Wiley & Sons Ltd, The Atrium, Southern Gate, Chichester, West Sussex, PO19 8SQ, UK

Editorial Offices
350 Main Street, Malden, MA 02148-5020, USA
9600 Garsington Road, Oxford, OX4 2DQ, UK
The Atrium, Southern Gate, Chichester, West Sussex, PO19 8SQ, UK

For details of our global editorial offices, for customer services, and for information about how to apply for permission to reuse the copyright material in this book please see our website at www.wiley.com/wiley-blackwell.

Library of Congress Cataloging-in-Publication Data
The Blackwell companion to natural theology / edited by William Lane Craig and J. P. Moreland.
    p. cm.
  Includes bibliographical references and index.
  ISBN 978-1-4051-7657-6 (hardcover : alk. paper) – ISBN 978-1-4443-5085-2 (paperback)
  1. Natural theology. I. Craig, William Lane. II. Moreland, James Porter, 1948– III. Title: Companion to natural theology.
  BL175.B53 2009
  212′.1–dc22

2008028316

A catalogue record for this book is available from the British Library.

This book is published in the following electronic formats: ePDFs 9781444308341; Wiley Online Library 9781444308334; ePub 9781444345421; Mobi 9781444345438

Set in 10/12.5pt Minion by Toppan Best-set Premedia Limited

Printed in the UK

Contents

List of Figures

Notes on Contributors

Robin Collins is professor of philosophy at Messiah College, Grantham, Pennsylvania, specializing in the intersection of science and religion. He is the author of over 25 articles/ book chapters, including "The Multiverse Hypothesis: A Theistic Perspective" in *Universe or Multiverse?* (edited by Bernard Carr and published by Cambridge University Press, 2007).

William Lane Craig is a research professor of philosophy at Talbot School of Theology in La Mirada, California. He is the co-author of *Theism, Atheism, and Big Bang Cosmology* (Clarendon, 1993).

Stewart Goetz is professor of philosophy at Ursinus College in Collegeville, Pennsylvania. He is the author of *Freedom, Teleology, and Evil* (Continuum Press, 2008).

Kai-man Kwan is professor of philosophy at Hong Kong Baptist University in Hong Kong. He is the author of several articles on religious experience in books and journals, including Macmillan's second edition of *Encyclopedia of Philosophy*.

Mark D. Linville is an independent philosopher living in Atlanta, Georgia. He has published articles in such journals as the *American Philosophical Quarterly*, *Religious Studies*, *The International Journal for Philosophy of Religion*, *Faith and Philosophy*, and *Philosophia Christi*.

Robert E. Maydole is professor emeritus of philosophy at Davidson College, Davidson, North Carolina. He is the author of several papers with new modal arguments for the existence of a supreme being.

J. P. Moreland is distinguished professor of philosophy at Talbot School of Theology in La Mirada, California. He is the author of *Consciousness and the Existence of God: A Theistic Argument* (Routledge, 2008) and *Universals* (McGill-Queen's, 2001).

Lydia McGrew is the author (with Timothy McGrew) of *Internalism and Epistemology* (Routledge, 2007).

Timothy McGrew is professor and chairman of the Department of Philosophy at Western Michigan University, Kalamazoo, Michigan. He is the author of *The Foundations of Knowledge* (Rowman and Littlefield, 1995) and (with Lydia McGrew) *Internalism and Epistemology* (Routledge, 2007).

Alexander R. Pruss is associate professor of philosophy at Baylor University, Waco, Texas. He is the author of *The Principle of Sufficient Reason: A Reassessment* (Cambridge, 2006) and coeditor, with Richard M. Gale, of *The Existence of God* (Ashgate, 2003).

Victor Reppert teaches philosophy at Glendale Community College and Grand Canyon University, Phoenix, Arizona. He is the author of *C. S. Lewis's Dangerous Idea: In Defense of the Argument from Reason* (IVP, 2003) and several articles about related themes.

James D. Sinclair is a senior warfare analyst with the U.S. Navy. He has authored numerous papers for symposia such as the Military Operations Research Society and the Combat Identification Systems Conference.

Charles Taliaferro is a professor of philosophy at St. Olaf College, Northfield, Minnesota, USA. He is the author of *Evidence and Faith: Philosophy and Religion since the Seventeenth Century* (Cambridge University Press, 2005).

Introduction

WILLIAM LANE CRAIG AND J. P. MORELAND

The collapse of positivism and its attendant verification principle of meaning was undoubtedly the most important philosophical event of the twentieth century. Their demise heralded a resurgence of metaphysics, along with other traditional problems of philosophy that verificationism had suppressed. Accompanying this resurgence has come something new and altogether unanticipated: a renaissance in Christian philosophy.

The face of Anglo-American philosophy has been transformed as a result. Theism is on the rise; atheism is on the decline. Atheism, although perhaps still the dominant viewpoint at the American university, is a philosophy in retreat. In a recent article in the secularist journal *Philo*, Quentin Smith laments what he calls "the desecularization of academia that evolved in philosophy departments since the late 1960s." He complains that:

> [n]aturalists passively watched as realist versions of theism . . . began to sweep through the philosophical community, until today perhaps one-quarter or one-third of philosophy professors are theists, with most being orthodox Christians. . . . in philosophy, it became, almost overnight, 'academically respectable' to argue for theism, making philosophy a favored field of entry for the most intelligent and talented theists entering academia today.[1]

Smith concludes, "God is not 'dead' in academia; he returned to life in the late 1960s and is now alive and well in his last academic stronghold, philosophy departments."[2]

The renaissance of Christian philosophy over the last half century has served to reinvigorate natural theology, that branch of theology that seeks to provide warrant for belief in God's existence apart from the resources of authoritative, propositional revelation. Today, in contrast to just a generation ago, natural theology is a vibrant field of

---

1. Smith (2001). A sign of the times: *Philo* itself, unable to succeed as a secular organ, has now become a journal for general philosophy of religion.
2. Smith (2001, p. 4).

study.[3] All of the various traditional arguments for God's existence, as well as creative new arguments, find prominent, intelligent proponents among contemporary philosophers. Moreover, genuinely new insights have been acquired into traditional problems raised by nontheists such as the problem of evil and the coherence of theism.

In this volume, we bring together some of the foremost practitioners of natural theology writing today and give them the opportunity to develop their arguments at length and to interact with the arguments' critics. The resulting volume is a compendium of theistic arguments on the cutting edge of philosophical discussion.

The volume opens with an essay on the *project of natural theology* by Charles Taliaferro. He not only provides a historical perspective on contemporary debates over theistic arguments but, even more, also emphasizes the importance of issues in the philosophy of mind for the viability of natural theology. To anyone who is not open to the notion of an immaterial mental substance distinct from a material substratum, the whole project of natural theology is abortive. For God just is such an unembodied mind, distinct from and the Creator of the physical universe. Taliaferro, therefore, seeks to show that we are far from warranted in being confident that substantial minds are impossible, so that we must be open to the project of natural theology.

Alexander Pruss explores the first theistic argument under discussion in this volume, the *argument from contingency* or the version of the cosmological argument classically associated with G. W. Leibniz. The argument attempts to ground the existence of the contingent realm of things in a necessarily existent being. Prominent contemporary proponents of theistic arguments of this sort include Richard Taylor, Timothy O'Connor, Robert Koons, Richard Swinburne, Stephen Davis, and Bruce Reichenbach, among others. Pruss identifies and discusses at length four key issues that any successful defense of such an argument must address:

1   the status of the Principle of Sufficient Reason;
2   the possibility of an infinite regress of explanations;
3   the applicability of the Principle of Sufficient Reason to the explanatory ultimate; and
4   the theological significance of the argument's conclusion.

A cosmological argument of a different sort, one largely neglected until recent decades, is the so-called *kalam cosmological argument*. Based upon the finitude of the temporal series of past events, the argument aspires to show the existence of a personal Creator of the universe, who brought the universe into being and is therefore responsible for the universe's beginning to exist. Philosophers such as G. J. Whitrow, Stuart Hackett, David Oderberg, and Mark Nowacki have made significant contributions to this argument. In their

---

3. The change has not gone unnoticed even in popular culture. In 1980, *Time* magazine ran a major story entitled "Modernizing the Case for God," in which it described the movement among contemporary philosophers to refurbish the traditional arguments for God's existence. *Time* marveled, "In a quiet revolution in thought and argument that hardly anybody could have foreseen only two decades ago, God is making a comeback. Most intriguingly, this is happening not among theologians or ordinary believers, but in the crisp intellectual circles of academic philosophers, where the consensus had long banished the Almighty from fruitful discourse" (*Time* 1980). The article cites the late Roderick Chisholm to the effect that the reason that atheism was so influential a generation ago is that the brightest philosophers were atheists; but today, in his opinion, many of the brightest philosophers are theists, using a tough-minded intellectualism in defense of that belief that was formerly lacking on their side of the debate.

treatment, William Lane Craig and James Sinclair examine afresh two classical philosophical arguments for the finitude of the past in light of modern mathematics and metaphysics and review remarkable scientific evidence drawn from the from the field of astrophysical cosmology that points to an absolute temporal origin of the cosmos. With this argument, we begin to see the intimate and fascinating links between natural theology and developments in contemporary science that philosophers cannot afford to ignore.

Those links are in full view in Robin Collins's treatment of the *teleological argument*. John Leslie, Paul Davies, Richard Swinburne, William Dembski, Michael Denton, and Del Ratzsch are among the many defenders of this argument today. Focusing on the fine-tuning of nature's laws, constants, and initial conditions, Collins asks how this amazing fine-tuning is best explained. In unfolding his answer, Collins carefully formulates a theory of probability that serves as the framework for his argument, addressing such key issues as the nature of probability, the principle of indifference, and the comparative ranges of life-permitting values versus assumable values for the finely tuned parameters. He argues that the evidence strongly confirms the hypothesis of theism over an atheistic single universe hypothesis and, moreover, that appeals to a multiverse or a many-worlds hypothesis in order to rescue the atheistic position are ultimately unavailing. Finally, he assesses the significance of his conclusion for the overall case for theism.

The argument from fine-tuning concerns the design of the universe with embodied moral agents in view. We focus on such agents in moving from the external world to the internal world of human persons in J. P. Moreland's essay on the *argument from consciousness*. Setting aside panpsychism on the grounds that, first, it is a label for the problem of consciousness' origin and not a solution and, second, theism and naturalism are the only live options for most Western thinkers, Moreland lays out the ontological constraints for a naturalist worldview that follow most plausibly from a naturalist epistemology, etiology, and core ontology, to wit, there is a burden of proof for any naturalist ontology that ventures beyond strict physicalism. Moreland then presents and defends the central premises in an argument for God from the existence of consciousness or its lawlike correlation with physical states (the argument for God from consciousness, here after abbreviated as AC). Given AC as a rival to naturalism, there is an additional burden of proof for a naturalist ontology that quantifies over *sui generis* emergent properties such as those constitutive of consciousness. After characterizing epistemically the dialectical severity of this burden, in the final section, Moreland rebuts the three most prominent naturalist theories of the existence of consciousness, namely, the views of John Searle, Colin McGinn, and Timothy O'Connor. Contemporary advocates of this argument include Charles Taliaferro, Richard Swinburne, and Robert Adams.

Partially due to the theistic connection between finite consciousness and God, a cottage industry of versions of physicalism has sprung up to eliminate consciousness in favor of or to reduce consciousness in one way or another to something physical. While this will be a hard sell to many, the existence and nature of reason cannot easily be treated along these lines on pain of self-referential inconsistence. Thus, Victor Reppert develops an *argument from reason* for God's existence based on the reality of reason in human persons. Similar arguments have been developed by C. S. Lewis and Alvin Plantinga. Although the argument takes a number of forms, in all instances, according to Reppert, it attempts to show that the necessary conditions of logical and mathematical reasoning, which undergird the natural sciences as a human activity, require the rejection of all broadly materialist worldviews. Reppert begins by examining the nature of the argument and identifying the central characteristics of a materialist worldview. In so doing, he lays out the general problem of materialism and how the argument from reason points to a single aspect of that broader problem. Second, he examines the argument's history, including the famous Lewis–Anscombe controversy. In so doing, Reppert indicates how the argument from reason can surmount Anscombe's objections. He also explains the transcendental structure of the argument. Third, he investigates three subarguments: the argument from intentionality, the argument from mental causation, and the argument from the psychological relevance of logical laws, showing how these demonstrate serious and unsolved difficulties for materialism. Finally, Reppert presents some popular objections and shows that these do not refute the argument.

Having laid out two features of anthropology that are recalcitrant facts for naturalists but which provide evidence for theism – consciousness and reason – a third theistic-friendly purported fact about human persons is that they are moral agents with intrinsic value. Thus, we next turn to metaethical issues, as Mark Linville presents a *moral argument* for God's existence. Contemporary philosophers who have defended various versions of the moral argument for theism include Robert Adams, William Alston, Paul Copan, John Hare, and Stephen Evans. Linville argues that naturalists, committed as they are to the blind evolutionary development of our cognitive faculties in response to the pressures to survive, cannot be warranted in their moral convictions, in contrast to theists, who see our moral faculties as under the suzerainty of God. Linville also contends that atheistic views of normative ethics, in contrast to theistic views, cannot adequately ground belief in human dignity. If we trust our moral convictions or believe in personal dignity, we should, then, be theists.

Moral considerations raise naturally the *problem of evil* in the world. In his chapter, Stewart Goetz distinguishes between the idea of a defense and that of a theodicy, and defends an instance of the latter. As a prolegomenon to his theodicy, Goetz examines the purpose or meaning of an individual's life. Although the vast majority of philosophers, including those who write on the problem of evil, have shown little or no interest in this topic for far too long, Goetz believes that an understanding of the purpose for which a person exists provides the central insight for a viable theodicy. This insight is that a person exists for the purpose of experiencing the great good of perfect happiness. Given that perfect happiness is an individual's greatest good, Goetz argues that it supplies the core idea for why God is justified in permitting evil. Main contemporary contributors to a theistic treatment of evil include Alvin Plantinga, William Alston, Richard Swinburne, Marilyn Adams, Peter van Inwag and Stephen Wykstra, among many others.

One aspect of the problem of evil is God's apparent inactivity in the presence of evil and in the midst of ordinary, daily life. On the other hand, it has been the testimony of millions of people that God Himself has shown up in their lives and that they have both experienced His presence and seen effects in and around their lives that only He could do. Human persons are not only moral agents, they are ineluctably religious. According to Kai-man Kwan, the *argument from religious experience* contends that given the appropriate premises, we can derive from the religious experiences of humankind a significant degree of epistemic justification for the existence of God. Kwan has no intention of arguing here that only one particular theistic tradition (such as Christianity) is correct. He focuses on a subclass of religious experiences, the experiences of God or theistic experience, and argues that theistic experiences provide significant justification for belief in God. Kwan does not claim that his argument is a conclusive argument on its own, but he does think that it is a reasonable argument that can contribute to the cumulative case for the existence of God.

Contemporary defenders of arguments from theistic religious experience include William Alston, Jerome Gellman, William Wainwright, and Keith Yandell.

The summit of natural theology is the famous *ontological argument*, which would infer God's existence starting from the concept of God as the greatest conceivable being. This argument, if successful, will give us God with all His superlative, great-making attributes. Recent defenders of the argument in various forms include Charles Hartshorne, Kurt Gödel, Norman Malcolm, Alvin Plantinga, Clement Dore, Stephen Davis, and Brian Leftow. In his essay, Robert Maydole, one of the most recent philosophers to enter the lists on behalf of the ontological argument, examines classical statements of the argument along with contemporary reformulations. He argues that some versions of the ontological argument are not only sound but also non-question-begging and are not susceptible to the parodies that detractors of the argument frequently offer.

Our final essay moves from generic theism to specifically Christian theism, as Timothy and Lydia McGrew develop in some detail an *argument from miracles*, the miracle in this case being the central Christian miracle of Jesus of Nazareth's resurrection. Scholars who have made significant contributions to an argument of this sort include Wolfhart Pannenberg, N. T. Wright, Gerald O'Collins, William Lane Craig, Stephen Davis, Richard Swinburne, Dale Allison, Gary Habermas, and a host of New Testament historians. McGrew and McGrew's contribution lies in their careful formulation of the argument in terms of Bayes's Theorem, showing how, *pace* David Hume, miracles are positively identifiable as the most probable hypothesis despite the prior improbability of a miracle claim. They argue that in the case of Jesus's putative resurrection, the ratio between the likelihoods of the resurrection hypothesis and its contradictory is such that one ought to conclude that the resurrection hypothesis is the most probable hypothesis on the total evidence.

The foregoing arguments, while not exhausting the range of arguments of contemporary natural theology, do serve as representative of the best work being done in the field today. It is our hope that the present *Companion* will serve as a stimulus to the discussion and further development of these arguments.

References

Modernizing the case for God. *Time*, April 7, 1980, 65–6.
Smith, Q. (2001) The metaphilosophy of naturalism. *Philo* 4: 2, 3–4.

1

The Project of Natural Theology

CHARLES TALIAFERRO

Natural theology is the practice of philosophically reflecting on the existence and nature of God independent of real or apparent divine revelation or scripture. Traditionally, natural theology involves weighing arguments for and against God's existence, and it is contrasted with *revealed theology*, which may be carried out within the context of ostensible revelation or scripture. For example, revealed theology may take as authoritative certain New Testament claims about Jesus and then construct a philosophical or theological model for understanding how Jesus may be human and divine. Natural theology, on the other hand, develops arguments about God based on the existence of the cosmos, the very concept of God, and different views of the nature of the cosmos, such as its ostensible order and value. Natural theology is often practiced in the West and the Near East with respect to the theistic view of God, and thus the God of Judaism, Christianity, and Islam. But natural theology has also been carried out by those who reject such religious traditions (e.g. Voltaire (1694–1778) endorsed theistic natural theology, but he put no credence in Christian revelation), and philosophers have employed natural theology to argue that God has attributes and a character that is either slightly or radically different from orthodox, religious concepts of God. The philosophy of God developed by Spinoza (1632–1677) is an example of a natural theology, according to which God is radically different from the theism of his Jewish and Christian contemporaries.

Plato (428–348 BCE), Aristotle (384–322 BCE), and their successors in ancient and medieval philosophy developed substantial arguments for the existence of God without relying on revelation. In the West, Anselm of Canterbury (1033–1109), Thomas Aquinas (1225–74), and Duns Scotus (1266–1308) are among the most celebrated contributors to natural theology. Muslim philosophy has also been a rich resource for natural theology, especially for cosmological theistic arguments. This may be due, in part, to the immense emphasis by philosophers such as Ibn Sina (or Avicenna, 980–1037) on the necessary, noncontingent reality of God in contrast to the contingent cosmos.

Natural theology played a major role in early modern philosophy. Some of the classics in the modern era, such as the *Meditations* by Descartes (1596–1650), *An Essay Concerning Human Understanding* by John Locke (1632–1704), *Three Dialogues between Hylas and Philonous* by George Berkeley, the *Theodicy* by Leibniz (1646–1716), the *Dialogues Concerning Natural Religion* by David Hume (1711–76), and the *Critique of Pure Reason* by Immanuel Kant

(1724–1804) all constitute major contributions to assessing reasons for and against theism, without making any appeal to revelation. The last two works are commonly thought to advance the most serious challenges to carrying out natural theology at all, but in point of fact, they still remain works in the tradition of natural theology, insofar as they reflect on the credibility of believing that there is a God, employing arguments that do not explicitly appeal to revelation. It is difficult to exaggerate the role of natural theology in the history of modern philosophy. The first substantial philosophical work published in English was a work in natural theology: *The True Intellectual System of the Universe* by Ralph Cudworth (1617–88).

In this chapter, I explore the prospects of employing natural theology in its traditional role of supporting a theistic understanding of God. In the first section, I bring together a series of arguments to the effect that a theistic natural theology is either unintelligible or, in principle, at a major disadvantage over against naturalism. These objections include critical arguments from Hume and Kant contra natural theology as employed to justify theism. I then address each of these, and bring to light reasons why today there is a renaissance in the field of natural theology in contemporary philosophy. I conclude with observations about the role of natural theology in addressing nontheistic accounts of God, along with a modest observation about the virtues of inquiry. The goal of this chapter is to address the general framework of natural theology in order to pave the way for the chapters that follow, which address specific strands in natural theology.

Does Theistic Natural Theology Rest upon a Mistake?

According to classical theism, there is a creator and sustainer of the cosmos who is omniscient, omnipotent, necessarily existing, nonphysical, essentially good, omnipresent, without temporal beginning or end, and everlasting or eternal. How these attributes are understood with precision is a matter of controversy. For example, some theists understand God as not temporally extended but transcending temporal passage (for God, there is no before, during, and after), while others see God as temporal and still others think that "prior" to God's creation of time, God is timelessly eternal, although temporal after the creation. In what follows, I shall not enter into such fascinating questions about the divine attributes. (For in-depth coverage, see Wierenga 1989; Swinburne 1994; Taliaferro 1994, 1999; Hoffman & Rosenkrantz 2002).

In the current intellectual climate, the closest competitor with theism, and the customary launching pad for antitheistic natural theology arguments, is naturalism. *Naturalism* has been variously described and is sometimes characterized so broadly as to be without substance. For current purposes, naturalism may be described as a scientifically oriented philosophy that rules out the existence of God, as well as the soul. Some naturalists do not deny that there are nonphysical processes or states (e.g. consciousness is not itself a physical process or state), but most embrace some form of physicalism, according to which there is no thing or process that is nonphysical. Here is a current description of naturalism by Richard Dawkins that seems to restrict reality to that which is physical or "natural."

> [A] philosophical naturalist is somebody who believes there is nothing beyond the natural, physical world, no *super*natural creative intelligence lurking behind the observable universe, no soul that outlasts the body and no miracles – except in the sense of natural phenomena

that we don't yet understand. If there is something that appears to lie beyond the natural world as it is now imperfectly understood, we hope eventually to understand it and embrace it within the natural. As ever when we unweave a rainbow, it will not become less wonderful. (Dawkins 2006, p. 14)

Far from becoming less wonderful, Dawkins and some (but not all) naturalists argue that the natural world is more accurately and deeply appreciated aesthetically, once theistic natural theology is set to one side. Four of the five arguments against a theistic natural theology that follow reflect some form of naturalism, a worldview that is advanced as more elegant and powerful than theism.

Argument I

There is no logical space for theism. According to D. Z. Phillips, theism can be faulted for its positing a reality that is independent of the structure of the world. He not only proposes that it makes no sense to think about what is beyond the world but also proposes theism can be faulted for its advancing what might be called a theory of everything. Phillips writes:

> What kind of theory is a theory about the structure of the world? If by "the world" one wants to mean "everything", there is no such theory. Certainly, science has no such theory, nor could it have. "Everything" is not the name of one big thing or topic, and, therefore, there can be no theory concerning a thing or topic of this kind. To speak of a thing is to acknowledge the existence of many things, since one can always be asked which thing one is referring to. Science is concerned with specific states of affairs, no matter how wide the scope of its questions may be. Whatever explanations it offers, further questions can be asked about them. It makes no sense to speak of a last answer in science, one that does not admit of any further questions. Science is not concerned with "the structure of the world", and there are no scientific investigations which have this as their subject." (Phillips 2005, pp. xv–xvi)

Phillips's critique of theories of everything may also be seen as cutting against naturalism insofar as it advances a theory covering all of reality. Physicalist forms of naturalism would seem to fit that description, for example, as physicalists hold that everything is physical. However, insofar as naturalism involves a negative thesis (there is no God not identical with the cosmos), Phillips's reasoning is very much in keeping with a naturalistic perspective.

For another representation of the *no logical space for theism argument*, consider Kai Nielsen's challenge:

> What does or could "transcendent to the universe" mean? Perhaps being "beyond the universe"? But how would that be other than just more universe? Alternatively, if you do not want to say that, try – thinking carefully about the sense of "beyond" – to get a handle on "going beyond the universe." Is not language idling here? (Nielsen 2004, p. 474)

If successful, this objection rules out any evidential case for theism in the offing from natural theology. Kai Nielsen counsels us to set aside the search for theistic evidence, even if such ostensible evidence were something fantastic like the claim "GOD EXISTS" appearing in the heavens.

We are no better off with the stars in the heavens spelling out GOD EXISTS than with their spelling out PROCRASTINATION DRINKS MELANCHOLY. We know that something has shaken our world [if "GOD EXISTS" appeared in the heavens], but we know not what; we know – or think we know, how could we tell which it was in such a circumstance? – that we heard a voice coming out of the sky and we know – or again think that we know – that the stars rearranged themselves right before our eyes and on several occasions to spell out GOD EXISTS. But are we wiser by observing this about what "God" refers to or what a pure disembodied spirit transcendent to the universe is or could be? At most we might think that maybe those religious people have something – something we know not what – going for them. But we also might think it was some kind of big trick or some mass delusion. The point is that we wouldn't know what to think. (Nielsen 2004, p. 279)

Argument II

Theism fails in terms of explanatory power. Some see theism as a quasi-scientific hypothesis. This is Richard Dawkins's position:

I pay religions the compliment of regarding them as scientific theories and . . . I see God as a competing explanation for facts about the universe and life. This is certainly how God has been seen by most theologians of past centuries and by most ordinary religious people today. . . . Either admit that God is a scientific hypothesis and let him submit to the same judgment as any other scientific hypothesis. Or admit that his status is no higher than that of fairies and river sprites. (Dawkins 1995, pp. 46–7)

But once we introduce theism as a scientific thesis, it seems utterly unable to carry out the kinds of work we expect in terms of science. This objection is articulated by Jan Narveson:

It ought to be regarded as a major embarrassment to natural theology that the very idea of something like a universe's being "created" by some minded being is sufficiently mind-boggling that any attempt to provide a detailed account of how it might be done is bound to look silly, or mythical, or a vaguely anthropomorphized version of some familiar physical process. Creation stories abound in human societies, as we know. Accounts ascribe the creation to various mythical beings, chief gods among a sizeable polytheistic committee, giant tortoises, super-mom hens, and, one is tempted to say, God-knows-what. The Judeo-Christian account does no better, and perhaps does a bit worse, in proposing a "six-day" process of creation.

It is plainly no surprise that details about just *how* all this was supposed to have happened are totally lacking when they are not, as I say, silly or simply poetic. For the fundamental idea is that some infinitely powerful mind simply willed it to be thus, and, as they say, Lo!, it was so! If we aren't ready to accept that as an explanatory description – as we should not be, since it plainly doesn't *explain* anything, as distinct from merely asserting that it was in fact done – then where do we go from there? On all accounts, we at this point meet up with mystery. "How are we supposed to know the ways of the infinite and almighty God?" it is asked – as if that put-down made a decent substitute for an answer. But of course it doesn't. If we are serious about "natural theology," then we ought to be ready to supply content in our explication of theological hypotheses just as we do when we explicate scientific hypotheses. Such explications carry the brunt of explanations. Why does water boil when heated? The scientific story supplies an analysis of matter in its liquid state, the effects of atmospheric pressure and heat, and so on until we see, in impressive detail, just how the thing works. An explanation's right to be called "scientific" is, indeed, in considerable part earned precisely by its ability to provide such detail. (Narveson 2003, pp. 93–4)

Matthew Bagger is equally convinced that theistic explanations should be discredited over against a naturalist alternative. He holds that no occasion can arise that would offer reason for questioning the adequacy of naturalism.

> We can never assert that, in principle, an event resists naturalistic explanation. A perfectly substantiated, anomalous event, rather than providing evidence for the supernatural, merely calls into question our understanding of particular natural laws. In the modern era, this position fairly accurately represents the educated response to novelty. Rather than invoke the supernatural, we can always adjust our knowledge of the natural in extreme cases. In the modern age in actual inquiry, we never reach the point where we throw up our hands and appeal to divine intervention to explain a localized event like an extraordinary experience. (Bagger 1999, p. 13)

Bagger's position closely resembles that of David Hume's on miracles, although his position is more comprehensive than explaining away events within the cosmos. Bagger thinks that there cannot, in principle, be any supernatural or theistic account of the cosmos itself. Accounts of what exist, according to Bagger, must be naturalistic, which he describes as amenable to scientific investigation. Because theism involves descriptions and explanations involving a reality that is not itself subject to scientific inquiry, it cannot be employed in accounting either for events in the cosmos (ostensible miracles or religious experience) or of the cosmos itself. Both Narveson and Bagger propose that theism fails because of its comparative paucity to explanations in the natural sciences.

Argument III

Theism and anthropomorphism – there are at least two versions of this line of reasoning. The first comes from Hume and maintains that theism receives whatever plausibility it has in natural theology by comparing God to a human person. In one version of the argument from design, for example, theists argue that God must be like us because the cosmos resembles artifacts we make intentionally. But, Hume reasons, is there not something grossly anthropomorphic (and anthropocentric) to suppose that the creator or cause of the cosmos must resemble us when there are so many other possible sources of causal explanation? There is an implicit charge that theism is too human-centered in the following lines:

> But allowing that we were to take the operations of one part of nature upon another for the foundation of our judgement concerning the origin of the whole (which never can be admitted), yet why select so minute, so weak, so bounded a principle as the reason and design of animals is found to be upon this planet? What peculiar privilege has this little agitation of the brain which we call thought, that we must make it the model of the whole universe? Our partiality in our own favor does indeed present it on all occasions, but sound philosophy ought carefully to guard against so natural an illusion. (Hume 1988, p. 19)

According to another version of this objection, theism is to be faulted not only for its somewhat hubristic identification of humanity as a model for the cause of the cosmos but also for a deeper reason: just as we have come to see in the philosophy of human nature that there is no sense to be made of humans having a nonphysical soul, we may similarly see that there is no sense to be made of the concept of the cosmos having a nonphysical creator. Bede Rundle has recently developed a version of this argument.

According to Rundle, our language and concepts that describe and explain intentional action are essentially references to material behavior. As God is nonphysical, the notion that God can act, hear, or know about the world is necessarily false or incoherent.

> We have no idea what it means to speak of God intervening in the affairs of the world. . . . We may well have to broaden our conception of what this universe contains; why should there not be many species of being more intelligent than us, some of whom make their presence felt locally from time to time? However, such a concession leaves us within the physical universe. The difficulty with a supernatural agent is that it requires one foot in both domains, so to speak. To qualify as supernatural it must be distanced from any spatio-temporal character which would place it in our world, but to make sense to us as explanatory of changes therein it must be sufficiently concrete to interact with material bodies, and the more convincingly a case is made for the former status, the greater the difficulty put in the way of the latter. (Rundle 2004, pp. 10, 27, 28)

Rundle contends that the very notion of nonmaterial intentions, knowledge, and so on is incoherent, and he takes particular aim at what he sees as the misuse of language in theistic religion.

> Someone who insists that God, though lacking eyes and ears, watches him incessantly and listens to his prayers, is clearly not using "watch" or "listen" in a sense in which we can recognize, so while the words may be individually meaningful and their combination grammatical, that is as far as meaningfulness goes: what we have is an unintelligible use of an intelligible form of words. God is not of this world, but that is not going to stop us speaking of him as if he were. It is not that we have a proposition which is meaningless because unverifiable, but we simply misuse language, making an affirmation which, in light of our understanding of the words, is totally unwarranted, an affirmation that makes no intelligible contact with reality. (Rundle 2004, p. 11)

Rundle's main justification for this stridently confident conclusion lies in ordinary language and a general materialism ("if there is anything at all, it must be matter" (Rundle 2004, p. ix)).

Rundle's appeal to ordinary language may seem strained over against linguistic and conceptual flexibility of contemporary science with its quarks, leptons, dark matter, energy, and so on. But Rundle's thesis may be bolstered by what appears to be an implicit *naturalism* in natural sciences. The sciences have not revealed clear marks of the divine, and theism as a hypothesis about reality does not help us with predictions. If theism is true, is it more or less likely that our sun will collapse in 4–5 billion years, turn into a red giant, and vaporize the earth? Daniel Dennett prizes physicalistic explanations that can answer such questions in terms of matter and energy, without bringing in theism or any kind of framework that privileges mental explanations that appeal to experience and intentions. For Dennett, Rundle's line of reasoning is sound. Theism is discredited for its extracting from the natural world intentional, mental terms (knowing, thinking, loving, and so on) and then projecting them on to a nonphysical, supernatural subject.

Argument IV

An argument from uniqueness – this argument received one of its most famous versions in Hume's *Dialogues Concerning Natural Religion*. According to this argument, the project of theistic natural theology cannot get off the ground because there is no framework in which we can test the plausibility of theism over against its alternatives. In the *Dialogues*, Hume reasons that we may well reach conclusions about the cause of some object, such as a house, because we have seen many houses built in the past. But when it comes to the cosmos itself, we have no reference point by which to weigh alternative hypotheses.

> But how this [design] argument can have place, where the objects, as in the present case, are single, individual, without parallel or specific resemblance, may be difficult to explain. And will any man tell me with a serious countenance, that an orderly universe must arise from some thought and art, like the human; because we have experience of it? To ascertain this reasoning, it were requisite, that we had experience of the origin of worlds; and it is not sufficient surely, that we have seen ships and cities arise from human art and contrivance. (Hume 1988, p. 21)

According to Hume, when we compare the cosmos itself to human artifacts and speculate about whether the cosmos resembles an artifact, we are simply moving from what we are familiar with in a commonsense context to form an analogy that is far beyond what we can properly evaluate.

> If we see a house, ... we conclude, with the greatest certainty, that it had an architect or builder; because this is precisely that species of effect, which we have experienced to proceed from that species of cause. But surely you will not affirm, that the universe bears such a resemblance to a house, that we can with the same certainty infer a similar cause, or that the analogy is here entire and perfect. The dissimilitude is so striking, that the utmost you can here pretend to is a guess, a conjecture, a presumption concerning a similar cause. (Hume 1988, p. 16)

This line of reasoning is used by Hume to undermine an argument from design.

Argument V

Natural theology is not enough. David Hume and Immanuel Kant both object to theistic natural theology on the grounds that the God that appears in natural theology is not sufficient to justify belief in the God of theistic tradition. So, while Kant is impressed by an argument from design, one of his objections is that the God evidenced by design would not thereby be shown to be omniscient, omnipotent, essentially good, and so on. Kant writes:

> The proof could at most establish a highest architect of the world, who would always be limited by the suitability of the material on which he works, but not a creator of the world, to whose idea everything is subject, which is far from sufficient for the great aim that one has in view, namely that of proving an all-sufficient original being. If we wanted to prove the contingency of matter itself, then we would have to take refuge in a transcendental argument, which, however, is exactly what was supposed to be avoided here. (Kant 1998, p. A627)

Hume also proposes that the tools of natural theology are unable to fashion a concept of a "supreme existence" that would befit the divine. Building a case for a God that resembles human minds would seem to be hopeless given the limited, elusive, and fluctuating nature of human minds.

All the sentiments of the human mind, gratitude, resentment, love, friendship, approbation, blame, pity, emulation, envy, have a plain reference to the state and situation of man, and are calculated for preserving the existence, and promoting the activity of such a being in such circumstances. It seems therefore unreasonable to transfer such sentiments to a supreme existence, or to suppose him actuated by them; and the phenomena, besides, of the universe will not support us in such a theory. All our ideas, derived from the senses, are confessedly false and illusive; and cannot, therefore, be supposed to have place in a supreme intelligence. (Hume 1988, p. 27)

A Foundation for Natural Theology

I believe that the most promising reply to these arguments is to start with a challenge to the physicalism that lies behind most (although not all) forms of naturalism. It is first essential to set up a nonphysicalist alternative before addressing the *no logical space for theism argument* and so on. The importance of linking the philosophy of mind with the philosophy of God is not apparent *only* in the arguments by Rundle and Narveson. Consider Anthony Kenny's observation:

If we are to attribute intelligence to any entity – limited or unlimited, cosmic or extra-cosmic – we have to take as our starting point our concept of intelligence as exhibited by human beings: we have no other concept of it. Human intelligence is displaced in the behavior of human bodies and in the thoughts of human minds. If we reflect on the active way in which we attribute mental predicate such as "know," "believe," "think," "design," "control" to human beings, we realize the immense difficulty there is [in] applying them to a putative being to which is immaterial, ubiquitous and eternal. It is not just that we do not, and cannot, know what goes on in God's mind, it is that we cannot really ascribe a mind to God at all. The language that we use to describe the contents of human minds operates within a web of links with bodily behavior and social institutions. When we try to apply this language to an entity outside the natural world, whose scope of operation is the entire universe, this web comes to pieces, and we no longer know what we are saying. (Kenny 2006, pp. 52, 53)

If Kenny is right, the most promising theistic starting point must be to question whether or not terms such as "consciousness," "know," "act," and so on are thoroughly physical or reducible to bodily states and behavior.

Given a thoroughgoing physicalism, theism is not likely to receive a friendly hearing. For some naturalists, theism and consciousness itself are in the same boat. Alisdair Hannay rightly recognizes how contemporary physicalists seek to marginalize consciousness, granting it only secondary or a provisional status to be explained away in nonconscious categories. Something even more negative can be said about the receptivity to theism.

The attitude of much physicalism [to consciousness] has been that of new owners to a sitting tenant. They would prefer eviction but, failing that, are content to dispose of as much of the paraphernalia as possible while keeping busy in other parts of the house. We should, I think, feel free to surmise that the current picture of consciousness eking out a sequestered life as a print-out monitor or raw feeler fails in a quite radical way to capture the facts. (Hannay 1987, p. 397)

How certain should we be that consciousness and other mental states are in fact marginal or thoroughly physical and identical to a bodily "web of links"? I suggest in what follows that once we recognize that some conscious, purposive explanations should count as *bona fide* accounts of human (and perhaps other animal) lives, one may see that the theistic appeal to consciousness, and the purposive account of the cosmos itself, should be taken seriously as well.

Consider first the project of marginalizing consciousness. To see the problem with treating consciousness as secondary to observable, bodily processes, witness the work of Daniel Dennett. Dennett has made a career seeking to displace what may be considered the apparent primacy of consciousness in terms of certitude. Early modern philosophy began with Descartes' stress on the indubitability of self-awareness. One early effort by Dennett to combat Cartesianism was to promote what he called "heterophenomenology," a method that did not completely dismiss introspection from the outset but treated people's reports on their states of consciousness as data that required additional scientific evidence before those reports could be taken seriously. Over the years, he has become increasingly hostile toward those who attribute to conscious experience an ineliminable, primary status. In a recent exchange, Dennett contends that David Chalmers needs "an independent ground for contemplating the drastic move of adding 'experience' to mass, charge, and space-time" (Dennett 2000, p. 35). Chalmers replies that "Dennett challenges me to provide 'independent' evidence (presumably behavioral or functional evidence) for the 'postulation' of experience. But this is to miss the point: conscious experience is not 'postulated' to explain other phenomena in turn; rather, it is a phenomenon to be explained in its own right . . ." (Chalmers 2000, p. 385)

I suggest that Chalmers is absolutely convincing in this reply. There can be no "contemplating" or observations of this or that evidence about behavior or functions or any theories about mass, charge, and space-time unless there is conscious awareness. Consciousness is antecedent to, and a presupposition of, science and philosophy. To emphasize the primacy of consciousness, note Drew McDermott's effort to defend Dennett against Chalmers. McDermott offers this analogy against Chalmers and in favor of Dennett: "Suppose a lunatic claims he is Jesus Christ. We explain why his brain chemicals make him think that. But he is not convinced. 'The fact that I am Jesus is my starting point, a brute explanandum; explaining why I think this is not sufficient.' The only difference between him and us is that he can't stop believing he's Jesus because he's insane, whereas we can't stop believing in phenomenal consciousness because we are not" (McDermott 2001, p. 147). But surely, this analogy is wide of the mark, ignoring the unique, radically fundamental nature of consciousness and experience. Without consciousness, we should not be able even to think that someone is sane or insane, let alone Jesus. Recognition of the reality of conscious awareness is not simply an obstinate belief; the reality of consciousness seems to be a precondition of inquiry. (As a side note, it is peculiar that in his defense of Dennett, McDermott implies that we are not insane because we believe in phenomenal consciousness.)

Once the existence of consciousness is conceded as no less and perhaps even more assured than Dennett's "mass, charge, and space-time," it becomes difficult to see how consciousness can turn out to be the very same thing as brain activity or other bodily states and behavior. The following observation by Michael Lockwood is telling:

Let me begin by nailing my colours to the mast. I count myself a materialist, in the sense that I take consciousness to be a species of brain activity. Having said that, however, it seems to me evident that no description of brain activity of the relevant kind, couched in the currently available languages of physics, physiology, or functional or computational roles, is remotely capable of capturing what is distinctive about consciousness. So glaring, indeed, are the short-comings of all the reductive programmes currently on offer, that I cannot believe that anyone with a philosophical training, looking dispassionately at these programmes, would take any of them seriously for a moment, were in not for a deep-seated conviction that current physical science has essentially got reality taped, and accordingly, *something* along the lines of what the reductionists are offering *must* be correct. To that extent the very existence of consciousness seems to me to be a standing demonstration of the explanatory limitations of contemporary physical science. (Lockwood 2003, p. 447)

There is a powerful, enduring argument against identifying consciousness and brain activity that is very much in favor now and that highlights the limitations of physicalist treatments of consciousness. A wide range of philosophers argue that it is possible for us to have an exhaustive observation of a person's physiology, anatomy, all outward behavior, and language use and still not know that the person is conscious (for a defense of this argument and reply to objections, see Taliaferro 1994, 2002; Swinburne 1997; Goetz & Taliaferro 2008; Moreland 2008).

It would be premature to refer to a consensus in philosophy of mind, but there is a strong, growing conviction that "solving" the problem of consciousness may require a revolution in the way that we conceive of both consciousness and the physical world. Thomas Nagel puts the matter as follows:

I believe that the explanatory gap [linking consciousness and physical processes] in its present form cannot be closed – that so long as we work with our present mental and physical concepts no transparently necessary connection will ever be revealed, between physically described brain processes and sensory experience, of the logical type familiar from the explanation of other natural processes by analysis into their physico-chemical constituents. We have good grounds for believing that the mental supervenes on the physical – i.e. that there is no mental difference without a physical difference. But pure, unexplained supervenience is not a solution but a sign that there is something fundamental we don't know. We cannot regard pure supervenience as the end of the story because that would require the physical to necessitate the mental without there being any answer to the question *how* it does so. But there *must* be a "how," and our task is to understand it. An obviously systematic connection that remains unintelligible to us calls out for a theory. (Nagel 1998, pp. 344–5)

Nagel's confidence that we will somehow bridge the gap and understand how consciousness may turn out to be brain activity does not inspire enthusiasm: "I believe," writes Nagel, "it is not irrational to hope that someday, long after we are all dead, people will be able to observe the operation of the brain and say, with true understanding 'That's what the experience of tasting chocolate looks like from the outside'" (Nagel 1998, p. 338).

The difficulty of explaining away the obstinate reality of consciousness, and the ostensible contingency of the relationship between consciousness and physical processes, should caution those who dismiss theism in light of a confident form of physicalism.

Reply to Argument I

I shall later reply in some detail to Rundle's argument that theism is incoherent, but I shall assume (provisionally) in my reply to the first argument that consciousness does indeed exist and that there are problems with explaining away what appears to be a contingent relationship between consciousness and physical states and processes. It seems that we can conceive of the one without the other, and we currently lack an explanatory scheme to show that there is an identity between them (see Taliaferro 1994, 1997, 2002). I do not assume here that some form of dualism is true; I am asserting, however, that physicalism is not known to be true and that it is problematic to beg the question about the successful prospects of nonphysical explanations at the outset. Granted this foundation, consider Argument I. If we cannot rule out that consciousness with respect to human beings is something nonphysical, how can we justifiably rule out that there may be a nonphysical theistic mode of consciousness (a God who knows, acts, and so on)? If it is possible that there is a nonphysical, purposive causal agent as conceived of in theism, is there not logical space for asking the theistic cosmic question that Phillips and Kai Nielsen seek to rule out?

Furthermore, the fundamental theistic cosmic question is actually slightly different than Phillips and Nielsen suppose. In standard forms of the cosmological argument, theists ask the question of why the contingent cosmos exists rather than not. This is not akin to asking why *everything* exists, assuming God (*ex hypothesi*) is a substantial reality or subject who would (if God exists) be referred to as one of the "things" that exists. So the question of the cosmological argument (addressed in Chapter 3) concerns the cosmos and its origin and continuation, not the cosmos plus God. Nielsen's objection to theism similarly seems to have purchase only if by "universe" we mean "everything." If, instead, the "universe" refers to the contingent cosmos we observe, it seems that it is perfectly sensible to ask why it exists and whether it has a sustaining, necessarily existing, conscious, nonphysical, purposive cause. The latter would be "beyond the universe" as such a being would not be identical to the contingent universe. It is worthy of note, too, that some naturalists have been led to posit abstract objects (propositions, properties, sets) that exist necessarily and are thus "beyond the contingent cosmos."

Consider, again, Nielsen's claim that "God exists" is akin to "procrastination drinks melancholy." Unless we charitably interpret the latter as a poetic report that, say, the tendency to delay projects promotes melancholy (which seems to hold in my case, on occasion), the latter report is profoundly different from the former. People and animals drink, but not tendencies or states of character. I suggest that the second phrase is meaningless, but the first expresses a proposition which may, in fact, be true and so ought to arouse our interest in its truth. If we have some reason to think human consciousness may not be physical and this opens up the question of whether there may be a nonphysical divine agent, then asking about (human or divine) causes of events is vital. A strict behaviorist who denies the possibility of any mental events may urge us to put to one side any search for a mental cause for my writing this sentence. But once strict behaviorism is put to one side, the search for causes can no longer be so contracted. (More on Phillips's claim about science and "the structure of the world" later in this chapter.)

Reply to Argument II

I first note that many of the arguments in natural theology do not treat theism as a scientific hypothesis. Dawkins seems to suppose that if God exists, God's existence should be evident in gravity, electromagnetism, nuclear forces, lumps of matter, rocks, asteroids, and black holes. But while theism (rightly, I think) can serve as a justified explanation of some events in the cosmos (I subscribe to a theistic argument from religious experience), the chief evidence of much theistic natural theology is the very existence and endurance of our contingent cosmos as a whole. Those of us who accept a version of the cosmological argument hold that to fully explain the existence and endurance of this cosmos requires appeal to the intentional agency of a necessarily existing, good being (see Chapter 10). Contrary to Dawkins et al., theism is better seen as a philosophical explanation *of the cosmos* rather than as a scientific account of events *in the cosmos*.

Let us now turn to Narveson's argument. Narveson wants scientific details *about* how divine agency works. He compares explanations that work (water boils because of molecules in motion) with those that do not (God commanded that there be light and, lo, there was light). But consider an example of human agency: You light a candle in order to see your beloved. Most of us assume that such acts are truly explanatory. There may be highly complex layers to such an intentional account, distinctions between basic and nonbasic actions, and there would be a physiological story to tell about muscles and brains and so on, but most would hold that the intention to see the beloved was part of the account (Searle 1983, 1992, 1997, 2004). I suggest that if intentions are truly explanatory, then there must be a sense in which they are not reducible to the physiologically detailed explanations. "I wish to see my beloved" may need backing in terms of other intentions such as "I like to see her golden hair," but I suggest that if agency is genuinely causal, there must be a sense in which it is basic in the sense that it is not fully accounted for in other terms (Danto 1965; Swinburne 1997). If every intentional explanation were acceptable only if it involved a further intentional explanation (I intended to turn on the lights A by intending action B, and I intended B by C *ad infinitum*), then I should never be able to undertake the first intentional act. I shall further spell out a positive account of agency in response to Rundle's work, but I now wish to make the further observation against Narveson that the physical sciences themselves are not inimical to basic explanations. In contemporary particle physics, objects without mass are posited with primitive charges or spins, which are presumed to be the basic foundations for explaining more complex events. Positing a basic power, terrestrial or divine, is not, *ipso facto*, explanatorily empty. On this point, Phillips's observation cited earlier about science seems curious. In the sciences, we may well claim that with respect to any explanation, further questions can be asked of it, but this is not the same thing as claiming that science does not or cannot posit basic powers and accounts that are not themselves explained by further powers or scientific accounts. If the sciences can allow that subatomic particles have basic powers, it is hard to see how we can rule out that intentional agents have basic powers. (Phillips's claim that science is "not concerned with 'the structure of the world'" also seems curious. The atomic theory of matter seems unintelligible unless it is interpreted as offering a description and explanation of the structure of the world.)

If Narveson's dismissal of theism is unsuccessful, it is hard to see how Bagger's *a priori* ruling out of theism is more promising. This is especially true because Bagger's form of naturalism does not seem linked to a strict naturalism or some form of reductive physicalism. Bagger's form of naturalism allows for almost anything but theism.

Despite the occasional references to natural law and science both here and in the final chapter which might suggest otherwise, I intend my use of "natural" to entail (1) no commitments to a physicalistic ontology; (2) no valorization of the specific methods, vocabularies, presuppositions, or conclusions peculiar to natural science; (3) no view about the reducibility of the mental to the physical; (4) no position on the ontological status of logic or mathematics; and

(5) no denial of the possibility of moral knowledge. Beliefs, values, and logical truths, for example, count as natural and folk psychological explanations, therefore, are natural explanations. The concept of the natural, in the sense I use it, has virtually no content except as the definitional correlative to the supernatural, taken here as a transcendent order of reality (and causation) distinct from the mundane order presupposed alike by the natural scientist and the rest of us in our quotidian affairs. (Bagger 1999, p. 15)

Imagine, however, that a physicalist ontology is found wanting and (as suggested earlier) that we need to be open to nonphysical states, processes, and the like. Imagine that the mental is irreducible to the physical and that we give no primary place to the natural sciences, and that we further allow that intentional explanations involving purposes are all permissible. Bagger seems to allow for all of this; but once such a wider framework is taken seriously, it is hard to see how one can (in principle) know that theistic explanations are never acceptable.

Reply to Argument III

Let us first consider Hume's disparaging observation about using human beings as a model for God.[1] The ways in which Hume denigrates consciousness is interesting because it is itself so laden with a narrow anthropomorphism. Why assume that if thought were the key to some cosmic metaphysic such as theism, then thought or a divine intention would be "minute"? Hume does not say that thought would have to be minute, but the passage implies that it is the minuteness of thought (in human life) that should dissuade us from thinking that it might be the key to a comprehensive account of nature. Thought (whether human or divine) would not be small in physical size because nonphysical and divine thought (if classical theism is true) would be neither "weak" nor "bounded." Cosmic theistic explanations would be in the form of appealing to the limitless knowledge and unsurpassable power of God. It may be that in constructing a theistic metaphysic, we employ the concepts of intentionality and consciousness that are used to describe our contingent and limited life, but in theism the concepts of intentionality and consciousness are then conceived in terms of a noncontingent, limitless, powerful, intentional, conscious Creator. To many naturalists, as we have seen, this is a matter of unwarranted projection, but, whether it is a mere projection or discovery, a theistic metaphysic needs to be seen as introducing a comprehensive, powerful, intentional account of the very existence and continuation of nature.

I believe that the basic point that is obscured in the passage from Hume is the way in which overall accounts of the cosmos should be contrasted. At the broadest level of description and explanation, theism and naturalism represent two of the more promising accounts of the cosmos. The one treats intentional, purposive explanations resting in a supreme agent as foundational, while the other accounts for the emergence of purpose and agency (if any) in terms of nonpurposive, nonconscious causal powers. The theistic account is no more to be disparaged if one of the reference points *of* teleological, conscious explanations is in human life than if one of the reference points in naturalistic accounts is water's boiling

---

1. Technically, the passage by Hume cited earlier occurs in his *Dialogues Concerning Natural Religion* as a claim advanced by one of the characters and not as a direct claim by Hume himself. In this context, I am following the practice of most philosophers in seeing the character, Philo, as a spokesperson for Hume's position.

(to use Narveson's example). (More on the topic under the section "Nontheistic Natural Theology" later in this chapter.)

Let us now consider Rundle's critique of theistic natural theology. Rundle's critique of divine agency is linked with his critique of human agency. He not only finds it puzzling to suppose that God's intentions could causally account for the origin and continued existence of light, he also doubts that human intentions play a causal role in human action. By taking this line, I suspect that Rundle winds up with his own version of "dualism," in which the apparent role played by our emotions and intentions *is* cut off from causal relations in the world. Because of the importance of Rundle's noncausal account of human agency and its bearing on the central attack on theism, I cite him at length.

> Suppose you are pleased at having won a game of bridge, or disappointed at having lost. These are not, surely, brute-factual relations, but there are conceptual connections: the responses *make sense* in the light of what has led to them. That is indeed so, but is the relevant relation one of causation? How do you know that it is your loss at bridge that disappoints you? There may be feelings akin to those of disappointment at whose source you can only conjecture, but there is no room for conjecture as to what you are disappointed at, so that you might say: I think it is because I lost at bridge that I am disappointed, but it may be my failure to win the lottery that is having this effect. The inappropriateness of mere conjecture is not because we are infallible when it comes to identifying a cause in this connection, but because the very notions of cause and effect, as these are understood in the natural sciences, are out of place here.
>
> Consider this in terms of reasons for action. You say that you are opening the door in order to let the cat out. If this is an explanation made in all sincerity, and with understanding of the words used, then the reason cited is indeed your reason for acting. Its being your reason just consists in its standing as an honestly made avowal, with no room for rival alternatives. It is not as with causal propositions, where one's honest say-so does not decide what caused what, but where it is always in principle possible that one's attribution of a cause will be overturned by further investigation. To say, for instance, "I think I am opening the door to let the cat out", would be to relocate what would ordinarily be a matter of one's reason for acting in an altogether different domain. It would be to treat one's avowal as a matter for conjecture on one's own part, much as if the act were involuntary, as with "I think I am sneezing because of the dust." Just the standing appropriate to a causal hypothesis, but a distortion of our conception of a reason. The conclusion is not that causal relations are, after all, a species of logical relation, but that we are concerned here with reasons rather than causes. (Rundle 2004, pp. 48–9)

Is Rundle's account plausible?

I do not think so and I suggest that, at the least, his position faces an enormous burden of proof. First, consider again Rundle's examples. Surely the whole idea that you are disappointed over a loss at bridge is that the realization that you lost and your desire to win is what (along with other factors) brings about (causally contributes to) your feeling disappointed. Rundle uses a humorous alternative (viz. losing the lottery) to cajole us into thinking there is no causation going on but adjust the example to something less remote (e.g. maybe the real cause of disappointment is that you are about to lose a friendship), and the example seems to resist Rundle's noncausal analysis. Surely you may be fully justified in believing that your disappointment stems from your belief that a friendship is on the rocks and not confusing this with your disappointment at failing to win 350 million dollars with your lottery ticket, which had a one in a trillion chance of winning. Consider also his case of letting the cat out. Plausible cases are readily described where a person's motives may be unclear, and this lack of clarity is owing to our not knowing what was the fundamental, intended cause of our action. Was the reason for opening the door to let the cat out or to welcome a visitor or to get fresh air or to interrupt a job interview? Rundle's noncausal account of reasoned, motivated action strikes me as promoting an intolerable dualism of sorts, whereby human action is cut off from the natural world. At least from a common sense or prephilosophical perspective, a person is a causal agent, one who brings about changes on the basis of reason. I am sympathetic with the claim that human agency involves more than "cause and effect, as these are understood in the natural sciences," if by the latter Rundle means nonintentional, nonmental processes. But once you allow the "natural sciences" to include things such as an agent's wanting there to be light (and other relevant desires and intentions), it is harder to see why these mental processes should not have causal roles.

It does not follow that if Rundle's noncausal account of human agency fails, then his case against divine agency fails. But as one looks more closely at some of Rundle's other examples, his overall case against theism wavers. Take, for example, the following critique of divine agency. He allows that *some* intentional control over remote objects may be imaginable or intelligible, but theism nonetheless faces an "intractable difficulty" with conceiving of the scope and precision of divine causation. Rundle shapes his objection against a proposal that psychokinesis could provide a model for thinking of divine agency.

> Those who believe in the reality of psychokinesis consider it possible to effect changes in the world merely through an act of will – Locke's account of voluntary action, we may note, amounts to regarding it as an exercise of psychokinesis directed at one's own limbs. It is not absurd to suppose that issuing a spoken command should have an effect on things in one's environment, nor even that formulating the command to oneself should likewise have external repercussions. Neural activity associated with such an act could conceivably harness larger forces which impacted upon things beyond the brain. Whether the command is delivered out loud or said to oneself, what is difficult to account for is the specificity of the effect. If a soldier is given the command "Attention!" or "Stand at ease!", his understanding of the words puts him in a position to comply. Even when the words are uttered *in foro interno*, we can imagine that some sort of signal should reach an inanimate object, but a seemingly intractable difficulty remains on the side of the object, which is not possessed of the understanding which would result in its moving to the left when told to move to the left, or rotating when told to rotate. Psychokinesis is not a promising model for making sense of God's action on a mindless cosmos, and God's supposed role as lawgiver. (Rundle 2004, p. 157)

This is puzzling. The cited passage suggests that theistic accounts of God's creative power rest on creation's understanding and then obeying divine commands. Clearly, this is a Pickwickean treatment of divine agency, although perhaps Rundle's observation bears on accounts of divine revelation when it is not clear what (or whether) God wills. All that to one side, once Rundle allows that an agent can have causal effects on remote objects (Rundle speaks of "some sort of signal"), why would it be incoherent to imagine that such causal efficacy is irresistible (necessarily, if God wills that there is light, there is light) and unsurpassed in specificity? Why suppose that God might only be able to set subatomic particles in motion but not be able to specify whether this be (in reference to some frame of reference) to the right or the left?

Let us now consider Rundle's charge that a nonphysical agent cannot hear prayers and so on. Rundle's work is reminiscent of the Wittgensteinian tactic (also employed by J. L.

Austin and G. Ryle) of professing bafflement over an opponent's position; Rundle maintains that he has "no idea" of theistic claims. "I can get no grip on the idea of an agent doing something where the doing, the bringing about, is not an episode in time . . ." (Rundle 2004, p. 77). One may well agree that he, Rundle, does, indeed, not understand the metaphysical claims he writes about, and yet challenge Rundle's charge that others also fail in this respect. Certainly, the line (presumably taken from Wittgenstein) that to talk of God's seeing requires (grammatically) that God have (literal) eyes seems open to question. I am tempted to ask the question, "Whose grammar?" Anselm of Canterbury and Ralph Cudworth (to pick two remote and otherwise quite different figures) held that God's cognition of the world and all its aspects did not require bodily organs. Perhaps they are mistaken, but it is hard to believe that they were merely making a mistake in Latin or English grammar. This is especially true if one adopts Rundle's view of meaning, according to which we fix the meaning of "God" and presumably words such as "to see" and "eyes." Rundle writes: "As with any other word, the meaning of 'God' is the meaning that our usage has conferred upon it, so what is true of God of necessity – that is, by dint of being required for the applicability of the term – is in principle something of which we know" (Rundle 2004, p. 101). In the seventeenth-century work *The True Intellectual System*, did Cudworth not use the terms "God" and "seeing" and "eyes" coherently in claiming God sees and knows without using eyes? Maybe "our usage" makes the claim problematic and we now know that it is impossible for there to be a nonphysical, cognitive agent. But what scientific account of (or conceptual investigation of) our eyes, brain, and so on led us to believe that a different form of agency and knowledge is metaphysically impossible? (It would be hard to argue that Cudworth was misusing the term "theism" since it appears that he coined the word in English.)

It is interesting that Rundle does not explicitly repudiate divine agency based on a form of contemporary physicalism. He writes:

> The idea that an ultimate source of being and becoming is to be found in the purely mental and non-physical is at odds with the conception of mind espoused by most contemporary philosophers. It is commonly held that mental states are to be characterized in terms of their causal role, but since such states are thought to be states of the brain, there is no lessening of a dependence on the physical. This is not a position I wish to invoke. It is doubtless true that we could not believe, desire, or intend without a brain, but any attempt to construe belief and the rest as states of that organ involves a serious mismatch between the psychological concepts and physical reality. Beliefs can be obsessive, unwavering, irrational, or unfounded, but nothing inside anyone's head answers to such descriptions. (Rundle 2004, pp. 76–7)

But given Rundle's (I believe correct) misgivings about the identity between mental and brain states, why be so sure that it is impossible for there to be nonphysical agency and cognition? All the theist needs here is the bare coherence of dualism, not its plausibility. And many materialists in philosophy of mind at least grant that dualism is intelligible though mistaken (Peter van Inwagon, Lynne Baker).

Reply to Argument IV

In reply to the argument from uniqueness, it has been argued that contemporary astrophysics and cosmology would not be carried out if Hume's objection were taken seriously.

Big Bang cosmology seems undeterred by the fact that our universe is the only one we experience; moreover, there seems to be little worry about the scientific use of analogies or the appeal to resemblance when it comes to referring to the cosmos as a whole. Richard Swinburne counters the uniqueness objection as follows:

> From time to time various writers have told us that we cannot reach any conclusions about the origin or development of the universe, since it is (whether by logic or just in fact) a unique object, the only one of its kind, and rational inquiry can only reach the conclusions about objects which belong to kinds, e.g. it can reach a conclusion about what will happen to this bit of iron, because there are other bits of iron, the behaviour of which can be studied. This objection of course has the surprising, and to most of these writers unwelcome, consequence, that physical cosmology cannot reach justified conclusions about such matters as the size, age, rate of expansion, and density of the universe as a whole (because it is a unique object); and also that physical anthropology cannot reach conclusions about the origin and development of the human race (because, as far as our knowledge goes, it is the only one of its kind). The implausibility of these consequences leads us to doubt the original objection, which is indeed totally misguided. (Swinburne 2004, p. 134)

I suggest that the most promising way to compare accounts of the cosmos is to appeal to such general criteria as explanatory scope, simplicity, compatibility with known science, support form other domains of inquiry including ethics or value theory, philosophy of mind, and so on. An analogy with assessing nonhuman animal mental life may prove helpful.

According to many philosophers, it is reasonable to believe that some nonhuman animals are conscious agents, and yet it is a commonplace observation that none of us will or can directly confirm the existence of nonhuman animal consciousness on the basis of the observation of nonhuman consciousness, anatomy, and behavior. No account of the animal brains and physiology, behavior, and language (or signals) has been accepted as definitive proof. Despite striking similarities to our own organic causes of suffering, and profound analogies with our own behavior when we are in pain, it is still possible to be a skeptic like Bob Bermond, who argues that animal emotions and behavior all occur without any conscious feeling (see Bermond 1997). Bermond reasons that in the case of humans, conscious feeling is correlated with certain brain states (a fully formed prefrontal cortex and right neocortex) not found among nonhuman animals. Because of this missing correlation and given the possibility that animals lack consciousness, we should not posit animal consciousness. In my view, this is a rationally defensible position, but in the wake of such profound analogies between human and nonhuman anatomy and behavior, it is more reasonable to believe that what appear to be symptoms of conscious suffering in great apes, chimps, dolphins, and many other animal species are the result of actual suffering. Bermond, for his part, has no positive reason for believing that conscious feeling occurs if – and only if – there is such and such brain developments. With support absent for such a strong claim, I think the reasonable stance is to accept that there is some nonhuman animal consciousness (Rollin 1990). To settle this debate (if it can be settled) would require a lengthy book of its own. Rather than establish my preferred position, my more modest point is that the debate over animal consciousness can and should take place, even though the debate would be undermined by Hume's objection about uniqueness. We are not in a position in which we can compare nonhuman animals, some of whom we *know* to be conscious and others not. Bernard does not recognize an uncontroversial case of nonhuman consciousness to get such a comparative study under way. But debate need not end. Which account does the best job in terms of explanatory power and what we know independently in terms of evolutionary history, and so on? A similar concern for scope and explanatory power befits the theism–naturalism debate.

Reply to Argument V

Consider the following three points in reply to Kant's objection to theistic natural theology.

First, what Kant thinks to be too modest an outcome in natural theology would be intolerable to many naturalists. Imagine that contemporary naturalists such as Narveson, Bagger, or Rundle become convinced that philosophical arguments "establish a highest architect of the world." This would not sit well with their central claims about the explanatory hegemony of naturalism.

A second point worth observing is that natural theology is one domain among others in which the justification of religious belief is assessed. There are extant treatments of religious belief that do not require natural theology in order for religious belief to be warranted (Plantinga 2000). Perhaps some religious believers would be uninterested in natural theology unless it can deliver a full commitment to a religious tradition, but this seems a matter for apologetics, not philosophy. In pursuing a philosophy of God, I suggest philosophers of all stripes should pursue natural theology and follow the arguments wherever they lead. More general accounts of justification and value might subsequently come into play about whether natural theology is sufficient in determining one's conviction about religious matters.

Third, while I began this chapter by noting the distinction between natural and revealed theology, that distinction has become less sharp. While a philosophical project that presupposed the authority of biblical or Qur'anic scripture would still not count as natural theology, philosophical arguments about the evidential value of religious experience now are treated in the domain of natural theology. This allows for greater material for theists and naturalists to argue for evidence that might or might not fill out a religious concept of the divine (Wainwright 1981; Davis 1989; Alston 1991; Yandell 1993; Gellman 1997, 2001). The current work on religious experience does not pass over into revealed theology so long as scriptural texts are not treated as presuppositions of inquiry.

Nontheistic Natural Theology

I conclude this chapter with a section on the virtues of inquiry, as I hope to encourage what I suggest is a golden rule in philosophy of religion. But before addressing the role of humility in philosophical inquiry, it is vital to note that the philosophical investigation into the divine without appeal to an authoritative scripture has historically included nontheistic accounts of a divine reality. I cited Spinoza earlier, who advanced a monistic view of God (or, as he put it, God or nature), according to which God is not an intentional, purposive agent. In the twentieth and early twenty-first centuries, there are developed accounts of the divine employing the process philosophy inspired by Alfred North Whitehead (1861–1947) and Charles Hartshorne (1897–2000). Feminist philosophers have developed views of God that have distinctive pantheistic forms (Rosemary Ruether). I believe this to be a sign of the healthiness of natural theology today, an indication of a growing interest in natural theology, whatever its specific religious implications.

The development of nontheistic natural theology is also an emerging new chapter in the dialogue about the relationship of science and religion. Rather than supporting a warfare model of science versus religion, works such as the Macmillan *Encyclopedia of Science and Religion* under the editorship of J. W. V. Van Huyssteen (2003) is a sign of the rich interplay on theistic and nontheistic natural theology.

As the field widens, I believe that more philosophers are appreciating the role of *cumulative arguments*, the combining of independent reasons for embracing a conclusion. Thus, a case for pantheism might be supported by an appeal to religious experience as well as a principle of simplicity. A leading philosopher of religion, Graham Oppy, has recently sounded a warning about cumulative arguments. Consider Oppy's somewhat complex analysis in his fine book *Arguing About Gods*:

> If we have two valid arguments, each of which entails the conclusion that a particular mono-theistic god exists, then we can form a disjunctive argument that also entails the same conclusion. More generally, if we have a large collection of valid arguments, each of which entails the conclusion that a particular monotheistic god exists, then we can form a multiply disjunctive argument that also entails that same conclusion. However, it should not be supposed that a "cumulative" argument that is formed in this way is guaranteed to be a better argument than the individual arguments with which we began (even if we are properly entitled to the claim that the arguments with which we are working are all valid). For, on the one hand, if all of the arguments are effective on grounds other than those of validity – for example, because they have false premises, or because they are question-begging – then the cumulative argument will also be defective. But, on the other hand, if even one of the arguments with which we began is not defective on any other grounds, then *it* is a cogent argument for its conclusion, and the cumulative argument is plainly worse (since longer and more convoluted). So, at the very least, we have good reason to be suspicious of talk about a cumulative case for the claim that a given monotheistic god does – or does not – exist that is based upon a collection of (alleg-edly) valid arguments for the claim that the god in question does – or does not – exist. (Oppy 2006, pp. 5, 6)

It is certainly right that simply having a greater number of arguments for one position (theism) rather than another (pantheism) is not, *ipso facto*, an advantage. The larger number of arguments may raise a larger number of good objections. But what Oppy's analysis may lead us to miss is that independent lines of reasoning can increase the *bona fide* cogency of their mutual conclusion. So if religious experience gives one some reason to embrace pantheism and an argument from simplicity gives one reason to embrace pantheism, then pantheism is better supported than if one only had one such argument. This is not a matter of a mere disjunction but a case of one argument supporting the other. To offer one other example, the moral theistic argument and ontological arguments are con-ceptually distinguishable (one may embrace one without embracing the other), but if both have some evidential force, then the evidence for the conclusion has grown greater than if only one had evidential force.

Consider a concrete case in which pantheistic and theistic arguments might together offer a cumulative case against naturalism. Without spelling out the details, John Leslie has developed a sustained argument for pantheism on the grounds that the cosmos is best explained in terms of values. Leslie is in the Platonic tradition, according to which the cosmos exists because it is good that it exists (in the *Republic*, Book VI, Plato proposes that the Good is what gives existence to things). And Leslie goes on to argue that the world itself is identifiable with "divine thought-patterns" (Leslie 2007, p. 3). Imagine that Leslie's argument has some, but not decisive, weight. Now, imagine that a moral theistic argument has some, but not decisive, weight. What follows? It may be that we are at a point where the evidential basis for theism and pantheism is on a par, but we would also be in a position (*ceterus paribus*) where there is more reason to question the sufficiency of secular naturalism. Both the nontheistic and theistic arguments would function as providing independent reasons for seeking a nonnaturalist account of the cosmos.

While my suggestion in the section that follows about the conduct of philosophy takes its focus to be the biggest debate in modern natural theology (theism versus naturalism), its broader point bears on the growing rich variety of viewpoints that are being developed by philosophers in natural theology today.

Virtues and Vices of Inquiry

In recent epistemology of religious beliefs, there has been great attention to the virtues of inquiry. Is there some overriding virtue that theists and naturalists can recognize as truly virtuous that will incline us to one or the other side? Anthony Kenny has recently developed an interesting case for humility, which he believes should incline us to agnosticism. This, in fact, is Kenny's current position: he thinks both atheism and theism are unwarranted:

> For my part I find the arguments for God's existence unconvincing and the historical evidence uncertain on which the creedal statements are based. The appropriate response to the uncertainty of argument and evidence is not atheism – that is at least as rash as the theism to which it is opposed – but agnosticism: that is the admission that one does not know whether there is a God who has revealed himself to the world. (Kenny 2004, p. 109)

He then develops the following argument, based on his view of humility as a virtue.

> If we look at [the debate over theism versus atheism] from the viewpoint of humility it seems that the agnostic is in the safer position. . . . The theist is claiming to possess a good which the agnostic does not claim to possess: he is claiming to be in possession of knowledge; the agnostic lays claim only to ignorance. The believer will say he does not claim knowledge, only true belief; but at least he claims to have laid hold, in whatever way, of information that the agnostic does not possess. It may be said that any claim to possess gifts which others do not have is in the same situation, and yet we have admitted that such a claim may be made with truth and without prejudice to humility. But in the case of a gift such as intelligence or athletic skill, those surpassed will agree that they are surpassed; whereas in this case, the theist can only rely on the support of other theists, and the agnostic does not think that the information which the theist claims is genuine information at all. Since Socrates philosophers have realized that a claim not to know is easier to support than a claim to know. (Kenny 2004, p. 109)

Does his argument succeed? I do not think so, but it opens up what I believe is a promising avenue for inquiry to note at the end of this first chapter.

Kenney structures his argument on the grounds that the theist claims to have a good (which he describes as a gift or information) that others lack, whereas the agnostic does not. Yet agnostics historically claim to have a good that theists and atheists lack: the good of intellectual integrity. If you like, they claim to have the information that we should withhold our consent both to theism and atheism. And, if it were successful, Kenny's argument would explicitly secure the idea that agnostics have a good that theists and atheists lack, namely, humility. There is a further problem about claiming that theists are only supported by theists. First, it is not just possible but commonplace for atheists to admire theists and theists to admire atheists. In this sense, there is mutual support and a massive amount of collaboration between the different parties. If by "support" Kenney means "belief," then (arguably) only agnostics support agnostics because if you support agnostics in the sense of *believing they are right*, you are yourself an agnostic.

I think humility in the context of the theism versus naturalism debate should be understood more along the lines of what may be described as the philosophical golden rule of treating other people's philosophies in the way you would like yours to be treated. I suggest that humility involves stepping back from one's own position and trying to evaluate and sympathetically consider the range of beliefs and evidence that can be arrayed in support for another position. If one employed such a rule in the debate between naturalism and theism, then I suggest that theistic philosophers should truly seek to see naturalism in its best, most comprehensive light, weighing the different ways in which consciousness and values and the very nature of the cosmos should be described and explained. Conversely, a naturalist philosopher needs to see theism in comprehensive terms. For example, rather than dismissing from the start the possibility that religious experience could provide evidence of a divine reality, one should consider such ostensible evidence in light of a comprehensive theistic account of the contingency of the cosmos, its apparent order, the emergence of cosmos and values. Claims to experience God look profoundly unreliable unless one takes seriously the whole pattern of such experiences across cultures and assesses their credibility in light of a comprehensive case for theism or some other religious philosophy.

The importance *of* what I am referring to as the philosophical golden rule may be seen as even more poignant when one appreciates that the field of natural theology involves not just theism and naturalism but a growing literature in nontheistic natural theology.

References

Alston, W. P. (1991) *Perceiving God: The Epistemology of Religious Experience*. Ithaca, NY: Cornell University Press.

Bagger, M. (1999) *Religious Experience, Justification, and History*. Cambridge: Cambridge University Press.

Bermond, B. (1997) The myth of animal suffering. In M. Dol, S. Kasanmoentalib, S. Lijmbach, E. Rivas and R. vandenBos (eds.), *Animal Consciousness and Animal Ethics Perspectives from the Netherlands*. Assen, The Netherlands: Van Gorcum, pp. 125–43.

Chalmers, D. J. (2000) Moving forward on the problem of consciousness. In J. Shear (ed.), *Explaining Consciousness – The "Hard Problem"*, 379–412. Cambridge, MA: MIT Press.

Danto, A. C. (1965) Basic actions. *American Philosophical Quarterly* 2, 141–8.

Davis, C. F. (1989) *The Evidential Force of Religious Experience*. Oxford: Clarendon Press.

Dawkins, R. (1995). *River Out of Eden: A Darwinian View of Life*. London: Phoenix.

Dawkins, R. (2006) *The God Delusion*. Boston: Houghton Mifflin Co.

Dennett, D. (2000) Facing backwards on the problem of consciousness. In J. Shear (ed.), *Explaining Consciousness – The "Hard Problem"*, 33–36. Cambridge, MA: MIT Press.

Gellman, J. I. (1997) *Experience of God and the Rationality of Theistic Belief*. Ithaca, NY: Cornell University Press.

Gellman, J. I. (2001) *Mystical Experience: A Philosophical Inquiry*. Aldershot, UK: Ashgate.

Goetz, S. and Taliaferro, C. (2008) *Naturalism*. Grand Rapids, MI: Eerdmans.

Hannay, A. (1987) The claims of consciousness: a critical survey. *Inquiry* 30, 395–434.

Hill, D. J. (2005) *Divinity and Maximal Greatness*. London: Routledge.

Hoffman, J. and Rosenkrantz, G. S. (2002) *The Divine Attributes*. Oxford: Blackwell Publishing.

Hume, D. (1988) *Dialogues Concerning Natural Religion: The Posthumous Essays of the Immortality of the Soul and of Suicide*, 2nd edn, Ed. Richard H. Popkin. Indianapolis: Hackett Publishing Co.

Kant, I. (1998) *Critique of Pure Reason*. Trans. and ed. P. Guyer and A. W. Wood. Cambridge: Cambridge University Press.

Kenny, A. (2004) *The Unknown God: Agnostic Essays*. London: Continuum.

Kenny, A. (2006) *What I Believe*. London: Continuum International Publishing Group.

Leslie, J. (2001) *Infinite Minds: A Philosophical Theology*. Oxford: Oxford University Press.

Leslie, J. (2007) *Immortality Defended*. Malden, MA: Blackwell Publishing.

Lockwood, M. (2003) Consciousness and the quantum worlds. In Q. Smith and A. Jokric (eds.), *Consciousness: New Philosophical Perspectives*, 447–467. Oxford: Clarendon.

McDermott, D. (2001) *Mind and Mechanism*. Cambridge, MA: MIT Press.

Moreland, J. P. (2008) *Consciousness and the Existence of God: A Theistic Argument*. London: Routledge.

Nagel, T. (1998) Conceiving the impossible and the mind-body problem. *Philosophy* 73: 285, 337–52.

Narveson, J. (2003) God by design? In N. A. Manson (ed.), *God and Design: The Teleological Argument and Modern Science*, 88–104. London: Routledge.

Nielsen, K. (2004) *Naturalism and Religion*. New York: Prometheus Books.

Oppy, G. (2006) *Arguing about Gods*. Cambridge: Cambridge University Press.

Phillips, D. Z. (2005) *The Problem of Evil and the Problem of God*. Minneapolis: Fortress Press.

Plantinga, A. (2000) *Warranted Christian Belief*. New York: Oxford University Press.

Rollin, B. E. (1990) *The Unheeded Cry: Animal Consciousness, Animal Pain, and Science*. Oxford: Oxford University Press.

Rundle, B. (2004) *Why There is Something Rather Than Nothing*. New York: Clarendon Press.

Searle, J. R. (1982) *Intentionality*. Cambridge: Cambridge University Press.

Searle, J. R. (1992) *The Rediscovery of Mind*. Cambridge, MA: MIT Press.

Searle, J. R. (2004) *Mind: A Brief Introduction*. New York: Oxford University Press.

Searle, J. R. (1997) *The Mystery of Consciousness*. New York: The New York Review of Books.

Swinburne, R. (1994) *The Christian God*. Oxford: Oxford University Press.

Swinburne, R. (1997) *The Evolution of the Soul*. Oxford: Clarendon Press.

Swinburne, R. (2004) *The Existence of God*, 2nd edn. Oxford: Clarendon Press.

Taliaferro, C. (1994) *Consciousness and the Mind of God*. Cambridge: Cambridge University Press.

Taliaferro, C. (1997) Possibilities in the philosophy of mind. *Philosophy and Phenomenological Research* 57, 127–37.

Taliaferro, C. (1999) *Contemporary Philosophy of Religion*. Oxford: Basil Blackwell.

Taliaferro, C. (2001) Sensibility and possibilia: a defense of thought experiments. *Philosophia Christi* 3, 403–20.

Taliaferro, C. (2005) *Evidence and Faith*. Cambridge: Cambridge University Press.

Van Huyssteen J. W. V. (ed.) (2003) *Encyclopedia of Science and Religion*. New York: Macmillan.

Wainwright, W. J. (1981) *Mysticism: A Study of Its Nature, Cognitive Value and Moral Implications*. Madison: The University of Wisconsin Press.

Wierenga, E. R. (1989) *The Nature of God*. Ithaca, NY: Cornell University Press.

Yandell, K. E. (1993) *The Epistemology of Religious Experience*. Cambridge: Cambridge University Press.

2

The Leibnizian Cosmological Argument

ALEXANDER R. PRUSS

1. Introduction

A cosmological argument takes some cosmic feature of the universe – such as the existence of contingent things or the fact of motion – that calls out for an explanation and argues that this feature is to be explained in terms of the activity of a First Cause, which First Cause is God. A typical cosmological argument faces four different problems. If these problems are solved, the argument is successful.

The first problem is that although some features, such as the existence of contingent things, *call* for an explanation, it can be disputed whether an explanation exists. I shall call this the Glendower Problem in honor of the following exchange from Shakespeare's *Henry IV, Part 1*, Act III:

> Glendower: I can call spirits from the vasty deep.
> Hotspur: Why, so can I, or so can any man;
> But will they come when you do call for them?
> (Shakespeare 2000, p. 59)

A typical solution to the Glendower Problem involves a causal or explanatory principle, such as the claim that all things have causes or that all contingent facts possibly have explanations, together with an argument that the principle applies to the cosmic feature in question and implies the existence of an explanation for it.

The second issue that must be faced in defending a cosmological argument is the Regress Problem – the problem of how to deal with an infinite regress of causes or explanations. Hume stated that if we had an infinite regress of explanations, E_1 explained by E_2, E_3, E_4, and so on, then everything in the regress would be explained, even if there were no *ultimate* explanation positing some First Cause.

The third difficulty is the Taxicab Problem, coming from Schopenhauer's quip that in the cosmological argument, the Principle of Sufficient Reason (PSR) is like a taxicab that once used is sent away. The difficulty here is in answering what happens when the explanatory principle that was used to solve the Glendower Problem gets applied to the First Cause. A popular formulation is: "If God is the cause of the universe, what is the cause of God?" Typical solutions argue that the case of the First Cause is different in some way that is not merely *ad hoc* from the cases to which the explanatory principle was applied.

The final difficulty for cosmological arguments is the Gap Problem.[1] Granted there is a First Cause, but does anything of religious interest follow? There is a gap between the statements that there is a First Cause and that there is a God. Aquinas, in his Five Ways, proves the existence of an unmoved mover and then says: "*et hoc omnes intelligent Deum*" ("and all understand this to be God"). Some critics have taken this to be his way of papering over the difficulty of moving from a First Cause to God; however, that reading is mistaken in light of the fact that succeeding sections of the *Summa Theologiae* give careful and elaborate arguments that the First Cause is wholly actual, unchanging, simple, one, immaterial, perfect, good, and intelligent. Rather, Aquinas is simply marking the fact that the *theist* will recognize the unmoved mover to be God. Aquinas knows that an argument that the First Cause has, at least, some of the attributes of the God of Western monotheism is needed and offers such an argument.

The solutions to the Glendower and Regress problems tend to go hand in hand and, probably, the best way to classify cosmological arguments is by how they address these problems. There are then three basic kinds of cosmological arguments: *kalam*, Thomistic, and Leibnizian. The *kalam* and Thomistic arguments posit an intuitively plausible Causal Principle (CP) that says that every item of some sort – for example, event, contingent being, instance of coming-into-existence, or movement – has a cause. The arguments then split depending on how they handle the Regress Problem. The *kalam* argument proceeds by arguing, on *a priori* or *a posteriori* grounds, that the past is finite and hence, in fact, no infinite regress occurred. The Thomistic argument, exemplified by Aquinas' first three ways, does not rule out the possibility of an infinite past but uses a variety of methods to argue against the hypothesis that there is an infinite regress of causes with no First Cause. The most distinctive of these methods is an attempt to show that there is an intrinsic distinction between intermediate and nonintermediate causes, where an intermediate cause of *E* is an item *C* that is itself caused by something else to cause *E*, and that this distinction is such that intermediate causes are, of necessity, dependent for their causal activity on nonintermediate causes, which then end the regress.

Leibnizian arguments, on the other hand, invoke a very general explanatory principle, such as the PSR, which is then applied to the cosmos or to some vast cosmic state of affairs, or else a nonlocal CP that can be applied to an infinite chain or the universe as a whole. In the PSR-based versions, the Regress Problem is typically handled by showing that an infinite chain of causes with no First Cause fails to explain why the *whole chain* is there. The main challenge for Leibnizian arguments here is to argue for an explanatory principle or CP that is (a) plausible, (b) applicable to the cosmic state of affairs in question, and (c) not so strong as to lead to implausible conclusions such as the denial of contingency or of free will. In this chapter, I shall defend several Leibnizian arguments.

The basic Leibnizian argument has the following steps:

(1) Every contingent fact has an explanation.
(2) There is a contingent fact that includes all other contingent facts.
(3) Therefore, there is an explanation of this fact.

---

1. I got the term from Richard Gale.

(4)   This explanation must involve a necessary being.

(5)   This necessary being is God.

We shall see, however, that the first step, the assumption of the PSR, can be modified in various ways, with the resulting argument maintaining the distinctive feature of Leibnizian arguments that the relevant explanatory principle or CP is to be applied to a global state or proposition.

2. The PSR

2.1. The scope of the PSR

For simplicity, I shall stipulatively use the term "fact" for a true proposition. The PSR states that every fact, or every contingent fact, has an explanation, and this is the standard tool in Leibnizian arguments for handling the Glendower and Regress problems.

Some authors restrict the PSR to contingent facts. The advantage of a restriction to contingent facts is that we do not know very much about how the explanation of necessary truths works and, hence, may not be in a position to justify the PSR for necessary truths. To explain the Pythagorean Theorem, presumably, I should prove it from the axioms. But which proof counts as explanatory? Which axioms are the right ones to start from? Is there a fact of the matter here?

On the other hand, maybe the case of necessary facts is not a real worry, for it might be that any necessary truth p can be explained by citing its necessity: p holds because p necessarily holds. This leads into a regress since that p necessarily holds will also be a necessary truth by Axiom S4 of modal logic; but perhaps this regress is somehow to be distinguished from vicious ones.

Alternatively, the defender of an unrestricted PSR can say that while we do not yet know how the explanation of necessary truths works, we do know some cases of it. For instance, it might be that the proposition that $1 = 1$ is self-explanatory, namely explained by the very same proposition $1 = 1$, while the proposition that, necessarily, $1 = 1$ is explained by the proposition that $1 = 1$ together with the fact that mathematical truths are necessary truths. The necessary truth that all dogs are mammals, assuming this is indeed metaphysically necessary, is explained by the genetic similarity between dogs and the first mammals, together with some necessary truths about how biological classification works. The necessary truth that making false promises is wrong might be explained by the fact that falsely promising treats the promisee as a mere means. In other words, while we have no general account of the explanation of necessary truths, we do have many examples. And, anyway, the requirement that we have a general account of explanation would also be a problem for a PSR restricted to contingent propositions, since it is not clear that we yet have a general account of explanation of contingent propositions, although we have many clear examples.

2.2. Why should we believe the PSR?

2.2.1. Self-evidence

Many of those who accept the PSR do so unreflectively because they take the PSR to be self-evident. I do not think that there is any good argument against the propriety of doing so. We are perfectly within our epistemic rights to accept the Law of Excluded Middle (LEM), namely the claim that for all p we have p or not-p, because of the self-evidence of LEM, without needing any further argument for it. However, it will be of no use to opponents of the PSR or of the LEM to be told that the claim they deny is self-evident to us. Presumably, the claim is not self-evident to them, and we can all agree that there are many things that people have *claimed* to be self-evident that, in fact, are false, so the fact that the claim is said by us to be self-evident does not provide these opponents with much reason to accept it. There may be a presumption that what people take to be self-evident is, in fact, more likely true than not, but this presumption is often easily defeated.

One might think that philosophical disagreement about the PSR shows that the PSR is *not* self-evident, or at least that those of us who take it as self-evident should not see this as providing any reason to believe it to be true. Otherwise, how could competent philosophers such as David Hume or Graham Oppy fail to see it as self-evident? Or, worse, how is it that some of these philosophers take as self-evident claims *incompatible* with the PSR?

If we think we should accept the LEM because of its self-evidence despite some brilliant intuitionist mathematicians' denials of it, we will be unimpressed by this argument. And it is not clear on what grounds we could accept the LEM other than self-evidence. Is there some inductive argument like: "For many propositions p, we have concluded that the LEM holds. Hence, the LEM holds for all propositions p"? I doubt it. The problem is that an inductive argument of the form "Many Fs are Gs, thus all Fs are Gs" is epistemically close to worthless by itself. Many dogs are spotted, thus all dogs are spotted? We would do slightly better if we could show that most Fs are Gs, although even that would be very weak ("Most humans are female, thus all humans are female"). But how would we check that the LEM holds for most propositions? To check that the LEM holds for a proposition is, presumably, to determine that this proposition is true or to determine that this proposition is false, since in either case, the truth of the LEM follows for the proposition. But most propositions are such that we cannot determine whether they are true or false.

In any case, the argument from philosophical disagreement is weak. It might be that our judgment as to what is or is not self-evident is fallible, and Hume and Oppy have simply judged wrongly. Or it might be that it is possible to be talked out of seeing something as self-evident, just as it is possible to be (rightly or wrongly) talked out of all sorts of commonsensical beliefs. Finally, it could be that the PSR's opponents have failed to grasp one or more of the concepts in it due to their substantive philosophical positions. Thus, Hume's equating constant conjunction with causation suggests that he does not have the same concept of causation as I do – that he is talking of something different – and the fact that he thinks causation *thus understood* yields explanations, as well as his belief that infinite regresses can be explanatory, show that his concept of explanation is different from mine. Differences in views of modality are also relevant. As a result, it is far from clear to me that Hume has even grasped the PSR in the sense that I assign to it. And if not, then his failure to see it as self-evident is irrelevant.

I can give a similar story about Hume's seeing as self-evident propositions that are incompatible with the PSR, such as that no being's existence is necessary.[2] Hume's concept of the necessity of p is that a contradiction can be proved from the denial of p. If LEM is

---

2. This is incompatible with the PSR, given the other ingredients in the cosmological argument.

true, this is equivalent to equating necessity with provability. But defenders of the Leibnizian cosmological argument typically use a notion of *broadly logical* necessity when they claim that God is a necessary being, and broadly logical necessity is weaker than provability.

At this point, it may seem as if the defense of the self-evidence of the PSR destroys all possibility of philosophical communication. If philosophers all mean different things by the same terms, how can they even disagree with one another? Two points can be made here. The first is that in many cases, when philosophers use a word such as "cause," they *both* mean by it what ordinary language does *and* they have an account of what the word says which they think is faithful to the ordinary meaning. And if this is true, then when one philosopher says "A causes B" and the other says "A does not cause B," there is a genuine disagreement between them even if their analyses of causation are different, since the first philosopher holds that A causes B in the ordinary English sense of "causes" (which he rightly or wrongly thinks is identical with his analysis of the term) and the second denies this. Second, disagreement is possible because even though philosophers may use the term "causes" differently, they will tend to agree on some entailments, such as that if A causes B, then both A and B occurred and B's occurrence can be explained, at least in part, in terms of A's occurrence. So differences in meaning do not undercut philosophical communication, but they seriously damage the argument against self-evidence.

Self-evidence might well give those of us to whom the PSR is self-evident a good reason to believe it. But if we want to convince others, we need arguments.

2.2.2. The epistemological argument

This argument is based on the ideas of Robert Koons (1997), although I am simplifying it. Starting with the observation that once we admit that some contingent states of affairs have no explanations, a completely new skeptical scenario becomes possible: no demon is deceiving you, but your perceptual states are occurring for no reason at all, with no prior causes.

Moreover, objective probabilities are tied to laws of nature or objective tendencies, and so if an objective probability attaches to some contingent fact, then that situation can be given an explanation in terms of laws of nature or objective tendencies. Hence, if the PSR is false of some contingent fact, no objective probability attaches to the fact.

Thus, we cannot even say that violations of the PSR are improbable if the PSR is false. Consequently, someone who does not affirm the PSR cannot say that Koons' skeptical scenario is objectively improbable. It may be taken to follow from this that if the PSR were false or maybe even not known *a priori*, we would not know any empirical truths. But we do know empirical truths. Hence, the PSR is true, and maybe even known *a priori*.

2.2.3. Evolution

One of my graduate students suggested in discussion that if one rejects the PSR, our knowledge of evolution may be undercut. We can use this insight to generate an *ad hominem* argument for the PSR. Most atheists and agnostics (and many theists as well, but it is to atheists and agnostics that the argument is addressed) believe that there is a complete naturalistic evolutionary explanation of the development of the human species from a single-celled organism. I claim that they are not justified in believing this if they do not accept the PSR.

For consider what could be the argument for thinking that there is such an explanation. We might first try an inductive argument. Some features of some organisms can be given naturalistic evolutionary explanations. Therefore, all features of all organisms can be given naturalistic evolutionary explanations. But this argument is as bad as inductive arguments can come. The error in the argument is that we are reasoning from a biased sample, namely those features for which we already have found an explanation. Such features are only a small portion of the features of organisms in nature – as is always the case in science, what we do not know far exceeds what we know.

Once we admit the selection bias, the argument becomes this: "all the features of organisms for which we know the explanation can be explained through naturalistic evolutionary means, and so all the features of organisms can be explained through naturalistic evolutionary means." There are at least two things wrong with this argument. The first is that it might just be that naturalistic explanations are easier to find than nonnaturalistic ones; hence, it is no surprise that we first found those explanations that are naturalistic. But even if one could get around this objection, it would not obviate the need for the PSR. For the argument, at most, gives us reason to accept the claim that those features *that have explanations* have naturalistic evolutionary explanations. The inductive data is that all the explanations of biological features that we have found are naturalistic and evolutionary. The only conclusion that can be drawn without the PSR is that all the explanations of biological features *that there are* are naturalistic and evolutionary, not that all biological features have naturalistic evolutionary explanations.

A different approach would be to suppose that natural occurrences have naturalistic explanations, and evolution is the only naturalistic form of explanation of biological features that we know of; therefore, it is likely that the development of the human race has a naturalistic evolutionary explanation. But what plausibility is there in the claim that natural occurrences have naturalistic explanations if one does not accept the PSR for contingent propositions? After all, if it is possible for contingent propositions to simply fail to have an explanation, what reason do we have for confidence that, at least, those contingent propositions that report natural occurrences have explanations? If "natural occurrence" is taken as *entailing* the existence of a naturalistic explanation, the argument for an evolutionary explanation of the development of the human race begs the question in its assumption that the development was a natural occurrence. But if "natural occurrence" is taken more weakly as a physical event or process, whether or not it has a natural explanation, then the naturalness of the occurrence does not give us reason to think that the occurrence has an explanation, much less a naturalistic one, absent the PSR. If we had the PSR in play, we could at least try to use a principle, perhaps defeasible, that the cause is ontologically like the effect, so that if the effect is natural, the cause is likely such as well. (It is interesting that this principle itself could be useful to theists with respect to the Gap Problem – see the perfection axiom in Section 5.4.)

Consider a final way to justify the evolutionary claim. We have good inductive reason to think that everything physical obeys the laws of physics. But everything that is governed by the laws of physics has a naturalistic explanation. Hence, the development of the human race has a naturalistic explanation, and an evolutionary one is the best candidate we have.

The claim that everything that obeys the laws of physics has a naturalistic explanation, however, has not been justified. The claim was more plausible back when we thought that everything could be explained in a Newtonian manner, but even then the claim could be falsified. Consider John Norton's (2003) ball-on-dome example. We have a rigid dome, on the exact top of which there sits a perfectly round ball, and the dome is in a constant downward gravitational field of acceleration g. The dome is rotationally symmetric, and its height as a function of the distance r from its central axis is $h = (2/3g)r^{3/2}$. It turns out to be consistent with Newtonian physics that the ball should either remain still at the top of the dome or start to roll down in any direction whatsoever, in the absence of any external forces. One might wonder how this squares with Newton's second law – how there could be an acceleration without an external force. It turns out, however, that because of the shape of the dome, in the first instant of the ball's movement, its acceleration would be zero, and after that it would have an acceleration given by the gravitational force. The physics would fail to explain the ball's standing still at the top of the dome or the ball's moving in one direction or another; it would fail to explain this either deterministically or stochastically. Thus, even Newtonian physics is not sufficient to yield the claim that every-thing that obeys the laws of physics can be explained in terms of the laws of physics.

And I doubt we do any better with non-Newtonian physics. After all, we do not actually right now know *what* the correct physics is going to be, and in particular we do not know whether the correct physics will make true the claim that everything that obeys the laws of physics can be explained in terms of the laws of physics. Besides, surely it would be an implausible claim that justification for the claim that the human race developed through evolutionary means depends on speculation about what the final physics will be like.

I do not have an argument that there is no other way of arguing for the evolutionary claim absent the PSR. But, intuitively, if one were not confident of something very much like the PSR, it would be hard to be justifiably confident that no biological features of the human species arose *for no reason at all* – say, that an ape walked into a swamp, and out walked a human, with no explanation of why.

2.2.4. Inference to best explanation

Suppose we have a phenomenon and several plausible explanations. We then reasonably assume that the best of these explanations is probably the right one, at least if it is signifi-cantly better than the runner-up. How we measure the goodness of an explanation is, of course, controverted: prior probability, simplicity, explanatory power, and so on are all candidates. Or, if we have ruled out all explanations but one, we take the remaining one to be true (White 1979) – this is what the maxim that "when you have eliminated the impossible, whatever remains, *however improbable*, must be the truth" comes down to in Sherlock Holmes's actual practice (Doyle 1890, p. 93; italics in the original).

But suppose we admit, contrary to the PSR, the possibility that the phenomenon has no explanation at all. What reason do we have to suppose that the best or the only explana-tion is likely to be true? To argue for that explanation, we compared it with its competitors. But the hypothesis that the phenomenon has no explanation at all was not one of these competitors. Indeed, we do not know how to compare this hypothesis with its competitors. The hypothesis that there is no explanation is, in one sense, simpler than any explanatory explanation. On the other hand, it altogether lacks explanatory power. Still, it is unfair to rule it out just because it lacks explanatory power unless one believes in the PSR.

Perhaps the no-explanation hypothesis can be ruled out, not because it is impossible, as the defender of the PSR will say, but because it is simply less probable than its competitors. But does it make any sense to assign a *probability* to the hypothesis that a brick comes to exist *ex nihilo* in midair in front of us for no reason at all, assuming this is possible? We certainly cannot assign a probability grounded in the laws of nature to a brick's coming into existence *ex nihilo*, in the way in which we can to the electron's moving upwards in the Stern–Gerlach experiment, since the brick's entry into existence would arguably not be governed by the laws if it happens "for no reason at all."

But maybe we can argue that such an arising *ex nihilo* is impossible, since it is contrary to the laws. However, the laws of nature only specify what happens in the absence of external influence. They do not, thus, exclude the possibility of a brick coming into existence by the power of a nonphysical being, say, God. But if the PSR does not hold, intuitively any laws that do not preclude the possibility of a brick coming into existence by the power of a nonphysical being should not exclude the possibility of the brick coming into existence *ex nihilo*. The possibility of a nonphysical being's producing such a brick shows that there is no innate contradiction between the brick's coming into existence and there being such-and-such laws of nature. And it would be odd indeed if the laws of nature entailed that any bricks that come into existence should have causes of some sort or other, *whether natural or not*. Furthermore, if my argument is taken seriously, then we may not have good reason to believe in the laws of nature in the first place (without the PSR, that is) – for the phenomena that we tried to explain in terms of them might just be lacking in explanation.

Suppose, however, that we grant that the laws of nature exist and entail that physical events have causes, natural or not, but continue to balk at the full PSR because we are not sure whether nonphysical facts have to have explanations. Then, at least on probabilistic grounds, we cannot exclude the following explanatory hypothesis, available for any phenomenon *F*: there came into existence, *ex nihilo* and for no reason at all, a nonphysical being whose only basic nonformal property was the disposition to cause *F* as soon as the being is in existence, a property that the being has essentially, and this being came into existence for precisely the amount of time needed for the activation of this disposition. Why did Jones fall asleep? Because a nonphysical being came into existence for no reason at all, a being characterized by an essential *dispositio dormitiva* and by nothing else. No nomic probabilities can be assigned to the hypothesis of such a nonphysical being's coming into existence. (It might be that there is some argument available that only God can create *ex nihilo*, and so such a being cannot create a brick *ex nihilo*. Fine, but at least it should be able to create it out of air.)

One might try to assign nonnomic probabilities to the no-explanation hypothesis and the hypothesis of *ex nihilo* creation by a nonnatural being. But then, the no-explanation hypothesis would be on par with each explanatory explanation. And there would be an infinitude of explanatory hypotheses in terms of nonnatural beings that came into existence *ex nihilo*, for we could suppose that, in addition to the disposition to cause *F*, they do have some other essential property (say, being happy or being beautiful), and they differ in respect of it. Why would we take a "normal" scientific explanation over one of these, then?

It is tempting here to say: "Well, we don't know anything either way about the likelihoods of these weird hypotheses that contradict the PSR. So we should just dismiss them all." As practical advice for doing our best in finding predictions, this may be fine. But if we are to hope for scientific *knowledge*, that surely will not do. A *complete* inability to estimate the likelihood of an alternate hypothesis is surely a serious problem.

It is easy not to take these odd hypotheses seriously. And that may well be because we do, in fact, have a deep commitment to the PSR and maybe even to a defeasible principle that causes have a resemblance to their effects. If I am right, the PSR is essential to the practice of science, even outside of evolutionary biology.

2.2.5. Why aren't there widespread violations of the PSR all around?

If the PSR were false, we would expect a profusion of events that would not appear to fit into any kind of nomic causal order. After all, for each way that things could go in accordance with the laws of nature, there is an uncountable infinity of ways – of arbitrary cardinality – that things could, for no reason at all, go contrary to the laws of nature. For instance, if we deny the PSR, then for no reason at all, a cloud of photons, $\aleph_{9314}$ in number, could suddenly appear *ex nihilo* just near the moon, heading for San Francisco. (Because the cardinality is so high, some of the photons would have to share the same quantum state; but photons are bosons, so they should be able to do that.) And the number of ways such things could happen seems to have no limit if the PSR fails. Or perhaps, $\aleph_{9314}$ nonnatural beings could come into existence, each of which could then produce one photon.

Our empirical observations suggest that the probability of such events is very low. On the other hand, if we get our probabilities *a priori* from some sort of principle of indifference, supposing all arrangements to be equally likely, the messy PSR-violating arrangements would seem much more probable. How to explain the fact that bricks and photon clouds do not show up in the air for no discernible reason? I suggest that the best explanation is that the PSR holds, and that whatever beings there may be (e.g. God) who are capable of causing bricks and photon clouds to show up in the air for no discernible reason are, in fact, disposed not to do so. We need both parts for the explanation: without the PSR, the possibility of this happening for no reason at all would be impossible to rule out, and without the claim that existing beings are unlikely to cause it, the PSR would be insufficient (this suggests that if the cosmological argument can establish the existence of a First Cause, there is reason to think that the First Cause has a predilection for order, a fact relevant to the Gap Problem).

It may seem that I am caught in a vicious circularity here. I have produced a phenomenon – the lack of weird, apparently causeless, events – and have suggested that its explanation needs to involve the PSR. But am I not invoking the PSR in supposing that there is an explanation here? No. I am only invoking inference to best, or only, explanation, an ampliative principle that we should all accept. Nor am I applying this principle to some strange fact such as the conjunction of all contingent states of affairs. I am applying the principle to the homely fact that bricks and photon clouds do not show up in the air *ex nihilo*. And the best explanation of this fact is that they, simply, cannot do that, absent some cause, and that there does not, in fact, exist a cause likely to produce such effects.

One might think that some physical law, say, a conservation law, would do the explanatory work here, a principle other than the PSR. But the logical possibility of miracles shows that it should be possible for a supernatural being to cause photon clouds to show up *ex nihilo*, and if the PSR is false, such supernatural beings could be coming into existence all the time, causing the weird effects. Our best explanation for why *this* is not happening is that there is nothing in existence that would be likely to cause such supernatural beings to come into existence, and by the PSR they cannot come into existence uncaused.

2.2.6. An argument from the nature of modality

2.2.6.1. Alethic modality

Alethic modality is a deeply puzzling phenomenon. Whence comes the difference between a golden mountain and a square circle? Why is it necessary that $2 + 2 = 4$, but merely contingent that horses exist? I could become a biologist, but I could never be a number or a point in space. What makes that so?

The question here is as to the ground of truth of these kinds of facts. I am not asking the explanatory question of *why* these facts obtain. That is easy to find in at least some cases. A square circle is contradictory, for instance, and had evolution gone somewhat differently, the niche occupied by horses would have been occupied by medium-sized and fast reptiles. But what features of reality make these alethic modal facts hold?

Five main kinds of nonrevisionist theories have been offered here: narrowly logical, Lewisian, Platonic, Aristotelian-essentialist, and Aristotelian-causal. The first three will be seen to be unsatisfactory, and only the Aristotelian theories will remain. Of these, the Aristotelian-essentialist account will have some serious problems with it and, moreover, seems to require theism, so the agnostic or atheist cannot embrace it as an alternative to the Aristotelian-causal one. The remaining theory, the Aristotelian-causal one, turns out to entail a PSR sufficiently strong to run a cosmological argument, given some plausible auxiliary assumptions. Hence, we should accept the PSR, unless we have a better account of alethic modality.

I shall now argue for the unsatisfactoriness of the first four theories. I have no argument that there is no better story possible than the Aristotelian-causal one. But until a good competitor is found, we should accept this account, and hence the PSR.

2.2.6.2. Narrowly logical account of modality

In a number of other early modern thinkers, we have the following "narrowly logical" account of modality, probably best developed in Leibniz. A proposition p is necessary if and only if a contradiction can be proved from its negation. Assuming classical logic, as these thinkers did, it follows that *necessity* is equivalent to *provability*. And a proposition is possible if and only if no contradiction can be proved from it.

There are counterexamples to this account.

First, we learn from Gödel that for any axiomatization within our reach (any set of axioms we can generate recursively), there will be truths of arithmetic that we cannot prove from the axiomatization. On the narrowly logical account, thus, there are contingent truths of arithmetic. This seems absurd. (For one, what kind of truthmakers would they have?)

Second, necessarily, all horses are mammals. But this is an empirical discovery. We cannot *prove* it by narrowly logical means. *A posteriori* necessities such as this provide a large family of counterexamples.

Third, it is impossible for anything to cause itself. (If, like Descartes, you disagree, choose another example – maybe, the claim that it is necessarily possible for something to cause itself.) But how would we go about proving this? We might start with some partial analysis of causation. Perhaps a cause has to temporally precede the effect (a dubious thesis in my opinion, but what I say will apply to any story we could fill in here). And nothing can temporally precede itself. But how could we *prove* that a cause has to temporally precede the effect, and how do we prove that nothing can temporally precede itself?

In two ways, I suppose. First, we might derive these claims from some *definitions*, say of causation or temporal priority. But, leaving aside the somewhat implausible suggestion that "causation" and "temporal priority" can *both* be defined, how do we *prove* that this definition is in fact the right way to define the terms? To show that a definition is correct is beyond the powers of logic narrowly conceived, unless the definitions are stipulative, in which case the proof is trivial. But a stipulative route is unsatisfactory for two reasons. First, the claim that nothing can cause itself is *not* just a claim involving a stipulative concept of "cause." Second, even if I have a stipulative definition, I need the principle that if D is stipulatively defined as E (where E is some linguistic expression), then necessarily anything that satisfies D satisfies E. But what grounds the latter necessity? If I say that I can prove it from the definition of "stipulated," then I go around in a circle – for either the definition of "stipulative" is nonstipulative, in which case it seems we need to go beyond logic narrowly conceived to prove the definition of "stipulative" correct, or else we have a stipulative definition of "stipulative," and to prove that anything that satisfies D *must* satisfy E whenever E is the stipulative definition of D, I need to know that, necessarily, whatever is stipulative has the properties in terms of which the word has been defined.

So the stipulative route to proving that nothing can cause itself will not work. The only other route is that among our *axioms* there are substantive axioms about the nature of causation or that there are substantive *rules of inference* in our logic. Without such axioms or rules of inference, we get nowhere when dealing with a nonstipulative concept. But now note that any axiom gets to be necessary *for free* on the narrowly logical account. So what would it be that would make it be the case that among our axioms is the claim that, say, *causes temporally precede their effects*, or whatever other truth it would be from which we were going to prove that nothing can cause itself, while the equally true claim that *there are horses* is not among the axioms? The intuitive answer is that the claim about causation is more plausibly a necessary truth, while the claim about horses is plainly contingent; but that would be viciously circular. Similarly, if there are substantive rules of inference in our logic, say, ones that allow us to infer from *x causes y* and *y causes z* that *x is not identical with z*, the question of what makes these but not other substantive rules of inference (say, the rule that one can derive *there are horses* from every statement) appropriate is equally problematic as the question of what gets to count as an axiom.

And so the narrowly logical account is of little help – a part of what makes a proposition an axiom seems to be that it is necessary, and a part of what makes a proposition be a rule of inference is that it embodies a necessary implication. Moreover, the necessity here is the same sort of necessity we were trying to explicate, so there is really very little gain. Alethic modality remains ungrounded.

Our last example has shown the general problem with narrowly logical accounts of modality: the grounding burden simply shifts to the question of the choice of the axioms and/or rules of inference and that question we cannot answer with the resources of the view in question.

An early modern answer one might try is this: we take as axioms all and only the claims that are clear and distinct. An anachronistic objection is that this does not solve the Gödelian problem. A counterexample-based answer is that the claim that I exist seems to be as clear and distinct as anything can be, and yet is contingent. Moreover, plausibly, there are necessary truths that are far beyond our ken and cannot be derived from clear and distinct truths within our ken. (If we assume the existence of God, this is very plausible: there surely are many such facts about him.) Besides, we no longer have much of a handle on the notion of clear and distinct claims, and to use them to ground necessity would be to confuse facts about our doxastic faculties with metaphysics.

The narrowly logical view is distinctly unsatisfactory. Let us thus continue our brief survey.

2.2.6.3. Lewisian account of modality

The Lewisian account, also known as Extreme Modal Realism (EMR), says that a proposition is possible if and only if it holds in some possible world, and necessary if and only if it holds in all possible worlds. This is only going to be of help if we have an independent account of possible worlds, and indeed EMR supplies one. A possible world is a maximal spatiotemporally interconnected aggregate of things. (We can also stipulate that abstract entities count as existing in every world.) We live in one of these worlds, the *actual* world, and there are infinitely many others. Every way that things could have been is a way that things are in some world. We then make a distinction between *existence* and *actuality*. Something *exists* provided it exists in some world or other. Something is *actual* provided it exists in the actual world.

EMR has a number of problematic consequences. For instance, if EMR holds, consequentialistic moral reasoning breaks down completely because no matter what I do, the overall consequences in reality are the same, since reality always already contains all possible worlds. Lewis thinks that we can restrict our concern to those who exist in our world and only count what happens to them as relevant. But this neglects the importance of overall consequences. Even deontologists need consequentialistic moral reasoning. If I am to give money to one of two charities, and everything is otherwise morally on par, I should choose the one giving to which will produce better consequences.

Lewis, however, thinks that what matters ethically is not just the consequences but that *I have produced them* (Lewis 1986, p. 127). I cannot affect what happens in other worlds, but I can be the cause of goods in our world. Of course, this makes no difference in the space of all possible worlds – in infinitely many of them, people very much like me are causes of goods and in infinitely many of them, people very much like me are not causes of goods, and the distribution of worlds is not affected by my action. But my relationship to the goods *is* affected.

However, this unacceptably reduces the moral weight of consequences. Suppose that either you or I can operate on a patient. The operation is perfectly safe, but I am better than you at this particular operation, and so the patient will recover somewhat faster after the surgery if I do it. I thus have good reason, when we are deciding which of us will perform the operation, to volunteer to do it. And if I do perform the operation, then I additionally gain the agent-centered good of *my* being the cause of the patient's improvement. However, the latter consideration is surely of very little moral weight. After all, the same kind of consideration would also give you reason to do the surgery, but this consideration should be trumped by the good of the patient. Even if my skill at this operation is only *slightly* better than yours, so that the patient will likely recover *slightly* better, all other things being equal this fact should trump your reason to be the cause of the patient's improvement. Thus, the agent-centered reason of wanting to be the cause of good is, in a case like this, of very low weight – the consequences are the *main* consideration.

This is not so in every case. When there is a close relationship between me and someone else, then it may matter very much that I be the one to benefit that person. However, when there is no particularly morally important relationship – and merely being spatiotemporally connected is very low on the scale of moral importance – it should not matter or at least matter much.

On Lewis's view, however, my reason to help strangers is *only* the agent-centered reason to be the cause of goods because the consequences are always the same. But since the agent-centered reason to be the cause of goods has extremely low weight, it follows that EMR radically lowers the weight of reasons to help strangers. If we accept a more traditional assessment of the weight of these reasons, we shall have to reject EMR.

Instead of cataloging further problems entailed by EMR, I shall give what I take to be one of the deepest criticisms, which I believe is due to van Inwagen. The criticism is simply that the existence of infinitely many maximally spatiotemporally interconnected aggregates has nothing to do with modality. If we found out that reality contains infinitely many maximally spatiotemporally interconnected aggregates, we would simply have learned that the *actual* world is richer than we thought – that it contains all of these island universes – rather than learning something about the space of possibilities.

Here is a variant on the objection. Suppose that there exist infinitely many maximally spatiotemporally interconnected aggregates, and some of them contain golden mountains but none contains unicorns.[3] It would follow that golden mountains are possible, simply because what is actual is also possible, but surely it would not follow from this fact that unicorns are impossible. And if there were only *one* spatiotemporally interconnected aggregate, namely ours, it would not follow that modal fatalism is true – that every actual truth is necessary. Yet on Lewis's view, if no unicorns were found in any island universe, it would follow that unicorns are impossible, and if there were only one island universe, it would follow that every actual truth is necessary since things could not be otherwise than they are then.

Now Lewis, of course, thought there was more than one universe, and indeed that there was a universe that contained unicorns. He believed this because he accepted a recombination principle that said that one can cut up the ingredients of one world and rearrange them in any geometrically available way, and the resulting rearrangement would be exemplified in some world or other. However, while he accepted the recombination principle, the recombination principle is not, on his view, a part of what makes alethic modal claims true. What makes alethic modal claims true on his view are just the facts about universes, and we have seen that that is not correct.

We should thus reject EMR and keep on searching for a good account of modality.

2.2.6.4. *Platonic account of modality*

The most promising contemporary realist alternative to Lewis's account of possible worlds are the abstract worlds accounts promoted by Robert M. Adams (1974) and Alvin Plantinga (1974). On their accounts, worlds turn out to be abstract Platonic entities, exactly one of which is instantiated by the universe, where "the universe" is defined to be the aggregate of all existing or occurring concrete entities, and this is the world that is absolutely actual. I will focus primarily on the Adams permutation of this account.

---

3. To avoid Kripkean worries as to what precise species a unicorn would belong to, we can stipulatively define a unicorn as any horselike mammal with one horn.

We thus start off by introducing *propositions* as theoretical abstract entities that are the bearers of truth-values and are needed to explain what it is that sentences express, what the objects of beliefs and propositional attitudes are, and what paraphrases preserve, somewhat as electrons are needed to explain various physical phenomena. Some propositions, namely the true ones, are related to things and events in the universe, with the relation being one of the propositions *being made true by* or *representing* these things and events in the universe. If things in the universe were otherwise than they are, then different propositions would stand in these relations to things in the universe – if there were unicorns, then the proposition that there are unicorns would stand in the relation of *being made true by* to some things, namely, the unicorns in the universe.[4]

Note that the theoretical reason for believing in these Platonic propositions is largely independent of issues of modality. Adams then constructs a possible world as a maximal consistent collection of propositions. (An argument is needed that such collections exist, but let that pass.) Exactly one world is then absolutely actual: it is the one all of whose propositions are true. A proposition can be said to be true *at* a world, providing it is one of the propositions that are members of the collection of propositions that the world is identical with. Note that because the worlds are Platonic entities, I had to distinguish between the concrete *universe*, which we physically inhabit, and the actual *world*, which is the collection of all true propositions.

One might object to the Platonic approaches on the grounds that they all involve queer entities. Not only are we required to believe in Platonic beings, but, as Lewis notes, we are to believe that there is a magical relation of representation holding between Platonic beings such as propositions and the concrete entities that make them true, with it being contingent which propositions enter into those relations since it is contingent which propositions are true. What is it, then, that picks out one relation in the Platonic heaven rather than another as *the* relation of representation?

The proponents of these Platonic worlds can argue, however, that they have no need to answer this question. The relation of representation is one of the primitive terms in their theory, and it is not a primitive chosen *ad hoc* to explain possible worlds but a primitive needed for other explanatory purposes, such as for making sense of our practices of claiming, believing, and paraphrasing. Nonetheless, if we had some way of pointing out this relation within the Platonic universe of all relations, we would be happier as theorists.

These Platonic theories are expressly nonreductive as accounts of possibility, unlike Lewis's theory. For Adams, a possible world is a maximal consistent collection of propositions, which is just the same as saying it is a maximal *compossible* collection of propositions. On this theory, there is a primitive abstract property of possibility or consistency that applies to individual propositions and to collections of them. One could also take necessity to be the primitive concept, but this would not change anything substantially.

That the Platonic accounts are nonreductive is only a problem if a reductive account of possibility is available. However, the most plausible account claiming to be reductive is Lewis's, which is too paradoxical to accept. But while a complete reduction is probably impossible, it could be desirable to give at least a partial reduction, on which the whole realm of

---

4. Lewis (1986) worries that the relation between the propositions and the things they are about is magical, but as van Inwagen (1986) notes, it is no more magical (although no less) than the relation between sets and their members, a relation that Lewis accepts.

alethic possibility would be seen to have its root in some more comprehensible subclass. An example of an otherwise implausible theory that would provide such a reduction would be an account on which a proposition is possible if and only if Alvin Plantinga could conceive its being true: all of modality would then be reduced to Alvin Plantinga's considerable powers of imagination. Claims about Plantinga's powers are still modal claims, but of a more comprehensible sort than claims about the possibilities of unicorns and zombies. However, these Platonic accounts do not succeed in performing this more limited reduction either.

Adams's theory is an *actualist* one. His possible worlds are built up out of things that are actual. These abstracta actually exist – indeed, necessarily so – and an actualist theory is one that grounds possibility in actually existent realities. On the other hand, Lewis's other worlds are not actual entities by Lewis's indexical criterion, as they are not the world in which my tokening of the word "actual" in this sentence occurred. If we think of possible worlds as possibilities for our universe, then there is a sense in which Adams and Plantinga have grounded possibilities in actuality, thereby answering to the Aristotelian maxim that actuality is prior to possibility.

However, in a deeper way, the Platonic approach is not faithful to what the Aristotelian maxim affirms. When Aristotelians say that a possibility is grounded in an actuality, they mean that actuality includes some powers, capacities, or dispositions capable of producing that possibility, which of course once produced would no longer be a mere possibility. This is clearest in the paradigm case where the actuality is temporally prior to the possibility. Aristotle's favorite illustration is how the actuality of one man makes possible the existence of a future man through the first man's capability for begetting a descendant. If we find attractive the idea that possibilities should be grounded in actuality in the stronger Aristotelian sense, then the Platonic approach will be unsatisfactory because Platonic entities, in virtue of their abstractness, are usually taken to be categorially barred from entering into causal relations, and hence cannot make possibilities possible by being capable of producing them. And if they make possibilities possible by being capable of producing them, then what we have is a variant on the Aristotelian-causal account.

Moreover, an Aristotelian can argue that in fact there *are* capabilities and dispositions sufficient to ground the truth of at least *some* possibility claims. That I could have been a biologist is very plausibly made true by my capacities and dispositions and those of various persons and things in my environment. These capacities and dispositions are concrete real-worldly things, albeit ones having modal force. Hence, in fact, we do not need a Platonic realm to make at least some possibility claims true. Indeed, the facts about the Platonic realm – about propositions' having or not having some primitive property – are interlopers here. Just as the statement that I could have been a biologist was not made true by what my Lewisian counterparts in other worlds do, so too it is not made true by abstract properties of Platonic abstracta. The common intuition behind both cases is that it is something in me and my concrete environment that makes the statement true.

This, however, creates a major problem for the Platonic approach. On the Platonic approach, what makes it possible that I have been a biologist is that the abstract proposition (an entity in the Platonic heaven) *that I have been a biologist* has the abstract property of possibility. But we have just seen that there are concrete capacities and dispositions in the universe that are by themselves sufficient to make it possible that I have been a biologist. We thus have two different ways of characterizing possibility: one is via the concrete this-worldly Aristotelian properties of concreta, which really do exist – the Platonist should not deny this – and the other is via the abstract Platonic primitive properties of abstracta.

Moreover, anything that is possible on Aristotelian grounds will be physically possible, and hence also logically possible, and thus possible on Platonist grounds (though *prima facie* perhaps not conversely). But now we can ask: Why is this so? Why is there this apparent coincidence that anything made possible by this-worldly powers and capacities and dispositions happens to correspond to a proposition in the Platonic realm that has a certain abstract property? The Platonist is unable to explain this coincidence between powers in our universe and abstract facts about the Platonic realm, given the lack of causal interaction between the two realms.

2.2.6.5. *Aristotelian-essentialist account of modality*

Aristotle's own account of modality seems to have been based on the idea that a sentence is necessarily true if and only if it holds always. Then, a sentence is possibly true if it holds at some time. I shall not consider this account further. It is not clear that in characterizing "necessarily" in this way, one is really talking of the same thing as we are when we say that *necessarily* there are no square circles. We certainly mean more by saying that there can be no square circle than that just that there have never been, nor are, nor ever will be any square circles. Granted, if we adopt some kind of principle of variety, on which given infinite time every possibility is realized, we might get out of this Aristotelian story an account that is extensionally acceptable. However, that account would still face many of the same problems Lewis's account faces – indeed, it would be just like Lewis's account, but with time-slices replacing universes. In particular, the objection that we are not talking about modality at all would be to the point. If it should turn out that the past, present, and future of our world contain no golden mountains, that would say nothing about whether golden mountains are possible.

But while Aristotle's own account of modality was flawed, two somewhat different accounts have been derived from ingredients of Aristotelian ontology. One of these grounds modality in the *essences* of things and takes necessity to be the primitive notion. The other account grounds modality in *causal powers* and takes *possibility* to be more primitive. I shall begin by discussing the account based on essences (cf. O'Connor 2008).

Things that exist have essences. These essences, on this account, constrain what properties these things can have. Thus, a horse cannot be immaterial, and a dog cannot become a cat. A proposition is impossible provided that it affirms something contrary to the essences of things.

There are several objections to this rough sketch of a view. First, maybe it is plausible that the essence of a horse encodes that a horse must occupy space. But what makes it necessary that horses must occupy space or be green? Do we really want to suppose that for every property *P*, the essence of a horse contains in itself the specification that a horse occupies space or has *P*? An affirmative answer appears implausible. Why should the essence of a horse include the specification that horses occupy space or are cats?

This objection is not just an incredulous stare. Horses could surely exist without any cats in existence. But the essence of a horse, on this view, in some way presupposes catness. It follows that it makes sense to talk of catness – the essence of cats – apart from cats, since horses could exist apart from cats, and hence the essence of a horse could exist apart from cats. The Aristotelian, however, cannot tolerate this, *unless* the Aristotelian is a theistic Aristotelian who accepts that all essences have some kind of an existence in the mind of God. Thus, unless one accepts theism, the theory seems to be unsatisfactory.

But maybe I was too fast. Perhaps it is not that the essence of a horse contains all the necessary truths about horses, but that all the necessary truths about horses can be *derived* from the essence of a horse as combined with all other essences there are. That every horse occupies space or is a cat can be derived from the essence of a horse and the essence of a cat.

But "derived" surely means "logically derived." And so it turns out that the Aristotelian-essentialist needs elements of the narrowly logical view. Once again, the same question comes up: what grounds the choice of axioms or rules of inference? However, the Aristotelian is better off here than the proponent of just the narrowly logical view because the truths contained in the essences of things provide a rich set of nonarbitrary axioms.

Aristotelian-essentialists might then be able just to specify, say, some plausible version of logic (e.g. some second-order quantified modal logic), and claim that our thought and language presupposes the truth of this logic. They could then say one of two things about the status of this logic. First, they could say that the basic rules of this logic are grounded in some or all essences. For instance, maybe every essence encodes the rules of logic, or maybe one could make the theistic move of saying that the essence of God encodes these rules. In this way, the rules of logic would be on par with other truths within the essences of things, such as the truth that horses occupy space that is encoded within the essence of a horse. This construal of the rules of logic would be to make the rules of inference effectively into facts or propositions written into essences, such as:

(6)   For all p and q, if it is the case that if p then q, and if it is the case that p, then it is the case that q.

But the rules of logic cannot be construed in this way without losing what is essential to them, namely their *applicability*. If *modus ponens* is just the fact (6) or maybe the necessary truth of (6), then how do you apply *modus ponens*? You have p, you have *if p then q*, and then you know that the antecedent of the big conditional in (6) is satisfied. But how do you know that the consequent of the big conditional in (6) holds, namely that it is the case that q? You know it by *modus ponens*. But *modus ponens* is just the truth (6), so you need to go back once more to (6) to apply it to the case where you have (6) and the antecedent of (6). In other words, you need *modus ponens* to apply *modus ponens* if *modus ponens* is just a truth like (6), and a vicious regress ensues. Applicability requires that the truths of logic be more than just statements.[5]

A better solution for advocates of the Aristotelian-essentialist account of modality would be to say that logic narrowly construed is something deeper than the necessities they are grounded in essences. One could, for instance, take the Tractarian line that narrowly logical impossibilities cannot even be thought.

But we have not exhausted all the objections to the Aristotelian-essentialist view. Consider truths that hold of all things no matter what essence they might have. No entity has a shape that is both a square and a circle (at the same time and in the same respect), and no entity is the cause of itself. What makes *these* be necessary truths? Granted, it may be encoded in the essence of every actually existing thing that nothing having that essence is a square circle, or is *causa sui*, or exists in a world where some (actually true) Gödelian

---

5. This argument goes back, at least, to Sextus Empiricus (1993, sec. II.11, para. 114).

unprovable arithmetical claim fails to hold, but a seemingly stronger claim is true: there could not be *anything*, whether with one of these essences or with some other essence, that is a square circle or that is *causa sui* or that exists in a world where some particular (actually true) Gödelian unprovable arithmetical claim fails to hold. Maybe the square circle case can be handled through a narrowly logical move as described earlier, but it may not be plausible that this can be done with the *causa sui* case, although perhaps there is some Tractarian line that one can take that self-causation cannot even be thought. But in any case, the Tractarian line does not seem to help much with the Gödelian worry.

Moreover, consider the question of what essences can possibly exist (in mind or reality). The story we have so far is that something is possible provided its existing is not contradictory to the truths encoded in those essences that exist. This, however, seems to let in so many essences that a certain amount of skepticism is engendered. For instance, it seems that there will be a possible world *w* that is just like this one, with this exception. The essence of human beings does not exist at *w*, but instead there are entities that physically behave just like human beings, except that instead of being a single natural kind, they are divided up into two natural kinds defined by different essences: there are those who have an even number of hairs on their bodies and there are those who have an odd number of hairs on their bodies. As soon as one of these beings gains or loses a hair, it perishes, and a new being comes to exist, physically and psychologically just like it, apart from that hair. Otherwise, everything is as it is in our world. After all the existence of such being and such essences does not seem to contradict the truths encoded in any of the essences that exist, such as the essence of the live oak or the photon. But once we allow that *w* is possible, do we have good reason to suppose that it is not *our* world, that in our world there are no different essences for people with even numbers of hairs and for people with odd numbers of hairs?

The problem, thus, is with what constrains what essences there could be. One answer, inspired by the static character of Aristotle's universe, would be that all the essences that can exist in fact do exist, or at least existed, exist, or will exist. However, a crucial difficulty remains as to what "can" could mean here. What constrains which essences *can* exist?

Some of these problems can be solved by going a theistic route. Perhaps there is a God whose essence encodes necessary truths not just about himself but about others, such as that there can be no square circles, and that certain weird essences cannot exist.

In fact, I think one can argue that only a necessarily exemplified essence can solve the difficulties here; for, on the present account, it seems very likely that an essence cannot in any way constrain what happens in any worlds in which that essence is not exemplified. An essence E can exclude some worlds containing an exemplification of it from including something incompatible with E, but it does not have anything to say about what things are like in worlds where there is no exemplification of E.

Suppose now that none of the essences that are exemplified in our world is necessarily exemplified. We should then be able to describe a world full of really, really weird things – beings with essences that make their kinds be defined by the number of hairs, self-caused beings, and the like – as long as we do not transgress narrowly logical norms and as long as we take care to include none of the beings of our world. And such a world will be possible since the essences that exist in our world will be irrelevant to what goes on in that world as our world's essences will be unexemplified there. Likewise, a completely empty world would be possible then – a world with no essences exemplified. In *that world*, it will be true that everything that is narrowly logically possible is metaphysically possible, since there will be no constraining essences at all. In particular, in that world it will be possible that Gödelian claims of arithmetic that are true at our world are false. And, of course, it would then be the case that S5 is false, but the Aristotelian-essentialist may not mind that consequence.

If we think that the space of all possible worlds is not such a slum as to include all such worlds, we have to think that at least one of the beings that exist in our world is such that its essence is *necessarily* exemplified, and that the essences of the necessary beings place constraints on what sorts of essences there can be, what sorts of arithmetical truths there can be, and so on.

There are now two difficulties. First, what does it mean that the essence of some being is *necessarily* exemplified? If an essence E cannot constrain what happens in worlds where it does not exist, it is unclear how E could prevent the actuality of worlds that do not contain an exemplification of E. Second, just *how* does an essence place such global constraints on worlds and on what essences are exemplified in them?

The first difficulty forces us, I think, to modify the account. Let N be one of the necessarily exemplified essences. Even if some necessities are grounded in essences, the necessity of Ns being exemplified cannot be grounded in an essence, at least not in the sense in which essences exclude their being exemplified together with something incompatible, since by doing so, the essences do not exclude their *not* being exemplified. So there is some other kind of necessity that the exemplification of N has. This is, in general, not going to be narrowly logical necessity, since unprovable arithmetic truths will follow from the exemplification of all the necessarily exemplified essences.

The account now becomes rather less attractive. It posits *three* kinds of modality as together yielding metaphysical alethic modality: the necessity of the exemplification of certain essences, the necessities encoded in essences, and narrowly logical necessity. Moreover, our best story as to what a necessarily exemplified essence that constrains reality outside of itself is like is that it is the essence of God, so this is not an escape an atheist is likely to want to take. And we have no story yet about what necessary exemplification is grounded in.

There is a way of making something similar to this story work. If we posit that all contingently exemplified essences must originate from something, then we might get the idea of an essence that does not itself originate from anywhere, an essence that is necessarily exemplified, so that the contingently exemplified essences get their reality from at least one necessarily exemplified essence or from the exemplifier of such an essence (in the case of God, if divine simplicity holds, the two options will come to the same thing). It will also be plausible that just as the essences originate from something, so do their exemplifications; on an Aristotelian view, essences are not completely independent of their exemplifications. All of this focuses the attention, however, on causation, and leads us to the last account of modality – the causal one.

Another thing that leads us away from the Aristotelian-essentialist account of modality is the intuition that I used against the Platonic view. One can give a simple account of why I could be a biologist in terms of my abilities and the powers of various entities in my environment. On the Platonic side, I wondered why there is this coincidence between what happens in the Platonic realm and earthly powers and capacities. Now one can wonder why there is a coincidence between powers and essences. Why is it that I cannot do anything that contradicts the essence of any entity in existence? Perhaps this question is somewhat less pressing than on the Platonic side. After all, maybe my powers are grounded in my essence. But it is still not clear why something could not have the power to act contrary to its essence.[6]

2.2.6.6. Aristotelian-causal account of modality

The critiques of the Platonic and Aristotelian-essentialist accounts point the way toward an account where causation is central. Here is a sketch of an account that does this. Say that a nonactual state of affairs S is merely possible provided that something – an event or substance or collection of events or substances, say – exists (in the tenseless sense: existed, exists presently, exists eternally, or will exist) with a causal power of bringing about S, or with a causal power of bringing about something with a causal power of bringing about S, or with a causal power of bringing about something with a causal power of bringing about something with a causal power of bringing about S, or more generally provided that something exists capable of originating a chain of exercises of causal power capable of leading to S. We then say that a state of affairs is possible if it is either actual or merely possible, and that it is necessary when its nonoccurrence is impossible. A proposition, then, is possible provided it describes a possible state of affairs, and necessary if it describes a necessary state of affairs.

This account has the advantage of reducing metaphysical possibility to causal possibility. One might think this is not much of a gain – we are still stuck with some primitive modality. Yes, but the primitive modality we are left with is a modality that we have a better handle on and a better epistemological story about. We ourselves exercise causal powers all day long and run up against the causal powers of other entities. Our scientific observation of the world gives us information as to what is and what is not within the powers of things. For instance, we know that unicorns[7] are possible because we know that it would be within the powers of natural selection and variation processes to have produced unicorns.

Moreover, we are probably going to need causal powers, or something like them, in our metaphysics even if we have an independent story about metaphysical alethic modality. It does, after all, seem to be a feature of the world that entities can produce effects. So by reducing metaphysical to causal modality, we seem to make a real gain in elegance and simplicity.

Furthermore, this account lets us handle a spectrum of modalities in a uniform framework by restricting the entities in the causal chains that define mere possibility and the

---

6. It is also worth noting, by the way, that essences function differently in the Aristotelian-essentialist account than they did in medieval Aristotelian views, and perhaps even in Aristotle himself, although this is not an objection to the Aristotelian-essentialist account. The essences that medieval Aristotelians have talked about were not understood as having the modal implications that the Aristotelian-essentialist accounts needs them to have. For instance, the Christian West took it for granted that it was possible for the second person of the Trinity to take on a human nature. But a human nature is an essence. So in one case at least – that of the second person of the Trinity – the possession of the essence of humanity was not an "essential property" in the modern, Kripkean sense of a property that the entity could not possibly lack, and it is this modern sense that would be needed to get the Aristotelian-essentialist account going.

7. See n. 3 above.

causal relations between them. For instance, a nonactual state of affairs is physically causally merely possible provided that it can be produced by a causal chain consisting purely of physical entities and starting with something physical. A state of affairs is temporally merely possible provided that it is not actual but can be produced by a chain of exercises of causal power starting with something in the present or future.

But what is of most relevance to this chapter is that, given some plausible assumptions, the Aristotelian-causal account, perhaps surprisingly, entails a version of the PSR: every contingent state of affairs has a causal explanation, that is, an explanation based on facts about contingent exercises of causal powers, perhaps combined with some necessary truths.

For the argument, I need a *prima facie* weaker version of the Brouwer Axiom. The Brouwer Axiom, in general, states that if p holds, then it is a necessary truth that p is possible. The weaker version of it that I need is:

(7)   If p holds contingently, then it is possible for p to be both possible and false.

This follows from the full Brouwer Axiom, since if p holds contingently, then p is possible, and so it is necessarily possible, but since it is contingent, it is possibly false, so possibly it is both false and possible. And Brouwer, in turn, follows from S5.

Suppose for a *reductio* that a contingent state of affairs E has no causal explanation. Let E^* be the state of affairs of E's obtaining without causal explanation. Then E^* is a contingent state of affairs. By the weaker version of the Brouwer Axiom, it is possible that E^* does not obtain but is nonetheless possible. Let us suppose a possible world w where that happens. Here, the use of possible worlds is inessential, but it helps make the argument clear. In w, E^* does not obtain but is possible. Thus, there is a cause C in w that could initiate a chain of exercises of causal powers capable of leading to E^*'s obtaining. But that is absurd, since in doing so, the chain would give a causal explanation of E as well as leading to E's not having a causal explanation!

One might deny Brouwer, as well as Brouwer's weaker cousin (7), and hold on to the Aristotelian-causal account in the absence of the PSR.[8] But the Brouwer Axiom is intuitively plausible: however else things might have gone than they did, it would still be true that they could have gone as they actually did.

Without the Brouwer Axiom, we can give an alternate argument for the PSR based on the following highly plausible material conditional:

(8)   If the PSR is true in all possible worlds with the possible exception of the actual world, then the PSR is in fact true in all possible worlds.

It would be incredibly bad luck for us to inhabit the one world where the PSR is false, if there were one. Moreover, if (8) is false, the following absurdity ensues: the PSR is false, but had I skipped breakfast this morning, it would have been true (since it is true in all possible worlds in which I skip breakfast this morning, as it is true in all possible worlds but the nonactual one, and in the actual one I had breakfast). And even someone who is

---

8. In earlier work (e.g. Pruss 2006, sec. 19.5.2), I said that S5, and hence Brouwer, can be proved from the Aristotelian-causal account of possibility. The sketch of an argument that I gave there does not seem to work, however, unless one assumes something like the PSR.

willing to embrace this absurdity should still accept the cosmological argument, since the cosmological argument could be run in the world where I skip breakfast this morning, and it would be an even greater absurdity to suppose that God does not in fact exist but would have existed had I skipped breakfast this morning. And this would in fact be a contradiction, not just an absurdity, if God is a necessary being.

To show the PSR to be true given (8), for a *reductio* suppose that there is a possible world w, distinct from the actual world, but in which the PSR does not hold. Let E be a state of affairs in w that has no causal explanation. If E does not obtain in the actual world, let $F = E$. Otherwise, let F be the conjunction of E with some other state of affairs obtaining in w that does not obtain in the actual world – there must be such, since w is not the actual world, and hence different states of affairs obtain in w than in the actual world. In either case, F is a state of affairs in w that has no causal explanation. Let F^* be the state of affairs of F's obtaining with no causal explanation. Then F^* is a possible state of affairs but is not actual, since F does not obtain in the actual world. But then there is something that can initiate a chain of causes leading to F^*, which, as in the Brouwer-based argument, is absurd, since the chain of causes will lead to F's obtaining, as well as to F's not having a causal explanation.

Thus, the Aristotelian-causal account of modality leads to the PSR, while the main alternatives to this account of modality are unsatisfactory and/or require something like theism anyway. This gives us a powerful reason to accept the PSR.

2.2.7. Philosophical argumentation

It is morally acceptable to redirect a speeding trolley from a track on which there are five people onto a track with only one person. On the other hand, it is not right to shoot one innocent person to save five. What is the morally relevant difference between the two cases? If we denied the PSR, then we could simply say: "Who cares? Both of these moral facts are just brute facts, with no explanation." Why, indeed, suppose that there should be some explanation of the difference in moral evaluation if we accept the denial of the PSR, and hence accept that there can be facts with no explanation at all?

Almost all moral theorists accept the supervenience of the moral on the nonmoral. But without the PSR, would we really have reason to accept that? We could simply suppose brute contingent facts. In this world, torture is wrong. In that world, exactly alike in every other respect, torture is a duty. Why? No reason, just contingent brute fact.

The denial of the PSR, thus, would bring much philosophical argumentation to a standstill.

An interesting thing about this argument is that it yields a PSR not just for contingent truths but also for necessary ones.

2.2.8. Justification via the sense of deity

If God exists, then the PSR for contingent propositions is true. Why? Because God's activity ultimately explains everything. This is going to be clearest on views on which God's activity *alone* explains everything, and that is going to be most plausible on Calvinist-type views but also seems correct on any theological account that has a strong view of divine concurrence with creaturely activity. Moreover, the inference from God's being the creator and sustainer of everything to the claim that divine activity provides the explanation of everything contingent, or at least of everything contingent that is otherwise unexplained (this variant might be needed to handle creaturely free will), is a highly plausible one. Thus, someone who has good reason to accept theism has good reason to accept the PSR.

Now one might think that this is a useless justification for the PSR if we are going to use the PSR to run a cosmological argument, since then the cosmological argument will be viciously circular: the conclusion will justify the PSR, whereas the PSR is a premise in the argument.

However, recently, Daniel Johnson (forthcoming) has come up with a very clever account showing that a cosmological argument based on the PSR could still be epistemically useful, even if the PSR is accepted because of the existence of God (he also applies the view to the possibility premise in the ontological argument). Suppose that, as Calvin and Plantinga think, there is a *sensus divinitatis* (SD), which, noninferentially, induces in people the knowledge that God exists – at least absent defeaters – and tells them something about God's power and nature.

Suppose that Smith knows by means of the SD that God exists. From this, Smith concludes that the PSR is true – this conclusion may not involve explicit reasoning, and it is one well within the abilities of the average believer. Smith then *knows* that the PSR is true. Next, Smith sinfully and without epistemic justification suppresses the SD in himself and suppresses the belief that God exists. If Calvin's reading of Romans 1 is correct, this kind of thing does indeed happen, and it is why nontheists are responsible for their lack of theism. However, the story continues, the suppression is not complete. For instance, Smith's worshipful attitude toward God turns into an idolatrous attitude toward some part of creation. It may very well happen, likewise, that Smith does not in fact suppress his belief in the PSR, although he forgets that he had accepted the PSR in the first place because he believed in God. Indeed, this situation may be common for all we know.

Johnson then claims that Smith remains justified in believing the PSR, just as we remain justified in believing the Pythagorean theorem even after we have forgotten from whom we have learned it and how it is proved. Thus, Smith continues to know the PSR. The cosmological argument then lets Smith argue to the existence of God from the PSR, and so Smith then can justifiably conclude that God exists. Of course, unless Smith has some additional source of justification for believing the PSR, Smith has no more justification for believing that God exists than he did when he learned about God from his SD. So the argument has not provided *additional* evidence, but it has restored the knowledge that he had lost.

We have a circularity, then, but not one that vitiates the epistemic usefulness of the argument. Irrational suppression of a part of one's network of belief can be incomplete, leaving in place sufficient beliefs allowing the reconstruction of the suppressed belief. A similar thing happens not uncommonly with memory. Suppose I am trying to commit to memory my hotel room number of 314. I note to myself that my hotel room number is the first three digits of π. Later I will forget the hotel room number, but remember that it is identical to the first three digits of π, from which I will be able to conclude that the number is 314. My reason for believing the number to be identical to the first three digits of π was that the number is 314, but then, after I lose, through a nonrational process of forgetting, the knowledge that the number was 314, I will be able to recover the knowledge by using a logical consequence of that very piece of knowledge. In doing so, I do not end up with any more justification for my belief about the room number than I had started out with, but still if I started out with knowledge, I end up with knowledge again.

This means that an argument where a premise was justified in terms of the conclusion *can* be useful in counteracting the effects of nonrational or irrational loss of knowledge. This means that the cosmological argument could be useful even if none of the arguments for the PSR given earlier worked, and even if the PSR were not self-evident, for some people may know that the PSR is true because they once knew that God exists. They lost the knowledge that God exists but retained its shadow, the entailed belief that the PSR is true.

2.3. Objections to the PSR

2.3.1. Modal imagination argument

One can, arguably, imagine that a brick pops into existence uncaused. Therefore, one might conclude that it is possible that a brick pops into existence uncaused, and hence that the PSR is not a necessary truth. This is a popular Humean argument against the PSR.

The defender of the PSR can, of course, simply insist that the inference from imaginability to possibility is defeasible. After all, someone might imagine that a certain straightedge and compass construction trisects an angle,[9] and if the inference from imaginability to possibility were indefeasible, it would follow that the construction *possibly* trisects an angle. But a mathematical construction *possibly* (in the metaphysical sense) trisects an angle if and only if it *actually* does so, and in fact we know that angles cannot be trisected with straightedge and compass. So the inference had better be defeasible. The defender of the PSR can then claim that the arguments for the PSR are so strong that the argument from imaginability of PSR failure, being defeasible, does little to shake our confidence in the PSR.

However, there is a better solution for the defender of the PSR, and this is to question the claim that the opponent has actually imagined a brick popping into existence uncaused. It is one thing to imagine something without simultaneously imagining its cause, and another to imagine something along with the absence of a cause. In fact, the task of imagining absences *as such* is a difficult one. If I tell an ordinary person to imagine a completely empty room, the subject is likely to imagine an ordinary room, with walls but no furniture. But has the subject really imagined an *empty* room? Likely not. Most likely the imagined room is conceptualized in a way that implies that it has *air* in it. For instance, we could ask our subject what it would be like to sit in that empty room for 8 hours, and our subject is unlikely to respond: "You'd be dead since the room has nothing in it, and hence no oxygen either."

Could one with more directed effort imagine a room without any air in it? I am not at all sure of that. While we have the *concept* of vacuum as the absence of anything, it is not at all clear that we can imagine vacuum. Our language may itself be a giveaway of what we imagine when we imagine, as we say, a room "filled" with vacuum – perhaps we are not really imagining an empty room, but one filled with some colorless, frictionless, zero-pressure substance. Moreover, most likely, we are imagining the room as embedded in a universe like ours. But a room in a universe like ours will be pervaded with quantum

---

9. In fact, many people have imagined just that (see Dudley 1987).

vacuum as well as with electromagnetic and other fields, and perhaps even with spatial or spatiotemporal points. Whether these "items" count as things or not is controversial, of course, but at least it is far from clear that we have really imagined a truly empty room.

It is true that philosophers sometimes claim that they can imagine a world that, say, consists only of two iron balls (Black 1952). But a claim to imagine that is surely open to question. First of all, the typical sighted person's imagination is visual. The balls are, almost surely, imagined visible. But if so, then it is an implicit part of what one is imagining that there are photons bouncing off the balls. Furthermore, unless one takes care to specify – and I do not know how one exactly one specifies this in the imagination – that the balls obey laws very different from those of our world, there will constantly be occasional atoms coming off the edges of the balls, and hence there will be a highly diffuse gas around the balls. Suppose all of this physics is taken care of by our careful imaginer. Still, have we really imagined a world containing only two balls? What about the proper *parts* of the billiard balls – does the world not contain those? What about properties such as *roundness*, or at least tropes such as *this ball's roundness*? And are there no, perhaps, spatial or other relations between the balls? We see that unless one is a most determined nominalist, the content of the imagined world is going to be rather richer than we initially said. There are details implicit in the imagined situation that we have omitted.

There may, however, be a way we can imagine an absence. We can probably imagine absences of particular kinds of things in a particular area of space-time. Certainly, I can imagine a room free of talking donkeys, or even of donkeys in general. Moreover, I can probably imagine a room with no particles or electromagnetic fields in it. But that is not the same as imagining a truly empty room. A truly empty room does not have any other kinds of fields in it, at least if fields are things; there are no points of space or space-time in it; and it certainly has no ghosts, angels, or demons in it. But no list of kinds of things that we imagine as absent from the room will assure us of the literal and complete emptiness of the room, for there may always be a different kind of being, one utterly beyond the powers of our imagination, whose absence from the room we have failed to imagine. Nor will it do to imagine "unimaginables" as missing since "unimaginables" are not a genuine kind of thing but, surely, a mix of very different kinds of possibilia – it seems highly plausible that there are many kinds of possible things beyond our wildest imagination.

Similarly, we can imagine a brick coming into existence in the absence of a brickmaker, a brick not resulting from the baking of clay, a brick not made by an angel, demon, or ghost. But that is not the same thing as imagining a brick that comes into existence completely causelessly. To imagine that, we would need to imagine every possible kind of cause – including the unimaginable ones – as absent. That seems to be a feat beyond our abilities. We can, of course, *say* the words "This is causeless" both with our lips and with our minds while imagining the brick, but the claim that whenever one can imagine an F and say of it, with lips or minds, that it is a G, then, possibly, there is an F that is a G, would not only be highly defeasible but would also surely be a nonstarter. I can imagine a circle and say the words "This is a square" while imagining it.

Moreover, in general, when we imagine a situation, we imagine not a whole possible world, but a part of one, and our imagination is neutral on whether there are further support structures. I imagine three billiard balls on a billiard table. Probably, it is part of my imagining that there is gravity. Something, then, has to hold the table up, but what it is is not a part of the imagined situation. But I am not imagining a table miraculously suspended in a gravitational field – I am simply not imagining what the outside of the situation has to be like to support the part I care about.

Maybe, with a lot of work, one can imagine a situation involving a brick and involving enough imagined detail that one can, with confidence, say that the situation is not only one where the ordinary causes of bricks are not present near the brick, but where nowhere in the universe are there any causes of the brick and where there are no nonphysical causes of the brick either. But now we see that the situation imagined took rather more effort, and the given examples of how there may be more to an imagined situation than one initially thought should severely reduce one's confidence that one has been successful at the task of imagining a causeless brick. And even if one has been successful at it, the inference to the possibility of a causeless brick is still defeasible.

I want to end this discussion by comparing the imaginability argument for a causeless brick with the imaginability argument against Platonism. One might claim that it is possible to imagine a brick that does not stand in an instantiation relation to any other entities. If one can, then defeasibly it follows that possibly a brick does not stand in an instantiation relation to any other entities. But that, of course, contradicts Platonism, which holds that, necessarily, all bricks instantiate brickness. While I am not a Platonist, this argument against Platonism strikes me as weak. The Platonist can answer as I did earlier: have we really imagined a brick that does not stand in an instantiation relation to another entity, or have we merely imagined a brick without imagining its standing in an instantiation relation?

But there is also a further answer the Platonist can make. The Platonist can say: "For all you know, by imagining it as a *brick* you have implicitly imagined a situation where it is related to brickness, although your description of the contents of what you imagined contradicts this." Compare this to the point one should make against someone who claims that to have imagined a cube without any space or spatial relations – surely, by imagining it as a cube, you have implicitly imagined it as occupying space or as involving spatial relations (say, between the vertices).

Can the defender of the PSR make this point too? Perhaps. The brick we allegedly imagine coming into existence *ex nihilo* is a contingent brick. But it might be that the nature of contingency involves being caused (cf. Section 2.2.6.6, above). Moreover, the brick has existence. But it seems implausible to claim that we have plumbed the depths of the nature of existence. It could, for instance, be that *to be* is either *to be necessary* or *to be caused* – that the *esse*, the *existence*, of a contingent being is its being caused (it may be that Thomas Aquinas thought this; I explore this kind of a view in Pruss 2006, chap. 12). It could even be that the *esse* of a contingent being is its being caused by that particular set of causes by which it is caused – that would cohere neatly with and explain the essentiality of origins.

A variant of the argument from modal imagination is to say that one can without overt logical contradiction state the claim that a brick exists without a cause:

(9) $\exists x(\text{brick}(x)\ \&\ \sim\exists y(\text{causes}(y,x)))$.

However, that is a bad argument. That one can state something without *overt* contradiction does not imply that there is no *hidden* contradiction. After all, compare (9) with:

(10) $\exists x(\text{sculpture}(x)\ \&\ \sim\exists y(\text{causes}(y,x)))$.

This claim is impossible since it is a necessary truth that sculptures have sculptors – that is what makes them be sculptures. In the case of (10) the contradiction lies pretty close to the surface. But how do we know that in (9), there is no contradiction somewhat further from the surface? Maybe there is even a hidden complexity in the concept represented by the existential quantifier.

2.3.2. Van Inwagen's modal fatalism argument

2.3.2.1. The basic argument

Peter van Inwagen (1983, pp. 202–4) has formulated an influential and elegant *reductio ad absurdum* of the PSR. Let p be the conjunction of all contingent truths. If p has an explanation, say q, then q will itself be a contingent truth, and hence a conjunct of p. But then q will end up explaining itself, which is absurd. We can formulate this precisely as follows:

(11)   No necessary proposition explains a contingent proposition. (Premise)
(12)   No contingent proposition explains itself. (Premise)
(13)   If a proposition explains a conjunction, it explains every conjunct. (Premise)
(14)   A proposition q only explains a proposition p if q is true. (Premise)
(15)   There is a Big Conjunctive Contingent Fact (BCCF), which is the conjunction of all true contingent propositions, perhaps with logical redundancies removed, and the BCCF is contingent. (Premise)
(16)   Suppose the PSR holds. (for *reductio*)
(17)   Then, the BCCF has an explanation, q. (by (15) and (16))
(18)   The proposition q is not necessary. (by (11) and (15) and as the conjunction of true contingent propositions is contingent)
(19)   Therefore, q is a contingent true proposition. (by (14) and (18))
(20)   Thus, q is a conjunct in the BCCF. (by (15) and (19))
(21)   Thus, q explains itself. (by (13), (15), (17), and (19))
(22)   But q does not explain itself. (by (12) and (19))
(23)   Thus, q does and does not explain itself, which is absurd. Hence, the PSR is false.

Versions of this argument has been defended by James Ross (1969, pp. 295–304), William Rowe (1975, 1984), and, more recently, Francken and Geirsson (1999).

The argument is plainly valid. Thus, the only question is whether the premises are true. Premise (14) is unimpeachable.[10]

Premise (13) bears some discussion. In favor of it, one might note that the explanation of the conjunction might have more information in it than is needed to explain just one of the conjuncts, but if it has enough information to explain the conjunction it also has enough information to explain the conjuncts. We may, however, worry about Salmon's remark that irrelevancies spoil explanations (Salmon 1990, p. 102). If we are worried about this, however, we can replace "explains" with "provides material sufficient for an explanation" throughout the argument, and whatever was plausible before, will remain plausible.

---

10. That aliens shot John F. Kennedy *would* be a good explanation of JFK's death *were it true*, but since it is false, it is not an explanation. False propositions can be *putative* explainers, but not *actual* explainers.

Alternately, we may say that if q explains a conjunction, then the only reason it might fail to explain a conjunct r is because q might contain irrelevant information. But, surely, when the conjunct r is equal to q itself, this worry will not be real – how could q contain information irrelevant *to itself*? So even if (13) is questioned, (21) still very plausibly follows from (15), (17), and (19).

This leaves the technical Premise (15) about the existence of a BCCF, and two substantive claims, (11) and (12), about explanation. Leibnizian cosmological arguments based on the PSR need something like a BCCF, so questioning (15) is probably not a fruitful avenue for questioning for a defender of the Leibnizian cosmological argument (see further discussion in Section 4.1.1.3, below, as well as in Pruss 2006, sec. 6.1).

But we should *not* accept (11). We shall see that the main reason for believing (11) rests on a misunderstanding of how explanation works. Moreover, I shall argue that someone who accepts the logical possibility of libertarian free will should deny at least one of (11) and (12).

2.3.2.2. Is (11) true?

Premise (11), that no necessary proposition can explain a contingent one, needs some justification. The main reason to accept (11) is the idea that if a necessary proposition q explained a contingent proposition p, then there would be worlds where q is true but p is false, and so q cannot give the reason why p is true. This sketch of the argument can be formalized as follows:

(24) If it is possible for q to be true with p false, then q does not explain p. (Premise)

(25) If q is necessary and p is contingent, then it is possible for q to be true with p false. (a theorem in any plausible modal logic)

(26) Therefore, if q is necessary and p is contingent, then q does not explain p.

Instead of attacking (11) directly, I shall focus my attack on (24). Without (24), Premise (11) in the modal fatalism argument does not appear to be justified. Now, granted, someone might one day find a powerful argument for (11) not dependent on (24), in which case more work will need to be done, but (24) seems to capture just about all the intuition behind (11).

By contraposition, (24) is equivalent to

(27) If q explains p, then q entails p.

Let me start with a quick *ad hominem* argument against (27). It seems a perfectly good explanation of why the dog did not bark that neither a stranger came by the dog nor did any other potential cause of the dog's barking occur. But the explanans here only entails the explanandum if we suppose that it is a necessary truth that if the dog barked, its barking had a cause. But opponents of the PSR are unlikely to grant that this is a necessary truth, unless they have some principled to reason to argue that dogs' barkings metaphysically require causes, but some other things do not need any explanation, whether causal or not. But I doubt that there is a good way of drawing the line between barkings and other states of affairs.

Now, (27) does seem to hold in the case of many conceptual explanations. These explain a state of affairs by saying what the state of affairs is constituted by or consists in. For instance, in *Metaphysics* Z, Aristotle suggests explaining an eclipse of the sun by noting that an eclipse of the sun is *identical with* the earth's entry into the moon's shadow. Likewise, one might explain a knife's being hot by noting that its being hot consists in, or maybe is constituted by, its molecules having high kinetic energy.

However, (27) is falsified by just about every modern scientific *nonconceptual* explanation that I know of. Scientific causal explanations, in general, simply do not give conditions that *entail* the explanandum. This is obvious in the case of statistical explanations, since in these, the explanans gives laws of nature and states of affairs that do not entail the explanandum but either render the explanandum more probable than it would otherwise be, or at least are explanatorily relevant to the explanandum. Why did the cream spread throughout the coffee cup? Because it is *very likely* that random molecular motion would disperse cream in this way.

But the falsity of (27) also follows in the case of nonstatistical explanations. Why are the planets moving in approximately elliptical orbits? Because the main gravitational influence on them is that of an approximate point mass (the sun), the secondary gravitational influences on them from other objects, including other planets, being weak. But what I just said does not entail that the planets move in approximately elliptical orbits. It only entails that *absent* other influences, the planets move in approximately elliptical orbits.

Perhaps we can build that proviso into the explanation. Why do the planets move in approximately elliptical orbits? Because the main gravitational influence is that of an approximate point mass, *and there are no other relevant influences.* But the word "relevant" is crucial here, for, of course, there are many other influences, such as electromagnetic ones. The word "relevant" here seems to mean "relevant to affecting the approximate shape of the planets' orbits." But that is not quite right. Electromagnetic influences of the sort that the planets undergo are, in general, relevant to affecting the approximate shape of the planets' orbits. They are just not relevant *in this case* because the gravitational influence of the sun swamps the other effects.

So what we are really saying when we give the proviso is that the main gravitational influence is that of an approximate point mass, *and no other influence prevents the orbits from having elliptical shape.* Perhaps now we have entailment? Actually, the objector to the PSR should not say so. For if the PSR is false, then surely things can come into existence for no reason at all and can likewise pop out of existence for no reason at all. Thus, it is quite possible for all of the aforementioned to be true, and yet for the planets to pop out of existence, thereby preventing them from having any orbits at all.

Do we add, then, to the our explanans the conjunct "and the planets remain in existence"? Perhaps then we will get entailment, although even that is not at all clear. For if the PSR is false, and if the laws of nature are of such a nature as not to rule out the possibility of external influence, then it seems likely that the laws of nature cannot rule out the possibility of a brute, unexplained departure from the laws of nature.

Or perhaps objectors to the PSR will admit that by their own lights (27) is false, but insist that the defenders of the PSR are committed to (27). Then the argument against the PSR becomes *ad hominem*. I have no objection against *ad hominem* arguments, but one would need to give an argument that while the opponents of the PSR can reasonably reject (27), for some reason the proponents of the PSR should accept (27). But then an argument is needed as to why the proponents of the PSR must accept a theory of the nature of explanation that requires (27) just because they happen to think that all contingent facts have explanations. Yet since the PSR is incompatible with (27) given some plausible other assumptions, this would be a hard case to make!

In any case, suppose that through a lot of careful work we have somehow managed to come up with an explanans that entails that the planets have approximately elliptical orbits. An easy point I can make here is that the resulting explanation is unlike *standard* scientific explanations in more than one way.

First, note that with the provisos we have loaded into the explanans, the explanation becomes logically odd. What we end up saying is essentially that the planets move in approximately elliptical orbits because the gravitational influence of an approximate point mass moves them in approximately elliptical orbits. The provisos all add up to saying that the gravitational influence of the sun *succeeds* in moving the planets in elliptical orbits. But now the explanandum is in effect there in the explanans, and our explanation is like "He died because he died of being stabbed." But that is not how we give explanations. He died *because he was stabbed*. The planets move approximately elliptically *because the sun gravitationally influences them*. He did not die because he died of being stabbed, and the planets do not move approximately elliptically because the sun moves them approximately elliptically.

Second, the proponents of the PSR have an epistemic right to reject the loading up of the explanation of provisos, a right grounded in reasons apparently independent of their need to reject the van Inwagen argument. Our provisoed explanation basically was: "The planets move approximately elliptically because the sun gravitationally influences them as an approximate point source and nothing prevents them from moving approximately elliptically." But if the PSR is a necessary truth, then that nothing prevents the planets from moving approximately elliptically *entails* that they in fact move approximately elliptically, since if they did not, there would have to be a reason why they do not. However, it is an odd sort of explanation where one of the conjuncts in the explanans is sufficient by itself to entail the explanandum. One wonders why one bothers mentioning the sun's gravitational influence at all! In fact, this worry may be there even for the PSR's opponent, if one of the provisos has to be something like "and the PSR is not relevantly violated in this case."

Third, the claim that *nothing* prevents the planets from moving approximately elliptically involves universal quantification over all entities in existence, whether natural or not. It is a claim that each of these entities is a nonpreventer of the planets' elliptical motion. But while scientific claims have *entailments* about nonnatural entities (e.g. that the planets are moving approximately elliptically entails that God is not making them move along logarithmic spirals), they should not quantify over nonnatural entities. Thus, our heavily provisoed explanation does not appear any longer to be a scientific one.

Let me end this section with the following argument for (27). The PSR had better understand "explains" as "gives a sufficient reason for." But a sufficient reason is, surely, a *logically* sufficient reason, that is, an entailing reason. And, indeed, Leibniz thought that the reasons said by the PSR to exist would be entailing.

A simple answer to this is to say that I am not defending Leibniz's PSR, but a PSR sufficient for the cosmological argument. We do not, in fact, need entailing reasons for the cosmological argument, as shall be clear when we discuss cosmological arguments. A fuller answer is that when I talk of the PSR, by "sufficient reasons" I mean reasons that are suffi-cient *to explain* the explanandum. Leibniz may have erroneously thought that a reason is only sufficient to explain something that it entails, but we do not need to follow him in his error – and should not, since that route leads to modal fatalism. But if the reader is not convinced, I can just rename the principle I am defending the "Principle of Good-Enough Explanation."

2.3.2.3. *Libertarian free choices*

Let me now offer an argument that someone who accepts the possibility of libertarian free will *must* reject the van Inwagen argument. Since van Inwagen is a libertarian, he too must reject his own argument. To make this more than an *ad hominem*, I would need to argue for the possibility of libertarian free will (or for its actuality), for which, of course, there is no space here.

Libertarian free will is nondeterministic. From the condition of the mind of the chooser prior to the choice, one cannot deduce what choice will be made. This has given rise to the *randomness* objection to libertarianism: libertarian free choices are not really caused by the person, but are merely *random* blips, as some people think quantum events are. We would not account a person free if acts of will occurred *randomly* in a person's mind or brain.

Libertarians are, of course, committed to a denial of the randomness objection. However they manage it, they must reject the claim that libertarian free actions are random – they may, for instance, insist that they are not random because they are caused by agent causa-tion. Now suppose that a libertarian allowed that in the case of a libertarian free choice between options A and B, where in fact A was chosen, there is no sufficient explanation of why A was chosen. Such a libertarian has succumbed to the randomness objection. If there is no explanation for why option A was chosen, then that A was chosen is a brute, unex-plained, uncaused fact – a *random* fact. Thus, the libertarian cannot allow that there is no explanation of why A was chosen.

Look at this from another direction. Suppose someone is externally determined to choose A instead of B, so that the explanation for why A was chosen was that some external puppet master has caused the agent to choose A rather than B. In that case, there would indeed be an explanation for why A was chosen rather than B – the causal efficacy of the puppet master. The libertarian will insist that in that case, there is no free will. Now take this situation and *subtract* the puppet master, without adding anything. We get a situation where there is no explanation for the choice of A rather than of B. We get a genuine case of randomness, having replaced the puppet master by nothing at all. And this mere removal of the puppet master does nothing to give freedom to the agent. Libertarian freedom is not supposed to be something purely negative, the lack of a puppet master, but something positive like self-determination. To go from the choice determined by the puppet master to a genuine libertarian free choice, we cannot merely delete the explanation of the action in terms of the puppet master: we must *add* something to the situation. It is plausible that what needs to be done is to substitute the free agent and/or her free will for the puppet master: the action must be explained in terms of the agent now, instead of in terms of something external. The basic intuition of a libertar-ian is that determinism places the ultimate point of decision outside the agent, in the environment that forms and influences the agent. This external determinism, to produce freedom, must not only be removed but must be replaced by something causal, though still indeterministic in the case of agents that have a cause of their existence,[11] within the agent.

Thus, the libertarian should hold that there is an explanation for why one rather than another choice was freely made. Otherwise, the randomness objection to libertarianism succeeds. This either forces the libertarian to say (a) that a description of a mind in a state that is equally compatible with either of two actions, A or B, can be used to explain why A was in fact freely chosen – a denial of (27) – or (b) that the claim that action A was freely chosen, or perhaps freely chosen for reason R, is "almost" a self-explanatory claim, despite its contingency, with the only thing unexplained being why the agent existed and was free and perhaps impressed by R. If the agent were a being that necessarily exists and is necessarily freely and omnisciently, then in case (b), nothing would be left unexplained, and we would have a counterexample to (12).

Nonetheless, how there can be explanation of exercises of libertarian free will is mysterious. I shall here defend option (a), that a choice of A can be explained in terms of a state that was compatible with choosing B. I shall defend this by offering a hypothesis about how libertarian free will works. If this hypothesis is false, perhaps another can do the same job, but I find this one plausible. For simplicity, I will assume a binary choice between A and B. On my hypothesis, free choices are made on the basis of reasons that one is "impressed by," that is, that one takes into consideration in making the decision. Some of the reasons are in favor of one choice, and others are in favor of another choice. Reasons that are neutral between the options are not taken into account by the agent in the choice between A or B.

I now suppose that when the agent x chooses A, there is a subset S of the reasons that favor A over B that the agent is impressed by, such that x freely chooses A on account of S. My explanatory hypothesis, then, is that x freely chooses A because x is making a free choice between A and B while impressed by the reasons in S. On my hypothesis, further, had the agent chosen B, the agent would still have been impressed by the reasons in S, but the choice of B would have been explained by x's freely choosing between A and B while impressed by the reasons in T, where T is a set of reasons that favor B over A. Moreover, in the actual world where A is chosen, the agent is also impressed by T. However, in the actual world, the agent does not act on the impressive reasons in T, but on the reasons in S.

This explanation fits well with how agents in fact describe their choices. They say things like: "I chose this graduate school because it was important to me that my spouse be able to study at the same institution." Sure, another school might have better fit with their academic interests, and that may also be important to them. But while the latter consideration is one they are also impressed by, they did not in fact choose on the basis of it, and hence it does not enter into the explanation.

---

11. The reason for the proviso is this: If agent x is caused by y to exist, and is *internally* determined to do A, then y by causing x to exist has caused x to do A. But if agent x has no cause of its existence, then this argument no longer works, and internal determinism may be compatible with freedom. This is important for the question whether a God who cannot choose evil can be free (see, for instance, Pruss 2003).

Note that I am not claiming that the same thing explains the choice of A as would have explained the choice of B. That sameness of explanation claim might seem absurd, so an opponent might try to push me to admit that there is a single explanation in both cases. Thus, one might say that if p (a proposition about the choice being made while impressed by the reasons in S) explains the choice of A, and q (which is like p but with T in place of S) is true, then p&q also explains the choice of A. However, "irrelevancies [are] harmless in arguments but fatal in explanations" (cf. Salmon 1990, p. 102). Thus, even though p explains the choice of A, and q is true, one can coherently deny that p&q explains the choice of A. If, on the other hand, this point is denied, I will regroup by saying that the idea that the same proposition should explain A in our world and an incompatible B in another world is defensible. Salmon (1990, pp. 178–9) argues that one *must* accept the possibility that the same kinds of circumstances can explain one event on one occasion and an incompatible kind of event on another occasion if one is to have any hope of explaining stochastic outcomes.[12] For instance, if a carcinogen causes cancer 12 percent of the time, with 60 percent of the time its being type A cancer and 40 percent of the time its being type B cancer, these statistical facts can explain both an occurrence of type A cancer in one patient and an occurrence of type B cancer in another.

For the cosmological argument, the most important case of libertarian choice is God's choice what world to create. In this case, I actually think it is a *necessary* truth that God is impressed by the reasons S on account of which he created the actual world, just as it is a necessary truth that God was impressed by a different set of reasons on account of which he might have created another world. After all, necessarily, an omniscient and morally perfect God is impressed by all and only the good reasons. What the reasons on the basis of which God created this world are is something largely beyond my ken, although we can say a few standard things about the value of beings that participate in God's life.

As a modification of my hypothesis, I should note that it might be that what matters explanatorily is not only the fact of the agent's being impressed by the reasons, but also the degree to which the agent is impressed by them. It is easy to modify the account to take this into account, by explaining not just in terms of a set of reasons but in terms of a set of reason–weight pairs.

There is, still, something uncomfortable about the proposed explanation of libertarian action. I think a reader is likely to have the sense that while it is correct to say that the choice of graduate school might be explained by what is better for a spouse, even though this reason would have equally been present had a choice not supported by this reason been made instead, this kind of explanation is explanatorily inferior to, say, deterministic causal explanation or explanation in terms of a necessitating metaphysical principle. That may be. But there is no need to take the PSR to say that there is always *the best* kind of explanation – the PSR I am defending merely says that there is *an* explanation of every contingent proposition. And that is all I need for the cosmological argument.

---

12. Note that Salmon's definition (Salmon 1990, p. 67) of a statistical relevance explanation of a fact as simply being an assemblage of statistically relevant facts implies the claim that the explanation of p in one world will be an explanation of ~p in another if we add the observation that sometimes, maybe even always, whatever is relevant to p will also be relevant to ~p.

2.3.3. A probabilistic version of van Inwagen's argument

But even if van Inwagen's argument fails, there is a probabilistic variant that does not rely on (11). This argument is inspired by some remarks I got from Peter Forrest. Instead of (11), the argument uses the following claim:

(28)   If q explains p, then $P(p|q) > 1/2$.

Instead of concluding that the BCCF *in fact* does not have an explanation, the argument will conclude that some worlds have a BCCF that does not have an explanation. We proceed as follows. Making use of all the other premises of van Inwagen's argument, generalized to hold in all worlds, we get the claim that in every possible world there is an explanation of the BCCF, and the explanans is a necessary proposition. Now, if q is a necessary truth, then $P(p|q) = P(p)$. Conditioning on necessary truth gets us no new probabilistic information beyond prior probabilities. Hence, in any world w, if the BCCF p of w is explained by a necessary truth, then $P(p) > 1/2$ by (28). Therefore, the BCCF of every possible world has probability greater than 1/2. But the BCCFs of different worlds are mutually exclusive, since any two worlds differ in the truth-value of some contingent proposition, and then the BCCF of one of the worlds will contain that proposition and that of the other will contain its denial. Hence, if p_1 and p_2 are the BCCFs of two distinct worlds, we have $P(p_1 \text{ or } p_2) = P(p_1) + P(p_2) > 1/2 + 1/2 = 1$. But no probability can be bigger than 1, and absurdity ensues again.

A defender of the PSR could, of course, deny (12), which this version of the argument presupposes, since otherwise we could have self-explanatory contingent explanations of the BCCF. A desperate, but not entirely unjustified, alternate measure would be to deny the assumption that if q is necessary, then $P(p|q) = P(p)$, perhaps allowing that this is true if q is a tautology, and maybe even any narrowly logically necessary truth, but not if it is a substantive necessary truth, such as that horses are mammals, that water is H_2O or that God values unity and happiness. It could, then, be the case that p_1 has probability greater than 1/2 given one necessary truth q_1, while a proposition p_2 incompatible with p_1 has probability greater than 1/2 given another necessary truth q_2. For instance, perhaps that the universe consisting only of a single particle has high probability given that God values unity, and that the universe containing infinitely many happy persons has high probability given that God values happiness, even though it is a necessary truth that God values *both* unity *and* happiness.

The best way out for the PSR's defender, however, seems to be to oppose (28). First of all, statistical relevance theories of explanation deny (28), and, more broadly, (28) may be a manifestation of the mistaken conflation of explanation with prediction that plagued both the deductive–nomological (Hempel & Oppenheim 1948) and inductive–statistical (Hempel 1962) models of explanation. A standard counterexample to these models is the syphilis/paresis case (Scriven 1959; see also the discussion in Salmon 1990, sec. 2.3), which is also a counterexample to (28). We can explain why a person has paresis in terms of the earlier having of latent untreated syphilis, even though latent untreated syphilis leads to paresis only in a minority of cases.

Second, it is plausible that citing the relevant actual cause of an event explains the event. Indeed, to give causes is a paradigmatic way of explaining. But causation can filter through indeterministic events of probability less than 1/2. This is particularly clear in the case of forensic explanations. George murderously pushes Maurice off a very high cliff. Maurice falls and drowns. Unbeknownst to George, Maurice is actually a cliff diver, and had a 75 percent chance of survival for the fall. Nonetheless, George's murderous push killed Maurice, and George's having pushed Maurice explains why Maurice died. Granted, in this case it does not explain *everything* about why Maurice died. It does not explain, for instance, why in this case Maurice did not manage to swim out or why lack of oxygen kills earthly vertebrates. But it is still a fine explanation. In any case, it could well be that even after we answered all of these questions, it would be that the explanans made the explanandum less than 50 percent probable – there could be indeterministic quantum events in Maurice's brain behind Maurice's inability to swim out.

Third, if libertarianism holds, and if a plausible account of action requires one to say that free choices are explained by the agent's reasons, we have reason to deny (28). For it seems likely that libertarian-free agents can act on reasons that they had probability less than 1/2 of acting on.

2.3.4. Quantum mechanics

A common objection to the PSR is that indeterministic quantum effects lack sufficient reasons. However, the PSR that I am defending concerns explanation, which is the giving of reasons sufficient *to explain* the explanandum, not the giving of reasons logically suffi-cient for entailing the explanandum.

Quantum mechanical events do, however, have explanations. The experimental setup in which they happen has the property of giving rise to emissions with certain probabilities (John Haldane makes this suggestion in Smart & Haldane 2003, p. 126). Granted, on inde-terministic accounts of quantum mechanics, this explanation does not entail the outcome, and will only be a statistical explanation, perhaps involving small probabilities, but as the syphilis/paresis case in the previous section showed, that should not be a problem.

Still, one might be somewhat dissatisfied with quantum mechanical explanations. One might say that, yes, they are explanatory, but they lack some feature that better explanations have. But that is fine for the defense of the PSR. The PSR does not say that for every con-tingent proposition there is the best possible kind of explanation, but just that there is *an* explanation, "an 'explanation enough'" in Haldane's words (Smart & Haldane 2003, p. 126). And the kind of explanation that our PSR provides will be, as we shall see, enough to yield a cosmological argument – and that is the point here.

2.3.5. Contrastive explanation and the PSR

Perhaps, though, we can formulate the dissatisfaction with statistical quantum mechanical and libertarian explanations as follows. Suppose we are dealing with an electron in a mixed |up> + |down> state, which in an appropriate magnetic field will either go up or down, with equal probability. Suppose it goes up. Why did it go up? Because of its state, the experimental setup, and the laws of nature. Maybe this is a fine explanation, but it does not seem to be a *contrastive* explanation. It does not explain why the electron went up *rather than* down.

The simplest move at this point is just to deny this intuition, and say that the same facts can explain why it went up rather than down, as would have explained why it went down rather than up. Alternatively, one might distinguish the quantum mechanical and libertarian cases. Perhaps one can take a deterministic interpretation of quantum mechanics, and in libertarian cases give contrastive explanations in terms of different sets of reasons, as in Section 2.3.2.3, above.

Another move available to the defender of the PSR is to admit the failure of contrastive explanations. But the PSR says that every contingently true proposition p has an explanation, not that for every pair of propositions p and q where p is contingently true and q is a relevant alternative to p, there is an explanation of why p rather than q holds. There may well be such a notion of explanation that would make explanation be a ternary relation, but there is also a perfectly fine notion of explanation that makes explanation a binary relation, and it is the latter that the PSR concerns.

Some do, however, believe that all explanation is contrastive (cf. Dretske 1972; van Fraassen 1980). The standard example is something like this. George ate a banana rather than eating an orange because he liked bananas. George ate a banana rather than putting it in his backpack because he was hungry. Without specifying a contrast, we cannot tell which explanation we are after.

Arguments like this do not, however, establish that explanation is *always* contrastive. If we do not specify a contrast, we can give an explanation along either set of lines. George ate a banana because he liked bananas and chose to eat. George ate a banana because he was hungry and chose a banana. Neither explanation tells the whole story. But we can elicit more of the story by applying the PSR again. Why did George like bananas and choose to eat? Granted, we might say that this is because he likes nonjuicy sweet fruit and chose to eat, leaving that second conjunct as yet unexplained. But if explanation comes to an end in an ultimate explanation, we cannot *just* keep on furthering the explanation of the first conjunct – eventually, we will be done with that side, and a further demand for explanation will force us to tackle the question why George chose to eat.

A different move is that *on its own terms* the PSR that I am defending requires contrastive explanation. After all, it requires an explanation of every contingent proposition and that the electron went up rather than going down, or that George ate a banana rather than eating an orange, is a perfectly good proposition.

There is room to be quite unsure here, though. For it might be argued that when we make a contrastive claim, we are doing two things. We are asserting a proposition with an "and . . . not" truth-functional connective, for example, that the electron went up and did not go down, and drawing the listener's attention to the contrast between the two claims joined by the truth-functional connective. The proposition asserted, however, is not contrastive in nature and can be explained straightforwardly. We can just give the statistical explanation of why the electron went up and explain that if it went up, it could not have gone down at the same time, so it went up and did not go down.

There is reason to think this is the right way to understand contrastive claims. First, note that whatever proposition is asserted by saying "p rather than q holds," necessarily, it is a proposition that is true if and only if p is true and q is false. To see this, begin by observing that if p is not true or q is not false, then whatever "p rather than q holds" expresses must be false.

The converse is more difficult to establish. There certainly are cases where the sentence "p rather than q holds" is not assertible even though "p holds" and "q does not hold" are assertible. These will be cases when there is no relevant contrast between p and q. Thus, in typical contexts, "The moon is spherical rather than Jupiter being cubical" is not assertible. However, the failure of assertibility is not due to facts about the objective situation being talked about, but due to one's concerns, interests, and epistemic position. There will be epistemic contexts involving no mistakes but where "The moon is spherical rather than Jupiter being cubical" is assertible. For instance, suppose that George has seen neither the moon or Jupiter, and nobody has told him anything about them, except that an epistemic authority testified to him that the moon is spherical or Jupiter is cubical. One day, George learns that Jupiter is spherical. He then correctly sums up his conclusions: "The moon is spherical rather than Jupiter being cubical!" Given knowledge that p and that not-q, the assertibility of "p rather than q holds" depends on nonalethic matters, and hence all we need for *truth* is p and not q.

One might object that "p rather than q holds" *asserts* something about the state of mind of the speaker – that it is a mind-dependent proposition. But that is completely mistaken, since, then, every "rather than" claim would entail the existence of a speaker saying that claim, but that the moon is spherical rather than Jupiter being cubical entails nothing about a speaker who is saying that the moon is spherical rather than Jupiter being cubical.

So if proposition r is expressed by "p rather than q holds," then, necessarily, r holds if and only if $p\&\sim q$. I think it is simplest to suppose that r is actually the same proposition as $p\&\sim q$.

But suppose this is denied, and it is said that there is "something more" in the proposition that p rather than q holds than in $p\&\sim q$ (for surely there is nothing less). Nonetheless, the contrastive explanation argument can be questioned. It is no coincidence that p rather than q holds if and only if $p\&\sim q$ holds – it is a necessary truth, in light of the said argument, that this is always the case. In fact, it seems right to say that what makes it be true that p rather than q holds is simply that p holds and q does not hold. The fact that $p\&\sim q$ seems to be the more basic, the more primitive, since the fact that p rather than q holds contains it and that mysterious "something more." But then, this provides a conceptual explanation of why it is the case that p holds rather than q: p holds rather than q because $p\&\sim q$ holds, and $p\&\sim q$ is more ontologically basic, and necessarily whenever $a\&\sim b$ holds, a rather than b holds. Granted, this is not a contrastive explanation; but that only shows that the attempt to assimilate contrastive explanations to explanations of contrastive propositions failed.

3. Nonlocal CPs

3.1. *From local to nonlocal CPs*

A local CP is a principle that every localized contingent item of a certain sort has a cause. Thus, a local CP about contingent substances holds that every *substance* has a cause. A cosmological argument making use of a local CP needs to rule out infinite regresses. On the other hand, a nonlocal CP lacks the restriction that the items be localized in the way substances and events are, and this allows one to get out of infinite regresses. Using a CP instead of the PSR has the advantage that avoiding the van Inwagen problem and its relatives is easier.

I shall argue that the intuitions that typically make local CPs plausible apply just as well to nonlocal CPs. The locality restrictions are objectionably *ad hoc*, and if we should accept a local CP, we should accept a nonlocal CP. I will then give an argument for a powerful CP.

Consider first a restriction of CPs to (localized) substances as opposed to substance-like aggregates such as heaps of sand or the mereological sum of all the contingent substances now existing. The basic intuition behind such CPs is that bricks and other objects cannot come into existence without cause. But suppose that we learned from the correct metaphysics that bricks are not actually substances but are heaplike (as is indeed what Aristotle's metaphysics says about bricks). That would not affect our commitment to the impossibility of bricks coming into existence *ex nihilo*.

Now, maybe, we could argue that a CP restricted to substances would suffice to show that nonsubstantial items such as bricks that are made up of a finite number of substances (maybe elementary particles are substances even if bricks are not) have causes. For we could just apply the CP separately to each of the component substances, and while some of them could be causes of others, it could not be true of all the component substances that they are caused by other component substances, since that would require either a causal loop or an infinity of component substances. Thus, the restricted CP is sufficient to do justice to our intuition that bricks do not causelessly pop into existence even if bricks are heaps.

But this argument only works if bricks are made up of a finite number of substances. However, suppose we found out that a brick was, in fact, made up of an infinite number of particles. It does not look right now as if physics is heading in the direction of positing an infinite number of particles in ordinary material objects, but unless there is some logical problem with actual infinities – which problem would then be grist for the *kalam* arguer's mill, so an atheist will probably not want to embrace that option – the possibility is not absurd. Finding this out would not, I think, shake our conviction that a brick cannot pop into existence. Should it not be, if anything, harder for more particles to pop into existence? Nor would we be impressed by being told that the brick made of infinitely many particles popped into existence by the following pattern. At time $t_0 + 1$ second, particle number 1 was caused to exist by particle number 2; at time $t_0 + 1/2$ second, particle number 2 was caused to exist by particle number 3; at time $t_0 + 1/3$ second, particle number 3 was caused to exist by particle number 4, and so on, with none of the particles existing at time t_0. That would still count as an objectionable causeless popping into existence of the brick. But if bricks are not substances, this possibility cannot be ruled out by a CP restricted to substances. However, our intuitions call for this to be ruled out.

Perhaps we can restrict the CP to entities that consist of less than the sum total of all contingent beings. But that will gain the opponent of global CPs nothing. For instance, let S_0 be any simple particle that has a contingent cause (there are in fact many such) and let S_1 be the aggregate of all other contingent beings now in existence. Let C_1 be a cause of S_1, by the restricted CP. As the contingent cause of S_0 is outside of S_0 (since a particle cannot be caused by itself), this cause must be a part of S_1, and hence is caused by C_1. By transitivity, C_1 will also be the cause of S_0. If there are no simple particles, the argument is slightly more elaborate and is left as an exercise to the reader (hint: just let S_0 be a cat, and note that the cat surely has a cause that is outside of it).

And, certainly, it will not do to restrict the CP based on size, absurdly as if objects that are less than 10 m in diameter needed causes, but larger objects like the universe did not. Here, it is worth recalling Taylor's example of the universe being like a walnut (Taylor 1974, chap. 10). If we accept that *then* it should have a cause, we should also accept it when it is much larger.

A different kind of restriction is diachronic in nature. Perhaps, the CP can only be applied to entities that exist all at one time and cannot be applied to causal chains of entities, or at least to infinite such chains. However, once again, such a CP will fail to rule out a brick's doing what intuitively should count as popping into existence causelessly. Suppose we saw a brick pop into existence in midair. We would be deeply puzzled. To allay our puzzlement, a scientist tells us that study of the phenomenon reveals that what actually happened was this. The brick popped into existence at $t_0 + 1$ millisecond. There was no cause at t_0. However, at $t_0 + 1/2$ milliseconds, the particles of the brick were caused by a set of earlier particles making up a brick, which then immediately annihilated themselves (or perhaps underwent substantial change into the new ones). At $t_0 + 1/3$ milliseconds, the earlier particles were caused by a yet earlier set. And so on, *ad infinitum*. The whole infinite sequence took 1 millisecond to complete, but nonetheless each synchronic collection of particles had an earlier cause.[13] Surely, this would still be as objectionable as a brick popping into existence causelessly. That there was an infinite sequence of bricks, or of sets of particles, in that millisecond does not seem to affect the idea that this cannot happen.

Thus, to rule out the popping of bricks into existence *ex nihilo*, we need a CP not restricted in a way that rules out infinite chains. Similar considerations rule out CPs concerning events that do not generalize to infinite chains of events. A fire could start for no cause via an infinite chain of events, each temporal part of the fire being caused by an earlier temporal part of the fire, and so on, with the whole infinite chain only taking a second, and the temporally extended conflagration having no cause. That is absurd, and CPs for events should rule it out.

But perhaps there is a difference between infinite chains that take an infinite amount of time and infinite chains, like the one in the previous examples, that take a finite amount of time. Maybe we can restrict CPs to chains of causes that take a finite amount of time?

I do not think this is plausible because an interval from minus infinity to a finite number is order-isomorphic to a finite interval. For instance, the function $f(t) = -1/(t-1)$ maps the half-infinite interval[14] $(-\infty, 0]$ onto the half-open finite interval $(0, 1]$, while preserving order relations so that $t_1 < t_2$ if and only if $f(t_1) < f(t_2)$ for t_1 and t_2 in $(-\infty, 0]$.

But perhaps there is something relevantly metaphysically disanalogous about infinite amounts of time as opposed to finite ones. One difference would be if infinite amounts of time were impossible. But if so, then the *kalam* argument again shows up, and in any case, if an infinite amount of time is impossible, then a restriction of the CP to chains that take a finite amount of time is no restriction at all.

Another potential difference is that one might argue that a finite temporal interval either is preceded by a time or at least *could* be preceded by a time (if time has a beginning at the start of the interval), but a temporal interval infinite at its lower end *could not* be preceded by a time. This would be in support of a restriction of the CP to causal chains that are not temporally infinite in the direction of the past.

Consider first the following version of this disanalogy: the interval $(-\infty, 0]$ is not preceded by an earlier time, while a finite interval $(0, 1]$ is. But suppose that we are dealing with a causal chain spread over a half-open finite interval that is *not* preceded by an earlier time, since time starts with this half-open finite interval. In that case, we need a cause for the chain as a whole just as much as in the case where the half-open finite interval *is*

---

13. Examples like this go back at least to Łukasiewicz (1961), who tried to use them to show how free will could be reconciled with determinism (see also Shapiro 2001).
14. Here I use the standard notation where $(a, b] = \{x : a < x \le b\}$.

preceded by an earlier time. Suppose that we have a chain of causes spread over $(0, 1]$, tending to being temporally positioned at 0 in the backwards limit, and suppose that there is no "time 0." Surely, the nonexistence of a time prior to the interval makes it, if anything, "harder" for a chain of causes to arise without an external cause. After all, if even time does not exist prior to the chain of causes, then the chain is even more a case of coming into existence *ex nihilo*, since there is even less there. The absence of an earlier time does nothing to make it easier for things to arise causelessly.

Maybe, though, the idea is that we should require causes where causes can be reasonably demanded. But, the argument continues, a cause can only be reasonably demanded if there is a prior time, since causes must be temporally prior to their effects. However, the latter thesis is dubious. Kant's example of a metal ball continually causing a depression in a soft material shows that simultaneous causation is conceivable. And apart from full or partial reductions of the notion of causation to something like Humean regularity and temporal precedence, I do not think there is much reason to suppose that the cause of a temporal effect must even be in time.

Now consider the second version: even if there is no "time 0," there *could* be one. The finite interval $(0, 1]$ could be preceded by a time, while the interval $(-\infty, 0]$ could not. But it is quite unclear why this alleged modal difference is at all relevant to the existence of a cause for the chain. The absence of the possibility of an earlier time does not seem relevant, unless perhaps one thinks that causation requires temporal priority, a thesis one should, I think, reject.

There is also another, more controversial, objection to such a restricted CP. An infinite interval $(-\infty, 0]$ can be embedded in a larger temporal sequence $[-\infty, 0]$ obtained by appending a point, which we may call $-\infty$, and which stands in the relation $-\infty < x$ to every point x of $(-\infty, 0]$. It may well be that such a sequence could be the temporal sequence of some possible world. And, if so, then the interval $(-\infty, 0]$ *could* be preceded by an earlier time, and the disanalogy disappears.

It appears, thus, that local CPs are restricted in an *ad hoc* way. If we have strong intuitions in favor of local CPs, then we likewise should accept unrestricted CPs that can be applied to infinite chains of global aggregates of entities.

3.2. A modal argument for the CP

3.2.1. The basic argument

3.2.1.1. The effect would not have occurred without the cause

I will formulate this argument in terms of the cause of a contingent state of affairs. "States of affairs" here are understood as concrete things that can stand in causal relations, rather than as abstracta, and that exist if and only if they obtain. Moreover, I shall assume that states of affairs are individuated in such a way that in every world where Socrates is sitting at t_0, his sitting at t_0 is the very same state of affairs, just as the proposition that he is sitting at t_0 is the same proposition in every world. States of affairs are, thus, fine-grained, and Kripkean essentiality of origins does not hold for them – the state of affairs of Socrates' sitting at t_0 is the same state of affairs regardless of what caused it.

The argument now bootstraps its way from the *possibility* of a cause to the *actuality* of a cause. Thomas Sullivan (1994) has tried to find an argument for the CP based on the idea that a cause was a necessary condition for the effect. While this requirement is too strong, something in the vicinity of the following fact should be true:

(29)   That *C* causes *E* entails that were *C* not to exist or take place, *E* would not have taken place.

Claim (29) is not meant to be a complete analysis of causation, and, anyway, it requires that in cases of causal overdetermination we describe *C* carefully, for instance, as a disjunctive state of affairs. But something like this counterfactual claim is certainly a part of our notion of causation. David Lewis thought that this counterfactual claim was at the root of a complete analysis of causation, but this further controversial claim will not be needed.[15]

Suppose now that an airplane crashes due to metal fatigue in the ailerons. Then the following nested counterfactual is true:

(30)   Were the plane earlier hit by a surface-to-air missile, then the plane would have crashed and it would have been the case that were the plane not hit by a surface-to-air missile, the plane would, or at least might, still have crashed.

The plane would or might still have crashed because of the metal fatigue in the ailerons. Analogously, one might say this. Suppose that an airplane crashes for no reason at all. Then the following nested counterfactual should be true by parallel to (30):

(31)   Were the plane hit by a surface-to-air missile, then the plane would have crashed and it would have been the case that were the plane not hit by a surface-to-air missile, the plane would, or at least might, still have crashed.

Presumably, the consequent of the inner counterfactual can be taken to say that the plane would or might still have crashed for no reason at all. But this results in the absurdity that in the counterfactual world *w* where the plane is hit by a surface-to-air missile, and where no other crash-inducing causes are available (since the counterfactual that moved us to that world presupposed only one added cause – the surface-to-air missile), it is the case that were the missile not to have hit, the plane would or might still have crashed, contradicting the fact that the missile is the cause in *w* of the plane's crashing. Therefore, we should reject the possibility of the assumption that an airplane crashes for no reason at all.

As it stands, the argument may be thought to rest on improperly assimilating the case where the plane crashes because of no reason at all to the case where the plane crashes for some specific reason. In the latter case, when we move to a counterfactual world by positing

---

15. One might argue as follows against Lewis's more general claim. The recently shown failure of Lewis's own semantics for counterfactuals to properly exclude absurd cases of backtracking counterfactuals where the consequent is in the antecedent's past (Elga 2001; Pruss 2004b) strongly suggests that a semantics for counterfactuals will have to presuppose an asymmetry between the past and the future. One might further argue that there are no scientific asymmetries to sufficiently ground an asymmetry of such philosophical significance, and this might lead one to the Kantian view that the asymmetry in time supervenes on the asymmetry of causation: the past is just that region of time where (at least most of) the causes of present events are situated and the future is just that region of time where (at least most of) the effects of present events are situated. But if the asymmetry of time is presupposed in a semantics for counterfactuals, and the asymmetry between cause and effect is presupposed in the asymmetry of time, then at the pain of circularity one cannot analyze causation in terms of counterfactuals.

a new cause, we generate a case of overdetermination, and hence a case where the effect would still happen even without the new overdetermining cause. But in the case where the plane crashes because of no reason at all, the counterfactual world where a cause is posited is a world where there is only one cause, and hence the counterfactual that were the cause not to have occurred the effect would not have taken place is intact.

3.2.1.2. What can have a cause, does

We will see, however, that we can make a variant of the said argument into a valid and plausible argument for a CP. We will need a certain precise version of the observation that were the cause to have taken place, the effect would not have. This version says that if a state of affairs E is in fact caused by C, then E would not have occurred were no cause of E to exist:

(32)   (C causes E) $\Rightarrow$ (($\sim\exists D$ (D causes E)) $\Box\!\!\longrightarrow E$ did not occur),

where "$p \Box\!\!\longrightarrow q$" stands for "were p to hold, q would hold," and where "$\Rightarrow$" marks entailment. We will also need a *might* operator: "$p \diamond\!\!\longrightarrow q$" will stand for "were p to hold, q might hold." The two operators are related as follows: $(p \Box\!\!\longrightarrow q) \Leftrightarrow \sim(p \diamond\!\!\longrightarrow \sim q)$.

Premise (32) takes into account the possibility of overdetermination, where more than one state of affairs takes place, each of which is sufficient to cause E. It also takes into account the possibility that perhaps, were C not to have occurred, some other state of affairs D would have caused E. For instance, if members of some group are asked to volunteer to execute a traitor, then it might well be that Jones's shooting the traitor causes the death of the traitor, although were Jones not to have shot the traitor, someone else would have, and hence the traitor would still have died.

I shall now argue that if E is a state of affairs that *can* have a cause, then E is a state of affairs that *does* have a cause. Since every step in the argument will be a conceptual truth if the argument works, it will follow that if E has a cause in one possible world, then in every world in which E takes place, E has a cause.

David Lewis proposed the following analysis of counterfactuals for a possible proposition p: $p \Box\!\!\longrightarrow q$ holds providing there is a ($p\&q$)-satisfying world that is more similar to the actual world than any ($p\&\sim q$)-satisfying world is (Lewis 1986, sec. 1.3). While this analysis is, doubtless, not correct in all its details,[16] the intuitive idea of a connection between counterfactuals and possible worlds should remain. When we try to see whether $p \Box\!\!\longrightarrow q$ is true, we move to worlds relevantly similar to our world, but in which p holds, and see whether q holds in all such worlds. What features we must carry over from the actual world to the counterfactual world for it to count as "relevantly similar" is a difficult question. One might well say that, to the extent that p allows, one needs to carry over laws of nature and the past of p, while Lewis insists that "relevant similarity" has to do with being as similar as possible to the actual world. If, on the other hand, we think that there is some world relevantly similar to our world in which p holds but q does not, then we say that were p to hold, q might not hold.

---

16. See, for instance, Edgington (1995), Elga (2001), and Pruss (2004b, 2007). See also Section 3.2.2.1, below.

In modal logic, the Brouwer Axiom, which is entailed by S5, says that if a proposition p is actually true, then necessarily that proposition is possible. In terms of accessibility, this says that if we were to move to a world accessible from the actual world, the actual world would be accessible from that world: the accessibility relation is symmetric. But perhaps the best intuitive way to think about the Brouwer Axiom is to think of it as encapsulating the observation that in any nonactual situation we might consider, the events of the actual world remain relevant as alternative possibilities.

There is an analogue of this observation in the case of counterfactuals:

(33) $(q \ \& \ p \ \& \ M{\sim}p) \supset ({\sim}p \ \square\!\!\!\rightarrow (p \ \diamond\!\!\!\rightarrow q))$,

where M indicates metaphysical possibility. If we actually have both p and q holding, and then move to a relevantly similar world w in which p does not hold, so as to evaluate a counterfactual with antecedent ${\sim}p$, the events of the actual world are going to be relevant for the evaluation of counterfactuals in w. Hence, if we ask in w what would happen were p to hold, we need to say that q might happen, since q in fact happens in the actual world.

Consider how (33) plays out in some paradigmatic cases. Suppose p claims that Jones freely chose to set fire to a barn and q claims that Jones was arrested. Then, were Jones not to have set fire to the barn, it would certainly have been true that were he to have set fire to the barn, he at least *might* have been arrested. In the case where p reports the occurrence or nonoccurrence of some punctual event in time, we can think of the space of possibilities as a branching structure. Were p not to have occurred, we would have gone on a different branch from the one we had in fact gone on. But were we to have gone on that branch, it would have been true that were p to have occurred, things *might* have gone just as they have *actually* gone. The fact that things *have* gone a certain way witnesses to the relevant possibility of them going this way. In this sense, (33) is an analogue to the Brouwer Axiom.

We also need two further obvious axioms dealing with counterfactuals, where "$\Rightarrow$" is entailment:

(34) $(p \Rightarrow q) \Rightarrow (p \ \square\!\!\!\rightarrow q)$
(35) $((p \ \square\!\!\!\rightarrow q) \ \& \ (p \ \square\!\!\!\rightarrow {\sim}q)) \Rightarrow {\sim}Mp.$

Entailment relations are stronger than counterfactual conditionals, and it cannot be that both q would hold were p to hold and ${\sim}q$ would happen were p to hold, unless p is itself impossible.

But now (33)–(35) imply that anything that can have a cause does have a cause. Let q be the true proposition that event E occurs, and suppose that E can have a cause. For a *reductio*, let p be the true proposition that there is nothing that causes E, that is, ${\sim}\exists D$ (D causes E). However, since E can have a cause, $M{\sim}p$. Thus, by the Brouwer analogue (33), we have:

(36) ${\sim}p \ \square\!\!\!\rightarrow (p \ \diamond\!\!\!\rightarrow q).$

Let w be any possible world at which ${\sim}p$ holds. Then, w is a world at which E has a cause. Since nonexistent and nonoccurrent things can neither cause nor be caused, E occurs at w, as does a cause, call it C. Applying (32), we see that it is true at w that were no cause of E to have existed, E would not have occurred, that is, it is true at w that $p \,\square\!\!\rightarrow \sim q$. Since this is true at every world at which E has a cause, that is, at every world at which $\sim p$ holds, it follows that:

(37) $\sim p \Rightarrow (p \,\square\!\!\rightarrow \sim q)$.

But $p \,\square\!\!\rightarrow \sim q$ is equivalent to $\sim(p \,\diamond\!\!\rightarrow q)$. Thus, by (34):

(38) $\sim p \,\square\!\!\rightarrow \sim(p \,\diamond\!\!\rightarrow q)$.

By (35) and (36) it follows that $\sim Mp$. But p was assumed to be true, and true propositions are possible, and hence absurdly $\sim Mp$ and Mp.

Thus, the assumption for the *reductio* is false, and so p is false. Hence, there is a cause of E.

This is enough to show that Humeans are wrong to think that a brick could come into existence for no cause at all. For it is plain that there *can* be a cause of the state of affairs of a brick's coming into existence at t, and hence by the argument, there *is* such a cause.

It is plausible that for any physical kind of object identified *de dicto* and in a positive way, such as *a galaxy containing exactly n stars and having total mass M*, the state of affairs of that kind of object existing can have a cause, and hence does. Similarly, if we have a positive *de dicto* description D of all the physical stuff in the universe, it seems that it ought to be possible for there to be a cause of the state of affairs described by D. For instance, we could imagine D being satisfied in a larger world w^* where D describes a proper part P of the contents of w^*, a proper part that has a cause in another proper part Q of the contents of w^*, where Q might not actually exist in the actual world. That the description D is positive is important, since a nonpositive description could rule out the existence of Q, for example, by saying that there is nothing outside of what D describes.

From such considerations, we get a CP for physical objects, and by the same reasoning for causal chains of physical objects (surely there could be a cause of the whole chain). And this can yield a cosmological argument for a nonphysical being (see Section 4.2, below).

But let us slow down for a moment, and try for a more expansive result.

3.2.1.3. Which contingent states of affairs can have a cause?

If I could argue that all contingent states of affairs can have causes, then a CP for contingent states of affairs would follow from the conclusion of the previous section. However, there are several concerns about this idea.

A contingent state of affairs that contains a part that obtains necessarily perhaps cannot be expected to possibly have a cause. We do not expect the state of Socrates' having existed in a world without square circles to have a cause. Consider now the notion of a wholly contingent state of affairs, that is, one that has no component part that is necessary. Thus, the state of affairs of Socrates' having existed is wholly contingent, but the state of affairs of Socrates' having existed in a world that has no square circles is not wholly contingent. On a plausible set of mereological axioms for states of affairs, one can establish that every contingent state of affairs S contains a maximal wholly contingent part S^* such that, necessarily, S obtains if and only if S^* does.[17] We can now reasonably expect the possibility of causes for the wholly contingent substates.

A second problem is that if essentiality of origins holds, then that the state of affairs of Socrates' existing *can* have a cause *immediately* implies that the state of affairs *does* have a cause, since a cause of the state of affairs will presumably have to be a cause of Socrates, and hence will have to exist in every world where Socrates does. So if essentiality of origins holds, the atheist is likely not to grant that all contingent states of affairs *can* have causes. (Note that essentiality of origins could, in principle, hold for an uncaused being – such a being would then be *essentially* uncaused.)

Likewise, the smart atheist is likely not to grant that, in general, nonpositive contingent states of affairs can have causes, since granting that would yield the existence of a necessarily existent, causally efficacious being too quickly. For instance, the atheist is likely to think that there is a possible world that consists of only a single photon, and no necessarily existent, causally efficacious beings. But then, consider the state of affairs of there being one photon and nothing else. That state of affairs *cannot* have a cause, since that cause could not be the photon on pain of circularity and could not be anything else on pain of contradiction.

Consider now the following pair of claims:

(39)   If all wholly contingent, positive states of affairs that do not *de re* involve entities for which essentiality of origins holds have causes, then all wholly contingent, positive states of affairs have causes.

(40)   Every wholly contingent, positive state of affairs that does not *de re* involve contingent entities for which essentiality of origins holds *can* have a cause.

Claim (40) is an extension of the observation that states of affairs of the existence of *de dicto* described physical entities all can have causes. There is no reason to limit that observation to physical entities. If there can be a ghost that is 7-feet tall, then there can be a 7-foot tall ghost with a cause.

---

17. Koons (1997, Lemma 2) shows that every contingent state of affairs ("fact" in his terminology) contains a wholly contingent part. Let S^* be the aggregate of all wholly contingent parts of S. Note that S^* must itself be wholly contingent. For suppose, for a *reductio*, that it has a necessary part N. Then N has to overlap at least one of the wholly contingent parts of S, since every part of an aggregate must overlap at least one of the aggregated things. Thus, N will have a part in common with a wholly contingent part P of S. Thus, there will be a part Q that N and P will have in common. Any part of a necessary state of affairs is necessary (Koons 1997, Lemma 1), and so Q is necessary, contrary to the claim that P is wholly contingent, which is absurd. So S^* is wholly contingent. Moreover, it is a maximal, wholly contingent part of S. The only remaining question is whether it is the case that, necessarily, S obtains if and only if S^* does. One direction is clear: necessarily, if a state of affairs obtains, so do its parts, so, necessarily, if S obtains, so does S^*. For the converse, let N be the aggregate of all necessary parts of S. Clearly, N is itself necessary. Let S^{**} be the aggregate of N and S^*. Since N is necessary, necessarily if S^* obtains, so does S^{**}. If we can show that $S^{**} = S$, it will follow that, necessarily, if S^* obtains, so does S. For a *reductio*, suppose that S^{**} is not equal to S; then there is a U that overlaps one but not the other (Koons 1997, Axiom 3). Since S^{**} is a part of S, it must be that U overlaps S but not S^{**}. But then, let V be a part that S and U have in common. If V is contingent, it will have a wholly contingent part (Koons 1997, Lemma 2), and this part will then be a part of S^{**}, and so V will overlap S^{**}, and hence so will U, which contradicts what was already said. So V must be necessary. But then V is a part of N, and hence overlaps S^{**}, and hence U overlaps S^{**}, which again contradicts what was already said.

I now argue for (39). Say that a kind of entity is "essentially origined" if essentiality of origins holds for that kind of entity. I claim that any contingent state of affairs S that does *de re* involve essentially origined entities has an associated state of affairs $S^\dagger$ that does not. We obtain $S^\dagger$ by taking a canonical description D of S in some ideal language and Ramseyfying it as follows. If the description D made reference to essentially origined entities $e_1, e_2, \ldots$, so that $D = D(e_1, e_2, \ldots)$, then let E_i be the maximally specific, positive description of e_i that does not involve the *de re* occurrence of any essentially origined entities (I shall assume there is a unique maximal description, since we can just conjoin any descriptions that meet the criteria other than maximality). A positive description is one such that the state of affairs of its being satisfied is a positive state of affairs. Descriptions that use words such as "unique" are not positive. And now we can Ramseyfy by letting $D^\dagger$ be:

(41) $\exists x_1 \exists x_2 \ldots (D(x_1, x_2, \ldots) \mathbin{\&} E_1(x_1) \mathbin{\&} E_2(x_2) \mathbin{\&} \ldots).$

Finally, let $S^\dagger$ be the state of affairs described by $D^\dagger$.

Say that a world is "nice" if every pair of distinct essentially origined entities in that world differs in the maximally specific, positive, definitive descriptions that do not involve the *de re* occurrence of any essentially origined entities. On a plausible way of understanding Leibniz's doctrine of identity of indiscernibles, any world for which identity of indiscernibles holds is a nice world. It is very plausible that our world is nice – it seems very likely that our world, in fact, lacks indiscernibles.

Now, plausibly, in a nice world, a cause C of $S^\dagger$ is also going to be a cause of S. First of all, C will be the cause of everything in S except maybe of the numerical identities of the satisfiers of D being what they, are since perhaps different individuals could play the same roles and satisfy $D(x_1, x_2, \ldots)$. But, plausibly, there is no *further* step in causing particular individuals to occupy roles. Sophroniscus and Phainarete were causes of the existence of a philosopher executed by hemlock. There was nothing further that they did to cause the existence of *Socrates*. Moreover, if we include *all* of the causes of $S^\dagger$ in C, then the numerical identities of the essentially origined individuals will also be taken care of, since it is plausible that for essentially origined entities, once their full causes have been given, their identity is thereby explained.

Therefore, (39) holds in nice worlds, and our world seems to be nice.

To amplify on the argument, observe that there are three plausible kinds of entities, with "entity" broadly understood, that might be essentially origined: substances, events, and some natural kinds. We might be a bit more worried about natural kinds. If *all* natural kinds were essentially origined, then the maximal descriptions introduced in the Ramseyfication would be unable to include reference to natural kinds, and that might make the descriptions not be specific enough to ensure niceness of our world. However, plausibly, only *some* natural kinds are essentially origined. The thesis of essentiality of origins for natural kinds is highly implausible for basic kinds such as *electron*, *star*, and *organism*. Suppose the first electron, star, or organism could have arisen from a different cause. It would perhaps be a numerically different electron, star, or organism (respectively) from the first one in our world, but it would nonetheless still be an electron, star, or organism (respectively). Let us suppose that electrons arose from collisions between certain other particles. Then even had these collisions happened earlier or later, and had different individuals been involved in the collisions, it would still be *electrons* that arose. The only natural kinds for which essentiality of origins is plausible are biological taxa defined in evolution-ary terms. It is somewhat plausible that had an animal with a different evolutionary history had the same DNA as the first horses, that animal would not have been a horse. But the limitation on descriptions that they do not involve taxa defined in evolutionary terms is not much of a limitation for our purposes – we can use phenotypic or genotypic descrip-tions instead, and if these are maximally specific, we will capture sufficient detail for the purposes of niceness.

And it seems that typical substances and events of our world can be captured by positive *de dicto* descriptions quite well. This may not capture their numerical identity, but it gives a maximal description strong enough that we would say that the cause of that description's being satisfied is the cause of the entity.

Now, given the conclusion of the previous section, together with (39) in nice worlds as well as (40), we get the claim that all wholly contingent, positive states of affairs in nice worlds have causes. But it is highly plausible that if the CP holds in nice worlds for wholly contingent, positive states of affairs, it also holds in non-nice worlds. The niceness condi-tion is a version of the identity of indiscernibles. It would be odd indeed if there could not be a world consisting of a single uncaused brick, but there could be a world consisting of two indiscernible uncaused bricks. Hence, plausibly, the CP holds in all worlds for all wholly contingent, positive states of affairs.

One objection to this line of argument is that if libertarianism holds, it seems that states of affairs such as of George's freely choosing *A* are wholly contingent and positive, but cannot have a cause. One may worry whether *freely* choosing can be part of a positive state of affairs, since perhaps it entails the absence of external compulsion; but whether that worry is a good answer to the objection is unclear because many libertarians may accept that freedom is an *intrinsic* property of an action, and the absence of external compulsion is only relevant insofar as external compulsion would remove something from the intrinsic character of the action. However, the libertarian *can* say that the state of affairs of George freely choosing *A* has a cause. Maybe George is the cause. Or maybe George's making a choice between *A* and *B* while impressed by reasons *R* is the cause. Whether this cause provides a sufficient *explanation* of George's freely choosing *A* is a further question (see Section 2.3.2.3, above), but the mere claim of the existence of a cause is plausible.

3.2.2. Back to the PSR

If we do grant that causes always yield explanations, we can do even better than a CP on the given assumptions – we can get the PSR, supposing that the arguments previously outlined have successfully established the following claim:

(42)   Necessarily, all wholly contingent, positive states of affairs have causes.

This is not only a CP, but it seems to entail the necessary truth of a PSR for positive propo-sitions, that is, propositions that report positive states of affairs. For if *p* is a proposition reporting a positive state of affairs *S*, we can let S^* be the maximal, wholly contingent part of *S*. Recall that, necessarily, *S* obtains if and only if S^* does, and by (42), S^* has a cause *C*. Hence, we can explain the obtaining of S^* as follows: *S* obtains because S^* has a cause *C* and because contingent states of affairs obtain if and only if their maximal, wholly contingent substates do. If one objects that the noncontingent substates of S have not been explained, we can instead say that their obtaining is explained by the necessity of their obtaining or that they are self-explanatory, or stipulate that we are talking about explaining things *modulo* necessary truths, or perhaps hope that there is some way in which ultimately even the necessary truths all have explanations in terms of self-explanatory necessary truths (such as that each thing is identical with itself).

But now the necessary truth of a PSR for positive contingent propositions entails the necessary truth of a PSR for negative contingent propositions, where a negative proposition is the denial of a positive one. For if p is a negative contingent proposition, we can explain why p holds as follows: p holds because (a) there is nothing to explain why not-p holds, and (b) not-p is a positive contingent proposition, while (c) necessarily all positive contingent propositions that hold have explanations. This explanatory scheme is a variant of the scheme: E did not take place because no cause of E took place (see the discussion of the dog that did not bark in Section 2.3.2.2).

Finally, it is plausible that once we have explained all the positive contingent propositions and all the negative ones, then *all* contingent propositions will thereby have been explained, since their truth-values should supervene, in an explanation-preserving way, on the truth-values of the positive and negative ones.

This argument has an interesting consequence. I have argued (Pruss 2004a) that if we reject the PSR because we think that it has some counterexamples, such as the BCCF according to the van Inwagen argument, we should instead accept the restricted PSR (R-PSR):

(R-PSR) Every proposition that possibly has an explanation actually has an explanation.

Now, since the R-PSR claims to be a metaphysical principle, we should take it to be a necessary truth. We are now, however, in a position to see that the necessity of the R-PSR actually entails the PSR, *if* the arguments of the preceding section are successful. The argument is easy. The previous section shows, independently of any CP, that every wholly contingent, positive state of affairs can have a cause. Hence:

(43)   Necessarily, every proposition reporting a wholly contingent, positive state of affairs can have an explanation.

The R-PSR then entails that it does have an explanation. But the same argument that shows that (42) entails the PSR also shows that (43) does so as well.

There is good news and bad news here for the cosmological arguer. The bad news is that if there are counterexamples to the PSR, there will be counterexamples to the R-PSR, and so the R-PSR does not make possible a cosmological argument that would work even if the PSR were false. The good news is that those whose intuitions lead them to accept that whatever is explainable is explained need to also accept the PSR for all contingent propositions.

If, on the other hand, the arguments of the preceding section are *not* successful, then it seems to be possible to accept the R-PSR without being committed to the PSR. In Section 4.4, I will show how to run a cosmological argument for a First Cause based only on the R-PSR.

3.2.2.1. The Brouwer analogue

The greatest difficulties in the given modal argument for the CP are with (33). The first difficulty is that (33) cannot be a conceptual truth on Lewis's semantics for counterfactuals. According to David Lewis, $p \,\square\!\!\rightarrow q$ is true if and only if either p is necessarily false, or there is a $p\&q$-world (i.e. a world where $p\&q$ holds) closer to the actual world than any $p\&{\sim}q$-world (i.e. a world where $p\&{\sim}q$ holds).

Write Aw for a proposition true at w and only at w. We might take Aw to be the BCCF of w, or we might take Aw to be the proposition that w is actual. Let $q = Aw_0$, where w_0 is the actual world. Let w_1 be any other world, and let $p = {\sim}Aw_1$. Then, $q \& p \& M{\sim}p$ holds. Consider the consequent of (33). This says that there is a ${\sim}p$-world w at which $p \,\diamond\!\!\rightarrow q$ and which is closer than any ${\sim}p$-world at which ${\sim}(p \,\diamond\!\!\rightarrow q)$. In fact, there is only one ${\sim}p$ world, namely w_1. Thus, the consequent of (33) says simply that $p \,\diamond\!\!\rightarrow q$ holds at w_1. Now, $p \,\diamond\!\!\rightarrow q$ is equivalent to ${\sim}(p \,\square\!\!\rightarrow {\sim}q)$. The proposition $p \,\square\!\!\rightarrow {\sim}q$ holds at w_1 if and only if there is a $p\&{\sim}q$-world that is closer to w_1 than any $p\&q$-world is. Now, there is only one $p\&q$-world, namely w_0, and a $p\&{\sim}q$-world is just a world different from w_0 and w_1. Thus, $p \,\square\!\!\rightarrow {\sim}q$ holds at w_1 if and only if there is a world different from w_0 and w_1 that is closer to w_1 than w_0 is. Thus, ${\sim}(p \,\square\!\!\rightarrow {\sim}q)$ holds if and only if no other world is closer to w_1 than w_0.

What we have shown is that if (33) holds, then for any world w_1 other than the actual world w_0, the closest world to w_1 is w_0. But this is most unlikely. Moreover, (33) is presented as a conceptual truth. If it is such, then the said argument should work in all possible worlds. It follows that for every pair of worlds w and w_1, no other world is closer to w than w_1. This is equivalent to the claim that one never has a chain of three distinct worlds w_1, w_2 and w_3 such that w_2 is closer to w_1 than w_3 is. But surely there are such chains, and thus the consequence is absurd. Hence, the assumption that (33) is a conceptual truth leads to absurdity on Lewis's semantics.

However, all we need (33) for is the special case where q reports a wholly contingent, positive state of affairs and p reports the nonexistence of a state of affairs under a certain description (namely, under the description of being a cause of the state of affairs reported by q), and it might well be that in those cases (33) could still hold on Lewis's semantics. The given counterexample was generated using very special propositions – the proposition q was taken to be true at exactly one world and the proposition p was taken to be false at exactly one world. Ordinary language counterfactuals do not deal with such special propositions, and hence it might be that the intuitions supporting (33) do not require us to make (33) hold for these propositions, and hence these intuitions are not refuted in the relevant case by the counterexample.

This, however, is thin ice. One might perhaps more reasonably take (33) to entail a refutation of Lewis's semantics. In any case, Lewis's semantics are known to be flawed, especially when applied to propositions like the ones in the given counterexample. To see one flaw in them, suppose that w_0 is the actual world, and we have an infinite sequence of worlds w_1, w_2, w_3, ... such that w_{n+1} is closer to the actual world than w_n is. For instance, these worlds could be just like the actual world except in the level of the background radiation in the universe, with this level approaching closer and closer to the actual level as n goes to infinity. Let p be the infinite disjunction of the Aw_n for $n > 0$. Fix any $n > 0$. On Lewis's semantics, we then have:

(44) $p \,\square\!\!\rightarrow {\sim}Aw_n$.

For w_{n+1} is a $p\&\sim Aw_n$-world that is closer than any $p\&Aw_n$-world, since there is only one $p\&Aw_n$-world, namely w_n, and w_{n+1} is closer than it. This implies that it is true for every disjunct of p that were p true, that disjunct would be false! But, surely, there has to be some disjunct of p such that were p true, that disjunct might also be true.

Like the counterexample to (33), this counterexample deals with propositions specified as true at a small (in the case of p here, infinite, but still only countably infinite and hence much "smaller" than the collection of possible worlds, which is not only not countably infinite but is not even a set[18]) set of worlds. This shows that there is something wrong with Lewis's semantics, either in general or in handling such propositions (see also Pruss 2007).

To see even more clearly, although making use of a slightly stronger assumption about closeness series, that there is a commonality between a problem with Lewis's semantics and the Lewisian counterexample to (33), suppose the following principle of density: for any nonactual world w, there is a nonactual world w^* closer to the actual world than w is. This should at least be an epistemic possibility: our semantics for counterfactuals should not rule it out. Let w_0 be the actual world and put $p = \sim Aw_0$. Then, by the principle of density, on Lewis's semantics, there is no possible world w such that were p true, w might be actual, that is, such that $p \diamond\!\!\longrightarrow Aw$. To see this, suppose that we are given a w. First, note that it is hopeless to start with the case where w is w_0 since p and Aw_0 are logically incompatible. Next, observe that if w is not w_0, then we have $p \Box\!\!\longrightarrow \sim Aw$. For let w^* be any world closer than w. Then, w^* is a $p\&\sim Aw$-world that is closer than any $p\&Aw$ world, there being only one of the latter, namely w. But if we have $p \Box\!\!\longrightarrow \sim Aw$ and p is possible, then we do not have $p \diamond\!\!\longrightarrow Aw$.

But, intuitively, if p is possible, then there is *some* world which is such that it might be actual were p to hold. Lewis's semantics fails because of its incompatibility with this claim, on the aforementioned not implausible principle of density, which should not be ruled out of court by a semantics of possible worlds. Note further that the failure here is precisely a failure in the case of a might-conditional $p \diamond\!\!\longrightarrow q$ with p of the form $\sim Aw_1$ and q of the form Aw_2, which is precisely the kind of might-conditional that appeared in the analysis of the putative counterexample to (33). Lewis's semantics makes too few might-conditionals of this sort true, and it is precisely through failing to make a might-conditional of this sort true that it gave a counterexample to (33).

Thus, rather than having run my argument within Lewisian possible worlds semantics, it was run on an intuitive understanding of counterfactuals, which intuitions do support (33). It would be nice to have a complete satisfactory semantics for counterfactuals. Lewisian semantics are sometimes indeed helpful: they are an appropriate model in many cases. But as we have seen, they do not always work. Other forms of semantics meet with other difficulties. We may, at least for now, be stuck with a more intuitive approach.

If we want some more precision here, we might speak as follows. To evaluate $p \Box\!\!\longrightarrow q$ and $p \diamond\!\!\longrightarrow q$ at a world w, we need to look at some set $R(w,p,q)$ of "q-relevant p-worlds relative to w" and check whether q holds at none, some, or all of these. If q holds at all of them, then $p \Box\!\!\longrightarrow q$ and $p \diamond\!\!\longrightarrow q$. If it holds at none of them, then neither conditional is true. If it holds at some but not all of them, then $\sim(p \Box\!\!\longrightarrow q)$ and $p \diamond\!\!\longrightarrow q$. The difficulty is

18. Pruss (2001).

with specifying the q-relevant p-worlds. Proposition (33) then follows from the claim that the actual world is a q-relevant p-world relative to every world w which is a relevant $\sim p$-world relative to the actual world. This is plausible, and somewhat analogous to the Brouwer Axiom. However, this does not let us embed the discussion in a precise semantics because we do not have an account of what $R(w, p, q)$ is.

David Manley (2002) has come up with the following apparent counterexample to (33), which I modify slightly. Suppose our soccer team wins 20 to 0. Then, it is true that the team won overwhelmingly in the actual world w_0. What would have happened had our team not won? Presumably, the score would have been rather different, say 20 to 20, or 0 to 5, or something like that. Suppose the score is one of these – that we are in a possible world w_1 where our team has lost. Then, it is *not* true that were our team to have won, it would have won overwhelmingly. If our team in fact failed to win, as at w_1, then worlds where the team wins *overwhelmingly* are much more distant from our world than worlds where it wins by a bit. Thus, it is true at w_1 to say that were our team to have won, it would have won by a tiny amount. Putting this together, we conclude that were our team not to have won, then were it to have won, it would have won by a tiny amount. But this is incompatible with (33), which claims that were our team not to have won, then were it to have won, it *might* have won by a tiny amount.

But this account of the situation also relies on David Lewis's semantics, and again does so in a context in which Lewis's semantics *fail*. For, by this reasoning, if we are in a world where our team has not won, then we should say that were it to have won, it would have won by exactly one point. But this need not be true. Perhaps were it to get ahead by a point at some point in the game, then the other team would have become disheartened and lost by more. We can even more clearly see the problem in the Lewisian reasoning if we substitute a game very much like soccer except that its scores can take on any real value: perhaps instead of a flat one point for a goal, one gets a real-valued additive score depending on how close to the middle of a goal one hits. Then, by this reasoning, were our team not to have won, it would be true that were it to have won, it would have won by no more than $1/10$ of a point. Worlds where one wins by no more than $1/10$ of a point are closer than worlds where one wins by more than that. But this reasoning is perfectly general, and the "$1/10$" can be replaced by any positive number, no matter how tiny. But this is absurd. It is absurd to suppose that were our team not to have won, it would be true that were it to have won, it would have won by no more than $10^{-1,000}$ points.[19]

3.3. An objection: causing the causing

While the van Inwagen objection applies specifically to the PSR, there is a related objection to CPs. Suppose that our CP applies to all wholly contingent, concrete, contingent states of affairs. Suppose that state of affairs C causes state of affairs E. It may be that C is necessary (e.g. C might be God's existing and having such and such values), and thus one cannot get a regress by asking for C's cause, but there is a different move available. We can form a third state of affairs, the state of affairs C_1 of C's causing E, and then can ask what causes C_1. It seems plausible that if C is wholly contingent, then so is C_1. The object in asking this question is to generate a vicious regress. Once we gave the cause of C_1, we would form the state of affairs of that cause's causing C and so on.

---

19. This is similar to the coat thief example cited in Edgington (1995).

This problem looks formidable, but the real difficulty lies in choosing from the abundance of possible solutions. For instance, the literature contains Koons's solution (Koons 1997) on which C_1 is not a *further* state of affairs. Instead, C_1 consists simply in the mereological sum of C and E. Or one might argue that C_1 is only partly contingent, since in the case that interests us C is necessary and in some way enters into C_1, and its wholly contingent part C_1^* might not actually be distinct from E. Further, the scholastics apparently liked to say that the actuality of the cause *qua* cause is the effect. A good translation of "the actuality of the cause *qua* cause" may be "the cause's causing," so if they are right, then the cause's causing may not actually be distinct from E.

A different solution is to allow for a regress but to claim that it is not vicious. Not all regresses are vicious. If p is true, then it is true that p is true and so on. There does not appear to be any philosophical consensus on which regresses are vicious. A plausible suggestion is that regresses are vicious if they involve a dependence, whether explanatory, causal, or grounding. Thus, we should reject a theory of truth on which what makes a proposition true is that it is true that it is true, for then the truth regress would be a grounding regress. But as long one does not take such a theory of truth, the truth regress is not vicious.

Now, one might think that the causal regress here is an objectionable causal or explanatory dependence regress. Why did E happen? Because of C. But why did C cause E? Because of C_1. But why did C_1 cause C's causing E? Because of C_2. And so on. But it is mistaken to think that viciousness always occurs. The following seems a coherent account. *Ex hypothesi*, the cause of E is C. In particular, the cause of E is not C's causing E, at least not if that is an event distinct from C (and if it is not an event distinct from C, the problem disappears). In the process from C to E, C's causing E transpires. It is not the case that C's causing E is more ultimate causally than C. In fact, one might reasonably say that C causes C's causing E, and C causes C's causing C's causing E, and so on. These epi-events are not a part of the causal explanation of E, however.

Granted, we may sometimes explain that E happened not just because of C but because of C's causing E. We might, however, question whether this is always a perspicacious expression of the explanation – recall the fact that we do not say that "He died because he died of being stabbed" (see Section 2.3.2.2, above).

Given that the question is most interesting in the ultimate case of causation by a First Cause, and that the cosmological arguer thinks the ultimate case of causation is a case of agency, it might be good to consider how, on one interpretation of the phrase "C's causing E," this looks for agency. Suppose that x does A on account of reason R. Then the cause of A is x-who-appreciates-R, or maybe x's appreciating R. We can now ask why it is that R was what moved x, or why it is that x who appreciates R does A. After all, x may well also appreciate other reasons, reasons in favor of some other action, say B. We might ask why R is the reason that in fact moves x, and one way of putting this question is to ask for the cause of x-who-appreciates-R's causing A.

This is at least sometimes a substantive question to which a substantive answer is possible. Jones joined the Antarctic expedition because he appreciated the value of scientific discovery. But why was it that his appreciation of the value of scientific discovery moved him to join the Antarctic expedition, when instead his appreciation of the value of a congenial climate might have moved him to stay in Kansas? Perhaps it was because of a higher-order reason. Maybe he judges warmth to be a private bodily good and scientific discovery to be a nonprivate intellectual good, and he appreciates the value of sacrificing private bodily goods to nonprivate intellectual ones. In that case, there is a substantive answer to the substantive question: the value of scientific discovery moved him to join the Antarctic expedition because of his appreciation of sacrificing primitive bodily goods to nonprivate intellectual ones. And, of course, there might be a further question about why the second-order reason moved Jones.

But it is clear that such explanation will have to come to an end. We do not in fact have an infinite chain of reasons for every action, finite creatures as we are. And in fact, it is plausible that sometimes x does A for R, and there is no further answer to the question why it was that x did A for R, why it was that x-who-appreciated-R did A, beyond the fact that x appreciated R. Kant's ideal of being moved by the respect for duty provides an example of this. Why it is that Kenya, a perfect Kantian agent, kept her promise? It is because of her respect for duty. And why was Kenya moved by her respect for duty? Because her respect for duty requires of her that she be moved by reasons of duty. This sounds circular, but in fact we can see it as a case where respect for duty not only moves the Kantian to keep her promise but also to keep her promise out of respect for duty. This would be a case like the one I suggested earlier, where C causes C's causing E: respect for duty causes her respect of duty to be the cause of her action. No vicious regress ensues here, since there is nothing further to explain about why respect for duty moved Kenya beyond her respect for duty. Respect for duty causes her respect of duty to be the cause of her concretely action, precisely in and through respect causing that action in the absence of other causes.

Nor is Kantianism the only kind of case where this happens. Suppose George does something out of love for his child. It seems quite plausible that not only is love moving him to benefit the child but also love is moving him to benefit the child out of love. So cases of agency can, plausibly, have a structure that evades the Regress Problem.

There is a final answer to our Regress Problem, which I think is the best, and it is to identify C's causing E with C's causal activity. Now, in some cases, we can ask for a further cause of C's causal activity – we can ask what moved the mover. But what if C's causal activity is a necessary being? Then C's causal activity does not itself fall within the purview of the CP. Those who accept divine simplicity, with its contention that God is God's activity, will likely accept this; if God is simple and a necessary being, his activity must itself be necessary, being identical with him.

One might say that this cannot be right, at least not in the case closest to the cosmological arguer's heart, the case of God's causing this universe. For if God's causal activity is necessary, then God's causing this universe is necessary, and hence this universe is a necessary being, which is absurd, besides being contrary to the assumptions of typical cosmological arguments. But this objection commits a *de re/de dicto* fallacy. Consider the argument written out:

(45) C_1 is God's causal activity and is a necessary being. (Premise)
(46) C_1 is God's causing E. (Premise)
(47)   Therefore, God's causing E is a necessary being.
(48)   Therefore, God necessarily causes E.

The fallacy is in the last step, which has essentially the following logical form:

(49)   The F is a necessary being.
(50)   Therefore, necessarily, the F exists.

But this is fallacious if "the F" in (50) is read *de dicto*, as it must be in the case where F is "God's causing E." The number of eyes of the tallest person is, let us suppose, the number two and, let us also suppose, that the number two is a necessary Platonic being. But it is incorrect to conclude that, necessarily, the number of eyes of the tallest person exists, since that would entail the falsehood that necessarily there is a tallest person (it could be that no person has a height or that there is a tie).

The inference from (49) to (50) requires that Fness be an essential property of the F. It is not an essential property of the number two that it be the number of eyes of the tallest person, and hence the inference fails in that case. Similarly, in the God case, the argument is only going to work if it is an essential property of God's activity that it be the same as God's causing E. But this proponents of divine simplicity should deny. They should instead insist that the same activity would count as God's causing E in those worlds where God causes E and as God's causing F in those worlds where God causes F. A very imperfect analogy for this is that the same act of writing down a sequence of numbers is, in some worlds, the filling out of a winning lottery ticket and in others the filling out of a losing lottery ticket. The reason for the imperfection in the example is that in the lottery case, it does not depend on the act which lottery tickets are drawn, but everything, in some way, depends on God's act. But it should be no surprise if there is no close analogue to doctrines coming from divine simplicity.

The reason for the multitude of responses to the objection is that it is just not clear what "C's causing E" picks out. It might pick out the mereological sum of C and E. It might pick out E. It might pick out something causally posterior to C. To some extent the details will depend on fine details in the theory of causation, and to some extent it may simply be a matter of choosing what one means by the ambiguous phrase "C's causing E."

4. Toward a First Cause

4.1. Overcoming the Regress and Taxicab Problems

I have defended three principles, each of which is sufficient to overcome the Glendower Problem: a PSR for contingent propositions, a CP for wholly contingent positive states of affairs, and a CP not just for individual events/substances but for chains of events/substances. Now the question is whether they are sufficient to overcome the Regress and Taxicab problems and yield the existence of a First Cause. I shall argue in the positive, thereby giving versions of three cosmological arguments by Leibniz, Koons (1997), and Meyer (1987), respectively. I shall follow these three by giving a fourth argument, due to White (1979), and another argument based on the ideas in Pruss (2004a), both of which arguments are based on restrictions of the PSR.

4.1.1. The PSR

4.1.1.1. The basic argument

Consider once again the BCCF p, which was the conjunction of all contingently true propositions, perhaps with truth-functional redundancy removed. By the PSR, p has an explanation, call it q. What is q like? There are two general options. Either q is necessary or q is contingent. If q is contingent, then it is contained in p, and since q explains p, it follows that q is self-explanatory. Thus, q must be necessary or else contingent and self-explanatory. (Here we are, of course, retracing a part of the van Inwagen argument from Section 2.3.2.1.)

Next, observe that it is plausible that contingent existential propositions ultimately can only be explained causally. Since p includes many contingent existential propositions, q must state the existence of one or more causes. If these causes are all contingent substances or events, then the existence of these causes will be among the contingent existential propositions in p that are to be explained. But given a set of contingent entities, these entities can neither collectively nor individually causally explain their own existence. Nothing can be a cause of itself, *pace* Descartes. The existence of a cause is explanatorily prior to the existence of the effect, but nothing can be explanatorily prior to itself.

So the cause must be something necessary, presumably either a necessarily existing substance or a necessarily occurring event. Plausibly, there can be no events without substances – events are what happens to substances. A necessarily existing event happens to a necessarily existing substance. So we do get to a necessarily existing substance.

Moreover, as far as we can tell, there are three ways that something can be explained. First, one can have a conceptual explanation that explains one fact in terms of a conceptually connected fact entailing it in an explanatorily relevant way, as when we say Pat's action was wrong because it was the breaking of a promise, or that a knife is hot because its molecules have high kinetic energy. A conceptual explanation of a contingent proposition will itself involve a contingent proposition, and a nonconceptual explanation will be needed. We can say that the Queen of England exists because Elizabeth of Windsor is the Queen of England, a conceptual explanation, but the explanation of the existence of Elizabeth of Windsor will involve the gametes of the Duke and Duchess of York, and this will not be a conceptual explanation. Since q is the ultimate explanation of all contingent propositions, it will not be a conceptual explanation, except perhaps in part.

Second, one can explain things scientifically by citing laws of nature and initial conditions. Now, on some accounts of laws of nature, the laws of nature are contingent and non-self-explanatory. They will thus have to enter into the explanandum p, but not the explanans q. Moreover, the most plausible account of laws of nature that makes them necessary grounds them in the essences of natural objects. But natural objects are contingent. Hence, even though the laws of nature will be necessary, which laws are *applicable* to a given situation will depend on the contingent question of which contingently existing natural objects are involved in the situation. The ultimate explanation q cannot involve laws grounded in the essences of contingently existing natural objects, since q explains the existence of contingently existing natural objects. Moreover, the initial conditions cited in scientific explanations are contingent and non-self-explanatory. But q is either necessary or contingent and self-explanatory. So q cannot be a scientific explanation.

The last kind of explanation we know of involves the causal activity of an agent or, more generally, a substance. The substance will have to be a necessary being, or else it will absurdly be a *causa sui*, something that causally explains its own existence (since it explains all of the BCCF). Hence, the ultimate explanation involves one or more causally efficacious necessary beings, whom we may call First Causes. Were it not for the Gap Problem, we could now say *et hoc dicimus deum*.

4.1.1.2. Objection 1: explanations in terms of a principle

The main objection here is that perhaps there is some *further* mode of explanation, one that is not conceptual, scientific, or agentive. The main actually proposed alternative is explanation in terms of a metaphysical principle. This principle would have to be different in kind from run-of-the-mill metaphysical principles such as the Principle of Identity of Indiscernibles or the Principle of Impossibility of Circular Causation: it must be a principle capable of explaining the existence of the apparently contingent denizens of our world.

The best candidate principle is due to John Leslie (2001) and Nicholas Rescher (2000). I will discuss Rescher's formulation here. The idea is to explain the BCCF in terms of the Principle of Optimality: of metaphysical necessity, the best narrowly logically possible world is actual. However, Rescher's suggestion is one that the defender of the cosmological argument need not worry about too much, since it is plausible that the best narrowly logically possible world is a world that contains God, considered as a maximally great being. Rescher himself thinks this. And so, in any case, we get the existence of God, albeit in a somewhat more roundabout way. Leslie does not agree – he opts instead for an infinity of divine knowers. I suspect Rescher is right in supposing a single deity – any particular number of deities other than one would seem *ad hoc* vis-á-vis optimality, while a world with a single deity has an elegant and valuable unity to it. This is true whether the number is finite, say 117, or infinite, say $\aleph_{117}$. And if the number is Cantorian "absolute infinity," then it does not seem as though one can make any sense of it.

Moreover, it is plausible (although Rescher denies it) that principles need to be made true by something, and this something must have being. A principle cannot by itself pull beings into existence out of a metaphysical magic hat, since a principle itself must be true *of* something and true in virtue of something.

4.1.1.3. Objection 2: can we form the BCCF?

Forming the BCCF may present set-theoretic concerns. Not every conjunction of propositions makes sense, as was shown by Davey and Clifton (2001). Modifying their construction slightly, let p be conjunction of all true propositions that do not contain themselves as proper subformulas. Then p is true. Let q be the proposition *that p is true*. Now, either q is a proper subformula of itself or not, and in either case a contradiction ensues. For if q is a proper subformula of itself, then it is not a conjunct of p. But the only way q could be a proper subformula of itself is if it is a subformula of p, since all proper subformulas of q are subformulas of p. Since q is not a conjunction, the only way it can be a subformula of p is if it is a subformula of one of the conjuncts of p. Now, q is not a conjunct of p, as we said. Hence, q must be a proper subformula of one of the conjuncts of p, say of p_1. But p is a proper subformula of q, and p_1 is a subformula of p, so it follows that p_1 is a proper subformula of itself, and hence not a conjunct of p, contrary to the assumption. Suppose on the contrary that q is not a proper subformula of itself. Then it is a conjunct of p, and hence a proper subformula of itself, and absurdity ensues again.

This argument is a challenge: if some conjunctions do not make sense, how do we know that the BCCF makes sense? One way to meet the challenge is to try to shift the burden of proof. A conjunction of propositions should be assumed to make sense unless it is proved not to.

Alternately, one might use the strategy of Gale and Pruss (2002) here. Replace the BCCF by the BCCF*, which is the conjunction of the following:

(a)   all true contingent atomic propositions,

(b)   a "that's all clause" that says that any true contingent atomic proposition is one of these ones (this clause will involve an infinite disjunction such as in: "for all p, if p is a true contingent atomic proposition, then p is a_1 or a_2 or . . ."),

(c)   all true propositions appearing in the explananda of contingent atomic propositions or of conjunctions thereof,

(d)   all true basic propositions reporting causal relations,

(e)   a "that's all clause" that says that all the actual explanatory relations supervene on the facts reported in the above conjuncts. (Gale & Pruss 2002, p. 95)

Here, "basic propositions" might be taken to be ones that are not true in virtue of some more basic propositions' being true, in the way in which the proposition that George is human or rhino is true in virtue of the more basic proposition that he is human. Plausibly, the truth of the BCCF supervenes on that of the BCCF*, and we could probably run our cosmological argument with the BCCF* in place of the BCCF.

Also, some PSR-based cosmological arguments are not subject to this objection. For instance, we could ask why there are any contingent beings. It is highly plausible that *that there are contingent beings* is itself a contingent proposition. For if it were a necessary proposition that there are contingent beings, then we would have odd necessary truths such as that, necessarily, if there are no contingent nonunicorns, then there are contingent unicorns. Moreover, the explanation of why there are contingent beings cannot involve the causal efficacy of contingent beings. But, plausibly, an existential proposition can only be explained by citing the causal efficacy of something, and hence of a necessary being.

Note that if there is no way of forming something relevantly like the BCCF, then the van Inwagen objection, which is the main objection to the PSR, fails. So it could be a service to a defender of the PSR if nothing like the BCCF could be formed, although harder work would be needed then for running the cosmological argument, perhaps along the lines of the Gale and Pruss (2002) strategy.

4.1.1.4. Objection 3: the Hume–Edwards–Campbell principle

Hume states:

> Did I show you the particular causes of each individual in a collection of twenty particles of matter, I should think it very unreasonable, should you afterwards ask me, what was the cause of the whole twenty. This is sufficiently explained in explaining the cause of the parts. (Hume 1907, p. 120)

Paul Edwards (1959) illustrates this with the case of five Inuit on a street corner in New York. If for each Inuit we gave an explanation of why he or she is there, we would thereby have explained why they are all there.

We can generalize this to the Hume–Edwards Principle (HEP):

(51)   (HEP) In explaining every conjunct of a proposition, one has explained the whole proposition.

If the HEP is true, the PSR-based cosmological argument can be blocked. The objector can simply suggest that one contingent proposition is explained by a second, and the second by a third, and so on *ad infinitum*, and thereby the whole BCCF is explained.

But the HEP is false. The first objection to HEP is that it does not take into account the fact that there can be more to explaining the conjunction than explaining the conjuncts. If there were a hundred Inuit on a street corner in New York, individual explanations of each one's presence would miss the point of explaining why there are a *hundred* Inuit all there. There is a coincidence to be explained. This kind of objection has been pressed, for example, by Gale (1999, p. 254).

This response is, however, insufficient. First of all, while *sometimes* explaining the conjuncts is unsatisfactory as an explanation of the whole, sometimes it is quite satisfactory. If there are two Inuit there on the corner, then to say that one is there to give a paper on the cosmological argument at a conference in the hotel at that corner and the other is there because New York City winter is preferable to Iqaluit winter is likely to be a fine explanation of the conjunction. The cosmological arguer might then be required to show that the BCCF is in fact a case where an explanation of the conjuncts is insufficient for an explanation of the whole. There are issues as to onus of proof here, but it is better for cosmological arguer to sidestep them if possible.

The second problem with this response is that while it provides a counterexample to the HEP, there is a weaker version of the HEP due to Campbell (1996) that these sorts of examples do not address. Campbell agrees that sometimes we need to do more than explain the parts to explain the whole. Indeed, there may be a further story, an Inuit conspiracy, say. However, it *might* be that the individual explanations of the parts are the whole story and are the explanation of the whole. If there are a hundred Inuit on the street corner, then it seems *likely* that there is a further explanation beyond individual ones. But there *might not be*. It could be that it is just a coincidence, and the whole is correctly explained solely in terms of the individual parts.

This suggests the following Hume–Edwards–Campbell Principle (HECP):

(HECP) For any proposition *p* such that one has explained every conjunct of a proposition, one might have thereby explained the whole.

We can take the "might" as epistemic possibility absent evidence of a further explanation. The HECP is sufficient for blocking the PSR-based cosmological argument. For the defender of the HECP can say we *might* have explained the whole of the BCCF by explaining one proposition in terms of another *ad infinitum*, and then the onus would be on the cosmological arguer to provide evidence that there is a further explanation of the BCCF. But if one can provide such evidence, one probably does not need the PSR-based cosmological argument.

However, the HECP is also subject to counterexample, and any counterexample to the HECP will automatically be a counterexample to the stronger HEP. Perhaps the simplest counterexample is the following (Pruss 1998). At noon, a cannonball is not in motion, and then it starts to fly. The cannonball flies a long way, landing at 12:01 p.m. Thus, the cannonball is in flight between 12:00 noon and 12:01 p.m., in both cases noninclusive.

Let p_t be a proposition reporting the state of the cannonball (linear and angular moment, orientation, position, etc.) at time t. Let p be a conjunction of p_t over the range

$12:00 < t < 12:01$. I now claim that p has not been explained unless we say what caused the whole flight of the cannonball, for example, by citing a cannon being fired. This seems clear. If Hume is right and it is possible for causeless things to happen, then it could be that there is no cause of the whole flight. But that is just a case where p has not been explained. To claim that there was no cause of the flight of the cannonball but we have explained the flight anyway would be sophistry.

But if the HECP is true, then there might be an explanation of p without reference to any cause of the flight of the cannonball. For take any conjunct p_t of p. Since $12:00 < t$, we can choose a time t^* such that $12:00 < t^* < t$. Then, p_t is explained by p_{t^*} together with the laws of nature and the relevant environmental conditions, not including any cause of the whole flight itself. By the HECP we *might* have explained all of p by giving these explanations. Hence, by the HECP we might have explained the flight of a cannonball without giving a cause to it. But that is absurd.[20]

Perhaps the defender of the HECP might say that it is relevant here that there was a time before the times described by the p_t, namely *noon*, and the existence of this time is what provides us with evidence that there is a further explanation. But that is mistaken, for if there were no noon – if time started with an open interval, open at noon – that would not make the given explanation of p in terms of its conjuncts, the laws, and the environmental conditions any better an explanation.

The HECP is, thus, false. But there is some truth to it. In the cannonball case, we had an infinite regress where each explanation involved another conjunct of the same proposition. Such a situation is bound to involve a vicious regress. The HEP and HECP fail in the case where the individual explanations combine in a viciously regressive manner. They also fail in cases where the individual explanations combine in a circular manner. If it should ever make sense to say that Bob is at the party because Jenny is and that Jenny is at the party because Bob is, that would not explain why it is that Bob and Jenny are at the party. A further explanation is called for (e.g. in terms of the party being in honor of George's birthday, and George being a friend of Bob), and if, contrary to the PSR, it is lacking, then that Bob and Jenny are at the party is unexplained. Likewise, if we could explain that Martha constructed a time machine because of instructions given by her future self, and that Martha's future self gave her instructions because she had the time machine to base the instructions on and travel back in time with, that would not explain the whole causal loop. How an explanation of the whole loop could be given is not clear – maybe God could will it into existence – but without an explanation going beyond the two circular causes, the loop as a whole is unexplained.

Thus, not only is the HECP false in general, but it is false precisely in the kind of cases to which Hume, Edwards, and Campbell want to apply it: it is false in the case of an infinite regress of explanations, each in terms of the next.

Interestingly, the HEP *may* be true in finite cases where there is no circularity. Indeed, if we can explain each of the 20 particles, and if there is no circularity, we will at some point in our explanation have cited at least one cause beyond the 20 particles, and have given a fine explanation of all 20. Granted, there may be worries about coincidence, about

---

20. This counterexample to HECP makes use of the density of time. Many of the best reasons for doubting the density of time involve the sorts of considerations about traversing infinity that are at the heart of conceptual versions of the *kalam* argument (the Grim Reaper Paradox is the main exception to this). Thus, some of the people who object to the density of time assumption here will therefore have to worry about the *kalam* argument, which is discussed in Chapter 3 of this book.

whether the *whole* has been explained, but these worries can, I think, be skirted. For if I have explained individually why each of a hundred Inuit is at the street corner, and done so in a noncircular manner, then I have explained why there are a hundred Inuit there. Now my explanation may not be the best possible. It may not tell me everything there is to know about how the hundred Inuit got there, for example, through the agency of some clever manipulator who wanted to get Inuit extras for a film, but it is *an* explanation. But that is because the explanation goes beyond the contingent hundred Inuit, if circularity is avoided.

At this point it is also worth noting that anybody who accepts the possibility that an infinite regress of contingent propositions be explained by the regressive explanatory relations between these propositions is also committed to allowing, absurdly, that we can have two distinct propositions r and q such that r has the resources to explain q, q has the resources to explain r, and where the explanatory relations here also have the resources to explain the conjunction $r\&q$. For suppose that we have a regress of explanations: p_1 explained by p_2, p_2 by p_3, and so on. Let r be the conjunction of all the odd-numbered p_i, and let q be the conjunction of all the even-numbered p_i. Since the conjunction of all p_i has been explained in terms of the individual explanatory relations, by the same token we can say that r is explained by means of the explanatory resources in q since each conjunct of r is explained by a conjunct of q (p_7 being explained by p_8 and so on), and q is explained by means of the resources in r since each conjunct of q is explained by a conjunct of r (p_8 being explained by p_9 and so on). And these relations, in virtue of which r has the resources to explain q and q to explain r, also suffice to explain $r\&q$.

Quentin Smith has argued that the universe can cause itself to exist, either via an infinite regress or a circle of causes. However, while he has claimed that such a causal claim would provide an answer to the question "why does the universe exist?" (Smith 1999, p. 136), he appears to have provided no compelling argument for that conclusion. Hence, it is possible to grant Smith that the universe can cause itself to exist via an infinite regress or a circle of causes while denying that this can provide an *explanation* of why the universe exists. Granted, in normal cases of causation, to cite the cause is to give an explanation. However, when we say that the universe "caused itself to exist" via a regress or a circle of causes, we are surely using the verb "to cause" in a derivative sense. The only *real* causation going on is the causes between the items making up the regress or the circle. If we have such a story, maybe we can say that the universe caused itself to exist in a derivative sense, perhaps making use of some principle that if each part of A is caused by a part of B, then in virtue of this we can say that A is caused by B, but this derivative kind of causation is not the sort of causation which must give rise to an explanation. For, in fact, regresses and circles do not explain the whole.[21]

21. It is worth noting that Smith's arguments for circular causation are weak. One argument relies on quantum entanglement. Smith seems to think that simultaneous but spatially distant measurements of entangled states could involve mutual causation between the states. But that is far from clear; circular causation is only one possible interpretation of the data, and how good an interpretation it is depends in large part precisely on the question whether circular causation is possible. Smith's more classical example in terms of Newtonian gravitation simply fails: "There is an instantaneous gravitational attraction between two moving bodies at the instant t. Each body's infinitesimal state of motion at the instant t is an effect of an instantaneous gravitational force exerted by the other body at the instant t. In this case, the infinitesimal motion of the first body is an effect of an instantaneous gravitational force exerted by the second body, and the infinitesimal motion of the second body is an effect of an instantaneous gravitational force of the first body. This is a case of the existence of a state $S1$ being caused by another state $S2$, with the existence of $S2$ being simultaneously caused by $S1$" (Smith 1999, pp. 579–80). This is

4.1.1.5. Objection 4: can there be a necessarily existent, causally efficacious being?

Perhaps a necessary being is impossible. Abstracta such as propositions and numbers, however, furnish a quick counterexample to this for many philosophers. However, one might argue further that there cannot be a *causally efficacious* necessary being, whereas the unproblematic abstracta such as propositions and numbers are causally inefficacious.

A radical response to this is to question the dogma that propositions and numbers are causally inefficacious. Why should they be? Plato's Form of the Good looks much like one of the abstracta, but we see it in the middle dialogues as explanatorily efficacious, with the *Republic* analogizing its role to that of the sun in producing life. It might seem like a category mistake to talk of a proposition or a number as causing anything, but why should it be? Admittedly, propositions and numbers are often taken not to be spatiotemporal. But whence comes the notion that to be a cause one must be spatiotemporal? If we agree with Newton against Leibniz that action at a distance is at least a metaphysical possibility, although present physics may not support it as an actuality, the pressure to see spatiality or even spatiotemporality as such as essential to causality is apt to dissipate – the restriction requiring spatiotemporal relatedness between causal relata is just as unwarranted as the restriction requiring physical contact.

Admittedly, a Humean account of causation on which causation is nothing but constant conjunction only works for things in time, since the Humean distinguishes the cause from the effect by temporal priority. But unless we are dogmatically beholden to this Humean account, to an extent that makes us dogmatically *a priori* deny the existence of deities and other nonspatiotemporal causally efficacious beings, this should not worry us.

Moreover, there is actually some reason to suppose that propositions and numbers enter into causal relations. The primary problem in the epistemology of mathematics is of how we can get to know something like a number, given that a number cannot be a cause of any sensation or belief in us. It is plausible that our belief that some item x exists can only constitute knowledge if either x itself has a causal role in our formation of this belief or if some cause of x has such a causal role. The former case occurs when we know from the smoke that there was a fire, and the latter when we know from the sound of a match struck that there will be a fire. But if something does not enter into any causal relations, then it seems that our belief about it is in no way affected by it or by anything connected with it, and hence our belief, if it coincides with the reality, does so only coincidentally, and hence not as knowledge. Of course, there are attempts to solve the conundrum on the books. But

---

simply not really a case of circular causation. The infinitesimal motion of each body at t does not cause the infinitesimal motion of the other body at t. Nor does the infinitesimal motion of either body at t cause the gravitational force of either body. Nor does the gravitational force of either body cause the gravitational force of the other. Rather, the gravitational force of each body partly causes the infinitesimal motion of the other body. Now, if we throw into the state of each body *both* its infinitesimal motion *and* its gravitational force, then we have a case where a part of the state of each body causes a part of the state of the other body. But that is not really circular causation, except maybe in a manner of speaking, just as it would not be circular causation to say that if I punch you in the shoulder while you punch me in the face, a part of my total state (the movement of my arm) causes a part of your total state (pain in your shoulder) and a part of your total state (the movement of your arm) causes a part of my total state (pain in my face). For there are four different parts of the total state involved, whereas in circular causation there would be only two.

the puzzle gives us some reason to rethink the dogma that numbers can neither cause or be caused.

But even if abstracta such as numbers and propositions are causally inefficacious, why should we think that there cannot be a nonabstract necessary being that is causally efficacious? One answer was already alluded to: some will insist that only spatiotemporal entities can be causally efficacious and it is implausible that a necessary being be spatiotemporal. But it was difficult to see why exactly spatiotemporality is required for causal connections. (See also Chapter 5 in this volume on the argument from consciousness.)

A different answer might be given in terms of a puzzlement about how there could be a nonabstract necessary being. The traditional way of expressing this puzzlement is that given by Findlay (1948), although Findlay may have since backpedaled on his claims. A necessary being would be such that it would be an analytic truth that this being exists. But it is never analytic that something exists. If $\exists x(Fx)$ is coherent, so is $\sim\exists x(Fx)$. Basically, the worry is caused by the Humean principle that anything that can be thought to exist can also be thought not to exist. But it is by no means obvious why this principle should be restricted, without thereby doing something *ad hoc*, to nonabstract beings.

Indeed, why should abstract beings alone be allowed as necessary? Why should its necessarily being true that $\exists x(x$ is a deity) be more absurd than its necessarily being true that $\exists x(x$ is a number)? Perhaps the answer is that we can *prove* the existence of a number. In fact, mathematicians prove the existence of numbers all the time. Already in ancient times, it was shown that there exist infinitely many primes.

However, these proofs presuppose axioms. The proof that there are infinitely many primes presupposes a number system, say, with the Peano axioms or set theory. But a statement of the Peano axioms will state that there *is* a number labeled "0" and there *is* a successor function s such that for any number n, sn is also a number. Likewise, an axiomatization of set theory will include an axiom stating the existence of some set, for example, the empty set. If our mathematical conclusions are existential, at least one of the axioms will be so as well. The mathematical theory $\sim\exists x(x = x)$ is perfectly consistent as a mathematical theory if we do not have an existential axiom. Thus, if we are realists about numbers, we are admitting something which exists necessarily and that does not do so simply in virtue of a proof from nonexistential axioms.

Of course, one might not be a realist about abstracta. One might think that we do not need to believe that there necessarily exist propositions, properties, or numbers to be able to talk about necessarily true propositions or necessarily true relations between numbers or properties. But if the critic of the PSR had to go so far as to make this questionable move, the argument against the PSR would not be very plausible.

In any case, not all necessity is provability. We have already seen that the work of Gödel questions the thesis that all necessity is provability or analyticity (cf. Section 2.2.6.2, above). Kripke (1980), too, has questioned the same thesis on different grounds. That horses are mammals is a proposition we discover empirically and not one we can prove *a priori*. But it is nonetheless a *necessary* thesis. So is the proposition that every dog at some point in its life contained a carbon atom.

Now, it is admittedly true that the Kripkean necessities are not necessities of the *existence* of a thing. But they provide us with an example of necessarily true but not analytic propositions. Another such example might be truths of a correct metaphysics, such as that it is impossible that a trope exists, or that it is necessary that a trope exists in any world containing at least two material objects that are alike in some way, or that there are properties, or that there are no properties. But, likewise, it could be that the true system of ontology entails the existence of God.

Another option for the defender of the epistemic possibility of a necessarily existing deity is provided by the ontological argument. The ontological argument attempts to show that from the concept of God one can derive the necessary existence of God. A necessary being could then be one for which there was a successful ontological argument, although perhaps one beyond our logical abilities. While the extant ontological arguments might fail (although see Chapter 10 in this volume), the best ones are valid and the main criticism against them is that they are question-begging. Thinking about such arguments gives us a picture of what it would be like for something to have a successful ontological argument for the existence of something. It could, thus, be that in fact God exists necessarily in virtue of an ontological argument that is beyond our ken, or perhaps the non-question-begging justification of whose premises is beyond our ken, while we know that he necessarily exists by means of a cosmological argument within our ken. We do not, after all, at present have any good in principle objection to the possibility that a sound ontological argument might one day be found (cf. Oppy 2006, chap. 2).

4.1.1.6. Objection 5: the Taxicab Problem

Since the First Cause that this cosmological argument arrives at is a necessary being, while the PSR as defended applies only to contingent states of affairs, the problem of applying the PSR to the existence of the necessary being does not arise. And even if one defended a PSR that also applies to necessary beings, one could simply suppose that the being's existence is explained by the necessity of its existence, or that there is a sound ontological argument that we simply have not been smart enough to find yet.

However, a different way to construe the Taxicab Problem is to ask about what happens when we apply the PSR to the proposition allegedly explaining the BCCF. But this issue has already been discussed when we discussed the van Inwagen objection to the PSR. There are two live options at this point. The proposition explaining the BCCF might be a contingent but self-explanatory proposition. For instance, it might be that the proposition *that a necessarily existing agent freely chose to do A for reason R* is self-explanatory in the sense that once you understand the proposition, you understand that everything about it has been explained: the choice is explained by the reason and the fact that the choice is free, and the necessity of the agent's existence is, perhaps, self-explanatory, or perhaps explanation is understood modulo necessary propositions. The other, I think preferable, option is that the BCCF is explained by a necessary proposition of the form: *a necessarily existing God freely chose what to create while impressed by reason R.*

One might continue to press a variant of the Taxicab Objection on this second option, using an argument of Ross (1969). Granted, it is necessary that God freely chose what to create while he was impressed by R. Let q be this necessary proposition. Let p be the BCCF. Then, even though q is necessary, it is contingent that q explains p (or even that q explains anything – for if God created something else, that likely would not be explained by his being impressed by R, but by his being impressed by some other reason). And so we can ask why q explains p.

But at least one possible answer here is not particularly difficult. The question comes down to the question of why God acted on R to make p hold. But God acted on R to make p hold because he was impressed by R. And God's acting on R to make p hold is explained by his making a decision while impressed by R, with its being a necessary truth that God's action is explained by R and by every other good reason. So, ultimately, q not only explains p, but also explains why q explains p. Had God acted on some other reason S that he is also impressed by to make not-p hold, then we could say that this was because he was impressed by S. (See Section 2.3.2.3, above.)

And so the PSR-based argument circumvents the Regress and Taxicab problems.

4.1.2. The CP for wholly contingent states

Following Koons (1997), suppose that each wholly contingent state of affairs has a cause. Form the maximal, wholly contingent state of affairs M as the mereological sum of all wholly contingent states of affairs. Then, M has a cause C by the CP. Moreover, plausibly, C is wholly disjoint from M. For suppose that C and M overlapped in some state J. Then, J would be caused by C. But J is a part of C, and although a substance can cause a part of itself, for example, by growing a new limb, it is absurd to suppose that a state of affairs as a whole can cause a part of itself. One difference here lies in the fact that states of affairs are nothing but the sums of their constituent states, while substances can cause parts of themselves by being more than the sum of their parts. So, C and M are wholly disjoint.

But if C and M are wholly disjoint, then C cannot be contingent. For if it were contingent, it would have a nonempty, wholly contingent part (see the argument in Koons 1997), and that part would then be a part of M.

Thus, the cause of M is a necessary state of affairs. As in the PSR case, plausibly only an existential state of affairs can cause an existential state of affairs. Hence, C involves the existence of something. Moreover, it had better involve the existence of a *necessary* being. The alternative is that C involves a quantificational state of affairs that says that some being satisfying a description D exists, where it is a necessary truth that some being satisfies D, but there is no being b such that it is a necessary truth that b satisfies D. However, such quantificational states of affairs are unlikely to be genuine causes, just as disjunctive states of affairs are not causes. Nor is this scenario, with its being necessary that some contingent being or other exist, plausible.

Hence, once again, we get to a necessary being. If, furthermore, we think that causes can only function through the causal efficacy of a being, then we get a causally efficacious necessary being, a First Cause.

The Taxicab Problem here takes the form of asking what causes C to cause M, and this question has already been discussed in Section 3.3.

We can also modify the argument by only assuming a CP for *positive* wholly contingent states of affairs. Assuming the cause of a positive state of affairs is found in a positive state of affairs, we can again get to a necessary being.

4.2. The CP for chains

We assume in this argument that we are dealing with a kind of causation such that the *causes* relation is transitive (if x causes y and y causes z, then x causes z) and irreflexive (x does not cause x). A *causal chain* of items is a set S of items totally ordered under the *causes* relation. In other words, if x and y are members of S, then either $x = y$, or x causes y, or y causes x. The relata of the causal relation can be concrete things or events or concrete states of affairs – I shall call these relata "items." The relevant CP now states that if S is a causal chain of contingent items, then there is a cause of every item in the chain. If S is a finite chain, this follows from a CP for individual items – we just take the first item in the chain and ask for its cause, which cause then is the cause of every item in the chain.

THEOREM 1. Assume the given CP, assume that causation is transitive and irreflexive, and assume the Axiom of Choice (AC). Suppose there is a set U of all items. Then, for any contingent item e, there is a necessary being G such that G causes e.

This Theorem was shown by Robert K. Meyer (1987) based on a suggestion of Putnam. The AC is a technical assumption needed for the proof. The AC states that if B is a nonempty set of disjoint nonempty sets, then there is at least one set C that has exactly one member from each of the members of B. The AC is obvious in finite cases. If $B = \{\{1,2\}, \{3,4\}, \{0,7,8,9\}\}$, we can just let $C = \{0,2,3\}$. Another way to put the AC is to say that the Cartesian product of nonempty sets is always nonempty. The AC is also equivalent to the claim that every set can be well ordered, that is, given a total ordering such that every subset has a least element. One direction of the proof of this equivalence is easy and illustrative of how the AC works: given a set B of disjoint nonempty sets, let B^* be the union of all the members of B; suppose there is a well ordering on B^*; let C be the set each of whose members is the *least* member of one of the members of B.

The AC is an assumption most working mathematicians are willing to grant as intuitively obvious, although mathematicians being who they are, if they can prove something without using the AC, they would rather do so. The AC is independent of the other axioms of Zermelo–Fraenkel set theory, so we cannot expect a proof of it. The difficulty in the AC is that no procedure for constructing C out of B is given – all we get is the fact that there is a C satisfying the requirements.

Theorem 1 follows quickly from Zorn's Lemma, which is equivalent to the AC. Zorn's Lemma says that if every nonempty chain (i.e. totally ordered subset) S in a nonempty partially ordered set V has an upper bound (i.e. an element y of V such that $x \leq y$ for all x in S), then V has a maximal element. To see that Theorem 1 follows, write "$x \leq y$" provided that either y causes x or $y = x$. Let $U(e)$ be the set of all items in U that cause e. Suppose for a *reductio* that all the members of $U(e)$ are contingent. By the CP, every nonempty chain S of items in $U(e)$ has a cause y in U. But every item in $U(e)$ is a cause of e, and hence by transitivity this y will be a cause of e, and thus a member of $U(e)$. Hence, every nonempty chain in $U(e)$ has an upper bound. Thus, $U(e)$ has a maximal element. Call that element c. Since every member of $U(e)$ is contingent, c is contingent. Thus, by the CP, c has a cause, say b. Then by transitivity, b is also a cause of e, and hence a member of $U(e)$. But then $c < b$, and hence c is not maximal, contrary to the assumption. Thus, the claim that all members of $U(e)$ are contingent must be rejected. Thus, e has a noncontingent cause.

As before, if the Taxicab Problem amounts to asking for the cause of G, the problem cannot get off the ground, since we only assumed that contingent things had causes. Now in the case where the items are events, if G's causing e counts as an event, we can still ask for the cause of G's causing e. For responses to this question, we can refer back to Section 3.3.

4.3. The Principle of Only Explanation (POE)

White (1979) has proposed a principle that if only one putative explanation can be given of a phenomenon, that putative explanation is correct. As already mentioned, this is what Sherlock Holmes means by "when you have eliminated the impossible, whatever remains, *however improbable*, must be the truth" (Doyle 1890, p. 93; italics in the original). But only a necessary being's causal efficacy can explain global explananda like the BCCF. Hence, a necessarily existing First Cause exists.

The difficulty with this principle is that it is not clear how one *counts* putative explanations. Suppose a coroner sees a woman with a wound and can rule out all explanations except a stabbing with a knife. Does the POE apply? After all, one might say that there is still more than one explanation available. Maybe the woman was stabbed with a knife for profit or maybe she was stabbed out of a revenge. If the latter two count as alternative explanations and make the POE not applicable, then POE does not apply to the cosmological case, since more than one set of motives could be assigned to the First Cause.

Suppose instead that POE still applies in the murder case. Then POE must be understood as follows. If at some specific level of generality only one putative explanation can be given, then that one explanation must be correct. At one level of generality, we have a stabbing with a knife. All alternatives to that have been ruled out. Hence, we need to accept that a stabbing with a knife happened.

However, now POE becomes much more controversial, and it is not clear that it is a gain over versions of the CP. In fact, for a wide class of items, it implies a CP. For at a very high level of generality that "a cause caused E" seems to be an explanation, and for a large class of items E it seems plausible to suppose that no other explanation would be possible. This last claim requires ruling out conceptual explanations. To do that we would have to work with the ontologically most basic items, where further conceptual explanations are impossible so only causal ones are available, and then say that if the most basic items have causes, so do the less basic ones.

Perhaps more specificity is required than just "a cause caused E." Maybe "a necessary being caused E" has that kind of specificity, or maybe we can prove that only *God's* activity could explain the BCCF. But significant amounts of work would be needed here.

And, besides, it is not clear why someone who accepts the POE would deny the PSR. Supposing that the coroner rules out all explanations other than being poisoned or having a heart attack, the inference to the claim that the person was either poisoned or had a heart attack would be just as good as the inference to the claim that she was poisoned if only that option remained.

4.4. The R-PSR

Recall the R-PSR, which claimed that every proposition that *can* have an explanation *does* have an explanation (see Section 3.2.2). The R-PSR enables a cosmological argument for one or more necessary beings whose existence explains why there is something contingent. It certainly does so if, as is claimed in Section 3.2.2, the R-PSR entails the PSR. But it also does so if that entailment argument fails.

I do, however, need a technical assumption:

(52)   There is a set Q of kinds such that: (a) for no x does x's being of K, where K is in
Q, depend on anything essentially originated, and (b) every contingent object x is a
member of at least one kind from K.

If the cosmos consists of finitely many contingent objects, as seems fairly plausible empirically, then (52) is trivially true. Here, "kind" is a technical term. It does not simply mean
a set of objects, but a classification falling under which is explanatorily prior to all
the exercises of the entity's causal power. Natural kinds like *animal* and *electron* are paradigm instances of this. Whether kind membership is essential is a question we can stay
neutral on.

Now, consider the proposition p that at least one of the kinds in Q has at least one
contingently existing member. I claim that there could be an explanation of p. All we need
to do to see this is to imagine a possible world that has a being that is not a member of
any of the kinds in Q and is not caused into existence by any member or members of any
of the kinds in Q, but which being causes at least one of the kinds in Q to have a member.
The being might be a contingent being, as long as it is not a contingent being that is a
member of any of the kinds exemplified in our world or dependent on any members of
the kinds exemplified in our world. For instance, that being might be an angel or a witch
that brings an electron into existence. Or it might be a necessary being, such as God.

Thus, possibly, p is explained. Thus, by the R-PSR there is an explanation for p. Assuming further that existential propositions about substances can only be explained by the
causal activity of one or more substances, we conclude that there is a set U of substances
whose causal activity explains p. If all of the members of U are contingent, then they are
each a member of at least one kind from Q. Moreover, their kind membership is explanatorily prior to their causal activity. Thus, no one of these members of U can explain why
it is a member of the kind (or kinds) it is a member of or why the kind (or kinds) that it
is a member of has (have) a member, and hence no one can explain p. Neither can they
collectively explain p, for collective causal powers derive from individual causal powers,
and I have assumed that being the kind of being one is is explanatorily prior to having of
the causal powers one does – one is able to thermoregulate *because* one is a mammal.

Therefore, at least one member of U is not contingent. But in fact, no contingent
member of U should enter into an explanation of why some kind from Q has a member,
since to have a contingent member of U exercising its causal powers, that contingent
member must already have existed, and thus been a member of some kind from Q. So all
the members of U are necessary beings. Therefore, in fact, one or more necessarily existing
substances explain p through their causal activity.

5. The Gap Problem

5.1. Introduction

The last 50 years have seen significant progress in clarifying the philosophical issues involved
in the Glendower, Regress, and Taxicab problems. Indeed, several rigorous versions of the
cosmological argument are available to overcome these. The Gap Problem has yet to see as

much progress. Perhaps the reason is merely sociological. The typical philosophical atheist or agnostic not only does not believe in God but also does not believe in a necessarily existing First Cause. The typical philosopher who accepts a necessarily existing First Cause is also a theist. Thus, there is not much of an audience for arguments that the necessarily existing First Cause is God. Moreover, it makes sense to proceed in order – first, get clear on the argument for a necessarily existing First Cause, and only then on the argument that this is God.

Probably the most important part of the Gap Problem is the question whether the First Cause is an agent. After all, if the First Causes would have to be nonagentive necessarily existing substances that randomly spit out island universes, then the conclusion of the cosmological argument would be incompatible with theism.

In addition to the problem of personhood, there is the question of the other attributes that God has traditionally been believed to have: uniqueness, simplicity, omniscience, omnipotence, transcendence, and, crucially, perfect goodness. At the same time, it is quite reasonable for a defender of the cosmological argument to stop deriving attributes of the First Cause at some point, and say that the other attributes are to be accepted by a combination of faith and data from other arguments for the existence of God. In any case, rare is the Christian cosmological arguer who claims to be able to show that the First Cause is a Trinity, and indeed Christian theologians may say this is good, since that God is a Trinity is a matter of faith. Nor does the inability to show by reasoned arguments that the First Cause has some attribute provide much of an argument *against* the claim that the First Cause has that attribute.

There are two general approaches for bridging the gap between the First Cause and God: inductive and metaphysical. Inductive arguments may claim that supposing that the First Cause exemplifies some attribute is the best explanation of some feature of the First Cause's effects, and in doing so the arguments may reprise the considerations of design arguments. Typical metaphysical arguments, on the other hand, argue that a First Cause must have some special metaphysical feature, such as being simple or being pure actuality, from which feature a number of other attributes follow.

Considerations of space do not, however, allow a full discussion of these arguments, and of objections to them, so I shall confine the discussion to the barest sketches.

5.2. Agency

One might argue for *agency* in the causal activity of the First Cause in several ways. In order to not beg the question as to the number of First Causes, simply stipulatively define "*the First Cause*" as the aggregate of all First Causes – it might be a committee or a heap, but that is fine at this point.

If we got to the First Cause by means of the PSR, then the First Cause's activity must in some way explain everything contingent. If one accepts that all explanations of contingent states of affairs are either scientific, agential, or conceptual – at least these are all the kinds of explanations we know of, and since the concept of explanation is a concept of ours, we have some insight into what can and cannot yield an explanation – then one can argue that the First Cause is an agent. For the First Cause's activity does not provide a *scientific* explanation. As far as we can tell, science explains things in terms of contingent causes. Nor does the First Cause's activity *conceptually* explain everything contingent. In contingent reality we find substances, and the existence of a substance is not conceptually explained by the activity of something other than that substance – substances are *self-standing*. At worst, the existence of a substance is conceptually explained by the existence of constituent parts, but if so, then these constituent parts will themselves be substantial. In the end we shall have to give a nonconceptual explanation, or else to find parts that are necessary. But it is false that goats and people are made up of necessarily existing parts. So, in the end, a nonconceptual explanation must be given. Hence, the explanation cannot be entirely conceptual. Since the explanation is not scientific either, it follows that it is at least in part agential, and hence the First Cause either is or contains a necessarily existing agent, unless there is some fourth relevant kind of explanation.

Alternately, one might argue that the only way to resolve the van Inwagen problem is to posit agency in the explanation of the BCCF. Perhaps only agential explanations in terms of a necessary being combine the two crucial features: contingency of effect and the impossibility of asking for a further explanation of some further contingent fact. However, if one thinks that nonagential statistical explanations can also have this feature, then this argument will not impress.

Finally, one can bring to bear the full panoply of design arguments available. The First Cause is an entity that has produced a universe apparently fine-tuned for life, containing beauty and creatures attuned to beauty, containing moral obligations and creatures aware of them; a universe containing conscious beings with free will; and a universe some of whose contents have objective functions (eyes are for seeing and so on – these kinds of functional attributions arguably cannot be reduced to evolutionary claims, although there is a large literature on this controversial claim). We have shown, let us suppose, that there is a First Cause. The further supposition that the First Cause is a highly intelligent and very powerful person acting purposively is highly plausible given all this data.

Finally, one might argue for agency on metaphysical grounds. If the metaphysical arguments show that the First Cause has every positive property, then the First Cause will in particular have knowledge and will, and hence be an agent.

5.3. Goodness

Whether we can argue on inductive grounds that the First Cause is good is a particularly difficult question in light of all the evil in the world. If the First Cause is an agent, we have three options to choose from: he is a good agent, an evil agent, or an agent morally in the middle. I will argue that at least we can dismiss the worst of these options on inductive grounds.

Here is one set of considerations. We might see evil as ontologically inferior to the good. For instance, we might see evil as a *privation* of the good. Or we might see evil as a *twisting* of the good: the good can stand on its own axiologically, but evil is metaphysically something parasitic. Seen from that point of view, evil can never be seen to be the victor. Whatever power evil has is a good power twisted to bad ends. Human cruelty is only an evil because human nature has a power of transcending cruelty. Evil can only mock the good but can never win.

Suppose we do indeed see things this way. Then evil only makes sense against a background of goodness. And hence, the cause that the universe originates in, since that cause is the ultimate background, cannot but be perfectly good. If, further, perfect good is *stable*, then we might think that this cause *still* is perfectly good. This will be a metaphysical argument.

Moreover, if we see evil as metaphysically inferior to the good, then the idea that the First Cause is an evil person makes the First Cause be rather stupid, and so we have an inductive argument against the worst of the three options under consideration. For whatever gets created, there will be more good than evil. Behind the twisting of human nature in a serial killer, there is the good of human nature – if it were not good, and if it were not in some way metaphysically superior to the evil so as to provide a standard against which that evil is to be measured, then the twisting would not be an evil. So by creating, the First Cause makes more good than evil come into existence, and if the First Cause is evil, then to do that is, well, stupid. But the fine-tuning of the universe suggests that the First Cause is highly intelligent.

Furthermore, I think it *is* fair to say that there is much more good than evil in the human world. Consider the constant opportunities available for malice, opportunities that would result in no punishment at all. We can assume, with almost total certainty, that if we ask strangers for the time, they will not look at the time and subtract 10 minutes just to make sure we are late for whatever appointment we are rushing. Is it not wondrous that I regularly find myself around many omnivorous animals armed with teeth and guns (I am in Texas!), but I have not yet suffered serious harm from them? At least on the assumption that these omnivorous animals were created by an evil being, there would be some cause for surprise. When the rules of morality are transgressed, rarely are they transgressed wantonly. Granted, there have been genocides of massive proportions. But it is noteworthy that even there, there tends to be a background that makes the cruelty not be *entirely* wanton: a destructive ideology or a vengeful, and often mistaken, justice. The victims are demonized. This demonization is itself an evil, but it is an evil that underscores the fact that the victims *need* to be seen as demonic before most of us will be induced to be cruel to them. The hypothesis that the First Cause is evil is not a very plausible one, then.

Whether the hypothesis that the First Cause is good is any more plausible will depend on how we evaluate the arguments of various theodicies. Some of the aforementioned considerations might possibly be the start of a theodicy, but that is not what I intended them for: I intended them merely as data against the hypothesis of an evil First Cause. On the theodicy front, on the other hand, we might see in freely chosen virtue a goodness outweighing the evils of vice, and that might lead us to suppose the First Cause is good.

5.4. *Simplicity and beyond*

It is at least plausible that if something has parts, then it makes sense to ask why these parts are united. If so, then the existence of a being with parts cannot be self-explanatory. The same is true of what one might call "metaphysical parts," like distinct powers, tropes, and so on. If we suppose that the First Cause's existence is self-explanatory, rather than explained in terms of some further metaphysical principles, then we might well conclude that there cannot be any composition in the First Cause. Taking this seriously leads to the well-known difficulties concerning divine simplicity (see Pruss 2008; Brower, 2008), but might also make possible Aquinas' solution to the Gap Problem as given in the *Prima Pars* of the *Summa Theologiae*. (Note that this approach requires that we got to the First Cause through a PSR strong enough to allow us to ask for an explanation of the First Cause's existence and of the composition of any elements in the First Cause.)

Such a Thomistic approach would start by noting that a strong doctrine of divine simplicity entails that there is no potentiality in the First Cause. Potentiality entails the possession of modally accidental intrinsic properties, that is, intrinsic properties that one might not have. But if the First Cause had any modally accidental intrinsic properties, then there would be the aspects of the First Cause that make true its having its particular contingent intrinsic properties and the aspects of the First Cause that make true its having its essential properties, and these aspects would have to be different because of the modal difference here. However, such a distinction would be contrary to a sufficiently strong doctrine of divine simplicity.

Moreover, Aquinas argues that one of the forms of simplicity that the First Cause has is a lack of a distinction between it, its essence and its existence, which is that by which it exists. This assures a kind of *aseity*: whereas our existence is at least dependent on our essence and conversely, in God there is no such dependency.

From lack of potentiality, Aquinas derives perfection in the sense of *completeness*. If there were something lacking in the First Cause, then the First Cause would have a potentiality for filling in that lack. But this is perhaps a kind of perfection that only metaphysicians will get excited about. If there were a particle that always had exactly the same intrinsic properties, and could have no others, it would count as perfect in this sense.

Aquinas' next step is to argue that "the perfections of all things" are found in God (Aquinas, forthcoming, I.4.2). Here we start to get something that the ordinary believer cares about. Aquinas offers two arguments. One of them depends on Aquinas' ontological system. Aquinas thinks each thing has existence, which gives it reality, and an essence that delimits the existence by specifying the kinds of reality that the object has. Thus, our essence specifies that we exist in respect of an ability to think and choose, as well as in respect of various physical abilities. In the First Cause, by divine simplicity, there is no essence distinct from existence to limit that existence, and so existence is found in an unlimited way: every "perfection of being" is found in the First Cause. Note that this argument not only yields the claim that the perfection of every actual being is found in the First Cause but also that the perfection of every possible being is found there. A full evaluation of this argument would require an evaluation of Thomistic ontology, and that is beyond the scope of this essay.

Aquinas' other argument relies on the scholastic axiom that:

> the same perfection that is found in an effect must be found in the cause, either (a) according to the same nature, as when a man generates a man, or (b) in a more eminent mode. . . . (Aquinas, forthcoming I.4.2)

This axiom is a staple of classic discussions of the existence of God, reappearing in Descartes' argument from our idea of God, and used by Samuel Clarke for the same purpose as in Aquinas. The idea is that a cause cannot produce something with a completely new kind of positive feature. A cause can produce combinations of positive features it has, as well as derivative forms of these. This would be a good axiom for cosmological arguers. But is it true?

Emergentist theories of mind are predicated precisely on a rejection of this axiom, but it will not do to use them as counterexamples to the axiom, since emergentism is controversial precisely because it allows for nonphysical properties to arise from physical ones in contravention of our axiom. One might try to find a counterexample to the axiom in evolutionary theory: beings that fly, see, think, walk, produce webs, and so on all come from unicellular beings that can do none of these things. But here we should separate out the mental and the physical properties. It might be argued that there is no qualitative difference between flying, walking, and making webs, on the one hand, and doing the kinds of things that unicellular organisms do, on the other. Indeed, perhaps, we can argue that biology shows that these behaviors just *are* a matter of lots of unicellular organisms going through their individual behavioral repertoire, since higher organisms are composed of cells. On the other hand, whether mental properties can arise from things without them is controversial, and some accounts on which they can do so manage this feat simply by supposing that mental properties reduce to physical ones. Accounts that do not allow such reduction make the arising mysterious, and our being mystified here is a testimony to the plausibility of the axiom.

A different kind of objection to the axiom is an *ad hominem* one: the axiom is incompatible with theism because the peculiar perfections of material objects can only be found in material objects. Thus, the cause of material objects, God, must either lack some of the perfections of material objects, in which case the axiom is false, or else God is material, contrary to theistic orthodoxy. However, the axiom as Aquinas understands it allows that a more eminent version of a perfection could be found in the cause than in the effect. It could be that omnipresence is helpful here. Thus, God's omnipresence could be a more eminent version both of perfections of shape and movement. Thus, the earth is spherical, and God is not spherical (*pace* Xenophanes), but God by his omnipresence is also everywhere where the earth is, and so he has a more eminent version of sphericity. The cheetah certainly can run fast, whereas God cannot run, but God is always already where the cheetah's run ends, while also being at the starting line.

Unfortunately, these are only defensive maneuvers. It may be that the axiom is self-evident, but simply asserting its self-evidence will not help those who do not see it as such. And there has been very, very little attempt in contemporary philosophy to give a good argument for the axiom. Historically, Samuel Clarke (1823) had tried. His argument was that if a perfection comes from something that does not have it, then the perfection comes from nothing, and it is absurd for something to come from nothing. But that argument misunderstands what opponents of the axiom think: they do not, presumably, think that the perfection comes from nothing, but from something different in kind from itself.

If we do accept this argument for the First Cause's having all the perfections of created things, we can proceed to argue further as follows. The First Cause either is or is not the First Cause in every nonempty possible world. If it is the First Cause in every possible world, and these arguments are sound and work in all possible worlds, then in every world, it is true that the First Cause has all the perfections of the things in that world. Assuming perfections are intrinsic properties, it follows that what perfections the First Cause has cannot differ between worlds, since there is no contingency in the First Cause, by simplicity. Therefore, any perfection the First Cause has in one world, it has in all worlds. Consequently, the First Cause not only has all the perfections of the things that exist in our world but also all the perfections of the things that exist in any possible world.

Can different worlds have different First Causes? One way to settle this is stipulatively. Just let the First Cause be the aggregate of all the necessary beings. Any First Cause is a necessary being, and now our First Cause is indeed the First Cause of every world, and hence has all the perfections of things that exist in any possible world.

This seems to imply that the First Cause of the Leibnizian cosmological argument is the same being who is found in the conclusion of ontological arguments for a being with all perfections. In particular, if we allow that personhood is a perfection, it follows that the First Cause either is a person, or has some quality that is even greater than personhood.

At the same time, the aggregation move that we had made raises the possibility that the First Cause is a polytheistic committee, having all perfections collectively but with no one deity having them all individually. If Aquinas is right that in any First Cause there must be identity between the thing and its existence, and that having all perfections follows from this identity, then the worry does not arise. If this is not a satisfactory solution, we may need to employ some other argument for the unity of the First Cause, such as that if there were multiple necessary beings, we would not expect to see a nomically unified world (Aquinas, forthcoming, I.11.3).

From being perfect and having all perfections of things, of course, the sailing is fairly smooth, just as it is after one has come to the conclusion of an ontological argument. Aquinas, thus, proceeds to goodness, infinity, omnipresence, immutability, eternity, unity, knowability, omniscience, and omnipotence.

5.5. Gellman's argument for oneness and omnipotence

Jerome Gellman (2000) has offered a clever argument from the claim that in every possible world there is a necessarily existing cause that explains all contingent truths (perhaps a different one in different worlds) to the claim that there is a necessarily existing cause that is *omnipotent* and that explains all contingent truths in every world. The argument is intricate, and here I shall give a variant that I think is in some ways superior.

If N is a necessary being that explains all the contingent truths of a world w, I shall call N "a creator in w." I shall assume the Iterativeness Postulate (IP):

(IP)   If x has the power to gain the power to do A, then x already has the power to do A, although x might have to take two steps to do A (first acquire a power to directly do A, and then exercise the power).

It follows from IP that if N is a creator in w, then the powers of N are necessary properties of N. To see this, for a *reductio* suppose that w is actual and N contingently has the power to do A. Then N's causal activity explains why N has the power to do A, since N's causal activity explains all contingent truths. But then explanatorily prior to N's causal activity, N had the power to bring it about that it had the power to do A. But by IP, N had the power to do A explanatorily prior to N's causal activity, which contradicts the claim that this causal activity explains the power.

Next, we show that a creator N_1 in w_1 and a creator N_2 in w_2 must be the same individual. Suppose first that w_1 and w_2 are distinct worlds. Let p be some contingent proposition true in w_1 but not true in w_2. Beings N_1 and N_2 exist necessarily, and hence both exist in w_1. Let q be the proposition that N_2's causal activity does not explain not-p. This proposition is true at w_1 since not-p is false at w_1 and only true propositions have explanations; on the other hand, q is false at w_2. Since N_1 is a creator in w_1, N_1's causal activity explains q. Therefore, N_1 in w_1 has the power to make q true, a power it exercises. By what we have already shown, N_1 *essentially* has the power to make q true, and hence it also has this power in w_2. Call this power P_1. We can now ask why it is the case at w_2 that N_1 fails to exercise this power. Since N_2 is a creator in w_2, we must be able to explain N_1's contingent failure to exercise P_1 in terms of N_2's causal activity. Therefore, N_2 at w_2 has the power to prevent N_1 from exercising P_1. Call this power P_2. By what has already been shown, N_2 has P_2 essentially.

Moreover, N_2 does not exercise P_2 at w_1, since at w_1 N_1 does exercise P_1. Why does N_2 fail to exercise P_2 at w_1? This must be explained in terms of N_1's causal activity, just like all other contingent facts about w_1. Hence, at w_1 N_1 has the power, P_3, of preventing N_2 from exercising P_2. Hence, N_1 has that power essentially and is prevented at w_2 from exercising it by N_2. Therefore, arguing as before, N_2 essentially has the power, P_4, of preventing N_1 from exercising P_3. And so on.

This regress seems clearly vicious, and so we conclude that N_1 cannot be distinct from N_2 (if $N_1 = N_2$, we can say that what explains N_2's not bringing it about that p at w_1 is simply that N_2 brings it about that not-p at w_1, and then we can reference our previous discussions of libertarian explanations in Section 2.3.2.3, above). But perhaps we can make the argument work even without going through with the regress. What explains at w_1, we may ask, why it is that N_2 exercised *none* of its powers to prevent N_1 from engaging in the kind of activity it engages in in w_1? It must be that the explanation lies in the exercise of some power P by N_1 in w_1. But then N_1 also had this power in w_2 and did not exercise it, and its failure to exercise it must be explained by N_2's exercise of some preventative power Q. But Q is one of the powers whose exercise in w_1 is prevented by N_1's exercise of P. Repeating the argument with the two entities and worlds swapped, we conclude that each of N_1 and N_2 has the power to prevent the other from its preventing the other. But that is, surely, absurd! (It might not be absurd if $N_1 = N_2$ since in having the power to do A, I have the power to prevent myself from not doing non-A, but that is likely just because my doing A is identical with my refraining from doing non-A.)

So, if N_1 is a creator in w_1 and N_2 is a creator in w_2, then $N_1 = N_2$. It also follows that each world has only one creator. For if N_1 and N_2 were each a creator in w_1, then we could choose any second world w_2, let N_3 be a creator in w_2, and use the said argument to show that $N_1 = N_3$ and $N_2 = N_3$, so that it would also follow that $N_1 = N_2$.

Thus, there is a unique being that essentially has the power to explain every contingent truth in every world via its causal activity. But, surely, having the power to explain every possible contingent truth via one's causal activity implies omnipotence. (We can stipulate this if need be, and the stipulation will not be far away from ordinary usage.)

There are two difficulties in this line of argument. The first is that it requires that each world have one being that *by itself* explains all contingent truth. What if one takes the cosmological argument only to establish the weaker claim that there is at least one necessary being and the necessary beings collectively explain all contingent truths? In that case, the said argument can still be applied, with "a creator" being allowed to designate a collective and not just an individual. The conclusion would be that the very same omnipotent collective explains contingent truth in every world. Can there be an omnipotent collective? It is tempting to quip that there is a conceptual impossibility in a committee's being omnipotent, since committees always suffer from impotence, say, due to interaction issues within the committee. There may be something to this quip. How, after all, could a collective collectively be omnipotent? How would the powers of the individuals interact with one another? Would some individuals have the power to prevent the functioning of others? These are difficult questions. It seems simpler to posit a single being.

The second difficulty is that on this argument, the creator's causal activity explains *all* contingent activity, including, presumably, any free choices by creatures. This problem infects other Leibnizian cosmological arguments. Probably, the way to handle it is to give a subtler and more careful definition of what it is to be a creator in *w*. Maybe the First Cause's activity does not have to explain all free choices made by everybody; it may simply have to explain both the *prerequisites* for all free choices made by any contingent beings, and everything that does not depend on the free choices of contingent beings? This is probably all we need for the crucial uniqueness argument.

6. Conclusions and Further Research

The cosmological argument faces the Glendower, Regress, Taxicab, and Gap problems. Cosmological arguments using a sufficiently comprehensive CP or an appropriate PSR are able to overcome the Regress and Taxicab Objections. The Glendower Problem of justifying the explanatory principle is an important one. However, in recent years, a number of arguments for such explanatory principles, as well as weaker versions of these principles still sufficient for the purposes of the cosmological argument, have been produced. There is, of course, still much room for research here: for examining arguments for or against the relevant explanatory principles, and for trying to produce cosmological arguments using yet weaker principles.

What contemporary analytic philosophers have not sufficiently worked on – and what is perhaps the most promising avenue for future research – is the Gap Problem. There are both inductive and deductive approaches here. The deductive ones that are currently known proceed through exciting metaphysical territory of independent interest. The metaphysics of existence/essence composition involved in Aquinas' bridging of the gap is fascinating, and the axiom that the perfections of the effect must be found in the cause is one that needs further exploration, both in connection with the cosmological argument, as well as in connection with emergentist theories of mind.

References

Adams, R. M. (1974) Theories of actuality. *Noûs* 8, 211–31.

Aquinas, T. (Forthcoming) *Summa Theologiae*. Trans. A. Freddoso. Also available online at http://www.nd.edu/~afreddoso/summa-translation/TOC.htm.

Black, M. (1952) The identity of indiscernibles. *Mind* 61, 153–64.

Brower, J. E. (2008) Making sense of divine simplicity. *Faith and Philosophy* 25, 3–30.

Campbell, J. K. (1996). Hume's refutation of the cosmological argument. *International Journal for Philosophy of Religion* 40: 159–73.

Clarke, S. (1823) *A Discourse concerning the Being and Attributes of God, the Obligations of Natural Religion, and the Truth and Certainty of the Christian Revelation*. Glasgow: Griffin and Co.

Davey, K. and Clifton, R. (2001) Insufficient reason in the 'new cosmological argument'. *Religious Studies* 37, 485–90.

Doyle, A. C. (1890) *The Sign of Four*. London: Spencer Blackett.

Dretske, F. (1972) Contrastive facts. *Philosophical Review* 81, 411–37.

Dudley, U. (1987) *A Budget of Trisections*. New York: Springer.

Edgington, D. (1995). On conditionals. *Mind* 104, 235–329.

Edwards, P. (1959) The cosmological argument. *The Rationalist Annual for the Year 1959*. London: Pemberton. Reprinted in D. R. Burrill (ed.), *The Cosmological Argument*, New York: Doubleday, 1967.

Elga, A. (2001) Statistical mechanics and the asymmetry of counterfactual dependence. *Philosophy of Science* 68, S313–24.

Empiricus, S. (1993) *Outlines of Pyrrhonism*. Trans. R. G. Bury. Cambridge, MA: Harvard University Press.

Findlay, J. N. (1948) Can God's Existence. Be Disproved? *Mind* 57, 176–183.

van Fraassen, B. (1980) *The Scientific Image*. Oxford: Oxford University Press.

Francken, P. and Geirsson, H. (1999) Regresses, sufficient reasons, and cosmological arguments. *Journal of Philosophical Research* 24, 285–304.

Gale, R. M. (1999) *On the Nature and Existence of God*. Cambridge: Cambridge University Press.

Gale, R. M. and Pruss, A. R. (2002) A response to Oppy and to Davey and Clifton. *Religious Studies* 38, 89–99.

Gellman, J. (2000) Prospects for a sound stage 3 of cosmological arguments. *Religious Studies* 36, 195–201.

Hempel, C. G. (1962) Deductive-nomological vs. statistical explanation. In H. Feigl and G. Maxwell (eds.), *Minnesota Studies in the Philosophy of Science*, vol. III, 98–169. Minneapolis: University of Minnesota Press.

Hempel, C. G. and Oppenheim, P. (1948) Studies in the logic of explanation. *Philosophy of Science* 15, 135–75.

Hume, D. (1907) *Dialogues concerning Natural Religion*. Edinburgh: Blackwood and Sons.

van Inwagen, P. (1983) *An Essay on Free Will*. Oxford: Oxford University Press.

van Inwagen, P. (1986) Two concepts of possible worlds. *Midwest Studies in Philosophy* 11, 185–213.

Johnson, D. (Forthcoming) The sense of deity and begging the question with ontological and cosmological arguments. *Faith and Philosophy*.

Koons, R. C. (1997) A new look at the cosmological argument. *American Philosophical Quarterly* 34, 193–212.

Kripke, S. (1980) *Naming and Necessity*. Cambridge, MA: Harvard.

Leslie, J. (2001) *Infinite Minds*. Oxford: Oxford University Press.

Lewis, D. (1986) *On the Plurality of Worlds*. Malden, MA: Blackwell.

Łukasiewicz, J. (1961) O determiniźmie. In J. Słupiecki (ed.), *Z zagadnień logiki i filozofii*. Warsaw. Trans. Z. Jordan in S. McCall (ed.), *Polish Logic*, Oxford: Clarendon, 1967.

Meyer, R. K. (1987) God exists! *Noûs* 21, 345–61.

Norton, J. D. (2003) Causation as folk science. *Philosopher's Imprint* 3, 1–22.

O'Connor, T. (2008) *Theism and Ultimate Explanation*. Malden, MA: Blackwell.

Oppy, G. (2006) *Arguing about Gods*. Cambridge: Cambridge University Press.

Plantinga, A. (1974) *The Nature of Necessity*. Oxford: Clarendon.

Pruss, A. R. (1998) The Hume-Edwards principle and the cosmological argument. *International Journal for Philosophy of Religion* 43, 149–65.

Pruss, A. R. (2003) A new free will defense. *Religious Studies* 39, 211–33.

Pruss, A. R. (2004a) A restricted principle of sufficient reason and the cosmological argument. *Religious Studies* 40, 165–79.

Pruss, A. R. (2004b) David Lewis's counterfactual arrow of time. *Noûs* 37, 606–37.

Pruss, A. R. (2006). *The Principle of Sufficient Reason: A Reassessment*. Cambridge: Cambridge University Press.

Pruss, A. R. (2007). Conjunctions, disjunctions and Lewisian semantics for counterfactuals. *Synthese* 156, 33–52.

Pruss, A. R. (2008) On two problems of divine simplicity. In J. Kvanvig (ed.), *Oxford Studies in Philosophy of Religion*, vol. 1, 150–167. Oxford: Oxford University Press.

Rescher, N. (2000) *Nature and Understanding: The Metaphysics and Method of Science*. Oxford: Clarendon.

Ross, J. F. (1969) *Philosophical Theology*. Indianapolis: Bobbs-Merrill.

Rowe, W. L. (1975) *The Cosmological Argument*. Princeton, NJ: Princeton University Press.

Rowe, W. L. (1984) Rationalistic theology and some principles of explanation. *Faith and Philosophy* 1, 357–69.

Salmon, W. (1990) *Four Decades of Scientific Explanation*. Minneapolis: University of Minnesota Press.

Shakespeare, W. (2000) *Henry IV: Part I*. Ed. Claire McEachern. New York: Penguin Bantam.

Shapiro, L. S. (2001) 'The transition from sensibility to reason *in regressu*': indeterminism in Kant's *Reflexionen*. *Kant-Studien* 92, 3–12.

Smart, J. J. C. and Haldane, J. J. (2003) *Atheism and Theism*, 2nd ed. Malden, MA: Blackwell.

Smith, Q. (1999) The reason the universe exists is that it caused itself to exist. *Philosophy* 74, 579–86.

Sullivan, T. D. (1994) On the alleged causeless beginning of the universe: a reply to Quentin Smith. *Dialogue* 33, 325–35.

Taylor, R. C. (1974) *Metaphysics*, 2nd ed. Englewood Cliffs, NJ: Prentice Hall.

White, D. E. (1979) An argument for God's existence. *International Journal for Philosophy of Religion* 10, 101–15.

3

The *Kalam* Cosmological Argument

WILLIAM LANE CRAIG AND JAMES D. SINCLAIR

Introduction

The cosmological argument is a family of arguments that seek to demonstrate the existence of a Sufficient Reason or First Cause of the existence of the cosmos. The roll of the defenders of this argument reads like a *Who's Who* of Western philosophy: Plato, Aristotle, ibn Sina, al-Ghazali, Maimonides, Anselm, Aquinas, Scotus, Descartes, Spinoza, Leibniz, and Locke, to name but some. Cosmological arguments can be conveniently grouped into three basic types: the *kalam* cosmological argument for a First Cause of the beginning of the universe; the Thomist cosmological argument for a sustaining Ground of Being of the world; and the Leibnizian cosmological argument for a Sufficient Reason why something exists rather than nothing.[1]

The *kalam* cosmological argument traces its roots to the efforts of early Christian theologians who, out of their commitment to the biblical teaching of *creatio ex nihilo*, sought to rebut the Aristotelian doctrine of the eternity of the universe. In his works *Against Aristotle* and *On the Eternity of the World against Proclus*, the Alexandrian Aristotelian commentator John Philoponus (d. 580?), the last great champion of *creatio ex nihilo* prior to the advent of Islam, initiated a tradition of argumentation in support of the doctrine of creation based on the impossibility of an infinite temporal regress of events (Philoponus 1987; Philoponus & Simplicius 1991). Following the Muslim conquest of North Africa, this tradition was taken up and subsequently enriched by medieval Muslim and Jewish theologians before being transmitted back again into Christian scholastic theology.[2]

In light of the central role played by this form of the cosmological argument in medieval Islamic theology, as well as the substantive contribution to its development by its medieval Muslim proponents, we use the word "*kalam*" to denominate this version of the argument. The Arabic word for speech, *kalam* was used by Muslim thinkers to denote a statement of

---

1. This typology has become somewhat standard (*Routledge Encyclopedia of Philosophy* 1998; cf. *Stanford Encyclopedia of Philosophy* 2004a).
2. For an exposition of the argument in its historical context, see Craig (1980), Wolfson (1966), Wolfson (1976), Davidson (1987), and Dales (1990).

theological doctrine and eventually a statement of any intellectual position or an argument supporting such a position. According to the fourteenth-century Muslim theologian al-Idji, *kalam* is "the science which is concerned with firmly establishing religious beliefs by adducing proofs and banishing doubts" (al-Idji 1971). Ultimately, *kalam* became the name of the whole movement within Muslim thought that might best be described as Islamic scholasticism. A practitioner of *kalam* is called a *mutakallim* (pl. *mutakallimun*). Jewish theologians in Muslim Spain, who rubbed shoulders both with the Arabic East and the Latin West, were the means by which the *kalam* cosmological argument found its way back into Christian thought. The subject of extended debate, the argument pitted al-Ghazali against ibn Rushd, Saadia ben Gaon against Maimonides, and Bonaventure against Aquinas. The debate was eventually enshrined during the modern era in the thesis and antithesis of Kant's First Antinomy concerning time.

After suffering several centuries of eclipse, the argument has enjoyed a resurgence of interest in recent decades, doubtlessly spurred by the startling empirical evidence of contemporary astrophysical cosmology for a beginning of space and time. *Kalam* philosophical argumentation for the finitude of the past played a key role in the philosophy of time propounded by mathematician and cosmologist G. J. Whitrow (1980). As a piece of natural theology, the *kalam* argument was revived by Stuart Hackett in his little-noted *The Resurrection of Theism* (1957) and subsequently brought into philosophical prominence by his student William Lane Craig (1979). Noting the widespread debate over the argument today, Quentin Smith observes, "The fact that theists and atheists alike 'cannot leave [the] Kalam argument alone' suggests that it may be an argument of unusual philosophical interest or else has an attractive core of plausibility that keeps philosophers turning back to it and examining it once again" (Smith 2007, p. 183).

What is the *kalam* cosmological argument? In his *Kitab al-Iqtisad*, the medieval Muslim theologian al-Ghazali presented the following simple syllogism in support of the existence of a Creator: "Every being which begins has a cause for its beginning; now the world is a being which begins; therefore, it possesses a cause for its beginning" (al-Ghazali 1962, pp. 15–6). In defense of the second premise, Ghazali offered various philosophical arguments to show the impossibility of an infinite regress of temporal phenomena and, hence, of an infinite past. The limit at which the finite past terminates Ghazali calls "the Eternal" (al-Ghazali 1963, p. 32), which he evidently takes to be a state of timelessness. Given the truth of the first premise, the finite past must, therefore, "stop at an eternal being from which the first temporal being should have originated" (al-Ghazali 1963, p. 33).

The argument, then, is extremely simple:[3]

1.0.   Everything that begins to exist has a cause.
2.0.   The universe began to exist.
3.0.   Therefore, the universe has a cause.

---

3. In view of the bewildering variety of complex issues raised by cosmological arguments, Oppy cautions that *even before looking at it*, we should conclude that so simple an argument cannot plausibly be held to establish its conclusion (Oppy 2006b, p. 173). But the complexity of the issues involved in assessing the truth of an argument's premises does not require, *pace* Oppy, that the argument itself have "dozens of complex premises." The supporting arguments and responses to defeaters of the argument's two basic premises can proliferate in an almost fractal-like fashion.

As a final step one may explore the relevance of this conclusion for theism by means of a conceptual analysis of what it is to be a cause of the universe. In the sequel we shall examine each of the steps of the argument, beginning with Premise (2.0), since this is clearly the more controversial claim and since some attempts to subvert (1.0) are based upon cosmogonic theories – the discussion of which would be premature prior to their introduction in our treatment of (2.0).

2.0. Did the Universe Begin to Exist?

The crucial second premise of the *kalam* cosmological argument has been supported by both metaphysical and physical arguments. We shall examine two traditional philosophical arguments against the existence of an infinite temporal regress of events, as well as scientific evidence in support of an absolute beginning of the universe.

2.1. Argument from the impossibility of an actual infinite

One of the traditional arguments for the finitude of the past is based upon the impossibility of the existence of an actual infinite. It may be formulated as follows:

2.11.   An actual infinite cannot exist.
2.12.   An infinite temporal regress of events is an actual infinite.
2.13.   Therefore, an infinite temporal regress of events cannot exist.

In order to assess this argument, we need to have a clear understanding of its key terms. First and foremost among these is "actual infinite." Prior to the revolutionary work of mathematicians Bernard Bolzano (1781–1848), Richard Dedekind (1831–1916), and, especially, Georg Cantor (1845–1918), there was no clear mathematical understanding of the actual infinite (Moore 1990, pt. I). Aristotle had argued at length that no actually infinite magnitude can exist (*Physics* 3.5.204^{b}1–206^{a}8). The only legitimate sense in which one can speak of the infinite is in terms of potentiality: something may be infinitely divisible or susceptible to infinite addition, but this type of infinity is potential only and can never be fully actualized (*Physics* 8.8. 263^{a}4–263^{b}3). The concept of a potential infinite is a dynamic notion, and strictly speaking, we must say that the potential infinite is at any particular time finite.

This understanding of the infinite prevailed all the way up to the nineteenth century. But although the majority of philosophers and mathematicians adhered to the conception of the infinite as an ideal limit, dissenting voices could also be heard. Bolzano argued vigorously against the then current definitions of the potential infinite (Bolzano 1950, pp. 81–4). He contended that infinite multitudes can be of different sizes and observed the resultant paradox that although one infinite might be larger than another, the individual elements of the two infinites could nonetheless be matched against each other in a one-to-one correspondence (Bolzano 1950, pp. 95–6).[4] It was precisely this paradoxical notion that Dedekind seized upon in his definition of the infinite: a system is said to be infinite if a part of

---

4. Despite the one-to-one correspondence, Bolzano insisted that two infinites so matched might nevertheless be nonequivalent.

that system can be put into a one-to-one correspondence with the whole (Dedekind 1963, p. 63). According to Dedekind, the Euclidean maxim that the whole is greater than a part holds only for finite systems.

But it was undoubtedly Cantor who won for the actual infinite the status of mathematical legitimacy that it enjoys today. Cantor called the potential infinite a "variable finite" and attached the sign ∞ (called a lemniscate) to it; this signified that it was an "improper infinite" (Cantor 1915, pp. 55–6). The actual infinite he pronounced the "true infinite" and assigned the symbol $\aleph_0$ (aleph zero) to it. This represented the number of all the numbers in the series 1, 2, 3, . . . and was the first infinite or transfinite number, coming after all the finite numbers. According to Cantor, a collection or set is infinite when a part of it is equivalent to the whole (Cantor 1915, p. 108). Utilizing this notion of the actual infinite, Cantor was able to develop a whole system of transfinite arithmetic. "Cantor's . . . theory of *transfinite* numbers . . . is, I think, the finest product of mathematical genius and one of the supreme achievements of purely intellectual human activity," exclaimed the great German mathematician David Hilbert. "No one shall drive us out of the paradise which Cantor has created for us" (Hilbert 1964, pp. 139, 141).

Modern set theory, as a legacy of Cantor, is thus exclusively concerned with the actual as opposed to the potential infinite. According to Cantor, a set is a collection into a whole of definite, distinct objects of our intuition or of our thought; these objects are called elements or members of the set. Fraenkel draws attention to the characteristics *definite* and *distinct* as particularly significant (Fraenkel 1961, p. 10). That the members of a set are distinct means that each is different from the others. To say that they are definite means that given a set S, it should be intrinsically settled for any possible object x whether x is a member of S or not. This does not imply actual decidability with the present or even future resources of experience; rather a definition could settle the matter sufficiently, such as the definition for "transcendental" in the set of all transcendental numbers.

Unfortunately, Cantor's notion of a set as any logical collection was soon found to spawn various contradictions or antinomies within the naive set theory that threatened to bring down the whole structure. As a result, most mathematicians have renounced a definition of the general concept of set and chosen instead an axiomatic approach to set theory, by means of which the system is erected upon several given, undefined concepts formulated into axioms. An infinite set in the Zermelo–Fraenkel axiomatic set theory is defined as any set R that has a proper subset that is equivalent to R. A proper subset is a subset that does not exhaust all the members of the original set, that is to say, at least one member of the original set is not also a member of the subset. Two sets are said to be equivalent if the members of one set can be related to the members of the other set in a one-to-one correspondence, that is, so related that a single member of the one set corresponds to a single member of the other set and vice versa. Equivalent sets are regarded as having the same number of members. This convention has recently been dubbed as Hume's Principle[5] (on the basis of Hume 1978, bk, I, pt. iii, sec. 1, p. 71). An infinite set, then, is one that is such that the whole set has the same number of members as a proper subset. In contrast to this, a finite set is a set that is such that if n is a positive integer, the set has n members. Because set theory does not utilize the notion of potential infinity, a set containing a potentially infinite number of members is impossible. Such a collection would be one in which the

---

5. The appellation is due to Boolos (1986–7).

membership is not definite in number but may be increased without limit. It would best be described as indefinite. The crucial difference between an infinite set and an indefinite collection would be that the former is conceived as a determinate whole actually possessing an infinite number of members, while the latter never actually attains infinity, although it increases perpetually. We have, then, three types of collection that we must keep conceptually distinct: finite, infinite, and indefinite.

When we use the word "exist," we mean "be instantiated in the mind-independent world." We are inquiring whether there are extratheoretical correlates to the terms used in our mathematical theories. We thereby hope to differentiate the sense in which existence is denied to the actual infinite in (2.11) from what is often called "mathematical existence." Kasner and Newman strongly differentiate the two when they assert, "'Existence' in the mathematical sense is wholly different from the existence of objects in the physical world" (Kasner & Newman 1940, p. 61). "Mathematical existence" is frequently understood as roughly synonymous with "mathematical legitimacy." Historically, certain mathematical concepts have been viewed with suspicion and, therefore, initially denied legitimacy in mathematics. Most famous of these are the complex numbers, which as multiples of $\sqrt{-1}$, were dubbed "imaginary" numbers. To say that complex numbers exist in the mathematical sense is simply to say that they are legitimate mathematical notions; they are in that sense as "real" as the real numbers. Even negative numbers and zero had to fight to win mathematical existence. The actual infinite has, similarly, had to struggle for mathematical legitimacy. For many thinkers, a commitment to the mathematical legitimacy of some notion does not bring with it a commitment to the existence of the relevant entity in the non-mathematical sense. For formalist defenders of the actual infinite such as Hilbert, mere logical consistency was sufficient for existence in the mathematical sense. At the same time, Hilbert denied that the actual infinite is anywhere instantiated in reality. Clearly, for such thinkers, there is a differentiation between mathematical existence and existence in the everyday sense of the word. We are not here endorsing two modes of existence but simply alerting readers to the equivocal way in which "existence" is often used in mathematical discussions, lest the denial of existence of the actual infinite in (2.11) be misunderstood to be a denial of the mathematical legitimacy of the actual infinite. A modern *mutakallim* might deny the mathematical legitimacy of the actual infinite in favor of intuitionistic or constructivist views of mathematics, but he need not. When Kasner and Newman say, "the infinite certainly does not exist in the same sense that we say, 'There are fish in the sea'" (Kasner & Newman 1940, p. 61), *that* is the sense of existence that is at issue in (2.11).

These remarks make clear that when it is alleged that an actual infinite "cannot" exist, the modality at issue is not strict logical possibility. Otherwise the presumed strict logical consistency of axiomatic set theory would be enough to guarantee that the existence of an actual infinite is possible. Rather what is at issue here is so-called metaphysical possibility, which has to do with something's being realizable or actualizable. This sort of modality, in terms of which popular possible worlds semantics is typically formulated, is often characterized as broadly logical possibility, but here a word of caution is in order. Insofar as by broadly logical possibility one means merely strict logical possibility augmented by the meaning of terms in the sentence within the scope of the modal operator, such a conception is still too narrow for the purposes of the present argument. Such a conception would enable us to see the necessity of analytic truths in virtue of logic and the meaning of sentential terms used in the expression of these truths (such as "All bachelors are unmarried"), but it will not capture the metaphysical necessity or impossibility of synthetic truths, whether these be known *a priori* (such as "Everything that has a shape has a size") or *a posteriori* (such as "This table could not have been made of ice"). Broad logical possibility, then, will not be broad enough for a proper understanding of the argument unless synthetic truths are among those truths that are classed as necessary.

The fact that the argument is framed in terms of metaphysical modality also has an important epistemic consequence. Since metaphysical modality is so much woollier a notion than strict logical modality, there may not be the sort of clean, decisive markers of what is possible or impossible that consistency in first-order logic affords for strict logical modality. Arguments for metaphysical possibility or impossibility typically rely upon intuitions and conceivability arguments, which are obviously much less certain guides than strict logical consistency or inconsistency. The poorly defined nature of metaphysical modality cuts both ways dialectically: on the one hand, arguments for the metaphysical impossibility of some state of affairs will be much more subjective than arguments concerning strict logical impossibility; on the other hand, such arguments cannot be refuted by facile observations to the effect that such states of affairs have not been demonstrated to be strictly logically inconsistent.

Premise (2.12) speaks of a temporal regress of events. By an "event," one means any change. Since any change takes time, there are no instantaneous events so defined. Neither could there be an infinitely slow event, since such an "event" would, in reality, be a changeless state. Therefore, any event will have a finite, nonzero duration. In order that all the events comprised by the temporal regress of past events be of equal duration, one arbitrarily stipulates some event as our standard and, taking as our point of departure the present standard event, we consider any series of such standard events ordered according to the relation *earlier than*. The question is whether this series of events comprises an actually infinite number of events or not. If not, then since the universe cannot ever have existed in an absolutely quiescent state, the universe must have had a beginning. It is therefore not relevant whether the temporal series had a beginning *point* (a first temporal instant). The question is whether there was in the past an event occupying a nonzero, finite temporal interval which was absolutely first, that is, not preceded by any equal interval.[6]

With these explications in mind, let us now turn to an examination of the argument's two premises.

2.11. Existence of an actual infinite

Premise (2.11) asserts that an actual infinite cannot exist in the real world. It is frequently alleged that this sort of claim has been falsified by Cantor's work on the actual infinite and by subsequent developments in set theory, which provide a convincing demonstration of the existence of actual infinites. But this allegation is far too hasty. It not only begs the question against denials of the mathematical legitimacy of the actual infinite on the part of certain mathematicians (such as intuitionists), but, more seriously, it begs the question against anti-Platonist views of mathematical objects. These are distinct questions, all too

---

6. This criterion allows that there may be events of shorter duration prior to the first standard event. By stipulating as one's standard event a shorter interval, these can be made arbitrarily brief.

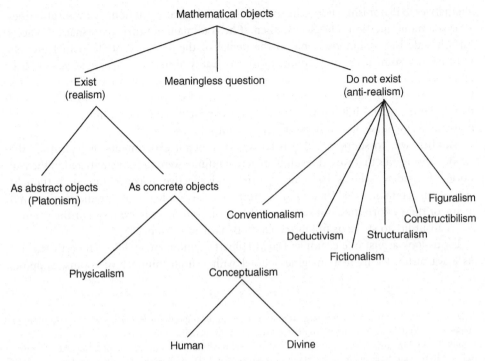

Figure 3.1 Some metaphysical options concerning the existence of abstract objects.

often conflated by recent critics of the argument (Sobel 2004, pp. 181–9, 198;9; Oppy 2006a, pp. 291–3; cf. Craig, 2008). Most non-Platonists would not go to the intuitionistic extreme of denying mathematical legitimacy to the actual infinite – hence, Hilbert's defiant declaration, "No one shall be able to drive us from the paradise that Cantor has created for us" (Hilbert 1964, p. 141) – rather they would simply insist that acceptance of the mathematical legitimacy of certain notions does not imply an ontological commitment to the reality of various objects. Thus, in Hilbert's view, "The infinite is nowhere to be found in reality. It neither exists in nature nor provides a legitimate basis for rational thought. . . . The role that remains for the infinite to play is solely that of an idea" (Hilbert 1964, p. 151). Cantor's system and axiomatized set theory may be taken to be simply a universe of discourse, a mathematical system based on certain adopted axioms and conventions, which carries no ontological commitments. In view of the plethora of alternatives to Platonism (Figure 3.1), critics of the argument cannot justifiably simply assume that the language of mathematics commits us ontologically to mind-independent entities, especially to such obscure objects as sets.

On antirealist views of mathematical objects such as Balaguer's fictionalism (Balaguer 1998, pt. II; 2001, pp. 87–114; *Stanford Encyclopedia of Philosophy* 2004b), Yablo's figuralism (Yablo 2000, pp. 275–312; 2001, pp. 72–102; 2005, pp. 88–115), Chihara's constructibilism (Chihara 1990, 2004; 2005, pp. 483–514), or Hellman's Modal structuralism (Hellman 1989; 2001, pp. 129–57; 2005, pp. 536–62), mathematical discourse is not in any way abridged, but there are, notwithstanding, no mathematical objects at all, let alone an infinite number of them. The abundance of nominalist (not to speak of conceptualist) alternatives to Platonism renders the issue of the ontological status of mathematical entities at least a moot question. The Realist, then, if he is to maintain that mathematical objects furnish a decisive counterexample to the denial of the existence of the actual infinite, must provide some overriding argument for the reality of mathematical objects, as well as rebutting defeaters of all the alternatives consistent with classical mathematics – a task whose prospects for success are dim, indeed. It is therefore open to the *mutakallim* to hold that while the actual infinite is a fruitful and consistent concept within the postulated universe of discourse, it cannot be transposed into the real world.

The best way to support (2.11) is by way of thought experiments that illustrate the various absurdities that would result if an actual infinite were to be instantiated in the real world.[7] Benardete, who is especially creative and effective at concocting such thought experiments, puts it well: "Viewed *in abstracto*, there is no logical contradiction involved in any of these enormities; but we have only to confront them *in concreto* for their outrageous absurdity to strike us full in the face" (Benardete 1964, p. 238).[8]

Let us look at just one example: David Hilbert's famous brainchild "Hilbert's Hotel."[9] As a warm-up, let us first imagine a hotel with a finite number of rooms. Suppose,

---

7. Ludwig Wittgenstein nicely enunciated this strategy when, in response to Hilbert's solemn declaration, he quipped, "I wouldn't dream of trying to drive anyone from this paradise. I would do something quite different: I would try to show you that it is not a paradise – so that you'll leave of your own accord. I would say, 'You're welcome to this; just look about you' . . ." (Wittgenstein 1976, p. 103). But here the strategy is employed on behalf of metaphysical, not mathematical, finitism. Oppy objects that such puzzles show, at most, that certain kinds of actual infinities cannot exist, but that this conclusion cannot be generalized (Oppy 2006b, p. 140). The difficulty with this attempt to blunt the force of the absurdities is twofold: (i) nothing in the various situations seems to be metaphysically impossible apart from the assumption of an actual infinite and (ii) the absurdities are not tied to the particular kinds of objects involved.

8. He has in mind especially what he calls paradoxes of the serrated continuum, such as the following:

> Here is a book lying on the table. Open it. Look at the first page. Measure its thickness. It is very thick indeed for a single sheet of paper – 1/2 inch thick. Now turn to the second page of the book. How thick is this second sheet of paper? 1/4 inch thick. And the third page of the book, how thick is this third sheet of paper? 1/8 inch thick, &c. *ad infinitum*. We are to posit not only that each page of the book is followed by an immediate successor the thickness of which is one-half that of the immediately preceding page but also (and this is not unimportant) that each page is separated from page 1 by a finite number of pages. These two conditions are logically compatible: there is no certifiable contradiction in their joint assertion. But they mutually entail that there is no last page in the book. Close the book. Turn it over so that the front cover of the book is now lying face down upon the table. Now – slowly – lift the back cover of the book with the aim of exposing to view the stack of pages lying beneath it. *There is nothing to see.* For there is no last page in the book to meet our gaze. (Benardete 1964, pp. 236–7).

To our mind this conclusion itself is evidently metaphysically absurd. Although Oppy, following Hazen (1993), offers expansions of the story so that someone opening the book will have some sort of visual experience, rather than as it were, a blank (Oppy 2006a, pp. 83–5), that does not negate the conclusion that there is nothing there to see since there is no last page. Benardete imagines what would happen if we tried to touch the last page of the book. We cannot do it. Either there will be an impenetrable barrier at $\omega + 1$, which seems like science fiction, or else our fingers will penetrate through an infinity of pages without first penetrating a page, which recalls Zeno's paradoxes in spades, since the pages are actual entities. What makes paradoxes such as these especially powerful, as Benardete points out, is that no process or supertask is involved here; each page is an actual entity having a finite thickness (none is a degenerate interval) which could be unbound from the others and all the pages scattered to the four winds, so that an actual infinity of pages would exist throughout space. If such a book cannot exist, therefore, neither can an actual infinite.

9. The story of Hilbert's Hotel is related in Gamow (1946, p. 17).

furthermore, that all the rooms are occupied. When a new guest arrives asking for a room, the proprietor apologizes, "Sorry, all the rooms are full," and that is the end of the story. But now let us imagine a hotel with an infinite number of rooms and suppose once more that *all the rooms are occupied.* There is not a single vacant room throughout the entire infinite hotel. Now suppose a new guest shows up, asking for a room. "But of course!" says the proprietor, and he immediately shifts the person in room #1 into room #2, the person in room #2 into room #3, the person in room #3 into room #4, and so on out to infinity. As a result of these room changes, room #1 now becomes vacant, and the new guest gratefully checks in. But remember, before he arrived, all the rooms were occupied! Equally curious, there are now no more persons in the hotel than there were before: the number is just infinite. But how can this be? The proprietor just added the new guest's name to the register and gave him his keys – how can there not be one more person in the hotel than before?

But the situation becomes even stranger. For suppose an infinity of new guests show up at the desk, asking for a room. "Of course, of course!" says the proprietor, and he proceeds to shift the person in room #1 into room #2, the person in room #2 into room #4, the person in room #3 into room #6, and so on out to infinity, always putting each former occupant into the room number twice his own. Because any natural number multiplied by two always equals an even number, all the guests wind up in even-numbered rooms. As a result, all the odd-numbered rooms become vacant, and the infinity of new guests is easily accommodated. And yet, before they came, all the rooms were occupied! And again, strangely enough, the number of guests in the hotel is the same after the infinity of new guests check in as before, even though there were as many new guests as old guests. In fact, the proprietor could repeat this process *infinitely many times* and yet there would never be a single person more in the hotel than before.

But Hilbert's Hotel is even stranger than the German mathematician made it out to be. For suppose some of the guests start to check out. Suppose the guest in room #1 departs. Is there not now one fewer person in the hotel? Not according to infinite set theory! Suppose the guests in rooms #1, 3, 5, . . . check out. In this case an infinite number of people has left the hotel, but by Hume's Principle, there are no fewer people in the hotel. In fact, we could have every other guest check out of the hotel and repeat this process infinitely many times, and yet there would never be any fewer people in the hotel. Now suppose the proprietor does not like having a half-empty hotel (it looks bad for business). No matter! By shifting guests in even-numbered rooms into rooms with numbers half their respective room numbers, he transforms his half-vacant hotel into one that is completely full. In fact, if the manager wanted double occupancy in each room, he would have no need of additional guests at all. Just carry out the dividing procedure when there is one guest in every room of the hotel, then do it again, and finally have one of the guests in each odd-numbered room walk next door to the higher even-numbered room, and one winds up with two people in every room!

One might think that by means of these maneuvers the proprietor could always keep this strange hotel fully occupied. But one would be wrong. For suppose that the persons in rooms #4, 5, 6, . . . checked out. At a single stroke the hotel would be virtually emptied, the guest register reduced to three names, and the infinite converted to finitude. And yet it would remain true that as many guests checked out this time as when the guests in rooms #1, 3, 5, . . . checked out! Can anyone believe that such a hotel could exist in reality?

Hilbert's Hotel is absurd. But if an actual infinite were metaphysically possible, then such a hotel would be metaphysically possible. It follows that the real existence of an actual infinite is not metaphysically possible.

Partisans of the actual infinite might concede the absurdity of a Hilbert's Hotel but maintain that this case is somehow peculiar and, therefore, its metaphysical impossibility warrants no inference that an actual infinite is metaphysically impossible. This sort of response might seem appropriate with respect to certain absurdities involving actual infinites; for example, those imagining the completion of a so-called supertask, the sequential execution of an actually infinite number of definite and discrete operations in a finite time. But when it comes to situations involving the simultaneous existence of an actually infinite number of familiar macroscopic objects, then this sort of response seems less plausible.[10] If a (denumerably) actually infinite number of things could exist, they could be numbered and manipulated just like the guests in Hilbert's Hotel. Since nothing hangs on the illustration's involving a hotel, the metaphysical absurdity is plausibly attributed to the existence of an actual infinite. Thus, thought experiments of this sort show, in general, that it is impossible for an actually infinite number of things to exist in reality.

At this point, the actual infinitist has little choice but, in Oppy's words, simply to "embrace the conclusion of one's opponent's *reductio ad absurdum* argument" (Oppy 2006a, p. 48). Oppy explains, "these allegedly absurd situations are just what one ought to expect if there were . . . physical infinities" (Oppy 2006a, p. 48).

Oppy's response, however, falls short: it does nothing to prove that the envisioned situations are not absurd but only serves to reiterate, in effect, that if an actual infinite could exist in reality, then there could be a Hilbert's Hotel, which is not in dispute. The problem cases would, after all, not be problematic if the alleged consequences would not ensue! Rather the question is whether these consequences really are absurd.

Sobel similarly observes that such thought experiments bring into conflict two "seemingly innocuous" principles, namely,

(i)   There are not more things in a multitude M than there are in a multitude M' if there is a one-to-one correspondence of their members.

and

(ii)   There are more things in M' than there are in M' if M' is a proper submultitude of M.

We cannot have both of these principles along with

(iii)   An infinite multitude exists.

---

10. Oppy, for example, makes the point that having a hotel with an infinite number of occupied rooms does not commit one to the possibility of accommodating more guests by shifting guests about – maybe the hotel's construction hinders the guests' movements or the guests die off before their turn to move comes round. But as a *Gedankenexperiment* Hilbert's Hotel can be configured as we please without regard to mere physical possibilities.

For Sobel, the choice to be taken is clear: "The choice we have taken from Cantor is to hold on to (i) while restricting the proper submultiplicity condition to finite multiplicities. In this way we can 'have' comparable infinite multitudes" (Sobel 2004, pp. 186–7; cf. Mackie 1982, p. 93).

But the choice taken from Cantor of which Sobel speaks is a choice on the part of the mathematical community to reject intuitionism and finitism in favor of axiomatic infinite set theory. Finitism would too radically truncate mathematics to be acceptable to most mathematicians. But, as already indicated, that choice does not validate metaphysical conclusions. The metaphysician wants to know why, in order to resolve the inconsistency among (i)–(iii), it is (ii) that should be jettisoned (or restricted). Why not instead reject or restrict to finite multiplicities (i), which is a mere set-theoretical convention? More to the point, why not reject (iii) instead of the apparently innocuous (i) or (ii)? It certainly lacks the innocuousness of those principles, and giving it up would enable us to affirm both (i) and (ii). Remember: we can "have" comparable infinite multiplicities in mathematics without admitting them into our ontology.

Sobel thus needs some *argument* for the falsity of (ii). Again, it is insufficient merely to point out that if (i) and (iii) are true, then (ii) is false, for that is merely to reiterate that if an actual infinite were to exist, then the relevant situations would result, which is not in dispute.

Take Hilbert's Hotel. Sobel says that the difficulties with such a hotel are practical and physical; "they bring out the physical impossibility of this particular infinity of concurrent real things, not its logical impossibility" (Sobel 2004, p. 187). But the claim is not that such a hotel is logically impossible but metaphysically impossible. As an illustrative embodiment of transfinite arithmetic based on the axiomatic set theory, Hilbert's Hotel will, of necessity, be as logically consistent as that system; otherwise it would be useless as an illustration. But it also vividly illustrates the absurd situations to which the real existence of an infinite multitude can lead. The absurdity is not merely practical and physical; it is ontologically absurd that a hotel exist which is completely full and yet can accommodate untold infinities of new guests just by moving people around.

Oppy is prepared, if need be, simply to bite the bullet: "There can, after all, be a hotel in which infinitely many new guests are accommodated, even though all the rooms are full, via the simple expedient of moving the guests in room N to room $2N$ (for all N)" (Oppy 2006a, p. 53). So asserting does nothing to alleviate one's doubts that such a hotel is absurd. And would Oppy say something similar about what would happen when an infinite number of guests depart?[11] In transfinite arithmetic, inverse operations of subtraction and division with infinite quantities are prohibited because they lead to contradictions; as Sobel says, "Of course, as operations and properties are extended from finite to transfinite cardinals, some arithmetic principles are left confined to the finite" (Sobel 2007). But in reality, one cannot stop people from checking out of a hotel if they so desire! In this case, one does wind up with logically impossible situations, such

11. Oppy suggests using J. Conway's recently developed constructions called surreal numbers to define operations of subtraction and division of transfinite numbers (Oppy 2006b, p. 140), but he explicitly denies that such non-canonical theories can be applied "to real-world problems, if one wishes to treat one's models with full ontological seriousness" (Oppy 2006a, p. 272). Oppy does not show, nor does he think, that the results of operations on surreals would be any less counterintuitive when translated into the concrete realm.

as subtracting identical quantities from identical quantities and finding nonidentical differences.[12]

In response to the absurdities springing from performing inverse operations with infinite quantities, David Yandell has insisted that subtraction of infinite quantities does not yield contradictions. He writes,

> Subtracting the even positive integers from the set of positive integers leaves an infinite set, the odd positive integers. Subtracting all of the positive integers greater than 40 from the set of positive integers leaves a finite (forty-membered) set. Subtracting all of the positive integers from the set of positive integers leaves one with the null set. But none of these subtractions could possibly lead to any other conclusion than each leads to. This alleged contradictory feature of the infinite seems not to generate any actual contradictions. (Yandell 2003, p. 132)

It is, of course, true that every time one subtracts all the even numbers from all the natural numbers, one gets all the odd numbers, which are infinite in quantity. But that is not where the contradiction is alleged to lie. Rather the contradiction lies in the fact that one can subtract equal quantities from equal quantities and arrive at different answers. For example, if we subtract all the even numbers from all the natural numbers, we get an infinity of numbers, and if we subtract all the numbers greater than three from all the natural numbers, we get only four numbers. Yet in both cases we subtracted the *identical number* of numbers from the *identical number* of numbers and yet did not arrive at an identical result. In fact, one can subtract equal quantities from equal quantities and get any quantity between zero and infinity as the remainder. For this reason, subtraction and division of infinite quantities are simply prohibited in transfinite arithmetic – a mere stipulation which has no force in the nonmathematical realm.

Sometimes it is said that we can find concrete counterexamples to the claim that an actually infinite number of things cannot exist, so that Premise (2.11) must be false. For example, Walter Sinnott-Armstrong asserts that the continuity of space and time entails the existence of an actually infinite number of points and instants (Craig & Sinnott-Armstrong 2003, p. 43). This familiar objection gratuitously assumes that space and time are composed of real points and instants, which has never been proven. Mathematically, the objection can be met by distinguishing a potential infinite from an actual infinite. While one can continue indefinitely to divide conceptually any distance, the series of subintervals thereby generated is merely potentially infinite, in that infinity serves as a limit that one endlessly approaches but never reaches. This is the thoroughgoing Aristotelian position on the infinite: only the potential infinite exists. This position does not imply that minimal time atoms, or chronons, exist. Rather time, like space, is infinitely divisible in the sense that division can proceed indefinitely, but time is never actually infinitely divided, neither does one arrive at an instantaneous point. If one thinks of a geometrical line as logically

---

12. It will not do, in order to avoid the contradiction, to assert that there is nothing in transfinite arithmetic that forbids using set difference to form sets. Indeed, the thought experiment assumes that we can do such a thing. Removing all the guests in the odd-numbered rooms always leaves an infinite number of guests remaining, and removing all the guests in rooms numbered greater than four always leaves three guests remaining. That does not change the fact that in such cases identical quantities minus identical quantities yields nonidentical quantities, a contradiction.

prior to any points which one may care to specify on it rather than as a construction built up out of points (itself a paradoxical notion[13]), then one's ability to specify certain points, like the halfway point along a certain distance, does not imply that such points actually exist independently of our specification of them. As Grünbaum emphasizes, it is not infinite divisibility as such which gives rise to Zeno's paradoxes; the paradoxes presuppose the postulation of an actual infinity of points *ab initio*. "... [A]ny attribution of (infinite) 'divisibility' to a Cantorian line must be based on the fact that *ab initio* that line and the intervals are already 'divided' into an actual dense infinity of point-elements of which the line (interval) is the aggregate. Accordingly, the Cantorian line can be said to be already actually *infinitely divided*" (Grünbaum 1973, p. 169). By contrast, if we think of the line as logically prior to any points designated on it, then it is not an ordered aggregate of points nor actually infinitely divided. Time as duration is then logically prior to the (potentially infinite) divisions we make of it. Specified instants are not temporal intervals but merely the boundary points of intervals, which are always nonzero in duration. If one simply assumes that any distance is *already* composed out of an actually infinite number of points, then one is begging the question. The objector is assuming what he is supposed to prove, namely that there is a clear counterexample to the claim that an actually infinite number of things cannot exist.

Some critics have charged that the Aristotelian position that only potential, but no actual, infinites exist in reality is incoherent because a potential infinite presupposes an actual infinite. For example, Rudy Rucker claims that there must be a "definite class of possibilities," which is actually infinite in order for the mathematical intuitionist to regard the natural number series as potentially infinite through repetition of certain mathematical operations (Rucker 1980, p. 66). Similarly, Richard Sorabji asserts that Aristotle's view of the potentially infinite divisibility of a line entails that there is an actually infinite number of positions at which the line could be divided (Sorabji 1983, pp. 210–3, 322–4).

---

13. See Craig (1985). Consider, for example, the many variations on the Grim Reaper Paradox (Benardete 1964, pp. 259–61; Hawthorne 2000; Oppy 2006a, pp. 63–6, 81–3). There are denumerably infinitely many Grim Reapers (whom we may identify as gods, so as to forestall any kinematic objections). You are alive at 12:00 p.m. Grim Reaper 1 will strike you dead at 1:00 p.m. if you are still alive at that time. Grim Reaper 2 will strike you dead at 12:30 p.m. if you are still alive then. Grim Reaper 3 will strike you dead at 12:15 p.m., and so on. Such a situation seems clearly conceivable but leads to an impossibility: you cannot survive past 12:00 p.m. and yet you cannot be killed at any time past 12:00 p.m. Oppy's solution to a similar paradox concerning infinitely many deafening peals, viz. that there is no particular peal responsible for your deafness but that the collective effect of infinitely many peals is to bring about deafness (Oppy 2006a, p. 83), not only involves a most bizarre form of retro-causation (Benardete 1964, p. 259) but is also in any case inapplicable to the Grim Reaper version since once you are dead no further Grim Reaper will swing his scythe, so that collective action is out of the question. The most plausible way to avert such paradoxes is by denying that time and space are constructions out of an actually infinite number of points. (My thanks to Alexander Pruss for drawing my attention to this version of the paradox.)

Moreover, on an A-Theory of time, according to which temporal becoming is an objective feature of reality, treating time as composed of instants (degenerate temporal intervals of zero duration) seems to land one in Zeno's clutches since temporal becoming would require the actualization of consecutive instants, which is incoherent. For a good discussion, see Grünbaum (1950–1, pp. 143–86). Grünbaum succeeds in defending the continuity of time only at the expense of sacrificing temporal becoming, which his interlocutors James and Whitehead would not do. See further Craig (2000c).

If this line of argument were successful, it would, indeed, be a *tour de force* since it would show mathematical thought from Aristotle to Gauss to be not merely mistaken or incomplete but incoherent in this respect. But the objection is not successful. For the claim that a physical distance is, say, potentially infinitely divisible does not entail that the distance is potentially divisible *here* and *here* and *here* and. . . . Potential infinite divisibility (the property of being susceptible of division without end) does not entail actual infinite divisibility (the property of being composed of an infinite number of points where divisions can be made). The argument that it does is guilty of a modal operator shift, inferring from the true claim

(1) Possibly, there is some point at which *x* is divided

to the disputed claim

(2)   There is some point at which *x* is possibly divided.

But it is coherent to deny the validity of such an inference. Hence, one can maintain that a physical distance is potentially infinitely divisible without holding that there is an infinite number of positions where it could be divided.

Rucker also argues that there are probably, in fact, physical infinities (Rucker 1980, p. 69). If the *mutakallim* says, for example, that time is potentially infinite, then Rucker will reply that the modern, scientific worldview sees the past, present, and future as merely different regions coexisting in space-time. If he says that any physical infinity exists only as a temporal (potentially infinite) process, Rucker will rejoin that it is artificial to make physical existence a by-product of human activity. If there are, for example, an infinite number of bits of matter, this is a well-defined state of affairs which obtains right now regardless of our apprehension of it. Rucker concludes that it seems quite likely that there is some form of physical infinity.

Rucker's conclusion, however, clearly does not follow from his arguments. Time and space may well be finite. But could they be potentially infinite? Concerning time, even if Rucker were correct that a tenseless four-dimensionalism is correct, that would provide no reason at all to think the space-time manifold to be temporally infinite: there could well be finitely separated initial and final singularities. In any case, Rucker is simply incorrect in saying that "the modern, scientific worldview" precludes a theory of time, according to which temporal becoming is a real and objective feature of reality. Following McTaggart, contemporary philosophers of space and time distinguish between the so-called A-Theory of time, according to which events are temporally ordered by tensed determinations of past, present, and future, and temporal becoming is an objective feature of physical reality, and the so-called B-Theory of time, according to which events are ordered by the tenseless relations of *earlier than*, *simultaneous with*, and *later than*, and temporal becoming is purely subjective. Although some thinkers have carelessly asserted that relativity theory has vindicated the B-Theory over against its rival, such claims are untenable. One could harmonize the A-Theory and relativity theory in at least three different ways: (1) distinguish metaphysical time from physical or clock time and maintain that while the former is A-Theoretic in nature, the latter is a bare abstraction therefrom, useful for scientific purposes and quite possibly B-Theoretic in character, the element of becoming having been abstracted out; (2) relativize becoming to reference frames, just as is done with simultaneity; and (3) select a privileged reference frame to define the time in which objective becoming occurs, most plausibly the cosmic time, which serves as the time parameter for hypersurfaces of homogeneity in space-time in the General Theory of Relativity. And concerning space, to say that space is potentially infinite is not to say, with certain constructivists, that it depends on human activity (nor again, that there are actual places to which it can extend), but simply that space expands limitlessly as the distances between galaxies increase with time. As for the number of bits of matter, there is no incoherence in saying that there is a finite number of bits or that matter is capable of only a finite number of physical subdivisions, although mathematically one could proceed to carve up matter potentially *ad infinitum*. The sober fact is that there is just no evidence that actual infinities are anywhere instantiated in the physical world. It is therefore futile to seek to rebut (2.11) by appealing to clear counterexamples drawn from physical science.

2.12. An infinite regress of events as an actual infinite

The second premise states that *an infinite temporal regress of events is an actual infinite*. The point seems obvious enough, for if there has been a sequence composed of an infinite number of events stretching back into the past, then the set of all events in the series would be an actually infinite set.

But manifest as this may be to us, it was not always considered so. The point somehow eluded Aristotle himself, as well as his scholastic progeny, who regarded the series of past events as a potential infinite. Aristotle contended that since things in time come to exist sequentially, an actual infinite never exists at any one moment; only the present thing actually exists (*Physics* 3.6.206^{a}25–206^{b}1). Similarly, Aquinas, after confessing the impossibility of the existence of an actual infinite, nevertheless proceeded to assert that the existence of an infinite regress of past events is possible (*Summa Theologiae* 1.a.7.4.). This is because the series of past events does not exist in actuality. Past events do not now exist, and hence do not constitute an infinite number of actually existing things. The series is only potentially infinite, not actually infinite, in that it is constantly increasing by the addition of new events.

These Aristotelian thinkers are clearly presupposing an A-Theory of time and an ontology of presentism, according to which the only temporal items which exist are those that presently exist. On a B-Theory of tenseless time, since there is ontological parity among all events, there can be no question that an infinite temporal regress of events is composed of an actually infinite number of events.[14] Since all events are equally real, the fact that they exist (tenselessly) at different times loses any significance. The question, then, is whether events' temporal distribution over the past on a presentist ontology precludes our saying that the number of events in a beginningless series of events is actually infinite.

Now we may take it as a datum that the presentist can accurately count things that have existed but no longer exist. He knows, for example, how many US presidents there have been up through the present incumbent, what day of the month it is, how many shots Oswald squeezed off, and so forth. He knows how old his children are and can reckon how many billion years have elapsed since the Big Bang, if there was such an event. The

---

14. Some philosophers of time, such as C. D. Broad and Michael Tooley, have defended a sort of hybrid A/B-Theory, according to which the past and present are on an ontological par, the past being a growing space-time block. On such a view, a beginningless series of past events is also, uncontroversially, actually infinite.

nonexistence of such things or events is no hindrance to their being enumerated. Indeed, any obstacle here is merely epistemic, for aside from considerations of vagueness there must be a certain number of such things. So in a beginningless series of past events of equal duration, the number of past events must be infinite, for it is larger than any natural number. But then the number of past events must be $\aleph_0$, for ∞ is not a number but an ideal limit. Aquinas' own example of a blacksmith working from eternity who uses one hammer after another as each one breaks furnishes a good example of an actual infinite, for the collection of all the hammers employed by the smith is an actual infinite. The fact that the broken hammers still exist is incidental to the story; even if they had all been destroyed after being broken, the number of hammers broken by the smith is the same. Similarly, if we consider all the events in an infinite temporal regress of events, they constitute an actual infinite.

The question arises whether on the A-Theory the series of future events, if time will go on forever, is not also actually infinite. Intuitively, it seems clear that the situation is not symmetrical, but this is notoriously difficult to express. It might rightly be pointed out that on presentism there are no future events and so no series of future events. Therefore, the number of future events is simply zero, not $\aleph_0$. (By this statement, one means not that there are future events, and that their number is 0, but that there just are no future events.) But on presentism, the past is as unreal as the future and, therefore, the number of past events could, with equal justification, be said to be zero. It might be said that at least there *have been* past events, and so they can be numbered. But by the same token there *will be* future events, so why can they not be numbered? Accordingly, one might be tempted to say that in an endless future there *will be* an actually infinite number of events, just as in a beginningless past there *have been* an actually infinite number of events. But in a sense that assertion is false; for there never will be an actually infinite number of events since it is impossible to count to infinity. The only sense in which there will be an infinite number of events is that the series of events will go toward infinity as a limit. But that is the concept of a potential infinite, not an actual infinite. Here the objectivity of temporal becoming makes itself felt. For as a result of the arrow of time, the series of events later than any arbitrarily selected past event is properly to be regarded as potentially infinite, that is to say, finite but indefinitely increasing toward infinity as a limit. The situation, significantly, is not symmetrical: as we have seen, the series of events earlier than any arbitrarily selected future event cannot properly be regarded as potentially infinite. So when we say that the number of past events is infinite, we mean that prior to today, $\aleph_0$ events have elapsed. But when we say that the number of future events is infinite, we do not mean that $\aleph_0$ events will elapse, for that is false. Ironically, then, it turns out that the series of future events cannot be actually infinite regardless of the infinity of the past or the metaphysical possibility of an actual infinite, for it is the objectivity of temporal becoming that makes the future potentially infinite only.

Because the series of past events is an actual infinite, all the absurdities attending the existence of an actual infinite apply to it. For example, if the series of past events is actually infinite, then the number of events that have occurred up to the present is no greater than the number that have occurred *at any point in the past*. Or again, if we number the events beginning in the present, then there have occurred as many odd-numbered events as events. If we mentally take away all the odd-numbered events, there are still an infinite number of events left over; but if we take away all the events greater than three, there are only four events left, even though in both cases we took away the same number of events.

2.13. Conclusion

Since an actual infinite cannot exist and an infinite temporal regress of events is an actual infinite, we may conclude that an infinite temporal regress of events cannot exist. Therefore, since the temporal regress of events is finite, the universe began to exist.

2.2. Argument from the impossibility of the formation of an actual infinite by successive addition

We now turn to a second philosophical argument in support of the premise that the universe began to exist, the argument from the impossibility of the formation of an actual infinite by successive addition. The argument may be simply formulated as follows:

2.21   A collection formed by successive addition cannot be an actual infinite.
2.22   The temporal series of events is a collection formed by successive addition.
2.23   Therefore, the temporal series of events cannot be an actual infinite.

This second argument is independent of the foregoing argument, for its conclusion is not incompatible with the existence of an actual infinite. It rather denies that a collection containing an actually infinite number of things can be *formed* by adding one member after another. If an actual infinite cannot be formed by successive addition, then the series of past events must be finite since that series is formed by successive addition of one event after another in time.

2.21. Formation of an actual infinite

Quite independent of the absurdities arising from the existence of an actually infinite number of things are the further difficulties arising as a result of the temporal formation of such a multitude through a process of successive addition. By "successive addition," one means the accrual of one new element at a (later) time. The temporality of the process of accrual is critical here. For while it is true that $1 + 1 + 1 + \ldots$ equals $\aleph_0$, the operation of addition signified by "+" is not applied successively but simultaneously or, better, timelessly. One does not add the *addenda* in temporal succession: $1 + 1 = 2$, then $2 + 1 = 3$, then $3 + 1 = 4, \ldots$, but rather all together. By contrast, we are concerned here with a temporal process of successive addition of one element after another.

The impossibility of the formation of an actual infinite by successive addition seems obvious in the case of beginning at some point and trying to reach infinity.[15] For given any finite number n, $n + 1$ equals a finite number. Hence, $\aleph_0$ has no immediate predecessor; it is not the terminus of the natural number series but stands, as it were, outside it and is the

---

15. This despite the speculation concerning the possibility of supertasks, various thought experiments involving the completion of an infinite number of tasks in a finite time by performing each successive task during half the time taken to perform its immediate predecessor. The fatal flaw in all such scenarios is that the state at $\omega + 1$ is causally unconnected to the successive states in the ω series of states. Since there is no last term in the ω series, the state of reality at $\omega + 1$ appears mysteriously from nowhere. The absurdity of such supertasks underlines the metaphysical impossibility of trying to convert a potential into an actual infinite.

number of all the members in the series. Notice that the impossibility of forming an actual infinite by successive addition has nothing to do with the amount of time available. Sometimes it is wrongly alleged that the only reason an actual infinite cannot be formed by successive addition is because there is not enough time.[16] But this is mistaken. While we can imagine an actually infinite series of events mapped onto a tenselessly existing infinite series of temporal intervals, such that each consecutive event is correlated with a unique consecutive interval, the question remains whether such a sequence of intervals can be instantiated, not tenselessly, but one interval after another. The very nature of the actual infinite precludes this. For regardless of the time available, a potential infinite cannot be turned into an actual infinite by any amount of successive addition since the result of every addition will always be finite. One sometimes, therefore, speaks of the impossibility of counting to infinity, for no matter how many numbers one counts, one can always count one more number before arriving at infinity. One sometimes speaks instead of the impossibility of traversing the infinite. The difficulty is the same: no matter how many steps one takes, the addition of one more step will not bring one to a point infinitely distant from one's starting point.

The question then arises whether, as a result of time's asymmetry, an actually infinite collection, although incapable of being formed by successive addition by beginning at a point and adding members, nevertheless could be formed by successive addition by never beginning but ending at a point, that is to say, ending at a point after having added one member after another from eternity. In this case, one is not engaged in the impossible task of trying to convert a potential into an actual infinite by successive addition. Rather at every point the series already is actually infinite, although allegedly successively formed.

Although the problems will be different, the formation of an actually infinite collection by never beginning and ending at some point seems scarcely less difficult than the formation of such a collection by beginning at some point and never ending. If one cannot count *to* infinity, how can one count down *from* infinity? If one cannot traverse the infinite by moving in one direction, how can one traverse it by moving in the opposite direction? In order for us to have "arrived" at today, temporal existence has, so to speak, traversed an infinite number of prior events.[17] But before the present event could occur, the event immediately prior to it would have to occur; and before that event could occur, the event immediately prior to it would have to occur; and so on *ad infinitum*. One gets driven back and back into the infinite past, making it impossible for any event to occur. Thus, if the series of past events were beginningless, the present event could not have occurred, which is absurd.

16. For example, Oppy's discussion of counting forward to infinity is predicated upon Dretske's assumption that if one never stops counting, then one does count to infinity (Oppy 2006a, p. 61; cf. Dretske 1965). Oppy fails so much as to mention, much less take account, of the difference between an actual and a potential infinite in this case. One who, having begun, never stops counting counts "to infinity" only in the sense that one counts potentially infinitely.

17. Richard Gale protests, "This argument depends on an anthropomorphic sense of 'going through' a set. The universe does not go through a set of events in the sense of planning which to go through first, in order to get through the second, and so on" (Gale 2007, pp. 92–3). Of course not; but on an A-Theory of time, the universe does endure through successive intervals of time. It arrives at its present event-state only by enduring through a series of prior event-states. Gale's framing the argument in terms of a "set of events" is maladroit since we are not talking about a set but about a series of events which elapse one after another.

It is unavailing to say that an infinite series of past events cannot be formed only in a finite time but that such formation is possible given infinite time, for that riposte only pushes the question back a notch: how can an actually infinite series of congruent temporal intervals successively elapse? Tenseless correlations are irrelevant here. Granted that the series of past events, if infinite, can be mapped one-to-one onto an equally infinite series of past temporal intervals, the question remains how such a temporal series can be lived through so as to arrive at the present.

The arguments against the formation of an actual infinite by successive addition bear a clear resemblance to Zeno's celebrated paradoxes of motion, in particular the Stadium and Dichotomy paradoxes, the Stadium in the case of beginning at some point and never ending and the Dichotomy in the case of never beginning and ending at some point. In the Dichotomy Paradox, Zeno argued that before Achilles could cross the stadium, he would have to cross halfway; but before he could cross halfway, he would have to cross a quarter of the way; but before he could cross a quarter of the way, he would have to cross an eighth of the way, and so on to infinity. It is evident that Achilles could not arrive at any point. In the case of the infinite past, we cannot speak meaningfully of halfway through the past or a quarter of the way, and so on since there is no beginning point, as there is in Achilles' case. But the metrical distances traversed are not essential to the conundrum insofar as the series of past events is concerned since the essential point holds that before traversing any interval there will always be a prior interval to be traversed first.

Now although Zeno's paradoxes have proved very stubborn, scarely anybody has really believed that motion is impossible. Is the argument against the impossibility of traversing an infinite past, as some critics allege, no more plausible than Zeno's paradoxes? This cannot be said because the allgation fails to reckon with two crucial disanalogies of the case of an infinite past to Zeno's paradoxes: whereas in Zeno's thought experimentsm the intervals traversed are *potential* and *unequal,* in the case of an infinite past the intervals are *actual* and *equal.* The claim that Achilles must pass through an infinite number of halfway points in order to cross the stadium already assumes that the whole interval is a composition of an infinite number of points, whereas Zeno's opponents, like Aristotle, take the line as a whole to be conceptually prior to any divisions which we might make in it. Moreover, Zeno's intervals, being unequal, sum to a merely finite distance, whereas the intervals in an infinite past sum to an infinite distance. The question is not whether it is possible to traverse infinitely many (progressively shorter) distances but whether it is possible to traverse an infinite distance. Thus, the problem of traversing an infinite distance comprising an infinite number of equal, actual intervals to arrive at our present location cannot be dismissed on the basis of the argument's resemblance in certain respects to Zeno's puzzles.

It is surprising that a number of critics, such as Mackie and Sobel, have objected that the argument illicitly presupposes an infinitely distant starting point in the past and then pronounces it impossible to travel from that point to today. But if the past is infinite, they say, then there would be no starting point whatever, not even an infinitely distant one. Nevertheless, from any given point in the past, there is only a finite distance to the present, which is easily "traversed" (Mackie 1982, p. 93; Sobel 2004, p. 182). But, in fact, no proponent of the *kalam* argument of whom we are aware has assumed that there was an infinitely distant starting point in the past. The fact that there is *no beginning* at all, not even an infinitely distant one, seems only to make the problem worse, not better. To say that the infinite past could have been formed by successive addition is like saying that someone has just succeeded in writing down all the negative numbers, ending at −1. And how is the claim that from any given moment in the past there is only a finite distance to the present even relevant to the issue? For the question is how the *whole* series can be formed, not a finite portion of it. Do Mackie and Sobel think that because every *finite* segment of the series can be formed by successive addition the whole *infinite* series can be so formed? That is as logically fallacious as saying that because every part of an elephant is light in weight, the whole elephant is light in weight, or in other words, to commit the fallacy of composition. The claim that from any given moment in the past there is only a finite distance to the present is simply irrelevant.

Wholly apart from these Zenonian arguments, the notion that the series of past events could be actually infinite is notoriously difficult. Consider, for example, al-Ghazali's thought experiment involving two beginningless series of coordinated events. He envisions our solar system's existing from eternity past, the orbital periods of the planets being so coordinated that for every one orbit which Saturn completes Jupiter completes 2.5 times as many. If they have been orbiting from eternity, which planet has completed the most orbits? The correct mathematical answer is that they have completed precisely the same number of orbits. But this seems absurd, for the longer they revolve, the greater becomes the disparity between them, so that they progressively approach a limit at which Jupiter has fallen infinitely far behind Saturn. Yet, being now actually infinite, their respective completed orbits are somehow magically identical. Indeed, they will have "attained" infinity from eternity past: the number of completed orbits is always the same. Moreover, Ghazali asks, will the number of completed orbits be even or odd? Either answer seems absurd. We might be tempted to deny that the number of completed orbits is either even or odd. But post-Cantorian transfinite arithmetic gives a quite different answer: the number of orbits completed is both even and odd! For a cardinal number n is even if there is a unique cardinal number m such that $n = 2m$, and n is odd if there is a unique cardinal number m such that $n = 2m + 1$. In the envisioned scenario, the number of completed orbits is (in both cases!) $\aleph_0$, and $\aleph_0 = 2\aleph_0 = 2\aleph_0 + 1$. So Jupiter and Saturn have each completed both an even and an odd number of orbits, and that number has remained equal and unchanged from all eternity, despite their ongoing revolutions and the growing disparity between them over any finite interval of time. This seems absurd.[18]

Or consider the case of Tristram Shandy, who, in the novel by Sterne, writes his autobiography so slowly that it takes him a whole year to record the events of a single day. Tristram Shandy laments that at this rate he can never come to an end.

According to Russell, if Tristram Shandy were immortal and did not weary of his task, "no part of his biography would have remained unwritten," since by Hume's Principle to each day there would correspond 1 year, and both are infinite (Russell, 1937, p. 358). Such an assertion is misleading, however. The fact that every part of the autobiography will be eventually written does not imply that the whole autobiography will be eventually written, which was, after all, Tristram Shandy's concern. For every part of the autobiography there

---

18. Oppy's discussion of al-Ghazali's problem just fails to connect with the problem as we understand it (Oppy 2006a, pp. 49–51), probably because Oppy takes its point to be that there is a logical contradiction with respect to the number of orbits completed (Oppy 2006a, p. 8), so that he spends most of his space arguing that given Cantorian assumptions there is no unequivocal sense in which the number of orbits both is and is not same. Temporal becoming is left wholly out of account.

is some time at which it will be completed, but there is not some time at which every part of the autobiography will be completed. Given an A-Theory of time, though he write forever, Tristram Shandy would only get farther and farther behind, so that instead of finishing his autobiography, he would progressively approach a state in which he would be infinitely far behind.

But now turn the story about: suppose Tristram Shandy has been writing from eternity past at the rate of 1 day per year. Should not Tristram Shandy now be infinitely far behind? For if he has lived for an infinite number of years, Tristram Shandy has recorded an equally infinite number of past days. Given the thoroughness of his autobiography, these days are all consecutive days. At any point in the past or present, therefore, Tristram Shandy has recorded a beginningless, infinite series of consecutive days. But now the question arises: Which days are these? Where in the temporal series of events are the days recorded by Tristram Shandy at any given point? The answer can only be that *they are days infinitely distant from the present.* For there is no day on which Tristram Shandy is writing which is finitely distant from the last recorded day.

This may be seen through an incisive analysis of the Tristram Shandy Paradox given by Robin Small (1986, pp. 214–5). He points out that if Tristram Shandy has been writing for 1 year's time, then the most recent day he could have recorded is 1 year ago. But if he has been writing for 2 years, then that same day could not have been recorded by him. For since his intention is to record consecutive days of his life, the most recent day he could have recorded is the day immediately after a day at least 2 years ago. This is because it takes a year to record a day, so that to record 2 days he must have 2 years. Similarly, if he has been writing 3 years, then the most recent day recorded could be no more recent than 3 years and 2 days ago. In other words, the longer he has written the further behind he has fallen. In fact, the recession into the past of the most recent recordable day can be plotted according to the formula (present date – n years of writing) + n – 1 days. But what happens if Tristram Shandy has, *ex hypothesi*, been writing for an infinite number of years? The most recent day of his autobiography recedes to infinity, that is to say, to a day infinitely distant from the present. Nowhere in the past at a finite distance from the present can we find a recorded day, for by now Tristram Shandy is infinitely far behind. The beginningless, infinite series of days which he has recorded are days which lie at an infinite temporal distance from the present. This is not in itself a contradiction. The infinite past must have in this case, not the order type of the negative numbers ω^*, but the order type $\omega^* + \omega^*$, the order type of the series . . . , –3, –2, –1, . . . , –3, –2, –1. But there is no way to traverse the temporal interval from an infinitely distant event to the present, or, more technically, for an event which was once present to recede to an infinite temporal distance. Since the task of writing one's autobiography at the rate of 1 year per day seems obviously coherent, what follows from the Tristram Shandy story is that an infinite series of past events is absurd.[19]

But suppose that such an infinite task could be completed by the present day. Suppose we meet a man who claims to have been counting down from infinity and who is now finishing: . . . , –3, –2, –1, 0. We could ask, why did he not finish counting yesterday or the

---

19. Oppy rightly observes that it is the whole scenario that is impossible, which includes the requirement that consecutive days be recorded (Oppy 2006a, p. 57, n. 3). But given that the task of writing one's autobiography at the rate of 1 day per year seems obviously coherent, it seem to us that the blame can be placed on the infinity of the past.

day before or the year before? By then an infinite time had already elapsed, so that he has had ample time to finish. Thus, at no point in the infinite past should we ever find the man finishing his countdown, for by that point he should already be done! In fact, no matter how far back into the past we go, we can never find the man counting at all, for at any point we reach he will already have finished. But if at no point in the past do we find him counting, this contradicts the hypothesis that he has been counting from eternity. This shows again that the formation of an actual infinite by never beginning but reaching an end is as impossible as beginning at a point and trying to reach infinity.

Conway and Sorabji have responded that there is no reason to think that the man would at any point have already finished (Sorabji 1983, pp. 219–22; Conway 1984). Sorabji thinks the argument confuses counting an *infinity* of numbers with counting *all* the numbers. At any given point in the past, the man will have already counted an infinity of negative numbers, but that does not entail that he will have counted all the negative numbers. Similarly, in Conway's analysis, the nub of the argument lies in the conditional

(*)   If an infinite number of numbers had been counted by yesterday, then the man will have finished by yesterday.

But Conway's conditional is quite ambiguous, and the arguments that he suggests in support of it have no apparent relevance to the reasoning behind the paradox. The *mutakallim* is not making the obviously false claim that to count infinitely many negative numbers is to count all the negative numbers! Rather, the conditional at the heart of the paradox is a counterfactual conditional like:

(**)   If the man would have finished his countdown by today, then he would have finished it by yesterday,

and the truth of this conditional seems plausible in light of Hume's Principle. It is on the basis of this principle that the defender of the infinite past seeks to justify the intuitively impossible feat of someone's counting down all the negative numbers and ending at 0. Since the negative numbers can be put into a one-to-one correspondence with the series of, say, past hours, someone counting from eternity would have completed his countdown. But by the same token, the man at any point in the past should have already completed his countdown, since by then a one-to-one correspondence exists between each negative number and a past hour. In this case, having infinite time does seem to be a sufficient condition of finishing the job. Having had infinite time, the man should have already completed his task.

Such reasoning in support of the finitude of the past and the beginning of the universe is not mere armchair cosmology. P. C. W. Davies, for example, utilizes this reasoning in explaining two profound implications of the thermodynamic properties of the universe:

> The first is that the universe will eventually die, wallowing, as it were, in its own entropy. This is known among physicists as the 'heat death' of the universe. The second is that the universe cannot have existed for ever, otherwise it would have reached its equilibrium end state an infinite time ago. Conclusion: the universe did not always exist. (Davies 1983, p. 11)

The second of these implications is a clear application of the reasoning that underlies the current paradox: even if the universe had infinite energy, it would in infinite time come to an equilibrium since at any point in the past infinite time has elapsed, a beginningless universe would have already reached an equilibrium, or as Davies puts it, it would have reached an equilibrium an infinite time ago. Therefore, the universe began to exist, *quod erat demonstrandum.*[20]

Oppy's response to the problem at hand is to say that the man's finishing his countdown when he does rather than earlier is just "a brute feature of the scenario, that is, a feature that has no explanation" (Oppy 2006a, p. 59; cf. p. 63; Oppy 2006b, pp. 141–2). It has always been the case that he will finish when he does, but why the man finishes when he does rather than at some other time is just inexplicable. Resting with inexplicability may seem unsatisfactory, however, especially in light of the respectable role such reasoning plays in scientific cosmological discussions. Oppy justifies his response on the basis that principles of sufficient reason requiring that there be an explanation in such a case are highly contentious. Oppy presents the typical objections to various versions of the Principle of Sufficient Reason such as the impossibility of providing an explanation of what has been called the "Big Contingent Conjunctive Fact" (BCCF), which is the conjunction of all the contingent facts there are, or of libertarian free choices (Oppy 2006a, pp. 279–80). The problem with this justification, however, is twofold. First, plausible defenses of the Principle of Sufficient Reason can be given.[21] Second, and more to the point, there is no reason to think that requiring the need for an explanation in the present case demands for its acceptability or plausibility the enunciation and defense of some general Principle of Sufficient Reason. Indeed, any such principle is apt to be tested inductively for its adequacy by whether cases like this constitute plausible counterexamples. The exceptions offered by Oppy, such as the inexplicability of the BCCF and libertarian choices, are simply irrelevant to the present case, for the BCCF is not at stake nor can a person counting from eternity at a constant rate choose arbitrarily when to finish his countdown. In the case under discussion, we have a good reason to think that the man should have finished his countdown earlier than any

---

20. See the similar reasoning of Barrow and Tipler (1986, p. 601–8) against inflationary steady-state cosmologies on the ground that any event which would have happened by now would have already happened before now if the past were infinite.

21. See Pruss' article in this volume. We shall leave to him the defense of principles of sufficient reason. Oppy himself thinks that it is "very plausible" that there are acceptable instances of the following schema for a Principle of Sufficient Reason:

O (for every **FG** of kind K, there is an **F′G′** that *partly* explains why the **GF**s rather than **Q** possible alternatives),

where O is an operator like "necessarily," "it is knowable *a priori*," etc., G is an ontological category such as a proposition, state of affairs, etc., F is a restriction such as true, contingent, etc., and Q is a quantifier like "any," "every," etc. (Oppy 2006a, p. 285, cf. pp. 275–6). But he thinks that it is not at all clear that there are acceptable instances of this schema that can be used to rule out scenarios like counting down from infinity. Although it is not clear what Oppy means by "**GF**s," the following principle would seem to be an instance of his schema: Necessarily, for any contingent state of affairs involving concrete objects there is a contingent state of affairs that partly explains why that state of affairs obtains rather than any other. Such a principle would require that there be some partial explanation for why the man finishes his countdown today rather than at some other time. But not even a partial explanation can be given, for regardless of how we vary such factors as the rate of counting, they will be the same regardless of the time that he finishes and so do not furnish even a partial explanation of why he finishes today. So why is this instance of the schema not acceptable?

time that he does, namely, he has already had infinite time to get the job done.[22] If we deny that infinite time is sufficient for completing the task, then we shall wonder why he is finishing today rather than tomorrow or the day after tomorrow, or, indeed, at any time in the potentially infinite future. It is not unreasonable to demand some sort of explanation for why, if he finishes today, he did not already finish yesterday. By contrast, if such a countdown is metaphysically impossible, then no such conundrum can arise. But clearly, there is no metaphysical impossibility in counting backward for all time, unless time is past eternal. It follows that the past cannot be infinite.

For all of these reasons, the formation of an actual infinite by successive addition is a notoriously difficult notion, even more so than the static existence of an actual infinite.

2.22. Successive formation of the series of past events

Premise (2.22) may seem rather obvious. The past did not spring into being whole and entire but was formed sequentially, one event occurring after another. Notice, too, that the direction of this formation is "forward," in the sense that the collection grows with time. Although we sometimes speak of an "infinite regress" of events, in reality an infinite past would be an "infinite progress" of events with no beginning and its end in the present.

As obvious as this premise may seem at first blush, it is, in fact, a matter of great controversy. It presupposes once again an A-Theory of time. On such a theory, the collection of all past events prior to any given event is not a collection whose members all tenselessly coexist. Rather it is a collection that is instantiated sequentially or successively in time, one event coming to pass on the heels of another. Since temporal becoming is an objective feature of the physical world, the series of past events is not a tenselessly existing manifold, all of whose members are equally real. Rather the members of the series come to be and pass away one after another.

Space does not permit a review of the arguments for and against the A- and B-Theories of time respectively. But on the basis of a case such as is presented by Craig (2000a,b), we take ourselves to be justified in affirming the objective reality of temporal becoming and, hence, the formation of the series of temporal events by successive addition. It is noteworthy that contemporary opponents of Zenonian arguments such as Grünbaum resolve those puzzles only by denying the objective reality of temporal becoming and treating time as a continuum of tenselessly existing point-instants. If moments of time and, hence, events really do come to be and elapse, then it remains mysterious how an infinite number of such event-intervals can be traversed or manage successively to elapse.

2.23. Conclusion

It follows, then, that the temporal series of events cannot be actually infinite. The only way a collection to which members are being successively added could be actually infinite would

---

22. Notice, too, that if there is *any* probability of his finishing in infinite time, then he will have already finished.

be for it to have an infinite tenselessly existing "core" to which additions are being made. But then, it would not be a collection *formed* by successive addition, for there would always exist a surd infinite, itself not formed successively but simply given, to which a finite number of successive additions have been made. Clearly, the temporal series of events cannot be so characterized, for it is by nature successively formed throughout. Thus, prior to any arbitrarily designated point in the temporal series, one has a collection of past events up to that point which is successively formed and completed and cannot, therefore, be actually infinite.

2.3. *Scientific confirmation*

The sort of philosophical problems with the infinity of the past, which have been the object of our discussion, are now being recognized in scientific papers by leading cosmologists and philosophers of science.[23] For example, Ellis, Kirchner, and Stoeger ask, "Can there be an infinite set of really existing universes? We suggest that, on the basis of well-known *philosophical* arguments, the answer is No" (Ellis, Kirchner, & Stoeger 2003, p. 14; emphasis added). Similarly, noting that an actual infinite is not constructible and, therefore, not actualizable, they assert, "This is precisely why a realized past infinity in time is not considered possible from this standpoint – since it involves an infinite set of completed events or moments" (Ellis, Kirchner, & Stoeger 2003, p. 14). These misgivings represent endorsements of both the *kalam* arguments defended earlier. Ellis and his colleagues conclude, "The arguments against an infinite past time are strong – it's simply not constructible in terms of events or instants of time, besides being conceptually indefinite" (Ellis, Kirchner, & Stoeger 2003, p. 14).

Apart from these philosophical arguments, there has emerged during the course of the twentieth century provocative empirical evidence that the universe is not past eternal. This physical evidence for the beginning of the universe comes from what is undoubtedly one of the most exciting and rapidly developing fields of science today: astronomy and astrophysics. Prior to the 1920s, scientists had always assumed that the universe was stationary and eternal. Tremors of the impending earthquake that would topple this traditional cosmology were first felt in 1917, when Albert Einstein made a cosmological application of his newly discovered gravitational theory, the General Theory of Relativity (Einstein 1917, pp. 177–88). In so doing, he assumed that the universe is homogeneous and isotropic and that it exists in a steady state, with a constant mean mass density and a constant curvature of space. To his chagrin, however, he found that General Relativity (GR) would not permit such a model of the universe unless he introduced into his gravitational field equations a certain "fudge factor" Λ in order to counterbalance the gravitational effect of matter and so ensure a static universe. Einstein's universe was balanced on a razor's edge, however, and the least perturbation – even the transport of matter from one part of the universe to another – would cause the universe either to implode or to expand. By taking this feature of Einstein's model seriously, the Russian mathematician Alexander Friedmann and the Belgian astronomer Georges Lemaître were able to formulate independently in the 1920s solutions to the field equations which predicted an expanding universe (Friedmann 1922; Lemaître 1927).

23. Besides the paper by Ellis et al., see Vaas (2004).

A "perfect" city

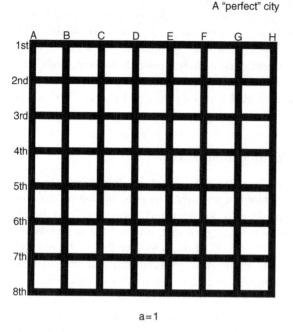

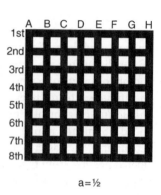

Figure 3.2 Analogy of the universe as a city laid out in a grid.

Friedmann's first equation is:

$$H^2 = \left(\frac{\dot{a}}{a}\right)^2 = \frac{8\pi G}{3}\rho + \frac{\Lambda}{3} - \frac{k}{a^2},$$

where H = Hubble parameter, a = scale factor, G = gravitational constant, ρ = mass density of universe, Λ = cosmological constant, k = curvature parameter.[24] By way of explanation, the scale factor, "a," of the universe is a global multiplier to universe size. Imagine the universe as a perfectly laid out city with streets that travel only north-south and east-west. Streets are spaced at equal-distance intervals. Street intersections then define perfectly symmetric city blocks. One could go further and think of buildings in the city as analogous with galaxies in the universe.

The distance from one city block to another is a function of two values: the originally laid out distance (call that the "normalized" distance) and the scale factor multiplier "a." Note that, as in Figure 3.2, when one multiplies by a scale factor of 1/2, one still has precisely the same city with the same number of city blocks. The only thing that has changed is the distance interval between the city blocks.

Now consider buildings within the city. If the city block distance were reduced to the size of buildings, clearly something must give. The buildings would be squeezed together and destroyed. This is analogous to what happens with matter in the real universe. The sizes of nonelementary particle mass structures such as protons, neutrons, atomic nuclei, and so on are fixed; they do not change with the scale factor. Other physical structures, such as massless particles, *do* adjust with the scale factor. The wavelength of radiation

---

24. This form of the equation assumes a unit system where the speed of light, "c," is equal to one. Otherwise the cosmological constant term and the curvature parameter term would be seen as multipled by c^2.

adjusts and, hence, would gain (in the case of contraction) or lose (in the case of expansion) energy as a result[25]. When one crowds these particles in upon themselves, one will see a transition to different physics.

Recall that the full city is always present regardless of the value of the scale factor. So now consider two additional situations. First, suppose that the scale factor were to shrink to zero. Space (and time) would disappear. Any structure that could not transform to zero size would be destroyed. If there were no physical process that would allow such a thing to happen, we should seem to have a paradox. Either there must be an undiscovered physical process or the scale factor cannot, in reality, assume a null value.

Second, imagine that the city is of infinite size. Conceptually, there is no problem with extending the streets north-south and east-west to infinity in each direction. What does it mean to scale the universe's size in such a situation? No matter what scale factor one adopts, the size of the universe remains infinite. Nevertheless, the idea of scaling still retains coherency in that we can apply a multiplier to the finite distance between city blocks. Yet what would be the meaning of applying a zero scale factor in this situation? Now it would appear that the size of the full universe is "zero times infinity," which, in general, can be any finite number (Barrow 2005, p. 160). What does this mean, given that the distance between *any* spot in the universe to *any* other spot must still be zero? GR simply breaks down at zero scale factor.

Whether or not the full universe is of infinite or finite size is given in the Friedmann equation by the curvature parameter "k." A positive k indicates that the universe, much like the surface of the Earth, is unbounded yet of finite size. Going back to the analogy, imagine that the city is laid out over Earth's entire curved surface. A traveler on 1st street would never come to the end; rather he would eventually come back to the location where he started. A positive k yields positive curvature and a closed universe. This is one type of "compact metric" within GR.

A zero value for "k" yields a "flat" universe. The 1st street is unbounded and of infinite length (in both directions). A similar situation obtains for a negative k value. Here one has negative, or "saddle-shaped," curvature. Two travelers moving east and side-by-side up 1st and 2nd streets would actually get laterally farther apart as the curvature of the surface causes the streets to diverge from each other. The latter case gives an infinitely sized "open" universe.

The components of the universe (all the energy, keeping in mind that $E = mc^2$) determine what type of curvature the universe possesses. The "strength" of gravity, included in the equation via the parameter "G," affects the magnitude of the curvature.

The parameters ρ and Λ indicate the type and magnitude of the different types of energy that cause the curvature. The parameter "ρ" represents the density (that is, the energy per unit volume) of the two types of "ordinary" energy: matter and radiation. It is "ordinary" in the sense that we are familiar with it in daily life and it is of a form that makes gravity an attractive force. Λ represents an exotic type of energy density which can transform gravity from an attractive to a repulsive force.

Friedmann's first equation tells us how the scale factor changes as time elapses. Mathematically, this is the first derivative of the scale factor "a," known as "a-dot," or $\dot{a}$. One can see that the increase (or decrease) in the scale factor is strongly a function of the universe's energy content. Now the "ordinary" energy density ρ will become smaller as the universe

---

25. Hence, the temperature of the universe would be seen to rise as one looked back in time.

expands, since one has the same amount of energy spread out over a greater volume. So its causal impact on the expansion will progressively diminish at ever later times (this works in reverse for contraction). By contrast, Λ, which represents the dark energy density, is constant. The dark energy does not become more dilute during expansion or concentrated during contraction. Hence, early in the life of an expanding universe, Λ is unimportant compared to ρ. But its impact "snowballs" as time goes on. As long as the impact of ρ in the early universe is not enough to overturn an expansion and begin a contraction, the effect of Λ will eventually lead to a runaway expansion of the universe. There will appear a moment in the history of the universe when the dark energy will begin to dominate the ordinary energy, and the universe's expansion will begin to accelerate. Recent observations, in fact, seem to show precisely this effect in our own universe, with a transition age at 9 billion years (Overbye 2006).

Friedmann's second equation gives the rate of change of the expansion rate:

$$\frac{\ddot{a}}{a} = -\frac{4\pi G}{3}(\rho + 3p) + \frac{\Lambda}{3}$$

It determines whether the expansion itself is slowing or accelerating. This acceleration is referred to as "a-double-dot," or $\ddot{a}$. A new term "p" appears in the equation. This is the pressure (similar to the pressure of a gas inside a balloon). Pressure itself can produce gravitational force. Pressure is normally negligible for ordinary matter, although it can play a role in radiation dominated universes. Pressure, however, can have a tremendous impact given a universe dominated by dark energy. As Friedmann's second equation shows, the rate at which the expansion of the universe accelerates is proportional to: $(-\rho - 3p)$. But the pressure in the vacuum is just equal to the negative of the energy density; this is called the equation of state. Hence, overall, the acceleration is positive (which will produce expansion) and proportional to twice the energy density.

Ordinary matter will exert positive pressure (which will keep a balloon inflated, for example). This type of pressure will produce an attractive gravitational force, which supplements the attractive gravity that accrues from mass. Dark energy has the bizarre property that it generates *negative* pressure. But dark energy, while it has a positive energy density (which contributes to attractive gravity) will, *on net*, produce a repulsive gravitational effect. Looking at Friedmann's second equation, one sees that an attractive gravitational contribution tends to slow down expansion (or accelerate contraction), while repulsive gravity will do the opposite.

The monumental significance of the Friedmann–Lemaître model lay in its historization of the universe. As one commentator has remarked, up to this time the idea of the expansion of the universe "was absolutely beyond comprehension. Throughout all of human history the universe was regarded as fixed and immutable and the idea that it might actually be changing was inconceivable" (Naber 1988, pp. 126–7). But if the Friedmann–Lemaître model is correct, the universe can no longer be adequately treated as a static entity existing, in effect, timelessly. Rather the universe has a history, and time will not be a matter of indifference for our investigation of the cosmos.

In 1929, the American astronomer Edwin Hubble showed that the redshift in the optical spectra of light from distant galaxies was a common feature of all measured galaxies and was proportional to their distance from us (Hubble 1929, pp. 168–73). This redshift, first observed by Vesto Slipher at the Lowell Observatory,[26] was taken to be a Doppler effect indicative of the recessional motion of the light source in the line of sight. Incredibly, what Hubble had discovered was the isotropic expansion of the universe predicted by Friedmann and Lemaître on the basis of Einstein's GR. It was a veritable turning point in the history of science. "Of all the great predictions that science has ever made over the centuries," exclaims John Wheeler, "was there ever one greater than this, to predict, and predict correctly, and predict against all expectation a phenomenon so fantastic as the expansion of the universe?" (Wheeler 1980, p. 354).

2.31. The standard Hot Big Bang model

According to the Friedmann–Lemaître model, as time proceeds, the distances separating the ideal particles of the cosmological fluid constituted by the matter and energy of the universe become greater. It is important to appreciate that as a GR-based theory, the model does not describe the expansion of the material content of the universe into a preexisting, empty, Newtonian space, but rather the expansion of space itself. The ideal particles of the cosmological fluid are conceived to be at rest with respect to space but to recede progressively from one another as space itself expands or stretches, just as buttons glued to the surface of a balloon will recede from one another as the balloon inflates. As the universe expands, its density progressively declines.

This has the astonishing implication that as one reverses the expansion and extrapolates back in time, the universe becomes progressively denser until one arrives at a state of infinite density at some point in the finite past. This state represents a singularity at which space-time curvature, along with temperature, pressure, and density, becomes infinite. To be more correct, the volume of the universe *approaches* zero in the limit as the *scale factor* of the universe approaches zero. The Friedmann–Lemaître model does not, in fact, describe what happens at the singularity, since Einstein's GR breaks down at this limit.

The initial cosmological singularity is, therefore, not in space-time but constitutes an edge or boundary to space-time itself. Robert Wald describes how singular space-times are to be properly characterized:

> By far the most satisfactory idea proposed thus far is basically to use the 'holes' left behind by the removal of singularities as the criterion for their presence. These 'holes' should be detectable by the fact that there will be geodesics which have finite affine length; that is, more precisely there should exist geodesics which are inextendible in at least one direction but have only a finite range of affine parameter. Such geodesics are said to be *incomplete*. (For timelike and spacelike geodesics, finite affine 'length' is equivalent to finite proper time or length so the use of affine parameter simply generalizes the notion of 'finite length' to null geodesics.) Thus, we could define a spacetime to be singular if it possesses at least one incomplete geodesic.
>
> Nevertheless, there is a serious physical pathology in any spacetime which is timelike or null geodesically incomplete. In such a spacetime, it is possible for at least one freely falling particle or photon to end its existence within a finite 'time' (that is, affine parameter) or to have begun its existence a finite time ago. Thus, even if one does not have a completely satisfactory general notion of singularities, one would be justified in calling such spacetimes

---

26. Slipher's early papers are now available online at http://www.roe.ac.uk/~jap/slipher/.

physically singular. It is this property that is proven by the singularity theorems to hold in a wide class of spacetimes. (Wald 1984, pp. 215–6)[27]

The existence of a boundary to space-time implies, not merely that the "stuff" of the universe begins to exist but that space and time do as well (for in the Friedmann–Lemaître model all past-directed geodesics terminate at the singularity). P. C. W. Davies comments:

> If we extrapolate this prediction to its extreme, we reach a point when all distances in the universe have shrunk to zero. An initial cosmological singularity therefore forms a past temporal extremity to the universe. We cannot continue physical reasoning, or even the concept of spacetime, through such an extremity. For this reason most cosmologists think of the initial singularity as the beginning of the universe. On this view the big bang represents the creation event; the creation not only of all the matter and energy in the universe, but also of spacetime itself. (Davies 1978, pp. 78–9)

The term "Big Bang," originally a derisive expression coined by Fred Hoyle to characterize the beginning of the universe predicted by the Friedmann–Lemaître model, is thus potentially misleading, since the expansion cannot be visualized from the outside (there being no "outside," just as there is no "before" with respect to the Big Bang).[28]

The standard Hot Big Bang model, as the Friedmann–Lemaître model came to be called, thus describes a universe which is not eternal in the past, but which came into being a finite time ago. Moreover – and this deserves underscoring – the origin it posits is an absolute origin *ex nihilo*. For not only all matter and energy but also space and time themselves come into being at the initial cosmological singularity. As Barrow and Tipler emphasize, "At this singularity, space and time came into existence; literally nothing existed before the singularity, so, if the Universe originated at such a singularity, we would truly have a creation *ex nihilo*" (Barrow and Tipler 1986, p. 442). On such a model the universe originates *ex nihilo* in the sense that it is false that something existed prior to the singularity.

---

27. A geodesic is the path that a freely falling particle traces out through space and time. A timelike geodesic is traveled by a massive particle. A null geodesic is traveled by a massless particle such as the photons that make up visible light.

28. As Gott et al. write:

> The universe began from a state of infinite density about one Hubble time ago. Space and time were created in that event and so was all the matter in the universe. It is not meaningful to ask what happened before the big bang; it is somewhat like asking what is north of the North Pole. Similarly, it is not sensible to ask where the big bang took place. The point-universe was not an object isolated in space; it was the entire universe, and so the only answer can be that the big bang happened everywhere. (1976, p. 65)

The Hubble time is the time since the singularity if the rate of expansion has been constant. The singularity is a point only in the sense that the distance between any two points in the singularity is zero. Anyone who thinks that there must be a place in the universe where the Big Bang occurred still has not grasped that it is space itself which is expanding; it is the two-dimensional *surface* of an inflating balloon which is analogous to three-dimensional space. The spherical surface has no center and so no location where the expansion begins. The analogy of the North Pole with the beginning of time should not be pressed, since the North Pole is not an edge to the surface of the globe; the beginning of time is more like the apex of a cone. But the idea is that just as one cannot go further north than the North Pole, so one cannot go earlier than the initial singularity.

2.32. Evidence for GR

The earliest evidence in favor of the Big Bang came from the consonance of theory and experiment. Einstein's early papers proposed two tests that could be performed immediately. It had been known for some time that Newton's gravitational theory could not adequately describe the orbit of the planet Mercury. The real orbit precessed around the sun (i.e. the ellipse itself rotates over time). In contrast to Newton's theory of gravity, GR "predicted" that this precession should take place. Einstein's theory also predicted that, since matter bends space, light rays should have their paths noticeably bent when they pass close to massive objects. A solar eclipse in 1919 provided the opportunity for a test of this prediction. An expedition led by Arthur Eddington confirmed that light rays were indeed deflected.

These tests were not sufficiently accurate[29] to ensure that small deviations from GR were not possible. It was also suspected that, since the real universe is not completely homogeneous and isotropic at all scales, Friedmann and Lemaître's prediction of a true singular beginning to the universe would ultimately fail. Perhaps a slight anisotropy could result in matter's "sling-shotting" past itself at a minimum (but nonzero) radius condition, so that the present expansion was preceded by a cosmic contraction, thereby avoiding the absolute beginning of the universe. In 1970, however, Stephen Hawking and Roger Penrose proved that the homogeneity/isotropy assumption was irrelevant. The Hawking–Penrose singularity theorems showed that so long as the universe is governed by GR (with a few technical exceptions, which will become prominent in our discussion later into the chapter), our past must include a singularity (Hawking & Penrose 1970). Wald comments:

> [Hawking–Penrose 1970] gives us strong reason to believe that our universe is singular . . . the observational evidence strongly suggests that our universe – or, at least, the portion of our universe within our causal past – is well described by a Robertson-Walker model [standard hot Big Bang theory] at least back as far as the decoupling time of matter and radiation. However, in these models, the expansion of the past directed null geodesics emanating from the event representing us at the present time becomes negative at a much more recent time than the decoupling time. Thus there is strong reason to believe that condition 4c of [Hawking–Penrose 1970] is satisfied in our universe. Since we expect that conditions (1)-(3) also are satisfied, it appears that our universe must be singular. Thus, it appears that we must confront the breakdown of classical general relativity expected to occur near singularities if we are to understand the origin of our universe. (Wald 1984, p. 241)

The conditions Wald mentions are:

1.   Satisfaction of the strong energy condition (typically obeyed by "normal" types of matter).

---

29. However, further experiments *did* definitively establish the correspondence between GR and nature. The 1993 Nobel Prize for Physics was awarded to two astronomers: Russell A. Hulse and Joseph H. Taylor, Jr. The award was given for their study of a distant solar system consisting of a binary pulsar – two neutron stars orbiting each other. GR predicted that the orbit would shrink over time due to the emission of gravitational waves. They proved that GR is accurate to a startling degree of one part in 10^{14}. This makes GR perhaps the best-proved theory in all of physics.

2. Satisfaction of the generic energy condition (there is no exotic property of the space-time that prevents gravitational focusing).
3. No closed time loops (the future does not bend back and become one's own past).
4. There is a point p such that past-directed worldlines emanating from p have negative expansion; that is, they are focused back on each other (the worldlines of observers do not trace into an infinite past given sufficiently concentrated matter but are "focused," as by a lens, into a singular condition within a finite time).

2.33. Exceptions to the Hawking–Penrose theorems

Four possible exceptions to the Hawking–Penrose singularity theorems conveniently distinguish four classes of nonstandard models that provide possible alternatives to the standard Big Bang model (Figure 3.3). The Hawking–Penrose Theorem also has the obvious, but implicit, condition that GR is fundamental; that is, it is a complete as well as correct description of conditions within our universe (thereby defining a 5th condition).

The first option (closed time loops) has been the subject of some exploration in cosmological circles. The next two – eternal inflation and quantum gravity – represent areas of fertile cosmological investigation which merit our attention. The last two exception conditions are not expected to be part of "reasonable" physical models of the universe. Hawking explains:

> Between 1965 and 1970 Penrose and I used the techniques I have described to prove a number of singularity theorems. These theorems had three kinds of conditions. First there was an energy condition such as the weak, strong or generic energy conditions. Then there was some global condition on the causal structure such as that there shouldn't be any closed time like curves. And finally was some condition that gravity was so strong in some region that nothing could escape. . . .

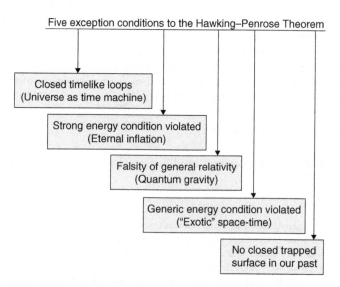

Figure 3.3 Model classes based on exceptions to the Hawking–Penrose singularity theorems.

[The generic energy condition] says that first the strong energy condition holds. Second, every timelike or null geodesic encounters some point where there is some curvature that is not specially aligned with the geodesic. The generic energy condition is not satisfied by a number of known exact solutions. But these are rather special. One would expect it to be satisfied by a solution that was "generic" in an appropriate sense [that is, a reasonable physical model]. If the generic energy condition holds, each geodesic will encounter a region of gravitational focusing. (Hawking & Penrose 1996, pp. 14–5)

We do expect our past to feature a closed, trapped surface, and there is no reason to postulate an exotic space-time construction that would just happen to have perfect defocusing characteristics so as to counter the effects of gravity. Hence, our discussion will revolve around the first three options.

I. Closed timelike curves (CTCs)

A first, exotic exception to the Hawking–Penrose theorems is the possible existence of CTCs. Permitted by Einstein's GR, CTCs represent an observer tracing out a circular path through space and time.

J. Richard Gott and Li-Xin Li have proposed a model according to which the early universe (only) is a closed time loop that occasionally gives "birth" to a universe like ours (Figure 3.4). They maintain that Alexander Vilenkin's "tunneling from nothing" model (see section IVc) should properly be taken as tunneling from a previous state. As will be seen in this chapter, most cosmological models assert that the past terminates at a boundary a finite time ago. One then wishes to explain what exists at that boundary. Vilenkin (and, independently, the team of Stephen Hawking and James Hartle) believes that the universe sprang into being "out of nothing." Gott and Li believe, instead, that there is a CTC at this boundary.

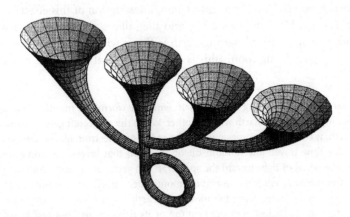

Figure 3.4 A Gott–Li universe time machine.

The region of closed timelike curves (CTC) exists at the bottom of the diagram. This region is separated from the future evolution of the universe by a Cauchy horizon (a boundary that separates space-time into CTC regions and non-CTC regions). The four branches to the top of the diagram can be thought of as inflationary bubbles undergoing a de Sitter-like expansion (see sections II and IIIa for a discussion of inflation and de Sitter spaces). (source: Gott & Li 1998)

The Gott–Li model could be an example of a universe timeline looping back upon itself to allow the universe, in Gott and Li's words, "to become its own mother." They explain:

> In this paper, we consider instead the notion that the Universe did not arise out of nothing, but rather created itself. One of the remarkable properties of the theory of general relativity is that in principle it allows solutions with CTCs. Why not apply this to the problem of the first-cause?
>
> Many inflationary models allow creation of baby inflationary universes inside black holes, either by tunneling across the Einstein-Rosen bridge, or by formation as one approaches the singularity. *If one of these baby universes simply turns out to be the universe we started with, then a multiply connected model with early CTCs bounded by a Cauchy horizon is produced.*
>
> ... Then the Universe neither tunneled from nothing, nor arose from a singularity; it created itself. (Gott & Li 1998, p. 39; emphasis added)

Some histories in our past were circular in nature (forming a multiply connected space-time) and recreating the Big Bang. Further, this is not a cyclic universe; *it is the same Big Bang.*

The CTC scenario raises interesting philosophical questions about the nature of time (see below, p. 191). But here, our interest is in the model's physical viability. The primary physical problem confronting CTC models in general is their violation of the so-called Chronology Protection Conjecture (CPC).

Gott and Li indicate that "the region of CTCs ... should be in a pure vacuum state containing no real particles or Hawking radiation and no bubbles"(Gott & Li 1998, p. 39). This is so because this stray radiation would destroy the CTC. The reason for this curious feature of a CTC model was discussed by Stephen Hawking (1992), where he formally suggested a "CPC." His theory was that a time machine (CTC) would have characteristics that were so unstable that it would quickly destroy itself. Hence, nature conspires to prevent time machines. A popular level (and entertaining) description of this effect is given by GR theorist Kip Thorne. He constructs a scenario that allows a local time machine to exist with one end on a spaceship departing Earth with his wife Carole and the other end on Earth with him in his living room (this is an exotic general relativistic structure called a wormhole).

> Imagine that Carole is zooming back to Earth with one wormhole mouth in her spacecraft, and I am sitting at home on Earth with the other. When the spacecraft gets to within 10 light-years of Earth, it suddenly becomes possible for radiation (electromagnetic waves) to use the wormhole for time travel: any random bit of radiation that leaves our home in Pasadena traveling at the speed of light toward the spacecraft can arrive at the spacecraft after 10 years' time (as seen on Earth), enter the wormhole mouth there, travel back in time by 10 years (as seen on Earth), and emerge from the mouth on Earth at precisely the same moment as it started its trip. The radiation piles right on top of its previous self, not just in space but in spacetime, doubling its strength. What's more, during the trip each quantum of radiation (each photon) got boosted in energy due to the relative motion of the wormhole mouths (a "Doppler-shift" boost).
>
> After the radiation's next trip out to the spacecraft then back through the wormhole, it again returns at the same time as it left and again piles up on itself, again with a Doppler-boosted energy. Again and again this happens, making the beam of radiation infinitely strong.

In this way, beginning with an arbitrarily tiny amount of radiation, a beam of infinite energy is created, coursing through space between the two wormhole mouths. As the beam passes through the wormhole ... it will produce infinite spacetime curvature [i.e. a singularity] and probably destroy the wormhole, thereby preventing [a time machine from coming into being in the first place]. (Thorne 1994, pp. 505–6)

Of interest to us is the general applicability of this effect to the Gott–Li model. Gott and Li are sensitive to this problem and have developed a solution[30]. They and others have found some specially constructed space-times that appear to elude Hawking's CPC. To avoid the CPC, they have constructed a special initial state for the universe: a zero-temperature empty space called an "adapted Rindler vacuum." It is specially built and balanced such that it does not develop the destructive effect suggested by Thorne earlier.

After the publication of Gott and Li's paper, William Hiscock developed a defense of the CPC that still appears to stand (Hiscock 2000). First, Hiscock argues that the Gott–Li choice of initial conditions is highly fine-tuned. In fact, Gott–Li's vacuum is of "measure zero" in the set of all possible Rindler vacuums. This means that the scenario is just about as unlikely as is possible without ruling it out summarily. D. H. Coule agrees in his summary of quantum gravity models, referring to the Gott–Li model as "rather contrived" (Coule 2005).[31] Second, Hiscock argues that the Gott–Li vacuum is not stable, given more realistic physical force fields. He writes:

... the (Rindler) vacuum stress-energy of a nonconformally coupled scalar field, or a conformally coupled massless field with a ... self-interaction will diverge on the chronology horizon for all values of the Misner identification scale [this is the parameter that Gott–Li have fine-tuned]. In addition, the vacuum polarization of [the scalar field considered in the Gott–Li model] diverges in all cases [leading to the Thorne effect cited earlier], even for the conformally invariant case examined by Li and Gott. Hence, the regular behavior found by Cassidy and Li and Gott holds only for a conformally invariant, non-interacting field, and only for the stress-energy tensor. While some fields in nature (e.g., the electromagnetic field, before interactions are added) are conformally invariant, others – notably gravity itself–are not; and interactions are the rule, not the exception. (Hiscock 2000, p. 4)

30. Gott indicates:

I think no one has been able to rule out CTC's. There have been no significant changes in quantum gravity since our paper. To understand whether one can create a time machine one may have to understand quantum gravity and we do not yet. Several loopholes in chronology protection have been found. Li Xin-Li and I and Cassidy, Hawking's student have found examples of quantum vacuum states that do not blow up on the cauchy horizon. Li Xin-Li's paper on the correct renormalization procedure [Phys. Rev. D. 084016 (1999)] showed that the vacuum field did not blow up for electromagnetic fields and other fields as well as for scalar fields. This means the action or entropy does not blow up either–solving a trouble Hawking and Cassidy thought existed. For matter obeying the weak energy condition instabilities are cured if the time loop occurs at the beginning of the universe, as we are proposing. (pers. comm., March 1, 2008)

31. Coule has some additional objections of his own. For example, he criticizes the nature of the vacuum, indicating that thermal fluctuations need to be of a precise form in order to avoid the radiation backreaction described earlier by Thorne. This expectation is inconsistent with the Planck scale physics employed by Gott and Li.

Coule adds: "... in Misner space this state [Gott–Li model] was only possible with identification scale $b = 2\pi$, or $b = 2\pi r0$ for the multiple de Sitter case. Such an exact value is itself inconsistent with notions of quantum uncertainty" (Coule 2005, p. 31). So the Heisenberg uncertainty principle of quantum mechanics (QM) would guarantee that the relevant parameter could not be "just-so." But if it is not "just-so," then the universe collapses into a singular condition in the presence of a time machine. Coule also suggests that this parameter, called the "Misner identification scale" is not a constant. Rather it is likely to change dynamically as a function of matter couplings or energy potentials. As soon as it does, the CTC will destabilize.

Interestingly, Gott and Li used similar objections when arguing for their model at the expense of the "creation from nothing" approach of Vilenkin and Hartle and Hawking [section IVc]. Gott and Li criticize the "creation from nothing" approach on the grounds of the uncertainty principle and the fact that their competitors are not using realistic force fields; that is to say, the Vilenkin approach is not close enough to what we expect for the real universe. Yet their own model appears to break down when similar objections are leveled against it.[32,33]

CTC physics is interesting, and while some theorists still pursue it, it occupies only a small minority of ongoing cosmological investigation. While it is true that no one has been able definitively to rule out CTCs, the evidentiary burden lies upon those defending the viability of such space-times and models predicated upon their reality.

II. Eternal inflation

Motivation

A more serious exception to the Hawking–Penrose singularity theorems is afforded by inflationary theory. Although the Friedmann–Lemaître model had a great deal of evidential support, there were, nonetheless, observational anomalies which suggested that there was more to the story. There were also theoretical reasons to think that the description was not quite complete. These difficulties, especially the horizon, flatness, and cosmic relic problems, prompted theorists to propose a modification of the standard Big Bang picture called "inflation."

With respect to the horizon problem, cosmologists lacked an explanation as to *why* the universe should be so homogeneous and isotropic.[34] Alan Guth explains:

The initial universe is assumed to be homogeneous, yet it consists of at least $\sim 10^{83}$ separate regions which are causally disconnected (*i.e.*, these regions have not yet had time to commu-

---

32. In fairness to Gott and Li, it should be noted that Hiscock's criticisms are based on a semiclassical approach (an approximation of quantum gravity), and it is possible that a full theory of quantum gravity could vindicate their idea.

33. Vilenkin has also criticized the Gott–Li model (see Vilenkin 2006, p. 219). He indicates that the Gott–Li space-time contains incomplete histories, so, "This means that the spacetime itself is past-incomplete, and therefore does not provide a satisfactory model of a universe without a beginning."

34. The universe does *appear* different at various distances as we look at it. But this is due to the fact that we observe distant galaxies as they were in the past, given the time it takes for their light to reach us.

nicate with each other via light signals) ... Thus, one must assume that the forces which created these initial conditions were capable of violating causality. (Guth 1981, p. 347)

Cosmology had an appropriate "organizing" principle at hand – thermodynamic equilibrium – yet mathematics showed that, in the limit, as one looked backward at the Big Bang, the different parts of the universe would lose causal communication. Without causal communication, all the parts of the observable universe could not have cooperated in energy transfer so as to make all parts look the same (in the present). Physicist Brian Greene describes the horizon problem:

> Physicists define a region's *cosmic horizon* (or *horizon* for short) as the most distant surrounding regions of space that are close enough to the given region for the two to have exchanged light signals in the time since the [Big] bang. ... The *horizon problem*, then is the puzzle, inherent in the observations, that regions whose horizons have always been separate – regions that could never have interacted, communicated, or exerted any kind of influence on each other – somehow have nearly identical temperatures. (Greene 2004, p. 289; emphasis in the original)
>
> ... imagine running the cosmic film in reverse while focusing on two regions of space currently on opposite sides of the observable universe – regions that are so distant that they are beyond each other's spheres of influence. If in order to halve their separation we have to roll the cosmic film more than halfway back toward the beginning, then even though the regions of space were closer together, communication between them was still impossible: they were half as far apart, but the time since the bang was *less* than half of what it is today, so light could travel only *less* than half as far. Similarly, if from that point in the film we have to run more than halfway back to the beginning in order to halve the separation between the regions once again, communication becomes more difficult still. With this kind of cosmic evolution, even though regions were closer together in the past, it becomes more puzzling – not less –that they somehow managed to equalize their temperatures. Relative to how far light can travel, the regions become increasingly cut off as we examine them ever farther back in time. This is exactly what happens in the standard big bang theory. (Greene 2004, p. 288; emphasis in the original)

A second problem was that the universe appears to be "flat" (i.e. space is Euclidian: the angles of a triangle add up to 180 degrees; parallel lines do not intersect), while GR predicts that that is a wildly improbable outcome.

> A typical closed universe will reach its maximum size on the order [of the Planck scale of 10^{-44} sec], while a typical open universe will dwindle to a ρ [density] much less than ρ_{cr} [critical density; the density for a long-lived universe]. A universe can only survive $\sim 10^{10}$ years [approximately the age of our universe] only by extreme fine tuning. ... For [the likely initial conditions for our universe] the value of H_0 [the initial expansion rate of the universe] must be fine tuned to an accuracy of one part in 10^{55}. In the standard model this incredibly precise initial relationship must be assumed without explanation. (Guth 1981, p. 348)

The third problem was that the supposition of an initial disorganized state of the universe led to the prediction of the presence of bizarre cosmic relics. Magnetic monopoles should appear in our universe at a density amenable to detection with our present means. In Guth's original paper on inflation, he indicates that standard particle physics predicts a monopole concentration 14 orders of magnitude greater than the upper bound observed in our universe. To date, we have seen none of these exotic structures.[35]

Guth's solution to these three problems was to postulate a period of exponential expansion very early in the history of the universe. Again Greene:

> In inflationary cosmology, there was a brief instant during which gravity was repulsive and this drove space to expand faster and faster. During this part of the cosmic film, you would have to wind the film less than halfway back in order to halve the distance between the two regions. . . . the increasingly rapid separation of any two regions of space during inflationary expansion implies that halving their separation requires winding the cosmic film less – *much less* – than halfway back toward the beginning. As we go farther back in time, therefore, it becomes *easier* for any two regions of space to influence each other, because, proportionally speaking, there is more time for them to communicate. Calculations show that if the inflationary expansion phase drove space to expand by at least a factor of 10^{30}, an amount that is readily achieved in specific realizations of inflationary expansion, all the regions in space that we currently see . . . were able to communicate . . . and hence efficiently come to a common temperature in the earliest moments of the universe. (Greene 2004, pp. 289–90; emphasis in the original)

This inflationary period began and ended in a fraction of a second, yet a typical inflationary event could lead to 70 "e-folds." An e-fold is a logarithmic measure of how large the universe grows during an inflationary event. Here, N is the number of e-folds, and $a(t)$ represents the scale factor of the universe at the beginning and end of inflation.[36]

$$N(t) \equiv \ln\left[a(t_{end})/a(t_{beginning})\right]$$

E-folds are a shorthand way of expressing the huge increase in size of the universe during an inflationary event (recall Greene's factor of 10^{30}).

Hence, prior to inflation all parts of the present, observable universe could be in causal communication with one another. Inflationary expansion would also smooth the curvature of the present-day universe to be flat or nearly flat, similar to the way the curvature of a basketball would appear to vanish if it suddenly grew to the size of the Earth. Further, since our present observable universe would be only a microscopic part of the original generic manifold, the density of exotic cosmic relics would be expected to be so small that we should not see them.

Inflation was a remarkable fix to a set of serious anomalies; but it also had one more feature in store. The Hawking–Penrose singularity theorems had as one of their requirements that gravity is always attractive – just as it is for ordinary matter. But the

---

35. To understand what these exotic structures represent, consider the analogy of a pond freezing in wintertime. If the pond starts freezing in one place and the ice simply grows until it encompasses the whole pond, you will have a smooth surface. But if different parts of the pond start freezing separately, ultimately, these growing "icebergs" must meet at a boundary. (Imagine taking big rocks and cracking holes in the ice; then letting it refreeze. The boundaries will be rough.) The early universe was similar. These boundaries are called "defects" and can be zero-, one-, or two-dimensional. Zero-dimensional defects are called magnetic monopoles. One-dimensional defects are called cosmic strings. Two-dimensional boundaries are called domain walls.
36. Definition of e-fold available at http://astro.uchicago.edu/~cunha/inflation/node4.html.

most likely physical candidate that could account for an inflationary event was a type of energy similar to the original cosmological constant that Einstein had proposed (Einstein 1917). This bizarre type of energy would act like repulsive gravity. This led to a philosophically desired outcome. If this "repulsive gravity" was present in the early universe and could dominate attractive gravity, then the possibility arises that the Hawking–Penrose singularity theorems did not apply to the real universe. Perhaps the universe is past eternal after all.

Inflationary theorizing eventually led to a yet grander theory, according to which the gravitationally repulsive material may, in fact, be the norm in the universe rather than the exception. Cosmologist Andrei Linde explains:

> This process, which I have called eternal inflation, keeps going as a chain reaction, producing a fractal-like pattern of universes. In this scenario the universe as a whole is immortal. *Each particular part of the universe may stem from a singularity somewhere in the past, and it may end up in a singularity somewhere in the future.* There is, however, no end for the evolution of the entire universe.
>
> The situation with the very beginning is less certain. There is a chance that all parts of the universe were created simultaneously in an initial big bang singularity. The necessity of this assumption, however, is no longer obvious.
>
> Furthermore, the total number of inflationary bubbles on our 'cosmic tree' grows exponentially in time. Therefore, most bubbles (including our own part of the universe) grow indefinitely far away from the trunk of this tree. Although this scenario makes the existence of the initial big bang almost irrelevant, for all practical purposes, one can consider the moment of formation of each inflationary bubble as a new 'big bang.' From this perspective, inflation is not a part of the big bang theory, as we thought 15 years ago. On the contrary, the big bang is a part of the inflationary model. (Linde 1998, p. 103; emphasis added)

Linde's chaotic inflation was one of two competing views for the theory. The competitor, called "new" inflation, featured the idea that there is a "false vacuum," which represents (meta)stable vacuum with a high Einstein-like cosmological constant (compared with the "true vacuum" in which we live). In "new inflation," this eternally expanding false vacuum regionally decays into the slower expanding true vacuum. It expands faster than it decays, so the process never stops.

Chaotic inflation is rather a different idea. Here, the universe starts from a "generic manifold," which is a state of maximal entropy chaos. An energy field of different regional values pervades this manifold. Where the field is large, inflation occurs. The field can undergo quantum fluctuation to high values as well; thereby giving onset to inflation. Locally, a region will have a tendency to seek out the minimum allowed value of the energy field. This leads to a process called "reheating," which creates the ordinary matter and energy that we see around us. Meanwhile, in locations of the universe where the field energy density is high, the quantum fluctuations will tend to offset the minimizing tendency and make perpetual (globally, but not regionally) the inflationary process (Figure 3.5).

Eternal inflationary models

The 1980s and 1990s witnessed a proliferation of inflationary models that theoretically allowed for a projection into an eternal past (Linde 2005). The inflationary phase mentioned earlier was not viewed in these models as an isolated event. Theorists began to describe the

Figure 3.5 In chaotic inflation, an initial generic manifold (a global space with random characteristics; that is, inhomogeneous and anisotropic in energy density and curvature) undergoes regional inflation. An observer sitting on an inflating spot will eventually see inflation come to a stop, but conditions are always suitable – somewhere – for inflation to proceed.

exotic energy that produces inflation as a field that pervades otherwise empty space. A key assumption was that the density[37] of the energy throughout space never changes, so that it resembles Einstein's cosmological constant. It does not depend on space or time, that is, it is constant. In that case, as space expands, more energy must continually be produced in order to maintain a constant energy density (where this energy comes from is still a matter of controversy). Space "clones" itself.[38] Occasionally, parts of this rapidly expanding space decay (convert) into the type of "empty" space that we live in. This space has a much lower energy density, so there is now a great deal of excess energy that pervades our new "bubble." This excess energy is thought to convert into the normal matter that we see around us.

In the latest version of inflationary theory (Figure 3.6), these decays take the form of quantum tunneling events. Every state that possesses a positive cosmological constant is "metastable." That means that, similar to a radioactive isotope, the state lasts for a while and then changes to a different (usually lower) allowed value of the cosmological constant. This lower-energy state is initially confined to a tiny portion of space, but given that the cosmological constant makes space expand, it becomes a rapidly growing bubble that is nested within the original space.

But what happens to the original space, part of which decayed to form our universe? It is still there, continuing to expand at enormous speed. Since it (usually) has a cosmological constant larger than the new bubble, its growth outpaces that of the new bubble. Since the false vacuum expands faster than it decays, inflation is eternal into the future. New bubbles of low-energy vacuum will continue to decay out of the expanding space.

37. In Linde's chaotic inflation, the energy field does feature quantum fluctuations that are critical to the onset of new inflationary patches.

38. Since only the "material" cause is missing, this process is an example of genuine *creatio ex nihilo* seen by physical theorists in the present day. Such recognition of efficient causation in the absence of material causation may serve to mute objections to theistic *creatio ex nihilo* as featured in the *kalam* cosmological argument.

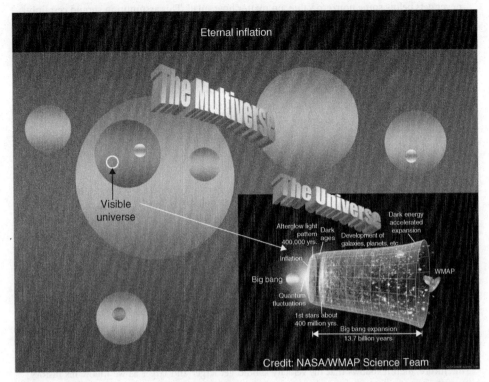

Figure 3.6 The String Landscape inflationary model. The Big Bang is just a regional event within a larger multiverse. There are different kinds of "empty space," which feature different values of the cosmological constant (different bubbles). The larger the constant, the faster the universe expands. Our universe decayed from one of these "false vacuum" regions. (inset adapted from the National Aeronautics and Space Administration, available at: http://map.gsfc.nasa.gov/news/index. html)

Theorists wondered whether this process could be infinitely extended into the past. Interestingly, Guth himself, along with collaborators Alexander Vilenkin and Arvind Borde, has likely closed the door on that possibility. In 2003, Borde, Guth, and Vilenkin published an updated singularity theorem far grander in scope than the Hawking–Penrose theorems. They explain,

> Our argument shows that null and time-like geodesics are, in general, past-incomplete in inflationary models, whether or not energy conditions hold, provided only that the averaged expansion condition $H_{av} > 0$ holds along these past-directed geodesics. (Borde, Guth, & Vilenkin 2003, p. 3)[39]
>
> A remarkable thing about this theorem is its sweeping generality. We made no assumptions about the material content of the universe. We did not even assume that gravity is described by Einstein's equations. So, if Einstein's gravity requires some modification, our conclusion will still hold. The only assumption that we made was that the expansion rate of the universe

---

39. H_{av} refers to the average value of the Hubble constant throughout history.

never gets below some nonzero value, no matter how small. This assumption should certainly be satisfied in the inflating false vacuum. The conclusion is that past-eternal inflation without a beginning is impossible. (Vilenkin 2006, p. 175)

Vilenkin affirms that any universe (including universes modeled by higher dimensional cosmology, pre–Big Bang cosmology, and so forth,) which, on average, expands has to connect, in a finite time, to a past boundary (pers. comm., March 4, 2004).

Intuitively, the reason that the universe must have a beginning in the finite past is that, in an expanding space, an observer tracing out a worldline (to the future) slows down. This is the redshift. Vilenkin explains:

> Let us now introduce another observer who is moving relative to the spectators [each of whom is motionless except for the expansion of space]. We shall call him the space traveler. He is moving by inertia, with the engines of his spaceship turned off, and has been doing so for all eternity. As he passes the spectators, they register his velocity.
>
> Since the spectators are flying apart [i.e. the universe is expanding], the space traveler's velocity relative to each successive spectator will be smaller than his velocity relative to the preceding one. Suppose, for example, that the space traveler has just zoomed by the Earth at the speed of 100,000 kilometers per hour and is now headed toward a distant galaxy, about a billion light years away. That galaxy is moving away from us at a speed of 20,000 kilometers per second, so when the space traveler catches up with it, the observers there will see him moving at 80,000 kilometers per second.
>
> If the velocity of the space traveler relative to the spectators gets smaller and smaller into the future, then it follows that his velocity should get larger and larger as we follow his history into the past. In the limit, his velocity should get arbitrarily close to the speed of light. (Vilenkin 2006)[40]

So, looking into the past, the observer must be seen to speed up. But one cannot exceed the speed of light. The implication of this is that the past worldline of this observer has a finite length. This is the symptom of singularity; the "pathology" that Robert Wald referred to earlier. The observer will have "begun its existence a finite time ago."

The Borde–Vilenkin–Guth (BVG) singularity theorem is now widely accepted within the physics community. As of this writing, it has gone largely unchallenged.[41] Instead a new round of model building has resulted based on exceptions to *this* theorem. Four alternatives present themselves (Figure 3.7).

---

40. Alan Guth, in a 2003 lecture at the University of California Santa Barbara's Kavli Institute, says: "If we follow the observer backwards in an expanding universe, she speeds up. But the calculation shows that if $H_{average} > 0$ in the past, then she will reach the speed of light in a finite proper time." (See http://online.kitp.ucsb.edu/online/strings_c03/guth/pdf/KITPGuth_2up.pdf.)

41. Andrei Linde has offered a critique, suggesting that BVG imply that all the individual parts of the universe have a beginning, but perhaps the WHOLE does not. This seems misconstrued, however, since BVG are *not* claiming that *each* past inextendible geodesic is related to a *regional* singularity. Rather, they claim that Linde's universe description contains an internal contradiction. As we look backward along the geodesic, it *must* extend to the infinite past if the universe is to be past eternal. But it does not (for the observer comoving with the expansion). Rather, past inextendible geodesics are the "symptom," not the "disease." As Robert Wald (1984, p. 216) says, "Unfortunately, the singularity theorems give virtually no information about the nature of the singularities of which they prove existence." So we do not know the nature of the singularity that the BVG Theorem indicates; we know only that Linde's description of an infinite past is in error.

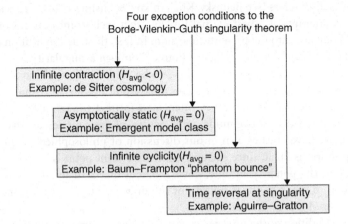

Figure 3.7 Post-2003 cosmological model building based on finding exceptions to the Borde–Vilenkin–Guth Theorem.

IIIa. Infinite contraction

Assume that a spatially infinite universe contracted down to a singularity and then "bounced" into our present expansion. In such a case, the universe cannot be said to be, on average, in a state of cosmic expansion throughout its history since the expansion phase, even if infinite, is canceled out by the contraction phase. While permissible under the BVG Theorem, this option is not, however, a popular option among contemporary cosmologists. George Ellis identifies two problems that bedevil such an approach:

> The problems are related: first, initial conditions have to be set in an extremely special way at the start of the collapse phase in order that it is a Robertson-Walker universe collapsing; and these conditions have to be set in an acausal way (in the infinite past). It is possible, but a great deal of inexplicable fine tuning is taking place: how does the matter in widely separated causally disconnected places at the start of the universe know how to correlate its motions (and densities) so that they will come together correctly in a spatially homogeneous way in the future??
>
> Secondly, if one gets that right, the collapse phase is unstable, with perturbations increasing rapidly, so only a very fine-tuned collapse phase remains close to Robertson-Walker even if it started off so, and will be able to turn around as a whole (in general many black holes will form locally and collapse to a singularity).
>
> So, yes, it is possible, but who focused the collapse so well that it turns around nicely? (pers. comm., January 25, 2006)

So there is a significant problem of *acausal* fine-tuning. One asserts not just brute contingency but also a rather curious form of it. In the face of apparent fine-tuning, physicists usually prefer to offer some type of explanation. Consider, for example, multiverse models as an explanation of the apparent fine-tuning of the fundamental physical constants, or Guth's inflationary resolution of the horizon problem (past thermodynamic equilibrium).

Second, there is the problem that the collapse becomes chaotic as it approaches the singularity. This will produce a preexpansion start condition that is known to be dramatically different from our actual "Big Bang." This phenomenon is referred to as "BKL chaos" after its discoverers (see Belinsky, Khalatnikov, & Lifshitz 1970).[42] This problem will appear for all attempts at a past-eternal timeline that seek to introduce a pre–Big Bang phase that "bounces" into the present expansion. In fact, the true implication of BKL may well be that it is physically impossible to "bounce" *through* a singularity.

In stating that the initial conditions "have to be set in an acausal way (in the infinite past)," Ellis puts his finger on a nettlesome philosophical issue in cosmological models featuring an infinite past, namely, they often *seem* to treat the infinite past as though it featured an infinitely distant beginning point. Several of these models are discussed in this essay. But, as we have already seen in our discussion of philosophical *kalam* arguments, such a supposition is illicit, since such an infinitely distant point is merely an ideal limit characteristic of the potential infinite, not a moment that actually once was present.[43] If we are allowed to speak of the condition of the universe at past infinity, then Zenonian paradoxes (see p. 119) are unavoidable.

If the past condition of the universe is acausal, then of course there was no "setting" of the condition; it just "is." Ellis is referring merely to the construction of the mathematical model. But suppose we do imagine that the boundary conditions were literally set at past infinity. Something like this was a feature of Charles Misner's old "Mixmaster" universe:

> In reality we don't expect universes to expand at exactly the same rate in every direction, and when they become asymmetrical like this they behave in a very complicated way. Although they expand in volume, one direction tends to contract while the other two expand, tending to create an expanding 'pancake'. But soon the contracting direction switches to expansion and one of the other two expanding directions switches into contraction. Over a long period of time, the effect is a sequence of oscillations ... The striking thing about the sequence of oscillations of the volume of the universe as it shrinks to zero, when one runs its history back into the Big Bang at time-zero, or on into the Big Crunch at crunch-time, is that an infinite number of oscillations occur. ... The difference between the Mixmaster Universe and Zeno's paradox is that an infinite number of physically distinct, real events happen in any finite interval of time that includes time-zero or crunch time. Measured by a clock that 'ticks' on this oscillatory time, the Mixmaster Universe would be judged to be infinitely old, because an infinite number of things have happened to the past in this time, and it will 'live' forever because an infinite number of things are still to happen in the future. (Barrow 2005, pp. 242–3)

The Mixmaster universe is interesting in that it appears to offer a past infinite timeline that nonetheless features a clear past boundary to that timeline; that is, an infinitely distant

---

42. Also, see Damour and Henneaux (2000): ". . . our findings suggest that the spatial inhomogeneity continuously increases toward a singularity, as all quasi-uniform patches of space get broken up into smaller and smaller ones by the chaotic oscillatory evolution. In other words, the spacetime structure tends to develop a kind of 'turbulence.'"

43. In response to the question, "Are c-boundaries [see Figure 3.8 and the following discussion for explanation of these terms] such as past and future timelike infinity and scri+ physically real edges to spacetime (real, as a black hole is an ontologically real entity) or are they merely mathematical conveniences? But if infinity is 'actual' and reachable, then a c-boundary must be an actual edge to spacetime, physically real in its ontology," Ellis (pers. comm.) responds curtly:

1. no
2. maths – after all a spacetime diagram is just a representation of physical reality
3. in my view infinity is neither actual nor reachable.

beginning point. There *is* a question of judging the most physically appropriate measure of time. By proper time, Mixmaster arose a finite time ago from a singularity and will end its existence a finite time to the future. Time measured by oscillatory "ticks" would report a timeline that is infinite to the past and future. Barrow and Tipler elucidate:

> It is always possible to find a conformal transformation which will convert an infinite universe to a finite one and vise-versa. One can always find a time coordinate in which a universe that exists for a finite proper time . . . exists for an infinite time in the new time coordinate, and a time coordinate in which a universe that exists for an infinite proper time . . . exists for only a finite time. The most appropriate *physical* time may or may not be the proper time coordinate. (Barrow & Tipler 1986, p. 636)

Physicists routinely consider an infinitely distant past "beginning" point, in effect bringing infinity into their physical models through a process called a conformal transformation. Consider Barrow and Tipler, here explaining simple Friedmann–Robertson–Walker (FRW) cosmological models using a device called a Penrose diagram.

> The boundaries of a Penrose diagram represent what are termed c-boundaries of the cosmological models. The c-boundaries are composed of the singularities and the points at infinity; the c-boundary of a cosmology is the edge of space-time, the 'place' at which space and time begin. By convention, singularities are represented by double lines in Penrose diagrams. [For example] the initial and final singularities are the only c-boundaries in a closed Friedmann universe. An open Friedmann universe, on the other hand, has four distinct c-boundary structures: an initial singularity out of which the entire space-time arose, a single point i^0 representing spatial infinity, a 45° line ϑ^+ (called 'scri plus') representing 'null infinity' which are the points at infinity that light rays (null curves) reach after infinite time, and a single point i^+ which all timelike curves approach for all finite times, and reach after infinite time (with the exception of those timelike curves that accelerate forever and thus approach arbitrarily close to the speed of light. These curves hit scri plus rather that i^+ at temporal infinity).
> A Penrose diagram allows us to define rigorously 'an achieved infinity', a concept whose logical consistency philosophers have been doubtful about for thousands of years. Using the c-boundary, it is possible to discuss the topology of the 'achieved infinity' and the 'beginning of time' in cosmological models. (Barrow & Tipler 1986, pp. 635–6)

Models such as Mixmaster, the problem of supertasks[44] in general, and the meaning of conformal transformations raise the question of whether an infinite past implies the absence of a past boundary.

Figure 3.8 shows a Penrose diagram for the universe type under consideration in this section; that is, one that contracts from infinite size down to a singularity, and then bounces into an expanding universe (see right side of the diagram). Figure 3.9 shows another type of simplified model (a de Sitter universe) that has this type of behavior. The de Sitter model includes "dark energy," while the contracting model in Figure 3.8 includes only ordinary matter. A more realistic physical model would include both ordinary matter and "dark energy." The behavior of the universe at large size would be dominated

---

44. A supertask is an infinite series of subtasks that can be completed in a finite time.

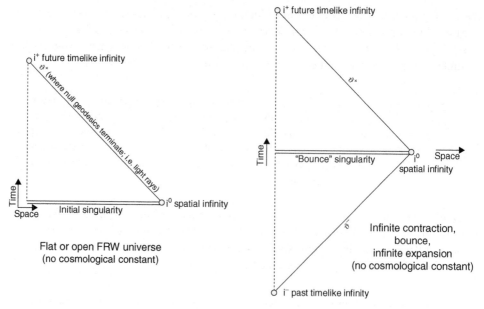

Figure 3.8 Penrose depiction of Friedmann–Robertson–Walker (FRW) cosmology.

de Sitter universe
A universe with no matter but with a positive cosmological constant Λ.

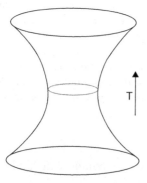

Contracts from infinite size to a minimum radius, then expands exponentially. A more realistic model would include radiation and matter, which would cause a singularity at time zero, while the distant past and future would behave like the de Sitter solution.

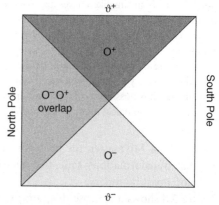

Penrose diagram: South and North "Pole" represent observers tracing out timelike paths. O⁻ indicates limits of causal past of North Pole observer. O⁺ indicates causal future. No observer sees the full space-time; hence the mystery of the acausal fine-tuning.

Figure 3.9 A more realistic rendering of a universe that infinitely collapses down to a Big Bang, and then expands. The de Sitter cosmology takes into account the dominant behavior of a cosmological constant for a universe of large size.

by the dark energy, and so a de Sitter model yields good insight into the behavior of an infinite contraction model for the asymptotic past. By contrast, the behavior of the universe at the Big Bang would be best described by the Friedmann–Lemaître models in Figure 3.8.

It appears there is a dilemma. On the one hand, one could have the reality of a past infinite timeline without a beginning. But then one must assert brute contingency. "Things are as they are because they were as they were."[45] Further, one must do this with respect to apparent fine-tuning. This seems implausible. One can at least say that it is unpopular, given that cosmologists are avidly seeking an *explanation* for apparent fine tuning in the form of a multiverse or a superdeterministic Theory of Everything. If we are going to give up *explanation*, then what was wrong with leaving cosmology as it was prior to 1980, namely, the standard Hot Big Bang model (with associated breakdown of physics at the singularity)?[46]

The other horn involves an infinitely distant beginning point and allows the possibility of an explanation. But it opens the door for a supernatural explanation of the beginning. The *kalam* cosmological argument's second premise would be upheld, for that premise does not require that the beginning lie in the finite past.

IIIb. Asymptotically static space-time

An asymptotically static space is one in which the average expansion rate of the universe over its history is equal to zero, since the expansion rate of the universe "at" infinity is zero. Hence, the universe, perhaps in the asymptotic past, is in a static state (neither expanding nor contracting). This allows the model to escape the BVG singularity theorem.

At first blush, it would seem that the universe could hardly be said to have zero average expansion throughout its history if, as we know from observation, it has indeed been expanding! Would not the average expansion rate have to be greater than zero? No, not when we include "infinity" in the average. Consider an analogy in which the local government decides that, henceforth, everyone will pay property taxes according to the average value of property (per acre) in the county instead of on one's individual assessment. This might be good or bad for you, depending on whether you live in the high end district. But suppose that your county suddenly expanded to include the Sahara Desert. The Sahara is worthless and big, hence the average value of property, by the square mile, dives precipitously. Further, the larger the Sahara is, the closer to zero one's property taxes will be. In the limit as the Sahara grows to infinite size, one's property taxes will go to zero. In a similar way, a zero expansion condition at infinity would have the same impact on the average expansion rate. And the BVG Theorem only applies to a positive *average* expansion universe. George Ellis and his colleagues have been active in this type of model building. Models of this sort belong to what is called the "Emergent" model class. They rehabilitate Einstein's static model by postulating that the universe initially existed in such a phase and then transitioned via an inflationary phase into the universe we see around us today. Ellis and Maartens explain:

---

45. Barrow and Tipler (1986, p. 408), attributed to cosmologist Thomas Gold.
46. See, for example, Earman and Mosterin (1999) for a related argument.

We show here that when K = +1 [recall the curvature parameter from Friedmann's equation] there are closed inflationary models that do not bounce, but inflate from a static beginning, and then reheat in the usual way. [Recall Guth's inflation] The inflationary universe emerges from a small static state that has within it the seeds for the development of the macroscopic universe, and we call this the "Emergent Universe" scenario. (This can be seen as a modern version and extension of the Eddington universe.) *The universe has a finite initial size, with a finite amount of inflation occurring over an infinite time in the past,* and with inflation then coming to an end via reheating in the standard way. (Ellis & Maartens 2004; emphasis added)[47]

As such, it is a manifestly nonsingular closed inflationary cosmology that *begins from a meta-stable Einstein static state* and decays into a de Sitter phase and subsequently into standard hot Big Bang evolution. (Ellis, Murugan, & Tsagas 2004; emphasis added)

A second, equally intriguing, possibility is that the initial Einstein static universe is created from "nothing" by some quantum tunneling process. Indeed, finiteness of the tunneling action requires that the universe created through instantonic tunneling be closed. It is not implausible, then, that through spontaneous quantum fluctuations, *a closed universe could be created in a long lived but transient Einstein static state* which then makes a transition to a finite lifetime de-Sitter and subsequent marginally closed FRW phase along the lines described above. (Ellis, Murugan, & Tsagas 2004; emphasis added)[48]

Now the question that interests us is whether the past of this model is perceived as eternal. A certain amount of ambiguity attends the answer. In some accounts (such as the above), it seems pretty clear that the Emergent models do have a beginning, namely, the Einstein static state (ESS). It is also stated explicitly that the model can be constructed with ESS occurring a finite time to the past (Ellis & Maartens 2004, sec. V). However, in the relevant papers ESS is usually described as asymptotically approached for past infinite time: "Here . . . we consider a universe filled with a dynamical scalar field, which is past asymptotic to an Einstein static model with a radius determined by the field's kinetic energy" (Ellis & Maartens 2004, p. 1). Some philosophers who have written on the topic have a problem with the contrived nature of the past infinity in models of this type. For example, Rüdiger Vaas characterizes the Emergent models as "soft-bang/pseudobeginning" in nature.

---

47. Now we just showed in the previous section that Ellis has a philosophical problem with models that suggest an infinitely distant beginning point and even, in fact, the notion of a realized infinity in nature. Yet here we have a family of models developed by Ellis et al. that seem to suggest precisely that. This is explained via the following:

1. Infinity is so deeply ingrained in GR that pure pragmatism demands that one include the concept within one's work.
2. It is not cognitively dissonant to consider that one might be wrong and research accordingly. In fact, good scientific procedure includes an attempt to falsify one's own theories.
3. Ellis's collaborators may not have the same philosophical commitments.
4. An infinity that appears due to a technical interpretation of GR can disappear given a generalization of the theory (say, by considering quantum gravity).

A full look at Ellis's recent work indicates a bias toward models with compact spaces (i.e. spatially finite either through closed curvature or topology), a skepticism with regard to infinite multiverses, and openness toward the idea of a "pseudobeginning" in the finite past. In short, the pseudobeginning idea is that there is timeless reality where time "switches on," producing our present state of affairs.

48. This is related to "creation from nothing" models; see section IVc.

He views the asymptotic approach toward ESS as something of a mathematical artifact (Vaas 2004, p. 18).

It is worth focusing on the issue of the instability of ESS. The Einstein static universe itself was originally viewed as past eternal. But there are obvious problems with this interpretation. The reason Einstein himself originally dropped the model was its feature of unstable equilibrium. Although, in pure nonquantum GR, one can consider a static state with worldlines that trace to negative infinite time, in reality we know that gravity is a quantum force. As Vilenkin notes, "Small fluctuations in the size of the universe are inevitable according to the quantum theory, and thus Einstein's universe cannot remain in balance for an infinite time" (Vilenkin 2006, p. 209).[49] On the other hand, the current observable universe is demonstrably *not* in a static state. A quantum (or perhaps a thermal) fluctuation is necessary to force a transition to an expanding universe. A fluctuation is, in fact, necessary for the two phase model to work. But this very mechanism implies that the *initial state* is not past eternal.

The best that can be done is the latest version of the Emergent model, which uses a "low-energy" solution of loop quantum gravity (LQG) to make the Einstein state stable against perturbations of a limited size (Figure 3.10). In response to the question, "Is the initial state metastable and therefore finite in its lifetime?," Ellis answers that the Einstein state can persist at most for a "long" but apparently *finite* time.[50]

LQG theorist Martin Bojowald explains that *any* perturbation, even if not of sufficient initial size to cause the system to escape the metastable potential, will *eventually* cause the system to escape it:

> Static solutions do not evolve, and so are clearly ill-suited as a model for the Universe. *But by introducing a perturbation to a static solution, one can slightly change it and thereby start a more interesting history.* Unfortunately, the classical solution [ESS] is unstable: any disturbance grows rapidly, leaving little of the initial state behind. The insight of Mulryne and colleagues is that quantum effects could supply all the necessary ingredients where classical solutions do not. Within the framework of loop quantum gravity, repulsion also implies static solutions at small size, but these – in contrast to the classical case – are stable. *According to the authors' model, perturbing such a state leads to small cycles of interchanging expansion and contraction.* During this process, matter will evolve slowly, and the cycles will gradually change their behavior. By itself, this perpetual recurrence and incremental change seems to lack the spark necessary for so momentous an event as the birth of the Universe. And indeed, Mulryne and colleagues identify one final theoretical ingredient that lights this spark: mediated through repulsive effects, *potential energy is gradually pushed into the matter during its slow evolution. At the point when potential energy starts to dominate kinetic energy, the mundane cycling is broken by a sudden, dramatic inflationary explosion – the emergent Universe.* (Bojowald 2005, pp. 920–1; emphasis added)

49. We note, as well, that a perturbation to a near-ESS state should be just as effective at disrupting the universe as a perturbation to a genuine ESS. Hence, a model which is only past asymptotic ESS does not escape the problem. In fact, given past infinite time, and the variety of exotic quantum universe transitions postulated throughout the cosmological literature, it seems inconceivable that any universe could possibly maintain a conserved structure over time periods "long" compared with the interval since the Big Bang.

50. He says, "note the later version of our model (astro-ph/0502589) based in the semi-classical approximation to loop quantum gravity where the static model is stable for a long while" (Private communication, January 24, 2006).

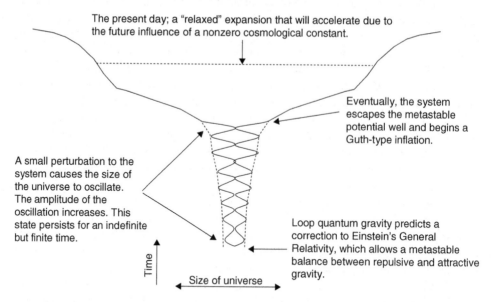

Figure 3.10 Evolution of an Emergent universe from a metastable loop quantum gravity state.

Metastability implies a finite life for the associated state. Either something must have come before it or it was "created." This issue of metastability is a general problem across a wide array of model classes. Vaas elaborates:

> Meta-stable states have a local, but not a global minimum in their potential landscape and, hence, they can decay; ground states might also change due to quantum uncertainty, *i.e.*, due to local tunneling events. Some still speculative theories of quantum gravity permit the assumption of such a global, macroscopically time-less ground state (*e.g.*, quantum or string vacuum, spin networks, twistors). *Due to accidental fluctuations, which exceed a certain threshold value, universes can emerge out of that state.* Due to some also speculative physical mechanism (like cosmic inflation) they acquire – and, thus, are characterized by – directed non-equilibrium dynamics, specific initial conditions, and, hence, an arrow of time. (Vaas 2004, p. 10; emphasis added)

It therefore seems that metastable (and, for that matter, unstable) states must have a merely finite lifetime. Metastable states leave unexplained how they came to exist. Universes with a metastable initial state must therefore have a beginning, consistent with the second premise of the *kalam* cosmological argument.

IIIc. Cyclic universe

According to these models, the universe goes through a cycle in which it grows from zero (or near-zero) size to a maximum and then contracts back to its starting condition. The universe itself is periodic, in the sense that it undergoes many such cycles, perhaps an infinite number. The average expansion of the universe would be zero in a "pure" cyclic model since cycle by cycle, one always experiences precisely equal amounts of expansion and contraction. Hence, a cyclic model evades the BVG Theorem. The past is featureless. Unlike the previous two model classes, it is not the case that the universe asymptotically approaches some particular state in the infinite past.

As Vilenkin indicates, however, cyclic models face a thermodynamic problem: "A truly cyclic universe has a problem with entropy increase: it should have reached thermodynamic equilibrium by now" (pers. comm., January 19, 2007). Our observation of the present day universe indicates that we are not at a condition of thermodynamic equilibrium – a good thing for us, as life requires nonequilibrium conditions to exist! As one looks into the past, the size of each cycle is also thought to decrease (due to radiation effect on entropy). Eventually the cycles are so small that one ends up with a different physics – which would preclude the cycling and imply a beginning to the universe.

So how does one overcome this problem? Paul Frampton and Lauris Baum have recently proposed an ingenious mechanism that breaks genuinely new ground in cosmological studies. It is surprising that they base their model on a scenario that is generally thought to imply quite the opposite of cycling. They assume that a type of dark energy pervades the universe where its equation of state (the ratio between pressure and energy density) is less than −1. This would be different from the cosmological constant mentioned earlier (equation of state equal to −1). This type of expansion is thought to lead to an event called the Big Rip. Dark energy (also called phantom energy in this context) causes the acceleration in the expansion of the universe to become so great that our visible horizon shrinks over time. Eventually, this causal horizon shrinks so much that cosmological objects of smaller and smaller size become causally unbound. Galaxies, solar systems, planets, and, eventually, even atoms get ripped apart as the expansion rate of the universe tends toward infinity. This would stop at a spatial singularity in the finite future. Baum and Frampton propose a "mosaic" model[51] to overcome the problem of entropy buildup in a single universe:

> We consider a model where, as we approach the rip, expansion stops due to a brane contribution just short of the big rip and there is a turnaround time $t = t_T$ when the scale factor is deflated to a very tiny fraction (f) of itself and only one causal patch is retained, while the other $1/f^3$ patches contract independently to separate universes. Turnaround takes place an extremely short time ($<10^{-27}$ s) before the big rip would have occurred, at a time when the Universe is fractionated into many independent causal patches. (Baum & Frampton 2007, p. 1)

What happens in the Baum–Frampton approach is that very close to the Big Rip event, the universe splits into noninteracting (causally disconnected) patches. The universe has expanded so much at this point that nearly all of these patches are empty of (normal) matter and radiation. They contain only phantom[52] energy. It turns out that the entropy content of the universe (which is what interferes with cycling) is contained within the thinly spread matter and radiation. Those patches that contain only phantom energy are supposed never to undergo the Big Rip. Instead they separately undergo a *deflation* event; contracting

---

51. Mosaic model: undesirable features of a model universe may be regional in scope; consideration of a multiverse may remove those features.

52. Phantom energy: dark energy with a supernegative equation of state, that is, $p/\rho < -1$.

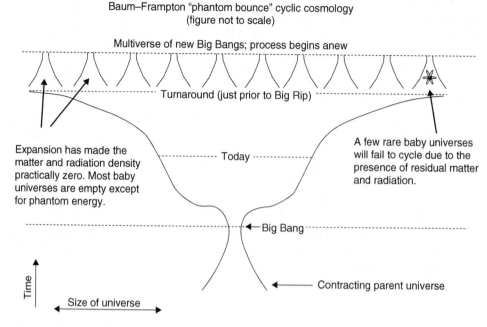

Figure 3.11 Baum–Frampton phantom bounce model.

an amount exactly equal to the expansion that the universe experienced since the Big Bang (thereby avoiding the implications of the BVG Theorem). Prior to reaching a singularity, the contracting patch rebounds due to the effects of phantom energy. It then repeats the same cycle endlessly. Every patch that undergoes this fractionates into new "universes" that themselves begin to propagate (think of dandelions spreading over your lawn). Hence, the Baum–Frampton model is said to feature an infinite multiverse in addition to a beginning-less cyclic behavior (Figure 3.11). But is the model viable?

Several challenges remain to be addressed if the model is to be a viable option. First, in order to avoid the BVG singularity theorem, the average contraction must equal exactly the average expansion (for every geodesic). But how is this to be done without introducing explicit fine-tuning? There is no reason that deflation of scale factor will exactly match post–Big Bang expansion. Frampton admits:

> I have no idea why it [the BVG constraint] is satisfied because it does relate expansion with dark matter to contraction without dark matter. . . . I suspect it is not fine tuning but that may ultimately depend on one's perspective: if BVG were not satisfied, infinite cyclicity is impossible. (pers. comm., February 5, 2007)

The problem has not yet been addressed.[53]

---

53. In June 2007, Paul Frampton did put a paper on the Web preprint (Frampton 2007a) that partially addressed the issue. But it appears to show only that a generic cyclic model avoids the BVG Theorem. That point was not in dispute. The original question still seems to persist.

Second, globally, entropy should have already grown to an infinite value. How is it that the various regions remain causally disconnected? The key factor in this model is the method for jettisoning the universe's entropy. As Baum and Frampton emphasize, if matter is retained during a contraction phase:

> ... presence of dust or matter would require that our universe go in reverse through several phase transitions (recombination, QCD and electroweak to name a few) which would violate the second law of thermodynamics. We thus require that our universe comes back empty! (Baum & Frampton 2007, p. 4)

Now, globally, over infinite past time, the model posits that an infinite amount of matter and radiation (hence, infinite entropy) has been produced. How is it, then, that the entropy density avoids achieving an infinite quantity? Frampton responds:

> It is true that if we retain all the separate patches entropy continues to increase. Our key idea is to retain only one causal patch for our universe whose entropy thereby drops precipitously in what we for obvious reasons call deflation. (pers. comm., February 5, 2007)

The sole mention of where this entropy goes occurs in the following passage: "The old problem confronting Tolman is avoided by removing entropy to an unobservable exterior region; one may say in hindsight that the problem lay in considering only one universe" (Frampton 2007a, p. 4).

Simply shoving the entropy into other "universes" raises the question whether, given infinite time, a static space and a countable infinity of realms within the multiverse, the realms must not eventually collide. Frampton responds:

> ... the 'causal patches' remain disjoint spawning separate universes which do not interact or collide again as they start out and remain causally disconnected. This more definite answer ... results from our better understanding of the turnaround from subsequent technical calculations. (pers. comm., October 10, 2007)

In our initial communication (February 2007), Frampton indicated that the problem of collision was a valid one and would be investigated. These calculations have not yet been published, hence the issue remains troubling.

Cosmologist Xin Zhang, in a recent paper (Zhang 2007a), argues that the causal disconnection mechanism at turnaround does not work precisely because the disconnected patches do come back into causal contact. Frampton has pointed out a possible error in Zhang's critique (Frampton 2007b). This appears, however, to have been rectified in a new communication (Zhang 2007b). Zhang's (new) critique is the following: Frampton uses the following form of the modified Friedmann equation:[54]

$$H^2 = \frac{8\pi G}{3}\rho\left(1 - \frac{\rho}{\rho_c}\right)$$

---

54. Phantom bounce models operate on the assumption that the standard Friedmann equation is no longer valid for universe conditions where the phantom energy density is near a critical value.

Here, "H" is the Hubble parameter, which is defined as the time derivative of the scale factor divided by the scale factor. Recall that the scale factor is the factor by which one multiplies the size of the universe in order to represent expansion or contraction.

Zhang clarifies:

> ... ρ_c is the critical energy density set by quantum gravity, which is the maximal density of the universe. Such a modified Friedmann equation with a phantom energy component leads to a cyclic universe scenario in which the universe oscillates through a series of expansions and contractions. In the usual universe [that is one governed by the ordinary Friedmann equation], the phantom dark energy leads to a "big rip" singularity; however, in this peculiar cyclic universe, the big-rip singularity can be avoided because when ρ reaches ρ_c the universe will turn around due to [the modified Friedmann equation]. (Zhang 2007b)

So the rate of change of the size of the universe is governed by the density of this special type of "phantom" energy. Zhang continues:

> When the universe approaches the turnaround point ($\rho \to \rho_c$), we have $H \to 0$. Therefore, obviously, at the turnaround, we have $H^{-1} \to \infty$. This implies that the Hubble radius becomes infinity at the turnaround point, because at that time the universe becomes static instantaneously (that is, it ceases to expand at the turnaround). Obviously, at the turnaround, the universe would not be fragmented into many disconnected causal patches. (Zhang 2007b)

The inverse of the Hubble parameter (H^{-1}, called the Hubble radius) governs the scale at which microphysics can act, that is, the scale of causal connection. While this is near zero as one nears a "Big Rip" event, it seems clear that as one approaches Baum and Frampton's turnaround, the Hubble radius grows again to an infinite value. This means that all the separate patches of the universe are not disconnected (i.e. light signals can now propagate among them and allow them to interact). Thus, a subsequent collapse phase should include all of the matter and radiation then present, which essentially prevents a working cyclic scenario (since all the ordinary matter and radiation from the previous expansion would now be included). Frampton offers the following comment with respect to Zhang's criticism: "deflation must occur at a time before turnaround when the Hubble radius is small, before it reaches its minimum value ($x = 1/2$). Deflation remains a plausible conjecture which still requires further technical calculation to confirm" (pers. comm., Feb 7, 2008).

This seems difficult to square, as it would seem deflation = contraction, and turnaround is the time at which expansion ends and contraction begins. Baum and Frampton, in fact, issued a preprint in 2006 entitled "Deflation at Turnaround for Oscillatory Cosmology," in which they state:

> A key ingredient in our cyclic model is that at turnaround $t = t_T \pmod{\tau}$ our universe deflates dramatically with scale factor $a(t_T)$ shrinking to $\hat{a}(t_T) = f a(t_T)$ where $f < 10^{-28}$. This jettisoning of almost all, a fraction $(1-f)$, of the accumulated entropy is permitted by the exceptional causal structure of the universe. (Baum & Frampton 2006, p. 4)[55]

Frampton clarifies:

> The beginning of contraction is the turnaround. Deflation is where the causal patches separate and our entropy drops to zero.

---

55. Here τ indicates periodicy; it indicates which cycle the universe is presently in.

By the way the time difference between deflation and later turnaround is a trillion trillionth of a second or less!!!

It [Hubble radius divergence at turnaround] does have the significance that each spawned universe is separately one causal patch at turnaround. (pers. comm., February 7, 2008)

So deflation is not contraction. Instead it refers to causal disconnection. The Hubble radius *does* diverge at turnaround. But for some reason the causal horizons frozen in at deflation remain intact. This seems problematic. After all, causal horizons are not *real* physical barriers. They are observer dependent. For example, we on Earth have a causal horizon that stretches out some 46 billion light years. So does a space traveler in orbit around Alpha Centauri. But the space traveler sees a different portion of the universe than we do here on Earth. There is not actually a physical barrier 46 billion light years away from each of us. This is distinct from the event horizon of a black hole, which *is* an objective physical barrier. How exactly do Baum and Frampton understand this causal disconnection? A study of Frampton's early work could perhaps clarify the situation:

... the time when a system becomes gravitationally unbound corresponds approximately to the time when the growing dark energy density matches the mean density of the bound system. For a "typical" object like the Earth (or a hydrogen atom where the mean density happens to be about the density of water $\rho_{H2O} = 1$ g/cm^3 since 10^{-24} g/$(10^{-8}$ cm$)^3 = 1$ g/cm^3) water's density ρ_{H2O} is an unlikely but practical unit for cosmic density in the oscillatory universe.

... the unimaginable dark energy density at turnaround of $\rho_\Lambda(tT) > 10^{27}\rho_{H2O}$. By the time the dark energy density reaches such a value, according to the Big Rip analysis,[56] the smallest known bound systems of particles have become unbound. Additionally the constituents will be causally disconnected, meaning that if *the expansion had, instead, continued to the Big Rip* the particles could no longer causally communicate. (Baum & Frampton 2006, pp. 3–4; emphasis added)

This is the key. If the density of the phantom energy is $\rho_\Lambda(tT) > 10^{27}\rho_{H2O}$, then *in a Big Rip scenario*,[57] the universe would be causally unbound. But we are not in a Big Rip scenario. Instead, according to Baum and Frampton, the laws of physics have changed (we now have a *modified* Friedmann equation) where *something* (perhaps extradimensional brane dynamics) acts to stop the expansion and leads to a contraction. In this case, it is hard to see why Frampton and Takahashi's analysis of causally unbound systems still applies. It is the runaway expansion in the Big Rip scenario that leads to and *maintains* shrinking causal horizons. If that stops, and even reverses, then it would appear reasonable to assume that the causal horizon grows along with it.

Frampton and Takahashi's explanation seems akin to a personal causal horizon as opposed to some physical barrier that results in permanent causal disconnection. What is lacking is a discussion of what causes "turnaround" and maintains causal disconnection. Without those details, it seems reasonable to entertain Zhang's misgiving concerning the viability of the universe-fractionating mechanism.

We should note Frampton's emphasis on the limited time between deflation, turnaround, and contraction. That would make the relevant issue the behavior of phantom

---

56. Frampton and Takahashi (2003, 2004).
57. In a "Big Rip," the expansion rate of the universe becomes infinite and leads to a future singularity.

energy right at turnaround (given that there is no time for ordinary matter and radiation to reestablish contact, given the amount of contraction that occurs in the first fraction of a second after turnaround). The question seems to be: given the *homogeneity* of the phantom energy at turnaround, and its ability to interact with its surroundings (given the unbounded Hubble horizon right at turnaround), why would the universe split into separate domains rather than precipitate a single, global contraction?

Third, the presence of *any* matter or radiation (during contraction) will prevent cycling. This could be a problem, given that spontaneous structure can form as thermal fluctuations (even if the contraction stage begins without any matter or radiation). Bousso and Freivogel explain:

> In a long-lived vacuum with positive cosmological constant, structure can form in two ways. Structure can form in the conventional way (through a period of inflation followed by reheating), or it can form spontaneously as a rare thermal fluctuation. Because deSitter space is thermal, if the vacuum is sufficiently long-lived spontaneous structure formation will occur. (Bousso & Freivogel 2007, p. 4)

The Baum–Frampton space is not a de Sitter space, but it is also thermal. Hence, one would expect that matter would still fluctuate into existence spontaneously. If so, then (at a reasonable probability) the Baum–Frampton cyclicity would not work.

Cosmologist Thomas Banks contends that a contracting space filled with quantum fields will have an "ergodic" property as the space shrinks. Its fields become highly excited as one approaches the end of contraction and these fields will produce chaotic fluctuations. Spontaneously created matter with a different equation of state will dominate the energy density. That, and the inhomogeneity of the fluctuations, will prevent cycling. Banks and Fischler even suggest that the fields will spontaneously produce a dense "fluid" of black holes leading to a condition they call a "Black Crunch" (Banks & Fischler 2002) for arbitrary states approaching full contraction.[58] Hence, it appears that the Baum–Frampton cyclicity will not work.[59]

58. Banks complains:

> I have a problem with ALL cyclic cosmologies. . . . The collapsing phase of these models always have a time dependent Hamiltonian for the quantum field fluctuations around the classical background. Furthermore the classical backgrounds are becoming singular. This means that the field theories will be excited to higher and higher energy states (define energy in some adiabatic fashion during the era when the cosmology is still fairly slowly varying, and use this to classify the states, even though it is not conserved). High energy states in field theory have the ergodic property–they thermalize rapidly, in the sense that the system explores all of its states. Willy Fischler and I proposed that in this situation you would again tend to maximize the entropy. We called this a Black Crunch and suggested the equation of state of matter would again tend toward p = ρ. It seems silly to imagine that, even if this is followed by a re-expansion, that one would start that expansion with a low entropy initial state, or that one had any control over the initial state at all. (pers. comm., October 12, 2007)

59. We note that Xin Zhang has his own competing cyclic model, in which he admits that thermal fluctuations pose a serious problem for phantom bounce cosmologies:

> It is noteworthy that the cyclic universe discussed in this paper is an ideal case, and there are still several severe obstacles existing in the cyclic cosmology, *such as the density fluctuation growth in the contraction phase*, black hole formation, and entropy increase, which can obstruct the realization of a truly cyclic cosmology. (Zhang, Zhang, & Liu 2007; emphasis added)

While phantom bounce cosmologies (such as Baum–Frampton and Xin Zhang's own model) do represent a frontier worth exploring, there seem to be unanswered questions as to the viability of such an approach. The field is too young to pass full judgment. But some questions that *can* be answered (such as the ergodic/chaotic approach to a singular bounce) seem to indicate that problems native to cyclic cosmologies remain.

IIId. A fourth alternative?: time deconstruction

As Borde et al. point out in their seminal paper, one of their primary assumptions was the following:

> The intuitive reason why de Sitter inflation cannot be past-eternal is that, in the full de Sitter space, exponential expansion is preceded by exponential contraction. Such a contracting phase is not part of standard inflationary models, and does not appear to be consistent with the physics of inflation. If thermalized regions were able to form all the way to past infinity in the contracting spacetime, the whole universe would have been thermalized before inflationary expansion could begin. In our analysis we will exclude the possibility of such a contracting phase by considering spacetimes for which the past region obeys an averaged expansion condition, by which we mean that the average expansion rate in the past is greater than zero: $H_{av} > 0$. (Borde, Guth, & Vilenkin 2003, p. 1)

In his 2003 lecture at the Kavli Institute at UCSB, Guth acknowledges, "[Anthony] Aguirre and [Steve] Gratton have proposed a model that evades our theorem, in which the arrow of time reverses at the $t = -$infinity hypersurface, so the universe 'expands' in both halves of the full de Sitter space."[60] It is possible, then, to evade the BVG Theorem through a gross deconstruction of the notion of time. Suppose one asserts that in the past contracting phase the direction of time is reversed. Time then flows in both directions *away* from the singularity. Is this reasonable? We suggest *not*, for the Aguirre–Gratton scenario (Aguirre & Gratton 2002) denies the evolutionary continuity of the universe which is topologically prior to t and our universe. *The other side of the de Sitter space is not our past.* For the moments of that time are not earlier than t or any of the moments later than t in our universe. There is no connection or temporal relation whatsoever of our universe to that other reality. Efforts to deconstruct time thus fundamentally reject the evolutionary paradigm.

Section III summary

Primarily, attempts to overcome the new singularity theorem of Borde, Vilenkin, and Guth center on generating universe models that do not feature average positive expansion in their past. This can be done by having average negative expansion (i.e. contraction) or by having zero average expansion (an asymptotically static model). Both attempts seem to encounter insurmountable difficulties. The contraction model features acausal fine-tuning to its asymptotic past and BKL chaos as the contraction nears a singularity in its pre–Big

---

60. Alan Guth, speech to the Kavli Institute for Theoretical Physics, October 2003. Available at: http://online.kitp.ucsb.edu/online/strings_c03/guth/.

Bang "bounce" into our present expanding reality. BKL chaos may, in fact, prove that it is impossible for a universe to pass through a singularity.

Zero average expansion models are usually constructed in two different ways. Either the expansion asymptotically approaches zero as time (looking backward) approaches negative infinity. One can also consider an infinite number of cycles where expansion and contraction exactly cancel for each cycle. The first case has the dilemma that it must begin static and then transition to an expansion. Hence, the static phase is metastable, which implies that it is finite in lifetime. The universe begins to exist.

Cyclic models usually fail due to the necessary buildup of entropy from cycle to cycle. If there were an infinite number of cycles, why is the universe not in a state of "heat death"? The entropy would also have the effect of making the amplitude of the cycles (the maximum size of the universe during a cycle) grow over time. Looking backward in time, then, this implies a first cycle to the finite past. One can attempt to overcome these problems, as Baum and Frampton do, by claiming that a single universe fractionates into a multiverse of contractions. Most of the contracting "children" from the parent universe will have shed the entropy developed from the preceding phase and hence permit cycling.

But as we have seen, their mechanism appears to fail to fractionate. Even if it did fractionate into separate entropy-free domains, even an initially empty daughter universe would develop BKL chaos when approaching a contraction and disrupt the scenario!

The last gambit, that of claiming that time reverses its arrow prior to the Big Bang, fails because the other side of the Big Bang is *not* the past of our universe.

Hence, these models either have a beginning or are not viable.

IV. Quantum gravity

A final, expected exception to the Hawking–Penrose theorems is a formulation known as "quantum gravity." The two great pillars of twentieth-century physics, Einstein's GR (the science of the very large) and QM (the science of the very small), both enjoy overwhelming observational support. However, if the standard Big Bang theory were correct in its prediction that the universe must approach a singularity in its distant past, then QM must eventually govern it. But GR is a classical theory, not a quantum field theory. For an extremely high-density early universe, where gravity acted both as the dominant force and as a quantum force, we must have a new theory – quantum gravity – to describe it. Further, in 2002,[61] the first observational evidence that gravity is indeed a quantum force was reported. One of the Hawking–Penrose assumptions for their singularity theorems, however, was that GR is a correct description of the universe. Since this is not true at the scale of singularities, perhaps singularities did not exist after all. Perhaps, extrapolating backward, the universe evolves smoothly *through* the Big Bang to an unknown past.

Here are three prominent candidates for a theory of quantum gravity (Figure 3.12). The main job of some quantum gravity models is to get one through the singularity to an (it is hoped) eternal past. Others will accept a "beginning" to the universe but will deconstruct the notions of time, nothingness, or causation.

---

61. Nesvizhevsky et al. (2001), see http://www.newscientist.com/article.ns?id = dn1801, or http://physicsworld.com/cws/article/news/3525. The experiment was done by bouncing supercold neutrons and noticing that the height of the bounce was quantized.

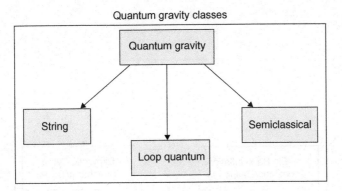

Figure 3.12 Families of quantum gravity cosmologies.

IVa. String models

String theory is by far the most popular method proposed so far to unify quantum theory with GR. Essentially, string theory proposes that the elementary entities of nature are not point particles (zero-dimensional objects) but are strings (one-dimensional objects). String theory eliminates many of the problems that occur in particle theories. Particle interactions can occur down to literally zero distance; where force laws blow up (recall, for example, that gravity's dependence on distance is $1/r^2$; that is, the force becomes infinite as range goes to zero) and predict infinite (i.e. nonsensical) answers. String theory calms this behavior by introducing a minimum distance (the "Planck" distance) to interactions. By "spreading out" string interactions, infinities are avoided.

Another advantage of string theory is that it can explain in a non–*ad hoc* manner the existence of different types of elementary "particles." Differing "particle" properties could be merely different types of vibrations that occur on a string (similar to musical notes). It was hoped (and still is by some) that the theory would naturally predict the characteristics of the elementary particles that are otherwise free parameters in the earlier theory (which is called the "Standard model").

The "minimum distance" feature of string theory is thought to be a desirable feature for cosmological models because, analogously to the case of particle interactions, the standard Big Bang model predicts that the scale factor of the universe shrinks to literally zero size. String theory could "calm" this feature of the model by suggesting a minimum size. This could even overcome the Hawking–Penrose theorems and suggest that there was a "before" to the singular condition. Perhaps the Big Bang was not an ultramundane event at which time itself came into being. If it was not, the door is open to a past eternal universe.

String theory has also given birth to "brane" cosmology, where the emphasis is on the background within which strings propagate rather than the strings themselves (Figure 3.13). These backgrounds, called *n*-branes, can be variable in the number of their dimensions. For example, it is normally proposed that our three-dimensional space is one of these "three-branes" which may or may not be floating around in a higher-dimensional space (usually called "the bulk").

Some string cosmologies

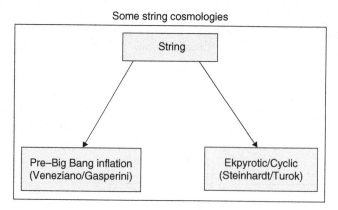

Figure 3.13 String cosmology models and proponents.

IVa(i). Pre–Big Bang inflation (PBBI)
There are two string models that can aspire to describe adequately a past infinite pre–Big Bang environment. These are the PBBI scenario of Gabriele Veneziano and Maurizio Gasperini and the Ekpyrotic/cyclic model of Paul Steinhardt and Neil Turok. The PBBI scenario is a classic version of an asymptotically static model. Here is how one of its authors describes it:

> According to the scenario, the pre-bang universe was almost a perfect mirror image of the post-bang one. If the universe is eternal into the future, its contents thinning to a meager gruel, it is also eternal into the past. Infinitely long ago it was nearly empty, filled only with a tenuous, widely dispersed, chaotic gas of radiation and matter. The forces of nature, controlled by the dilaton field, were so feeble that particles in this gas barely interacted. As time went on, the forces gained in strength and pulled matter together. (Veneziano 2004, p. 63)

Through gravitational contraction, regions of the pre–Big Bang universe turned into black holes. Due to quantum effects, once the density of a black hole reached a critical value, it underwent a "bounce" into a Big Bang. Our universe then persists within this otherwise closed surface (with respect to the 'outer' background space where everything began).

In his popularization in *Scientific American*, Veneziano seems to suggest that his beginning is an infinitely distant but never reachable (i.e. ideal) point. The article implies that the model is to be interpreted realistically.[62] But one must be wary in interpreting the infinity of the past for this model, as it is easy to misuse the concept of an infinite limit, as well to ignore the distinction between a realist and an instrumentalist interpretation of the model. The problems in interpreting this model are similar to those encountered when assessing the Emergent model class. It is worth noting that the coauthor of the PBBI model, Maurizio Gasperini, indicates that the entire asymptotic past (or future) should not be taken as real:

---

62. Or is it *Scientific American* that has inserted the realist interpretation?

... I find it misleading to talk of a 'future of the PBB scenario,' because the PBB scenario only (possibly) applies to describe some (more or less extended) portion of the past history of our cosmos, and is expected to smoothly join the standard cosmological scenario at an early enough epoch, so as to reproduce standard results on nucleosynthesis, baryogenesis, structure formation, and so on. In other words, the PBB scenario can be regarded as a model for explaining the initial conditions of our standard cosmological configuration, in a way which is string-theory consistent, but it cannot be extrapolated towards the future without further assumptions, which at present have not been fully worked out (with the exception of the dilaton model of dark energy proposed by Piazza, Veneziano and myself on PRD 65, 023508 (2002)). (pers. comm., January 10, 2006)

Can one build a realist interpretation of this model? It is interesting to contrast the depiction of PBBI as proving "the myth of the beginning of time" in a setting where sensational conclusions are encouraged (*Scientific American*) with the characterization of PBBI as a "toy model" in a setting where scientists are naturally conservative (peer-reviewed academic journals).[63]

As described in the academic literature, the model appears to have an initial phase. The relevant phases are:

(1)   A static (Milne) universe, or string perturbative vacuum (SPV) phase. This means that the universe is empty (energy and energy density is zero) and is static, that is, neither expanding nor contracting globally or locally.

(2)   A quasi-Milne phase, which constitutes a "perturbed" SPV. Here "H is (small and) positive in the String frame, (small in modulus and) negative in the Einstein frame, and tends to zero as t goes to minus infinity, and the Universe approaches the SPV configuration (where H is identically zero, since the spacetime is flat)" (M. Gasperini, pers. comm., January 16, 2007).

(3)   An "inflationary" phase. In one set of coordinates (the Einstein frame), matter collapses into trapped surfaces, or black holes. In another set of coordinates (the string frame), this can be viewed as a spatial expansion. This happens regionally rather than globally.

(4)   A post–Big Bang FRW phase that is typical of the standard Hot Big Bang model.

The authors begin building the model at a finite time in the past where a condition called "asymptotic past triviality" (APT) obtains (Veneziano & Gasperini 2002, p. 54). APT represents the boundary between phase (2) and phase (3). The period of contraction (inflation in the string frame) is itself finite.

The authors then project this state into the future, and asymptotically evolve it into the past. Similar to the Maartens version of the Emergent model, one takes the APT past-directed duration of phase (2) to be infinite (Figure 3.14).

Unlike the Emergent model, perturbed SPV lasts for a while and then individual patches that meet the Hawking–Penrose condition for a closed trapped surface begin *regional*

---

63. "The so-called 'pre-big bang' scenario described in this report has to be seen in the above perspective as a possible example, even just as a toy model of what cosmology can look like if we assume that the sought for standard model of gravity and cosmology is based on (some particular version of) superstring theory" (Veneziano & Gasperini 2002, p. 4).

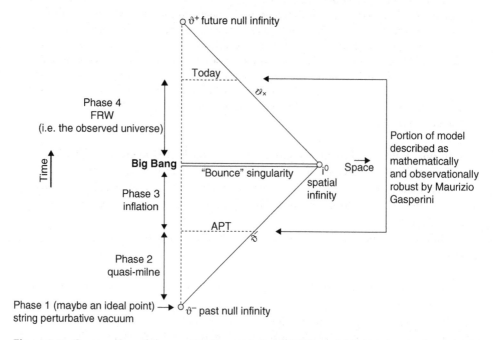

Figure 3.14 Construction of the pre–Big Bang inflation (PBBI) model is given at the "asymptotic past triviality" or APT point. From here, the model is projected forward in time to give the Big Bang universe. It is also projected backwards to past infinity. Note that the APT data is given at a finite time in the past in the diagram. The proposed string perturbative vacuum era would be at "past null infinity" or the lower point marked "ϑ^-." The past infinite is "null" rather than "timelike" because the gravidilaton waves that embed it are massless. FRW = Friedmann–Robertson–Walker.

contraction (inflation in string coordinates) (Figure 3.15). Should we treat SPV like ESS? Gasperini observes that a significant feature of SPV is that it is unstable:

> ... the SPV is unstable already at the classical level ... it [decay of the SPV] can be described as a quantum transition, but it is a process which is also classically allowed. (pers. comm., January 4, 2007)

> ... the instability of the SPV is similar to the instability of a classical ball placed exactly at the top of a perfectly symmetric hill. In principle, if the system starts initially in the unique equilibrium configuration, and there are no external perturbations, the system might remain static forever. In practice, however, there are physical perturbations removing the system from equilibrium, sooner or later, with a probability which is chaotically (or randomly) distributed. In the case of the SPV the perturbations removing it from equilibrium are the quantum fluctuations of the background fields (in particular of the dilaton). In addition, the exact equilibrium configuration can only be achieved as an asymptotic extrapolation, in the limit in which the cosmic time goes to minus infinity: in practice, at any given finite physical time, the system is always displaced a bit from equilibrium. (pers. comm., January 9, 2007)

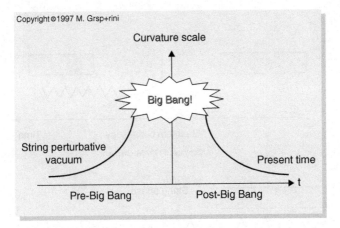

Figure 3.15 Rate of universe expansion versus time in the pre–Big Bang inflation model. (source: Maurizio Gasperini, available at: http://www.ba.infn.it/~gasperin/)

I would say that the SPV is not a phase extended in time, it is only an asymptotic initial state which is approached, however, in an infinite time. In practice, the physical description never starts "exactly" from that state, but from a state which represents an arbitrarily small perturbation of the SPV. (pers. comm., February 27, 2007)

... if I live in the initially collapsing portion of spacetime, then I have a chance to go through the bounce, at some epoch in the future. But this does not concern the entire spacetime. There are spacetime regions which are collapsing and eventually bouncing into a FRW like Universe, and others which do not. It is possible, in principle, to live in regions of spacetime never experiencing the bouncing nor the collapse, and staying for ever in a configuration well described by the string perturbative vacuum (or by a quantum perturbation of it). (pers. comm., January 9, 2006)

So if the SPV were real, it would be a state with a finite lifetime. Some time after decay, random portions will be sufficiently dense to form closed trapped surfaces and begin gravitational contraction. Other regions could remain indefinitely in the post-SPV state (i.e. already perturbed from an equilibrium condition).

Veneziano and Gasperini's language at times suggests treating SPV as an ultimately unrealized extrapolation similar to what is described in the *Scientific American* article. But here and elsewhere, they seem to suggest that the SPV is quite real (if the asymptotic past of the model were taken seriously):

The whole process may be seen as the slow, but eventually explosive, decay of the string perturbative vacuum (the flat and interaction-free asymptotic initial state of the pre-big bang scenario), into a final, radiation-dominated state typical of standard cosmology. (Veneziano & Gasperini 2002, p. 21)

The PBBI model is described as a "decay" or a quantum "tunneling" event similar to the semiclassical models of Hawking–Hartle and Vilenkin (see section IVc) (Figure 3.16). But:

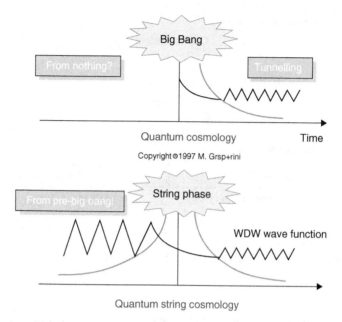

Figure 3.16 Pre–Big Bang inflation as a string quantum transition. The figure contrasts "creation from nothing" models such as the Hawking–Hartle no-boundary approach or the Vilenkin "tunneling from nothing" (see section IVc) with a string approach. Here, a prior state quantum tunnels into our current Friedmann–Robertson–Walker universe. WDW = Wheeler–DeWitt equation, which is the basis for the semiclassical cosmologies to be discussed in section IVc (source: Maurizio Gasperini, available at: http://www.ba.infn.it/~gasperin/)

> [PBBI] can also be interpreted as a tunneling process, not "from nothing", however [which is how the Hawking–Hartle and Vilenkin models are interpreted; see section IVc], but "from the string perturbative vacuum." (Veneziano & Gasperini 2002, p. 208)

It is reasonable to presume that if there is a physical transition from state "A" to state "B," and state "B" is ontologically real, then state "A" must be taken to be ontologically real.[64] Significant as well is that the state right after SPV decay (if SPV were a realized physical state) would obtain only a finite time ago to the past, given that Gasperini's description of the decay product is identical to the following:

> The generic regular solution thus approaches Milne as t [approaches negative infinity] but, *at any finite large* [negative time], *also contains small dilatonic (and gravitational-wave) perturbations* giving $0 < \Omega \ll 1$. As t→ −∞, $\Omega \to 0$. As time goes forward, instead, Ω tends to grow until, at some critical time $-T_0$, Ω becomes $O(1)$, in some region of space. From that moment on, in that "lucky" patch, the metric starts to deviate from Milne and dilaton-driven inflation

---

64. If state "A" is unreal, then no transition at all takes place but rather an absolute "coming into being" of state "B." On this interpretation, the universe began to exist.

sets in, pushing Ω extremely close to 1 in that patch. (Veneziano 1998, p. 10; emphasis added)[65]

So if the SPV state were real, there could only be a finite timeline from it to the present. Only if the perturbation itself were unreal would the past eternal nature of the model survive. Is this realistic? As we look backward from the APT point, what would the significance be of a real quantum perturbation to a state which was arbitrarily close to SPV? Would not one have a situation that was virtually identical to simply starting with "real" SPV? This is essentially a "pseudobeginning" scenario.

Vaas classifies this cosmology as "soft bang/pseudobeginning" just as he does the Emergent models.[66] Although the behavior of perturbed SPV is ultimately different from ESS (or perturbed ESS), the similarity with respect to classical (and quantum) instability should be the controlling one. The two models are mathematically similar with respect to the asymptotic approach to an infinitely distant unstable state. Vaas argues that there is no obvious arrow of time and hence the asymptotic past is likely a mathematical artifact.

Perhaps the past infinite timeline is only *technical* in nature: the duration from the APT point extrapolated *backward* is infinite, but that is to be understood *instrumentally*. In response to the question, "if the SPV is unstable, and within a finite time quantum fluctuations of the dilaton will disturb its equilibrium, does that not imply that the past must be finite?" Gasperini answers:

> From a physical point of view, a spacetime manifold has an infinite (past) extension if its timelike or null geodesics can be (past) extended for infinite values of their affine parameter, without ending into a singularity. This property is satisfied by the past extension of the pre-big bang solutions, so, in this sense, they are past eternal. (pers. comm., January 17, 2007)

As Gasperini indicates, it is true that, *in a sense*, the solutions are past eternal. In pure GR, it is true that backward-directed geodesics will trace all the way to past infinity. In fact, in pure GR, even if one assumed a *real* SPV state, it would still be the case that, technically speaking, backward-directed geodesics are past eternal for the same reason that a real ESS is technically past eternal.

But the relevant question seems to be this: do all past-directed geodesics from a quasi-Milne state (or a quasi-ESS) intersect with a significant system perturbation, or would

---

65. For clarification, a Milne universe is a special state where the critical density parameter Ω is exactly equal to zero; the universe is empty. Recall that the critical density parameter Ω determines if an FRW cosmology will have a closed, flat, or open geometry. It is closed if $\Omega < 1$, flat if $\Omega = 1$, and open if $\Omega > 1$. If the cosmological constant is zero, then a closed universe will recollapse, and a flat or open universe will be ever-expanding.

66. Vaas elaborates:

> A related problem refers to the pre-big bang model (Veneziano & Gasperini 2003). Here the string vacuum – where a local collapse in the Einstein frame (which corresponds to a dilaton-driven inflation in the string frame) before the big bang occurs – is quite simple, homogeneous, almost empty and does not have an overall arrow of time. But, mathematically, the origin of the pre-big bang – or, to be more precise, any pre-big bang, for the model does also imply a multiverse scenario – traces back to a maximally simple, static condition only in the infinite past (principle of asymptotic past triviality). But this can also be interpreted just as a local predecessor of a big bang and not a feature characterizing the infinite string vacuum as a whole. (Vaas 2004, pp. 18–9)

at least one geodesic trace, undisturbed, to past infinity? Consider the following comparison:

A.   Suppose that the SPV (or ESS) were viewed as ontologically real rather than just ideal-ized points at past infinity. Within a finite time, a quantum perturbation would disturb the state and the resultant timeline to the present would also be finite. The model would not be past infinite.

B.   Suppose, instead, that ESS or SPV are taken to be asymptotic ideal points. For analysis' sake, start at the present and look backward. Within a finite time, one is arbitrarily close to the ideal condition. Now consider any (new) quantum fluctuation that occurs to the quasi-SPV (or quasi-ESS) state while one is tracing the backward timeline. The probability of this is essentially 1.

What meaningful difference is there between the universe in case A and case B (at the "new" fluctuation point)? Looking backward, there will be an unbounded number of all types of fluctuations of all sizes, any one of which will arrest the supposed asymptotic development of the SPV (or ESS). The proposed past infinite extrapolation seems to be a mathematical artifact (or at least explanatorily vacuous). Even taken seriously (i.e. not as a "toy" model), the model does not predict that the past is infinite.

IVa(ii). Ekpyrotic/cyclic

The Ekpyrotic model is a cyclic model, but not in the old sense of a universe that undergoes an eternal periodic sequence of expansion and collapse. The Ekpyrotic model makes use of the extradimensional nature of string theory to propose that cycling occurs, but in a higher dimension. Authors Paul Steinhardt and Neil Turok view the new model as prefer-able to the post–Big Bang inflationary model because it has fewer *ad hoc* features. For example, (present-day) dark energy is an add-on to the earlier model but is a natural and necessary feature of their new cycling model. String theory allows entities called "branes" that could be representative of what we would otherwise call our three (spatial)-dimensional universe. String theory demands six extra dimensions of space in order to be self-consistent. It is thought that these extra dimensions are (usually) tightly curled up around the three macroscopic dimensions and hence usually unobservable. (Think of a soda straw versus a one-dimensional line. The circle formed by looking at the straw edge-on could be thought of as a second dimension curled around the first.)

The Ekpyrotic model proposes that one of these extra dimensions (the "bulk" dimen-sion) is of macroscopic size. Within this extra dimension lie two three-branes, either of which could represent our universe. These three-branes periodically collide, just as if they were connected by a spring. When they do so, the energy of the collision is transferred to the branes (Figure 3.17).

This energy is converted into the matter (and radiation) that ultimately gravitates into galaxies. The rest of the normal Big Bang sequence follows (stars, planets, and so on). As the branes separate from each other, the branes themselves are always expanding. (There are versions of the model where the branes undergo limited contraction, but always expand, on net, with each cycle.) Eventually, stars burn out, the galaxies recede beyond each galaxy's visual horizon, and the universe enters a period of cold, burned-out cinders. Meanwhile, the branes cycle toward another collision.

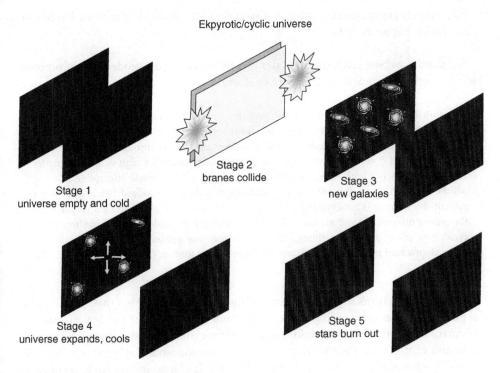

Figure 3.17 Pictorial description of the Ekpyrotic cycle.

The universe is then renewed with a new cycle. The energy that is released into the branes during each collision is replenished by an inexhaustible supply – gravitational potential energy. In this way, Ekpyrosis is an "open" system. There is always a limitless supply of free energy. This feature of cosmology as an open system (as opposed to the old "heat death" scenario) is new but widespread in contemporary cosmology.

Despite avoiding the "heat death" scenario, however, there is now a new problem to solve. If new energy is dumped onto the brane for infinite time, then either the entropy density or the energy density at each point must be infinite. This would obviously be contrary to observation. The continual expansion of the infinite-sized branes, however, keeps the entropy density constant. So (net) expansion is a critical model feature.

Steinhardt recognizes that his model of the universe is not truly beginningless. Here are the relevant comments from his Web site:

- Has the cyclic model been cycling forever?
- In principle, it is possible that the universe has undergone a semi-infinite number of cycles in its past during which the volume increases from cycle to cycle. Even though this would take an infinite time according to ordinary clocks, this cannot be the full story. This cycling regime would not cover all space-time. Something must have preceded the cycles.
- A similar issue arises in inflationary cosmology. In both cases, this is an open question. The issue is referred to as the problem of geodesic incompleteness referring to the fact

that a purely expanding phase does not span the entire space-time and one has to consider what happened before.[67]

Steinhardt's website FAQ page indicates that the model is past geodesically incomplete. Here the authors comment in their published work:

> The most likely story is that cycling was preceded by some singular beginning. Consider a universe that settles into cycling beginning from some flat slice in the distant past many bounces ago. Any particles produced before cycling must travel through an exponentially large number of bounces, each of which is a caustic surface with a high density of matter and radiation at rest with respect to the flat spatial slices. Any particle attempting this trip will be scattered or annihilated and its information will be thermalized before reaching a present-day observer. Consequently, the observer is effectively insulated from what preceded the cycling phase, and there are no measurements that can be made to determine how many cycles have taken place. Even though the space is formally geodesically incomplete, it is as if, for all practical purposes, the universe has been cycling forever. (Steinhardt & Turok 2005, p. 5)

Steinhardt and Turok suggest the universe began in a singularity but that "for all practical purposes" it has been cycling forever. This claim is based on the fact that virtually no information as to the initial conditions of the universe could have survived to the present. Steinhardt explains that photons carrying this information would be "semi-infinitely redshifted" (pers. comm., January 27 and 30, 2004). There is a "semi-infinite" number of cycles between that boundary and the present. How are we to understand this? The description of the model as "de Sitter like" and the associated "semi-infinite" past timeline is nearly the same situation seen earlier with the discussion of the Misner "Mixmaster" universe (section IIIa). The key difference between Mixmaster and the Ekpyrotic model is that Mixmaster is intrinsically chaotic at its singularities (so not necessarily a good physical model of our universe), while the Ekpyrotic model avoids BKL chaos by having a positive equation of state (which is a unique feature of this cosmology) (pers. comm., January 17, 2006).[68]

Within the Ekpyrotic model an observer would see an infinite number of bounces with roughly a trillion years per bounce. So on ordinary clocks, past time is infinite (pers. comm., January 27 and 30, 2004). Yet there is clearly a past boundary (an infinitely distant beginning point?) preceding this behavior. One should note that the reason this model has a beginning is precisely because it falls under the previously mentioned BVG Theorem. Borde et al. explicitly apply their theorem to the Ekpyrotic model of Steinhardt and Turok (Borde, Guth, & Vilenkin 2003).

That implies, among other things, that the "past boundary" must be reached in a finite amount of time. So Steinhardt seems to be mistaken in his prediction of a semi-infinite number of cycles, unlike the Emergent and PBBI models, which evade the BVG Theorem (in proper time; i.e. if "an ordinary clock" is the most appropriate measure of physical time).

---

67. Cosmologist Paul Steinhardt's internet site; FAQ section for the Ekpyrotic model http://web.archive.org/web/20041231000425/http://wwwphy.princeton.edu/~steinh/cyclicFAQS/index.html#eternal
68. Recall that the equation of state is negative (for a cosmological constant pressure = minus density) for a typical inflationary model. For Ekpyrosis, the collision singularity occurs in the "bulk" dimension between the two branes; not within the brane that we ourselves would live on.

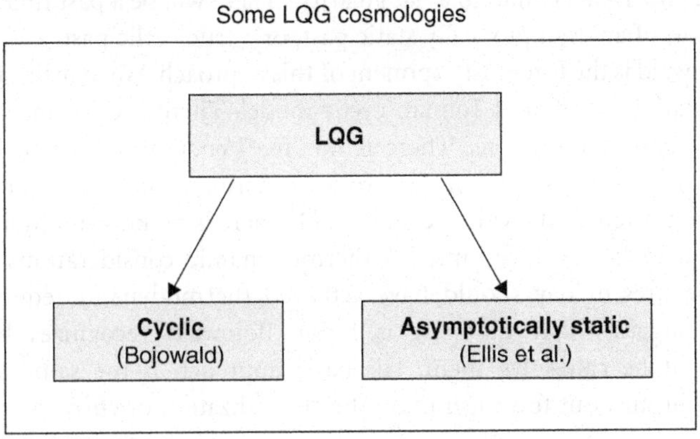

Figure 3.18 Candidate loop quantum gravity (LQG) cosmologies.

Steinhardt indicated to us that measuring the distance between the present and the beginning is ambiguous. What is not ambiguous, however, is that there is a boundary. And are the infinite cycles a necessary feature of the theory? In personal communication, he recognized that the theory does not require an infinite number of cycles.

Steinhardt, similar to Maurizio Gasperini, suggested to us a pragmatic view of his model. The model's description of the approach to the past boundary (and the boundary) is not (yet) rigorous. The boundary referenced by the BVG Theorem could be the mark of something fundamental, such as a singularity, or instead be the marker for a transition to different physics. If one asserts that the boundary merely marks the transition to different physics, then the issue as to the age of the precycling configuration asserts itself. Significantly, Steinhardt argues the cyclic solution is a dynamic attractor (this *is* rigorous) (pers. comm., January 27 and 30, 2004). What this means is that if one sets up the system with generic initial conditions within the twin-brane configuration, it will automatically, within a finite time, converge to the cyclic solution. Thus, the precycling configuration would have a finite lifetime. Thus, there is still an unexplained origin. So the Ekpyrotic universe (whether the boundary represents a genuine singularity or not) can safely be said to begin to exist.[69]

IVb. Loop Quantum Gravity (LQG)

Another theory of quantum gravity is the loop quantum approach (Figure 3.18). LQG takes the view that space-time itself is quantized; that is to say, space-time is divided into discrete constituent parts. It is a theory that aims to fill in the gap in standard GR by answering the question, what really happens at a singularity?

According to LQG, singularities do not really exist. As in string theory, there is a minimum size to nature that prevents microscopic mathematical infinities. Hence, time and space do

---

69. Rüdiger Vaas has suggested that, while the cycling in the Ekpyrotic model had an origin, the brane components themselves could be past eternal. As we have seen, however, an explanation is necessary as to how they got into their initial noncycling state a finite time to the past. Vaas does not provide one (Vaas 2004, p. 17).

not come to an end as one comes to a "singularity." There will be a past timeline. This leads to the conclusion of an asymptotically static past, or a true cyclic past.

Martin Bojowald is the foremost exponent of this approach. We may think of Bojowald's model as a variation on the old Tolman cyclic model. There is only one universe. There are only three spatial dimensions. There is no "free" energy injected into the situation (such as there is in inflationary or Ekpyrotic scenarios). The Tolman model had two problems which prevented its wide acceptance: (1) there is no known physical mechanism for producing a cyclic "bounce" and (2) thermodynamic considerations show that the universe of the present day should have achieved thermodynamic equilibrium ("heat death"). This suggests that the past is finite. Bojowald recognizes both problems and believes that he can solve them. His basic approach is the same to both issues; the problems will turn out to vanish upon the generalization of current "classical" theory into LQG.

With regard to the first problem, the major difficulty has been resolving a type of chaos predicted to occur near classical singularities[70]. This chaos, named "BKL" after its discoverers (Belinsky, Khalatnikov, and Lifshitz) has been shown to be "calmed" by a loop quantum approach. As of 2007, some loop quantum theorists have been able to show that, for certain idealized models, a transition through a Big Bang condition is feasible (Ashtekar, Pawlowski, & Singh 2006). So, while a generalized proof is still lacking, the project seems promising.

The second condition is more daunting. How can there be truly cyclic behavior (one cycle looks pretty much like the last one, although there is not an event-by-event recurrence) when the second law of thermodynamics predicts that entropy must increase from cycle to cycle? Using a semiclassical approach to calculate entropy, Penrose finds that the end of our current cycle (the "Big Crunch") should differ in entropy from the Big Bang singularity by the stupendous factor of 10^{22} (Penrose 2005, p. 730).[71] Given no energy input from outside (and Bojowald argues that the system is truly closed), how can this outcome be avoided? There seem to be three possibilities:

1. The problem is epistemic only. In a 2004 paper, Bojowald and his colleagues appear to favor this solution:

   While the effective dynamics is consistent with our expectations for both the beginning and the end of the universe, the apparent time reversal asymmetry remains. This is explained by the fact that the situation is, in fact, time asymmetric due to our own position in the universe. We can see only some part of it, not the whole space-time, and in particular we see only a small part of the beginning. With the current understanding, the observable part of our universe can well be part of a classical space-time with a very inhomogeneous initial singularity.

---

70. This is the same type of chaos that Ellis mentioned as an obstacle to infinite contraction models in section IIIa and is related to the problem mentioned by Banks for oscillating models (section IIIb).

71. Penrose considers that there are 10^{80} baryons in the observable universe. He then suggests that the maximum entropy for the universe is equivalent to a black hole with this mass. Should the fate of the universe be to ultimately collapse in a "Big Crunch," this would be the entropy contributed by these 10^{80} baryons. Penrose uses the Hawking–Bekenstein formula for the entropy of a black hole, and in natural units (where constants of nature such as the speed of light are set to unity), finds that this entropy is approximately 10^{123}. The entropy of our universe in the current day is far lower than this by about 22 orders of magnitude.

Since most of the initial singularity is unobservable, however, it is not discussed further. The final singularity, on the other hand, is completely unobservable until it is reached. If we compare only observable properties from within the universe, we simply cannot possibly know enough to tell whether past and future singularities are similar. If we compare the theoretical structure of a space-time from outside, then we conclude that in fact there is no conceptual difference between the beginning and the end of a generic spacetime.

Only if we compare the observable part of the initial singularity with the theoretical expectation for a final singularity does the time asymmetry appear. (Bojowald & Hossain 2004, p. 38)[72]

2. Our current "classical" understanding of entropy is misleading. Bojowald suggested this possibility in personal communication:

The interpretation of entropy is as a measure for the lack of information an outside observer can obtain if he just knows macroscopic parameters such as the total mass or angular momentum.

The situation in non-equilibrium thermodynamics is more complicated, which would be relevant, *e.g.*, for colliding black holes or violent stages of cosmology. For cosmology, it is also not so clear what the total entropy should be associated with mathematically, so a counting is difficult. For black holes, on the other hand, entropy refers to degrees of freedom in the black hole region, which can be identified and counted within the theory.

Black hole entropy then describes the lack of information in classical stages of black holes (how many quantum states there are for given mass and other parameters). This is an absolute lack of knowledge in classical gravity because the black hole region is concealed from outside observers.

With quantum theory, however, black holes evaporate and thus reveal information at later stages (although it is still disputed to what degree this is realized). *The lack of information is then only temporary and apparent because an outside observer is simply not patient enough to wait until he can recover all information. In other words, entropy in this context is observer dependent and not an absolute quantity.* Since it includes only the black hole but not the observer or anything outside, it is also not the entropy relevant for cosmology.

The usual intuitive picture in cosmology is as follows: When there are many black holes, this apparent entropy is very high for outside observers. *But if all degrees of freedom are considered, including those in the black holes which will re-emerge after evaporation, or one waits until after the black holes have evaporated one would obtain a smaller amount. This does not mean that entropy decreases; the accessibility of information by observers just changes.* (pers. comm., February 28, 2006; emphasis added)

3. Cycle by cycle, the entropy state is genuinely reversible. Again, this alternative emerges in personal communication:

Sinclair: 'What it sounds to me you are saying in this last communication is that (with regard to the cyclic model) the same energy is endlessly recycled. This is a closed system, unlike some other cosmological proposals out there. Hence you are talking about a system that is fully reversible. This isn't a case where there are dissipative, irreversible processes that build up over time and produce the "heat death" scenario.'

72. Note that the terms "initial" singularity and "final" singularity refer to the states that begin and end our current cosmological cycle. Bojowald *et al.* are not referring to the beginning and end of time.

Bojowald: 'At least in the cyclic version. If there is no recollapse at large volume, the universe would just have gone through a single bounce and will keep expanding. The end may be such a heat death, but since we don't know the field content of our universe (as evidenced by the dark matter and dark energy puzzles) the far future may be quite different from what it appears to be now'. (pers. comm., February 28, 2006)

It is important to note that Bojowald (and his colleagues) are not committed to a model with a past-infinite number of cycles, as his last response shows. He is open to the possibility of an irreversible rise in entropy as a function of time. So the fact that entropy rises, cycle by cycle, and would trip up a proposed past infinite cyclic model is not, *per se*, a test of the viability of the loop quantum approach as a candidate for quantum gravity. Instead our interest (in this section) is limited to beginningless cyclic models.

Considering the first solution, Bojowald's reply to Penrose would be that there is a large, unobservable part of the initial singularity that is a genuine generic manifold, that is, a state of maximum entropy featuring random inhomogeneity and anisotropy. Hence, the entropy of the initial and final singularities would be similar. An inflation mechanism (of a small patch of this manifold) would then produce the requisite homogeneity and isotropy of the current FRW universe. Penrose, however, had anticipated this objection. Using an anthropic observer selection argument, he argues that the size of the inflationary patch we should expect to see should be much smaller based on thermodynamic criteria (by the factor $10^{(10^{123})}$) (Penrose 2005, p. 763).

Penrose suggests that life might need a universe only 1/10 the size of our current (visible) universe. He obtains the probability of an appropriately sized initial patch of a generic manifold using the Hawking–Bekenstein equation for the entropy of a black hole. The exponent "123" in Penrose's formula is based on the square of the mass within the observable universe. So multiplying the radius of the universe by a tenth would have the following effect: the mass within this smaller sized universe would be reduced by a factor of 10^{-3} (since volume is proportional to r^3), and mass is squared in the entropy formula. Hence, the exponent is reduced by 6; so the overall entropy is reduced from (10^{123}) to (10^{117}). The probability of finding ourselves in either state would be approximately 10 raised to the appropriate power.[73]

How many more inflationary events in a multiverse, then, would produce a life amenable but smaller universe? This is obtained from dividing out the probabilities:

$$E = 10^{-(10^{117})}/10^{-(10^{123})}.$$

Take the logarithm of both sides and simplify:

$$LOG(E) = -10^{117} + 10^{123} = 10^{123}.$$

Here -10^{117} is negligible compared with the larger 10^{123}. Hence, $E = 10^{(10^{123})}$. The reciprocal of this represents the likelihood of finding ourselves *in a big universe* versus a small one.

---

73. The entropy is related to the number of possible configurations of a system of particles. The number of configurations is approximately equal to the exponential of the entropy. Given the size of the numbers involved, there is essentially no difference between e^x and 10^x. So Penrose uses base 10 for convenience.

So it is exceedingly improbable to find ourselves as the product of an inflationary event of a generic manifold, as Bojowald et al. originally proposed. Hence, Penrose argues, the entropy of the initial manifold must be exceedingly low.

Aside from this, the epistemic argument takes no account of entropy generation during the cycle. Over infinite time, this would have to be a factor, although it may be negligible for a single cycle. Eggs break, people get old, stars burn out. This entropy may be negligible compared to black hole formation. But over infinite cycles, it would add up.

The second solution – that the "classical" understanding of entropy is misleading – mitigates the problem of entropy growth but does not resolve it. While entropy as classically calculated may be too high (i.e. Penrose's estimation overestimates entropy due to contextual lack of information), the quantum approach still recognizes entropy (and entropy growth) as a genuine physical quantity. Black holes are still highly entropic. So their formation during a cycle, especially if one lands in a Big Crunch, would still cause a final manifold to have more entropy than an initial manifold. One would still expect that this situation would imply a beginning, since it implies a heat death given infinite cycles. Hence, Bojowald is only being realistic in opting for the third solution, that the cyclic LQG model does, indeed, need to be fully reversible.

But opposing the second law of thermodynamics is a formidable task; one recalls the words of early twentieth-century cosmologist Sir Arthur Eddington:

> If someone points out to you that your pet theory of the universe is in disagreement with Maxwell's equations – then so much the worse for Maxwell's equations. If it is found to be contradicted by observation – well, these experimentalists do bungle things sometimes. But if your theory is found to be against the second law of thermodynamics I can give you no hope; there is nothing for it but to collapse in deepest humiliation. (Eddington 1948, p. 74)

So the question is, can LQG really prove reversibility? We must await further developments in the field. It is fair to say that the prevailing view in cosmological community at large disagrees with Bojowald. As Bojowald himself admits, the jury is still out:

> **Sinclair:** 'Is the assumption of entropy reversal: a) an initial assumption around which a self-consistent LQG model is built, or b) a natural fallout of LQG models?'

> **Bojowald:** 'It is definitely b), as far as we can see it currently. Many details have to be filled in, but we do not make any a priori assumptions about entropy. Since entropy is not a fundamental object but a measure for our ignorance of what is happening microscopically, it is not even possible to make such an assumption in a theory like loop quantum gravity. We can only make assumptions on microscopic objects, and then see what this implies for more common quantities. What we don't know yet is how entropy changes balance out exactly. *So we are not sure if entropy does not increase from cycle to cycle. We can only say that the usual black hole arguments are not as strong as usually assumed*'. (pers. comm., March 29, 2006; emphasis added)

To his credit, Bojowald has not simply assumed zero net entropy in his model. He is using the right approach; allowing the physics to predict entropy accrual over time. So far, however, the only reliable conclusion is that LQG may show that Penrose's entropy arguments must be modified from their semiclassical orientation (what we have called option 2). This has failed to show, however, that universe entropy does not increase cumulatively cycle-by-cycle. The force of Penrose's argument remains intact even if his quantitative assessment of entropy must change.

Aside from the entropy issue, there remains the issue of dark energy, which may have the potential to stop cycling and induce an open-ended expansion. The current empirically observed dark energy effect, for example, appears adequate to produce an open-ended accelerated expansion. This result would be definitive if the dark energy were of the form of a cosmological constant (i.e. its value were independent of space and time; see Barrow & Dabrowski 1995).[74] As related earlier (Overbye 2006), this does appear to be the fate of the present day universe. But if an entropy gain (cycle-to-cycle) is denied, one can never have more than one "cycle." The cosmological constant would have led to open-ended expansion *the first time*. Hence, the initial singularity (our Big Bang) represents an absolute beginning.

If the dark energy were of the form of "quintessence" (i.e. had a value that is dependent on space and/or time), however, then it would be possible that its value could reverse and be consistent with a collapse phase, even given the current observational evidence. But then a new problem could intrude. Bojowald recognizes that after the bounce and the following energy transfer, different modes of the matter fields will become excited such that the next bounce will differ from the preceding one. But if the quintessence term changes, then perhaps the most generic model of LQG would be a hybrid between the cyclic and single-bounce models. On some particular cycle a value for the quintessence term would be such that it would lead to an open-ended expansion. Bojowald responds,

> If there is just a cosmological constant, it would be fixed for all cycles and not change. But if there is some kind of quintessence, you are right that its initial conditions for the classical phase would be affected by the bounce transition. So your scenario can be realized in suitable quintessence models. However, what people usually prefer are quintessence models which have an attractor behavior at late times, or the so-called tracking solutions. This allows one to avoid too much fine-tuning, and it makes the dynamics less sensitive to changes in initial values. For such models one thus does not generically expect big changes between cycles. On the other hand, since the effect would be quite dramatic if open-ended expansion can be realized, even a non-generic possibility can be important. (pers. comm., March 9, 2006)

Given an infinite number of rolls of the dice, any nonzero probability that quintessence could produce an open-ended expansion would be sufficient to do so. An open-ended expansion implies that that the overall number of cycles has been finite, and hence, the model would not be beginningless.[75]

In general, LQG looks like a promising alternative to string theory as a candidate for quantum gravity. But building a genuinely beginningless cyclic LQG model seems to be a far more difficult challenge.[76]

---

74. According to the National Aeronautics and Space Administration (NASA) (http://map.gsfc.nasa.gov/m_mm/mr_limits.html), their current data tends to favor the cosmological constant theory for dark energy as opposed to quintessence, although the latter is not ruled out.

75. Barrow and Dabrowski do indicate that if the dark energy were of the type to decay away into matter and radiation; that is, if it is impermanent, then cycling would recommence after the decay.

76. We note that there are other LQG models that feature Vaas-type pseudobeginnings and seem to us to be viable.

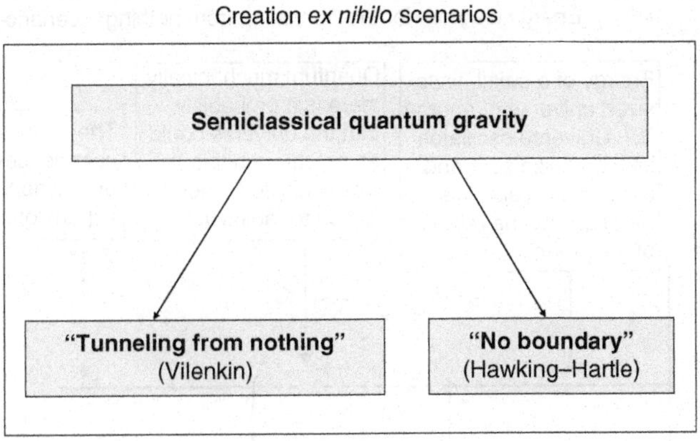

Creation *ex nihilo* scenarios

Figure 3.19 Quantum models with an explicit beginning to the finite past.

IVc. Semiclassical creation ex nihilo *models*

When inflation was first explored as a concept, it was understood to be a phase in the history of our universe that occurred sometime after the origin event and ended long ago. This naturally led to the question: "How could inflation itself have started?" (Figure 3.19).

That understanding has changed with the work of cosmologists such as Andrei Linde (chaotic inflation) and the recent work on the String Landscape by pioneers such as Susskind, Bousso, and Polchinski (and many others). Here, inflation is not viewed just as a phase in development but instead as the dominant feature of a larger multiverse, within which our "universe" is just a regional phenomenon. Nevertheless, given the singularity theorems developed by Borde, Vilenkin, and Guth, inflation itself is viewed as not past eternal.[77] Hence, the old question still persists: How did inflation get started? Vilenkin (1982) explains an approach he initiated to address this question:

> Many people suspected that in order to understand what actually happened in the beginning, we should treat the universe quantum-mechanically and describe it by a wave function rather than by a classical spacetime. This quantum approach to cosmology was initiated by DeWitt and Misner, and after a somewhat slow start received wide recognition in the last two decades or so. *The picture that has emerged from this line of development is that a small closed universe can spontaneously nucleate out of nothing, where by 'nothing' I mean a state with no classical space and time.* The cosmological wave function can be used to calculate the probability distribution for the initial configurations of the nucleating universes. Once the universe nucleates, it is expected to go through a period of inflation, driven by the energy of a false vacuum. The vacuum energy is eventually thermalized, inflation ends, and from then on the universe follows the standard hot cosmological scenario. (Vilenkin 2002, p. 2; emphasis added)

Vilenkin uses quantum tunneling of a particle through a potential well as an analogy for the whole universe. In Figure 3.20, the '$E > 0$' line represents an ordinary, closed FRW

---

77. One remembers, of course, exceptions such as asymptotically static models and Linde's objection that the behavior of the whole may not be the same as its parts.

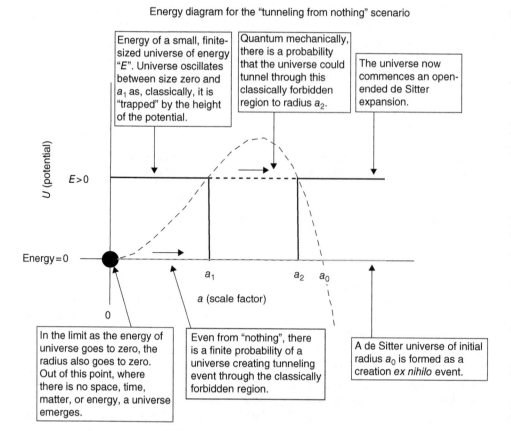

Figure 3.20 Creation *ex nihilo* of a universe.

universe, which (classically) does not have enough energy to escape into an open-ended expansion. Hence, it goes through continued Big Bang/Big Crunch cycles. In classical physics (GR), this state of affairs would persist forever.[78] But quantum gravity provides a way out. There is a finite probability that, instead of a recollapse, the universe will "tunnel" through the energy barrier and commence an inflationary expansion instead.

This approach still does not solve the problem of creation; rather it has moved the question back one step: to the initial, tiny, closed, and metastable universe. This universe state can have existed for only a finite time. Where did it come from?

Vilenkin's solution was to consider what happens in the limit as the energy of this initial closed universe becomes zero. The scale factor of the universe becomes zero as well. This is the genesis of the claim that the universe is created from "nothing." There is no space, time, matter, or energy. This constitutes a topological transformation: "Creation of a universe from nothing . . . is a transition from the null topological sector containing no universes at all to the sector with one universe of topology S^3" (Vilenkin 1994, p. 23). Vilenkin grants that nothingness so conceived is not the same as the *absence* of being:

---

78. Assuming, of course, that the problems of cyclic cosmologies (entropy buildup, bounce physics, etc.) were solvable.

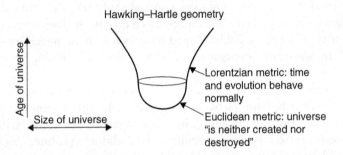

Figure 3.21 Transition to "normal" time in a Hartle–Hawking approach. This is really just a mathematical technique called *analytic continuation*, which is useful for problems with "badly behaved" functions, but which does not imply ontological commitment.

> I understand that a universe of zero radius is not necessarily the same thing as no universe at all. But mathematically my quantum tunneling from nothing is described by the same "shuttlecock" geometry as Hartle and Hawking [NB Figure 3.21]. (In fact, the shuttlecock first appeared in my 1982 paper.) This geometry is certainly not past-eternal, and there is no point on the Euclidean sphere which you can identify as the initial universe of zero size. So, if the Hartle-Hawking approach avoids the "paradoxes of creation", I don't see why my mine doesn't. (pers. comm., October 23, 2006)

> The mathematical description of a tunneling universe suggests that time, space and matter came into being a finite time ago. "Nothing" refers to the "prior" state. (pers. comm., October 30, 2006)

The universe clearly has a beginning in this approach. But the claim seems to go beyond this: the universe "came into being" from a "prior" state of "nothing." This latter claim (that the universe comes into being) is significant because the notion of time becomes ill defined in these models near the beginning.

A similar approach to Vilenkin's is the "no-boundary proposal" of James Hartle and Stephen Hawking. Hartle and Hawking make use of Richard Feynman's approach to QM. Feynman's (1985) approach is to find the probability for a certain final quantum state by a path integral, a "sum over histories." In quantum terms, this is a superposition of states. Every possible universe history is part of the wave function; each possible end state has an associated probability of realization (alternatively, one can view all the possible states as existing "somewhere" in a realized multiverse). The path integral of the universe, as one might imagine, presents an intractable problem; hence, Hartle and Hawking make an educated guess as to a subset of possible universes that are expected to dominate the calculation and assert compact spaces only in order to solve the problem that path (or contour) integrals often are badly behaved. They tend to diverge and give nonsense answers (such as "infinity" for a probability).

To rectify the divergence problem, Hartle and Hawking make use of Euclidean metrics to describe the earliest phases of the universe's existence. This is a mathematical technique called analytic continuation (or more specifically, a Wick rotation), which allows one to analyze a better behaved function in the domain of interest. A "normal" or "Lorentzian" metric has signature $(-,+,+,+)$, indicating a special character to the time dimension. A Euclidean metric $(+,+,+,+)$ treats time the same as it does the space dimensions. The Wick rotation takes the real time variable "T" and replaces it with the imaginary quantity "$I \times T$". Here "i" is the square root of negative one. Thus, Hartle and Hawking are said to employ "imaginary time" in their model.

The use of a Euclidean metric has the effect of removing the initial singularity predicted by "pure" GR – hence the term "no boundary proposal." There is, in general, no ontological commitment associated with this change in metric signature. But Hawking, in his popular writings, appears to assert the physical reality of the Euclidean signature. This is the genesis of Hawking's claim that "[the universe] would neither be created nor destroyed. It would just BE" (Hawking 1988, p. 141). Hawking goes on to ask "What place, then, for a creator?" Yet, curiously, Hartle and Hawking also claim their universe can be interpreted to have come into being out of "nothing":

> One can interpret the functional integral over all compact four-geometries bounded by a given three-geometry as giving the amplitude for that three-geometry to arise from a zero three-geometry; that is, a single point. In other words, the ground state is the probability for the Universe to appear from nothing. (Hawking & Hartle, 1983, p. 2961) [They then refer to Vilenkin's "tunneling from nothing" paper.][79]

A third interpretation of these results exists as well. Recall that Gott and Li have criticized the creation *ex nihilo* approach on two grounds. (1) Transitions in QM are always between allowed classical states (Vilenkin and Hartle–Hawking's approach has a transition from a classically forbidden region to a classically allowed region). (2) The Vilenkin and Hartle–Hawking approaches should contain realistic energy fields (something closer to what we actually see in nature). If they did, then Heisenberg's uncertainty principle would require that the initial state of their models have a finite and nonzero energy. It that is the case, then semiclassical quantum models actually start in a classically allowed metastable state, rather than "nothing." Gott and Li elaborate:

> The problem with this model [Vilenkin and Hawking–Hartle] is that it ignores the "zero-point energy." If there is a conformal scalar field ϕ, then the "energy" levels should be $E_n = n + 1/2$. Even for $n = 0$ there is a "zero-point-energy." The potential makes the system behave like a harmonic oscillator in the potential well near $a = 0$. A harmonic oscillator cannot sit at the bottom of the potential well – the uncertainty principle would not allow it. There must be some zero-point-energy and the particle must have some momentum, as it oscillates within the potential well when the field ϕ is included. Thus, when the "zero point-energy" is considered, we see that the initial state is not a point but a tiny oscillating $(0 < a < a_1)$ big bang universe, that oscillates between big bangs and big crunches (though the singularities at the big bangs and big crunches might be smeared by quantum effects). This is the initial *classical* state from which the tunneling occurs. *It is metastable, so this oscillating universe could not have existed forever: after a finite half-life, it is likely to decay.* It reaches maximum radius a_1, and then tunnels to a classical de Sitter state at minimum radius a_2 where $a_2 < a_0$. (Gott & Li 1998, p. 38; emphasis added)

---

79. Note that in Vilenkin's comment (above), he indicates that the geometry of his model can be understood in terms of an initial Euclidean metric (which would represent the "forbidden" region of the energy diagram (Figure 3.20).

The relevant question for the interpretation of these models, then, is: Is the universe (i) created from nothing, (ii) neither created not destroyed but, in effect, timelessly subsistent, or (iii) left ultimately unexplained, since the existence of the initial, metastable, closed, Planck-sized universe out of which our universe was born is not itself accounted for? Option (i), if adopted, clearly implies that the universe began to exist. Nonetheless, as even Vilenkin himself recognizes, "nothing" as he describes it is not the same as absence of being. Whatever reality underlies the laws of QM must exist at least, so as to transform the null topological sector into an FRW universe. The laws themselves, if they exist, are mere abstract objects of a propositional nature and so do not stand in causal relations to anything. As such they are irrelevant to what happens in the world; it is the reality that corresponds to them that distinguishes merely logical from real possibility. As Heinz Pagels once remarked: "This unthinkable void converts itself into the plenum of existence–a necessary consequence of physical laws. Where are these laws written into that void? What "tells" the void that it is pregnant with a possible universe? It would seem that even the void is subject to law, a logic that exists prior to space and time" (Pagels 1985, p. 347). Option (i), then, is mistaken, being based upon an idiosyncratic use of the word "nothing." That initial state is clearly not nothing, but something.

As for option (ii), Hawking himself seems to give good grounds for treating their proposal as an instrumental approach only. In his collaboration with Roger Penrose, *The Nature of Space and Time* (Hawking & Penrose 1996), he demonstrates the same mathematical approach (analytic continuation) to describe pair production of electron–positron pairs in a strong electric field. This is a standard mathematical technique sometimes used when complex analytic functions are better behaved in a certain domain than their real counterparts. It does not imply ontological commitment to the alternative description, however. It seems to us that given the unintelligibility of the "imaginary time" region in these models, it is most reasonable to treat this approach as nonrealist in character.

As for option (iii), we seem to have the same sort of situation that we encountered with the Emergent and PBBI models with their associated metastable ESS and SPV states. The universe cannot be past eternal because the initial metastable state can have had only a finite lifetime. This seems to us to be the most reasonable option to take for a realist interpretation of these models. It employs known, meaningful interpretations of physical phenomena from "classical" quantum theory and extends them to the quantum gravity models. One avoids the problems associated with the novelty of asserting a zero-energy condition for the initial state (denied by the Heisenberg uncertainty principle), the novelty of asserting a quantum transition from a forbidden to a classically allowed state (normal quantum theory only includes transitions over or through forbidden regions from one allowed state to another), and it is consistent with more realistic energy fields. Option (iii) is also consistent with the second premise of the *kalam* cosmological argument.

2.34. Summary

Taking as a springboard challenges to the Hawking–Penrose singularity theorems, we have surveyed the historical development of three research programs each pursuing known exceptions to the theorems:[80] (1) CTCs; (2) violation of strong energy condition (eternal

---

80. The fourth and fifth conditions, viz., satisfaction of a generic energy condition and the existence of a closed trapped surface in our past are easily met.

inflation); and (3) falsity of GR (quantum gravity). Major theoretical developments concerning options (2) and (3) were inflationary theory (repulsive gravity) and semiclassical quantum gravity.

CTCs, while interesting, seem to fail given the CPC. Counterexamples to the conjecture can be found, but they seem to be unphysical and/or infinitely fine-tuned toy models.

As for inflation, an exotic type of energy field possesses the bizarre property of *negative* pressure. This energy wants to collapse in on itself due to pressure, yet according to Einstein's equations, pressure also produces a gravitational force. If the pressure is negative, the gravitational force is *repulsive*. It turns out that the repulsion is the stronger of the two tendencies; *greatly* so. The universe can expand many orders of magnitude in a fraction of a second; from invisibly small to bigger than the entire observable sky. This development permitted a reappraisal of the question of origins that lasted two decades. Finally, a new singularity theorem, developed by Arvind Borde, Alexander Vilenkin, and Alan Guth showed that this model – the inflationary universe – still had a beginning in the finite past.

It is fascinating to note that the recent history of cosmology can be mapped by attempts to overcome these singularity theorems. Following the BVG Theorem in 2003, attempts to build models have been based on exceptions to *that* theorem. These were (1) average past expansion of universe is negative (contraction-bounce), (2) average past expansion is zero (asymptotically static universe), (3) average past expansion is zero (cyclic universe), and (4) exotic space-time.

The first, somewhat akin to the de Sitter universe, featured an infinite contraction into a bounce at the singularity, followed by our current expansion. But it featured a Hobson's choice between an acausally fine-tuned contraction or an infinitely distant beginning point. In either case, the bounce was predicted to be chaotic (due to BKL oscillations), and hence its "Big Bang" would look nothing like the one we actually measure.

The second case, exemplified by the Emergent model class, features an unstable or metastable initial state followed by an inflationary expansion. But an unstable state (ESS) or a metastable state (the LQG addition to the Emergent model) has a finite lifetime. So the beginning of the universe reasserts itself.

The third case has long been known, since the original models of Richard Tolman, to be problematic on entropy grounds. Baum and Frampton have sought to solve this problem through an approach dubbed "the phantom bounce." Here, the universe undergoes a superexpansion aided by the effects of "phantom" energy, which accelerates the expansion with effects similar to inflation. The universe would then fractionate into a multiverse, with almost all of the daughter universes having jettisoned their entropy given the initial expansion. Could this work? It does not appear so, the chief difficulty being that causal reconnection of universe likely occurs at the "turnaround" point (when expansion goes over to contraction) leading to *one* contraction, rather than to many. A more certain conclusion is that, even given an "empty" universe[81] undergoing contraction, chaotic fluctuations as the contraction nears a singularity would *create* matter, thereby leading to a chaotic crunch, which would prevent cycling.

The fourth case features a deconstruction of time itself. It postulates two mirror-image, inflationary expansions, where the arrows of time lead *away* from a past boundary. Thus,

---

81. That is, except for the zero entropy phantom energy.

the mirror universe is not our past. This is just a case of a double Big Bang. Hence, the universe *still* has an origin.

What about the attempts at quantum gravity models (many of which overlap with those previously discussed)? They include (1) string models, (3) LQG models, and (3) semiclassical quantum gravity models.[82]

The most popular new field is the class of string models. Two prominent approaches are the Ekpyrotic/cyclic and PBBI models. But the first is subject to the BVG singularity theorem and hence has a beginning. The second is probably to be interpreted instrumentally only and seems in any case to have the characteristics of the Emergent class with respect to the initial state. Hence, it has a metastable beginning phase, called the SPV, which cannot be eternal in the past. The most popular string model is the generalization of inflationary theory known as the String Landscape. This scenario, however, is known to have a beginning to the finite past due to the same BVG Theorem.

LQG is a competitor to string theory. We saw one such application when LQG was incorporated into the Emergent model class. Another LQG approach is to try to build a viable cyclic model. LQG seems a promising approach to address the issue of BKL chaos, hence, perhaps, providing a justification for a bouncing model. But the cyclic LQG still seems to fail to account for the entropy effects that usually doom infinite cyclicity. Even if it did, current observations show that our universe is in an open-ended expansion rather than a Big Bang/Big Crunch cycle. So current LQG attempts do not appear to support a past eternal universe.

The semiclassical quantum gravity models have, in their very approach, a beginning to the finite past. The beginning has been described in three possible (and not consistent) ways. Either:

1. The universe came into being from a prior state of null topology (but somehow containing the laws of physics themselves) to a Lorentzian metric (the normal universe). Hence, the universe "tunneled from nothing" into existence.
2. The initial state of the universe is uncreated. This is due to the nature of time in a Euclidean metric. It is equivalent to a spatial dimension.
3. Because the initial state of the geometry must have a zero point energy, it is in a classical state with a Lorentzian metric. It is a metastable closed universe. Hence, this state could not have existed forever and, in a manner unexplained by the model, began to exist.

The second description seems to be purely instrumental in character. The first and third imply that the universe began to exist. Hence, semiclassical models are supportive of the universe's having a beginning.

Our survey shows that contemporary cosmology is quite supportive of the second premise of the *kalam* cosmological argument. Further, this conclusion is not reached through ferreting out elaborate and unique failure conditions for scores of individual

82. In interests of economy, we have not discussed earlier attempts to postulate a regional, immanent status for the Big Bang which leave the origin of the initial space in question. It would seem that this space cannot contract, expand, or be static without violating criteria mentioned earlier (singularity theorems, chaotic bounces, metastable beginnings, etc.). Thus, these models proved to be untenable.

Table 3.1 Effective principles in ruling out a beginningless model

Model average expansion history	Condition requiring a beginning
1) Expanding models	Singularity theorems
2) Asymptotically static models	Metastability
3) Cyclic models	Second law of thermodynamics
4) Contracting models	Acausal fine-tuning

models. Rather, the repeated application of simple principles seems effective in ruling out a beginningless model.[83] They are found in Table 3.1.

It seems that the field of cosmology, therefore, yields good evidence that the universe began to exist.

1.0. Everything That Begins to Exist Has a Cause

To return, then, at length to the first premise of the *kalam* cosmological argument

1.0.   Everything that begins to exist has a cause,

we take (1.0) to be obviously true – at the least, more plausibly true than its negation. Three reasons can be given in its support.

1.1. Ex nihilo nihil fit

First and foremost, the principle is rooted in the metaphysical intuition that something cannot come into being from nothing. For to come into existence without a cause of any sort is to come into being from nothing.[84] To suggest that things could just pop into being uncaused out of nothing is to quit doing serious metaphysics and to resort to magic. Nobody *sincerely* believes that things, say, a horse or an Eskimo village, can just pop into being without a cause. But if we make the universe an exception to (1.0), we have got to think that the whole universe just *appeared* at some point in the past for no reason whatsoever.

Sometimes it is said that quantum physics furnishes an exception to the claim that something cannot come into being uncaused out of nothing, since on the subatomic level,

83. This does not exhaust the list of possible model formulations. Different types of mosaic models are likely to be the next thing to come down the pike. Nor did we survey every model that exists in the present (nor could we). There is also the complaint of philosopher James Brian Pitts: "What rights do unborn theories possess?"

84. See Oppy's suggestion that we construe the first premise to assert that everything that begins to exist has a cause of some sort, whether efficient or material (Oppy 2006b, p. 153). His protest that the cause of the universe could then be a material cause is not troubling because the incoreality of the First Cause plausibly follows from a conceptual analysis of what it is to be a cause of the space-time universe, on which see further discussion below.

so-called "virtual particles" come into being from nothing. In the same way, certain cosmogonic theories are interpreted as showing that the universe could have sprung into being out of the quantum vacuum or even out of nothingness. Thus, the universe is said to be the proverbial "free lunch."

This objection, however, is based on misunderstanding. In the first place, wholly apart from the disputed question of whether virtual particles really exist at all,[85] not all physicists agree that subatomic events are uncaused. A great many physicists today are quite dissatisfied with the traditional Copenhagen interpretation of quantum physics and are exploring deterministic theories like that of David Bohm.[86] Indeed, most of the available interpretations of the mathematical formalism of QM are fully deterministic. Quantum cosmologists are especially averse to Copenhagen, since that interpretation in a cosmological context will require an ultramundane observer to collapse the wave function of the universe. Thus, quantum physics hardly furnishes a proven exception to (1.0). Second, even on the indeterministic interpretation, particles do not come into being out of nothing. They arise as spontaneous fluctuations of the energy contained in the subatomic vacuum, which constitutes an indeterministic cause of their origination. Third, the same point can be made about theories of the origin of the universe out of a primordial vacuum. Popularizers touting such theories as getting "something from nothing" apparently do not understand that the vacuum is not nothing but is a sea of fluctuating energy endowed with a rich structure and subject to physical laws. Such models do not, therefore, involve a true origination *ex nihilo*.[87]

Neither do theories such as Vilenkin's quantum creation model. Vilenkin invites us to envision a small, closed, spherical universe filled with a so-called false vacuum and containing some ordinary matter. If the radius of such a universe is small, classical physics predicts that it will collapse to a point; but quantum physics permits it to "tunnel" into a state of inflationary expansion. If we allow the radius to shrink all the way to zero, there still remains some positive probability of the universe's tunneling to inflation. As we have seen, Vilenkin equates the initial state of the universe explanatorily prior to tunneling with nothingness. But postulating such an equivalence is grossly misleading. As Vilenkin's own diagram illustrates (Vilenkin 2006, p. 180), quantum tunneling is at every point a function from something to something (Figure 3.22). For quantum tunneling to be truly from nothing, the function would have to have only one term, the posterior term. Another way of seeing the point is to reflect on the fact that to have no radius (as is the case with nothingness) is not to have a radius, whose measure is zero. Thus, there is no basis for the claim that quantum physics proves that things can begin to exist without a cause, much less that universe could have sprung into being uncaused from literally nothing.

A more pertinent objection to the justification of (1.0) on the basis of the metaphysical principle that something cannot come from nothing issues from the partisans of the B-Theory of time (Grünbaum 1967, p. 153; 2000, p.16). For B-Theorists deny that in beginning to exist the universe *came into being* or *became actual.* They thereby focus attention on the theory of time underlying the *kalam* cosmological argument. From start to finish, the *kalam* cosmological argument is predicated upon the A-Theory of time. On a B-Theory

---

85. See Weingard (1982) for doubts.
86. See Cushing (1994) and Cushing (1998).
87. See remarks by Kanitscheider (1990).

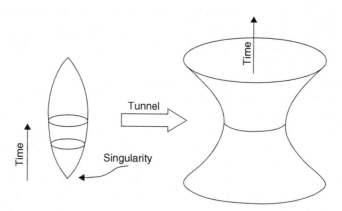

Figure 3.22 Quantum tunneling of the universe to an inflationary condition. Note that the tunneling is at every point from something to something; the origin of the initial point remains unexplained. (source: Vilenkin 2006)

of time, the universe does not in fact come into being or become actual at the Big Bang; it just exists tenselessly as a four-dimensional space-time block that is finitely extended in the *earlier than* direction. If time is tenseless, then the universe never really comes into being, and, therefore, the quest for a cause of its coming into being is misconceived. Although G. W. F. Leibniz's question, *Why is there* (tenselessly) *something rather than nothing?*, should still rightly be asked, there would be no reason to look for a cause of the universe's beginning to exist, since on tenseless theories of time the universe did not begin to exist in virtue of its having a first event anymore than a meter stick begins to exist in virtue of having a first centimeter. In affirming that things which begin to exist need a cause, the *mutakallim* assumes the following understanding of that notion, where "*x*" ranges over any entity and "*t*" ranges over times, whether instants or moments of nonzero finite duration:

A. *x* begins to exist at *t* iff *x* comes into being at *t*.
B. *x* comes into being at *t* iff (i) *x* exists at *t*, and the actual world includes no state of affairs in which *x* exists timelessly, (ii) *t* is either the first time at which *x* exists or is separated from any *t*′ < *t* at which *x* existed by an interval during which *x* does not exist, and (iii) *x*'s existing at *t* is a tensed fact.

By presupposing an A-Theory of time, according to which temporal becoming is real, the *mutakallim* justifiably assumes that the universe's existing at a first moment of time represents the moment at which the universe came into being. Thus, the real issue separating the proponent of the *kalam* cosmological argument and critics of the first premise is the objectivity of tense and temporal becoming.

It is worth recalling that having a beginning does not entail having a beginning point, lest someone should essay to avert the beginning of the universe by asserting that the series of past states of the universe might converge toward *t* = 0 in the metrically finite past as a merely ideal limit.[88] On such a proposal, it is alleged, the universe lacks a beginning point and can therefore be said to have no earliest time of its existence. Hence, it does not, despite its past temporal finitude, begin to exist, and so no cause of the universe's origin need be postulated.

It is not clear that such a proposal is even physically possible;[89] but let that pass. The fundamental philosophical shortcoming of this proposal is its gratuitous assumption that having a beginning entails having a beginning point. This is not, in fact, how the locution "begins to exist" is typically understood.[90] Contemporary cosmologists frequently "cut out" the initial cosmological singularity as a merely ideal point on the boundary of space-time, so that the universe has no first instant of its existence; but they do not therefore think that the universe no longer begins to exist or that the mystery of the origin of the universe has thereby been solved.

Granted a tensed theory of time, the key criterion for determining if something has a beginning is its past metrical finitude.[91] Something has a beginning just in case the time during which it has existed is finite. Time itself may be said to begin to exist just in case for any nonzero, finite interval of time that one picks, there are only a finite number of congruent intervals earlier than it. Or, alternatively, time begins to exist just in case for some specified nonzero, finite interval of time, there are no congruent intervals earlier than it. In either case beginning to exist does not entail having a beginning point.

So understood, deleting the beginning point of a thing's existence does not imply that that thing no longer begins to exist and therefore came into being uncaused. As mentioned, cosmologists continue to puzzle over the origin of the universe out of nothing, whether or not it had an initial instant of its existence. One is reminded in this connection of the ancient sorites-style problems of starting and stopping.[92] If there is a last instant at which some object is at rest, then when does it begin to move? The answer can only be

---

88. Quentin Smith suggested as much on the occasion of the forum "Science and Religion," University of California, Santa Barbara, January 30, 2004, featuring William Lane Craig, Richard Gale, Alvin Plantinga, and Quentin Smith, available in DVD format through www.veritas-ucsb.org. See also Grünbaum (2000, pp. 16–7).

89. It will depend crucially on one's theory of quantum gravity. A typical approach to marrying quantum theory to GR involves describing the evolution of space-time as a path integral (a sum over all possible paths) in superspace, which is a space of points representing three-dimensional configurations of the universe. The points of this configuration space can be regarded as instantaneous states or even as instants, but the fact that in the quantum theory one has a path integral, rather than a single path, makes it impossible to "stack" these instants into a unique history constituting a space-time. So, eventually, the dividing process becomes ill-defined in the theory. The fact that the first split second of the universe's existence as measured in cosmic time is not resolvable into a unique sequence of ever briefer states is not inconsistent with there being a first second of its existence.

90. We might mention as well that the proposal commits us to the reality of points, which surely overloads the expression "begins to exist" with unintended ontological commitments. Such metaphysical issues should be decided by argument, not definition.

91. Oppy seems ready to concede that the second premise of the *kalam* cosmological argument is true if we accept that something begins to exist iff it is finite in the past (Oppy 2006b, p. 147). Given a tensed theory of time, we think that that biconditional holds for wholly temporal entities. So the remaining question, as Oppy says, is whether everything that begins to exist in this sense has a cause. While not denying the causal principle, Oppy denies that that premise is either obviously true or supported by experience (Oppy 2006b, pp. 150–3).

92. See Sorabji (1983, pp. 403–21).

that there is no first instant of its motion. Nonetheless, the object does begin to move and plausibly requires a cause to set it in motion. Similarly, if a thing has not always existed, then it is plausible that that thing began to exist and requires a cause to bring it into being, whether or not there was a first instant at which it existed.

In view of the seemingly evident metaphysical absurdity of something's coming into being without a cause, one would not anticipate that naturalists would deny the first premise of the *kalam* cosmological argument and assert that the universe sprang into existence uncaused out of nothing. It is therefore surprising how many nontheists, confronted with the evidence of the universe's beginning, have taken this route. For example, Quentin Smith, commenting that philosophers are too often adversely affected by Heidegger's dread of "the nothing," concludes that the most reasonable belief is that we came "from nothing, by nothing, and for nothing"(Craig & Smith 1993, p. 135)[93] – a nice ending to a sort of Gettysburg address of atheism, perhaps. Such a confession merely expresses the faith of an atheist. For it is, we repeat, literally worse than magic.

1.2. Why only universes?

Second, if things really could come into being uncaused out of nothing, then it becomes inexplicable why just anything or everything does not come into existence uncaused from nothing. Why do bicycles and Beethoven and root beer not pop into being from nothing? Why is it only universes that can come into being from nothing? What makes nothingness so discriminatory? There cannot be anything about nothingness that favors universes, for nothingness does not have any properties. Nothingness is the absence of anything whatsoever. As such, nothingness can have no properties, since there literally is not anything to have any properties. Nor can anything constrain nothingness, for there is not anything to be constrained. How silly, then, when popularizers say things such as "Nothingness is unstable to quantum fluctuations" or "The universe tunneled into being out of nothing"!

Some critics have responded to this problem by asserting that while (1.0) is true with respect to things *in* the universe, it is not true *of* the universe itself. But this proposed differentiation misconstrues the nature of the Causal Principle. Premise (1.0) does not state a merely physical law such as Boyle's law or the second law of thermodynamics, which are contingent laws of nature. Premise (1.0) is not a physical principle. Rather, it is a metaphysical principle: being cannot come from nonbeing; something cannot come into existence uncaused from nothing. Such claims are not contingent upon the properties, causal powers, and dispositions of the natural kinds of substances which happen to exist. Critics have given no good reason for construing such claims as merely physical rather

---

93. Smith's most recent criticism of the *kalam* cosmological argument is also a denial of the first premise, despite Smith's avowal that he now accepts the conclusion that the universe has a cause of its existence (Smith 2007, pp. 182–98). Smith's most recent published position is that the initial singular point of the universe is not real and that, therefore, the sequence of instantaneous states of the universe is a beginningless series converging toward zero as a limit. Each state is caused by its prior states and there is no first state. Any nonzero interval or state, such as the first second of the universe's existence, "is not caused by any or all of its instantaneous states and is not caused by any external cause" (Smith 2007, p. 189). Smith takes "the beginning of the universe" to refer to the Planck era, that state which lasts until 10^{-43} seconds after the singularity. As a state of nonzero duration, the beginning of the universe therefore has no cause of any sort. The universe therefore comes into being uncaused out of nothing.

than as metaphysical claims. The Causal Principle plausibly applies to all of reality, and it is thus metaphysically absurd that the universe should pop into being uncaused out of nothing.

Second, why think in any case that the universe is an exception to the rule? As Arthur Schopenhauer once remarked, the Causal Principle is not something we can dismiss like a cab once we have arrived at our desired destination. Sometimes critics will say that while it is impossible for things to come into being uncaused *in* time, things can come into being uncaused *with* time, that is, at a first moment of time. But until the premise's detractors are able to explain the relevant difference between embedded moments of time and a first moment of time, there seems to be no reason to think it more plausible that things can come into being uncaused at a first moment than at a later moment of time. If something cannot come into existence uncaused at *t*, where *t* is preceded by earlier moments of time, why think that if we were to annihilate all moments earlier than *t*, then that thing could come into existence uncaused at *t*? How could the existence of moments earlier than an uncaused event be of any possible relevance to the occurrence of that event?

Indeed, given a pure A-Theory of time, according to which only the present exists, every moment of time is a fresh beginning, qualitatively indistinguishable from a first moment of time, for when any moment is present, earlier moments have passed away and do not exist. Thus, if the universe could exist uncaused at a first moment of time, it could exist uncaused at any moment of time. There just does not seem to be any relevant difference. It follows that if the latter is metaphysically impossible, so is the former.

Third, the objection stifles scientific exploration of cosmological questions. The absolute beginning of time predicted by the standard Friedmann–Lemaître model was the crucial factor in provoking not only the formulation of the Steady-State model of continuous creation, but a whole series of subsequent models all aimed at avoiding the origin *ex nihilo* of our universe predicted by the standard model. Both philosophers and physicists have been deeply disturbed at the prospect of a beginning of time and an absolute origination of the universe and so have felt constrained to posit the existence of causally prior entities such as quantum vacuum states, inflationary domains, imaginary time regimes, and even timelike causal loops. The history of twentieth-century astrophysical cosmology would be considerably different if there were thought to be no need of a causal explanation of the origin of time and the universe.

By contrast, the *mutakallim* cannot be similarly accused of stifling science because it is only with the conceptual analysis of the argument's conclusion that he is able to identify the cause of the universe as a being of religious significance, and the *mutakallim* will in any case welcome attempts to falsify his theistic hypothesis in hopes of corroboration of his preferred hypothesis by the failure of such naturalistic explanations.

1.3. Experiential confirmation

Finally, (1.0) is constantly confirmed in our experience. Scientific naturalists thus have the strongest of motivations to accept it. It is precisely on the strength of the role played by the Causal Principle in science that the naturalist philosopher of science Bernulf Kanitscheider warns, "If taken seriously, the initial singularity is in head-on collision with the most successful ontological commitment that was a guiding line of research since Epicurus and Lucretius," namely, *out of nothing nothing comes*, which Kanitscheider calls "a metaphysical hypothesis which has proved so fruitful in every corner of science that we are surely well-advised to try as hard as we can to eschew processes of absolute origin" (Kanitscheider 1990, p. 344). Doubtless, as mentioned earlier, this same conviction inspired many of the efforts to craft cosmological models aimed at averting the absolute beginning of the universe. If we do have good reasons for accepting the fact of the universe's absolute origin, that fact in no way entails that the Causal Principle is false. *Qua* physicists, we may refuse to draw the inference implied by the two premises on the quite reasonable grounds that one thereby crosses the threshold of science into the realm of metaphysics, but *qua* philosophers, we are free to draw whatever inferences the premises logically imply.

Wesley Morriston opposes two other empirical generalizations to the Causal Principle which he thinks enjoy comparable support but are allegedly incompatible with the *kalam* argument, to wit, (i) *everything that begins to exist has a material cause* and (ii) *causes always stand in temporal relations to their effects* (Morriston 2002, p. 162). Notice, however, that neither of these principles is incompatible with the Causal Principle enunciated in (1.0). They form a consistent triad. Morriston, in truth, offers no defeater at all for the argument's causal premise, taken as an empirical generalization.

What is true is that the conjunction of (1.0) and (2.0) will imply the falsity of at least (i), if not (ii). As putative defeaters of the conclusion (3.0) of the *kalam* argument, however, (i) and (ii) are not compelling. The evidence for (i) is, indeed, impressive. But it is not unequivocal or universal.[94] More importantly, (i) may be simply overridden by the arguments for the finitude of the past. For if it is impossible that there be an infinite regress of past events, it is impossible that the First Cause be a material object, since matter/energy is never quiescent.[95] If (2.0) commends itself to us, then, we must reject (i), and it would

---

94. Morriston himself takes our own power to control our actions to be the paradigm of causality. But, as J. P. Moreland argues, such control plausibly requires some sort of dualism (Moreland 1998b, pp. 68–91), in which case we have a clear counterexample to the claim that every effect has a material cause. For not only do I cause effects in my physical body, but my mental states are causally connected.

Again, many philosophers believe that immaterial, abstract objects such as numbers, sets, propositions, and so on exist necessarily and eternally. But there are also many abstract objects which seem to exist contingently and noneternally, for example, the equator, the center of mass of the solar system, Beethoven's *Fifth Symphony*, Leo Tolstoy's *Anna Karenina*, and so forth. None of these is a material object. Tolstoy's novel, for example, is not identical to any of its printed exemplars, for these could all be destroyed and replaced by new books. Nor can Beethoven's *Fifth* be identified with any particular series of ink marks or any performance of the symphony. Now these things all began to exist: the equator, for example, did not exist before the earth did. But if they began to exist, did they have a cause or did they come into being out of just nothing? (Notice that it makes sense to ask this question even though these entities are immaterial and so have no material cause.) Many philosophers would say that these objects did indeed have causes: it was Tolstoy, for example, who created *Anna Karenina*. So in cases such as these (and they are legion), we do, indeed, have instances of efficient causation without material causation. We may not agree that such abstract objects really exist; but charity demands that we say that the view defended by our philosophical colleagues is a coherent one.

Moreover, in the realm of physics itself, we have already alluded to the creation of space in the expanding universe as a case of the efficient causation of something real in the absence of any material cause. Moreover, some physicists have taken background fluctuation models to be a counterexample to (i), since if the total energy of the universe is on balance zero, the universe did not borrow any energy from the vacuum and so has no material cause, even though it was spawned by the vacuum as its efficient cause. (See Craig 1998, pp. 332–59).

95. See Craig (1991, pp. 104–8).

be the height of folly then to go on to reject (1.0) as well. For if coming into being without a material cause seems impossible, coming into being with neither a material nor an efficient cause is doubly absurd.

As for (ii), it appears to be merely an accidental generalization, akin to *Human beings have always lived on the Earth*, which was true until 1968. There does not seem to be anything inherently temporal about a causal relationship. More importantly, however, (ii) is not at all incompatible with the *kalam* argument's conclusion, since its defender may hold that God exists timelessly sans creation and temporally at and subsequent to the moment of creation, so that His act of causing the beginning of the universe is simultaneous with the universe's beginning to exist.[96]

1.4. Objections

J. L. Mackie, in response to the *kalam* cosmological argument, reserved his chief criticism for its first premise. He complains, "there is *a priori* no good reason why a sheer origination of things, not determined by anything, should be unacceptable, whereas the existence of a god [*sic*] with the power to create something out of nothing is acceptable" (Mackie 1982, p. 94). Indeed, he believes *creatio ex nihilo* raises problems: (i) If God began to exist at a point in time, then this is as great a puzzle as the beginning of the universe. (ii) Or if God existed for infinite time, then the same arguments would apply to his existence as would apply to the infinite duration of the universe. (iii) If it be said that God is timeless, then this, says Mackie, is a complete mystery.

Now it is noteworthy that Mackie never *refutes* the principle that whatever begins to exist has a cause. Rather, he simply demands what good reason there is *a priori* to accept it. He writes, "As Hume pointed out, we can certainly conceive an uncaused beginning-to-be of an object; if what we can thus conceive is nevertheless in some way impossible, this still requires to be shown" (Mackie 1982, p. 89; cf. Oppy 2006b, p. 151). But, as many philosophers have pointed out, Hume's argument in no way makes it plausible to think that something could really come into being without a cause. Just because I can imagine an object, say a horse, coming into existence from nothing, that in no way proves that a horse really could come into existence that way. The *mutakallim* plausibly claims that it is ontologically impossible for something to come uncaused from nothing. Does anyone really believe that, however vivid his imagination of such an event, a raging tiger, say, could suddenly come into existence uncaused, out of nothing, in the room right now? The same applies to the universe: if there was absolutely nothing prior to the existence of the universe – no God, no space, no time – how could the universe possibly have come to exist?[97]

---

96. Craig (2001, pp. 275–80).

97. Elsewhere, Mackie reveals his true sentiments: "I myself find it hard to accept the notion of self-creation *from nothing*, even *given* unrestricted chance. And how *can* this be given, if there really is nothing?" (Mackie 1982, p. 126). It seems inconceivable that the space-time universe could have come into being without a cause, for in that case there was not even the potentiality of the universe's existence prior to the beginning (since there was no "prior"). But how could the universe become actual if there was not even the potentiality of its existence? It seems more plausible to hold that its potentiality lay in the power of its cause to create it.

In fact, Mackie's appeal to Hume at this point is counterproductive. For Hume himself clearly believed in the Causal Principle. In 1754, he wrote to John Stewart, "But allow me to tell you that I never asserted so absurd a Proposition as *that anything might arise without a cause*: I only maintain'd, that our Certainty of the Falsehood of that Proposition proceeded neither from Intuition nor Demonstration, but from another source" (Grieg 1932, 1: p. 187). Even Mackie confesses, "Still this [causal] principle has some plausibility, in that it is constantly confirmed in our experience (and also used, reasonably, in interpreting our experience)" (Mackie 1982, p. 89). So why not accept the truth of the Causal Principle as plausible and reasonable – at the very least more so than its denial?

Because, Mackie thinks, in this particular case the theism implied by affirming the principle is even more unintelligible than the denial of the principle. It makes more sense to believe that the universe came into being uncaused out of nothing than to believe that God created the universe out of nothing.

But is this really the case? Consider the three problems Mackie raises with *creatio ex nihilo*. Certainly, the *mutakallim* will not hold (i) that God began to exist or (ii) that God has existed for an infinite number of, say, hours, or any other unit of time prior to creation. But what is wrong with (iii), that God is, without creation, timeless? This may be "mysterious" in the sense of "wonderful" or "awe inspiring," but it is not, so far as we can see, unintelligible; and Mackie gives us no reason to think that it is.

Moreover, there is also an alternative that Mackie failed to consider, namely, (iv) prior to creation God existed in an undifferentiated time in which hours, seconds, days, and so forth simply do not exist.[98] Because this time is undifferentiated, it is not incompatible with the *kalam* arguments against an infinite regress of events. This alternative would require us to distinguish between time as it plays a role in physics and time as a metaphysical reality, a distinction famously defended by Isaac Newton on the basis of God's eternal duration independent of any physical measures thereof (Newton 1966, I: p. 6). Even apart from theism, the distinction between time and our physical measures thereof is one that is quite plausible and intuitive, and, given theism, it becomes nearly incumbent, since God could experience a temporal succession of contents of consciousness in the absence of any physical world at all. Mackie, then, is quite unjustified in rejecting the first premise of the argument as not being intuitively obvious, plausible, and reasonable.

So it seems that the Causal Principle enunciated in (1.0) has considerable warrant for us and that putative defeaters of the principle can be undercut or rebutted.

3.0. The Cause of the Universe

From the two premises, it follows logically that the universe has a cause. This is a staggering conclusion, for it implies that the universe was brought into existence by a transcendent reality.

Or does it? As we have seen, Gott and Li have sought to avoid this conclusion by defending the extraordinary hypothesis that *the universe created itself*. Noting that GR allows for the possibility of CTCs, they hypothesize that as we trace the history of the universe back through an original inflationary state, we encounter a region of CTCs prior to inflation (Figure 3.4). According to one possible scenario, a metastable vacuum inflates, producing

---

98. Such a view is defended by Padgett (1992).

an infinite number of (Big Bang type) bubble universes. In many of these a number of bubbles of metastable vacuum are created at late times by high-energy events. These bubbles usually collapse and form black holes, but occasionally one will tunnel to create an expanding, metastable vacuum or baby universe. One of these expanding, metastable vacuum baby universes "turns out to be the original inflating metastable vacuum we began with." Gott and Li conclude that "the laws of physics may allow the universe to be its own mother" (Gott & Li 1998, p. 023501–1).

We have seen that even on the physical level Gott and Li's model is probably not a plausible account of the universe's origin. But the Gott–Li hypothesis raises even more fundamental metaphysical issues about the nature of time which render their hypothesis either metaphysically impossible or else superfluous. For all instances of causal influence over the past which have been suggested – whether we are talking about CTCs, time travel, tachyonic antitelephones, or whatever – presuppose the truth of the B-Theory of time. For on the A-Theory, at the time at which the effect is present, the cause is future and therefore literally nonexistent. Thus, the effect just comes into being from nothing. Not only is this scenario metaphysically absurd, but it also defeats the claim that the universe is self-caused. Rather the universe just came uncaused from nothing.

Thus, the Gott–Li hypothesis presupposes the B-Theory of time. But if one presupposes such a view of time, then Gott and Li's hypothesis becomes superfluous. For, as we have seen, on a B-Theory of time the universe never truly comes into being at all.[99] The whole four-dimensional space-time manifold just exists tenselessly, and the universe has a beginning only in the sense that a meter stick has a beginning prior to the first centimeter. Although the space-time manifold is intrinsically temporal in that one of its four dimensions is time, nonetheless it is extrinsically timeless, in that it does not exist in an embedding hypertime but exists tenselessly, neither coming into nor going out of being. The four-dimensional space-time manifold is in this latter sense eternal. Thus, there is no need for the device of causal loops or CTCs at the beginning to explain how it came into being.

Given the truth of the A-Theory of time, the idea that the universe is self-created, that is to say, that it brought itself into being via CTCs, is metaphysically impossible because it reduces to the notion that the universe sprang into existence uncaused out of nothing. The universe, then, must have an ultramundane cause.

Properties of the First Cause

Conceptual analysis of what it is to be a cause of the universe enables us to recover a number of striking properties which this ultramundane cause must possess and which are of theological significance. For example, the cause must be uncaused, since, as we have seen, an

---

99. This is the salient point of Grünbaum's most recent salvo against the inference to a First Cause of the origin of the universe (Grünbaum 2000). As a B-Theorist, Grünbaum does not believe that the universe ever came into being, even if it had a first temporal interval. As he elsewhere writes, "coming *into* being (or 'becoming') is *not* a property of *physical* events themselves but only of human or conscious awareness of these events" (Grünbaum 1967, p. 153). What Grünbaum fails to see, however, is that the claim that an absolute beginning of the universe entails that the universe came into being is rooted, not in the presupposition of the so-called Spontaneity of Nothingness, but in an A-Theory of time.

infinite regress of causes is impossible. One could, of course, arbitrarily posit a plurality of causes in some sense prior to the origin of the universe, but ultimately, if the philosophical *kalam* arguments are sound, this causal chain must terminate in a cause which is absolutely first and uncaused. There being no reason to perpetuate the series of events beyond the origin of the universe, Ockham's Razor, which enjoins us not to posit causes beyond necessity, strikes such further causes in favor of an immediate First Cause of the origin of the universe. The same principle dictates that we are warranted in ignoring the possibility of a plurality of uncaused causes in favor of assuming the unicity of the First Cause.

This First Cause must also be beginningless, since by contraposition of Premise (1.0), whatever is uncaused does not begin to exist. Moreover, this cause must be changeless, since, once more, an infinite temporal regress of changes cannot exist. We should not be warranted, however, in inferring the immutability of the First Cause, since immutability is a modal property, and from the Cause's changelessness we cannot infer that it is incapable of change. But we can know that the First Cause is changeless, at least insofar as it exists sans the universe. From the changelessness of the First Cause, its immateriality follows. For whatever is material involves incessant change on at least the molecular and atomic levels, but the uncaused First Cause exists in a state of absolute changelessness. Given some relational theory of time, the Uncaused Cause must therefore also be timeless, at least sans the universe, since in the utter absence of events time would not exist. It is true that some philosophers have argued persuasively that time could continue to exist even if all events were to cease (Shoemaker 1969; Forbes 1993), but such arguments are inapplicable in the case at hand, where we are envisioning, not the cessation of events, but the utter absence of any events whatsoever. In any case, the timelessness of the First Cause sans the universe can be more directly inferred from the finitude of the past. Given that time had a beginning, the cause of the beginning of time must be timeless.[100] It follows that this Cause must also be spaceless, since it is both immaterial and timeless, and no spatial entity can be both immaterial and timeless. If an entity is immaterial, it could exist in space only in virtue of being related to material things in space; but then it could not be timeless, since it undergoes extrinsic change in its relations to material things. Hence, the uncaused First Cause must transcend both time and space and be the cause of their origination. Such a being must be, moreover, enormously powerful, since it brought the entirety of physical reality, including all matter and energy and space-time itself, into being without any material cause.

Finally, and most remarkably, such a transcendent cause is plausibly taken to be personal. Three reasons can be given for this conclusion. First, as Richard Swinburne (1991, pp. 32–48) points out, there are two types of causal explanation: scientific explanations in terms of laws and initial conditions and personal explanations in terms of agents and their volitions. For example, in answer to the question, "Why is the kettle boiling?" we might be told, "The heat of the flame is being conducted via the copper bottom of the kettle to the water, increasing the kinetic energy of the water molecules, such that they vibrate so violently that they break the surface tension of the water and are thrown off in the form of steam." Or alternatively, we might be told, "I put it on to make a cup of tea. Would you like some?" The first provides a scientific explanation, the second a personal explanation. Each

---

100. This needs some qualification, since the *kalam* argument strictly demonstrates only that metric time had a beginning. Perhaps the cause exists changelessly in an undifferentiated time in which temporal intervals cannot be distinguished. On this view, God existed literally before creation, but there was no moment, say, 1 hour or 1 million years before creation.

is a perfectly legitimate form of explanation; indeed, in certain contexts it would be wholly inappropriate to give one rather than the other. Now a first state of the universe *cannot* have a scientific explanation, since there is nothing before it, and therefore, it cannot be accounted for in terms of laws operating on initial conditions. It can only be accounted for in terms of an agent and his volitions, a personal explanation.

Second, the personhood of the First Cause is already powerfully suggested by the properties which have been deduced by means of our conceptual analysis. For there appear to be only two candidates which can be described as immaterial, beginningless, uncaused, timeless, and spaceless beings: either abstract objects or an unembodied mind. Abstract objects such as numbers, sets, propositions, and properties are very typically construed by philosophers who include such things in their ontology as being precisely the sort of entities which exist necessarily, timelessly, and spacelessly. Similarly, philosophers who hold to the possibility of disembodied mind would describe such mental substances as immaterial and spaceless, and there seems no reason to think that a Cosmic Mind might not also be beginningless and uncaused. No other candidates which could be suitably described as immaterial, beginningless, uncaused, timeless, and spaceless beings come to mind. Nor has anyone else, to our knowledge, suggested any other such candidates. But no sort of abstract object can be the cause of the origin of the universe, for abstract objects are not involved in causal relations. Even if they were, since they are not agents, they cannot volitionally exercise a causal power to do anything. If they were causes, they would be so, not as agents, but as mindless events or states. But they cannot be event-causes, since they do not exist in time and space. Even if we allow that some abstract objects exist in time (e.g. propositions which change their truth-value in virtue of the tense of the sentences which express them), still, in view of their abstract nature, it remains utterly mysterious how they could be causally related to concrete objects so as to bring about events, including the origin of the universe. Nor can they be state-causes of states involving concrete objects, for the same reason, not to mention the fact that in the case at hand we are not talking about state-state causation (i.e. the causal dependence of one state on another), but what would amount to state-event causation (namely, the universe's coming into being because of the state of some abstract object(s)), which seems impossible. Thus, the cause of the universe must be an unembodied mind.

Third, this same conclusion is also implied by the fact that only personal, free agency can account for the origin of a first temporal effect from a changeless cause. We have concluded that the beginning of the universe was the effect of a First Cause. By the nature of the case, that cause cannot have any beginning of its existence nor any prior cause. Nor can there have been any changes in this cause, either in its nature or operations, prior to the beginning of the universe. It just exists changelessly without beginning, and a finite time ago it brought the universe into existence. Now this is exceedingly odd. The cause is in some sense eternal, and yet the effect which it produced is not eternal but began to exist a finite time ago. How can this be? If the necessary and sufficient conditions for the production of the effect are eternal, then why is not the effect eternal? How can all the causal conditions sufficient for the production of the effect be changelessly existent and yet the effect not also be existent along with the cause? How can the cause exist without the effect?

One might say that the cause came to exist or changed in some way just prior to the first event. But then the cause's beginning or changing would be the first event, and we must ask all over again for its cause. And this cannot go on forever, for we know that a beginningless series of events cannot exist. There must be an absolutely first event, before which there was no change, no previous event. We know that this first event must have been caused. The question is: How can a first event come to exist if the cause of that event exists changelessly and eternally? Why is the effect not coeternal with its cause?

The best way out of this dilemma is agent causation, whereby the agent freely brings about some event in the absence of prior determining conditions. Because the agent is free, he can initiate new effects by freely bringing about conditions which were not previously present. For example, a man sitting changelessly from eternity could freely will to stand up; thus, a temporal effect arises from an eternally existing agent. Similarly, a finite time ago a Creator endowed with free will could have freely brought the world into being at that moment. In this way, the Creator could exist changelessly and eternally but choose to create the world in time. By "choose" one need not mean that the Creator changes his mind about the decision to create but that he freely and eternally intends to create a world with a beginning. By exercising his causal power, he therefore brings it about that a world with a beginning comes to exist.[101] So the cause is eternal, but the effect is not. In this way, then, it is possible for the temporal universe to have come to exist from an eternal cause: through the free will of a personal Creator.

A conceptual analysis of what properties must be possessed by an ultramundane First Cause thus enables us to recover a striking number of the traditional divine attributes. An analysis of what it is to be cause of the universe reveals that:

4.0.   If the universe has a cause, then an uncaused, personal Creator of the universe exists, who sans the universe is beginningless, changeless, immaterial, timeless, spaceless, and enormously powerful.

From (3.0) and (4.0), it follows that:

5.0.   Therefore, an uncaused, personal Creator of the universe exists, who sans the universe is beginningless, changeless, immaterial, timeless, spaceless, and enormously powerful.

This, as Thomas Aquinas was wont to remark, is what everybody means by "God."

---

101. Such an exercise of causal power plausibly brings God into time, if He was not temporal already. As Moreland explains, in the case of personal causal explanations, the salient factors are the existence of an agent with his relevant properties and powers, the agent's intention to bring about some result, an exercise of the agent's causal powers, and in some cases a description of the relevant action plan. So "a personal explanation (divine or otherwise) of some basic result R brought about intentionally by person P where this bringing about of R is a basic action A will cite the intention I of P that R occur and the basic power B that P exercised to bring about R" (Moreland 1998b, p. 75; see further Moreland 1998a). Notice that it is insufficient for P to have merely the intention and power to bring about R. There must also be a basic action on the part of P, an undertaking or endeavoring or exercise of P's causal powers. Thus, it is insufficient to account for the origin of the universe by citing simply God, His timeless intention to create a world with a beginning, and His power to produce such a result. There must be an exercise of His causal power in order for the universe to be created. That entails, of course, an intrinsic change on God's part which brings Him into time at the moment of creation. For that reason He must be temporal since creation, even if He is timeless sans creation.

We should not say that in agent causation the agent causes his causing of some effect. Partisans of agent causation typically say that the agent's causing some effect is not an event requiring a cause, either because it is not itself an event, but just a way of describing an agent's causing an event, or if it is an event, then it is not further caused (O'Connor 2000, chap. 3). Neither alternative requires revision of Premise (1.0), which concerns, not events, but substances which come into being.

Objections

Certain thinkers have objected to the intelligibility of this conclusion. For example, Adolf Grünbaum has marshaled a whole troop of objections against inferring God as the Creator of the universe (Grünbaum 1990b). As these are very typical, a brief review of his objections should be quite helpful.

Grünbaum's objections fall into three groups. Group I seeks to cast doubt upon the concept of "cause" in the argument: (1) When we say that everything has a cause, we use the word "cause" to mean something that transforms previously existing materials from one state to another. But when we infer that the universe has a cause, we must mean by "cause" something that creates its effect out of nothing. Since these two meanings of "cause" are not the same, the argument is guilty of equivocation and is thus invalid. (2) It does not follow from the necessity of there being a cause that the cause of the universe is a conscious agent. (3) It is logically fallacious to infer that there is a *single* conscious agent who created the universe.

But these objections do not seem to present any insuperable difficulties: (1) The univocal concept of "cause" employed throughout the argument is the concept of something which brings about or produces its effects.[102] Whether this production involves transformation of already existing materials or creation out of nothing is an incidental question. Thus, the charge of equivocation is groundless. (2) The personhood of the cause does not follow from the two premises of the cosmological argument proper, but rather from a conceptual analysis of the notion of a First Cause of the beginning of the universe, as we have seen. (3) The inference to a single cause of the origin of the universe seems justified in light of the principle, commonly accepted in science, that one should not multiply causes beyond necessity. One is justified in inferring only causes such as are necessary to explain the effect in question; positing any more would be gratuitous.

The objections of Group II relate the notion of causality to the temporal series of events: (1) Causality is logically compatible with an infinite, beginningless series of events. (2) If everything has a cause of its existence, then the cause of the universe must also have a cause of its existence.

Both of these objections, however, seem to be based on misunderstandings. (1) It is not the concept of causality which is incompatible with an infinite series of past events. Rather the incompatibility, as we have seen, is between the notion of an actually infinite number of things and the series of past events. The fact that causality has nothing to do with it may be seen by reflecting on the fact that the philosophical arguments for the beginning of the universe would work even if the events were all spontaneous, causally unconnected events. (2) The argument does not presuppose that everything has a cause. Rather the operative Causal Principle is that *whatever begins to exist has a cause*. Something that exists eternally and, hence, without a beginning would not need to have a cause. This is not special pleading for God, since the atheist has always maintained the same thing about the universe: it is beginningless and uncaused.

Group III objections are aimed at the alleged claim that creation from nothing surpasses all understanding: (1) If creation out of nothing is incomprehensible, then it is irrational to believe in such a doctrine. (2) An incomprehensible doctrine cannot explain anything.

---

102. That is to say, an efficient cause. Alternatively, we could leave the question of material causation open by taking "cause" to mean either an efficient or a material cause. Then our conceptual analysis of what it is to be a cause of the universe will eliminate the alternative that the cause is a material cause, leaving us with an ultra-mundane efficient cause.

But with regard to (1), creation from nothing is not incomprehensible in Grünbaum's sense. By "incomprehensible," Grünbaum appears to mean "unintelligible" or "meaningless." But the statement that a finite time ago a transcendent cause brought the universe into being out of nothing is clearly a meaningful statement, not mere gibberish, as is evident from the very fact that we are debating it. We may not understand *how* the cause brought the universe into being out of nothing, but such efficient causation without material causation is not unprecedented, as we have seen, and it is even more incomprehensible, in this sense, how the universe could have popped into being out of nothing without *any* cause, material or efficient. One cannot avert the necessity of a cause by positing an absurdity. (2) The doctrine, being an intelligible statement, obviously does constitute a purported explanation of the origin of the universe. It may be a metaphysical rather than a scientific explanation, but it is no less an explanation for that.

Grünbaum has one final objection against inferring a cause of the origin of the universe: the cause of the Big Bang can be neither *after* the Big Bang (since backward causation is impossible) nor *before* the Big Bang (since time begins at or after the Big Bang). Therefore, the universe's beginning to exist cannot have a cause (Grünbaum 1990a, 1991; cf. Craig 1994a). But this argument pretty clearly confronts us with a false dilemma. For why could not God's creating the universe be *simultaneous* (or coincident) with the Big Bang? God may be conceived to exist timelessly (or in an undifferentiated time) without the universe and in time from the moment of creation. Perhaps an analogy from physical cosmology will be illuminating. The initial Big Bang singularity is not considered to be part of physical time, but to constitute a boundary to time. Nevertheless, it is causally connected to the universe. In an analogous way, we could say that God's timeless eternity is, as it were, a boundary of time which is causally, but not temporally, prior to the origin of the universe. It seems, therefore, that it is not only coherent but also plausible in light of the *kalam* cosmological argument that God existing changelessly alone without creation is timeless and that He enters time at the moment of creation in virtue of His causal relation to the temporal universe. The time of the first event would be not only the first time at which the universe exists but also, technically, the first time at which God exists, since sans the universe God exists timelessly.[103] The moment of creation is, as it were, the moment at which God enters time. His act of creation is thus simultaneous with the origination of the universe.

Conclusion

The first premise of the *kalam* cosmological argument is obviously more plausibly true than its contradictory. Similarly, in light of both philosophical argument and scientific evidence, its second premise, although more controversial, is again more plausibly true than its negation. The conclusion of the argument involves no demonstrable incoherence and, when subjected to conceptual analysis, is rich in theological implications. On the basis of the *kalam* cosmological argument, it is therefore plausible that an uncaused, personal Creator of the universe exists, who sans the universe is beginningless, changeless, immaterial, timeless, spaceless, and enormously powerful.

---

103. Leftow (1991, p. 269, cf. p. 201) captures this idea nicely. Senor has dubbed such a model of divine eternity "accidental temporalism" (Senor 1993, p. 88). See further Craig (2001, pp. 256–80).

References

Aguirre, A. and Gratton, S. (2002) Steady state eternal inflation. *Physical Review D* 65, 083507, preprint http://arxiv.org/abs/astro-ph/0111191 (accessed July 11, 2008).

Al-Ghazali (1962) *Kitab al-Iqtisad fi'l-Iqtiqad.* Ankara, Turkey: University of Ankara Press.

Al-Ghazali (1963) *Tahafut al-Falasifah.* Trans. S. A. Kamali. Lahore: Pakistan Philosophical Congress.

Al-Idji (1971) *Mawakif.* Cited in *Encyclopaedia of Islam,* s.v. "Ilm al-Kalam" (by L. Gardet).

Ashtekar, A., Pawlowski, T., and Singh, P. (2006) Quantum nature of the Big Bang. *Physical Review D* 74, 084003, preprint: http://arxiv.org/abs/gr-qc/0602086v2.

Balaguer, M. (1998) *Platonism and Anti-Platonism in Mathematics.* New York: Oxford University Press.

Balaguer, M. (2001) A theory of mathematical correctness and mathematical truth. *Pacific Philosophical Quarterly* 82, 87–114.

Banks, T. and Fischler, W. (2002) Black crunch. http://arxiv.org/abs/hep-th/0212113v1 (accessed July 11, 2008).

Barrow, J. and Dabrowski, M. (1995) Oscillating universes. *Monthly Notices of the Royal Astronomical Society* 275, 850–62.

Barrow, J. D. (2005) *The Infinite Book.* New York: Pantheon Books.

Barrow, J. D. and Tipler, F. (1986) *The Anthropic Cosmological Principle.* Oxford: Clarendon Press.

Baum, L. and Frampton, P. H. (2006) Deflation at turnaround for oscillatory cosmology. http://arxiv.org/abs/astro-ph/0608138 (accessed July 11, 2008).

Baum, L. and Frampton, P. H. (2007) Turnaround in cyclic cosmology. *Physical Review Letters* 98, 071301, p. 1, preprint: http://arxiv.org/abs/hep-th/0610213.

Belinsky, V. A., Khalatnikov, I. M., and Lifshitz, E. M. (1970) Oscillatory approach to a singular point in the relativistic cosmology. *Advances in Physics* 19, 525–73.

Benardete, J. A. (1964) *Infinity: An Essay in Metaphysics.* Oxford: Clarendon Press.

Bojowald, M. (2005) Original questions. *Nature* 436, 920–1.

Bojowald, M., Date, G., and Hossain, G. M. (2004) The Bianchi IX model in loop quantum cosmology. *Classical and Quantum Gravity* 21, 3541, preprint: http://arxiv.org/abs/gr-qc/0404039.

Bolzano, B. (1950) *Paradoxes of the Infinite.* Trans. Fr. Prihonsky. London: Routledge & Kegan Paul.

Boolos, G. (1986–7) Saving Frege from contradiction. *Proceedings of the Aristotelian Society* 87, 137–51.

Borde, A., Guth, A., and Vilenkin, A. (2003) Inflationary spacetimes are not past-complete. *Physical Review Letters* 90, 151301, preprint: http://arxiv.org/abs/gr-qc/0110012.

Bousso, R. and Freivogel, B. (2007) A paradox in the global description of the multiverse. *Journal of High Energy Physics* 6, preprint: http://arxiv.org/PS_cache/hep-th/pdf/0610/0610132v2.pdf.

Cantor, G. (1915) *Contributions to the Founding of the Theory of Transfinite Numbers.* Trans. and Intro. P. E. B. Jourdain. New York: Dover.

Chihara, C. S. (1990). *Constructibility and Mathematical Existence.* Oxford: Clarendon Press.

Chihara, C. S. (2004) *A Structural Account of Mathematics.* Oxford: Clarendon Press.

Chihara, C. S. (2005) Nominalism. In S. Shapiro (ed.), *The Oxford Handbook of Philosophy of Mathematics and Logic,* 483–514. Oxford: Oxford University Press.

Conway, D. A. (1984) "It would have happened already": on one argument for a first cause. *Analysis* 44, 159–66.

Coule, D. H. (2005) Quantum cosmological models. *Classical and Quantum Gravity* 22, R125–2308, p. 31, preprint: http://arxiv.org/abs/gr-qc/0412026v3.

Craig, W. L. (1979) *The Kalam Cosmological Argument.* London: Macmillan.

Craig, W. L. (1980) *The Cosmological Argument from Plato to Leibniz.* London: Macmillan & Co.

Craig, W. L. (1985) Critical notice of *Time, Creation and the Continuum,* by Richard Sorabji. *International Philosophical Quarterly* 25, 319–26.

Craig, W. L. (1991) The *Kalam* Cosmological argument and the hypothesis of a quiescent universe. *Faith and Philosophy* 8, 104–8.

Craig, W. L. (1992) The origin and creation of the universe: a reply to Adolf Grünbaum. *British Journal for the Philosophy of Science* 43, 233–40.

Craig, W. L. (1994a) Prof. Grünbaum on creation. *Erkenntnis* 40, 325–41.

Craig, W. L. (1994b) A response to Grünbaum on creation and Big Bang cosmology. *Philosophia Naturalis* 31, 237–49.

Craig, W. L. (1998) Design and the cosmological argument. In W. Dembski (ed.), *Mere Creation*, 332–59. Downers Grove, Ill.: Inter-Varsity.

Craig, W. L. (2000a) *The Tensed Theory of Time: A Critical Examination.* Synthese Library 293. Dordrecht, the Netherlands: Kluwer Academic Publishers.

Craig, W. L. (2000b) *The Tenseless Theory of Time: A Critical Examination.* Synthese Library 294. Dordrecht, the Netherlands: Kluwer Academic Publishers.

Craig, W. L. (2000c) The extent of the present. *International Studies in the Philosophy of Science* 14, 165–85.

Craig, W. L. (2001) *God, Time and Eternity.* Dordrecht, the Netherlands: Kluwer Academic Publishers.

Craig, W. L. (2008) Critical notice of *Philosophical Perspectives on Infinity*, by G. Oppy. *Philosophia Christi* 10, 435–52.

Craig, W. L. and Moreland, J. P. (2003) *Philosophical Foundations of a Christian Worldview.* Downer's Grove, Ill.: Inter-Varsity Press.

Craig, W. L. and Sinnott-Armstrong, W. (2003) *God?: A Debate between a Christian and an Atheist.* Oxford: Oxford University Press.

Craig, W. L., and Smith, Q. (1993) *Theism, Atheism, and Big Bang Cosmology.* Oxford: Clarendon Press.

Dales, R. C. (1990) *Medieval Discussions of the Eternity of the World.* Brill's Studies in Intellectual History 18. Leiden, the Netherlands: E. J. Brill.

Damour, T. and Henneaux, M. (2000) Chaos in superstring cosmology. *Physical Review Letters* 85, 920–3, preprint: http://aps.arxiv.org/abs/hep-th/0003139.

Davidson, H. A. (1987) *Proofs for Eternity, Creation, and the Existence of God in Medieval Islamic and Jewish Philosophy.* New York: Oxford University Press.

Davies, P. (1978) Spacetime singularities in cosmology. In J. T. Fraser (ed.), *The Study of Time III*, 78–9. Berlin: Springer Verlag.

Davies, P. (1983) *God and the New Physics.* New York: Simon & Schuster.

Dedekind, R. (1963) The nature and meaning of numbers. In Richard Dedekind (ed.), W. W. Beman (trans.), *Essays on the Theory of Numbers*, 29–115. New York: Dover.

Dretske, F. (1965) Counting to infinity. *Analysis* 25, 99–101.

Earman, J. and Mosterin, J. (1999) A critical look at inflationary cosmology. *Philosophy of Science* 66, 1–49.

Eddington, A. S. (1948) *The Nature of the Physical World.* New York: Macmillan.

Einstein, A. (1917) Cosmological considerations on the general theory of relativity. With notes by A. Sommerfeld, translated by W. Perrett and J. B. Jefferey, *The Principle of Relativity*, 177–88. Reprint, New York: Dover Publications, 1952.

Ellis, G. F. R. and Maartens, R. (2004) The emergent universe: inflationary cosmology with no singularity. *Classical and Quantum Gravity* 21, 223, preprint: http://arxiv.org/abs/gr-qc/0211082.

Ellis, G. F. R., Kirchner, U., and Stoeger, W. R. (2003) Multiverses and physical cosmology. http://arXiv.org/abs/astro-ph/0305292 (accessed July 11, 2008).

Ellis, G. F. R., Murugan, J., and Tsagas, C. G. (2004) The emergent universe: an explicit construction. *Classical and Quantum Gravity* 27, 233, preprint: http://arxiv.org/abs/gr-qc/0307112.

Feynman, R. (1985) *QED, The Strange Theory of Light and Matter.* Princeton, NJ: Princeton University Press.

Forbes, G. (1993) Time, events, and modality. In R. Le Poidevin and M. MacBeath (eds.), *The Philosophy of Time*, 80–95. Oxford: Oxford University Press.

Fraenkel, A. A. (1961) *Abstract Set Theory.* Studies in Logic and the Foundations of Mathematics. 2nd rev. edn. Amsterdam, the Netherlands: North-Holland.

Frampton, P. (2007a) Cyclic universe and infinite past, preprint http://arxiv.org/abs/0705.2730 (accessed July 11, 2008).

Frampton, P. (2007b) Comment on "Can black holes be torn up by a phantom in cyclic cosmology?" by X. Zhang, preprint http://arxiv.org/abs/0709.1630 (accessed July 11, 2008).

Frampton, P. H. and Takahashi, T. (2003) The fate of dark energy. *Physical Letters B* 557, 135, preprint: http://arxiv.org/abs/astro-ph/0211544.

Frampton, P. H. and Takahashi, T. (2004) Bigger rip with no dark energy. *Astropart. Phys.* 22, 307, preprint: http://arxiv.org/abs/astro-ph/0405333.

Friedmann, A. (1922) Über die Krümmung des Raumes. *Zeitschrift für Physik* 10, 377–86.

Gale, R. (2007) The failure of classic theistic arguments. In M. Martin (ed.), *The Cambridge Companion to Atheism*, Cambridge Companions to Philosophy, 86–101. Cambridge: Cambridge University Press.

Gamow, G. (1946) *One, Two, Three, Infinity*. London: Macmillan.

Gott, J. R. III, Gunn, J. E., Schramm, D. N., and Tinsley, B. M. (1976) Will the universe expand forever? *Scientific American*, March, 65.

Gott, J. R. III and Li, L.-X. (1998) Can the universe create itself? *Physical Review D* 58: 2, 023501–1.

Greene, B. (2004) *The Fabric of the Cosmos*. New York: Alfred A. Knopf.

Grieg, J. (ed.) (1932) *The Letters of David Hume*, 2 vols. Oxford: Clarendon Press.

Grünbaum, A. (1950–1) Relativity and the atomicity of becoming. *Review of Metaphysics* 4, 143–86.

Grünbaum, A. (1967) The anisotropy of time. In T. Gold (ed.), *The Nature of Time*, 49–186. Ithaca, NY: Cornell University Press.

Grünbaum, A. (1973) *Philosophical Problems of Space and Time*, 2nd ed. Boston Studies for the Philosophy of Science 12. Dordrecht, the Netherlands: D. Reidel.

Grünbaum, A. (1990a) Pseudo-creation of the Big Bang. *Nature* 344, 821–2.

Grünbaum, A. (1990b) The pseudo-problem of creation in physical cosmology. In J. Leslie (ed.), *Physical Cosmology and Philosophy*, Philosophical Topics, 92–112. New York: Macmillan.

Grünbaum, A. (1991) Creation as a pseudo-explanation in current physical cosmology. *Erkenntnis* 35, 233–54.

Grünbaum, A. (2000) A new critique of theological interpretations of physical cosmology. *British Journal for the Philosophy of Science* 51, 1–43.

Guth, A. H. (1981) Inflationary universe: a possible solution to the horizon and flatness problems. *Physical Review D* 23: 2, 347–56.

Hackett, S. (1957) *The Resurrection of Theism*. Chicago: Moody Press.

Hawking, S. (1988) *A Brief History of Time*. New York: Bantam Books.

Hawking, S. (1992) The chronology protection conjecture. *Physical Review D* 46, 603–11.

Hawking, S. and Hartle, J. (1983) The wave function of the universe. *Physical Review D* 28: 12, 2960–75.

Hawking, S. and Penrose, R. (1970) The singularities of gravitational collapse and cosmology. *Proceedings of the Royal Society of London A* 314, 529–48.

Hawking, S. and Penrose, R. (1996) *The Nature of Space and Time*. Princeton, NJ: Princeton University Press.

Hawthorne, J. (2000) Before-effect and Zeno causality. *Noûs* 34, 622–33.

Hazen, A. (1993) Slicing it thin. *Analysis* 53, 189–92.

Hellman, G. (1989) *Mathematics without Numbers: Towards a Modal-Structural Interpretation*. Oxford: Oxford University Press.

Hellman, G. (2001) Three varieties of mathematical structuralism. *Philosophia Mathermatica* 3, 129–57.

Hellman, G. (2005) Structuralism. In S. Shapiro (ed.), *The Oxford Handbook of Philosophy of Mathematics and Logic*, 536–62. Oxford: Oxford University Press.

Hilbert, D. (1964) On the infinite. In P. Benacerraf and H. Putnam (eds.), *Philosophy of Mathematics*, 183–201. Englewood Cliffs, N J: Prentice-Hall.

Hiscock, W. A. (2000) Quantized fields and chronology protection, preprint: http://arxiv.org/abs/gr-qc/0009061v2 (accessed July 11, 2008).

Hubble, E. (1929) A relation between distance and radial velocity among extra-galactic nebulae. *Proceedings of the National Academy of Sciences* 15, 168–73.

Hume, D. (1978) *A Treatise of Human Nature*, 2nd edn. Edited and with notes by P. H. Nidditch. Oxford: Clarendon Press.

Kanitscheider, B. (1990) Does physical cosmology transcend the limits of naturalistic reasoning? In P. Weingartner and G. Doen (eds.), *Studies on Marco Bunge's "Treatise,"* 337–50. Amsterdam: Rodopi.

Kasner, E. and Newman, J. (1940) *Mathematics and the Imagination*. New York: Simon & Schuster.

Leftow, B. (1991) *Time and Eternity*. Cornell Studies in Philosophy of Religion. Ithaca, NY: Cornell University Press.

Lemaître, G. (1927) Un univers homogène de masse constante et de rayon croissant, rendant compte de la vitesse radiale des nébuleuses extragalactiques. *Annales de la Société scientifique de Bruxelles* 47, 49–59.

Linde, A. (1998) The self-reproducing inflationary universe. *Scientific American*, May, 103.

Linde, A. (2005) Inflation and string cosmology. *Journal of Physics: Conference Series 24* 151–60, preprint: http://arxiv.org/PS_cache/hep-th/pdf/0503/0503195v1.pdf.

Mackie, J. L. (1982) *The Miracle of Theism*. Oxford: Clarendon Press.

Moore, A. W. (1990) *The Infinite*. London: Routledge.

Moreland, J. P. (1998a) Libertarian agency and the Craig/Grünbaum debate about theistic explanation of the initial singularity. *American Catholic Philosophical Quarterly* 71, 539–54.

Moreland, J. P. (1998b) Searle's biological naturalism and the argument from consciousness. *Faith and Philosophy* 15, 68–91.

Morriston, W. (2002) Craig on the actual infinite. *Religious Studies* 38, 147–66.

Naber, G. L. (1988) *Spacetime and Singularities: An Introduction*. Cambridge: Cambridge University Press.

Nesvizhevsky, V., Börner, H. G., Petukhorv, A. K., et al. (2001) Quantum states of neutrons in the Earth's gravitational field. *Nature* 415, 297–99.

Newton, I. (1966) *Sir Isaac Newton's "Mathematical Principles of Natural Philosophy" and his "System of the World."* 2 vols. Trans. A. Motte. Rev. Florian Cajori. Los Angeles: University of California Press.

O'Connor, T. (2000) *Persons and Causes: The Metaphysics of Free Will*. Oxford: Oxford University Press.

Oppy, G. (2006a) *Philosophical Perspectives on Infinity*. Cambridge: Cambridge University Press.

Oppy, G. (2006b) *Arguing about Gods*. Cambridge: Cambridge University Press.

Overbye, D. (2006) 9 billion-year-old "dark energy" reported. *The New York Times*, January 15, 2008.

Padgett, A. (1992) *God, Eternity, and the Nature of Time*. New York: St. Martin's.

Pagels, H. (1985) *Perfect Symmetry: The Search for the Beginning of Time*. New York: Simon & Schuster.

Penrose, R. (2005) *The Road to Reality*. New York: Alfred A. Knopf.

Philoponus, J. (1987) *Against Aristotle, on the Eternity of the World*. Trans. C. Wildberg. London: Duckworth.

Philoponus, J. and Simplicius (1991) *Place, Void, and Eternity*. Trans. D. Furley and C. Wildberg. Ithaca, NY: Cornell University Press.

Routledge Encyclopedia of Philosophy (1998) s.v. "God, Arguments for the Existence of," (by A. Plantinga).

Rucker, R. v. B. (1980) The actual infinite. *Speculations in Science and Technology* 3, 63–76.

Russell, B. (1937) *The Principles of Mathematics*, 2nd edn. London: George Allen & Unwin.

Senor, T. D. (1993) Divine temporality and creation *ex nihilo*. *Faith and Philosophy* 10, 86–92.

Shoemaker, S. (1969) Time without change. *Journal of Philosophy*. 66, 363–81.

Small, R. (1986) Tristram Shandy's last page. *British Journal for the Philosophy of Science* 37, 213–6.

Smith, Q. (2007) Kalam cosmological arguments for atheism. In M. Martin (ed.), *The Cambridge Companion to Atheism*, Cambridge Companions to Philosophy, 182–98. Cambridge: Cambridge University Press.

Sobel, J. H. (2004) *Logic and Theism: Arguments for and against Beliefs in God*. Cambridge: Cambridge University Press.

Sobel, J. H. (2007) Online revisions of chapter V of *Logic and Theism*. http://www.scar.utoronto.ca/~sobel/OnL_T/ (accessed March 7, 2008).

Sorabji, R. (1983) *Time, Creation and the Continuum*. Ithaca, NY: Cornell University Press.

Stanford Encyclopedia of Philosophy (2004a) s.v. "Cosmological Argument" (by B. Reichenbach).

Stanford Encyclopedia of Philosophy (2004b) s.v. "Platonism in Metaphysics" (by M. Balaguer), http://plato.stanford.edu/archives/sum2004/entries/platonism/ (accessed March 7, 2008).

Steinhardt, P. and Turok, N. (2005) The cyclic model simplified. *New Astronomy Reviews* 49, 43–57, preprint: http://arxiv.org/abs/astro-ph/0404480.

Swinburne, R. (1991) *The Existence of God*, rev. edn. Oxford: Clarendon Press.

Thorne, K. (1994) *Black Holes and Time Warps*. New York: W.W. Norton & Co.

Vaas, R. (2004) Time before time: classifications of universes in contemporary cosmology, and how to avoid the antinomy of the beginning and eternity of the world. In W. Löffler and P. Weingartner (eds.), *Knowledge and Belief. Papers of the 26th International Wittgenstein Symposium*, 351–3. Kirchberg am Wechsel: Austrian Ludwig Wittgenstein Society, preprint: http://arXiv.org/abs/physics/0408111.

Veneziano, G. (1998) A simple/short introduction to pre-big-bang physics/cosmology, preprint: http://arxiv.org/abs/hep-th/9802057 (accessed July 11, 2008).

Veneziano, G. (2004) The myth of the beginning of time. *Scientific American*, May, 63.

Veneziano G. and Gasperini, M. (2002) The pre big bang scenario in string cosmology. *Physics Reports* 373, 1, preprint: http://arxiv.org/abs/hep-th/0207130.

Vilenkin, A. (1982) Creation of universes from nothing. *Physics Letters B* 117, 25–28.

Vilenkin, A. (1994) Approaches to quantum cosmology. *Physical Review D* 50, 2581–94, preprint: http://lanl.arxiv.org/abs/gr-qc/9403010v1.

Vilenkin, A. (2002) Quantum cosmology and eternal inflation. *The Future of Theoretical Physics and Cosmology*, Proceedings of the Conference in Honor of Stephen Hawking's 60th birthday, preprint: http://arxiv.org/abs/gr-qc/0204061 (accessed July 11, 2008).

Vilenkin, A. (2006) *Many Worlds in One*. New York: Hill & Wang.

Wald, R. M. (1984) *General Relativity*. Chicago, Ill.: The University of Chicago Press.

Walton, K. L. (1990) *Mimesis as Make–Believe*. Cambridge, Mass.: Harvard University Press.

Wheeler, J. A. (1980) Beyond the hole. In H. Woolf (ed.), *Some Strangeness in the Proportion*, 354–75. Reading, Mass.: Addison-Wesley.

Whitrow, G. J. (1980) *The Natural Philosophy of Time*, 2nd edn. Oxford: Clarendon Press.

Wittgenstein, L. (1976) *Lectures on the Foundations of Mathematics*. Ed. C. Diamond. Sussex, England: Harvester.

Wolfson, H. A. (1966) Patristic arguments against the eternity of the world. *Harvard Theological Review* 59, 354–67.

Wolfson, H. A. (1976) *The Philosophy of the Kalam*. Cambridge, Mass.: Harvard University Press.

Yablo, S. (2000) A paradox of existence. In A. Everett and T. Hofweber (eds.), *Empty Names, Fiction, and the Puzzles of Non-Existence*, 275–312. Stanford, Cal.: Center for Study of Language and Information.

Yablo, S. (2001) Go figure: a path through fictionalism. In P. A. French and H. K. Wettstein (eds.), *Figurative Language*, Midwest Studies in Philosophy 25, 72–102. Oxford: Blackwell.

Yablo, S. (2005) The myth of the seven. In M. E. Kalderon (ed.), *Fictionalism in Metaphysics*, 88–115. Oxford: Clarendon Press.

Yandell, D. (2003) Infinity and explanation, damnation and empiricism. In S. Wallace (ed.), *The Existence of God*, 131–40. Aldershot, Hampshire: Ashgate.

Zhang, J., Zhang, X., and Liu, H. (2007) Holographic dark energy in a cyclic universe. *European Physical Journal C* 52, 693–9, preprint: http://arxiv.org/PS_cache/arxiv/pdf/0708/0708.3121v2.pdf.

Zhang, X. (2007a) Can black holes be torn up by phantom in cyclic cosmology?, preprint: http://arxiv.org/PS_cache/arxiv/pdf/0708/0708.1408v1.pdf.

Zhang, X. (2007b) Comment on "Turnaround in Cyclic Cosmology" by Paul Frampton and Lauris Baum, preprint: http://arxiv.org/abs/0711.0667v1.

4

The Teleological Argument: An Exploration of the Fine-Tuning of the Universe

ROBIN COLLINS

1. Introduction: Setting Up the Argument

1.1. Nature of project and summary of sections

Historically, the argument from design probably has been the most widely cited argument for the existence of God, both in the West and the East (such as in theistic schools of Hinduism). Modern scientific discoveries, particularly the discovery beginning around the 1950s that the fundamental structure of the universe is "balanced on a razor's edge" for the existence of life, have given this argument significant new force in the last 30 years, with several books and many essays written on it.[1] This precise setting of the structure of the universe for life is called the "fine-tuning of the cosmos." This fine-tuning falls into three major categories: that of the laws of nature, that of the constants of physics, and that of the initial conditions of the universe, each of which we shall explore in Section 2. As will become clear in Section 5.2, the sort of life that is most significant for the argument is that of embodied moral agents, of which humans are one example.

This chapter is a highly abridged version of an in-process book-length project in which I argue for the existence of God based on this fine-tuning of the cosmos for life along with the beauty and intelligibility of the laws of nature. The main purpose of the book is to put this argument on as rigorous as possible scientific and philosophical foundation. Although this chapter has the same purpose, it will focus solely on the argument based on the fine-tuning for life, although in my judgment the argument based on beauty and intelligibility is as strong.

The sections of this chapter are arranged as follows. In Section 1.2, I present some key terms and definitions for easy reference. In Section 1.3, I present the basic form of what I call the *core* fine-tuning argument for the existence of God. This argument is explicated in terms of what I call the *restricted version of the Likelihood Principle*. In Section 1.4, I present an alternative way of formulating the argument using what I call the *method of probabilistic*

---

1. For shorter versions of the fine-tuning argument appropriate for undergraduates, see Collins (2002, 2007, 2008), Leslie (1988, 1998), and Collins (www.fine-tuning.org). For other book-length treatments of the fine-tuning argument, see Leslie (1989) and Holder (2004).

tension. In Sections 2.1–2.6, I present the evidence for fine-tuning and consider some of the main criticisms of this evidence.

Since I shall formulate the argument in Sections 1.3 and 1.4 in terms of certain *conditional epistemic probabilities*, I need to develop an account of conditional epistemic probability and a general method for determining the degree of conditional epistemic probability that one proposition has on another. I do this in Sections 3.1–3.3. In Sections 4.1–4.5, I address some further critical issues for my formulation of the fine-tuning argument, namely, the appropriate background information to use in the argument and the appropriate comparison range of values for the constants of physics. In Sections 5.1 and 5.2, I complete the core fine-tuning argument by using the results of the previous sections to derive the premises of the main argument presented in Sections 1.3 and 1.4.

In Sections 6.1–6.3, I address the so-called multiverse hypothesis as an alternative explanation of the fine-tuning, or at least as a way of undermining the fine-tuning argument for theism. The multiverse hypothesis is widely considered the leading alternative to a theistic explanation. In Sections 7.1–7.5, I reply to various miscellaneous objections to the fine-tuning argument, such as the so-called "who designed God?" objection. Finally, in Section 8, I conclude the entire argument.

My overall approach will be to present a version of the fine-tuning argument that is more rigorous than its predecessors by presenting the argument in a step-by-step fashion and then justifying each step using widely used principles of reasoning. This way of developing the argument will not only show that the argument can be developed in a philosophically principled way, but it automatically will answer many of the criticisms that have been raised against it; it also will help us go beyond a mere "battle of intuitions" between advocates and critics of the argument. Further, as much as possible, I shall avoid using theories of confirmation that attempt to account for everyday and scientific forms of reasoning but whose claims go significantly beyond what these forms of reasoning demand. Thus, for instance, I will avoid appealing to *prior* probabilities and to notions of purely logical probability that claim that relations of probability exist completely independently of human cognizers (see e.g. Sections 1.3 and 3.2).

1.2. *Some key definitions, terminologies, and abbreviations*

In this section, I shall define some key terminologies and abbreviations that are used in more than one section. This will help the reader keep track of my terms and symbolisms.

1 **Embodied moral agents.** An "embodied moral agent" will be defined as an embodied conscious being that can make morally significant choices, without prejudging the status of moral truths. Our main concern, however, will be with embodied beings that are relevantly similar to humans – that is, who exist in a world with fixed laws and who can significantly affect each other for good or ill. Thus, whenever I talk about embodied moral agents, this is the type of agent I shall have in mind.

2 **The existence of a life-permitting universe (LPU).** This will always mean the existence of a material spatiotemporal reality that can support embodied moral agents, not merely life of some sort. Indeed, in every case where I use the word "life," I shall have in mind embodied moral agents as the relevant kind of life. The reason that embodied moral agents are the relevant kind of life will become clear in Section 5.2, where I argue that LPU is not improbable under theism. Throughout, it will be

assumed that the existence of such beings requires a high degree of organized material complexity, such as we find in the brains of higher-order animals.

3   **Fine-tuning of the universe; existence of a fine-tuned universe; fine-tuning evidence; fine-tuning data.** To stay in conformity with the literature, I shall mean by the "fine-tuning of the universe" or the "existence of a fine-tuned universe" the conjunction of the following two claims: (i) the claim that the laws and values of the constants of physics, and the initial conditions of any universe with the same laws as our universe, must be set in a seemingly very precise way for the universe to support life; and (ii) the claim that such a universe exists, or when the background information includes the information that there is only one universe, the claim that *this* universe is life-permitting, where *this* is an indexical that picks out the one universe that actually exists. When I speak of the "fine-tuning evidence (data)," or "the evidence (data) of fine-tuning," or variations of these, I shall be referring only to claim (i). The reason for this is that "evidence" and "data" implicitly refer to what physicists have discovered. Clearly, physicists have not discovered that the laws, constants, and initial conditions are life-permitting since we always knew that based on our existence. Rather, they have discovered claim (i). When I attempt rigorously to formulate the argument, the distinction between claim (i) and claim (ii), and the distinction between the "fine-tuning of the universe" and the "fine-tuning evidence (or data)" should be kept in mind.

4   **Fine-tuning of a constant C of physics.** When discussing a constant C of physics (see Sections 2.3 and 4.2), I shall use the term "fine-tuning" specifically to refer to the claim that the life-permitting range of C – that is, the range of values that allows for life – is very small compared with the some properly chosen "comparison range" for that constant. (For how to choose this comparison range, see Sections 4.3 and 4.4.) In connection with a constant C, the term "fine-tuning" will never be used to include the claim that it has a life-permitting value.

5   **Constant C has a life-permitting value (Lpc).** This denotes the claim that the value of a constant C is such that, given the laws of nature, the initial conditions of the universe, and the values of the other constants, the universe would allow for the existence of the relevant type of life – namely, embodied moral agents.

6   **The Theistic hypothesis (T).** According to this hypothesis, there exists an omnipotent, omniscient, everlasting or eternal, perfectly free creator of the universe whose existence does not depend on anything outside itself.

7   **The naturalistic single-universe hypothesis (NSU).** This is the hypothesis that there is only one universe, the existence of which is an unexplained, brute given, and that within that universe the laws and constants of physics do not significantly vary from one space-time region to another. NSU does not build in any hypothesis about the structure of the universe that does exist, other than that it is some sort of material, spatiotemporal reality that obeys physical laws; it also excludes any transcendent explanation of the universe, be that explanation theistic or nontheistic.

8   **Multiverse hypothesis.** This is the hypothesis that there are many universes or regions of space-time in which the constants and initial conditions of the universe, and in some versions the laws themselves, vary from universe to universe. The *naturalistic multiverse hypothesis* is the hypothesis that there is no transcendent explanation for such a multiverse.

9   **P(A|B) and conditional epistemic probability.** P(A|B) represents the *conditional epistemic probability* of a Proposition A on another Proposition B. See Sections 3.1 and 3.2 for details.

10   **Background information k and k′.** k refers to our total background information, whereas k′ refers to some appropriately chosen background information – for example, for the case of the fine-tuning of the constants, k′ is the total background information minus the fact that a particular constant C has a life-permitting value. (See Sections 4.1–4.4 for how to determine k′ for the fine-tuning argument.)

11   **Other symbols.** ≪ will always mean "much, much less than" – for example, $P(A|B) \ll 1$ will mean that $P(A|B)$ is very close to zero since $P(A|B)$ cannot have a negative value. $\sim P(A|B) \ll 1$ will mean that it is not the case that $P(A|B) \ll 1$. W_r will usually refer to the width of the life-permitting range of a particular constant C of physics, and W_R will usually refer to the width of the "comparison range" for that constant, which we argue is typically the EI region (see Section 4.4). The EI region for a constant will refer to the "epistemically illuminated" region – that is, the region of values for C for which we can determine whether they are life-permitting. A constant is fine-tuned if $W_r/W_R \ll 1$; "BB" stands for "Boltzmann brain" (see Sections 6.3.3 and 6.3.4).

1.3. The basic argument presented: likelihood approach

My basic argument first claims that, given the fine-tuning evidence, LPU strongly supports T over the NSU. I call this the *core* fine-tuning argument. After developing this argument in Sections 2 through 5, I then present arguments for preferring T over the multiverse hypothesis (Section 6). Finally, in Section 8, I shall briefly consider other possible alternative explanations of the fine-tuning.

The core fine-tuning argument relies on a standard Principle of Confirmation theory, the so-called *Likelihood Principle*. This principle can be stated as follows. Let h_1 and h_2 be two competing hypotheses. According to the Likelihood Principle, an observation e counts as evidence in favor of hypothesis h_1 over h_2 if the observation is more probable under h_1 than h_2. Put symbolically, e counts in favor of h_1 over h_2 if $P(e|h_1) > P(e|h_2)$, where $P(e|h_1)$ and $P(e|h_2)$ represent the *conditional probability* of e on h_1 and h_2, respectively. Moreover, the degree to which the evidence counts in favor of one hypothesis over another is proportional to the degree to which e is more probable under h_1 than h_2: specifically, it is proportional to $P(e|h_1)/P(e|h_2)$.[2]

The Likelihood Principle appears to be sound under all interpretations of probability. The type of probability that we shall be concerned with is what is called conditional *epistemic* probability. The conditional epistemic probability of a Proposition A on a Proposition B can be defined roughly as the degree to which Proposition B, in and of itself,

---

2. There are many reasons why the Likelihood Principle should be accepted (e.g. see Edwards 1972; Royall 1997; Forster & Sober 2001; Sober 2002); for the purposes of this chapter, I take what I call the *restricted version of the Likelihood Principle* (see further discussion) as providing a sufficient condition for when evidence e supports a hypothesis, h_1, over another, h_2. For a counterexample to the Likelihood Principle's being a necessary condition, see Forster (2006). For an application of the Likelihood Principle to arguments for design, see Sober (2005). (I address Sober's main criticism of the fine-tuning argument in Sections 3.2, 5.2, and 7.5.)

   The Likelihood Principle can be derived from the so-called odds form of Bayes's Theorem, which also allows one to give a precise statement of the degree to which evidence counts in favor of one hypothesis over another. The odds form of Bayes's Theorem is $P(h_1|e)/P(h_2|e) = [P(h_1)/P(h_2)] \times [P(e|h_1)/P(e|h_2)]$. The Likelihood Principle, however, does not require the applicability or truth of Bayes's Theorem and can be given independent justification by appealing to our normal epistemic practices.

supports or leads us to expect A to be true. In Section 3.2, I shall explicate this notion of probability in much more detail. Put in terms of epistemic probability, the Likelihood Principle can be reworded in terms of degrees of expectation instead of probability, in which case it becomes what I call the *Expectation Principle*. According to the Expectation Principle, if an event or state of affairs e is more to be expected under one hypothesis, h_1, than another, h_2, it counts as evidence in favor of h_1 over h_2 – that is, in favor of the hypothesis under which it has the highest expectation. The strength of the evidence is proportional to the relative degree to which it is more to be expected under h_1 than h_2. Rewording the Likelihood Principle in terms of expectation is particularly helpful for those trained in the sciences, who are not familiar with epistemic probability and therefore tend to confuse it with other kinds of probability even when they are aware of the distinction.

Because of certain potential counterexamples, I shall use what I call the *restricted version* of the Likelihood Principle, although I shall often refer to it simply as the Likelihood Principle. The restricted version limits the applicability of the Likelihood Principle to cases in which the hypothesis being confirmed is non-*ad hoc*. A sufficient condition for a hypothesis being non-*ad hoc* (in the sense used here) is that there are independent motivations for believing the hypothesis apart from the confirming data e, or for the hypothesis to have been widely advocated prior to the confirming evidence. To illustrate the need for the restricted version, suppose that I roll a die 20 times and it comes up some apparently random sequence of numbers – say 2, 6, 4, 3, 1, 5, 6, 4, 3, 2, 1, 6, 2, 4, 4, 1, 3, 6, 6, 1. The probability of its coming up in this sequence is one in 3.6×10^{15}, or about one in a million billion. To explain this occurrence, suppose I invented the hypothesis that there is a demon whose favorite number is just the aforementioned sequence of numbers (i.e. 26431564321624413661), and that this demon had a strong desire for that sequence to turn up when I rolled the die. Now, if this demon hypothesis were true, then the fact that the die came up in this sequence would be expected – that is, the sequence would not be epistemically improbable. Consequently, by the standard Likelihood Principle, the occurrence of this sequence would strongly confirm the demon hypothesis over the chance hypothesis. But this seems counterintuitive: given a sort of commonsense notion of confirmation, it does not seem that the demon hypothesis is confirmed.

Now consider a modification of the demon case in which, prior to my rolling the die, a group of occultists claimed to have a religious experience of a demon they called "Groodal," who they claimed revealed that her favorite number was 26431564321624441366, and that she strongly desired that number be realized in some continuous sequence of die rolls in the near future. Suppose they wrote this all down in front of many reliable witnesses days before I rolled the die. Certainly, it seems that the sequence of die rolls would count as evidence in favor of the Groodal hypothesis over the chance hypothesis. The relevant difference between this and the previous case is that in this case the Groodal hypothesis was already advocated prior to the rolling of the die, and thus the restricted Likelihood Principle implies that the sequence of die rolls confirms the Groodal hypothesis.[3]

---

3. The restricted version of the Likelihood Principle is not the only way of dealing with the sort of counterexample raised by the first demon case. Another way is to claim that, contrary to our intuitions, in the appropriate technical sense given by Bayes's Theorem, the sequence really does confirm the demon hypothesis, but never enough to make it probable since its prior probability is so low. For the purposes of this chapter, however, I am trying to stay as close to our intuitions about evidence as possible and hence prefer restricting the Likelihood Principle to deal with these purported counterexamples.

Using the restricted version of the Likelihood Principle, the core fine-tuning argument can be stated as follows:

(1) Given the fine-tuning evidence, LPU is very, very epistemically unlikely under NSU: that is, $P(LPU|NSU \ \& \ k') \ll 1$, where k' represents some appropriately chosen background information, and $\ll$ represents much, much less than (thus making $P(LPU|NSU \ \& \ k')$ close to zero).

(2) Given the fine-tuning evidence, LPU is not unlikely under T: that is, $\sim P(LPU|T \ \& \ k') \ll 1$.

(3) T was advocated prior to the fine-tuning evidence (and has independent motivation).

(4) Therefore, by the restricted version of the Likelihood Principle, LPU strongly supports T over NSU.

This argument is a valid argument since the conclusion (4) follows from the premises. Accordingly, the key issues for the argument will be justifying the premises and assessing the significance of the conclusion. Premise (3) seems obviously true since T was advocated long before the fine-tuning evidence came to light.[4] Supporting Premises (1) and (2) in as rigorous a way as possible will require delving into and resolving several further issues. First, we shall need to be more precise on what we mean by "epistemic" probability (Section 3.2) and to develop a preliminary theory of what it is that will be usable for our main argument. Second, we shall need to consider how epistemic probability is justified (Section 3.3). In particular, in Section 3.3.2, I argue for what I call the *restricted Principle of Indifference*. Third, we shall need to carefully determine what the appropriate background information k' is (Sections 4.1–4.6). If, for example, we were to include in k' everything we know about the world, including our existence, then both probabilities in Premises (1) and (2) will turn out to be 1.0 since our existence entails LPU. Determining k' will also provide a comparison region of law structures (or values for the constants) to which we are comparing the life-permitting region (Section 4.4). Having done this, we shall be ready to complete the argument for Premises (1) and (2) in Sections 5.1 and 5.2 – for example, we shall justify Premise (1) for the case of the fine-tuning of the constants by appealing to the restricted version of the Principle of Indifference defended in Sections 3.3.1 and 3.3.2.

Finally, given that we can establish the conclusion, what is its significance? Even if LPU counts as strong evidence in favor of T over NSU, that does not itself establish that T is likely to be true, or even more likely to be true than NSU. In this way, LPU is much like fingerprints found on a murder weapon. Via the Likelihood Principle, a defendant's fingerprints' matching those on the weapon typically provide strong evidence for guilt because the jury correctly judges that it is very unlikely for this matching to occur if the defendant is not guilty (and claims to have never seen the murder weapon), whereas it is not unexpected if the defendant actually used the murder weapon. Although such a

---

4. There is one worry about Premise (3) though: T was not advocated prior to the evidence of LPU since the life-permitting character of our universe follows from our existence and all the motivations for T are intertwined with the fact that we exist. If this is a real difficulty, one might need to use my alternative version of the fine-tuning argument, the method of *probabilistic tension* (Section 1.4), for which this problem clearly does not arise.

match can provide strong evidence that the defendant is guilty, one could not conclude merely from this alone that the defendant is guilty; one would also have to look at all the other evidence offered. Perhaps, for instance, ten reliable witnesses claimed to see the defendant at a party at the time of the shooting. In that case, by the restricted version of the Likelihood Principle, the matching would still count as significant evidence of guilt, but this evidence would be counterbalanced by the testimony of the witnesses. Similarly, we shall claim that the evidence of fine-tuning significantly supports T over NSU; this, however, neither shows that, everything considered, T is probably true, nor that it is the most plausible explanation of existence of the universe, nor even that it is more probable than NSU. In order to show that any hypothesis is likely to be true using a likelihood approach, we would have to assess the prior epistemic probability of the hypothesis, something I shall not attempt to do for T.

Our more limited conclusion is nonetheless highly relevant to the rationality of and justification for belief in God, even though it does not itself establish that, all things considered, T is more probable than NSU. One could argue, for example, that in everyday life and science we speak of evidence for and against various views, but seldom of prior probabilities. For example, if one were to ask most physicists why they (tentatively) believe in General Relativity's approximate truth (or at least its future empirical fruitfulness), they probably would cite the evidence in favor of it, along with some of Einstein's motivations. They probably would not cast these considerations – such as Einstein's motivations – into talk of prior probability, either epistemic or otherwise. Of course, at the end of the day, some might say things such as "Einstein's theory is likely to be true," which is a notion of epistemic probability. But I can imagine them saying, "I have no idea what the prior probability of Einstein's theory is; all I will say is that Einstein had motivations for considering it and there are at least three strong pieces of empirical evidence in its favor." Indeed, I think it would be very difficult to estimate the prior probability of General Relativity's approximate truth (or future empirical fruitfulness) in any objective manner, since we should have to weigh incommensurable factors against each other – the simplicity of the mathematical framework of General Relativity against such things as the philosophically puzzling character of the idea of a four-dimensional space-time's being curved. Arguably, this is analogous to the case of T.

One way of putting my approach in perspective is to note that one of the most common philosophical objections to T is an updated version of one offered by Kant, in which the methods of theoretical reason are restricted to justifying only the existence of natural causes. Unlike Kant, however, modern atheistic philosophers often reject God as a necessary hypothesis of practical reasoning. Typically, these philosophers claim that by analyzing the notion of explanation, particularly as exemplified in natural science, we find that to explain something involves citing overarching laws, mechanical causes, and the like; thus, they assert, the very notion of explanation involves a restriction to purely naturalistic explanations. The idea of God as providing a complete explanation of all contingent reality is therefore rejected as being empty, an improper extension of the notion of "explain" to places where it cannot apply. Another attack is to argue that even if God could be said to explain contingent reality, God's own existence would be as much in need of explanation.

Richard Swinburne (2004, chaps. 2–4) has responded to these critics by offering an alternative analysis of ordinary explanation. He claims that these critics have neglected the notion of personal explanation and then goes on to claim that God provides the best personal explanation of everything we know about the universe. His argument rests on the dual claim that the simplicity of an explanation is the ultimate criterion of its adequacy and that God provides the simplest explanation of the universe. There are many places one might object to Swinburne's project, particularly these two claims about simplicity. Further, by basing his project on the notion of explanation used in everyday life, Swinburne leaves God's own existence entirely unexplained. Indeed, Swinburne claims that God is the ultimate contingent brute fact and could be said to necessarily exist only in the limited sense that God is without beginning and that, in principle, nothing could explain God's existence.

The approach I am taking avoids this question of how best to analyze the notion of explanation or whether God ultimately provides the best explanation of the universe. Rather, it simply attempts to establish the more limited claim that various features of the universe offer strong evidence in favor of T over its major naturalistic alternatives. I believe that establishing this more limited claim in a careful, principled way would alone be a great accomplishment. In Section 7.1, however, I address how this more limited claim fits into an overall argument for the existence of God. In that section, I also briefly address the issue of God's providing an ultimate explanation and respond to the claim that God is as much in need of a designer as the universe itself. A fuller discussion of this issue, however, is beyond the scope of this chapter.

1.4. Alternative version of argument: method of probabilistic tension

One problem with using simply the Likelihood Principle is that whether or not a hypothesis is confirmed or disconfirmed depends on what one builds into the hypothesis. For example, single-universe naturalists could prevent disconfirmation of their hypotheses by advocating *the elaborated naturalistic single-universe hypothesis* (NSUe), defined as NSU conjoined with the claim that the universe that exists is life-permitting: that is, NSUe = NSU & LPU. Similarly, theists could avoid any question about whether LPU is probable on T by constructing an elaborated theistic hypothesis (Te) which builds in the claim that God desired to create such a universe: Te = T & God desires to create a life-permitting universe.

One could attempt to deal with these sorts of moves by finding some principled way of restricting what can be built into the theistic and naturalistic hypotheses – for example, by requiring that the theistic and naturalistic hypotheses be some sort of "bare" theism and "bare" single-universe naturalism, respectively. This, however, is likely to run into difficulties not only in justifying the principle, but in defining what "bare" theism and "bare" single-universe naturalism are supposed to be. A simpler way of addressing the issue is by means of a concept I call *probabilistic tension*. A hypothesis h suffers from probabilistic tension if and only if h is logically equivalent to some conjunctive hypothesis, h_1 & h_2, such that $P(h_1|h_2) \ll 1$: that is, one conjunct of the hypothesis is very unlikely, conditioned on the other conjunct. Among other things, a hypothesis h that suffers from probabilistic tension will be very unlikely: since $P(h) = P(h_1 \& h_2) = P(h_1|h_2) \times P(h_2) = P(h_2|h_1) \times P(h_1)$, it follows that if $P(h_1|h_2) \ll 1$ or $P(h_2|h_1) \ll 1$, then $P(h) \ll 1$.

I claim that significant probabilistic tension is an epistemic black mark against a hypothesis, and thus offers us a reason to reject it. To see this, consider the fingerprint example discussed earlier. We noted that based on the Likelihood Principle, the matching of a defendant's fingerprints with those on a murder weapon often strongly confirms the guilt hypothesis over the innocence hypothesis. Such matching, however, does not confirm the guilt hypothesis over what could be called an "elaborated innocence hypothesis" – that is, an innocence hypothesis constructed in such a way that the matching of the fingerprints is implied by the hypothesis. An example of such a hypothesis is the claim that the defendant did not touch the murder weapon conjoined with the claim that someone else with almost identical fingerprints touched the weapon. This hypothesis entails that the fingerprints will appear to match, and hence by the Likelihood Principle the apparent matching could not confirm the guilt hypothesis over this hypothesis.

Nonetheless, this elaborated innocence hypothesis suffers from severe probabilistic tension: one conjunct of the hypothesis (that some other person with almost identical fingerprints touched the weapon) is very improbable on the other conjunct (that the defendant is innocent) since it is extremely rare for two people to happen to have almost identical fingerprints. Given that the guilt hypothesis does not suffer from a corresponding probabilistic tension, the high degree of probabilistic tension of the elaborated innocence hypothesis gives us strong reason to reject it over the guilt hypothesis, even though this elaborated hypothesis is not itself disconfirmed by the matching of the fingerprints.

This idea of probabilistic tension allows us to eliminate any arbitrariness with regard to how we choose the theistic and naturalistic hypotheses that we are confirming or disconfirming.[5] For example, both the theist and the naturalist can build into their respective hypotheses whatever is necessary for them to entail the relevant data. Then one can apply the method of probabilistic tension to these elaborated hypotheses. Consider, for instance, the NSUe and the Te defined earlier: that is, NSUe = NSU & LPU and Te = T & God desires to create a life-permitting universe. Both of these hypotheses entail LPU, and hence neither is confirmed (via the Likelihood Principle) with respect to the other by LPU.

Now given the truth of Premise (1) of our main argument in Section 1.3, NSUe clearly exhibits a high degree of probabilistic tension relative to background information k', since one conjunction of the hypothesis, LPU, is very improbable conditioned on the other conjunct, NSU: that is, $P(LPU|NSU \& k') \ll 1$.[6] Given the truth of Premise (2), elaborated theism will not suffer any corresponding probabilistic tension. The reason is that according to Premise (2), it is not the case that $P(LPU|T \& k') \ll 1$, and hence it follows that it is *not* unlikely that the God of "bare theism" would desire to create a life-permitting universe. This means there will be no probabilistic tension between "bare" theism and the claim that God desires to create such a universe. This will be true even if the probability of $P(LPU|T \& k')$ is merely indeterminate, since such a probabilistic tension would exist only if $P(LPU|T \& k') \ll 1$. Thus, the fine-tuning evidence causes NSUe to suffer from a severe probabilistic tension without causing a corresponding probabilistic tension in Te. Thus, because it creates this probabilistic tension, we could say that the fine-tuning evidence (but not LPU itself) gives us strong reason to reject NSUe over Te.

In practice, any sufficiently elaborated hypothesis will suffer from severe probabilistic tension somewhere. For instance, the elaborated guilt hypothesis mentioned earlier could

---

5. Later, in Section 4.3, we shall see that the method of probabilistic tension also helps eliminate a potential arbitrariness problem that arises with the choice of the appropriate background information k'.

6. This probabilistic tension, of course, makes NSUe very unlikely. Since $P(LPU|NSU \& k') \ll 1$ and $P(LPU\&NSU) = P(LPU|NSU) \times P(NSU)$, it follows that $P(NSUe) = P(NSU \& LPU) \ll 1$. One cannot conclude, however, that NSUe is less likely than Te, unless one can determine various prior probabilities, which I am avoiding doing.

include that the knife used in the murder was green, had a certain shaped scratch mark on its handle, had a weight of 0.15679876675876 kg, and the like. The corresponding elaborated innocence hypothesis would include the same data. Both would suffer from severe probabilistic tension with respect to each piece of data – for example, the murder knife having a weight of 0.15679876675876 kg is very improbable under both the "bare" guilt and "bare" innocence hypothesis. The lesson here is that only the probabilistic tension that one hypothesis has and that another lacks relative to some specified domain can be used as evidence in favor of one hypothesis over another. In our case, the relevant specified domain causing probabilistic tension is that of the fine-tuning data. Elaborated naturalism might do better in other areas with regard to probabilistic tension, but to say that the fine-tuning data counts against elaborated naturalism with respect to elaborated theism, all we have to show is that the fine-tuning evidence creates a probabilistic tension within elaborated naturalism without creating a corresponding tension within elaborated theism.

2. The Evidence for Fine-Tuning

2.1. Introduction

The evidence for fine-tuning of the universe for life falls into three categories:

(i)   The fine-tuning of the laws of nature.
(ii)   The fine-tuning of the constants of nature.
(iii)   The fine-tuning of the initial conditions of the universe.

We shall present examples of each type of fine-tuning further in the discussion. Before we begin, we should note that each of the aforementioned types of fine-tuning presupposes that a necessary requirement for the evolution of embodied moral agents is that there exist material systems that can sustain a high level of self-reproducing complexity – something comparable to that of a human brain. Given what we know of life on Earth, this seems a reasonable assumption.

2.2. Laws of nature

The first major type of fine-tuning is that of the laws of nature. The laws and principles of nature themselves have just the right form to allow for the existence embodied moral agents. To illustrate this, we shall consider the following five laws or principles (or causal powers) and show that if any one of them did not exist, self-reproducing, highly complex material systems could not exist: (1) a universal attractive force, such as gravity; (2) a force relevantly similar to that of the strong nuclear force, which binds protons and neutrons together in the nucleus; (3) a force relevantly similar to that of the electromagnetic force; (4) Bohr's Quantization Rule or something similar; (5) the Pauli Exclusion Principle.

If any one of these laws or principles did not exist (and were not replaced by a law or principle that served the same or similar role), complex self-reproducing material systems could not evolve. First, consider gravity. Gravity is a long-range attractive force between all material objects, whose strength increases in proportion to the masses of the objects and falls off with the inverse square of the distance between them. In classical physics, the amount of force is given by Newton's law, $F = Gm_1m_2/r^2$, where F is the force of attraction between two masses, m_1 and m_2, separated by a distance r, and G is the gravitational constant (which is simply a number with a value of 6.672×10^{-11} N·m^2/kg^2). Now consider what would happen if there were no universal, long-range attractive force between material objects, but all the other fundamental laws remained (as much as possible) the same. If no such force existed, then there would be no stars, since the force of gravity is what holds the matter in stars together against the outward forces caused by the high internal temperatures inside the stars. This means that there would be no long-term energy sources to sustain the evolution (or even existence) of highly complex life. Moreover, there probably would be no planets, since there would be nothing to bring material particles together, and even if there were planets (say because planet-sized objects always existed in the universe and were held together by cohesion), any beings of significant size could not move around without floating off the planet with no way of returning. This means that embodied moral agents could not evolve, since the development of the brain of such beings would require significant mobility. For all these reasons, a universal attractive force such as gravity is required for embodied moral agents.

Second, consider the strong nuclear force. The strong nuclear force is the force that binds nucleons (i.e. protons and neutrons) together in the nucleus of an atom. Without it, the nucleons would not stay together. It is actually a result of a deeper force, the "gluonic force," between the quark constituents of the neutrons and protons, a force described by the theory of quantum chromodynamics. It must be strong enough to overcome the repulsive electromagnetic force between the protons and the quantum zero-point energy of the nucleons. Because of this, it must be considerably stronger than the electromagnetic force; otherwise the nucleus would come apart. Further, to keep atoms of limited size, it must be very short range – which means its strength must fall off much, much more rapidly than the inverse square law characteristic of the electromagnetic force and gravity. Since it is a purely attractive force (except at extraordinarily small distances), if it fell off by an inverse square law like gravity or electromagnetism, it would act just like gravity and pull all the protons and neutrons in the entire universe together. In fact, given its current strength, around 10^{40} stronger than the force of gravity between the nucleons in a nucleus, the universe would most likely consist of a giant black hole.

Thus, to have atoms with an atomic number greater than that of hydrogen, there must be a force that plays the same role as the strong nuclear force – that is, one that is much stronger than the electromagnetic force but only acts over a very short range. It should be clear that embodied moral agents could not be formed from mere hydrogen, contrary to what one might see on science fiction shows such as *Star Trek*. One cannot obtain enough self-reproducing, stable complexity. Furthermore, in a universe in which no other atoms but hydrogen could exist, stars could not be powered by nuclear fusion, but only by gravitational collapse, thereby drastically decreasing the time for, and hence probability of, the evolution of embodied moral agents.

Third, consider electromagnetism. Without electromagnetism, there would be no atoms, since there would be nothing to hold the electrons in orbit. Further, there would be no means of transmission of energy from stars for the existence of life on planets. It is doubtful whether enough stable complexity could arise in such a universe for even the simplest forms of life to exist.

Fourth, consider Bohr's rule of quantization, first proposed in 1913, which requires that electrons occupy only fixed orbitals (energy levels) in atoms. It was only with the development of quantum mechanics in the 1920s and 1930s that Bohr's proposal was given an adequate theoretical foundation. If we view the atom from the perspective of classical Newtonian mechanics, an electron should be able to go in any orbit around the nucleus. The reason is the same as why planets in the solar system can be any distance from the Sun – for example, the Earth could have been 150 million miles from the Sun instead of its present 93 million miles. Now the laws of electromagnetism – that is, Maxwell's equations – require that any charged particle that is accelerating emit radiation. Consequently, because electrons orbiting the nucleus are accelerating – since their direction of motion is changing – they would emit radiation. This emission would in turn cause the electrons to lose energy, causing their orbits to decay so rapidly that atoms could not exist for more than a few moments. This was a major problem confronting Rutherford's model of the atom – in which the atom had a nucleus with electrons around the nucleus – until Niels Bohr proposed his *ad hoc* rule of quantization in 1913, which required that electrons occupy fixed orbitals. Thus, without the existence of this rule of quantization – or something relevantly similar – atoms could not exist, and hence there would be no life.

Finally, consider the Pauli Exclusion Principle, which dictates that no two fermions (spin-½ particles) can occupy the same quantum state. This arises from a deep principle in quantum mechanics which requires that the joint wave function of a system of fermions be antisymmetric. This implies that not more than two electrons can occupy the same orbital in an atom, since a single orbital consists of two possible quantum states (or more precisely, eigenstates) corresponding to the spin pointing in one direction and the spin pointing in the opposite direction. This allows for complex chemistry, since without this principle, all electrons would occupy the lowest atomic orbital. Thus, without this principle, no complex life would be possible.[7]

2.3. Constants of physics

2.3.1. Introduction

The constants of physics are fundamental numbers that, when plugged into the laws of physics, determine the basic structure of the universe. An example of a fundamental constant is Newton's gravitational constant G, which determines the strength of gravity via Newton's law $F = Gm_1m_2/r^2$. We will say that a constant is fine-tuned if the width of its life-permitting range, W_r, is very small in comparison to the width, W_R, of some properly chosen comparison range: that is, $W_r/W_R \ll 1$. A more philosophically rigorous way of determining this comparison range will be presented in Section 4.4. Here we shall simply use certain standard comparison ranges that naturally arise in physics and hence are used by physicists when they speak of cases of anthropic fine-tuning.[8]

---

7. The Pauli Exclusion Principle also applies to the nucleus. It prevents an indefinite number of neutrons from falling into the lowest nuclear shell, thereby putting a limit on the atomic weight of atoms, a limit which appears necessary for life.

8. Physicists often speak of a requirement that there be "no fine-tuning" in a way that is independent of considerations regarding the existence of life. Two versions of this requirement are (i) that "all dimensionless parameters should be of the order of unity" (Narkilar 2002, pp. 479–80), and (ii) that the value of a constant should not be much, much smaller than the quantum corrections to its bare value, since otherwise the bare value

There are many examples of the anthropic fine-tuning of the fundamental constants of physics. Elsewhere, I have more thoroughly examined six of what I considered the most well-established cases, carefully articulating the physical lines of evidence offered in support of these cases along with correcting some incorrect and often-repeated claims regarding fine-tuning (Collins 2003). For purposes of illustration, here I shall explicate in some detail only two constants of physics – the strength of gravity and the cosmological constant.[9]

2.3.2. Fine-tuning of gravity

Using a standard measure of force strengths – which turns out to be roughly the relative strength of the various forces between two protons in a nucleus – gravity is the weakest of the forces, and the strong nuclear force is the strongest, being a factor of 10^{40} – or 10 thousand billion, billion, billion, billion times stronger than gravity (Barrow & Tipler 1986, pp. 293–5). Now if we increased the strength of gravity a billionfold, for instance, the force of gravity on a planet with the mass and size of the Earth would be so great that organisms anywhere near the size of human beings, whether land-based or aquatic, would be crushed. (The strength of materials depends on the electromagnetic force via the fine-structure constant, which would not be affected by a change in gravity.) Even a much smaller planet of only 40 ft in diameter – which is not large enough to sustain organisms of our size – would have a gravitational pull of 1,000 times that of Earth, still too strong for organisms with brains of our size to exist. As astrophysicist Martin Rees notes, "In an imaginary strong gravity world, even insects would need thick legs to support them, and no animals could get much larger" (2000, p. 30). Based on the evidence from Earth, only organisms with brains of a size comparable to our own have significant moral agency. Consequently, such an increase in the strength of gravity would render the existence of embodied moral agents virtually impossible and thus would not be life-permitting in the sense that we defined.

Of course, a billionfold increase in the strength of gravity is a lot, but compared with the total range of the strengths of the forces in nature (which span a range of 10^{40}), it is very small, being one part in 10 thousand, billion, billion, billion. Indeed, other calculations show that stars with lifetimes of more than a billion years, as compared with our Sun's lifetime of 10 billion years, could not exist if gravity were increased by more than a factor of 3,000 (Collins 2003). This would significantly inhibit the occurrence of embodied moral agents.

would have to be fine-tuned to be almost exactly opposite of the quantum correction to yield such a relatively small value for the constant (see Donoghue 2007, pp. 234–6). It is important, therefore, not to naively equate discussions of fine-tuning in the physics literature with anthropic fine-tuning, although, as John Donoghue (2007) shows, they are often closely related.

9. Some other examples of fine-tuning of the constants are the following: if the mass of the neutron were slightly increased by about one part in 700, stable hydrogen burning stars would cease to exist (Leslie 1989, pp. 39–40; Collins 2003); if the weak force were slightly weaker by one part in 10^9 of the range of force strengths, then the existence of complex life would be severely inhibited (Collins 2003); finally, if the "vacuum expectation value" of the Higgs field were not within a few times its present strength, complex atoms (with atomic numbers greater than hydrogen) could not exist (see Donoghue 2007, pp. 237–8). All these cases, however, need more explication and analysis than can be given here.

The case of fine-tuning of gravity described is relative to the strength of the electro-magnetic force, since it is this force that determines the strength of materials – for example, how much weight an insect leg can hold; it is also indirectly relative to other constants – such as the speed of light, the electron and proton mass, and the like – which help determine the properties of matter. There is, however, a fine-tuning of gravity relative to other parameters. One of these is the fine-tuning of gravity relative to the density of mass-energy in the early universe and other factors determining the expansion rate of the Big Bang – such as the value of the Hubble constant and the value of the cosmological constant. Holding these other parameters constant, if the strength of gravity were smaller or larger by an estimated one part in 10^{60} of its current value, the universe would have either exploded too quickly for galaxies and stars to form, or collapsed back on itself too quickly for life to evolve.[10] The lesson here is that a single parameter, such as gravity, participates in several different fine-tunings relative to other parameters.

2.3.3. The cosmological constant

Probably the most widely discussed case of fine-tuning for life is that of the cosmological constant. The cosmological constant, Λ, is a term in Einstein's equation of General Relativity that, when positive, acts as a repulsive force, causing space to expand and, when negative, acts as an attractive force, causing space to contract. Einstein's equation implies that if the vacuum – that is, space-time devoid of normal matter – has an energy density, then that energy density must act in a mathematically, and hence physically, equivalent way to a cosmological constant. The seeming need for fine-tuning of the cosmological constant arises from the fact that almost every field within modern physics – the electromagnetic field, the Higgs fields associated with the weak force, the *inflaton* field hypothesized by inflationary cosmology, the *dilaton* field hypothesized by superstring theory, and the fields associated with elementary particles – each contributes to the vacuum energy far in excess of the maximum life-permitting amount. These contributions to the vacuum energy can be either negative or positive. If the total effective cosmological constant is positive and larger than some positive value $\Lambda+_{max}$, or negative and smaller than some negative value $\Lambda-_{max}$, then the universe would have expanded (if positive), or collapsed (if negative), too quickly for stars or galaxies to form. Thus, for life to occur, the cosmological constant must be between $\Lambda-_{max}$ and $\Lambda+_{max}$. I shall let Λ_{max} designate the larger of the two absolute values of $\Lambda-_{max}$ and $\Lambda+_{max}$. Since the absolute values of $\Lambda-_{max}$ and $\Lambda+_{max}$ are within one or two orders of magnitude of each other, I shall explain the cosmological constant problem for the case in which Λ is assumed to be positive, but the same analysis will apply for the case in which Λ is negative.

---

10. This latter fine-tuning of the strength of gravity is typically expressed as the claim that the density of matter at the Planck time (the time at which we have any confidence in the theory of Big Bang dynamics) must have been tuned to one part in 10^{60} of the so-called critical density (e.g. Davies 1982, p. 89). Since the critical density is inversely proportional to the strength of gravity (Davies 1982, p. 88, eqn. 4.15), the fine-tuning of the matter density can easily be shown to be equivalent to the aforementioned claim about the tuning of the strength of gravity. Of course, if one cites this fine-tuning of gravity, one cannot then treat the fine-tuning of the force of the Big Bang or matter density of the Big Bang as an independent fine-tuning. (See Section 5.1.1 for how to combine cases of fine-tuning.)

Einstein originally hypothesized the existence of the cosmological constant so that his theory would imply a static universe. Thus, the original cosmological constant that Einstein postulated was not associated with contributions to the vacuum energy of the various fields of physics. If we let Λ_{vac} represent the contribution to the cosmological constant from the vacuum energy of all the fields combined, and Λ_{bare} represent the intrinsic value of the cosmological constant apart from any contribution from these fields, then the total value, Λ_{tot}, of the cosmological constant is $\Lambda_{tot} = \Lambda_{vac} + \Lambda_{bare}$. The contributions to Λ_{vac} can be further divided into those contributions arising from various forms of potential energy, V, as the universe passes through different phases along with those arising from the zero-point energies of the vacuum fluctuations of the quantum fields of the fundamental forces and elementary particles.

Finally, there have been various proposals for a new and highly speculative type of energy, called *quintessence*, whose defining feature is that it acts like a cosmological constant in the way it causes space to expand or contract, but unlike the cosmological constant it can change with time as the universe evolves from the Big Bang onward. Consequently, we can define the total *effective* cosmological constant as the sum of all these contributions that *function in the same way* as the cosmological constant with regard to causing space to expand or contract: that is, $\Lambda_{eff} = \Lambda_{vac} + \Lambda_{bare} + \Lambda_q$, where Λ_q designates the contribution resulting from quintessence. *The fine-tuning problem can now be stated as follows: without fine-tuning or some new principle of physics, Λ_{eff} is expected to be at least 10^{53} to 10^{120} times larger than the maximum life-permitting value Λ_{max}.* The smallness of the cosmological constant compared to its non-fine-tuned, theoretically expected value is widely regarded as the single greatest problem confronting current physics and cosmology.

To understand this fine-tuning problem more fully, it will be helpful to consider the three major types of contribution to the vacuum energy term, Λ_{vac}, of the cosmological constant in modern cosmology. Following standard terminology, we will let ρ_{vac} designate the vacuum energy density, and ρ_{max} the maximum vacuum energy density compatible with the existence of life, given that the vacuum energy is the only contribution to the cosmological constant.[11] The first contribution we shall consider arises from the Higgs field postulated as part of the widely accepted Weinberg–Salem–Glashow electroweak theory. According to this theory, the electromagnetic force and the weak force acted as one force prior to symmetry breaking of the Higgs field in the very early universe when temperatures were still extremely high. Before symmetry breaking, the vacuum energy of the Higgs field had its maximum value V_0. This value was approximately $10^{53} \rho_{max}$. After symmetry breaking, the Higgs field fell into some local minimum of its possible energy density, a minimum which theoretically could be anywhere from zero to $10^{53} \rho_{max}$, being solely determined by V_0 and other free parameters of the electroweak theory.[12]

Now either this local minimum is less than ρ_{max}, or it is greater than ρ_{max} and the other contributions to the cosmological constant offset its contribution to Λ_{eff} so that $\Lambda_{eff} < \Lambda_{max}$. In either case, the fine-tuning would have to be in one part in 10^{53}. In the former case, for instance, the local minimum of energy would have to be between zero and ρ_{max}, which would be one part in 10^{53} of its possible range of values.

---

11. Choosing units in which the speed of light, c, is equal to one (as is commonly done), it follows from Einstein's equation that $\rho_{vac} = 8\pi G\Lambda_{vac}$ and $\rho_{max} = 8\pi G\Lambda_{max}$, where G is Newton's constant of gravity. Hence, the vacuum energy and the cosmological constant are strictly proportional to each other.

12. See Collins (2003, p. 196, endnote 9) for more analysis of this case.

The second contribution to the vacuum energy is the postulated inflaton field of inflationary cosmology. Inflationary universe models hypothesize that the inflaton field had an enormously high energy density in the first 10^{-35} to 10^{-37} seconds of our universe, resulting in an effective cosmological constant that caused space to expand by a factor of around 10^{60} (Guth 1997, p. 185). By around 10^{-35} seconds or so, however, the value of the inflaton field fell to a relatively small value corresponding to a *local minimum* of its energy.[13] Now, in order to start inflation, the initial energy density of the inflaton field, ρ_i, must have been enormously larger than ρ_{max}: $\rho_i \gg \rho_{max}$. Theoretically, however, the local minimum of the inflaton field could be anything from zero to ρ_i (see Sahni & Starobinsky 1999, sec. 7.0; Rees 2000, p. 154). The fact that the effective cosmological constant after inflation is less than ρ_{max} requires an enormous degree of fine-tuning, for the same reason as the Higgs field mentioned – for example, neglecting other contributions to the cosmological constant, the local minimum of energy into which the inflaton field fell must be between zero and ρ_{max}, a tiny portion of the its possible range, zero to ρ_i.

The final contribution results from the so-called *zero-point energies* of the fields associated with forces and elementary particles, such as the electromagnetic force and electrons and protons. If we calculate this contribution using quantum field theory and assume that space is a continuum, the contribution turns out to be infinite. Physicists, however, typically assume that quantum field theory is valid only up to a certain very large cutoff energy (see Section 4.5), in which case the contribution turns out to be extraordinarily large, but finite, with the actual value depending on the cutoff energy below which quantum field theory is taken as valid. The so-called Plank energy is often assumed to be the energy scale that quantum field theory breaks down, in which case the energy contribution of the zero-point energy for the various fields would be expected to be $10^{120} \rho_{max}$ (see Sahni & Starobinsky 1999, p. 44). To reduce this contribution to within an order of magnitude of the life-permitting range (thus eliminating any significant fine-tuning) would require an extremely low cutoff energy, which most physicists consider very unlikely (Donoghue 2007, p. 236).

One solution to the cosmological constant problem is to claim that God, or some other intelligence, fine-tuned the various contributions to the cosmological constant, $\Lambda_{vac} + \Lambda_{bare} + \Lambda_q$, in such a way that $\Lambda_{eff} < \Lambda_{max}$. Another much discussed solution is an appeal to multiple universes and some anthropic selection effect, which we shall discuss in Section 6. Is there a nondivine, nonanthropic solution to the fine-tuning of the cosmological constant? Physicist Victor Stenger, the leading critic of the data appealed to by advocates of the fine-tuning argument, claims that there is. According to Stenger:

> ... recent theoretical work has offered a plausible non-divine solution to the cosmological constant problem. Theoretical physicists have proposed models in which the dark energy is not identified with the energy of curved space-time but rather with a dynamical, material energy field called *quintessence*. In these models, the cosmological constant is exactly 0, as suggested by a symmetry principle called *supersymmetry*. Since 0 multiplied by 10^{120} is still 0, we have no cosmological constant problem in this case. The energy density of quintessence is not constant but evolves along with the other matter/energy fields of the universe. Unlike the cosmological constant, quintessence energy density need not be fine-tuned. (2004, p. 182)

13. Although the Higgs fields and the other fields of physics could contribute to inflation, for various technical reasons inflationary cosmology requires a distinct energy field that helps create a very large effective cosmological constant in the very early universe. There is currently no candidate for this field that is "deeply rooted in well-established theories of fundamental physics" (Albrecht 2004, p. 381).

Although in a later publication, Stenger (2007, pp. 151–3) does not mention supersymmetry, he still claims that a hypothesized new form of energy, quintessence, could solve the cosmological constant problem and that it "requires no fine-tuning" (Stenger 2007, p. 152).

Stenger's proposal can be summarized in three steps: (1) postulate some natural symmetry or principle that requires that the cosmological constant, $\Lambda_{tot} = \Lambda_{vac} + \Lambda_{bare}$, be zero; (2) postulate some additional quintessential field to account for what appears to be a small positive value of the *effective* cosmological constant today;[14] and (3) postulate that there is some natural equation that implies that $\Lambda_q < \Lambda_{max}$ in the early universe, an equation which itself does not require fine-tuning. Since $\Lambda_{eff} = \Lambda_{vac} + \Lambda_{bare} + \Lambda_q$, those three steps would guarantee in a natural way that $\Lambda_{eff} < \Lambda_{max}$.

A well-known proposal that would go part way to making $\Lambda_{tot} = 0$ is the appeal to the speculative hypothesis of supersymmetry. Supersymmetry requires that for each bosonic field there exist a corresponding fermionic field, where bosonic fields are those associated with spin-1 particles, such as the photon, and fermionic fields are those associated with spin-½ particles, such as electrons and protons. It further requires that the positive zero-point energy contribution associated with each bosonic field is exactly canceled by the negative zero-point energy contribution associated with the corresponding fermionic field. Consequently, it requires that the total zero-point energies associated with the various fields of physics sum to zero, resulting in a net contribution of zero to the total cosmological constant. This solution faces a major difficulty: even if supersymmetry exists, it is presently a broken symmetry and thus cannot solve the cosmological constant problem. As astrophysicist John Peacock notes, "supersymmetry, if it exists at all, is clearly a broken symmetry at present day energies; there is no natural way of achieving this breaking while retaining the attractive consequence of a zero cosmological constant, and so the Λ problem remains as puzzling as ever" (1999, p. 268).

Further, even if some other symmetry could be discovered that would force the contributions of the bosonic or fermionic fields to cancel each other out, the first two contributions to the cosmological constant mentioned earlier would remain – that is, those arising from the Higgs field and the inflaton field. In order to get a zero cosmological constant, one would have to postulate some law, symmetry, or other mechanism that forced the sum of *all* contributions to the cosmological constant to be zero. In order to get this suggestion to work, physicists would have to either (a) abandon inflationary cosmology, which requires that the effective cosmological constant be initially very large and then fall off to near zero, or (b) invoke some special law, symmetry, or "mechanism" that selectively requires that the cosmological constant be zero at the end of the inflationary period. If options (a) and

---

14. The assumption that $\Lambda_{eff} > 0$ is regarded by most physicists as the best way of accounting for the evidence, based on redshifted light from distant supernovae, that the universe is accelerating. An effective cosmological constant is not the only way of explaining the cosmic acceleration, however. Olga Mena and José Santiago (2006) have recently developed a modification of Einstein's theory of gravity that explains the acceleration of the universe without appealing to an effective cosmological constant. Their model, however, still must assume some nonmaterial substance in addition to normal matter. As stated in their abstract, "the inverse-curvature gravity models considered *cannot* explain the dynamics of the Universe just with a baryonic matter component." If a successful non-*ad hoc* and non-fine-tuned modification of General Relativity could be developed that would account for the acceleration of the universe, it could serve as an alternative to steps (2) and (3) in an attempt to avoid the fine-tuning of the cosmological constant.

(b) are both rejected, one will be left with the fine-tuning problem generated by a large effective cosmological constant required for inflation that must drop off to near zero after inflation in order for life to exist.

Further, supposing that option (a) or (b) are chosen, steps (2) and (3) are still required to account for the small, nonzero effective cosmological constant today. In typical models of quintessence, Λ_q "tracks" the matter and radiation density of the universe – that is, Λ_q is some function of these densities. One problem here is that unless the function is both natural and simple, without any adjustable parameters needed to make $\Lambda_q < \Lambda_{max}$, the problem of fine-tuning will simply re-arise: if that function is not simple or natural, or such a parameter is needed, then the question will arise as to why that function or parameter is such that the value of the effective cosmological constant is within the life-permitting range instead of falling outside the life-permitting range. So far, no such natural function has been found, and it is widely argued that current models of quintessence require fine-tuning, especially when combined with inflationary cosmology.[15] Further, quintessential energy must have special characteristics to act as an effective cosmological constant. As noted by physicists Robert R. Caldwell and Paul J. Steinhardt (2000), "The simplest model proposes that the quintessence is a quantum field with a very long wavelength, approximately the size of the observable universe." The long wavelength of the field means that its energy is dominated by potential energy, which in turn allows for it to act as an effective cosmological constant.

In sum, it is conceivable that by postulating the right set of laws–symmetries–mechanisms, physicists will be able to explain the fine-tuning of the effective cosmological constant in a non-*ad hoc* way. Nonetheless, two points should be made. First, any such explanation will require the hypothesis of just the right set of laws. At best, this will merely transfer the fine-tuning of the cosmological constant to that of the laws of nature; even if those laws of nature are deemed "natural," one would still have to have the right set of laws to eliminate the fine-tuning of the cosmological constant. Consequently, other than eliminating the ability to quantify the degree of fine-tuning, it is unclear how much such a move undercuts the need for some anthropic explanation. Second, it is unclear at what point we should continue searching for such an explanation in terms of physical laws when no plausible candidates have been forthcoming in the last 20 years. Atheists such as Stenger claim that we should continue searching until we can be absolutely sure that no scientific explanation can be found. In Section 2.5.2, where I consider the "God of the gaps" objection, I argue that such a requirement begs the question against T.

Finally, one way of avoiding the fine-tuning of the cosmological constant is to claim that one day the current framework of modern physics will be superseded in such a way as to avoid the fine-tuning problem. For example, one could claim that Einstein's theory of General Relativity will be superseded by a future theory that retains the verified predictions of General Relativity but does not predict that vacuum energy will cause space to

---

15. For example, physicists Christopher Kolda and David H. Lyth note that "an alternative to a cosmological constant is quintessence, defined as a slowly-varying scalar field potential $V(\varphi)$.... In contrast with ordinary inflation, quintessence seems to require extreme fine tuning of the potential $V(\varphi'')$" (1999, abstract). Further, as physicist Gabriela Barenboim notes, models that combine inflation and quintessence "require significant *ad hoc* tuning to simultaneously produce the features of inflation and quintessence" (2006, p. 1).

expand.[16] Or one could claim that this prediction is an artifact of General Relativity that is not to be taken realistically, in analogy to how most physicists reject waves that travel backward in time, even though such waves are one mathematically legitimate solution to the equations of electromagnetism. Such moves, however, will involve giving up inflationary cosmology or radically reformulating it (since it depends on this prediction of General Relativity), and they would present difficulties for explaining the compelling evidence that the expansion of the universe is accelerating. Further, such moves clearly will not work for the fine-tuning of other constants, since many of them depend on facts so basic that they certainly will not be superseded. For example, the fine-tuning of the strength of gravity, as discussed in Section 2.3.2, only depends on the fact that bodies with masses typical of planets and stars attract each other with a force approximately given by Newton's law, and that if the gravitational pull of a planet is too large, most organisms would be crushed. Thus, as a general strategy, this way circumventing the fine-tuning of the cosmological constant is of limited value.

2.4. Initial conditions of the universe

One other fundamental type of fine-tuning should be mentioned, that of the initial conditions of the universe. This refers to the fact that the initial distribution of mass-energy – as measured by entropy – must fall within an exceedingly narrow range for life to occur. Some aspects of these initial conditions are expressed by various cosmic parameters, such as the mass density of the early universe, the strength of the explosion of the Big Bang, the strength of the density perturbations that led to star formation, the ratio of radiation density to the density of normal matter, and the like. Various arguments have been made that each of these must be fine-tuned for life to occur (see e.g. Rees 2000; Davies 1982, chap. 4). Instead of focusing on these individual cases of fine-tuning, I shall focus on what is arguably the most outstanding special initial condition of our universe: its low entropy. According to Roger Penrose, one of Britain's leading theoretical physicists, "In order to produce a universe resembling the one in which we live, the Creator would have to aim for an absurdly tiny volume of the phase space of possible universes" (Penrose 1989, p. 343). How tiny is this volume? According to Penrose, if we let $x = 10^{123}$, the volume of phase space would be about $1/10^x$ of the entire volume (1989, p. 343). This is vastly smaller than the ratio of the volume of a proton – which is about 10^{-45} m^3 – to the entire volume of the visible universe, which is approximately 10^{84} m^3. Thus, this precision is much, much greater than the precision that would be required to hit an individual proton if the entire visible universe were a dartboard! Others have calculated the volume to be zero (Kiessling 2001).

Now phase space is the space that physicists use to measure the various possible configurations of mass-energy of a system. For a system of particles in classical mechanics, this phase space consists of a space whose coordinates are the positions and momenta (i.e. mass × velocity) of the particles, or any other so-called "conjugate" pair of position and momenta variables within the Hamiltonian formulation of mechanics. Consistency requires that any probability measure over this phase space remain invariant regardless of which conjugate positions and momenta are chosen; further, consistency requires

---

16. Apart from General Relativity, the absolute value of the energy has no physical consequences, only the relative differences in energy from one space-time point to another.

that the measure of a volume $V(t_0)$ of phase space at time t_0 be the same as the measure that this volume evolves into at time t, $V(t)$, given that the laws of physics are time-reversal invariant – that is, that they hold in the reverse time direction.[17] One measure that meets this condition is the standard "equiprobability measure" in which the regions of phase space are assigned a probability corresponding to their volume given by their position and momenta (or conjugate position and momenta) coordinates. Moreover, if an additional assumption is made – that the system is ergodic – it is the only measure that meets this condition.[18] This measure is called the *standard measure* of statistical mechanics, and forms the foundation for all the predictions of classical statistical mechanics. A related probability measure – an equiprobability distribution over the eigenstates of any quantum mechanical observable – forms the basis of quantum statistical mechanics.

Statistical mechanics could be thought of as the third main branch of physics, besides the theory of relativity and quantum theory, and has been enormously successful. Under the orthodox view presented in physics texts and widely accepted among philosophers of physics, it is claimed to explain the laws of thermodynamics, such as the second law, which holds that the entropy of a system will increase towards its maximum with overwhelming probability.

Applying this measure to the initial state of the universe, we could then say that under the standard measure, it is enormously improbable, having a probability equal to the minute portion of phase space compatible with it. Indeed, in discussions of the issue, it is typically assumed that this state is enormously improbable. The probability here is not the probability of the particles' (or fields') being in the exact microstate that they were in; that is always zero. Rather, it is the state specified by the requirement that the entropy be low enough for the occurrence of stars and ultimately life. An infinite number of microstates meet this requirement, but they all must be in that tiny region of phase space that Penrose mentions. Finally, it is important to note that the standard measure of statistical mechanics must imply a corresponding epistemic probability measure. The reason is that statistical mechanics is supposed to tell us what *to expect* a system's behavior to be. For instance, the calculation that an increase in entropy for a physical system in the next 5 minutes is enormously improbable leads us to be almost certain that it will not occur – that is, it generates a very low epistemic probability for its occurrence. Thus, applying the standard measure to the initial condition of our universe implies that it has an enormously low unconditional epistemic probability of occurring.

Many points could be disputed in the aforementioned argument and I cannot adequately enter into the debate here. Rather, I shall just summarize three of the major

17. The reason that the statistical mechanics measures are assumed to be time-invariant is easy to see, given that the laws of physics are deterministic and time-reversal invariant. Let $C(t_0)$ be some class of possible initial states of a system. Each member $m(t_0)$ of $C(t_0)$ will evolve into some particular state $m(t)$ at time t. Call $C(t)$ the class of all such states $m(t)$. If the laws of physics are time reversal invariant, any state $m^*(t) \in C(t)$ could have come from only one state $m^*(t_0) \in C(t_0)$ at time t_0. Thus, there is a one-to-one correspondence between microstates in $C(t_0)$ and microstates in $C(t)$. Consequently, if the probability of some system having a microstate in a class $C(t_0)$ is x%, then it must be the case that the probability of the system having a microstate in the corresponding class $C(t)$ of states at time t is x%.

18. An ergodic system is one in which in the limit as time goes to infinity, the average proportion of time a system spends in a given region of phase space with finite volume is the same as the standard equiprobability measure for that region.

ways to avoid assigning an extremely low epistemic probability to the initial state of the universe. First, as suggested by David Albert (2000, pp. 150–62), one could attempt to ground the standard probability measure of statistical mechanics in postulated inde‾terministic quantum processes that have just the right probability distribution to yield this measure. As Albert (2000, p. 160–1) recognizes, such a procedure would still require the postulation of an enormously special, low-entropy macroscopic state at the beginning of the universe but would not require that one postulate a probability measure over the states of its phase space. Second, one could simply restrict all statements of probability in statistical mechanics to statements of conditional probability, where the statement being conditioned on is that that the universe started out in this special macrostate of exceedingly low entropy. Then one could treat the measure over phase space as applying only to those scattered points in phase space consistent with this initial assumption. Doing this would recover all the predictions of statistical mechanics, although it might seem an arbitrary restriction imposed to avoid treating the initial state as improbable. Third, one could point out, as John Earman (2006) has, that no one has been able to develop an even near-adequate mathematical measure for the degrees of freedom of the gravitational field, which is thought to play an essential role in the low entropy of the initial state of the universe.

In light of these responses, how should we view the purported improbability of the initial state? First, we can point out that the improbability assigned by the standard measure is the same as the one that we should assign using the method outlined in Sections 3.3.2 and 3.3.3, in which we argue that scientific confirmation requires that we place an epistemic equiprobability measure over the natural variables in a theory. In statistical mechanics these natural variables turn out to be the position and momenta, or other conjugate variables, used to construct phase space. Thus, it demonstrates a certain consistency in the method we proposed for arriving at epistemic probabilities. Second, all these responses admit that the initial state is in some sense enormously special in some way, while denying the degree of "specialness" can be quantified or physically explained. This leaves us with a strong qualitative, although nonquantifiable, form of fine-tuning.

2.5. Stenger's objections

As mentioned when we discussed the fine-tuning of the cosmological constant, in the last 15 years Victor Stenger has emerged as one of the leading critics of the evidence for fine-tuning. In the next two subsections, we shall look at two of his objections.

2.5.1. Stenger's "Monkey God" objection

One major way in which Stenger has attempted to cast skepticism on fine-tuning arguments is by constructing a computer program that shows that random selections of the constants of physics generally produce viable, life-permitting stars. He calls his computer program "Monkey God." Based on his program, Stenger concludes that:

> No basis exists for assuming that a random universe would not have some kind of life. Calculations of the properties of universes having different physical constants than ours indicate that long-lived stars are not unusual, and thus most universes should have time for complex systems of some type to evolve. (2000, p. 50)

Stenger calculates the lifetime of stars using the equation $t_s = (\alpha^2/\alpha_G) (m_p/m_e)^2 \hbar/(m_p c^2)^{-1}$, where α is the dimensionless electromagnetic interaction strength, α_G is the dimensionless gravitational binding energy, m_p is the mass of the proton, m_e is the mass of the electron, $\hbar$ is Plank's constant divided by 2π, and c is the speed of light.

Using this equation and a program that randomly selects values for the relevant parameters in the aforementioned equation, Stenger concludes that long-lived stars are not unusual among these randomly selected universes and takes this to count as evidence against claims of fine-tuning. The first criticism of his approach is that he does not address the question of whether these universes would have other life-inhibiting features relative to ours. For example, if one decreases the strength of the strong nuclear force by more than 50 percent (while keeping the electromagnetic force constant), carbon becomes unstable, and with a slightly greater decrease, no atoms with atomic number greater than hydrogen can exist (Barrow & Tipler 1986, pp. 326–7). This would make it virtually impossible for complex life forms to evolve. That Stenger ignores these other life-inhibiting features is clear from his equation for the lifetime of a star (which is unaffected by changes in the strong nuclear force, since none of the parameters he uses depends on this strength), and is also obvious from what he says elsewhere regarding his "Monkey God" calculations:

> I find that long-lived stars, which could make life more likely, will occur over a wide range of these parameters. . . . For example, if we take the electron and proton masses to be equal to their values in our universe, an electromagnetic force any stronger than its value in our universe will give a stellar lifetime of more than 680 million years. The strength of the strong interaction does not enter into this calculation. (Stenger 2004, pp. 179–80)

Obviously, if we increased the electromagnetic force by very much while keeping the strong interaction the same, the nuclei of atoms other than hydrogen would break apart due to the increased electromagnetic repulsion of the protons in the nuclei. In this case, there could be no nuclear fusion in stars, and hence no stars.

Second, the equation he uses is based on a simple star model of stellar evolution. The equation does not take into account the complexities of a stellar evolution, such as whether the energy transport from the center of the star to the surface is by convection or radiative diffusion. More importantly, it assumes that the star is made mostly of hydrogen, which would not be the case if the strong force were increased beyond a small amount (see Collins 2003, p. 192 and references therein); further, it does not take into account the effects on star stability of quantum degeneracy, which require much more sophisticated codes to take into account. No simple equation could incorporate these sorts of complexities. As I have shown elsewhere (Collins 2003, pp. 192–3), *using a simple star model*, one can increase the strength of gravity a million- or a billionfold, and still obtain stable, long-lived stars with around the same surface temperature as our Sun. When one takes into account quantum degeneracy effects, however, one can only increase the strength of gravity by around a thousandfold before significantly decreasing the lifetime of stars (Collins 2003, pp. 193–4). Presumably, if one also changed one of the other constants, one could increase the strength of gravity by more than 3,000-fold and still obtain a stable, long-lived star, since it would change when electron degeneracy kicks in. In sum, life-prohibiting effects related to stellar lifetimes and stability only come to light when one begins to consider the complexity of the physics involved in stellar evolution, something Stenger has not done.

2.5.2. Stenger's "God of the gaps" objection

Another common objection to the fine-tuning argument is that it is a variation of the "God of the gaps" argument, and so it should be rejected. Victor Stenger raises this objection with regard to the fine-tuning of the cosmological constant. According to Stenger:

> While quintessence may not turn out to provide the correct explanation for the cosmological constant problem, it demonstrates, if nothing else, that science is always hard at work trying to solve its puzzles within a materialistic framework. The assertion that God can be seen by virtue of his acts of cosmological fine-tuning, like intelligent design and earlier versions of the argument from design, is nothing more than another variation on the disreputable God-of-the gaps argument. These rely on the faint hope that scientists will never be able to find a natural explanation for one or more of the puzzles that currently have them scratching their heads and therefore will have to insert God as the explanation. As long as science can provide plausible scenarios for a fully material universe, even if those scenarios cannot be currently tested they are sufficient to refute the God of the gaps. (2004, p. 182)

Elsewhere, Stenger claims that one would be justified in invoking God only if "the phenomenon in question is not only currently scientifically inexplicable but can be shown to forever defy natural description" (2007, pp. 13–4). As he recognizes, this requirement of proof is exceptionally strong. Although he qualifies his assertion regarding God as a scientific hypothesis, the question that arises is the level of proof that we need regarding the nonexistence of a plausible scientific explanation before we are justified in invoking God as an explanation of the fine-tuning, regardless of whether it is considered a scientific or a metaphysical explanation.

To answer this latter question, we must consider the reasons for thinking that a "God of the gaps" sort of explanation is in principle something to be avoided. The reasons partly depend on whether one is a theist or an atheist; and if one is a theist, it will depend on how one understands the nature of divine action. Many theists will claim that ultimately we should avoid a God of the gaps explanation because it is bad theology. According to these theists, God would be greater if God created a material order that could function on its own without God's needing to intervene and fill various gaps. If these theists are correct, then for theological reasons one should strenuously avoid appealing to divine intervention in the natural order to explain phenomena that science has not yet explained and instead trust that God has created a material world with its own integrity. *Such theological reasons, however, will not apply to the structure of the cosmos itself – its basic laws, its initial conditions, and the values of its constants – since these do not require any intervention in the natural order.* Other theists, such as intelligent design theorists, will be even more lenient concerning those cases in which it is appropriate to invoke God as an explanation.

Of course, atheists who are fully committed to a naturalistic account of the cosmos will always claim that it is illegitimate to appeal to God, since God does not exist. In order for the God of the gaps objection to avoid begging the question against the theist, however, it has to be framed in such a way as to carry force even on theistic assumptions. Such an argument does carry force, at least on the assumption of many theists, when God or some other transcendent designer is invoked to explain, for instance, seemingly irreducibly complex biological systems, since in such cases it implies that nature lacks sufficient integrity to produce the systems on its own. Stenger and others have not shown that it carries any non-question-begging force for the case of the structure of the universe as a whole.

One might object to this response by claiming that the history of science provides independent grounds for rejecting any appeal to God to fill in the apparent gaps left by science. The failure of such appeals, however, can be explained as well by the theist as the naturalist: for example, many theists would claim that Newton's famous invocation of God to keep the planetary orbits stable implies a less than satisfactory picture of a constantly intervening God. The key question is how one inductively extrapolates from these historical incidences, and that all depends on one's background assumptions – that is, whether one is an atheist or a theist, and what kind of theist one is. In themselves, these incidences can tell us nothing about whether we can be justified in appealing to God for explaining the fine-tuning.

But what about the scientific strictures of methodological naturalism? These would be relevant only if the appeal to God were considered as a *scientific* explanation, something that I am not assuming. Rather, God should be considered a philosophical or metaphysical explanation of LPU. So where does this leave us with regard to the burden of proof? The advocate of the fine-tuning argument will only need to argue that it is unlikely that all the cases can be given a natural explanation that removes their epistemic improbability without transferring that improbability up one level. And as argued in Sections 6.3.1 and 7.2, even if the fine-tuning of the constants of physics can be explained in terms of some set of deeper physical laws, as hypothesized by the so-called "theory of everything" or by an inflationary multiverse, this would simply transfer the improbability up one level to the existence of these deeper laws.

2.6. Conclusion

There are many other cases of fine-tuning that I have not discussed, such as those extensively discussed by biochemist Michael Denton (1998). These latter consist of various higher-level features of the natural world, such as the many unique properties of carbon, oxygen, water, and the electromagnetic spectrum, that appear optimally adjusted for the existence of complex biochemical systems (Denton 1988, chaps 3–6, pp. 19–140). Presumably, these higher-level features of the universe are ultimately grounded in the laws, constants, and initial conditions of the universe. Nonetheless, they provide additional evidence that the fundamental structure of the universe is fine-tuned for life.

As illustrated by the case of Victor Stenger discussed earlier (Section 2.5), it should be pointed out that some physicists and scientists have been skeptical of some of the prominent cases of fine-tuning in the literature. As I have shown in detail elsewhere, in some cases this skepticism is warranted, but in other cases the physical arguments offered for fine-tuning are solid (see Collins 2003). Nonetheless, even if there are no cases of fine-tuning that are sufficiently established to be beyond doubt, the argument would still have significant force. As philosopher John Leslie has pointed out, "clues heaped upon clues can constitute weighty evidence despite doubts about each element in the pile" (1988, p. 300). This is especially true given that the clues in this case fall into a variety of distinct types – there are not only three distinct fundamental types of fine-tuning, but there are many distinct cases under each type. The only plausible response that a skeptic could give to the multitude of different cases of fine-tuning is to find one or two overarching reasons that would undercut almost all the cases of fine-tuning in a single stroke. Given the diversity of the cases of fine-tuning, it is very unlikely that this will happen. In any case, in Section 7.2, I will address one such attempt, an attempt I call the "more fundamental law" objection, according to which there might be some fundamental law (or principle) that entails all the cases of fine-tuning.

3. Epistemic Probability

3.1. The need for epistemic probability

According to atheist Keith Parsons:

> If atheism is correct, if the universe and its laws are all that is or ever has been, how can it be said that the universe, with all of its 'finely tuned' features, is in any relevant sense probable or improbable? *Ex Hypothesi* there are no antecedent conditions that could determine such a probability. Hence, if the universe is the ultimate brute fact, it is neither likely nor unlikely, probable nor improbable; it simply is.
>
> Further, even if the universe were somehow improbable, it is hard to see on the hypothesis of atheism how we could ever know this. If we were in the position to witness the birth of many worlds – some designed, some undesigned – then we might be in a position to say of any particular world that it had such-and-such a probability of existing undesigned. But we simply are not in such a position. We have absolutely no empirical basis for assigning probabilities to ultimate facts. (1990, p. 182)

Although commonly raised, Parson's objection is deeply mistaken. It fails to recognize a common, nonstatistical kind of probability that some philosophers have called *epistemic probability* and others have called *inductive probability* (e.g. Swinburne 2001, p. 62).[19] As Ian Hacking notes in his excellent study of the history of probability theory, the idea of probability was Janus-faced from its emergence in seventeenth-century Europe, with one side being the notion of statistical probability and the other side being the notion of epistemic probability:

> On the one side it [the conception of probability] is statistical, concerning itself with stochastic laws or chance processes. On the other side it is epistemological, dedicated to assessing reasonable degrees of belief in propositions quite devoid of statistical background. (Hacking 1975, p. 12)

So, for instance, when people say that the Thesis of Common Ancestry is probably true given the fossil and genetic evidence we currently have, they are clearly not talking about statistical probability, since this thesis is about a unique event in Earth's history. The same holds for any claim about the probable truth (or "empirical adequacy") of a scientific theory. In his treatise, *A Treatise on Probability* (1921), John Maynard Keynes further developed this conception, and there have been several recent attempts to provide a more precise account of this sort of probability (e.g. Swinburne 2001, chaps. 3 and 4; Plantinga 1993, chap. 9).

In conjunction with the Likelihood Principle, this sort of probability is extensively used in scientific confirmation. Consider, for example, the arguments typically offered in favor

---

19. Swinburne (2001, p. 68), for instance, reserves the term "epistemic probability" for inductive probability that takes into account human cognitive limitations. I will use it more broadly to refer to what Swinburne calls "inductive probability."

of the Thesis of Common Ancestry, continental drift theory, and the atomic hypothesis. The Thesis of Common Ancestry is commonly supported by claiming that a variety of features of the world – such as the structure of the tree of life – would not be improbable if this thesis is true, but would be very improbable under other contending, nonevolutionary hypotheses, such as special creation. Consider, for instance, the following quotation from evolutionary biologist and geneticist Edward Dodson, in which he summarizes the case for evolution, understood as the Thesis of Common Ancestry:

> All [pieces of evidence] concur in *suggesting* evolution with varying degrees of cogency, but most can be explained on other bases, albeit with some damage to the law of parsimony. The strongest evidence for evolution is the concurrence of so many *independent probabilities*. That such different disciplines as biochemistry and comparative anatomy, genetics and biogeography should all point toward the same conclusion is very difficult to attribute to coincidence. (1984, p. 68; italics added)

Similar lines of reasoning are given for accepting continental drift theory. For example, the similarity between the animal and plant life on Africa and South America millions of years ago was considered to provide significant support for continental drift theory. Why? Because it was judged very unlikely that this similarity would exist if continental drift theory were false, but not if it were true.

Finally, consider the use of epistemic probability in the confirmation of atomic theory. According to Wesley Salmon (1984, pp. 219–20), what finally convinced virtually all physical scientists by 1912 of the atomic hypothesis was the agreement of at least 13 independent determinations of Avogadro's number based on the assumption that atomic theory was correct.[20] For example, one method of determining Avogadro's number is through observations of Brownian motion, that is, the random motion of very small particles suspended in a liquid, a motion that was postulated to be caused by the unequal, random impact of the molecules in the liquid. From this motion and the kinetic theory of heat, one can calculate what the mass of each molecule must be in order to account for the observed motion, and then using that value one can obtain Avogadro's number.

The scientists reasoned that *if atomic theory were false, then such an agreement between thirteen different determinations of Avogadro's number would be exceedingly epistemically improbable* – in Salmon's words, an "utterly astonishing coincidence" (1984, p. 220). Indeed, if scientists had not judged the agreement to be exceedingly improbable if atomic theory were false, it is difficult to see why they would take it to count as strong evidence in its favor. On the other hand, the scientists reasoned, if atomic theory were true, such an agreement would be expected. Thus, by implicitly using the *Likelihood Principle*, they reasoned that these independent determinations of Avogadro's number strongly confirmed atomic theory.

It should be noted that one could not avoid this sort of reasoning simply by rejecting scientific realism, since even though antirealists reject the truth or approximate truth of certain types of well-confirmed hypotheses, they still accept them as being reliable bases for future explanations and predictions – that is, in Bas van Fraassen's (1980) terminology,

---

20. Avogadro's number = 6.02252×10^{23}. Avogadro's number is defined as the number of atoms in 12 grams of carbon 12 and by definition is equal to the number of elementary entities in one mole of any substance.

they accept them as being "empirically adequate." Consequently, instead of interpreting the confirming evidence as evidence for a hypothesis' truth, they accept it as evidence for the hypothesis' empirical adequacy. This means that insofar as realists need to appeal to epistemic probabilities to support the approximate truth of a theory, antirealists will need to appeal to those same probabilities in support of a theory's empirical adequacy – for example, antirealists would need to claim that it is highly improbable for the determinations of Avogadro's number to agree if atomic theory were not empirically adequate.

Since some of the probabilities in the aforementioned examples involve singular, non-repeatable states of affairs, they are not based on statistical probabilities, nor arguably other non-epistemic probabilities. This is especially evident for the probabilities involved in the confirmation of atomic theory since some of them involve claims about probabilities conditioned on the underlying structure and laws of the universe being different – e.g. atoms not existing. Hence, they are not based on actual physical propensities, relative frequencies, or theoretical models of the universe's operation. They therefore cannot be grounded in theoretical, statistical, or physical probabilities. Similar things can be said about many other related types of confirmation in science, such as the confirmation of quantum electrodynamics (QED) by its extraordinarily precise prediction of the gyromagnetic moment of the electron, which we shall discuss later in this chapter. Such cases, I contend, establish the widespread use of purely epistemic probabilities in scientific confirmation that are neither grounded in other types of probability nor in experience – e.g. the probabilities invoked in atomic theory clearly are not grounded in experience, since nothing like such an agreement had ever occurred before. We shall return to this in Sections 3.3.2 and 3.3.3 when I discuss the Principle of Indifference.

3.2. An account of epistemic probability

Having established the need for epistemic probability, we now turn to developing an account of it. Accounts of epistemic probability range from the so-called subjective theory to the logical theory. According to the subjective theory, epistemic probability amounts to nothing more than our purely subjective degree of belief in a claim with the only restriction on the rationality of our degrees of belief is that they obey the probability calculus and conform to our own personal inductive standards. In contrast, according to the logical theory, epistemic probability refers to some human-mind independent relation analogous to that of logical entailment. Despite its popularity, I shall say nothing more here about subjective theory, other than that it seems to lead to an extreme form of epistemic relativism. The reason is that it does not distinguish between rational and irrational inductive criteria. Given the right inductive criteria almost any set of beliefs can be made to cohere with the probability calculus – for example, the belief that the Sun and stars revolve around the Earth can be made to cohere with all the current evidence we have to the contrary. (For a further critique, see Swinburne (2001, pp. 73f) and Plantinga (1993, pp. 143f)).

On the other hand, at least two major problems confront the purely logical theory of epistemic probability. First, it is doubtful that we need to hypothesize a metaphysics of human-mind independent relations of logical probability between propositions to ground the rationality of all of our statements involving epistemic probability. As Keynes (1921, pp. 4, 32) pointed out, all we need is the existence of relations of rational support or expectation that are independent of merely personal or cultural beliefs and standards. Consequently, allowing for the relations of epistemic probability to be dependent on the contingent construction of human cognitive faculties fits much better with my overall approach of trying to stay as close as possible to the principles of reasoning that are part of everyday and scientific practice (see Section 1.1).

Second, purely logical probability would guide the expectations only of logically omniscient agents – that is, agents that could see all logical relations between propositions, including the relations of logical probability. Humans, however, are limited to a partial grasp of such relations, which is reflected in the relevant usage of epistemic probability in science. For example, as Swinburne acknowledges, based on the current mathematical evidence, Goldbach's conjecture (that every even number greater than two is the sum of two prime numbers) is probably true, but not certainly true. That is, the current evidence – such as that Goldbach's conjecture has been shown to be true for the first trillion numbers and was claimed to be proven by some otherwise truthful mathematician – supports this conjecture, but not enough to justify our being certain that it is true. Since it is a mathematical claim, however, Goldbach's conjecture is either necessarily true, or it is necessarily false, and thus its logical probability is either one or zero. The epistemic probability being invoked here, therefore, is not purely logical probability. Even if one does not agree that this sort of epistemic probability arises in mathematics, nonetheless it is clear that when judging the evidential support for a scientific theory, we are not aware of all the relevant logical relations between the evidence and the theory. Keynes, who made the degree of logical/epistemological probability of one proposition on another relative to human powers, recognized this issue. According to him:

> If we do not take this view of probability, if we do not limit it in this way and make it, to this extent, relative to human powers, we are altogether adrift in the unknown; for we cannot ever know what degree of probability would be justified by the perception of logical relations which we are, and must always be, incapable of comprehending. (1921, p. 33)

Following Swinburne, one could still attempt to take logical probability as the primary kind of epistemic (or what he calls *inductive*) probability, and then attempt to accommodate human limitations. The problem with this approach is that in order to use logical probability to make statements about the rational degree of credence one ought to place in a theory, or the amount by which we should take a body of evidence to increase our confidence in a theory, one would need some account of how to translate degrees of logical probability to rational degrees of credence for beings subject to our limitations. Consequently, one would still need an account of another more human-centered type of epistemic probability that is relative to human cognitive powers to grasp these human perceptions of logical probability; in itself, logical probability only stipulates what the rational degrees of belief of a logically omniscient agent ought to be, not that of a mere human being. As far as I know, Swinburne does not provide any account that links the two together.

I call the conception of epistemic probability that is grounded in our perceptions of logical relations between propositions, *episto-logical* probability. In contrast to the episto-logical account of epistemic probability, Alvin Plantinga (1993, chap. 9, pp. 159–75) has developed an account in which the relations of probability are grounded in the contingent construction of our cognitive faculties, which in many cases need not involve perceptions of logical relations. In his account, for instance, we think that the future will resemble the past, since those aspects of properly functioning human cognitive faculties that are aimed at truth normally incline us to believe that the future will resemble the past. Similarly, we accept simpler theories over complex ones for the same reason. Because of their stress on the contingent construction of our cognitive faculties, I call views such as Plantinga's *noetic conceptions* of epistemic probability.

The account of epistemic probability that I favor is one in which epistemic probabilities are grounded in some combination of both the contingent construction of our cognitive faculties and the perceived logical relations among propositions. For the purposes of this chapter, I will leave it as an open question which of these conceptions of epistemic probability – the logical, the epistological, the noetic, or some combination thereof – is ultimately correct. A word, however, needs to be said about a problem with Plantinga's account of epistemic probability that is relevant for our purposes. Plantinga defines the conditional epistemic probability of a Proposition A on a Proposition B as follows:

> **Plantinga's Definition of Conditional Epistemic Probability:** $P(A|B) = <x,y>$ iff $<x,y>$ is the smallest interval which contains all the intervals which represent the degree to which a rational human being S (for whom the conditions necessary for warrant hold) could believe A if she believed B, *had no undercutting defeater for A, had no other source of warrant either for A or for -A, was aware that she believed B, and considered the evidential bearing of B on A.* (1993, p. 169; italics added)

Plantinga's account of conditional epistemic probability is a counterfactual account that defines epistemic probability in terms of the degree of warrant a rational human being would have in A if she believed B and had no other sources of warrant for A or –A. The italicized portion, which we shall call Plantinga's *condition of epistemic probability* (CEP), primarily does the job of excluding contributions to our warrant which arise from our epistemic circumstances and other information besides B that is part of our background information k.

We cannot go into a detailed analysis of this account of conditional epistemic probability here. However, we shall consider one major objection that is relevant to the way in which we shall be using epistemic probability. As Bas van Fraassen has pointed out, Plantinga's account does not account for those cases in which B could not be the sole source of warrant for A, an objection that Plantinga attempts to address (1993, p. 168–9). This problem arises in the case of the fine-tuning argument, since we claim that the epistemic probability of LPU is very small under NSU. Our own existence in a body, however, provides a source of warrant for LPU, and it is a source that we cannot eliminate without severely altering our cognitive faculties (or epistemic conditions) in a way that would undermine our rationality.

More recently, Richard Otte has given new teeth to the objection to Plantinga's account raised by van Fraassen. Among other examples, Otte asks us to consider the following variation of one of Plantinga's examples:

P (people are sometimes appeared to redly | I am appeared to redly)

According to Otte:

> Intuitively this probability is 1; if I am appeared to redly, it must be the case that people are sometimes appeared to redly. But Plantinga claims that it is not possible for a rational person's sole source of warrant for *people are sometimes appeared to redly* to be *I am appeared to redly*.

Thus this probability is undefined according to CEP, even though it obviously has a value of 1. This example shows that CEP does not account for our intuitive notion of conditional epistemic probability. (2006, p. 87)

Otte locates the problem with Plantinga's account in his use of counterfactuals, claiming that spelling out conditional epistemic probability in terms of counterfactuals is the wrong approach. Some sort of counterfactual element, however, is essential to any account of conditional epistemic probability if we are to connect degrees of conditional epistemic probability with actual rational degrees of belief, which we need to do if judgments of conditional probability are to serve as guides to life. This requirement, however, does not imply that we must provide a purely counterfactual analysis of conditional epistemic probability; all it demands is that counterfactuals will play some role in connecting conditional epistemic probability with rational degrees of belief.

Although I cannot develop this idea in detail here, I propose that conditional epistemic probability should be conceived as a relation between propositions that is in part determined by the contingent nature of our cognitive faculties. Through introspection, we have partial access to this relation. We typically determine the epistemic probability, $P(A|B)$, of Proposition A on Proposition B – that is, the degree of rational inclination B should give us for A – by artificially creating in our own minds Plantinga's conditions for CEP – that is, by "bracketing out" all other sources of warrant for A or –A, and any undercutting defeaters for A. Thus, for instance, suppose I see it raining outside but want to access the conditional epistemic probability of "it will rain today" (Proposition A) on Proposition B, where B is the conjunction of the claim that "www.weather.com has predicted a 25 percent chance of rain" and other background information, such as that www.weather.com is reliable weather predictor. In assessing this conditional probability, I block out all other sources of warrant for its raining today (such as seeing dark clouds on the horizon), except for Proposition B, and arrive at the correct conditional probability, $P(A|B) = 0.25$. The fact that, for the cases when CEP applies, I come to know these counterfactual degrees of warrant by means of this "bracketing procedure" strongly suggests that epistemic probability should not be identified with counterfactual degrees of belief. *Rather, it should be considered a non-reducible relation of support or warrant existing between propositions that comes in degrees, is partially dependent on our cognitive faculties, and which we can know by introspection via the "bracketing procedure." This relation in turn gives rise to the corresponding counterfactual degrees of warrant when CEP is met.*

The fact that conditional epistemic probability should be considered such a relation existing between propositions that we determine by the "bracketing procedure" is supported by other examples. Consider, for instance, the conditional epistemic probability, $P(A|B \& k')$, of the claim that "human beings exist today" (claim A) based on the claim that the asteroid that supposedly killed the dinosaurs missed planet Earth (claim B) and certain relevant scientific theories (k') regarding the conditions necessary for the evolution of hominids. Given B and k', I might judge it would be very unlikely that the dinosaurs would have become extinct, and hence very unlikely that humans would exist: that is, I would judge $P(A|B \& k') \ll 1$. The procedure I would go through is that of bracketing out all other sources of warrant for A except the relevant scientific theories, k', and claim B, and then access the degree to which the remaining information warranted or supported A. For instance, I would bracket out all those everyday pieces of information that imply the existence of human beings. Since CEP cannot be met in this case, the existence of a conditional epistemic probability in this case shows that identifying epistemic probability with counterfactual degrees of warrant (or belief or credence) cannot be right.

Part of the purpose of this section is to provide a theoretical underpinning for both the existence of conditional epistemic probability and the claim that $P(A|B \& k')$ can exist for those cases in which the Proposition B & k' cannot be the sole source of warrant for A. Such a claim is crucial to the likelihood (and probabilistic tension) formulation of the fine-tuning argument, since LPU will be improbable only on background information k' in which the information that embodied, conscious observers exist is subtracted out of our background information k (see Sections 4.3 and 4.4). Since all rational people believe that they are embodied, it is impossible for k' & NSU to be the sole source of warrant for LPU. Hence, Plantinga's CEP cannot be met for $P(LPU|k' \& NSU)$. Despite these theoretical underpinnings, some still might question whether there can exist relations of epistemic probability in those cases in which the antecedent (B & k') cannot be the sole source of warrant for the consequent (A).

To further support the existence of epistemic probabilities in these cases, consider the sorts of cases, such as those mentioned earlier, in which scientific confirmation appears to depend on claims that some state of affairs S – such as the agreement of the various methods of determining Avogadro's number – is expected under a certain hypothesis h, but very epistemically improbable under the negation of that hypothesis, ~h. Suppose we discovered for one of these cases that S was also necessary for our own existence. It seems clear that such a discovery would not itself undermine the confirmation argument in favor of the approximate truth (or empirical adequacy) of the theory. If it did, then we could undermine the support based on the Likelihood Principle for many theories of physics simply by discovering that the state of affairs S predicted by the theory – for example, the degree of bending of light around the Sun predicted by General Relativity – was necessary for embodied conscious life. This seems clearly wrong. Thus, there must be a probability for $P(S|\sim h \& k')$ in these cases, where k' is some appropriately chosen background information that does not implicitly or explicitly include the fact that humans exist. (If k' included that humans exist, then $P(S|\sim h \& k') = 1$, destroying any likelihood confirmation; see Section 4.3 for more discussion on choosing k' in cases like this.)

As a specific example, consider QED's precise prediction of the deviation from 2 of the gyromagnetic moment of the electron to nine significant digits, as discussed in Section 3.3.3. In terms of the Likelihood Principle, the reason this prediction has been thought to significantly confirm QED is that such a precise, correct prediction seems very epistemically unlikely if QED is *not* approximately true (or at least empirically adequate), but it is epistemically likely if QED is true.[21] Suppose we discovered that this precise magnitude of deviation was necessary for the evolution of life in our universe. It seems clear that this would not undermine the confirmation that this precise prediction gives to QED.

Finally, since no rational person could doubt LPU, it will often be useful to use the following conceptual device to intuitively grasp the relations of conditional epistemic probability for LPU conditioned on NSU & k' and conditioned on T & k'. The device is to

---

21. The importance of this example, and others like it, is that insofar as the confirmation in question admits a likelihood reconstruction, it clearly involves epistemic probabilities that cannot be reduced to statistical or theoretical probabilities (since the predicted value has to do with the basic structure of our universe), and it is one in which we can plausibly conceive of it as having some anthropic significance.

imagine an unembodied alien observer with cognitive faculties structurally similar to our own in the relevant ways, and then ask the degrees of credence that such a being would have in LPU given that he or she believes in NSU & k′ or in T & k′. This device of the unembodied alien observer should remove any lingering doubts about the existence of a conditional epistemic probability on background information k′ that we could not have – for example, when k′ does not implicitly or explicitly include the existence of embodied conscious beings. Given that such an alien is possible, it could have k′ as its background information and thus would not have the aforementioned problem regarding the existence of an epistemic probability for LPU on k′; hence, the existence of LPU could significantly confirm T over NSU for that being. It seems clear that if we met such a being and if we discovered that LPU confirmed T over NSU for that being, then it should do so for us too.[22]

I believe the various arguments I have offered establish both the crucial role of epistemic probabilities in scientific confirmation and their existence between some Propositions A and B & k′ in those cases in which B & k′ could never be the sole source of warrant (or justification) for A. Our next question is how to determine P(A|B & k′).

3.3. Determining epistemic probability

3.3.1. Introduction

Now that we know what we mean by epistemic probability, it is time to consider how it is justified. In science, many times epistemic probability is determined by an appeal to intuition, such as many of the epistemic probabilities considered in the last section – for example, those arising in conjunction with the Thesis of Common Ancestry, continental drift theory, and atomic theory. These probabilities clearly were not justified by an appeal to statistical improbability – for example, we have no statistics regarding the relative frequency of life on a planet having those features cited in favor of evolution either under the evolutionary hypothesis or under some nonevolutionary hypothesis. Indeed, these judgments of epistemic probability were never rigorously justified in any way. Rather, after (we hope) doing their best job of looking at the evidence, scientists and laypersons made judgments of what kind of world we should expect under each hypothesis, and then they simply trusted these judgments. This sort of trust in our judgments of epistemic probability is a pervasive and indispensable feature of our intellectual life. It is these sorts of intuitive judgments, I contend, that ultimately ground the claim that, given the evidence for the first type of fine-tuning we discussed in Section 2.2 – that of the laws of nature – it is very epistemically unlikely that such a universe would exist under NSU & k′.

Of course, the more widely shared these judgments are by those who are relevantly informed, the more seriously we take them. In this regard, it should be noted that, given the fine-tuning data, the judgment that LPU is surprising under naturalism is widely shared by intelligent, informed individuals, as evidenced by the various attempts to account for

---

22. For a denial of the kind of claim that I make here – namely, that the confirmation must be the same for the unembodied being and us – see Sober (2005, pp. 137–40). For a critique of Sober, see footnote in Section 7.5. Even if Sober is correct, my other arguments still hold for thinking there could exist an epistemic probability of LPU on k′ & NSU and k′ & T. Further, these arguments show that confirmation can still occur even when there is an observer selection effect, such as the aforementioned thought experiments in which we discovered that the data in support of atomic theory or QED had anthropic significance.

it, such as the multiverse hypothesis. Of course, the skeptic might object that scientific theories are testable, whereas the theistic explanation is not. But why should testability matter with regard to the acceptability of our judgments of epistemic probability? After all, testability is about being able to find evidence for or against a theory in the future, not about the present likelihood of the theory or the likelihood of some body of data's being the case if the theory is false or not empirically adequate. Thus, I contend, the merely intuitive judgments of epistemic probability in the case of fine-tuning are on as solid ground as many of those accepted in science that cannot be rigorously justified. It is dishonest, therefore, to accept one sort of inference without rigorous justification but reject the other merely because it purportedly lacks such justification. At any rate, we shall present such justification for judgments of epistemic probability in the case of the fine-tuning of the constants of physics, regarding which I shall argue that we can go beyond a mere appeal to intuition. Instead, we can provide a solid, principled justification based on what I shall call the restricted Principle of Indifference, which we shall discuss in the next two subsections.[23]

3.3.2. Restricted Principle of Indifference

According to the *restricted Principle of Indifference*, when we have no reason to prefer any one value of a variable p over another in some range R, we should assign equal epistemic probabilities to equal ranges of p that are in R, given that p constitutes a "natural variable." A variable is defined as "natural" if it occurs within the simplest formulation of the relevant area of physics. When there is a range of viable natural variables, then one can only legitimately speak of the range of possible probabilities, with the range being determined by probabilities spanned by the lower and upper bound of the probabilities determined by the various choices of natural variables.

Since the constants of physics used in the fine-tuning argument typically occur within the simplest formulation of the relevant physics, the constants themselves are natural variables. Thus, the restricted Principle of Indifference entails that we should assign epistemic probability in proportion to the width of the range of the constant we are considering. We shall use this fact in Section 5.1 to derive the claim that $P(Lpc|NSU \& k') \ll 1$, where Lpc is the claim that the value for some fine-tuned constant C falls within the life-permitting range.

To see why the restriction to a natural variable is needed, consider the case in which we are told that a factory produces cubes between 0 and 10 meters in length, but in which we are given no information about what lengths it produces. Using our aforementioned principle, we shall now calculate the epistemic probability of the cube being between 9 and 10 meters in length. Such a cube could be characterized either by its length, L, or its volume, V. If we characterize it by its length, then since the range [9,10] is one-tenth of the possible range of lengths of the cube, the probability would be 1/10. If, however, we characterize it by its volume, the ratio of the range of volumes is: $[1,000 - 9^3]/1,000 = [1,000 - 729]/1,000 = 0.271$, which yields almost three times the probability as for the case of using

---

23. A rigorous justification of the epistemic improbability of the initial conditions of the universe is a little trickier, since it presupposes that one can apply the standard measure of statistical mechanics to the initial state of the universe, something John Earman and others have questioned (see Section 2.4). We cannot pursue this issue further in this chapter, however.

length. Thus, the probability we obtain depends on what mathematically equivalent variable we use to characterize the situation.

In the case of the constants of physics, one can always find some mathematically equivalent way of writing the laws of physics in which W_r/W_R is any arbitrarily selected value between zero and one. For example, one could write Newton's law of gravity as $F = U^{100}m_1m_2/r^2$, where U is the corresponding gravitational constant such that $U^{100} = G$. If the comparison range for the standard gravitational constant G were from 0 to $10^{100}G_0$, and the life-permitting range were from 0 to $10^9 G_0$, that would translate to a comparison range for U of 0 to $10U_0$ and a life-permitting range of 0 to $1.2U_0$, since $10U_0 = 10^{100}G_0$ and $1.2U_0 = 10^9G_0$. (Here G_0 is the present value of G and U_0 would be the corresponding present value of U.) Thus, using G as the gravitational constant, the ratio, W_r/W_R, would be $10^9G_0/10^{100}G_0 = 1/10^{91}$, and using U as the "gravitational constant," it would be $1.2U_0/10U_0$, or 0.12, a dramatic difference! Of course, $F = U^{100}m_1m_2/r^2$ is not nearly as simple as $F = Gm_1m_2/r^2$, and thus the restricted Principle of Indifference would only apply when using G as one's variable, not U.

Examples such as that of the cube mentioned have come to be known as the Bertrand Paradoxes (see e.g. Weatherford 1982, p. 56). Historically, this has been thought of as the fatal blow to the general applicability of the Principle of Indifference, except in those cases in which a natural variable can be determined by, for instance, symmetry considerations such as in statistical mechanics. In the next section, however, we shall see that for purposes of theory confirmation, scientists often take those variables that occur in the simplest formulation of a theory as the natural variables. Thus, when there is a simplest formulation, or nontrivial class of such formulations, of the laws of physics, the restricted Principle of Indifference circumvents the Bertrand Paradoxes.

Several powerful general reasons can be offered in defense of the Principle of Indifference if it is restricted in the ways explained earlier. First, it has an extraordinarily wide range of applicability. As Roy Weatherford notes in his book, *Philosophical Foundations of Probability Theory*, "an astonishing number of extremely complex problems in probability theory have been solved, and usefully so, by calculations based entirely on the assumption of equiprobable alternatives [that is, the Principle of Indifference]" (1982, p. 35). Second, in certain everyday cases, the Principle of Indifference seems the only justification we have for assigning probability. To illustrate, suppose that in the last 10 minutes a factory produced the first 20-sided die ever produced (which would be a regular **icosahedron**). Further suppose that every side of the die is (macroscopically) perfectly symmetrical with every other side, except for each side having different numbers printed on it. (The die we are imagining is like a fair six-sided die except that it has 20 sides instead of six.) Now, we all immediately know that upon being rolled the probability of the die coming up on any given side is one in 20. Yet we do not know this directly from experience with 20-sided dice, since by hypothesis no one has yet rolled such dice to determine the relative frequency with which they come up on each side. Rather, it seems our only justification for assigning this probability is the Principle of Indifference: that is, given that every side of the die is macroscopically symmetrical with every other side, we have no reason to believe that it will land on one side versus any other. Accordingly, we assign all outcomes an equal probability of one in 20.[24]

---

24. A full-scale defense of the restricted Principle of Indifference is beyond the scope of this chapter. See Schlesinger (1985, chap. 5) for a lengthy defense of the standard Principle of Indifference.

In the next section, I shall first offer a powerful reason for epistemically privileging those variables that occur in the simplest overall formulation of the relevant domain of physics. I shall then show how this reason offers a further, strong support for the restricted Principle of Indifference based on scientific practice.

3.3.3. Natural variable assumption

Typically, in scientific practice, precise and correct novel predictions are taken to significantly confirm a theory, with the degree of confirmation increasing with the precision of the prediction. We shall argue, however, that the notion of the "precision" of a prediction makes sense only if one privileges certain variables – the ones that I shall call the *natural variables*. These are the variables that occur in the simplest overall expression of the laws of physics. Thus, epistemically privileging the natural variables as required by the restricted Principle of Indifference corresponds to the epistemic practice in certain areas of scientific confirmation; if scientists did not privilege certain variables, they could not claim that highly precise predictions confirm a theory significantly more than imprecise predictions.

We begin our argument by considering only cases in which the predictions of a theory are accurate to within experimental error. In such cases, the known predictive precision will be equal to the *experimental precision* of the measured quantity. Our fundamental premise will then be that everything else being equal, the confirmation that a prediction offers a theory increases with the *known precision* of a prediction.

The experimental precision of a measurement of a quantity is dependent on the experimental error. In standard scientific notation, the experimental value of a quantity is often expressed as $V \pm e$, where e indicates that one's measuring apparatus cannot distinguish between values that differ by more than e. More precisely, to say that the experimentally determined value is $V \pm e$ indicates that we have a certain set degree of confidence – usually chosen to be 95 percent – that the actual value is within the interval $[V + e, V - e]$. So, for example, one might measure the weight of a person as $145.3 \text{ lb} \pm 0.1$: that is, the experiment gives us a 95 percent confidence that the person's weight is within the interval $[145.4 \text{ lb}, 145.2 \text{ lb}]$.

Scientists often speak of experimental accuracy/precision in terms of significant digits. Thus, in the above example, the precision is three significant digits since one's measuring apparatus cannot determine whether the person weighs 145.4 lb or 145.2 lb, and thus only three digits (i.e. 145) can be relied on to give one the value of the weight. Because sometimes zeroes can be "placeholder" digits that determine the order of magnitude of a quantity, these digits are not considered significant. For example, the zeroes in 0.000841 are placeholder digits. To eliminate counting placeholder digits as significant, one can simply express the measured value in terms of scientific notation, and then count the number of digits that are within the margin of error. Thus, a measurement of 0.000841 ± 0.000002 meters for the length of a piece of steel expressed in scientific notation becomes $8.41 \pm 0.02 \times 10^{-4}$ meters, which yields an accuracy of two significant digits. This measure of precision will not work for those cases in which the measured value is zero, nor should it even be applied to those cases in which the measured value is less than the error.

A more precise way of thinking about this kind of precision is in terms of the ratio of the width, W_p of the confidence interval $[V + e, V - e]$ to the value of V, with the restriction that $V > e$. Under this notion of precision, to say that the experimental value has a precision of δ means that $\text{Abs}[W_r/V] < \delta$, where Abs denotes the absolute value of the quantity in brackets, and W_r denotes the width of the range $[V + e, V - e]$ – that is, $2e$. There is a rough correspondence between precision expressed in terms of this ratio and in terms of significant digits: a precision of n significant digits roughly corresponds to a ratio of one in 10^n. Thus, in our weight example, $W_r = 2e = 0.2$, and hence $W_r/V = 0.2/145 \sim 1/1{,}000$.

A more careful analysis would reveal that scientists only consider significant digit (SD) precision as a guide to what I call W_R precision, which is the ratio of the width, W_r, of the experimentally determined/predicted range for a variable to what is estimated to be the width of the expected range, W_R, for the variable given the background information. The actual value, V, is then taken as a guide to the width of the theoretically possible range, and hence $W_r/W_R \sim \text{Abs}[e/V]$, where $\sim$ means approximately. We shall return to this issue when we discuss QED, but for the purposes of this chapter, we are concerned only with showing that determining the degree of precision of a prediction – whether SD or W_R precision – depends on privileging the natural variable(s) as defined.

Finally, one might wonder why we cannot define precision simply as the amount that, with a set degree of probability, the actual value could differ from the experimental value. We could, but it would be a useless notion when it came to the question of experimental confirmation. For example, how could we compare the confirmatory value of a predictive precision of 1 kg with that of 1 μm? Or, is it really plausible to say that, for instance, a predictive precision of 20 significant digits of the mass of the universe has less confirmatory significance than a prediction of one significant digit of the mass of a hydrogen atom because the former is less accurate in terms of number of kilograms by which the actual value could differ from the predicted value?

We shall now argue that if either the degree of SD precision or the degree of W_R precision is epistemically relevant, it follows that one must privilege variables that are closely tied with the natural variables. We shall start by showing that SD experimental precision depends on the variable one uses to represent the quantity being measured; consequently, in order to speak of precision in a nonrelative sense, one must specify the variable one is using to express the physical situation. To illustrate, consider the case of a cube discussed in the last section. The volume of a cube is equal to the third power of the length of its side: $V = L^3$. Suppose we determine the length of the cube is 10 μm, to within a precision of 1 μm. Thus, expressed as a ratio, the SD precision is $\text{Abs}[e/V] < 1/10$, or one part in 10. Roughly, this means that the length of the cube could be anywhere from 9 to 11 μm. In terms of volume, however, the cube can vary between $9^3 = 729$ μm^3 and $11^3 = 1{,}331$ μm^3. This means that the experimental precision is $(1{,}331 - 1{,}000)/1{,}000 \sim 1/3$, or one part in three, if we take volume as our variable.

Now consider a theory that predicts that the length of the side of the cube is 10 μm. This is equivalent to the theory predicting the volume of the cube to be 1,000 μm. In this case, the predicted value agrees with the experimental value to within experimental precision. If we ask what the known precision of the prediction is, however, we do not get a definite answer. If we consider the theory as predicting the length of the cube, we get one value for the known precision, whereas if we consider the theory as predicting the volume, we get another value for the precision. (Remember, since we are assuming that the theory predicts the correct value to within experimental error, the known predictive precision is equal to the experimental precision.) The moral here is that the known precision of a prediction depends on the mathematical variable – for example, L^3 or L in the said example – under which one is considering the prediction. Put differently, *one can speak of precision of an experimentally correct prediction only relative to the variable one uses to represent the predicted result.* In analogy to Bertrand's Cube Paradox for the Principle of Indifference, in the case of the aforementioned cube it seems that we have no *a priori* way of choosing between expressing the precision in terms of volume or in terms of length, since both seem equally natural. At best, all we can say is that the predicted precision is somewhere between that determined by using length to represent the experimental data and that determined by using volume to represent the experimental data.

For an illustration from actual physics, consider the case of QED's astoundingly accurate prediction of the correction of the gyromagnetic ratio – called the *g*-factor – of the electron due to its self-interaction. QED predicted that, because of the self-interaction of the electron, the *g*-factor (gyromagnetic moment) of the electron differs from 2 by a small amount: $g/2 = 1.001\,159\,652\,38 \pm 0.000\,000\,000\,26$. Very accurate experimental measurements yielded: $g/2 = 1.001\,159\,652 \pm 0.000\,000\,000\,20$. The precision of the said prediction of $g/2$ is one part in a billion.

Now determining the experimental value for $g/2$ is equivalent to determining the experimental value of some arbitrarily defined function $U(g/2)$ of $g/2$, say $U(g/2) = (g/2)^{100}$. Moreover, if QED predicted the value of $g/2$ to within experimental error, then it follows that it also predicted the correct value of U to within experimental error. The precision by which U is known, however, is one in 10 million instead of one in a billion, as in the case of $g/2$. Thus, in analogy to the case of probability, even to speak of the precision of QED's prediction, we must already assume a certain natural variable. It seems that the only non-arbitrary choices are the natural variables defined earlier, which is what scientists actually use.

From examples like the one cited earlier, it is also clear that W_R precision also depends on the choice of the natural variable, as we explained for the case of fine-tuning. So it seems that in order to speak of the predictive SD or W_R precision for those cases in which a theory predicts the correct experimental value for some quantity, one must assume a natural variable for determining the known predictive precision. One could, of course, deny that there exists any nonrelative predictive precision, and instead claim that all we can say is that a prediction has a certain precision relative to the variable we use to express the prediction. Such a claim, however, would amount to a denial that highly accurate predictions, such as those of QED, have any special epistemic merit over predictions of much less precision. This, however, is contrary to the practice of most scientists. In the case of QED, for instance, scientists did take the astounding, known precision of QED's prediction of the *g*-factor of the electron, along with its astoundingly accurate predictions of other quantities, such as the Lamb shift, as strong evidence in favor of the theory. Further, denying the special merit of very accurate predictions seems highly implausible in and of itself. Such a denial would amount to saying, for example, that the fact that a theory correctly predicts a quantity to an SD precision of, say, 20 significant digits does not, in general, count significantly more in favor of the theory than if it had correctly predicted another quantity with a precision of two significant digits. This seems highly implausible.

Of course, strictly speaking, to make these sorts of comparisons of relative degrees of confirmation, one need not privilege one particular variable for expressing the experimental result and calculating its precision, since one need not be committed to a specific degree of precision. Nonetheless, one must put some significant restrictions on the functions of a given variable on which one bases one's calculation of precision, for otherwise one cannot make any significant comparisons. For example, in some cases, there might be several different equally simple ways of writing the laws of physics, giving rise to several different candidates for natural variables. In that case, one would simply say that the degree of precision fell into a certain range covering the different choices of natural variables.

Finally, consider a Likelihood Principle reconstruction of the confirmation that QED received from its correct, precise prediction of the correction to the g-factor of the electron. Let QED represent the claim that QED is approximately true or at least empirically adequate; let ~QED represent the negation of this claim; finally, let e represent the fact that the correction to the g-factor of the electron falls within the experimentally determined range. Now, $P(e|QED \& k') = 1$, since QED entails that it will fall into the experimentally determined range. (Since e was old evidence at the time of QED's prediction, k' is our background minus this old evidence). The value of $P(e|\text{~QED} \& k')$ will depend on the comparison range one chooses – that is, the range of plausible values for the correction to the g-factor given ~QED & k'. There is no precise way of determining this range, but given that without any correction, the g-factor is 2, it is reasonable to suppose that most physicists would have expected it to be no larger than 2. Suppose that it were reasonable to expect the correction to be no greater than ± 0.01, with no preference for any value between 0 and ± 0.01. This would yield a width, W_R, for the comparison range of 0.02. If we let W_r be the range of the experimentally determined value of correction, and we used the restricted Principle of Indifference, we would arrive at $P(e|\text{~QED} \& k') = W_r/W_R \sim 10^{-7}$, yielding a large likelihood confirmation of QED over ~QED.

The lesson here is that any support that correct, precise predictions provide for QED over ~QED via the Likelihood Principle will involve using something similar to the restricted Principle of Indifference, with the epistemically privileged natural variables being those in the simplest formulation of the area of physics in question. The same can be said for the likelihood reconstruction of other cases of confirmation based on precise predictions. Such likelihood reconstructions, if plausible, strongly support the epistemic role of the restricted version of the Principle of Indifference in scientific practice.

4. Determining k' and the Comparison Range

4.1. Introduction

To complete the philosophical groundwork for our argument, we shall need to provide some way of determining k'. Determining k' will automatically determine the "possible universes" to which we are comparing the life-permitting ones – that is, what we called the "comparison range." We shall focus on the constants of physics, but everything we say applies to the laws and initial conditions of the universe with minor modifications. First, however, we need to get clear on what it means to vary a constant of physics.

4.2. What it means to vary a constant of physics

Intuitively, there is a distinction between laws and constants, and physicists usually suppose such a distinction. In current physics, most laws can be thought of as mathematical descriptions of the relations between certain physical quantities. Each of these descriptions has a mathematical form, along with a set of numbers that are determined by experiment. So, for example, Newton's law of gravity ($F = Gm_1m_2/r^2$) has a mathematical form, along with a number (G) determined by experiment. We can then think of a world in which the relation of force to mass and distance has the same mathematical form (the form of being proportional to the product of the masses divided by the distance between them squared), but in which G is different. We could then say that such worlds have the same law of gravity, but a different value for G. So when we conceive of worlds in which a constant of physics is different but in which the laws are the same, we are conceiving of worlds in which the mathematical form of the laws remains the same, but in which the experimentally determined numbers are different. It should be noted that the distinction between laws and constants need not be a metaphysical distinction, but only a conceptual distinction.

Now these constants of physics are relative to our current physical models, since these constants only occur within a model. Thus, any probabilities we calculate will only be relative to a certain model. Ian Hacking (1987, pp. 119–227) and Bas van Fraassen (1980, pp. 178–95), among others, have emphasized this model-relativism with regard to the relative frequency interpretation of probabilities. Under this interpretation, probabilities are understood as the limit of the ratio of the favorable outcomes to the total number of outcomes as the number of trials goes to infinity. Since for most, if not all, cases these infinite long-run frequencies do not exist in the real world, they ultimately must make reference to frequencies in idealized models, as van Fraassen has worked out in detail (1980, pp. 190–3). Similarly, I shall assume, epistemic probabilities exist only relative to our models of the world and our other background information.

At least in the case of epistemic probabilities, this should come as no surprise, since it has to do with rational degrees of belief, which, of course, are relative to human cognition. If one denies the model dependence of epistemic probabilities, then it is hard to see how any statements of epistemic probabilities will ever be justified. One reason is that they are almost always grounded in conceptualizing alternative possibilities under some measure, as illustrated in Section 3.1 by the sort of epistemic probabilities used to justify the Thesis of Common Ancestry, continental drift theory, or the atomic hypothesis. But such conceptualizations typically involve implicit reference to some (often vague) model of how those possibilities are spread out. In fact, this was illustrated by use of natural variables in science discussed in Section 3.3.3.

The relevant models for the fine-tuning hypothesis are just the models given to us by our best theories in physics, just as if we calculated relative frequencies we should do so using the best models that we had in the relevant domain. At present, the best model we have is the Standard Model of particle physics. Sometimes, however, we can calculate the life-permitting range only for a constant that is less than fundamental, either because we do not have a fundamental theory or because of limitations on our ability to calculate. In that case, the most sensible thing to do is to go with the best model for which we can do calculations, as long as we consider only variations in the constant that fall within the limits of applicability of the model established by the deeper theory –for example, we could sensibly consider the consequences of varying mass using the model of Newton's theory of gravity as long as the variation were within the range of validity of Newtonian mechanics dictated by Einstein's theory of General Relativity.

Because we are considering only one reference class of possible law structures (that given by variations of the constants within our best theories and/or the ones we can perform calculations for), it is unclear how much weight to attach to the values of epistemic probabilities one obtains using this reference class. Hence, one cannot simply map the epistemic probabilities obtained in this way onto the degrees of belief we should have at the end of the day. What we can do, however, is say that given that we choose our reference class in the way suggested, and assuming our other principles (such as the restricted Principle of Indifference in Section 3.3.2), we obtain a certain epistemic probability, or range of probabilities. Then, as a second-order concern, we must assess the confidence we have in this probability based on the various components that went into the calculation, such as the representative nature of the reference class. Given that there is no completely objective procedure for addressing this secondary concern, I suggest that the probability calculations should be thought of as providing supporting confirmation, based on a plausible, nonarbitrary procedure, of the common intuitive sense that given the fine-tuning evidence, LPU is very epistemically improbable under NSU. This evidence will be strengthened by the fact that there are many different fine-tuned constants of physics, and many different kinds of fine-tuning, so that the fine-tuning argument does not depend on one highly specific reference class. In light of this, we must keep in mind that our goal is not to provide some exact degree by which the fine-tuning evidence supports T over NSU. Rather, it is to show that the intuitive sense that LPU supports T over NSU is not based on some mistake in thinking or perception, or on some merely subjective interpretation of the data, but rather can be grounded in a justified, nonarbitrary procedure.[25]

4.3. Determining k′: old evidence problem

In Premises (1) and (2) of our main argument in Section 1.3, the probability of LPU is conditioned on background information k′. As we mentioned in Section 1.3, we cannot simply take k′ to be our entire background information k, since k includes the fact that we exist, and hence entails LPU. To determine what to include in k′, therefore, we must confront what is called the "problem of old evidence." The much-discussed problem is that if we include known evidence e in our background information k, then even if an hypothesis h entails e, it cannot confirm h under the Likelihood Principle, or any Bayesian or quasi-Bayesian methodology, since $P(e|k \& h) = P(e|k \& \sim h)$. But this seems incorrect: General Relativity's prediction of the correct degree of the precession of the perihelion of Mercury (which was a major anomaly under Newton's theory of gravity) has been taken to confirm General Relativity even though it was known for over 50 years prior to the development of General Relativity and thus entailed by k.

An attractive solution to this problem is to subtract our knowledge of old evidence e from the background information k and then relativize confirmation to this new body of information $k′ = k - \{e\}$. As Colin Howson explains, "when you ask yourself how much support e gives [hypothesis] h, you are plausibly asking how much knowledge of e *would* increase the credibility of h," but this is "the same thing as asking how much e boosts h relative to what else we know" (1991, p. 548). This "what else" is just our background knowledge k minus e. As appealing as this method seems, it faces a major problem: there

---

25. Given the multiplicity of possible references classes, one could simply decide not to assign any epistemic probability to LPU. As with skepticism in general, such a practice would also undercut any sort of rational commitment to the approximate truth or empirical adequacy of a theory, since the epistemic probabilities used in justifying these theories also lack a complete fundamental justification. Given that we are not skeptics, the best we can do is use the least arbitrary procedure available to assign epistemic probabilities.

is no unambiguous way of subtracting e from k. Consider the case of the fine-tuning of the strength of gravity. The fact, Lpg, that the strength of gravity falls into the life-permitting range entails the existence of stable, long-lived stars. On the other hand, given our knowledge of the laws of physics, the initial conditions of the universe, and the value of the other constants, the existence of stable, long-lived stars entails Lpg. Thus, if we were to obtain k′ by subtracting Lpg from our total background information k without also subtracting our knowledge of the existence of long-lived stable stars from k, then $P(Lpg|k') = 1$.

To solve such problems, Howson says that we should regard k as "in effect, an independent axiomatization of background information and $k - \{e\}$ as the simple set-theoretic subtraction of e from k" (1991, p. 549). That is, Howson proposes that we axiomatize our background information k by a set of sentences {A} in such a way that e is logically independent of the other sentences in {A}. Then k′ would simply consist of the set of sentences {A} − e. One serious problem with this method is that there are different ways of axiomatizing our background information. Thus, as Howson recognizes, the degree to which e confirms h becomes relative to our axiomatization scheme (1991, p. 550). Howson argues that in practice this is not as serious a problem as one might expect, since in many cases our background information k is already represented to us in a partially axiomatized way in which e is logically isolated from other components of k. As he notes, "the sorts of cases which are brought up in the literature tend to be those in which the evidence, like the statements describing the magnitude of the observed annual advance of Mercury's perihelion, is a logically isolated component of the background information." (1991, p. 549). In such cases, when we ask ourselves how much e boosts the credibility of h with respect to what else we know, this "what else we know" is well defined by how we represent our background knowledge. Of course, in those cases in which there are alternative ways of axiomatizing k that are consistent with the way our background knowledge is represented to us, there will be corresponding ambiguities in the degree to which e confirms h. I agree with Howson that this is not necessarily a problem unless one thinks that the degree of confirmation e provides h must be independent of the way we represent our background knowledge. Like Howson, I see no reason to make this assumption: confirmation is an epistemic notion and thus is relative to our epistemic situation, which will include the way we represent our background information.

In the case of fine-tuning, our knowledge of the universe is already presented to us in a partially axiomatized way. Assuming a deterministic universe, the laws and constants of physics, along with the initial conditions of the universe, supposedly determine everything else about the universe. Thus, the set of propositions expressing these laws, constants, and initial conditions constitutes an axiomatization of our knowledge. Further, in scientific contexts, this represents the *natural* axiomatization. Indeed, I would argue, the fact that this is the natural axiomatization of our knowledge is part of our background knowledge, at least for scientific realists who want scientific theories to "cut reality at its seams."[26] Furthermore, we have a particularly powerful reason for adopting this axiomatization when considering a constant of physics. The very meaning of a constant of physics is only defined

---

26. One might object that this procedure is only justified under the assumption that we live in a deterministic universe, since, otherwise, the k we have chosen is not a true axiomatization of our knowledge. This is true, but it is difficult to see how the thesis that the world is indeterministic could be relevant to the legitimacy of the fine-tuning argument.

in terms of a particular framework of physics. Saying that the strong force constant has a certain value, for instance, would be meaningless in Aristotelian physics. Accordingly, the very idea of subtracting out the value of such a constant only has meaning relative to our knowledge of the current set of laws and constants, and hence this constitutes the appropriate axiomatization of our relevant background information k with respect to which we should perform our subtraction.

Using Howson's method, therefore, we have a straightforward way of determining $k - \{e\}$ for the case of the constants of physics: we let k be axiomatized by the set of propositions expressing the initial conditions of the universe and the laws and fundamental constants of physics within our currently most fundamental theory which we can do calculations. *Since the constants of physics can be considered as given by a list of numbers in a table, we simply subtract the proposition expressing the value of C from that table to obtain k'. Thus, k' can be thought of as including the initial conditions of the universe, the laws of physics, and the values of all the other constants except C.*

It should be noted that although Howson's method was developed in the context of subjective Bayesian conception of probability, his argument for this method does not depend on this conception. All it depends on is the claim that "when you ask yourself how much support e gives [hypothesis] h, you are plausibly asking how much knowledge of e *would* increase the credibility of h," and that this is "the same thing as asking how much e boosts h relative to what else we know" (1991, p. 548). Anyone who subscribes to a probabilistic confirmation account of evidence, according to which e counts as evidence for h if and only if knowledge of e increases our degree of confidence in h, should at least be sympathetic to the underlying premises of his argument.

Finally, it is worth considering how the old evidence problem plays out in the method of probabilistic tension. As mentioned earlier, the major problem with Howson's method is that the background information k' depends on the subtraction procedure one uses. If we cast the fine-tuning argument in terms of probabilistic tension, as elaborated in Section 1.4, this problem can be avoided; we do not need to privilege any particular subtraction procedure. According to that method, both NSU and T should be elaborated in such a way that each of them entails LPU. (We called these elaborated hypotheses NSUe and Te, respectively.) Thus, LPU does not directly confirm one of these elaborated hypotheses over the other. Nonetheless, the fine-tuning evidence creates severe probabilistic tension for NSUe but not for Te. Thus, it gives us a significant reason to prefer Te over NSUe: if with respect to some domain, one hypothesis h_1 has much more probabilistic tension than another, h_2, then the probabilistic tension gives us strong reason to prefer h_2 over h_1, everything else being equal.

To determine the degree of probabilistic tension generated for NSUe by the fine-tuning evidence, we need to probe NSUe & k for hidden probabilistic tension related to the fine-tuning evidence. Now, when considering only a single constant C, the fine-tuning evidence only generates probabilistic tension because of the data Lpc. To bring this probabilistic tension out, we first note that NSUe & k = NSU & k = NSU & k' & Lpc, since $k' = k - \{Lpc\}$ and hence k = Lpc & k', *where no particular subtraction procedure is specified for* $-\{Lpc\}$. Then, we must consider all k' such that k = k' & Lpc, and take the true probabilistic tension of NSUe & k to be given by the lower bound of P(Lpc|NSU & k'), for all possible k'. We then follow a similar procedure for the probabilistic tension of Te & k. Using the lower bound guarantees that the information that a constant fell into the life-permitting range is not implicitly left in the k' one uses to assess probabilistic tension, as we saw in our given example for the fine-tuning of gravity where the existence of long lived, stable stars was left in k'. This is a determinate procedure that does not depend on any choice of subtraction procedure and demonstrates the power of the idea of probabilistic tension. (As an alternative to Howson's method, one might also use this approach to determine k' for the Likelihood Principle method mentioned, although we will not pursue this further here.)

4.4. Determining k': the EI region

Next, for any given fine-tuned constant C, we must determine the comparison range of values for C. My proposal is that the primary comparison range is the set of values for which we can make determinations of whether the values are life-permitting or not. I will call this range the *epistemically illuminated* (EI) range.[27] Thus, given that the EI range is taken as our comparison range, we will say that a constant C is fine-tuned if the width, W_r, of the range of life-permitting values for the constant is very small compared with the width, W_R, of the EI range.

To motivate the claim that the comparison range, W_R, should be taken as the EI range, we shall consider a more mundane case of a very large dartboard with only some small, finite region around the bull's eye that is illuminated, with the bulk of the dartboard in darkness. In this case, we know neither how far the dartboard extends nor whether there are other bull's eyes on it. If we saw a dart hit the bull's eye in the illuminated (IL) region, and the bull's eye was very, very small compared with the IL region, we would take that as evidence that the dart was aimed, even though we cannot say anything about the density of bull's eyes on other regions of the board.

One way of providing a likelihood reconstruction of the confirmation of the aiming hypothesis is to include the fact that the dart fell into the IL region as part of the information being conditioned on: that is, include it in the background information k'. We could then use the Likelihood Principle to argue as follows: given that we know that the dart has fallen into the IL region, it is very unlikely for it to have hit the bull's eye by chance but not unlikely if it was aimed; hence, its falling in the bull's eye confirms the aiming hypothesis over the chance hypothesis. Similarly, for the case of fine-tuning, we should include the fact that the value of a constant is within the EI region as part of our background information k'.

Is including in k' the fact that C falls into the EI range an adequate procedure? The case of the dartboard, I believe, shows that it is not only a natural procedure to adopt, but also arguably the only way of providing a Likelihood Principle reconstruction of the inference in this sort of mundane case. First, it is clearly the ratio of the area taken up by the bull's eye to the IL region around the bull's eye that leads us to conclude that it was aimed. Second, one *must* restrict the comparison range to the IL range (i.e. include IL in k') since one does not know how many bull's eyes are in the unilluminated portion of the dartboard. Thus, if one expanded the comparison range outside the IL range, one could make no estimate as to the ratio of the area of the bull's eye regions to the non-bull's eye regions, and thus could not provide a likelihood reconstruction. Yet it seems intuitively clear that

---

27. This is a different approach than in one of my earlier papers on the issue (Collins 2005b), where the range was constrained by what values are consistent with a universe's existing – for example, too high of a value for the gravitational constant would reduce the whole universe to a singularity and so forms a natural bound of the range. The "universe existing constraint" is still valid (since NSU & k' presuppose the existence of a universe), but it is typically trumped by the EI region constraint, since the latter is more stringent.

the dart's hitting the bull's eye in this case does confirm the aimed hypothesis over the chance hypothesis.

Another way of seeing why the comparison range should be equal to the EI range is in terms of the rational degrees of credence in Lpc of the fictional unembodied alien observer introduced at the end of Section 3.2. In accordance with the method of dealing with old evidence, we imagine our alien observer holding background information k', in which the knowledge of the value of C is subtracted out. Then we imagine that our alien observer learns that C falls into the EI range. Call this new information Q. Even assuming that it makes sense to speak of C as possibly having any value between minus infinity and infinity, the alien observer would not know whether the sum of the widths of all the life-permitting regions outside of the EI region are finite or infinite. Hence, it would not know the value of $P(Q|T \& k')$, since to say anything about the chance of God's creating C in the EI region, it would have to know if there are other life-permitting regions besides the ones in EI. Hence, $P(Q|NSU \& k')/P(Q|T \& k')$ would be indeterminate. This means that knowledge of Q neither confirms nor disconfirms T relative to NSU.

Suppose our alien observer learns the additional information, Lpc, that C falls into the life-permitting region of EI. Since our observer knows Q, assessing whether this additional information confirms T with respect to NSU will depend on the ratio $P(Lpc|k' \& Q \& T)/P(Lpc|k' \& Q \& NSU)$. Now, since $k' \& Q \& NSU$ implies nothing about where C falls in the EI region, it would leave our alien observer indifferent as to where it fell in this region. Hence, assuming the validity of the restricted Principle of Indifference (see Section 3.3.2), $P(Lpc|k' \& Q \& NSU) = W_r/W_R$, where W_R is equal to width of the EI region. Thus, including the information Q that C falls into the EI region in our background information k' is equivalent to choosing our comparison range as the EI range.

At this point, one might question the legitimacy of including Q in our background information k': that is, choosing k' such that $k' \to k' \& Q$. Besides appealing to examples such as the previously discussed dartboard case, in general when comparing hypotheses, we can place into the background information any evidence that we have good reason to believe neither confirms nor disconfirms the hypothesis in question. In some cases this is obvious: for example, when assessing the ratio of the probabilities of the defendant's fingerprints' matching those on the gun under the guilt and innocence hypothesis, respectively, the fact that Jupiter has over 62 moons would be irrelevant information. Thus, jurors would be free to include it as part of their background information.

Another way of thinking about this issue is to note that k' determines the reference class of possible law structures to be used for purposes of estimating the epistemic probability of Lpc under NSU: the probability of Lpc given $k' \& NSU$ is the relative proportion of law structures that are life-permitting in the class of all law structures that are consistent with $k' \& NSU$. (The measure over this reference class is then given by the restricted Principle of Indifference.) Thinking in terms of reference classes, the justification for restricting our reference class to the EI region is similar to that used in science: when testing a hypothesis, we always restrict our reference classes to those for which we can make the observations and calculations of the frequencies or proportions of interest – what in statistics is called the sample class. This is legitimate as long as we have no reason to think that such a restriction produces a relevantly biased reference class. Tests of the long-term efficacy of certain vitamins, for instance, are often restricted to a reference class of randomly selected doctors and nurses in certain participating hospitals, since these are the only individuals that one can reliably trace for extended periods of time. The assumption of such tests is that we have no reason to think that the doctors and nurses are relevantly different than people who are neither doctors nor nurses, and thus that the reference class is not biased. As discussed in Section 4.2, the justification for varying a constant instead of varying the mathematical form of a law in the fine-tuning argument is that, in the reference class of law structures picked out by varying a constant, we can make some estimate of the proportion of life-permitting law structures. This is something we probably could not do if our reference class involved variations of mathematical form. The same sort of justification underlies restricting the class to the EI range.

It is also important to keep things in perspective by noting that there are really two separate issues here. First is the issue of the existence of a meaningful probability for $P(Lpc|Q \& k' \& NSU)$. That question reduces to whether there is an epistemic probability measure over the EI region; this will uncontroversially be the case if the EI region is finite and the restricted Principle of Indifference is true and applies. The second question is whether $Q \& k'$ is the appropriate background information. If one allowed for prior probabilities and the full use of Bayes's Theorem, then any choice is appropriate as long as one also has meaningful prior probabilities for $P(NSU|Q \& k')$, $P(T|Q \& k')$, and $P(Lpc|Q \& k' \& T)$.[28] Since I have attempted to avoid the use of prior probabilities, it became important to have some procedure of determining the appropriate background information k'. So this issue arises only for the likelihood version of the argument that avoids prior probabilities. It does not arise for other versions, including the secondary method of probabilistic tension, since, as we saw earlier, that does not depend on the particular choice of appropriate background information.

Including Q in k' provides a Likelihood Principle reconstruction of John Leslie's "fly on the wall" analogy, which he offers in response to the claim that there could be other unknown values for the constants of physics, or unknown laws, that allow for life:

> If a tiny group of flies is surrounded by a largish fly-free wall area then whether a bullet hits a fly in the group will be very sensitive to the direction in which the firer's rifle points, even if other very different areas of the wall are thick with flies. So it is sufficient to consider *a local area of possible universes*, e.g., those produced by slight changes in gravity's strength. . . . It certainly needn't be claimed that Life and Intelligence could exist *only if* certain force strengths, particle masses, etc. fell within certain narrow ranges. . . . All that need be claimed is that a lifeless universe would have resulted from *fairly minor changes* in the forces etc. with which we are familiar. (1989, pp. 138–9).

Finally, notice how our methodology deals with a common major misunderstanding of the fine-tuning argument based on the constants of physics. On this misunderstanding, advocates of the fine-tuning argument are accused of implicitly assuming the laws somehow existed temporally or logically prior to the constants, and then afterwards the values of the constants were determined. Then one imagines that if NSU is true, the values occur by

---

28. According to the odds form of Bayes's Theorem, $P(NSU|Lpc \& k)/P(T|Lpc \& k) = P(NSU|Lpc \& Q \& k')/P(T|Lpc \& Q \& k') = P(NSU|Q \& k')/P(T|Q \& k') \times P(Lpc|Q \& k' \& NSU)/P(Lpc|Q \& k' \& T)$. [Lpc & Q & k' = Lpc & k, since (i) Lpc & k' = k and (ii) the life-permitting range is part of the EI range, and hence Lpc entails Q, which means Lpc & k' = Lpc & k' & Q. I am assuming none of the probabilities in the denominators are zero.]

"chance," and hence it is very, very unlikely for them to fall into the life-permitting range. Thus, critics of the fine-tuning argument, such as Ian Hacking (1987, pp. 129–30) and John Earman (2006), have claimed that it begs the question, since it already presupposes the existence of a creator. According to Earman, talk of the existence of a fine-tuned universe's being improbable "seems to presuppose a creation account of actuality: in the beginning there is an ensemble of physically possible universes – all satisfying the laws of our universe but with different values of the constants – awaiting to be anointed with the property of actuality by the great Actualizer . . ." (2006). It should be clear that the way in which I spell out the argument makes no such metaphysical assumption. We simply consider the ratio of epistemic probabilities $P(Lpc|T \& k')/P(Lpc|NSU \& k')$, where Lpc denotes the claim that a constant fell into the life-permitting range; this does not presuppose a creation account of the laws any more than does a likelihood reconstruction of the confirmation that old evidence e provides a scientific theory, in which a similar procedure of subtracting old evidence is involved.[29]

4.5. Examples of the EI region

In this section, we shall consider how to estimate the EI region for the force strengths and some other constants. In doing this, we first note that, as argued in Section 4.2, we must make our estimates of epistemic probability relative to the best calculation-permitting models we have, as long as those models are reasonable approximations of the best current overall models. Consider, for instance, the strong nuclear force, which is only defined in a specific model. We know that this model has only limited applicability since the strong nuclear force is ultimately the byproduct (or residue) of the "color force" between the quarks of which neutrons and protons are composed. Further, the physical model, quantum chromodynamics, describing the color force is thought to have only limited range of applicability to relatively low energies. Thus, the EI region will be finite, since we can only do valid calculations for those values of the strong nuclear force or color force that stay within a relatively low-energy regime.

This limitation of energy regime does not apply just to the theory of strong interactions, but to all of the fundamental quantum theories of nature. In the past, we have found that physical theories are limited in their range of applicability – for example, Newtonian mechanics was limited to medium-sized objects moving at slow speeds relative to the speed of light. For fast-moving objects, we require special relativity; for massive objects, General Relativity; for very small objects, quantum theory. When the Newtonian limits are violated, these theories predict completely unexpected and seemingly bizarre effects, such as time dilation in special relativity or tunneling in quantum mechanics.

There are good reasons to believe that current physics is limited in its domain of applicability. The most discussed of these limits is energy scale. The current orthodoxy in high-

29. Those, such as McGrew, McGrew, and Vestrup (Section 4.6), who claim that the entire possible range of constants is the only nonarbitrary comparison range, also appear to be in the grip of the mistaken idea that the relevant probabilities are determined by a model of "universe creation" in which first the laws come into existence, and then the constants are "chosen" from the range of possible values that they could have. Since within such a conceptualization, the constants could have had any value, one is erroneously led to think that the only adequate comparison range is minus infinity to plus infinity.

energy physics and cosmology is that our current physics is either only a low-energy approximation to the true physics that applies at all energies or only the low-energy end of a hierarchy of physics, with each member of the hierarchy operating at its own range of energies.[30] The energy at which any particular current theory can no longer to be considered approximately accurate is called the *cutoff* energy, although (despite its name) we should typically expect a continuous decrease in applicability, not simply a sudden change from applicability to nonapplicability. In contemporary terminology, our current physical theories are to be considered *effective field theories*. The limitation of our current physics directly affects thought experiments involving changing the force strengths. Although in everyday life we conceive of forces anthropomorphically as pushes or pulls, in current physics forces are conceived of as interactions involving exchanges of quanta of energy and momentum.[31] The strength of a particular force, therefore, can be thought of as proportional to the rate of exchange of energy-momentum, expressed quantum mechanically in terms of probability cross sections. Drastically increasing the force strengths, therefore, would drastically increase the energy-momentum being exchanged in any given interaction. Put another way, increasing the strength of a force will involve increasing the energy at which the relevant physics takes place. So, for instance, if one were to increase the strength of electromagnetism, the binding energy of electrons in the atom would increase; similarly, an increase in the strength of the strong nuclear force would correspond to an increase in the binding energy in the nucleus.[32]

The limits of the applicability our current physical theories to below a certain energy scales, therefore, translates to a limit on our ability to determine the effects of drastically increasing a value of a given force strength – for example, our physics does not tell us what would happen if we increased the strong nuclear force by a factor of $10^{1,000}$. If we naively applied current physics to that situation, we should conclude that no complex life would be possible because atomic nuclei would be crushed. If a new physics applies, however, entirely new and almost inconceivable effects could occur that make complex life possible, much as quantum effects make the existence of stable atomic orbits possible, whereas such orbits were inconceivable under classical mechanics. Further, we have no guarantee that the concept of a force strength itself remains applicable from within the perspective of the new physics at such energy scales, just as the concept of a particle's having a definite position and momentum, lost applicability in quantum mechanics; or the notion of absolute time lost validity in special relativity; or gravitational "force" (versus curvature of space-

---

30. See, for instance, Zee (2003, pp. 437–8), Cao (1997, pp. 349–53), and Teller (1988, p. 87). For example, Zee says that he espouses "the philosophy that a quantum field theory provides an effective description of physics up to a certain energy scale Λ, a threshold of ignorance beyond which physics not included in the theory comes into play" (p. 438).

31. Speaking of gravitational force as involving energy exchange is highly problematic, although speaking of gravitational binding energy is not nearly as problematic. One problem is that in General Relativity, gravity is not conceived of as a force but as curvature of space-time. Another problem is that there is no theoretically adequate definition for the local energy of a gravitational field or wave. (See, for instance, Wald, 1984, p. 70, n. 6; p. 286.) Finally, although physicists often speak of gravitons as the carriers as the carrier of the gravitational force, the quantum theory of gravity out of which gravitons arise is notoriously non-renormalizable, meaning that infinities arise that cannot be eliminated. Nonetheless, since gravitational waves cause changes in the energy of material objects at a certain rate, we can still meaningfully speak of energy scales at which a particular gravitational "force" is operating, which is all that is needed for this argument.

32. The weak force does not involve binding energies but is an interaction governing the transmutation of particles from one form to another, and so this last argument would not apply to it.

time) in General Relativity.[33] Thus, by inductive reasoning from the past, we should expect not only entirely unforeseen phenomena at energies far exceeding the cutoff, but we even should expect the loss of the applicability of many of our ordinary concepts, such as that of force strength.

The so-called Plank scale is often assumed to be the cutoff for the applicability of the strong, weak, and electromagnetic forces. This is the scale at which unknown quantum gravity effects are suspected to take place thus invalidating certain foundational assumptions on which current quantum field theories are based, such a continuous space-time (see e.g. Peacock 1999, p. 275; Sahni & Starobinsky 1999, p. 44). The Plank scale occurs at the energy of 10^{19} GeV (billion electron volts), which is roughly 10^{21} higher than the binding energies of protons and neutrons in a nucleus. This means that we could expect a new physics to begin to come into play if the strength of the strong force were increased by more than a factor of $\sim 10^{21}$. Another commonly considered cutoff is the grand unified theory (GUT) scale, which occurs around 10^{15} GeV (Peacock 1999, pp. 249, 267). The GUT scale is the scale at which physicists expect the strong, weak, and electromagnetic forces to be united. From the perspective of the currently proposed GUT, these forces are seen as a result of symmetry-breaking of the united force that is unbroken above 10^{15} GeV, where a new physics would then come into play. Effective field theory approaches to gravity also involve General Relativity's being a low-energy approximation to the true theory. One common proposed cutoff is the Plank scale, although this is not the only one (see e.g. Burgess 2004, p. 6).

Where these cutoffs lie and what is the fundamental justification for them are controversial issues. The point of the previous discussion is that the limits of our current theories are most likely finite but very large, since we know that our physics does work for an enormously wide range of energies. Accordingly, if the life-permitting range for a constant is very small in comparison, then $W_r/W_R \ll 1$, which means that there will be fine-tuning. Rigorously determining W_r/W_R is beyond the scope of this chapter. Almost all other purportedly fine-tuned constants also involve energy considerations: for example, because of Einstein's $E = mc^2$, the rest masses of the fundamental particles (which are fundamental constants) are typically given in terms of their rest energies – for example, the mass of the proton is 938 MeV (million electron volts). Further, the cosmological constant is now thought of as corresponding to the energy density of empty space. Thus, the considerations of energy cutoff mentioned will play a fundamental role in defining the EI region, and hence W_R, for many constants of physics.

4.6. Purported problem of infinite ranges

Finally, let us suppose that the comparison range is infinite, either because of some new theory that applies at all energy scales or because the reasoning in the last two subsections is incorrect. Timothy McGrew, Lydia McGrew, and Eric Vestrup (2001) and, independently, Mark Colyvan, Jay Garfield, and Graham Priest (2005) have argued that if the comparison range is infinite, no meaningful probability can be assigned to a constant's landing in

---

33. More generally, since constants are only defined with respect to the theories of physics in which they occur, their range of applicability, and thus the EI range, is restricted to the range of applicability of those theories.

the life-permitting region. (They also mistakenly assume that the only nonarbitrary comparison range for the constants of nature consists of all possible values ($-\infty$ to ∞).) These authors first assert that (i) the total probability of a constant's being somewhere in the infinite range of possible values has to be 1 (since it must have some value), and (ii) if we assume an equiprobability distribution over the possible values – which they claim is the only nonarbitrary choice – the probability of its being in any finite region must be zero or undefined. Finally, (iii) they consider any arbitrary way of dividing up the entire range into a countably infinite set of finite, nonoverlapping regions, and assert that the total probability of its being in the entire region must the sum of the probabilities of its being in each member of the set. For example, the probability of its being in the entire region is the sum of the probabilities of its being between 0 and 1, of its being between 1 and 2, of its being between 2 and 3, *ad infinitum*, plus the sum of the probabilities of its being between 0 and -1, between -1 and -2, *ad infinitum*. But since no matter how many times one adds zero together, one gets zero, this sum turns out to be zero. Hence, if we assume that each probability is zero, we get a contradiction since the probability of the constant having a value somewhere in the entire region is 1. Therefore, it must be undefined.

The problem with this argument is the assumption that the epistemic probability for the entire region is the sum of the individual probabilities of each finite disjoint region. In cases where the number of alternatives is finite, this is true: the sum of the probabilities of a die landing on each of its sides is equal to the probability of the die landing on some side. This is a fundamental principle of the probability calculus called *finite additivity*. When finite additivity is extended to a countably infinite number of alternatives, it is called *countable additivity*, which is the principle that McGrew and Vestrup implicitly invoke.

This latter principle, however, has been very controversial for almost every type of probability, with many purported counterexamples to it. Consider, for example, the following situation. Suppose that what you firmly believe to be an angel of God tells you that the universe is infinite in extent and that there are a countably infinite number of other planets with civilizations on each planet. Finally, the "angel" tells you that within a billion miles of one and only one of those planets is a golden ball 1 mile in diameter and that it has delivered the identical message to one person on each of those planets. Finally, you decide on the following arbitrary numbering system to identify the planets: you label Earth 1, the planet that is closest to Earth 2, the planet that is next farther out 3, and so forth. Since within current Big Bang cosmology an infinite universe would have no center, there is nothing special about Earth's location that could figure into one's probability calculation. Accordingly, it seems obvious that, given that you fully believe the "angel", for every planet k your confidence that the golden ball is within a billion miles of k should be zero. Yet this probability distribution violates countable additivity. One cannot argue that the scenario I proposed is in any way self-contradictory, unless one wants to argue that an infinite universe is self-contradictory. This, however, ends up involving substantive metaphysical claims and is arguably irrelevant, since the issue is the degree to which the propositions delivered by the "angel" justifies, or warrants, the belief that the ball is within a billion miles of our planet, not whether these propositions ultimately could be true.

McGrew and McGrew (2005) have responded to these sorts of arguments by claiming that when the only nonarbitrary distribution of degrees of belief violates the axiom of countable additivity, the most rational alternative is to remain agnostic. They point out that one need not assign epistemic probabilities to all propositions. I do not believe this is an adequate response, since I think in some cases it would be irrational to remain agnostic. For example, it would be irrational for a billionaire who received the aforementioned message to spend millions, or even hundreds, of dollars in search of the golden planet, even if it were entirely rational for him to believe what the "angel" told him; it would even be irrational for him to hope to discover the planet. This is radically different than cases where people are legitimately agnostic, such as perhaps about the existence of extraterrestrials or the existence of God; for example, it seems rationally permitted at least to hope for and seek evidence for the existence of extraterrestrials or God.

The implausibility of being agnostic in the "golden planet case" is further brought out when one considers that if the billionaire were told that the universe was finite with exactly $10^{10,000}$ planets with civilizations, clearly he should be near certain that the golden planet is not near Earth. But, clearly, if the billionaire is told that there are even more planets – infinitely many – the billionaire should be at least as confident that the planet is not near Earth; and, certainly, it should not become more rational for him to search for it than in the $10^{10,000}$ planets case, as it would if he should switch to being agnostic.

So the McGrews and others are wrong in claiming that there would be no epistemic probability if the range is infinite. However, they are correct in claiming that this would turn the fine-tuning argument into what McGrew, McGrew, and Vestrup (2001) have called *the course-tuning argument* (CTA). As they correctly point out, if the comparison range is infinite, then no matter how large the life-permitting range is, as long as it is finite the ratio W_r/W_R will be zero. This means that the narrowness of the range becomes irrelevant to our assessment of degree of fine-tuning. The McGrews and Vestrup, reiterating a point made by Paul Davies (1992, pp. 204–5), claim that it is obvious that CTA is not a good argument since CTA would have the same force no matter how "un-fine-tuned" a constant is, as long as the life-permitting range is finite. Thus, they argue, this would render the appeal to physics, and the narrowness of the life-permitting range, completely superfluous.

In response, an appeal to physics would still be necessary: we still should have to have good physical reasons to think the life-permitting range to be finite, which itself would involve having a model that we had good reasons to believe was accurate for all values of the parameter in question. This would involve a substantial appeal to physics. Of course, if it turned out that the comparison range were infinite, the restrictiveness of the life-permitting range would no longer play a role, and thus the popular presentation of the argument would have to be modified. Nonetheless, the formal presentation of the argument, based on the claim that $W_r/W_R \ll 1$ and the restricted Principle of Indifference, would remain. As is, I suggest that the reason we are impressed with the smallness is that we actually do have some vague finite comparison range to which we are comparing the life-permitting range, namely the EI range.

Finally, rejecting CTA for the reasons the McGrews and Vestrup give is counterintuitive. Assume that the fine-tuning argument would have probative force if the comparison range were finite. Although they might not agree with this assumption, making it will allow us to consider whether having an infinite instead of finite comparison range is relevant to the cogency of the fine-tuning argument. Now imagine increasing the width of this comparison range while keeping it finite. Clearly, the more W_R increases, the stronger the fine-tuning argument gets. Indeed, if we accept the restricted Principle of Indifference (Section 3.32), as W_R approaches infinity, $P(Lpc|NSU \& k')$ will converge to zero, and thus $P(Lpc|NSU$

& k') = 0 in the limit as W_R approaches infinity. Accordingly, if we deny that CTA has probative force *because* W_R is purportedly infinite, we must draw the counterintuitive consequence that although the fine-tuning argument gets stronger and stronger as W_R grows, magically when W_R becomes actually infinite, the fine-tuning argument loses all probative force.[34]

5. Justifying Premises (1) and (2)

5.1. Justifying premise (1)

The justification of Premise (1) of our main argument in Section 1.3 will depend on which fine-tuned feature of the universe is being considered. For the fine-tuning of the laws of nature, Premise (1) would be justified by an appeal to widely shared intuitions, as explained in Section 3.3.1. For the fine-tuning of the initial conditions of the universe, we have two choices. First, we could appeal to the standard measure of statistical mechanics (as is typically done). Second, if we have qualms about the applicability of the standard measure discussed in Section 2.4, we could appeal to the compelling reasons given in that section for thinking that the universe started in an extraordinarily special state; hence, in some real sense it is still epistemically enormously improbable, even if we cannot provide a rigorous mathematical grounding for that probability.

Finally, for the fine-tuning of the constants of physics, we shall appeal to the restricted Principle of Indifference (Section 3.3.2). This is the case we shall elaborate in detail. We shall begin by justifying Premise (1) for the case of individual constants that are fine-tuned and then consider the case in which the constants are combined. The argument has two steps:

(i)   Let C be a constant that is fine-tuned, with C occurring in the simplest current formulation of the laws of physics. Then, by the definition of fine-tuning, $W_r/W_R \ll 1$, where W_r is the width of the life-permitting range of C, and W_R is the width of the comparison range, which we argued was equal to the width of the EI range.

(ii) Since NSU and k' give us no reason to think that the constant will be in one part of the EI range instead of any other of equal width, and k' contains the information that it is somewhere in the EI range, it follows from the restricted Principle of Indifference that $P(Lpc|NSU \& k') = W_r/W_R$, which implies that $P(Lpc|NSU \& k') \ll 1$.

5.1.1. Combining constants

Some have faulted the fine-tuning arguments for only varying one constant at a time, while keeping the values of the rest fixed. For example, Victor Stenger claims that, "One of the many major flaws with most studies of the anthropic coincidences is that the investigators vary a single parameter while assuming all the others remain fixed!" (2007, p. 148).

---

34. For an argument showing that various inferences in contemporary cosmological speculation use infinite ranges, and for some mathematical justification of these, see Koperski (2005).

This issue can be easily addressed for a case in which the life-permitting range of one constant, C_1, does not significantly depend on the value that another constant, C_2, takes within its comparison range, R_2. In that case, the joint probability of *both* C_1 and C_2 falling into their life-permitting ranges is simply the product of the two probabilities. To see why, note that by the method explicated in Sections 4.3 and 4.4, the appropriate background information, k'_{12}, for the joint conditional probability of Lpc_1 & Lpc_2 on NSU is $k'_{12} = k - Lpc_1$ & $Q_1 - Lpc_2$ & $Q_2 = k'_1$ & k'_2. Here, $-Lpc_1$ and the $-Lpc_2$ represent the subtraction of the information that C_1 and C_2 have life-permitting values, respectively; Q_1 and Q_2 represent, respectively, the knowledge that they each fell into their respective EI regions (which is added back in, as explained in Section 4.4); and $k'_1 = k - Lpc_1$ & Q_1 and $k'_2 = k - Lpc_2$ & Q_2 represent the appropriate background information for C_1 and C_2, respectively, when they are considered separately.

By the definition of conditional probability, $P(Lpc_1$ & $Lpc_2|NSU$ & $k'_{12}) = P(Lpc_1|NSU$ & k'_{12} & $Lpc_2) \times P(Lpc_2|NSU$ & $k'_{12})$. Now, Q_2 & $Lpc_2 = Lpc_2$ since the claim that C_2 fell into its (known) life-permitting region entails that it fell into its EI region: that is, $Lpc_2 \rightarrow Q_2$. Hence, k'_{12} & $Lpc_2 = k - Lpc_1$ & $Q_1 - Lpc_2$ & Q_2 & $Lpc_2 = k - Lpc_1$ & $Q_1 - Lpc_2$ & $(Q_2$ & $Lpc_2) = k - Lpc_1$ & $Q_1 - Lpc_2$ & $Lpc_2 = k - Lpc_1$ & $Q_1 = k'_1$. It follows, therefore, that $P(Lpc_1|NSU$ & k'_{12} & $Lpc_2) = P(Lpc_1|NSU$ & $k'_1)$, which was merely the probability we calculated for Lpc_1 on the background information in which we held all the other constants fixed. So, our next question is, what is the value of $P(Lpc_2|NSU$ & $k'_{12})$? Now, k'_{12} includes the values of all the other constants besides C_1 and C_2. For C_1 and C_2 it only includes the information that they are in their respective EI regions. Thus, if the width, W_{r2}, of the life-permitting range of C_2 is not significantly dependent on the value of C_1 in C_1's EI region, then by the restricted Principle of Indifference, $P(Lpc_2|NSU$ & $k'_{12}) \sim W_{r2}/W_{R2} = P(Lpc_2|NSU$ & k'_2), where W_{R2} is the width of EI region for C_2 when all other constants are held fixed.[35] This means that $P(Lpc_1$ & $Lpc_2|NSU$ & $k'_{12}) \sim P(Lpc_1|NSU$ & $k'_1) \times P(Lpc_2|NSU$ & $k'_2)$. *Thus, we can treat the two probabilities as effectively independent.*

When will two constants be independent in this way? Those will be cases in which the factors responsible for C_1's being life-permitting are effectively independent of the factors responsible for C_2's being life-permitting. For example, consider the case of the fine-tuning of the cosmological constant (C_1) and the fine-tuning of the strength of gravity (C_2) relative to the strength of materials – that is, the first case of the fine-tuning of gravity discussed in Section 2.3.2. The life-permitting range of gravity as it relates to the strength of materials does not depend on the value of the cosmological constant, and hence $P(Lpc_2|k'_{12}$ & $NSU) = P(Lpc_2|k'_2$ & $NSU)$. This means that the joint probability of both gravity and the cosmological constant's falling into their life-permitting ranges is the product of these two probabilities: W_r/W_R for gravity times W_r/W_R for the cosmological constant. This same analysis will hold for any set of fine-tuned constants in which the life-permitting range for each constant is independent of the values the other constants take in their respective EI ranges: e.g., the set consisting of the fine-tuning of the strong nuclear force needed for stable nuclei and the previously discussed example of the fine-tuning of gravity.

35. If W_{r2} is dependent on the value C_1 takes in its EI region, then one would have to take the average value of W_{r2} over C_1's EI region. This would cover those cases for which the two constants are not independent, although we are not considering those cases here. We are also assuming that W_{R2} is not significantly dependent on the value C_1 takes in its EI region; otherwise, we would also have to take the average of W_{R2}.

5.2. Justifying premise (2)

In order to justify Premise (2) of our main argument in Section 1.3, we shall need to argue that God has some reason to bring about LPU.[36] For definiteness, we shall first consider the case of the fine-tuning of the constants under the assumption that T is true and that there is only one universe. That is, we shall attempt to justify the claim that for any constant C that is fine-tuned, $\sim P(Lpc|TSU \& k') \ll 1$, where TSU is the theistic single-universe hypothesis and k' is the background information defined in Sections 4.3 and 4.4. It should then be clear how this case generalizes to cases in which the constants are combined, and for the two other fundamental types of fine-tuning discussed in Section 2. Finally, we shall indicate how this argument generalizes for the theistic multiverse hypothesis (TMU).

To determine $P(Lpc|TSU \& k')$, let us invoke our imaginative device (Section 3.2) of an unembodied, alien observer with cognitive faculties relevantly similar to our own and who believes TSU and k'. This observer would designate our universe as "the universe that is actual" – which we shall abbreviate as U – and would know that U has the laws that our universe has and the values of all the other constants, except that it only would know that constant C had a value in the EI region. Now if this unembodied being could perceive no reason for God to create the universe with C in the life-permitting region instead of any other part of the EI region, then $P(Lpc|TSU \& k') = W_r/W_R \ll 1$. *So the claim that $\sim P(Lpc|TSU \& k') \ll 1$ hinges on this unembodied being's (and hence our) perceiving some reason why God would create a life-permitting universe over other possibilities.*

As Richard Swinburne has argued (2004, pp. 99–106), since God is perfectly good, omniscient, omnipotent, and perfectly free, the only motivation God has for bringing about one state of affairs instead of another is its relative (probable) contribution to the overall moral and aesthetic value of reality.[37] Simple forms of life, such as bacteria, do not seem in and of themselves to contribute to the overall moral value of reality, although it is possible that they might contribute to its overall aesthetic value. On the other hand, embodied moral agents seem to allow for the realization of unique types of value. Hence, it is this form of life that is most relevant for arguing that $\sim P(Lpc|k' \& T) \ll 1$, and thus the most relevant for the fine-tuning argument.

Now let EMA represent the claim that the universe contains embodied moral agents, and let Wh represent whatever else God must do over and above creating the universe with the right laws, constants, and initial conditions to ensure that it contains such agents, such as God's intervening in the unfolding of the universe. Now $P(EMA|TSU \& k') = P(Lpc \& Wh|TSU \& k') = P(Wh|Lpc \& k' \& TSU) \times P(Lpc|TSU \& k')$, given that these probabilities have well-defined values or ranges of value. Since $P(Wh|Lpc \& k' \& TSU) \leq 1$, it follows that $P(Lpc|TSU \& k') \geq P(EMA|TSU \& k')$, once again assuming that these probabilities have well-defined values or ranges of value. Thus, if we can establish that $\sim P(EMA|TSU \& k') \ll 1$, we shall have established that $\sim P(Lpc|TSU \& k') \ll 1$ (which will automatically

---

36. For the specific case of the fine-tuning argument, this section will answer a major objection that is often raised more generally against the design argument (e.g. by Sober 2005): namely, that for the features F that these arguments appeal to, we have no way of determining the probability of God's creating a world with those features, since we have no way of determining God's desires.

37. "Probable" is parenthetically inserted before "value" here and elsewhere to allow for open theism, in which God cannot predict with certainty human free choices and hence the overall value of reality.

be true if the probabilities are not well defined). In order for $\sim P(EMA|TSU \ \& \ k') \ll 1$, it must be plausible to suppose that on balance, God has more reason to make U in such a way that EMA is true than to make it in such a way that EMA is false. We must be very careful about what is required here. Since we are dealing with epistemic probabilities, which are relative to human cognitive faculties and limitations, to establish that $\sim P(EMA|TSU \ \& \ k') \ll 1$ does not require that we show that God actually has more reason, only that it is plausible to suppose that God does.

This will require first that we perceive, however dimly, that it is plausible to think that the existence of embodied creatures like us – that is, finite, vulnerable, embodied moral agents –has a (probable) overall positive value, thus giving God a reason to create a world in which such beings could come about. One cannot merely argue for the value of personal agents in general. The reason is that God's fine-tuning universe U to make EMA true will result in various forms of moral and natural evil, unless God constantly intervenes to prevent it, which clearly does not happen in our world.[38] Thus, in order for God to have a reason to adjust C so that U contains our type of embodied moral agents, there must be certain compensatory goods that could not be realized, or at least optimally realized, without our type of embodiment. This brings us directly to the problem of evil.

If we have an adequate theodicy, then we could plausibly argue that our unembodied alien observer would have positive grounds for thinking that God had more reason to create the universe so that EMA is true, since it would have good reason to think that the existence of such beings would add to the overall value of reality. In that case, we could argue that $P(Lpc|TSU \ \& \ k') > 0.5$.[39] On the other hand, if we have no adequate theodicy, but only a good defense – that is, a good argument showing that we lack sufficient reasons to think that a world such as ours would result in more evil than good – then our unembodied being would both lack sufficient reason to expect that God would make U so that EMA would be true and lack sufficient reason to expect God to create U so that EMA would be false. Hence, there would be no conditional epistemic probability of EMA on TSU & k' and therefore no conditional epistemic probability for $P(Lpc|TSU \ \& \ k')$. It would still follow, however, that Lpc is not epistemically improbable under TSU: that is, $\sim P(Lpc|TSU \ \& \ k') \ll 1$. Hence, Lpc would still give us good reason to believe TSU over NSU.[40]

38. I would like to thank Paul Draper for making me aware of the need to address the problem of evil as part of the fine-tuning argument. (See Draper 2008.)

39. One such theodicy (Collins, unpublished manuscript) that I believe explains much of the evil in the world is what I call the "connection building theodicy," in which the greater goods are certain sorts of deep eternal, ongoing relations of appreciation and intimacy created by one person's helping another – for example, out of moral and spiritual darkness, in times of suffering, and so on.

40. One might challenge this conclusion by claiming that both the restricted Likelihood Principle and the method of probabilistic tension require that a positive, known probability exist for Lpc on T & k'. This seems incorrect, as can be seen by considering cases of disconfirmation in science. For example, suppose some hypothesis h conjoined with suitable auxiliary hypotheses, A, predict e, but e is found not to obtain. Let $\sim E$ be the claim that the experimental results were $\sim e$. Now, $P(\sim E|h \ \& \ A \ \& \ k) \ll 1$, yet $P(\sim E|h \ \& \ A \ \& \ k) \neq 0$ because of the small likelihood of experimental error. Further, often $P(\sim E|\sim (h \ \& \ A) \ \& \ k)$ will be unknown or indeterminate, since we do not know all the alternatives to h nor what they predict about e. Yet, typically we would take $\sim E$ to disconfirm h & A in this case because $P(\sim E|h \ \& \ A \ \& \ k) \ll 1$ and $\sim P(\sim E|\sim (h \ \& \ A) \ \& \ k) \ll 1$.

Thus, unless the atheist can show that it is highly improbable that God would create a world which contained as much evil as ours, it will still be the case that, given the evidence of the fine-tuning of the constants, the *conjunction* of the existence of evil and the fact that the constants have life-permitting values strongly confirms TSU over NSU. This means that theism is still confirmed when the strongest evidence that atheists typically offer for their position (i.e. the existence of evil) is combined with the evidence of the fine-tuning of the constants. Specifically, if we let Ev denote the existence of the kinds and degrees of evil we find in the world, then, for all fine-tuned constants C, Lpc & Ev gives us good reason to believe in TSU over NSU.[41]

What about the case of TMU – that is, the hypothesis that God exists and created many universes. One possibility is to consider the evidence, Lpc*, where Lpc* = "the value of the constant C of *this* universe falls into the life-permitting range," where "this universe" refers to our universe by some means other than "the one and only actual universe": for example, by means of some sort of indexical, such as "the universe that contains *this* electron," where the unembodied being has some way of referring to "this electron" other than by a definite description that uses only purely qualitative properties. Now, some might worry here that given the existence of multiple universes, God would have no reason to make this universe life-permitting, and thus that $P(\text{Lpc*}|\text{TMU \& k}') \ll 1$. For example, Roger White claims that, "It is only the assumption that there are no other options that we should expect the designer to fine-tune *this* universe for life" (2000, p. 243). I disagree. Given that the existence of our type of embodied moral agents is a (probable) overall good, it would contribute to the overall value of reality even if there were such beings in other universes. Thus, God would still have a reason for fine-tuning this universe, and hence $\sim P(\text{Lpc*}|\text{TMU \& k}') \ll 1$. Yet, $P(\text{Lpc*}/\text{NSU \& k}') = P(\text{Lpc}/\text{NSU \& k}') \ll 1$, and hence Lpc* would confirm TMU over NSU.

Even if White is correct, however, our unembodied alien would still have the same reason as offered earlier for thinking that God would create *some* life-permitting universe. Thus, $\sim P(\text{LPU*}|\text{TMU \& k}') \ll 1$, where LPU* is the claim that "some life-permitting universe exists." Nonetheless, since for every constant C, NSU & k' & LPU* entails Lpc & NSU & k', $P(\text{LPU*}|\text{NSU \& k}') \le P(\text{Lpc}|\text{NSU \& k}') \ll 1$. Thus, by the restricted version of the Likelihood Principle, LPU* confirms TMU over NSU. If White is right, therefore, the relevant confirmatory evidence for TMU versus NSU would become "some life-permitting universe exists" instead of "this universe has life-permitting values for its constants."

6. The Multiverse Hypothesis

6.1. Introduction

The multiverse hypothesis is the hypothesis that there exist many regions of space-time – that is, "universes" – with different initial conditions, constants of physics, and even laws of nature. It is commonly considered the major alternative to the competing hypotheses

---

41. Finally, in a worst-case scenario in which an atheist offered good reason to believe that Ev is unlikely under T, it would still probably be the case that Lpc & Ev would disconfirm NSU over TSU, not only because the improbability of Lpc is so great under NSU that it would be less than $P(\text{Ev}|\text{TSU \& k}')$ but also because $P(\text{Lpc}|\text{NSU \& k}') \ll 1$ receives a principled justification – via the restricted Principle of Indifference – whereas the arguments offered for $P(\text{Ev}|\text{T \& k}) \ll 1$ are typically based on highly controversial intuitions.

of T and NSU. Just as in a lottery in which all the tickets are sold, one is bound to be the winning number, so given a varied enough set of universes with regard to some life-permitting feature F, it is no longer surprising that there exists a universe somewhere that has F. Multiverse hypotheses differ both in the features that vary from universe to universe – for example, the initial conditions, the constants of physics, and so on – and what physical process, if any, produced them.

The multiverse objection can be interpreted as either claiming that the multiverse provides an alternative explanation of the fine-tuning of the cosmos, or that it simply eliminates the epistemic improbability of the fine-tuning. We shall focus primarily on the latter objection, since such an objection would undermine any argument based on the Likelihood Principle that the fine-tuning provides evidence for T over a naturalistic version of the multiverse hypothesis. Put precisely, this version of the multiverse objection is that $\sim P(LPU|NMU \& k') \ll 1$, where k' is some appropriately chosen background information and NMU is the relevant naturalistic multiverse hypothesis. Thus, it is claimed, LPU does not provide evidence via the Likelihood Principle for T over an appropriately chosen multiverse hypothesis.

To address this objection, we first need to get clear on exactly how multiverse hypotheses are supposed to explain, or take away the seeming improbability of, the fine-tuning. To begin, we need to distinguish between three facts with regard to the fine-tuning that are candidates for explanation: (1) what I call the *observer-relative* life-permitting (LP) fact that we, or I, observe a life-permitting universe instead of a non-life-permitting universe; (2) what I call the *indexical* LP fact that *this* universe is life-permitting – or has some life-permitting feature F, where "this" is an indexical that picks out the universe we inhabit; and (3) what I call the *existential* LP fact that a life-permitting universe exists, a fact that is equivalent to what we have been referring to by "LPU". The so-called *Weak Anthropic Principle*, which states that the universe we inhabit must have a life-permitting structure, appears to be enough to make the observer-relative LP fact unsurprising. With regard to the indexical LP fact, some philosophers claim that we cannot make a purely indexical reference to our universe but can only refer to our universe via an implicit description. Thus, for instance, one could claim that "this universe" is reducible to "the universe we inhabit," where the "we" is in turn reducible to some other description such as "conscious observers with characteristics X," where X refers to some set of purely qualitative properties. If this analysis is correct, then the claim that "this universe is life-permitting" would be a tautology, and hence have an epistemic probability of one. Even if one rejected this analysis, one could still claim that the life-permitting character of our universe is a defining, or at least an essential, feature of it, so the indexical LP fact is a necessary truth and thus not surprising. Consequently, it is questionable whether this indexical fact is in any way improbable. In any case, it is clear that the multiverse hypothesis does not itself explain or render probable this indexical LP fact, since whether or not other universes exist is irrelevant to the features *our* universe might have.

So the only place where the multiverse hypothesis could help in explaining the fine-tuning or undercutting its improbability is by explaining or undercutting the apparent improbability of LPU – that is, of the existential LP fact expressed by (3). A hypothesis postulating a sufficiently varied multiverse will entail LPU; hence, purportedly it will not only explain why some such universe exists but will also undercut any claim that the existence of such a universe is improbable. It is here, and only here, that the multiverse could do any work in undercutting the fine-tuning argument for T. The so-called observer-selection effect, often considered an essential part of the multiverse explanation, does not itself contribute at all; this effect only explains the observer-relative LP fact given by (1) and is already taken into account by the Weak Anthropic Principle.

Now it is important to distinguish between two categories of multiverse hypotheses: the *unrestricted* version (which I shall label UMU) and various types of *restricted* versions. The unrestricted version is the hypothesis that all possible worlds exist, a version famously advocated by philosopher David Lewis as an account of modal claims. According to Lewis, every possible world actually exists (as a region of space-time) parallel to our own. Thus, for instance, there exists a reality parallel to our own in which objects can travel faster than the speed of light. Dream up a possible scenario, and it exists in some parallel reality, according to Lewis. These worlds, however, are completely isolated from ours, and there are no spatiotemporal or causal relations between the worlds – for example, things in one world do not happen before, at the same time, or after things in our world. Further, they do not overlap in any way, except for the possibility of sharing immanent universals. (1986, p. 2).

Lewis advocates his hypothesis as an account of modal statements – that is, statements that make claims about possibility and impossibility, such as "it is possible that Al Gore won the US presidential election in 2004," and "it is impossible for an object to be a perfect cube and a perfect sphere at the same time." Thus, Lewis calls his view modal realism, with the term "realism" indicating that every possible world exists in as real a way as our own. This term, however, is a misnomer, since it implies that other accounts of modal claims are antirealist, which they are not. The other major advocate of a similar view is Massachusetts Institute of Technology astrophysicist Max Tegmark (1998, 2003). According to Tegmark, "everything that exists mathematically exists physically" (1998, p. 1), by which he means that every self-consistent mathematical structure is in one-to-one correspondence with some physical reality (1998, pp. 1–3). Unlike Lewis, Tegmark's primary argument for his view is to explain LPU. Further, it is unclear whether Tegmark is claiming that every possible universe exists, or only that every possible universe that can be described purely mathematically; in the latter case it would not be a completely unrestricted multiverse hypothesis.

In contrast to Lewis's and perhaps Tegmark's hypothesis, restricted multiverse hypotheses postulate some restriction on the possible universes (or worlds) that actually exist. The most widely discussed versions are those that claim that a multitude of varied universes are generated by some physical process (what I will call a "multiverse generator"). We shall discuss these in Section 6.3. The important point here is that such a restriction will run the danger of reinstantiating the problem of fine-tuning at the level of the restrictions placed on the set of existing universes. In Section 6.3, I shall argue in detail that this is what happens in the case of the most widely discussed multiverse-generator hypothesis, the inflationary-superstring multiverse hypothesis.

Unlike the restricted versions of the multiverse hypothesis, the unrestricted version does not run any danger of reinstantiating the problem of fine-tuning. As I shall argue in the next subsection, however, it faces the following devastating dilemma as an alternative to a theistic explanation of the fine-tuning: *it either undercuts almost all scientific reasoning and ordinary claims of improbability, or it completely fails to undercut the fine-tuning argument for T.*[42]

---

42. Here, I am simply making rigorous an argument suggested by others, such as William Lane Craig (2003, p. 173) and cosmologist Robert Mann (2005, pp. 308–9).

6.2. Critique of the unrestricted multiverse

To begin our argument, consider a particular event for which we would normally demand an explanation, say, that of Jane's rolling a six-sided die 100 times in a row and its coming up on six each time. Call the type of sequence "coming up 100 times on six" type Tx. Further, let "D" denote the particular die that Jane rolled and DTx the state of affairs of D's falling under type Tx for the particular sequence of die rolls: that is, DTx is the state of affairs of D's coming up 100 times in a row on six for that particular sequence of die rolls. Normally, we should not accept that DTx simply happened by chance; we should look for an explanation. The reason is that DTx is *both* very improbable, having a one in 6^{100} chance of occurring, and in some way "special." The quality of being "special" is necessary for our seeking an explanation since all 100 sequences of rolls are equally improbable, but they are not all in need of an explanation. In general, what makes an improbable occurrence special, and thus a *coincidence* in need of explanation, is difficult to explicate precisely. John Leslie, for example, has proposed that this specialness consists of our being able to glimpse a simple, unified explanation of the occurrence (Leslie, 1988, p. 302). In whatever way one explicates being "special," however, certainly, a six-sided die coming up 100 times in a row on six qualifies.

Now, for any possible state of affairs S – such as DTx – UMU entails that this state of affairs S is actual. Thus, with regard to explanation, for all possible states of affairs S, advocates of UMU must claim that the fact that UMU entails S either (i.a) undercuts all need for explanation, or (i.b) it does not. Further, with regard to some state of affairs S (such as DTx) that we normally and uncontroversially regard as improbable, they must claim that the fact that UMU entails S either (ii.a) undercuts the improbability of S (since it entails S), or (ii.b) it does not. Both (i.a) and (ii.a) would constitute a *reductio* of UMU, since it would undercut both all justifications in science based on explanatory merits of an hypothesis and ordinary claims of probability, such as in our die example. If advocates of UMU adopt (i.b) and (ii.b), however, then the mere fact that UMU entails LPU undercuts neither the need to explain LPU nor its apparent improbability.[43]

Part of what gives rise to the temptation to think that UMU can explain, or render unsurprising, LPU (without doing the same for every other occurrence) is the existence of other "many-trials" scenarios that appear to be analogous but which are really crucially disanalogous. The way in which they are disanalogous is that they only entail the occurrence of a very limited number of states of affairs that we find highly surprising, without entailing the existence of all such states of affairs. What drives inferences of epistemic probability in these cases is what I call the *Entailment Principle*. This principle states that if h & k′ is *known* to entail S, or *known* to render the statistical probability of S near 1, then the conditional epistemic probability of S on h & k′ is near 1: that is, $P(S|h \& k') \sim 1$.[44] For limited multiple-trial hypotheses the Entailment Principle can render epistemically

---

43. Lewis (1986, pp. 131–2) explicitly adopts (i.b).

44. In standard presentations of the logical and subjective accounts of conditional probability, the fact that h & k′ entails S is sufficient to render $P(S|h \& k') = 1$, whether or not we know that h & k′ entails S. The account of epistemic probability that I developed in Section 3.2, however, assumes that epistemic probability is relative to human cognitive limitations. Thus, the fact that h & k′ entails S would only make $P(S|h \& k') = 1$ if we knew that fact.

probable the actuality of some state of affairs whose actuality would otherwise be considered highly improbable, without at the same time rendering the actuality of other states of affairs probable that we normally consider improbable. Consider, for example, what could be called the multiple-die-roll hypothesis (MDR), according to which an enormous number of dice are being rolled at every moment throughout the galaxy, in fact so many that the statistical probability that some sequence of 100 die rolls will come up all sixes is almost one. By the Entailment Principle, it follows that it is highly epistemically probable under MDR that *some* 100-member sequence of die rolls will come up all sixes. The conjunction of MDR and the Entailment Principle, however, does not change the probability of other states of affairs whose improbability is critical for everyday inferences, such as that of some particular sequence of die rolls coming up all sixes.

Now, advocates of UMU could affirm the Entailment Principle and still retain the claim that for some states of affairs S, the actuality of S is epistemically improbable under UMU. As we saw earlier, if S is a possible state of affairs, then UMU entails that S is actual. If we can know that S is possible without knowing that S is actual, then the claim that S is possible would be part of our background information k', and hence $P(S|UMU \& k') = 1$. Suppose that for some cases, however, we cannot know whether S is possible apart from S's actually occurring. In those cases, the Entailment Principle could be true and yet for some S, $P(S|UMU \& k') < 1$, even though UMU entails S. In the case of the die D in our earlier example, the particular die D exists only as part of the world W it occupies, and thus the only possible sequence of rolls of D are those that it has in W.[45] Consequently, unless we know the sequences of rolls of D that have actually occurred in W, we cannot know whether it is *possible* for D to fall in sequence type Tx without knowing whether D has *actually* fallen in type Tx. This means that even though UMU might entail that D lands in type Tx, we could not deduce this from UMU, and, hence, the conditional epistemic probability of D's falling in Tx could be less than 1. The epistemic probability of $P(DTx|k' \& UMU)$ would then be given by the degree to which $k' \& UMU$ of itself rationally justifies the proposition, DTx, that die D came up in sequence type Tx. Call this the *nondeducibility loophole*, since it arises from the fact that even though UMU entails the actuality of all actual states of affairs S, we cannot always *derive* S's actuality from UMU.

Now the nondeducibility loophole will work only if we can refer to D in W in a way that is not equivalent or reducible to providing some qualitative description that uniquely picks it out from among all dice that exist across worlds, since such a qualitative description would have to include everything about D that distinguishes it from its counterparts in other worlds, including DTx, or ~DTx. Put differently, it will work only if we can make statements about the die that *essentially* involve the use of indexicals – that is, involve the use of indexicals, such as "this die," in a way that cannot be translated in terms of statements that only use qualitative descriptions such as "the die with properties P," where the properties P are purely qualitative properties.[46]

---

45. Of course, Lewis would want to affirm the ordinary claim that it possible for D to land in a different sequence than it actually does in world W. He would interpret that ordinary claim, however, as really saying that there are certain relevantly similar counterparts to D in other worlds that landed in a different sequence, not that it was possible for the *particular die D* to have landed differently.

46. It is hard to see how such essentially indexical claims are possible under UMU, since such claims seem to imply unrealized alternative possibilities, which would contradict UMU. For example, if die D is not defined by the conjunction of all its qualitative properties, then it seems that it could have had different qualitative properties, such as landing on a different sequence of numbers.

If we allow such essentially indexical propositions about particular objects in the universe, such as the die, then it seems we can also make such essentially indexical statements about the universe we inhabit: we could simply specify that universe U (or "this universe") refers to the universe that contains some particular object – for example, some particular electron – that we are referring to in an essentially indexical manner. This will allow us to adopt the same loophole to the Entailment Principle as adopted by advocates of UMU. Put differently, what I called the *indexical LP fact* – that is, the fact that universe U is life-permitting – could no longer be simply dismissed as needing no explanation (or lacking improbability) because it is purportedly a defining or essential feature of this universe that it is life-permitting. The reason is that even though it would be an essential feature of this universe, we could not deduce it from UMU without already knowing that it is possible for universe U to be life-permitting, just as we could not deduce DTx from UMU without knowing that DTx is possible.

Finally, to exploit the nondeducibility loophole for the indexical LP fact, we simply apply our standard procedure for subtracting out old evidence – such as that the universe has life-permitting values for its constants – to obtain background information k'. Now, although k' and UMU entail that universe U is life-permitting, a being with cognitive faculties relevantly similar to our own could not deduce that simply by knowing k' and UMU: for example, if our unembodied being introduced at the end of Section 3.2 were given the information k' and UMU, it would not know whether U was life-permitting or not. Consequently, by the same argument used for the case of the NSU, P(Universe U is life-permitting|UMU & k') $\ll 1$ and P(Lpc|UMU & k') $\ll 1$.[47] Of course, one might argue against this subtraction procedure, but this sort of argument is a direct challenge to my version of the fine-tuning argument itself, not a challenge arising from UMU. (See Section 4.3 for a defense of the subtraction procedure.)[48]

A general lesson to be gained from this analysis is that any multiverse hypothesis that purportedly undercuts the fine-tuning argument by entailing LPU will have to be restricted in the right way: specifically, it will have to be such that it does not entail states

---

47. Further, the probability, P(Lpc|TSU & k'), discussed in Section 5.2 would be unaffected, although now its interpretation would be different: Lpc in both P(Lpc|UMU & k') and P(Lpc|TSU & k') would refer to the fact that *this* universe U has a life-permitting value for its constant C instead of the fact that the "universe that is actual" has a life-permitting value, as it did in Sections 5, where Lpc* denoted the former use of Lpc. If we had strong independent reasons for believing in multiple universes (of some sort of restricted variety, not UMU), then we should have to consider whether ~P(Lpc*|TMU & k') $\ll 1$ since TSU would no longer be a viable hypothesis. (TMU is the theistic multiverse hypothesis.) See the end of Section 5.2 for brief discussion of ~P(Lpc*|TMU & k') $\ll 1$.

48. Lewis could also attempt to appeal to statistical probability in defense of the improbability of DTx by claiming that D should be considered a part of a reference class of all relevantly similar dice in nearby worlds. This, however, opens the door to an advocate of the fine-tuning argument to make a similar claim about the improbability of the fine-tuning of our universe: namely, we should consider our universe part of a reference class of worlds with the same mathematical form for the laws of nature but with constants that are allowed to differ. Then, by the restricted Principle of Indifference, P(Lpc*|UMU & k') = $W_r/W_R \ll 1$. (See note 47 for definition of Lpc*.)

Another major objection that can be raised against UMU is that the overwhelming majority of worlds are deceptive worlds and worlds in which induction fails. For example, Peter Forrest has argued that there are a vastly greater proportion of worlds in which observers exist with the same past and the same subjective experiences as ours, but in which the future does not in any way resemble the past. Purportedly, this raises an enormous skeptical problem for UMU. I tend to agree with Forrest, but I also agree with Lewis's response to Forrest that without a measure over the class of other worlds, one cannot make this objection rigorous (Lewis, 1986, pp. 115–21). Thus, I have not pursued this objection here.

of affairs S that we normally take to be improbable. Consider, for example, a multiverse hypotheses M that attempts to explain the special initial conditions of our universe by hypothesizing that it is part of a vast array of universes all of which have the same laws L but in which every possible initial condition is realized. The standard inflationary-superstring scenario discussed in the next section contains such a multiverse as a subset. So do standard multiverse theories based on the existence of an infinite universe with widely varying initial conditions. Assuming that universes lack haecceities – which in this case implies that they are distinguished only by their initial conditions – and assuming the laws are deterministic, then M will entail the existence of our universe along with all of its properties. For example, M will entail DTx. Hence, the mere fact that M entails the existence of our universe and its life-permitting structure cannot be taken as undercutting the claim that it is improbable without at the same time undercutting claims such as that DTx is improbable. Of course, an advocate of M could always use the nondeducibility loophole discussed earlier to save the improbability of the actuality of these states of affairs, but that will open the door to the advocate of the fine-tuning argument's using the same loophole.[49] If this analysis is correct, it will spell trouble for those who claim that the multiverses discussed in contemporary cosmology – such as the inflationary multiverse – can undercut the improbability of the extraordinarily special initial conditions of our universe by claiming that every possible initial condition is realized in some universe or another.

6.3. The inflationary-superstring multiverse explained and criticized

As mentioned in Section 6.1, by far the most commonly advocated version of the restricted multiverse hypothesis is the "multiverse-generator" version that claims that our universe was generated by some physical process that produces an enormous number of universes with different initial conditions, values for the constants of nature, and even lower-level laws. Many scenarios have been proposed – such as the oscillating Big Bang model and Lee Smolin's claim that many universes are generated via black holes (Smolin 1997). Among these, the one based on inflationary cosmology conjoined with superstring theory is by far the most widely discussed and advocated, since this is the only one that goes beyond mere speculation. According to inflationary cosmology, our universe started from an exceedingly small region of space that underwent enormous expansion due to a hypothesized *inflaton* field that both caused the expansion and imparted a constant, very large energy density to space as it expanded. The expansion caused the temperature of space to decrease, causing one or more so-called "bubble universes" to form. As each bubble

---

49. If universes have haecceities, then M would not necessarily entail the existence of our universe but only one qualitatively identical with it. In that case, M would not necessarily entail DTx, but only that a die qualitatively identical to D came up on six 100 times in a row. Allowing for haecceities, however, means that one must consider the improbability of purely indexical LP facts about our universe, since the essential features of our universe no longer must include all of its qualitative properties, such as its initial conditions. In that case, the fine-tuning argument could be relocated to the indexical fact regarding the improbability of *our* universe's having life-permitting initial conditions, since M no longer entails that *our* universe U has the initial conditions it does. (The earlier argument was formulated on the assumption that the laws are deterministic; I believe that a similar argument also works if the laws are indeterministic, but I cannot pursue it here.)

universe is formed, the energy of the inflaton field is converted into a burst of "normal" mass-energy, thereby giving rise to a standard Big Bang expansion of the kind we see in our universe.

In *chaotic inflation* models – widely considered the most plausible – space expands so rapidly that it becomes a never-ending source of bubble universes. Thus, an enormous number of universes naturally arise from this scenario. In order to get the parameters of physics to vary from universe to universe, however, there must be a further physical mechanism/law to cause the variation. Currently, many argue that this mechanism/law is given by superstring theory or its proposed successor, M-Theory, which are widely considered the only currently feasible candidates for a truly fundamental physical theory. It should be stressed, however, that both inflationary cosmology and superstring/M-Theory are highly speculative. For example, Michio Kaku states in his recent textbook on superstring theory, "Not a shred of experimental evidence has been found to confirm . . . superstrings" (1999, p. 17). The same remains true today. The major attraction of superstring/M-Theory is its mathematical elegance and the fact that many physicists think that it is the only game in town that offers significant hope of providing a truly unified physical theory of gravitation with quantum mechanics (Greene 1999, p. 214).

6.3.1. Inflationary-superstring multiverse requires right laws

One major possible theistic response to the multiverse generator scenario, whether of the inflationary variety or some other type, is that the laws of the multiverse generator must be just right – fine-tuned – in order to produce life-sustaining universes. To give an analogy, even a mundane item such as a bread machine, which only produces loaves of bread instead of universes, must have the right structure, programs, and ingredients (flour, water, yeast, and gluten) to produce decent loaves of bread. Thus, it seems, invoking some sort of multiverse generator as an explanation of the fine-tuning reinstates the fine-tuning up one level, to the laws governing the multiverse generator. So, at most, it could explain the fine-tuning of the constants and initial conditions. (Even the latter will be problematic, however, as we shall see in the next two sections.)

As a test case, consider the inflationary type multiverse generator. In order for it to explain the fine-tuning of the constants, it must hypothesize one or more "mechanisms" or laws that will do the following five things: (i) cause the expansion of a small region of space into a very large region; (ii) generate the very large amount of mass-energy needed for that region to contain matter instead of merely empty space; (iii) convert the mass-energy of inflated space to the sort of mass-energy we find in our universe; and (iv) cause sufficient variations among the constants of physics to explain their fine-tuning.

Glossing over the details, in inflationary models, the first two conditions are met via two factors. The first factor is the postulated inflaton field that gives the vacuum (that is, empty space), a positive energy density. The second factor is the peculiar nature of Einstein's equation of General Relativity, which dictates that space expand at an enormous rate in the presence of a large near-homogenous positive energy density (see Section 2.3.3). Finally, because the inflaton field gives a constant positive energy density to empty space, as space expands the total vacuum energy within the space in question will increase enormously. This, in turn, generates the needed energy for the formation of matter in the universe. As one text in cosmology explains, "the vacuum acts as a reservoir of unlimited energy, which can supply as much as is required to inflate a given region to any required size at constant energy density" (Peacock 1999, p. 26).

So, to achieve (i)–(ii), we effectively have a sort of "conspiracy" between at least two different factors: the inflaton field that gives empty space a positive energy density, and Einstein's equation. Without either factor, there would neither be regions of space that inflate nor would those regions have the mass-energy necessary for a universe to exist. If, for example, the universe obeyed Newton's theory of gravity instead of Einstein's, the vacuum energy of the inflaton field would at best simply create a gravitational attraction causing space to contract, not to expand.

The conversion of the energy of the inflaton field to the normal mass-energy of our universe (condition (iii)) is achieved by Einstein's equivalence of mass and energy, $E = mc^2$, along with the assumption that there is a coupling between the inflaton field and the matter fields. Finally, the variation in the constants (and to some extent the laws) of nature is typically claimed to be achieved by combining inflationary cosmology with superstring/M-Theory, which purportedly allows for an enormous number (greater than 10^{500}) possible combinations of values for the constants of physics. The important point here is that the laws underlying the inflationary scenario must be just right in order to cause these variations in the constants of physics from one universe to another. If the underlying laws are those given by superstring/M-Theory, arguably there is enough variation; this is not the case, however, for the typical grand unified theories that have been recently studied, which allow for only a very limited number of variations of the parameters of physics, about a dozen or so in the case of the simplest model (Linde 1990, p. 33). As Joseph Polchinski notes in his textbook on superstring theory (1998, vol. II, pp. 372–3), there is no reason to expect a generic field to have an enormous number of stable local minima of energy, which would be required if there is to be a large number of variations in the constants of physics among universes in inflationary cosmology.

In addition to the four factors listed, the fundamental physical laws underlying a multiverse generator – whether of the inflationary type or some other – must be just right in order for it to produce life-permitting universes, instead of merely dead universes. Specifically, these fundamental laws must be such as to allow the conversion of the mass-energy into material forms that allow for the sort of stable complexity needed for complex intelligent life. For example, as elaborated in Section 2.2, without the Principle of Quantization, all electrons would be sucked into the atomic nuclei, and, hence atoms would be impossible; without the Pauli Exclusion Principle, electrons would occupy the lowest atomic orbit, and hence complex and varied atoms would be impossible; without a universally attractive force between all masses, such as gravity, matter would not be able to form sufficiently large material bodies (such as planets) for life to develop or for long-lived stable energy sources such as stars to exist.

Although some of the laws of physics can vary from universe to universe in superstring/M-Theory, these fundamental laws and principles underlie superstring/M-Theory and therefore cannot be explained as a multiverse selection effect. Further, since the variation among universes would consist of variation of the masses and types of particles, and the form of the forces between them, complex structures would almost certainly be atomlike and stable energy sources would almost certainly require aggregates of matter. Thus, the said fundamental laws seem necessary for there to be life in *any* of the many universes generated in this scenario, not merely in a universe with our specific types of particles and forces.

In sum, even if an inflationary-superstring multiverse generator exists, it must have just the right combination of laws and fields for the production of life-permitting universes: if one of the components were missing or different, such as Einstein's equation or the Pauli Exclusion Principle, it is unlikely that any life-permitting universes could be produced. Consequently, at most, this highly speculative scenario would explain the fine-tuning of the constants of physics, but at the cost of postulating additional fine-tuning of the laws of nature.

6.3.2. Low-entropy problems for inflationary cosmology

Inflationary cosmology runs into a major problem in explaining the low entropy of the universe. This is a critical problem, since unless it can do this, arguably much, if not all, of the motivation for inflationary cosmology vanishes. Further, this problem will cast severe doubt on the ability of an inflationary multiverse to explain the fine-tuning. The problem is that, applied to the universe as a whole, the second law of thermodynamics demands that the entropy of the universe always increase. Indeed, even if one has doubts about the applicability of the second law to the universe as a whole, inflation invokes a thermalization process, and thermalization is known to be a paradigmatic entropy-increasing process. As Oxford University physicist Roger Penrose states:

> Indeed, it is fundamentally misconceived to explain why the universe is special in *any* particular respect by appealing to a thermalization process. For, if the thermalization is actually doing anything (such as making temperatures in different regions more equal than they were before), then it represents a definite increasing of entropy. Thus, the universe would have had to be more special before the thermalization than after. This only serves to increase whatever difficulty we might have had previously in trying to come to terms with the initial extraordinarily special nature of the universe.... invoking arguments from thermalization, to address this particular problem [of the specialness of the universe], is worse than useless! (2004, p. 756)

Based on this sort of argument, it is now widely accepted that the preinflationary patch of space-time that inflated to form our universe must have had lower entropy than the universe right after inflation. For example, Andreas Albrecht, a defender of inflationary cosmology, admits that inflationary cosmology must hypothesize a special initial low entropy state: "For inflation, the *inflaton field* is the out-of-equilibrium degree of freedom that drives other subsystems. The inflaton starts in a fairly homogeneous potential-dominated state which is certainly not a high-entropy state for that field ..." (2004, p. 382). Elsewhere, he says the preinflation patch must have been in a "very special state" (2004, p. 380).

6.3.3. Albrecht's "dominant channel" response

So, how does inflation explain the special initial conditions of the Big Bang, which is the primary aim of the theory? According to Albrecht, it explains the initial conditions by a two-stage process, via the "chaotic inflation" models mentioned in Section 6.3. First, as Albrecht explains, "One typically imagines some sort of chaotic primordial state, where the inflaton field is more or less randomly tossed about, until by sheer chance it winds up in a very rare fluctuation that produces a potential-dominated state ..." (Albrecht 2004, p. 384). Potential-dominated states are those in which the potential energy of the inflaton field is enormous compared to the rate of change of the inflaton field with respect to time and space. That is, in order for inflation to occur, the inflaton field must be almost uniform both spatially and temporally relative to the total energy density of the field (Peacock 1999, p. 329). Although macroscopic uniformity of matter is typically a state of very high entropy (such as perfume spread throughout a room), it is generally accepted that in the case of the gravitational field and the inflaton field, greater uniformity entails lower entropy. This is said to explain why the universe becomes more and more inhomogeneous as it expands (with matter clustering into galaxies and stars forming), and yet at the same time its entropy increases. Entropy increases because the gravitational field becomes less uniform. Since the gravitational field would play a significant role in the space-time of the early universe, a near uniform inflaton field would correspond to extremely low entropy.

Now a general requirement for inflation is that the inflaton field be nearly uniform, in the potential-dominated sense defined earlier, over some very small patch. Although these states will be extremely rare, given a large enough initial inflaton field, or enough time, they are likely eventually to occur in some small patch of space simply as a result of thermal fluctuations. Once they occur, inflation sets in, enormously expanding the patch. Eventually, because of the postulated nature of the inflaton field, in one or more regions of this expanded space, the field decays, resulting in reheating that produces a bubble universe with ordinary matter. So, in effect, because inflation can only occur in highly uniform states of the inflaton field, any universe produced from an inflated region will have initially low entropy.

Accordingly, Albrecht proposes that inflation explains the low entropy of our universe by a two-stage process: (i) a low-entropy patch occurs as a result of a statistical fluctuation, and then (ii) that patch inflates into our universe. As John Barrow and Frank Tipler pointed out over 20 years ago (1986, p. 437), however, if the right special initial conditions must be stumbled upon by a statistical fluctuation, why not simply hypothesize a very large, or infinite, material field that undergoes a random fluctuation that produces a universe relevantly like ours? Why invoke the additional mechanism of inflation?

The answer requires looking at the standard objection to "random fluctuation models." The objection is that universes being produced by such a fluctuation (without inflation) would almost certainly lead to small islands of observers surrounded by chaos, not one with a low degree of entropy throughout. Even more ominously, a random observer most likely would be a so-called Boltzmann brain (BB). A BB is a small region of mass-energy with the same structure as our brains (including the same sort of apparent memory and sensory experiences), but with the surrounding regions of space and time in a chaotic, high-entropy state. Although the experiences of such brains would be highly ordered for a brief time, they would not in any way correspond to reality, and any sort of inductive reasoning would fail.

The BB concept was originally articulated as part of an objection raised against the proposed anthropic-selection-effect explanation of the low initial entropy offered by Ludwig Boltzmann, one of the principal founders of statistical mechanics. Boltzmann attempted to explain the relatively low entropy of the universe by claiming that it was the result a fluctuation from the normal "chaotic," equilibrium state, and that a fluctuation with a high degree of order was necessary for the existence of observers. As theoretical physicist Paul Davies and many others have pointed out in response to Boltzmann's anthropic explanation, a fluctuation "the size of the solar system would be sufficient to ensure the existence of life on Earth, and such a fluctuation is *far* more probable than one of cosmic proportions" (Davies 1974, p. 103). Indeed, fluctuations of even smaller dimensions – ones in which matter has the same organization as the brain with all its apparent memories and sense experiences but in which the surrounding space-time was chaos – would be even more likely. Consequently, insofar as a random fluctuation world contained observers, any randomly selected observer would almost certainly be a BB.

To intuitively see why Davies's statement is correct, consider an analogy of a very large scrabble board. If we were to shake the scrabble board at random, we would be much more likely to get an ordered, meaningful arrangement of letters in one small region, with the arrangement on the rest of the board essentially chaotic, than for all the letters on the entire board to form meaningful patterns. Or, as another analogy, consider a hundred coins lined up in a row, which are then shaken at random. Define a local island of order to be any consecutive sequence of five coins which all are on the same side – that is, either all heads or all tails. It is much more likely for the sequence of a hundred coin tosses to contain one or more subsequences of five consecutive heads or tails than for it to be all heads or all tails. Indeed, it is likely that such a sequence of coins will have at least one such island of five consecutive heads or tails; the probability of the coins coming up all heads or all tails, however, is around one in 10^{30}, or one in a thousand, billion, billion, billion.

The same argument applies to the mass-energy configurations of our visible universe, with the argument being grounded in probability calculations based on the standard probability measure of statistical mechanics over phase space. Roger Penrose's calculations show that among all possible configurations, it is enormously more likely (by a factor of around 1 in 10^x, where $x = 10^{123}$) for local islands of low entropy to form than the whole visible universe to be in a low-entropy state (see e.g. Penrose 2004, pp. 762–5). Indeed, if we consider the set of all configurations of mass-energy that would result in an observer – for example, an organized structure with the same relevant order as our brain – the subset of such configurations that are dominated by BB observers would be far, far larger than those configurations that are dominated by non-BB observers.

Some people attempt to draw from these calculations the conclusion that if the random fluctuation model is correct, we should then expect ourselves to be BBs. This assumption, however, is difficult to justify. We can, however, derive the more limited conclusion that under the random fluctuation model it is epistemically very likely that we are BBs conditioned on only our purely subjective experiences: that is, $P(BB|k' \& RF) \sim 1$, where BB represents the hypothesis that "I am a BB," RF the claim that the random fluctuation model is correct, and k' includes all of one's own "purely subjective" experiences but no claim that these experiences correspond to reality.

Many have argued, however, that we have noninferential knowledge of the existence of the external world – that is, knowledge of the external world that cannot be deduced from k'. If this is right, then $P(BB|k \& RF) = 0$, where $k^* =$ there is an external world that generally corresponds to our subjective experiences, and $k = k' \& k^*$ is our relevantly complete background information. This is the reason we cannot derive the skeptical conclusion that if the random fluctuation model is true, we should expect ourselves to be BBs. However, since $P(\sim BB \& k^*|RF \& k') \ll 1$, the elaborated RF hypothesis, $k \& RF = \sim BB \& k' \& k^* \& RF$, suffers from a severe probabilistic tension that the elaborated $\sim RF$ hypothesis, $k \& \sim RF = \sim BB \& k' \& k^* \& \sim RF$, does not. (Here, $\sim BB$ is the claim that we are not BBs, and $\sim RF$ is the denial of the RF model.) This probabilistic tension gives us strong reasons to accept $\sim RF$ over RF, given that that we are not BBs. Or, given that $\sim RF$ is not *ad hoc* in the sense defined in section 1.3, the restricted version of the Likelihood Principle implies that

~BB & k* strongly confirms ~RF over RF, since $P(\sim BB\ \&\ k^*|RF\ \&\ k') \ll 1$ and $\sim P(\sim BB\ \&\ k^*|\sim RF\ \&\ k') \ll 1$.[50]

A major question for a chaotic inflationary multiverse model is whether it can circumvent the BB problem that plagues the random fluctuation model. If not, such a model will encounter the same disconfirmation as RF, thus giving us strong reasons to reject it. According to Albrecht, the inflationary model can avoid the BB problem, and this is its key advantage. Says Albrecht:

> Inflation is best thought of as the "dominant channel" from random chaos into a big bang-like state. *The exponentially large volume of the Big Bang-like regions produced via inflation appear to completely swamp any other regions that might have fluctuated into a Big Bang-like state via some other route.* So, if you went looking around in the universe looking for a region like the one we see, it would be exponentially more likely to have arrived at that state via inflation, than some other way, and is thus strongly predicted to have the whole package of inflationary predictions. (Albrecht 2004, p. 385; italics added)[51]

The idea here is that inflation takes small, low-entropy regions and expands them into enormously large regions with enough order so that they will be dominated by non-BB observers (if they have observers). The assumption is that the regions that undergo inflation are so small that they are much more likely to occur than regions that generate observers by random fluctuations; further, because of inflation, these initially small regions become so large that they dominate over those regions that produce observers by means of random fluctuations. Albrecht admits, however, that his argument that inflation would be the dominant channel "rests on very heuristic arguments" and that "the program of putting this sort of argument on firmer foundations is in its infancy" (2004, p. 396).

Several articles have been written in recent years arguing that inflation will generate universes in which BBs enormously dominate among observers in the far future (Bousso & Freivogel 2006; Banks 2007).[52] These arguments, however, might only present a problem if one adopts a block universe view, according to which future events have the same ontological status as present and past events. Although advocates of inflation typically assume such a view, they need not. If one adopts a metaphysical view in which the future is not yet real, these arguments will not themselves show that inflation leads to a present dominance of BB universes. Further, as cosmologist Don Page (2006) has pointed out, the same dominance of BBs occurs for long-lived single universes; further, the evidence at present strongly suggests that our universe will continue existing for an enormously long time, if not forever, if there is no supernatural intervention. In any case, I shall next present a powerful reason

50. The claim that $P(\sim BB\ \&\ k^*|RF\ \&\ k') \ll 1$ assumes that one can separate out a "purely subjective" element of experience (corresponding to k') from other aspects of experience that essentially involve reference to the external world. Some deny this assumption, although it seems very plausible to me. I also should note that the aforementioned argument provides a more rigorous way of proceeding than invoking the so-called "typicality" assumption – that we are in some ill-defined sense "typical observers" – so often invoked in discussions of the BB problem.

51. See Albrecht (2004) for a more detailed presentation of this argument, especially pages 385–87 and 390.

52. I would like to thank James Sinclair for pointing out some of these articles to me. For a recent review of the literature, see Banks (2007, ref. 4).

for thinking that Albrecht's argument is flawed and that without assuming highly special initial conditions, inflationary cosmology leads to a dominance of BBs for *any* period of time in which observers exist. Since there are many versions of inflationary cosmology, my argument will be very general.

6.3.4. A BB objection to the inflationary multiverse

There is a simple argument that if the BB problem exists for the random fluctuation multiverse, then the same problem exists for the inflationary multiverse. Define a *megaverse* as some very large finite, or even infinite, region of space-time of a universe or multiverse that has some configuration of mass-energy in it.[53] The BB problem arises for a random fluctuation multiverse because, when the standard measure M of statistical mechanics is applied to the phase space of an arbitrary megaverse, the measure of configurations dominated by non-BB observers is much, much smaller than that of those configurations dominated by BB observers. Further, if this is true for the entire megaverse, then it will have to be true for any arbitrarily chosen spacelike hypersurface, hp, of constant time t of the megaverse. Thus, if we let $M_t(BB)$ designate the measure of volume, $V_t(BB)$, of the phase space of hp corresponding to those configurations dominated by BB observers, and $M_t(\sim BB)$ designate the measure of volume, $V_t(\sim BB)$, of hp corresponding to configurations dominated by non-BB observers, then $M_t(\sim BB)/M_t(BB) \ll 1$.[54] That is, the measure for the possible mass-energy-momentum configurations of hp that are non-BB dominated will be much, much smaller than the measure for those configurations that are BB dominated. Assuming that the laws of physics are deterministic and time-reversal invariant, then the measure is time-invariant, as explained in Section 2.4. If we consider the mass-energy-momentum configurations of hp as evolving with time, this means that for any volume of phase space $V(t_0)$ of measure $M_{V(t_0)}$ at time t_0, $V(t_0)$ will evolve into a volume $V(t)$ of the same measure at time t: that is, $M_{V(t)} = M_{V(t_0)}$.

Now, consider the initial conditions of the megaverse defined on some spacelike hypersurface of constant time t_0. Let $V_{t_0}(BB)$ and $V_{t_0}(\sim BB)$ represent the volume of phase space of that hypersurface that evolves into configurations dominated by BB observers and by non-BB observers, respectively, for some later hypersurface at time t. Since the statistical mechanics measure m is time-invariant, the ratio of the measure of $V_{t_0}(\sim BB)$ to $V_{t_0}(BB)$, that is, $M_{t_0}(\sim BB)/M_{t_0}(BB)$, will remain the same. Consequently, $M_{t_0}(\sim BB)/M_{t_0}(BB) = M_t(\sim BB)/M_t(BB) \ll 1$. This means that the measure of initial states that give rise to a universe dominated by non-BB observers at some arbitrarily chosen later time t is much, much smaller than the measure of initial states that give rise to a universe dominated by BB observers at t. Consequently, unless the initial state of the megaverse is in a very special low-probability state – that corresponding to volume $V_{t_0}(\sim BB)$ – it will not give rise to a universe dominated by ~BBs. This is true for any megaverse in which the laws of physics are deterministic and time-reversal invariant. Inflationary cosmology denies neither of these assumptions. Further, even

---

53. I use the idea of a megaverse to avoid problems arising from defining a measure if the multiverse is infinite. If the multiverse is infinite, we could avoid such potential problems by making our megaverse finite but large enough to include many observers.

54. A universe is dominated by non-BB observers (~BBs) if and only if it contains at least one observer, and in some well-defined sense there is a greater proportion of non-BB observers than BB observers.

though the laws of physics are not strictly speaking time-reversal invariant – since time-reversal symmetry is broken in weak interactions, notably the decay of neutral kaons – the argument offered by Albrecht and others that was explicated in Section 6.3.3 does not, in any way, exploit this lack of invariance, nor does it exploit any sort of quantum indeterminacy. Thus, without assuming highly special initial conditions, inflationary cosmology cannot do better with regard to the BB problem than the random fluctuation multiverse.

To illustrate this argument, consider the following analogy. Let a highly ordered, low-entropy non-BB-dominated megaverse of finite volume containing observers be represented as a black-and-white TV screen with rows and rows of O's throughout, and let a megaverse dominated by BBs be represented by occasional O's with large patches of "snow" – that is, "random" configurations of black-and-white pixels. We shall call the former arrangement the ordered, non-BB-pixel arrangement, and the latter the BB-pixel arrangement. For simplicity, suppose there are only a finite number of pixels on the TV screen. In that case, the number of ordered non-BB-pixel arrangements would be very small compared with BB-pixel arrangements. Further, suppose the image on the TV screen is being generated by some small magnetic patch on a videocassette recorder (VCR) tape that the VCR head is reading. Finally, suppose that there is a one-to-one correspondence between arrangements of magnetic particles on the patch and the possible configurations of black-and-white pixels on the screen.

Because of the one-to-one correspondence, the ratio of possible configurations of magnetic particles on the patch of tape that give rise to non-BB-pixel arrangements to those that give rise to BB arrangements will be the same as the ratio of non-BB-pixel arrangements to BB-pixel arrangements on the TV screen. Thus, if the latter ratio is enormously small, so will the former ratio. This is analogous to what happens in the inflationary megaverse: because the laws of physics are deterministic and time-reversal invariant, every microstate $m(t_0)$ at time t_0 evolves into one and only one microstate, $m(t)$, at time t, and, hence, they can be put into a one-to-one correspondence. Consequently, just as the ratios of the number of non-BB-pixel configurations to the BB-pixel configurations is preserved from VCR patch to TV screen, the ratio of the measure of initial configurations that lead to non-BB-dominant universes to the measure of those that lead to BB-dominant universes is the same as the corresponding ratio at a later time t.[55]

---

55. The fundamental error in Albrecht's reasoning can be illustrated by another analogy. Consider a balloon that is being unevenly inflated. Suppose some patches of its two-dimensional surface are massively blown up – say by a trillionfold in each of its two dimensions (e.g. one-trillionth of a meter becomes a meter). This corresponds to the space out of which bubble universes form, some parts of which are inflated and other parts of which are not. Now, suppose one of the blown-up patches is one square meter in volume and is completely covered by adjacent black Os that are one centimeter in diameter, with the space in between simply consisting of random mix of black-and-white dots. The *scale of the order* on this patch is one centimeter; at a level of less than one centimeter, there is a random mix of black-and-white dots. The crucial thing to note, however, is that scale of order of the pre-blown-up patch will be much, much smaller: one-trillionth of a centimeter.

Now it is true that for any two patches, larger patches of the same order and scale of order will be much less likely to occur at random than small patches with the same order and scale – for example, a patch covered with adjacent Os of 1 cm in diameter that has an area of one square meter is much more likely to occur at random than a patch covered with the same pattern of Os that has an area of a thousand square meters. This kind of consideration misleads Albrecht into thinking that very small patches of space-time that inflate into large observer filled, non-BB dominated universes are vastly more likely to occur than large patches of space-time that form

Some might try to dispute one or more of the assumptions of this argument. The most vulnerable assumptions are the problems of nonarbitrarily dealing with the possible infinities that might arise when one attempts to define a measure for the entire megaverse, along with the additional problem of making rigorous the claim that in the entire phase space, the measure of non-BB-dominated hypersurfaces is much, much less than that of BB-dominated hypersurfaces. These problems, however, are as much a problem for making Albrecht's argument rigorous. The whole point of Albrecht's argument is that inflation does better with regard to BBs than the random fluctuation multiverse. In order for this claim to be true, there must be some "correct" measure M for the possible mass-energy states of the multiverse (or at least for arbitrarily chosen very large finite subsets of it) such that non-BB-observer-dominated states have a much, much smaller measure than those of BB-observer-dominated states for the random fluctuation model.

In response, perhaps Albrecht could appeal to some notion of a "generic" initial state that is not dependent on the existence of a measure over phase space. Such an appeal, however, will immediately run afoul an objection Penrose has raised. Consider an enormously large universe that eventually collapses back on itself and assume that all the special laws that are required by inflation hold in that universe. (We could even have an infinite universe with a negative cosmological constant to ensure collapse.) Suppose that this universe had many domains, some of which are highly irregular. In fact, we can suppose that it is chock full of BBs. As Penrose points out, the collapse of such a universe will result in "a generic *space-time singularity*, as we can reasonably infer from precise mathematical theorems" (2004, p. 756). Assuming that the laws of physics (including those of inflation) are time-symmetric (as is typically assumed in these contexts), if we now reverse the direction of time in our model, we shall "obtain an evolution which starts from a general-looking singularity and then becomes whatever irregular type of universe we may care to choose" (2004, p. 757). Since the laws governing inflation will hold in this time-reversed situation, it follows that one cannot guarantee that a uniform or non-BB-dominant universe will arise from generic initial conditions. Thus, inflationary cosmology can explain such a universe only by effectively presupposing those subsets of generic initial conditions that will lead this type of universe. As Penrose notes, "The point is that whether or not we actually have inflation, the physical possibility of an inflationary period is of no use whatever in attempts to ensure that evolution from a generic singularity will lead to a uniform (or spatially flat) universe" (2004, p. 757).

a non-BB-observer-filled universe via a thermal fluctuation. Consequently, Albrecht is misled into thinking that inflation can help overcome the BB problem confronting the RF model by increasing the relative proportion of non-BB observers. The problem for Albrecht's reasoning is that in order to produce a non-BB observer-dominant universe, the order of the patch that inflates would have to be at a vastly smaller scale – for example, inversely proportional to the factor by which the patch inflated– and hence contain a vastly higher degree of order per unit of volume than a corresponding non-BB-observer patch of the size of our universe that did not inflate. The decrease in likelihood resulting from the higher degree of order compensates for the increase in probability resulting from the size of the patch, as can be seen by our more rigorous argument offered earlier based on the time-invariance of the standard measure. In terms of our balloon analogy, a square patch with sides one-trillionth of a meter in length filled with adjacent Os one-trillionth of a centimeter in diameter is no more likely to occur at random than a square patch with sides of 1 m in length filled with Os that are 1 cm in diameter.

6.3.5. Conclusion

The aforementioned arguments do not show that inflationary cosmology is wrong or even that scientists are unjustified in accepting it. What they do show is that the inflationary multiverse offers no help in eliminating either the fine-tuning of the laws of nature or the special low-entropic initial conditions of the Big Bang. With regard to the special low-entropic initial conditions, it can explain the special conditions of the Big Bang only by hypothesizing some other, even more special, set of initial conditions. Although a chaotic inflationary model might lead one to expect a universe like ours, unless highly special initial conditions are assumed across the entire multiverse, it will not lead to a multiverse dominated by ~BBs for later times and thus does no better than a random fluctuation model. It also runs into the generic problems faced by multiverse hypotheses discussed at the end of Section 6.2. If we find the existence of a BB-dominated multiverse unacceptable, it follows that an inflationary-superstring multiverse at best eliminates only the need to explain the life-permitting values of the constants of physics (and perhaps other nonentropic types of special initial conditions). Because of the highly speculative extra laws and conditions required to make an inflationary multiverse work, one could not be blamed if one judged that such purported explanatory ability were far too costly.

7. Miscellaneous Objections

7.1. The "who designed God?" objection

Perhaps the most common objection that atheists raise to the argument from design is that postulating the existence of God does not solve the problem of design but merely transfers it up one level to the question, "Who or what designed God?" The eighteenth-century philosopher David Hume hinted at this objection:

> For aught we can know *a priori*, matter may contain the source or spring of order originally within itself, as well as mind does; and there is no more difficulty conceiving that the several elements, from an internal unknown cause, may fall into the most exquisite arrangement, than to conceive that their ideas, in the great universal mind, from a like unknown cause, fall into that arrangement. (Hume 1980, pp. 17–8)

A host of atheist philosophers and thinkers, such as J. L. Mackie (1982, p. 144), Graham Oppy (2006, pp. 183–4), J. J. C. Smart (1985, pp. 275–6), Richard Dawkins (1986, p. 316), and Colin McGinn (1999, p. 86) have also repeated this objection. For example, J. J. C. Smart claims that:

> If we postulate God in addition to the created universe we increase the complexity of our hypothesis. We have all the complexity of the universe itself, and we have in addition the at least equal complexity of God. (The designer of an artifact must be at least as complex as the designed artifact). (1985, pp. 275–6)

As an objection to our version of fine-tuning argument, it is flawed on several grounds. I have addressed this objection in detail elsewhere (Collins 2005a). Here I shall present a brief response. To begin, this objection would arise only if either T were constructed *solely* to *explain* the fine-tuning, without any independent motivation for believing it, or one considered these other motivations as data and then justified T by claiming that it is the best explanation of all the data. Our main argument, however, is not that T is the best explanation of all the data, but only that given the fine-tuning evidence, LPU strongly confirms T over NSU.

Further, we have substantial reasons for *not* treating the other motivations for T like data, which we then combine with the fine-tuning evidence to infer to the best explanation. To illustrate, let me focus on one such motivation. Many theists have claimed that for most people at least, belief in God is grounded in a fundamental intuition regarding the existence of God, an intuition relevantly similar to moral intuitions or the intuitions regarding epistemic norms. If this is right, then, as Keith Ward and others have noted, treating the existence of God like a scientific hypothesis that needs to be justified by some form of inference to the best explanation is "like trying to justify moral belief by reference to the findings of the natural sciences" (1987, p. 178). On this view, faith can be seen as itself "a response to one who claims my loyalty by showing the true nature of my present mode of being and the way of salvation" (Ward 1987, p. 178). It is "a basic and distinctive mode of human thought and activity" (Ward 1987, p. 180). Thus, in analogy to our ethical intuitions, faith should be considered a mode of knowing, not just a mere leap of belief under insufficient evidence. Plantinga (2000) has provided one way of carefully developing this view and shows it has been commonplace in the Christian tradition – for example, Thomas Aquinas and John Calvin (Plantinga 2000, chap. 6). From this point of view, the religious mode of knowing or justification involved in faith, therefore, should *not* be treated as providing data for an inference to the best explanation but rather as analogous to our ethical intuitions, or even our intuitions regarding epistemic virtues – for example, that, everything else being equal, simpler theories are more likely to be true or empirically adequate than complex theories. Clearly, one cannot ground our belief in these epistemic virtues in an inference to the best explanation, since all such inferences presuppose the virtues. Finally, William Alston (1993) and others have made similar claims with regard to our knowledge of God based on religious experience, claiming it is relevantly analogous to our knowledge of the material world, which they claim is not justified by appeal to an inference to the best explanation.

If we do not treat these other motivations for T as part of a body of data for which we employ the strategy of inference to the best explanation, then the "who designed God?" objection largely evaporates. The existence of God is not a hypothesis that is being offered as the best explanation of the structure of the universe, and hence it is not relevant whether or not God is an explanatorily better (e.g. simpler) terminus for ultimate explanation than the universe itself. Nonetheless, via the restricted version of the Likelihood Principle (Section 1.3), the various features of the universe can be seen as providing *confirming* evidence for the existence of God. One advantage of this way of viewing the situation is that it largely reconciles the views of those who stress a need for faith in coming to believe in God and those who stress reason. They each play a complementary role.

To illustrate this point, consider the following analogy. Suppose that in the year 2050 extraterrestrials visit Earth, and we find that they share the same fundamental ethical beliefs as we do – for example, that it is wrong to torture others for no compelling ethical reason. Further, suppose that we were able to show that it is very epistemically unlikely that such an agreement would occur under ethical antirealism – for example, because we have good reason to believe both that unguided naturalistic evolution would not produce these beliefs and that ethical antirealism is not compatible with viable, alternative explanations of human beings based on design (such as T). Finally, suppose we could show that it is not unlikely for this agreement to occur under ethical realism.[56] The discovery that these aliens shared the same ethical beliefs as we do would therefore confirm ethical realism, even though we would not believe ethical realism because it provided the best explanation of some set of phenomena. In fact, I believe it would decisively tip the balance in favor of ethical realism. I suggest that the evidence of fine-tuning does the same for T.

Apart from rejecting the claim that the justification for the existence of God is based on some sort of inference to the best explanation, however, one can also object to the atheist's key assumption, articulated by J. J. C. Smart in the aforementioned quotation, that the "designer of an artifact must be at least as complex as the artifact itself." This assumption is not even clearly true in the human case, since it is at least conceivable that one could produce a computer that is more complicated than oneself, which is a common theme of science fiction. In the case of God, however, we have even less reason to believe it. If the theist were hypothesizing an anthropomorphic God, with a brain and a body, then this objection would be much stronger: one would then be tempted to ask, is that not God's brain and body as much in need of an explanation as the universe itself? Thus, this objection might seem to have significant bite against such a conception of God. Within traditional theism, however, God has always been claimed to lack any sort of significant internal complexity. In fact, most of the Western medieval tradition claimed that God was absolutely simple in every way – God did not even have complexity with regard to God's properties. Aquinas, for instance, claimed that all of God's properties (such as God's omnipotence and perfect goodness) were absolutely identical; these were, in turn, identical with God's essence and existence. Although I do not think that this view of God as being absolutely simple is coherent, the point here is that the "who designed God?" objection begs the question against traditional theism, by assuming a type of God which traditional theists would all disavow. Even the heirs to traditional Western theism who deny absolute divine simplicity, such as Richard Swinburne (2004), claim that God's overall being is extraordinarily simple. Thus, what these atheists really need to show is that the God of all varieties of traditional theism is logically incoherent insofar as those versions of theism hold on to some form of divine simplicity. This, however, is a very different objection – and a much harder task – than simply raising the "who designed God?" objection and then claiming that one has eliminated the theistic explanation in a single stroke.

7.2. The more fundamental law objection

One criticism of the fine-tuning argument is that, as far as we know, there could be a more fundamental law that entails both the current laws of physics and the values of the constants of physics. Thus, given such a law, it is not improbable that the laws and constants of physics fall within the life-permitting range. Besides being entirely speculative, three problems confront such an objection. First, although many physicists had hoped that superstring theory would entail all the current laws and constants of physics, that hope has

---

56. For example, we might argue that it is not unlikely under ethical realism because ethical realism entails some form of ethical Platonism and because Platonism requires that the mind has some sort of direct access to Platonic truths.

almost completely faded as string theorists have come to recognize that superstring theory (and its proposed successor, M-Theory) has many, many solutions, estimated at 10^{500} or more. Consequently, the prospects of discovering such a fundamental law are much dimmer than they once were. Second, such a fundamental law would not explain the fine-tuning of the initial conditions of the universe. Finally, hypothesizing such a law merely moves the epistemic improbability of the fine-tuning of the laws and constants up one level, to that of the postulated fundamental law itself. Even if such a law existed, it would still be a huge coincidence that the fundamental law implied just those lower-level laws and values of the constants of physics that are life-permitting, instead of some other laws or values. As astrophysicists Bernard Carr and Martin Rees note "even if all apparently anthropic coincidences could be explained [in terms of some fundamental law], it would still be remarkable that the relationships dictated by physical theory happened also to be those propitious for life" (1979, p. 612). It is very unlikely, therefore, that the fine-tuning of the universe would lose its significance even if such a law were verified.

To illustrate the last response, consider the following analogy. Suppose that superdeterminism is true: that is, everything about the universe, including its initial conditions, is determined by some set of laws, although we do not know the details of those laws. Now consider a flip of a coin and let L_h and L_t denote the claims that the laws are such as to determine the coin to come up heads and tails, respectively. We would have equal reason to believe that L_h as that L_t. Hence, since L_h entails that the coin will come up heads, and L_t that the coin will come up tails, the epistemic probability of heads remains 50 percent, and likewise for tails. This would be true even though each of their physical probabilities would be one or zero. The fact that the laws of nature determine the initial conditions, instead of the initial conditions' not being determined by any law, has no influence on the epistemic probability. This can be seen also by the fact that when Laplacian determinism was thought to be true, everyone nonetheless gave a fair coin a 50 percent chance of coming up heads.

A similar sort of response can be given to the claim that fine-tuning is not improbable because it might be *logically necessary* for the constants of physics to have life-permitting values. That is, according to this claim, the constants of physics must have life-permitting values in the same way $2 + 2$ must equal 4, or the interior angles of a triangle must add up to 180 degrees in Euclidian geometry. Like the "more fundamental law" proposal mentioned, however, this postulate simply transfers the epistemic improbability up one level: of all the laws and constants of physics that conceivably could have been logically necessary, it seems highly *epistemically* improbable that it would be those that are life-permitting, at least apart from some sort of *Axiarchic* Principle discussed in Section 8.[57]

7.3. Other life-permitting laws objection

According to what I call the "other life-permitting laws objection," there could be other life-permitting sets of laws that we know nothing about. This objection is directly answered by the way in which I have formulated the fine-tuning argument. As I formulated it, the fine-tuning argument does not assume that ours is the only possible set of life-permitting

---

57. As explained in Section 3.2, necessarily true propositions can still have an epistemic probability of less than one.

laws. Rather, it only assumes that the region of life-permitting laws (or constants or initial conditions) is very small compared with the region for which we can determine whether the laws, constants, or initial conditions are life-permitting – that is, what I called the EI region (see Section 4.5). In the case of the constants of physics, it assumed only that given our current laws of nature, the life-permitting range for the values of the constants (such as gravity) is small compared to the *surrounding* EI range for which we can determine whether or not a value is life-permitting.

7.4. *Other forms of life objection*

As raised against the fine-tuning argument based on the constants of physics, the "other forms of life objection" claims that as far as we know, other forms of non-carbon-based life could exist even if the constants of physics fell outside the purported life-permitting region. So, it is claimed, the fine-tuning argument ends up presupposing that all forms of embodied, conscious life must be based on carbon (e.g. Stenger 2004, pp. 177–8). Besides the extreme difficulty of conceiving of how non-carbon-based material systems could achieve the sort of self-reproducing material complexity needed to support embodied moral agents, another problem with this objection is that many cases of fine-tuning do not presuppose that all life must be carbon based. Consider, for instance, the cosmological constant. If the cosmological constant were much larger than it is, matter would disperse so rapidly that no stars could exist. Without stars, however, there would be no stable energy sources for complex material systems of any sort to evolve. So, all the fine-tuning argument presupposes in this case is that the evolution of embodied moral agents in our universe require some stable energy source. This is certainly a very reasonable assumption.

7.5. *Weak Anthropic Principle objection*

According to the weak version of so-called *Anthropic Principle*, if the laws of nature were not fine-tuned, we should not be here to comment on the fact. Some have argued, therefore, that LPU is not really *improbable or surprising* at all under NSU, but simply follows from the fact that we exist. In response, we simply restate the argument in terms of our existence: our existence as embodied moral agents is extremely unlikely under NSU, but not improbable under T, and therefore our existence confirms T over NSU. As explained in Section 4.3, this requires that we treat LPU and our existence as "old evidence," which we subtract from our background information. This allows us to obtain an appropriate background information k' that does not entail LPU. The other approach was to use the method of probabilistic tension, which avoided the issue entirely (see Sections 1.4, 4.3, and 4.4).

The methods used in Section 4 deal with this problem of old evidence, and our arguments in Section 3.2 for the existence of conditional epistemic probabilities for P(A|B & k') for some cases in which our own existence entails A, provide the formal underpinnings in support of the intuitions underlying the "firing-squad" analogy offered by John Leslie (1988, p. 304) and others in response to this objection. As Leslie points out, if 50 sharpshooters all miss me, the response "if they had not missed me I would not be here to consider the fact" is inadequate. Instead, I would naturally conclude that there was some reason why they all missed, such as that they never really intended to kill me. Why would I conclude this? Because, conditioned on background information k' that does not include my continued existence – such as the background information of a third-party observer watching the execution – my continued existence would be very improbable under the hypothesis that they intended to kill me, but not improbable under the hypothesis that they did not intend to kill me.[58]

8. Conclusion: Putting the Argument in Perspective

As I developed in Sections 1.3 and 1.4, the fine-tuning argument concludes that, given the evidence of the fine-tuning of the cosmos, LPU significantly confirms T over NSU. In fact, as shown in Section 5.2, a good case can be made that LPU *conjoined* with the existence of evil significantly confirms T over NSU. This does not itself show that T is true, or even likely to be true; or even that one is justified in believing in T. Despite this, I claimed that such confirmation is highly significant – as significant as the confirmation that would be received for moral realism if we discovered that extraterrestrials held the same fundamental moral beliefs that we do and that such an occurrence was very improbable under moral antirealism (see Section 7.1). This confirmation would not itself show that moral realism is true, or even justified. Nonetheless, when combined with other reasons we have for endorsing moral realism (e.g. those based on moral intuitions), arguably it tips the balance in its favor. Analogous things, I believe, could be said for T.

I also considered the challenge raised by the two most widely advocated versions of the multiverse hypothesis – what I called the unrestricted multiverse hypothesis, advocated by Lewis and Tegmark, according to which all possible universes exist, and the *restricted* multiverse hypothesis arising out of inflationary cosmology. I argued that neither of these is able adequately to explain away the fine-tuning or undercut the fine-tuning argument.

Finally, one might wonder whether there are other viable alternative explanations of LPU to that offered by T, NSU, or the multiverse hypothesis. One such possibility is various nontheistic design hypotheses – either nontheistic supernatural beings or aliens in some meta-universe who can create bubble universes. The postulated designer, D, could

---

58. Sober rejects this sharpshooter analogy (2005, pp. 137–40). He admits, however, that for a bystander, the sharpshooters' missing (evidence E) would strongly support the "fake-execution" hypothesis (FE) that the captors never really intended to shoot the prisoner. He then goes on to claim that for the prisoner, E does not support FE, claiming that "the bystander and prisoner are in different epistemic situations, even though their observation reports differ by a mere pronoun" (p. 138). To see the problem with Sober's claim, suppose that: (i) the prisoner and bystander had exactly the same prior probabilities for the FE hypothesis (say, 0.01); (ii) they had relevantly the same cognitive faculties; and (iii) they both had all the same information that could be expressible in sentences, except the difference in the pronouns each would use. Finally, suppose they had to make a practical decision whether to risk their lives with a dangerous escape attempt or to bet that the captors did not intend to kill them. How should the bystander advise the prisoner? Attempt to flee, because P(FE) < 0.5 from the prisoner's perspective? Do not attempt to flee because P(FE) ~1 for the bystander? And, if they wanted to flee together, whose perspective do they go with? Surely, the bystander should not go with the prisoner's perspective, since the bystander's perspective involves nothing suspicious – there is no observational selection effect for the bystander. Furthermore, it seems clear that the prisoner cannot support his probability claim over that of the bystander's by appeal to special insight based on experiencing the attempted execution, since both would agree that this does not give special insight. (This is one way this case differs from religious and other kinds of fundamental disagreement.) Thus, if there is any course of action which is rational regarding fleeing together, it is that given by the bystander's perspective. So, contrary to Sober, there cannot be two radically different rational degrees of belief in FE.

not be a merely "generic" designer but must be hypothesized to have some motivation to create a life-permitting universe; otherwise P(LPU|D & k′) = P(LPU|NSU & k′), as explained in Section 5.2. Unless these non-generic hypotheses were advocated prior to the fine-tuning evidence, or we had independent motivations for them, they would not pass the non-*ad hocness* test of the restricted version of the Likelihood Principle (Section 1.3). Furthermore, from the perspective of probabilistic tension, these alternative design hypotheses typically would generate a corresponding probabilistic tension between the claim that the postulated being had a motive to create a life-permitting world instead of some other type of world and the beings' other attributes, something that does not arise for classical theism (see Section 5.2). Finally, for some of these postulated beings, one could claim that even if LPU confirms their existence, we lack sufficient independent reasons to believe in their existence, whereas for T we have such reasons; or one could claim that they simply transfer the problem of design up one level (see Section 7.1).

The only one of these alternatives that I consider a serious contender is the *axiarchic* hypothesis, versions of which have been advanced in the last 30 years by John Leslie (1989, chap. 8) and recently by Hugh Rice (2000) and others, wherein goodness or ethical "required-ness" has a direct power to bring about concrete reality. Whatever the merits of this hypothesis, it is likely to entail T. Since God is the greatest possible being, it is supremely good that God exists (Leslie 1989, pp. 168–9). Therefore, it is unclear that the axiarchic hypothesis actually conflicts with T.[59] In any case, this chapter has shown that we have solid philosophical grounds for claiming that given the fine-tuning evidence, LPU provides significant support for T over its nonaxiarchic contenders.

References

Albert, D. (2000) *Time and Chance*. Cambridge, MA: Harvard University Press.

Albrecht, A. (2004) Cosmic inflation and the arrow of time. In J. D. Barrow, P. C. W. Davies, and C. L. Harper (eds.), *Science and Ultimate Reality: Quantum Theory, Cosmology and Complexity*, 363–401. New York: Cambridge University Press.

Alston, W. (1993) *Perceiving God: The Epistemology of Religious Experience*. Ithaca, NY: Cornell University Press.

Banks, T. (2007). Entropy and initial conditions in cosmology. http://arxiv.org/PS_cache/hep-th/pdf/0701/0701146v1.pdf (accessed May 1, 2008).

Barenboim, G. (2006) The dark(er) side of inflation. http://arxiv.org/PS_cache/hep-ph/pdf/0605/0605111v1.pdf (accessed May 1, 2008).

Barrow, J. and Tipler, F. (1986) *The Anthropic Cosmological Principle*. Oxford: Oxford University Press.

Bousso, R. and Freivogel, B. (2006) A paradox in the global description of the multiverse. http://arxiv.org/PS_cache/hep-th/pdf/0610/0610132v2.pdf (accessed May 1, 2008).

Burgess, C. P. (2004). Quantum Gravity in Everyday Life: General Relativity as an Effective Field Theory. *Living Rev. Relativity* 7, 5. http://www.livingreviews.org/lrr-2004–5 (accessed March 15, 2005).

59. I would like to thank the John Templeton Foundation for a grant to support this work, William Lane Craig for comments on an earlier draft of this chapter and final editorial comments, David Schenk for comments on the next-to-the-final version, physicists Don Page and Robert Mann for comments on an earlier version of the section on inflationary cosmology, and many other people, such as Alvin Plantinga, who have encouraged me in, raised objections to, and offered comments on my work on the fine-tuning argument over the years.

Caldwell, R. and Steinhardt, P. (2000) Quintessence. *Physicsworld.com*, November 1. http://physicsworld.com/cws/article/print/402 (accessed May 1, 2008).

Cao, T. Y. (1997) *Conceptual Developments of 20th Century Field Theories*. Cambridge: Cambridge University Press.

Carr, B. J. and Rees, M. J. (1979) The anthropic cosmological principle and the structure of the physical world. *Nature* 278, 605–12.

Collins, R. (2002) God, design, and fine-tuning. In R. Martin and C. Bernard (eds.), *God Matters: Readings in the Philosophy of Religion*, 54–65. New York: Longman Press.

Collins, R. (2003) Evidence for fine-tuning. In N. Manson (ed.), *God and Design: The Teleological Argument and Modern Science*, 178–99. London: Routledge.

Collins, R. (2005a) Hume, fine-tuning and the "who designed God?" objection. In J. Sennett and D. Groothius (eds.), *In Defense of Natural Theology: A Post-Humean Assessment*, 175–99. Downers Grove, IL: Inter Varsity Press.

Collins, R. (2005b) How to rigorously define fine-tuning. *Philosophia Christi* 7, 382–407.

Collins, R. (2007) The teleological argument. In P. Copan and C. V. Meister (ed.), *Philosophy of Religion: Contemporary Issues*, 98–111. Oxford: Wiley-Blackwell.

Collins, R. (2008) The case for cosmic design. *God or Blind Nature? Philosophers Debate the Evidence (2007–2008)*. Available at: http://www.infidels.org/library/modern/debates/great-debate.html (accessed May 1, 2008).

Colyvan, M., Garfield, J., and Priest, G. (2005) Some problems with the "fine tuning argument." *Synthese* 145: 3, 325–38.

Craig, W. L. (2003) Fine-tuning of the universe. In Neil Manson (ed.), *God and Design: The Teleological Argument and Modern Science*, 155–77. London: Routledge.

Davies, P. (1974) *The Physics of Time Asymmetry*. Berkeley: University of California Press.

Davies, P. (1982) *The Accidental Universe*. Cambridge: Cambridge University Press.

Davies, P. (1992) *The Mind of God: The Scientific Basis for a Rational World*. New York: Simon and Schuster.

Dawkins, R. (1986) The Blind Watchmaker. Why the Evidence of Evolution Reveals a Universe without Design. New York: W. W. Norton.

Denton, M. (1998) *Nature's Destiny: How the Laws of Biology Reveal Purpose in the Universe*. New York: The Free Press.

Dodson, E. (1984) *The Phenomena of Man Revisited: A Biological Viewpoint on Teilhard de Chardin*. New York: Columbia University Press.

Donoghue, J. (2007) Fine-tuning problems of particle physics. In B. Carr (ed.), *Universe or Multiverse?*, 231–46. Cambridge: Cambridge University Press.

Draper, P. (2008) Collins' case for cosmic design. *God or Blind Nature? Philosophers Debate the Evidence (2007–2008)*. Available at: http://www.infidels.org/library/modern/debates/great-debate.html (accessed May 1, 2008).

Earman, J. (2006) The improbable universe. Talk delivered at the APA Central Division Symposium: "Fine Tuning and the Improbable Universe," April 26–9.

Edwards, A. W. F. (1992) *Likelihood*. Baltimore: Johns Hopkins University Press.

Forster, M. (2006) Counterexamples to a likelihood theory of evidence. *Minds and Machines* 16: 3, 319–38. Available at: http://philosophy.wisc.edu/forster (accessed May 6, 2008).

Forster, M. and Sober, E. (2001) Why likelihood? In M. Taper and S. Lee (eds.), *The Nature of Scientific Evidence*. Chicago: University of Chicago Press. Available at: http://philosophy.wisc.edu/forster (accessed May 6, 2008).

van Fraassen, B. (1980) *The Scientific Image*. Oxford: Clarendon Press.

Greene, B. (1999) *The Elegant Universe: Superstrings, Hidden Dimensions, and the Quest for the Ultimate Theory*. New York: W. W. Norton and Co.

Guth, A. (1997) *The Inflationary Universe: The Quest for a New Theory of Cosmic Origins*. New York: Helix Books.

Hacking, I. (1975) *The Emergence of Probability: A Philosophical Study of Early Ideas about Probability, Induction and Statistical Inference*. Cambridge: Cambridge University Press.

Hacking, I. (1987) Coincidences: mundane and cosmological. In J. M. Robson (ed.), *Origin and Evolution of the Universe: Evidence for Design*, 119–38. Montreal: McGill-Queen's University Press.

Holder, R. (2004) *God, the Multiverse, and Everything: Modern Cosmology and the Argument from Design*. Burlington, VT: Ashgate.

Howson, C. (1991) Discussion: the old evidence problem. *The British Journal for the Philosophy of Science* 42, 547–55.

Hume, D. (1980) *Dialogues concerning Natural Religion and the Posthumous Essays*. Ed. R. Popkin. Indianapolis, IN: Hackett Publishing Co.

Kaku, M. (1999) *Introduction to Superstrings and M-Theory*, 2nd edn. New York: Springer-Verlag.

Keynes, J. M. (1921) *A Treatise on Probability*. London: Macmillan.

Kiessling, M. (2001) How to implement Boltzmann's probabilistic ideas in a relativistic world? In J. Bricmont, D. Dürr, M. C. Galavotti, G. Ghirardi, F. Petruccione, N. Zanghi (eds.), *Chance in Physics*, 83–102. Berlin: Springer-Verlag.

Kolda, C. and Lyth, D. (1999) Quintessential difficulties. http://arxiv.org/PS_cache/hep-ph/pdf/9811/9811375v3.pdf (accessed April 10, 2008).

Koperski, J. (2005) Should we care about fine-tuning? *The British Journal for the Philosophy of Science* 56: 2, 303–19.

Leslie, J. (1988) How to draw conclusions from a fine-tuned cosmos. In R. J. Russell W. R. Stoeger, G. V. Coyne (eds.), *Physics, Philosophy and Theology: A Common Quest for Understanding*, 297–312. Vatican City State: Vatican Observatory Press.

Leslie, J. (1989) *Universes*. New York: Routledge.

Leslie, J. (1998) Cosmology and philosophy. *Stanford Encyclopedia of Philosophy*. Available at: http://plato.stanford.edu/archives/fall1998/entries/cosmology-theology/ (accessed October, 2007).

Lewis, D. (1986) *On the Plurality of Worlds*. New York: Basil Blackwell.

Linde, A. (1990) *Particle Physics and Inflationary Cosmology*. Trans. M. Damashek. Longhorne, PA: Harwood Academic Publishers.

Mackie, J. L. (1982) *The Miracle of Theism*. Oxford: Clarendon Press.

Mann, R. (2005) Inconstant multiverse. *Perspectives on Science and the Christian Faith* 57: 4, 302–10.

McGinn, C. (1999) *The Mysterious Flame: Conscious Minds in a Material World*. New York: Basic Books.

McGrew, T. and McGrew, L. (2005) A response to Robin Collins and Alexander R. Pruss. *Philosophia Christi* 7, 425–43.

McGrew, T., McGrew, L., and Vestrup, E. (2001) Probabilities and the fine-tuning argument: a skeptical view. *Mind* 110, 1027–38.

Mena, O. and Santiago, J. (2006) Constraining inverse-curvature gravity with supernovae. *Physical Review Letters* 96, 041103.

Narlikar, J. V. (2002) *An Introduction to Cosmology*, 3rd edn. Cambridge: Cambridge University Press.

Oppy, G. (2006) *Arguing about Gods*. Cambridge: Cambridge University Press.

Otte, R. (2006) Counterfactuals and epistemic probability. *Synthese* 152: 1, 83–94.

Page, D. (2006) Is our universe decaying at an astronomical rate? http://arxiv.org/abs/hep-th/0612137 (accessed April 10, 2008).

Parsons, K. (1990) Is there a case for Christian theism? In J. P. Moreland and K. Nielsen (eds.), *Does God Exist? The Great Debate*, 177–96. Nashville, TN: Thomas Nelson.

Peacock, J. (1999) *Cosmological Physics*. Cambridge: Cambridge University Press.

Penrose, R. (1989) *The Emperor's New Mind: Concerning Computers, Minds, and the Laws of Physics*. New York: Oxford University Press.

Penrose, R. (2004) *The Road to Reality: A Complete Guide to the Laws of the Universe*. New York: Alfred A. Knopf.

Plantinga, A. (1993) *Warrant and Proper Function*. Oxford: Oxford University Press.

Plantinga, A. (2000) *Warranted Christian Belief*. Oxford: Oxford University Press.

Polchinski, J. (1998) *String Theory*, vols. I and II. Cambridge Monographs in Mathematical Physics. Cambridge: Cambridge University Press.

Rees, M. (2000) *Just Six Numbers: The Deep Forces that Shape the Universe*, New York: Basic Books.

Rice, H. (2000) *God and Goodness*. Oxford: Oxford University Press.

Royall, R. (1997) *Statistical Evidence – A Likelihood Paradigm*. London: Chapman and Hall.

Sahni, V. and Starobinsky, A. (1999) The case for a positive cosmological lambda-term. http://arxiv.org/abs/astro-ph/9904398 (accessed March 15, 2008).

Salmon, W. (1984) *Scientific Explanation and the Causal Structure of the World*. Princeton, NJ: Princeton University Press.

Schlesinger, G. (1985) *The Intelligibility of Nature*. Aberdeen, Scotland: Aberdeen University Press.

Smart, J. C. (1985) Laws of nature and cosmic coincidence. *The Philosophical Quarterly* 35: 140, 272–80.

Smolin, L. (1997) *The Life of the Cosmos*. Oxford: Oxford University Press.

Sober, E. (2002) Bayesianism – its scope and limits. In R. Swinburne (ed.), *Bayes's Theorem*, 21–38. Oxford: Oxford University Press.

Sober, E. (2005) The design argument. In W. Mann (ed.), *The Blackwell Guide to the Philosophy of Religion*, 117–48. Oxford: Blackwell.

Stenger, V. (2000) Natural explanations for the anthropic coincidences. *Philo* 3: 2, 50–67.

Stenger, V. (2004) Is the universe fine-tuned for us. In M. Young and T. Edis (eds.), *Why Intelligent Design Fails: A Scientific Critique of the New Creationism*, 172–84. New Brunswick, NJ: Rutgers University Press.

Stenger, V. (2007) *God: The Failed Hypothesis: How Science Shows That God Does Not Exist*. Amherst, NY: Prometheus Books.

Swinburne, R. (2001) *Epistemic Justification*. Oxford: Clarendon Press.

Swinburne, R. (2004) *The Existence of God*, 2nd edn. Oxford: Oxford University Press.

Tegmark, M. (1998) Is the theory of everything merely the ultimate ensemble theory? *Annals of Physics* 270, 1–51.

Tegmark, M. (2003) Parallel universes. *Scientific American*, May, 41–51. (Also see Parallel universes. In J. D. Barrow, P. C. W. Davies, and C. L. Harper (eds.), *Science and Ultimate Reality: From Quantum to Cosmos*. Cambridge University Press, 2003. Also available at: http://arxiv.org/abs/astro-ph/0302131).

Teller, P. (1988) Three problems of renormalization. In R. Harré and H. Brown (eds.), *Philosophical Foundations of Quantum Field Theory*, 73–89. Oxford: Clarendon Press.

Wald, R. (1984) *General Relativity*. Chicago: University of Chicago Press.

Ward, K. (1987) *Concepts of God: Images of the Divine in Five Religious Traditions*. Oxford: Oneworld Publications.

Weatherford, R. (1982) *Foundations of Probability Theory*. Boston: Routledge and Kegan Paul.

White, R. (2000) Fine-tuning and multiple universes. *Nous* 34, 260–76. Reprinted in N. Manson (ed.), *God and Design: The Teleological Argument and Modern Science*, 229–50. London: Routledge, 2003).

Zee, A. (2003) *Quantum Field Theory in a Nutshell*. Princeton, NJ: Princeton University Press.

5

The Argument from Consciousness

J. P. MORELAND

Section One: The Backdrop for Locating Consciousness in a Naturalist Ontology

Consciousness is among the most mystifying features of the cosmos (see Moreland 2008). During the emergence of the mechanical philosophy in the seventeenth century, Leibniz wrote the following as a challenge to mechanistic materialism:

> It must be confessed, moreover, that *perception*, and that which depends on it *are inexplicable by mechanical cause*, that is by figures and motions. And supposing there were a machine so constructed as to think, feel and have perception, we could conceive of it as enlarged and yet preserving the same proportions, so that we might enter it as a mill. And this granted, we should only find on visiting it, pieces which push one against another, but never anything by which to explain a perception. This must be sought for, therefore, in the simple substance and not in the composite or in the machine. (Leibniz 1979, p. 536)

And while different bells and whistles have been added to our conception of matter since Leibniz's time, scientific naturalist explanations for the emergence of consciousness are as inadequate today as they were when Leibniz threw down his gauntlet. As Geoffrey Madell opines, "the emergence of consciousness, then is a mystery, and one to which materialism signally fails to provide an answer" (Madell 1988, p. 141).

Not only are adequate naturalistic explanations for irreducible consciousness hard to come by, there is a widespread suspicion, if not explicit acknowledgement that irreducible consciousness provides evidence for theism. Thus, Crispin Wright notes:

> A central dilemma in contemporary metaphysics is to find a place for certain anthropocentric subject-matters—for instance, semantic, moral, and psychological—in a world as conceived by modern naturalism: a stance which inflates the concepts and categories deployed by (finished) physical science into a metaphysics of the kind of thing the real world essentially and exhaustively is. On one horn, if we embrace this naturalism, it seems we are committed either to reductionism: that is, to a construal of the reference of, for example, semantic, moral and psychological vocabulary as somehow being within the physical domain—or to disputing that

the discourses in question involve reference to what is real at all. On the other horn, if we reject this naturalism, then we accept that there is more to the world than can be embraced within a physicalist ontology—and so take on a commitment, it can seem, to a kind of eerie supernaturalism. (Wright 2002, p. 401)

Similarly, William Lyons claims that:

[physicalism] seem[s] to be in tune with the scientific materialism of the twentieth century because it [is] a harmonic of the general theme that all there is in the universe is matter and energy and motion and that humans are a product of the evolution of species just as much as buffaloes and beavers are. Evolution is a seamless garment with no holes wherein souls might be inserted from above. (Lyons 1995, p. lv)

Souls being "inserted from above" is a veiled reference to theism's explanatory power for consciousness: If "souls" exist, they would have to be "inserted from above", since natural processes by themselves are "seamless." Some argue that, while certain features of finite mental entities may be inexplicable on a naturalist worldview, they may be explained by theism, thereby furnishing evidence for God's existence. For some time, mental entities have been recalcitrant facts for naturalists. Indeed, for philosophers who take the issues and options in philosophy of mind to be significantly influenced by empirical consider-ations, the proliferation of a wild variety of physicalist specifications of a naturalist treat-ment of mental phenomena may fairly be taken as a sign that naturalism is in a period of Kuhnian paradigm crisis. The argument from consciousness for God's existence (hereafter, AC) provides a way of dethroning the naturalist hegemony. Moreover, by giving a more adequate analysis of and explanation for mental entities, it provides a way out of the crisis and, together with other lines of evidence, offers materials for a cumulative case argument for theism.[1]

For decades, versions of naturalism have multiplied like rabbits, so before we examine AC and its chief rivals, it is important to clarify two factors that constitute the dialectical background for what follows. First, I shall unpack the ideational structure of a version of naturalism that follows most plausibly from taking it as a worldview that claims explana-tory, epistemic superiority to its rivals. Second, I shall lay out the central epistemic condi-tions relevant to assessing the force of AC vis-à-vis naturalism.

While there will be different nuances given to naturalism by different thinkers, it is still possible to give an accurate characterization of a specific form of philosophical natu-ralism (hereafter, simply naturalism or scientific naturalism) that is currently enjoying widespread acceptance (cf. Rosenberg 1996; Moreland & Craig 2000). And by clarifying the relationship between a naturalist ontology on the one hand, and its epistemology and creation account on the other, a picture will emerge as to what *ought* to constitute that ontology. This picture will allow us to identify a substantial burden of proof for alternative naturalist ontologies that bloat naturalist metaphysical commitments beyond what is justifiable within the constraints that follow from the other two aspects of a naturalist worldview.

1. Graham Oppy offers a brief critique of AC, especially as formulated by John Locke and Richard Swinburne. See *Arguing about Gods* (Oppy 2006, pp. 382–401). Unfortunately, he rejects all-too-briefly cumulative case argu-ments (Oppy 2006, pp. 5–6) and, thus, in my view does not give them sufficient consideration.

Naturalism is the view that the spatiotemporal universe of entities postulated by our best current (or ideal) theories in the physical sciences, particularly physics, is all there is. It includes (1) a naturalist epistemic attitude (e.g. a rejection of so-called first philosophy); (2) an etiological account of how all entities whatsoever have come to be, constituted by an event-causal story described in natural scientific terms; and (3) a general ontology in which the only entities allowed are ones that bear a relevant similarity to those thought to characterize a completed form of physics. Whether this ontology should also include *sui generis* emergent properties will occupy our attention shortly.

The ordering of these is important. The epistemic attitude justifies the etiology, which together justify the ontological commitment. Also, naturalism requires coherence among these three areas. David Papineau claims that we should set philosophy within science in that philosophical investigation should be conducted within the framework of our best empirical theories. It follows that "… the task of the philosophers is to bring coherence and order to the set of assumptions we use to explain the empirical world" (Papineau 1993, p.3). Thus, there should be coherence among third-person scientific ways of knowing, a physical, evolutionary account of how our sensory/cognitive processes came to be, and an analysis of those processes themselves. Any entities that are taken to exist should bear a relevant similarity to those characterizing our best (or ideal) physical theories, their coming-to-be should be intelligible in light of the naturalist causal story, and they should be knowable by scientific means.

The naturalist epistemic attitude

Scientism constitutes the core of the naturalist epistemology. Wilfrid Sellars said that "in the dimension of describing and explaining the world, science is the measure of all things, of what is that it is, and of what is not that it is not" (Sellars 1963, p.173). Contemporary naturalists embrace either weak or strong scientism. According to the former, nonscientific fields are not worthless nor do they offer no intellectual results, but they are vastly inferior to science in their epistemic standing and do not merit full credence. According to the latter, unqualified cognitive value resides in science and in nothing else. Either way, naturalists are extremely skeptical of any claims about reality that are not justified by scientific methodology in the hard sciences.

For example, that methodology is a third-person one that sanctions only entities capable of exhaustive description from a third-person perspective. Skepticism prevails for entities that require the first-person perspective as their basic mode of epistemic access. For such naturalists, the exhaustive or elevated nature of scientific knowledge entails that either the only explanations that count or the ones with superior, unqualified acceptance are those employed in the hard sciences.[2] At least two philosophical theses elaborate the naturalistic epistemic and methodological constraints for philosophy. First, there is no such thing as first philosophy; rather, there is continuity between philosophy and natural science. Second, scientific theories that are paradigm cases of epistemic/explanatory success, for example, the atomic theory of matter, evolutionary biology, employ combinatorial modes of explanation. Thus, any process that constitutes the Grand Story and any entity in the naturalist ontology should exhibit an ontological structure analyzable in terms that are isomorphic

---

2. I am assuming here a realist construal of explanation.

with such modes of explanation. Colin McGinn has defended this idea along with what he takes it to entail, viz., the inability of naturalism to explain genuinely unique emergent properties:

> Can we gain any deeper insight into what makes the problem of consciousness run against the grain of our thinking? Are our modes of theorizing about the world of the wrong shape to extend to the nature of mind? I think we can discern a characteristic structure possessed by successful scientific theories, a structure that is unsuitable for explaining consciousness. . . .
>
> Perhaps the most basic aspect of thought is the operation of *combination*. This is the way in which we think of complex entities as resulting from the arrangement of simpler parts. There are three aspects to this basic idea: the atoms we start with, the laws we use to combine them, and the resulting complexes . . . I think it is clear that this mode of understanding is central . . . [and] our scientific faculty involves representing the world in this combinatorial style. (McGinn 1999, pp.55–6; cf. pp.54–62, 90, 95)

The naturalist Grand Story

Let us call the naturalist creation account "the Grand Story": All of reality – space, time, and matter – came from the Big Bang and various heavenly bodies developed as the universe expanded. On at least the Earth, some sort of prebiotic soup scenario explains how living things came into being from nonliving chemicals. And the processes of evolution, understood in either neo-Darwinian or punctuated equilibrium terms, gave rise to all the life forms we see including human beings. Thus, all organisms and their parts exist and are what they are because they contributed to (or at least did not hinder) the struggle for reproductive advantage, more specifically, because they contributed to the tasks of feeding, fighting, fleeing, and reproducing.

The Grand Story has three key features. First, at its core are two theories that result from combinatorial modes of explanation: the atomic theory of matter and evolutionary theory. If we take John Searle to be representative of naturalists here, this means that causal explanations, specifically, bottom-up but not top-down causal explanations, are central to the (alleged) explanatory superiority of the Grand Story (Searle 1994, p.83–93).

Second, it expresses a scientistic philosophical monism, according to which everything that exists or happens in the world is susceptible to explanations by natural scientific methods. *Prima facie*, the most consistent way to understand naturalism in this regard is to see it as entailing some version of strong physicalism: everything that exists is fundamentally matter, most likely, elementary "particles" (whether taken as points of potentiality, centers of mass/energy, units of spatially extended stuff/waves, or reduced to/eliminated in favor of fields), organized in various ways according to the laws of nature. By keeping track of these particles and their physical traits, we are keeping track of everything that exists. No nonphysical entities exist, including emergent ones. When naturalists venture away from strong physicalism, however, they still argue that additions to a strong physicalist ontology must be depicted as rooted in, emergent from, and dependent on the physical states and events of the Grand Story.

Third, the Grand Story is constituted by event causality and eschews both irreducible teleology and agent causation (AGC) in which the first relatum of the causal relation is in the category of substance and not event. And the Grand Story is deterministic in two senses:

diachronically, such that the state of the universe at any time t coupled with the laws of nature determine or fix the chances for the state of the universe at subsequent times; and synchronically, such that the features of and changes regarding macrowholes are dependent on and determined by microphenomena.

The naturalist ontology

Weak versus strong naturalism

There is a distinction between strong/strict and weak naturalists. Strong naturalists (e.g. Papineau) accept a strict version of physicalism (all individuals, events, states of affairs, properties, relations, and laws are entirely physical) for the natural world, while weak naturalists (e.g. Searle) embrace various emergent entities.

The location problem

A good place to start a more detailed analysis of a naturalist ontology is with what Frank Jackson calls the location problem (Jackson 1998, pp. 1–5). On the basis of the superiority of the naturalist epistemology, naturalists accept a fairly widely accepted physical story about how things came to be (the Grand Story) and what they are. The location problem is the task of locating some entity (e.g. semantic contents) in that story.

For Jackson, the naturalist must either locate a problematic entity in the basic story or eliminate it. Roughly, an entity is located in the basic story just in case it is entailed by that story. Otherwise, the entity must be eliminated. At this point, it is worth recalling that Kim and others have complained that one does not *explain* a phenomenon by labeling it supervenient. Likewise, one might think that someone has not really "located" a puzzling phenomena if all one has done is point out that it necessarily covaries with this or that sort of physical phenomenon. In any case, Jackson provides three examples of location. First, just as density is a different property from mass and volume, it is not an additional feature of reality over and above mass and volume in at least this sense: an account of things in terms of mass and volume implicitly contains, that is, entails the account in terms of density. Second, Jones's being taller than Smith is not an additional feature of reality besides Jones's and Smith's heights because the relational fact is entailed, and in this sense located by the latter.

More importantly, Jackson focuses on the location of macrosolidity. He acknowledges that prior to modern science, there was a widely accepted commonsense notion of macrosolidity, viz., being everywhere dense. However, due to modern science, this notion has been replaced with being impenetrable. Thus, macrosolidity may be located in the basic microstory: given a description of two macro-objects in terms of their atomic parts, lattice structures, and subatomic forces of repulsion, this description entails that one macro-object is impenetrable with respect to the other.

Jackson believes mental properties are troublesome entities for the naturalist to locate, and the naturalist must argue that they globally supervene on the physical. He unpacks this claim with two clarifications. First, he defines a minimal physical duplicate of our world as "a world that (a) is exactly like our world in every physical respect (instantiated property for instantiated property, law for law, relation for relation), and (b) contains nothing else in the sense of nothing more by way of kinds or particulars than it *must* to satisfy (a)"

(Jackson 1998, p. 13). Second, he advocates B*: any world that is a minimal physical duplicate of our world is a psychological duplicate of our world.

The logic of the mereological hierarchy

Jackson correctly grasps the connection between accepting the epistemic superiority of
naturalism and deciding between weak and strong naturalism. For Jackson, if naturalism
is to have superior explanatory power, this entails strong naturalism. Jackson understands
that there are at least three constraints for developing a naturalist ontology and locating
entities within it: (a) entities should conform to the naturalist epistemology; (b) entities
should conform to the naturalist Grand Story; (c) entities should bear a relevant similarity
to those found in chemistry and physics or merely be capable of one-to-one or one-
to-many correlation with entities in chemistry or physics or be shown to depend necessarily
on entities in chemistry and physics.

Further in the discussion, we will see why these constraints disallow explanations for
the existence of emergent properties. Regarding emergent properties, the second disjunct
of (c) "solves" the so-called explanatory gap by simply naming the problem and dismissing
the need for a naturalist to do any further explanatory work. For many philosophers,
including many naturalists, this strategy is inadequate. The second disjunct also suffers
from the difficulty of justifying the existence of *sui generis* emergent entities in light of
criteria (a) and (b). The third disjunct of (c) suffers from this latter problem and also from
difficulties with justifying the claim that emergent entities are "necessitated" by their subvenient physical bases. Defending these claims are central to the desiderata of this chapter.
But it may be useful at this stage of reflection to show how (a) and (b) justify the standard
mereological hierarchy as the proper naturalist ontology.

Construing the hierarchy in terms of individual entities and properties rather than in
terms of concepts or linguistic descriptions, it consists in an ascending level of entities in
the category of individual such that for each level above the ground level of elementary
microphysics (at which entities have no further physically significant separable parts),
wholes at that level are composed of the separable parts at lower levels. Thus, from bottom
to top we get microphysical entities, subatomic parts, atoms, molecules, cells, living organisms, and so on. The relationship between individuals at level n and n + 1 is the part/whole
relation.

Here is a key point about the hierarchy in the category of individual and property (see
further discussion): *the "hierarchy" is not really a hierarchy*. There is no ascending anything.
Rather, the levels form spatiotemporally wider and wider wholes. So we should think of
the "hierarchy" as going out, not up.

Moreover, there are ontological constraints for what sorts of properties a naturalist
should include in the hierarchy. As typically presented, the hierarchy entails the causal
closure of the basic microphysical level along with the ontological dependence of entities
and their activities at supervenient levels on entities and their activities at that basic level.
Causal closure and top/down causation are controversial. But acceptance of closure and a
rejection of top/down causation are hard for a naturalist to avoid. The basic naturalist
argument for causal closure is that if it is rejected, then

> you are ipso facto rejecting the in-principle completeability of physics—that is, the possibility
> of a complete and comprehensive physical theory of all physical phenomena. For you would

be saying that any complete explanatory theory of the physical domain must invoke nonphysical causal agents. . . . It is safe to assume that no serious physicalist could accept such a prospect. (Kim 1998, p. 40)

The completeability of physics is not arbitrary. It follows naturally from the Grand Story, according to which one begins at the Big Bang with a small number of physical entities and explains the origin and behavior of everything else in terms of the laws of physics and new combinations of microphysical entities. The Story itself gives pride of place to microphysical entities and it is bottom/up at its core. The completeability of physics is essential to the explanatory superiority of the Story. The causal closure principle (no physical event has a nonphysical cause) is not arbitrary nor is it an additional postulate naturalists are intellectually free to reject. It follows from the combinatorial mode of causal explanation and the Grand Story's commitment to the sort of micro-macro constitution and determination at the core of the atomic theory of matter, evolutionary biology, and other central theories of how things have come to be. If a naturalist rejects closure, he or she will have to accept *sui generis*, contingent brute facts. In turn, this undermines the claim that a naturalist worldview is superior to rivals because it can explain how all things have come to be.

Besides closure, a related issue for deciding what sorts or properties should populate the hierarchy is the problem of top/down causation. There is severe intellectual pressure from naturalism itself for rejecting top/down causation for genuinely emergent *sui generis* properties. Moreover, the only way to save top/down causation is to reduce it to outside/in causation that occurs with respect to structural wholes at the same level as their parts via causal feedback. I also think that the price to be paid for retaining causal laws in the special sciences is to disallow emergent properties and allow only microphysically based structural properties constituted by microphysical parts, properties, and relationships. If this is right, it follows that an adequate treatment of these desiderata (to preserve "top/down" causation and causal laws in the special sciences) entails that a naturalist ontology constituted by the standard mereological hierarchy can countenance structural wholes in the category of individual and structural supervenient properties in the category of property, but it cannot countenance genuine emergent properties, especially causally active emergent properties. All emergent properties, if such there be, must be epiphenomenal.

An emergent property is a completely unique, new kind of property different from those that characterize its subvenient base. Accordingly, emergent supervenience is the view that the supervenient property is a simple, intrinsically characterizable, novel property different from and not composed of the parts, properties, relations, and events at the subvenient level. We may characterize "novel" as follows:

Property P is a *novel* emergent property of some particular x at level l_n just in case P is an emergent property, x exemplifies P, and there are no determinates P' of the same determinable D as P such that some particular at level $l_{i=1-(n-1)}$ exemplifies P or P'. (Haldane 1996)

A structural property is one that is constituted by the parts, properties, relations, and events at the subvenient level. A structural property is identical to a configurational pattern among the subvenient entities. It is not *sui generis*.

The existence of emergent mental properties presents two problems for naturalism. First, for those who accept a causal criterion of existence, emergent mental properties are epiphenomenal and, thus, do not exist. One is then faced with a dilemma: accept phenomenal consciousness as emergent and reject causal closure or retain closure and reject phenomenal consciousness on the grounds that it is epiphenomenal. In the subsequent sections, we shall examine versions of naturalism that accept emergent mental properties. These versions must address epiphenomenalism.

Second, it is pretty obvious that mental states are causal factors in our behavior. Knowledge and agency are hard to salvage if this is denied. Indeed, if an analysis of mental states entails epiphenomenalism, this is widely recognized as fodder for a *reductio* against that analysis. Thus, many naturalists think that the only way to save mental causation is to identify it with the physical. Not all naturalists reject top/down causation. But since bottom/up but not top/down causation follows most naturally from (1) the central theories that constitute the Grand Story and (2) the mereological hierarchy with the dependency of lower on higher levels, there is a burden of proof on those naturalists who accept genuine top/down (and not merely outside/in) causation.

Here is one final constraint for a naturalist ontology. If we limit ourselves to macro-properties, an appropriate limitation because consciousness is a macrofeature, then the following principle seems to be *prima facie* justified:

Principle of Naturalist Exemplification (PNE): (x) Px → Ex

P stands for any property whatever and E stands for the property of being extended. Moreover, x ranges over and only over property instances. Elsewhere I have defended a constituent ontology in which property instances are complex entities, and I shall merely assume this ontology here (see Moreland 2001b). According to this ontology, when some concrete particular e exemplifies a property P, then the-having-of-P-by-e is a property instance that is modally distinct from both P and e. Thus, x is neither identical to P nor e. So understood, property instances are certain sorts of states of affairs and, moreover, if the instantiation of P by e is temporal, then the property instance becomes an event.

Note that P and e are constituents of x. If we focus on paradigm cases that satisfy PNE, it becomes reasonable to hold that the spatial extension of x is grounded in, obtains in virtue of the spatial extension of e. For example, when an apple is red, the-having-of-red-by-the-apple is a property instance spread out through the extended region occupied by the apple. It is in virtue of the apple's extension that the particular instance of red is extended. This may be seen, for example, by noting that it is because the apple has a particular shape that its instance of red has that shape as well.

PNE says that if a property in the naturalist ontology is to be exemplified, then a necessary condition is that both the concrete particular that exemplifies P and the property instance that results have spatial extension.

PNE seems to capture nicely the wide range of properties in macrophysics, chemistry, geology, neuroscience, and so forth. It could be objected that PNE fails because certain entities, for example, some quantum entities or the point particles of Roger Boscovich were unextended and provide counterexamples to PNE. I do not think this objection works. Regarding quantum entities, there are at least eight different empirically equivalent philosophical models of quantum reality and, it is irresponsible to make dogmatic claims about the ontology of the quantum level (Herbert 1987, p. 15–29). And since I have limited PNE to the macrolevel, we may set aside the quantum world for our purposes. Regarding entities such as Boscovich's particles, rather than conclude that they are counterexamples to PNE, their lack of spatial dimensionality may be taken as a *reductio* against them. Indeed, this is how the history of physics ran. Boscovichian particles fit more easily into a spiritual-ist ontology (e.g. Berkeley's) than in a straightforward version of materialism, and like action at a distance, they were rejected.

There is a debate about whether individual mental states such as pains and thoughts are extended. I cannot enter that debate here. But on the basis of PNE, if it turns out that mental states are not extended, then PNE banishes them and their constituent properties from a naturalist ontology. In this case, PNE counts against any naturalist ontology that quantifies over emergent mental properties.

It is time to summarize what a naturalist ontology should look like (cf. Moreland 1998b). In the category of individual, if we reject an eliminativist strategy, then all wholes "above" the microphysical level are structural, relational entities constituted by the parts, properties, and relations at the microphysical level. Such wholes stand in a constituent/ whole relation to these microphysical entities and are actually wider entities at the basic level. Regarding the category of property, consider the following:

Emergence$_0$: new features that can be deduced from base (e.g. fractals)

Emergence$_1$: ordinary structural properties (e.g. being water, solidity)

Emergence$_{2a}$: *sui generis*, simple, intrinsically characterizable, new kinds of properties relative to base that are also epiphenomenal (e.g. being painful construed epiphenomenally)

Emergence$_{2b}$: *sui generis*, simple, intrinsically characterizable, new kinds of properties rela-tive to base with new causal powers construed as passive liabilities (e.g. being painful understood as having top/down causal liabilities)

Emergence$_{2c}$: *sui generis*, simple, intrinsically characterizable, new kinds of properties with active power

Emergence$_3$: an emergent, suitably unified mental ego with active power

Clearly, Emergence$_0$ and Emergence$_1$ fit nicely in the mereological hierarchy and conform to the naturalist epistemology (e.g. combinatorial explanation) and Grand Story. But Emergence$_{2a}$ through Emergence$_3$ should be disallowed for reasons we have already inves-tigated. It would seem that all a naturalist could do with them is simply to label them as contingent brute facts and assert that they are not a problem for the naturalist. We will look at different attempts to handle some of these sorts of properties in subsequent sec-tions. But we have already examined reasons to be highly suspicious of a naturalist view that accepts one or more of these sorts of properties and also claims that naturalism is explanatorily and epistemically superior to alternative worldviews.

Moreover, there is an increasingly heavy burden of proof on a naturalist ontology as one moves from Emergence$_{2a}$ to Emergence$_3$. All types of emergence fall prey to previous arguments against emergent entities. Emergence$_{2a}$ requires less justification than stronger forms of emergence because it does not require a rejection of closure. Emergence$_{2b}$ is subject to these arguments and additional difficulties with top/down causation and causal closure. But relative to Emergence$_{2c}$ and Emergence$_3$, it has the advantage of exhibiting the same sort of causal power − passive liability subject to law − that characterizes causal par-ticulars at the microphysical level.

Emergence$_{2c}$ has all the problems exemplified by Emergence$_{2b}$ and it also suffers from having a unique sort of active causal power different from causal powers of the naturalist ontology besides agent-causal events. Emergence$_3$ shares difficulties with Emergence$_{2c}$ and it also suffers from two further facts not easily accommodated in the naturalist ontology if they are taken as irreducible and uneliminable facts about the world: the indexical fact associated with "I" and difficulties with explaining how one can get a sort of primitive, substantial unity in which its various inseparable parts/faculties are internally related to the substantial subject from a mereological aggregate constituted by a structural arrangement of separable parts that stand in external relations to each other and their mereological whole.

Serious metaphysics, simplicity, and emergent properties

Frank Jackson begins his attempt to develop a naturalistic account of the mental by contrasting two very different approaches to metaphysics. The first he calls serious metaphysics. Serious metaphysics is not content to draw up large pluralistic lists of *sui generis* entities. Advocates of serious metaphysics tend to approach the discipline with a prior epistemic commitment of some sort which functions as a criterion of knowledge or justified belief for quantifying over some entity. Thus, naturalist commitment to serious metaphysics usually includes epistemological methodism constituted by the naturalist epistemic attitude. Accordingly, serious metaphysics is primarily *explanatory* and not *descriptive* metaphysics. Thus, advocates seek to account for all entities in terms of a limited number of basic entities and in this way serious metaphysics is inherently reductionistic. For naturalists, these entities will constitute those at the core of the Grand Story: A property/event/object x exists iff it is contained within (truth functionally entailed by) the Grand Story.

The second perspective we may call a "shopping-list" approach whose primary goal is a careful description and categorial analysis of reality. Advocates usually employ epistemological particularism, and it is no accident that Roderick Chisholm is the paradigm case of epistemological particularism and shopping-list metaphysics (cf. Chisholm 1989a,b, pp. 162–8).

Jackson correctly claims that the scientific naturalist will prefer serious metaphysics. His naturalist approach to metaphysics expresses a certain form of the principle of simplicity and provides material content for that principle of simplicity most suited for a philosophical naturalist. To see this, let us compare two versions of the principle of simplicity, an epistemic and ontological version, respectively:

Simplicity$_E$: entities must not be multiplied beyond necessity
Simplicity$_O$: our ontology/preferred theory about the world should be simple

Of course, there are various ways to state each principle, but these will do for our purposes. Simplicity$_E$ may not be easy to apply (one rival may be simple in one respect and the other in a different respect; one rival may be simpler and the other may be more empirically accurate), but its rationale is fairly straightforward. All things being equal, if a simpler theory does the epistemic job, then the more complicated theory has baggage that serves no important epistemic function. Ontological simplicity is quite different from epistemic simplicity, and some philosophers conflate the two principles. For example, Kim rightly advocates epistemological simplicity for the same reason just mentioned. But he then passes over into ontological simplicity, apparently without noticing the equivocation. After embracing "entities must not be multiplied beyond necessity," he urges with no justification or further explanation that "we expect our basic laws to be reasonably simple, and we expect to explain complex phenomena by combining and iteratively applying these simple laws" (Kim 1996, p. 91).

Ontological simplicity does not follow from epistemic simplicity. In fact, it sometimes happens that progress in an area of science entails adopting a more complicated ontology even though both the simpler and more complicated ontologies are epistemically simple. The shift from the simpler ideal gas equation to the more complicated van der Waals equation is a case in point. That said, I believe that the naturalist should adopt both principles of simplicity, and Kim and Jackson give the reason why. Each makes reference to the Grand Story (which, in turn, is justified by the naturalist epistemology), which is inherently reductionistic.

Moreover, if naturalists claim to have epistemic/explanatory superiority over rivals, then their employment of the Grand Story must be done such that entities that cannot be identified with some structural combination of fundamental microphysical entities must be eliminated. Kim and Jackson both understand this, and while Jackson seeks to carry out this way of understanding the location project, Kim has abandoned it in recent months (see Kim 2005, chap. 6; cf. 1998, chap. 4). Still, Kim's appeal to ontological simplicity ever bit as much as Jackson's provides a representative naturalist employment of the principle.

And their characterization of it provides a way of transforming the merely formal principle Simplicity$_0$ into a related version with material content. For Kim, we begin with simple, basic laws – and presumably microphysical particulars governed by them – and allow more complex entities into one's ontology only if they are subject to combinatorial modes of explanation that involve the iterative application of the basic laws. Similarly, Jackson says one should start with the Grand Story and allow entities into one's ontology only if they are entailed by that ontology (Jackson 1998, pp. 24–7).[3] For Jackson, this means accepting only structural entities that are Emergence$_0$ or Emergence$_1$. Expressed in terms of the appropriate naturalist material principle of simplicity, we have

Simplicity$_{ON}$: our ontology or preferred theory about the world should be simple in the sense that it contains the microphysical entities of an ideal physics or entities whose existence can be explained by the naturalist epistemology (e.g. combinatorial modes of explanation) applied to the microphysical entities that constitute the Grand Story. Simplicity$_{ON}$ would seem to rule out entities that are Emergence$_2$ or Emergence$_3$.

A realist view of causation and emergent properties

We have seen reasons for adopting a *prima facie* burden of proof on any naturalist ontology that includes emergent entities. If such entities are accepted, then a naturalist would owe us a causal account of their coming-to-be. In closing this section, it is important to state

---

3. By "entails" here, Jackson means the ordinary truth-functional connective. Jackson actually thinks physicalism *a priori* entails the psychological and that this is a necessary truth. If physicalism φ is true, then, of necessity, the psychological truths ψ follow *a priori*. Jackson employs a version of two-dimensional semantics to defend the claim that instances of $\varphi \rightarrow \psi$ are *a priori* necessary. But this is a stronger claim and many naturalists would not follow him in this, so I shall employ the weaker truth-functional version in what follows. I am indebted to Shaun McNaughton for pointing this out to me.

certain constraints on such an account. In the sections to follow, we shall look at naturalist views that seek to conform to or disregard these constraints. But these constrains seem *prima facie* justified because they follow naturally from the naturalist epistemology, Grand Story, and other aspects of the naturalist ontology.

Regarding emergent properties, although some demur, at least five reasons have been proffered for the claim that causal explanations in the natural sciences exhibit a kind of causal necessity, that on a typical realist construal of natural science, physical causal explanations must show – usually by citing a mechanism – why an effect must follow given the relevant causal conditions:

(1) Causal necessitation unpacks the deepest, core realist notion of causation, namely, causal production: a cause "brings about" or "produces" its effect.
(2) Causal necessitation fits the paradigm cases of causal explanation central to the core theories that constitute a naturalist worldview and in terms of which it is purported to have explanatory superiority to rival worldviews.
(3) Causal necessitation provides a way of distinguishing accidental generalizations or coincidences from true causal laws or sequences.
(4) Causal necessitation grounds the derivation of counterfactuals.
(5) Causal necessitation clarifies the direction of causality.

Three points of clarification are in order. First, minimally, the sort of modality involved may be taken as physical necessity, a form of necessity that runs throughout possible worlds relevantly physically similar to our actual world (e.g. in having the same physical particulars, properties, relations, and/or laws). Second, strong conceivability is the test that is used to judge causal necessitation (given the lattice structures and so forth of two macro-objects impenetrable with respect to each other, it is strongly inconceivable that one could penetrate the other).

Finally, Principles (3)–(5) have sometimes been offered as additions to a covering law form of explanation to provide an adequate natural scientific causal explanation. Strictly speaking, a covering law "explanation" is just a description of what needs to be explained and not an explanation. But by adding a causal model that underwrites it and that exhibits causal necessitation, the total package provides explanations for both what and why the phenomena are as they are. For brevity's sake, I will talk as if a covering law explanation is an explanation, but when I speak of a covering law explanation I mean to include in it an underwriting causal model.

In this section, we have examined the limitations on a naturalist ontology that follow from naturalism itself taken as a worldview epistemically/explanatorially superior to its rivals. Let N stand for the truth of naturalism. In the terms of epistemic appraisal proffered by Chisholm, it seems that – (N & Emergence$_{2a}$) is at least *epistemically in the clear* where a proposition is *epistemically in the clear* provided only that subject S is not more justified in withholding that proposition than in believing it. Alternatively, it is at least *reasonable to disbelieve* (N & Emergence$_{2a}$) (S is not more justified in withholding that proposition than in disbelieving it) (Chisholm 1977, p. 16).

However, there are additional limits for a naturalist ontology when a plausible rival worldview is brought into the picture. As Timothy O'Connor points out, emergent properties, especially mental properties, must be shown to arise by way of causal necessitation from a microphysical base if we are to "render emergent phenomena naturalistically explicable" (O'Connor 2000, p. 112). Among his reasons is the idea that if the link between microbase and emergent properties is a contingent one, then the only explanation for the existence and constancy of the link is a theist explanation (O'Connor 2000, pp. 70–1, n. 8). O'Connor claim seems to me to be correct, and to probe this matter further, we turn to an examination of the theistic argument for God's existence from consciousness.

Section Two: The AC

In this section, I shall clarify and defend this AC by describing three issues in scientific theory acceptance relevant to assessing AC's force, presenting three forms of AC and offering a brief defense of its premises. I hope to show that an important factor in theory acceptance – scientific or otherwise – is whether or not a specific theory has a rival. If not, then certain epistemic activities, for example, labeling some phenomenon as basic for which only a description and not an explanation is needed, may be quite adequate not to impede the theory in question. But the adequacy of those same activities can change dramatically if there is a sufficient rival. Section one presented reasons for denying emergent mental properties/events that follow solely from naturalism. In this section, we shall discover additional reasons for naturalists to eschew emergent mental entities that follow because of the presence of AC. The combined force of sections one and two place a severe (and increasing) burden of proof on any naturalist who seeks to reconcile the existence of emergent mental entities (from Emergence$_{2a}$ to Emergence$_3$) with naturalism.

Three issues in scientific theory acceptance

Basicality

While theism and naturalism are broad worldviews and not scientific theories, three issues that inform the adjudication between rival scientific theories are relevant to AC. The first issue involves deciding whether it is appropriate to take some phenomenon as *basic* such that only a description and not an explanation for it is required, or whether that phenomenon should be understood as something to be explained in terms of *more basic* phenomena. Attempts to explain uniform inertial motion are disallowed in Newtonian mechanics because such motion is basic on this view, but an Aristotelian had to explain why a particular body exhibited uniform inertial motion. Thus, what is basic to one theory may be derivative in another.

Naturalness

Issue two is the *naturalness* of a postulated entity in light of the overall theory of which it is a part. The particulars, properties, and relations postulated should be at home with other entities in the theory and, in this sense, be natural for the theory. Some entity (particular thing, process, property, or relation) e is natural for a theory T just in case either e is a central, core entity of T or e bears a relevant similarity to central, core entities in e's category within T. If e is in a category such as substance, force, property, event, relation, or cause, e should bear a relevant similarity to other entities of T in that category. This is a formal definition and the material content given to it will depend on the theory in question. In section one, I argued that the basic entities constituitive of the Grand Story provide the material content for naturalism.

Moreover, given rivals R and S, the postulation of e in R is *ad hoc* and question-begging against advocates of S if e bears a relevant similarity to the appropriate entities in S, and in this sense is "at home" in S, but fails to bear this similarity to the appropriate entities in R. The notion of "being *ad hoc*" is difficult to specify precisely. It is usually characterized as an inappropriate adjustment of a theory whose sole epistemic justification is to save the theory from falsification. Such an adjustment involves adding a new supposition to a theory not already implied by its other features. In the context of evaluating rivals R and S, the principle just mentioned provides a sufficient condition for the postulation of e to be *ad hoc* and question-begging.

Naturalness provides a criterion for advocates of a theory to claim that their rivals have begged the question or adjusted their theory in an inappropriate, *ad hoc* way. Naturalness is also useful for deciding the merits of accepting R, which depicts phenomenon e as basic, versus embracing S, which takes e to be explainable in more basic terms. If e is natural in S but not in R, it will be difficult for advocates of R to justify the bald assertion that e is basic in R and that all proponents of R need to do is describe e and correlate it with other phenomena in R as opposed to explaining e. Such a claim by advocates of R will be even more problematic if S provides an explanation for e.

Epistemic values

Issue three involves *epistemic values*, normative properties which confer some degree of justification on a theory possessing them. Examples are theories should be simple, descriptively accurate, predicatively successful, fruitful for guiding new research, capable of solving their internal and external conceptual problems, and use certain types of explanations or follow certain methodological rules and not others (e.g. "appeal to efficient and not final causes"). Studies in scientific theory assessment have made it clear that two rivals may solve a problem differently depending on the way each theory depicts the phenomenon to be solved.

It is possible for two rivals to rank the relative merits of epistemic values in different ways or even give the same virtue a different meaning or application. Rivals can differ radically about the nature, application, and relative importance of a particular epistemic value. Thus, in arguing against B, it may be inappropriate for advocates of A to cite its superior comportment with an epistemic value when B's proponents do not weigh that value as heavily as they do a different one they take to be more central to B. For example, given rivals A and B, if A is simpler than B but B is more descriptively accurate than A, then it may be inappropriate – indeed, question-begging – for advocates of A to cite A's simplicity as grounds for judging it superior to B. I am not suggesting that rivals are incommensurable. In fact, I believe that seldom, if ever, is this the case. Only on an issue-by-issue basis can one appropriately make judgments about the epistemic impact of the conflict of disparate epistemic values.

The AC

The deductive form of the argument

Theists (e.g. Robert Adams (1992, pp. 225–40) and Richard Swinburne (1979, chap. 9; 1986, p. 183–96)) have advanced a different theistic argument from consciousness. The argument may be construed as an inference to the best explanation, a Bayesian-style argument, or a straightforward deductive argument in which its premises are alleged to be more reasonable then their denials. Setting the inductive forms aside, AC becomes the following:

(1) Mental events are genuine nonphysical mental entities that exist.
(2) Specific mental and physical event types are regularly correlated.
(3) There is an explanation for these correlations.
(4) Personal explanation is different from natural scientific explanation.
(5) The explanation for these correlations is either a personal or natural scientific explanation.
(6) The explanation is not a natural scientific one.
(7) Therefore, the explanation is a personal one.
(8) If the explanation is personal, then it is theistic.
(9) Therefore, the explanation is theistic.

Overview of deductive premises

In my view, Premises (3) and (6) are the most crucial ones for the success of AC, since they are the premises most likely to come under naturalist attack. Let us set them aside for the moment. We are assuming the truth of Premises (1) and (2). All the naturalist rivals of AC we are considering agree with them.

The main justification for Premise (4) is the difference between libertarian and event causal theories of agency. J. L. Mackie rejected (4), claiming that personal explanation is simply a subclass of event causal explanation. Moreover, divine action in Swinburne's account of personal explanation involves the direct fulfillment of an intention on the part of God. But, argued Mackie, since human action is a type of efficient event causality between the relevant prior mental state, for example, an intending, and a fulfillment which runs through and depends on a number of intermediate events which are part of a complex physical mechanism, there is a disanalogy between human intentional acts in which intentions are fulfilled indirectly and those of a god in which, supposedly, intentions are directly fulfilled. On Mackie's view, this disanalogy makes alleged divine action and the relevant sort of personal explanation mysterious and antecedently improbable. Thus, (4) is false and, even if it is true, it makes theistic personal explanation less, not more probable.

Is Mackie's argument successful against (4)? I do not think so. For one thing, *pace* Mackie, it is not at all clear that libertarian agency and the associated form of personal explanation are not to be preferred as accounts of human action to event-causal accounts. Obviously, we cannot delve into this issue here, but if libertarian agency is correct, then Mackie is wrong in his claim that (4) is false.

Secondly, a defense of (4) may only require a *concept* of libertarian agency and personal explanation, even if we grant an event-causal theory of action for human acts. If we have such a clear conception, then even if human acts do not fall under it, under the right circumstances, it could be argued that a form of explanation clearly available to us is now to be employed. What those circumstances are and whether they obtain are more centrally related to Premises (3) and (6) of AC and not (4). But since Mackie criticized (4) on the grounds that if true it would make theistic explanation antecedently improbable, I want briefly to say something about what could justify the claim that a personal explanation of the libertarian sort should actually be used.

Many have tried to state necessary and sufficient conditions for personal action in event-causal terms with John Bishop's account being the most sophisticated to date. But Bishop admits that our concept of agency is different from and irreducible to event causality and is, in fact, libertarian (Bishop 1989, pp. 58, 72, 69, 95–6, 103–4, 110–1, 126–7, 140–1, 144). For Bishop, the pervasiveness and power of the libertarian conception of agency places the burden of proof on the defender of a causal theory of action. Bishop claims that his own causal theory works only for worlds relevantly similar to ours in being naturalistic worlds. He does not offer an analysis of action true across all possible worlds because he admits that our concept of action is libertarian and there are worlds in which it is satisfied. His justification of this minimal task is a prior assumption of naturalism, but such an assumption is clearly question-begging against AC. So if we have a clear, powerful, and *prima facie* justified libertarian conception of agency, Mackie's point about the mysteriousness and antecedent improbability of anything answering to this concept is seriously overstated.

Granting the nonphysicality of mental states, a causal theory of personal action will boil down to the claim that person P does some act e (raising one's hand to vote) if and only if some event b (the hand going up), which instantiates the type of state intrinsic to e-ing is caused by the appropriate mental state in the appropriate way. Note carefully that, regardless of the details of such an account, it will amount to nothing more that a causal correlation between certain physical states and the relevant mental events. According to Premises (2) and (3) of AC, these correlations need and have an explanation. A causal theory of action will not do for the origin, regularity, and precise nature of these correlations, since these are what constitute a causal theory of action in the first place. If a causal theory of action presupposes mental states, then it will be impotent to explain the existence, regularity, and precise nature of those mental states themselves unless, of course, a divine causal theory of action is used. If this is so, and if we possess a clear concept of libertarian agency and personal explanation, then there is no good reason why a theist cannot use this type of explanation in this case.

However, a defender of (4) could deny a libertarian view of agency and personal explanation. After all, some Christian theists (e.g. certain Calvinists) employ a causal theory for divine action. One could argue that there is some difference between normal physical event causality and a causal theory of personal action. Minimally, the latter utilizes appropriately related mental states as parts of causal chains. Since (4) simply notes that there is a distinguishable difference between personal and natural scientific explanation, the alternative we are now considering may be all that AC needs to rebut Mackie. Bishop claims that for a naturalist causal theory of action must be combined with a strong physicalist theory of mental states (Bishop 1989, pp. 8, 43, 103). But setting this aside, since we are assuming the reality of mental states, Bishop's physicalist rendition of the causal theory of action simply does not apply here and a suitable statement of the nature and role of mental states in a causal theory could be all that is needed to distinguish personal from natural scientific explanation according to (4).

The presence of personal explanation as a unique argument form means that when it comes to explaining emergent properties such as those constituitive of consciousness, one does not need to acquiesce with Samuel Alexander's dictum that such properties are "to be accepted with the natural piety of the investigator." Thus, it is more than curious to find naturalists jump straightaway from the recognition that mental properties are genuinely emergent and incapable of naturalist explanation to the conclusion that we must take then as brute facts.

There are two sides to (5): is personal explanation different from natural scientific explanation and are there other explanations for the facts mentioned in (1) and (2) besides these two? We have already dealt with the first question in conjunction with (4). Regarding question two, I think it is safe to say that, given the current intellectual climate, a personal theistic or a naturalistic explanation would exhaust at least the live, if not the logical, options. It is true that Thomas Nagel suggested that panpsychism may be necessary to explain the mental (Nagel 1986, pp. 49–53). But it is widely recognized that panpsychism has serious problems in its own right – for example, explaining what an incipient or protomental entity is or how the type of unity that appears to characterize the self could emerge from a mere system of parts standing together in various causal and spatiotemporal relations (cf. Moreland 2008, chap. 6). Moreover, panpsychism is arguably less reasonable than theism on other grounds, although I cannot pursue this point here. Further, it is not clear that panpsychism is an *explanation* of the phenomena in question. As Geoffrey Madell notes,

> the sense that the mental and the physical are just inexplicably and gratuitously slapped together is hardly allayed by adopting . . . a panpsychist . . . view of the mind, for [it does not] have an explanation to offer as to why or how mental properties cohere with physical. (Madell 1988, p. 3)

For these and other reasons, I shall not consider panpsychism further except as part of Timothy O'Connor's project.

Premise (7) follows from previous steps in the argument and asserts the adequacy of a personal explanation for the facts expressed in (1) and (2). One may reject (7) (or (5)) on the grounds that personal explanation, theistic or otherwise, does not give us any real understanding of an explanandum, especially one like (1) and (2). Sometimes this objection assumes that an explanation must cite a mechanism before it can count as adequate. My response to this problem centers on the difference between libertarian and event causality and their associated forms of explanation.

Advocates of libertarian agency widely employ the following form of personal explanation (that stands in contrast to a covering law model): A personal explanation (divine or otherwise) of some basic result R brought about intentionally by person P where this bringing about of R is a basic action A will cite the intention I of P that R occur and the basic power B that P exercised to bring about R. P, I, and B provide a personal explanation of R: agent P brought about R by exercising power B in order to realize intention I as an irreducibly teleological goal.

By way of application, the adequacy of a personal explanation does not consist in offering a mechanism, but rather, in correctly citing the relevant person, his intentions, the basic power exercised, and in some cases, offering a description of the relevant action plan. Thus, if we have some model of God and His intentions for creating a world suitable for human persons (from revelation or otherwise), we can make reference to God, His intentions for creating a world with persons with mental states regularly correlated with their environment, and the adequacy of His power to bring about the basic results captured in (1) and (2).

Premise (8) seems fairly uncontroversial. Humean style arguments about the type, size, and number of deities involved could be raised, but these issues would be intramural theistic problems of small comfort to someone committed to naturalism (cf. Martin 1990,

p. 220). And if we take live options only, then it seems fair to limit our alternatives in (5) to theistic or naturalistic. If that is acceptable, at least for the purposes of arguing against Searle and other naturalists like him, then (8) should not be objectionable.

In the terms of epistemic appraisal proffered by Chisholm, it seems that, given AC and what we have seen about the naturalist ontology from section one, – (N & Emergence$_{2a}$) is at least *beyond reasonable doubt* where a proposition is *beyond reasonable doubt* for a subject S means that S is more justified in believing that proposition than in withholding it. Alternatively, given AC, (N & Emergence$_{2a}$) is at least *reasonable to disbelieve* (S is more justified in disbelieving that proposition than in withholding it) (Chisholm 1989a, pp. 10–7). However, it would be premature to conclude that this is the correct epistemic appraisal of (N & Emergence$_{2a}$). We still need to look at Premises (3) and (6). Rather than doing so directly, I shall examine them in sections three through five in the context of naturalist attempts that, if successful, would defeat (3) and (6).

Preview of sections three through five

We have seen reasons that follow from the nature of naturalism itself and from the presence of AC as a rival for why a naturalist ought to be a strong physicalist. Unfortunately, strong physicalism is a tough sell, and a growing number of philosophers are dissatisfied with it. Perhaps our conclusion that a naturalist ought to be a strong physicalist is premature. Maybe there are adequate naturalist accounts of the mental. In sections three through five, we will look at representative samples of the major strategies employed to provide such an account. I will conclude that none of these solutions is adequate and that AC is to be preferred. If I am right about this, then the existence of finite mental states provides good evidence that God exists. The best thing for a naturalist to do in this case it to opt for a strong form of physicalism.

Section Three: John Searle and Contingent Correlation

The weakest position for a naturalist who accepts emergent mental properties and events is one according to which all the naturalist must do adequately to explain the mental is to establish contingent correlations between physical and mental states and leave it at that. Searle's view is the most prominent attempt to flesh out this approach.

Searle's position

Contingent correlation

Actually, Searle acknowledges that correlations are not enough and an adequate account should include the transformation of correlations into causal relations by showing that the manipulation of the physical state alters the mental state and by providing a mechanism as to how this works. But for three reasons, I believe it is appropriate to take him as an example of a contingent correlation position. First, he takes such correlations to be adequate to justify the superiority of biological naturalism, so they are sufficient conditions for a naturalist account of consciousness. Second, he claims that a causal explanation of consciousness may be, in principle, beyond our abilities to obtain; even so, biological naturalism remains standing. Third, he argues against the need for a naturalist to meet some necessitation requirement, according to which one can show that the relevant mental state *must* occur given a certain physical state. That leaves us with correlations for which the establishment of counterfactual covariance would be nice but not necessary for biological naturalism to be adequate.

Biological naturalism

Searle says harsh things about the last 50 years or so of work in the philosophy of mind (Searle 1994, chaps. 1 and 2; cf. Burge 1992).[4] He says that the field has contained numerous assertions that are obviously false and has cycled neurotically through various positions because of the dominance of strong physicalism as the only option for a naturalist. For these naturalists, if one abandons strong physicalism one has rejected a scientific naturalist approach to the mind/body problem and opened himself up to the intrusion of religious concepts and arguments about the mental such as AC.

Searle offers his analysis of the mind as a naturalistic account because, he says, no one in the modern world can deny ". . . the obvious facts of physics–for example, that the world is made up entirely of physical particles in fields of force ..." (Searle 1994, p. 28). Naturalism is constituted by the atomic theory of matter and evolutionary biology both of which allow for micro-to-micro or micro-to-macro causal explanations, but not macro-to-micro ones. Dualism in any form is widely rejected because it is correctly considered to be inconsistent with the scientific worldview. People educated in the scientific worldview know how the world works, and the existence of God is no longer a serious candidate for truth. But a commitment to naturalism and a concomitant rejection of dualism have blinded people to the point that they feel compelled to reject what is obvious to experience, namely, the obvious nature of consciousness and intentionality.

Searle's own solution to the mind/body problem is biological naturalism: consciousness, intentionality, and mental states, in general, are emergent biological states and processes that supervene upon a suitably structured, functioning brain. Brain processes cause mental processes that are not reducible to the former. Consciousness is just an ordinary (i.e. physical) feature of the brain and, as such, is merely an ordinary feature of the natural world. Despite the frequent assertions by a number of philosophers that Searle is a property dualist, he denies the charge and seems puzzled by it. However, in my view, Searle is indeed a property dualist and an epiphenomenalist one at that, although he also denies the latter charge as well. To show this, let us consider the charge of property dualism first. Searle's characterization of neurophysiological and mental states are exactly those of the property dualist who insists that mental and physical properties are to be characterized in a certain way and that they are two, different types of properties. In light of Searle's descriptions of the mental and physical, it is obvious why most philosophers charge him with property dualism, and the burden of proof is on him to show why he is not.

---

4. Since the publication of *The Rediscovery of the Mind*, Searle has restated his views on these topics, but he continues to cite this earlier work as his most thorough treatment on the topic from which he has not deviated. See his works *The Mystery of Consciousness* (1995, p. 194) and *Mind* (2004, p. 2). Thus, I will rely on *The Rediscovery of the Mind* in explicating Searle's views and supplement them when needed.

Searle's response is twofold. First, he seems to think that a property dualist must accept the entire Cartesian metaphysics. Second, he says that dualists accept a false dichotomistic vocabulary in which something is either physical or mental but cannot be both. So biological naturalism is to be distinguished from property dualism in that the former does not include the entire Cartesian apparatus and it rejects this dichotomistic vocabulary. If this is how Searle distinguishes biological naturalism from property dualism, his response is inadequate. For one thing, it is absurd to claim that one must accept the entire Cartesian metaphysics to be a property dualist. Thomas Aquinas was a certain sort of property (and substance) dualist, but obviously, he did not accept the Cartesian apparatus (cf. Moreland 1995; Moreland & Wallace 1995). Swinburne defends Cartesian property and substance dualism without accepting Descartes' entire metaphysical scheme (Swinburne 1986, chap. 8). Moreover, Searle's own view has a dichotomistic vocabulary in which he distinguishes normal physical (e.g. neurophysiological) properties from emergent biological "physical" (i.e. mental) properties. So he has simply replaced one dualism with another one.

But perhaps there is a different and deeper distinction between (at least) Cartesian property dualism and biological naturalism for Searle. For the property dualist, mental and physical properties are so different that it is inconceivable that one could emerge from the other by natural processes. However, for the biological naturalist, biological physical properties are normal physical properties in this sense: they are like solidity, liquidity, or the properties of digestion or other higher-level properties that can emerge by means of natural processes. I do not wish to comment further on this claim here except to say that Searle's employment of it to distinguish biological naturalism from property dualism amounts to nothing more than a mere assertion combined with a few undeveloped examples (e.g. liquidity) that are supposed to be good analogies to emergent mental states. But this assertion is simply question-begging in light of AC and, as I will show later, it amounts to an abandonment of naturalism. At the very least, one should stop and ask why, if Searle's solution to the mind/body problem is at once obvious and not at all problematic for naturalists, a field of philosophy dominated by naturalists for 50 years has missed this obvious solution?

Searle's three reasons why biological naturalism is not a threat to naturalism

Why are there no deep metaphysical implications that follow from Searle's biological naturalism? Why is it that biological naturalism does not represent a rejection of scientific naturalism which, in turn, opens the door for religious concepts about and arguments from the mental? Searle's answer to this question is developed in three steps. First, he cites several examples of emergence (e.g. liquidity) that he takes to be unproblematic for a naturalist and argues by analogy that the emergent properties of consciousness are likewise unproblematic.

Step two is a formulation of two reasons why, appearances to the contrary notwithstanding, consciousness is not a problem for naturalists. First, Searle says that naturalists are troubled by the existence of irreducible mental entities because they are misled into thinking that the following is a coherent question that needs an answer: "How do unconscious bits of matter produce consciousness?" (Searle 1994, p. 55; cf. pp. 32, 56–7). Many "find it difficult, if not impossible to accept the idea that the real world, the world described by physics and chemistry and biology, contains an ineliminably subjective element. How could such a thing be? How can we possibly get a coherent world picture if the world contains these mysterious conscious entities?" (Searle 1994, p. 95).

For Searle, the question of how matter produces consciousness is simply a question about how the brain works to produce mental states even though individual neurons in the brain are not conscious. This question is easily answered in terms of specific, though largely unknown, neurobiological features of the brain. However, Searle thinks that many are misled into thinking this question is about something deeper and more puzzling. Setting consciousness aside, in all other cases of entities arranged in a part/whole hierarchy of systems, we can picture or image how emergent features arise because these systems and all their features are objective phenomena. Our problem is that we try to image how consciousness could arise from a system of unconscious bits of matter in the same way, but this is not possible because consciousness itself is not imageable and we cannot get at it through a visual metaphor. Once we give up trying to imagine consciousness, any deep puzzlement about the emergence of consciousness, given naturalism, evaporates, and the only question left is one about how the brain produces mental states.

There is another reason Searle offers as to why the emergence of consciousness has no deep metaphysical significance. In standard cases of reduction, for example, heat and color, an ontological reduction (color is nothing but a wavelength) is based on a causal reduction (color is caused by a wavelength). In these cases, we can distinguish the appearance of heat and color from the reality, place the former in consciousness, leave the latter in the objective world, and go on to define the phenomenon itself in terms of its causes. We can do this because our interests are in the reality and not the appearance. The ontological reduction of heat to its causes leaves the appearance of heat the same. However, when it comes to mental states such as pain, even though an ontological reduction cannot be found, there is a similar causal pattern; for example, pain is caused by such and such brain states.

So why do we regard heat as ontologically reducible but not pain? In the case of heat, we are interested in the physical causes and not the subjective appearances, but with pain it is the subjective appearance itself that interests us. If we wanted to, we could reduce pain to such and such physical processes and go on to talk about pain appearances analogous to the heat case. However, in the case of consciousness, the reality is the appearance. Since the point of reductions is to distinguish and separate reality from appearance in order to focus on underlying causes by definitionally identifying the reality with those causes, the point of a reduction for consciousness is missing, since it is the appearance itself that is the reality of interest. Therefore, the irreducibility of consciousness has no deep metaphysical consequences and is simply a result of the pattern of reduction that expresses our pragmatic interests.

In step three, Searle claims that an adequate scientific explanation of mental emergence is a set of very detailed, even lawlike correlations between specific mental and physical states.

Critique

Searle versus Nagel on causal necessitation

Searle rejects an argument by Thomas Nagel which denies that mere correlations amount to a scientific explanation. In terms of AC, Nagel would accept Premise (6) (the explanation is not a natural scientific one) and deny that Searle's correlations count as scientific explanations. Searle rejects (6) and believes such correlations count as adequate scientific explanations. Nagel claims that in other cases of emergence such as liquidity, a scientific explanation does not just tell us what happens, it explains why liquidity *must* emerge when a collection of water molecules gather under certain circumstances. In this case, scientific explanation offers physical causal necessity: given certain states of affairs, it is causally necessary that liquidity emerge and it is inconceivable that it not supervene. But, argues Nagel, no such necessity and no answer to a why question is given by a mere correlation between mental states and physical states in the brain.

Searle's response to Nagel is threefold. First, he says that some explanations in science do not exhibit the type of causal necessity Nagel requires; for example, the inverse square law is an account of gravity that does not show why bodies have to have gravitational attraction. This response is question-begging against Nagel because the inverse square law is merely a description of what happens and not an explanation of why it happens. Interestingly, Newton himself took the inverse square law to be a mere description of how gravity works but explained the nature of gravity itself (due to his views about action at a distance, the nature of spirit, and the mechanical nature of corpuscularian causation by contact) in terms of the activity of the Spirit of God. The point is not that Newton was right, but that he distinguished a description of gravity from an explanation of what it is and his explanation cannot be rebutted by citing the inverse square law. Rather, one needs a better explanatory model of gravity. So Searle's own example actually works against him.

Moreover, even if we grant that mere covering law explanations are, in fact, explanations in some sense, they are clearly different from explanations that offer a model of why things must take place given the model and its mechanisms. Since the AC assumes the correlations and offers an answer to the why question, Searle's solution here is not really a rival explanation but merely a claim that such correlations are basic, brute facts that just need to be listed. In light of what we have already seen, there are at least two further difficulties with Searle's claim.

First, given AC and the nature of theory adjudication among rivals, it is question-begging and *ad hoc* for Searle to assert that these correlations are basic, since the correlations themselves, along with the entities and properties they relate are natural and bear a relevant similarity to other entities, properties, and relations in theism (e.g. God as spirit who can create and causally interact with matter), but are unnatural given the naturalist epistemology, Grand Story, and ontology. As we saw in section one, self-reflective naturalists understand this. Thus, Terence Horgan says that "in any metaphysical framework that deserves labels like 'materialism', 'naturalism', or 'physicalism', supervenience facts must be explainable rather than being *sui generis*" (Horgan 1993, pp. 313–4). And D. M. Armstrong's admits:

> I suppose that if the principles involved [in analyzing the single all-embracing spatio-temporal system which is reality] were completely different from the current principles of physics, in particular if they involved appeal to mental entities, such as purposes, we might then count the analysis as a falsification of Naturalism. But the Naturalist need make no more concession than this. (Armstrong 1978b, p. 262)

Horgan and Armstrong say this precisely because mental entities, the supervenience relation, or a causal correlation between mental and physical entities simply are not natural given a consistent naturalist paradigm. Nor can they be located in Jackson's sense in the Grand Story. Their reality constitutes a falsification of naturalism for Horgan and Armstrong and, given AC, they provide evidence for theism. It is question-begging and *ad hoc* simply to adjust naturalism as does Searle, given the presence of AC as a rival explanation.

Naturalists have long criticized Cartesian dualism on the grounds that the causal relation it posits is so bizarre and its relata so disparate that the relation is virtually unintelligible. Many Cartesian dualists are theists and have sought to rebut this claim by appealing to the alleged clarity of divine miraculous activity in the natural world as a counterexample. However, the dialectical situation worsens if the Cartesian is a naturalist for she must now try to render interaction intelligible solely in light of the resources of the Grand Story, and that cannot be done if the interaction relation is taken to be a natural entity at home in the naturalist ontology. It clearly does not bear a relevant similarity to other entities in that ontology. However, this problem is not a function of the ontological category of the relata. Specifically, it is not a problem that arises for naturalism only if the relata are in the category of individual. It applies equally to the category of property. This is why this problem is sometimes called "Descartes' Revenge." Thus, Searle's employment of a supervenience relation – causal or otherwise – between the brain and consciousness is a serious difficulty for his biological naturalism, one he does not adequately address.

Second, Swinburne's version of AC points out that a correlation can be either an accidental generalization or a genuine law (which exhibits at least physical necessity), and we distinguish the two in that laws are (but accidental correlations are not) noncircular correlations that fit naturally into theories that (1) are ontologically simple, (2) have broad explanatory power, and (3) fit with background knowledge from other, closely related scientific theories about the world. By "fit," Swinburne means the degree of naturalness of the correlation and entities correlated in light of both the broader theory of which the correlation is a part and background knowledge. Now Searle admits that mental phenomena are absolutely unique compared to all other entities in that they "have a special feature not possessed by other natural phenomena, namely, subjectivity" (Searle 1994, p. 93) Unfortunately, it is precisely this radical uniqueness that makes mental phenomena unnatural for a naturalist worldview and which prevents Searle from distinguishing an accidental correlation from a genuine law of nature regarding mental and physical correlations.

So much, then, for Searle's first response to Nagel. His second response is that the apparent necessity of some scientific causal explanations may just be a function of our finding some explanation so convincing that we cannot conceive of certain phenomena behaving differently. Medievals may have thought modern explanations of the emergence of liquidity mysterious and causally contingent. Similarly, our belief that specific mind/brain correlations are causally contingent may simply be due to our ignorance of the brain.

It is hard to see what is supposed to follow from Searle's point here. Just because one can be mistaken in using conceivability as a test for causal necessity, it does not follow that conceivability is never a good test for it. Only a case-by-case study can, in principle, decide the appropriateness of its employment. Now when it comes to things such as liquidity or solidity, Nagel is right. Precisely because of what we know about matter, we cannot conceive of certain states of affairs obtaining and these properties being absent. That Medievals would not be so convinced is beside the points, since they were ignorant of the relevant atomic theory. If they possessed the correct theory, their intuitions would be as are ours. But when it comes to the mental and physical, they are such different entities, and the mental is so unnatural given the rest of the naturalist ontology that there is no clearly conceivable necessity about their connection. And this judgment is based, not on what we do not know about the two types of states, but on what we do know.

Moreover, a more detailed correlation in the future will not change the situation one bit. There is no noncircular or non–*ad hoc* way to formulate such a correlation and we will merely be left with a more detailed dictionary of correlations that will leave intact the same type of problem of causal necessity true of less detailed correlations. Our current lack of belief in such a causal necessity is not due to ignorance of more and more details of the very thing that lacks the necessity in the first place. Rather, it is based on a clear understanding of the nature of the mental and physical, an understanding that Searle himself accepts.

This is why it will not do for naturalists to claim that they are not committed to anything ultimately or utterly brute (such as the divine will), just to their being something unexplained at any given time but which can be explained through deeper investigation. No scientific advance in our knowledge of the details of mental/physical correlations will render either the existence of mental entities or their regular correlation with physical ones anything other that utterly brute for the naturalist.

But Searle had another line of defense against Nagel: even if we grant Nagel's point about the lack of causal necessity in the mental/physical case, nothing follows from this. Why? Because in the water and liquidity case, we can picture the relation between the two in such a way that causal necessity is easily a part of that picture. But since consciousness is not picturable, we are not able to imagine the same sort of causal necessity. Yet that does not mean it is not there.

Here Searle simply applies his earlier point that, given naturalism, our puzzlement about the emergence of consciousness from unconscious bits of matter is due to our attempt to picture consciousness. Now it seems to me that this point is just false and egregiously so. I, for one, have no temptation to try to picture consciousness. And other naturalists have put their finger on the real difficulty about the emergence of consciousness. Paul Churchland says:

> The important point about the standard evolutionary story is that the human species and all of its features are the wholly physical outcome of a purely physical process. . . . If this is the correct account of our origins, then there seems neither need, nor room, to fit any nonphysical substances or properties into our theoretical account of ourselves. We are creatures of matter. And we should learn to live with that fact. (Churchland 1984, p. 21)

Regarding need, I take it he means that everything we need in order to explain the origin and workings of human beings can be supplied by physicalist causal explanations. Regarding room, entities do not come into existence *ex nihilo* nor do radically different kinds of entities emerge from purely physical components placed in some sort of complex arrangement. What comes from the physical by means of physical processes will also be physical.

Searle is simply wrong about the problem being the imageability of consciousness. The problem here for naturalism is ontological, not epistemological.

Searle versus McGinn on causal necessitation

Searle has one final line of defense against those who place a necessitation requirement on an adequate naturalist explanation for "emergent" properties. Searle seeks to rebut an argument by Collin McGinn to the effect that such a necessitation requirement is both essential for and unavailable to a strictly naturalist account of consciousness (Searle 1994, pp. 104–5). We will investigate the details of McGinn's position in section five, but for present purposes, Searle focuses on the following aspects of McGinn's position: consciousness is a kind of "stuff" that is known by introspection, things known by introspection are nonspatial, an adequate solution to the mind/body problem requires understanding the "link" between matter and consciousness, but given our noetic limitations, it is in principle beyond our ability to know that link and, therefore, there is no naturalist account of consciousness. Searle rebuts McGinn on the grounds that (1) consciousness is a property not a stuff; (2) introspection is a confused notion and should be abandoned; given (1) and (2), there is no reason to deny that consciousness is spatial; and moreover (3) there is no link between consciousness and the brain anymore than there is a link between liquidity and H_2O.

Setting aside until section five the issue of whether or not Searle has adequately rebutted McGinn's particular formulation of this argument, the more important point is whether or not Searle has rebutted this form of argument if it is stated in more plausible dualist terms. This is a fair approach to Searle's rebuttal because he explicitly takes McGinn's premises to represent broad Cartesian-style commitments (except for McGinn's claim that the link is *in principle* unknowable) and his own rebuttal to be successful against Cartesian dualism in general. Given this broader context, I believe Searle's rebuttal fails. Consider Premise (1). I do not know of a single property dualist (Cartesian or otherwise) who would take mental properties to be a sort of stuff that, for example, should be referred to by mass terms. Even with respect to mental substances, a framework of stuff is not usually employed. To be sure, some Cartesian dualists may believe in soul stuff, but most substance dualists, including me, employ a substance/attribute ontology to characterize a mental substance as an individuated mental essence; they do not use a separable part/whole framework or the notion of stuff. So Searle is guilty of arguing against a straw man in (1).

What about (2)? Searle's argument against introspection is as follows:

(1_1) If the standard model is true, then there is a distinction (presumably, not a distinction of reason) between the thing seen and the seeing of it.
(2_1) The standard model is true.
(3_1) Therefore, there is a distinction between the thing seen and the seeing of it.
(4_1) If introspection occurs, then there is no distinction between the thing seen and the seeing of it.
(5_1) Therefore, introspection does not occur.

There are at least two problems with this argument and they involve (2_1) and (4_1). Let us begin with (4_1). Searle gives no good reason to accept it and, in fact, there are sufficient reasons to reject it. Let us assume as is standardly granted that in introspection, we have a second-order mental state directed upon a first-order mental state. For example, in introspection the self – whatever it is – is directly aware of a sensation of red or a feeling of pain by directing a second-order mental state onto a first-order one. This is a perfectly intelligible account of introspection and it provides the distinction required to reject (4_1).

If someone rejects this model of introspection, then one can still rebut Searle's argument by rejecting (2_1). That is, one can grant (1_1) for the sake of argument and deny that it applies to introspection on the grounds that it begs the question. After all, why apply the standard model to introspective acts? Recall that in section two I claimed that at least a certain range of mental states relevant to introspection are self-presenting properties. And according to a standard characterization of them, a self-presenting property presents to a subject the intentional object of that property (e.g. an apple's surface) and the self-presenting property itself (being-an-appearing-of-red). Such properties present other things to a subject intermediately by means of them, and they present themselves to a subject directly simply in virtue of the fact that he has them. Introspective awareness of being-an-appearing-of-red could be understood as the exemplification of a self-presenting property.

In this case, introspection provides a counterexample to the standard model. And while Searle does not mention the self, I see no reason why one cannot be directly aware of oneself. On a certain understanding of intentionality, according to which it is a monadic property, when one is aware of oneself (as opposed to a mental state one has), in direct self-awareness, one simply directs one's intentionality onto oneself and the subject and object of awareness stand in the identity relation to each other. Nothing Searle says comes close to undermining such an understanding of self-awareness.

Searle similarly attacks a spatial metaphor associated with "privileged access" that he alleges to go proxy for introspection: when I spatially enter something, there is a distinction among me, the act of entering, and the thing entered. No such distinction obtains in alleged acts of "private access" and, thus, "private access" should be rejected. The appropriate rebuttal analogously follows the lines of response given to the argument against introspection.

This brings us to (3). As we shall see further in the discussion, liquidity is a bad analogy with conscious properties. Liquidity may be understood as the property of flowing freely, which, in turn, may be characterized in terms of friction, flexibility of bonding angles, degree of spatial compactness, and so forth. In short, liquidity is a structural property and, as such, liquidity constitutively supervenes "upon" a collection of water molecules. There is no causal relation here. Liquidity just is a feature of nonrigid motion constituted by a subvenient base. Thus, it is plausible to deny a "link" between liquidity and a swarm of water molecules. But Searle is clear that conscious properties are simple, *sui generis* emergent properties and, as such, are causally supervenient on the brain. In this case, there is indeed a causal "link" between the brain and consciousness and Searle's analogy employed in (3) is a failure, even in terms of his own views.

I conclude, therefore, that Searle has not succeeded in undermining Nagel: Premise (6) of AC (the explanation is not a natural scientific one) is correct and Searle's correlations are not examples of scientific explanation which count against (6). But what about Premise (3) (there is an explanation for these correlations)? Why is it not reasonable to take mental entities and their regular correlations with physical entities to be utterly brute natural facts for which there is no explanation? The answer is provided by the arguments just mentioned about why Searle's correlations are not really scientific explanations. Mental entities are not natural or at home in the naturalist epistemology, etiology, and ontology. Given theism and AC as a rival explanatory paradigm, and given the fact that mental entities and correlations are natural for theism, it is question-begging and *ad hoc* simply to announce that these entities and correlations are natural entities.

Searle could reply that biological naturalism is not question-begging because we already have reason to believe that naturalism is superior to theism prior to our study of the nature of the mental. The only support Searle gives for this claim, apart from a few sociological musings about what it means to be a modern person, is that it is an obvious fact of physics that the world consists *entirely* of physical particles moving in fields of force. It should be clear, however, that this claim is itself question-begging and clearly false. When there is a statement in a physics text about the world in its entirety, it is important to note that this is not a statement of physics. It is a philosophical assertion that does not express any obvious fact of physics. Moreover, it is a question-begging assertion by naturalists prior to a consideration of the evidence and arguments for theism, including AC. If Searle denies this, then he should inform advocates of AC of exactly what obvious fact of physics they deny in their employment of the argument.

Most naturalists have seen this and have opted for strong physicalism in order to avoid abandoning naturalism and legitimizing the introduction of religious concepts and explanations into the picture. It may be "neurotic" to deny consciousness, as Searle points out. But it is far from "neurotic" to be driven to do so in terms of a prior commitment to naturalism, and AC makes clear why this is the case.

Mackie on Locke and thinking matter

But perhaps there is a naturalist rejoinder at this point in the form of a *tu quoque* against theists and AC. J. L. Mackie advanced just such an argument (Mackie 1982, pp. 120–1; Williams 1996; cf. Moreland 1998a, 2000, 2001a). According to Mackie, theists such as John Locke admitted that God could superadd consciousness to systems of matter fitly disposed and, therefore, as a result of divine intervention, matter may give rise to consciousness after all. Thus, Locke leaves open the possibility that a mere material being might be conscious given theism. Mackie then asks this question: "But if some material structures could be conscious, how can we know *a priori* that material structures cannot *of themselves give rise to* consciousness?" (Mackie 1982, p. 121). He concludes that this Lockean admission opens the door for the naturalist to assert the emergence of consciousness from fitly disposed matter as a brute fact.

In my view, Mackie's argument carries no force against AC because a main part of AC consists in the recognition that mental/physical correlations exist, they are not explicable within the constraints of scientific naturalism, and they require a personal theistic explanation if they are to be explained at all. In this sense, the idea that, in one way or another, God could "superadd" thinking or other mental states to matter is required for AC to go through.

However, as I have tried to show, it does not follow from this "Lockean admission" that it is a brute, naturalistic fact that material structures of themselves can give rise to consciousness or that adequate naturalistic explanations can be given for this. Indeed, Locke himself constructed detailed arguments to show that mental states such as thinkings are not within the natural powers of matter nor could they arise from material structures without an original mind to create and attach those mental states to matter (Locke 1959, pp. 313–9). Locke's view that God could superadd thinking to a material substance just as easily as to a spiritual substance was a conclusion he drew from the omnipotence of God along with the claim that "thinking matter" is not a contradiction and, thus, possible for God to bring about.

I am not defending Locke's way of arguing that God could superadd thinking to matter. In fact, I do not think it is correct as he formulated it but, clearly, Locke would not have believed that Mackie's naturalistic conclusion can justifiably be drawn from his own (Locke's) admission of the possibility of divine omnipotence adding a faculty of thought to a material structure.

Mackie cannot simply assert that material structures have the power to give rise to consciousness and also claim to be operating with a naturalistic depiction of matter. According to David Papineau, matter with emergent mental potentiality is not the sort of matter countenanced by naturalists. This is why when Papineau attempts to characterize the physical in terms of a future ideal physics, he places clear boundaries on the types of changes allowed by naturalism for developments in physical theory. According to Papineau, the naturalist will admit that future physics may change some features of what we believe about matter, but in light of a naturalist commitment and the past few hundred years of development in physics, future physics will not need to be supplemented by psychological or mental categories (Papineau 1993, pp. 29–32).

Given theism, we cannot say *a priori* just what capacities or states God will correlate with specific physical states. But given naturalism, and the commitment to the role of physics in naturalism, along with a view of the physical that is required by physics, we can say that mental potentiality is just not part of matter. Thus, it is question-begging and *ad hoc* against AC for Mackie to adjust naturalism to allow that material structures of them-selves can give rise to consciousness.

Consciousness, liquidity, solidity, and digestion

There is one final issue in Searle's defense of biological naturalism that needs to be addressed, viz., his claim that the emergence of consciousness fits a broad pattern of emergence, for example, cases of liquidity, solidity, digestion, and, therefore, since the latter present no problem for naturalism, neither does the former. I offer three responses. First, if we take liquidity or solidity to be the degree of rigidity, flexibility, or viscosity of a collection of particles, then these properties are not good analogies to consciousness because they turn out to be nothing more than group behavior of particles placed in a relatively compressed, stable, ordered structure for solids or a more viscous, less compact arrangement for liquids. So there is no problem about emergence here, since we can easily understand how liquidity and solidity are related to groups of material particles as they are depicted in physical theory.

Second, when we are dealing with genuinely emergent properties that are categorially different from what physical theory takes to characterize subvenient entities, I think that it could be argued that the naturalist has the same difficulty here as with the emergence of consciousness. Recall Searle's point about the pragmatics of reduction: we reduce heat to its causes because we happen to be interested in the objective causes and not the subjective appearances, but in cases of, for example, pain, we are interested in the painful appearance itself, so we do not reduce pain to its causes. In my view, the decision to reduce heat to its causes is not primarily a scientific matter nor is it a matter of our pragmatic interest. I think it has been a function of two things.

First, if we take heat, color, liquidity, or solidity to be identical to the qualia we experience in certain circumstances (e.g. heat is identical to warmth, red is a color not a wavelength, liquidity is wetness), then an ontological puzzle arises analogous to the one about the emer-gence of mental states: how could warmth emerge in a physical structure as a result of increased atomic agitation? Second, there was a way of avoiding this question in light of a widely held Lockean view of secondary qualities and sense perception. We can locate these secondary quali-ties in consciousness and identify them as appearances of the real objective phenomena, viz., the objective causes for our experiences of secondary qualities. John Yolton has shown that during late seventeenth- and early eighteenth- century debates about materialism, immaterialist philosophers (e.g. Ralph Cudworth) regularly argued against the idea that mental entities could emerge from properly structured matter (Yolton 1983, pp. 4–13). A standard rebuttal to this claim was that light and heat were very different from matter but could be generated in material bodies given the right conditions. So mind could likewise emerge. Cudworth and others responded by asserting that light, heat, and other secondary qualities were not in material bodies but were sensations in minds and, thus, the problem does not arise as to how they could arise in a material structure devoid of such qualities prior to the right conditions obtaining. It is clear from this debate at the very beginning of the emergence of modern materialism that one philosophical motive for locating secondary qualities in consciousness was to avoid a straightforward metaphysical problem: *ex nihilo nihil fit*.

If I am right about this, then the ontological puzzle is really the driving force behind what Searle calls normal naturalist cases of emergence. The problem is that these cases are not natural any more than the emergence of consciousness and that is why they were located in consciousness. For example, both secondary qualities such as redness or warmth and painfulness are dissimilar to the properties that constitute an ideal physics. Jaegwon Kim has argued that in Nagel-type reductions, the relevant bridge laws should be taken as biconditionals and not as conditionals because we need materially equivalent correlations between entities (or terms) in the reduced and base theories in order to assert identities between the entities in question (Kim 1996, p. 91). Moreover, says Kim, the identity of reduced and base entities is preferable to mere correlations because the latter raise potentially embarrassing questions as to why such precise correlations arise in the first place.

Kim's point is not confined to mental and physical correlations. All a naturalist can do with them (if we keep these so-called secondary qualities or other categorially distinct emergent qualities in the external world) is to offer a detailed correlation to describe regular relations between physical structures and emergent entities. No amount of knowledge whatever of subvenient entities would take us one inch toward predicting or picturing why these particular entities regularly emerge in such and such circumstances and not others. In discussions of emergence over a century ago, it was precisely their unpredictability from knowledge of subvenient entities that was identified as the hallmark of an emergent property.

In more modern terms, it is the inability to either image or understand why warmth emerges regularly here and not somewhere else, or why it emerges at all given our knowledge of molecular agitation. Note carefully that Searle himself seems to accept picturability as a necessary condition for the acceptance of a claim that one entity emerges from another in the "normal" cases, but picturability is no more available for heat (warmth) emerging from matter than it is for mental states (Searle 1994, pp. 102–3). Nagel's conceivability test applies here just as it does for mental states.

However, even if I am wrong about this, there is a third response that can be given to Searle. There are two features of mental states that make their emergence disanalogous to, say, the properties of digestion. First, mental states are so unique and different from all other entities in the world that it is far more difficult to see how they could emerge from physical states than it is for the so-called normal cases. Second, mental states are quite natural in a theistic world view and have a higher prior probability given theism over against naturalism even if we agree that, say, the emergence of the properties of digestion are equally natural and probable on both world hypotheses.

In my view, these two features of mental states make them more analogous to value properties than to characteristics of digestion. Mackie argued that the supervenience of moral properties would constitute a refutation of naturalism and evidence for theism: "Moral properties constitute so odd a cluster of properties and relations that they are most unlikely to have arisen in the ordinary course of events without an all-powerful god to create them" (Mackie 1982, p. 115; cf. Moreland & Nielsen 1993, chap. 8–10). Presumably, Mackie's reasons for this claim involve some of the points I have just made earlier: moral properties have the two features that make them natural for theism but unnatural for naturalism. No matter how far future physics advances our understanding of matter, it will not make the emergence of moral properties the least bit more likely, more picturable, or more natural. And the same claim could easily be made for mental properties even if features of digestion are granted equally natural for theism and naturalism.

Searle himself admits that of all the entities in the world, mental states are absolutely unique and radically different from all the others. And as we saw earlier, Armstrong is willing to accept that more ordinary physical or biological properties could emerge when the nervous system reaches a certain level of complexity. But he could not accept the natural emergence of mental states from matter because mental states are of "a quite different nature" from states accepted by naturalists. The jump from physical states to mental states was too far for Armstrong's naturalism to allow, so he adopted strong physicalism as the only acceptable naturalist solution.

The problem with my third response is that it requires one to weigh the difference between acceptable and unacceptable cases of emergence. But to the degree that mental entities are taken as radically unique from all other physical or biological entities, then to that degree the analogy between the emergence of mental states and other cases of emergence is weakened. And to that degree, the emergence of the mental would be radical as Nagel calls it or unnatural as Adams and Swinburne claim.

After all, naturalists have not spent the last fifty years trying to eliminate or reduce solidity or the properties of digestion like they have mental states. This is because the latter are rightly seen as a threat to naturalism even if the former are not. As B. F. Skinner noted just before his death:

> Evolutionary theorists have suggested that 'conscious intelligence' is an evolved trait, but they have never shown how a nonphysical variation could arise [in the first place] to be selected by physical contingencies of survival. (Skinner 1990, p. 1207)

Indeed. The constraints on a naturalist ontology discussed in sections one and two place a severe burden of proof on adding emergent mental properties to that ontology, a burden that Searle has singularly failed to meet.

Section Four: Timothy O'Connor and Emergent Necessitation

The vast majority of friends and foes of agent-causal versions of libertarian freedom agree that it is either inconsistent or not plausibly harmonized with a naturalistic view of the world, including a physicalist depiction of particulars taken to populate the naturalist ontology. Thus, naturalist John Bishop claims that:

the idea of a responsible agent, with the 'originative' ability to initiate events in the natural world, does not sit easily with the idea of [an agent as] a natural organism. . . . Our scientific understanding of human behavior seems to be in tension with a presupposition of the ethical stance we adopt toward it. (Bishop 1989, p. 1)

In his excellent and penetrating development of an agent-causal count of freedom, *Persons & Causes*, Timothy O'Connor acknowledges that this is the case: "A great many contemporary philosophers will dismiss [an agent-causal account of freedom] as pointless, since it blatantly contradicts 'the scientific facts'" (O'Connor 2000, p. 108; cf. Moreland 1997; O'Connor 2003). However, O'Connor is actually puzzled by the majority view on this issue, and claims that a robust version of AGC, including his own, may be very plausibly harmonized with the emerging naturalist picture of the world, including a physicalist view of the agent. O'Connor's puzzlement is odd in light of the considerations we noted in sections one and two. In any case, for O'Connor, agent-causal power is an emergent property. To support this claim, O'Connor defends what I shall call the Harmony Thesis: the emergence of agent-causal power may be plausibly located within a widely accepted naturalist ontology, including a physicalist depiction of the agent.

To explain why I think O'Connor has failed to substantiate this claim, I shall describe features of his model and offer three lines of criticism. First, I will expose problems in O'Connor's description of the agent. Second, I will show why a certain model of causation is crucial for O'Connor's project and argue that, given this model, it is not true that consciousness in general, and active power in particular, are emergent properties. Third, I will try to show that certain epistemic features that characterize O'Connor's own case for AGC, if applied consistently, provide adequate grounds for rejecting the Harmony Thesis. Besides problems intrinsic to O'Connor's view, in light of considerations of sections one and two there is a substantial burden of proof – made precise in those sections and shown to be far from arbitrary – that he must meet to be successful. I believe it will become obvious that he fails to meet this burden.

O'Connor is a Christian theist, not a naturalist. Nevertheless, he is concerned to show that AGC, including active power, may be plausibly located in a widely accepted naturalist ontology, and it this claim that I wish to clarify and dispute.

AGC and the emerging naturalist picture of the world (N)

To assess the Harmony Thesis, it is important to get clear on the central features of O'Connor's understanding of AGC and N that are relevant to our present concerns. According to O'Connor, although it may be difficult to do so, AGC may be reconciled with the *Causal Unity of Nature Thesis*, but not with the *Constitution Thesis* (O'Connor 2000, p. 109):

> *The Causal Unity of Nature Thesis*: Macro-level phenomena arise through entirely natural microphysical causal processes and the existence of macro-level phenomena continues to depend causally on microphysical processes.
> *The Constitution Thesis*: All macro-level phenomena are constituted by micro-level phenomena.

AGC

Regarding AGC, O'Connor claims that the core of every free act is an irreducible causal relation between a person and some appropriate internal event that triggers latter elements of the action. O'Connor holds to a realist view of causation, according to which the essence of causality is causal production or the bringing about of an effect. Active power constitutes a special type of causal event that is intrinsically active, that cannot be caused, even by the agent, and that is intrinsically a case of the agent directly causing/controlling his behavior, or at least, the action trigger. Agent causes bring about immediately executive states of intention to act in various ways.

What kind of agent is required for this account? Such an agent must have "rather special properties in her constitution" (O'Connor 2000, p. 49). To elaborate, entities that exhibit event causation are such that the capacity to generate a particular effect is exercised as a matter of course: given the right circumstances, the cluster of properties that ground the capacity directly give rise to the effect. By contrast, having the properties that subserve an agent-causal capacity does not produce the effect; it enables the agent to do so (O'Connor 2000, pp. xiv, 75). Such an agent is a "not wholly moved mover" (O'Connor 2000, p. 67) and an enduring continuant, but not a different kind of substance radically diverse from physical substances (O'Connor 2000, p. 73). Personal agents are biological entities with irreducible emergent properties, where properties are construed as universals that have essentially their dispositional tendencies (O'Connor 2000, p. 73). Sometimes O'Connor uses substance talk to describe the agent (O'Connor 2000, p. 73). However, he also describes the agent as a "complex system regulated by dynamic processes" (O'Connor 2000, p. 95) with a structured capacity, structured by tendency-conferring states of having reasons to act in specific ways (O'Connor 2000, pp. 97–8).

In various places, O'Connor describes the emergent properties essential to AGC. Only entities with more basic attributes can have free will, viz., volition, understanding, practical judgment and the power to believe the act is within one's power (O'Connor 2000, pp. 45–6). Thus, agent causes must possess conscious awareness (O'Connor 2000, p. 122). An agent must be able to represent to himself possible courses of action and have belief/desire sets relevant to each (O'Connor 2000, p. 72). Moreover, given that intentions are action triggers internal to the agent, an agent must be able to cause directly an event internal to the agent (O'Connor 2000, p. 72). In accounting for the role of reasons in AGC, O'Connor claims that an agent directly causes an action-triggering intention the content of which is that an action of a specific sort be performed for certain reasons the agent had at the time. Thus, an agent must have the potentiality to have intrinsic events that exemplify a twofold internal relation of direct reference and of similar content (O'Connor 2000, pp. xiv, 85–6).

Four relevant aspects of naturalism

There are four aspects of N relevant to our discussion. First, O'Connor accepts the mereological hierarchy: physics is the basic level of reality and, in the category of individual, all wholes above the fundamental level are systems constituted by parts at lower levels. On this view, the world is fundamentally event causal in nature (O'Connor 2000, p. 107). This seems to mean two things: (1) all strictly physical entities exhibit event causality; and (2) all macrowholes with or without emergent properties exhibit event causality except for libertarian agents. O'Connor's view of the hierarchy is fairly standard, but it does have an aspect that would be considered controversial among those who accept N, namely, O'Connor rejects the causal closure of the physical (2000, p. 79).

Second, all particulars are physical objects. When discussing N, O'Connor calls the agent "a macrophysical object or system" (2000, pp. 95, 109, 111, 118), and a physical substance (2000, p. 73). According to O'Connor, N requires substance monism (2000, p. 121).

Third, there are genuinely emergent properties (cf. O'Connor 1994). For O'Connor, an emergent property has three important traits: It is (1) a simple, intrinsically characterizable, new kind of property qualitatively different from and not composed of subvenient parts, properties, relations; (2) a property which has its own ontologically basic type of causal influence; and (3) a property which is necessitated by and causally grounded in its base (O'Connor 2000, pp.70, 110–5, 117–8). Trait (3) requires further elaboration. According to O'Connor, the causal powers of properties are essential aspects of those properties and, thus, belong to properties with an absolute, metaphysical necessity. The causal potentialities of a property are part of what constitutes the property's identity (O'Connor 2000, pp. 70–1, 117–8). It is in this sense, that in the right circumstances, a subvenient property necessitates an emergent property. Thus, properties constitutive of consciousness, including the property of active power, are emergent (O'Connor 2000, pp. 115–23).

Finally, O'Connor embraces Causal Unity but rejects the Constitution Thesis (O'Connor 2000, pp. 108–10). While recognizing that most naturalists take N to require both, he claims that only the former is required. The Constitution Thesis allows only structural macro-properties. In rejecting it, O'Connor accepts emergent properties. And by accepting the Causal Unity Thesis, he believes that he can harmonize AGC with N.

Problems with O'Connor's description of the agent

There are two problems with O'Connor's agent: it is no mere physical particular, and O'Connor cannot justify naturalism over panpsychism as the appropriate ontological framework for locating the agent. Let us consider these in order.

O'Connor's agent is not a purely physical particular

When he speaks of the self *qua* agent, it is essentially mental in nature. When O'Connor describes the self from the perspective of N, he talks as though it were a physical object (O'Connor 2001, p. 51). Galen Strawson claims that a necessary condition for free agency is that one have a concept of oneself as single just *qua* mental, quite independently of whether one also has a concept of oneself as an indissolubly psychophysical thing:

> In some very strong and straightforward sense, we intuitively require that there be a *mental subject* in the case of any free agent, a mental subject that is in some way or other properly distinguishable from all its particular thoughts . . . ; a mental subject that is moreover present to itself as such in some way. Whether or not there can correctly be said to *be* such a thing, we require at the very least that any free agent's thought or experience be such that it is overwhelmingly natural for us (and for it) to talk in terms of such a subject. . . . (Strawson 1986, pp. 161–2; cf. 146–69, 323–9)

All that follows from this, says Strawson, is that the concept of the self as a mental particular is a necessary condition for taking the self to be a free agent, not that there actually are mental substances. O'Connor's description of the agent seems to present it as a subject essentially characterized by a range of mental properties necessary for agency. Since O'Connor offers a characterization of agents themselves, and not simply an analysis of our common sense concept of agents, O'Connor's agent appears to be a mental particular, an essentially mental particular *qua* agent cause.

It is not clear how he can hold that the agent self is a physical substance necessarily characterized by emergent mental properties. If the agent self is essentially mental, and if we recognize that a particular's actual and potential properties are both relevant for characterizing the kind of entity the particular is, then the agent self would seem to be essentially a mental/physical particular, and not simply a physical particular with emergent mental properties attached to it. When John Locke argued that thinking matter was possible, some of his critics (Edward Stillingfleet, S. G. Gerdil, Malcolm Flemyng) responded by pointing out that a "material" substance whose essence was constituted in part by mental potentialities was no longer simply a "material" substance (Yolton 1983). I believe O'Connor's agent is subject to the same criticism.

Perhaps in response to arguments such as these, O'Connor has developed his view of the agent beyond what appeared in *Persons & Causes* and now advances the idea that persons are material substances in a qualified sense (O'Connor & Jacobs 2003; O'Connor & Wong 2005). Working within a framework of immanent universals, O'Connor uses these descriptors for the person-as-agent: a biological organism with emergent properties (in his three senses, including top/down active power) that are as basic as the negative charge of an electron; a three-dimensional continuant with a mental life grounded in its physical nature; a cluster of immanent universals with its own unique particularity not reducible to that of the mereological aggregate from which it arises; an emergent biological organism with a new thisness; a new composite that exhibits an objective substantial unity. These descriptors express O'Connor's desire to steer a via media between a mere ordered mereological aggregate on the one hand and a view such as William Hasker's, according to which a brand new emergent mental whole exists and is in no way composed of subvenient entities (Hasker 1999).

O'Connor claims that the standard mereological aggregate is inadequate to ground an enduring continuant, one that is needed to satisfy the requirements for a responsible libertarian causal agent. He also rejects a Haskerian view on the grounds that only a theistic solution along the lines of AC could account for how a complex physical system could give rise all in one go to a brand-new emergent mental entity.[5] O'Connor wants to avoid universalism regarding composite objects, so he specifies conditions, under which a new emergent individual arises, and he offers an ontological account of how such an individual could arise in the first place. Regarding the former, emergent properties are the best candidates for emergent individuals (and the only clear evidence we have for such properties is consciousness). All other macrowholes are merely mereological aggregates. So in the category of individual, O'Connor's ontology includes atomic simples, mereological aggregates, emergent biological organisms (and as a Christian theist, at least one purely spiritual substance – God).

---

5. O'Connor rejects this move because it suffers from the causal pairing problem for which most plausible solution to that problem – singular causation – is bogus. O'Connor seems unfamiliar with Thomistic solutions. See Moreland and Wallace (1995).

When it comes to offering an account of all this, O'Connor is not clear about his task, and it is sometimes hard to tell which of these two questions he is answering: (1) How are we to explain ontologically how emergent individuals could come about? (2) When should we judge that an emergent individual has come about? Questions (1) and (2) are ontological and epistemological, respectively, and I shall take (1) to be O'Connor's focus. So understood, he claims that subvenient entities are always trying to bring about the emergent individual, but it is only when a certain threshold level of complexity is reached that conditions are right for that base to cause the emergent individual to come into being. When emergent mental properties appear, they constitute holistic mental states – perhaps enduring baseline mental states – and these, in turn, confer on persons their substantial unity as thinking biological substances, presumably by bringing about through top/down causation a new particularity over and above that of the series of subvenient mereological aggregates that are in a constant state of flux. This "composition-conferred-by-holism" view produces an emergent individual that is somehow composed by its parts yet has a new thisness all its own.

Why should we believe any of this? First, according to O'Connor first-person direct awareness justifies the view that consciousness is emergent in his three senses and this justification overrides any *a posteriori* ascriptions of microstructure to conscious states. All empirical knowledge, he tells us, presupposes this knowledge. Second, we should limit our account to the constraints provided by the naturalist mereological hierarchy and the grounds we have for accepting it, we should avoid a theistic explanation of emergent individuals, and on the basis of theoretical simplicity, we should adopt a view of the emergent individual that does two things: grounds endurance and agency beyond the flux of change in a mere ordered aggregate and is as close to the mereological aggregate as possible in order to fit the naturalist viewpoint.

What should we make of O'Connor's modified view? I believe the objections raised against his earlier position apply with equal or greater force to the modified view. For example, it is still not clear how a particular with basic mental potentialities is a physical object. To his credit, O'Connor seems to recognize this and, thus, he calls persons material substances "in a qualified form." Moreover, O'Connor's new view is more clearly a version of panpsychism, and it is far from clear that this is a legitimate specification of positive naturalism. For example, when he claims that consciousness is just as basic as negative charge, this claim is closer to theism than to naturalism and it will be a hard pill for naturalists to swallow. This view also renders impossible a strict naturalist explanation of emergence as, for example, in the Causal Unity Thesis. Instead, mental potentialities and their causal interaction with physical conditions are required, and this is a long way from (positive) naturalism.

Besides retaining difficulties from the earlier position, the modified view suffers from some new problems not present in the older version. I mention two. First, there are deep metaphysical problems with O'Connor's emergent individuals. For one thing, the framework of immanent universals renders unintelligible the claim that the emergent individual has its own thisness while at the same time being constituted by the relevant mereological complex. The framework of immanent universals depicts property instances as states of affairs (the so-called thick particular) – in the case of O'Connor's persons, states of affairs that are substantial continuants – with three constituents: the universal, the nexus of exemplification, and an individuator (the thin particular, in my view, a bare particular). Whatever conditions ground the exemplification of the universal are external to (not constituents of) the instance itself. And since the person can endure even though the mereological aggregate is in constant flux, it would seem that the aggregate is accidental to the continuant. To the degree that his emergent individuals provide what is needed (e.g. being enduring continuants), they look strangely like Hasker's emergent mental ego rather than some via media.

Moreover, there just is no baseline conscious state that is constant throughout a person's life and apt for grounding endurance. The property of being conscious cannot provide such a baseline because it is both a universal and a second-order property of mental properties (being a sensation) that comes-to-be and ceases-to-be exemplified when first-order states come and go. Our mental lives team with flux as does the "underlying" aggregate. There seems to be no account of the individual that grounds its endurance unless we treat the individual as a state of affairs constituted by a mental essence, exemplification, and particularity with the aggregate its cause but outside the being of its effect. But, again, this is Hasker's view, not O'Connor's. Finally, in criticizing Hasker, he claims that unless one appeals to a theistic explanation, one cannot explain how a complex physical system could give rise, all in one go, to unique emergent whole. As an advocate of AC, I am cheered by this admission. Unfortunately, this argument has been repeatedly raised against emergent properties themselves.

Second, I find O'Connor's composition-conferred-by-holism to be deeply troubling. He apparently accepts the dictum that "thought implies a thinker," or more generally, that consciousness requires a particular to possess it. So far so good. But it seems to me that this is so because the bearer of consciousness is more basic ontologically that the mental properties it exemplifies or the mental states that obtain within it. But O'Connor's view has this backward. If I understand him correctly, when the mereological aggregate reaches the proper threshold, emergent consciousness arises and this, in turn, causes the conscious individual to come into existence via top/down conferral (by generating a new thisness). Thus, thinkings cause thinkers, but it seems to me that something like the converse is true – the dependence goes the other way.

O'Connor also claims that emergent states are caused by temporally prior subvenient states and, thus, emergence is diachronic and not synchronic (see O'Connor & Wong 2005). Thus, the following scenario seems to arise: at t_1 subvenient conditions cause emergent conscious state C_1 to obtain at t_2 which, in turn brings about emergent individual I_1 at t_3. Two things seem to follow. First, the very first mental state in one's life (C_1) seems clearly ownerless, since at t_2 there is no individual to possess it.

Second, beyond the very first conscious state, the following would seem to hold: for all C_{N+1} (for N greater than zero) at t_{N+2}, the individual I_{N+1} conferred by and, thus, ontologically tied to C_{N+1} exists at t_{N+2}. I see no further relevant ontological relationship between a conscious state and an emergent individual other than the conferral relation. If this is correct, then it is hard to see how a continuing "self" can exist, since there just is no single, ongoing "baseline mental state" throughout one's life. Since conscious states are in flux, so are the instantaneous individuals upon whom they confer existence. In this case, for any time t greater than one, there may be an emergent individual that exists while a particular conscious state obtains, but it is the wrong one. In general, each emergent individual at a time is ontologically associated with a mental state that obtained instantaneously earlier and, thus, is ownerless.

Additionally, his modified view is even less compatible with naturalism than his earlier view. In light of the ontology-constraining factors surfaced in section one and their associated graded burden of proof on any ontology that goes beyond them, O'Connor exceeds those factors (e.g. the mental is as basic as negative charge, the emergence of active power and a new individual, neither emergent entity satisfies the "entry by entailment" condition, top/down causation, epistemic authority given to first-person introspection that trumps *a posteriori* considerations) and fails to meet the burden of proof required for his position to be a plausible version of naturalism. Moreover, given the presence of AC which O'Connor himself acknowledges, his dismissive attitude toward theistic explanation begs the question at several points and fails to take into account adequately the epistemic impact of AC for his project.

O'Connor and panpsychism

So much for O'Connor's depiction of the agent. Here is the second difficulty with his account: As McGinn points out, in the contemporary setting, a "material" substance such as O'Connor's would properly be characterized according to weak panpsychism (McGinn 1999, pp. 95–101). The vast majority of naturalists take panpsychism to be a rival to a naturalist understanding of matter and not a permissible version of N. We will examine this issue in more detail in this section. For present purposes, recall that according to N, the fundamental level of reality is strictly physical and emergent entities "up" the hierarchy depend for their existence, or at least instantiation, on strictly microphysical entities. However, according to panpsychism, mental properties (either potential or actual properties) are fundamental and *sui generis*, and this conflicts with the naturalist hierarchy according to which the fundamental level is strictly physical.

O'Connor can simply disagree here that panpsychism is a rival to naturalism. He acknowledges that his view implies that "the presence of agent-causal capacities in select complex entities has always been among the potentialities of the world's primordial building blocks ..." (O'Connor 2001, p. 58). Elsewhere he argues that "[t]he basic properties and relations of our world will be those properties whose instantiation does not even partly consist in the instantiation of distinct properties by the entity *or its parts. It is the thesis of emergentism that some basic properties are had by composite individuals*" (O'Connor & Wong 2005, p. 665; italics in the original). Again, "[e]mergent features are as basic as electric charge now appears to be, just more restricted in the circumstances of their manifestation" (O'Connor & Jacobs 2003, pp. 541). I suspect that these are hard sayings for most naturalists. In order for O'Connor to justify the claim that this assertion is a permissible version of N, two things seem to be required.

First, he must show that the emergence of active power is causally necessitated by the relevant physical base. This is a necessary condition for him to show that the actual emergence of active power is consistent with the Causal Unity Thesis. Further in the discussion, I argue that O'Connor fails in this regard. Even if he successfully shows that strictly natural microphysical entities are necessary causal conditions for the emergence of active power, this would not show that his view is an appropriate revision of N and not an abandonment of N in favor of panpsychism as a rival framework because O'Connor's view requires abandonment of the Causal Unity Thesis. Recall that this thesis states that macrolevel phenomena arise through and continue to depend on *entirely* natural microphysical causal processes. On O'Connor's treatment of emergent active power (and consciousness in general), emergence depends on the actualization of nonphysical mental potentialities which are not themselves "natural micro*physical* properties," even if strictly natural microphysical entities are necessary causal conditions for such emergence. Second, he could argue that we have prephilosophical intuitions for taking mental properties in general, and active power in particular, to be emergent properties in his specific sense of emergence. I shall consider these moves in what follows.

The Harmony Thesis, mental properties, and the causal grounding condition

Emergent necessitation and contingency

For two reasons, to justify the Harmony Thesis, O'Connor needs the "necessitation" of emergent active power by the subvenient base. The best way to clarify "necessitation" is to characterize it in the context of presenting the first reason. To get at that reason, it will be useful to begin by reviewing insights from Frank Jackson that were presented in section one (Jackson 1998).

According to Jackson, advocates of N should take naturalism to be a piece of serious metaphysics because in so doing, they pattern the epistemic justification of N on that of good scientific theories, and they provide grounds for preferring N to its rivals on the basis of N's superior explanatory power. Accordingly, one must face the location problem: the task of finding a place for some entity (e.g. agency) in the Grand Story. The mereological hierarchy results from serious metaphysics. For Jackson, some entity is located iff it is entailed by the basic account. Thus, if Φ is true of the actual world and all of its minimal physical duplicates told in purely physical terms, and Ψ is the corresponding true description of the actual world told in psychological terms, then Φ entails Ψ. In this way, the physical may be said to "necessitate" the psychological. It is important to keep this framework in mind for what follows.

Although he does not mention it explicitly, O'Connor seems concerned to take N as an expression of serious metaphysics, and he understands this to require the location of emergent properties, including mental properties such as active power, in terms of the understanding of "necessitation" just mentioned. Since he is concerned to show that those who accept N are not thereby given adequate grounds for rejecting AGC, O'Connor must be assuming that AGC may be adequately located in N and, moreover, that AGC does not provide evidence for a rival to N, say theism, along with substance dualism as a component of theism. As O'Connor admits, many – perhaps most – have seen AGC as evidence against N and reject the Harmony Thesis. Thus, O'Connor argues that if one is going to have a scientific understanding of an emergent property, one cannot merely accept a property as emergent without explaining its existence. Rather, one must require that an emergent property be causally grounded in its base properties if it is to be naturalistically explicable (O'Connor 2000, pp. 111–2).

O'Connor also claims that if an emergent property is contingently linked to the base properties causing it to emerge, then apart from an appeal to God's contingent choice that things be so and to God's stable intention that they continue to be so, there will be no explanation for the link itself or its constancy (O'Connor 2000, pp. 70–1). In short, if the link is contingent, the Harmony Thesis is false and AGC provides evidence for theism, and there is less need to preserve physicalism in the category of individual.

The second reason why O'Connor needs the "necessitation" of emergent active power by the subvenient base involves O'Connor's view of causation: The causal powers of properties are essential aspects of those properties and, thus, belong to properties with an absolute, metaphysical necessity. The causal potentialities of a property are part of what constitutes the property's identity (O'Connor 2000, pp. 70–1, 117–8). O'Connor's realist view of causation – event and agent – entails that a cause produces or brings about its effect in virtue of the properties of the cause, and properties are universals that have essentially their causal powers (O'Connor 2000, p. 73). Since most philosophers identify the supervenience relation with the causal relation in the case of emergent properties, it is in this causal sense that in the right circumstances, the instantiation of a subvenient property necessitates the instantiation of its associated emergent property.

Since an emergent property is the actualization of causal potentialities in the right circumstances, the emergent property seems to be a part of its causal property's identity as well. Thus, an emergent property seems to require its base property to exist. In an earlier account, O'Connor accepted this robust claim about emergent properties because he took an emergent property to be an expression of the very nature of the subvenient base causing it. However, in *Persons & Causes* he says that the notion that an emergent property could not exist without its subvenient base is "possibly gratuitous" (O'Connor 2000, p. 112). His concession seems to result from his desire to offer as minimalist an account of emergence as possible to increase its chances of being accepted by critics and, thus, he leaves open the sort of modality (metaphysical, nomological) required for a minimalist account of emergence. But O'Connor himself continues to accept the more robust account of causality, and this would seem to require that he also continue to accept the stronger notion of emergence.[6]

Unfortunately, while the Harmony Thesis requires the relevant physical circumstances to necessitate emergent mental properties, including active power, the link between mental properties and the relevant physical circumstances seems utterly contingent. Grounded in strong conceivability, thought experiments that provide strong justification for this claim proliferate throughout the literature. For example, inverted qualia and Chinese Room scenarios seem to be coherent and entirely possible. No strictly physical proposition of N employing solely physical terms for particulars, properties, relations, or laws renders these thought experiments broadly logically impossible, even in worlds that resemble ours in every physical respect.

Again, different forms of the well-known knowledge argument seem to be quite plausible. Since O'Connor himself accepts a property dualist interpretation of the argument, given this interpretation, no knowledge whatever of merely physical facts gives one any information at all about the presence, absence, or nature of mental facts. If this is so, it is difficult to see how one could justify the claim that Φ entails Ψ. No amount of information about the former entails anything at all about the latter. Φ is consistent with our world and with inverted qualia and zombie worlds that are minimal physical duplicates of our world. The physical/mental link seems contingent indeed.

Further, the modal argument for substance dualism seems plausible. If so, then at least certain versions of the argument imply that physical entities are not necessary for the instantiation of mental properties. Indeed, theism itself presents (at least) one case in which

6. If I am correct about this, then O'Connor cannot simply argue that the emergence of active power is merely metaphysically copossible with N. Rather, the existence of active power would seem to require N. Thus, the existence of substance dualism as a rival position is a crucial aspect of evaluating the Harmony Thesis, since the presence of substance dualism as a coherent rival counts against this stronger claim.

active power is not dependent upon a physical base. Surely, the existence of God or angels with libertarian power is metaphysically possible, and if so, it is just not clear why the property of active power is causally tied to a physical base.

These thought experiments have been around a long time and there is no sign that they are going away. They provide evidence against the necessitation claim that is central to the Harmony Thesis. As far as I know, O'Connor does not consider the force of the modal argument. I wonder how he would handle cases in which the agent cause is a pure spirit (God). If he says that the presence of the relevant physical base necessitates the emergence of active power but that the latter could obtain without the former, then this would amount to a denial that an emergent property is an essential aspect of the subvenient property whose potentialities actualize it.

Given a functionalist analysis of mental kinds, it may be that a type of mental state could be "realized" in spirits and brains and this fact is consistent with certain brain states in certain circumstances necessitating the realization of a mental state by being sufficient for such a realization. But this admission would not provide O'Connor with a rejoinder to my argument from the instantiation of active power in spirits. Given that active power is a simply, intrinsically characterized property that is instantiated, and not a structural property that is realized, O'Connor depicts active power as a disposition of its metaphysical base as a matter of metaphysical necessity, and it is hard to see how this disposition could be actualized without its categorical base. Further, most naturalists do not cash out emergent supervenience merely as the logical sufficiency of the subvenient base. They spell out emergence in terms of two other principles which, together with logical sufficiency, constitute minimal physicalism:

(1) The anti-Cartesian principle: there can be no purely mental beings (e.g. substantial souls) because nothing can have a mental property without having a physical property as well.
(2) Mind-body dependence: what mental properties an entity has depend on and are determined by its physical properties (cf. Kim 1996, pp. 9–13).

Naturalists employ (1) and (2) in their analysis of emergence precisely because they want to ensure that emergent properties are located in the naturalist ontology by guaranteeing that such properties require, depend on, and are causally determined by their entirely physical subvenient bases. If most naturalists are correct about this requirement for locating an emergent property in the ontology of N, then the actuality, or even the metaphysical possibility of the instantiation of active power in a pure spirit is a problem for the Harmony Thesis. It is one thing to reject the existence of God and angels. It is another thing altogether to claim that God or angels are metaphysical impossibilities, even if the modal status of such a claim is limited to possible worlds with the same physical particulars, properties, relations, and laws as the actual world.

O'Connor does address the knowledge argument and inverted qualia thought experiments. Regarding the former, he opts for a dualist interpretation of the argument and claims that two features of many mental phenomena are emergent properties causally necessitated by the appropriate physical bases: the phenomenal feature and subjectivity which he interprets as the fact that one can come into contact with a conscious property only by having it (O'Connor 2000, p. 116). What about the apparent contingency of the mental/physical causal link? O'Connor simply denies that all causal necessity must be transparent. He says that there is no good reason to think that when we come to have a scientific understanding of some phenomenon, we will just be able to see that a causal effect had to follow from its cause. In the case of conscious properties, although they are necessitated by their causal bases, we just cannot see the necessity of the causal connection. Regarding inverted qualia, O'Connor adopts the same dismissive strategy, claiming that inverted qualia thought experiments "implausibly drive a wedge between a phenomenal property's qualitative features and its causal role" (O'Connor 2000, p. 120).

O'Connor's rejoinder to these arguments sounds very much like a denial that there is a problem, but the intuitions of contingency that lie behind the various dualist arguments in focus are rooted deep within our prephilosophical intuitions, and surely, there is a burden of proof on O'Connor that is not met by his dismissive strategy.

Four arguments against consciousness as emergent

Four additional considerations cumulatively undercut O'Connor's claim that conscious properties are emergent. First, O'Connor himself admits that "there are no widely accepted working theories that are committed to the existence of emergent properties . . . " (O'Connor 2000, p. 114), and "there is a lack of hard evidence in favor of emergence in areas that are well understood . . . " (O'Connor 2000, p. 115). He does not find this particularly troubling, however, because he believes that our scientific knowledge is so incomplete that the absence of emergent properties is far from empirically established. But the burden of proof lies in the other direction, and the proper conclusion to draw is that, currently, "the hypothesis of emergence" is yet to be justified.

Second, it is false to claim that "there is convincing evidence" (O'Connor 2000, p. 116) that mental properties are emergent. For three reasons, it is difficult and may be impossible to justify their emergence empirically. (1) The emergent hypothesis and substance dualism are empirically equivalent models and no empirical evidence counts in favor of one over the other. (2) To correlate mental and physical properties as a first step toward justifying emergence, one of the two correlates is not available for empirical inspection, and this makes straightforward empirical justification of emergence more difficult. (3) It is only in the case of fairly simple mental states (e.g. specific sorts of pains) that we have any hard evidence of specific mental/physical correlations. There is no evidence whatever that complex mental properties, such as the property thinking-about-the-history-of-skepticism, are correlated with specific base physical properties, much less emergent on them. Part of the problem here is the difficulty of providing criteria for individuating complex mental states in an empirically testable way, a problem that O'Connor himself acknowledges (O'Connor 2000, p. 118). On a fine-grained theory of properties, this may be an impossible task, not just a difficult one. Thus, many strong physicalists adopt a course-grained view of mental properties as a response to inverted qualia arguments, but this move requires that mental properties be identified with functional roles, and it is not available to O'Connor.

Third, even if mental properties are, in some sense, emergent, that does not entail that they are emergent in O'Connor's sense. Recall that for O'Connor, emergent properties have these three features: (1) they are simple, intrinsically characterizable, new kinds of properties; (2) they have their own ontologically basic type of causal influence; and (3) they are causally necessitated by their subvenient physical base.

Roughly, the first two features correspond to what John Searle calls Emergence$_1$ and Emergence$_2$, respectively (Searle 1994, pp. 111–2). Now Searle is typical of those naturalists who accept emergent properties as merely emergence$_1$ and not Emergence$_2$. Since we have seen reasons for this in section one, I will not rehearse them here. But one point needs to be emphasized. O'Connor claims that mental properties are the best examples of emergent properties, since they exhibit subjectivity and a phenomenal nature, and he claims that we have "direct evidence" of emergence in the case of consciousness (O'Connor 2000, p. 114).

I agree that we have direct access to and introspective knowledge by acquaintance of our own mental states, but naturalists such as Searle claim that this "direct evidence" merely justifies conscious properties as Emergence$_1$ and not Emergence$_2$. As I will argue next, the sort of introspective evidence that might be cited to support the claim that some mental properties, especially active power, have their own causal powers also supports substance dualism and, thus, that evidence provides a defeater for the claim that mental properties are emergent. At the very least, this additional introspective evidence goes beyond the sort of direct evidence O'Connor cites to justify consciousness as Emergence$_2$. At best, it merely justifies them as Emergence$_1$.

However, even if this "direct evidence" justifies taking active power to be emergent in the first two senses, it utterly fails to justify the third sense. The vast majority of people agree that in introspection they are completely unaware of anything physical. They have no introspective acquaintance with their brain or any other strictly physical object, or with any subvenient physical properties. When philosophers argue that consciousness is a set of emergent properties, they do not appeal to first-person introspection to justify the claim. No inspection of the brain or any other candidate for the subvenient physical base from either a first- or third-person perspective provides "direct evidence" for treating any conscious property as emergent in sense three.

This is an important conclusion that O'Connor apparently fails to see. In a publication subsequent to *Persons & Causes*, O'Connor acknowledges that:

> [t]he emergentist can and should allow that there is an epistemological presumption against emergentist hypotheses for systems of currently-untested complexity levels *absent special reason to suspect that they are different from run of the mill cases.* (O'Connor & Wong 2005, p. 674)

But right after this concession, O'Connor attempts to refute a claim by Brian McLaughlin to the effect that, while emergence is a coherent concept, it is enormously implausible that there are any such properties, and least for those with ostensible scientific sobriety.

O'Connor's response consists in two claims: (1) a person's experiences and other conscious mental states are *sui generis* simple emergent properties and (2) claim (1) is defeasibly justified by direct first-person awareness of conscious states with an epistemic strength that precludes the *a posteriori* ascription to them of hidden microstructure hidden to introspection. But O'Connor is simply mistaken about this. Direct first-person awareness completely fails to provide any justification whatsoever for his third characterization of emergent properties, and this is the sense he needs to justify conscious properties as emergent in the sense needed for his Harmony Thesis.

Finally, given O'Connor's employment of "direct evidence" to justify the claim that conscious properties are emergent ones, the epistemic grounds for this claim derive from first-person introspection and not from empirical research. As we have just seen, O'Connor insists on this. Given that this evidence provides accurate information about the intrinsic nature of mental properties (his sense one of emergence), and given that we have a fairly good idea of the nature of physical properties, most have seen their connection to be contingent, and that is why naturalists have had such a hard time "locating" them in light of the necessitation condition discussed earlier.

The contingency of the link between mental/physical properties stands in stark contrast to paradigm cases of located macroproperties. Jackson cites macrosolidity, understood as impenetrability, as something easily construed as necessitated by subvenient base traits (e.g. intermolecular forces, lattice structures) (Jackson 1998, pp. 3–4). Jackson also points out that the prescientific notion of macrosolidity as being everywhere dense has been rejected by those who accept N. The reason for this rejection is clear. If real, the latter notion of solidity would be a macroproperty only contingently connected to its microphysical base and, thus, it would not be located in N.

Irreducible mental properties are like the prescientific notion of solidity. Since they cannot be located, our dualistic prescientific conception of them must be revised according to some strict physicalist strategy. If mental properties are emergent, they fail to resemble paradigm cases of located macroproperties (e.g. solidity as impenetrability), and O'Connor has failed to provide an adequate justification for assimilating them to the paradigm cases. Interestingly, he acknowledges that:

> [r]eductionism nowadays is much disparaged. Yet by our lights, the most plausible variety of physicalism is reductionist, as it does not require one to make dubious moves in the underlying metaphysics of physical properties. (O'Connor & Wong 2005, p. 661)

It is no accident that strong physicalism is (and ought to be) the ontology of naturalism precisely because it does not require such dubious moves. For self-reflective positive naturalists, the Constitution Thesis is an essential component that fits naturalism like a hand in a glove.

AGC, the Harmony Thesis, and the epistemic features of O'Connor's case

In contending for his views, O'Connor makes implicit or explicit reference to certain epistemic features of his case both for AGC and the Harmony Thesis. I shall focus on two of these features and argue that, if applied consistently, they place a burden of proof on O'Connor's defense of the Harmony Thesis – specifically, the harmony of AGC and a physical agent – that he has failed to meet: the role of prephilosophical intuitions in his case, and his view of the nature of prephilosophical intuitions about mental properties.

O'Connor and the role of prephilosophical intuitions

In arguing for AGC, O'Connor accepts two important epistemic requirements: (i) one's view of agency should be guided by and justified in light of prephilosophical, commonsense intuitions, which place a burden of proof on views that abandon them; (ii) these intuitions justify beliefs about the nature of human action itself, and not merely about our concept of human action (O'Connor 2000, pp. xii–xiii, 3–5, 42). O'Connor uses these intuitions to place a burden of proof on compatibilists and on critics of the Harmony Thesis. Thus, his task in both areas of debate is to rebut and not refute his interlocutors. Applied to agency, O'Connor claims that incompatibilism is *prima facie* justified by these intuitions, they ground a modal argument for incompatibilism, and compatibilists fail to overturn the argument based on these *prima facie* justified intuitions. Applied to the Harmony Thesis, given N and the prephilosophical intuitive justification of AGC, O'Connor says that the burden is on those who reject the Harmony Thesis and accept the Constitution Thesis. Since the latter is neither entailed by the Causal Unity Thesis nor empirically established, then we are not required to accept it. Failure to meet this burden, coupled with positive grounds for emergent properties (see further discussion), means that there is no good reason to reject the Harmony Thesis.

How does one know one's prephilosophical intuitions have sufficient justification to do the work required by O'Connor's case? There are two features of such intuitions. First, they should be held widely and deeply by normal folk with no ideological axe to grind. Throughout the literature, friends, and foes of incompatibilism acknowledge that it enjoys this sort of intuitive support, and O'Connor makes explicit use of this fact in his case (O'Connor 2000, pp. 4–5; cf. Kane 1996, p. 4; Foster 2001, p. 267). Second, both sides of a dispute employ concepts derived from or based on those intuitions. John Bishop is typical of many compatibilists when he explicitly employs a libertarian concept of agency to develop his own compatibilist model that falls under that concept "closely enough" to be adequate (Bishop 1989, pp. 58, 69, 72, 95–7, 103–4, 114, 120, 126–7, 140–4, 177–80). Bishop allows a libertarian conception of agency to guide the development of his own account, and to be the legitimate source both of counter arguments in the form of thought experiments and of the sense of adequacy for his responses to those counterarguments. Libertarian intuitions seem pervasive in debates about agency.

Both characteristics seem present for intuitions on behalf of substance dualism and against physicalist views of the self. Friends and foes of dualism admit that it is the commonsense view, and the vast majority of people throughout history have been dualists about the self in one form or another. Jaegwon Kim acknowledges that:

> We commonly think that we, as persons, have a mental and bodily dimension. . . . Something like this dualism of personhood, I believe, is common lore shared across most cultures and religious traditions . . . (Kim 2001, p. 30)

Along similar lines, Frank Jackson says that ". . . our folk conception of personal identity is Cartesian in character . . ." (Jackson 1998, p. 45).

Prephilosophical intuitions in support of a substantial, immaterial self are widely and deeply held, and they ground the modal argument for substance dualism. These intuitions seem expressed in the concepts and arguments used by dualists and physicalists. The intelligibility of near-death experiences, arguments from the unity of one's conscious field, thought experiments about personal identity to the effect that the person is merely contingently related to his body or psychological traits, and responses to these thought experiments (e.g. various causal chain analyses of personal identity) seem to employ a substantial, immaterial conception of the self.

O'Connor could respond that in the case of substance dualism, grounds for N justify a rejection of these prephilosophical intuitions, but in light of his own employment of similar prephilosophical intuitions for AGC and the Harmony Thesis, this response seems arbitrary. After all, most naturalists employ N to justify a rejection of the intuitions in support of AGC, a fact that O'Connor acknowledges. Most naturalists agree that prephilosophical intuitions are on the side of AGC and substance dualism, but they adopt a consistent attitude – rejection – toward both sets of intuitions. While strictly consistent with the grounds for N, most naturalists believe that AGC and substance dualism are not as plausible as compatibilism (or noncausal versions of incompatibilism) and physicalism in light of those grounds.

Moreover, just as the Causal Unity Thesis fails to entail the Constitution Thesis and the latter has not been empirically established, so the empirical grounds for N fail to entail or empirically establish a physical agent. If O'Connor thinks otherwise, he is invited to cite the empirical evidence that accomplishes this feat. In the absence of such evidence and in light of his own epistemic characterization of the requirements placed on those who would reject the Harmony Thesis, it is hard to see what O'Connor would say to the same claim made by substance dualists about the epistemic status of physicalism, given the presence of prephilosophical intuitions for substance dualism.

O'Connor and the nature of prephilosophical intuitions

In addition to the role of prephilosophical intuitions in O'Connor's case for AGC and the Harmony Thesis, the nature of those intuitions is also of crucial importance. Philosophers differ about the nature of intuitions, for example, some hold that they are merely dispositions to believe certain things. However, the traditional view of intuitions takes them to be cases of first-person direct awareness of a relevant intentional object reported by way of the phenomenological use of "seems" or "appears." O'Connor seem to agree: intuitions in support of AGC are the way things "seem" to people (O'Connor 2000, p. 4); people have "direct evidence" of the nature of conscious properties themselves. Thus, one has direct first-person access to one's own mental states and, indeed, if this is so, such access seems to provide nondoxastic justification for prephilosophical beliefs about/concepts of mental properties, including the nature of active power. He also claims to experience himself directly bringing about the formation of an intention (O'Connor 2000, p. 124). If one accepts this account of intuitions, then one has the resources to explain why certain beliefs are so widely and deeply held.

But the same claim is often made by dualists regarding intuitions about the self. Stewart Goetz has argued that we are directly aware of ourselves and, on this basis, we are justified in believing substance dualism (see Goetz 2001, pp. 89–104). It is on the basis of such first-person self-awareness that people have the prephilosophical dualist beliefs they do, and this is why these beliefs (or, at least, dualist concepts) play such a regulative role in philosophical arguments about personal identity and related topics.

Of course, it is fashionable to claim that people have direct access to their mental states but not to their selves. Since Hume, the major strategy employed to justify this assertion is the claim that people just are never aware of themselves. I believe that dualists have provided adequate responses to this strategy, but that is beside the present point because I do not believe that O'Connor can avail himself of this strategy. To see why, we need to examine his response to an epistemological objection raised against his version of AGC. The objection is that we cannot know whether any events are produced in the manner that AGC postulates, since agent-caused events would be indistinguishable from ones that were essentially random (O'Connor 2000, pp. 123–4).

O'Connor points out that this Humean type objection would be equally telling against his realist version of event causation (event causes produce their effects). The Humean allows direct evidence for the pattern of relations among events, but not of the causal event bringing about its effect. O'Connor says that in some cases we seem to observe directly the causal connectedness between cause and effect. He illustrates this by pointing out that we do not merely observe the movement of the hammer followed by the movement of the nail; rather, we see the hammer's moving the nail.

Now it is not clear how one can directly see the hammer's moving the nail without directly seeing the hammer. Similarly, it is hard to see how one could directly be aware of one's own self producing an intention to act without being directly aware of one's own self. Indeed, O'Connor acknowledges that:

> ... in the deliberate formation of an intention, the coming to be of my intention doesn't seem to me merely to occur at the conclusion of my deliberation; I seem to experience myself directly bringing it about. (O'Connor 2000, p. 124)

This would seem to imply that people are able to be directly aware of their own selves. If so, and given that prephilosophical intuitions are widely acknowledged to be of a substance dualist sort, the very nature of intuitions as first person forms of direct access seems to offer defeasible justified beliefs of a substance dualist sort.

Perhaps O'Connor has other reasons for rejecting the use of first-person direct awareness of the self as grounds for substance dualism. To my knowledge, he has not addressed the topic in writing. If he does, there seem to be two requirements for such response. First, without begging the question, he is going to have to provide sufficient grounds for rejecting first-person awareness of the self and the role such awareness plays in justifying substance dualism in such a way that he does not undermine his own use of first-person awarenesses as a source of justification for AGC. For example, he cannot simply assert that naturalism makes substance dualism implausible, so we must reject the force of this dualist argument, because the same thing is widely said about the epistemic impact of naturalism on the justification of AGC.

Second, he would need to offer an explanation of the origin and justification of the various dualist intuitions that are a part of O'Connor's own characterization of the agent, one I accept. From where did it come and why we should believe it. I believe there is a good answer to these questions – first-person awareness of the self – but these questions would need to be answered in a way that avoids lending support to substance dualism. For example, it seems implausible to suggest that we have first-person awareness of ourselves as physical substances. If we are physical substances, yet we lack first-person awarenesses that this is so and, in fact, seem to have awarenesses that support substance dualism, we would need to know the source of and justification for dualist intuitions that form an essential part of the self *qua* agent.

The fact is that it does not seem to most folks that they are macrolevel objects. On the contrary, it seems to them from the first-person perspective – the perspective upon which O'Connor draws to justify AGC – that they are mental subjects who fail to be aware of exemplifying any physical properties. The issue then becomes whether there is any good reason to think we are physical objects, although we are not aware of being such. As far as I know, O'Connor never gives us any reason to think we are physical objects, and he must provide such an argument. When he does, he runs the danger of bringing forth considerations of a kind (e.g. from the third-person perspective) that, if persuasive, could also undermine our conviction that we have libertarian freedom. If he simply breaks rank with most people and says that he is, in fact, aware of being a material object by first-person introspection, then this would at best justify locating his view within panpsychism and not within naturalism.

Section Five: Colin McGinn and Mysterian "Naturalism"

Unsatisfied with strong physicalism on the one hand and the various extant naturalist solutions for the origin of consciousness on the other, Colin McGinn has offered the most radical "naturalist" alternative to date (McGinn 1999).[7] It is so bizarre that it is fair to question whether, even if successful, it is a naturalist position in any meaningful sense of the term. In this section, I shall describe and seek to rebut McGinn's position.

McGinn's mysterian "naturalism"

According to McGinn, given the radical difference between mind and matter, due to our epistemic limitations inherited from evolution, there is, *in principle*, no knowable naturalistic solution to the origin of consciousness or its regular correlation with matter that stays within the widely accepted naturalist epistemology and ontology. Nor is there a plausible nonnatural alternative. What is needed is a solution radically different in kind from anything previously offered, one that must meet two conditions: (i) it must be a naturalistic solution; and (ii) it must depict the emergence of consciousness and its correlation with matter as necessary and not contingent facts. More specifically, there must be three kinds of unknowable natural properties that solve the problem. We can unpack McGinn's position by examining four different aspects of his view.

McGinn and property/event dualism

First, McGinn is committed to property/event dualism. He defines consciousness by giving first-person, introspective, ostensive definitions of particular phenomenal states. He also believes that a fairly simple form of the knowledge argument is conclusive.

McGinn on standard naturalist solutions

He also rejects all other naturalist solutions for many of the reasons mentioned in section one: the uniformity of nature, the inadequacy of Darwinian explanations, the centrality for naturalism and inadequacy of combinatorial modes of explanation along with the bottom/up combinatorial processes constituitive of the Grand Story, the acceptance of a necessitation requirement for an adequate naturalist account.

---

7. Unless otherwise noted, my description of McGinn's position is taken from *The Mysterious Flame*. McGinn first thought of his mysterian naturalism in the late 1980s [see his *The Problem of Consciousness* (1991, p. vii; cf. chaps. 1–4)], and his view has remained largely unchanged until the present [see his *Consciousness and its Objects* (2004, reprinted unchanged in 2006, p. 1)].

McGinn on antinaturalist solutions

Third, various antinaturalist solutions must be rejected. He evaluates and rejects three of them: theistic dualism and AC, hyperdualism, and panpsychism. For present purposes, let us examine McGinn's treatment of theistic dualism and AC.

McGinn says that AC is a plausible argument and that there is no plausible naturalist rival outside of his own. But for six reasons, AC is a bad argument. For one thing, if we appeal to a conscious God to explain finite consciousness, we generate a vicious infinite regress for we will have to explain why God Himself is conscious. And if we stop the regress with an unexplainable conscious God, we could just as easily do the same thing by taking finite consciousness as an unexplainable brute fact.

Second, the God hypothesis dignifies consciousness with the word "soul" as an independent thing that uses the body, and thereby generates unanswerable questions that undercut AC: Do rats have souls? Why does God give souls to rats and not worms? Third, theists exaggerate the gap between minds and brains. Mind depends on brain. Why would this be so if mind depends on God? Fourth, the existence of causally powerful substantial souls that are dependent upon brains to which they are contingently connected implies that zombie worlds possible. Now, such a world seems *prima facie* possible, says McGinn, but on further inspection it faces an insurmountable difficulty. It means that consciousness is epiphenomenal and any view that entails epiphenomenalism must be rejected. Epiphenomenalism ensues because if a zombie world is possible if follows that the physical will chug along just the same regardless of whether or not consciousness obtains. Fifth, we do not know how God produces consciousness, so at best AC is a stalemate vis-à-vis naturalism.

Finally, AC gets off the ground only if consciousness is a mystery for which we need an explanation. But, claims McGinn, his account provides a deflationary explanation for why consciousness is a mystery and, in so doing, it becomes obvious that the sort of mystery involved is not of the right kind needed to justify AC.

McGinn's solution

Finally, McGinn offers his own "solution" to the problem. He begins by claiming that while evolutionary processes formed noetic faculties in us apt for doing science, it did not develop faculties capable of doing philosophy. Thus, we have cognitive closure regarding philosophical topics, where an organism has cognitive closure with respect to some domain of knowledge just in case that domain is beyond the organism's faculties to grasp. An area of inquiry in which there is no progress is a good sign of cognitive closure, and philosophy in general, and the mind/body problem in particular are cognitively closed to human faculties due to their limitations that follow from the evolutionary processes that generated them. Thus, the mystery of consciousness would not exist if we did not have the cognitive limitations we do.

What we can do, however, is characterize the kinds of conditions that must be true of any adequate solution: (i) There must be some order underlying the heterogeneous appearances of mind and matter because nature abhors a miracle. (ii) It must be a naturalistic solution. (iii) It must depict the emergence of consciousness and its regular correlation with matter as necessary and not contingent facts. More specifically, there must be three kinds of unknowable natural properties that solve the problem: some general properties of matter that enter into the production of consciousness when assembled into a brain (thus, all matter has the potentiality to underlie consciousness); some natural property of the brain he calls C* that unleashes these general properties under the right conditions; just as the brain must have a hidden unknowable structure that allows consciousness to emerge from it, so consciousness must have a hidden unknowable essence that allows it to be embedded in the brain.

There is one final aspect to McGinn's position that provides a naturalistic solution to the apparent nonspatiality of the mental. According to McGinn, ours is a spatial world, yet conscious states have neither spatial extension nor location. This raises a problem: If the brain is spatial but conscious states are not, how could the brain cause consciousness? This seems like a rupture in the natural order. The nonspatiality of consciousness raises serious problems for emergence and causal interaction. McGinn proffers two solutions to this problem. First, he argues that the Big Bang had to have a cause, this cause "operated" in a state of reality temporally prior to the creation of matter and space, and this reality existed in a nonspatial mode. So the cause of the Big Bang was not spatial or material, yet it obeyed some laws in the prior state. At the Big Bang, we have a transformation from nonspatial to spatial reality, and at the appearance of consciousness we have a converse transformation. The nonspatial dimension continued to exist in matter after the Big Bang, lurking behind the scene until brains evolved, at which time this dimension showed itself again.

McGinn's second solution focuses on our concept of space. Typically, we think we are correct to depict space as a three-dimensional manifold containing extended objects. But perhaps this depiction is wrong. Maybe its not that consciousness is nonspatial; perhaps it is spatial according to the real nature of space that is quite different from the commonsense view. If we define "space" as "whatever is out there as a containing medium of all things," then it may be that the real nature of space allows it to contain consciousness and matter in a natural way. Here the Big Bang was a transformation of space itself and not a transition from nonspace to space.

Critique

I do not believe that McGinn's position will be widely accepted and that for good reason. In this section, I will criticize his evaluation of theistic dualism and AC and reserve discussion of McGinn's view of the mystery of consciousness for latter.

Theistic dualism and AC

McGinn argues that by appealing to God to explain finite consciousness, one generates a vicious infinite regress and if the regress is stopped with divine consciousness as a brute fact, then one could just as easily stop with finite consciousness. This sort of argument has been around a long time and McGinn appears to be ignorant of what many believe is a long-standing, successful rebuttal to it. Let us consider the first horn of McGinn's dilemma. McGinn seems to think that if we acknowledge there is a problem with cases of finite consciousness that must be solved by appealing to other finite consciousness, then this problem generalizes and applies equally to a conscious God. Unfortunately, McGinn is wrong about this and fails to appreciate what motivates the relevant regress and the sort of regress it is.

For one thing, the infinity of the regress is impossible because it involves traversing an actual infinite and, arguably, that cannot be done. To illustrate, one cannot count from one to $\aleph_0$ for no matter how far one has counted, he will still have an infinite number of items to count. Such a task can begin, but it cannot be completed. Moreover, trying to count from $-\aleph_0$ to 0 can neither be completed (it involves the same number of tasks as going from one to $\aleph_0$) nor begun for the following reason: trying to reach any number in the past will itself require an infinite traversal as a preliminary step. Now in a *per se* regress (see further discussion), the transitivity of the relation ordering the regress implies that the dependence among members runs from the earlier to latter members. Thus, such regresses are precisely like traversing from $-\aleph_0$ to 0. Space considerations forbid me to discuss this line of argument further, but in philosophy of religion it is part of what is called the *kalam* cosmological argument. I believe the argument is sound, and I refer the reader to some relevant sources that provide a more thorough evaluation of it than can be done here (cf. Craig & Smith 1993; see also Moreland 2004).

If this is correct, the regress must be finite, and this requires there to be a first member. I shall describe next some necessary conditions that must be satisfied if one is to select an adequate first member. For now, I merely note that it is not an arbitrary decision to stop the regress because it is vicious, indeed.

The first problem with the existence of an infinite regress of the sort McGinn mentions is, as it were, its *length* – it involves traversing an actual infinite series of members. Besides the problem of traversing an actual infinite, there is another problem with the regress that McGinn fails to note: by its very *nature* it is vicious. To see this, let us ask how should "vicious" be characterized here? At least four characterizations have been offered. Roderick Chisholm says that, "One is confronted with a vicious infinite regress when one attempts a task of the following sort: Every step needed to begin the task requires a preliminary step" (Chisholm 1996, p. 53). For example, if the only way to tie together any two things whatever is to connect them with a rope, then one would have to use two ropes to tie the two things to the initial connecting ropes, and use additional ropes to tie them to these subsequent ropes, and so on. According to Chisholm, this is a vicious infinite regress because the task cannot be accomplished.

D. M. Armstrong claims that when a reductive analysis of something contains a covert appeal to the very thing being analyzed, it generates a vicious infinite regress because the analysis does not solve anything, but merely postpones a solution (Armstrong 1978a, pp. 19–21). No advance has been made. He says that this is like a man without funds who writes checks from an empty account to cover his debts, and so on, forever.

Chisholm and Armstrong's analyses are helpful. But far and away, the most sophisticated treatment of regresses, including vicious ones, was provided by Thomas Aquinas and Duns Scotus. According to Thomas Aquinas a vicious regress is a *per se* regress which exhibits two key features (see Brown 1976): (1) it is not just a list of members, but an ordering of members in the sequence; and (2) the relationship among the members of the series is transitive. If a stands in R to b and b in R to c, then a stands in R to c, and so on. According to Aquinas, if there is no first member in the series that simply has the relevant feature in itself, no other member of the series will have that feature, since each subsequent member can only "pass on" that feature if it first receives it.

Consider a chain of people borrowing a typewriter. Whether or not the chain is vicious depends on one's view of the correct description of entities at each stage in the chain. Suppose *a* goes to *b* to borrow a typewriter and *b* complies, claiming to have just what *a* needs. If asked how *b* has a typewriter to loan, he claims to have borrowed it from *c* who, having already borrowed one from *d*, has one to give to *b*. Allegedly, at each stage in the chain, the relevant entity can be described as "a possessor of a typewriter who can loan it to another." Thus, it is alleged, the regress is not vicious.

But it is incomplete to describe each person as "a possessor of a typewriter who can loan it to another." Rather, each person is "a possessor of a typewriter who can loan it to another who first had to borrow it from another." At each stage, the person *qua* lender is such only because he is also a borrower. Thus, given the nature of the series, each stage cannot be adequately described without reference to the earlier stage. Because each member is a borrowing lender, no one will ever get a typewriter unless the regress stops with someone who differs from all the other members of the series in being a lender who just has a typewriter without having to borrow it.

Analogously, because finite conscious beings are contingent, before each such being can give what it has (consciousness) to another, it must first undergo the preliminary step of receiving finite conscious being first. In Armstrong's terms, each member of the chain exhibits the same problematic feature, namely, being a lender of consciousness who must himself "borrow" consciousness from another. In Aquinas' terms, the members of the regress *qua* conscious lenders stand in a transitive relationship to the relevant other members in the chain, so without a member who just has consciousness without lending it, there would be no consciousness.

Finally, Duns Scotus offered detailed analyses of various regresses some of which is relevant for present purposes (Cross 2005, pp. 17–28). According to Scotus, there are two very different sorts of ordered sequences involving causal or other sorts of dependence relations: an essentially ordered or *per se* regress and an accidentally ordered or *per accidens* regress. The former are irreflexive (if reflexive, Scotus says one will have self-causation, which is absurd), asymmetrical (if symmetrical, then a member will be both a cause and an effect of the same member in the series), and, most importantly, transitive. In some essentially ordered regresses, an earlier member actually causes a latter member to cause: either *a* causes effects in *b* sufficient for *b* to cause the relevant effect in *c* (*a* effects *b*) or *a* causes *b*'s causing *c* (*a* affects *b*). In various sorts of *per se* dependency chains, the ordering of dependency is (at least) an ordering of necessary dependency conditions from earlier to latter members in the chain.

Scotus identifies three essentially ordered regresses relevant to our discussion: existence, getting the power to operate, and exercising the power to operate. Scotus' main argument against the infinity of such regresses is crafted to avoid a fallacy of composition (e.g. since each member of the series is dependent, the whole must be dependent). His argument is that there is something in the final effect, the last member of the chain about which we are puzzling and seeking an adequate explanation (existence, causal power, consciousness), that is missing in all the other members precisely as essentially ordered with respect to each other, and that requires a first member which is (1) not a part of the chain and (2) simply has the feature of the final effect in itself without having to get it elsewhere.

But why must we stop with God and not some particular finite conscious being? The decision to stop with God is not arbitrary for this reason. The sort of regress we are considering is one such that in the respect relevant to the ordering of the regress's members, the stopping place must be unique and different from all others. In the typewriter case, the relevant respect is that each member does not simply have a typewriter; he is himself one who must borrow before he lends. The proper stopping place is with a "first mover" who simply has a typewriter with no need to borrow one before lending it. Now, each finite conscious being is contingent in two senses: with respect to its existence and with respect to the fact that consciousness was actualized in it. These types of contingency disqualify finite conscious beings from being the proper first mover. Being a necessary being in both senses, God is such a proper First Mover.

This kind of dialectic occurs frequently in philosophy. In agency theory, an advocate of AGC begins with certain concerns about human action and responsibility, opts for AGC, and confronts a problem, viz., what does the agent do to bring about an action? Desiring to avoid a vicious infinite regress, the advocate of AGC concludes that an agent cause is a first cause, a first mover, an entity that may bring about a change without having to change first or be changed to do so. In this sense, agent causes are *sui generis* compared with ordinary event causes in that the latter are changed changers characterized by passive liabilities; and agents, being characterized by *sui generis* active power, cannot be caused to act freely.

In epistemology, foundational beliefs are discovered to be such that they provide justification for nonfoundational beliefs without having to receive their entire justification from their relationship with other beliefs. In one way or another, foundationalists stop the epistemic regress with an epistemic first mover, for example, a nondoxastic self-presenting property. In ontology, discussions of relations and Bradley's famous regress lead to the notion that relations are discovered to be able to relate relata without having themselves to stand in a different relation to those relata. They are unrelatable relaters. AC is an argument form relevantly analogous to these.

McGinn's second critique of theistic dualism and AC is the claim that it uses "soul" to dignify consciousness, and this generates serious difficulties (do rats have souls and, if so, why rats and not worms?). As it stands, this is not much of an argument. For one thing, it is simply false. AC does not quantify over souls in any of its premises, and Premise (1) launches AC on the basis of the existence of consciousness or its lawlike correlations with the brain.

Second, the question "Why do rats have souls and not worms?" is an ambiguous question. If it is the question "Why would God, if He exists, give souls to rats and not worms?," presumably, the answer would be along the lines of why I painted my dining room walls and not the bathroom yellow: I wanted to. What is so problematic about that? If He exists, presumably, God wanted to create certain things and give them certain accidental attributes, and He did not wish to do so for other possible beings He refrained from creating or giving certain accidental attributes. If, instead, the question is about why some things are conscious and others are not, one could say that this is just part of the nature of different things. It is part of the nature of a rat to be conscious and not part of the nature of, say, a tree or rock. Obviously, such an answer involves a commitment to some form of essentialism, but whether or not essentialism is a plausible metaphysical framework is not specifically a theistic concern. This theistic response could employ "nature" in a variety of ways and still be successful.

Finally, focusing on consciousness and not souls, McGinn may be claiming that there is a sort of arbitrariness about theistic dualism such that it entails that at some point, God rather arbitrarily decided to create beings with consciousness and others without it. In response, the sort of "arbitrariness" that seems to underlie this claim is precisely what one would expect if property dualism is true. On a widely accepted dualist understanding of the knowledge of other minds, one starts with first-person acquaintance of one's own mental states and is justified in attributing to other minds whatever mental states are needed to explain the organism's behavior. Ontologically, an organism either is or is not conscious, it either does or does not have some specific mental state. But epistemologically, as organisms become increasingly disanalogous to humans, one is less and less justified in attributing specific mental states or consciousness itself to the organism. Thus, one is increasingly less justified in such attributions applied to another normal human, a rat, or a worm. As with other cases involving degreed properties (in this case, "being justified to such and such a degree"), sorites-style difficulties surface about drawing precise lines among the relevant ordered entities. However, far from being a problem, this is precisely what one would expect from a dualist perspective and McGinn is mistaken if he thinks otherwise.

McGinn also criticizes theistic dualism and AC on the grounds that, if true, it entails that consciousness depends entirely on God's will but this is not true, since consciousness clearly depends on the brain. Again, McGinn's objection is ambiguous. I can see two interpretations each of which is fairly easy to rebut. His question assumes that if something depends entirely on God, then it will not depend on something else in any sense. But this is a bizarre view of divine providence and God's act of sustaining contingent beings in existence. No matter what the precise theistic formulation of these matters is, theists agree that there is a relevant distinction between primary and secondary causality. For example, just because God created and continually sustains the physical universe and its laws, and is in this sense that upon which they "depend entirely," it hardly follows that lightning does not causally depend on certain antecedent conditions within the cosmos. Various causal relations and dependencies within the created order are consistent with the view that if God had not created and does not continually sustain the universe (or some feature within it), then the universe (or some feature within it) would not exist. Clearly, there is no problem here.

Alternatively, the question may be asking why, if the creation of consciousness is a contingent act, there is a covarying dependence among life forms according to which as brains become less and less complex, consciousness does so as well. Note the sort of question this is. It is a theological question about why God would arrange things in this way. So understood, the question is not a request for a scientific answer or even a distinctively philosophical one. It is a question whose answer requires reference to God's possible intentions and motives for arranging things in this way. As I see it, the question is part of a larger one about why there are bodies in the first place.

What are the adequacy requirements for a theological answer to this question? In my view, we have a situation parallel to the difference between a theodicy and defense regarding the problem of evil for theism. A theodicy aims at providing an account of why God actually permits evil in the world. By contrast, a defense offers no such account but seeks merely to show that atheists have failed to carry their case that evil is inconsistent with the existence of God. A defense seeks to undercut the atheist's argument by providing a possible solution on the grounds that there is a substantial burden of proof on the atheist for which a defense is adequate.

It is hard to see the force of this problem. McGinn would need to give reasons for thinking that the dependency of mind on the brain in the manner specified earlier (and the dependency goes in both directions) is such that there is no reason God would have for creating such a situation. To be successful, McGinn would have to assume that there is no possible reason for God to make things this way. But it is hard to see why this would be the case. The theist could easily hold that God has reasons for doing things this way and even if the details of those reasons are not available to us, the mere fact that God could easily have them is sufficient to undercut this objection.

Moreover, according to a theology of the body that I favor, God created bodies to provide a source of power for living things so they could act in ways independent of God's own exercise of efficient causal power. Bodies provide power for action in the created world. Further, the more complicated an animal's consciousness is, the more complex and finely tuned the body would need to be to be responsive to the fine-graded mental states in causal interaction with it. Consider a form of consciousness with a complexity sufficient to engage in a variety of quite specific actions associated with precise nuances in thought, believe, emotion, desire, and so forth. On this view, if such a consciousness were causally connected to a material object without the physical complexity needed to register in the physical world the appropriate mental complexity, that mental complexity would be wasted. Such a theology of the body is clearly a possible reason God could have for making things the way he has, and it is sufficient for the purposes of defense required to undercut McGinn's objection.

McGinn's fourth criticism of theistic dualism is that, if true, it entails the possibility of zombie worlds that imply an implausible epiphenomenalism regarding conscious states. But the latter entailment is not the case. One could consistently embrace a form of dualism that entails the possibility of zombie worlds, and also believe that causal interaction between consciousness and matter in the actual world is contingent. From this, it follows that an epiphenomenal world is, indeed, a possible world, but it does not follow that the actual world is an epiphenomenal one. One could go on to unpack "brings about" in "mental state M brings about brain state B" in terms of causal necessitation, viz., "M brings about B in all interactionist worlds relevantly similar to the actual world." All this is clearly consistent with zombie worlds.

I am among those dualists who believe that the causal relation (and any other relevant relations, e.g. the emergent supervenient relation construed in noncausal terms) between consciousness and matter is a contingent one. If God wished, He could have created an epiphenomenal world. Inverted qualia worlds, zombie worlds, the metaphysical possibility of body switches, or disembodied existence are part of the case for the contingency of the relevant mind/matter relations. Since McGinn's objection assumes that dualism entails such contingency, I need not defend it in the present dialectic. Rather, I am arguing that if we grant this contingency and the possibility of both zombie and epiphenomenal worlds, it does not follow that our word is an epiphenomenal one. The dualist will hold that as a matter of contingent fact we live in a world of causal interaction and nothing McGinn says threatens this claim.

McGinn's fifth objection is that the theistic solution does not solve anything because it does not tell us *how* God created consciousness. Without providing such a mechanism, the God hypothesis is vacuous and fails to be an advance over a naturalistic explanation which likewise fails to answer the *how* question.

There are two things to be said in response to this argument. First, McGinn's claim simply fails to understand the logic of personal explanation. I will not repeat here our discussion in section two of the nature of personal explanation. I make one simple point: a personal explanation can be epistemically successful without making any reference to a mechanism or other means by which the hypothesized agent brought about the state of affairs in the explanandum. I can explain the existence and precise nature of a certain arrangement of objects on our dinner table by saying that my wife brought it about so we could have an Italian dinner with the Isslers. That explanation is informative (I can tell its Italian food we are having, that we are having the Isslers over and not the Duncans, that my wife did this and not my daughter, that natural processes are inadequate). And the adequacy of such a personal explanation is quite independent of whether or not I know exactly how my wife did it.

There are many sciences that involve formulating criteria for inferring intelligent agent causes to explain certain phenomena and for refraining from inferring such causes. And in these sciences, such an inference is usually both epistemically justified and explanatorily significant completely independently of knowledge as to how the agent brought about the phenomena. In forensic science, the Search for Extraterrestrial Intelligence (SETI), psychology, sociology, and archeology, a scientist can know that an intelligent agent is the best explanation of a sequence involving the first 20 prime numbers in a row or that such and such is an intelligently designed artifact used in a culture's religious sacrifices without having so much as a clue as to how the sequence or artifact was made.

Furthermore, an appeal to a particular epistemic value, in this case to the requirement that a necessary condition for successful explanation is that a theory explains how a certain phenomenon was produced, is question-begging against AC and represents a naive understanding of the role various epistemic values play in adjudicating between rival explanations of some phenomenon.

For one thing, two rivals may solve a problem differently depending on the way each theory depicts the phenomenon to be solved. Thus, the epistemic values for assessing one theory may differ substantially from those relevant to its rival. Thus, it is often more complicated to compare rivals than McGinn seems to assume. It is possible for two rivals to rank the relative merits of epistemic virtues in different ways or even give the same virtue a different meaning or application. Rivals can differ radically about the nature, application, and relative importance of a particular epistemic virtue. Thus, it is question-begging to claim that a criterion P set by one hypothesis should be most important for its rival such that if it fails to satisfy P it is explanatorily inferior.

Finally, sometimes one rival will consider a phenomenon basic and not in need of a solution, empirical or otherwise. It may, therefore, disallow questions about how or why that phenomenon occurs and, thus, can hardly be faulted for not being fruitful in suggesting lines of empirical research for mechanisms whose existence is not postulated by the theory. By way of application, a theistic dualism could take God's creation of consciousness and its precise causal correlation with the brain to be a basic action for which there is no further "how" question to be asked. And the theistic dualist can also claim that, given the nature of personal explanation, the epistemic value of citing a mechanism in answer to a "how" question is not as important as other epistemic values. Thus, failure to answer such a question is not a significant issue in light of its own inner logic. But the same cannot be said for naturalism, and given the way physical explanation works, the importance of answering "how" questions by citing a mechanism is, indeed, quite high. Thus, the naturalist's failure to answer this question is a serious one but the same cannot be said for theistic dualism.

Four problems with mysterian "naturalism"

We come to an evaluation of McGinn's own position – mysterian "naturalism." For at least four reasons, it must be judged a failure. First, given McGinn's agnosticism about the properties that link mind and matter, how can he confidently assert some of their features? How does he know they are nonsensory, prespatial, or spatial in an unknowable way? How can he confidently assert that we are naturally constituted from smoothly meshing materials, as seamless as anything else in nature? How does he know some of these properties underlie all matter? These seem unanswerable.

The only one he proffers is that we must provide a naturalistic solution and all ordinary naturalistic ones either deny consciousness or fail to solve the problem. But given the presence of AC, McGinn's claims are simply question-begging and *ad hoc* according to criteria developed in section two. Indeed, his agnosticism seems to be a convenient way of hiding behind naturalism and avoiding a theistic explanation. Given that theism enjoys a positive degree of justification prior to the problem of consciousness, he should avail himself of the explanatory resources of theism.

In a related fashion, it is sometimes argued, and not without some justification, that attempts to draw a line between what we can and cannot know requires that one must first cross the line to draw it. McGinn comes close to doing the very thing he claims cannot be done. Whether or not one accepts this claim about drawing lines, McGinn's view seems self-refuting. He tells us that we did not evolve with faculties apt for doing philosophy, that when confronted with a lack of progress we should draw the conclusion that we are cognitively closed to the subject matter in question, and so on. Yet McGinn's entire book is a species of philosophical argument, and he explicitly states that his purpose is to develop and defend his viewpoint over against rivals. He also derives philosophical theses (e.g. skeptical theses in areas for which we have cognitive closure) by philosophically studying the history of philosophy, he gives an analysis of the nature of human knowledge, he offers philosophical – not scientific – arguments against positions that rival naturalism. I may be missing something here, but it is hard to avoid the conclusion that McGinn's own project is refuted, or at least undercut by his own views that constitute the core of that very project.

Second, it is not clear that his solution is a version of naturalism. His hypothesized properties cannot be known by employment of the naturalist epistemology, nor are they relevantly similar to the rest of the naturalist ontology. McGinn may appropriately call these "naturalistic" properties in the sense that they are (1) not created by God and (2) are regularly involved in giving rise to consciousness in organisms. However, it is vacuous to call these properties "naturalistic" in the only sense relevant to theistic dualism and AC, namely, as entities whose nature, existence, and activity can be located in a natural ontology and given a naturalistic explanation. Given that naturalism is a worldview that claims superior explanatory power to its rivals, these are bizarre, *sui generis* brute facts on a naturalist view. Indeed, McGinn's ontology is so bizarre that it may be taken as a *reductio* against naturalism if McGinn is correct that no other naturalist solution is available. McGinn's solution is actually closer to an agnostic form of panpsychism than to naturalism, he is clear that panpsychism is a rival to and not a legitimate specification of naturalism.

Third, McGinn does not solve the problem of consciousness, he merely relocates it. Rather than having two radically different entities, he offers us three unknowable properties with radically different aspects, for example, his links contain the potentiality for ordinary spatiality and nonspatiality, for ordinary materiality, and for mentality. Moreover, these aspects of the linking properties are just as contingently related as they seem to be without a linking intermediary. The contingency comes from the nature of mind and matter as naturalists conceive it. It does not remove the contingency to relocate it as two aspects of unknowable intermediaries with both.

Finally, there are difficulties with McGinn's solution to the problem of the nonspatiality of mental states. According to his first option, the Big Bang had to have a cause, this cause "operated" in a state of reality temporally prior to the creation of matter and space, this reality existed in a nonspatial mode, and while the cause of the Big Bang was neither spatial nor material, it still obeyed some laws in the prior state.

There is much in this solution that brings a smile to the theist: the Big Bang had to have a cause, presumably because either events *per se* or those in which something comes-to-be must have causes, the cause is not spatial nor is it material. This cause shares important features with the God of classic theism. At the very least, it is hard to see how the hypothesized state of affairs satisfies the conditions for location in a naturalist ontology specified in section one. The presence of temporality is not sufficient to claim this is a naturalistic state of affairs because on the basis of strong conceivability there are possible worlds in which angels alone exist temporally. As Kant argued, finite consciousness entails temporality, so such worlds are temporal but hardly apt for appropriation by a naturalist.

Nor is the presence of law sufficient. In discussing constituent/whole relations, Edmund Husserl described a host of (*a priori*) laws that he claimed governed the coming-to-be and perishing of various entities, and changes that take place among them (Moreland 2002a). However, these laws are not physical laws of nature. Even if Husserl is wrong, his ontology and many others like it demonstrate that the mere presence of laws that govern change in some purported ontological model is far from sufficient to claim that the model is a naturalistic one. Moreover, it seems reasonable to hold that the nature of a relation is constituted by the nature of its relata – spatial, musical, odor, and logical relations are such because they can relate certain kinds of entities and not others. If this is right, it is hard to see how the laws envisaged by McGinn are natural laws.

Finally, McGinn seems unfamiliar with the *kalam* cosmological argument (see chapter 3). It is safe to say that the argument is sufficiently robust to require inclusion in any discussion of the beginning of the spatiotemporal physical universe. If successful, it justifies the claim that time itself had a beginning that was caused by something that can exist without time. And on the assumption that laws of nature govern temporal processes and, thus, require events to be instantiated, it becomes clear that the cause of the first event was not governed by a law of nature. At the very least, McGinn's speculations regarding his first option are grossly incomplete and, moreover, they open the door for considerations quite favorable to theism.

What about McGinn's second option, that we are wrong to think of space as a three-dimensional manifold containing extended objects? Perhaps the real nature of space is "whatever is out there as a containing medium of all things." If this is correct, then the real nature of space allows it to contain consciousness and matter in a natural way.

I do not have a knockdown argument against this option, but I do find it highly counterintuitive and, in fact, unintelligible. And it may be useful to say why. I begin with an observation about the difference between formal concepts and certain material concepts. In my view, formal concepts are capable of being expressed adequately by way of definite descriptions. To illustrate, the formal concept of a substance is "whatever is an essentially characterized continuant"; the formal concept of justice is "whatever outcome is fair and accords with the maxim 'treat equals equally and unequals unequally'." Functional concepts are good examples of formal concepts. By contrast, material concepts, at least those defined by ostensive definition, are defined by rigid designation. If we limit ourselves to sense perceptible entities with which we may be acquainted, then "red," "sour," and "middle C" seem to express material concepts.

Now I take the notion of extension to be such a material concept. If I am right, then the only intelligible notion of a spatial dimension is the material concept of "extended one-directional magnitude," which must be defined ostensively. Along similar lines, "space" is a material concept defined by acquaintance as "extended three-directional magnitude." I, for one, have no idea what it means to use spatial language to speak of multidimensionality or in the way McGinn does. When a scientist claims that a three-dimensional object can be "*spatially* rotated" into other spatial dimensions, I can give no material content to the claim and, thus, I cannot understand what is being said. Likewise, when McGinn tell us that space is "whatever is *out there* as a *containing medium* of all things," "out there," "containing," and "medium" are either used in the ordinary way characterized earlier, in which case the definition is circular and seems to require ostensive definition to give these terms intelligible content, or else they are used equivocally in which case they are unintelligible, at least to me.

I recognize that physicists talk about a multitude of spatial dimensions. In my view, the scientific notion of an extra dimension of space is a mere mathematical devise, a formal definition with no material content that can intelligibly be ascribed to reality, and theories that employ such language should be understood in antirealist terms. When scientists speak of multidimensionality with respect to space, they say things such as the following: there are millions of dimensions of space; there could be an infinitely small volume; mass and space are literally interchangeable; triangles can be identical to circles; that a one-dimensional line (a string) could literally have clockwise vibrations in 10 dimensions of space and counterclockwise vibrations in 26 space dimensions (Ross 1996). I find such language unintelligible, and while the problem may my lack of imagination, I suspect that others may agree with me.

I have argued that McGinn's position is not as plausible as AC and is not a legitimate version of naturalism. Long ago, Thomas Kuhn taught us that there are certain telltale signs of a paradigm in crisis, among which are the proliferation of epicycles and of rival specifications of the paradigm formulated to preserve that paradigm in the face of stubborn, recalcitrant facts. Especially significant are specifications so bizarre that it is hard to recognize them as specifications of the paradigm. I take McGinn's mysterian "naturalism" to be an indication that naturalism is in serious crisis with respect to consciousness. Kuhn also taught us that as bizarre and *ad hoc* as some of the specifications may be, if there is no rival paradigm, then an advocate of the degenerate paradigm must simply do the best he or she can with the recalcitrant facts and leave it at that. But if there is a plausible rival, a paradigm shift may well be in order. In my view, McGinn's position, coupled with theism and AC as a rival, serve as evidence that such a paradigm shift away from naturalism toward theism is past due.

Conclusion

Strong naturalism/physicalism has been in a period of Kuhnian paradigm crisis for a long time, and physicalist epicycles have multiplied like rabbits in the last two decades. Moreover, the various versions of physicalism are in a stagnating period of stalemate. Increasingly, naturalists are turning to emergentist views of consciousness.

The truth is that naturalism has no plausible way to explain the appearance of emergent mental properties in the cosmos. Ned Block confesses that we have no idea how consciousness could have emerged from nonconscious matter: "we have nothing—zilch—worthy of being called a research programme. . . . Researchers are stumped" (Block 1994, p. 211). John Searle says this is a "leading problem in the biological sciences" (Searle 1995, p. 61). Colin McGinn observes that consciousness seems like "a radical novelty in the universe" (McGinn 1999, p. 14); he wonders how our "technicolour" awareness can "arise from soggy grey matter" (McGinn 1991, pp. 10–1). David Papineau wonders *why* consciousness emerges: "to this question physicalists 'theories of consciousness' seem to provide no answer" (Papineau 1993, p. 119). Papineau's solution is to deny the reality of consciousness as a genuinely mental phenomenon (Papineau 1993, pp. 106, 114–8, 120, 121, 126). He correctly sees that strong physicalism is the only real alternative for a naturalist.

If one is a positive naturalist who embraces emergent mental properties, then he or she should admit defeat as Frank Jackson acknowledges:

> Our primary concern is with physicalism as a doctrine of the *kind* of world we are in. From this perspective, attribute dualism is not more physicalistically acceptable than is substance dualism. (Jackson 1998, p. 6, n. 5)

Emergence, in particular, is a mere name for a problem to be solved, and it is consistent with substance dualism, double-aspect theory, certain forms of personalism, and epiphenomenalism. This is not a result most naturalists will want to accept.

Jaegwon Kim observes that:

> if a whole system of phenomena that are prima facie not among basic physical phenomena resists physical explanation, and especially if we don't even know where or how to begin, it would be time to reexamine one's physicalist commitments. (Kim 1998, p. 96)

For Kim, emergent mental entities are the paradigm case of such a system of phenomena. Not long ago, Kim's advised fellow naturalists to simply admit the irreality of the mental and recognize that naturalism exacts a steep price and cannot be had on the cheap (Kim 1998, chap. 4, especially pp. 118–20).[8] If feigning anesthesia is the price to be paid to retain naturalism, then the price is too high. Fortunately, the theistic argument from consciousness reminds us that it is a price that does not need to be paid.

Further Reading

Armstrong, D. M. (1999) *The Mind-Body Problem: An Opinionated Introduction.* Boulder, CO: Westview Press.

Bealer, G. (1996) On the possibility of philosophical knowledge. In J. E. Tomberlin (ed.), *Philosophical Perspectives 10: Metaphysics*, 1–34. Cambridge, MA: Blackwell.

8. Curiously, Kim has become an emergent epiphenomenal dualist regarding phenomenal consciousness. See his *Physicalism or Something Near Enough* (2005). It is likely that his ontology has many brute facts, a curious situation for one who accepts ontological simplicity as a guide for ontology.

Beauregard, M. and O'Leary, D. (2007) *The Spiritual Brain: A Neuroscientist's Case for the Existence of the Soul*. New York: HarperCollins.

Beilby, J. (ed.) (2002) *Naturalism Defeated? Essays on Plantinga's Evolutionary Argument against Naturalism*. Ithaca, NY: Cornell University Press.

Churchland, P. (1988) *Matter and Consciousness*, rev. edn. Cambridge, MA: MIT Press.

Clayton, P. (2004) *Mind & Emergence*. Oxford: Oxford University Press.

Connell, R. (1988) *Substance and Modern Science*. Houston, TX: Center for Thomistic Studies.

Martin, M. (ed.) (2007) *The Cambridge Companion to Atheism*. Cambridge: Cambridge University Press.

Menuge, A. (2004) *Agents under Fire*. Lanham, MD: Rowman & Littlefield.

Moreland, J. P. (2003) The argument from consciousness. In P. Copan and P. Moser (eds.), *Rationality of Theism*, 204–20. London: Routledge.

Moreland, J. P. (2008) *Consciousness and the Existence of God: A Theistic Argument*. London: Routledge.

Moreland, J. P. and Rae, S. (2000) *Body & Soul*. Downers Grove, IL: InterVarsity Press.

Nagel, T. (1997) *The Last Word*. New York: Oxford University Press.

O'Hear, A. (1997) *Beyond Evolution: Human Nature and the Limits of Evolutionary Explanation*. Oxford: Clarendon.

Robinson, H. (ed.) (1993) *Objections to Physicalism*. Oxford: Clarendon.

Skrbina, D. (2005) *Panpsychism in the West*. Cambridge, MA: MIT Press.

Swinburne, R. (1997) *The Evolution of the Soul*, rev. edn. Oxford: Clarendon Press.

Swinburne, R. (2004) *The Existence of God*, 2nd edn. Oxford: Clarendon Press.

Wagner, S. J. and Wagner, R. (1993) *Naturalism: A Critical Appraisal*. Notre Dame, IN: University of Notre Dame Press.

References

Adams, R. (1992). Flavors, colors, and God. In R. Douglas Geivett and B. Sweetman (eds.), *Contemporary Perspectives on Religious Epistemology*, 225–40. New York Oxford University Press.

Armstrong, D. M. (1978a) *Universals & Scientific Realism Vol. I: Nominalism & Realism*. Cambridge: Cambridge University Press.

Armstrong, D. M. (1978b) Naturalism, materialism, and first philosophy. *Philosophia* 8, 261–76.

Bishop, J. (1989) *Natural Agency*. Cambridge: Cambridge University Press.

Block, N. (1994) Consciousness. In S. D. Guttenplan (ed.), *A Companion to the Philosophy of Mind*, 210–9. Malden, MA: Blackwell.

Brown, P. (1976) Infinite causal regression. In A. Kenny (ed.), *Aquinas: A Collection of Essays*, 214–36. Notre Dame, IN: University of Notre Dame Press.

Burge, T. (1992) Philosophy of language and mind: 1950–1990. *The Philosophical Review* 101: 1, 3–51.

Chisholm, R. M. (1977) *Theory of Knowledge*, 2nd edn. Englewood Cliff, NJ: Prentice-Hall.

Chisholm, R. M. (1989a) *Theory of Knowledge*, 3rd edn. Englewood Cliff, NJ: Prentice-Hall.

Chisholm, R. M. (1989b) *On Metaphysics*. Minneapolis: University of Minnesota Press.

Chisholm, R. M. (1996) *A Realistic Theory of the Categories*. Cambridge: Cambridge University Press.

Churchland, P. (1984) *Matter and Consciousness*. Cambridge, MA: MIT Press.

Craig, W. L. and Smith, Q. (1993) *Theism, Atheism, and Big Bang Cosmology*. Oxford: Clarendon Press.

Cross, R. (2005) *Duns Scotus on God*. Hants, England: Ashgate Publishing Ltd.

Foster, J. (2001) *The Immaterial Self*. London: Routledge.

Goetz, S. (2001) Modal dualism: a critique. In K. Corcoran (ed.), *Soul, Body and Survival*, 89–104. Ithaca, NY: Cornell University Press.

Haldane, J. (1996) The mystery of emergence. *Proceedings of the Aristotelian Society* 96, 261–7.

Hasker, W. (1999) *The Emergent Self.* Ithaca, NY: Cornell University Press.

Herbert, N. (1987) *Quantum Reality.* Garden City, NY: Anchor Press/Doubleday.

Horgan, T. (1993) Nonreductive materialism and the explanatory autonomy of psychology. In S. J. Wagner and R. Warner (eds.), *Naturalism*, 295–320. Notre Dame, IN: University of Notre Dame Press.

Jackson, F. (1998) *From Metaphysics to Ethics: A Defence of Conceptual Analysis.* Oxford: Clarendon Press.

Kane, R. (1996) *The Significance of Free Will.* New York: Oxford.

Kim, J. (1996) *Philosophy of Mind.* Boulder, CO: Westview Press.

Kim, J. (1998) *Mind in a Physical World. An Essay on the Mind-Body Problem and Mental Causation.* Cambridge, MA: MIT Press.

Kim, J. (2001) Lonely souls: causality and substance dualism. In K. Corcoran (ed.), *Soul, Body and Survival*, 30–43. Ithaca, NY: Cornell University Press.

Kim, J. (2005) *Physicalism or Something Near Enough.* Princeton, NJ: Princeton University Press.

Leibniz, G. (1979) Monadology 17. In P. P. Weiner (ed.), *Leibniz Selections*, 533–551. New York: Charles Scribner's Sons.

Locke, J. (1959) *An Essay concerning Human Understanding.* New York: Dover Publications.

Lyons, W. (1995) Introduction. In W. Lyons (ed.), *Modern Philosophy of Mind*, xlv–lv. London: Everyman.

Mackie, J. L. (1982) *The Miracle of Theism.* Oxford: Clarendon Press.

Madell, G. (1988) *Mind and Materialism.* Edinburgh: Edinburgh University Press.

Martin, M. (1990) *Atheism: A Philosophical Justification.* Philadelphia: Temple University Press.

McGinn, C. (1991) *The Problem of Consciousness: Essays toward a Resolution* Oxford: Basil Blackwell.

McGinn, C. (1999) *The Mysterious Flame: Conscious Minds in a Material World.* New York: Basic Books.

McGinn, C. ([2004] 2006) *Consciousness and Its Objects.* Oxford: Clarendon Press.

Moreland, J. P. (1995) Humanness, personhood, and the right to die. *Faith and Philosophy* 12, 95–112.

Moreland, J. P. (1997) Naturalism and libertarian agency. *Philosophy and Theology* 10, 351–81.

Moreland, J. P. (1998a) Locke's parity thesis about thinking matter: a response to Williams. *Religious Studies* 34, 253–9.

Moreland, J. P. (1998b) Should a naturalist be a supervenient physicalist? *Metaphilosophy* 29, 35–57.

Moreland, J. P. (2000) Christian materialism and the parity thesis revisited, *International Philosophical Quarterly* 40, 423–40.

Moreland, J. P. (2001a) Topic neutrality and the parity thesis: a surrejoinder to Williams. *Religious Studies* 37, 93–101.

Moreland, J. P. (2001b) *Universals.* Canada: McGill-Queen's University Press.

Moreland, J. P. (2002a) Naturalism, nominalism, and Husserlian moments. *The Modern Schoolman* 79, 199–216.

Moreland, J. P. (2002b) Timothy O'Connor and the harmony thesis: a critique. *Metaphysica* 3: 2, 5–40.

Moreland, J. P. (2004) A response to a Platonistic and set-theoretic objection to the kalam cosmological argument. *Religious Studies* 39, 373–90.

Moreland, J. P. (2008) *Consciousness and the Existence of God: A Theistic Argument.* London: Routledge.

Moreland, J. P. and Craig, W. L. (eds.) (2000) *Naturalism: A Critical Analysis.* London: Routledge.

Moreland, J. P. and Nielsen, K. (1993) *Does God Exist? The Debate between Theists & Atheists.* Buffalo, NY: Prometheus.

Moreland, J. P. and Wallace, S. (1995) Aquinas vs. Descartes and Locke on the human person and end-of-life ethics. *International Philosophical Quarterly* 35, 319–30.

Nagel, T. (1986) *The View from Nowhere*. New York: Oxford.

O'Connor, T. (1994) Emergent properties. *American Philosophical Quarterly* 31, 91–104.

O'Connor, T. (2000) *Persons & Causes*. New York: Oxford University Press.

O'Connor, T. (2001) Causality, mind, and free will. In K. Corcoran (ed.), *Soul, Body, and Survival: Essays on the Metaphysics of Human Persons*, 44–58. Ithaca, NY: Cornell University Press.

O'Connor, T. and Jacobs, J. D. (2003) Emergent individuals. *The Philosophical Quarterly* 53, 540–55.

O'Connor, T. and Wong, H. Y. (2005) The metaphysics of emergence. *Nous* 39: 4, 658–78.

Oppy, G. (2006) *Arguing about Gods*. Cambridge: Cambridge University Press.

Papineau, D. (1993) *Philosophical Naturalism*. Oxford: Blackwell.

Rosenberg, A. (1996) A field guide to recent species of naturalism. *British Journal for the Philosophy of Science* 47, 1–29.

Ross, H. (1996) *Beyond the Cosmos: The Extra-Dimensionality of God*. Colorado Springs, CO: NavPress.

Searle, J. (1994) *The Rediscovery of the Mind*. Cambridge, MA: MIT Press.

Searle, J. (1995) The mystery of consciousness: part II. *New York Review of Books* 16, 60–6.

Searle, J. (2004) *Mind: A Brief Introduction*. Oxford: Oxford University Press.

Sellars, W. (1963) *Science, Perception, and Reality*. London: Routledge & Kegan Paul.

Skinner, B. F. (1990) Can psychology be a science of mind? *American Psychologist* 45, 1206–10.

Strawson, G. (1986) *Freedom and Belief*. Oxford: Clarendon Press.

Swinburne, R. (1979) *The Existence of God*. Oxford: Clarendon.

Swinburne, R. (1986) *The Evolution of the Soul*. Oxford: Clarendon.

Williams, C. (1996) Christian materialism and the parity thesis. *International Journal for Philosophy of Religion* 39, 1–14.

Wright, C. (2002) The conceivability of naturalism. In T. S. Gendler and J. Hawthorne (eds.), *Conceivability and Possibility*, 401–39. Oxford: Clarendon.

Yolton, J. W. (1983) *Thinking Matter: Materialism in Eighteenth-Century Britain*. Minneapolis: University of Minnesota Press.

6

The Argument from Reason

VICTOR REPPERT

Introduction

In this chapter, I will be considering the argument from reason. The argument, as we shall see, takes a number of forms, but in all instances it attempts to show that the necessary conditions of logical and mathematical reasoning, which undergird the natural sciences as a human activity, require the rejection of all broadly materialist worldviews. I will begin by examining the nature of the argument, identifying the central characteristics of a materialist worldview. In so doing, I will examine the general problem of materialism, and how the argument from reason points to a single aspect of a broader problem. Second, I will examine the argument's history, including the famous Lewis–Anscombe controversy. In so doing, I will indicate how the argument from reason can surmount Anscombe's objections. I will also explain the transcendental structure of the argument. Third, I will examine three subarguments: the argument from intentionality, the argument from mental causation, and the argument from the psychological relevance of logical laws, showing how these demonstrate serious and unsolved difficulties for materialism. Finally, I will examine some popular objections and show that these objections do not refute the argument.

The Nature of the Argument

Materialistic and mentalist worldviews

"In the beginning was the word." Although this statement, in its context, is laden with Christological implications, we can also use this statement to illustrate a central feature of various worldviews, including Christian theism. The central idea is that fundamental to reality is that which is intelligible and rational. The metaphysical systems of Plato, Aristotle and the Stoics, Hindu pantheism, and Confucian philosophy as well, share this essential conception, as do the metaphysics of Spinoza and absolute idealism. The intelligible is fundamental to reality, the unintelligible is, perhaps, a by-product of the created order, or perhaps a product of our own ignorance and lack of understanding.

We might describe these worldviews as mentalistic worldviews. The mental is fundamental to reality; the nonmental is perhaps a creation, or perhaps a product of ignorance. Reality in mentalistic worldviews has a top-down character to it. The higher, mental levels create the lower levels, or the lower levels emanate from the higher levels. Alternatively, perhaps the lower levels are an illusion generated by the higher levels.

As science has progressed for the last few centuries, a move away from this kind of mentalistic worldview has emerged. According to broadly materialistic worldviews, it would be appropriate to say that in the beginning the word was not. Reason and intelligence are the by-product of centuries of evolution. As the higher primates evolved, they developed large brains, which provided them with true knowledge of the world around us, and this was an effective survival tool for them.

A good deal of debate within Western philosophy between worldviews has taken place between broadly mentalistic and broadly materialistic worldviews. (Sometimes people use the word naturalistic here, but for purposes of this discussion "broadly materialistic" will encompass all doctrines, that one could plausibly call naturalistic.) Christian theism has been the most popular, although by no means the only mentalistic worldview. Among broadly materialistic worldviews, there are options as well. Some proponents of material-istic views are eliminativist with respect to certain features of the mental lives that we commonsensically suppose ourselves to have. Other people in the materialistic camp main-tain that we can account for many aspects of our mental lives through a reductive analysis of mind to the material. Still others believe that we can maintain a materialistic worldview by claiming that although we cannot reduce the mind to the material, the mind supervenes on the physical level.

Nevertheless, I am convinced that a broadly materialist view of the world must possess three essential features. First, for a worldview to be materialistic, there must be a mecha-nistic base level. Now by mechanistic I do not mean necessarily deterministic. There can be brute chance at the basic level of reality in a mechanistic worldview. However, the level of what I will call "basic physics" is free of purpose, free of meaning or intentionality, free of normativity, and free of subjectivity. If one is operating within a materialistic framework, then one cannot attribute purpose to what happens at the basic level. Purpose talk may be appropriate for macrosystems, but it is a purpose that is ultimately the product of a pur-poseless basic physics. Second, what something means cannot be an element of reality, as it appears at the most basic level. Third, there is nothing normative about basic physics. We can never say that some particle of matter is doing what it is doing because it ought to be doing that. Rocks in an avalanche do not go where they go because it would be a good idea to go there. Finally, basic physics is lacking in subjectivity. The basic elements of the universe have no "points of view," and no subjective experience. Consciousness, if it exists, must be a "macro" feature of basic elements massed together.

Second, the level of basic physics must be causally closed. That is, if a physical event has a cause at time t, then it has a physical cause at time t. Even that cause is not a deter-mining cause; there cannot be something nonphysical that plays a role in producing a physical event. If you knew everything about the physical level (the laws and the facts) before an event occurred, you could add nothing to your ability to predict where the particles will be in the future by knowing anything about anything outside of basic physics.

Third, whatever is not physical, at least if it is in space and time, must supervene on the physical. Given the physical, everything else is a necessary consequence. In short, what the world is at bottom is a mindless system of events at the level of fundamental particles, and everything else that exists must exist in virtue of what is going on at that basic level. This understanding of a broadly materialist worldview is not a tendentiously defined form of reductionism; it is what most people who would regard themselves as being in the broadly materialist camp would agree with, a sort of "minimal materialism." Not only that, but I maintain that any worldview that could reasonably be called "naturalistic" is going to have these features, and the difficulties that I will be advancing against a "broadly materialist" worldview thus defined will be a difficulty that will exist for any kind of naturalism that I can think of.

A metamodel for philosophical arguments

Before launching into the discussion of the argument from reason, some preamble about what we can expect philosophical arguments to do is in order. To do this we must consider the scope and limits of arguments. What at maximum one can hope for, in presenting an argument, is that the argument will be a decisive argument in favor of one's conclusion. A decisive argument is an argument so strong that, with respect to all inquirers, the argument is such that they ought to embrace the conclusion. Even when a decisive argument is present, some may remain unpersuaded, but these are cases of irrationality.

The difficulty here is that by this standard very few philosophical arguments can possibly succeed. This is largely because in assessing the question of, say, whether God exists, numerous considerations are relevant. Since we can concentrate on only one argument at a time, it is easy to get "tunnel vision" and consider only the piece of evidence that the argument puts forward. However, a person weighing the truth of theism must consider the total evidence. Therefore, I propose to advance a different concept of what an argument can do. I will assume, for the sake of argument, which people will differ as to their initial probabilities concerning the probability that God exists. The question I will then pose is whether the phenomenon picked out by the argument makes theism more likely, or makes atheism more likely. If it makes theism more likely to be true than it would otherwise be before we started thinking about the phenomenon in question, then the argument carries some weight in support of theism. If it makes atheism more likely, then it provides inductive support for atheism.

The model I am proposing is a Bayesian model with a subjectivist theory of prior probabilities. We begin by asking ourselves how likely we thought theism was before we started thinking about the argument in question. We then ask how likely the phenomenon is to exist given the hypothesis of theism. We then ask how likely the phenomenon is to exist whether or not theism is true. If the phenomenon is more likely to exist given theism than it is to exist whether or not theism is true, then the argument carries some inductive weight in favor of theism.

I should add that one could be an atheist and admit that there are some facts in the world that confirm theism. You can also be a theist and maintain that some atheistic arguments enhance the epistemic status of atheism. Some theists have made just this sort of claim on behalf of the argument from evil. That is, they are prepared to concede that the argument from evil does provide some epistemic support for atheism, but not enough epistemic support to make atheists out of them.

The argument from reason and natural theology

We might ask the following question: in what sense is the argument from reason a piece of natural theology? The job of natural theology is supposed to be to provide epistemic support for theism. However, the argument from reason, at best, argues that the ultimate causes of the universe are mental and not physical. This is, of course, consistent with various worldviews that other than traditional theism, such as pantheism or idealism.

It is a good idea to look at what happened in the case of the argument from reason's best-known defender, C. S. Lewis, to see how the argument contributed to his coming to belief in God. Lewis had been what philosophers of the time called a "realist," accepting the world of sense experience and science as rock-bottom reality. Largely through conversations with Owen Barfield, he became convinced that this worldview was inconsistent with the claims we make on behalf of our own reasoning processes (Lewis 1955, p. 208). In response to this, however, Lewis became not a theist but an absolute idealist. It was only later that Lewis rejected absolute idealism in favor of theism, and only after that that he became a Christian (Lewis 1955, pp. 212–29).

So, did the argument from reason that Lewis accepted make theism more likely in his mind? It certainly did. In his mind, it gave him a reason to reject his previously held naturalism. Now you might not think of absolute idealism as an atheistic worldview, but it does deny the existence of the theistic God as traditionally understood. However, this considerably narrowed the playing field.

In fact, most arguments for theism actually establish some attributes of the theistic God, but very often they do not establish the existence of all such attributes. Cosmological arguments establish the existence of a cause of the universe, but they do not establish the existence of a designer or establish anything with respect to the moral character of the being they prove. So while the result that the argument from reason seeks to establish is a substantial one, it is not one that establishes theism uniquely even if it is successful.

Consider the following argument:

1   Either at least some of the fundamental causes of the universes are more like a mind than anything else, or they are not.
2   If they are not, then it is either impossible or extremely improbable that reason should emerge.
3   All things being equal, worldviews that render it impossible or extremely improbable that reason should emerge should be rejected in favor of worldviews according to which it is not impossible and not improbable that reason should emerge.
4   Therefore, we have a good reason to reject all worldviews that reject the claim that the fundamental causes of the universe are more like a mind than anything else.

Now if you want to hold out the idea that an idealist worldview is nevertheless atheistic, then my argument merely serves to eliminate one of the atheistic options. However, suppose someone originally thinks that the likelihoods are as follows:

Naturalism, 50 percent likely to be true
Idealism, 25 percent likely to be true
Theism, 25 percent likely to be true

In addition, suppose that someone accepts a version of the argument from reason, and as a result, naturalism drops 30 percentage points. Then those points have to be divided among theism and idealism. Therefore, the epistemic status of theism is enhanced by the argument from reason, if the argument is successful in defeating naturalism.

The general problem of materialism

The argument from reason is best understood as an instance of what I call the general problem with materialism. The difficulty here is that the materialist holds, at the rock-bottom level, that the universe is an empty universe. As Lewis observes:

> The process whereby man has come to know the universe is from one point of view extremely complicated; from another it is alarmingly simple. We can observe a single one-way progression. At the outset, the universe appears packed with will, intelligence, life, and positive qualities; every tree is a nymph and every planet a god. Man himself is akin to the gods. The advance gradually empties this rich and genial universe, first of its gods, then of its colours, smells, sounds and tastes, finally of solidity itself as solidity was originally imagined. As these items are taken from the world, they are transferred to the subjective side of the account: classified as our sensations, thoughts, images or emotions. The Subject becomes gorged, inflated, at the expense of the Object. But the matter does not rest there. The same method which has emptied the world now proceeds to empty ourselves. The masters of the method soon announce that we were just mistaken (and mistaken in much the same way) when we attributed "souls" or "selves" or "minds" to human organisms, as when we attributed Dryads to the trees. Animism, apparently, begins at home. We, who have personified all other things, turn out to be ourselves mere personifications. Man is indeed akin to the gods, that is, he is no less phantasmal than they. Just as the Dryad is a "ghost," an abbreviated symbol for certain verifiable facts about his behaviour: a symbol mistaken for a thing. And just as we have been broken of our bad habit of personifying trees, so we must now be broken of our habit of personifying men; a reform already effected in the political field. There never was a Subjective account into which we could transfer the items which the Subject had lost. There is no "consciousness" to contain, as images or private experiences, all the lost gods, colours, and concepts. Consciousness is "not the sort of noun that can be used that way." (Lewis 1986, pp. 81–2)

When Lewis says the universe is empty, he means that it is empty of many of the things that are part of our normal existence. As I indicated, at the rock-bottom level, reality is free of normativity, free of subjectivity, free of meaning, and free of purpose. All of these features of what makes life interesting for us are, on a materialist view, late products of the struggle for survival.

On the materialist view, purpose must reduce to Darwinian function. The purposeless motion of matter through space produced beings whose faculties perform functions that enhance their capacity to survive and pass on their genes. The physical is, on even the broadest of materialist views, a closed, nonpurposive system, and any purpose that arises in such a world must be a by-product of what, in the final analysis, lacks purpose. As Daniel Dennett puts it,

> Psychology of course must not be question-begging. It must not explain intelligence in terms of intelligence, for instance assuming responsibility for the existence of intelligence to the munificence of an intelligent creator, or by putting clever homunculi at the control panels of

the nervous system. If this were the best psychology could do, the psychology could not to the job assigned to it. (Dennett 1976, p. 171)

In the final analysis, "purpose" exists in the world not because there is, ultimately, any intended purpose for anything, but rather because things serve Darwinian functions. The claim that this type of analysis fails to adequately capture the kinds of purposiveness that exist provides the basis for arguments from design based on, for example, irreducible complexity.

Just as clearly, according to materialist worldviews, reality is free of subjectivity. The facts about the physical world are objective facts that are not relative to anyone's subjectivity. Moreover, once again, arguments from consciousness are advanced to try to show that a physicalist perspective on the world is going to leave out subjective inner states. Hence, we have arguments that point out that when all the physical facts about pain are given, we do not seem to have the grounding for, say, the state of what it is like to be in pain. We can imagine a possible world in which all the physical states obtain but whatever it is like to be in pain is missing. Arguments from consciousness arise from these considerations.

Moreover, there is the fact that normativity is absent at the physical level. There is the notorious difficulty of getting an "ought" from an "is." Let us begin with all the naturalistic facts about, let us say, the homicides of Ted Bundy. We can include the physical transformations that took place at that time, the chemical changes, the biology of the death process in each of these murders, the psychological state of the killer and his victims, the sociology how membership in this or that social group might make one more likely to be a serial killer of a serial killer victim, and so on. From all of this, can we conclude that these homicides were morally reprehensible acts? We might know that most people believe them to be morally reprehensible acts, but whether they are reprehensible acts or not does not follow from any of this information. So, if all facts supervene on the physical facts, how can it be true that these actions were morally wrong?

However, there are other types of norms. In addition to the norms of morality, there are the norms of rationality. Some patterns of reasoning are correct and others are not correct. We ought to draw the conclusion if we accept the premises of a valid argument, and it is not the case that we ought to draw the conclusion of an argument if the argument is invalid. Some people have raised the question of how these norms can exist if naturalism is true. As William Lycan observed,

It's interesting that this parallel [between ethics and epistemology] goes generally unremarked. Moral subjectivism, relativism, emotivism, etc. are rife among both philosophers and ordinary people, yet very few of these same people would think even for a moment of denying the objectivity of epistemic value; that is, of attacking the reality of the distinction between reasonable and unreasonable belief. I wonder why that is? (Lycan 1985, p. 137)

Hence, there are antimaterialist arguments that ask how it is possible for rational norms to exist. Thomas Nagel wrote,

Reason, if there is such a thing, can serve as a court of appeal not only against the received opinions and habits of our community, but also against the peculiarities of our personal perspective. It is something each individual can find within himself, but at the same time has universal authority. Reason provides, mysteriously, a way of distancing oneself from common opinion and received practices that is not a mere elevation of individuality—not a determination to express one's idiosyncratic self rather than go along with everyone else. Whoever appeals to reason purports to discover a source of authority within himself that is not merely personal, societal, but universal, and that should persuade others who are willing to listen to it. (Nagel 1997, p. 3)

Further, on the face of things at least, physical states are not about other physical states. Physics suggests that particles and states have relations to one another, but it does not seem to be part of physics to say that one state is about another state. Hence, arguments from intentionality are advanced to challenge materialistic worldviews. What is more, there is certainly no propositional content at the physical level. It does seem to be possible to entertain a proposition. Here I am not even talking about belief (I think that p is true) or desire (I want p to be true) but just the process of entertaining the proposition and knowing what it means. It seems possible for propositions to be true or false, and for certain propositions to follow from others.

Error theories and the argument from reason

At this point I am not endorsing these arguments; I am only saying that arguments of this sort are possible. One way for the skeptic to respond to those arguments is with an error theory. We think there are objective moral norms, but we are mistaken: moral norms are subjective. We think conscious, subjective states really exist, but strictly speaking, they do not. As Susan Blackmore puts it:

> ... each illusory self is a construct of the memetic world in which it successfully competes. Each selfplex gives rise to ordinary human consciousness based on the false idea that there is someone inside who is in charge. (Blackmore 1999, p. 236)

By referring to the self as illusory, she is saying that what we ordinarily think of as consciousness does not exist. As we think of consciousness, we think of some center in which all mental states inhere. According to the *Stanford Encyclopedia of Philosophy*, consciousness has these characteristics: a first-person character, a qualitative character, a phenomenal structure, subjectivity, a self-perspectival organization, unity, intentionality, and dynamic flow (Van Gulick 2007). Error theories of consciousness such as Blackmore's – instead of showing how these aspects of consciousness can exist in a materialist world – suggest that we are mistaken in thinking that these elements which we thought of as consciousness really exist.

Defenders of materialism usually use three general types of arguments to criticize the family of arguments I presented earlier. They use Error replies if they think the item that the antimaterialist is setting up for explanation can be denied. They use Reconciliation objections if they suppose that the item in question can be fitted within a materialist ontology. Moreover, they also use Inadequacy objections to argue that whatever difficulties there may be in explaining the matter in materialist terms, it does not get us any better explanations if we accept some mentalistic worldview such as theism. We can see this typology at work in responses to the argument from objective moral values. Materialist critics of the moral argument can argue that there is really no objective morality, they can say objective morality is compatible with materialism, or they can use arguments such as the Euthyphro dilemma to argue that whatever we cannot explain about morality in materialist terms cannot better be explained by appealing to nonmaterial entities such as God.

However, it is important to notice something about materialist philosophies. They not only believe that the world is material, they also perforce believe that the truth about that material world can be discovered, and is being discovered, by people in the sciences. Furthermore, there are philosophical arguments that ought to persuade people to eschew mentalistic worldviews in favor of materialistic ones. They do think that we can better discover the nature of the world by observation and experimentation than by reading tea leaves. Arguments from reason are arguments that appeal to necessary conditions of rational thought and inquiry. Thus, they have what on the face of things is an advantage over other arguments, in that they have a built-in defense against error theory responses. If there is no truth, they cannot say that materialism is true. If there are no beliefs, then they cannot say we ought to believe that materialism is true. If there is no mental causation, then they cannot say that our beliefs ought to be based on supporting evidence. If there are no logical laws, then we cannot say that the argument from evil is a good argument. If our rational faculties as a whole are unreliable, then we cannot argue that religious beliefs are formed by irrational belief-producing mechanisms. Hence, arguments from reason have what I call a transcendental impact – that is, appeal to things that, if denied, undermine the most fundamental convictions of philosophical materialists. There cannot be a scientific proof that scientists do not exist. That would undermine the scientific enterprise that constitutes the very foundation of materialism.

The reality of rational inference

The argument from reason focuses on cases where we infer one proposition from another proposition. I will not deny that there are other ways of acquiring true and justified beliefs. Many have argued that, for example, I can have a justified belief that my eyeglasses are here on my computer table without drawing any inferences at all, but rather, just by perceiving my glasses. I should add that this "direct realist" view of perception is by no means universal among philosophers; there are many who maintain that what we are directly aware of are "sense data" and that we infer physical objects from sense data. John Beversluis, for example, has argued that Lewis's argument from reason relies on an inference-from-sense-data theory of the knowledge of physical objects, and fails unless that theory is defensible (Beversluis 2007, pp. 148–9). However, even if Lewis himself held such a position, (and I think he probably did, although the evidence is less than crystal clear), the argument does not *need* to rely on inferential theories of sensory knowledge. The reason that even if we concede that there is some knowledge that is not inferred from sensations and therefore does not depend on the validity of reasoning, advocates of materialistic worldviews are committed to the existence of *at least some* inferential knowledge. They must hold that *scientists* make rational and mathematical inferences, they must hold that they accept materialism because there is good reason to believe it. Even if we accept the "direct realist" view with respect to physical objects, there is a whole lot of rationally inferred knowledge that no materialist can dare deny, on pain of undermining both science and naturalism. The claim that rational inferences are essential to the possibility of science even though there maybe other sources of justified beliefs is sometimes overlooked by persons who respond to the argument from reason, so I will name this argument the critical subset argument. Thus, I do not need to agree with C. S. Lewis that "*All* possible knowledge . . . depends on the validity of reasoning" (italics added). Even if only a subclass of knowledge depends on the validity of reasoning, that subclass of knowledge is a subclass critical to the materialist's enterprise.

Materialists maintain, of course, that what is real are the sorts of things that lend themselves to scientific analysis, but they also cannot escape believing that there are scientists and mathematicians whose minds are capable of performing those scientific analyses. Consider, for example, a doctrine I call "hyper-Freudianism," the view that all beliefs are the product on unconscious drives, and that no one believes anything they believe for the reasons that they think they believe it. An atheist could say of the theist, "You think you believe in God because of the arguments of Christian apologists, but you really believe it because you are searching for a cosmic father figure to calm your fears." Alternatively, a theist can say "You think you are an atheist because of the evidence of evolution and the problem of evil, but I know that you just want to kill your father." However, this, of course, can be pushed still further to include all beliefs. However, that is just the trouble, if it is pushed that far, then it has to be extended to the belief in hyper-Freudianism itself. If someone tries to present evidence for hyper-Freudianism, he is doing something that can only be done if hyper-Freudianism is false.

Consider the following classic syllogism:

1   All men are mortal.
2   Socrates is a man.
3   Therefore, Socrates is mortal.

If it is a consequence of naturalism that nothing like this ever happens, that no one ever draws these types of conclusions from premises, then the belief that naturalism is true is in a lot of trouble.

Consider, for example, the role of mathematics in science. Mathematical inferences were critical in making it possible for Newton to discover the theory of gravity and Einstein to discover relativity. If we believe that natural science gets the truth about the world, then we must not deny that mathematical inferences exist. If we are persuaded that the argument from evil is a good argument against theism, then we must not accept a position that entails that no one is ever persuaded by an argument.

The History of the Argument

Antecedents of Lewis's argument from reason

The argument from reason did not originate with Lewis. Something like it can be traced all the way back to Plato, and Augustine had an argument that said that our knowledge of eternal and necessary truths showed that God exists. Descartes maintained that the higher rational processes of human beings could not be accounted for in materialistic terms, and while Kant denied that these considerations provided adequate proof of the immortality of the soul, he did think they were sufficient to rule out any materialist account of the mind (Allison 1989). However, naturalism or materialism as a force in Western philosophy increased considerably in 1859, when Charles Darwin published the *Origin of Species*.

The earliest post-Darwinian presentation of the Argument from Reason that I am familiar with, and one that bears a lot of similarities to Lewis's argument, is found in Prime

Minister Arthur Balfour's *The Foundations of Belief*. Lewis never mentions *The Foundations of Belief* in his writings, but he does say in one place that Balfour's subsequent book *Theism and Humanism* is "a book too little read (Balfour 1906, 1915; Lewis, 1962)." Also, J. B, Pratt, in his book *Matter and Spirit*, presented a version of the argument from reason as an argument for mind–body dualism (Pratt 1922).

Lewis's first edition argument

In the first edition of *Miracles*, Lewis presents the version of the argument from reason that Anscombe criticized. We can formalize it as follows:

1 No thought is valid if it can be fully explained as the result of irrational causes.
2 If naturalism is true, then all beliefs can be explained in terms of irrational causes.
3 Therefore, if naturalism is true, then no thought is valid.
4 If no thought is valid, then the thought "materialism is true" is not valid.
5 Therefore, if materialism is true, then the belief "materialism is true" is not valid.
6 A thesis whose truth entails the invalidity of the belief that it is true ought to be rejected, and its denial ought to be accepted.
7 Therefore, naturalism ought to be rejected, and its denial accepted. (Lewis 1947, pp. 26–31)

This is the argument that drew the criticisms of Roman Catholic philosopher and Wittgenstein student Elizabeth Anscombe. This critique is significant because of the way in which it forced Lewis to develop and refine his arguments. We will examine three challenges Anscombe put to Lewis's argument to see how the argument needs to be refined to meet the challenges.

Anscombe's first objection: irrational versus nonrational

Is it correct for Lewis to talk about physically caused events as having irrational causes? Irrational beliefs, one would think, are beliefs that are formed in ways that conflict with reason: wishful thinking, for example, or with fallacious arguments. On the other hand, when we speak of a thought having a nonrational cause, we need not be thinking that there is any conflict with reason (Anscombe 1981, pp. 224–5).

This distinction, while legitimate, is hardly sufficient to refute Lewis's argument. Remember, a materialist philosopher not only believes that some beliefs are justified; a materialist, if she thinks that science is true, thinks that some people do draw correct logical and mathematical inferences. While not all justified beliefs are inferred from other beliefs, a contemporary materialist is not in a position to maintain that beliefs are formed as a result of rational inferences.

For that reason, it is possible to restate Lewis's argument in such a way that it does not make reference to irrational causes, and indeed in Lewis's revised chapter the phrase "irrational causes" does not appear (Lewis's argument was against naturalism, but I am presenting it here as an argument against materialism, keeping in mind my previous claim that all recognizable forms of naturalism suffer from the same kind of difficulties as does materialism).

1 No belief is rationally inferred if it can be fully explained in terms of nonrational causes.

2   If materialism is true, then all beliefs can be fully explained in terms of nonrational causes.
3   Therefore, if materialism is true, then no belief is rationally inferred.
4   If any thesis entails the conclusion that no belief is rationally inferred, then it should be accepted and its denial accepted.
5   Therefore, materialism should be rejected and its denial accepted.

However, it seems that I could go a bit farther in defending Lewis against Anscombe's critique here. In my 1989 essay "The Lewis-Anscombe Controversy: A Discussion of the Issues," and in my work *C. S. Lewis's Dangerous Idea* (Reppert 2003a), I discussed Anscombe's insistence that Lewis distinguish between irrational causes and nonrational causes. Irrational causes would be things such as being bitten by a black dog as a child gives you a complex and causes you to believe that all black dogs are dangerous. Nonrational causes are physical events or physical causes. Interestingly enough, the following passage from *The Abolition of Man*, (written before Anscombe criticized Lewis) makes the distinction that Anscombe insisted upon between nonrational and irrational, but in this passage Lewis instead distinguishes two senses of irrational:

> Now the emotion, thus considered by itself, cannot be either in agreement or disagreement with Reason. It is irrational not as a paralogism is irrational, but as a physical event is irrational: it does not rise even to the dignity of error. (Lewis 1947, p. 30)

Now, in this passage, Lewis draws the exact distinction on which Anscombe insisted. The only difference here is that Lewis distinguishes two senses of the term "irrational" instead of distinguishing between irrational and nonrational. Nevertheless, was Lewis's usage of the term "irrational" wrong? Going to a dictionary definition of "irrational," I think not. The first dictionary entry for "irrational" in www.dictionary.com is "without the faculty of reason; deprived of reason." Nevertheless, Lewis changed from "irrational" to "nonrational" to accommodate Anscombe's criticism. However, physical causes are, by nature, irrational causes in the sense presented in the dictionary definition, so his use of "irrational" was not mistaken.

Anscombe's second objection: paradigm cases and skeptical threats

Anscombe also objected to the idea that Lewis had argued that, if naturalism were true, then reasoning would not be valid. She asks, "What can you mean by valid beyond what would be indicated by the explanation you give for distinguishing between valid and invalid reasoning, and what in the naturalistic hypothesis prevents the explanation form being given or meaning what it does" (Anscombe 1981, p. 226). This is a paradigm case argument, and the point is this: we can ask whether this particular argument is a good one, but does it really make sense to argue that reasoning might itself be invalid? Anscombe maintains that, since the argument that some particular piece of reasoning is invalid involves contrasting it with some other kinds of reasoning that are valid, the question "Could reasoning really be valid?" is really a nonsense question.

One way of using the argument from reason would be to use it as a skeptical threat argument. The idea is that if naturalism is true we will be unable to refute skeptical arguments against reasoning in general. The problem here is that it is far from clear that anyone, naturalist or not, can refute skepticism about reasoning, nor is it considered any great merit for any metaphysical theory that it would be possible to refute this kind of thoroughgoing skepticism. And, if we need to refute skepticism in order to accept some worldview, then it is not at all clear that theism will do that either. If we use our theistic beliefs to defend the basic principles of reasoning, then we would have to formulate that into an argument and then *presuppose* our ordinary canons of logical evaluation in the presentation of that very argument, thereby begging the question.

In my previous writings on the subject, I present the argument from reason as a best explanation argument. One should assume, at least to begin with, that human beings do reach true conclusions by reasoning, and then try to show, given the fact that people do reach true conclusions by reasoning, that this is best explained in terms of a theistic metaphysics as opposed to a naturalistic metaphysics. Now if we present the argument in this way and then an opponent comes along and says, "I see that your argument presupposes that we have beliefs. I do not think we do, so your argument fails," then we can reply to him by saying that if there are no beliefs then you do not believe what you are saying. Consequently, the status of your own remarks as *assertions* is called into question by your own thesis that there are no beliefs, and that this is going to end up having a devastating effect on the very sciences on which you base your arguments. Presenting the argument in this way, it seems to me, gets around the problems based on the paradigm case argument.

William Hasker, however, while previously endorsing the gist of my claim that the argument should be a best explanation argument rather than a skeptical threat argument, offered another suggestion in his mostly friendly response to me in *Philosophia Christi*. He wrote:

> However, if the Skeptical Threat strategy claims too much for the Argument from Reason, there is a danger that the Best Explanation strategy may claim too little. On the face of it, this strategy seems to invite the following kind of response: "It may be true that we naturalists have not, so far, produced a satisfying explanation for the process of rational inference. But there is nothing especially surprising or alarming about this fact. Finding good scientific explanations is hard work and often takes considerable time, and the relevant sciences are still in their infancy. We must simply be prepared to wait a bit longer, until we reach the stage where the desired explanations can be developed. (Hasker 2003, p. 61)

He then makes the following recommendation:

> The objection is not merely that naturalism has not yet produced an explanation of rational inference and the like, as though this were a deficiency that could be remedied by another decade or so of scientific research. The problem is that the naturalist is committed to certain assumptions that preclude in principle any explanation of the sort required. The key assumptions are three in number: mechanism (the view that fundamental physical explanations are nonteleological), the causal closure of the physical domain, and the supervenience of the mental on the physical. So long as these assumptions remain, no amount of ingenious computer modeling can possibly fill the explanatory gap. In order to bring out this feature of the situation, I propose that the first two stages of the Argument from Reason are best viewed as a transcendental argument in roughly the Kantian sense: They specify the conditions which are required for experience of a certain sort to be possible—in this case the kind of experience found in the performance of rational inference. (Hasker 2003, p. 61)

I have already discussed the transcendental impact of the arguments from reason, and I think Hasker's suggestion is a good one.

In my previous treatment of the argument from reason, I presented nine presuppositions of rational inference. Consider the following list of presuppositions of reason. These presuppositions have transcendental justifications. The justification goes from the fact that there is at least one person who has made a rational inference (such as a mathematical calculation) and establishes that these conditions must obtain if that rational inference has taken place.

1   States of mind have a relation to the world we call intentionality, or aboutness.
2   Thoughts and beliefs can be either true or false.
3   Human can be in the condition of accepting, rejecting, or suspending belief about propositions.
4   Logical laws exist.
5   Human beings are capable of apprehending logical laws.
6   The state of accepting the truth of a proposition plays a crucial causal role in the production of other beliefs, and the propositional content of mental states is relevant to the playing of this causal role.
7   The apprehension of logical laws plays a causal role in the acceptance of the conclusion of the argument as true.
8   The same individual entertains thoughts of the premises and then draws the conclusion.
9   Our processes of reasoning provide us with a systematically reliable way of understanding the world around us. (Reppert 2003a, p.73)

Unless all of these statements are true, it is incoherent to argue that one should accept naturalism based on evidence of any kind. Nor would it be possible to accept the claim that one should accept evolution as opposed to creationism because there is so much evidence for evolution. Nor could one argue that one should be supremely confident that the use of the scientific method will result in an accurate understanding of reality. Unless all these statements are true, there are no scientists and no one is using the scientific method.

To see how the transcendental justification works, consider the possibility that reality consists of nothing but a turnip with whipped cream on top. Of course this flies in the face of all the empirical evidence, but we can argue further that if this were so no one would be able to reason to that conclusion. Given the way this argument is structured, one could not use the paradigm case argument to argue that, since there has to be a contrast between valid and invalid inference, inference would also have to be possible in the turnip-world. No, the very fact that we can make such a distinction provides a transcendental basis for believing that we do not live in the turnip-world.

Anscombe's main objection: the ambiguity of "why," "because," and "explanation"

The third and main Anscombe objection to Lewis's argument is that he fails to distinguish between different senses of the terms "why," "because," and "explanation." There are, she suggests, four explanation-types, which have to be distinguished:

1   Naturalistic causal explanations, typically subsuming the event in question under some physical law
2   Logical explanation, showing the logical relationship between the premises and the conclusion
3   Psychological explanations, explaining why a person believes as he or she does
4   Personal history explanations, explaining how, as a matter of someone's personal history, that person came to hold a belief

She suggests that explanations of different types can be compatible with one another. Thus, a naturalistic causal explanation might be a complete answer to one type of question with respect to how someone's belief came to be what it was, but that explanation might be compatible with a "full" explanation of a different type (Lewis 1978, pp. 16–7).

Now what is interesting is that Lewis, in reformulating his own argument, not only draws the distinctions on which Anscombe had insisted; he actually makes these distinctions the centerpiece of his revised argument. He makes a distinction between cause-and-effect relations on the one hand, and ground-and-consequent relations on the other. Cause-and-effect relations say how a thought was produced, but ground-and-consequent relations indicate how thoughts are related to one another logically. However, in order to allow for rational inference, there must be a combination of ground–consequent and cause–effect relationships, which, Lewis says, cannot exist if the world is as the naturalist says that it is.

Claiming that a thought has been rationally inferred is a claim about how that thought was caused. Any face-saving account of how we come to hold beliefs by rational inference must maintain that "One thought can cause another thought not by being, but by being, a ground for it" (Lewis 1978, p. 17).

However, there are a number of features of thoughts as they occur in rational inference that set them apart from other beliefs.

> Acts of thinking are no doubt events, but they are special sorts of events. They are "about" other things and can be true or false. Events in general are not "about" anything and cannot be true or false. . . . Hence acts of inference can, and must be considered in two different lights. On the one hand they are subjective events in somebody's psychological history. On the other hand, they are insights into, or knowings of, something other than themselves. (Lewis 1978, p. 17)

So here, we already have three features of acts of thinking as they occur in rational inference. First, these thoughts have to be about something else, and second, they can be true or false. Third, their propositional contents must cause other thoughts to take place. But there is more:

> What from the first point of view is a psychological transition from thought A to thought B, at some particular moment in some particular mind is, from the thinker's point of view a perception of an implication (if A, then B). When we are adopting the psychological point of view we may use the past tense, "B followed A in my thoughts." But when we assert the implication we always use the present – "B *follows from* A." If it ever "follows from" in the logical sense it does so always. Moreover, we cannot reject the second point of view as a subjective illusion without discrediting human knowledge. (Lewis 1978, p. 17)

So now, in addition to the three features of thoughts as they occur in rational inference, we can add a fourth, that is, that the act of inference must be subsumed under a logical law. Moreover, the logical law according to which one thought follows another thought is true always. It is not local to any particular place or time; indeed, laws of logical obtain in all possible worlds.

Lewis then argues that an act of knowing "is determined, in a sense, by what is known; we must know it to be thus because it is thus" (Lewis 1978, p. 18). P's being true somehow brings it about that we hold the belief that P is true. Ringing in my ears is a basis for knowing if a ringing object causes it; it is not knowledge if it is caused by a tinnitus.

> Anything that professes to explain our reasoning fully without introducing an act of knowing thus solely determined by what it knows, is really a theory that there is no reasoning. But this, as it seems, is what Naturalism is bound to do. It offers what professes to be a full account of our mental behaviour, but this account, on inspection, leaves no room for the acts of knowing or insight on which the whole value of our thinking, as a means to truth, depends. (Lewis 1978, p. 18)

If a broadly materialist, or what Lewis calls a naturalist worldview, is true, how is it possible for our acts of rational inference to occur because reality has a feature that corresponds to that inferential process? That is the question Lewis thinks a materialist cannot answer.

Unlimited explanatory compatibility and the noncausal view of reasons

This is a point at which Anscombe, in her brief response to Lewis's revised argument, objects, claiming that Lewis did not examine the concept of "full explanation" that he was using. Anscombe had expounded a "question relative" conception of what a "full explanation" is; a full explanation gives a person everything they want to know about something. What this appears to result in is the idea of an unlimited explanatory compatibilism. It is further supported if one accepts, as Anscombe did when she wrote her original response to Lewis, the Wittgensteinian doctrine that reasons-explanations are not causal explanations at all. They are rather what sincere responses that are elicited from a person when he is asked what his reasons are. As Anscombe puts it:

> It appears to me that if a man has reasons, and they are good reasons, and they genuinely are his reasons, for thinking something–then his thought is rational, whatever causal statements can be made about him. (Anscombe 1981, p. 229)

Keith Parsons adopted essentially the same position in response to my version of the argument from reason when he wrote:

> My own (internalist) view is that if I can adduce reasons sufficient for the conclusion Q, then my belief that Q is rational. The causal history of the mental states of being aware of Q and the justifying grounds strike me was quite irrelevant. Whether those mental states are caused by other mental states, or caused by other physical states, or just pop into existence uncaused, the grounds still justify the claim. (Parsons 2000, p. 101)

However, the claim that reasons-explanations are not causal explanations at all seems to me to be completely implausible. As Lewis puts it:

> Even if grounds do exist, what have they got to do with the actual occurrence of belief as a psychological event? If it is an event it must be caused. It must in fact be simply one link in a causal chain which stretched back to the beginning and forward to the end of time. How could such a trifle as lack of logical grounds prevent the belief's occurrence and how could the existence of grounds promote it? (Lewis 1978, p. 16)

If you were to meet a person, let us call him Steve, who could argue with great cogency for every position he held, you might be inclined to consider him a very rational person. However, suppose that on all disputed questions Steve rolled dice to fix his positions permanently and then used his reasoning abilities only to generate the best-available arguments for those beliefs selected in the above-mentioned random method. I think that such a discovery would prompt you to withdraw from him the honorific title "rational." Clearly, we cannot answer the question of whether or not a person is rational in a manner that leaves entirely out of account the question of how his or her beliefs are produced and sustained.

There do seem to be limits on explanatory compatibility. Consider how we explain how presents came to appear under the Christmas tree. If we accept the explanation that, in spite of the tags on the presents that say Santa Claus, Mom and Dad in fact put the presents there, this would of course conflict with the explanation in terms of the activity of Santa Claus. An explanation of disease in terms of microorganisms is incompatible with an explanation in terms of a voodoo curse. In fact, naturalists are the first to say, "We have no need of that hypothesis" if a materialistically acceptable explanation can be given where a supernatural explanation had previously been accepted.

Further, explanations, causal or noncausal, involve *ontological commitments*. That which plays an explanatory role is supposed to *exist*. Therefore, if we explain the existence of the presents under the Christmas tree in terms of Santa Claus, I take it means that Santa Claus exists in more than just a nonrealist "Yes, Virginia" sense. Anscombe seemed to think that all that is involved in naturalism is that every event can be given a naturalistic explanation. But either naturalism or materialism are typically defined in ontological terms. The main page of the Internet Infidels Web site quotes the philosopher Paul Draper:

> The hypothesis that the physical world is a 'closed system' in the sense that nothing that is neither a part nor a product of it can affect it." More simply, it is the denial of the existence of supernatural causes. In rejecting the reality of supernatural events, forces, or entities, naturalism is the antithesis of supernaturalism.[1]

What this means is that even if reasons-explanations do not exclude physical explanations, even if reasons-explanations are somehow not causal explanations, the naturalist is not out of the woods. The materialist maintains that the universe, at its base, is governed by blind matter rather than reasons. So if reasons-explanations are true, we still need to know why they are true and why reasons exist in a world that is fundamentally nonrational.

---

1. Paul Draper, as quoted on the Internet Infidels home page (www.infidels.org).

In her final response to Lewis, Anscombe made two complaints: one was that Lewis did not repair the concept of a "full explanation," and that he did not adequately explore the idea of "an act of knowing solely determined by what is known." On the other hand, she admitted that, "We haven't got an answer" to the question "Even if grounds do exist, what have they got to do with the actual occurrence of belief ?" (Anscombe 1981, pp. ix–x).

Because of the ambiguities connected with the idea of "full explanation," my own development of the argument from reason has avoided talk about full explanations, but has instead focused on the ideas of mechanism, causal closure, and supervenience. Given these three doctrines, it seems as if some kinds of explanations face the prospect of being ruled out. Even the most nonreductive forms of materialism maintain that there can be only one kind of causation in a physicalist world, and that is physical causation. It is not enough simply to point out that we can give different "full" explanations for the same event. Of course, they can. Nevertheless, given the causal closure thesis of materialism, there cannot be causal explanations that require nonmaterialist ontological commitments. The question that is still open is whether the kinds of mental explanations required for rational inference are compatible with the limitations placed on causal explanations by materialism. If not, then we are forced to choose between saying that there are rational inferences and accepting materialism. However, materialism is invariably presented as the logical conclusion of a rational argument. Therefore, the choice will have to be to reject materialism.

Second, Anscombe insisted that Lewis needed to clarify his conception of "an act of knowing" determined by "what is known." Now, in one sense, this can be made clear by reflecting on the correspondence theory of truth. If I am in the state of believing that the cat is on the mat, which corresponds to some state of the world, what makes it a case of knowledge instead of just a lucky guess or something like that? If the cat is on the mat, and I know that, then somehow the cat's being on the mat has to play some role in producing the belief in me that the cat is on the mat. Otherwise, the cat could be anywhere but on the mat and I would still think it was there. However, in place of this concept, I prefer to employ the set of transcendentally established presuppositions of reason and science that I listed earlier.

How could reason emerge?

Lewis maintains that if we acquired the capability for rational inference in a naturalistic world, it would have to have arisen either through the process of evolution or because of experience. However, he says that evolution will always select for improved responses to the environment, evolution could do this without actually providing us with inferential knowledge. As he says:

> Once, then, our thoughts were not rational. That is, all our thoughts once were, as many of our thoughts still are, merely subjective events, not apprehensions of objective truth. Those which had a cause external to ourselves at all were (like our pains) responses to stimuli. Now natural selection could operate only by eliminating responses that were biologically hurtful and multiplying those which tended to survival. But it is not conceivable that any improvement of responses could ever turn them into acts of insight, or even remotely tend to do so. The relation between response and stimulus is utterly different from that between knowledge and the truth known. Our physical vision is a far more useful response to light than that of the cruder organisms which have only a photo-sensitive spot. But neither this improvement nor

any possible improvements we can suppose could bring it an inch nearer to being a knowledge of light. It is admittedly something without which we could not have had that knowledge. But the knowledge is achieved by experiments and inferences from them, not by refinement of the response. It is not men with specially good eyes who know about light, but men who have studied the relevant sciences. In the same way our psychological responses to our environment-our curiosities, aversions, delights, expectations-could be indefinitely improved (from the biological point of view) without becoming anything more than responses. Such perfection of the non-rational responses, far from amounting to their conversion into valid inferences, might be conceived as a different method of achieving survival—an alternative to reason. A conditioning which secured that we never felt delight except in the useful nor aversion save from the dangerous, and that the degrees of both were exquisitely proportional to the degree of real utility or danger in the object, might serve us as well as reason or in some circumstances better. (Lewis 1978, p. 19)

In addition, while experience might cause us to expect one event to follow another, to logically deduce that we should expect one effect to follow another is not something that could be given in experience. Experience can show us that A succeeds B, but it cannot show us that A follows necessarily from B. As Lewis writes:

My belief that things which are equal to the same thing are equal to one another is not at all based on the fact that I have never caught them behaving otherwise. I see that it 'must' be so. (Lewis 1978, p. 20)

Lewis then makes his case that theism, at least, can avoid the kinds of problems that the Naturalist faces:

On these terms the Theist's position must be a chimera nearly as outrageous as the Naturalist's. (Nearly, not quite; it abstains from the crowning audacity of a huge negative). But the Theist need not, and does not, grant these terms. He is not committed to the view that reason is a comparatively recent development moulded by a process of selection which can select only the biologically useful. For him, reason–the reason of God–is older than Nature, and from it the orderliness of Nature, which alone enables us to know her, is derived. For him, the human mind in the act of knowing is illuminated by the Divine reason. It is set free, in the measure required, from the huge nexus of non-rational causation; free from this to be determined by the truth known. And the preliminary processes within Nature which led up to this liberation, if there were any, were designed to do so. (Lewis 1978, pp. 22–3)

The argument since Lewis

Lewis's argument has been echoed in various places since the debate with Anscombe. One of the lesser-known developments in the argument was a defense of Lewis against Anscombe in his book *Christian Theology and Natural Science* by Eric Mascall (1956, pp. 214–6). The argument appeared in various other essays. J. R. Lucas claims that the central argument of his book *Freedom of the Will* was inspired by Lewis's argument, although he imports Godel's theorem to defend his central argument (Lucas 1970). Perhaps the best defense of the argument between the 1960s and the 1990s came in William Hasker's essay "The Transcendental Refutation of Determinism" (1973). John Beversluis, in a book highly critical of all of Lewis's arguments, including the argument from reason, was the first to use that term to designate the argument (1985).[2] My own efforts with respect to the argument were begun when I wrote my doctoral dissertation in defense of it entitled "Physical Causes and Rational Belief: A Problem for Materialism?" (Reppert 1989). The second chapter of my dissertation became my original essay on the Lewis–Anscombe controversy. Shortly thereafter, Alvin Plantinga published his first defense of what came to be known as the Evolutionary Argument against Naturalism, which first appeared in his book *Warrant and Proper Function* (1993) and was developed in more detail in *Warranted Christian Belief* (2000). In 1999, William Hasker published a chapter-long defense of the argument entitled "Why the Physical Isn't Closed," in his book *The Emergent Self* (1999, pp. 58–80). I returned to the defense of the argument starting in 1999 with an exchange in *Philo* that spilled over into *Philosophia Christi*. (Reppert 1999, 2000, 2001, 2003b,c). Then my book *C. S. Lewis's Dangerous Idea: In Defense of the Argument from Reason*, was published in 2003, and I have engaged in further development and discussion of the argument since (Reppert 2007). In addition, other defenders of the argument have emerged, such as Darek Barefoot (2001), Angus Menuge (2004, chap. 6), and Michael Rea (2002).

Subdividing the Argument

One aspect of my own discussion of the argument that has, I think, influenced the discussion of the argument the most is my subdivision of the argument from reason into six subarguments. In examining the argument, I found that the argument focused on different elements of the reasoning process, and that one could find difficulties for naturalism at more than one step along the way.

Perhaps Lewis himself also noticed that there are different elements to the process of rational inference. Consider this description of inference, which, interestingly enough, occurs in a critique of pacifism, not in a presentation of the argument from reason:

> Now any concrete train of reasoning involves three elements: Firstly, there is the reception of facts to reason about. These facts are received either from our own senses, or from the report of other minds; that is, either experience or authority supplies us with our material. But each man's experience is so limited that the second source is the more usual; of every hundred facts upon which to reason, ninety-nine depend on authority. Secondly, there is the direct, simple act of the mind perceiving self-evident truth, as when we see that if A and B both equal C, then they equal each other. This act I call intuition. Thirdly, there is an art or skill of arranging the facts so as to yield a series of such intuitions, which linked together produce, a proof of the truth of the propositions we are considering. This in a geometrical proof each step is seen by intuition, and to fail to see it is to be not a bad geometrician but an idiot. The skill comes in arranging the material into a series of intuitable "steps". Failure to do this does not mean idiocy, but only lack of ingenuity or invention. Failure to follow it need not mean idiocy, but either inattention or a defect of memory which forbids us to hold all the intuitions together." (Lewis 1962, p. 34)

So Lewis isolates three steps in the reasoning process: (1) the reception of facts to think about; (2) the perception of a self-evident truth of rule that permits the inference; and (3)

---

2. A revised and considerably improved edition was published in 2007 (Amherst, NY: Prometheus Books).

arranging the fact to prove a conclusion. Sometimes, in developing the argument from reason, advocates point out the difficulty the naturalist has in giving an account of how it is a thought can be *about* something. This aspect of thought, which philosophers since Brentano have called *intentionality*, has often been thought to be profoundly problematic for the philosophical naturalist. The next step in the process seems problematic as well: how is that that purely natural creatures completely embedded in the space-time continuum could possibly not only know something that is true but also must be true. Our physical senses might perceive what is, but how could physical beings know what aspects of what they experienced could not be otherwise? And then, finally what happens when we arrange statements to prove a conclusion? It seems that our understanding of the propositional content of one statement has to be the deciding factor in our being able to conclude the conclusion. As Lewis asked in his revised chapter, "Even if grounds do exist, what exactly have they got to do with the actual occurrence of belief as a psychological event?" Hence, it looks as if the naturalist, in order to affirm the existence of rational inference, must accept the existence of mental causation in which the state of accepting the content of one statement causes the acceptance of the content of another statement. How mental causation can fit into a naturalistic world has been widely regarded as a problem.

In order to keep the strands of the argument straight, I divided the argument from reason into the following six subarguments:

(1)   The argument from intentionality
(2)   The argument from truth
(3)   The argument from mental causation in virtue of propositional content
(4)   The argument from the psychological relevance of logical laws
(5)   The argument from the unity of consciousness
(6)   The argument from the reliability of our rational faculties

I will analyze just three of the arguments here: the argument from conscious, propositional intentional states; the argument from mental causation; and the argument from the psychological relevance of logical laws.

Intentional states and rational inference

Why reduction fails

Intentional states are at the heart of the argument from reason. In the philosophy of mind, the term "intentionality" refers to "aboutness." Our thoughts are about other things, surely. The first thing that we notice about our mental states is that they are about certain other things. If there is to be rational inference, there has to be something to reason about.

However, intentionality is a rather complex phenomenon. Consider the following passage by Lewis:

> The strength of the critic lies in the words "merely" or "nothing but". He sees all the facts but not the meaning. Quite truly, therefore, he claims to have seen all the facts. There *is* nothing else there, except the meaning. He is therefore, as regards the matter at hand, in the position of an animal. You will have noticed that most dogs cannot understand *pointing*. You point to a bit of food on the floor; the dog, instead of looking at the floor, sniffs at your finger. A finger is a finger to him, and that is all. His world is all fact and no meaning. (Lewis 1962, p. 71)

What is interesting about this passage is that although it is clear enough the dogs don't *understand* pointing, it is equally true that dogs can be very good at tracking things. There are certainly states of the dog that link up to previous positions of a fox. The dog certainly can "track" a fox, and in one important sense we can say that the dog has states that are "about" the fox. Nevertheless the dog doesn't *understand* pointing. It does not *recognize* the "aboutness" of our mental states. It does not understand the relation between its own fox-tracking activities and the fox.

So we might distinguish between simple representation on the one hand, with representation that is understood by the agent, what I will call *understood representation*. Clearly, the latter type of intentionality is necessary for the kind of rational inference employed by the natural sciences. We have to know what we mean when we think, if we are to infer one claim from another. Consider the following joke syllogism, invented by a freshman student at the University of Illinois years ago.

1. Going to class is pointless.
2. An unsharpened pencil is pointless.
3. Therefore, going to class is an unsharpened pencil.

Recognizing that this is not a good argument is a matter of seeing that the meaning of the term "pointless" does not remain invariant between the first and second premises. As a recent US President once observed, even the meaning of the word "is" does not remain constant from context to context. No rational inference, in or out of a scientific context, could occur if we never know what we mean when we use words.

But there is another characteristic of intentional states that is critical to their use in rational inference, and that is states of mind that are about other things are formulated together to provide us with a state with propositional content. This is a further development, which results in agents who have beliefs, desires, and other propositional attitudes. If we have propositional attitudes, not only do we understand what our thoughts are about but we also are able to formulate those thoughts in a sentential format. Hence, we might want to introduce the concept of *propositionally understood representation* as another essential feature of rational inference.

Lewis wrote this in his essay "De Futilitate":

> We are compelled to admit between the thoughts of a terrestrial astronomer and the behaviour of matter several light-years away that particular relation which we call truth. But this relation has no meaning at all if we try to make it exist between the matter of the star and the astronomer's brain, considered as a lump of matter. The brain may be in all sorts of relations to the star no doubt: it is in a spatial relation, and a time relation, and a quantitative relation. But to talk of one bit of matter as being true about another bit of matter seems to me to be nonsense. (Lewis 1967, pp. 63–4).

Of course, materialists are going to say that it is not a bit of matter that is about another bit of matter, it is a state of the brain (along, perhaps, with a set of causally related items outside the brain) that is about something else.

In virtue of what is some physical state about some other physical state? This is the familiar worry about intentionality, a worry made more difficult by my claim that the kind of intentional states involved in rational inference are states in which the content is understood by the agent and put into a propositional format. Is there a set of necessary and sufficient conditions which are physical in the sense in which we are understanding it here, and which jointly entail the conclusion that agent A is in the state of believing, or doubting, or desiring, or fearing, the proposition P is true? Reductive analyses of mind hope to provide this kind of account of mental states.

When we consider material entities that exhibit intentionality, we see that they do not have their intentional content inherently, but have it relative to human interests. The marks on paper that you are reading now are just marks, unless they are related to a set of users who interpret it as such. In other words, it possesses a "derived intentionality" as opposed to an "original intentionality." As Feser points out:

> More to the point, brain processes, composed as they are of meaningless chemical components, seem as inherently devoid of intentionality as soundwaves or ink marks. Any intentionality they would also have to be derived from something else. But if anything physical would be devoid of intrinsic intentionality, whatever does have intrinsic intentionality would thereby have to be *non*-physical. Sine the mind is the source of the intentionality of physical entities like sentences and pictures, and doesn't get its intentionality from anything else (there's no one "using" our minds to convey meaning) it seems to follow that the mind has intrinsic intentionality, and thus is non-physical. (Feser 2005, p. 136)

For example, clearly, the relationship between brain states and states of affairs cannot be a matter of resemblance. If what I perceive is a pine tree, then what I see is green, but there is nothing green in the gray matter of the brain that corresponds to the green tree in the world. So there must be something that connects the brain states to the mental states. But what could that be?

James Ross, in his essay "Immaterial Aspects of Thought", presents an argument against a physicalist account of propositional content that I will call the argument from determinate content. He writes:

> Some thinking (judgment) is determinate in the way no physical process can be. Consequently, such thinking cannot be a (wholly) physical process. If all thinking, all judgment, is determinate in that way, no physical process can be the (the whole of) any judgment at all. Furthermore, "functions" amng physical states cannot be determinate enough to be such judgments, either. Hence some judgments can be niether wholly physical processes nor wholly functions among physical processes. (Ross 1992)

Yet, he maintains, we cannot deny that we perform determinate mental operations. He writes:

> I propose now, with some simple cases, to reinforce the perhaps already obvious point that pure function has to be wholly realized in the single case, and cannot consist in the array of "inputs and outputs" for a certain kind of thinking. Does anyone count that we can actually square numbers? "4 times 4 is sixteen"; a definite form $(N \times N = N^2)$ is "squaring" for all relevant cases, whether or not we are able to process the digits, or ralk long enough to give the answer. To be squaring, I have to be doing some thing that works for all the cases, something for which any relevant case can be substituted without change in what I am doing, but only in which thing is done. (Ross 1992)

I should add that if we do not literally add, subtract, divide, multiply, square numbers, and take their square roots, not to mention perform all the complicated mathematical operations involved in, say, Einstein's theory of relativity, then physicalism, which not only says that reality is physical but that physics, at least approximately, gets it right, is up the creek without a paddle.

Ross's argument can be formalized as follows.

1   Some mental states have determinate content. In particular, the states involved in adding, subtracting, multiplying, dividing, squaring numbers, and taking their square roots are determinate with respect to their intentional content.
2   Physical states are indeterminate with respect to intentional content. Any physical state is logically compatible with the existence of a mulitplicity of propostionally defined intentional states, or even with the absence of propositionally defined intentional states entirely.
3   Therefore, the mental states involed in mathematical operations are not and cannot be identical to physical states.

Some naturalistic theories have been developed to provide a physicalist account of intentionality. Feser delineates four types of theories of this nature: conceptual role theories, causal theories, biological theories, and instrumentalist theories.

Conceptual role theories explicate intentional states in terms of their conceptual roles, that is, in relation to other intentional states. Of course, this does not explain why there is a network of intentional states in the first place.

A more popular approach to coming up with a naturalistic account of intentionality is causal theories of intentionality. These appeal to the causal relations that intentional states stand to items in the external world. Thus, if I believe that there is a computer monitor in front of me as I type these words, there is a causal connection between the monitor and my visual cortex, which causes states of my brain to be affected by it.

However, there are some fairly obvious difficulties which must be confronted by any causal theories. First of all, how would we explain our relationship to nonexistent objects? How could we meaningfully refer to Superman if Superman does not exist? How could a cat cause us to form the belief that a dog is on the mat? This is frequently called the misrepresentation problem. These are problems that causal theorist have been frequently discussed in the literature, and various responses have been proposed. I will not put primary focus on these difficulties; I am merely pointing them out to develop a contrast.

Now if we are working on the level of simple representation, then perhaps some solution to the problem of misrepresentation can be generated. Let us consider, for example, the case of bee dances. Bees perform dances which "represent" the positions of flowers in a garden. The bees, based on this information, go out to the garden only to find no flowers because in the intervening time between the bees' discovery of the flowers and the time when the bees performed the dance, a child had picked all the flowers and taken them indoors. We might be able to cash out this fact of misrepresentation in causal terms: there is a normal casual relationship between the bees' dance and the location of pollinated flowers, so the bees represented flowers in that location, but the representation was incorrect, because the flowers had been picked in the meantime.

However, other kinds of misrepresentation seem more difficult to deal with at the level of simple representation. Let us consider the kind of misrepresentation that goes on in, say, a used-car dealership. Can we really imagine a bee from a competing hive "sneaking in," giving a dance which would send the swarm of bees to a place where there are no pollinated flowers, in order to secure the real flowers for its own hive? This kind of misrepresentation seems to require that the fifth-columnist bee, like the used-car dealer, know that the dance was misleading, in other words, understand what it is that their own dance and know that it was a misrepresentation. This seems to be beyond the capabilities of bees, and requires a radically different set of abilities. Can we account for the difference between being sincerely mistaken and lying in terms of causal relationships? I rather doubt it. In order to misrepresent in the "used-car salesman" sense (i.e. to lie), one has to be in an inner state of believing that not-P is true and to assert P.

There have, certainly, been causal theories of reference that have been advanced. But these do not suggest that causal relationships alone are sufficient to fix reference. On a Kripkean view of the causal theory of reference, a name's referent is fixed by an original act of naming (also called a "dubbing" or, by Kripke, an "initial baptism"), whereupon the name becomes a rigid designator of that object. Later uses of the name succeed in referring to the referent by being linked to that original act via a causal chain. In other words, what causation explains, according to this theory, is how references is *transmitted* once an initial act of naming, an intentional (both in the sense of being intended and in the sense of possessing "aboutness") is performed. How such actions could be performed in the first place is not accounted for in causal terms (Kripke 1980).

When we move from simple representation to intended representation, one question I have is how any specification of causal relations can possibly entail the existence of meaning at all. Let us say a bird is hardwired to let out a certain squawk when something approximately the shape of a hawk is nearby. There is a regular causal relation between the appearance of a hawk and the occurrence of the squawk. In one sense, we can say that the squawk is about the hawk. Something could, of course, touch off the "hawk" signal and the subsequent evasive action without being a hawk. It does not mean that the bird has the ability to distinguish a hawk from various nonhawks. Expecting fire when one sees smoke is not the same as inferring fire from smoke. We say "smoke means fire," but what this amounts to is that smoke and fire are often conjoined in experience. We quite often experience smoke before we experience fire, but it turns out upon examination of the causal relations that fire causes smoke and not vice versa. We say "smoke means fire," but that means that smoke and fire are conjoined in our experience. The "meaning" is imposed by human understanding, not in the world as it is in itself.

As Feser writes:

> Any account of such theories that could give the relevant causal relations holding between a particular mental state and a particular object in the external world will require picking out a particular object in the beginning point of the causal series (call it A) and a particular end point (B) as the mental state doing the representing. . . . Nothing in the flux objectively either the determinate starting point or a particular sequence or the determinate ending point. It is we who pick certaub events and count them as beginnings and endings; their status as beginnings and endings is relative certain purposes and interests of ours. (Feser 2005, p. 145)

In short, there is a difference between causing action appropriate to something being the case (causing the bees to go where the nectar is) and declaring it to be the case that the nectar is in such-and-such place. Science is inherently declarative and requires understanding. It is, in my view, tempting, but erroneous, to attribute a declarative character to bee dances and birdsongs. Casual connections are invariably insufficient to provide determinacy of propositional content. Without determinacy of propositional content, the type of rational inference in science cannot occur.

Another theory looks to biological role or function as a basis of determining content. However, I believe that Dennett has successfully argued that biological function also leaves propositional content indeterminate. Evolutionary function is essentially fluid in nature, and to get something as determinate as propositional content out of biological function is asking too much of it. (What is *the* biological function of feathers on a bird?)

John Searle writes:

> So far no attempt at naturalizing content has produced an explanation (analysis, reduction) of intentional content that is even remotely plausible. A symptom that something is radically wrong with the project is that intentional notions are inherently normative. They set standards of truth, rationality, consistency, etc., and there is no way that these standards can be intrinsic to a system consisting entirely of brute, blind, nonintentional causal relations. There is no mean [middle] component to billiard ball causation. Darwinian biological attempts at naturalizing content try to avoid this problem by appealing to what they suppose is the inherently teleological [i.e. purposeful], normative character of biological evolution. But this is a very deep mistake. There is nothing normative or teleological about Darwinian evolution. Indeed, Darwin's major contribution was precisely to remove purpose, and teleology from evolution, and substitute for it purely natural forms of selection. (Searle 1992, 50–1)

Or as Feser puts it:

> Talk of purposes and functions, if taken literally, seems to presuppose intentionality; in particular it seems to presuppose the agency of an intelligence of one who design something for a particular purpose. But the aim of Darwinian evolutionary theory is to explain biological phenomena in a manner that involves no appeal to intelligent design. . . . Just as modern physics has tended to explain phenomena by carving off the subjective qualitative appearances of things and relocating them into the mind, so to did the Darwinian revolution in biology push purpose and function out of the biological realm, making them out to be mind-dependent and devoid of objective reality. (Feser 2005, p. 149)

In point of fact, the ruthless naturalist W. V. Quine has argued that the reference of our terms is indeterminate, and that there is no fact of the matter as to what our words refer to (Quine 1960, chaps. 1 and 2). However, this has a disastrous consequence on the practice of science. Only if our terms have determinate reference can we reason to conclusions. Consider once again the aforementioned argument about the unsharpened pencil. Our ability to reason logically can exist only if we are able to identify sameness of meaning. Dennett's view of the mind essentially affirms the Quinian thesis of indeterminacy, and indeed Dennett thinks that this kind of indeterminacy is a consequence of philosophical naturalism.

> And why not? Here, I think, we find as powerful and direct an expression as could be of the intuition that lies behind the belief in original intentionality. This is the doctrine Ruth Millikan calls *meaning rationalism*, and it is one of the central burdens of her important book, *Language,*

Thought, and Other Biological Categories, to topple it from its traditional pedestal (Millikan, 1984. See also Millikan forthcoming) Something has to give. Either you must abandon meaning rationalism–the idea that you are unlike the fledgling cuckoo not only having access, but in having privileged access to your meanings–or you must abandon the naturalism that insists that you are, after all, just a product of natural selection, whose intentionality is thus derivative and hence potentially indeterminate. (Dennett 1987, p. 313)

If meanings are indeterminate then it is indeterminate what Dennett means by anything he says. No one can possibly determine whether any argument is valid or not because if, say, it is a categorical syllogism, there is no way to determine whether we have got three, four, five or six terms.

So let us have a look at Dennett's argument.

1   If naturalism is true, then meaning is indeterminate.
2   Naturalism is true.
3   Therefore, meaning is indeterminate.

And here is mine.

1   If naturalism is true, then meaning is indeterminate.
2   Meaning is determinate (a presupposition of reason and science).
3   Therefore, naturalism is false.

Perhaps, it might be suggested that the indeterminacy of meaning is benign and not such that it undermines science in the radical way in which I have described. Consider Kripke's distinction between addition and what he calls "quaddition," where addition has the form $x + y$ but quaddition has the form $x + y$ if x,y are less than 57, 5 otherwise (Kripke 1970). If mathematics is indeterminate between addition and quaddition, science is in trouble.

Another approach to intentionality, attributed to Dennett, regards propositional states in instrumental terms. That essentially makes all intentionality derived intentionality. But, we would have to then say, "derived from what?" If we have intentionality because we take ourselves to have intentionality, then how to we account for our the intentional state of taking ourselves to have intentionality.

There have been a number of arguments presented against the possibility of *reducing* determinate beliefs and desires to physical states. Quine's argument for the indeterminacy of translation, Kripke's adapted Wittgenstein argument, Davidson's argument against psychophysical laws (Davidson 1970), and Nagel's discussions in *The Last Word* (1997) all have this implication. However, different philosophers have drawn different conclusions from the arguments for irreducibility. Since reason cannot be reduced to physical relations, materialists have to use other strategies to fit reason into a physicalist world.

Why propositional attitudes cannot be eliminated

Eliminative materialism is a frequently misunderstood position according to which there are no propositional attitudes. Its primary advocates have been Paul and Patricia Churchland (1986, 1989). If would be a mistake to say, as some commentators have, that eliminative materialism is the view that there are no mental states. Nor, at least in some significant sense, can it be said that eliminative materialists deny the existence of intentionality. What I have described earlier as simple representation will certainly not be denied by eliminative materialists. What the eliminative materialist denies is the existence of *propositional attitudes*. These would include believing a proposition, doubting a proposition, fearing that a proposition is true, and desiring that a proposition be true. So it is true that eliminative materialist claims that there are no beliefs.

To be fair, the eliminativist position is somewhat more complex than that. Eliminativism maintains that "belief" and "desire" are not mental states we are directly aware of, as "seeing red" or "feeling sick" would be, but are posits of a theory called "folk psychology." In the history of science, "folk" theories have been succeeded by scientific theories. Sometimes the scientific theories absorb the "folk" theories in such a way that the "folk" theory is taken to be fundamentally right; just standing in need of some development by the scietific theory. In other cases, such as the move from Ptolemaic astronomy to Copernican, the succeeding theory showed the previous theory to be dead wrong, and the posits of the theory to be nonexistent. The Churchlands maintain that when neuroscience "looks under the hood" of the brain, it will not find objects in it corresponding to "belief" and "desire." Hence, the right thing for science to do given this state of affairs is to deny the existence of beliefs and desires in much the way present-day science denies the existence of phogiston and ether.

The self-referential rebuttal is pretty obvious. "Come on Paul, you expect me to believe that, Paul?" Or, we could even present an argument that if eliminative materialism were true, no one could possibly know that it was true.

1   Knowledge is justified, true, belief (plus maybe a fourth condition).
2   If eliminativism is true, then no one believes that eliminative materialism is true, since there are no beliefs.
3   Hence, if eliminativism is true, no one knows that eliminativism is true (consequence of 1 and 2).

Here the Churchlands would reply that our standard definitions of knowledge are, of course, laden with folk-psychological assumptions, and when those are overthrown and a new theory based on neuroscience is developed, a fully adequate conception of knowledge will emerge.

Now the promise of successor concepts seems to be, to many people, at best, a huge promissory note drawn on future science, and we are told very little about that the successors are actually going to look like. The successor concepts are going to have to do everything for us that we thought propositional attitudes did, except that these will be a more neurophysiologically accurate way of talking about human behavior and will not be propositional states.

Now propositional attitude psychology does a lot of work for us, in everyday life, and in science as well. Lynne Baker makes this point:

> Suppose I dialed your phone number and said "Would you join us for dinner at our house on Saturday at 7:00?" You replied "yes." On Saturday, I act in the way I should act if I believed that you were coming to dinner. But if neither of us had any beliefs, intentions, or other states attributed by "that"-clauses, it would be amazing if I actually prepared dinner for you and if you actually showed up. (Baker 1987, p. 130)

Consider the whole practice of political polling, which is very often able to predict the outcome of elections before they occur. Pollsters ask respondents who they intend to vote for, or who they believe is best equipped to deal with health care or terrorism.

What is most critical, however, is that if science is what every naturalist I know says that it is – a rational method for discovering the truth – then it we have to be able to know the precise content of the terms and concepts we are using. This is especially true in the area of mathematical reasoning, which is at the heart of physics. We have to be adding, not quadding. The definite integral has to be definite if it is to do the job assigned to it. There has to be some state of the person that recognizes the mathematical content of, say, Maxwell's equations (which to me is the propositional attitude of understanding that p), and if there has to be such a state, why should we not call this a propositional attitude.

It seems to me that there is an introspectively accessible state of knowing what one means when one says something. Now it may be that the full and complete content of what we know when we say it is not known to us. For example, I can say "I want a glass of water" without having any idea of the exact chemical composition of water. But there has to be an internally accessible content of the term "water" which will allow me to recognize whether I have been given a glass of water or a glass of coke. Of course there can be errors here, if it turns out that "What he thought was H_2O was H_2SO_4." But one might be tempted to think that sulfuric acid was water, but it would be unlikely to be tempted by the likelihood that Coca-Cola is water, because Coke does not look at all like water, but sulfuric acid sort of does. All of which suggests to me that we do have internally understood concepts of what we mean by words, and if we did not we would not be able to get through life. I do not see how you can accept the existence of internally understood concepts of what we mean by words without also accepting propositional attitudes. I also fail to see the possibility that further brain-mapping is going to change this situation. This seems to me to be an insuperable difficulty for eliminative materialism.

Intentionality and the supervenience strategy

Another very popular view, which has even been accepted by some Christians, is a nonreductive materialist position. On this view, intentional states are not eliminated, they are not reducible to physical states, they are, however, supervenient upon physical states. Mental states are not identical to physical states, but given the state of the physical, there is only one way the mental can be.

Of course, earlier I indicated that supervenience of all non-physical states on physical states is part of what it takes for a worldview to be naturalistic. However, if mental states can be reductively analyzed in terms of physical states, then the supervenience is simply obvious. A difference in B requires a difference in A because, in the final analysis, Bs just *are* As. Again, if the B-states are eliminated from the ontology, then we do not have to worry about a difference in B that is not guaranteed by a difference in A. However, for many, perhaps most, philosophers who believe in a broadly materialist worldview, the reductionist and eliminativist positions are both implausible. For these philosophers, the supervenience relation has a job to do, it explains how it is possible for everything to be in the final analysis physical while at the same time maintaining the irreducibility and the autonomy of the mental realm.

Philosophers often distinguish between weak supervenience and strong supervenience. According to weak supervenience, B-properties weakly supervene on A-properties if and only if things that are alike in their A-properties are always alike in their B-properties. What this establishes is a constant conjunction between A-properties and B-properties. It does not really show that there is anything about the A-properties that guarantees that the B-properties will always be the same. Nevertheless, we must remember what caused problems for reductionist accounts of mental states. The physical, I maintained, is incurably indeterminate with respect to propositonal states. Whatever story we tell at the physical level is compatible with a multiplicity of stories at the mental level. This kind of constant conjunction claim, however, explains little. There is, for example, a constant conjunction between increases in the homicide rate in New York City and increases in the rate of ice cream consumption. We could say that the homicide rate supervenes on the rate of ice cream consumption, but we will have explained nothing. We will not have shown that ice cream consumption is responsible for homicides, or vice versa, or whether these are just two unrelated effects of a common cause (an increase in the city's temperatures) (Stump 2006, p. 67).

I should add that a good deal of confusion in the discussion of neuroscientific discoveries and their relation to the philosophy of mind often occurs at this point. What neuroscience is often able to do is provide correlations between certain mental states and activity in certain parts of the brain. These are often taken as proof of materialism, but there is no good reason why dualists should not expect these correlations to exist. Further, it must be emphasized that correlation between mental states and physical states is not the same as identification of mental states with physical states.

Strong supervenience is the claim that B-properties strongly supervene on A-properties just in case things that are alike in A-properties must be alike in B-properties. On this view, the supervenience is not just a brute conjunction; it is necessarily so. However, as an attempt to explain anything, this seems inadequate as well. Religious explanations are often taken to task as being God-of-the-gaps explanations, this just seem to me to be a necessity-of-the-gaps explanation. "We might ask this question: Why, if Jones's beliefs could be five or six different ways given the physical, or perhaps, given the physical, Jones could be a zombie with no beliefs at all, does Jones have the beliefs he has?" If the answer is "Well, there is this strong supervenience relationship that exists between the physical and the mental, so it is necessary, it looks as if we are taken no closer to an explanation as to why Jones has the beliefs he has.

Why does the supervenience relation exist, if it does? It is pure dumb luck? Is it a Leibnizian preestablished harmony set up before the foundation of the world by God? (This might not be naturalistically acceptable.) Presumably, it is not a physical relation, so why does it exist? Unless there is something about the physical that guarantees that the mental be only one way, the supervenience relation needs to be explained. There is what James Stump calls a "classic reflexivity problem" for the supervenience theorist. For superevenience theory, everything is either physical, or supervenes on the physical (Stump 2006, p. 70). So, the supervenience relation is going to have to be either physical or supervene on the physical, if supervenient physicalism is true. But does it. Stump summarizes an argument originally presented by Lynch and Glasgow to contend that the supervenience relation itself cannot be admitted into the supervenient materialism's ontology, which I have altered slightly for the sake of congruence with previous discussion:

1   For physicalists, all facts must be materialistically acceptable. That is, they are facts about physical things, or about things which are ontologically distinct from the physical, but strongly supervene on the physical.

2   There must be some fact – the explanation – in virtue of which B-properties supervene on A-properties; call the S-facts. What kind of facts are S-facts? There are two options for materialistically respectable facts:

(a)   They themselves could suprevene on A-properties. But then there is an infinite regress problem, for now we have to explain this new supervenience relations, which in turn needs to be explained, and so on *ad infinitum*. So this is no good.

(b)   Or, the S-facts could not just be further A-properties, that is, facts about the physical entity. But then these facts do not bridge the explanatory gap between the B-facts and the A-facts. (Stump 2006)

Perhaps the supervenience theorist can simply accept the supervenience relation as an unexplained brute fact. However, as J. P. Moreland argues, this is also deeply problematic for the supervenience theorist. First, he highlights the claim that in a materialist *universe* it must be explainable rather than *sui generis*. As Horgan points out, if there are going to be any brute unexplainable givens in a materialist *universe* it must be the the physical facts themselves, not some fact concerning interlevel supervenience (Horgan 1994). Second, the truth of supervenience does not look like something science could possibly have discovered, and so to accept supervenience as a brute fact would be to accept the idea that there are truths about the world that can be figured out by philosophical, rather than scientific means, and this is anathema to most contemporary naturalists (Moreland 1988). Also, this position begs the question against people such as Swinburne and Robert Adams, who maintain that the supervenience of the mind stands in need of a theistic explanation (Moreland 1988).

Second, debate about just what kind of supervenience holds between physical and mental states is not a scientific question, and cannot be settle by scientific theorizing. Further, supervenience theory involves terms and concepts that are not the terms and concepts of natural science. As Moreland puts it:

> Naturalists criticize Cartesian dualism and its problem of interaction between radically different sorts of entities. In my view, the dualist has the resources to answer this problem because of her commitment to entities, relations, and causation that go beyond those in the physical sciences. But the same cannot be said for naturalism, and what is sauce for the goose is sauce for the gander. Naturalists have the very same kind of problem that they claim as a difficulty for the Cartesian. And given the philosophical constraints that follow from accepting the naturalist epistemology, etiology, and ontolgy, it is more difficult to see how a naturalist could accept metaphysical supervenience than it is to understand how a Cartesian without those constraints could accept mental/physical interaction. (Moreland 1988)

Intentionality is more than just a puzzle for broadly materialist views, it is a deep and profound problem distinct from, and as serious as, the "hard problem" of consciousness. Reduction of understood intentional states to the physical seems to be inherently impossible. Elimination of those states eliminates states essential to the operation of the natural sciences on which the credibility of naturalism is founded. Nonpropositional successors to propositional attitudes cannot do the job assigned to them. Supervenient materialism commits the materialist to a materialistically unacceptable relation between the physical and the mental and, as we shall see, presents serious problems in accounting for mental causation.

Theories of the universe that make the mental a basic fact of reality, such as theism, pantheism, or idealism, do not have the problem of unacceptably terminating explanatory chains with non-mental states. Thus the problem of intentionality provides one good reason for preferring a broadly mentalistic world-view to a broadly materialist world-view.

Angus Menuge suggests the following argument in support of the claim that our intentionality is the result of a prior intentionality:

1 If something has a purpose, then it is designed.
2 Intentionality has the purpose of guiding behavior.
3 So intentionality is designed. (1 and 2)
4 But clearly, our intentionality was not designed by us, although it does enable us to convey our own designs.
5 Thus, our intentionality is the result of prior design. (3 and 4)
6 But ... if something is designed, then it is the product of intentionality.
7 So our intentionality is the product of prior intentionality. (Menuge 2004, p. 82)

If this argument is correct, then intentionality can be grounds for thinking that our intentionality is the product of a prior intentionality.

Mystery and materialism

In his book *God and the Reach of Reason*, Erik Wielenberg attempts to respond to Lewis's argument from reason, using a parallel with some Christian responses to the argument from evil. In response to the argument from evil, Christian philosophers have sometimes attempted to produce theodicies which explain God's reason for permitting various of the world's evils. Other Christians, however, have argued that our inability to explain this, that, or the other instance of evil in suffering is not the end of the world for theists. We are, after all, human beings with limited understanding, and it would be surprising if God were to exist and we could understand God's ways well enough to know why some particular instance of suffering was permitted. In the same way, the fact that no analysis of intentional states in physical terms need not be fatal for materialism because it could be that our brains are simply not well suited to understand the connections between the mental and the physical. If we cannot figure out how the mental could possibly be, in the last analysis, physical, that need not be because the mental is really nonphysical, it could be simply that we have trouble solving philosophical problems. The response he gives to the argument from reason is very much akin to the "mysterian" view in the philosophy of consciousness put forward by Colin McGinn (Wielenberg 2007).

In response, I would begin by saying that as I have been presenting the argument from intentionality, it does not seem to rest on anything being mysterious. Rather it has rested on clearly reflecting on what propositional states are in certain key cases, namely that they must have determinate mental content in order to do their jobs, and that the physical is indeterminate with respect to mental content. Mark Twain once said, "It isn't the parts of the Bible that I don't understand that trouble me, it's the parts that I do." Similarly, in considering physicalism, it is my understanding of physical states and mental states that leads me to the conclusion that any attempt to bring the sorts of mental states involved in rational inference into a physicalistic universe are going to involve confusion and the fudging over of critical distinctions.

Further, responding to the argument from evil in the terms delineated earlier, it does seem to me that the theist is engaging in a damage control project rather than a project that actually refutes the argument from evil. If an atheistic worldview can come up with an explanation for the suffering in the world that makes more sense than theism can possibly offer, then it seems to me that the argument from evil still counts in favor of atheism. Some theists are prepared to admit that the existence of suffering counts against theism, but just think that there is better reason to be a theist nonetheless. Of course, it would be another matter if the atheists' explanation for suffering could be shown to be fundamentally inadequate. If that were the case, then the force of the atheistic argument could be blunted completely. On my view, we have to consider the fact that on a broadly materialist worldview, the existence of qualia such as pain, as well as the existence of a moral standard by which to judge something to be evil, are both problematic, so I am not fully convinced that the argument from evil really points to an explanatory advantage for atheism. However, it may be that it does show an explanatory advantage for atheism, in which case I would argue that the explanatory disadvantage for theism need not be fatal.

Everytime I have presented the argument from reason, I have put it forward as a factor that should count in favor of theism, but not necessarily decisively. In evaluating particular arguments, it is important not to get "tunnel vision" and think that the argument now being considered is the only consideration for or against theism. So I can easily imagine someone saying, "Yes, reason is tough for atheists to explain, but theists have worse problems, so I am not going to go there." In fact, I introduced the comparison between the argument from reason and the argument from evil in my book's penultimate paragraph. I wrote:

> However, I do contend that the arguments from reason do provide some substantial reasons for preferring theism to naturalism. The "problem of reason" is a huge problem for natuarlism, as serious or, I would say, more serious, than the problem of evil is for theists. But while theists have expended considerable effort in confronting the problem of evil, the problem of reason has not as yet been acknowledged as a serious problem for naturalism. (Reppert 2003a, p. 128)

Now, once again, the force of the argument from reason could be blunted if it could be shown that whatever the weaknesses of the various materialistic accounts of reason, a non-naturalistic account of reason would have to be, by its very nature, inadequate. However, theism does offer a way, whereby we can say that we need not be saddled with the problem of how reason might arise in a universe that lacked it to begin with, or how rational states can supervene on lower-level states that lack rationality entirely. If we ask "Why does reason exist at all?," the theist can answer "It is on the ground floor of reality. Its existence is more fundamental to the ultimate causes of the universe than the existence of matter itself.

Others have argued that whatever theistic explanations are always inadequate explanations, and that we are better off saying "I don't know" than attributing anything to God. That is the force of what I call the Inadequacy objection, and it is an argument that I will take up later in this chapter.

The argument from mental causation

Hasker's counterfactual argument from mental causation

The third argument, and a very significant one, is the argument from mental causation. Recall for a moment Lewis's discussion of how rationally inferred beliefs must be caused.

He says, "One thought can cause another not by being, but by being seen to be, a ground for it" (Lewis 1978). So besides the existence of facts to think about, and our capacity to perceive a self-evident rule that permits the inference (which we will get to when we talk about logical laws), we also must be able to arrange these facts to prove a conclusion, and it must be possible for new beliefs to be brought into existence by this kind of a process of reasoning. To those who, like Anscombe, are inclined to think that reasons-explanations are always noncausal in nature, I would like to ask how we are to understand words like "convince" or "persuade"? Presumably, rational convincing and persuading is the goal of argumentative discourse, but if reasons are in no sense causal in nature, this is impossible.

Suppose we were to answer Lewis's question "Even if grounds do exist, what have they got to do with the actual occurrence of belief as a psychological event" by saying, "Nothing. Beliefs (if they exist at all given naturalism – of course this is denied by eliminativists) are strictly epiphenomenal. It seems to us that we hold beliefs for good reasons, but if we examine how these beliefs are produced and sustained, we find that reasons have nothing to do with it. We think they do, but this is just one more example of the 'user illusion.'" If we were to say that, it seems to me that the possibility of science as an operation would have to be called into question. As Jerry Fodor once put it:

> If it isn't literally true that my wanting is causally responsible for my reaching, and my itching is causally responsible for my scratching, and my believing is causally responsible for my saying . . . if none of that is literally true, then practically everything I believe about anything is false and it's the end of the world. (Hasker 1999, p. 69–75)

Further, we have to look at just what is involved when we talk about causal transactions. Only some properties of an object are casually relevant to the production of the effect. For example, if I take the baseball that Luis Gonzalez hit to win the 2001 World Series for the Arizona Diamondbacks over the New York Yankees, and throw it at the window, it would break the window only in virtue of the force it applied to the window. It does not break the window in virtue of its having been the ball Gonzo hit against Mariano Rivera. When Lewis says "One thought can cause another not by being, but by being seen to be, a ground for it," obviously not only must one mental event cause another mental event, but it must do so in virtue of its propositional content and, in fact, in virtue of the kind of logical relationships between the relevant propositions.

There are a couple of arguments that have been developed to show that given the causal closure of the physical, rational inference is impossible. In William Hasker's third chapter of *The Emergent Self*, entitled "Why the Physical Isn't Closed," Hasker uses a counterfactual argument to show that the kinds of counterfactuals involved in mental causation will turn out false if the physical is closed (Hasker 1999, pp. 69–75). Let us just take what it is to be persuaded by the evidence for some claim. Let us say that Marcia believes that O. J. Simpson is guilty of murder on the basis of the blood evidence, along with other considerations. What this would have to mean is that if there were no evidence in favor of O. J.'s guilt, she would not think him guilty. If it turns out she was hardwired or sufficiently prejudiced to think of African-American former football stars as guilty of murder regardless of the state of the evidence, this would make your claim to believe on the basis of evidence false. So for someone to claim to believe that O. J. is guilty (or innocent) on the basis of evidence, the following conditionals must be true.

1   If strong evidence supporting O. J.'s guilt exists, then Marcia would believe that O. J. is guilty.

2   If strong evidence supporting O. J.'s innocence exists, then Marcia would believe that O. J. is innocent.

If physicalism is true, then sufficient physical causes for one's forming the belief that O. J. is guilty must exist if you are to believe that O. J. is guilty. Thus, if the physical conditions exist for you to form the belief that O. J. is guilty, then you will form that belief, and if they do not, you will not. Yet those physical conditions contain nothing about blood evidence or any other kind of evidence. After all, it could be a similar world in which the evidence-thoughts do not occur, but the belief is formed anyway. As Hasker explains:

> Following John Pollock, we assume that a counterfactual conditional is true if and only if the consequent is true in all those worlds minimally changed from the actual world in which the antecedent is true. Would a world minimally changed from the actual world in which she doesn't see that her belief is supported by good reasons, be one in which she would not accept the belief? No doubt there are a number of different ways in which the world could be changed just enough to satisfy the antecedent of the conditional; in some of these she accepts the belief while in others she doesn't. And there is no basis for saying that those in which she doesn't accept it are less changed from the actual world in which she does, or *vice versa*. (Hasker 1999, p. 70)

I am assuming here, on the basis of my discussion of intentionality earlier, that mental states are not type-reducible to physical states. However, let us suppose that the mental state supervenes on the physical state. It is true, that, according to strong supervenience, the mental state must exist if the physical state does. Still, we can imagine the truths of supervenience being different from what they are, and if those truths of supervenience are different, the belief is formed in the absence of evidence. Further, if the universe is fundamentally physical, that means that the physical facts are the most fundamental facts in existence, more fundamental, surely, than the truths of supervenience.

Hasker considers the possibility that the truths of supervenience are metaphysically necessary truths. If the laws governing objects in the world are metaphysically necessary truths, then we can take a world of objects similar to this world, except with regard to the psychophysical connections that obtain in this world. Such a world would be a zombie-world, in which the basic properties of matter would be zombie-protons, zombie-neutrons, zombie-electrons, zombie-quarks, or zombie-strings. In such a world, again, the appropriate beliefs could be formed in the absence of the relevant evidence. The mental states are irrelevant to physical events, which have physical causes and only physical causes, according to materialism, and whatever mental states might exist, exist in virtue of the physical states (Hasker 1999, p. 71).

Another important point is that very often, naturalists appeal to evolution in order to explain the existence of reason. The idea is that surely evolution would select for good reasoning methods over bad reasoning methods. However, this will work only if the mental states involved in rational inferences are causally effective. As Hasker says:

> If we accept the physicalist premises of causal closure and the supervenience of the mental, Darwinist epistemology flunks out completely: it has no ability whatever to explain how any of our conscious mental states have even the most tenuous hold on objective reality. (Hasker 1999, p. 76)

On top of this, I should revert to what I said earlier, that the claim that given the physical, the mental necessarily supervenes seems to me just plain ungrounded. Given the physical, why does there have to be just these mental states? Why do there have to be intentional states at all. Appeal to supervenience in this context is just a mask for a lack of understanding, it seems to me.

Barefoot and the four corollary argument

Darek Barefoot, in response to some criticisms of my book by Richard Carrier, has developed a version of the argument from mental causation based on two corollaries of naturalism and two corollaries of reason. The corollaries of naturalism must be true if naturalism is true, the two corollaries of reason must be true if there is to be the sort of rational inference we find in the sciences.

The following are the two corollaries of naturalism:

1   To the extent that changes in natural systems have causes, those causes are potentially available to the senses either directly or by scientific instruments.
2   Every belief accompanies a natural (physical) state, and the properties of a belief are wholly dependent upon and determined by the natural state that it accompanies.

The following are the two corollaries of reason:

1   Reason includes, although it is not limited to, the acceptance of a belief due to the accurate, conscious perception that true premises logically entail it.
2   A belief may be considered to be held rationally only to the extent that what are consciously perceived by the holder to be the reasons for his accepting the belief are in fact the reasons for his doing so. (Barefoot 2007)

It should be noted that the corollaries of reason need not be true of all beliefs. We might believe some things noninferentially because we perceive the objects in question. Thus, perhaps my belief that my glasses are one the table does not require me to draw any inferences in order to be justified. If I have a hunch that Smith will not betray my secret if I tell it to him, this may not have to be due to some traceable reasoning process. However, if we deny that there is rational inference of the kind that I have been talking about in this chapter, which conforms to the two cited corollaries of reason, then the heart of science is ripped out. If physics is a true source of knowledge about the physical, then some people have to be able to draw precise mathematical inferences.

What lies at the heart of naturalism is the idea that we can apply the methods of science, of observation and measurement to every type of reality. In the last analysis, everything is at least potentially available to the senses and we can analyze it in scientific terms. If there are features of reality that we can only reach through introspection, which in principle someone could not figure out looking at it from the outside, then something has escaped the nets of naturalistic analysis.

If a broadly materialist worldview is true, then only physical states can have any causal efficacy. If could provide necessary and sufficient conditions for propositional states by specifying physical states, then we would be able to bring propositional contents into the web of causal interaction in a naturalistic world. However, the trouble is we cannot do that.

The following is an adaptation of an argument Barefoot provides against the reconcilability of the corollaries of reason with the corollaries of naturalism.

1   Only the physical properties of representations can generate functional states in computational systems.
2   Propositional contents cannot be identified with the physical properties and their representations.
3   Therefore, propositional contents cannot generate functional states in computational systems.
4   Propositional contents generate some beliefs in some minds.
5   Therefore, some beliefs in minds cannot be identified with, or wholly dependent upon, functional states in computational systems.

The argument from indeterminate causes

I would put the argument from physicalism to epiphenomenalism in the following way, using the discussion of the indeterminacy of the physical discussed earlier as a basis.

1   Physical states are indeterminate with respect to intentional content.
2   If a broadly materialist worldview is correct, then the physical is causally closed. Nothing over and above the physical state of the world can be responsible for a subsequent physical or mental state.
3   Therefore, if there are mental states, and those mental states have determinate mental content, then that determinate mental content is causally irrelevant to the future course of nature.

I conclude, therefore, that the problem of mental causation is still a serious difficulty for materialism, and failure to solve it calls into question the very scientific enterprise which alone provides the foundations for naturalism. We still have no good materialist answer to the question "Even if grounds do exist, what exactly have they got to do with belief as a psychological event," and, to be honest, I do not think we are going to ever get one.

The argument from the psychological relevance of logical laws

It is not enough that one mental event cause another mental event in virtue of its propositional content. Someone who engages in rational inference must recognize the correctness of the principle of sound reasoning, which one applies to one's inference. *Modus ponens* works, affirming the consequent does not. Our inferences are supposed to be governed by the rules of reasoning we recognize to be correct. However, can these rules of inference ever really govern our reasoning processes? According to physicalism, all of our reasoning processes are the inevitable result of a physical substrate that is not governed by reasons.

So we might ask this question: "Which laws govern the activity we call rational inference?" We might stipulate, for the purposes of this discussion, the idea that laws of physics are accounts of the powers and liabilities of the objects in question. If the materialist claim that laws other than the laws of physics apply to the assemblage of particles we call human beings, then those particles are not what (mechanistic) physics says they are, and we have admitted a fundamental explanatory dualism. If however, the laws are the laws of physics, then there are no powers and liabilities that cannot be predicted from the physical level. If this is so there can be a sort of emergence, in that the basic laws governing a sleeping pill will not mention that the pills tend to put you to sleep. Nevertheless, the pill's soporific effectiveness can be fully and completely analyzed in terms of its physical powers and liability. If this is so, then we will be rational if and only if the physical configurations of matter guarantee that we are physical, and in the last analysis, the laws of logic do not govern our intellectual conduct.

This is especially difficult for the naturalist if you are inclined to think, as I am, that laws of logic pick out ways of thinking that are correct regardless of place, time, or even possible, world. Not only are there no true logical contradictions in Arizona, in Texas, in Georgia, in Iraq, or even in Southern California, there are none on the moon or even in other possible worlds. How could truths that are not local to any space and time affect the brains of those who are in space and time and whose thoughts are under the complete causal influence of a mechanistic physical order. We can certainly imagine, for example, a possible world in which the laws of physics are different from the way they are in the actual world. We can imagine, for example, that instead of living in a universe in which dead people tend to stay dead, we find them rising out of their graves on a regular basis on the third day after they are buried. Nevertheless, we cannot imagine a world in which, once we know which cat and which mat, the cat can be both on the mat and not on the mat. Now can we imagine there being a world in which 2 + 2 is 5 and not 4? I think not.

It is one thing to suggest that brains might be able to "track" states of affairs in the physical world. It is another thing to suggest that a physical system can be aware, not only that something is the case but also that it must be the case; that not only is it the case but also that it could not fail to be the case. Brain states stand in physical relations to the rest of the world, and are related to that world through cause and effect, responding to changes in the world around us. How can these brain states be knowings of what must be true in all possible worlds?

Arguing that such knowledge is trivial because it merely constitutes the "relations of ideas" and does not tell anything about the world outside our minds seems to me to be an inadequate response. If, for example, the laws of logic are about the relations of ideas, then not only are they about ideas that I have thought already but also they are true of thoughts I have not even had yet. If contradictions cannot be true because this is how my ideas relate to one another, and it is a contingent fact that my ideas relate to one another in this way, then it is impossible to say that they will not relate differently tomorrow.

Richard Carrier responds somewhat differently. He says:

> For logical laws are just like physical laws, because physical laws describe the way the universe works, and logical laws describe the way reason works—or, to avoid begging the question, logical laws describe the way a truth-finding machine works, in the very same way that the laws of aerodynamics describe the way a flying-machine works, or the laws of ballistics describe the way guns shoot their targets. The only difference between logical laws and physical laws is that the fact that physical laws describe physics and logical laws describe logic. But that is a difference both trivial and obvious. (Carrier 2004)

What this amounts to, it seems to me, is a denial of the absolute necessity of logic. If the laws of logic just tell us how truth-finding machines work, then if the world were different a truth-finding machine would work differently. I would insist on a critical distinction between the truths of mathematics, which are true regardless of whether anybody thinks them or not, and laws governing how either a person or a computer ought to perform computations. I would ask, "What is it about reality that makes one set of computations correct and another set of computations incorrect?"

If we are completely physical systems, we will "follow" the laws of logic exactly when the physics results in logically correct thought, and we will violate the laws of logic, contradict ourselves, and commit fallacies when the physics governing our brain has us doing that. The laws of logic, or rather, the principles of sound reasoning, are inoperative when it comes to the formation of our beliefs. Ground-and-consequent relationships can, on this view, have nothing to do with what beliefs are caused.

Five Popular Objections

The argument from computers

Some people think it is easy to refute any argument from reason just by appealing to the existence of computers. Computers, according to the objection, reason, they also are undeniably physical system, but they are also rational. So whatever incompatibility there might be between mechanism and reason must be illusory. However, in the case of computers, the compatibility is the result of mental states in the background that deliberately create this compatibility. Thus, the chess computer Deep Blue was able to defeat the world champion Garry Kasparov in their 1997 chess match. However, Deep Blue's ability to defeat Kasparov was not the exclusive result of physical causation, unless the people on the programming team (such as Grandmaster Joel Benjamin) are entirely physical results of physical causation. To assume that, however, is to beg the question against the advocate of the argument from reason. As Hasker points out:

> Computers function as they do because they have been constructed by human beings endowed with rational insight. A computer, in other words, is merely an extension of the rationality of its designers and users, it is no more an independent source of rational insight than a television set is an independent source of news and entertainment. (Hasker 1983, p. 49)

The argument from reason says that reason cannot emerge from a closed, mechanistic system. The computer is, narrowly speaking, a mechanistic system, and it does "follow" rational rules. But not only was the computer made by humans, the framework of meaning that makes the computer's actions intelligible is supplied by humans. As a set of physical events, the actions of a computer are just as subject as anything else to the indeterminacy of the physical. If a computer plays the move Rf6, and we see it on the screen, it is our perception and understanding that gives that move a definite meaning. In fact, the move has no meaning to the computer itself, it only means something to persons playing and watching the game. Suppose we lived in a world without chess, and two computers were to magically materialize in the middle of the Gobi desert and go through all the physical states that the computers went through the last time Fritz played Shredder. If that were true they would not be playing a chess game at all, since there would be no humans around to impose the context that made those physical processes a chess game and not something else. Hence, I think that we can safely regard the computer objection as a red herring.

The problem of interaction

One of the most popular arguments for materialism is the argument that dualism saddles the dualist with the problem of interaction: the problem of seeing how something non-physical can interact with something physical. William Lycan, for example, provides four arguments against mind–body dualism (Lycan 2002, p. 168; quoted in Parsons 2003, p. 72).

First, Lycan argues that Cartesian minds do not fit in with our otherwise physical and scientific picture of the world. However, I have been arguing that a truly scientific under-standing of the world has to include scientists who engage in mathematical and scientific reasoning, and that we need something nonphysical to explain the existence of scientists. Absent an effective reply to my arguments on this score, I can maintain that my dualism, not his materialism, is the truly science-supporting worldview. Further, it is not the case that we know nothing about such a soul. We know that it is the sort of thing whose essence it is to act for reasons, possibly because it was created to do so.

Second, Lycan argues that human beings evolved over aeons through a purely physical process of natural selection and random mutation. However, it is the thrust of my argu-ment that our minds could not be the product of "blind watchmaker" evolution, and it begs the question against my argument to insist that it does, absent a good explanation of how reason is possible in a physicalistic universe. Hence, to insist that our minds are the product of "blind watchmaker" evolution in the face of an argument that suggests other-wise is to beg the question.

Third, according to Lycan, if minds are nonspatial, how could they interact with physical objects in space? However, I did not argue that minds are nonspatial, I am just arguing that the basic explanation of their activity is rational rather than nonrational. Second, if nothing nonspatial can interact with anything spatial, then we would have an argument that a creator God is impossible. Have atheists been missing out on a good argument here? Nev-ertheless, where is the analysis of cause that shows that an effect in space can only have a cause in space? It certainly seems logically possible for something that is not in space to interact with something that is. The claim that it is impossible is often simply made as a bald assertion, without supporting argumentation.

Fourth, Lycan argues that a soul interacting with the body would be a violation of con-servation laws. However, I do not see a problem here either because the conservation laws tell us only what will happen within a closed physical system all things being equal, and cannot tell us what will happen in something outside the physical system interferes. So once again, the argument assumes the truth of physicalism, and so begs the question.

Jaegwon Kim has asked what connects a soul with a body, so as to enable causal con-nections between them (Kim 2001). Now, my argument, as I have indicated earlier, does not actually contend that the soul must be nonspatial. What I have been arguing is that something must exist who can act independently of the nexus of nonrational causation so as to be determined by reasons and not physical causes. It could be in space or not in space.

If the soul is not spatial, then the body might have some identifying characteristic, unique to itself throughout its career, that the soul can identify. Or perhaps God creates and sustains the causal interaction between the soul and the body. Another option is a Thomistic form of dualism, according to which the person is a single thing that is a combination of form (the soul) and matter (the body). On a Aristotelian–Thomistic view, there are, in the final analysis, no purely material objects, and everything is a combination of matter and form. There is also Hasker's emergent dualism (Hasker 1999), which involves the matter having potentialities to produce a soul distinct from itself. If the soul is somehow produced by the body, then the soul should be able to identify the body that produced it. Of course, these sorts of potentialities in matter would be hard to accept within a naturalistic framework, although if theism is accepted, the antecedent probability is lessened.

I do not want to underestimate the difficulties that Kim is posing here. However, I have argued that there must be something inherently rational that is responsible for the rationality we find in the world. It seems that that can be cashed out in a variety of ways, all of which have the advantage of not requiring us to somehow identify our reason with a set of mechanistically defined, inherently nonrational states.

Armchair science

Richard Carrier, in his critique of my book, accused me of doing armchair science maintaining that a materialist account of reasoning would invariably be inadequate. Science is continuously expanding our knowledge of the mind and its capabilities, and while present science may not yet have all the answers as to how the mind works, it is the height of presumption to assume that an adequate physicalist analysis of the mind will not be forthcoming. To make matters worse, my argument contains no discussion of current work in cognitive science and neuroscience (Carrier 2004).

First of all, my argument never denies that brain science can discover a great deal about how the mind works. However, we need to ask what exactly we are expecting science to discover here. Scientific analyses of cognition give us numerous correlations between mental states and brain states. As Moreland puts it:

> It will do no good for the naturalist to claim that once we know more about the brain, we will be able to explain how mental states emerge in the developing brain. At best, such a so-called explanation would merely state a correlation about the fact that such emergence regularly obtains and dualists are happy with such correlation. But a correlation that answers a question is not the same thing as saying how the emergence is exemplified. (Moreland 1988, p. 52)

I have been arguing that there is a logicoconceptual chasm between the physical and the intelligible world. On my view, physical analyses, by their very nature, must perforce be compatible with a multiplicity of mental states, or with the absence of mental states entirely. Success in finding correlations will not solve this problem. Bridging the chasm is not going to simply be a matter of exploring the territory on one side of the chasm. What neuroscience is going to have to come up with is an intertheoretic reduction between the mental and the physical. However, even many naturalists are convinced that such a reduction will not be forthcoming.

Consider the frequently maintained assertion that no "ought" statement can be derived from an "is" statement. Whatever you think of this argument, it seems an inadequate response to say that this claim is guilty of armchair science, that somehow if we mapped the brain and the rest of the physical world well enough we could figure out what moral norms are true and which are not. The kind of assertion made by normative ethics is something that we can see cannot possibly follow logically from scientific claims about the physical world, however comprehensive or sophisticated.

God of the gaps

Another argument frequently advanced against virtually any piece of natural theology is the God of the gaps charge. In fact, this is one of the most popular items in the atheist playbook. We know from the history of science that many things were thought in the past to require an explanation in terms of divine agency are now known to have naturalistic explanations. Rainbows, for example, were once thought to have been put in the sky as a sign, we now know that they can be naturalistically explained in terms of light refraction. Various biological systems show a harmony between means and ends which in the past was cannon fodder for the design argument, but is now explicable in terms of random variation and natural selection. So if there is something that we think cannot be explained in physical terms, just give science some time, and they will figure it out sooner or later.

An instance where the God of the gaps objection appears strong is in the case of Newton's account of the orbits of the planets. His theory would have expected the orbits to go somewhat differently from the way they go, and so he postulated God as the one who keeps the planets in line. Laplace later developed a theory that did not require this kind of divine tinkering, and when asked about Newton's theistic theory, he said "I have no need of that hypothesis."

However, I am not sure that every argument that points to an explanatory difficulty for the naturalist can be effectively answered with a "God of the gaps" charge. Consider, for example, being at a dinner party with someone who is given a large amount of water and creates from it an equal volume of wine. Can we reasonably say that we just have a gap in our understanding. As Robert Larmer points out, our understanding of how wine is made is precisely what makes it so difficult to explain naturalistically.

> What should be at issue in assessing "God of the gaps" arguments is whether they have met these conditions. Claims regarding events traditionally described as miracles and claims regarding the origin and development of life are where "God of the gaps" arguments are most commonly met. In the case of events traditionally described as miracles, it seems very evident that our increased knowledge of how natural causes operate has not made it easier, but more difficult, to explain such events naturalistically. The science underlying wine-making is considerably more advanced today than it was in first century Palestine, but our advances have made it even more difficult to explain in terms of natural causes how Jesus, without any technological aids, could, in a matter of minutes, turn water into high quality wine. Indeed, it is the difficulty of providing a naturalistic account of such events that leads many critics to deny that they ever occurred; though this looks suspiciously like begging the question in favour of naturalism. It is clear that if such events have occurred, the advance of science has made them more, rather than less, difficult to explain in terms of natural causes. Employing a "God of the gaps" argument that the occurrence of such events would constitute good evidence for supernatural intervention within the natural order seems entirely legitimate. (Larmer 2002)

Perhaps even Newton has been given a bad rap, as Plantinga points out:

> Newton seems ... to have suffered a bum rap. He suggested that God made periodic adjust-
> ments in the orbits of the planets; true enough. But he didn't propose this as a reason for
> believing in God; it is rather that (of course) he already believed in God, and couldn't think
> of any other explanation for the movements of the planets. He turned out to be wrong; he
> could have been right, however, and in any event he wasn't endorsing any of the characteristic
> ideas of God-of-the-gaps thought. (Plantinga 1997, footnote 52)

So, I would maintain that there are gaps and there are gaps. It is not just pointing to an
unsolved engineering problem in nature. First of all, the categories of the mental and the
physical are logically incompatible categories. You start attributing mental properties to
physics and you might end up being told that you are no longer describing the physical at
all. Purpose, normativity, intentionality, or aboutness, all these things are not supposed to
be brought in to the physical descriptions of things, at least at the most basic level of
analysis.

Let us consider the gap between the propositional content of thought and the physical
description of the brain. My claim is that no matter in how much detail you describe the
physical state of the brain (and the environment), the propositional content of thought
will invariably be undetermined. This is not my claim or C. S. Lewis's, this argument was
made by the archnaturalist W. V. Quine. As I see it, it is not a matter of getting a physical
description that will work. In my view, the logicoconceptual gap is always going to be there
regardless of how extensively you describe the physical. As I said earlier, bridging the chasm
is not going to simply be a matter of exploring the territory on one side of the chasm.

Second, to a very large extent, the gap between the mental and the physical was caused
by science in the first place. The way physics got going in the early days of modern science
was to attribute such things as colors, tastes, smells to the mind while explaining the physics
of it without having to consider these things. So, for example, in reducing heat to the
mean kinetic energy of gases, science "siphoned off" the feeling of warmth caused by heat
to the mind, and explained heat without reference to how heat feels to us. As Swinburne
put it:

> There is a crucial difference between these two cases. All other integrations into a super-
> science, or sciences dealing with entities and properties apparently qualitatively distinct, was
> achieved by saying that really some of the entities and properties were not as they appeared
> to be; by making a distinction between the underlying (not immediately observable) entities
> and properties and the phenomenal properties to which they give rise. Thermodynamics was
> conceived with the laws of temperature exchange; and temperature was supposed to be a
> property inherent in an object. The felt hotness of a hot body is indeed qualitatively distinct
> from particle velocities and collisions. The reduction was achieved by distinguishing between
> the underlying cause of the hotness (the motion of the molecules) and the sensations which
> the motion of molecules cause in observers. The former falls naturally within the scope of
> statistical mechanic—for molecules are particles' the entities and properties are not of distinct
> kinds. But this reduction has been achieved at the price of separating off the phenomenal from
> its causes, and only explaining the latter. All reduction from one science to another dealing
> with apparently very disparate properties has been achieved by this device of denying that the
> apparent properties (i. e. the 'secondary qualities" of colour, heat, sound, taste, etc.) with which
> one science dealt belonged to the physical world at all. It siphoned them off to the world of
> the mental. But then, but when you come to face the problem of the sensations themselves,

you cannot do this. If you are to explain the sensations themselves, you cannot distinguish between them and their underlying causes and only explain the latter. In fact the enormous success of science in producing an integrated physico-chemistry has been achieved at the expense of separating off from the physical world colours, smells, and tastes, and regarding them as purely private sensory phenomena. *The very success of science in achieving its vast integrations in physics and chemistry is the very thing which has made apparently impossible any final success in integrating the world of mind into the world of physics.* (Swinburne 1986, p. 191, italics mine)

If Swinburne is correct here, the very thing that made reduction possible in many historic cases is going to make it impossible in the case of the mind and matter.

I conclude, therefore, that the "God of the gaps" or even a "soul of the gaps" response to the argument from reason does not work. I am not saying that we just cannot figure out right now why the mental states involved in rational inference are really physical, I am suggesting on principled grounds that a careful reflction on the nature of mind and matter will invariably reveal that there is a logical gap between them that in principle cannot be bridged without fudging categories.

The inadequacy objection

This objection is also extremely popular. It claims that appealing to God or any or any other supernatural entity provides only a pseudoexplanation for the phenomena in question. So, if something cannot be explained naturalistically, it is better to simply say we do not have an explanation than to appeal to something beyond our outside of nature.

So for example, if we were to explain the existence of reason in terms of the theistic God, that would not be to explain the existence of reason at all. The only way reason could be genuinely explained would be if reason could be explained interms of something that is without reason, something like, say, a blind evolutionary process. As Keith Parsons put it:

> Creationist "explanations" do not explain. When we appeal to the inscrutable acts and incomprehensible powers of an occult being to account for mysterious phenomena, we only deepen the mystery. Like Nagel . . . I regard such "explanations" as mere markers for our ignorance, placeholders for expalantion we hope someday to get. (Parsons 1999, p. 84)

However, what we are calling "supernatural" explanations are primarily intentional, teleological, or person explanations that cannot in principle be reduced to impersonal mechanistic explanations. And it is just false to say that in the absence of a further mechanistic explanation, all we have is a "placeholder." Consider my cheering and pumping my fist when Steve Nash hits Amare Stoudemire with a alley-oop pass that results in a slam dunk for Amare against the San Antonio Spurs. The explanation that makes sense of that action on my part is that I am a fan of the Phoenix Suns who especially likes to see them beat the San Antonio Spurs. Having given that explanation, which is intentional in nature, I have not indicated whether or not there is some further explanation available in terms of neurophysiology. No doubt neurophysiology is part of the account (no dualist wants to deny that), but whatever may be involved in that further account, or even if there is no further account and the intentional explanation is all we are ever going to have, nevertheless we do have an explanation and not just a placeholder. Indeed, a detailed analysis of my brain states would be far less explanatory in terms of what anyone wants to know about my state of mind after seeing that slam dunk than the simple intentional explanation that I gave earlier.

If, as I believe, God is a rational, personal being, surely that makes it more likely that rational creatures should arise in a world God creates because persons by nature are interested in communicating with other persons. So the probability that rational beings should emerge looks to me pretty good; the emergence of rational beings in a naturalistic universe seems very unlikely if not impossible.

While we do not know any strict laws concerning God's conduct, we certainly think we know various things regarded God's character which make some divine acts more likely than others. If God were to resurrect someone from the dead who lived in the twenty-first century, it would more likely be Mother Teresa than Adolf Hitler.

The inadequacy objection gratuitously assumes that matter is what is clearly understandable, and that "mind" is something mysterious, the very existence of which has to be explained in terms of unmysterious matter. This seems just false. According to Galen Strawson:

> This is the assumption that we have a pretty good understanding of the nature of matter—of matter and space—of the phsyical in general. It is only relative to this assumption that the existence of consciousness in the material world seems mystifying. For what exactly is puzzling about consciousness, once we put the assumption aside? Suppose you have an experience of redness, or pain, and consider it to be just as such. There doesn't seem to be any room for amything that could be called a failure to understand what it is. (Strawson 1999, p. 13)

On the other hand, matter is described by modern physics in the most mystifying terms imaginable. The philosopher of science Bas van Fraassen writes: "Do concepts of the soul . . . baffle you? They pale beside the unimaginable otheriness of closed space-times, event horizons, EPR correlations, and bootstrap models" (Churchland & Hooker 1985, p. 285).

Parsons says, "When I am told that consciousness and reasoning are due to the inscrutable and miraculous operations of occult powers wielded by an undetectable entity that exists nowhere in the physical universe, I am not enlightened." I will not comment on whether or not this description of mind/body dualism backed up by theism is an apt one, although I consider it to be actually misleading. Nonetheless, I would simply point out that to be enlightened is to discover the truth, and if this is the truth, then it is enlightening, even though it may be epistemically frustrating to someone like Parsons. Second, the "obscurantism" I am advocating may be necessary to preserve science itself, while (if I am right) a mechanistic account of mind undermines the scientific enterprise. Parsons's own theory makes Einstein's theory of relativity and Darwin's theory of evolution the result of blind physical causes. In the last analysis, whose theory is more obscurantist?

Therefore, I maintain that the inadequacy objection gratuitously assumes that the only real explanations are mechanistic explanations, and that this is evidently false. It is supposed to be part of God's nature to be rational. If we explain one thing in terms of something else, and that something else in terms of something else again, the chain of explanation will have to terminate somewhere. The theist explains the existence of rationality in the universe by appealing to the inherent rationality of God. It cannot be the case that the materialist can actually argue that one ought never to explain anything in terms of something having such and such a nature. One cannot go on giving reductive explanations forever. If, as I have argued, we have good reason to suppose that reason cannot be built up out of nonintentional and nonteleological building blocks, then in order to preserve reason and the logical foundations of science, we have good reason to accept a nonmaterialist understanding of the universe. If my argument in this chapter is correct, then explaining reason in terms of unreason explains reason *away*, and undercuts the very reason on which the explanation is supposed to be based.

References

Allison, H. (1989) Kant's refutation of materialism. *The Monist* 79, 190–209.

Anscombe, G. E. M. (1981) *The Collected Papers of G. E. M. Anscombe, Vol. 2. Metaphysics and the Philosophy of Mind*. Minneapolis: University of Minnesota Press.

Baker, L. R. (1987) *Saving Belief*. Princeton, NJ: Princeton University Press.

Balfour, A. (1906) *The Foundations of Belief: Notes Introductory to the Study of Theology*, 8th edn. New York: Longmans.

Balfour, A. (1915) *Theism and Humanism*. New York: Hodder and Stoughton.

Barefoot, D. (2001) "A Response to Nicholas Tattersall's 'A Critique of *Miracles* by C. S. Lewis'," http://www.secweb.org/index.aspx?action=viewAsset&id=89 (accessed December 27, 2007).

Barefoot, D. (2007) "A Response to Richard Carrier's Review of *C.S. Lewis's Dangerous Idea* http://www.infidels.org/library/modern/darek_barefoot/dangerous.html (accessed December 27, 2007).

Beversluis, J. (1985) *C. S. Lewis and the Search for Rational Religion*. Grand Rapids, MI: William B. Eerdmans.

Beversluis, J. (2007) *C. S. Lewis and the Search for Rational Religion*. Amherst, NY: Prometheus Books.

Blackmore, S. (1999) *The Meme Machine*. Oxford: Oxford University Press.

Carrier, R. (2004) "Critical Review of Victor Reppert's Defense of the Argument from Reason," http://www.infidels.org/library/modern/richard_carrier/reppert.html (accessed December 27, 2007).

Churchland, P. (1986) *Neurophilosophy: Toward a Unified Science of the Mind-Brain*. Cambridge, MA: MIT Press.

Churchland, P. (1989) *A Neurocomputational Perspective: The Nature of Mind and the Structure of Science*. Cambridge, MA: MIT Press.

Churchland, P. and Hooker, C. (1985) *Images of Science: Essays on Realism and Empiricism, with a Reply from Bas C. van Fraassen*. Chicago: University of Chicago Press.

Davidson, D. (1970) Mental events. In L. Foster and J. W. Swanson (eds.), *Experience and Theory*. London: Duckworth.

Dennett, D. (1976) Why the law of effect will not go away. *Journal for the Theory of Social Behavior* 5: 2, 171.

Dennett, D. (1987) Evolution, error and intentionality. In *The Intentional Stance*, 287–321. Cambridge, MA: MIT Press.

Feser E. (2005) *Philosophy of Mind: A Short Introduction*. Oxford: Oneworld Press.

Hasker, W. (1973) Transcendental refutation of determinism. *Southern Journal of Philosophy* 9, 175–83.

Hasker, W. (1983) *Metaphysics*. Downer's Grove, IL: InterVarsity Press.

Hasker, W. (1999) Why the physical isn't closed. In *The Emergent Self*, 58–80. Ithaca, NY: Cornell University Press.

Hasker, W. (2003) What about a sensible naturalism: a response to Victor Reppert. *Philosophia Christi* 5, 61.

Horgan, T. (1994) Non-reductive materialism and the explanatory autonomy of psychology. In S. J. Wagner and R. Warner (eds.), *Naturalism*, 295–320. Notre Dame, IN: University of Notre Dame Press.

Kim, J. (2001) Lonely souls: causality and substance dualism. In K. Corcoran (ed.), *Soul, Body, and Survival*, 30–43. Ithaca, NY: Cornell University Press.

Kripke, S. (1980) *Naming and Necessity*. Cambridge, MA: Harvard University Press.

Kripke, S. (1982) *Wittgenstein on Rules and Private Language*. Cambridge, MA: Harvard University Press.

Larmer, R. A. (2002) Is there anything wrong with "God of the gaps" reasoning? *International Journal for Philosophy of Religion* 52, 129–42.

Lewis, C. S. (1947a) *The Abolition of Man*. New York: Macmillan.

Lewis, C. S. (1947b) *Miracles: A Preliminary Study*. New York: Macmillan.

Lewis, C. S. (1955) *Surprised by Joy*. San Diego, CA: Harcourt Brace.

Lewis, C. S. (1962) *The Weight of Glory and Other Essays*. New York: Macmillan.

Lewis, C. S. (1967) *Christian Reflections*. Grand Rapids, MI: William. B. Eerdmans.

Lewis, C. S. (1978) *Miracles: A Preliminary Study*, rev edn. New York: Macmillan.

Lewis, C. S. (1986) The empty universe. In W. Hopper (ed.), *Present Concerns*, 81–2. San Diego, CA: Harcourt Brace.

Lucas, J. R. (1970) *Freedom of the Will*. Oxford: Oxford University Press.

Lycan, W. G. (1985) Epistemic value. *Synthese* 62: 2, 137.

Lycan, W. G. (2002) Philosophy of mind. In N. Bunnin and E. P. Tsui-James (eds.), *The Blackwell Companion to Philosophy*, 168. Oxford: Blackwell.

Mascall, E. L. (1956) *Christian Theology and Natural Science*. New York: Longmans.

Menuge, A. (2004) *Agents under Fire: Materialism and the Rationality of Science*. Lanham, MD: Rowman and Littlefield.

Moreland, J. P. (1998) Should a naturalist be a supervenient physicalist? *Metaphilosophy* 29: 1/2, 35–57.

Nagel, T. (1997) *The Last Word*. Oxford: Oxford University Press.

Parsons, K. (1999) Defending objectivity. *Philo* 2, 84.

Parsons, K. (2000) Further reflections on the argument from reason. *Philo* 3: 1, 101.

Parsons, K. (2003) Need reasons be causes: a further reply to Victor Reppert's argument from reason. *Philosophia Christi* 5: 1, 72.

Plantinga, A. (1993) *Warrant and Proper Function*. Oxford: Oxford University Press.

Plantinga, A. (1997) Methodological naturalism, part II. *Origins and Design* 18: 2, 22–34.

Plantinga, A. (2000) *Warranted Christian Belief*. Oxford: Oxford University Press.

Pratt, J. B. (1922) *Matter and Spirit*. New York: Macmillan Books.

Quine, W. V. (1960) *Word and Object*. Cambridge, MA: MIT Press.

Rea, M. (2002) *World without Design: The Ontological Consequences of Naturalism*. Oxford: Oxford University Press.

Reppert, V. (1989a) The Lewis-Anscombe controversy: a discussion of the issues. *Christian Scholar's Review* 19: 3, 32–48.

Reppert, V. (1989b) *Physical Causes and Rational Belief: A Problem for Materialism?* PhD Dissertation, University of Illinois at Urbana – Champaign.

Reppert, V. (1999) The argument from reason. *Philo* 2: 1, 33–46.

Reppert, V. (2000) Reply to Parsons and Lippard on the argument from reason. *Philo* 2: 1, 76–89.

Reppert, V. (2001) Causal closure, mechanism, and rational inference. *Philosophia Christi* 3: 2, 473–84.

Reppert, V. (2003a) *C. S. Lewis's Dangerous Idea: In Defense of the Argument from Reason*. Downer's Grove, IL: Inter-Varsity Press.

Reppert, V. (2003b) Several formulations of the argument from reason. *Philosophia Christi* 5: 1, 9–34.

Reppert, V. (2003c) Some supernatural reasons why my critics are wrong: a reply to Drange, Parsons, and Hasker. *Philosophia Christi* 5: 1, 77–92.

Reppert, V. (2005) The argument from reason and Hume's legacy. In J. Sennett and D. Groothuis (eds.), *In Defense of Natural Theology*, 253–70. Downer's Grove, IL: InterVarsity Press.

Reppert, V. (2007) *Miracles*: C. S. Lewis's critique of naturalism. In B. L. Edwards (ed.), *C. S. Lewis: Life Works and Legacy*, vol. 3, 153–82.

Ross, J. (1992) Immaterial aspects of thought. *The Journal of Philosophy* 89, 136–50.

Searle, J. (1992) *The Re-Discovery of the Mind*. Cambridge: Cambridge University Press.

Strawson, G. (1999) Little grey cells. *New York Times Book Review*, July 11, 13.

Stump, J. B. (2006) Non-reductive materialism: a dissenting voice. *Christian Scholar's Review* 36: 1, 67.

Swinburne, R. (1986) *The Evolution of the Soul*. Oxford: Clarendon Press.

Van Gulick, R. (2007) "Consciousness." Stanford Encyclopedia of Philosophy, http://plato.stanford.edu/archives/spr2007/entries/consciousness/ (accessed December 27, 2007).

Wielenberg, E. (2007) *God and the Reach of Reason*. Cambridge: Cambridge University Press.

7

The Moral Argument

MARK D. LINVILLE

G. K. Chesterton once remarked that Nietzsche was unable to laugh but could only sneer. I believe his point was that all good satire is animated by moral vision or conviction. Attempts at satire without such conviction never rise above mere sarcasm – sneering. Whether all of this is so is beyond the purpose of this chapter. But we certainly do find Nietzsche sneering in places, and in some of those places, that sneering is directed at moral conviction itself. When in the midst of a tirade against nearly anyone and everyone ever to put pen to paper, Nietzsche heaped scorn upon "G. Eliot" and her fellow "English flat-heads." Eliot – whose actual name was Mary Anne Evans – had long since rejected theistic belief, but she held fast to a sense of moral duty that she regarded as "peremptory and absolute" (Myers 1881, p. 62). Morality, she thought, simply did not require a religious foundation. Indeed, the religious impulse *dilutes* the moral, as thoughts of another world distract from the duties of the present, and hope of an eternal reward reduces moral motivation to a form of egoism. Instead, hers was a "Religion of Humanity," involving "the expansion of the sense of human fellowship into an impulse strong enough to compel us to live for others, even though it be beneath the on-coming shadow of an endless night" (Myers 1881, p. 61). At this, Nietzsche complained, "They are rid of the Christian God and now believe all the more firmly that they must cling to Christian morality" (1968, p. 69). But this "English consistency," he argued, is altogether inconsistent. He urged that, in giving up the Christian faith, "one pulls the right to Christian morality out from under one's feet." The "duty" to which Eliot and her freethinking friends appealed, was actually part and parcel of the system that is Christianity. "By breaking one main concept out of it, the faith in God, one breaks the whole: nothing necessary remains in one's hands" (Nietzsche 1968, pp. 69–70). Indeed, the moral "intuitions" to which Eliot and others appealed were nothing more than the lingering effects of Christianity upon that society – fading echoes of the late deity's voice, whose churches remained as his "tombs and sepulchers" (Nietzsche 1982, pp. 181–2).

If Eliot held out for the reality of a moral law over against the illusion of religion, Nietzsche countered with the exclamation, "Moral judgments agree with religious ones in believing in realities which are no realities" (1968, p. 55). Nietzsche's moral nihilism is handily summarized with his assertion, "*There are altogether no moral facts*" (1968, p. 55). And there are no such facts precisely because neither are there any theological ones.

Nietzsche observed that few of his contemporaries seemed to comprehend the full implications of the death of God – the fact that "belief in the Christian God has ceased to be believable." But once that belief was undermined, all that was built upon it would inevitably collapse, notably "our whole European morality" (1982, p. 447). Morality "has truth only if God is the truth—it stands or falls with faith in God" (Nietzsche 1968, p. 70). For Eliot and the English, "morality is not yet a problem" only for want of discernment.

The moral argument for the existence of God essentially takes Nietzsche's assertion as one of its premises: if there is no God, then "there are altogether no moral facts." But it urges with Evans and against Nietzsche that we have, in our moral experience, good reason to suppose that there are indeed moral facts. And so our moral experience provides some reason for belief in God. The argument may take a variety of forms, some more plausible than others. Popular versions of the argument abound. Some have argued, for instance, that wherever there are laws there is a Lawgiver, so that the existence of moral laws calls for someone who bears a strong resemblance to Moses's Host atop Sinai. Others have argued that without a carrot and a stick – heaven and hell – there is no sufficient incentive for behaving morally. Some might even be heard to argue either that belief in God is required in order to have a *knowledge* of right and wrong, perhaps through some sort of special revelation, or that such explicit belief is required in order to become virtuous – there can be no virtuous atheists, it might be said. Similarly, it is sometimes urged that a society that abandons faith in God is doomed to destruction from within due to moral decay.

More sophisticated, perhaps, is the sort of argument for which Immanuel Kant is famous. If there is no God, then the moral law makes objective demands that are not possibly met, namely, that the moral good of virtue and the natural good of happiness embrace and become perfect in a "highest good" (Kant 1956). But then those demands appear to be empty and, in the face of such an "antinomy," we might come to think of moral requirement as null and void.

For Kant, although God is not the *Author* of the moral law, he is required as a sort of Director of the screenplay. Kant also argued, promisingly, I think, that if "one vast tomb" finally engulfs both the righteous and the wicked, then it is hard to see why moral behavior ultimately matters (Kant 1987, p. 342). But if moral requirements are genuine, it seems that they *ought* to matter in some ultimate sense.[1]

Whatever merits such arguments may or may not have (and some, I think, have no merit at all), none is on offer in the essay that follows. Actually, there are two essays, each a relatively independent version of the moral argument. The first, "An Argument from Evolutionary Naturalism (AEN)," argues that theists can, where naturalists cannot, offer a framework on which our moral beliefs may be presumed to be warranted. In particular, the naturalist's commitment to a Darwinian explanation of certain salient features of human psychology presents an undercutting defeater for our moral beliefs taken as a whole. The argument is thus chiefly epistemological in nature, and seldom strays from the discipline of metaethics. The second essay, "An Argument from Personal Dignity," argues, first, that something like the Kantian notion of human or personal dignity is implicated by the sorts of moral beliefs with which we begin moral reflection. Here, it weighs various competing theories in normative ethics and finds them wanting. Second, theists can, where naturalists cannot, offer a worldview that accommodates the notion of personal dignity.

---

1. George Mavrodes develops an argument along similar lines in Audi and Wainwright (1986).

An Argument From Evolutionary Naturalism

Edward O. Wilson and Michael Ruse have agreed together that "ethics as we understand it is an illusion fobbed off on us by our genes in order to get us to cooperate" (Ruse & Wilson 1989, p. 51). The sociobiologists tell a familiar evolutionary story to justify this striking assertion. The pressures of natural selection have had an enormous influence on human psychology, including the hardwiring of *epigenetic rules*. According to Wilson and Ruse, these are widely distributed propensities to believe and behave in certain ways, and such rules have developed through the interaction of human genetics and human culture. "Epigenetic rules giving us a sense of obligation have been put in place by selection, because of their adaptive value" (Ruse 1998, p. 223). Such rules have adaptive value because they incline us toward adaptive behaviors, and a behavior is adaptive insofar as it tends toward reproductive success. The resulting "sense of obligation" is thus in place, not because it detects any actual moral obligations but because the perceived obligatory behavior is adaptive. Strictly speaking, experiences of, say, moral obligation or guilt are nonveridical: their seeming objects are illusory. Ruse explains:

> The Darwinian argues that morality simply does not work (from a biological perspective), unless we believe that it is objective. Darwinian theory shows that, in fact, morality is a function of (subjective) feelings; but it shows also that we have (and must have) the illusion of objectivity. (Ruse 1998, p. 253)

The belief in moral objectivity is a useful fiction, and its utility is in the name of reproductive fitness. Evolutionary theory is thus wed to some variety of moral antirealism. Ruse thinks Darwin's theory complements Hume's subjectivism.

Hume, of course, maintained that belief in objective moral properties is, at best, unwarranted, and talk of them is, in fact, meaningless. In a pivotal passage, Hume challenges his reader to produce the moral property of some putatively immoral action, such as willful murder, over and above the natural properties that we perceive. "The vice entirely escapes you, as long as you consider the object" (Hume 1978, p. 468). But a closer look does reveal a matter of fact that *is* the object of experience: one's own *sentiment* that is excited by the deed.

> Here is a matter of fact; but 'tis the object of feeling, not of reason. It lies in yourself, not in the object. So that when you pronounce any action or character to be vicious, you mean nothing, but that from the constitution of your nature you have a feeling or sentiment of blame from the contemplation of it. Vice and virtue, therefore, may be compar'd to sounds, colours, heat and cold, which, according to modern philosophy, are not qualities in objects, but perceptions in the mind. (Hume 1978, p. 469)

The mind has a "great propensity to spread itself on external objects" (Hume 1978, p. 167), so that the subjective feelings which, given our constitution, result from the contemplation of some act, are mistaken for perceptions of objective properties of the act itself. As Michael Ruse (1998) sees it, Darwin explained the origins of that constitution.

Some have seized upon these apparent implications of Darwin's theory in order to argue that naturalism – the view that reality is pretty much exhausted by the stuff of the empirical sciences – implies an unpalatable moral skepticism. To take a noteworthy example, C. S.

Lewis argued that if naturalism is true, and human moral beliefs are ultimately the product of our evolution, then the "transcendental pretensions" of morality are "exposed for a sham" (Lewis 2001b, p. 59). Let's call the combination of naturalism and an overall Darwinian account of the origin of species *evolutionary naturalism* (EN). According to Lewis, on EN, the dictates of conscience are little more than an aggregate of subjective impulses, which, although distributed widely throughout our species, are no more capable of being true or false "than a vomit or a yawn" (2001b, p. 58). "If the naturalist really remembered his philosophy out of school," then he would realize that his saying "I ought" is on a par with "I itch," and "my impulse to serve posterity is just the same sort of thing as my fondness for cheese" (Lewis 2001b, p. 59). Morality is thus an "illusion" (Lewis 2001b, p. 56), little more than a "twist of the mind" (Lewis 1996b, p. 18).

Lewis scores an apologetic point when he observes that the very people who defend such a variety of subjectivism are often later found promoting some moral cause. "A moment after they have admitted that good and evil are illusions, you will find them exhorting us to work for posterity, to educate, revolutionise, liquidate, live and die for the good of the human race" (Lewis 2001b, p. 58). Elsewhere, writing with these same thinkers in mind, he quips, "We castrate and bid the geldings to be fruitful" (Lewis 1996a, p. 37). Lewis believes that he has identified a practical inconsistency in such persons: their considered theories entail that morality is an illusion, but they nevertheless *live* as though there are objective moral facts that are the appropriate objects of our serious concern. Moral skepticism is impracticable, but it appears to be implied by a naturalistic worldview. If this is so, then, all other things being equal, we have some reason to reject naturalism.

An argument – call it the argument from evolutionary naturalism (AEN) – thus emerges from such considerations. Perhaps the following is in the spirit of what Lewis has in mind:

(1)   If EN is true, then human morality is a by-product of natural selection.
(2)   If human morality is a by-product of natural selection, then there are no objective moral facts.
(3)   There are objective moral facts.
(4)   Therefore, EN is false.

Of course, AEN, even if successful, is not an argument for the existence of God, but only for the falseness of EN. But it might be employed as an important component of such an argument were one to go on and argue that theism accommodates moral facts in a way that naturalism does not, that, all other things being equal, a worldview that makes sense of moral facts is preferable to one that does not, and so, all other things being equal, theism is preferable to naturalism.

Does AEN succeed? Off the bat, one might note that the falseness of EN is not thereby an argument for the falseness of naturalism, and the latter is the real target of such arguments. Might one be a naturalist without being an *evolutionary* naturalist? Does naturalism *entail* Darwinism? Strictly speaking, it seems possible to affirm the worldview of naturalism without also endorsing the scientific theory of evolution, and so there is no strict entailment. But as Alvin Plantinga, a theist, and Alex Rosenberg, a naturalist, agree, for the naturalist, "Darwinism is the only game in town." Indeed, Richard Dawkins was recently seen sporting a T-shirt that read, "*Evolution: The Greatest Show on Earth, The Only Game in Town.*" Perhaps Dawkins's shirt reflects his more careful comment elsewhere that, "Although atheism might have been *logically* tenable before Darwin, Darwin made it possible to be an intellectually fulfilled atheist" (Dawkins 1986, p. 6). Before Darwin, the inference to Paley's Watchmaker seemed natural, if not inevitable, given a world filled with things "that give the appearance of having been designed for a purpose" (Dawkins 1986, p. 1). Naturalism *sans* Darwinism – like Tarzan *sans* loincloth – is lacking in essentials. It is a worldview at a loss for explanation. While it is conceivable that a critic of AEN might object by driving a wedge between the worldview and the theory, we will retain the focus on the evolutionary version of naturalism.

As we shall see, there are substantial objections to each of the three premises. Premise (3) is an assertion of the truth of moral realism, and, of course, there are a variety of extant antirealist traditions. Antirealists will tell us either that there are no moral facts whatever, or that the moral facts that obtain are not objective – that is, they are not mind-independent or *stance-independent*. When C. S. Lewis originally advanced his argument, perhaps the majority of his philosophical detractors would have embraced noncognitivism, thus denying that there are moral facts. But, at least for the present, I am more interested in those philosophers (of increasing number) who embrace (3), and thus some form of moral realism, but aim to conjoin that commitment to moral realism with EN.

I am primarily interested, then, in objections to (1) and (2). One might object to (1) by denying that natural selection is solely (or even partly) responsible for the emergence of "human morality." Theists are permitted nonsupernatural explanations of some things. Might not the Darwinian be permitted nonevolutionary explanations here and there? And (2) moves rather quickly from an account of the *origins* of human morality to the assertion that its claims to objectivity are false. But why think this? First, such a move might be thought guilty of a well-known fallacy. And should we not at least give an ear to what the evolutionary naturalist may have to say about the possible connections between the workings of natural selection and the truth of our moral beliefs?

AEN and the genetic fallacy

Let us begin with an objection to (2). At first blush, at least, the move there appears guilty of the *genetic fallacy*. At least in standard cases, the fact that a given belief B is the product of some cause C, entails nothing whatsoever regarding its truth or falsity. And (2) concludes that widespread beliefs in moral facts are false if such beliefs have an evolutionary explanation. But some forms of genetic argument may be correct. Suppose we can show that the explanation of someone's belief is *epistemically independent* of whatever would make the belief true. In a discussion that has direct bearing upon the assessment of AEN, Elliot Sober offers an example of such an ill-formed belief (Sober 1994, pp. 93–113). Consider Sober's eccentric colleague, Ben, who believes that he has 73 students in his class because he drew the number 73 from an urn filled with slips of paper numbered from 1 to 100. Presumably, there are no esoteric connections between class attendance and such random drawings. Ben's resulting belief is thus epistemically independent of its would-be truth-maker in that Ben would believe that this was his enrollment *regardless of the actual number* of students in the class. According to Sober, Ben's belief is "probably false."

Might we offer a similar evolutionary argument for moral skepticism? Sober suggests that such an argument is a tall order because one would first have to identify (a) the processes of moral belief formation and (b) the would-be truth-makers for moral beliefs, and then show that (a) and (b) are independent. Call this the *Independence Thesis*. A defense of the Independence Thesis would call for a considerable project in metaethics for which the simple observation that our moral beliefs have evolutionary origins is no substitute.

As Sober sees things, such an evolutionary argument aims to show that "subjectivism" is true. (He identifies subjectivism as the view that "no normative ethical statement is true," and thus seems to have in mind something more akin to noncognitivism or error theory.) That is, such an argument would attempt to establish the Wilson–Ruse assertion that ethics is an *illusion*. But to say that ethics is an illusion is to advance a positive thesis regarding the ontological status of putative moral facts or properties. Presumably, such an argument would call for some positive reason for thinking that the Independence Thesis is true.

Of course, even the truth of the Independence Thesis does not entail that morality is an illusion. At best, we might conclude that it is safe to treat moral beliefs as though they are false on the grounds that it is unlikely that beliefs formed independently of their truth conditions will be true. After all, and all other things equal, we should grant the possibility that Ben's enrollment *is* precisely 73, and the possibility should be conceded even where we have a compelling argument for thinking that urns and numbered slips of paper have absolutely nothing to do with student enrollment decisions. Ben's belief about the number of students in his class is "probably false" only because we suppose that he has about a 1 in 100 chance of drawing a number that corresponds to his enrollment. And, assuming the truth of the Independence Thesis, our moral beliefs are "probably false" in that the odds that truth and adaptiveness would happen to embrace are slim. Sharon Street compares such odds to "setting out for Bermuda and letting the course of your boat be determined by the wind and tides" (Street 2006, p. 13). Well, *bon voyage!*

But we need not argue for the falseness or probable falseness of our moral beliefs. Nor is it necessary to argue for the truth of the Independence Thesis. It is one thing to suggest that there are positive reasons for asserting epistemic independence; it is quite another to say that we *lack* any reason for thinking that a relevant *dependence* relation obtains. We would have a reason for thinking there *is* such a relation just in case the best explanation for a person's having a given belief essentially involves the *truth* of that belief. One might thus argue that belief in objective moral facts is *warranted* only if there is reason for thinking that a relation of epistemic dependence obtains between our beliefs and their truth-makers.

It seems that a plausible Darwinian yarn may be spun in such a way as to offer a complete and exhaustive explanation of our various moral beliefs without ever supposing that any of them are true. According to this story, some behaviors (feeding one's babies, fleeing from large predators) are adaptive, and others (feeding one's babies to large predators) are not. Any predisposition or prompting that increases the probability of the adaptive behavior will thus also be adaptive. A predisposition to make moral judgments or form moral beliefs enforced corresponding behaviors, and so was adaptive for such reasons. Richard Joyce asks, "Can we make sense of its having been useful for our ancestors to form beliefs concerning *rightness* and *wrongness* independently of the existence of rightness and wrongness?" The answer, he thinks, is "a resounding 'Quite possibly'" (Joyce 2006, p. 183).

In review of the "whole complex story" of the evolution of altruism and "helping behavior" as well as the predisposition to form moral beliefs, Joyce notes, "It was no background assumption of that explanation that any actual moral rightness or wrongness existed in the ancestral environment" (Joyce 2006, p. 183). The observation finds support, I think, when we look around at the behaviors of many nonhuman social animals. Individual animals display the predisposition for social behavior – what Darwin called social instincts

– but, presumably, without *judgments* of any sort regarding the appropriateness of the behavior. We explain their behavior – and the *impulse* toward the behavior – by appeal to adaptiveness. Moral properties are not included in the cast of characters. Rightness and wrongness do not even come up. On this Darwinian story, *conscience* is what arises in a social creature once the social instincts are overlain with a sufficient degree of rationality. As Darwin asserted:

> The following proposition seems to me in a high degree probable—namely, that any animal whatever, endowed with well-marked social instincts, the parental and filial affections being here included, would inevitably acquire a moral sense or conscience, as soon as its intellectual powers had become as well, or nearly as well developed, as in man. (Darwin 1882, p. 98)

Wolves in a pack know their place in the social hierarchy. A lower-ranked wolf feels compelled to give way to the alpha male. Were he endowed with the intellectual powers that Darwin had in mind, then, presumably, his "moral sense" would tell him that obeisance is his moral duty. He would regard it as a moral fact that alpha interests trump beta or omega interests. Lupine moral philosophers might even wrangle over the question of whether there *are* such moral facts, and, if so, whether the legitimacy of the ancient hierarchical social system is one of them. But we need not suppose that the moral realists among them have it right in order to understand the genealogy of lupine morals.

Arguably, given an evolutionary account of *human* moral beliefs, there is no reason for thinking that a relation of epistemic dependence obtains, and so, given an evolutionary account, belief in moral facts is unwarranted (Joyce 2006, p. 183). If our moral beliefs are without warrant, then they do not amount to moral knowledge. We might thus modify AEN so that (2) gives way to

(2*)   If human morality is a by-product of natural selection, then there is no moral knowledge.

There is moral knowledge only if there are warranted moral beliefs, and the suggestion under consideration is that an evolutionary account serves to *undercut* whatever warrant we might have had for those beliefs.

Bertrand Russell allegedly once observed, "Everything looks yellow to a person suffering from jaundice." Actually, I believe the truth of the matter is that *people* suffering from jaundice *look* yellow. But suppose that *both* are right: jaundiced people both appear and are appeared to yellowly. Jones enters Dr. Smith's office, complaining of various and vague discomforts. Smith takes one look at Jones and exclaims, "Your skin has a very tawny appearance!" He diagnoses Jones with jaundice and prescribes accordingly. Later, it occurs to Smith that *all* of his patients have a yellowish tint, as do his charts, the floor tiles, once-white pills, and the nurses' uniforms. A simple blood test determines that *he* is suffering from jaundice. It dawns on the doctor that Jones would have appeared yellow to him *regardless* of Jones' actual condition. Has Smith now a reason for supposing *Jones is jaundiced* is false in the way that, say, a negative blood test would provide such a reason? It seems not. Perhaps Jones *is* jaundiced. Smith simply lacks any reason for thinking that Jones' appearance was caused by Jones' condition, or that the belief that Jones was jaundiced is epistemically dependent upon any medical facts about Jones. And this is to suggest that facts about Dr. Smith's own condition have now supplied him with an *undercutting defeater* for his belief regarding Jones' condition.

As we have seen, Wilson and Ruse (and Lewis, hypothetically) draw the inference that ethics is an *illusion* – there are no objective moral facts. And they draw this conclusion from a consideration of the evolutionary function of our moral beliefs. We have the beliefs that we do, they suppose, because of their reproductive advantage, and not because of their truth. Thus, they think, Darwinism poses a *rebutting* defeater for our moral beliefs, as well as for moral realism itself. But it seems to me that the proponent of AEN might back off from the stronger claim that Darwinism entails that there are no moral facts, speaking instead of whether we are *warranted* in our ordinary moral beliefs. In this way, AEN becomes an *epistemological* argument for moral skepticism.

Judith Thomson (Harman & Thomson 1996) suggests that any red-blooded moral realist should seek to defend the *Thesis of Moral Objectivity* (TMO):

(TMO)   It is possible to find out about some moral sentences that they are true.

Of course, one may challenge TMO either by arguing that moral sentences never express true propositions or that it is not possible to find out. The former route involves advancing a positive metaethical theory that either denies that "moral sentences" ever express moral propositions *at all* (because there just *are* no moral propositions), or denies that moral propositions are ever *true*, or else denies that their truth is mind-independent. The latter route simply involves advancing an epistemological argument to the effect that no one is in a position to *know* whether any moral proposition is ever true. In challenging the warrant of our moral beliefs, AEN takes this route. As Richard Joyce observes, the conclusion that our moral beliefs are "unjustified" is "almost as disturbing a result" as an argument for the actual falseness of those beliefs (Joyce 2006, p. 180).

The suggestion, then, is that Darwinism presents us with an undercutting defeater for such beliefs. And so, instead of (3), perhaps we want:

(3*)   There is moral knowledge.

And this takes us to our conclusion.

(4)   EN is false.

What we lack is some reason for thinking that the adaptiveness of a moral belief depends in any way upon its being true. Perhaps, then, the tables may be turned. Instead of Sober's suggestion that the AEN defender must show that moral beliefs are independent of any truth-makers, perhaps the onus is on those who assert dependence. Why, given EN, should we suppose the world to include anything more than natural facts and properties and our subjective *reactions* to those properties? We will return to this question momentarily, and consider some possible replies. But first, let us consider a challenge to our Premise (1).

AEN and "greedy reductionism"

The evolutionary naturalist is saddled with the task of explaining the connection between adaptiveness and truth only if they accept our first premise.

(1)   If EN is true, then human morality is a by-product of natural selection.

In fact, (1) is widely rejected. Consider first a homely example illustrating the reason for this rejection.

I once attended a university lecture given by a noted animal ethologist who was convinced that evolutionary psychology applies to human behavior just as surely as it applies to the canines with which she specialized. She had a good stock of examples of how widespread human behaviors betray their evolutionary and genetic roots. Suppose, she said, you are sitting on your sofa in your living room. The front door opens, and in walks a stranger, uninvited. You bristle with fear, anger, and resentment, and experience a rush of adrenalin. On the other hand, suppose that, as you are sitting there, a bird flies in through an open window and lights on a curtain rod. While, out of a concern for your new upholstery, you might take measures to shoo the bird outside, you experience none of the emotions triggered by the human intruder. Why the difference? She answered: because of our evolutionary heritage, we have been hardwired to be *territorial* toward conspecifics – members of our own species – and more tolerant of the company of other species. The difference in the two reactions is thus predicted on a sociobiological reckoning of human psychology.

But is there not a simpler, more straightforward and "cognitive" explanation? In the case of the human intruder, it is reasonable to think that harm is intended. As a moral agent, he is presumably capable of understanding and acting upon societal laws as well as the rules of morality and etiquette, and his intrusion likely signals a willful breach of all of these in order to have gained entry. And then there is that ski mask.

Arguably, *resentment* is properly directed only at *persons* in the event that they cause or intend some harm. I may be unhappy that the wind has toppled a tree, causing property damage. I may lament the fact that termites have made a meal of my guitar collection. But resentment would be misplaced and would perhaps indicate misunderstanding or emotional immaturity on my part. Lacking such moral agency, the invading bird is incapable of *intending* harm, and he is likely already showing signs of regret for what seemed at first a good idea. And, in any case, it is easy to imagine that fear, resentment, anger, and adrenalin would present themselves in the event that my door is darkened not by an intruding human but by an Alpha Centaurian who, although a person, shares no Linnaean rank whatsoever with me.

I have been instructed more than once that the sociobiological assumptions of an argument such as AEN have been "widely discredited." Sociobiologists are often accused of forcing genetic and evolutionary explanations for widespread human behaviors and thereby supplanting more plausible cultural or "cognitive" or otherwise nonevolutionary explanations. Daniel Dennett charges Wilson and others with a biological form of "greedy reductionism," for their apparent assumption that the genes have human behavior and culture reined-in on a sort of leash. As Dennett (1995) wryly puts it, the fact that tribesmen have everywhere and always thrown their spears pointy-end first does not suggest a "pointy-end-first gene." Many such traits are instead to be attributed to "the general nonstupidity of the species." C.S. Lewis's character, Ransom, in *Out of the Silent Planet*, was surprised to discover that a boat constructed on Malacandra (Mars) was very much like a human-built boat. "Only later did he set himself the question, 'What else could a boat be like?'" (The astute Lewis reader might also have noticed that Malacandran hunters throw *their* spears pointy-end first, as Dennett would have predicted.) Some ideas are just better than others and, assuming a minimal degree of rationality, perhaps we have been equipped to discover and implement them.

The point applies forcefully in our assessment of AEN. The argument, as stated, seems to assume that our "moral beliefs" have an evolutionary explanation. We generally view deception, theft, and violence as wrong. We believe that good parents care for the welfare of their children and that kindness calls for reciprocation. We have an urge to help those who need help that we are capable of rendering. We tend to share the belief that basically equitable arrangements are *just* or manifest the moral property of justness. But, for one thing, it is just implausible to think that any fairly determinate *belief* has somehow been fashioned at the genetic level and then lodged, intact, within the human brain. Of his belief, "I ought to reciprocate to Mary for picking me up at the airport," Richard Joyce asks, "What does natural selection know of *Mary* or *airports*?" (Joyce 2006, p. 180). It would be like asserting that an unfortunate Tourette's-like disease resulted cross-culturally and through-out history in some determinate and meaningful combination of ejaculated words: "*Peter Piper picked a peck!*"

Further, do all of these traits find their explanation in the selection pressures that were at work when we came down from the trees? Is this not akin to the suggestion that all human problems stem from the trauma of early potty training? Is it not possible that certain moral beliefs are widespread because, like the hunting techniques of Dennett's tribesmen, they simply *make sense*? Philip Kitcher writes:

> All that selection may have done for us is to equip us with the capacity for various social arrange-
> ments and the capacity to formulate ethical rules. Recognizing that not every trait we care to
> focus on need have been the target of natural selection, we shall no longer be tempted to argue
> that any respectable history of our ethical behavior must identify some selective advantage for
> those beings who first adopted a system of ethical precepts. It is entirely possible that evolution
> fashioned the basic cognitive capacities—*alles übriges ist Menschenwerk*. (Kitcher 1985, p. 418)

Thus, our evolution may have provided us with the intellectual tools required for building cathedrals, playing chess, and drawing up social contracts. But might not these activities be more or less *autonomous* as far as the genes are concerned?

Let us agree, at least provisionally, that there are extremes to be avoided when seeking evolutionary explanations for human behavior. Thus, "It's all about the genes, stupid" expresses a form of greedy reductionism. Mary Midgley's own term for such reductionistic explanations is the "hydraulic approach," after the simpleminded person who, in seeking an explanation for rising damp, seeks a single place where the water is coming in (Midgley 1979, p. 57).

But extremes tend to come in pairs. Is it reasonable, given a background acceptance of evolutionary theory, to suppose that our evolution has had *nothing* to do with the distribution of widespread moral beliefs?

For one thing, one might have thought that to appeal to natural selection to explain incisors and libidos but to exclude the deepest springs of human behavior from such an account would seem rather a tenuous position to hold. Moral behavior is not the sort of thing likely to be overlooked by natural selection because of the important role that it plays in survival and reproductive success (Sommers & Rosenberg 2003, p. 659). Early ancestors who lacked the impulse to care for their offspring or to cooperate with their fellows would, like the celibate Shakers, have left few to claim them as ancestors.

Midgley refers to the wholesale rejection of evolutionary psychology as the "blank paper view" – a notion of humans as "totally plastic" and "structureless." Stephen Gould, she thinks, assumes a view implying that "newborn babies [are] what bear cubs were once supposed to be—indeterminate lumps of animal protoplasm, needing to be licked into shape by their elders" (Midgley 1979, p. 66). To B. F. Skinner's claim that the capability for abstract thought arises not from some "cognitive faculty" but from "a particular kind of environment," she quips, "So why can't a psychologist's parrot talk psychology?" (Midgley 1979, p. 20). To the blank paper view in general, which would deny that we humans come equipped with any innate tendencies whatsoever, she asks, "How do all the children of eighteen months pass the news along the grapevine that now is the time to join the sub-culture, to start climbing furniture, toddling out of the house, playing with fire, breaking windows, taking things to pieces, messing with mud, and chasing the ducks?" (Midgley 1979, p. 56). More recently, Richard Joyce has argued forcefully that this *tabula rasa* view "is obviously wrong." Indeed, "broadly speaking, no sensible person can object to evolutionary psychology." (He also observes that many of the objections are *politically* motivated and may even evince an unfortunate willingness to treat science as a wax nose, shaped to suit particular political agendas.)

Midgley maintains that the standard "nature versus nurture" debate presents a false dichotomy between two implausible extremes, and Joyce adds to this that the dichotomy "is so dead and buried that it is wearisome even to mention that it is dead and buried." If the extreme version of the blank paper view says, paraphrasing Locke, that there is nothing in human nature that is not put there by experience, Midgley, in effect replies after Leibniz, "*except for human nature itself.*"

If "instincts" refers to basic predispositions, drives, or "programs," then humans have instincts, but the more interesting of these are, by and large, "*open* instincts" or "programs with a gap." She suggests that the more complex an animal, the greater the "gap" in the program. The gap, where it exists, leaves it to the intelligence – rational reflection and culture in general in the case of humans – of the individual or the species to fill in the details. Migratory waterfowl come equipped with a basic drive to follow the sun south in the winter, but the programming itself need not specify the details of the itinerary. While the dances of bees or the songs of some birds may be due almost exclusively to their pro-gramming, so that the *precise patterns* are genetically choreographed, the dancers and singers displayed on, say, *American Bandstand*, might be supposed to have a bit more lati-tude. And this remains true even if there proves to be an evolutionary answer to the ques-tion, "Why are people fond of such things as singing and dancing?" (My minister in childhood insisted that dancing is "foreplay set to music." In this he may have found one point of agreement with the evolutionary psychologists.)

That latitude – the gap in Midgley's open instincts – would seem to leave ample room for Kitcher's *Menschenwerk*, whether it involves composing a piece of 12-bar blues or forging a social contract. Joyce notes that, "By claiming that human morality is genetically 'programmed,' one doesn't deny the centrality of cultural influence, or even imply that any manifestation of morality is inevitable" (Joyce 2006, p. 8). The "development of ethical precepts" of which Kitcher speaks, thus may well be the result of careful deliberation and rational reflection, but perhaps these are in response to proclivities that come with our programming. Such programming *may* be rather more determinate than a mere *capacity* for programming. Mammalian mothers are provided with both the capacity for mother-hood and a *nearly* irresistible impulse to nurture offspring.

Along these lines, Sharon Street (2006) distinguishes between *basic evaluative tendencies* and *full-fledged evaluative judgments*. The latter include our specific moral beliefs that might be formulated as moral principles or rules, and they may be explained by appeal to a variety of influences, cultural and otherwise. The former are "proto" forms of evaluative judgment that are unreflective and nonlinguistic impulses towards certain behaviors that seem "called for." She argues that "relentless selection pressure" has had a *direct* and "tremendous" influence on our basic evaluative tendencies and these, in turn, have had a major – but not necessarily overriding – *indirect* effect on our actual moral beliefs or full-fledged evaluative judgments.

If such programming and predispositions provide our basic moral orientation, then *it is within their scaffolds that all moral reflection takes place*. Our *reflective beliefs* about the duties of parenthood or of friendship, for instance, arise from more basic parental and altruistic drives that predate and are presupposed by all such reflection. While this evolutionary account provides a role for reason, that reason is in effect, to borrow from Hume, the slave of the passions. Those "passions" – Street's basic evaluative tendencies – are almost certainly *not* cultural artifacts. Evolutionary theory requires, and the experiences of common life suggest, that they are not. Human mothers sometimes require instruction on *how* to care for their newborns. But this typically presupposes *that* they care, and that such caring comes as a part of the mother's standard equipment.

Bottlenose dolphins off Australia have been spotted wearing sea sponges on their snouts. Hardly a fashion statement, the sponges presumably protect them from sharp objects and stinging marine animals while foraging on the bottom. Further, the behavior appears to be passed on exclusively from mothers to daughters. Biologists see here clear evidence of *cultural transmission* among the dolphins. It is highly unlikely that this behavior is the product of a "sponge-on-the-snout gene." It is, with apologies to Kitcher, *Delfinwerk*. But it is *equally* unlikely, I think, that the mammalian drive to nurture offspring, seen in these mother–daughter sessions among dolphins, is *also* a feature of dolphin culture. Here, it is exceedingly reasonable to suppose that they *are* "compelled by their genes."

The sponge trick and the task of mother–daughter instruction are the result of intelligence set to work at solving problems posed, respectively, by the instincts of self-preservation and motherhood. Were the local conditions of survival different, the "idea" might never have occurred. And, presumably, were the circumstances of dolphin evolution relevantly different, mother-daughter sessions of *any* kind might have been unnecessary, and delphine maternal instincts might have been nonexistent. "Teach your children well," after all, is a precept happily ignored by the female sea turtle, whose maternal "duties" are discharged along with her eggs.

Similarly, human culture is responsible for great accomplishments that assuredly are not the direct product of our evolution. And these may well include complex systems of moral precepts. Perhaps human social contracts – like sponges on the snout – are Good Tricks in that they solve problems posed by some combination of genetics plus environment plus intelligence. Rationality – *Menschenwerk* – is certainly employed. But it is an *instrumental* rationality.

We are now in a position to refine our claim at (1). "Human morality" is a by-product of natural selection in that a fundamental moral orientation – Street's "basic evaluative tendencies" and Midgley's "programming" – is in place because it was adaptive for our ancestors given the contingencies of the evolutionary landscape. Thus, the "program" provides *general* directives or tendencies. The "gap" allows room for rational reflection regarding our moral beliefs, but their very rationality is conditional or hypothetical: *given* the program that has been bequeathed to us by our genes, some policies are better than others. The program itself – with the general "moral" orientation that it determines – is precisely as it is due to its adaptive value given the contingencies of the evolutionary land-scape. Even if the gap is positively *cavernous* for humans, allowing for rational and moral deliberation, it is nevertheless found within the scope of our programming that is directly explained by appeal to natural selection. Moral reasoning would then appear to be *means-end* reasoning, where the ends have been laid down for us by natural selection.

Counterfactually, had the programming been relevantly different, so would the range of intelligent choices. As we saw, Darwin was of the opinion that the moral sense is the result of a sort of recipe – what you get when you begin with a set of social instincts and throw in a sufficient degree of intelligence. There may be "forced moves" through evolu-tionary design space, as Daniel Dennett (1995) has observed. For instance, given locomo-tion, stereoscopic vision is highly predictable. But Darwin did not think that any determinate set of moral precepts or dictates of conscience was among them. Consider what he described as an "extreme example" and what I will call a *Darwinian counterfactual*.

> If . . . men were reared under precisely the same conditions as hive-bees, there can hardly be a doubt that our unmarried females would, like the worker-bees, think it a sacred duty to kill their brothers, and mothers would strive to kill their fertile daughters, and no one would think of interfering. (Darwin 1882, p. 99)

Given the actual conditions of our "rearing," we have come to believe that our children and siblings are deserving of our care and respect, and that equitable bargaining outcomes are just. But here we are asked to imagine a world in which the resulting fundamental moral orientation – Midgley's open instincts – is different. Darwin appears to countenance the possibility of a species that is prompted, *even upon reflection*, to behave in ways that are inequitable and, from our standpoint, unjust. If rational and moral reflection takes its cue from a more primitive predisposition, then have we any reason for supposing that such reflection – the product of culture – would inevitably settle upon equitable treatment?

Recall our lupine philosophers who find themselves strongly inclined to think in terms of a social hierarchy and to regard anything like Bentham's dictum – "Each to count for one, none to count for more than one" – an absolute *howler*. Lacking opposable thumbs and all, they do not write books. But if they did, one learned treatise might be titled, *Our Caste System of Justice*, with chapters on "Duties of Obeisance" and "Beta Encounters Alpha: Rules of Engagement." If humans as a species have come to regard equitable arrangements as fair or just (have they?), then perhaps this is only because their initial programming was wired as it was given the circumstances of human evolution. We have the actual moral orientation that we do because it was adaptive. Had the circumstances been different, some other set would have conferred fitness. Is there any plausible reason to suppose that such a moral orientation is adaptive because its resultant moral beliefs are *true*? Does this not return us to Joyce's observation, "It was no background assumption of that explanation that any actual moral rightness or wrongness existed in the ancestral environment" (2006, p. 183)?

Of course, one might reply to this line of argument by insisting that a wedge be driven between Street's "basic evaluative tendencies" and her "full-fledged moral judgments." Have we not just acknowledged that the results of such programming are not inevitable?

Following Dennett and others, might we not suggest that, with the advent of culture it became possible for us to "snap" Wilson's "genetic leash" and strike out on our own? Perhaps, then, morality is autonomous, engaging in reflection that is independent of the drives of human nature. Such a reply, however, is just implausible. Our considered judgments regarding duties of parenthood or kinship or friendship clearly find their wellspring in our psychology, just as beliefs about the sacred duties of Darwin's hive bees or our wolves would find their respective sources in apiarian or lupine psychologies. And these respective psychologies appear to be what they are because of the circumstances of evolution in each case.

There is reason, then, to accept AEN Premise (1).

(1)   If EN is true, then human morality is a by-product of natural selection.

It is time to return to the question that we raised just before our assessment of (1). If human morality is a by-product of natural selection, is there any reason to suppose that there is a relevant dependence relation between (a) the processes of belief formation and (b) the would-be truth-makers for such beliefs? We can sharpen the question by simply asking whether there is a reason to suppose that the *belief-producing mechanisms* of our moral beliefs are *truth-aimed*? Is there a plausible defense of the Dependence Thesis available to the naturalist?

Epistemological arguments and the Dependence Thesis

I have characterized AEN as an *epistemological* argument for moral skepticism. The aim is to show that, on EN, our moral beliefs are without warrant. This is because the mechanisms responsible for our moral beliefs appear to be *fitness*-aimed, and such an account of those mechanisms seems not to require our thinking that they are also truth-aimed. As Tamler Sommers and Alex Rosenberg (2003) have put it, "if our best theory of why people believe P does not require that P is true, then there are no grounds to believe P is true" (p. 667). In this, AEN resembles a much-discussed argument urged by Gilbert Harman (1977).

Harman's so-called "problem with ethics" is that moral facts, if such there are, appear to be explanatorily irrelevant in a way that natural facts are not. Hitler's behavior, for example, may be fully explained by appealing only to certain natural facts about him, such as his anti-Semitism, monomania, and will to power. According to Harman, we need not suppose that, over and above such natural facts, there is a moral fact of Hitler's depravity. Nor must we appeal to his actual depravity in order to explain our *belief* that he was depraved. "You need only make assumptions about the psychology or moral sensibility of the person making the moral observation" (Harman 1977, p. 6). Harman may thus be viewed as arguing in his own manner that we "have no reason to believe that the best explanation for our moral beliefs involves their truth." We have no good reason to suppose that the causes of those beliefs are dependent upon whatever would make them true.

Nicholas Sturgeon has replied first by noting that moral facts *are* commonly and plausibly thought to have explanatory relevance. Both Hitler's behavior and our belief that he was depraved are handily explained by his actual depravity, and this is, in fact, the default explanation. He observes, "Many moral explanations appear to be good explanations ... that are not obviously undermined by anything else we know." "Sober people frequently offer such explanations of moral observations and beliefs," and "many of these explanations look plausible enough on the surface to be worth taking seriously" (Sturgeon 1988, p. 239).

Citing Quine's naturalized epistemology – what Sturgeon elsewhere (1992, p. 101) refers to as the method of reflective equilibrium – he notes, "We cannot decide whether one explanation is better than another without relying on beliefs we already have about the world" (Sturgeon 1988, p. 249). Reflective equilibrium, a method employed in both science and ethics, begins with certain considered judgments, and with the assumption that our theories, scientific and otherwise, are roughly correct, then moves "dialectically in this way between plausible general theses and plausible views about cases, thus seeking a reflective equilibrium" (Sturgeon 1992, p. 101). Sturgeon notes that, whereas he allows for the inclusion of moral beliefs among the initial set, Harman does not. But, he argues, there is no non-question-begging justification for singling out moral beliefs as unwelcome in the initial set while allowing those of a scientific or commonsense nature.

In particular, Harman's argument requires us to consider the conditional, *If Hitler had done just what he did but was not morally depraved, we would, nevertheless, have believed that he was depraved.* But this calls for our entertaining the possibility that

(H)   Hitler would have done just what he did even had he not been morally depraved.

(H), in turn, presupposes that there is a possible world in which Hitler does what he did but is not morally depraved. One will seriously entertain such a counterfactual only in the event that one accepts that

(H*)   There is a possible world W in which Hitler's natural properties are identical to those that he possesses in the actual world but in which Hitler is not depraved.

But Sturgeon's own moral theory invokes the *supervenience* of moral properties upon natural properties. On standard accounts, if some moral property M supervenes upon some natural property (or, more likely, some *set* of natural properties) N, then it is *impossible* for N to be instantiated unless M is also instantiated. Thus, we appear to have the following implication:

(S)   For every world W, every natural property N and every moral property M, if M supervenes upon N in W, then for all worlds W*, if N obtains in W*, then M is exemplified and supervenes upon N in W*.

Allowing that there is a world that includes N but not M requires either denying that M *actually* supervenes upon N or holding that (S) is false. And so (H*) and (S) together entail that there is *no possible world* in which Hitler's having the personality and displaying the behavior that he did constitutes depravity. To get off the ground, Harman's argument tacitly *assumes* that there *are* no moral facts or properties, which, of course, is the very point at issue.

Further, Harman must be understood to suppose that we would have *believed* that Hitler was depraved even if, despite having done all of the things that we know him to have done, he was *not*, in fact, depraved. One should be prepared to grant this point only if one has already granted that our whole moral theory is "hopelessly mistaken" (Sturgeon 1988,

p. 251). But the fact that our theory *would* be wrong *were* this possible is no reason for either abandoning the theory or embracing the possibility. Thinking otherwise provides a recipe for skepticism of a more global variety. Thus, "We should deny that any skeptical conclusion follows from this. In particular, we should deny that it follows that moral facts play no role in explaining our moral judgments" (Sturgeon 1988, p. 251).

Sturgeon's appeal to reflective equilibrium thus plays a crucial role in his reply to Harman. We begin moral reflection with a fund of considered judgments that may serve as the initial data for the construction of ethical theories. And, Sturgeon suggests, these beliefs are "not obviously undermined by anything else we know." Since *all* theorizing has these same humble origins, how can one nonarbitrarily single out a particular domain of beliefs for suspicion? Indeed, David Brink goes to some length in arguing that "Harman fails to demonstrate any explanatory disanalogy between the scientific and moral cases" (Brink 1989, p. 185). A scientist's belief that a proton has just passed through a cloud chamber *might* be explained merely by appeal to his background beliefs and theoretical commitments. For example, his theory has it that the appearance of a vapor trail is evidence of proton activity, and so, *of course*, when he sees, or *believes* that he sees, a vapor trail, he forms the belief in the proton. But here, we are required to be realists about protons only if we have assumed that the scientist's theory is "roughly correct." Indeed, my conviction that I have a head, and my belief that *other* heads involve other minds are best explained by the actual existence of such heads and minds only on the assumption that a common theory of life is generally on the right track. But, again, why extend this courtesy in these cases while being decidedly *discourteous* in the case of morality?

To my mind, Sturgeon's reply to Harman succeeds. Why, indeed, should our considered moral beliefs be excluded at the outset? Nearly a century ago, in his Gifford Lectures, W. R. Sorley cited "Lotze's Dictum," after the nineteenth-century German philosopher Rudolph Hermann Lotze: "The true beginning of metaphysics lies in ethics" (Sorley 1935, p. 3). Sorley observed that "the traditional order of procedure" – business as usual in metaphysics – was to construct an interpretation of reality – a worldview – that drew exclusively upon nonmoral considerations, such as the deliverances of the sciences. Not until the task of worldview construction was complete did one "go on to draw out the ethical consequences of the view that had been reached" (Sorley 1935, p. 1). Sorley thought it likely that such a method would result in an artificially truncated worldview, and that moral ideas would be given short shrift. And the exclusion of our moral experience was simply arbitrary. "If we take experience as a whole, and do not arbitrarily restrict ourselves to that portion of it with which the physical and natural sciences have to do, then our interpretation of it must have ethical data at its basis and ethical laws in its structure" (Sorley 1935, p. 7). Harman seems to be following that traditional procedure that Sorley criticized, and he thus manifests that same arbitrariness. His results are achieved only by begging the question against the moral realist.

But even Sorley would, in principle, admit that the initial "ethical data" must prove to be compatible with everything else that is included in our final interpretation of reality. In fact, in the same year that Sorley delivered his Gifford Lectures, George Santayana published *Winds of Doctrine*. There, he complained that Bertrand Russell's then-held moral realism was the result of Russell's "monocular" vision. "We need binocular vision to quicken the whole mind and yield a full image of reality. Ethics should be controlled by a physics that perceives the material ground and the relative status of whatever is moral" (Santayana

1957, p. 115). Russell took notice of Sorley's "ethical data" – "the ideas of good and evil as they appear in man's consciousness" (Sorley 1935, p. 1), but, according to Santayana, he simply refused to "glance back over the shoulder" to see that "our moral bias is conditioned" and has its basis "in the physical order of things" (Santayana 1957, p. 115). Indeed, Russell had made frequent appeals to common moral sense – not at all unlike the contemporary appeal to reflective equilibrium – in the course of his arguments. But Santayana would have none of this.

> Mr. Russell . . . thinks he triumphs when he feels that the prejudices of his readers will agree with his own; as if the constitutional unanimity of all human animals, supposing it existed, could tend to show that the good they agreed to recognize was independent of their constitution. (1957, p. 166)

Clearly, Santayana thought that human moral beliefs are a function of the human constitution, and the latter had taken its shape as the result of processes with no concern for the truth. An appeal to those very constitutional beliefs hardly offsets this skeptical conclusion. Interestingly, Santayana's arrows found their mark. Russell eventually abandoned his moral realism, crediting these very arguments.

The lesson carries over to our current discussion. While Harman seems not to have provided any good reason for challenging those initial ethical data – the initial moral beliefs with which we are equipped – our vision has been "monocular." AEN calls for a glance over the shoulder, and what we see poses a challenge to Sturgeon's reflective equilibrium despite his assertion that widely held judgments are "not obviously undermined by anything else we know." An appeal to those considered judgments that tip off the process of reflective equilibrium would hardly assuage Sharon Street's worry:

> If the fund of evaluative judgments with which human reflection began was thoroughly contaminated with illegitimate influence . . . then the tools of rational reflection were equally contaminated, for the latter are always just a subset of the former. (2006, p. 125)

What we require, then, is some assurance that our original fund is *not* contaminated. And so, we return to our question, what reason have we for supposing that the mechanisms responsible for those judgments are *truth-aimed*? What reason have we for supposing that the Dependence Thesis is true?

Santayana suggested an answer to this question that he knew was unavailable to the atheist Russell: if God exists and has fashioned the human constitution with the purpose of discerning moral truth, then we have reason to embrace the Dependence Thesis. "If the good were independent of nature, it might still be conceived as relevant to nature, by being its creator or mover; but Mr. Russell is not a theist after the manner of Socrates; his good is not a power" (Santayana 1957, p. 136). Alas, neither is Sturgeon a theist. And so he and other metaphysical naturalists shall have to seek assurance of the Dependence Thesis in nature itself.

In order to inspire confidence in those initial evaluative judgments of which Street speaks, the moral realist owes us some account of their origin that would lead us to suppose that they are reliable indicators of truth. On some externalist theory of justification, such as a causal theory, one might have, as Norman Daniels puts it, a "little story that gets told about why we should pay homage ultimately to those [considered] judgments and indirectly to the principles that systematize them" (Daniels 1979, p. 265). For the evolutionary naturalist, the account might follow that which is offered on behalf of ordinary perceptual or memory beliefs, or the everyday conclusions that we reach by induction. Quine offers such a story with a Darwinian spin to inspire confidence in our ability to acquire knowledge of the world around us. "Creatures inveterately wrong in their inductions have a pathetic but praiseworthy tendency to die before reproducing their kind," he suggests (Quine 1969, p. 126). Natural selection is unkind to those exhibiting particular behaviors that plausibly stem from either false beliefs or profound stupidity. Witness the so-called "Darwin Awards," given posthumously to people who met their fate as a result of bolting jet engines to automobiles or climbing – naked and inebriated – into bear cages. The suggestion, then, is that we should expect our cognitive faculties to be truth-aimed and generally reliable given such selection pressures.

Alvin Plantinga, of course, has challenged such stories with what he calls "Darwin's Doubt." The connection between fitness-conferring behavior and true belief might not be so certain as Quine suggests (Plantinga 2000, pp. 218–40; Beilby 2002, pp. 1–14, 204–276). If he is correct, then evolutionary naturalism is saddled with a far-ranging skepticism that takes in much more than our moral beliefs. And AEN would merely amount to a particular application of Plantinga's evolutionary argument. In that case, one might note, after the manner of Brink's comment on Harman, that there is no significant "explanatory disanalogy between the scientific and moral cases." But this would cut against the naturalist; not the proponent of AEN who rejects the evolutionary naturalism that apparently yields such untoward results.[2] However, Plantinga's argument has met with stiff resistance (Beilby 2002). Despite his many ingenious examples in which adaptive behavior results from *false* beliefs (e.g. Paul's belief that tigers are cuddly and the best way to get to know them is to run away), many people just find the link between true belief and adaptive behavior plausible. And, in any event, the two cases, moral and nonmoral, appear to be significantly different, as Street, Joyce, and others have argued.

The core of Sharon Street's paper is her "Darwinian Dilemma" that she poses to "value realists" such as Sturgeon. Our moral beliefs are fitness-aimed. Are they also truth-aimed? Either there is a fitness–truth relation or there is not. If there is not, and if we suppose that evolution has shaped our basic evaluative attitudes, then moral skepticism is in order. If there *is* a relation, then it is either that moral beliefs have reproductive fitness *because* they are true (the "tracking" relation), or we have the moral beliefs that we have simply because of the fitness that they conferred (the "adaptive link" account). But the adaptive link account suggests some variety of non-realism, such as the constructivism that Street endorses. The realist requires the tracking account in order to provide an account of warranted moral belief. Here, fitness follows *mind-independent* moral truths. But the tracking account, which, Street observes, is put forth as a *scientific* hypothesis, is just implausible from a scientific standpoint. While there is a clear and parsimonious *adaptive link* explanation of why humans have come to care for their offspring – namely, that the

2. As Joyce (2006, p. 183) observes, Peter Railton has argued that any argument taking the form of AEN "hammers itself into the same ground into which it had previously pounded morality." His reason for saying this is that the very faculties employed in constructing such an argument are just as much a product of natural selection as are the moral faculties being pounded. Because Joyce embraces EN, his strategy is to drive a wedge between the cases of moral and nonmoral belief. Those of us who reject EN need not bother with the wedge, being content to allow the evolutionary naturalist to wield Railton's hammer.

resulting behavior tends toward DNA preservation – the *tracking* account must add that basic paternal instincts were favored because it is independently true that parents *ought* to care for their offspring.

Ethical nonnaturalists, who hold that moral properties are *sui generis* and thus distinct from any natural properties, might be thought to have the worst time of it. Unlike the environmental hazards that Quine had in mind – predators, fires, precipices, and the like – "a creature cannot run into them or fall over them or be eaten by" nonnatural properties (Street 2006). Ethical naturalists, on the other hand, view moral properties as being constituted by natural properties with causal powers, so that it may be more plausible to suggest that creatures could interact with them profitably or unprofitably. But even here, insofar as the naturalist affirms a *bona fide* version of moral realism, the answers are far less plausible than is had in a straightforward adaptive link account. Why not just say that our ancestors who had a propensity to care for their offspring tended to act on that propensity and thus left more offspring – particularly when, as we noted earlier, we witness such propensities among nonhuman animals? Do dolphin mothers care for their daughters because they *ought* to do so? But, of course, Street's adaptive link account fails to provide what we have sought in this discussion: some defense of the Dependence Thesis.

Darwinian counterfactuals and ethical naturalism

A dilemma similar to that urged by Street arises if we return to consider the *Darwinian counterfactuals*. Consider the sorts of worlds that Darwin envisioned. Had the circumstances of human evolution been more like those of hive bees or Galapagos boobies or wolves, then the directives of conscience may have led us to judge and behave in ways that are quite foreign to our actual moral sense. Our wolfish philosophers defend justice as *inequality*, and their erudite reasonings take their cue from the fund of judgments bequeathed to them by their genes. Bees and boobies graced with intellect would judge that siblicide and infanticide are morally required under certain conditions. Presumably, those beliefs are *fitness-aimed* in those worlds. Are the beliefs also *true* there?

Consider Sturgeon's version of ethical naturalism, discussed earlier. One might expect that a straightforward implication of Sturgeon's Supervenience Thesis would be that such beliefs are false. We learned earlier that there is *no possible world* in which Hitler (or anyone) has just those natural properties that Hitler actually displays but is not depraved. Indeed, Sturgeon is of the Kripkean conviction that moral terms *rigidly designate* natural properties. Thus, moral terms function in much the same way as natural kind terms in that they pick out natural properties and track those same properties across worlds. "Gold" rigidly designates that metal with an atomic number of 79 and thus *necessarily* refers to all and only substances with that atomic number. We can readily imagine a Twin Earth scenario in which some other metal – of a different atomic number – with all of the *phenomenal* qualities of gold is scarce and valued, plundered by pirates and prospected by dreamers, and is even referred to as "gold." But for all of that, Twin Earth "gold" is not gold.

If "justice" picks out some natural property or properties, such as the *equity* displayed in the distribution of societal goods, then we might expect an ethical naturalist such as Sturgeon to conclude that inequitable arrangements are unjust. And this will be true even, say, in those lupine worlds in which such inequities are thought to be just, as surely as "all is not golde that glistereth" on Twin Earth.

But to insist that our moral terms rigidly designate specific earthly natural properties to which human sentiments have come to be attached appears to be an instance of what Judith Thomson has called *metaphysical imperialism*. In seeking the reference of "good" as used in "this is a good hammer," Thomson suggests that the natural property that best serves here is "being such as to facilitate hammering nails in in manners that conduce to satisfying the wants people typically hammer nails in to satisfy." She opts for this property as opposed to the more determinate properties of "being well-balanced, strong, with an easily graspable handle, and so on" (Thomson in Harman & Thomson 1996, p. 135). Even though *we* may find that the latter set of properties coextends with those that "conduce to satisfying the wants that people typically hammer nails in to satisfy," there are all sorts of "odd possible worlds" in which people typically have quite different wants for which deviant hammers come in handy. There are worlds in which "large slabs of granite" do the best job in this regard. And so we are being metaphysical imperialists if we presume to impose *our* nail hammering wants upon denizens of those worlds. She thus fixes upon a property that is *less determinate* than those that characterize hammers of earthly goodness: it is good insofar as it *answers to wants*, and chunks of granite serve well in this respect in some possible worlds.

The ethical *non*naturalist might very well maintain that the "justice" in such worlds is ill conceived and that natural selection has had an unfortunate and distorting influence there, alleging that some transcendent principle of justice as equality is among the verities. Perhaps entire *species* can get their moral facts wrong, as might entire societies. Russ Shafer-Landau, for instance, compares moral laws to mathematical or logical laws, and asks why the former should be any more problematic than the latter (2004, p. 77). If Twin Earth logicians have a penchant for affirming the consequent, then *Earthly* logicians might regard Twin Earth as a veritable mission field. There is certainly nothing "imperialistic" about that. But our ethical *naturalist* has identified justice as a particular set of natural properties upon which human evolution has, in fact, converged. Whatever circumstances of justice have obtained on Earth are contingent and fail to obtain in those Darwinian worlds. It seems that we have no more reason to think that *Earthly* justice is normative there than we have for denying that those denizens, who lack C-fibers, ever experience pain.

Should the ethical naturalist allow that such beliefs are *true*, as well as fitness-conferring, in such worlds? Suppose so. Then it would seem that either the Supervenience Thesis is false, since the world in question is one in which justice fails to supervene upon the relevant natural properties,[3] or the *actual* supervenience base is something different from what we might have imagined. Perhaps, for instance, the sacredness of infanticide is *in virtue* of the fact that it is conducive to fitness, so that *truth follows fitness*, so to speak. Or infanticide may be fitness-conferring *because* it is indeed a "sacred duty" in such worlds. Either way, Sturgeon's own ethical theory will be in for some readjustment along unexpected and, I think, implausible, lines. Whatever we say of the truth conditions of *infanticide is a sacred duty* in that Darwinian world will function as a universal acid, bearing implications for the shared moral beliefs of the actual world – *if* the actual world is similarly Darwinian.

If the truth-maker there is the belief's conduciveness to reproductive fitness, then, presumably, *our own* moral beliefs, opposed as they are to those in that Darwinian world, will

---

3. Is there, after all, a world in which someone behaviorally indiscernible from our Hitler – *Schitler*, perhaps – is a moral saint?

be true in virtue of *their* conduciveness to fitness *here*. This is a Dependence Thesis of sorts that may guarantee that truth and fitness may be found together. But it is hardly what we were seeking.[4] Did Sturgeon wish to say, implausibly, that the moral properties of an action supervene upon the overall reproductive advantage that it confers?

If, on the other hand, the counterfactual beliefs in those Darwinian worlds are fitness-conferring *because* they are true, then, given the Supervenience Thesis, it would seem that the moral properties that obtain in that world supervene upon natural properties found in common with the actual world. Presumably, this would be some natural property that is common to both equitable and inequitable social arrangements and to both the nurturing and the strangling of babies.[5] In that case, the natural properties upon which justice and injustice or depravity and saintliness supervene, are neither equity nor inequity, cruelty or kindness but something that is *less determinate* and serves as the genus for these seemingly opposed species of moral properties. One unhappy result here is that those more determinate natural properties that are favored by reflective equilibrium would prove to be merely accidental and coextensive features of morality. If there is some natural property N that is common to both equitable and inequitable bargaining outcomes, and upon which justice supervenes, then N, and not equity, defines the essence of justice. This would appear to be the metaethical equivalent of the suggestion that water is *whatever fills a world's oceans*, so that Earthly H_2O and Twin-Earthly XYZ both qualify as water. But then *being H_2O* is not the essence of the stuff that we call "water." (Note that N *could* be conduciveness to reproductive fitness, so that our two earlier suggestions would seem to converge.) One might thus offer a *functionalist* account of moral properties. Perhaps, for instance, "justice" picks out *whatever* natural properties tend toward societal stability. We happen to live in a world in which, given, as Kant put it, "the nature of man and the circumstances of the world in which he is placed," *equity* has this effect. But there are worlds in which *inequity* does the trick. In addition to signaling a significant departure from the sort of account that naturalists such as Sturgeon wish to offer, such a move would seem to offer a precarious footing for any robust account of moral realism.

Taking a line from the imperishable Jeremy Bentham, Daniel Dennett has suggested that, from a Darwinian perspective, the notion of *rights* is "nonsense on stilts." But, unlike Bentham, he thinks it is *"good* nonsense," and it is good precisely because it is on stilts (Dennett 1995, p. 507). "Rights" language is *instrumentally* good in that it functions as a "conversation stopper," thus putting an end to otherwise paralyzing deliberation. It is a variety of "rule worship," and obeisance to such rules is conducive to societal stability. But from this perspective, the *content* of the rules is of no more inherent importance than the contents of varying traffic laws. Things will go smoothly in Cambridge, UK, so long as everyone keeps to the left, but they are just as smooth in the New England namesake so long as everyone does the opposite. A realism indifferent to such content is a realism in name only.

We might pursue, if only briefly, one possible route suggested by something Sturgeon says in his exchange with Alan Gibbard. Gibbard (1990) offers a possible evolutionary

---

4. It is akin to saying that God is "necessarily good" in the sense that, necessarily, *whatever* God does is "good" for the simple reason that it is God who is doing it.

5. The set of natural properties that form the supervenience base might, after all, be rather complex, taking into account more than a bare description of an action, but the action performed under varying sets of circumstances.

account of human morality that he thinks is suggestive of expressivism. Perhaps our notion of justice, for instance, emerged from early "bargaining situations" in which some form of cooperation between self-interested individuals proves beneficial for all involved. Here, "beneficial" means, roughly, getting what one wants out of a bargain, and the assumption is that getting what one wants has some reproductive advantage. The problem is that, unless self-interest is checked in some way, the bargaining – and thus, the beneficial cooperation – breaks down. There is a stable outcome in which each is satisfied with getting his share, that is, an outcome that is least likely to prompt retaliation on the part of any members leading to a breakdown in the bargaining. There would thus be selection pressure in favor of a certain disposition to be satisfied with that outcome. With the advent of language, humans came to use words that were functionally equivalent to our words "just" or "fair" to express the positive sentiment attached to an outcome in which goods are distributed in some roughly equal manner. Thus, there is fitness in a particular sentiment that would likely be distributed widely. Moral language describes or expresses this sentiment. The result is a form of noncognitivism, or, at least, a variety of antirealism with regard to moral properties.

Sturgeon replies that there is nothing in Gibbard's admittedly speculative account that requires us to see morality as having been undercut. "Perhaps," Sturgeon suggests, "our ancestors sometimes called bargaining outcomes *just* because they really were" (1992, p. 105). In this case, people have come to "care about justice" and "are also able to resolve disputes about it." And perhaps "achieving consensus in debate might be a way . . . of detecting a property" (Sturgeon 1992, p. 105). Why, then, should we not think that Gibbard's bargainers are "referring to a real property that they care about, and about which their views are often correct?" (Sturgeon 1992, p. 105).

Further, moral explanations that appeal to justice enjoy the same plausibility as do appeals to, say, Hitler's depravity.

> The justice of a society . . . is supposed to stabilize it; and people are alleged to prosper precisely because of their justice. Of course, there is also a tradition that attacks this latter claim as a pious fiction. But the most prominent opposing view also treats justice as explanatory. That justice always pays, and that justice sometimes costs, are both views that cast justice as a property with causal efficacy. (Sturgeon 1992, p. 105)

We may discern here echoes of Sturgeon's exchange with Harman. We are entitled to regard moral properties as real in the event that they play an explanatory role. If an equitable distribution of goods tends toward societal stability, and people have come to believe that such equity is just, then why not conclude that the fact that the bargaining outcome *is*, in fact, just, explains both the belief and the stability? Why not suppose that the nonmoral evolutionary explanation *amplifies* rather than *undermines* the moral explanation? Sturgeon claims that Gibbard's account "does *nothing* whatever" to favor the "irrealist" account over the realist one. His general conclusion is that "nothing we know of our evolutionary history" supplies us with an undermining nonmoral explanation "or makes irrealism any more plausible than the moral realism that I am prepared to defend" (Sturgeon 1992, p. 112).

But is this so? Justice as equality has a stabilizing effect upon Gibbard's group of bargainers because of what the parties to the bargain are and are not prepared to accept. That is, stability is achieved because each bargainer leaves the table with the belief, "I got what I deserved." Gibbard's story includes a cast of characters who are self-interested individualists, each of whom imports assumptions about his relative worth within the community. Given these conditions, there is pressure in the direction of equitable arrangements. But might we imagine a different set of initial conditions? Would *lupine* "bargainers" instead come to "detect" the natural property of *inequity*? Might some come away with a disproportionately smaller share *plus* the belief, "I got what I deserved"? *That* "justice" would then be causally efficacious. Would it then be real?[6] Not if a property's being real requires its being *mind-independent*. For in each of these worlds, actual and lupine, if justice supervenes upon certain natural facts, these will essentially include facts about the psychological constitution of the respective bargainers.

Perhaps Sturgeon or some other ethical naturalist can offer some account that sits comfortably with the implications of Darwinian counterfactuals. My present argument is *not* that there is no possibly true story that can be told. However, in considering the sorts of circumstances that Darwin describes, it seems that the most plausible explanation is that such counterfactual moral beliefs are formed as the result of selection pressures that are themselves in place due to the contingencies of the evolutionary landscape – contingencies that are morally indifferent. Such beliefs are evolutionary means to nonmoral reproductive ends. While ethical naturalists in those worlds no doubt argue for the supervenience of the moral upon the natural, the efficacy of moral explanations, and the existence of corresponding moral facts, we should, I think, regard them as mistaken. But if the moral beliefs of the actual world have also taken their cue from predispositions that were fitness-conferring, then it is hard to see why our own ethical naturalists are in any better position so to argue.

Darwinian counterfactuals, ethical nonnaturalism, and theism

I suggested earlier that the ethical nonnaturalist might have a ready reply to the argument from Darwinian counterfactuals. For the nonnaturalist may be in a position to maintain that certain natural properties bear a *necessary* relation to the moral properties that they exemplify, regardless of any evolutionary possibilities.

But nonnaturalists who are also *metaphysical* naturalists seem to have problems of their own in the face of such Darwinian counterfactuals. Here, Santayana's criticism of Russell resurfaces. If "man is a product of causes that had no prevision of the end they were achieving" and moral beliefs are ultimately the product of whatever selection pressures were in place given the contingencies of the evolutionary landscape; if there is a vast range of possible outcomes, how is it that unguided human evolution on earth has resulted in just those moral beliefs that accord with the verities? The circumstances of evolution have likely

---

6. David Copp (1990) has argued that the sort of explanatory role to which Sturgeon and other "confirmation theorists" appeal falls short of the sort of justification that the moral skeptic demands. One might explain Stalin's behavior by observing that he is an *Ubermensch*. Indeed, the notion may come to be useful in identifying a particular personality type. But such explanations hardly take us in the direction of providing a *standard of behavior*. Similar things may be said of the "justice" that prevails in the Darwinian world under consideration. But, then, why suppose that things are different in the *actual* world?

been shaped by everything from plate tectonics to meteorological fluctuations to terrestrial collisions with asteroids. As Stephen Gould (1989) argued, everything about us, including our very existence, is *radically* contingent so that, were we to imagine "rewinding the reel," so to speak, and allowing it to play again, it is highly unlikely that evolution would again attempt the experiment called *Homo sapiens*. What a fortuitous chain of events that resulted in the actual existence of the kinds of creatures to whom eternally and necessarily true, but causally impotent, principles apply![7] The Dependence Thesis in the hands of the nonnaturalist seems highly improbable. A sort of "moral fine-tuning argument" is suggested. The theist may have an advantage just here. For, on theism, as Santayana put it, the Good is also nature's Creator.[8]

The theist, like the nonnaturalist, is in a position to say why there is a necessary connection between certain natural properties and their supervenient moral properties. Robert Adams, for example, has recently suggested that things bear the moral properties that they do – good or bad – insofar as they resemble or fail to resemble God. As he notes, "Natural things that resemble God do so, in general, by virtue of their natural properties" (Adams 1999, p. 61). A theist who accepts such a view can thus agree with Sturgeon that there is no possible world in which anyone does just what Hitler did but is not depraved. And this is precisely because there is no possible world in which such actions fail to be an affront to the divine nature.

But the theist also has an account of the development of human moral faculties – a theistic genealogy of morals – that allows for something akin to Street's "tracking relation": we have the basic moral beliefs we do because they are true, and this is because the mechanisms responsible for those moral beliefs are *truth-aimed*. Adams again says:

> If we suppose that God directly or indirectly causes human beings to regard as excellent approximately those things that are Godlike in the relevant way, it follows that there is a causal and explanatory connection between facts of excellence and beliefs that we may regard as justified about excellence, and hence it is in general no accident that such beliefs are correct when they are. (1999, p. 70)

The theist is thus in a position to offer Daniels' "little story" that would explain the general reliability of those considered judgments from which reflective equilibrium takes its cue. Certain of our moral beliefs – in particular, those that are presupposed in all moral reflection – are truth-aimed because human moral faculties are designed to guide human conduct in light of moral truth.

---

7. Apparently, Kant's Principle of Humanity, as it appeared in the empyrean and before the foundation of the world, read, "Should, against all probability, there be stars, and should, also improbably, those stars align in such a way as to permit the emergence of life, and should, against overwhelming odds, some of those living things turn out to be 'human,' then they are to be treated as ends-in-themselves and never as means to ends, and this even in the event that the contingencies of evolution direct them to think otherwise. Disregard this directive in those universes in which these conditions fail to obtain."

8. Of course, another option – one that earns "raised eyebrows, incredulous stares, or worse" – is John Leslie's recent suggestion that the best explanation for the existence of the world as it is, is simply that it is *good* for there to exist such a world. Leslie thus rousts Plato's Forms from their impotent repose and puts them directly to work in matching is for ought (Leslie 2001).

Humean skepticism or Reidean externalism?

Both the evolutionary naturalist and the theist may be found saying that certain of our moral beliefs are by-products of the human constitution: we think as we do largely as a result of our programming. Whether such beliefs are warranted would seem to depend upon who or what is responsible for the program. And this calls for some account of the metaphysical underpinnings of those beliefs and the mechanisms responsible for them.[9] With this point in mind, perhaps we may tidily summarize our discussion by comparing the perspectives of David Hume and his critic, Thomas Reid.

We saw that Michael Ruse claims Hume as one of his own in that Hume seems to have defended a variety of moral subjectivism – and a *Humean* one at that! But I am not convinced that this is right. I see Hume's discussion of moral beliefs as a part of a seamless whole that includes his discussion of the beliefs of common life. And there, I do not think that Hume should be read as advancing the positive metaphysical theses that causal connections fail to obtain or that the world is devoid of both material substances and substantial selves. Rather, his is a skeptical epistemological argument to the effect that we *lack any warrant whatsoever* for thinking that there *are* such connections. To be sure, in the final analysis, all that we are *warranted* in accepting are perceptions and the various ways in which we find them conjoined or otherwise related. But determining whether there is or is not anything more calls for speculation that exceeds the limits of Hume's skepticism. In each discussion – causality, substance, personal identity – he aims to show both that the belief in question is without any epistemic credentials and that relevant human propensities explain the belief without making any assumptions about the truth of the belief.

Things are no different when Hume turns to the question of morality. We are no more warranted in believing in objective moral properties than we are in thinking that there is any necessary connection among events. And a propensity account waits in the offing to explain the persistence of moral beliefs despite their lack of warrant. Moral beliefs are the by-products of human psychology. "Morality is more properly felt than jug'd of" (Hume 1978, p. 470). But then, so is just about everything else. "All probable reasoning is nothing but a species of sensation. 'Tis not solely in poetry and music, we must follow our taste and sentiment, but likewise in philosophy" (Hume 1978, p. 103). As I read him, Hume was no more a subjectivist than he was a bundle theorist regarding persons. He offered positive theories in neither metaethics nor metaphysics.[10] From a Humean perspective, we lack positive reasons for accepting *either* the dependence or independence theses. Thus, his is a variety of *epistemological* moral skepticism and, in this, resembles the version of AEN defended earlier.

---

9. Here, the advice of Hastings Rashdall is apt: "So long as he is content to assume the reality and authority of the moral consciousness, the Moral Philosopher can ignore Metaphysic; but if the reality of Morals or the validity of ethical truth be once brought into question, the attack can only be met by a thorough-going enquiry into the nature of Knowledge and of Reality" (Rashdall 1907, p. 192).

10. This assertion is, of course, complicated by Hume's unfortunate assertion that we do not even have the *idea* of objective moral properties, and talk of them is meaningless – which seems to place him in the noncognitivist camp. But neither do we have the ideas of necessary connection, material substance, or substantial selves, according to Hume, and for precisely the same reasons. If he is, say, an "expressivist" in the one area, then he is equally so in the other.

Thomas Reid countered the conclusions of Hume's *Treatise* by appeal to "common sense." Reid compares the course of modern philosophy, which began with Descartes and ended with Hume, to a traveler who, upon finding himself "in a coal-pit," realizes that he has taken a wrong turn. Upon hearing the skeptical musings of some of the modern philosophers, the average person, confident in the deliverances of common sense, takes them to be "either merry or mad." Indeed, Reid suggests that anyone who is a true *friend* of the man who seriously entertains doubts regarding, say, his own mind or of a world of things that endure over time, will "hope for his cure from physic and regimen, rather than metaphysic and logic" (Reid 1983, pp. 4–5). He places his hope in the doctor of medicine rather than the doctor of philosophy precisely because the beliefs in question do not admit of the sort of proof that the philosopher would vainly offer. As G. K. Chesterton (1986) put it, curing a madman is not arguing with a philosopher but casting out a devil. There is no set of premises more certainly known from which such beliefs follow. Hume is right: the beliefs of common life are not endorsed by reason, but, instead, are the inevitable by-products of our constitution. But Hume is mistaken in inferring from this that such beliefs are, therefore, without warrant. Why, after all, trust the rational faculties to which Hume appeals, but not trust the faculties responsible for our commonsense beliefs? After all, both "came from the same shop" (Reid 1983, p. 85). As Nicholas Wolterstorff notes, according to Reid, that "shop" was "divine creation by fiat" (Wolterstorff 2001, p. 199).

As Reid had it, the commonsense beliefs that arise spontaneously and noninferentially given our constitution are warranted even though they fail to measure up to the exacting standards of epistemic justification assumed by foundationalists after the Cartesian fashion. My belief, *I have a head,* is not *logically* self-evident: I am free to deny it without pain of contradiction (although perhaps not without pain of running it into a post). There are logically possible scenarios that would explain my having the belief even if it were false, though, of course, none of these is commended to me. Further, *I have a head* is not *incorrigible* in the way that *I am being appeared-to headly* is. Nor have I *inferred* the former from the latter or from any other belief. Nevertheless, I am warranted in believing it, and, what is more, I *know* that I have a head just in case I have one.

These days we might say that such beliefs are *properly basic.* My belief in my head is basic in that it is noninferential. And my accepting this belief in this basic way constitutes no epistemic impropriety on my part. The belief is properly basic just in case the faculty through which it is acquired (which, presumably, *involves* my head) is functioning as it ought. More specifically, as Alvin Plantinga (1993) has refined Reid's original view, a belief is warranted just in case it is the product of a belief-producing mechanism that is truth-aimed and functioning properly in the environment for which it was designed. This account accommodates those perceptual, memorial, testimonial, and even metaphysical beliefs that are the guides of common life and, closer to our purposes, are among the fund of native beliefs with which we begin in theory assessment. Even closer to our purposes, such an account accommodates those *moral* beliefs employed in reflective equilibrium.

Reid appealed to a set of "first, or 'self-evident' principles" of morality discerned through faculties that he thought were wrought in the same shop as reason and perception. Just as there is no reasoning with the man who, despite apparent evidence to the contrary, is convinced that his head is a gourd, neither is there advantage in engaging in moral argument with a man who fails to recognize self-evident principles of morality.

> If a man does not perceive that he ought to regard the good of society, and the good of his wife and children, the reasoning can have no effect upon him, because he denies the first principle upon which it is grounded. (Reid 1983, p. 322)

The details of Reid's own candidates for such first principles need not concern us in the present context. What is of significance is the suggestion that there are moral beliefs to which "we should pay homage," as Norman Daniels has put it. We pay such homage when we utilize them as data for the construction of moral theories or as a kind of court of appeal in assessing them. This is business as usual in moral philosophy. We may suppose, with Nicholas Sturgeon, that Adolf Hitler was depraved, or with Kai Nielsen (1990, p. 10) that wife beating or child molesting is vile, and go on to agree with the latter that such beliefs are "bedrock."

But our confidence in these constitutional beliefs is wisely invested only in the event that we have reason to believe the faculties responsible for them to be truth-aimed. Reid's theism provided him with such a reason: the moral faculties were forged in the same shop as our other cognitive faculties. They are designed by God for the purpose of discerning moral truth. "That conscience which is in every man's breast, is the law of God written in his heart, which he cannot disobey without acting unnaturally, and being self-condemned" (Reid 1983, p. 355). Hume, on the other hand, finding only the faculties but pretending to no knowledge of their origin, placed no such confidence in their reliability. The evolutionary naturalist may have added an account of origins, but it is one that inspires no more confidence than that displayed by Hume.

An Argument from Personal Dignity

In *The Brothers Karamazov*, one of Dostoevsky's characters relates a chilling tale of unspeakable acts of cruelty committed by soldiers at war. Among other things, he describes soldiers snatching babies from the arms of their mothers and tossing them into the air to catch them on the points of their bayonets. Presumably, bayoneting babies for fun (and for any other reason) is wrong. Indeed, we might suppose the belief that it is wrong to be included in that fund of moral beliefs with which we begin moral reflection. Employing the method of reflective equilibrium, we might appeal to such a belief as we seek to construct or assess theories of morality. We may well suppose that any ethical theory that implies the permissibility of recreational baby-bayoneting is worthy of the dustbin.

But competing ethical theories may be found to have significant overlap regarding which classes of actions are deemed right or wrong. One might imagine a group of three attempting to save a beached whale. Subsequent interviews reveal that one is a Deep Ecologist whose primary concern is the preservation of biological diversity, and this whale is a specimen of an endangered species. His collaborators include an animal rights activist who is acting from a direct concern for the welfare of the animal itself, and a theist who views the rescue as a duty of stewardship. Almost certainly, we could find other issues where the entailments of these respective views clash, but here they are in agreement. As they say, philosophy makes for strange bedfellows.

Similarly, competing grounds may be offered for the wrongness of baby-bayoneting. Consider, for example, the probable assessment of philosopher Mary Anne Warren. In a widely anthologized essay, Warren argues that all and only persons have rights, fetuses are not persons, and so fetuses do not have rights (Warren 2005). Her reason for thinking that fetuses are disqualified is that there is a set of faculties or capacities, X, Y, and Z, some subset of which all persons possess, fetuses display none of X, Y, or Z, and so fetuses are not persons. The upshot, of course, is that abortion does not involve a violation of any fetal right to life, and so the only rights at stake in the abortion issue are those of the woman.

In a postscript to the essay, Warren anticipates an objection. *Infants* fail to display the requisite faculties and so Warren's argument has perhaps proved more than she intended: we now have before us an argument for the moral permissibility of *infanticide*. Have we not the makings of an *ad absurdum* for her original argument?

Her reply is to acknowledge that her argument does indeed imply that infants do not have a right to life, and so the killing of an infant can never amount to *murder*, since murder essentially involves the violation of such a right. But she maintains that it does not follow that infanticide is *permissible*. The moral wrongness of killing a baby may be made out without invoking rights – at least not those of the baby.

> The needless destruction of a viable infant inevitably deprives some person or persons of a source of great pleasure and satisfaction, perhaps severely impoverishing their lives. (Warren 2005, p. 124)

On Warren's view, infanticide is wrong not because it violates any direct duties owed the infant. Rather, we have direct duties to other *persons* – individuals with traits X, Y, and Z – and these direct duties imply indirect duties *regarding* infants. Even if you do not care for babies, there are other people who do, and the wanton destruction of infants deprives those other people of the pleasure and satisfaction of having a child. In this respect, Warren's view of the wrongness of infanticide displays the same structure as Kant's account of the wrongness of animal cruelty. Kant (1981) maintained that we have direct duties to all and only persons. But it does not follow that we may deal with animals as we please. Animal cruelty works as a corrosive on one's character, resulting in callousness or even cruelty to our fellow humans. Because we have direct duties of kindness to people, we should cultivate those character traits that give us a propensity for such kindness. Animal cruelty is simply counterproductive in this regard.

I suspect that most people find both Warren's and Kant's views to be inadequate. In fact, Warren acknowledges that many will regard her conclusion on infanticide as "morally monstrous." Indeed, if infants do not have rights *at all*, then not only do they not have a right not to be killed, but neither do they have a right not to be *tortured*. And so, were we to imagine Dostoevsky's scenario or (assuming there can be such a thing) worse, Warren's position entails that the wrongness of the torture of infants is contingent upon the effect that it has upon actual persons. If infants, as nonpersons, have no rights whatsoever, then even such horrific instances of cruelty cannot be understood as violating any direct duty owed the infant. They are afforded no moral standing, and any moral concern regarding their treatment must look to other grounds. Perhaps it is wrong because of the suffering that it causes the mothers or other people. Perhaps it is wrong because of some other bad societal consequence, proximate or remote. If Kant is correct in thinking that animal abuse spawns cruelty to other humans, how much easier might be the move from infant torture to the torture of "actual" persons? Or we might suppose that it is wrong in that it manifests wickedness or vice in the extreme. Thomas E. Hill (1991) offers a potentially usable model here. He asks, if we do not think that, say, natural environments or works of art enjoy moral standing in their own right, might we explain our "moral unease" on contemplating their destruction by asking the question, "*What sort of person would do a thing like that?*" Our attention is thus shifted from a question of rights or direct duties owed anyone or anything, to an assessment of *character*. Surely, an even harsher judgment is appropriate regarding Dostoevsky's soldiers. Perhaps some combination of those mentioned can work together to arrive at the conclusion that infanticide is impermissible.

But such answers, even taken together, seem altogether unsatisfactory. Surely, if bayoneting babies for fun is morally wrong, the wrongness must be explained chiefly in terms of what is done *to the baby*. Consider Mary Midgley's objection to G. R. Grice's contract theory. Grice's theory implied that animals, young children, and the mentally impaired have no natural rights due to their nonparticipation in the contract out of which rights arise. He anticipated that some readers would chafe at such implications and urged that, for the sake of consistency with the theory, we "should be willing to accept" them even if they seem "harsh." Presumably, Grice, no more than Warren, was advocating a slaughter of the innocents. Nevertheless, Midgley will have none of this. She observes that, here, "harsh" just means "unjust." She insists, "An ethical theory which, when consistently followed through, has iniquitous consequences is a bad theory and must be changed" (Midgley 1986, p. 157). The so-called "iniquitous consequences" of the theory are seen not only in what actions would be permitted if the principle were accepted but also in the *grounds* for saying that a given action is required, permitted, or prohibited. It is along similar lines that Richard Joyce, in contemplating an example of "Jack," who treats those around him with brutality, remarks, "It is surely grotesque to think that what is wrong with Jack's actions is the self-harm being generated. The wrongness of torture, for example, surely derives chiefly from the harm being inflicted on *others*! (Joyce 2006, p. 60).

One lesson to be gleaned from the discussion thus far is that, for any proposed theory of morality to be plausible, it must not only carry implications that do justice to certain of our deep-seated moral convictions, but it must also offer a satisfactory account of those implications. After all, when told that his proposed theory implies the moral permissibility of baby-bayoneting, it is always open to the theorist to reply, "If my theory implies the permissibility of baby-bayoneting, well, then, baby-bayoneting is permissible! Let your 'intuitions' be hanged!" The fact that this is rarely done demonstrates the force of those "intuitions." In the face of such objections, most theorists will argue that, properly understood, their theories do not entail the permissibility of rape, genocide, or slavery. But if, as Norman Daniels (1979) has it, we are to "pay homage" to certain considered judgments about which acts are permissible or impermissible, and to the principles that would systemize those judgments, the honor should be extended to take in judgments about what qualifies as an acceptable explanation.

Another lesson to be gathered is that the considered judgments in question appear to call for our according *moral standing* to individuals – in the case of our considered example, human infants. I understand *S has moral standing* to mean *S is the appropriate object of direct moral duties*. And to say that S is the object of a direct moral duty is to imply that a violation of that duty would entail *wronging*, or doing an injustice to *S*.

Suppose that you carelessly park your car in the lot adjacent to the mathematics department at your university. When you return to your vehicle, you find that delinquent mathematicians have left the car on blocks and spray painted mathematical graffiti from bumper to bumper: the Pythagorean Theorem, the Triangular Inequality, Cantor's Theorem – it is all there. Have they done something wrong? Presumably. But, this side of the Bay area, we are not likely to find people suggesting that they have wronged *the car*, done it an injustice or violated its rights. Cars are not plausibly thought to have moral standing – not even Bentleys. Rather, we might suppose that the wrongness of such vandalism stems from the violation of a direct duty *to you* to respect your property rights or the like. And that direct duty carries with it an indirect duty *regarding* the car.

Consider the wrongness of rape as a test case. Any theory worthy of consideration even as a contender will imply the wrongness of rape. But any theory that essentially and wholly explains the wrongness of that act by regarding the rape victim in the way that we regard the car in the vandalism case, where our *direct* concern is for someone or something other than the victim, is, I think, equally implausible. Generally, in the case of harms brought to persons, we have, I think, an implausible explanation if it is reducible to the form:

(ID)   *A's harming B is wrong solely because A's harming B affects C.*

Here, I will understand C to be anyone not identical to B – including A.

Moral standing and egoism

There is some reason to doubt whether philosophical egoism is to be regarded as an ethical theory.[11] But let us regard it as such, at least provisionally, in order to put the present point into sharp relief. Using our distinction between direct and indirect duties, we may classify egoism as any theory holding that agents have *direct* duties only to *themselves* and indirect duties, if there are any duties at all, regarding anyone else. An initial reaction to the egoist's proposal is to think that the principle involved entails the precept, *Do whatever you can happily get away with.* An egoist might pillage and plunder and rifle and loot like a pirate, and, so long as it serves his interests and he is able to sleep nights (and why would he not, since he is acting in accord with the only moral principle he takes to be true?) then he may well be on his way to canonization.

Of course, one might distinguish between "nasty" and "nice" egoism. The former was just described. Proponents of the latter might fold in claims about the interdependence of individuals and the societies in which they are found. Perhaps, as Jerome K. Jerome suggested, "We are so bound together that no man can labor for himself alone. Each blow he strikes in his own behalf helps to mold the universe" (Jerome 2005, p. 47). Bishop Butler maintained in earnest that "self-love" and "benevolence" (by which he meant a concern for others and the public good in general) are so intricately related that, "we can scarcely promote the one without the other" (Butler 1983, p. 27). Were this true (is it?), one might have the resources for arguing that a world full of calculating but truly circumspect egoists would be like one big Hallmark greeting card commercial, featuring smiling people exchanging kindnesses. And, of course, rape is never depicted on greeting cards.

But even "nice" egoism is not nice enough. If the egoist concludes, happily, that rape is wrong, then he can only conclude this because he has determined that it wrongs *the rapist.* Such a verdict is, as Joyce (2006) says, "grotesque." While it is no doubt true that

---

11. See Kurt Baier's discussion of egoism in Singer (1991).

agents who engage in horrific acts of violence do damage to themselves in the process, this concern is, or ought to be, peripheral to the direct concern that one has for the *victim*. Rape is wrong, if wrong at all, because it violates a direct duty owed the victim. The victim is *wronged* by the act and done an injustice. Egoism cannot accommodate this insight. Any attempt to do so signals the abandonment of egoism for some other, perhaps more plausible, theory of morality. Egoism satisfies the criterion that a theory must countenance the moral standing of individuals. The trouble is that the only individual who enjoys such standing is the agent. And so we have but to add the clause, *in addition to the agent*.

Moral standing and utilitarianism

Are there more plausible theories? Consider utilitarianism, which is a theory that most certainly looks beyond a concern for the good of the agent. Generically stated, the principle of utility tells us that right actions are those that have good consequences for the community. This is "generic" because a great deal of variation is possible in defining what "good" and "community" mean here. Classical utilitarians in the tradition of Jeremy Bentham and J. S. Mill have held to a hedonist theory of value, so that *pleasure* is viewed as of intrinsic value. As Mill put it, "Pleasure, and freedom from pain, are the only things desirable as ends; and . . . all desirable things (which are as numerous in the utilitarian as in any other scheme) are desirable either for the pleasure inherent in themselves, or as means to the promotion of pleasure and the prevention of pain" (Mill 2001, p. 7). But there are other, nonhedonistic theories of value that *could* be plugged in here, from the plausible (e.g. human flourishing or the meeting of interests) to the bizarre (e.g. the maximization of back hair or of plastic Elvis figurines). As for the question of what is meant by the "community," classical utilitarians have taken an anthropocentric approach, equating the community with "humanity." But, following a clue from Bentham, Peter Singer has urged that the moral community should consist of all and only *sentient* creatures. His resulting utilitarianism would thus have it that our aim should be to maximize utility for the set of all sentient animals, including, of course, sentient humans. On this latter point, we might say, then, that utilitarians may differ with regard to the *scope of the moral community*. This issue, as with the theory of value, admits of much variety, including both the plausible (e.g. humanity, sentient creatures) and the implausible or bizarre (e.g. all and only those people who are Neil Young, all and only flatworms).

We might suppose that the utilitarian's question concerning the scope of the moral community is identical to the question of who or what has moral standing. However, I believe this is a mistake. The utilitarian's "moral community" is not identical to the set of individuals who enjoy moral standing. Utilitarianism does not accord moral standing to individual members of the moral community.

Jeremy Bentham, that imperishable proponent of utilitarianism, famously said that the notion of natural rights is "nonsense on stilts." In fact, the broader context of that quote is useful for our present purpose. Bentham's subject was the *Declaration of Rights* published by the French National Assembly in 1791. That declaration included a number of articles that Bentham thought demonstrably false. Article II, in particular, asserted, "The end in view of every political association is the preservation of the natural and imprescriptible rights of man. These rights are liberty, property, security, and resistance to oppression." On analysis, Bentham suggests that the article manifests confusion and that what it asserts is not only nonsense but also "dangerous nonsense" (2001, p. 500). In particular, Bentham challenges the notion of *natural* and *imprescriptible* rights, thought to exist, "anterior to the establishment of government." The notion is as fantastic as it is mischievous.

> How stands the truth of things? That there are no such things as natural rights – no such things as rights anterior to the establishment of government – no such things as natural rights opposed to, in contradistinction to, legal: that the expression is merely figurative; that when used, in the moment you attempt to give it a literal meaning it leads to error, and to that sort of error that leads to mischief – to the extremity of mischief. (Bentham 2001, p. 500)

Where that French document maintains that "the ignorance, neglect, or contempt of the rights of man are the sole cause of public calamities and of the corruption of governments," Bentham notes that this is little more than wishful thinking. "Reasons for wishing there were such things as rights, are not rights; – a reason for wishing that a certain right were established, is not that right – want is not supply – hunger is not bread" (Bentham 2001, p. 501). And whereas the document is motivated by a concern to preserve the natural rights of people, Bentham reasons that things that do not exist are in no danger of being destroyed and, therefore, cannot call for preservation. One might as well add unicorns and griffins to the list of endangered species. This sets the context for Bentham's well-known "nonsense" quip: "*Natural rights* is simple nonsense: natural and imprescriptible rights, rhetorical nonsense, – nonsense upon stilts" (Bentham 2001, p. 501).

Bentham's argument, then, is with the notion of rights that are *inherent* and *imprescriptible* (i.e. "inalienable"). Both features of such rights are rejected by means of one parsimonious explanation: whatever rights exist are contingent upon the circumstances of society. And those "circumstances" are determined by the question of what is "advantageous to society," that is to say, the notion of utility.

> In proportion as it is *right* or *proper, i.e.,* advantageous to the society in question, that this or that right – a right to this or that effect – should be established and maintained, in that same proportion it is *wrong* that it should be abrogated: but that as there is no *right*, which ought not to be maintained so long as it is upon the whole advantageous to the society that it should be maintained, so there is no right which, when the abolition of it is advantageous to society, should not be abolished. (Bentham 2001, p. 501)

Bentham's view does clearly entail that there are no natural or moral rights that are anterior to and independent of the civil rights that are accorded by society, and so the former are unavailable as the grounds for the latter. But it is worth highlighting here what may be obvious: this does not leave him in a position of saying that there are no anterior *moral grounds* for the granting of civil rights. Although there are no anterior and inherent rights, it may still be the case that individuals within a society *ought* to be accorded certain rights – perhaps even that list of rights delineated in the Declaration. And, of course, the court of appeal will be found in the Principle of Utility. But whether rights are extended or abrogated will be determined by the circumstances of utility, and this is always with a view to the advantage of society. There cannot be "imprescriptible" rights precisely because a concern for social utility may call for their abrogation. If there were such rights, then there would be occasions on which it is morally inappropriate to calculate consequences. But if the Principle of Utility is true, then it is always appropriate so to calculate. Whether you eat or drink, or whatsoever you do, do all to the benefit of society.

With this bit of exegesis behind us, we may see that John Stuart Mill did not veer sharply from the course already plotted by Bentham once Mill got around to discussing the notion of rights. Chapter five of *Utilitarianism* is Mill's attempt to show that utility and justice embrace, despite the criticisms of the theory's detractors. Mill identifies duties of justice with those "perfect duties"[12] discussed by philosophers. Unlike so-called "imperfect duties," these involve the rights of individuals, so that the violation of such a duty involves the *wronging* of the individual whose rights are involved. Thus, the notions of *justice* and individual *rights* are inextricably bound. "Justice implies something which it is not only right to do, and wrong not to do, but which some individual person can claim from us as his moral right" (Mill 2001, p. 50).

The ascription of any individual right, in turn, implies a claim that society ought to defend in the individual. To say, for instance, that I have a right to property is to imply that, through either legislation or education or both, society ought to defend me in my possession of that property. And it is here where Mill makes the connection between justice and utility clear:

> To have a right, then, is, I conceive, to have something which society ought to defend me in the possession of. If the objector goes on to ask, why it ought? I can give him no other reason than general utility. (Mill 2001, p. 54)

Nothing here would be likely to cause Mill's forbear, Bentham, to turn over in his booth. Mill, like Bentham, maintains that the sole basis for according rights to individuals is the effect that doing so has upon the advantage to society. He, no more than Bentham, has "anterior" or "inherent" rights in mind. But are Mill's rights "imprescriptible"?

Where Mill may offer some advance beyond Bentham is in his account of the seeming *inviolability* of such rights. As we have seen, Daniel Dennett (1995) suggests that "rights language" tends to serve as a "conversation stopper." The rights card is thought to trump any and all other considerations. Reading Bentham, one may come away with the impression that whatever "rights" we enjoy are tenuous at best, contingent as they are upon the fortuitous circumstances of social utility. We are prepared for Mill's argument in chapter five by some of the elements of his theory that are presented in earlier chapters. By the end of chapter two, it is clear that Mill is advancing a variety of rule utilitarianism. For example, he suggests at one place that there are occasions on which one must abstain from an action, even though "the consequences in the particular case might be beneficial" because "the action is of a class which, if practised generally, would be generally injurious" (Mill 2001, p. 19). And in what, at 178 words, is surely a contender for the longest sentence in the history of the English language, Mill argues for the wrongness of lying even when the lie is immediately expedient because lying undermines the trustworthiness of human assertion, ". . . which does more than any one thing that can be named to keep back civilisation, virtue, everything on which human happiness on the largest scale depends" (Mill 2001, p. 23). Lying thus falls under a rule of "transcendent expediency." He speaks of "corollaries

---

12. "Imperfect" duties are typically thought to correspond to "duties of benevolence," and these leave it to the discretion of the agent just when, under what circumstances, for which beneficiaries and to what degree the duties will be carried out. "Perfect" duties leave no such latitude. My duty to refrain from lying to you is not open to my own discretion to determine *when* to lie or be truthful, and so on.

from the Principle of Utility," "intermediate generalizations," "subordinate principles," and "secondary principles," which, clearly, are moral rules derived from the "first principle" – utility. And he closes the chapter with a discussion of moral quandaries in which two or more "secondary principles" are brought into conflict. "We must remember that only in these cases of conflict between secondary principles is it requisite that first principles should be appealed to" (Mill 2001, p. 26).

Each moral rule has its place in this scheme because of the utility derived from abstaining from tokens of the act type (in the case of wrong actions) or performing such act tokens (in the case of permissible or obligatory actions). But, as with any plausible theory of morality, Mill's rule utilitarianism treats such derivative rules as posing presumptive, rather than absolute, obligations, which may be overturned by rules weightier than themselves. Relative weight is determined by direct appeal to the principle of utility. We might thus speak of a weightier rule *trumping* its less substantial competitor. Mill's account of justice focuses on a set of moral rules which, because of the supreme importance of the human goods or interests that they are designed to protect, tend to trump any rules with which they may be found to compete. Thus, "Justice is a name for certain classes of moral rules, which concern the essentials of human well-being more nearly, and are therefore of more absolute obligation, than any other rules for the guidance of life" (Mill 2001, p. 59). And again:

> Justice is a name for certain moral requirements, which, regarded collectively, stand higher in the scale of social utility, and are therefore of more paramount obligation, than any others; though particular cases may occur in which some other social duty is so important, as to overrule any one of the general maxims of justice. (Mill 2001, p. 63)

Thus, those moral rules which are designed to safeguard our fundamental security or well-being derive their supreme importance and impose paramount obligations due to the weight of the goods that they protect *as weighed on the scale of social utility*. Individual "rights" are thus claims that people have to those goods, and, as we have seen, the claims themselves are sustained by that same concern for utility.

Mill takes nothing away from Bentham. The notion of inherent or natural rights is just as fantastic by Mill's reckoning as by Bentham's. He, like Bentham, "dispute(s) the pretensions of any theory which sets up an imaginary standard of justice not grounded on utility" (Mill 2001, p. 59). A concern for individual rights or for justice is at once a concern for social utility. This is no more to say that utilitarians must act from a *conscious concern* for general utility, overlooking the individual concerned, than that advocates of the "selfish gene" theory are committed to denying consciously altruistic motives. Perhaps the utilitarian has the resources for arguing that there is greater social utility to be had in a society of individuals who consciously and mutually *value* the other intrinsically. A Kantian respect-for-persons ethic could prove to be a useful fiction on a utilitarian reckoning. But, if Mill is to be believed, it is a fiction, useful or not, and it must be so precisely *because* of that utilitarian reckoning.

Mill's chapter is motivated from a concern to answer a familiar objection to utilitarian theory. We might call that objection the *problem of justice*. The worry is that there appears to be no necessary connection between an action's maximizing utility and its being fair or just. It is sometimes urged that the consistent utilitarian would be in a position of justifying, say, slavery, the torture of innocent persons, or even rape should the circumstances of utility call for it. I am supposing for the sake of argument that Mill's development of rule utilitarianism and account of utility-based justice offers a satisfactory solution to the problem of justice.[13] Let us assume with Mill, then, that even where it is determined that slavery or rape would produce beneficial consequences in a particular case, "it would be unworthy of an intelligent agent not to be consciously aware that the action is of a class which, if practised generally, would be generally injurious, and that this is the ground of the obligation to abstain." Indeed, let us leave the door open to Mill and to later utilitarians to demonstrate that the Principle of Utility, rightly understood, has none of these "iniquitous consequences." Nevertheless, I maintain that any and all versions of utilitarianism worthy of the name must fail to account for that portion of commonsense morality that we are holding up as a criterion: that individuals have moral standing.

Consider our test case of rape. Surely, rape is immoral if any act is immoral. And we may suppose that Mill has offered us grounds for saying why. Rape violates a moral rule that concerns "the essentials of human well-being more nearly" than other rules to such a degree that we find it difficult to imagine any competing rule trumping the rule against rape. And because justice is a name for rules in this class, and, further, justice always involves individual rights, we may say that, on Mill's view, rape involves the violation of the victim's *rights*. And, as we have seen, Mill suggests that, in such cases, the individual is *wronged* or done an injustice. Why, then, is this not sufficient for allowing that his view accords moral standing to individuals within the moral community?

The answer is that, upon analysis, the explanation for the wrongness of rape appeals to the "generally injurious" consequences for the community rather than the simple fact that the person who is the victim simply ought not to be treated in that manner. Again, Mill, no more than Bentham, offers us an account that permits the existence of inherent rights. If there is a right not to be raped, it is, therefore, derivative and contingent upon the circumstances of social utility. The structure of the utilitarian explanation of the wrongness of rape is reducible to that of (ID) mentioned earlier, and bears a strong resemblance to the explanation required of the egoist, not to mention our account of the wrongness of vandalism. And, while Mill employs language suggestive of direct duties to the holders of rights, we must not lose sight of the logic of the utilitarian analysis. William Paley, a divine command moralist who moonlighted as a utilitarian, seemed not particularly troubled over the prospect of convicting innocent persons, suggesting that "he who falls by a mistaken sentence may be considered as falling for his country" (Paley 1785, p. 369). Mill's "rights utilitarian" might endorse *Blackstone's Formulation*: "Better that ten guilty persons go free than that one innocent suffer."[14] This may call for extending certain civil rights to the obviously guilty and perhaps even acquitting in the event that those rights are deemed to have been violated in the process. Indeed, the resulting view has been aptly put by one economist: "The disutility of convicting an innocent person far exceeds the disutility of finding a guilty person to be not guilty" (Volokh 1997). But where this occurs, it is not out of a direct concern for the guilty person but for the preservation of an institution essential to social utility, and this is so despite a language of civil rights

13. I am, in fact, persuaded by the argument that rule utilitarianism is reducible to act utilitarianism – act utilitarianism in a rented tux, so to speak.

14. Bentham, of course, referred to Blackstone's work – or perhaps the man himself – as "ignorance on stilts." Were Blackstone to join company with the French delegates – whose views were, in Bentham's estimation, of similar artificial stature – we would have the beginnings of a small circus.

that may seem to suggest otherwise. And should the utilitarian *insist* otherwise, a dilemma awaits.

To the question of why society ought to defend the rights of individuals, Mill's answer was "social utility." But this invites a further question. Why should we concern ourselves over social utility? Is it for the sake of anything beyond itself – in particular, for the sake of the individuals who make up the community – or is it not? If not, then the argument of the present chapter succeeds: the utilitarian does not act ultimately out of a regard for the moral standing of individuals. But if so, then it would appear that our utilitarian has something beyond utility in mind – perhaps something more laudable. After all, the believer in natural rights might well evince a concern for social utility in that the flourishing of the community is conducive to the flourishing of people.

When a British captain and eight soldiers were to be tried, each for his role in the Boston Massacre, John Adams hazarded "a popularity hardly earned" and incurred "a clamour and popular suspicions and prejudices" by accepting an invitation to mount their defense. Reading accounts of the defense itself, as well as Adams' own memoirs concerning the trial, it is evident that he believed his clients were innocent. "Judgment of Death against those Soldiers would have been as foul a Stain upon this Country as the Executions of the Quakers or Witches, anciently. As the Evidence was, the Verdict of the Jury was exactly right," he said (Adams & Adams 2007, p. 317). The John Adams whose name is affixed to a document asserting inalienable human rights might well be thought to have been motivated by a direct concern for innocent soldiers, Quakers, and witches, as their natural and imprescriptible rights were at stake. But had he later read and been convinced by Bentham's critique, his interest may have been diverted to the importance of avoiding the "foul Stain" for its own sake rather than for the sake of those who would endure it. As Bernard Williams notes, "consequentialism attaches value ultimately to states of affairs" (Smart & Williams 1973, p. 95). This "ultimacy" calls for those states of affairs being pursued for their own sake rather than for the sake of anyone who appreciates them.[15] Perhaps man was made for the Sabbath after all.

The point coincides with the so-called "receptacle problem" that Tom Regan has urged against utilitarianism. According to Regan, it is not *individuals* that are valued by the utilitarian, but their *mental states*. Mill, for instance, made it clear that *pleasure* is the *only* thing desirable as an end, and the desirableness of anything else is contingent upon the pleasure that it produces. Other utilitarians might substitute satisfaction of the interests of individuals as the one thing of intrinsic value. Either way, this invites the question of where *persons* fit into such a scheme. According to Regan, persons are important because they are the vessels that are laden with this treasure. Consider his following example:

> Here is an analogy to help make the philosophical point clearer: a cup contains different liquids – sometimes sweet, sometimes bitter, sometimes a mix of the two. What has value are the liquids: the sweeter the better; the bitterer the worse. The cup – the container – has no value. It's what goes into it, not what they go into, that has value. For the utilitarian, you and I are like the cup; we have no value as individuals and thus no equal value. What has value is what goes into us, what we serve as receptacles for; our feelings of satisfaction have positive value; our feelings of frustration have negative value. (Regan in Pierce & VanDeVeer 1995, p. 75)

---

15. Marcus Singer has pointed out in his lectures that the utilitarian's direct duty proves to be an odd abstraction: it is to maintain a number in the universe – something like a GNP on a cosmic scale – representing net utility, and this not for the sake of anyone's enjoyment.

There is no direct concern to see to it that individuals are satisfied rather than frustrated, pleased rather than pained – at least, not for the individual's own sake. The principal concern is to maintain the greatest possible net pleasure or satisfaction. And this net pleasure is not for the sake of any individual persons. Rather, the reverse is true: any regard for the individual is ultimately out of a concern for increasing net utility. Utilitarianism fails to accord moral standing to individuals.

Moral standing and virtue ethics

Virtue Ethics (VE) is often distinguished from both consequentialist and deontological theories of morality on the grounds that, whereas those theories emphasize the rightness of acts, VE places a premium upon the goodness of agents. Thus, Roger Crisp and Michael Slote write, "Certainly it is characteristic of modern VE that it puts primary emphasis on aretaic or virtue centered concepts rather than deontic or obligation-centered concepts" (Crisp & Slote 1997, p. 3). And Rosalind Hursthouse (2007) helpfully observes:

> Suppose it is obvious that someone in need should be helped. A utilitarian will point to the fact that the consequences of doing so will maximise well-being, a deontologist to the fact that, in doing so the agent will be acting in accordance with a moral rule such as "Do unto others as you would be done by" and a virtue ethicist to the fact that helping the person would be charitable or benevolent.

Aristotle maintained that excellence or right action should be understood in terms of how a good person, one of practical wisdom, would choose to act. As Monika Betzler has it, "The standard of right action is to do whatever an entirely virtuous person would do" (Betzler 2008, p. 2) and, as Robert N. Johnson suggests, such theories make "an ideal of the person, rather than duty or value" the "foundation of ethics" so that "what makes an action a moral duty and what makes something of value is its relationship to some ideal of the person" (Johnson 2008, p. 58).

It is sometimes suggested that Aristotle faces a circularity problem here. Rightness is whatever a good person would do. But what makes a good person good? One cannot say, in turn, that good people are those who perform right actions. Consider, for example, a point made by Vasilis Politis in a review of Theodore Scaltsas's *The Golden Age of Virtue: Aristotle's Ethics*. Politis observes that Scaltsas attempts to break the circle by suggesting that good people are to be understood as those who choose things that are "good by nature" (*phusei*), and that these are good by nature insofar as they contribute to a "harmonic whole." But, Politis thinks, this signals an abandonment of Aristotle's position:

> I am not sure how the proposed solution is really a solution to the problem. Aristotle thinks that right action must be determined in terms of how the good person would choose. But Scaltsas' proposal, if I am not mistaken, means that right action is determined without appeal to how the good person would choose: right action is right by virtue of contributing to the 'harmony among a variety of elements in the character of the person. (Politis 1995, p. 259)

I do not wish to spend any time in worry over this problem. Instead, I will assume that the Aristotelian is able to answer the question, "What makes good people good?" without being drawn into this vortex. Perhaps an account of human flourishing may be offered so that the virtues amount to character traits that either conduce to or are manifestations of such flourishing – they are among the good-making traits for the kind. There is much that the virtue ethicist may plausibly say along these lines. Robert Johnson offers a formal account of VE that takes such a notion of flourishing into direct consideration.

> (VE)   For all actions φ and all persons S, it is right (to be done, ethical, correct, etc.) for S to φ in C at t if and only if φ-ing in C at t is or would be characteristic of a flourishing human life (Johnson 2008, p. 60).

But Politis' criticism raises an important point for our purposes. He is, after all, analyzing the structure of moral explanation regarding the moral properties of rightness and goodness – what Johnson calls the "form" of the theory (Johnson in Betzler 2007, p. 58) – and this is our task. Does the moral standing of persons factor in to the virtue ethicist's account?

Consider how a VE account might look in explaining the wrongness of an action in a context where we do not suppose that any direct duties are being violated.[16] Richard Routley (1973) has offered a counterexample – his "Last Man" example – to the anthropocentric view that our environmental duties are indirect, derivative of direct duties owed other humans. You are literally the last person on earth and, for whatever reason – perhaps just for the hell of it – you are considering some action that will have disastrous environmental effects,[17] say, setting multiple and massive wildfires in the Redwoods. In this scenario, there are no other human persons whose well-being could be either harmed or helped by anything that you do, and so an anthropocentric theory cannot account for the apparent wrongness of the act. But it does seem to most of us (does it not?) that it would, nevertheless, be wrong. Does this not implicate an ethic of direct environmental duties – the according of moral standing to nature itself?

I agree that Routley's Last Man behaves badly. But I am equally willing to censure him in other contexts. Suppose the Last Man were to set off on a kind of iconoclastic rampage. We find him in Paris defacing *Mona Lisa*, then on to Florence to have a go at Michelangelo's *David*. I squirm at such thoughts just as I do when he is targeting trees. But I do not think it is at all plausible to extend moral standing to paintings or statues.

Thomas Hill has suggested that there is a perfectly sensible way in which we may account for environmental wrongs independently of our positing direct duties to the environment itself. In the sorts of cases considered earlier, Hill would have us ask, "What kind of person would *do* a thing like that?" His is an application of a virtue ethic to the question of environmental responsibility. With this emphasis, there is a shift – characteristic of VE – away from the question of the rightness or wrongness of the actions in question and to the issue

---

16. Much of what I say here follows my discussion in Linville (1998).

17. Of course, there must *be* such a thing as a "disastrous environmental effect" in its own right in order to get the argument up and running. This seems to presuppose that the notion of *proper function* is applicable when thinking about ecosystems, and that assumption may be challenged. The Missoula Valley has been the location of Lake Missoula many times over in the course of the natural history of the area, as ice dams have formed and subsequently melted with "catastrophic" effects downstream. Is there any good sense in which we may identify the flooded condition of the valley as better or worse than its present state independently of the interests of, say, those Missoulians who now work and live there? In order to be able to say that there are some things that we ought not to do to the environment, we would seem to require the prior claim that some natural states are better than others. But the claim seems problematic given an ecocentric perspective. See Chase (2001).

of *excellence of character* – or lack thereof – of the person in question. He writes, "Sometimes we may not regard an action as wrong at all though we see it as reflecting something objectionable about the person who does it" (Hill 1991, p. 108). On this view, the "moral discomfort" that we experience at the thought of the Last Man destroying the world's natural or cultural treasures is explained primarily by the fact that we find ourselves assessing the character of a person who is capable of such an action, rather than the action itself. The ability to do such things reveals something dark about a person's basic moral disposition.

Hill reasons that, while environmentally destructive behavior "does not *necessarily* reflect the absence of virtues, it often signals the absence of certain traits which we want to encourage because they are, in most cases, a natural basis for the development of certain virtues" (Hill 1991, p. 109). Such destructive behavior may reflect, among other things, a lack of the kind of humility that one develops with a full realization of his place in the scheme of things, or it may betray a lack of an aesthetic sense. Since these are human excellences that we value, we recognize character flaws in those who have failed to develop them. Routley's Last Man may be thought to have an overinflated sense of self-importance – a kind of *hubris*. The same may be said of grave robbers, vandals, and iconoclasts. A lack of love and respect for our natural environment may be evidence of a lack of the more "generic" virtues that have application in other areas of life as well. And so, if Hill's account holds up, then perhaps we may account for the moral intuitions to which Routley appeals without being required to extend moral standing to stands of trees.

I find Hill's application of this account of human excellences to environmental concerns to be highly plausible. But a parallel application to explain our "moral discomfort" in cases of rape or genocide – certainly nothing that Hill himself would countenance – would be highly implausible. As I write, a particularly brutal and grotesque case of kidnapping and murder along the Appalachian Trail is in the news. A suspect has been arrested, and he is allegedly linked to three other recent murders in bordering states. I *do* find myself asking Hill's question, "What kind of person would *do* a thing like that?" It is a monumental understatement to observe that the killer "lacks excellence of character." He is, in fact, a moral monster. But, clearly, such observations do not adequately account for the "moral discomfort" that one feels on hearing news of rapes, murders, and decapitations. To appropriate Hill's formula, intended only for the environmental contexts, and employ it here would result in a bad parody at best or an outright perversity. Nor do we find an adequate resource in an adaptation of Hursthouse's explanation given earlier of the virtue ethicist's analysis of why one ought to help a person in need: "helping the person would be charitable or benevolent." We ought not to explain why one should refrain from rape by pointing to the fact that "raping a person would be *uncharitable* and malevolent." It *is* these things, of course, but it is very much more. Things are no better if we invoke Johnson's VE: it is right to refrain from rape (in C at t) just in case so refraining (in C at t) "is or would be characteristic of a flourishing human life." Moral standing is clearly implicated in the case of rape, but appears to have no place in formulations such as VE. The reason rape is wrong, and, indeed, the reason that it is committed only by bad people, is that persons ought never to be treated in that way.

My objection does not amount to what Hursthouse refers to as the "egotism objection," namely, that consistent virtue ethicists, in behaving generously or benevolently are, in fact, acting out of a concern for their own characters. Imagining a view with such implications, Mary Midgley observes:

> Anyone who refrained from cruelty merely from a wish not to sully his own character, without any direct consideration for the possible victims, would be frivolous and narcissistic. (Midgley 1986, p. 157)

And so we might imagine the would-be rapist refraining from that sordid deed solely because he wishes not to be a rapist. Or consider the *M*A*S*H** episode in which, upon learning that he nearly lost a patient through some oversight, Major Winchester, always the egotist, reacts in horror: "That would have been the worst thing ever to happen to me." To such objections, Hursthouse (2007) replies, "The virtuous agent acts as she does because she believes that someone's suffering will be averted, or someone benefited, or the truth established, or a debt repaid, or . . . thereby." I see no more reason to suppose that the egotism objection sticks here than I saw earlier for supposing that consistent utilitarians must always have "social utility" consciously before their minds and not the welfare of individuals. Surely, we can see our way to the view that generosity may be consciously altruistic regardless of what we learn about the metaethics involved in VE. But the devil is in the metaethical details.

A virtue ethic that is ultimately grounded in a notion of respect-for-persons may prove to be a rich and plausible theory. One likely interpretation of Confucianism has it as an account of human flourishing. But, whereas Aristotle defined humans as "rational animals" (which, on one standard interpretation, has the implausible result that one flourishes insofar as one basically leads the life of the philosopher), Confucius defined them as "moral animals" (Koller & Koller 1998, p. 239). On this reading, we flourish insofar as we fulfill that nature. The chief virtue lauded by Confucius is *jen*, or "human-heartedness." *Jen* amounts to a "love of humanity." One flourishes insofar as one cultivates this virtue and the complex character that is its corollary. In one place, Confucius instructs, "If a superior man departs from humanity (*jen*), how can he fulfill that name? A superior man never abandons humanity even for the lapse of a single meal. In moments of haste, he acts according to it. In times of difficulty and confusion, he acts according to it" (Analects 4:5). Allowing for obvious differences in detail, the concept of the "superior man" functions in the Confucian scheme in much the same way that the "man of practical wisdom" does in Aristotle's thought. He is the person who lives well by manifesting the desired character traits. In asking, "How can he fulfill that name?" Confucius is invoking one of his central doctrines, the Rectification of Names: "Let the ruler be a ruler, the minister a minister, the father a father and the son a son" (Analects 12:11). The idea is that each named thing has an essential function that must be fulfilled. To "fulfill the name" of "superior man" is thus to fulfill the function, and this is done, he says, by coming to love humanity. Confucianism thus folds the concept of respect-for-persons into its account of flourishing so that our question, "What makes a good person good?" is answered by reference to the person's regard for humanity and the role that such regard plays in the overall cultivation of character.

Assuming that I am correct in thinking that Confucian moral philosophy may fruitfully be regarded as a variety of VE, it would seem to differ from standard theories. Hursthouse (2007) notes that virtue ethicists largely "have eschewed any attempt to ground virtue ethics in an external foundation," and this observation is perhaps illustrated by Politis's criticism of Scaltsas's proposed ground. The "external foundation" that appears in Confucianism is a principle of respect-for-persons, and it compares favorably with the celebrated Kantian formulation of such a principle. Sandra A. Wawrytko (1982), for example, notes that "both revolve around the seminal concept of respect as the root of any system of ethics, as well as the *sine qua non* of moral practice" (p. 237). And Stuart Hackett's explanation of the role of personal worth in the thought of Confucius would work equally well were he discussing Kant's Principle of Humanity: "Personal being is intrinsically valuable, and the locus of ultimate, intrinsic worth; while love, as recognizing and implementing the actualization of that worth, is the essential principle of ultimate moral requirement" (Hackett 1979, p. 51). This agreement between the two moral theories would seem to put both "at odds" with classical views in the Aristotelian tradition. Robert Johnson writes in the *Stanford Encyclopedia of Philosophy* (2004):

> Kant's account of virtue presupposes an account of moral duty already in place. Thus, rather than treating admirable character traits as more basic than the notions of right and wrong conduct, Kant takes virtues to be explicable only in terms of a prior account of moral or dutiful behavior. He does not try to make out what shape a good character has and then draw conclusions about how we ought to act on that basis. He sets out the principles of moral conduct based on his philosophical account of rational agency, and then on that basis defines virtue as the trait of acting according to these principles.

I conclude, then, that standard accounts of VE have no conceptual room for the moral standing of individuals, and, as I have been arguing, this counts against such theories. We should be able to say simply that rape and genocide are wrong because people ought neither to be raped nor exterminated.

Moral standing and personal dignity

Immanuel Kant's Principle of Humanity instructs, "Act in such a way that you always treat humanity, whether in your own person or in the person of any other, never simply as a means, but always at the same time as an end" (Kant 1964, p. 96). The Principle of Humanity is informed by the idea that persons are of ultimate and unconditional worth, and to treat them as "ends" is just to respect their autonomy as persons who have wills and ends of their own, and thus to act toward them in a way that is consistent with that worth. Kant maintained that there are two ways in which something may be said to have value: either it has a *dignity* or it has a *price*. A thing has a (mere) price if it has a "market value," that is, its worth may, in principle, be expressed in terms of something else. Our various possessions pretty obviously fall into this category. One feature of such value is that it is *mind-dependent*: such objects have value only insofar as they are valued. The market value of your home, automobile, or Fender Stratocaster is strictly determined by what someone is willing to pay for it. We can readily imagine a possible world in which gold is valued by no one and is therefore of no value. The dollar in your pocket is *worth* a dollar only so long as someone *believes* that it is.

Something has dignity just in case it resists such valuation in terms of some market value so that its worth is intrinsic. Any property is intrinsic to a thing just in case that property involves no essential reference to any *other* thing, which is to say that it is *nonrelational*. Each and every individual human possesses the property *being human* intrinsically. Each and every individual *husband*, however, is such in virtue of a relation that he bears to his wife. Kantian dignity is a moral value or worth that individual persons possess intrinsically *as* persons. Since it is a nonrelational property, its value is mind-independent, and thus not reducible to or derivative of the valuings of some agent or other. If persons have dignity, then they *ought* to be valued for their own sake even if, in fact, they are not. And because dignity is nonrelational, neither is it reducible to any sort of instrumental value.

Dignity thus constitutes the unconditional worth of its possessor. The worth of persons is unconditional in that it derives from their intrinsic nature as persons and is in no way contingent upon their performance or their contribution or usefulness to anyone or anything. It is certainly possible to find people who are of little or no instrumental worth, or "useless." Consider Otis, the town drunk, who divides his time between being face up under a bottle and face down in the gutter. But there are no worthless people, because worth is not conditioned by usefulness.

Kant's principle prohibits treating persons simply as means to ends precisely because this amounts to treating a person as though his or her value is merely instrumental, or determined by their relation to something else. And this, in turn, is to treat a person as a mere thing. The injunction to treat people as "ends" thus amounts to an imperative to act from a respect for their dignity as persons with ends of their own. Kant's Principle of Humanity has it that the essence of an immoral action is that it treats persons as though they are mere things.

Pretty clearly, such a respect-for-persons ethic attributes moral standing to individual persons in the way that we have sought here. The theoretical form of the theory grounds the wrongness of such actions as rape in direct duties owed the person. Rape is straightforwardly a case in which a person is treated "merely as a means to an end he does not share" (Kant 1964, p. 97). Slavery is an example in which a person is regarded *quite literally* as having a market value.

Kant's notion of dignity is a natural basis for according those natural, inherent, and imprescriptible rights denied by Bentham. Persons are *entitled* to be treated *as* persons and are wronged, or treated unjustly, when treated as mere things. To Mill's question, "Why ought society to defend the rights of individuals?," the Kantian answer is not "social utility" but "personal dignity." The explanation need look no farther than a concern for the person whose rights are in question.

I have argued that moral standing of the sort capable of explaining certain of our moral beliefs requires that the duties in question not be derived from any concerns deemed more basic than or peripheral to a regard for the individuals themselves. A respect-for-persons ethic appears to be sufficient to such an explanatory task. Is it necessary? Is the intrinsic worth of the individual implied by that individual's moral standing? It is hard to see what moral standing *can* mean if it does not involve such value. We are told that we have a direct duty to some individual person S so that a violation of that duty involves *wronging* or doing an injustice to S. I have argued that Mill's notion of justice, with its attending idea of rights, does not amount to moral standing, derivative as it is from the more basic concern for social utility. Likewise, VE as commonly articulated appears to neglect moral standing, as the foundational concern is with the flourishing of the agent. Moral standing is thus not contingent upon anything extrinsic to the nature of persons *qua* persons, and so is unconditional. What is it to have such unconditional regard if it is not to value the person *intrinsically*? And to be told that one ought to value persons intrinsically would seem to imply that persons just *are* of intrinsic moral worth.[18]

---

18. That is, if the imperative so to value is categorical. As noted earlier, there might be utilitarian reasons for valuing persons or other things intrinsically, although I would argue that the resulting imperatives would be hypothetical, and so the regard itself would not be unconditional. ("You may stop valuing Pete intrinsically now as your doing so is no longer useful.")

Personal dignity and worldview assessment

Assuming that the argument of this chapter has succeeded to this point, we have arrived at the conclusion that personal dignity is implicated by the sorts of pre-theoretical moral beliefs to which we typically appeal in reflective equilibrium. We turn now to another question. Should we suppose that whether persons have dignity is indifferent to questions of metaphysics? That is, are we entitled to believe that persons enjoy intrinsic value regardless of what worldview we take to be true? It would be surprising if this were the case.

To make a rather obvious point, the belief that persons have dignity would seem to involve the belief that there are persons, just as surely as "penguins are comical" presupposes penguins. As such, the belief in personal dignity would not seem to be a natural component of a worldview that denies that there are persons. I suppose we might begin by noting that the committed solipsist need not lose sleep over his dealings with "others" except insofar as imaginary persons are capable of retaliating by placing him in an imaginary asylum.

But to take a more serious example, Advaita Vedanta appears to deny the real existence of persons, as discrete selves are said to be no more real than discrete spaces within jars. Just as there is only one universal Space, there is only the Self of Brahman (Radakrishnan & Moore 1967, p. 513). Such a worldview might easily accommodate the advice, "Neither a borrower nor a lender be" as neither party to the would-be transaction exists. But it is hard to see what to make of an injunction to treat others with respect when, strictly speaking, there is no one either to respect or to do the respecting.

On Theravada Buddhism, the question of whether there are such things as persons is at least problematic. There, we are offered a view of persons as bundles of instantaneous constituents (dharmas). A person at a given time just is a bundle of these constituents. Personal identity over time is spelled out in terms of a series of bundles in a causal relation so that the earlier self is a causal ancestor of the later self. But at no time is there anything substantial that may be identified as the self. There are only the nonpersonal constituents. One might wonder whether a bundle of nonpersonal constituents is the sort of thing that may plausibly be ascribed dignity and taken to be the appropriate object of respect.

The naturalist may be faced with a similar problem. Can the existence of persons be accounted for on naturalism? One might have thought so. But consider this "astonishing hypothesis":

> The Astonishing Hypothesis is that 'You,' your joys and your sorrows, your memories and your ambitions, your sense of identity and free will, are in fact no more than the behavior of a vast assembly of nerve cells and their associated molecules. As Lewis Carroll's Alice may have phrased it: 'You're nothing but a pack of neurons.' This hypothesis is so alien to the ideas of most people alive today that it can be truly called astonishing. (Goetz & Taliaferro 2008, p. 22)

Francis Crick here offers a sort of bundle theory of his own, suggesting that there is no substantive, personal, and conscious element that constitutes the self. Rather, what we call "persons" are actually vast assemblages of neurons and the like.

Of course, Crick is also notorious for his one-time advocacy of "directed panspermia," which has it that human DNA was transported to the earth by a race of superintelligent aliens. But before it is supposed that his bundle theory is likewise a fringe view, we should note that it is a direct implication of what Stewart Goetz and Charles Taliaferro call "strict naturalism," the idea that "nature is all that exists and nature itself is whatever will be disclosed by the ideal natural sciences, especially physics" (Goetz & Taliaferro 2008). As these authors note, this appears to be what Arthur Danto has in mind when he describes naturalism as "repudiating the view that there exists or could exist any entities or events which lie, in principle, beyond the scope of scientific explanation" (Goetz & Taliaferro 2008, p. 14). Unfortunately, *persons* as substantive selves that essentially possess a first-person point of view appear to lie, in principle, beyond the scope of third-person scientific explanation. It is for this reason that Daniel Dennett writes:

> We now understand that the mind is not, as Descartes confusedly supposed, in *communication with* the brain in some miraculous way; it *is* the brain, or, more specifically, a system or organization within the brain that has evolved in much the way that our immune system or respiratory system or digestive system has evolved. Like many other natural wonders, the human mind is something of a bag of tricks, cobbled together over the eons by the foresightless process of evolution by natural selection. (Dennett 2006, p. 107; emphasis in the original)

Unless the conscious is explained without remainder by reference to the nonconscious, the personal by way of the nonpersonal, or the first person in third-person terms, the task of explanation has not been accomplished. A final physical theory will be exhaustive and it will give no quarter to persons.

> You've got to leave the first person out of your final theory. You won't have a theory of consciousness if you still have the first person in there, because that was what it was your job to explain. All the paraphernalia that doesn't make any sense unless you've got a first person in there, has to be turned into something else. You've got to figure out some way to break it up and distribute its powers and opportunities into the system in some other way. (Dennett quoted in Blackmore 2006, p. 87)

For her part, Susan Blackmore seems to have followed Dennett's advice. "I long ago concluded that there is no substantial or persistent self to be found in experience, let alone in the brain. I have become quite uncertain as to whether there really is anything it is like to be me" (Blackmore 2006, p. 9). Thus, as Jaegwon Kim notes, consciousness has been "oddly absent" from both philosophy and scientific psychology in much of the work of the past century (Kim 2005, p. 8). For that matter, consciousness has been "oddly absent" even in twentieth-century works bearing such promising titles as *Consciousness Explained*. It is rather like picking up a title such as *Europe Explored* and finding that the author has serious doubts of the existence of that continent and devotes himself to explaining how putative Europeans might mistakenly think themselves to live there.[19]

The strict naturalist's inability to discover the self in either the laboratory or the field is, as Yogi Berra might have put it, like déjà vu all over again. David Hume similarly and famously failed to find himself despite careful search. His introspective attempts at perceiving himself as the subject of his various perceptions uniformly turned up only the

---

19. Of Dennett's efforts, Mary Midgley has written, "Suggestions that Dennett should be prosecuted for his title under the Trades Description Act are attractive, but might call for action over too many other books to be practicable" (Midgley 1994, p. 186). Thanks to Dave Werther for alerting me to this note from Midgley.

perceptions themselves, say, the appearance of the room about him, the feeling of the air against his skin, the pressure of chair to buttocks or floor to feet. The conclusion that he drew from his enquiry was that the only concept of a "self" that we have is that of a kind of aggregate of perceptions but not of any subject of those perceptions (Hume 1978, p. 259). At this, Thomas Reid expressed surprise over learning that the *Treatise of Human Nature* was without an author! (Reid 1983, p. 21). Similarly, Goetz and Taliaferro observe, "[*T*]*here would be no knowledge of mass, electric charge, or space-time unless we are enduring selves which have experiences.* The very practice of science itself is unintelligible unless persons exist and have observations and thoughts, and presumably *observing* and *thinking* are experiences" (Goetz & Taliaferro 2008, p. 50; emphasis in the original).

Owen Flanagan (2002) has said recently that we must "demythologize persons," and by this, he means that the Cartesian beliefs of the soul and of libertarian free will must be abandoned. But the project seems to have resulted instead in the *mythologizing* of persons so that they have come to be regarded in just the way that Flanagan and Dennett regard the Trinity. G. K. Chesterton once quipped of the secularization of society and the consequent erosion of confidence in the reliability of human reason, "With a long and sustained tug we have attempted to pull the mitre off pontifical man; and his head has come off with it" (Chesterton 1986, p. 237). A similar procedure seems to have taken place here. Flanagan's "de-souling" operation was a success; the patient vanished.

C. S. Lewis seems to have had such a view in mind as he worked through his grief over the loss of his wife. He pondered the question of whether she continued on as a person, and observed that if she "is not," "then she never was. I mistook a cloud of atoms for a person. There aren't, and never were, any people. Death only reveals the vacuity that was already there" (Lewis 2001a, p. 28). Elsewhere, he notes that we would then have mistaken "boxes of fireworks" for persons. In this, Lewis was not far from Dennett's own suggestion that human minds are "bags of tricks." In fact, Dennett might have attempted to console the grieving widower, as he has recently ventured his own observations on grief. Evolution has wired us to assume the "intentional stance," which amounts to a predisposition to view certain other things in the world as *intentional systems* – agents with beliefs and desires. The death of a loved one confronts one with "a major task of cognitive updating: revising all our habits of thought to fit a world with one less familiar intentional system in it" (Dennett 2006, p. 112). Lewis confessed that his grief felt like fear and that he refused to be consoled by religion because, even on the most optimistic account, he longed for something that was now irretrievably lost. Dennett would have advised that such are symptoms of this cognitive updating, and it is all to be expected due to the difficulty of simply "deleting the file" (2006, p. 122) in our memory banks. This prompted Leon Wieseltier, in his review of *Breaking the Spell*, to comment, "So steer clear of 'we materialists' in your dark hours. They cannot fortify you, say, after the funeral of a familiar intentional system" (Wieseltier 2006).

Insofar as the intentional stance is a propensity to ascribe irreducibly conscious states and teleological purposes to "intentional systems," it is, as we have learned earlier, misleading – much as our programmed propensity to ascribe rights to such systems is misleading according to Dennett (1995, p. 507). And a revised Kantian ethic – call it a "respect-for-intentional-systems" ethic – would be equally misleading: *Always treat intentional systems, whether in your own nonsubstantial self or that of another, as ends-in-themselves and never merely as means to ends.* Such would be misleading, I say, because given the eliminability of teleological purposes on strict naturalism, it is strictly false to say that intentional systems are autonomous and thus have ends of their own. On strict naturalism, Kant's famous distinction between things that are governed by law and those that *act* in accordance with their *idea* of law breaks down, as the latter category collapses into the former. And, presumably, there is nothing that it is *like* to represent a moral law to oneself.

But neither is it clear that moral agency or autonomy may be preserved on a more relaxed version of naturalism. The past few decades of work in philosophy of mind have included efforts on the part of physicalists to reconcile mental causation to an otherwise unyielding physicalism. "Broad naturalism" (Goetz & Taliaferro 2008) or "minimal physicalism" (Kim 2005) describe varieties of physicalism that appeal to some form of supervenience of the mental upon the physical. The aim is to allow room for the irreducibly mental within an exclusively physical world – property dualism. Here, one significant difference between a human brain and a slab of granite – both strictly physical objects – is that, while the latter is possessed only of physical properties, the former is qualified by both the physical and the mental. Kim suggests that as "seductive" as the possibility is, allowing physicalists to remain true to their name but also to declare amnesty for all of those valuable and obvious mental concepts that have lived in exile throughout much of the previous century, it is also a "piece of wishful thinking" (Kim 2005, p. 15).

Kim urges a compelling argument – "the supervenience/exclusion argument" – for thinking that the *irreducibility* of the mental is at odds with the *causal efficacy* of the mental. Physicalists – and naturalists in general – are committed to the *Causal Closure Principle*, which insists that all causes are physical in nature. And a Principle of *Causal Exclusion* has it that where any event has a sufficient cause c, then (barring causal overdetermination) no event distinct from c can be a cause of the event. Clearly then, if all physical events have physical causes, and mental events are irreducibly mental, then no mental event can be a cause of any physical event (Kim 2005, p. 19). The result is epiphenomenalism. If the *idea of law* is irreducibly mental in nature, it is difficult to see how it may result in moral behavior, despite observed correlations between *Jones thinks the maxim of act A cannot be willed to become a universal law* and *Jones refrains from A.*

> These observed correlations give us an impression of causation; however, that is only an appearance, and there is no more causation here than between two successive shadows cast by a moving car. (Kim 2005, p. 21)

In one fell swoop, we seem to have eliminated – or at least seriously compromised – both the Kantian grounds and the means of treating persons as ends-in-themselves. The latter suffers because the attitude of respect – whether for a person or the law itself – presupposes the sort of mental causation that is precluded by the supervenience/exclusion argument. The former is eclipsed by the fact that intentional systems, just like digestive and immune systems, are mechanistic. Autonomy presupposes teleology, and the latter has no purchase in the world described by naturalism, strict or broad.

The jam is created by attempting to affirm causal closure, the exclusion principle, mental–physical supervenience, and mental–physical property dualism. The first three are nonnegotiable, and so it appears that mental causation and consciousness can be salvaged only by denying property dualism, that is, reducing the mental to the physical. But, Kim warns, "reductionism may not be true" (2005, p. 22). Some might suppose that Kim, like Dickens or Twain, is a master of understatement. Consider Michael Lockwood's disparaging assessment of such reductionist programs:

It seems to me evident that no description of brain activity of the relevant kind, couched in the currently available languages of physics, physiology, or functional or computational roles, is remotely capable of capturing what is distinctive about consciousness. So glaring, indeed, are the shortcomings of all the reductive programmes currently on offer, that I cannot believe that anyone with a philosophical training, looking dispassionately at these programmes, would take any of them seriously for a moment, were it not for a deep-seated conviction that current physical science has essentially got reality taped, and accordingly, *something* along the lines of what the reductionists are offering *must* be correct. To that extent, the very existence of consciousness seems to me to be a standing demonstration of the explanatory limitations of contemporary physical science. (Lockwood 2002, p. 447)

As Kim notes, the prospects for a successful reduction either by way of so-called "bridge laws" that would establish a lawlike connection – necessary correlations – between mental and physical properties, or through strict identity are bleak. No amount of information regarding the physical goings-on of the brain would seem to give us a glimpse of the intrinsic features of a conscious experience. And we appear to have two irreducibly different kinds of things with different sets of properties. Conscious states, for example, defy description in terms of the spatial and compositional properties that are essential to accounts of physical states and processes.

Indeed, despite his own efforts at a *functional* identity of a limited class of cognitive properties (e.g. "To be in pain, by definition, is to be in a state which is caused by tissue damage and which in turn causes winces and groans" (Kim 2005, p. 28)), Kim suggests that *qualia* resist such a functional reduction. And, echoing Lockwood, we might wonder what, other than an attempt to salvage physicalism, would motivate anyone to offer such a functional reduction. Is there not more to pain – something that it is *like* to be in pain – than a system of inputs and outputs?

It is not the aim of this chapter to settle these complex issues in the philosophy of mind.[20] But we have seen a glimpse of the difficulty that confronts the naturalist in attempting to account for conscious moral agents. Consciousness is either eliminated altogether, reduced to the physical, or held to be emergent and irreducible. But eliminativism is altogether implausible and of dubious coherence, reductionist programs seem doomed to failure, and property dualism cannot account for mental causation and consciousness. And regarding the latter, we might observe with Goetz and Taliaferro that the assertion that there are irreducibly mental properties introduces a pluralist ontology and signals a departure from the spirit and letter of the scientific naturalism that is assumed by such philosophers. It begins to appear that supernaturalism must be avoided at all costs – even the cost of an unparsimonious and possibly *ad hoc* metaphysic. Bertrand Russell observed:

A strange mystery it is that Nature, omnipotent but blind, in the revolutions of her secular hurryings through the abysses of space, has brought forth at last a child, subject still to her power, but gifted with sight, with knowledge of good and evil, with the capacity of judging all the works of his unthinking Mother. (Russell 1957, p. 107)

It is indeed a "strange mystery," and the mystery remains. Just a few years before Russell penned these lines, William James confessed that, of the relation between thought and the

---

20. See THE ARGUMENT FROM CONSCIOUSNESS and THE ARGUMENT FROM REASON in this volume for a more detailed discussion.

workings of the brain, "no glimmer of explanation is yet in sight" (Kim 2005, p. 12). Kim has recently updated that confession, noting that qualia resist reduction so that "there is still no glimmer of explanation" (Kim 2005, p. 28). Colin McGinn is also less than impressed by the success of any attempts at naturalizing the mind. But, he says, the choices are "either eliminativism or miracles or hidden structure." Eliminativism denies the undeniable. An appeal to "miracles" amounts to "wallowing in the supernatural." But, of course, "we cannot allow a Divine Foot in the door," as Richard Lewontin once warned. And so McGinn opts for naturalism plus "hidden structure," or "noumenalism," where the latter involves a monkish appeal to mystery and the assertion, without explanation, that consciousness is a natural phenomenon (Goetz & Taliaferro 2008, p. 83). It is a shame that Descartes did not think to avail himself of this "hidden structure" option in his correspondence with Princess Elizabeth.

Generally speaking, it is difficult to see how conscious and autonomous persons could be engineered from Big Bang debris – particularly when the would-be engineer is truant. The insistence that such a feat has been accomplished appears merely to be a function of an entrenched antisupernaturalism combined with the commonsense recognition that there is consciousness and that it sometimes plays a causal role. We know that the world includes persons. What we do not know is how this could be the case if naturalism were true.

But if the naturalist is confronted with a *Weltknoten* when attempting to derive the personal from the nonpersonal, a similar knot is involved in attempts to derive the intrinsically valuable from the valueless. In a world that fits Russell's description earlier in "A Free Man's Worship," a world in which the human species is the product of blind forces "that had no prevision of the ends they were achieving," in which our noblest sentiments and passions are "but the outcome of accidental collocations of atoms," and in which those collocations – those "bags of tricks" – that have come to be called "persons" are aberrant and fleeting exceptions to the rule of otherwise insentient arrangements of matter, it is hard to see why any special and intrinsic value should be assigned to the species as a whole, much less to each and every individual specimen. Russell asks, "How, in such an alien and inhuman world, can so powerless a creature as Man preserve his aspirations untarnished?" (1957, p. 107). How, indeed?

Moral agency and personal dignity

Russell thought that our dignity is found in the human ability, during our "brief years," to "examine, to criticize, to know, and, in imagination, to create. To him alone, in the world with which he is acquainted, this freedom belongs; and in this lies his superiority to the resistless forces that control his outward life" (Russell 1957, p. 107). But, as we have seen, Russell later abandoned the moral realism that is implied in the "knowledge of good and evil," which would allow us to criticize our unthinking Mother. And now, as we have further seen, we have good reason to suppose that, on Russell's naturalism, those forces that reign over our outward life are just as "resistless" on the interior as well.

Immanuel Kant was similarly confronted by a universe without that threatened to tarnish his aspirations, but he also similarly claimed to find the ground of personal dignity within himself. Contemplation of the "starry heavens above" – the immensity of a universe in which he is "a mere speck" – seems to "annihilate" his significance as a creature who, after a brief tenure here, "must give back the matter of which it was formed." But reflection upon "the moral law within" has the opposite effect, as it "infinitely elevates my worth" (Kant 1956, p. 166). That infinite worth is thus secured by our autonomy as moral agents capable of understanding and acting upon moral principle. Moral agency is thus what we might call a *dignity-conferring* property.

If such an argument is to succeed at all, one requirement is that morality itself must be of intrinsic rather than instrumental value.[21] It is no mere coincidence that Kant identified *two* sorts of things that have dignity rather than a mere price: human persons and the moral law itself. Kant saw that genuine respect for persons requires respect for the law. My respecting you calls for my acting for the sake of certain direct duties *to you*. I should respect you because it is the right thing to do; and it is the right thing to do because you are deserving of respect. If, however, my fair treatment of you is only a happy by-product of my concern for some further end, then I am merely acting in accordance with those duties owed you. This is to behave as though I have, at best, certain indirect duties *regarding* you, and such behavior hardly qualifies as respect. But, further, suppose that morality itself is only valuable as a means to some nonmoral end. Then it is hard to see why anyone should conclude that moral agency, which would then also be of instrumental value, is a ground for attributing dignity to moral agents. The whole thing unravels unless Kant is correct in affording dignity to the moral law. Has the naturalist, then, sufficient reason for supposing that morality itself enjoys the sort of dignity that Kant ascribes to it? Given all that we have considered, it is hard to see why one should think so. Here is where the argument of the previous essay may be brought to bear. There, we saw reasons for thinking that, on evolutionary naturalism, human morality has emerged as an evolutionary device; a strategy aimed at reproductive fitness. One might as well argue for human dignity by appeal to the opposable thumb or to featherless bipedalism.

Personal dignity: some dead ends

Michael Martin has recently suggested a novel foundation for personal dignity. Martin defends an ideal observer theory, which analyzes moral judgments in terms of the feelings of approval or disapproval of a perfectly impartial and informed observer. Thus, "Rape is wrong" is analyzed as "An ideal observer would contemplate rape with a feeling of disapproval," and so forth. In an exchange with Martin, Paul Copan has charged that Martin's ideal observer theory, combined with his commitment to naturalism, has an inadequate ontology for grounding the notion of the intrinsic value of persons. Martin replies:

> It is not clear why Copan thinks that the Ideal Observer Theory cannot substantiate "the requisite metaphysics of personhood and its intrinsic dignity or value." After all, such values would be analyzed in terms of the feeling of approval or disapproval of an Ideal Observer. Moreover, the properties of an Ideal Observer are natural properties. So, metaphysically speaking, the attribute of intrinsic dignity would be a natural property. To be sure, such an analysis may be unsuccessful, but nothing Copan has said shows this. (Martin 2002, p. 92)

Perhaps we may say a few things here to show why such an analysis *must* be unsuccessful.

---

21. I attempt a defense of such an argument in Linville (2000).

Recall that a property is *intrinsic* only if, among other things, it is *nonrelational* and *mind-independent*. On the face of it, it is difficult to see why Martin supposes that sense can be made of *Kim has the property of intrinsic value* by analyzing it in terms of the *feelings* of anyone nonidentical to, or, for that matter, identical to Kim. If the property is intrinsic, then it is identical to or supervenient upon something true of Kim's intrinsic nature, and thus to analyze language describing that property in the way that Martin suggests is hardly more plausible than an analysis of *Kim is a person* or *Kim is trapezoidal* in terms of either the cognitive or noncognitive propositional attitudes of an ideally situated Someone. If this is intrinsic value, then it is of the extrinsic variety.

And it is a bit puzzling just how the analysis of *Kim has the property of intrinsic value* would go. I think I understand how the analysis of *X is wrong* comes out. Our ideal observer – call him Ivan – given his exhaustive knowledge of all of the relevant nonmoral facts, as well as his impartiality, has a feeling of disapproval upon contemplating the action. But *about what* does Ivan have feelings of approval in the case of intrinsic value? Kim herself? *I* have feelings of approval when I contemplate, say, Kim Basinger, but these are not necessarily an analysis of her intrinsic value as a person. Is it particular *actions* that either are or are not consonant with Kim's dignity? But this either (a) analyzes dignity in terms of some disjunction of things that it would be right or wrong to do to Kim, or (b) it *presupposes* dignity and thus leaves it unanalyzed. If (a), then we find that we have reversed the roles of dignity and direct duties: *Kim has dignity because she ought to be treated in certain ways* instead of *Kim ought to be treated in certain ways because she has dignity*. If (b), then Martin's proposal is simply unsuccessful. Is it the *proposition* itself, *Kim has the property of intrinsic value* that engenders the positive feelings? But in this case, either it is the cognitive content of the proposition that does the work, or it is some non-cognitive feature of the proposition that delights our observer. If the former, then is this not simply to say that Ivan takes the proposition to be *true*, and thus approves of it? But then moral facts obtain logically prior to Ivan's approval so that they may not be analyzed in terms of that approval. If the latter, then what, exactly, could it be? Is it in the rhythm or rhyme or the shapes of the letters on a page? *Kim carried carrots to Cambridge* might elicit noncognitive approval in some, but it seems an unlikely candidate for a moral foundation. Perhaps *Kim has the property of intrinsic value* is to be analyzed as *An ideal observer would value Kim intrinsically*. But then we have come to the heart of the matter.

The ideal observer theory faces a Euthyphro problem that has lurked in the preceding paragraphs. Does Ivan value Kim intrinsically because Kim is intrinsically valuable, or is she intrinsically valuable because Ivan values her intrinsically? Clearly, the first option is precluded as it would signal the abandonment of the ideal observer theory for a straightforward respect-for-persons ethic. Of course, if persons possess intrinsic value, and Ivan is an ideal observer, then he would, I suppose, value persons intrinsically. And that would be a good thing too because to do less than that would be less than ideal, which is unbecoming of an ideal observer. So is Kim intrinsically valuable *because* Ivan values her intrinsically? Presumably, this is what is called for. But why suppose that Ivan, impartial as he is and possessed of all of the relevant nonmoral facts *would* value Kim intrinsically unless she actually *is* intrinsically valuable? Russ Shafer-Landau has argued that such ideal observer theories face this dilemma: either they smuggle in moral facts that play a role in determining the ideal observer's feelings of approval or disapproval, or they admit only a knowledge of nonmoral facts, in which case there is no reason to suppose that the outcome is the morally desired one (Shafer-Landau 2003, p. 43). I think Copan is correct. Martin's ideal observer theory is doomed to failure because there is no room for a robust account of the intrinsic value of persons. If such an account of dignity is to be had at all, it must be rooted in the metaphysics of personhood.

Kai Nielsen thinks that no special account of persons is required in order to make sense of the requirements of justice. Much less is a *religious* account required. Anticipating the sort of argument being developed in this chapter, he observes that the "religious apologist" will argue that the principle of respect-for-persons is rooted in "the ancient religious principle that men are creatures of God, each with an infinite worth" (Nielsen 1990, p. 123). Indeed, the apologist may go on to urge that even the naturalist subscribes to the core idea of respect-for-persons, but he is "surreptitiously drawing on Christian inspiration" in so doing. Interestingly, Nielsen allows that, as a matter of historical fact, the idea of personal dignity may have a religious genesis, but, he observes, the validity of an idea is independent of the circumstances of its first occurrence. The religious apologist would need to show – but "has not shown" – that respect-for-persons can *only* be supported on religious grounds. But, he insists, "there is a purely secular rationale for treating people fairly, for regarding them as persons" (Nielsen 1990, p. 124). Essentially, Nielsen proposes that Kantian respect may be drawn out of Hobbesian egoism.

> Each Hobbesian egoist would want others to treat him with respect, for his very happiness is contingent upon that; and he would recognize that he could attain the fullest cooperation of others only if other rational egoists knew or had good grounds for believing that their interests and their persons would be respected. Such cooperation is essential for each egoist if all are to have the same type of community life that would give them the best chance of satisfying their interests to the fullest degree. Thus, even if men were thorough egoists, we would still have rational grounds for subscribing to a principle of respect for persons. (Nielsen 1990, p. 125)

Now, Nielsen considers the problem of the "powerfully placed egoist" – that egoist who, for whatever reason, need not worry about retaliation or consequences to himself for riding roughshod over the "rights" of others. Here, he acknowledges that, in the final analysis, there may just be no egoist rationale for respecting others. Here, reasoning reaches the end of its tether and "we must simply decide what sort of person we shall strive to become" (Nielsen 1990, p. 125).

The latter is an odd thing to say in a book promising to secure a place for ethics without God. First, plenty of egoists have decided to be nasty. Plato's Glaucon left no doubt that, were he to be so "powerfully placed" – in this case, by possession of a ring that renders its wearer invisible – he would rape, pillage, and plunder by day and then sleep like a baby by night. Indeed, Glaucon thought that anyone granted such a power who continued to work for justice would be universally regarded as an idiot. But, further, if moral values are embraced by "subscription," then the values themselves are a facade. The structure of one's system of values rests upon the arbitrary choice itself. Where preferences clash with chosen values, there is a built-in opt-out clause. Any imperatives that Nielsen's agent agrees to obey will thus be conditional, hypothetical, and not categorical, as their force is always contingent upon whatever ends the agent has selected. Nielsen makes the decision to live the Good Life sound like a career choice. "And what do you wish to be when you grow up?" "I want to be either a terrorist or a torturer."

As it happens, Nielsen's earlier suggestion that certain moral beliefs are "bedrock" is misleading, as it is suggestive of a variety of foundationalism lending itself to moral realism.

But in a later book, Nielsen rejects foundationalism and suggests that moral realism is a "myth" (Martin 2002, p. 82). And so, Nielsen's project assures us that we may have ethics without God, but there is fine print. The "torturing of innocents" is not *really* evil, nor is "wife beating or child molesting" *actually* vile (Nielsen 1990, p. 10), but, rest assured, "God or no God," one is free to subscribe to a set of values that allows one to suppose that such things are evil or vile. Well, indeed. God or no God, one is free to suppose all sorts of things that are not true. One might even suppose that Kai Nielsen has written a book that accomplishes the purpose implied by its title.

What of Nielsen's proposal to pull a Kantian rabbit from a Hobbesian hat? We have the makings of the criticism behind us in our critique of "nice egoism." On Hobbesian egoism, one has direct duties only to oneself. Thus, any duties involving others are indirect and never direct. But, then, there is no room for affording moral standing to other people. If "torturing innocents" is "evil" on egoism, it can only be because of some evil that is incurred by the torturer. Hobbesian "respectful behavior" is a far cry from Kantian respect.

Personal dignity and the imago dei

Perhaps there are other potential bases for dignity to which the naturalist may appeal. Darwin quotes Kant on precisely our topic: "I will not in my own person violate the dignity of humanity" (Darwin 1909, p. 86). And he does suggest that this noblest of sentiments is most likely found in the civilized person rather than the barbarian or "uncultivated man." And this is because reason has a role to play in arriving at such a maxim. But the admission of a role for reason to play does not nullify the main point of Darwin's discussion: the initial social impulse is very much the product of natural selection. And it is in this immediate context that Darwin offers his hive bee example – what I have earlier called "Darwinian counterfactuals." At bottom, Dennett (1995) is likely correct in his observation that, given the Darwinian account, the belief in rights, and, here, dignity, is actually a "conversation stopper." "Rule worship" – even where those rules are, strictly speaking, "nonsense on stilts" – is adaptive in that it permits us to get on with the business of social intercourse.

Stephen Gould (1989) found a basis for something such as dignity in the radical contingency of the existence of *Homo sapiens*. It is wildly improbable that we should be here at all, and so there is wonder in this fact. Were natural history somehow rewound to play over again it is astonishingly improbable that anything like ourselves would form any of the branches on the evolutionary tree. Given Gould's naturalism, this is almost certainly true. And reflection upon the radical contingency of our existence is, I think, a spiritual discipline that results in a kind of astonishment which, in turn, may yield gratitude. Chesterton compared the world to the few items that Crusoe managed to salvage from the wreck, which are all the more precious for the fact that they might not have been. It was said of Chesterton that he never quite got over the fact of his own existence, and this is surely correct, as his essays everywhere evince wonder and even astonishment over the fact that there is a creation and he *happens to be in on it*. But if *Homo sapiens* is astonishingly improbable, so are *Ursus horribilis* and *Rhododendron arboretum*. So are the Himalayas, the Isle of Crete, and, for that matter, each and every Mississippi towhead as well as the Milky Way itself. Improbability alone is not sufficient for singling out persons as having any special significance. And the difference between the worldviews of Chesterton and Gould is that the former has Someone to thank for purposely gifting him with wonderful life.

The naturalist's obstacles in accounting for the dignity of persons are at least threefold, and they are interlocked: how to derive the personal from the impersonal, how to derive values from a previously valueless universe, and how to unite the personal and the valuable with the result of a coherent and plausible notion of personal dignity. But suppose that the personal and the valuable are not emergent features of reality at all, but, rather, are basic. Indeed, suppose that personhood is the most basic feature of reality and, that, in fact the impersonal ultimately derives from the personal. Suppose that the one thing that is both metaphysically and axiologically ultimate is a person, so that personhood and value are necessarily united in that Being. Theists, of course, maintain precisely this and believe that Being to be God. Thus, "At the heart of 'the natural order of things' is a divine consciousness" (Goetz & Taliaferro 2008, p. 84).

Recall that Dennett and others have insisted that any explanation of consciousness that is not in terms of the nonconscious is question-begging. But one might suggest that this very assertion begs the question. Consider two kinds of explanations for some given event: *teleological*, which "explains a phenomenon by reference to the intentional actions of an intelligent agent" (Yandell 1984, p. 62), and *mechanistic*, which "explains a phenomenon by reference to physical events and a theory that relates physical events to one another by means of lawlike statements" (Yandell 1984, p. 63). Dennett assumes that all *ultimate* explanations must be mechanistic, so that the teleological, where it occurs, must be explained in mechanistic terms. But this is just to take naturalism as a kind of axiom, and it is far from clear that such an assumption is warranted. And it is precisely here that the theist reverses Dennett's order of explanation. The most ultimate explanations – including an explanation of why we observe lawlike relations that obtain among physical things – are teleological in nature because the world exists due to the creative activity of God. On theism, teleological explanations are irreducible and more basic than mechanistic explanations. And the justification for taking them as irreducible in this way is found precisely in the resulting implausibility and possible incoherence of attempting such reductions. We simply cannot explain all that calls for explanation unless there is a place for irreducible teleology in the scheme of things. For the theist, teleology factors in principally at the level of divine purpose and activity, but theism also offers an account of human persons that permits the irreducibility of human consciousness and purposes. Note, by the way, that the theist can afford to be a pluralist when it comes to explanation. Whereas Dennett's brand of naturalist must banish all teleology from the universe, the theist finds a place for mechanistic explanations within the world, and the latter seems a better fit with what we know.

According to the theist, then, God is personal and is the source of all value so that the value of personhood is found in the fact that the metaphysically, axiologically, and explanatorily ultimate Being is a person.

Kant compared the Christian command to love one's neighbor and even one's enemy to central features of his view, including the idea of respect, whether this is respect for a person or a reverence for the law. His immediate aim is to distinguish between actions that are done from duty and those that are merely from inclination. He writes:

> It is doubtless in this sense that we should understand too the passages from Scripture in which we are commanded to love our neighbor and even our enemy. For love out of inclination

cannot be commanded; but kindness done from duty – although no inclination impels us, and even although natural and unconquerable disposition stands in our way – is *practical*, and not *pathological* love, residing in the will and not in the propensions of feeling, in principles of action and not of melting compassion; and it is this practical love alone which can be an object of a command. (Kant 1964, p. 67)

Kant's distinction between duty and inclination is widely thought to be problematic. After all, the promptings of inclination in Aristotle's virtuous person who is "pleased by the right things" would seem to result in actions of supreme moral worth. And it is not strictly true that one cannot be held morally responsible for one's inclinations. Aristotle spoke of "rational emotions," and the idea is that inclinations may themselves be either rationally or morally appropriate or inappropriate. C. S. Lewis confessed to not being fond of small children, but also acknowledged this as a defect. If I am responsible for cultivating a certain sort of character, and if my inclinations proceed from my underlying character, then I might be thought to be responsible for my inclinations. Actually, Kant was clearly aware of such possibilities, as he suggested that we have a duty to cultivate a "moral feeling" (Kant 1956, p. 40).

But though there seem to be no extant copies of any commentaries on the gospels with Kant as their author, he appears to have this bit of exegesis right. Christ's command to love even one's enemies is clearly not the demand that we conjure feelings of affection for, say, terrorists and tyrants. Rather, Christian charity (αγαπη) is, I believe, favorably comparable to the Kantian idea of respect in that it is an attitude of unconditional regard for the worth of its object. As such, it "does not seek its own," or, is not contingent upon reciprocation. It is called for regardless of the behavior of the person who is its object. As I see it, the rationale for Christ's command to love persons unconditionally is found in the unconditional *value* of such persons. Because each person enjoys a worth that is categorical in nature – independent of any extrinsic considerations – the morally appropriate attitude to take toward them is one of a categorical regard for that worth. In this we seem to have a parallel between the Christian concept of charity and the Kantian notion of respect – and the Confucian idea of *jen*, for that matter. In each case, there is the affirmation of an unconditional personal worth paired with an injunction to value persons accordingly. And, in each case, the value and the valuing are together at the very heart of the ethical system. The centrality of Christian charity is seen in an exchange between Jesus and a lawyer as recorded by Luke (10:25–7, NIV).

> On one occasion an expert in the law stood up to test Jesus. "Teacher," he asked, "what must I do to inherit eternal life?" "What is written in the Law?" he replied. "How do you read it?" He answered: "'Love the Lord your God with all your heart and with all your soul and with all your strength and with all your mind'; and, 'Love your neighbor as yourself.'" "You have answered correctly," Jesus replied. "Do this and you will live."

The conjunction of a love for God and neighbor is no coincidence, as the rationale for loving one's neighbor – humanity in general – is grounded in the very reasons for loving God with the entirety of one's being. And this is because the *value* of persons is, in turn, grounded in the personhood of God. Persons *qua* persons are created in the image of God in that God himself is a person. On a Judeo-Christian worldview, *human* personal dignity, though intrinsic, is derivative. The value of human persons is found in the fact that, as bearers of the *imago dei*, they bear a significant resemblance to God in their very personhood.[22] God and human persons share an overlap of kind membership in person-hood itself, and human dignity is found precisely in membership in that kind.

Consider the theist's answer to a modified version of the dilemma that we urged against Martin's ideal observer theory. Are (human) persons valuable because God values them, or does God value them because they are valuable? I argued that Martin cannot say that his ideal observer values persons because they are valuable, as this would signal the abandonment of the ideal observer theory for something more like a respect-for-persons approach. But this is precisely the option that the theist embraces: God values human persons because they are intrinsically valuable. Further, they have such value because God has created them after his own image as a Person with a rational and moral nature.

On theism, human persons have been fashioned, in one morally relevant respect, after the most ultimate and sacred feature of reality and thus participate in that sacredness. Further, the personal is at home in such a universe. Nietzsche remarked that, contrary to a popular conception of Darwinism, "man" is actually "the most unsuccessful animal, the sickliest, the one most dangerously strayed from its instincts" (Nietzsche 1982, p. 580). I take it that the straying that he has in mind involves those very human aspirations that Russell sought to preserve untarnished. These involve a straying – and a dangerous one at that – because they have no place in a Nietzschean or Rusellian universe. Albert Camus had these same aspirations in mind when he wrote of the absurd. The absurd is born of a tension between two incongruent things. When a man armed only with a sword charges a well-armed machine gun nest, the absurdity is found not simply in the swordsman and his intentions, or in the arsenal that awaits him, but in the tension that is created by his inten-tions set against the reality that he is sure to face. Similarly, Camus thought, human exis-tence is absurd because of a confrontation between "the human need" on the one hand, and "the unreasonable silence of the world" on the other" (Camus 1955, p. 21). The uni-verse is simply silent and indifferent to our concerns.

The absurd serves in Camus' writings as the springboard for asking what he regards as the most fundamental philosophical question, the question of suicide. Of course, the whole point of existentialism is to attempt to conjure meaning where none otherwise exists. The theist, on the other hand, finds no such "confrontation" or "tension" at all, and this is because human persons find themselves in a world that is, at bottom, personal in nature. If Camus thought that suicide was a serious option, the theist G. K. Chesterton described suicide – particularly the *philosophical* suicide that results from a despair of human exis-tence – not simply as *a* sin but as *the* sin. And he saw it as such precisely because it implies a profound ingratitude for and disdain of a wondrous creation. "There is not a tiny creature in the cosmos at whom his death is not a sneer. When a man hangs himself on a tree, the leaves might fall off in anger and the birds fly away in fury: for each has received a personal affront" (Chesterton 1986, p. 276). Where Camus found only an unreasonable silence, Chesterton discovered, and rejoiced over, an "eternal gaiety in the nature of things"

---

22. Resemblance is, of course, a relation between two or more things. And so an initial puzzle may seem to arise. Have we not said that if a property is intrinsic it is not also relational? How, then, can the intrinsic value of persons be found in their resemblance to God? But a moment's reflection will clear this up. Consider Plato's scheme in which a horse is what it is in virtue of its participation in, or exemplification of, the Form of equinity or "horsey-ness." Horses are intrinsically what they are even if being such involves such a relation to the Form. Indeed, twins bear a mutual resemblance *in virtue of* their respective intrinsic properties.

(Chesterton 1986, p. 96) for he had the belief that, when people dance a *pas de quatre*, "the stars are dancing to the same tune" (p. 96).[23]

23. I wish to thank Paul Copan, William Lane Craig, and, especially, David Werther for their helpful feedback on earlier versions of this chapter. Thanks also to Robert N. Johnson for graciously sharing helpful materials on Kantian ethics.

References

Adams, C. and Adams, J. (2007) *The Works of John Adams*, vol. 2. Kila, MT: Kessinger Publishing.

Adams, R. (1999) *Finite and Infinite Goods*. Oxford: Oxford University Press.

Audi, R. and Wainwright, W. J. (eds.) (1986) *Rationality, Religious Belief, and Moral Commitment*. Ithaca, NY: Cornell University Press.

Beilby, J. K. (ed.) (2002) *Naturalism Defeated? Essays on Plantinga's Evolutionary Argument against Naturalism*. Ithaca, NY: Cornell University Press.

Bentham, J. (2001) *The Works of Jeremy Bentham*, vol. 2. Boston: Adamant Media Corp.

Betzler, M. (ed.) (2008) *Kant's Ethics of Virtue*. Berlin: De Gruyter Verlag.

Blackmore, S. (2006) *Conversations on Consciousness*. Oxford: Oxford University Press.

Brink, D. (1989) *Moral Realism and the Foundations of Ethics*. Cambridge: Cambridge University Press.

Butler, J. (1983) *Five Sermons*. Indianapolis, IN: Hackett Publishing Co.

Camus, A. (1955) *The Myth of Sisyphus and Other Essays*. New York: Vintage Books.

Chase, A. (2001) *In a Dark Wood: The Fight Over Forests and the New Tyranny of Ecology*. New York: Houghton Mifflin.

Chesterton, G. K. (1986) *Collected Works*, vol. 1. San Francisco: Ignatius Press.

Copp, D. (1990) Explanation and justification in ethics. Ethics 100: 2, 237–58.

Crisp, R. and Slote, M. (eds.) (1997) *Virtue Ethics*. Oxford: Oxford University Press.

Daniels, N. (1979) Wide reflective equilibrium and theory acceptance in ethics. Journal of Philosophy 76: 5, 256–82.

Darwin, C. (1882) *The Descent of Man and Selection in Relation to Sex*, 2nd edn. New York: D. Appleton & Co.

Dawkins, R. (1986) *The Blind Watchmaker*. New York: W. W. Norton & Co.

Dennett, D. (1995) *Darwin's Dangerous Idea*. New York: Simon and Schuster.

Dennett, D. (2006) *Breaking the Spell*. New York: Viking.

Flanagan, O. (2002) *The Problem of the Soul*. New York: Basic Books.

Gibbard, A. (1990) *Wise Choices, Apt Feelings*. Cambridge, MA: Harvard University Press.

Goetz, S. and Taliaferro, C. (2008) *Naturalism*. Grand Rapids, MI: William B. Eerdmans Publishing Co.

Gould, S. J. (1989) *Wonderful Life*. New York: W. W. Norton & Co.

Hackett, S. (1979) *Oriental Philosophy*. Madison: University of Wisconsin Press.

Harman, G. (1977) *The Nature of Morality: An Introduction to Ethics*. Oxford: Oxford University Press.

Harman, G. and Thomson, J. J. (1996) *Moral Relativism and Moral Objectivity*. Oxford: Blackwell Publishers.

Hill, T. E. (1991) *Autonomy and Self-Respect*. Cambridge: Cambridge University Press.

Hume, D. (1978) *A Treatise of Human Nature*. Oxford: Oxford University Press.

Hursthouse, R. (2007) "Virtue Ethics." *Stanford Encyclopedia of Philosophy*, http://plato.stanford.edu/entries/ethics-virtue/ (accessed February 29, 2008).

Jerome, J. K. (2005) *Idle Thoughts of an Idle Fellow*. Mumbai: Wilco Publishing House.

Johnson, R. N. (2004). "Kant's Moral Philosophy." *Stanford Encyclopedia of Philosophy*, http://plato. stanford.edu/entries/kant-moral/ (accessed February 29, 2008).

Johnson, R. N. (2008) Was Kant a virtue ethicist? In M. Betzler (ed.) *Kant's Ethics of Virtue*. Berlin: De Gruyter Verlag.

Joyce, R. (2006) *The Evolution of Morality*. Cambridge, MA: MIT Press.

Kant, I. (1956) *Critique of Practical Reason*. Trans. L. W. Beck. Indianapolis, IN: Bobbs-Merrill.

Kant, I. (1964) *Groundwork of the Metaphysics of Morals*. Trans. H. J. Paton. New York: Harper & Row.

Kant, I. (1981) *Lectures on Ethics*. Trans. L. Infield. Indianapolis, IN: Hackett Publishing Co.

Kant, I. (1987) *Critique of Judgment*. Trans. W. Pluhar. Indianapolis, IN: Hackett Publishing Co.

Kim, J. (2005) *Physicalism or Something Near Enough*. Princeton, NJ: Princeton University Press.

Kitcher, P. (1985) *Vaulting Ambition*. Cambridge, MA: MIT Press.

Koller, J. M. and Koller, P. (1998) *Asian Philosophies*, 3rd edn. Englewood Cliffs, NJ: Prentice-Hall.

Leslie, J. (2001) *Infinite Minds*. Oxford: Oxford University Press.

Lewis, C. S. (2001a) *A Grief Observed*. New York: HarperCollins.

Lewis, C. S. (2001b) *Miracles*. San Francisco: Harper Books.

Lewis, C. S. (1996a) *The Abolition of Man*. New York: Touchstone Books.

Lewis, C. S. (1996b) *The Problem of Pain*. New York: Touchstone Books.

Linville, M. D. (1998) A little lower than the angels: Christian humanism and environmental ethics. *Christian Scholar's Review* XXVIII: 2, 283–97.

Linville, M. D. (2000) A defense of human dignity. *Faith and Philosophy* 17: 3, 318–30.

Martin, M. (2002) *Atheism, Morality, and Meaning*. Amherst, NY: Prometheus Press.

Midgley, M. (1979) *Beast and Man*. London: Routledge Press.

Midgley, M. (1986) Duties concerning islands. In C. Pierce and D. VanDeVeer (eds.) *People, Penguins and Plastic Trees*, 156–164. Belmont, CA: Wadsworth Publishing.

Midgley, M. (1994) *The Ethical Primate: Humans, Freedom and Morality*. London: Routledge.

Mill, J. S. (2001) *Utilitarianism*. Indianapolis, IN: Hackett Publishing Co.

Myers, F. W. H. (1881) George Eliot. *The Century* 23, 1.

Nielsen, K. (1990) *Ethics without God*. Amherst, NY: Prometheus Press.

Nietzsche, F. (1968) *Twilight of the Idols and the Anti-Christ*. New York. Penguin Books.

Nietzsche, F. (1982) *The Portable Nietzsche*. Trans. and ed. W. Kaufmann. New York. Penguin Books.

Paley, W. (1785) Of crimes and punishments. Excerpt from *The Principles of Moral and Political Philosophy* in M. Singer, *Morals and Values*. New York: Charles Scribners and Sons, 1977.

Pierce, C. and VanDeVeer, D. (eds.) (1986) *People, Penguins and Plastic Trees*. Belmont, CA: Wadsworth Publishing.

Pierce, C. and VanDeVeer, D. (eds.) (1995) *People, Penguins and Plastic Trees*. Belmont, CA: Wadsworth Publishing.

Plantinga, A. (1993) *Warrant and Proper Function*. Oxford: Oxford University Press.

Plantinga, A. (2000) *Warranted Christian Belief*. Oxford: Oxford University Press.

Politis, V. (1995) Review of *The Golden Age of Virtue: Aristotle's Ethics*, by Theodore Scaltsas. The *Philosophical Quarterly* 45: 179, 258–60.

Quine, W. V. O. (1969) *Ontological Relativity and Other Essays*. New York: Columbia University Press.

Radakrishnan, S. and Moore, C. A. (eds.) (1967) *A Source Book in Indian Philosophy*. Princeton, NJ: Princeton University Press.

Rashdall, H. (1907) *The Theory of Good and Evil*. Oxford: Clarendon Press.

Regan, T. (1995) The case for animal rights. In C. Pierce and D. VanDeVeer (eds.) *People, Penguins and Plastic Trees*. Belmont, CA: Wadsworth Publishing, 1995.

Reid, T. (1983) *Inquiry and Essays*. Eds. R. E. Beanblossom and K. Lehrer. Indianapolis, IN: Hackett Publishing Co.

Routley, R. (1973) Is there a need for a new, an environmental, ethic? *Proceedings of the XVth World Congress of Philosophy* 1, 205–10.

Ruse, M. (1998) *Taking Darwin Seriously*. Amherst, NY: Prometheus Books.

Ruse, M. and Wilson, E. O. (1989) The evolution of ethics. *New Scientist* 17, 108–28.

Russell, B. (1957) *Why I Am Not a Christian & Other Essays*. New York: Simon and Schuster.

Santayana, G. (1957) *Winds of Doctrine*. New York: Harper and Brothers.

Sayre-McCord, G. (ed.) (1988) *Essays on Moral Realism*. Ithaca, NY: Cornell University Press.

Shafer-Landau, R. (2003) *Moral Realism: A Defence*. Oxford: Oxford University Press.

Shafer-Landau, R. (2004) *Whatever Happened to Good and Evil?* Oxford: Oxford University Press.

Singer, M. (ed.) (1977) *Morals and Values*. New York: Charles Scribners & Sons.

Singer, P. (ed.) (1991) *A Companion to Ethics*. Oxford: Blackwell Publishing.

Smart, J. J. C. and Williams, B. (1973) *Utilitarianism: For and Against*. Cambridge: Cambridge University Press.

Sober, E. (1994) *From a Biological Point of View*. Cambridge: Cambridge University Press.

Sommers, T. and Rosenberg, A. (2003) Darwin's nihilistic idea: evolution and the meaninglessness of life. *Biology and Philosophy* 18: 5, 653–88.

Sorley, W. R. (1935) *Moral Values and the Idea of God*, 3rd edn. Cambridge: Cambridge University Press.

Street, S. (2006) A Darwinian dilemma for realist theories of value. *Philosophical Studies* 127, 109–66.

Sturgeon, N. (1988) Moral explanations. In G. Sayre-McCord (ed.) *Essays on Moral Realism*. Ithaca, NY: Cornell University Press.

Sturgeon, N. (1992) Non-moral explanations. *Philosophical Perspectives* 6, 97–117.

Volokh, A. (1997) n guilty men. *University of Pennsylvania Law Review* 146: 1, 173–216.

Warren, M. A. (2005) The moral and legal status of abortion. In J. E. White (ed.) *Contemporary Moral Problems*, 114–125. Belmont, CA: Wadsworth Publishing.

Wawrytko, S. A. (1982) Confucius and Kant: the ethics of respect. *Philosophy East and West* 32: 3, 237–57.

White, J. E. (ed.) (2005) *Contemporary Moral Problems*. Belmont, CA: Wadsworth Publishing.

Wieseltier, L. (2006) The God genome: review of *Breaking the Spell* by Daniel Dennett. *New York Times*, February 19.

Wolterstorff, Nicholas. (2001). *Thomas Reid and the story of epistemology*. Cambridge: Cambridge University Press.

Yandell, K. (1984) *Christianity and Philosophy*. Grand Rapids, MI: William B. Eerdmans Publishing Co.

8

The Argument from Evil

STEWART GOETZ

Evil and Contemporary Philosophical Orthodoxy

The argument from or problem of evil concludes that the existence of evil is, in one way or another, incompatible with the existence of an omnipotent, omnibenevolent, and omniscient being (God).[1] For anyone who is a student of or familiar with modern philosophical orthodoxy in metaphysics, the philosophy of mind, and the philosophy of action (I will simply refer to the three together as "modern philosophical orthodoxy"), the problem of evil can be likened to the skeletal remains of dinosaurs that are housed in the back room of a museum and occasionally brought out for reexamination and public viewing. This is the case for four reasons.

First, the problem of evil is fundamentally, in the words of C. S. Lewis, the problem of pain (Lewis 1962), where an experience of pain is an irreducible, conscious feeling or quale that hurts. The occurrence of such a psychological event is, however, vigorously contested by many adherents of modern philosophical orthodoxy. Given the seemingly outlandish nature of their position, some defenders of this orthodoxy vehemently insist they do not deny that we experience pain. Nevertheless, when one reads their accounts of pain, one cannot help but be suspicious. Almost invariably, they talk about the "functional role" of pain, which is cashed out in terms of pain's extrinsic or relational features in the form of causal inputs and outputs. And these defenders of modern philosophical orthodoxy make clear that this functional role *exhausts* what pain is. The problem here is that while no one who is sane will deny that an experience of pain has certain relational features (e.g. other things being equal, one who is experiencing pain will act for the purpose that the pain be mitigated), no one who is sane will hold that an experience of pain is nothing more than its relational features. After all, pain *feels* a certain way. It has an intrinsic nature for which the only adequate description is that it hurts. And it is precisely because pain has this kind of intrinsic nature that it also has the relational features that it has. It is this irreducible, intrinsic qualitative nature of pain that modern philosophical orthodoxy is intent on either

---

1. The meanings of these concepts are widely debated, but I will assume that sense can be made of them.

reducing to something else or outright eliminating. Were their efforts to prove successful, there would be no problem of evil because there would be no quale that is evil. Jaegwon Kim, who is one of the most articulate spokespersons for modern philosophical orthodoxy, describes the nature of the contemporary philosophical milieu as follows:

> For most of us, there is no need to belabor the centrality of consciousness to our conception of ourselves as creatures with minds. But I want to point to the ambivalent, almost paradoxical, attitude that philosophers have displayed toward consciousness. . . . [C]onsciousness had been virtually banished from the philosophical and scientific scene for much of the last century, and consciousness-bashing still goes on in some quarters, with some reputable philosophers arguing that phenomenal consciousness, or 'qualia,' is a fiction of bad philosophy. And there are philosophers . . . who, while they recognize phenomenal consciousness as something real do not believe that a complete science of human behavior, including cognitive psychology and neuroscience, has a place for consciousness in an explanatory/predictive theory of cognition and behavior. . . .
>
> Contrast this lowly status of consciousness in science and metaphysics with its lofty standing in moral philosophy and value theory. When philosophers discuss the nature of the intrinsic good, or what is worthy of our desire and volition for its own sake, the most prominently mentioned candidates are things like pleasure, absence of pain, enjoyment, and happiness. . . . To most of us, a fulfilling life, a life worth living, is one that is rich and full in qualitative consciousness. We would regard life as impoverished and not fully satisfying if it never included experiences of things like the smell of the sea in a cool morning breeze, the lambent play of sunlight on brilliant autumn foliage, the fragrance of a field of lavender in bloom, and the vibrant, layered soundscape projected by a string quartet. . . . It is an ironic fact that the felt qualities of conscious experience, perhaps the only things that ultimately matter to us, are often relegated in the rest of philosophy to the status of 'secondary qualities,' in the shadowy zone between the real and the unreal, or even jettisoned outright as artifacts of confused minds. (Kim 2005, pp. 10–2)

The second reason for likening the problem of evil to the skeletal remains of dinosaurs arises out of contemporary philosophical orthodoxy's commitment to materialism. Given the lowly status of the felt experience of pain in the contemporary philosophical climate, it is not at all surprising that the concept of an immaterial soul is viewed as an erroneous idea of a bygone, nonscientific age. Thus, even if one can get an adherent of contemporary philosophical orthodoxy to concede the reality of consciousness and qualia, he will insist that a soul cannot be that which is conscious and experiences pain. For example, Owen Flanagan claims that the existence of the soul simply has no place whatsoever in what he calls the "scientific image" of persons:

> There is no consensus yet about the details of the scientific image of persons. But there is broad agreement about how we must construct this detailed picture. First, we will need to demythologize persons by rooting out certain unfounded ideas from the perennial philosophy. Letting go of the belief in souls is a minimal requirement. In fact, desouling is the primary operation of the scientific image. (Flanagan 2002, p. 3)

To most individuals who have not been influenced by contemporary philosophical orthodoxy, Flanagan's attitude toward the soul's existence is just as counterintuitive and puzzling as denying that people are conscious and pain hurts. As William Lyons has written, the view "that humans are bodies inhabited and governed in some intimate if mysterious way by minds (souls), seemed and still seems to be nothing more than good common sense" (Lyons 2001, p. 9). Confirmation of the existence of this common sense is found in the extremely successful Harry Potter books, where the author J. K. Rowling makes effective use of dualism (the idea that a human being is a body–soul combination) in portraying the worst death one can die as one where one's soul is sucked out of one's body by the kiss of a being called a dementor. And the contemporary nondualist philosopher John Searle reports that "[w]hen I lectured on the mind-body problem in India [I] was assured by several members of my audience that my views must be mistaken, because they personally had existed in their earlier lives as frogs or elephants, etc." (Searle 1992, p. 91).

Just as there cannot be a problem of evil if no one is conscious and experiences pain, so also there cannot be a satisfactory solution to the problem of evil if souls do not exist and survive death. And not only must souls exist, but I will also maintain they must be free in the libertarian sense (have libertarian free will) to make undetermined choices for purposes (reasons). Not surprisingly, however, modern philosophical orthodoxy views the belief in libertarian free will as just another misguided idea bequeathed to us by our unscientific ancestors. The doctrinal position on free will at present is the view known as compatibilism, which is the idea that freedom and determinism are compatible and that one and the same event can be both free and determined. When adherents of contemporary philosophical orthodoxy do talk about mental actions, they almost to a person assume that the entirety of our mental lives is determined by nonmental events. Thus, even Searle, who is an outspoken critic of those who deny the reality of consciousness and qualia, insists that "all mental phenomena whether conscious or unconscious, visual or auditory, pains, tickles, itches, thoughts, indeed, all of our mental life, are caused by processes going on in the brain" (Searle 1984, p. 18). And while Francis Crick, the codiscoverer of the molecular structure of DNA, acknowledges that we have an "undeniable feeling that our Will is free," he also maintains "that our Will only appears to be free" (Crick 1994, p. 10). In whatever sense it is true to say that we choose, Crick believes that a choice is completely determined to occur. Daniel Dennett agrees with Crick. According to Dennett, any kind of freedom that we have must be a kind of freedom that is compatible with the truth of determinism. While he concedes that we are not aware of the causes of our choices, there is an explanation of this ignorance:

> Whatever else we are, we are information-processing systems, and all information-processing systems rely on amplifiers of a sort. Relatively small causes are made to yield relatively large effects. . . . Vast amounts of information arrive on the coattails of negligible amounts of energy, and then, thanks to amplification powers of systems of switches, the information begins to do some work . . . leading eventually to an action whose pedigree of efficient . . . causation is so hopelessly inscrutable as to be invisible. We see the dramatic effects leaving; we don't see the causes entering; we are tempted by the hypothesis that there are no causes. (Dennett 1984, pp. 76–7; see also Dennett 2003)

In short, from our failure to be aware of the causes of our choices, we cannot reasonably conclude that there are none. This is because the causes are beyond our ken. Therefore, our lack of awareness of them is to be expected and in no way supports or justifies a belief in their absence, just as the failure to observe from afar a needle on the floor of a field house with bleachers in it does not justify a belief that no needle is lying on that floor. Flanagan summarizes this point nicely:

[T]he myth of a completely self-initiating ego, an unmoved but self-moving will, [is] simply a fiction motivated by our ignorance of the causes of human behavior. [There is] no need for the notion of a metaphysically unconstrained will or of an independent ego as an unconstrained primal cause in order to have a robust conception of free agency. For there to be agency we need the ego as a cause, possibly even the proximate cause of what we do. But the ego may serve as the proximate cause of action and still itself be part of the causal nexus. (Flanagan 2002, p. 112)

The fourth and last reason that explains contemporary philosophical orthodoxy's attitude toward the problem of evil stems from its commitment to the nonexistence of an irreducible teleological explanation of mental actions. Evidence of the rejection of a teleological explanation is often found in discussions of philosophical naturalism (naturalism, for short). For example, according to David Armstrong, naturalism is "the doctrine that reality consists of nothing but a single all-embracing spatio-temporal system" (Armstrong 1978, p. 261). Contemporary materialism is a form of naturalism and maintains that the single all-embracing temporal system contains nothing but the entities recognized by the most mature physics. Irreducible teleological explanation has no place in this (or any other) spatiotemporal system because it entails the existence of explanations by purposes (reasons), and explanations by purposes imply the falsity of naturalism. Thus, Armstrong says that "if the principles involved [in analyzing the single, all-embracing spatiotemporal system that is reality] were completely different from the current principles of physics, in particular if they involved appeal to mental entities, such as purposes, we might then count the analysis as a falsification of Naturalism" (Armstrong 1978, p. 262).

Now if there really are no purposes, then it is folly to spend one's time trying to discover God's purpose for choosing to allow evil. God could not choose to allow evil for a purpose because, ultimately, nothing can be adequately explained teleologically. Any account of God's purpose for choosing to allow evil will be rejected, not because it fails to state correctly what that purpose is but because, ultimately, there simply are no irreducible purposeful explanations of anything. The nonexistence of such explanations has a similar implication for human choices: Given that human beings cannot make choices that are ultimately explained in terms of irreducible purposes, they cannot possess libertarian free will.

It is not my purpose in this chapter to rebut modern philosophical orthodoxy and arguments against the reality of qualia, the soul, libertarian free will, and irreducible teleological explanation. I have done so elsewhere (see Goetz 2005; Goetz & Taliaferro 2008a,b). Rather, my purpose in raising these four issues at the outset of this chapter is simply to alert the reader to the fact that if you think that there is a problem of evil, then you must, if you are consistent, break ranks with contemporary philosophical orthodoxy. At a minimum, you must think that views in the philosophy of mind such as functionalism and eliminativism are wrong and that pain is an irreducible quale with an intrinsic nature. Moreover, even if you do not believe that souls exist and make undetermined choices that are irreducibly teleologically explained in terms of purposes, you must at least be willing to give someone who believes in these things a serious hearing. You must be willing to do this because chances are that those who think that the problem of evil can be reasonably answered believe in these things and invoke their reality in their response. If you are not willing to make such a concession, then there is not much point in your reading further in this chapter.

Defense versus Theodicy

As I stated at the outset of the previous section, the problem of evil is the argument that the existence of evil is, in some way, incompatible with the existence of an omnipotent, omnibenevolent, and omniscient being. Because the problem of evil is a philosophical argument that God's existence is incompatible with the existence of evil, it is a theoretical problem. There is, to be sure, a practical problem of evil, which is, broadly speaking, the practical difficulty of learning how to cope with one's own experience of evil (e.g. the pain experienced from either the loss of a loved one or a severe bodily injury). There is, unfortunately, no guarantee that a plausible response to the theoretical problem of evil (assuming that there is such a response) will prove practically helpful. Indeed, when in the throes of sorrow, silence is often far more appropriate or fitting than words. But while silence sometimes suits us better than words, many if not most of us are all too aware that the theoretical problem will abide silence for only so long before it once again raises its voice and demands our attention. Hence, it must be dealt with in its own time and place.

A moment ago, I wrote that the problem of evil is the argument that the existence of evil is, *in some way*, incompatible with the existence of God. Over the course of the last 50+ years, it has become common practice to distinguish between two kinds of incompatibility, namely, the logical and the evidential. According to the logical problem of evil, the mere existence of evil is inconsistent with or logically contradicts the existence of God. The evidential problem of evil, while it concedes that the existence of evil is logically compatible with God's existence, maintains that the amount and/or kinds of evil in this world provide evidence against the existence of God such that belief that God exists is unjustified and probably false.

In response to the logical and evidential arguments from evil against the existence of God, a forceful line of argument has been developed by some theists (I will assume that a theist is a person who affirms that God is omnipotent, omnibenevolent, and omniscient) to the effect that while it is desirable to know God's justification for permitting evil, reasonable theists (I will call them "defenders") need not[2] and ought not[3] do any more than provide a defense, which is a statement of what God's justification for permitting evil might be. Because of our limited epistemic powers, a defender believes that God's justification for permitting evil is beyond our ken.[4] As Peter van Inwagen has recently pointed out, it

---

2. "No doubt the theist would rather know what God's reason *is* for permitting evil than simply that it's possible that He has a good one. But in the present context (that of investigating the logical consistency of [God is omnipotent, wholly good, and evil exists], the latter is all that is needed" (Plantinga 1974, p. 28; emphasis in the original).

3. Plantinga says the following: "If God is omnipotent, omniscient, and wholly good, why is there any evil? ... The Christian theist must concede that she doesn't know – that is, she doesn't know in any detail. ... And here I must remark that many of the attempts to explain why God permits evil – theodicies, as we might call them – seem to me shallow, tepid, and ultimately frivolous" (Plantinga 1996a, p. 70). Peter van Inwagen notes that "Plantinga is rather down on theodicies. I have heard him say that to give a theodicy is 'presumptuous'" (van Inwagen 1988, p. 161).

4. "Our grasp of the fundamental way of things is at best limited; there is no reason to think that if God *did* have a reason for permitting the evil in question, we would be the first to know" (Plantinga, 1996a, p. 70; emphasis in the original). Stephen Wykstra explains that our supposed ignorance of the goods that outweigh instances of suffering is expected because God's wisdom in relationship to ours in this matter is analogous to that of an adult human's and that of a 1-month old infant's. "So for any selected instance of intense suffering, there is good reason to think that if there is an outweighing good ... we would not have epistemic access to [it] ..." (Wykstra 1990, p. 156).

has become quite common for defenders initially to treat the argument from evil by showing that the belief that both God and evil exist is free from internal logical contradiction (there is no logical problem of evil). Once they have successfully done this, however, they usually see the need to respond to the evidential problem of evil by providing a defense that is a real as opposed to a mere logical possibility. Van Inwagen illustrates his point about the difference between these two kinds of defense in terms of a defense counsel in a court of law:

> If defense counsels followed a parallel strategy in courts of law, they would first try to prove that their clients innocence was logically consistent with the evidence by telling stories (by presenting 'alternative theories of the crime') involving things like twins separated at birth, operatic coincidences, and mental telepathy; only after they had shown by this method that their clients' innocence was logically consistent with the evidence, would they go on to try to raise *real* doubts in the minds of jurors about the guilt of their clients. (van Inwagen 2006, p. 67; emphasis in the original)

As a defender, van Inwagen seeks to present a defense that is a real possibility, one that there is some reason to think might very well be true (and, thus, is stronger than a defense that stops with mere logical consistency). His defense is in the form of a story in which God exists and has reasons for allowing the existence of evil of the kind that occurs in the actual world. The story is a real possibility in the sense that upon hearing it one would respond with "'Given that God exists, the rest of the story might very well be true. I can't see any reason to rule it out'" (van Inwagen 2006, p. 66). There is, however, a response to the problem of evil that is yet more robust than one that presents a defense that is a real as opposed to a mere logical possibility. This response claims to know not only that a justification for evil's existence is a real possibility but also that this real possibility is God's *actual* justification for permitting evil. I will call theists who believe they know (in part or in whole) God's justification for permitting evil "theodicists." If we stick with van Inwagen's illustration from a court of law, a theodicist is like a defense counsel who convinces jurors of the innocence of his client by presenting facts about where his client actually was at the time of the crime, which make clear that it was impossible for his client to have committed the crime. A theodicist presents God's (his client's) actual reason for allowing evil with the result that it is clearly seen that evil does not present evidence against God's existence.

Now it is no doubt true that a defender might know God's reason for permitting evil and yet be under no obligation to disclose it to someone else or refer to it in an argument about the problem of evil. For whatever reason, a person might be a defender in public and a theodicist in private. This is not the position of the defenders whom I will discuss in this chapter. The assumption behind their defensive position is that if they knew God's justification for permitting evil, they would gladly refer to it in their response to the problem of evil, regardless of whether or not they were obligated to do so. Moreover, as Eleonore Stump has pointed out, knowing God's justifying reason and, thereby, being a theodicist, can be important to some theists outside the context of responding to the problem of evil:

> The problem with [the defender's] arguments and strategies . . . is that they leave people on both sides of the issue unsatisfied. . . . [F]or the theist struggling with the problem of evil,

even if he entertains no anxieties about the rationality of his theistic belief in consequence of the existence of evil, he may well still be weakened in his religious belief by the consideration that the deity in whom he is to place his *trust* seems to act in ways which are unintelligible to him at best and apparently evil at worst. (Stump 1985, pp. 394–5; emphasis in the original)

Given this brief overview of the distinction between a defense and a theodicy, I develop a theodicy in the rest of this chapter. A theodicy requires knowledge of a good that is great enough to justify God's permission of evil. Knowledge of that good is found, I believe, through consideration of the question of the purpose of life. In essence, I argue in the section "Life's Purpose and Perfect Happiness" that the purpose of an individual's life is that he experience the great good of perfect or complete happiness, and it is the possibility of his experiencing this great good that justifies God's allowing him to experience evil. To set the stage for my discussion of the purpose of life in the said section, I briefly summarize and discuss in the next section one theodicist's attempt to persuade a prominent defender to become a theodicst. While I conclude that this theodicist's particular argument fails, I believe that the general form of his argument is worth remembering when it comes time to develop my own theodicy in the section "Developing a Theodicy."

The Free Will Defense

As part of an argument to show that God's existence and the existence of evil are logically compatible, the defender Alvin Plantinga develops the free will defense, which maintains that "[a] world containing creatures who are significantly free (and freely perform more good than evil actions) is more valuable, all else being equal, than a world containing no free creatures at all" (Plantinga, 1974, p. 30). Given that this is the case, we know that the existence of evil is compatible with persons possessing significant freedom (libertarian free will) and that the possession of this freedom *might be* God's justification for permitting evil. The aim of the free will defense, however, is not to say that we know that the possession of this freedom *is* God's justification or reason for permitting evil.

The theodicist Jerry Walls has argued that contrary to what Plantinga maintains, the free will defense requires a commitment to the reality of libertarian free will as God's actual justification for permitting evil, thereby making Plantinga a theodicist. Walls argues that Plantinga is committed to the truth of the principle (call it *P*) that in all worlds where persons are either not free or have compatibilist free will, God could eliminate all moral evil, where moral evil is the experience of pain and/or deprivation of pleasure that results from morally wrong choices and/or actions of free beings, whether human or nonhuman. In other words, in a world that lacks persons with libertarian free will it is impossible for moral evil to exist. A certain *kind* of evil requires a certain kind of justification, and any possible world that contains moral evil must also contain beings with libertarian free will. Given that we know there is moral evil in our world, the only possible justification God can have for permitting the existence of this moral evil is the existence of beings with libertarian free will. Walls concludes that Plantinga is committed to a theodicy where he knows that God permits moral evil in our world because God knows that "[libertarian] freedom and its related goods outweigh the [moral] evil in our world" (Walls 1992b, p. 333). Plantinga can avoid moving from a defense to a theodicy only by unreasonably refusing to affirm that it is impossible for God to allow persons to experience moral evil and those individuals not have libertarian free will.

In response to Walls, Plantinga claims that it is not obvious to him that P is true. For all he knows:

> [m]aybe a certain amount of evil is necessary to every really good possible world. Perhaps among the really good possible worlds, there are some in which there is no creaturely freedom, but there are creatures capable of knowledge. Perhaps it is a good thing that those creatures be able to appreciate the great value of the world in question; but perhaps they couldn't appreciate its great value unless there were some evil with respect to which to contrast that value; and perhaps that evil could be of several kinds, including evil due to the free (in the compatibilist sense) activity of creatures. (Plantinga 1992, pp. 336–7)

Plantinga concludes that if a certain amount of evil is necessary to every really good possible world in the way that he suggests, then libertarian freedom is not necessary in order for God to be justified in permitting the existence of moral evil in a world. Perhaps, then, our possession of libertarian free will is not God's justification for allowing moral evil in our world.

At this point, Plantinga recognizes that Walls might grant, for the sake of argument, that any really good possible world requires the existence of some evil, and maybe some of the evil in those worlds includes moral evil produced by beings with compatibilist free will. Thus, we do not know that the possession of libertarian free will by creatures is God's justification for permitting moral evil *per se*. But what about a world such as our own which contains moral evils of a horrendous or very terrible sort? Must it not be the case that worlds with such terrible moral evils must also contain beings with libertarian free will, where that free will is the justification for permitting such horrible moral evils? In other words, while it might generically be the case that any really good possible world requires the existence of some evil, when we get down to the specific evil(s) of a particular really good possible world such as ours, theodicy becomes inevitable.

Plantinga concedes the force of this line of thought: while it might be the case that some evil is necessary for the existence of any really good possible world, it is implausible to believe that the horrific moral evils of this world are necessary, say, for the proper appreciation of what is good. Thus, he says that he is inclined to think that some principle analogous to P, which makes reference to appalling moral evils, is true. That is, he is inclined to believe that in all worlds in which persons either are not free or are free only in the compatibilist sense, God could and would eliminate all horrendous moral evil. But being inclined to believe that something is true is not the same thing as being committed to its truth. Thus, even with respect to the appalling moral evils of this world, Plantinga maintains that he is not committed to the truth of an analog of P in giving his free will defense. Granted, he fails to see a justifying good other than libertarian free will that God could have for permitting the horrific moral evils we find in our world. He points out, however, that "there is a big difference between failing to see that something is possible and seeing that it is impossible" (Plantinga 1992, p. 338). Therefore, for all he knows, there may be a justification other than libertarian free will that God has for allowing the appalling moral evils in our world.

Life's Purpose and Perfect Happiness

Given their shared assumption that libertarian free will is either itself a good that can, at least in part, justify God's permission of both nonhorrendous (nonappalling) and horrendous (appalling) moral evil (henceforth, moral evil, for short) or is required for the preponderance of morally good actions that can justify God's allowance of moral evil,[5] it seems to me that Plantinga has given a persuasive response to Walls. Although I think that Walls's argument fails, I will follow his theodical strategy and argue that defenders can avoid moving from a defense to a theodicy only by unreasonably refusing to acknowledge that a certain scenario is impossible. [Walls thinks Plantinga can avoid moving from a defense to a theodicy only by unreasonably refusing to acknowledge the impossibility of God allowing moral evil (or moral evil of a horrendous sort) without libertarian free will.] In my argument against defenders, I assume, like Plantinga and Walls, that created persons possess libertarian free will, but unlike them I explicitly deny that this freedom is a good that can, even in part, justify God's permission of moral evil.[6]

To understand why the move from defense to theodicy is rationally required, it is necessary to spend some time considering the question of the purpose of life, where I will always understand the "purpose of life" as the purpose of an *individual's* life. The issue of the purpose of life is one that defenders rarely, if ever, address. Perhaps the explanation for their not doing so is the same as that which explains their reluctance to become theodicists, namely, that we humans possess only limited epistemic powers. This limitation ensures not only that God's justification for permitting moral evil is beyond our ken but also that the purpose for our existence is epistemically inaccessible to us. It is perhaps of some consequence that defenders such as Plantinga and Stephen Wykstra are Protestant philosophers in the Calvinist tradition, a tradition that understands the effects of Adam's fall to include the fact that the human mind is darkened.[7] As Alasdair MacIntyre has pointed out, with the rise of Protestantism, the view developed that "[r]eason can supply ... *no* genuine comprehension of man's true end; that power of reason was destroyed by the fall of man. 'Si Adam integer stetisset' [If Adam has stood or remained whole or upright], on Calvin's view, reason might have played the part that Aristotle assigned to it" (MacIntyre 1981, p. 51; emphasis in the original). The part that Aristotle assigned to reason

---

5. "A world containing creatures who are significantly free (and freely perform more good than evil actions) is more valuable, all else being equal, than a world containing no free creatures at all" (Plantinga 1974, p. 30); and "[I]f we are so free [in the libertarian sense], then it naturally follows that God must think that freedom and its related goods outweigh the evil in our world" (Walls 1992b, p. 333).

6. Thus, I agree with the following comment by the atheist William Rowe: "The first question we need to ask is whether the possession of free will is something that is *in itself* of such great value as to merit God's permission of the horrendous moral evils in the world. I think the answer must be no. We should distinguish the intrinsic value of possessing free will from its extrinsic value. The mere possession of free will does not strike me as itself having much in the way of intrinsic value" (Rowe 1996, p. 279; emphasis in the original). My only quibble with Rowe is that I believe that free will does not have *any* intrinsic value.

7. It is important to make clear that I do not consider pointing out that Plantinga and Wykstra are philosophers in the Calvinist tradition as any kind of argument against defenders. After all, Calvinism, or certain elements of it, might be correct. My purpose in pointing out Plantinga's and Wykstra's association with Calvinism is only to make clear that their approach to the problem of evil is consistent with the more general Calvinist position that the powers of the human mind have been seriously undermined by sin.

included knowing man's telos or end. But Adam did not stand or remain whole, and the result according to Protestant thought was that unaided reason can no longer know man's true end.

What if, however, the result of the fall was not as epistemically disastrous as Protestantism maintains and it is possible to know the purpose of life? And what if knowledge of life's purpose is not only available but also provides insight into God's actual reason for permitting moral evil? Because I am a lapsed Protestant when it comes to the doctrine of the Fall, I believe it is possible to know the purpose of life, and I also believe this knowledge gives us insight into God's actual justification for permitting evil. Therefore, in the rest of this section I state what I think the purpose of life is and consider several objections to my view. Given a successful treatment of the issue of life's purpose, I will turn in the next section to developing a theodicy.

What, then, is the purpose of life? I believe that the answer is fairly obvious: the purpose of life is to experience perfect or complete happiness. What, however, is perfect happiness? Intuitively, it is an experience of what is intrinsically good (what is sometimes thought of as subjectively felt happiness), where something is intrinsically good if it is good and does not derive its goodness from the goodness of something else to which it is related. Because the problem of evil fundamentally concerns the experience of pain, where pain is a fundamental (first-order), metaphysical (nonmoral, where nonmoral ≠ immoral), intrinsic evil that does not derive its evil nature from the evil of something else to which it is related, it is plausible to think that an experience of pleasure is a fundamental, metaphysical, intrinsic good that does not derive its goodness from the goodness of something else to which it is related. Happiness, then, is related to the intrinsic goodness and evilness of pleasure and pain, respectively, in a way that makes it the case that the less pain and more pleasure that a person experiences, the happier he is. So there are degrees of happiness, and perfect or complete happiness is a condition in which a person experiences nothing but pleasure (a quale), where this positively good qualitative state continues without end.

That perfect happiness is the purpose for which a person exists is indirectly supported by the existence of the problem of evil itself. After all, what is the problem of evil except the quest for an explanation as to why, if God does exist, this apparent purpose for a person's existing (that he experience perfect happiness) is not fulfilled or realized? Given that God has the requisite attributes to guarantee the fulfillment or realization of this purpose, why is it not accomplished? Thus, when an atheist such as J. L. Mackie asks "why could [God] not have made men such that they always freely choose the good?" (Mackie 1990, p. 33), he assumes that always freely choosing the good is more in keeping with the achievement of perfect happiness, where the experience of that happiness is a person's purpose for existing.[8]

I assume, then, in what follows, that an individual's well-being is or consists of subjectively felt happiness, which is to say that happiness in its complete or perfect form is essentially experiences of pleasure (a positive hedonic state) and the absence of pain (a

8. In criticizing a solution to the problem of evil, which claims that the universe is better with some evil in it than it could be if there were no evil, Mackie is explicit about the connection in his own mind between pleasure, happiness, and the good: "Let us call pain and misery 'first order evil' or 'evil (1)'. What contrasts with this, namely pleasure and happiness, will be called 'first order good' or 'good (1)'" (Mackie 1990, p. 31).

negative hedonic state). During the course of my examination of the problem of evil in subsequent sections, I will make various points in support of this assumption. For now, I simply emphasize that on the understanding of happiness that informs this chapter, it simply is not possible that a life largely devoid of felt happiness is worth living *for its subject*. I realize that not everyone will agree with me about this point. For example, Flanagan has suggested that "[p]erhaps happiness is not necessary even [for a worthwhile life]. One might live a life largely devoid of happiness but still live a good and worthwhile life – even as seen from the subjective point of view" (Flanagan 1996, p. 5). The argument of this chapter simply assumes that Flanagan is mistaken.

Because (perfect) happiness is intrinsically good, it is a feature of human nature that a person cannot help but desire it for himself. St Augustine expressed this point quite succinctly when he wrote that "It is the decided opinion of all who use their brains that all men desire to be happy" (Augustine 1993, 10.1). One might, however, raise the following objection:

> [T]he desire satisfaction theory of human welfare [a person's well-being is a function of his satisfying his strongest desires concerning his own experiences] has counterintuitive implications. Suppose that (for whatever reason) a person strongly wanted to suffer mental anxiety and physical torment for the sake of satisfying no other want. The desire satisfaction theory implies that such a person would be doing quite well for having such a desire fulfilled, which seems absurd. (Metz 2003, p. 168)

This implication of the desire satisfaction theory is absurd. I am not, however, presupposing the desire satisfaction theory. Rather, I am assuming that a person's well-being consists of his experiencing happiness and that it is because this is the case that he ultimately desires his perfect happiness. In other words, the intrinsic goodness of happiness constrains what a person can and does desire for himself. No individual can desire that he suffer mental anxiety and physical torment for their own sakes because no one can desire what is intrinsically evil or bad for its own sake. Desire is necessarily ultimately directed at the intrinsic goodness of perfect happiness.

If the experience of perfect happiness is the purpose of life, a meaningless or absurd life is one in which a person fails to experience that degree of happiness. As Thomas Nagel has pointed out, the idea of absurdity is essentially the idea of a discrepancy or mismatch, which is illustrated by both a scenario in which a notorious criminal is made president of a major philanthropic foundation and a romantic moment in which one declares one's love over the telephone to a recorded announcement (Nagel 2000, p. 178). So if the purpose of life is to have a certain experience and a person fails to have it, there is a discrepancy or mismatch in that individual's life.

On the view of the purpose of life I am setting forth, life is not necessarily absurd. While some lives might be absurd, others might not. Nagel thinks otherwise, and his argument deserves careful consideration. According to him, we are beings who take things, including our lives, seriously. We have, however, the capacity to step back and survey ourselves and the lives that we take seriously and inevitably exercise that capacity. For example, an individual like Mother Theresa took seriously a life of helping the poor and destitute in Calcutta. And, like anyone else, she had the capacity to step back and survey her life. According to Nagel, when she stepped back and surveyed her life she was inevitably led to ask the question, "Is a life of helping the poor and destitute in Calcutta worth taking seriously?" Or take a person who lives for trying to impress other people. He too has the capacity to step back and survey his life. When he does so, he will ask, "Is a life of trying to impress others worth taking seriously?" What makes Nagel's argument important is that he believes no question asked by a person about the worthwhile nature of the life that he takes seriously has an answer that is immune to unanswerable doubt. Every answer to such a question is, therefore, ultimately unjustified. In other words, Nagel believes that no matter what kind of life an individual takes seriously, it will always be subject to a discrepancy in the form of a question about that life that does not have a justified answer. No matter what kind of life one has lived, it is not worth taking seriously: "There does not appear to be any conceivable world (containing us) about which unsettlable doubts could not arise" (Nagel 2000, p. 181). Therefore, *any* kind of life involving us is ultimately absurd or meaningless, even one involving perfect happiness. Thus, if we assume for the sake of discussion that a person both takes seriously the idea of being perfectly happy and actually experiences this happiness, Nagel's point is that such a person will realize, upon stepping back and asking, "Is a life of being perfectly happy worth taking seriously?" that he will always have unanswerable doubt about an affirmative answer. No affirmative answer to his question will ultimately justifiably settle his doubt.

Nagel's argument, however, surely fails when it is directed at the life of perfect happiness. Given that perfect happiness is intrinsically good, someone who asks whether it is worth taking seriously and believes that there is no good reason to think that it is is seriously confused. As Paul Edwards points out, "It makes sense for a person to ask about something 'Is it really worthwhile?' or 'Is it really worth the trouble?' if he does not regard it as intrinsically valuable. . . . It does not make sense [however] to ask such a question about something he regards as valuable in its own right. . . ." (Edwards 2000, p. 141). Thus, on the understanding of the purpose of life that I am assuming, the most serious discrepancy or mismatch involving an individual would be a failure on his part to give perfect happiness the utmost attention that it is due. If anything is absurd, such a failure is.

Because perfect happiness is intrinsically good, an argument that is sometimes raised against God's existence can be answered. This argument is a variant of Euthyphro's dilemma and asks, "Is perfect happiness good because God commands or says that it is good or does God command or say that perfect happiness is good because it is good?"[9] Given that perfect happiness is intrinsically good, its goodness has essentially nothing to do with what God commands or says. It just is good, period. Of course, if God is omnibenevolent, then He will want to provide us with perfect happiness because it is intrinsically good. But for that to be the case, it is not necessary that the goodness of perfect happiness depend upon what God commands or says about it.

Given, therefore, that complete or perfect happiness is the purpose of life, there is a sense in which God has something to say about its being so and a sense in which He does not. The sense in which God does have something to say has to do with God's granting perfect happiness to those who deserve it, and I will take up this issue in subsequent sections. The sense in which God has nothing to say has to do with the fact that because perfect happiness is intrinsically good, it does not derive its goodness from anything else, where 'anything else' includes anything God might command or say about the matter. Perfect

---

9. See West and West (1998, p. 52; 10a), where Socrates asks Euthyphro "Is the pious loved by the gods because it is pious, or is it pious because it is loved?"

happiness just is good and it does not take the command or word of anyone, including God, to make it so.

If it is the case that perfect happiness is intrinsically good and that God creates human persons for the purpose that they experience this happiness, then another objection sometimes raised against theism can be answered. According to Kurt Baier, there are two senses of the word "purpose":

> In the first and basic sense, purpose is normally attributed only to persons or their behaviour as in 'Did you have a purpose in leaving the ignition on?' In the second sense, purpose is normally attributed only to things, as in 'What is the purpose of that gadget you installed in the workshop?' The two uses are intimately connected. We cannot attribute a purpose to a thing without implying that someone did something, in the doing of which he had some purpose, namely to bring about the thing with that purpose. Of course, *his* purpose is not identical with *its* purpose. In hiring labourers and engineers and buying materials and a site for a factory and the like, the entrepreneur's purpose, let us say, is to manufacture cars, but the purpose of the cars is to serve as a means of transportation. . . . To attribute to a human being a purpose in [the second] sense is not neutral, let alone complimentary: it is offensive. It is degrading for a man to be regarded as merely serving a purpose. If, at a garden party, I ask a man in livery, 'What is your purpose?' I am insulting him. I might as well have asked, 'What are you *for*?' Such questions reduce him to the level of a gadget, a domestic animal, or perhaps a slave. I imply that *we* allot to *him* the tasks, the goals, the aims which he is to pursue; that *his* wishes and desires and aspirations and purposes are to count for little or nothing. We are treating him, in Kant's phrase, merely as a means to our ends, not as an end in himself. (Baier 2000, pp. 11–120; emphases in the original)

The two senses of purpose to which Baier calls our attention are real and important. Some of the conclusions he draws from the distinction between these two senses, however, are highly questionable. For example, it is not necessarily offensive or degrading to regard a man as merely serving a purpose. Whether or not it is offensive to regard a person as serving a purpose depends upon what the purpose is. If that purpose is the experience of perfect happiness, then its bestowal is not degrading but ennobling. Moreover, why cannot it be the case, contrary to what Baier claims, that an individual's purpose in acting, the goal at which he aims in acting, is identical with God's purpose for him? The two purposes can be the same when a person's wishes and desires and aspirations are the same as God's wishes and desires and aspirations for him. Lewis had no problem understanding this point: "God not only understands but *shares* . . . the desire for complete and ecstatic happiness. He made me for no other purpose than to enjoy it" (Lewis 2004, p. 123; emphasis in the original).

In addition to his objection stemming from the two senses of "purpose," Baier raises two other concerns that intersect with the understanding of life's purpose that I am defending. The first problem "is to find a purpose grand and noble enough to explain and justify the great amount of undeserved suffering in this world" (Baier 2000, p. 122). Now if the experience of perfect happiness is the great good that it is and the greatest good possible for an individual, it would seem that if any good is good enough to justify the great amount of undeserved suffering of this world, then it is this good. Whether or not a theodicy that makes use of this greatest possible good is defensible will be the subject matter of the subsequent sections of this chapter.

The second difficulty raised by Baier presupposes that perfect happiness is an individual's greatest good. The trouble as Baier sees it is that this good is too good:

The Christian evaluation of earthly lives is misguided because it adopts a quite unjustifiably high standard. Christianity singles out the major shortcomings of our earthly existence: there is not enough happiness; there is too much suffering; the good and bad points are quite unequally and unfairly distributed; the underprivileged and underendowed do not get adequate compensation; it lasts only a short time. It then quite accurately depicts the perfect or ideal life as that which does not have any of these shortcomings. Its next step is to promise the believer that he will be able to enjoy this perfect life later on. And then he adopts as its standard of judgment the perfect life, dismissing as inadequate anything that falls short of it. . . .

This procedure is as illegitimate as if I were to refuse to call anything tall unless it is infinitely tall, or anything beautiful unless it is perfectly flawless, or anyone strong unless he is omnipotent. Even if it were true that there is available to us an after-life which is flawless and perfect, it would still not be legitimate to judge earthly lives by this standard. (Baier 2000, p. 127)

In response to Baier, it is important to point out that in "adopting" the experience of perfect happiness as the purpose of life one is not making a choice of any kind, let alone an arbitrary choice (one made for no purpose or reason whatsoever). One is simply recognizing perfect happiness for what it is, namely, a great intrinsic good. And as I have already pointed out in reference to Euthyphro's dilemma, the goodness of perfect happiness is not a matter of what anyone commands, says, or chooses.

As to whether perfect happiness is a legitimate standard for judging the goodness of this life, it seems that Baier is trying to have it both ways. On the one hand, he seems to assume this standard himself when he raises the problem of evil and claims that there is no purpose that is good enough to justify God's permitting the amount of evil that is present in this world. Presumably, Baier believes that had our Earthly existence been thoroughly pleasurable and free of pain and suffering (perfectly happy), then there would not have been a problem of evil. That quality of existence would have been good enough to preclude any such problem. And it remains to be seen in following sections whether it is also good enough to answer the problem of evil that we actually face. On the other hand, when someone else makes use of this standard to judge the quality of our Earthly lives, Baier asserts that that person is guilty of setting the bar too high. If Baier is right, one is damned if one does and damned if one does not use the standard of perfect happiness. In the end, the facts of the matter are as follows: no one makes a choice about whether or not perfect happiness is good. It just is good and is intrinsically so. Moreover, it is the experience of the goodness of happiness in this life, imperfect as it may be because of the existence of evil, which makes us yearn for that which is perfect.

Perfect happiness, then, is just that: perfect. It excludes all experiences of what is intrinsically evil and includes only experiences of what is intrinsically good. I have, however, also claimed that perfect happiness includes another aspect, which is that it is unending. The consideration which leads to the inclusion of this aspect of perfect happiness is twofold in nature.

First, because perfect happiness is intrinsically good, one cannot help but desire its continuation. In other words, the idea of desiring a temporally finite complete happiness or an unending but incomplete happiness is conceptually suspect, if not incoherent. Because desire is conceptually ultimately aimed at the experience of what is intrinsically good and the avoidance of the experience of that which is intrinsically evil for their own sakes, no sane person can desire the cessation of perfect happiness or prefer the experience of an imperfect happiness over that which is perfect, given the availability of the latter. As Thomas Talbott has written, "[i]t is simply not possible . . . not to desire supreme happiness for its own sake" (Talbott 2001, p. 423). Walls adds the following thoughts in support of this point:

> Nothing short of [endless joy and satisfaction] will suffice to give us what we most deeply crave. The fact that we seek happiness is axiomatic. . . . Clearly, if some partial experience of happiness is desirable, perfect happiness is even more so. Either we have such happiness, or we do not. If we do not, then it is something we want, and if we never get it, our lives will end in some degree of frustration. On the other hand, if we have it, we would not want it to end. If it did end, then again, our lives would end in frustration. The only alternative to a frustrating end to our lives is perfect happiness, happiness without end. (Walls 2002, p. 195)

A comment by the atheist Kai Nielsen provides additional confirmation of the present point: "As I am now in possession of the normal powers of life, with things I want to do and experience, with pleasure in life and with people I very much care for and who care for me, I certainly do not want to die. I should very much like, in such a state, to go on living forever" (Nielsen 2000, p. 154).

The second reason for believing that perfect happiness is unending presupposes the first point about the kind of happiness that we desire and assumes that God is omnibenevolent. Given God's omnibenevolence, He cannot help but wish for us our greatest good, which is perfect happiness. Talbott puts the point quite succinctly: "If God is supremely loving, then He wills for us exactly what, at the most fundamental level, we want for ourselves; He wills that we should experience supreme happiness. . . ." (Talbott 2001, p. 421).

While a perfect happiness that does not end is what we desire, some have questioned whether what we desire is intelligible. One of the most well-known challenges is that of Bernard Williams in his essay "The Makropulos Case: Reflections on the Tedium of Immortality" (Williams 1973). In summarizing and discussing Williams's essay, I draw heavily from John Martin Fischer's paper "Why Immortality Is Not So Bad" (Fischer 1994).

Williams sets forth two necessary conditions of immortality: (1) that the future person must be numerically identical with the individual concerned, and (2) that the future life of that individual must be attractive to him in the sense that his future goals and projects and values and interests must be suitably related to his present goals and projects and values and interests. If they are not suitably related, then there is a risk that he will now (in the present) find it difficult to regard them as sufficiently interesting to support a present desire that he have them as his own in the future.

Given that I am assuming that souls exist and are capable of persisting self-identical from this life into the next, condition (1) is fulfilled. What about condition (2)? Can it be fulfilled? Williams thinks not. With regard to (2), Williams poses a dilemma: either an individual's fundamental desires, interests, purposes, and projects (his character) remain the same over time, or they do not. If they do remain the same, then given that their number is finite they will eventually be satisfied or fulfilled and boredom will ensue. If they do not remain the same (they change too much), then Williams suggests that the individual's future desires, interests, purposes, and projects will not be similar enough to his present psychological makeup and the projects it supports to make him now desire to survive to be the subject of what is so different. The person will simply prefer to go out of existence.

What about the first alternative? As Fischer points out, there is a distinction between self-exhausting and repeatable pleasures. A self-exhausting pleasure is one associated with an activity, the performance of which terminates any further need to do it again. An example Fischer provides is of an activity that you desire to do just once to prove to yourself that you can do it:

> Imagine ... that you are somewhat afraid of heights, and you have been working hard to overcome this phobia. You form the goal of climbing Mt Whitney just to show yourself that you have overcome the fear – just to show yourself that you can control your life and overcome obstacles. Upon climbing the mountain, you may in fact be very pleased and proud. Indeed, you may be deeply satisfied. But also you may have absolutely no desire to climb Mt Whitney (or any other mountain) again. You have accomplished your goal, but there is no impetus toward repeating the relevant activity or the pleasure that issues from it. (Fischer 1994, pp. 262–3)

Although Fischer does not mention the following point in response to Williams, it does seem coherent to suppose that even if there were no other kind of pleasure than that which is self-exhausting, the intelligibility of the idea of perfect happiness would still not be undermined. What would be required for perfect happiness would be a potentially infinite number of unrepeatable activities, each of which provided its subject with pleasure. And given that there is nothing incoherent in this concept, it would be possible for a person to be perfectly happy for eternity by means of the performance of an unending series of unrepeatable activities with their accompanying self-exhausting pleasures.

But as Fischer notes, there is another kind of pleasure. There are repeatable pleasures:

> Here an individual may well find the pleasure highly fulfilling and completely satisfying at the moment and yet wish to have more (i.e., to *repeat* the pleasure) at some point in the future (not necessarily immediately). Certain salient sensual pleasures leap immediately to mind: the pleasures of sex, of eating fine meals and drinking fine wines, of listening to beautiful music, of seeing great art, and so forth. ... Given the appropriate distribution of such pleasures, it seems that an endless life that included some (but perhaps not only) repeatable pleasures would *not* necessarily be boring or unattractive. (Fischer 1994, pp. 263–4; emphases in the original)

As Fischer goes on to point out, religious persons (and who is more likely to believe in perfect happiness than a religious person?) can experience not only repeatable pleasures of the sort just mentioned but also repeatable pleasures that come with the repeatable activities of worship of and thanks to God. Thanking God for the repeatable pleasures that He has granted is itself a source of additional pleasure.

Consider, now, the second alternative, which is that an individual's future goals and projects and values and interests must be suitably related to his present goals and projects and values and interests in life so that the former will now (in the present) be attractive to him. If they are not presently attractive, then he will now fail to find them sufficiently interesting to desire to have them as his own in the future. Without such an interest, non-existence will seem preferable to immortality. In response to this horn of the dilemma, Fischer writes that:

> it seems that an individual could value such an [unending] existence if he or she felt that the change in character would result from *certain sorts of sequences*. ... Surely in our ordinary,

finite lives we envisage certain changes in our values and preferences over time. For example, one may currently value excitement and challenge; thus, one might wish to live in an urban area with many career and avocational opportunities (but with lousy weather and a high crime rate). Still, one might envisage a time in the future when one will be older and will prefer warm weather, serenity and security. . . . Thus, there are quite ordinary cases in our finite lives in which we envisage changes in our characters – our values and preferences – and which are not so unattractive as to render death preferable. Why, then, could not the same be true of immortal existence? (Fischer 1994, pp. 267–8; emphasis in the original)

While what Fischer says is surely correct, I think it is important to note that Christians (and, I would assume, Jews and Islamists) actually expect a significant change in character in the afterlife that will not render unending existence unattractive. Indeed, if such a change did not occur something would be amiss. What Christians expect is not only that they will experience perfect happiness, which is in and of itself sufficiently attractive now to make immortality desirable, but that they will also experience this happiness without their present sinful nature and its vices. Indeed, it is the absence of sin and vice that will, in part, make perfect happiness possible.

Williams, then, provides no convincing reason to think that the idea of perfect happiness is unintelligible. Indeed, rather than change threatening the intelligibility of the idea of perfect happiness, the experience of that happiness is linked to a significant change in moral character. At this point, the relevance of libertarian free will to the problem of evil begins to emerge because the significant change in moral character that is a prerequisite for the experience of complete happiness comes about because of a choice. What kind of choice is it that implies such a profound change in a person's future character, values, and interests?

Christians describe the relevant choice as the mental act of repentance. Repentance involves a renunciation of an old way of life of unrestrained pursuit of what is good and an embracing of a new way of life of restraint in pursuit of what is good. Such a choice is an instance of the kind of choice that Robert Kane has termed a "self-forming willing" (Kane 1996, pp. 124–5) and that I will term a "self-forming choice" or SFC. In light of the concept of repentance and a renunciation of a former way of life with its character traits, I think a reasonable case can be developed for the view that an agent's most broadly influential SFC ultimately has a bearing on *when* he will maximize his happiness and the kind of life plan he will adopt in pursuit of that happiness. Moreover, because happiness is intrinsically *good*, I will term this most wide-ranging SFC a *good-seeking* SFC. To illustrate what I have in mind here, consider the case of St Augustine, who lived at the end of the fourth and the beginning of the fifth centuries. The following quote from Flanagan about Augustine's life nicely illustrates by example what I have in mind with the idea of a good-seeking SFC:

> St. Augustine was the ultimate party animal until his early thirties, at which point he changed his ways and became an exemplary moral person, a great philosopher, a bishop, and eventually a saint. We might say that Augustine was ruled by his passions until he saw the light in his early thirties. But according to the [libertarian] picture, we would not mean that he *couldn't* control himself. We would mean that he chose not to control himself or chose to control himself badly. (Flanagan 2002, p. 58; emphasis in the original)

What Flanagan is suggesting about Augustine's life is something like the following. At a certain point in his life, Augustine made a good-seeking SFC that entailed he would *not* restrain himself from pursuing certain means to maximizing his immediate or short-term happiness. Then some years later, he made a different good-seeking SFC that implied he would restrain his pursuit of goods that promoted his short-term happiness, where exercising this restraint involved his avoiding the performance of certain kinds of actions. Augustine's own account of this latter good-seeking SFC supports Flanagan's description of it. While Augustine says he was converted to God, in whom he believed he would find long-term, perfect happiness, it is clear from his summary of the events leading up to that conversion that he understood that this good-seeking SFC entailed that he would no longer seek to satisfy certain desires for goods that would promote his short-term happiness.

> But now . . . as I heard how [two men] had made the choice that was to save them by giving themselves up entirely to your care, the more bitterly I hated myself in comparison with them. . . . [N]o more was required than an act of will. But it must be a resolute and whole-hearted act of the will. . . . I was held back by mere trifles, the most paltry inanities, all my old attachments. They plucked at my garment of flesh and whispered, 'Are you going to dismiss us? From this moment we shall never be with you again, for ever and ever. From this moment you will never again be allowed to do this thing or that, for evermore.' (Augustine 1961, VIII, 7, 8, 11)

It is plausible, then, to understand Augustine's conversion as a good-seeking SFC, in which he chose a life plan that he believed would maximize his later experience of happiness (this belief, which is implicit in Augustine's comment that the choice of the two men would save them, will be made explicit a few paragraphs hence), where that choice entailed a commitment on his part to restrain himself from pursuing his short-term happiness in certain ways. Although Augustine's good-seeking SFC involved a conversion to Christianity, there is nothing essentially Christian about the idea of a good-seeking SFC that requires restrained pursuit by an agent of his short-term happiness for the sake of that which lies in the future. This is because *any* individual, as or *qua* human being, has a desire for his short-term happiness. Given his desire for his happiness in the short term, he has a reason to act for the sake of (to promote) his own immediate well-being. If, however, such an individual also believes that other persons exist who have a similar desire for their own short-term happiness, then in certain circumstances he will believe that were he to act in certain ways he would undermine their opportunity to satisfy their desire for their own short-term well-being, an opportunity to which they have as much right as he has to his own. As a result of what he believes about the potential impact of his actions on the immediate well-being of others, he comes to have beliefs about the moral impermissibility of performing certain kinds of actions. The upshot of this line of reasoning is that a person, as or *qua* human being, comes to possess beliefs about morally permissible and impermissible ways of pursuing what he believes is good and will promote his short-term happiness, where he views the former ways of pursuing what is good as *just* and the latter ways as *unjust*.

Given these ideas about just and unjust ways of pursuing what is good, a person forms ideas about two corresponding life plans, one which consists of ongoing restraint in pursuit of what conduces to his short-term happiness and the other which does not. A good-seeking choice of the former kind of life plan, which is the kind that Augustine made in his early 30s, is what I will call a just-good-seeking SFC, while a good-seeking choice of the latter way of life is what I will term an unjust-good-seeking SFC. In simplest terms, a just-good-seeking SFC is a choice (a) to live a life of restraint in pursuit of what is good, where this restraint includes avoiding as best as one can situations in which one believes one will be tempted to pursue what one believes is a morally wrong way of obtaining what is good; (b) to give thanks to God for the good that one experiences, assuming one has a belief that one is created by God; (c) to ask for forgiveness from those whom one wrongs when one chooses to pursue what one believes is a morally wrong way of obtaining what is good; and (d) to forgive others who ask for forgiveness when they freely wrong one in their pursuit of what is good. An unjust-good-seeking SFC is for all intents and purposes one which entails the denial of each of (a)–(d).

Before proceeding, it is important to answer one objection. It might be protested at this juncture that what a person believes about permissible and impermissible ways of pursuing what he takes to be good could be erroneous. In other words, what a person subjectively regards as just and unjust might not be objectively so. Hence, it is possible for a person to choose a life plan that he believes (subjectively) is just when in reality (objectively) it is (in whole or in part) unjust, and for a person to choose a life plan that he thinks (subjectively) is unjust when in reality (objectively) it is (in whole or in part) just.

While the distinction referred to in this objection is a real one, it is not relevant to the issue at hand. What is important is the fact that a person makes a just- or an unjust-good-seeking SFC in light of his beliefs about what is just and unjust, regardless of whether those beliefs are true or false, and he understands that he is obligated to make a just-good-seeking SFC in light of those beliefs by virtue of what is appropriately called his conscience, where his conscience is best thought of as an inner voice or judge that pronounces a verdict of innocence or guilt upon him depending on whether he makes a just- or an unjust-good-seeking SFC. St Paul frequently appealed to this notion of conscience, as in the following comments in his letter to the Romans: "When Gentiles who have not the law do by nature what the law requires, they are a law to themselves, even though they do not have the law. They show that what the law requires is written on their hearts, while their conscience also bears witness and their conflicting thoughts accuse or perhaps excuse them. . . ." (Romans 2:14–5). Kant, too, recognized the importance of conscience:

> [T]he accusation of conscience cannot be . . . readily dismissed, neither should it be; it is not a matter of the will. . . . Conscience is an instinct to judge with legal authority according to moral laws; it pronounces a judicial verdict, and, like a judge who can only punish or acquit but cannot reward, so also our conscience either acquits or declares us guilty and deserving of punishment. (Kant 1963, p. 131)

And as Austin Farrer noted, "Conscience claims absolute authority, if you are to have it at all; you can't tell conscience not to speak out of turn" (Farrer 1973, p. 78).

By way of summary, then, a person desires the happiness that by nature constitutes his well-being and is his ultimate end. Given this human nature, he must make a good-seeking SFC that is concerned with *how* and *when* he will maximize the happiness he cannot help but desire to experience. A just-good-seeking SFC will delay through restraint maximizing satisfaction of his desire for happiness, where this maximization is perfect happiness, until the next life. An unjust-good-seeking SFC will seek to maximize satisfaction of his desire for happiness in the short term, even at the expense of undermining the short-term happiness of others and, as I will argue in the section "Adams and Horrendous Evil," his own experience of perfect happiness in the future.

As a way of closing this section and transitioning to the development of my theodicy in the following section, I consider an objection of Marilyn Adams which, if sound, would undermine that theodicy. The theodicy that I will develop in the next section will make use of the idea of complete or perfect happiness that I have developed in this section. This idea includes the value claim that perfect happiness is intrinsically good. Adams believes, however, that once one starts to theorize about possible justifications for God's allowance of evil:

> the hope of universal agreement in value theory is shattered. . . . Insofar as the highest human happiness is usually conceived of as involving some relation to the best good(s), . . . different ontologies will produce different accounts of the human good. . . . Secular value theories can offer only packages of immanent goods; some religious theories posit an infinite transcendent good and invite relationship to it; while mainstream Christianity believes the infinite good to be personal and locates the happiness of finite persons in loving personal intimacy with the divine persons. (Adams 1999, pp. 11–2)

While it is true that there are differences among theories about where and how the experience of happiness is to be found – what the source of this good is (e.g. philosophizing, worshipping God, playing the horses, engaging in sexual escapades) – it is doubtful that the concept of happiness itself as an experience that is intrinsically good varies significantly in its essentials (e.g. it includes the absence of pain and the experience of pleasure) from theory to theory. In her own writings about the problem of evil, Adams assumes that all individuals recognize the evilness of pain, and she explicitly insists that the concept of horrendous evil (evil, the participation in which provides *prima facie* reason to doubt whether the participant's life is a great good to him on the whole such that it would be worth living) is an objective or religion-neutral value (Adams 1999, p. 27). If evil is objective and neutral in this way, however, then why think that good is any less so? Mackie, in setting forth his argument against the existence of God, had no trouble in seeing that pleasure and happiness are what contrast with pain and misery (Mackie 1990, p. 31), and I will follow Mackie and assume that pleasure and happiness, like pain and misery, are objective or religion-neutral values. Because they are religion-neutral, the concept of perfect happiness is values objective or value neutral.

In conclusion, I will henceforth assume that experiences of pleasure and pain are, respectively, intrinsically good and evil. I will also assume that a necessary condition of there being a problem of evil is that individuals who experience pain *be aware of themselves* as experiencing that pain. It is in virtue of this self-awareness that they can have higher-order mental attitudes (e.g. thought, belief, fear) about themselves as the subjects of experiences of pain. Furthermore, I will assume that it is in virtue of this self-awareness that it is possible for experiences of pain to be unjustified. For subjects of pain who lack such self-awareness, it is not possible for experiences of pain to be unjustified. The matter of self-awareness will be of utmost importance when I discuss the suffering of beasts (animal pain) in the last section.

Developing a Theodicy

Although I will have a few more comments to make about the concept of complete happiness in this section, what I have said about it in the previous sections will suffice for the purpose of constructing a theodicy in this section. By way of brief summary, at a minimum, the concept of perfect happiness involves the idea of a person existing forever or eternally in a state of beatitude or bliss which, at the least, involves the absence of all pain and the experience of pleasure. Such a state is an intrinsic good that satisfies or fulfills a person's most basic desire and is *his* greatest possible good.

Given the nature of perfect happiness, it is the case that it decisively *outweighs* or *over-balances* any moral evil that a person experiences in this life. If we think of an individual's experiencing perfect happiness because he makes a just-good-seeking SFC as the intrinsic good of his retributively *justly* experiencing complete happiness, then the central idea of this section is that a justification for God's permitting a person to experience moral evil is that that person justly experience perfect happiness. Because the just experience of complete happiness is conditional in nature – a person will justly experience complete happiness, *if* he chooses rightly – I will sometimes say that a justification for God's permission of moral evil is the possibility of a person's experiencing perfect happiness.

It is important to underscore at this juncture that while throughout this section I will often talk about God's purpose of granting to *persons* the just experience of perfect happiness, this purpose is a good for each person as an *individual*. Thus, if one thinks of the possibility of experiencing perfect happiness as a good that justifies God's permission of moral evil (which is the kind of evil that will occupy my attention in this section), what justifies God's permitting a particular person P to experience moral evil is God's purpose (good) for P, which is that P experienced perfect happiness.

Why think that the possibility of experiencing perfect happiness is a justifying good for permitting a person to experience moral evil? The following remark by William Rowe provides the rationale for such a belief:

> [I]t is reasonable to believe that the goods for the sake of which [God] permits much intense human suffering are goods that either are or include good experiences of the humans that endure the suffering. I say this because we normally would not regard someone as morally justified in permitting intense, involuntary suffering on the part of another, if that other were not to figure significantly in the good for which that suffering was necessary. We have reason to believe, then, that the goods for the sake of which much human suffering is permitted will include conscious experiences of these humans, conscious experiences that are themselves good. . . . So if such goods do occur we are likely to know them. (Rowe 1986, p. 244)

As I have already pointed out, perfect happiness is a person's greatest possible good because it consists of his endlessly experiencing nothing except what is intrinsically good. In light of the eminently reasonable nature of Rowe's remarks, it is plausible to think that if the possibility of experiencing complete happiness were not at least part of God's justification for permitting moral evil, something would be amiss. In support of this position, suppose the following scenario S obtains: I am a defender who can provide a possible justification (such as either the goodness of libertarian free will itself or the preponderance of morally good over bad actions that it makes possible) that God has for allowing moral evils to be experienced by human beings (persons) with libertarian free will. For all I know, however, there might be some other possible justification of these moral evils. I am now told that all of these possible justifications are compatible with the truth that no persons with libertarian freedom will experience complete happiness,[10] regardless of the kinds of choices they make in this life, even a just-good-seeking SFC.

---

10. Strictly speaking, the existence of only one such person is sufficient for my argument, but for the sake of sim-plicity of presentation, I will assume that no person experiences complete happiness.

Unlike a scenario in which a free will defender such as Plantinga can concede the possibility of God's having, for all he can see, a justification other than libertarian freedom for allowing moral evils, I believe that a defender who is reasonable must maintain it is impossible both that God has a justification for permitting the moral evils that human beings with libertarian free will experience and that none of these persons will experience perfect happiness, regardless of how he has chosen. It is reasonable to think that a defender must deny this possibility because of a belief of his that God's permitting moral evils would be unjustified in such a scenario. And this belief can itself plausibly be thought to be grounded in a defender's knowledge that God's actual justification for creating persons with libertarian free will and allowing them to experience moral evil includes[11] the possibility of their experiencing complete happiness.[12] In short, a defender knows that the possibility of experiencing complete happiness is included in God's justification for permitting moral evils because, like anyone else, he knows that experiencing perfect happiness is a person's greatest good that outweighs any moral evil he might experience. Thus, it seems that a defender must move to being a theodicist, if he is to maintain the impossibility of scenario S.

In the spirit of Plantinga's response to Walls's attempt to move him (Plantinga) from defense to theodicy (see the third section), a defender might say in response to my argument that while he fails to see how S is possible (maybe it is, although he does not see how it is), he does not see that it is impossible. At this point, I can only say that I believe that a *reasonable* defender will maintain that he sees that S is not possible. This is because a reasonable defender believes that God is concerned with bringing about a person's greatest possible good and S describes a situation in which that good is not realized.

Or consider the following suggestion: in an effort to avoid the extreme position of claiming to know nothing about God's justification for allowing moral evils while at the same time avoiding the theodicy I am suggesting, a defender might claim to know something about what God's justifying reasons are not. For example, a defender might confidently state that God's reason for allowing a horrific act of rape is not so that the rapist could experience pleasure from his act. Beyond knowing what some of God's justifying reasons are not, however, a defender is ignorant about what God's justification for permitting moral evils is.[13]

Is this *via negativa* theodicy plausible? Can a defender know what some of God's justifying reasons for permitting moral evils are not without knowing what any of them are? I believe that such a position is suspect. To see why, consider a version of scenario

---

11. I say "includes" and not "is" at this point because my argument so far leaves open the possibility that there are other reasons God has for permitting created persons to experience moral evil. Later in this section, I provide an argument that suggests that the purpose of giving to persons the just experience of complete happiness is God's only justification for allowing them to experience moral evil.

12. There is evidence that Walls is sympathetic with the idea that it is the purpose of granting to persons the just experience of complete happiness that justifies God's allowing persons to experience moral evil. In addressing the issue of hell, he states that "[i]t is because the good [the extraordinary opportunity to live before God in conscious relationship to him] is so wonderful that something as objectively terrible as hell is possible" (Walls 1992a, p. 137). Because the problem of hell is just a logical extension of the problem of evil, if the good of a possible conscious relationship with God (i.e. complete happiness) justifies God's permission of hell, it justifies His allowing human beings to experience moral evil in this life.

13. Michael Bergmann suggested this possible response to me on behalf of a defender.

S: a defender knows what some of God's justifying reasons for allowing moral evils are not and also that any justifying reason He has is compatible with created persons, for reasons that have nothing to do with how they choose, either (1) spending an eternity in hell (for the sake of argument, I assume that hell is a form of existence in which there are significant experiences of pain), (2) spending a finite period of time in hell after which they are annihilated, or (3) being annihilated at death (no afterlife of any kind). On the one hand, if a defender maintains that any justification God has for permitting moral evils is compatible with one or more of these alternatives, then he is a defender, but not a reasonable one. On the other hand, if he maintains that God's justification for allowing moral evils is not compatible with any of these alternatives, then it is plausible to think that this is because he knows that God's justifying reason for permitting moral evils includes the possibility of persons experiencing perfect happiness.

At this juncture, a defender might claim that while it is true that God cannot justifiably permit moral evils under any scenario such as (1), (2), or (3), it does not follow that he knows that God's justification for allowing moral evils is what I have proposed. Consider two versions of such a claim.

First, a defender might claim not to know that God's granting to persons the just experience of complete happiness is the justification for permitting moral evils because it is not clear that the greatest possible good for a person is the experience of complete happiness. After all, it might be the case that the experience by a person of complete happiness is not possible. For example, William Hasker has suggested to me that the experience of complete happiness might not be possible if created persons have a finite capacity for absorbing new experiences such that after a few thousand or million years, the further existence of those persons becomes pointless.

For the reasons that I mentioned in the previous section when discussing Williams's "The Makropulos Case: Reflections on the Tedium of Immortality" (Williams 1973), it seems to me (and, as I will point out in a moment, to several prominent defenders) that the experience of perfect happiness is possible. Even if I am wrong about this, however, it is still plausible to maintain that a defender must become a theodicist. This is because the essence of my argument is as follows: In order not to move from a defense to a theodicy, a defender must refuse to acknowledge the impossibility of a scenario in which there is a possible justification for permitting moral evils and it is the case that no persons with libertarian freedom will experience the greatest possible happiness for them regardless of what kinds of choices they make in this life. In other words, even if the greatest possible happiness for an individual cannot (for some reason) be perfect happiness, then whatever that greatest possible happiness is, a defender can avoid becoming a theodicist only by refusing to acknowledge the impossibility of a scenario S specified in terms of that happiness. I believe this shows that a defender knows that God's justification for permitting moral evils includes the possibility of persons experiencing their greatest possible happiness.

Second,[14] a defender might claim that even if the experience of eternal, complete happiness is the greatest possible happiness for a person, it is not clear that God must grant it

---

14. Michael Bergmann suggested the following argument to me on behalf of a defender.

to created persons who choose rightly by making a just-good-seeking SFC. Perhaps God only need be committed to the purpose of granting to a person who chooses rightly a degree of happiness in the afterlife that makes his life such that on balance it is a good thing. Although it is true that the possibility of justly experiencing perfect happiness is a possible justification for God's permission of moral evils in this life, perhaps the possibility of justly experiencing either a temporally finite complete happiness in the afterlife (where the good experienced in it outweighs the evil experienced in this life) or a temporally unlimited incomplete happiness with a modicum of pain[15] might also be God's justification for allowing moral evils. Thus, because we do not know that the possibility of experiencing eternal, complete happiness is included in God's actual justification, a defender need not become a theodicist.

I believe that this argument, like the first, is inadequate, and for a similar reason. A defender who makes this argument must at least know that the possibility of experiencing a certain degree of happiness is included in God's justification for permitting persons to experience moral evils. To this extent, he is a theodicist. There is, however, a reason for thinking that a defender knows that the possibility of experiencing eternal, perfect happiness is included in God's justification for permitting moral evils. This reason is that eternal, complete happiness is what persons actually desire and they desire this because (as I argued in the previous section) a desire for a temporally finite complete happiness or a temporally infinite but incomplete happiness is conceptually suspect, if not incoherent. If one finds the idea of an experience of happiness desirable, then one cannot fail to desire its eternality and completeness. One must desire that it be unending and complete. Given that it is only the desire for eternal, complete happiness that makes sense and this kind of happiness is possible, then provided a defender believes that God is omnibenevolent (completely morally good) and will fulfill our deepest desire (which He gave us) if we choose rightly, it is reasonable to think that he knows that it is the just experience of this kind of happiness that is God's justification for allowing moral evils.

Up until now, I have spoken about what reasonable defenders would say regarding the idea of perfect happiness. It is now appropriate to examine what some of them actually say about it. Consider what Plantinga says that relates to the issue of complete happiness. In response to the evidential argument from evil, he writes "I also believe in eternal life. The precise contours of this are certainly obscure, but it includes an eternity of bliss for

---

15. Thomas Flint has suggested to me that some persons might well question whether the absence of all pain is possible or desirable for a creature that has sinned. Even in heaven, should not such a creature have some memory of having freely done moral evil? And should not that memory continue to cause it at least some discomfort? Such a memory does not seem to be incompatible with genuine complete happiness, but it is on my account. Would it not be enough for my theodicy to say that complete happiness would involve the kind of bliss that would make pain, if present at all, seem very mild in comparison?

My claim that complete happiness involves the absence of all pain is rooted in the fact that this conception of happiness seems to me to describe the purpose for which I was created. It is without question the kind of existence that I ultimately desire. Even if complete happiness includes memories of having freely done moral evil, it seems to me that they need not cause discomfort (compare how time affects the impact of our memories on us in this life) and that they should not (God's forgiveness requires no suffering by us for our moral wrongs). If readers do not share my point of view about the nature of complete happiness, then they can, as Flint suggests, think of this happiness as a kind of bliss that makes pain, to the extent that it is experienced, mild in comparison.

enormous numbers of God's creatures" (Plantinga 1996b, p. 257).[16] Plantinga writes as a Christian theist, but it is reasonable to maintain that the points he makes relating to complete happiness are part of theism *per se* and not just of Christian theism. This is because the idea of an omniscient, omnibenevolent, and omnipotent being who created persons with the desire to experience complete happiness is at the heart of any reasonable theism, and such a being has the knowledge, moral goodness and power to ensure the satisfaction of that desire (provided that the necessary conditions of its satisfaction are met). Now suppose that Plantinga is told by a fellow defender that it is true that his suggested free will defense is thoroughly reasonable, and that it is possible that libertarian free will (or something else) is God's justification for allowing moral evils and that no persons who have this freedom will experience complete happiness regardless of how they choose. I think Plantinga would respond that his fellow defender is surely mistaken.[17] Provided that he would answer in this way, I believe this indicates that he must become a theodicist who believes that God's justification for allowing the moral evils that human beings experience includes the possibility of their experiencing complete happiness.

William Alston is another defender who comments on the issue of perfect happiness. According to Alston, Christian theism maintains that:

> one's life on earth is only a tiny proportion of one's total life span.... [W]hy suppose that we are entitled to judge that justifying goods, if any, would be realized during the sufferer's earthly life, unless we have specific reasons to the contrary? ... Why is the burden of proof on the suggestion of the realization of the goods in an afterlife? (Alston 1996b, pp. 104, 123, endnote 17)

For present purposes, it is important that Alston believes that the goods of the afterlife include "experiencing complete felicity in the everlasting presence of God" (Alston 1996a, p. 324). According to him, the problem for formulating a theodicy is that these goods of the afterlife belong to the kinds of goods of which we have no experience and only a minimal grasp of their value. Thus, "we are in a bad position to determine whether the magnitude of [complete felicity in the everlasting presence of God] is such as to make it worthwhile for God to permit a certain evil in order to make its realization possible" (Alston 1996a, p. 324).

How would Alston respond to the possible scenario where moral evils experienced by human beings have a justification and it is the case that no person will experience complete happiness even if he makes the requisite just-good-seeking SFC? Given the belief that we

---

16. Although he believes in perfect happiness, Plantinga does not invoke it in his free will defense. Andrew Chignell notes that "[m]any versions of the Free Will approach are not concerned with the problem of God's goodness to *individuals*.... Plantinga is less worried about how all horrors can be defeated in an individual's life than with how the maximal state of affairs that includes these horrors may be the best that can be actualized" (Chignell 1998, p. 213; emphasis in the original). Charles Seymour points out that Plantinga does not mention the afterlife in giving the free will defense and that the silent implication is that libertarian free will is of such value that it outweighs all the evil in the world, even if there were no afterlife to look forward to (Seymour 1997, p. 259).

17. Cf. the following comment of Plantinga's: "[T]he Christian theist will no doubt concur with St. Paul: 'For I reckon that the sufferings we now endure bear no comparison with the splendor, as yet unrevealed, which is in store for us.' (Romans 8:18).... From a Christian point of view, there is immortality and the expectation of a better world...." (Plantinga 1979, pp. 46–7; quoted in Adams 1999, pp. 23–4).

do not have an adequate grasp of the value of complete felicity in God's presence, it seems that he could not rule this out as a possible scenario. If Alston were to deny that it is a possible scenario, however, this would seem to indicate that he knows the value of complete happiness and that he is committed to the theodicy that maintains that God's actual justification for permitting persons to experience moral evils includes the possibility of their experiencing perfect happiness.

In response to my argument, a defender might argue that I have moved too fast. He might maintain that while it is true that any defender would deny that it is possible for God to have a justification for allowing moral evils and it be the case that no person will experience perfect happiness regardless of how he has chosen, it does not follow from this denial that a defender must become a theodicist who knows that God's actual justification for permitting moral evil includes the justification I have proposed. For example, a defender might claim that while the possibility of experiencing perfect happiness is a possible justification for God's permitting moral evil, it is also possible that it is no more than a necessary condition of any other possible justification God has for permitting moral evils. Indeed, Alston might advocate this view. As I noted two paragraphs back, Alston recognizes that experiencing complete happiness might be a good in virtue of which God is justified in permitting moral evils. Yet, he also claims that it might not be a justifying good. Even if it is not, there are other possible justifications (Alston 1996b, pp. 104–10). One other possible justification is the value of soul making: God allows moral evils as a means to the end of developing persons who exhibit moral virtues such as courage, patience, compassion, and so on. Another possible justification is the value of libertarian free will. Still other possible justifications might involve goods that are totally beyond our intellectual grasp. Even if one (or more) of these other possible justifications for allowing moral evils is God's actual justification, Alston seems to believe that a necessary condition of its being such must be that God justly provide persons the experience of complete happiness:

> [A] perfectly good God would not wholly sacrifice the welfare of one of His intelligent creatures simply in order to achieve a good for others, or for Himself. This would be incompatible with His concern for the welfare of each of His creatures. Any plan that God would implement will include provision for each of us having a life that is, on balance, a good thing, and one in which the person reaches the point of being able to see that his life as a whole is a good for him. Or at least, where free creaturely responses have a significant bearing on the overall quality of the person's life, any possible divine plan will have to provide for each of us to have the chance (or perhaps many chances) for such an outcome, if our free responses are of the right sort. (Alston 1996b, p. 111)

Why maintain, like Alston, that the provision that each of us have the opportunity for a life that is, on balance, a good thing (and perfect happiness is such a good) must be a necessary condition of whatever is God's justification for permitting moral evils? The only plausible answer is because the possibility of such a life *is* a justification for permitting moral evils in so far as it makes available to a person a good that outweighs any of his experiences of moral evil. Stated slightly differently and more generally, my point is that it is implausible to think that perfect happiness is no more than a necessary condition of whatever it is that justifies God's permission of moral evil. This is because the reason for thinking that it must be a necessary condition of this justification is that it itself is a *good* for a created person. And the fact that it must be a good for a created person makes one suspicious of the view that it is no more than a necessary condition of God's justification for permitting moral evil.

For purposes of simplicity and continuity, I will assume that what Alston calls "a life that is, on balance, a good thing" is one that ends in perfect happiness and that the possibility of perfect happiness is a justification God has for permitting moral evils. Is, however, the possibility of experiencing complete happiness not only *a* justification for permitting moral evils but also *the* justification? Because an agent might perform an action for more than one reason, I do not know of an argument that shows that the possibility of experiencing perfect happiness is more than just included in God's justification for permitting moral evils. If it is assumed, however, that this justification obtains and that none other does, it seems to be the case that God's permission of moral evils would be justified. For this reason, in what follows, I will assume that the possibility of experiencing perfect happiness is *the* justification for God's permitting moral evils.

Like Alston, Michael Bergmann is a defender who believes that "we have no good reason to oppose the suggestion that the goods we know of are representative of only a minor portion of the goods there are and that many (or even most) of the goods beyond our ken are far greater than and significantly different from any of the goods with which we are familiar" (Bergmann 2001, p. 284). He believes that this point applies to the goods of conscious experience. Thus, he defends the *prima facie* plausibility of the thesis that we have no good reason for thinking that the possible goods we know of that involve conscious human experience are representative of the possible goods that there are that involve conscious human experience. An implication of Bergmann's thesis is that a defender should not become a theodicist who invokes the concept of complete happiness in his theodicy. He should remain a defender.

The development earlier in this section of a version of scenario S where a person, for reasons that have nothing to do with how he chooses, either (1) spends an eternity in hell, (2) spends a finite period of time in hell after which he is annihilated, or (3) is annihilated at death, can be used to make clear the implausibility of Bergmann's position. If a defender such as Bergmann affirms the impossibility of this version of S, it would seem to be because he believes that the evils of this world constitute or are representative of the evil that cannot be included in the final chapter of a person's existence irrespective of how he chooses. If Bergmann believes this, however, what reason might he have for thinking that we have no good reason for believing that complete happiness, which is a good of conscious experience and a person's greatest possible good, is included in God's justification for permitting moral evil? If the evils of this life are representative of what a person who makes a just-good-seeking SFC cannot experience in the last chapter of his existence, why not think that the happiness that we enjoy in this life is representative or a foretaste of the perfect happiness, that will be experienced in the afterlife by those who make just-good-seeking SFCs? Bergmann says "it may be that enjoyment of goods that are very different from those with which we are familiar would lead to conscious experiences that are very different from – and far more enjoyable than – those with which we are familiar" (Bergmann 2001, p. 285). In support of this claim, he asks us to consider someone who has experienced no greater pleasure than the temporary absence of pain:

> Suppose that no one has ever told her of a more pleasant experience and that she cannot even imagine one. That person would be *mistaken* to conclude that the possible positive conscious experiences she is aware of are representative of the possible positive conscious experiences

there are. She would be *unreasonable* to draw such a conclusion for she has no good reason to endorse it. But the same point applies to us. (Bergmann 2001, p. 285; emphases in the original)

But does the very same point apply to us? As Bergmann notes, our actual conscious experience is more positive than the woman's (Bergmann 2001, p. 285). Although he does not explicitly say so, what Bergmann presumably means is that our experience includes experiences of pleasure, where experiencing pleasure is more than the mere absence of pain. Now it is no doubt the case that there are sources of pleasure beyond those known to us. The point that is relevant, however, is that those additional sources are sources of experiences of *pleasure* the concept of which is *not* beyond our ken. Moreover, the experience of complete happiness surely is, in Bergmann's words, "more enjoyable" than the happiness available in this life insofar as it contains no experiences of pain and is more pleasurable. The concept of enjoyment, however, like that of pleasure, is *not* beyond our ken. It seems, then, that all Bergmann does in trying to justify the idea that there may be goods of conscious experience beyond our ken is appeal to the idea of more enjoyable/pleasant experiences than those we experience in this life. This idea itself, however, seems to be nothing other than the idea of perfect happiness for an individual person.

Nevertheless, for the sake of discussion, let us assume that Bergmann is correct: we have no good reason to oppose the idea that there is a good of conscious experience that is greater than the experience of pleasure. Call this good of conscious experience "pleasure+." One can now think of the concept of perfect happiness as that of a person's greatest possible good that includes experiences of either pleasure or pleasure+. My point is this: given our knowledge about perfect happiness, when presented with scenario S, a defender can avoid moving from a defense to the theodicy I have set forth only by unreasonably refusing to acknowledge that S is impossible.

If the possibility of experiencing complete happiness is God's justification for permitting moral evils, what is the nature of the relationship between this justification and the experience of moral evils (pain resulting from morally wrong choices)? It is important to point out that one thing it is not is a *means–end* relationship. In other words, the possibility of experiencing perfect happiness is not a purpose or end to which the experience of moral evils is *intended* by God as a means. What this entails with respect to God's creative action is that the experience of moral evils by persons with libertarian free will is at most *foreseen* and permitted by God, but not intended.

To make clear the distinction between intending an end and merely foreseeing its occurrence, consider the following two stories about bombers. First, there is Terror Bomber. He is trying to ascertain the best way to achieve military victory over Enemy. After considering various alternatives, he concludes that the best way to defeat Enemy is to terrorize Enemy's population by bombing a school that is filled with children. Terror Bomber has some moral scruples about killing innocents but chooses to bomb the school anyway. He believes that by doing so he will promote victory. In virtue of making this choice, Terror Bomber intends to bomb the school and kill children in order to promote victory. His reason for so choosing and intending is that he promote victory.

Second, there is Strategic Bomber. He intends to bomb the munitions plant of Enemy in order to bring about the defeat of Enemy. Strategic Bomber is also aware, however, that next to the munitions plant is a building filled with innocent children. He also believes that when he bombs the plant he will kill the children. While for Terror Bomber killing the children is an intended means to the defeat of Enemy, for Strategic Bomber their deaths are not intended as a means but are foreseen as a side effect of the bombing.

God is like Strategic Bomber when it comes to permitting moral evils. Although He foresees that moral evils might (will) occur as a result of His creating persons with libertarian free will and for the purpose that they justly experience perfect happiness, He does not intend that the moral evils that occur serve as a means to that purpose. Indeed, when all is said and done, those moral evils might very well be pointless in the sense that they do not serve as means to any purpose. Because this is the case, one should beware of wasting one's time by asking of every moral evil why (for what purpose) God has allowed it to happen. One certainly should not routinely interpret a moral evil one experiences as God's means of punishment. While a moral evil might be a divinely intended punishment, it also might be no more than a foreseen but pointless side effect in the divine plan for our just experience of complete happiness.[18] Moreover, while God can bring something good out of a moral evil one experiences (St Paul reminds Christians in his Epistle to the Romans 8:28 that in everything God works for good for those who love Him), one must not confuse the idea of His doing so with that of His intending that one experience that moral evil as a means to the end that one justly experience perfect happiness or any other end.

Because God does not intend that the moral evils He permits serve as means to the end (purpose) of a person's justly experiencing complete happiness, it is not the case that there is a certain amount of moral evil that God may permit in order for Him to accomplish this purpose such that the occurrence of more than that amount of evil would be unjustified.

---

18. Compare van Inwagen's recommendation to students of the problem of evil: "Do not attempt any solution to this problem that entails that every particular evil has a purpose, or that ... God has some special reason for allowing it. Concentrate rather on the problem of what sort of reasons a loving and providential God might have for allowing His creatures to live in a world in which many of the evils that happen to them happen to them for no reason at all. ... Such things are a part of God's design in the sense that the ticking sound made by a clock is a part of the watchmaker's design: not intended, necessitated by what is intended. ..." (van Inwagen 1988, pp. 180, 182; emphasis in the original). What is intended by God for human beings? What is their purpose? According to van Inwagen, "human beings were designed for union with God. ..." (van Inwagen 1988, p. 170). Thus, "[e]very human being has an eternal future ... [w]hen ... there will never again be undeserved suffering or any other sort of evil" (van Inwagen 1988, p. 165).

Michael J. Murray and Glenn Ross agree that not every particular evil has a purpose: "[W]e prefer to cast [a discussion of the problem of evil] in terms of evil types rather than evil tokens. In brief, the reason is that we think that it is consistent with and likely on theism that token evils are pointless. ... [T]he theist should never, in treating the issue of evil, aim to give reasons for token instances of evil. For all we know, there are no such reasons. As a result, the theist should stick to showing why the permission of various types of good are necessary for securing outweighing benefits" (Murray and Ross 2006, p. 187, endnote 6). While I agree with Murray's and Ross's main point that token instances of evil might very well be pointless in the sense that they are not intended by God as means to ends, I do not think that this point entails that the theist should stick to God's permission of *types* of good when thinking about the justification for His permission of moral evil. If my theodicy is correct, the justifying good is a token of a type: it is *a particular individual's* possibility of experiencing perfect happiness, which justifies *his* experience of moral evil.

And given that created persons have libertarian free will, it is also the case that they might have chosen in ways that would have produced (much) less moral evil than that produced by the choices that they have actually made (e.g. more people might have made just-good-seeking SFCs).

In light of the fact that God does not intend that moral evil serve as a means to the good that justifies His allowance of moral evil and this has the implication just noted for the amount of moral evil that He may justifiably allow, it is helpful to consider the following objection raised by the defender Daniel Howard-Snyder against *any* proposed justifying good of which we are aware (Howard-Snyder 1996a, pp. 289f). According to this objection, for any justifying good of which we are cognizant, we cannot see how it would fail to be realized if God permitted a lot less horrific moral evil (examples here might be the Stalinist purges and the Holocaust). As applied to the justifying good that I am proposing, this objection can be posed in the form of a question: would not the possibility of experiencing perfect happiness have been achievable, if God had permitted a lot less horrific moral evil? Because we cannot see how this purpose would fail to be realized if God were to permit a lot less horrific moral evil, there is inscrutable moral evil; that is, there is moral evil for which we cannot see the justification.

In response to this objection, it is true to say that we cannot see how the possibility of experiencing perfect happiness would fail to be realized if there were a lot less horrific moral evil. The reason, however, that we cannot see how this great good would fail to be realized with a lot less horrific moral evil is that we actually see that the possibility of experiencing complete happiness would have been achieved with a lot less horrific moral evil. And we actually see this because, given that created persons have libertarian free will, they might have chosen differently than they did and produced significantly less moral evil. It is also possible that they might have chosen differently than they did and produced significantly more moral evil. Either way, we see that the moral evil produced would be justifiably permitted by God's purpose of granting to created persons the just experience of perfect happiness. Indeed, given that created persons have libertarian free will, the granting of which is itself justified by this purpose, we see that *any* amount of moral evil would also be justified by this purpose.[19] Thus, contrary to what Howard-Snyder claims, there is no

---

19. What if God has middle knowledge? Might it not, then, be the case that something roughly like the following is true: God is considering creating a world that includes persons who make just-good-seeking SFCs so as to experience perfect happiness. In addition, God is aware of two worlds, W and W*, each of which contains persons A, B, and C who make just-good-seeking SFCs. Moreover, W and W* are identical in all relevant respects except that in W, A, B, and C experience less moral evil than in W*. Is God not morally obligated to create W?

If God has middle knowledge, then my point is as follows: *whatever* the amount of moral evil is in W, God's permission of it is justified by the purpose that created persons justly experience perfect happiness. Thus, even if the amounts of moral evil in both W* and W had been greater and God created W because it contained less moral evil than W*, God's allowance of moral evil in W would still have been justified by the purpose that created persons have the possibility of experiencing perfect happiness. Moreover, while it is no doubt true, as Plantinga says, that although "we can imagine or in some sense conceive of worlds in which the only things that exist are persons always in excruciating pain" (Plantinga 2004, p. 6), no such world is possible "if God, as we are assuming, is a necessary being who has essentially such properties as unlimited goodness . . . ." (Plantinga 2004, p. 6).

inscrutable moral evil. There is no moral evil that God has actually permitted for which we do not know the justification.[20]

If the theodicy I am suggesting is correct, then God's granting to a person the experience of complete happiness is justly conditioned upon that individual exercising his libertarian free will in the right way (making a just-good-seeking SFC). What a critic might ask now is why, given the vast array of possible persons, did God create those who have libertarian free will, if such freedom is not itself a justifying good? Why did God not create from the array of possible persons those who do not have libertarian free will and who, thereby, always act deterministically but from the first moment of their existence and continuously thereafter experience nothing but the great good of complete happiness?

It is important to make two points in answering this question. First, it is doubtful that merely possible beings are entities to which God has an obligation to bring into existence. As Robert Adams has said, "A merely possible being cannot be (actually) wronged or treated unkindly. A being who never exists is not wronged by not being created, and there is no obligation to any possible being to bring it into existence" (Adams 1992, p. 277).

Second, the critic seems to assume that the intrinsic goodness of an experience such as perfect happiness imposes no constraints upon the one who chooses to give it as to whom it might be given. This assumption is itself questionable. For a created person who is self-conscious and aware of himself as a potential recipient of what is for him his greatest good, namely, the intrinsic good of complete happiness, it is necessary for purposes of justice that the giver of this possible good provide him with the libertarian freedom to make a just-good-seeking SFC. In other words, because complete happiness is such a great good, the experience of it must be deserved, and while being self-conscious is a necessary condition of its being deserved, it is not sufficient. What are needed for desert are the existence of libertarian freedom and the making of a choice about a life plan in the form of either a just- or an unjust-good-seeking SFC. W. D. Ross expressed this point about desert as follows:

> If we compare two imaginary states of the universe, alike in the total amounts of virtue and vice and of pleasure and pain present in the two, but in one of which the virtuous were all happy and the vicious miserable, while in the other the virtuous were miserable and the vicious happy, very few people would hesitate to say that the first was a much better state of the universe than the second. It would seem then that . . . we must recognize as a[n] . . . independent good, the apportionment of pleasure and pain to the virtuous and the vicious respectively. (Ross 1930, p. 138; cf. Lemos 1994, pp. 40–5)

---

20. There is evidence that Howard-Snyder implicitly recognizes the purpose of perfect happiness as I have described it for theodicy. For example, he states that "[t]he theist's hypothesis and its implications provide me and many others with a great source of comfort. . . ." (Howard-Snyder 1996a, p. 294). I do not think it is misguided to speculate that the great source of comfort to which Howard-Snyder refers is the great good of perfect happiness that he believes he will ultimately experience for choosing rightly. Dan Cohn-Sherbok (Cohn-Sherbok 1990) argues that without otherworldly reward, there is simply no way to make sense out of particular moral evil such as the Holocaust as part of a world that is the creation of an all-good and all-powerful God. Cohn-Sherbok's understanding of reward includes the idea of the experience of perfect happiness or, in his words, "the realm of eternal bliss" (Cohn-Sherbok 1990, p. 289).

At this juncture, it is helpful to explore a bit more the necessary conditions of making a choice about a life plan in the form of either a just- or an unjust-good-seeking SFC. Upon reflection, it is clear that a choice of a life plan requires a world of goods that are its (the choice's) subject matter. These goods, which in our world include material objects that are instruments of pleasure, must have natures whose properties are what I will call "iffy" or conditional in character, where a property that is conditional in nature is a property that is specified in terms such that if such-and-such is done to object O (e.g. a cause C is exerted on O), then so-and-so will occur to O. In terms of our experiences of pleasure, the goods of this world must be stable objects of the kind which are such that if such-and-such is done to or with them, then so-and-so will result so as to produce pleasure. Consider sugar as a simple, first example of a material object with an iffy nature. It is a material substance whose nature makes it such that if a healthy person ingests it, it will taste sweet and produce an experience of pleasure. Another example of objects with iffy natures is that of the human sexual organs. Men and women who choose to fulfill their sexual appetites do so with the assumption that stimulation of their sexual organs will yield experiences of pleasure and, provided they did not use birth control and their reproductive systems are functioning properly, offspring. Or consider a tyrant who solidifies his power and promotes his pleasure through stealth and brutality. He must rely on the nature of his weapons that are such that if he wields them, they will produce death and destruction.[21]

The iffy nature of material goods of our world helps provide an answer to the following questions that arise out of a consideration of moral evil. Why, it is sometimes asked, does not God intervene in the material world of objects with iffy natures to prevent moral evil? For example, why does not God cause the gun of the murderer to jam when the latter pulls the trigger? Or why does not God cause the knife in the hand of the would-be robber to turn to rubber? Or why does not God cause the tongue of the would-be slanderer to become limp when the latter goes to speak?

While God is certainly able (has the power) to intervene in the material world to perform the actions in question, regular intervention of this kind is not consistent with the purpose of our existence in this world, which is that we make a just- or unjust-good-seeking SFC that is either deserving of or not deserving of perfect happiness. In the world as conceived by the objector, a human being would quickly learn that his choice of a way of life (a life plan) would count for nothing because he could never perform the actions that flowed from that choice. What point would there be, then, in choosing a life plan? Every time he went to perform an action that ensued from an unjust-good-seeking SFC, God would intervene to prevent the occurrence of moral evil. Moreover, as Lewis points out, "if the [objector's] principle were carried out to its logical conclusion, evil thoughts [and, I would add, unjust-good-seeking SFCs] would be impossible, for the cerebral matter

---

21. It is relevant to note that David Chalmers provides an "iffy" characterization of microscopic, theoretical entities: "Basic particles . . . are largely characterized in terms of their propensity to interact with other particles. Their mass and charge is specified, to be sure, but all that a specification of mass ultimately comes to is a propensity to be accelerated in certain ways [moved at certain rates] by forces, and so on. . . . Reference to the proton is fixed as the thing that causes interactions of a certain kind that combines in certain ways with other entities, and so on . . ." (Chalmers 1996, p. 153). And the Nobel physicist Richard Feynman says, scientific questions are "questions that you can put this way: 'if I do this, what will happen?' . . . And so the question 'If I do it what will happen?' is a typically scientific question" (Feynman 1998, pp. 16, 45).

which we use in thinking would refuse its task [because of God's intervention] when we attempted to frame them" (Lewis 1962, p. 33). In short, if God were to intervene to eliminate the pain and suffering that result from unjust libertarian choices, He would end up eliminating the choices themselves.

At this point, an objector might insist that he never meant to suggest that God, if He exists, would frustrate every unjust choice by tampering with our brains or turning every knife into butter. Such a policy on God's part would undermine the entire objective order of events involving material objects with their iffy natures. Rather, God would intervene only some of the time and thereby reduce the *quantity* of moral evil. In other words, it is not the mere existence of moral evil that results from our choices that is problematic for God's existence. It is the amount of such evil. Surely, if God existed we would find much less moral evil in this world than we do.

The problem with this argument is that for all we know God already does the very thing that the objector says He should do. Sometimes He does interfere with human choice and prevents moral evil. For example, if God has answered even one prayer to protect the innocent from an aggressor by, say, altering the latter's thoughts and (thereby) his action, then He has done what the objector suggests. In the end, it seems as if there is no way to answer the present argument to the objector's satisfaction because it essentially has nothing to do with the actual amount of moral evil in the world. For any quantity X of moral evil, it will always be possible to say that God, if He existed, would have intervened to permit only X − 1 instances of such evil. If X were to equal 1, the objector would want to know why God did not eliminate moral evil altogether. And the same point can be made with respect to what some might think of as the *quality* or kind of moral evil that results from free choices (the quality of a moral evil is the pain and suffering that result from a *kind* of action an agent chooses to perform). For example, the objector might ask, 'Would not God have intervened to stop the mad choices of Hitler and/or Stalin and their equally demented minions to send millions of people to the concentration camps and the forced-labor camps of the Gulag?' Once again, for all we know, God did intervene to stop choices that would have resulted in actions to commit worse kinds of atrocities than Auschwitz, Buchanwald, Dachau, and the Gulag. Our failure to be aware that He did does not amount to an awareness that he did not. Furthermore, the logical problem with the objector's suggestion is that one kind of moral evil is "over the top" only in relation to another kind that is typical or normal. Thus, unless God eliminates every kind of moral evil by getting rid of such evil altogether (or somehow allows only one kind), there will always be some kinds which God could and should eliminate because they are worse than others. Thus, if God were to have prevented Hitler and Stalin from carrying out their kinds of madness, then the objector would bring forth some other type of moral evil as evidence that God does not exist.

If what I have argued so far in this and the previous section of this chapter is correct, the idea of a moral or virtuous choice is fundamentally that of making a just-good-seeking SFC. Among other things, the making of this kind of SFC implies that its subject (assuming the person is a theist) will express gratitude to God for his experiences of pleasure in this life and the possibility of his experiencing perfect happiness in the future. Thus, an implication of my proposed theodicy is that while we must take our experiences of moral evil with utmost seriousness, we err if we neglect to take our possible experience of perfect happiness with the same degree of seriousness. Adams points out that in the Judeo-Christian tradition, a person who worships God is typically not encouraged to praise Him for His moral rectitude and good judgment for creating him. Rather, he is encouraged to express gratitude to God for his existence (Adams 1992, pp. 275–8). I believe that what explains this encouragement of gratitude to God by a created person for his existence are the created person's present experiences of pleasure and, if he chooses rightly, his future experience of the great good of perfect happiness. The libertarian freedom to choose rightly (make a just-good-seeking SFC), however, entails the freedom to choose wrongly (make an unjust-good-seeking SFC). Thus, in order for God to have acted *justly* in choosing to provide created self-conscious creatures with the possible experience of the intrinsic good of complete happiness, He had to allow for the possibility of moral evil.

Ultimately, then, giving created persons libertarian free will is itself a necessary condition of the possibility of experiencing the intrinsic goodness of perfect happiness. As Rowe has rightly pointed out, "the free-will theodicy needs to be included within . . . a theodicy that stresses some intrinsic goods for which free will is a necessary condition" (Rowe 1996, p. 285). In addition, however, the intrinsic good of justice introduces constraints on choices not only for those self-conscious creatures who are provided the possible experience of perfect happiness,[22] but also for the self-conscious Creator who provides that opportunity for the experience of that happiness. Because God must act justly, He must provide self-conscious creatures who are the potential recipients of perfect happiness with the libertarian freedom that makes possible the choice that makes His granting of that happiness just.

Rowe is an atheist who has argued that we have reason to believe that God does not exist in light of the occurrence of certain moral evils. For example, he asks us to consider the case of a 5-year-old girl being viciously beaten, raped, and, finally, strangled by her mother's boyfriend (Rowe 1988, pp. 119–22). He notes that the girl's experiencing complete felicity in the eternal presence of God does apparently outweigh the moral evil that she suffers. Indeed, he states that it apparently outweighs almost *any* horrendous moral evil that may befall her in her earthly life (Rowe 1996, p. 277). Rowe believes it strains credulity, however, to think that it is beyond the power of God to realize this great good without having to permit the girl's being brutally beaten, raped, and murdered.

Two points are in order here. First, while I agree with Rowe that complete felicity in the eternal presence of God outweighs any[23] moral evil experienced in this life, I have not maintained that God's justification for allowing moral evil is simply the experience of perfect happiness. Rather, it is the possibility of experiencing perfect happiness. The fact that God's justification for permitting moral evil is the possibility of experiencing perfect happiness helps to answer an additional point raised by Rowe in another context. While he defends the view (as was pointed out earlier in this section) that a justificatory good

---

22. Seymour says that "we cannot embrace the . . . extreme of rejecting free choice altogether as an important good . . . , for if eternal happiness is the only good God is concerned to actualize, one could ask . . . why God does not create everyone in heaven. . . ." (Seymour 1997, p. 260). According to the theodicy I am proposing, eternal happiness is not the only intrinsic good, but this fact does not require that free choice also be an intrinsic good. Justice in the form of justly experiencing perfect happiness is the other intrinsic good and free choice is a necessary condition of achieving it. It is because of the existence of the intrinsic good of justice that God does not create everyone in heaven. He cannot create everyone in heaven without acting unjustly.

23. I have removed Rowe's qualification of "almost" from "almost any."

must include good, conscious experiences of those who suffer, Rowe also maintains that "[i]n the absence of any reason to think that [God] would need to postpone these good experiences, we have reason to expect that many of these goods would occur in the world we know" (Rowe 1986, p. 245). Given what I have argued so far in this section, the answer to Rowe's point is that it is because not just any person deserves to experience perfect happiness that it is reasonable to think that it must be delayed to another life. In order to determine who does and who does not deserve to be completely happy, God gives a period of time (e.g. this life) wherein a person is free to make a choice that serves as the basis of justly granting or denying to him the experience of perfect happiness.[24]

Second, given that moral evils are not a means to the purpose (end) that justifies permitting them, it does not strain credulity to think that God would have to permit the moral evils experienced by the girl in virtue of this justifying good. God has to permit their occurrence in virtue of this justifying good in so far as He has created persons with libertarian free will who are free to choose wrongly and produce moral evils. Moreover, given that God's purpose is to grant the just experience of complete happiness to persons and that the girl presumably did not live long enough to be justly granted or denied complete happiness, it is reasonable to hypothesize that she will somehow be granted this opportunity, perhaps in another life.[25]

Creating persons with libertarian free will is justified by the fact that if individuals exercise it rightly, they will experience the intrinsic good of complete happiness. Having the freedom to choose rightly, however, entails having the freedom to choose wrongly and produce moral evil. We can see, then, why it is necessary for God to permit moral evil even though the experience of that moral evil is not a means to the purpose of giving to persons the just experience of complete happiness. God must permit moral evils in order to achieve the purpose for which He created persons with libertarian free will. Some of the evils that humans suffer, however, do not appear to be explained by the exercise of human libertarian free will. For example, natural events such as earthquakes and tornadoes are evils in virtue

24. It is interesting to note at this point that Rowe maintains concerning any instance s_1 of intense suffering that "[p]erhaps preventing s_1 would preclude certain actions prescribed by the principles of justice. I shall allow that the satisfaction of certain principles of justice may be a good that outweighs the evil of s_1" (Rowe 1990, p. 128, footnote 3). The disagreement, then, between Rowe and me comes down to whether or not it is unjust to bestow the great good of perfect happiness on someone regardless of either what kind of good-seeking SFC that person has made or whether that person has made any good-seeking SFC at all. Because the good of perfect happiness is so great, there would be a problem of justice if making the right kind of good-seeking SFC were not a necessary condition of experiencing perfect happiness.

25. Chignell (1998, p. 216) notes that infants like those who are brutally murdered in Dostoyevsky's *The Brothers Karamazov* are perhaps reincarnated, if they fail to satisfy a necessary condition for union with God. Concerning the idea of reincarnation, Nathan Nobis says "we need to find a greater good that could 'balance out' [a] tortured infant's suffering and death. . . . It seems that there could be a balancing-off good for the infant in this case only if . . . the infant *herself* benefits from these events. . . . [T]he death by torture has to be a *necessary* component of the greater good, otherwise the torture is gratuitous" (Nobis 2001, p. 106; emphases in the original). On my theodicy, an infant's torture is neither a means to nor a component of the good end – the just experience of perfect happiness – that justifies God's permission of it. It need not be either of these because a justification for permitting moral evil need not be means–end in nature. According to the theodicy I am proposing, it is also the case that a tortured infant cannot be translated immediately to heaven where it is conscious of itself as a recipient of perfect happiness that is intrinsically good. It must somehow be given the opportunity to make a just- or an unjust-good-seeking SFC.

of the pain and suffering they produce, but they are not traceable by us to wrong human choices as their ultimate source. Is it possible to be a theodicist with respect to such evils (call them "natural evils")?

Although natural evils do not appear to us to be moral in nature, perhaps they are. Perhaps some of them are caused by human choices, even though we are not able to discern how they are. The present debate in the public square about whether or not human activity is responsible for global warming and the disturbances in weather that go with it should make us all too aware that many individuals are receptive to the idea that natural evils can be ultimately moral in nature. Perhaps the choices of nonhuman beings (e.g. fallen angels) with libertarian free will and the desire for complete happiness are ultimately responsible for some occurrences of natural evil. As Plantinga points out, the mere fact that this idea is unpopular at present with some is perhaps an interesting sociological fact but hardly relevant to the argument from evil (Plantinga 1974, pp. 58–62), and the idea is surely no more bizarre than the suggestion by Crick that life on our earth originally came from that of other intelligent beings in other planetary systems (Crick 1981). Or, perhaps the events that produce natural evils inevitably occur just as a part of nature, and what happened is that human persons lost an ability to protect themselves from these events when the first humans sinned (made an unjust-good-seeking SFC) (van Inwagen 1988, pp. 168–71; cf. Lewis 1962, chap. 5). Even in this last scenario, what do not appear to be moral evils are. What is clear is that we simply do not know what the ontological status of natural evils is because we do not know what their ultimate explanation is. As a defender would rightly say in this context, the explanation of natural evils is a matter that is beyond our intellectual purview.

While the ultimate explanation of natural evils that do not appear to be moral in nature is a matter that is beyond our epistemic wherewithal, the justification for God's permitting them is not. Regardless of whether or not natural evils are ultimately moral in nature, the theodicy I have set forth maintains that their permission is justified by the possibility of our experiencing perfect happiness. This is the justification of natural evils for the same reason that it is the justification of moral evils. Because experiencing perfect happiness is a person's greatest good and as such decisively outweighs any evil, moral or natural, that he might experience, the possibility of experiencing it is God's justification for permitting him to experience that evil.

If natural evils are ultimately moral in nature, then we not only understand *what* their justification is but also *how* that justification explains their permission, because we understand how the possibility of experiencing perfect happiness requires giving created persons libertarian free will whose wrong exercise produces moral evil. If natural evils are ultimately not moral in nature, then while we know what the justification for permitting them is, we do not presently understand (we fail to be aware of) how that justification explains their permission. Thus, what makes natural evils different from moral evils is not that we are ignorant about what justifies God's permission of the former, whereas we know what justifies His permission of the latter, but that we are ignorant about how that justification explains the permission of the former.

In closing this section, it is relevant to note that a proponent of the problem of evil might argue that if God did exist, we would now understand whether natural evils are ultimately moral or not moral in nature and, if the latter, how the possibility of experiencing complete happiness explains their permission. Our ignorance regarding these matters is itself an instance of evil that does not appear to be moral in nature. Surely, this ignorance is itself an instance of unjustified evil.

I cannot see any good reason to believe that we would now understand the matters that the proponent of the argument claims we would understand, if God exists. While it is plausible to believe that we know what God's justification for permitting our experience of evil is, given that knowledge about these matters is not required for knowledge of this justification, our ignorance about these issues is not surprising. As defenders are wont to point out, if theism is true, one would expect that God's knowledge would dwarf that of created persons. Ignorance about many things is part and parcel of being a created person.

Adams and Horrendous Evil

If the argument of the preceding section is correct, a defender must become a theodicist. Marilyn Adams is a theodicist who has recently maintained that the free will defense is inadequate because it defends God's goodness as a producer of libertarian free will, which in her terms is a "global" or "generic" good, to the neglect of the good of individual persons (Adams 1999, chap. 2). She believes that if God were to create for this purpose alone, He would at best be indifferent to individual persons and at worst cruel. In the spirit of the justification for permitting evils developed in the fifth section of this chapter, Adams believes that an adequate theodicy of God's goodness must take into consideration the good of persons as individuals. As she understands the issue of justification, there are two ways in which God might justify permitting evil that is experienced by a person.

First, God might ensure that the good in an individual's life balances off the evil in his life: "The balancing-off relation is arithmetical and additive: value-parts are balanced off within a larger whole if other parts of opposite value equal or outweigh them" (Adams 1999, p. 21). Adams claims that the problem with this theodical approach is that some individuals' lives are afflicted with horrendous evils, where a horrendous evil is one "the participation in which constitutes prima facie reason to doubt whether the participant's life could ... be a great good to him/her on the whole. ... [H]orrendous evils seem prima facie, not only to balance off but to engulf any positive value in the participant's life. ..." (Adams 1999, p. 26). Examples of horrendous evils include:

> the rape of a woman and axing off of her arms, psycho-physical torture whose ultimate goal is the disintegration of personality, betrayal of one's deepest loyalties, child abuse of the sort described by Ivan Karamazov, child pornography, parental incest, slow death by starvation, the explosion of nuclear bombs over populated areas. ... [W]hat makes horrendous evils so pernicious is their life-ruining potential, their power prima facie to degrade the individual by devouring the possibility of positive personal meaning in one swift gulp. (Adams 1999, pp. 26–8)

To present an adequate defense against horrendous evils, Adams claims that a theist must invoke a second form of justification which, following Roderick Chisholm, she terms "the defeat of evil" (Adams 1999, p. 21).[26] Evil is defeated by good in an individual's life when it is integrated into the whole of his life by means of a nonadditive relation or what

---

26. Chisholm's discussion of the idea of the defeat of evil is found in Chisholm (1990).

G. E. Moore called an "organic unity" (Moore 1968, pp. 27–36). With an organic unity, not only may the whole have a different value than a part but also a negatively (or positively) valued part can contribute to a great overall positive (or negative) value in the whole. Insofar as defeated horrendous evils make a positive contribution to the overall good of an individual's life by being integrated in this way, they provide that life with a unity and harmony that it would otherwise lack. To help clarify the idea of the defeat of horrendous evil, Adams appeals to aesthetic examples:

> Aesthetic examples illustrate this principle – for example, in Monet's study of Rouen cathedral in early morning, the ugliness of the bilious green color patches is defeated by their integration into the vast beauty of the artistic design. Obviously, if the value-parts were networked to the whole possible world only by additive relations, it would be impossible that the best of all possible worlds should contain evils. (Adams 1999, p. 21)

Adams maintains that in order for God to justify permitting a person to suffer horrendous evils, He must defeat them by weaving them into a life that is overall worth living (Adams 1999, p. 168). They must be defeated in this way because otherwise they would engulf an individual's life and defeat it by making it a life not worth living as a whole. Adams claims that there are different aesthetic scenarios under which horrendous evils are defeated. One scenario is where the sufferer has a vision of God that has enough aesthetic value to defeat its correlated horror. Another scenario is where the sufferer by means of his sufferings identifies with Christ's suffering, most notably his crucifixion. On this second scenario, the fact that God became incarnate in Christ enables a sufferer to identify with Christ's participation in horrific evils so that a positive aspect is conferred on the sufferer's experience of such evils ensuring their defeat (Adams 1999, chap. 8).

While Adams maintains that horrendous evils must be defeated, she believes that they must also be overbalanced by the experience of complete happiness in the afterlife if God's permission of them is justified: "Divine goodness to created persons includes an eventual and permanent over balance of concrete well-being" (Adams 1999, p. 158). In light of her conviction that divine goodness will not allow anyone to suffer eternal damnation because that would entail an ultimate and decisive defeat of good by evil in an individual's life (Adams 1999, p. 41), it follows that not only would horrendous evils remain unjustified if it were not possible for an individual to experience complete happiness but also that they would remain unjustified if an individual were not guaranteed the experience of such happiness. Thus, Adams says that:

> [i]f postmortem, the individual is ushered into a relation of beatific intimacy with God and comes to recognize how past participation in horrors is thus defeated, and if his/her concrete well-being is guaranteed forever afterward so that concrete ills are balanced off, then God will have been good to that individual despite participation in horrors. (Adams 1999, p. 168)

According to my theodicy, all evils, moral and natural (assuming that there are natural evils that are ultimately not moral in nature), horrendous and nonhorrendous, have the possibility of being decisively overbalanced or outweighed by perfect happiness, but in order to be outweighed in this way they must first be defeated. On my view, the defeat of evil is accomplished through justice, where justice is understood as the organic unity in which those who make a just-good-seeking SFC experience perfect happiness and those who make an unjust-good-seeking SFC do not experience it.[27] In the fourth section, I said that choosing rightly included choosing a way of life in which one seeks to avoid situations that are likely to produce temptation. One's best-laid plans sometimes fail, however, and when one is tempted and chooses wrongly, the defeat of evil is accomplished (as part of one's chosen way of life) through the expression of sorrow (the asking for forgiveness) for what one has done. Moral evils that are suffered by oneself at the hands of others are defeated (again, as part of one's chosen way of life) by not returning evil for evil, but instead by overcoming evil with good (cf. Romans 12:17, 21). If there are natural evils that are not ultimately moral in nature, then to the extent that they can be overcome by good (e.g. virtuous responses to victims of an earthquake or tidal wave), they too can be defeated. Most generally, on my theodicy, any evil we suffer at the hands of either moral agents other than ourselves or nature, insofar as it can be responded to in a virtuous manner, can be defeated.

Like me, Adams recognizes the need for a decisive overbalance or outweighing of evil by good. Her theodicy, however, ultimately excludes the just defeat of evil by good. On Adams's view, every person must ultimately experience perfect happiness, regardless of how he chooses. Thus, she maintains that in order to prevent a person's never experiencing complete happiness (hell), God will causally determine a person's will so that he chooses rightly. As she puts it, "I flatter the Creator with enormous resourcefulness to enable human agency ... to recognize and appropriate positive meanings sufficient to defeat its own participation in horrors. If this should mean God's causally determining some things to prevent everlasting ruin, I see this as no more an insult to our dignity than a mother's changing a baby's diaper is to a baby" (Adams 1999, p. 157). According to my theodicy, God's causally determining an individual's will to ensure the enjoyment of complete happiness would itself be unjust and amount to the defeat of good by evil because it would violate the idea that perfect happiness must be experienced justly. The matter of what a person's choosing wrongly (making an unjust-good-seeking SFC) implies about the duration of his failure to experience perfect happiness (the duration of his stay in hell) is a topic that is beyond the scope of this chapter. A few comments, however, are in order.

To begin, I can see nothing incoherent in the idea that a created person who has made an unjust-good-seeking SFC never reverses course. Because hell (whatever it is like) contains evil and no one can choose what is evil for its own sake, no one can choose to go to hell for the sake of the evil that it contains. What a person can do, however, is choose to pursue what is intrinsically good in a way that casts the restraint that is a prerequisite for experiencing perfect happiness to the winds (again, see the example of Augustine in the fourth section) and which, when all is said and done, results in his justly being excluded from heaven (justly denied the experience of perfect happiness) and confined to hell. Such a choice is an unjust-good-seeking SFC.

---

27. Chisholm (1990, p. 61) gives as an example of the defeat of good by evil the state of affairs where a wicked man experiences pleasure and good men do not (they need not experience displeasure, although presumably they might). Ross claims that the following is the one clear case of an organic unity: "Few people would hesitate to say that a state of affairs in which A is good and happy and B bad and unhappy is better than one in which A is good and unhappy and B bad and happy. ... The surplus value of the first whole arises not from the value of its elements but from the co-presence of goodness and happiness in one single person, and of badness and unhappiness in another." (Ross 1930, p. 72)

But how could eternal separation from God be just? The answer to this question depends upon how one thinks of retributive justice in this context. Consider, for example, the principle of an eye for an eye and a tooth for a tooth (*lex talionis* or literally "law of the claw") found in Deuteronomy 19:21. As Adams has pointed out, some who accept this principle look for an immoral deed or deeds performed in this life for which the just punishment is hell (Adams 1975). They think of the issue of retributive justice in terms of proportionality and wonder what human act or acts deserve hell as a proportionate punishment. To illustrate the idea that they have in mind, consider a man named "Smith" who makes another individual named "Jones" unhappy for every moment of the latter's 70-year life, and that Jones never "gets even" with Smith who lives out his years with more than his fair share of happiness. On the "eye for an eye" principle, God should make Smith unhappy to the same degree and for as long as Jones was unhappy, which was for 70 years. Suppose now that Smith not only made Jones unhappy for 70 years but also made a million other people unhappy for various lengths of time. On the "eye for an eye" principle as presently construed, God should sum up the years of unhappiness caused by Smith and make him unhappy to the same degree as everyone else and for the same cumulative amount of time.

It is fairly easy to construct other examples like the ones just mentioned involving Smith (Adams does just this in Adams 1975) and I will leave it to the reader to consider other examples like those I have just set forth. If we stick with my examples involving Smith, then thinking of retributive justice in the way suggested implies that no matter how much unhappiness Smith causes others, that unhappiness will always be finite in amount and Smith will deserve to be unhappy for only a finite period of time. Thus, there seems to be no way to make sense out of the idea of someone's going to hell for a potentially infinite or unending period of time if the justification for going is thought of in terms of the "eye for an eye" principle.

Perhaps, however, the issue at this point is not with the "eye for an eye" principle *per se* but with how it is being construed. Perhaps we should stop thinking of it too literally. For example, while eyes and feet are sources of pleasure and pain, it is highly doubtful that the amount of pleasure and pain that one person gets from his intact eyes and feet equals the amount of pleasure and pain that another gets from his. Hence, it seems as if there is no way of guaranteeing that a guilty person who unjustly causes the loss of an eye or a foot in someone else will by the loss of his own eye or foot be deprived of the same amount of pleasure and suffer the same amount of pain as his victim. It is perhaps for this and other reasons that biblical scholars believe the Israelites did not in general literally employ the "eye for an eye" principle as a form of retributive justice but instead intended it as an expression of the idea that punishment should be commensurate with the harm that is unjustly caused.[28] Perhaps the idea of punishment being expressed in the "eye for an eye" principle is that there are outer limits of retributive justice that might be meted out to a guilty party and that excessive punishment is itself unjust.

What, then, about hell? Is there any interpretation of the "eye for an eye" principle that makes intelligible the idea of a person spending a potentially infinite future in hell? I believe that there is and that it is a function of the freedom of the will and the choice of a life plan.

---

28. Rick Hess has pointed out to me in correspondence the virtual absence of examples in the Hebrew Bible of applications of the "eye for an eye" principle. The only kind of case in which it seems to have been literally enforced involved "life for life," where the most famous invocation of the principle is the prophet Nathan's parable and subsequent indictment of David for the incident with Bathsheba and the killing of Uriah, although even in this case it was not literally carried out.

In simplest terms, retributive justice in this context is the idea of a separation of persons on the basis of their choices about life plans into two separate camps or modes of existence, where this separation leaves both parties permanently isolated from each other to do as they please. Heaven (the domain of perfect happiness) is occupied by those who have made a just-good-seeking SFC and hell is inhabited by those who have made an unjust-good-seeking SFC. Thus, heaven and hell are ultimately about how a person chooses to live his life in pursuit of what is intrinsically good. Will an individual choose a life of restraint and deference to others who are created by God for the purpose of experiencing perfect happiness? Or will he insist on pursuing what is good on his own terms, which means without restraint and at the expense of the well-being of others? It is a not uncommon experience in life that those who make an unjust-good-seeking SFC and reject the exercise of restraint in pursuit of what is good want to have nothing to do with those who make a just-good-seeking SFC, because the latter insist upon exercising restraint in their pursuit of what is good. The former also want nothing to do with God in this life, and for the same reason. Given that the former cannot be perfectly happy in the presence of the latter and God in this life, they couldn't be perfectly happy in the presence of the latter and God in the afterlife. Thus, God will justly give the former their wish to be left alone to live with others according to the unjust-good-seeking SFC that has informed each of their lives in this world. As the *Catechism of the Catholic Church* states, hell is the "state of definitive self-exclusion from communion with God and the blessed" (*Catechism of the Catholic Church* 1995, sec. 1033). No one makes this point about self-exclusion better than Lewis:

> Either the day must come when joy prevails and all the makers of misery are no longer able to infect it: or else for ever and ever the makers of misery can destroy in others the happiness they reject for themselves. (Lewis 2001, p. 136)
>
> [T]he damned are, in one sense, successful, rebels to the end; that the doors of hell are locked on the *inside*. . . . In the long run the answer to all those who object to the doctrine of hell, is itself a question: 'What are you asking God to do?' To wipe out their past sins and, at all costs, to given them a fresh start, smoothing every difficulty and offering every miraculous help? But He has done so, on Calvary. To forgive them? They will not be forgiven. To leave them alone? Alas, I am afraid that is what He does. (Lewis 1962, pp. 127–8)

There are, then, in the end only two kinds of people: "those who say to God, 'Thy will be done,' and those to whom God says, in the end, '*Thy* will be done'" (Lewis 2001, p. 75; emphasis in the original). In the end, certain people go to hell and remain there because they choose to pursue what is good on their own terms and to have nothing to do with others who insisted on pursuing it on other terms. What is the case is that in order to experience complete happiness, a person must (freely) choose rightly. He must make a just-good-seeking SFC. Only then can evil ultimately be defeated by good because an experience of what is a person's greatest good must be had only by those who deserve it. It is this point that Adams overlooks in her theodicy.

Plantinga's "*O Felix Culpa*" Theodicy

After maintaining for some time that theodicies struck him "as tepid, shallow, and ultimately frivolous" (Plantinga 1996a, p 70), Plantinga has recently had a change of mind and embraced a theodicy in which God's justification for allowing created persons to experience evil is that the great goods of incarnation and atonement be instantiated (Plantinga 2004). He is careful to make clear that atonement, which presupposes incarnation, is a matter of created persons being saved from the consequences of their sin (morally wrong choices). Thus, if there were no moral evil and the pain and suffering that come with it, there could and would be no atonement. Moral evil and pain and suffering are necessary conditions of atonement, and because God wanted to create a world with a certain level of goodness, and every world with that or a greater level of goodness contains incarnation and atonement, our world includes evil.

Plantinga considers various objections to his theodicy. In light of the theodicy developed in the fifth section of this paper, it is most helpful to consider Plantinga's response to what he terms the "Munchausen syndrome by proxy." The Munchausen syndrome captures the idea of parents who mistreat or abuse their children for the purpose that they (the parents) act virtuously and save their children from their mistreatment and abuse. Does not Plantinga's theodicy describe a divine parent who mistreats His children by creating them for the purpose that they choose immorally and experience pain and suffering so that He can then virtuously become incarnate and atone for their moral wrongdoing? Would God really play around with a created person's well-being in this way for the sake of creating a world with the great goods of incarnation and atonement? Is this theodicy not a proxy of the Munchausen syndrome?

In answer to the Munchausen-syndrome-by-proxy objection, Plantinga maintains that a necessary condition of God's justification for allowing evil is that the final condition of created persons be a good one, although that final good is not part of the justification for His allowing evil. Although not part of this justification, it is the case that the final condition of created persons in a world that includes the goods of incarnation and atonement "is better than it is in the worlds in which there is no fall into sin but also no incarnation and redemption" (Plantinga 2004, p. 25). The idea seems to be that God is not morally blameworthy for creating persons for the purpose that the goods of incarnation and atonement be realized, so long as the stated necessary condition of His so doing (that the final condition of created persons be a good one) is fulfilled.

What might one say about Plantinga's theodicy? Early on in his essay, he asks "[W]hat are good-making qualities among worlds – what sort of features will make one world better than another" (Plantinga 2004, p. 6)? Plantinga's first words in response are "Here one thinks . . . of creaturely happiness. . . ." (Plantinga 2004, p. 6). This is a perfectly natural response. Why, however, does one think of this? Although Plantinga does not answer this question, he does state that "Suffering is an intrinsically bad thing" (Plantinga 2004, p. 15). If it is, it only stands to reason that happiness is an intrinsically good thing, and because God knows that it is and He is perfectly good and loving, He creates persons for the purpose that they experience this great good. Thus, as Plantinga says, while "we can imagine or in some sense conceive of worlds in which the only things that exist are persons always in excruciating pain" (Plantinga 2004, p. 6), no such world is possible "if God, as we are assuming, is a necessary being who has essentially such properties as unlimited goodness . . ." (Plantinga 2004, p. 6).

Given that God, because of His essential properties, cannot create conceivable worlds in which creatures are always in excruciating pain, and given that it is natural to think of creaturely happiness when one thinks of good-making features of a world, it is no surprise that Plantinga maintains that any world with incarnation and atonement will include the experience of a final good condition (or at least the possibility of the experience of such a good condition) for created persons. Plantinga claims, however, not only that a world with incarnation and atonement will include a final good condition for created persons, but also, as was already quoted, that this condition "is better than it is in worlds in which there is no fall into sin but also no incarnation and redemption" (Plantinga 2004, p. 25). What justifies this claim? Intuitively, an earthly life that includes only happiness and runs seamlessly into perfect happiness in the afterlife is on the whole better than one that includes Earthly pain and suffering and ends with perfect happiness in the afterlife. Plantinga, however, is favorably disposed toward the idea that it is by suffering that we can achieve an intimacy with God ("enjoying solidarity with [Christ]"; Plantinga 2004, p. 18) that cannot be achieved in any other way. Perhaps, then, he believes that his claim about worlds with incarnation, atonement, sin and suffering being better in terms of their final good condition for created persons than ones without incarnation, atonement, sin, and suffering is justified by the idea that sin and suffering make possible a level or kind of happiness (enjoyment) that cannot be experienced without them.

If this is Plantinga's reasoning, it is less than persuasive. After all, atheists and theists alike find it quite easy to conceive of a world in which created persons have perfect happiness without the preparatory work of sin and suffering. Indeed, it is because such a world seems better than one in which created persons experience this happiness but do sin and suffer that the problem of evil presents the intellectual challenge that it does. Moreover, if one turns to scripture for possible insight into the problem of evil, something which Plantinga is not averse to doing, one can easily come away from reading the story about the garden of Eden (as many down through the ages have done) with the impression that Adam and Eve had ongoing access to the tree of life (continued happiness and no pain and suffering), access that would not have been lost had they not eaten of the tree of the knowledge of good and evil. In short, while one can agree with Plantinga that a world with incarnation, atonement, sin and suffering includes the possibility of a final and exceedingly great, good condition for created persons (i.e. perfect happiness), there seemingly is no reason to think that these things are a necessary means to the achievement of this exceedingly great, good condition.

Finally, what about Plantinga's claim that, while it is a necessary condition of a world that includes incarnation and atonement that it also include (the possibility of) a final good condition for human beings, this necessary condition is not part of God's justification (reason) for permitting evil? In the fifth section, I stated that it was hard to see how the possibility of experiencing perfect happiness could be a necessary condition of God's justification for allowing evil, without being (at least a part of) that justification. Has Plantinga shown us a way in which this is possible?

I doubt it. To see why, consider what Plantinga says about the relationship between incarnation, atonement, sin, and suffering.

> The priority [of incarnation and atonement over sin and suffering] isn't temporal, and isn't exactly logical either; it is a matter, rather, of ultimate aim as opposed to proximate aim. God's ultimate aim, here, is to create a world of a certain level of value. That aim requires that he aim to create a world in which there is incarnation and atonement – which, in turn, requires that there be sin and evil. (Plantinga 2004, p. 12)

In other words, while sin and suffering are a *conceptually* necessary condition of incarnation and atonement in the sense that atonement just is salvation from the consequences of sin ("if there were no evil, there would be no sin, no consequences of sin to be saved from"; Plantinga 2004, p.12), in the order of explanation, God's ultimate purpose that the goods of incarnation and atonement be instantiated explains the subsidiary purpose that sin and suffering be allowed. Now the (possible) achievement of a final good condition for created persons is also a necessary condition of creating a world that includes incarnation and atonement. Why, however, is the former a necessary condition of the latter? Plantinga would have us believe that it is because God is essentially perfectly good and loving and, therefore, must provide a final, good existence for persons in every world that He creates, but it is not because the idea of a final, good existence for created persons is conceptually related to the idea of incarnation and atonement. Is it not the case, however, that just as atonement conceptually presupposes sin (and the suffering that it causes) because it by definition is salvation from that sin (and suffering), so also atonement conceptually presupposes the idea of a final, good condition for created persons because it is by definition *for that good*? In other words, is it not the case that just as "atonement is among other things a matter of creatures being saved from the consequences of their sin" (Plantinga 2004, p. 12), so also atonement is first and foremost a matter of creatures being saved *for the final good end* for which they were created? Moreover, is it not the case that in terms of ultimate and proximate aims, which is a matter concerning the order of explanation, God's ultimate justification for allowing libertarian free will and moral evil, namely, that created persons have the possibility of experiencing perfect happiness, also explains the proximate or subsidiary aim that the great goods of incarnation and atonement be realized?

The intuitively plausible answer to these questions is "Yes." Why so? Although we are, to use a favorite expression of Plantinga's, in deep waters here, it seems reasonable to think that the purpose that incarnation and atonement be realized is a subsidiary purpose in relation to God's ultimate purpose for allowing libertarian free will and moral evil because God will do what is necessary as a means to achieve this ultimate purpose. If acting justly is a conceptually necessary condition of achieving that purpose, as I suggested is the case in the fifth section, then perhaps incarnation and atonement are a function of God's acting justly and, thereby, are necessary as means to accomplishing that purpose. Perhaps acting justly itself requires that God submit Himself to what he submits His creatures to, namely, pain and suffering. If this is the case, then God must become incarnate. Or, if we follow a traditional Protestant understanding of the atonement, God atones for our sins by vicariously suffering the punishment due to us because the demands of justice must be satisfied (Aulén 1969, pp. 128–33). In the end, by according the possibility of experiencing perfect happiness primary place as God's justification for allowing evil, we are able to provide a more adequate conceptual integration than Plantinga does of the concepts of perfect happiness, incarnation and atonement, and sin (moral evil).

Beasts and the Problem of Evil

Finally, what about the beasts that it seems also experience pain? What is God's justification for permitting them to experience evil? With regard to this issue, it is reasonable for the theist to be a defender and answer these questions with "I do not know," because the matter is one that lies outside our cognitive purview. One thing that is important to understand is *why* it is beyond our ken. The explanation for this ignorance has to do with our lack of knowledge of both a beast's nature and the purpose for which a beast exists. Consider the problem of evil as it relates to created persons. In general terms, the theodicy proposed and defended in the fifth section identifies God's justification for permitting a person to experience evil with this individual's purpose for existing, where knowledge of this purpose requires awareness of a person's nature and what is intrinsically good. Given our knowledge that a person is an entity whose nature includes libertarian free will and a desire for perfect happiness, where this happiness is intrinsically good, it is possible to know what God's justification for permitting created persons to experience evil is. When it comes to beasts, we lack knowledge of their purpose for existing because we lack adequate knowledge of their natures. We simply do not know enough about their psychological makeups and what the structures, if any, of their wills is like.

It is important to stress at this point that being a defender with regard to the sufferings of beasts does not require that one deny that they experience pain. As Michael J. Murray and Glenn Ross have recently pointed out, a defender can consistently embrace the following principle (I will dub it 'SA') concerning the sufferings of animals:

> SA: Some non-human creatures have states that have intrinsic phenomenal qualities analogous to those possessed by humans when they are in states of pain. These creatures lack, however, any higher order states of being aware of themselves as being in first-order states. They have no access to the fact that they are having a particular feeling, though they are indeed having it. Since phenomenal properties of states of pain and other sensory states are intrinsic to the states themselves, there is no difference on this score between humans and other creatures. (Murray & Ross 2006, p. 176)

As Murray and Ross note, one might object to SA by arguing that there is moral disvalue in a world that contains experiences of pain, even where the subjects of those experiences do not possess the relevant higher order states of awareness of themselves as in those first-order states. "Access to these states, the critic might contend, is irrelevant to whether it is bad to be in the state itself. Clearly, if a state is intrinsically bad, it is not made better merely in virtue of the fact that the creature does not know about it" (Murray & Ross 2006, p. 176). Murray and Ross rightly respond that a defender of SA need not deny that the pain experienced by a beast is intrinsically evil. What is crucial for this response is the distinction between kinds of evils. In particular, it is important to distinguish between a metaphysical (nonmoral), intrinsic evil such as pain and a moral evil such as unjustly allowing a sentient creature to experience a metaphysical, intrinsic evil such as pain. The truth of SA helps bring to light that there is nothing morally unjust about allowing a beast that is not self-conscious and is unable to represent itself as experiencing pain to experience such a quale and its intrinsic, metaphysical evilness. If we use the terms of thought from Thomas Nagel's "What is it like to be a bat?" (Nagel 1979, pp. 165–80), then it is because a beast lacks higher-order access to its own first-order experiences of pains that "there is simply no victim, no subject for whom it can be said that there is a way it is like for it to be in such a state of pain" (Murray & Ross 2006, p. 177).

In light of this discussion of SA, consider Rowe's example of a fawn:

> Suppose in some distant forest lightning strikes a dead tree, resulting in a forest fire. In the fire a fawn is trapped, horribly burned, and lies in terrible agony for several days before death relieves its suffering. So far as we can see, the fawn's intense suffering is pointless. For there does not appear to be any greater good such that the prevention of the fawn's suffering would require either the loss of that good or the occurrence of an evil equally bad or worse. Nor does

there seem to be any equally bad or worse evil so connected to the fawn's suffering that it would have had to occur had the fawn's suffering been prevented. . . . An omnipotent, omniscient being could have easily prevented the fawn from being horribly burned, or, given the burning, could have spared the fawn the intense suffering by quickly ending its life, rather than allowing the fawn to lie in terrible agony for several days. Since the fawn's intense suffering was preventable and, so far as we can see, pointless, doesn't it appear . . . that there do exist instances of intense suffering which an omnipotent, omniscient being could have prevented without thereby losing some greater good or permitting some evil equally bad or worse? (Rowe 1990, pp. 129–30)

How can Rowe reasonably conclude, as he does, from the fawn's suffering that we are justified in believing that God's permission of that suffering is unjustified on the grounds that we cannot see what the point of its suffering is (Rowe 1990, pp. 127–32)? After all is said and done, does any one of us have adequate knowledge of a fawn's psychology? Does any one of us know whether a fawn is self-aware and in possession of a concept of itself as a persisting entity that remains self-identical through time? Does any one of us know that a fawn desires the experience of perfect happiness for itself like a person desires this experience for himself? Does any one of us know whether or not a fawn's existence ends with its death?[29]

I think it is reasonable to hold that if some beasts are like us in terms of being self-conscious and desirous of perfect happiness, then the justification for allowing them to experience evil is the same as that which justifies allowing us to experience evil. But I also believe that if we are honest it is correct to say that, while we might believe some things about a beast's psychology (e.g. that beasts experience qualia such as pain and pleasure just as we do), we must admit that none of us knows the answers to the kinds of questions posed in the previous paragraph. But if we do not, then how can the claim that the fawn's suffering appears unjustified (on the grounds that we cannot see any justification for permitting its occurrence) itself be justified? Is it not the case that the fawn's suffering as such neither appears justified nor unjustified because we simply do not know what a fawn's nature and purpose for existing are? Is it not the case that considered by itself, the fawn's suffering appears to be suffering, and that is it, the issue of whether its suffering is justified or unjustified being beyond our ken? With regard to instances of suffering of beasts, is it not reasonable to be a defender? It would certainly appear so.[30]

References

Adams, M. M. (1975) Hell and the God of justice. *Religious Studies* 11, 433–47.

Adams, M. M. (1999) *Horrendous Evils and the Goodness of God*. Ithaca, NY: Cornell University Press.

Adams, R. M. (1992) Must God create the best? In M. Peterson (ed.), *The Problem of Evil: Selected Readings*, 275–288. Notre Dame, IN: University of Notre Dame Press.

29. Philip L. Quinn has recently advocated the following for solving the problem of evil for at least some beasts: "I would . . . adopt the assumption that an afterlife is possible for at least some nonhuman animals. An afterlife for chickens? Well, why not?" (Quinn 2001, p. 398)

30. Thanks to Michael Bergmann, Andrei Buckareff, Douglas Geivett, William Hasker, and Nathan Nobis for reading earlier drafts of this paper and making several helpful comments. I owe a special debt of gratitude to Thomas Flint for numerous suggestions about the content of the paper.

Alston, W. (1996a) Some (temporarily) final thoughts on evidential arguments from evil. In D. Howard-Snyder (ed.), *The Evidential Argument from Evil*, 311–32. Bloomington: Indiana University Press.

Alston, W. (1996b) The inductive argument from evil and the human cognitive condition. In D. Howard-Snyder (ed.), *The Evidential Argument from Evil*, 97–125. Bloomington: Indiana University Press.

Armstrong, D. (1978) Naturalism, materialism, and first philosophy. *Philosophia* 8, 261–76.

Augustine. (1961) *Confessions*. Trans. R. S. Pine-Coffin. New York: Penguin Books.

Augustine. (1993) *The City of God*. Trans. M. Dods. New York: The Modern Library.

Aulén, G. (1969) *Christus Victor*. New York: Macmillan Publishing Co.

Baier, K. (2000) The meaning of life. In E. D. Klemke (ed.), *The Meaning of Life*, 2nd edn., 101–32. Oxford: Oxford University Press.

Bergmann, M. (2001) Skeptical theism and Rowe's new evidential argument from evil. *Nous* 35, 278–96.

Catechism of the Catholic Church (1995) New York: Image/Doubleday.

Chalmers, D. (1996) *The Conscious Mind: In Search of a Fundamental Theory*. New York: Oxford University Press.

Chignell, A. (1998) The problem of infant suffering. *Religious Studies* 34, 205–17.

Chisholm, R. (1990) The defeat of good and evil. In M. M. Adams and R. M. Adams (eds.), *The Problem of Evil*, 53–68. Oxford: Oxford University Press.

Cohn-Sherbok, D. (1990) Jewish faith and the Holocaust. *Religious Studies* 26, 277–93.

Crick, F. (1981) *Life Itself: Its Origin and Nature*. New York: Simon and Schuster.

Crick, F. (1994) *The Astonishing Hypothesis: The Scientific Search for the Soul*. New York: Charles Scribner's Sons.

Dennett, D. (1984) *Elbow Room: The Varieties of Free Will Worth Wanting*. Cambridge, MA: MIT Press.

Dennett, D. (2003) *Freedom Evolves*. New York: Viking.

Edwards, P. (2000) The meaning and value of life. In E. D. Klemke (ed.), *The Meaning of Life*, 2nd edn., 133–52. Oxford: Oxford University Press.

Farrer, A. (1973) *The End of Man*. London: SPCK.

Feynman, R. (1998) *The Meaning of It All*. Reading, MA: Perseus Books.

Fischer, J. M. (1994) Why immortality is not so bad. *International Journal of Philosophical Studies* 2, 257–70.

Flanagan, O. (1996) *Self Expressions: Mind, Morals, and the Meaning of Life*. Oxford: Oxford University Press.

Flanagan, O. (2002) *The Problem of the Soul*. New York: Basic Books.

Goetz, S. (2005) Substance dualism. In J. Green and S. L. Palmer (eds.), *In Search of the Soul*, 33–68. Downers Grove, IL: InterVarsity Press.

Goetz, S. and Taliaferro, C. (2008a) *Naturalism*. Grand Rapids, MI: William B. Eerdmans Publishing Co.

Goetz, S. and Taliaferro, C. (2008b) The prospect of Christian materialism. *Christian Scholars Review*, 37, 303–21.

Howard-Snyder, D. (1996a) The argument from inscrutable evil. In D. Howard-Snyder (ed.), *The Evidential Argument from Evil*, 286–310. Bloomington: Indiana University Press.

van Inwagen, P. (1988) The magnitude, duration, and distribution of evil: a theodicy. *Philosophical Topics* 16, 161–88.

van Inwagen, P. (2006) *The Problem of Evil*. Oxford: Clarendon Press.

Kane, R. (1996) *The Significance of Free Will*. Oxford: Oxford University Press.

Kant, I. (1963) *Lectures on Ethics*. Trans. L. Infield. New York: Harper Torchbooks.

Kim, J. (2005) *Physicalism, or Something Near Enough*. Princeton, NJ: Princeton University Press.

Lemos, N. M. (1994) *Intrinsic Value*. Cambridge: Cambridge University Press.

Lewis, C. S. (1962) *The Problem of Pain.* New York: MacMillan.

Lewis, C. S. (2001) *The Great Divorce.* New York: Harper Collins.

Lewis, C. S. (2004) *The Collected Letters of C. S. Lewis,* vol. II. Ed. W. Hooper. New York: Harper San Francisco.

Lyons, W. (2001) *Matters of the Mind.* New York: Routledge.

MacIntyre, A. (1981) *After Virtue.* Notre Dame, IN: University of Notre Dame Press.

Mackie, J. L. (1990) Evil and omnipotence. In M. M. Adams and R. M. Adams (eds.), *The Problem of Evil,* 25–37. Oxford: Oxford University Press.

Metz, T. (2003) The immortality requirement for life's meaning. *Ratio* 6, 161–77.

Moore, G. E. (1968) *Principia Ethica.* Cambridge: Cambridge University Press.

Murray, M. J. and Ross, G. (2006) Neo-Cartesianism and the problem of animal suffering. *Faith and Philosophy* 23, 169–90.

Nagel, T. (1979) *Mortal Questions.* Cambridge: Cambridge University Press.

Nagel, T. (2000) The absurd. In E. D. Klemke (ed.), *The Meaning of Life,* 2nd edn., 176–85. Oxford: Oxford University Press.

Nielsen, K. (2000) Death and the meaning of life. In E. D. Klemke (ed.), *The Meaning of Life,* 2nd edn., 153–59. Oxford: Oxford University Press.

Nobis, N. (2001) "Balancing out" infant torture and death: a reply to Chignell. *Religious Studies* 37, 103–8.

Plantinga, A. (1974) *God Freedom and Evil.* Grand Rapids, MI: William B. Eerdmans Publishing Co.

Plantinga, A. (1979) The probabilistic argument from evil. *Philosophical Studies* 35, 1–53.

Plantinga, A. (1992) Ad walls. In M. L. Peterson (ed.), *The Problem of Evil: Selected Readings,* 335–8. Notre Dame, IN: University of Notre Dame Press.

Plantinga, A. (1996a) Epistemic probability and evil. In D. Howard-Snyder (ed.), *The Evidential Argument from Evil,* 69–96. Bloomington: Indiana University Press.

Plantinga, A. (1996b) On being evidentially challenged. In D. Howard-Snyder (ed.), *The Evidential Argument from Evil,* 244–61. Bloomington: Indiana University Press.

Plantinga, A. (2004) Supralapsarianism, or 'O felix culpa' In P. van Inwagen (ed.), *Christian Faith and the Problem of Evil,* 1–25. Grand Rapids, MI: William B. Eerdmans Publishing Co.

Quinn, P. L. (2001) Review of Richard Swinburne's *Providence and the Problem of Evil. Faith and Philosophy* 18, 394–8.

Ross, W. D. (1930) *The Right and the Good.* Oxford: Clarendon Press.

Rowe, W. (1986) The empirical argument from evil. In R. Audi and W. J. Wainwright (eds.), *Rationality, Religious Belief, and Moral Commitment,* 227–47. Ithaca, NY: Cornell University Press.

Rowe, W. (1988) Evil and theodicy. *Philosophical Topics* 16, 119–32.

Rowe, W. (1990) The problem of evil and some varieties of atheism. In M. M. Adams and R. M. Adams (eds.), 126–37. *The Problem of Evil.* Oxford: Oxford University Press.

Rowe, W. (1996) The evidential argument from evil: a second look. In D. Howard-Snyder (ed.), *The Evidential Argument from Evil,* 262–85. Bloomington: Indiana University Press.

Searle, J. (1984) *Minds, Brains and Science.* Cambridge, MA: Harvard University Press.

Searle, J. (1992) *The Rediscovery of the Mind.* Cambridge, MA: MIT Press.

Seymour, C. (1997) On choosing hell. *Religious Studies* 33, 249–66.

Stump, E. (1985) The problem of evil. *Faith and Philosophy* 2, 392–423.

Talbott, T. (2001) Freedom, damnation, and the power to sin with impunity. *Religious Studies* 37, 417–34.

Walls, J. (1992a) *Hell: The Logic of Damnation.* Notre Dame, IN: University of Notre Dame Press.

Walls, J. (1992b) Why Plantinga must move from defense to theodicy. In M. Peterson (ed.), *The Problem of Evil: Selected Readings,* 331–4. Notre Dame, IN: University of Notre Dame Press.

Walls, J. (2002) *Heaven: The Logic of Eternal Joy.* Oxford: Oxford University Press.

West, T. G. and West, G. S. (1998) *Four Texts on Socrates, Plato and Aristophanes*, rev edn. Ithaca, NY: Cornell University Press.

Williams, B. (1973) The Makropulos case: reflections on the tedium of immortality. In B. Williams (ed.), *Problems of the Self*, 82–100. Cambridge: Cambridge University Press.

Wykstra, S. (1990) The Humean obstacle to evidential arguments from suffering: on avoiding the evils of 'appearance'. In M. M. Adams and R. M. Adams (eds.), 138–60. *The Problem of Evil*. Oxford: Oxford University Press.

9

The Argument from Religious Experience[1]

KAI-MAN KWAN

One of the main concerns of natural theology is whether there are rational arguments for the existence of God. The argument from religious experience (ARE) contends that given the appropriate premises, we can derive from the religious experiences (REs) of humankind a significant degree of epistemic justification for the existence of God. In this chapter, I will defend the ARE, but I have no intention to argue that only a particular theistic tradition (such as Christianity) is correct here. My strategy will focus on a subclass of RE, the experiences of God or theistic experience (TE), and argue that TEs provide significant justification for the belief in God. I do not claim that it is a conclusive argument, but I think it is a reasonable argument that can contribute to the cumulative case for the existence of God.

Some clarification of terms is needed. By an *RE*, I mean an experience that the subject takes to be an experience of God, or some supernatural being or state of affairs. (By "God" I roughly mean the supremely powerful, all-loving, and personal Ground of Being.) Such an experience is *veridical* if what the subject took to be the object of his experience actually existed, was present, and caused him to have that experience in an appropriate way.[2] The claim that "S has an experience of God" does not entail "God exists." So the fact that REs have happened does not prejudge the issue of the existence of God.

The Experiential Roots of Religion

God is not just a hypothesis for the religiously devoted. He is a Living Reality who permeates all their lives. REs sometimes convey such a heightened sense of reality that the conviction they instill transforms the lives of the experients. Furthermore, REs are often world

---

1. I have used a significant part of my essay published in *Philosophy Compass* in this chapter (Kwan, 2006b). I am grateful for the permission given to me by the journal to do that.
2. The last phrase is added to safeguard against the so-called deviant causal chains. This condition is hard to specify in details. The same problem occurs for the explication of the concept of veridical sensory perception (see Grice in Dancy 1988, chap. III). It should also be noted that this is offered as a sufficient condition for veridicality, and this may not be identical to its necessary condition.

transforming as well – just contemplate the immense impact of people such as Moses, St. Paul, Augustine, Wilberforce, and others on Western civilization. Let me follow with some concrete cases of RE.

Cases of TE

Case 1. The story of Christiana Tsai: queen of the dark chamber

Christiana Tsai was a Chinese lady who was born into a traditional Chinese society in the nineteenth century. She came from a Chinese family that was antagonistic toward Christianity, but she was converted after such an experience: one day she was playing in the backyard, and she noticed a stone that looked very smooth on the surface. She turned it over by a stick and discovered that there was a big lizard and many bugs under the stone. Suddenly, she heard a voice in her heart: "You are just like this stone, looking beautiful from the outside but full of evil inside!" She knelt down and prayed to God for forgiveness. Immediately, she found peace and felt that the burden of sin on her was lifted. Since then, the world appeared to her as the Lord's beautiful garden. She found a source of love in her heart, and felt that even the inanimate objects in the surroundings were singing praise to the Creator with her.

She shared the gospel with friends and relatives and many were converted as well. However, her mother was very resistant and was addicted to opium. One night, her mother had a vision of Jesus appearing in front of her in His glory. After that, her mother was also converted and found it easy to quit opium altogether. One time, Tsai was struggling over a decision concerning her relationship with her boyfriend. Suddenly, she seemed to see Jesus in Gethsemane. She was filled with the Holy Spirit. She felt the pain of Christ and knew that Christ could also understand her pain. She decided to let go of that relationship. Since then, she felt that the love of the Lord had never left her, and her communion with Him became sweeter and sweeter. However, the most severe trial was still to come.

One day a strange disease suddenly started to inflict immense sufferings on her. Even light would make her feel like being stabbed by a knife. For many days she just could not eat, move, speak, or open her eyes. Doctors said she would die soon. However, she saw a vision of a beautiful crown rising up to heaven one night, but a voice told her it was not yet the time. Then she started to recover. To cut the story short, although she survived the sickness, she had to stay in the dark chamber for the next 24 years, and tremendous pain still visited her. However, through such a long period and in darkness, she continued to feel strongly the love of God and the illumination of His light. She continued to have communion with God, and her life did show a kind of peace and joy that were almost palpable for her visitors. Many of them would say they could see God in her life.[3]

Case 2. Experience of Chinese Christians under persecution

Since the Communists have taken hold of China, many Chinese Christians were cruelly persecuted, but many of them courageously held on to their faith even though, sometimes, just a verbal denial of faith would easily secure their release. One believer said, "I am a

3. This story is told in Tsai (1953), and my account is extracted from the Chinese version of this book (Tsai 2000).

prisoner but my spirit cannot be imprisoned. I can freely have communion with the Lord from time to time. . . . Although my hands are handcuffed, and my body feels indescribable pain, my heart is still filled with peace and joy" (Xi 1990, p. 4). He was only released after 20 years in the labor camp, but he continued to experience the presence of God and His abundant grace (Xi 1990, p. 8). Another believer was arrested and brought before the crowd to receive criticisms. He felt like he was near the end of his life but suddenly he had a vision of Jesus bearing the cross and walking on the road to Calvary. Immediately, he felt a kind of relief all over his body, and all fear was driven out of his heart. He was then able to face the fierce crowd calmly (Xi 1990, p. 54). Many similar stories were told in the same book.

Case 3. Sheila's experience

"'The One, losing nothing from itself, overflows'. . . . I simply saw that it was so . . . The only bodily symptoms were tears of joy. . . . It seemed for a moment as though I stood 'in the great hand of God'. . . . Any distinction of subject and object, active and passive, noun and verb was lost. . . . That it was not an hallucination is, however, the most abiding conviction that I have" (quoted in Wall 1995, p. 47).

Case 4. Mark's experience

This experience lasted over 9 months: "The experience included a sublime consciousness of a personalized sustaining power which defies description. I recall wondering whether I had found God or had God found me. I was infinitely more concerned with and aware of people and my environment. Mental perception and originality of thought were heightened. Living reached undreamed of levels of sheer joy. . . . I was at first surprised to discover little correlation between my experience and the Church's beliefs and behaviour" (quoted in Wall 1995, p. 50).

Case 5. Simone Weil's experience

"In moment of intense suffering, when I was forcing myself to feel love, but without desiring to give a name to that love, I felt, without in any way prepared for it (for I had never read the mystical writers) a presence more personal, more certain, more real than that of any human being, though inaccessible to the senses and the imagination." Weil remarks: "I had never foreseen the possibility of that, of a real contact, person to person, here below, between a human being and God. I had vaguely heard tell of things of this kind, but I had never believed in them" (quoted in Layman 2007, p. 42).

Case 6. Angelique's experience

Angelique is a psychiatrist. She writes, "as far back as I can remember I 'knew' of the existence of God. Whatever gradually developing sense I had of myself as an entity was accompanied by a sense of someone other, invisible and infinitely greater than any other 'person' and different from them, a kind of all-powerful, pervasive force within the world but far from being impersonal was loving and beneficent with a real interest in me. . . . I never used any word for this person- after all I never needed to- but other people's use of the word 'God' or 'Creator' seemed to fit pretty well. I never saw or heard anything that I recall but the knowledge was as certain as the knowledge that other people continued to exist when they left the room . . . my parents were both agnostic and anti-church. I don't remember religion ever being a topic of conversation at home. Apart from a few flirtations with Sunday School I did not attend church until at 13 years old" (quoted in Wall 1995, p. 77).

Angelique claims that the experiences "have the quality of being not only self-authenticating but being the ground or standard by which everything else in my subjective experience can be, and is judged. This phenomenon itself is not unknown in abnormal states of delusion and hallucination," which "invariably leads to progressive mental deterioration, pain, and eventually psychological and social disintegration, whereas the only objective test of spiritual experiences is that they show fruit in enhanced sensitivity and maturity, and lead to growth in all areas of the personality" (Wall 1995, p. 78).

Case 7. A completely surprising RE

"The experience itself is very difficult to describe. It took me completely by surprise. I was about to start shaving at the time, of all things. I felt that my soul was literally physically shifted-for quite a number of seconds, perhaps 15 to 20 from the dark into the light. I saw my life, suddenly, as forming a pattern and felt that I had, suddenly, become acquainted with myself again . . . I must stress here that prior to this experience I used never to use the words such as 'soul' or 'salvation' or any such 'religiously coloured' words. But in order to make even the slightest sense of what happened to me I find it imperative to use them" (quoted in Hay 1994, p. 21).

Case 8. Experience of design

"My mind suddenly started thinking about the beauty around me, and I considered the marvelous order and timing of the growth of each flower, herb and the abundance of all the visible growth going on around, I remember thinking 'Here is mind'. . . . For a few moments I really did feel at one with the Universe or the Creative Power we recognize. . . . I must have been confronted with the source of all being" (quoted in Hay 1994, p. 23).

The ARE in the Twentieth Century

Earlier defenders of RE included both theologians and philosophers, for example, Farmer, Frank, Waterhouse, and Knudson. Some of them claimed that REs provide immediate knowledge of God, which was *self-authenticating*. However, philosophers tended to be critical of such claims (C. B. Martin, chap. 5; Flew 1966, chap. 6). Keith Yandell (1993, chap. 8), himself a defender of RE, was highly critical of this notion. No matter if these criticisms were cogent or not, they were influential and accounted for the rise of a form of ARE that did not rely on claims to self-authentication.

C. D. Broad anticipated the contemporary ARE:

> The practical postulate which we go upon everywhere else is to treat cognitive claims as veridical unless there be some positive reason to think them delusive. This, after all, is our only guarantee for believing that ordinary sense-perception is veridical. We cannot *prove* that what people agree in perceiving really exists independently of them; but we do always assume that ordinary waking sense-perception is veridical unless we can produce some positive ground for

thinking that it is delusive in any given case. I think it would be inconsistent to treat the experiences of religious mystics on different principles. So far as they agree they should be provisionally accepted as veridical unless there be some positive ground for thinking that they are not. (Broad 1953, p. 197)

From the fifties to the seventies, able defenders of RE include A. C. Ewing, John Hick, H. D. Lewis, Elton Trueblood, John Baillie, Rem Edwards, and H. P. Owen. However, at that time, verificationism, roughly the doctrine that only in principle verifiable sentences were cognitively meaningful, was still influential, and hence even the meaningfulness of religious language was in doubt. The situation by now is very different. First, verificationism is effectively dead. Second, starting from the end of 1970s, a number of analytic philosophers had produced increasingly sophisticated defenses of RE. Richard Swinburne (1979, chap. 13) defended RE via his Principle of Credulity (PC), which said that it was rational to treat our experiences (including RE) as innocent until proven guilty. In other words, REs were treated as *prima facie* evidence for the existence of God until there were reasons for doubting them. This attracted a lot of attention in philosophy of religion. There were of course many critics (e.g. William Rowe, Michael Martin), but Swinburne had also inspired the support of quite a few professional philosophers (e.g. Gary Gutting).

Many books were written on RE that basically followed Swinburne's line of reasoning: Davis (1989), Wall (1995), and Gellman (1997). Other philosophers (e.g. Wainwright and Yandell) also worked independently toward a similar conclusion. One landmark of this debate is William Alston's *Perceiving God* (1991), which skillfully defended a doxastic-practice approach to epistemology. This approach said that it was practically rational to trust our socially established doxastic practices, including the Christian mystical practice. His arguments were widely discussed and taken seriously in general.

Defenders of the ARE have made considerable progress in the twentieth century. When Swinburne first propounded his ARE via his PC in the late seventies, he was greeted with incredulity. At that time, the prevailing opinion among professional philosophers seemed to be that this kind of argument was hopeless and beyond the pale for respectable philosophers. So not even Mary Hesse, who was kind of sympathetic toward religion, could stomach it at that time. In response to Swinburne, although she thought his paper was "tightly argued," she could dismiss it in a few words: "such appeals to RE . . . are not common nor intellectually persuasive nor even intelligible in the current secular climate" (Hesse 1981, p. 288). Swinburne replied, "The suggestion that they are not common seems just false . . . The argument of my paper was that appeals to RE *ought* to be intellectually persuasive . . . As to the claim that appeals to RE are not intelligible- I can only suggest that he who finds them so should familiarize himself with the literature of religion in order to see what the appeals mean" (Swinburne 1981, pp. 303–4). This is a bit amusing.

Nowadays, on the whole, even critics among professional philosophers of religion treat it with some respect. It is now regularly treated in texts on philosophy of religion, and I think it is going to become one of the classical arguments for the existence of God. The old defenders continue to update their case (Yandell 1999; Gellman 2001; Hick 2006), and it has also drawn new supporters (Garth Hallett, Stephen Layman, Grahame Miles, T. J. Mawson, Douglas Geivett). Of course, the ARE also have able detractors (Richard Gale, Matthew Bagger, Nicholas Everitt, James Harris), but I think even they will concede that their opponents are their epistemic peers. After all, Alston and Swinburne are active researchers in the field of epistemology (and related fields), and they cannot be dismissed as amateur philosophers. No consensus exists yet but the ARE seems to be alive and well.

The ARE is also exciting and fascinating because it helps us rethink deep issues in epistemology. I think the contemporary defenders of ARE are exploring a new paradigm. There are also independent and consonant developments in the field of epistemology in recent decades. When Swinburne first boldly proposed his PC, it was quite novel and radical, and he did make apparently shocking statements such as "if it seems to me Poseidon exists, then it is good evidence that Poseidon exists." True, it was similar to Chisholm's critical commonsensism but few would imagine applying it directly to RE. At that time, the deficiencies of traditional foundationalism have already been made apparent to many epistemologists but perhaps they were still hoping for a quick fix. Now they are more open to radically different epistemological frameworks. Epistemic principles such as Swinburne's PC have been accepted by diverse philosophers such as Gary Gutting, William Lycan, Robert Audi, and Michael Huemer (but they do not entirely agree on its scope of application). Things such as presumptive data and defeasible reasoning are now stock-in-trade of contemporary epistemologists. Moreover, they are exploring theories which resemble more or less Alston's doxastic practice approach, for example, Catherine Elgin's (very) weak foundationalism, Susan Haack's foundherentism, or Nicholas Rescher's methodological pragmatism. This kind of epistemological development certainly enhances the initial plausibility of the ARE.

The Decline of Traditional Foundationalism and Stock Objections to RE

Traditional foundationalists believe that our knowledge has to be built upon the *sole* foundation of sense experiences (SEs) because only they are the indubitable given free from interpretations, and are open to public confirmation. RE, if they are to be trusted, have to be vindicated on the basis of this foundation – SE. Although the ARE has strong intuitive force for many people, for Western philosophers steeped in the tradition of empiricism, the trustworthiness of REs is hard to swallow. In introductory books on philosophy, the ARE is usually dismissed on the basis of stock objections such as the following:

1   The logical gap objection: We have to distinguish the experience and the subjective conviction it produces from the objectivity (or *veridicality*) of the experience, for example, a very "real" hallucination or dream is a live possibility. Critics such as Antony Flew and Alasdair MacIntyre (p. 72) admit that REs often produce subjective certitude in the subjects. However, there is a logical gap between the psychological data and the ontological claim of the REs. To bridge the gap, we need independent certification of the religious belief. For example, Flew challenges the defenders of REs to answer this basic question:

> How and when would we be justified in making inferences from the facts of the occurrence of religious experience, considered as a purely psychological phenomenon, to conclusions about the supposed objective religious truths? (Flew 1966, p. 129)[4]

---

4. Although Flew has now become a kind of theist (Flew & Varghese 2007), the ARE is not cited as the major reason for his conversion to theism (or, better yet, deism).

2   The theory-ladenness objection: The REs are heavily (or even entirely) shaped by the conceptual framework of the experients. Hence they are not useful as evidence for ontological claims (Donovan 1979, chap. 5). Indeed, a recent critic Graham Oppy thinks that, since:

> cases of revelation and selective ('private') religious experiences" are "rarely reported by those who are not already religious believers - or by those who are not embedded in a community in which there is considerable religious fervour, . . . there are good reasons for non-believers to suspect that there is pollution by prior theory in these cases as well. (2006, p. 350, n. 4)

3   The privacy objection: According to Rem Edwards, "the foremost accusation leveled at the mystics is that mystical experiences are private, like hallucinations, illusions, and dreams, and that like these 'nonveridical' experiences, religious experience is really of no noetic significance at all" (1972, p. 318).

Evaluation of the logical gap objection

Many theists have provided reasonable responses to these objections. First, we should note that the logical gap objection to REs basically conforms to the structure of the general skeptical argument. This can be seen from Gutting's parody of Flew's question:

> How and when would we be justified in making inferences from the facts of the occurrence of experiences of material objects, considered as a purely psychological phenomenon, to conclusions about the supposed objective truths about material objects? (Gutting 1982, p. 147)

The certitude/certainty distinction applies to almost all kinds of experience, including SE. A hallucination is exactly an unveridical SE, which, nevertheless produces subjective conviction. If the certitude/certainty distinction *in itself* threatens REs, it will also threaten SE. Why, then, is the theological gap not damaging in other cases? If the critics only apply the objection to REs but not to other experiences, it would be extremely arbitrary. This would also confirm Alston's charge that critics of REs often adopt a double standard with regard to SEs:

> The objections . . . involve unfavorable epistemic comparisons between mystical perception and sense perception; . . . they either condemn the former for features it shares with the latter (double standard) or unwarrantedly require the former to exhibit features of the latter (imperialism). (Alston 1991, p. 255; a list of double standards is provided on pp. 249–50)

Evaluation of the theory-ladenness objection

The theory-ladenness objection again raises a general problem in epistemology. Even ordinary perception is theory-laden (Papineau 1979), and a similar problem plagues scientific realism. The empiricists and the positivists have searched hard for the rock-bottom "given" that is free of interpretation. In this way, it can be the neutral arbiter of different theories or interpretations. However, the development of modern philosophy and, especially, contemporary philosophy of science bespeak the downfall of this project. All the major philosophers of science (e.g. Popper, Hanson, Kuhn, Lakatos, and Feyerabend) agree that all observations are, to some extent, theory-laden. For example, Nancy Cartwright writes:

> We can be mistaken about even the most mundane claims about sensible properties, and once these are called into question, their defense will rest on a complicated and sophisticated network of general claims about how sensations are caused, what kinds of things can go wrong in the process, and what kinds of things can and cannot be legitimately adduced as interferences. (p. 259)

Some authors also suggested that modern psychology confirms the idea that interpretation "is absolutely essential to there occurring a perceptual experience at all. . . . We are not passive recipients of ready-made representations of our environment; rather, stimuli from that environment must be processed by various interpretive mechanisms before they can have any significance for us" (Davis 1989, p. 149). Ralph Baergen, after surveying the empirical study, concludes that the:

> psychological evidence shows that the operation of the human visual system certainly is influenced by beliefs, assumptions, expectations, and so on. Moreover, "the processing involved is, to some extent, top-down . . . our beliefs, expectations, and so on influence our visual presentations, and not merely their interpretation. (Baergen 1993, p. 16)

That means even our sensations are "polluted."

Now let us examine Oppy's claim that in the case of REs, there is likely to be "pollution by prior theory." I think this allegation at least involves two claims. First, believers' prior theory has significant influence on the content of their RE. Second, this influence tends to "pollute" the experience, rendering it unveridical. The former claim is not implausible in light of the given considerations. It is not likely that RE can be the sole exception to a general rule about our experiences. However, it is not clear whether the prior theory in fact totally constrains the content of their RE. If it is not the case, then, at most, we can say that the interpretation of RE is fallible, and we cannot conclude that they are cognitively worthless. In fact, there is evidence that prior theory does not entirely determine the content of TE:

> many people have experiences which are highly individualistic . . . some . . . feel the arms of God wrapped around them; others sense Jesus' love gradually coming into their body from head to toe or from toe to head; . . . many experience Jesus or God in ways not clearly derived from Scripture or from reports in the church or elsewhere . . . at one time they have a fairly standard experience of Jesus and at another have an Eastern form of experience (we may think of Joy, who first of all had a Nirvana-type experience, which then developed into an experience in which she felt herself to be a participant with Jesus on the cross, sensing the meaning of his death. (Wall 1995, p. 302)

See also Cases 3, 4, and 7 given earlier. Oppy really needs to adduce more real cases to support his sweeping claim.

The more important point is that the second does not follow from the first: the influence of a prior conceptual framework in experience is not necessarily cognitively debilitating. In fact, after pointing out the top-down way of processing in human visual system, Baergen goes on to say that:

it is "the top-down aspects of vision which allow us, for example, to recognize objects under poor viewing conditions or when only a small part of them is visible . . . certain forms of agnosia arise when our knowledge about objects is prevented from influencing perceptual processing." (Baergen 1993, p. 16)

In other words, in our common experience, prior theory, even built-in our visual system, does not necessarily pollute. It may aid our perception instead. (Of course, we cannot noncircularly prove this point. What is said earlier is said within the critical trust framework.)

Gwen Griffith-Dickson presses the question: "Does one say that the humiliation a rape victim feels in the attack is just 'her interpretation' of the event, distinct from the physical sensations, or is it an integral part of it?" (2005, p. 400). If it seems to be mislead-ing, then the assumption that the less interpretation, the better is dubious. As the phenom-ena of agnosia in vision show, it is just as possible to miss the genuine significance of an experience through underinterpretation as it is through overinterpretation. Experience only becomes "knowledge" when our basic experiences of the world are transformed by "quite elaborate theoretical interpretations." Might this be true of mystical experiences as well? If we accept making such rich use of interpretative techniques in science, art, and everyday life, is it fair to refuse the same toleration to RE? After all, the "commonsense *physical objects dispersed in space* conceptual scheme is inculcated in a thousand subtle and not so subtle ways in the course of socialization. Does this imply that we are not proceeding rationally in forming perceptual beliefs in the standard way?" (Griffith-Dickson 2005, p. 402).

Perhaps the critic will still insist that this deprives RE of an independent evidential force. Namely, the interpretive elements of RE have to be independently supported before we can deem the experiences reliable. However, since SEs also have interpretive elements, "if we were always required to provide independent evidence that the beliefs in terms of which we had unconsciously 'interpreted' a perceptual experience were probably true before we could take the perceptual experience to be probably veridical, we would be trapped in [skepticism]" (Davis 1989, p. 144). If the critic is to avoid the charge of double standard, he needs to explain in what way this is a special problem for REs.

So, again, the theory-ladenness objection *in itself* is not decisive. Perhaps to avoid skepti-cism, the wiser policy is to treat the incorporated interpretations in our experiences as *prima facie* justified. I call it the top-down approach. Furthermore, prior religious frame-works need not be corrupting; they may instead help to "tune" people to perceive a reality that they would otherwise miss.

Evaluation of the privacy objection

Let us examine the privacy objection, the allegation that unlike SE, RE is private and sub-jective. In what sense is an SE public? My *experience* of a chair occurs essentially in my mind- it is every bit as private as other experiences in this aspect. I cannot directly experi-ence how you experience the chair and vice versa. What makes an SE public is that verbal reports of different persons can be compared. However, reports of people having REs can also be compared. For example, experiences of God are present in almost all ages, all places, and all cultures. The reports, to a considerable extent, match. The experience also develops in a tradition. So, in these aspects, RE is also public. As Edwards emphasizes:

the experience of the Holy seems to be very much *unlike* dreams and hallucinations. Extremely large numbers of people from extremely diverse cultural backgrounds claim to experience the Holy One, and there is a significant amount of transcultural agreement about what the experienced object is like. This is not the case with the objects of hallucinations- most hallucinators do not see pink elephants ... *Pink elephant* is simply a convenient symbolic abbreviation for the immense variety of weird entities encountered by people having hallucinations. (1972, pp. 320–1)

Vestiges of traditional foundationalism

The force of many stock objections to RE depends upon the traditional foundationalist framework. However, although "a narrowly empiricist and foundationalist position is rarely found now outside discussions of religious experience," the philosopher of religion comes up time and again against this outdated assumption (Davis 1989, p. 143).

Unfortunately, what Davis says is still true of some recent discussions. For example, James Harris's severe critique of the ARE basically follows the foundationalists' line of attack. He thinks that when a subject S has an RE, "it is not reasonable to attribute to S the power of determining that x is God who is seeming to appear rather than a near-god, an intelligent alien from some distant galaxy, or Satan" (2002, p. 153). However, it is also not clear that when S has an SE, it is reasonable to attribute to S the power of determining that x is a physical object which is seeming to appear rather than an alien superscientist or Satan manipulating his brain/mind. *Ex hypothesi*, phenomenologically indistinguishable experiences can be produced by a physical object, an alien superscientist or Satan. How can S determine which is the case on the basis of his experience alone? An appeal to further experiences will not help because similar problems plague those experiences as well.

Again, Harris insists that "S must make an inference from the experience of being appeared to by those properties or powers to the claim it is God doing the appearing" (2002, p. 153). This betrays a lack of understanding of the severe problems afflicting even ordinary SEs, and the rationales for the PC. True, some philosophers do think that when S is having an experience of a tree (being appeared to treely), S must justify an inference from the experience of being appeared to treely to the claim it is a tree doing the appearing. However, it is notoriously difficult how any such inference can be justified. The spirit of PC contends that typically perceivers do not make such an inference, and they do not need to. They are rational to trust their experience unless there are positive reasons to the contrary.

The decline of foundationalism does not mean an automatic victory for the ARE. However, the critics of RE should make sure their case is not based on problematic epistemological positions. Of course, the defenders also need to spell out and defend their epistemological framework. Swinburne has exactly attempted to do this.

The ARE via the Principle of Critical Trust (PCT)

Swinburne's ARE

Swinburne proposes a defense of REs by espousing an epistemological principle that accord REs with *prima facie justification* (PFJ). An experience has PFJ if the claims of the experience are probably true unless there are positive reasons to the contrary. The idea is that all experiences should be treated as innocent until proven guilty. REs should also be accorded PFJ then; that is, the claims of REs should be trusted unless counterevidence can be brought forward. This epistemological principle is the PC:

(PC)   If it seems (epistemically) to me that x is present on the basis of experience, then probably x is present unless there are special considerations to the contrary.

We need to understand Swinburne's distinction between "epistemic seeming" and "comparative seeming." For him, "to use 'looks', etc. in the comparative use is to compare the way an object looks with the way other objects normally look" (1979, p. 246). So a coin may look elliptical (comparatively) to me, but on the basis of this experience I am inclined (more or less) strongly to believe that the coin is round. The latter is how it seems epistemically. When I describe my experience of a chair as an epistemic seeming that the chair is present, it does not mean I only hold tentatively to the judgment that there is a chair. On the contrary, it means that on the basis of my experience I am spontaneously and strongly inclined to believe that the chair is there.

Then, Swinburne formulates the following argument:

(A)   It seems (epistemically) to me that God is present.
(B)   There is no good reason to think either God is nonexistent or not present; nor any good reason to think the experience unveridical.
(C)   Hence, probably God is present.

The PC does not stand alone in Swinburne's epistemological approach. It has to be used together with other epistemological principles such as the following:

(a)   The Principle of Testimony: other things being equal, others' experiences are likely to be as they report them to be.
(b)   The Principle of Simplicity: "in a given field, we take as most likely to be true the simplest theory which fits best with other theories of neighbouring fields to produce the simplest set of theories of the world" (Swinburne 1986, pp. 13–5).

These principles are important. Swinburne's approach has to be distinguished from an "anything goes" approach. It is recognized that man's ability to know is far from perfect: his initial epistemic seemings are fallible. The hope lies in the ability of man to sift and correct these initial data. For example, an erroneous epistemic seeming can be corrected by other epistemic seemings by applying the Principle of Simplicity.

So Swinburne's approach includes a way to sift the data and establish an orderly noetic structure. I call this the critical trust approach (CTA). The PC is renamed the PCT. I am glad that my terminology is at least accepted by Hick: "The term 'the critical trust approach' has been introduced by Kai-man Kwan (2003), and I use it in preference to the earlier 'principle of credulity'... and my own 'principle of rational credulity'" (Hick 2006, p. 210).

Each version of PCT can be formulated variously in descriptive or normative terms, involving claims about probability, rationality, or justification. I will mainly use the concept "justification" in this chapter. My basic contention is only that TE is also a basic source of justification (BSJ), and will eschew the controversy about knowledge. The concept of justification is also controversial, and we have the great debate between internalism and externalism. I think the PCT is more at home within the framework of internalism, which requires what justifies a belief to be internal to the subject *in some way*. I cannot settle the debate here. I suspect that structurally similar AREs can be argued using different epistemological vocabularies.

The formulation of PCT

A PCT can be formulated in diverse ways. The PCT is supposed to apply to epistemic seemings. Sometimes epistemic seemings are about necessary truths, and these are typically produced by rational intuitions. If we think that rational intuitions have PFJ, then we can say that the PCT is applicable to rational intuitions – we can represent this claim by PCT(intuition). The content of the bracket after "PCT" stands for the scope of that PCT. On the other hand, we also have epistemic seemings about the world, and they can be produced by intentional experiences (experiences of something external) and introspection as well as memory. These three are often recognized to be BSJs for our epistemic seemings about contingent states of affairs in the actual world, for example, about physical objects, one's own mental states, and the past. They have similarities but also a lot of dissimilarities and cannot all be subsumed under the category of SE or even perception (unless in a very loose sense). However, they are all broadly speaking experiential sources of justification. I would call all these noetic experiences.

If PCT(noetic experience) is true, then noetic experience is a BSJ. That would also entail that many kinds of RE (including TE) are also BSJ, possessing PFJ. Whether this is true is exactly the main controversy around the ARE. Defenders want to say that PCT(noetic experience) is true, but the critics either reject the entire CTA, or they want to restrict it to only SE or memory (some would also want to add introspection in the scope covered by the PCT but others, e.g. eliminativists, want to say that introspection is not a BSJ). If the scope of a PCT covers all epistemic seemings, including intuitions, I will call it the wider PC. In this chapter, the default version propounded is the PCT(noetic experience).

Formulations of PCT can also vary according to the epistemic force it possesses. We can distinguish the following types:

- Moderate PCT
  If it seems (epistemically) to a subject S that p on the basis of a noetic experience E, then S has PFJ for belief that p, which is sufficient for justified belief that p *simpliciter* in the absence of defeaters.

- Weak PCT
  If it seems (epistemically) to a subject S that p on the basis of a noetic experience E, then S has *some* defeasible justification for his belief that p which is less than sufficient justification for justified belief that p *simpliciter*.

The moderate PCT is incompatible with the weak PCT. (I think strong forms of PCT that grant infallibility or incorrigibility to our epistemic seemings are, on the whole, implausible.) Swinburne's formulation of his PC, and Gellman's (1997) formulation of

PCT are moderate versions. In contrast, the formulation by William Lycan is a weak one: "Accept at the outset each of those things that seem to be true" (1988, p. 165). However, the initial weight of those spontaneous beliefs are only minimal and they can be overridden by "almost anything: new input, noncoherence with other beliefs in a minimal way, slight explanatory advantage to be gained elsewhere, or whatever. The justification conferred on a spontaneous belief by the Principle of Credulity is flickering and feeble" (1988, pp. 166–7).

Some defenders of ARE favor the weak form over the moderate form. For example, Gutting thinks that:

> an of-**X** experience in general provides *prima facie* evidence of **X**'s existence only in the sense of supplying some (but not sufficient) support for the claim that **X** exists. For belief in the claim to be warranted, the solitary of-**X** experience requires supplementation by additional corroborating experiences. . . . In cases of kinds of objects of which we have frequently had veridical experiences, we can of course rightly believe that they exist, without further corroboration beyond our seeming to see them. But this is because we have good inductive reason to expect that the further corroborations will be forthcoming. With relatively unfamiliar objects . . . this sort of inductive reason is not available; and warranted assent must await further corroboration. (1982, p. 149)

He gives an example of an experience of apparition. He suggests that even if we cannot find cogent defeaters of this isolated experience, such an experience, although not completely without force, still cannot be deemed veridical. He then draws the conclusion that "we should think of an individual of-God experience as providing significant but not sufficient evidence for God's existence, needing to be included in a cumulative body of diverse evidence that can warrant the claim that God exists" (Gutting 1982, pp. 149–50). Several writers also have similar complaints, for example, Michael Martin (1990, p. 175) and Davis (1989, pp. 101–5).

This suggests we can further distinguish a Token PCT which applies to every token experience,[5] and a Type PCT which applies to a *type* of experience. All the formulations of PCT given earlier are Token PCTs. Now, suppose the weak Token PCT is true but the moderate Token PCT is not. There is still the possibility that when a token coheres with many other tokens, that is, it falls within a type of experience, then it can possess a degree of justification sufficient for PFJ. This idea will be captured by the Type PCT, which will be explicated further in the discussion.

Argument for TE via the Type PCT

The prior question is: by what principles do we group token noetic experiences together as one type? I suggest two main criteria:

(a)   Phenomenology: what kinds of sensations or feelings are involved in this kind of experience?

---

5. From now on, the word "noetic" would usually be dropped and "experience" would, by default, mean "noetic experience." So when I say "an experience is justified," it means "the truth of the epistemic seeming embodied in that noetic experience is justified."

(b) Ontology: what kinds of thing, process, or property are typically supposed to be the objects of experience?

I think that the ontological criterion should take primacy over the phenomenological criterion. For example, SE is the most clearly demarcated kind of experience. However, if the phenomenological criterion is primary, SE is not actually one type but a collection of many types: visual, auditory, tactile, olfactory, gustatory, and so on. It seems better to see SE as an epistemological unit and its unity explained by the common ontology shared by all these experiences: they all have physical objects as objects of experience. So, according to this understanding, SE should be taken to be an experience of a physical thing or event. Sensations or sense data would come in as the *qualitative character* of SE.[6]

- Type PCT
  If it seems (epistemically) to S that p on the basis of a noetic experience E, and E belongs to a well-established type of experience, then S has PFJ for belief that p, which is sufficient for justified belief that p *simpliciter* in the absence of defeaters.

When we can identify an experience as belonging to a well-established type, this means:

(a) Shared experiences: This experience is not altogether idiosyncratic. Similar experience occurs repeatedly and is shared by a substantial amount of people, preferably across cultures and eras.
(b) Common ontology: The tokens of the type have to largely cohere with one another before they can be grouped into a kind. Namely, the group of tokens does not have massive internal contradictions. They also need to share a common ontology such that different tokens can be mapped onto that ontology, exhibiting different sorts of epistemic relation among themselves (e.g. mutual support, explanatory dependence).
(c) Conceptual coherence: To enable mutual communication of the experiences, which is the prerequisite of our identification of a type of nonsolipsistic experience, the experiences have to be, *to some extent*, describable. It also requires a conceptual framework which is not obviously incoherent.

The degree of PFJ provided by a type of experience is also a variable because the degree to which each type is established is different. When a type of experience exhibits a significant degree of intracoherence, I would call it a well-established type. The factors contributing to the degree of *intracoherence* of a type of experience are summarized in the following:

---

6. Everitt writes, "MP [mystical practice] is supposed to be a practice directed at mind-independent entities - but so is SP [sensory practice]. Why then count MP as a separate practice? Surely MP should be classed as simply one branch of SP, analogous to VP (visual perception practice), AP (auditory perception practice), etc" (2004, p. 168). In the main text, I have given some reasons why I would not agree with Everitt's classification, which is not even common among atheistic critics. His major purpose seems to be that by subsuming MP under SP, he can deny the relative autonomy of MP's checking process, and so on.

Criteria of Intracoherence

The degree of intracoherence of a type of experience E would increase with the following factors, *ceteris paribus*:

(a) the number of people sharing E,
(b) the frequency of occurrence of E to an individual,
(c) the variability of the situations in which E occurs,
(d) the explanatory coherence between the tokens of E, and
(e) the conceptual coherence of E's ontological framework.

We can now formulate the following argument for TE:

(A) Type PCT is correct.
(B) TE is a well-established type of experience.
(C) It seems (epistemically) to S that God exists on the basis of a TE, E.
(D) The TE, E, is not defeated.

Therefore,

(E) S is justified to believe that God exists.

The argument seems valid. Premise (C) just states the fact of TEs and should not be controversial. If Premise (B) is also correct, then the conditions in the antecedent clause of Type PCT (applying to the case at hand) are satisfied. So if Type PCT is correct (Premise (A)), then it follows that S has PFJ for belief in God. Further, granting the truth of Premise (D), then it means S is not faced with defeaters. It follows that S's belief in God is sufficiently justified. The crucial premises are (B), (A), and (D), which will be defended in that order.

The ARE can be defended via different routes, and some authors defend ARE on the basis of an analogy with SE. However, although Swinburne and Alston do appeal to considerations of analogy to illustrate and strengthen their arguments, they are in fact proposing a kind of ARE on the basis of first principles in epistemology. The argument I defend is of this type.

RE and TE

The phenomenon and typology of RE

Since time immemorial, human beings as we know it are already religious. Throughout all periods of human history, and in all of the major cultures or societies, there have been a great many reports of a great variety of REs. The evidence for this claim can be garnered from the entire corpus of the religious literature in human history, which is evidently too voluminous to be summarized here. I trust that numerous basic texts on religious studies would substantiate this claim.

The experience of God is not confined to Westerners. A kind of God was known to the ancient Chinese. The most common Chinese translations of the word "God" are Shang-ti

(上帝), which means "the Emperor above," and the Lord of Tien (which means Heaven) (天主). Both Shang-ti and Tien are not terms created by the missionaries. They are in fact widely used in the ancient Chinese classics, and point to the belief in a kind of personal God. The name Shang-ti has already appeared in the oracle bones, and it stands for the Supreme Lord of the universe.

In the *Doctrine of the Mean*, Confucius said, "By the ceremonies of the sacrifices to Heaven and Earth they served Shang-ti." In the *Book of Poetry*, there is a Hymn of Zhou (《周頌》), which praised Shang-ti, "Lord Wu with mighty power, Above all else will tower, Cheng the lord and Kang lord, Shang-ti likewise will laud." Another poem said, "A good crop of barley and wheat, Will soon be ready to reap, Oh by Glorious Shang-ti blest."

Shang-ti is One who can receive sacrifice, One who can bless. He is also One whom we should serve. Shang-ti or Tien (Heaven) cannot just mean the physical nature or some impersonal force because He was regarded as a fearful God who had a moral will. Besides being the source of judgment, Shang-ti is also the source of goodness or happiness: "The great emperor of heaven grants happiness (or goodness) to the people below. The one who can follow the human nature of the people and make the people follow the instruction single-heartedly is not other but the sovereign."

So a contemporary Chinese scholar, He Guang-hu, thinks that the said view of Shang-ti and Heaven is the root of Confucianism, which believes in a personal God who is the Maker of the world and humankind, who is powerful, righteous, loving, and willing to communicate with human beings. So Chinese also have experiences of God, although the theistic tradition cannot be said to be very strong (Kwan & Han 2007).

REs can be further divided into the following types:

(A) TE – a noetic experience whose intentional object is God, the personal and supremely perfect creator of the world

(B) Ecstasy and peak experience (Abraham Maslow)

(C) Encounter of the Light Being in a near-death experience (Moody)

(D) Experience of evil spirit (Hay 1990, p. 49), angels, or departed saints

(E) Experience of contingency – a spontaneous feeling that the world is not ultimate and is somehow dependent on something beyond

(F) Experience of design – experience of being struck by the beauty and intricacy of the natural order and the feeling that this order is ultimately due to Intelligence or Mind

(G) Nature mysticism or cosmic consciousness – a spontaneous feeling that the universe and oneself are one. It is usually induced by contemplation of nature, but a similar experience can also be induced by drugs (e.g. mescalin)

(H) Pure consciousness event (PCE): a pure state of consciousness without *any* intentional object and uncontaminated by any concept. This event should be distinguished from the monistic mystical experience which may include a PCE as a part

(I) Experience of minor deities (e.g. visions of Kali or Buddha or Apollo)

(J) Monistic mysticism (e.g. the intuitive apprehension that Atman is Brahman and that All is One)

(K) Experience of Nirvana – experience of Nothingness or No-self as the Ultimate

RE and TE in contemporary world

According to the secularization theory, the decline (and perhaps ultimate demise) of religion is inevitable as a result of the process of modernization. For the secularists, RE is just a vestige of premodern civilization, society, and worldview. Since religion no longer plays any essential role in modern society, and the religious worldview has been largely discredited or at least thrown in doubt by modern science and knowledge, it stands to reason that the phenomenon of RE will also fade out in the long run.

Although I have doubts about the secularization theory (Kwan 2001), the secularists are correct to point out that modern life is hardly supportive of religious life and RE. In fact, Hay points out that the "contemporary culture . . . is uncertain about religion. Ambivalence about religion and the question of whether it is an illness . . . appears to have been part of the European consciousness for a long time . . . Repeated findings of modern research into religious experience" have testified to "a shyness or 'taboo' on admitting to religious experience." Many "respondents said they had never told anyone else about their experience, even relatives as close as their husbands or wives" for "fear of being thought mentally unbalanced, or . . . stupid" (Hay 1994, pp. 10–1).

In such a kind of inhibitive culture, it is indeed extremely surprising how religious faith and RE have held up quite well. The distribution of religious faith according to Schaffer and Lamm (1995, p. 393) is shown in Table 9.1.

Religious believers are still the overwhelming majority of the world's population (84 percent), while nonreligious people are the minority (16 percent). It is certainly true that many 'believers" counted here are not much more than nominal believers. However, it is reasonable to believe that a substantial portion of the religious people have had some form of RE (past studies of RE show that people who do not profess to any religion sometimes have RE). Note that Christians and Muslims together constitute 52 percent of the population, and the dominant form of RE in these theistic traditions is certainly TE. Hindus and Buddhists together amount to 19 percent of the population. However, we cannot conclude that the major form of their RE has to be monistic. In fact, the Advaita is just one among many schools in Hinduism, and there are theistic and panentheistic traditions in Hinduism (Madvha and Ramanuja). More to the point, many ordinary Hindus are not enthusiastic about the abstruse theory of monism, and their religious life in fact also consists of the worship of God or deities (bhakti).

Table 9.1 Distribution of religious faith (Schaffer & Lamm 1995)

Religion	Percentage of total population
None	16
Christianity	34
Islam	18
Hinduism	13
Buddhism	6
Other religions	13

We have some quantitative data about the situation in the Western world. For example, the "BBC's 'Soul of Britain' survey in 2000 found that 76 per cent of the population ... had some kind of spiritual experience" (Hick 2006, p. 17). The category of spiritual experience is considerably broader but other statistics show that the proportion of people having RE (largely theistic) is not low:

> In the United States a 1975 National Opinion Research Center inquiry in which people were asked 'Have you ever felt as though you were close to a spiritual force that seemed to lift you out of yourself?' found that 35 per cent of those asked said that they had, and a Princeton Research Center ... survey in 1978 also recorded 35 per cent. In Britain at the same time a National Opinion Poll of a sample of 2000 reported 36 per cent. (Hick 2006, p. 35)

The real proportion may be higher because of the taboo factor I have mentioned. The said results were obtained with the more impersonal method of a poll. Hay and Morisy find out that when they interview people and try to build up mutual trust and let them take time to recall, the positive response rate rises dramatically to 62–67 percent (Hay 1994, p. 11).

Quantitative data about TE in other countries are not available. But Christianity is nowadays truly a world religion, and there are a large number of Christians in every continent. For example, there are at least, say, 30–40 million Chinese Christians. I know from my own experience (treated as a kind of informal sampling) that a significant proportion of them have TEs, some of them quite a lot and quite dramatic (see Cases 1 and 2). I cannot offer any exact figure, but no one can deny that many Christians living in very diverse places in the contemporary world, perhaps running up to hundreds of million, have had at least one TE. If we factor in the experiences of Muslims and people in other theistic traditions, and TEs even in cultures not particularly theistic (e.g. the Chinese culture), the figure will be even more impressive.[7] In short, TE indeed has a broad base across cultures, eras, and even religious traditions.

Some critics charge that TE is a kind of odd experience (Vardy 1990, p. 103; Draper 1992, p. 159), and hence it should be subjected to initial skepticism. However, it seems wrongheaded to label a kind of experience shared by at least tens of million of people odd. Again Hay has got it right:

> post-Enlightenment, secular models of reality have come to dominate contemporary understanding," and this leads to "a failure on the part of many scientists to attend seriously to the phenomenology of religious experience. This has produced a distorted understanding and dismissal of what appears to be a *widespread and normal field of human experience*. (1994, p. 1; italics added)

---

7. For some people in a more specific theistic tradition, for example, Christianity, they may want to dismiss the theistic experiences in other traditions *in toto*. The CTA I adopt does not advise us to do that, and I do not think a Christian theist need to do that. He can appeal to the concept of general revelation or common grace in the Christian tradition. I submit indeed it is plausible to think that God can be experienced in different cultures (e. g. the Chinese culture) at least as the Creator, Supreme Being in the universe, or just a very powerful divine being. Moreover, we are only talking about the PFJ here. That we should not dismiss the TEs in other traditions or cultures from the very beginning does not entail that we will accept all of them as veridical in the end. Especially in this chapter, I mainly want to defend a less specific subtype of TE, such as the sense of presence of God, and the awareness of the transcendent being implicit in different forms of TE.

Typology of TE

Numinous experience

Otto's description of the numinous is still a good one: *mysterium tremendum et fascinans.* Yandell spells it out in this way: the subject "seems to experience an awesome . . . majestic and overpowering being and the subject . . . has a feeling of being a creature in the presence of the creator . . . the subject seems to experience a being who is unique in kind and intensely alive" (1984, pp. 9–10).

Theistic mysticism

Whereas in a numinous experience God is felt to be other than the subject, in theistic mysticism, God is experienced in a union of the soul with God. God is searched from within in this type of love mysticism (e.g. Teresa of Avila) (Pike).

Sense of presence of God

It is the more commonplace intuitive awareness of God. This awareness is often fused with a feeling of calm assurance and peace (Baillie, Beardsworth). Whereas extraordinary types of TE usually last for a relatively short duration, it is possible for some to maintain the sense of presence of God for a relatively long period (Brother Lawrence).

Divine–human encounter

In this type of TE, God is experienced as the Eternal Thou. Farmer has laid his fingers on the crucial features: "First, central in the living awareness of God as personal is something which happens . . . in the sphere of the *will*. The religious man is aware of a certain peculiar type of resistance . . . the resistance, namely, of absolute, sacred, unconditional values" (1935, p. 23). Second, there is also the awareness of God as the "final succour. . . . The unconditional demands, the values of God, are apprehended as pointing the way to the highest self-realisation, the final security of man" (1935, p. 25). These experiences of encounter are fused with characteristic emotions which accompany personal interaction (e.g. warmth, gratitude, joy of communication, sense of being personally addressed).

Experience of grace

Awareness of God's unconditional demands may also occasion awareness of one's moral failings as "sinning against God" and awareness of one's moral impotence as "spiritual death." This may also open up the possibility of experiencing divine forgiveness of sin and renewal of moral personality through reconciliation with God. Characteristic emotions are sense of guilt, peace of forgiveness, and joy of liberation.

Experience of personal growth in God

We should also note the personalizing character of some TEs (Cases 6 and 7). A person who experiences God may also experiences personal growth at the same time: heightened sensitivity to people and moral values, a revitalized conscience, a greater concern for people and willingness to sacrifice, and so on. In a word, he finds himself becoming more like an (integrated) person and his *telos* fulfilled in his life in God.

Baptism in the Spirit

It is "an overwhelming sense of being set free from sinful selfishness ... deep interior peace.... the gift of tongues" (Dorr 1978, p. 40). There are a lot of these nowadays, since the charismatics constitute one of the fastest growing groups in contemporary world.

Conversion

The content of a conversion experience actually overlaps with the aforementioned types of TEs and it is only marked out by the dramatic and sudden change that is caused by the experience. There may be a drastic change in personality, beliefs, and direction of life.

Corporate TE

Many TEs occur in the context of the "flight of the alone to the Alone." However, in Christianity, the corporate nature of these experiences is always emphasized:

> after Pentecost, the Spirit descends on the disciples.... then it is said that the disciples were all "of one heart and soul".... So the descent of the Spirit forms the community and the community is such that in it everything is shared, even at the economic level. (Griffiths 1989, p. 223)

So experience of God and experience of community are often inseparable, and I would call this kind of TE a corporate TE. To different degrees, I think a religious community in corporate worship and prayer (sometimes) is having similar experiences.

Mediated TE

Sometimes a person can have a TE that is mediated by other kinds of experience, for example, experiences of nature, art, conscience, fellowship with others, and saintliness of others. Sometimes the subject has focal awareness of God through subsidiary awareness of something else, for example, awareness of God through awareness of the beauty of nature. At other times the awareness of God may just be present in the background while the person is focally aware of some other thing. We then have an oblique perception of God instead.

Sensory TE

A sensory TE is an experience of God that is mediated by sensory experiences (e.g. visions, auditions, dreams, stigmata).

Interpretive TE

It is a spontaneous interpretation of an event as God's action or message but the event can be clearly described without using religious concepts. Experiences of God through answered prayers, guidance, miracles, healing, tongues, and so on are examples of interpretive TE.

Intuitive apprehension of God

All the aforementioned types are more or less mediated by some feelings, but some mystics also report a nonsensory awareness or intellectual vision of God in which all phenomenal content is absent. I call this an intuitive apprehension.

TEs within a common ontology

All the given kinds of TE are actually experienced by believers. It is foolish to elevate a certain kind of TE to the exclusion of other kinds. God's relations to the world and to man are so multifaceted that it is unreasonable to think there is only one way to approach Him. Consider an experience of drinking a cup of coffee, which is actually consisted of visual, olfactory, tactile, and gustatory experiences of the coffee. Considered in themselves, the smell of coffee and the visual sensations of a brown liquid are as diverse as any two things can be. Yet they are connected as modalities of the same SE of the same object. Similarly, God can be approached in many directions and manifested in diverse ways; yet the whole lot can be coherently explained by the categoreal nature of the same God:

(a)   Since God is the transcendent and holy creator, numinous experience and experience of contingency are to be expected.
(b)   If man is created in the image of God and their selves are ultimately grounded in God's sustaining activity, then God can also be approached from within (theistic mysticism).
(c)   Since God is Himself the Absolute Good, it is no surprise to have experiences of His unconditional imperative as well as love and succor, and also mediated TEs through conscience and morality.
(d)   Since God is personal, we can have experiences of personal encounter, divine speech, emotional healing, and so on.
(e)   God's wisdom and power over nature makes it possible for Him to reveal His purposes through providential and miraculous acts (mediated and interpretive TE).
(f)   God as the source of personality and community nicely explains the personalizing character of TEs and the occurrence of corporate TEs.
(g)   God as Redeemer is correlated with our experiences of grace and conversion.
(h)   God can act directly on the mind, and hence intuitive apprehension is possible.

So the experience of God is marked by a rich diversity in unity. Arguably, this pattern is already there in the Biblical portrayal of the divine interaction with man. For example, the Old Testament scholar Rowley says,

> His voice is still heard in Nature and in history, in individual experience and in the personality of men and women who are attuned to his spirit . . . Of greater significance than any of these separately, however, is that combination of factors dovetailing into one another. (1956, p. 47)

In the New Testament, Paul talks about a God who is above us, inside us, and among us (Ephesians). These descriptions can be nicely correlated with numinous experience, mystical or oblique experience of God, and corporate TE. Paul's own experience of God reflects the same rich diversity in unity: a conversion experience, experience of grace and self-transformation, experiences of providence and miracles, and probably some mystical experience (see 2 Corinthians 5).

The same intricate pattern of experience of God is also reported by persons in contemporary secular society. Consider Jackie Pullinger's experience of God. She experienced God's calling to serve Him and, finally, she settled down inside the Walled City of Hong Kong, trying to preach the gospel to the drug addicts, Triad gangsters, and the prostitutes. Now it is still an expanding ministry. Her story consists of many "inner" and "private" experiences of God, and experiences of guidance, providence, comfort, and illumination that result in practical actions of social concern. She herself undergoes self-transformation while many drug addicts experience conversion. There are also many experiences of tongues, healing, and miracles. Above all, all these experiences fit nicely together in her lifelong experience of God that manifests beauty and an overarching purpose.

It is really important to keep sight of the *whole* of this evidential base. All these experiences are of God and the various types are to be expected once the nature of God is given. So they are not like the links in a chain which is as weak as the weakest link. Instead, they are like the strands which are woven into a cable. The full evidential force of TE can only be seen when the rich diversity and coherence of TEs are simultaneously recognized.

Conceptual Coherence of TE

To be a well-established type of experience, the concept of TE needs to be conceptually coherent. Assuming the coherence of the concept of God, TE can still be incoherent because experience of God can be shown to be impossible. Several reasons have been adduced for this claim: Jonathan Harrison rejected TE "partly on the grounds that one cannot have immediate experience of dispositional characteristics, partly on the grounds that we can have immediate experience only of the contents of our own mind" (1999, pp. 257–8). Forgie takes "theistic experience" to mean "an experience which is phenomenologically of God, i.e. an experience which, if veridical, would *have to* constitute an accurate perception of God and *nothing else instead*" (Forgie 1998, p. 317; italics added). But no experience can be phenomenologically of God. So TE is impossible. Some other critics put the emphasis on the alleged impossibility to recognize the infinite attributes of God in experience (Davies).[8]

Initially, it sounds plausible to think it rather problematic to say the finite can experience the infinite, or the transcendent can be wholly given in the immanent. Simply put, God is just too big for humans to experience. However, puzzles immediately arise when we realize similar questions can be raised about the possibility of seeing a physical object. We think we can see the Yellow River or the Great Wall of China but is it not equally obvious that the Yellow River or the Great Wall are also too big for humans to see? I can see a physical object, and a physical object is essentially a three-dimensional object, having a front and a

---

8. Everitt also thinks that God "is not even a possible object of sensory experience" (2004, p. 172). I think his objection basically hinges on a kind of favoritism toward SE, which is widely criticized in this chapter.

back, which cannot be given in our visual experience at the same time. So can I really see the object? Moreover, suppose Kripke is right that water is essentially H_2O. Then we need to ask: when we see water, how can the property of being H_2O be given in our experience?

The basic problem about these kinds of questions about experience of God or physical objects is that they have presupposed this requirement:

For S to have an experience of an object O having an attribute F, either the whole being of O (or at least O's essential properties) has to be *given* in the experience, or that an infallible indicator of the state of affairs (O is F) is present (and perceived as such) in the experience.

Similar requirements such as that mentioned are in fact made by the traditional foundationalists. If experience is our only access to the external world, once we allow a gap between the experience and the world, how then can we guarantee the possibility of empirical knowledge? However, the lessons of epistemology in recent decades tell us that these requirements simply cannot be met even in our SE.

Consider our visual experience of water. What are given in the experience are two kinds of content: the propositional content of our epistemic seeming ("there is water over there"), and the nonconceptual content, which can be described in various ways: being appeared to waterly, this and that kind of qualia or sense data. The direct realists also contend that, when the experience is veridical, there is the direct awareness of water in virtue of water appearing to us. Water as a physical object cannot be, in any literal sense, be given in our experience, which is a mental event. Indeed this is a good ground for raising the question whether any experience of a physical object is possible. This worry is further aggravated by the realization that the concept of a physical object is the concept of something which can exist independent of all our experiences – how can this property be given in our experience? This ability to exist independently is also a dispositional property. How can we perceive that? What features of our experience tell us that physical objects can do that? More experiences only tell us those objects can *continue to be perceived and experienced*, and it does not entail that they can exist *independently* of our stream of experience.

Contemporary understanding of physical objects further complicates matters. For example, Russell thinks that "if physics is true there must be so little resemblance between our percepts and their external causes that it is difficult to see how, from percepts, we can acquire a knowledge of external objects" (1948, p. 213). Since the "table as a physical object, consisting of electrons, positrons, and neutrons, lies outside my experience" (1948, p. 236), "I do not 'see' the furniture in my room except in a Pickwickian sense. When I am said to 'see' a table, what really happens is that I have a complex sensation which is, in certain respects, similar in structure to the physical table. The physical table, consisting of electrons, positrons, and neutrons, is inferred" (1948, pp. 237–8).

The problem then arises: if the physical table is inferred, then how do we justify this inference? The sensations certainly are not infallible indicators of the presence of the table. Even the alleged direct awareness of the table can be faked. As Alston admits "the intrinsic indistinguishability of hallucinations and the real thing," he has to concede that "even if hallucinations do not prove that perceptual experience is never a direct awareness of external objects, they certainly prove that it isn't always that" (1999, p. 238). Of course, the propositional content of our experience can also be mistaken.

At this point, I think it is pertinent to ask what kind of approach we should adopt in relation to these questions. I suggest we cannot decide what capacities for experience and recognition are possible in an *a priori* manner. Instead it is more fruitful to look and see what are the actual experiences people claim to have and what sort of things they claim to recognize. If a concept of experience renders most of our actual experiences impossible, then what needs to be changed perhaps is the concept itself. In this spirit, I would suggest there is no need to insist on too strong a connection between experience and its object. As long as the appearance of a transparent colorless liquid reliably indicates the presence of water (H_2O) *in our context*, and the water causes in an appropriate way our visual experience, then we can see water (H_2O). Our experiences are fallible, and its reliability cannot be guaranteed. Suppose, unknowingly, we have been transported to Putnam's Twin Earth. The appearance of water may then be misleading but this does not mean that here on Earth we cannot see water. The said analysis is used to explicate the *concept* of "experience of something." I do not suppose it can be proved apart from our actual experiences.

It follows that when we have an experience of O, we do not need to require that O's essential properties be given in the experience. Schoen argues that encountering maples does not require any knowledge, perception, or even detection of the essential nature of maples, which:

> presumably . . . are tied somehow to matters of genetics . . . If perceived or detected objects are to be recognized as maples, reliable indicators must be processed more specifically. Such indicators . . . need bear no special relation to essences . . . Furthermore, it is not necessary that everyone use the same indicators. (1990, p. 9)

In this way, experiences of the Yellow River, the Great Wall, or a three-dimensional object are no longer puzzling.[9]

We can now come back to the question about the possibility of the experience of God. Forgie's concept of TE is certainly too strong. As he admits, his concept will render impossible SEs which are phenomenologically of individuals, or many ordinary objects such as a coffee maker. He also admits his concept of the phenomenological content of experience is not the only possible one, and that "on . . . an alternative account theistic experience would thus be possible" (Forgie 1998, p. 323). I have offered an alternative account earlier which is also similar to Layman's account: "one can have a reliable experience of God without experiencing all of God's features (though of course the experience must include reliable indicators of a divine presence, such as infinite power and goodness)" (Layman 2007, p. 54).

Similarly, Harrison's objection depends on a very narrow understanding of experience. The concept of a physical object entails a lot of dispositional characteristics. Take the experience of color as example:

> In reporting that I saw a red flower, I am normally reporting that I had a visual experience of a physical object having certain powers or dispositions, i.e. that under normal lighting, normal perceivers (in general) would also see something red if they looked at the flower . . . And of course, being very powerful . . . is a power or capacity. So, at least in principle, a direct

9. Even a critic of theism, Everitt, agrees here (2004, p. 173).

awareness of an entity as very powerful-or even almighty-seems to be possible. (Layman 2007, p. 54)

We can also use this model to understand how the content of a TE can convey the presence of God: "God might have created us in such a way that when He appears to us what appears to us phenomenologically is secondary qualities of God which emerge when God is so experienced" (Gellman 1994, p. 55). These secondary qualities may consist of some unique phenomenal properties of the appearance of God such as the "taste" of God that some mystics have reported. Our feelings and emotions can also be used as indicators of divine presence:

> our own subjective, emotional reactions figure into our recognition of certain types of features. Sometimes upon meeting a person we regard him as less than trustworthy primarily because he invokes in us a feeling of uneasiness. In this type of case, our subjective, emotional reactions serve (in combination with presentations made through sense experience) as indicators of certain types of qualities, and these indicators are very important in dealing with social realities . . . in the theistic mystical experiences . . . subjects were presented with personal presence, and they had an immediate impression of its infinite power and goodness. Their subjective, emotional reactions were of profound awe, of feeling very "small" or finite, of being loved, of extraordinary peace, and so on. All in all, I think that's what one might expect an experience of God to be like. (Layman 2007, p. 54)

For example, consider the experience of God's infinite love. According to Harrison, it is both a disposition as well as a mental state of other minds, and hence cannot be presented in immediate experience. However, making use of the given model, there can be an awareness of the love of God mediated by feelings of feelings of warmth and bliss – feelings which are analogous with what we feel in our interpersonal experience.[10] *Pace* Harrison, when we attend to our concrete experiences, there is reason to believe we can feel the love, joy, sadness, or other mental states of other persons.[11] Alternatively, we can be told by God about His love. Philosophers sometimes ignore the communication model because they are obsessed with the visual model. However, the former model is especially important in interpersonal experience: a lot of experiences of other minds are mediated by verbal and informal communication (e.g. symbolic acts) – say, God can give us a vision of the Cross of Jesus and impress on our mind or tells us by a "voice" the meaning of this event. Something like this has in fact happened to many believers (Case 2).

Since it is an empirical fact that an awful lot of people seem to have experiences of God, in the absence of a good reason to think otherwise, one should conclude that TEs are indeed possible.

---

10. I think epistemologists are still bound by a narrow understanding of human knowing, and underestimate the cognitive role of emotions in human life. Wynn's recent book (2005) defends the thesis that "emotional feelings can function as modes of value perception- in relation to God, the world, and individual human beings . . . they can also function as 'paradigms', and can therefore properly direct the development of our discursive understanding, in religious and other contexts . . ." (2005, p. xi). He explicitly applies this understanding to TE, and argues that even a TE's phenomenal content is purely affective, this will not necessarily be epistemically dubious (2005, pp. 8ff).

11. Hallett has a good defense of this possibility, and use this as analogy for TE.

Intracoherence of TE

Of course, mere possibility is not sufficient. We need to judge whether TEs deserve PFJ by the criteria of intracoherence formulated earlier. As for clauses (a), (b), and (c) in that criteria, we have noted that many people in almost every age, culture, and in many religions seem to have at least some plainer TE such as the sense of presence of God. Even nowadays, in some countries, the majority has some TEs. In other countries, TEs are at least shared and communicated to one another within theistic communities, which are significant minorities in the society. So conditions (a) and (c) are certainly satisfied.

For many persons who have had TEs, they may have just a few of them. However, we have also mentioned the dramatic experiences of God, which quite a number of individuals (e.g. Christiana Tsai, Jackie Pullinger) have throughout their lives, and many more somewhat in the middle of these two groups. So condition (b) is reasonably satisfied for many, and eminently satisfied for a smaller number. I have also argued for the explanatory coherence between the TEs, and the conceptual coherence of TE. If my arguments are correct, conditions (d) and (e) are also satisfied. So barring the demonstration of conceptual incoherence of theism itself, we can conclude that TE is a relatively well-established type of experience.

The critics may argue that our criterion of intracoherence of a type of experience has too low a requirement. For example, TEs still fall short of being universal and are much less frequent to many people than other established types of experience such as SE or memory. However, the critics' requirements are too stringent here. First, universality among human beings is certainly not a necessary condition for PFJ. Obviously, a kind of experience shared just by a minority of people can nevertheless still be veridical. Actually, not all people can see or hear. Conceivably, a nuclear war can happen which causes all but one to be blind. Furthermore, many are tone-deaf. It seems to be quite clear that even if much fewer people share the SEs we have, they are still at least *prima facie* justified for us.

If we count all the people in the whole history, people having TE may outnumber those who have none. Moreover, in view of the fact that TEs occur to many diverse kinds of person, it is not implausible to say that the capacity for TE is at least potentially universal. If it is true, the contingent fact that TEs are not actually universal is not that damaging. The near universality of our current SEs is also contingent. Suppose there are aliens in many different places in the universe, and they all possess very distinct types of sense. Humankind is only a particular community of perceivers. So our SE may not be really universal in the universe. Would this hypothetical fact show that our SE cannot even be regarded as having PFJ?

Furthermore, in most of our cognitive situations, when we have some initial presumption for the reliability of the experients, a sufficient number short of the entire community are adequate to convince us their reports are at least worthy of initial support. Take science as example, the majority of people in fact do not know how to give reasons for the existence of black holes or quarks. However, as long as the science community agrees that they have good reasons to believe those exotic entities, I am reasonable to trust them even though the scientists involved are just the minority among human beings. It is also the case for testimony to events one has not witnessed. Suppose one person tells me that he has seen a rare bird species in Hong Kong. It has some weight for me but I may still doubt it (even not having strong reasons to doubt his integrity or reliability as a witness). However, when 30 people tell the same story to me, I think my initial worry should be sufficiently dispelled. Suppose I later learn of 300 people who also give the same testimony. The degree of PFJ of that testimony will be further enhanced, but it does not seem to be essential for its PFJ.

I suggest the critics often commit the superreliability fallacy, which strictly requires a BSJ to reach the level of superreliability before it can be regarded as having PFJ. Gellman rightly points out that we should not tie our notion of confirming evidence to that associated with sensory perception. It is because:

> Our ordinary physical-object beliefs are way overjustified by confirming evidence. We have extremely luxurious constellations of confirming networks there. Hence it does not follow that were mystical claims justified to a lesser degree than that, or not by similar procedure, that they would be *un*justified. (Gellman 2001, p. 27)

The critics are right in pointing out the ways in which TE differs from sensory experience, and it indeed follows that TE has intracoherence *to a lesser extent* than sensory experiences. However, the hasty inference that TE is, therefore, not well established is a *non sequitur*, and is like arguing that, since a scientist is less brilliant than Einstein, he must be an incompetent scientist. The superreliability requirement will not only endanger the PFJ of TEs but also that of moral experience, aesthetic experience, and so on. This consequence is also implausible.

We are not yet arguing for the veridicality of TEs: we are only asking that they deserve similar kinds of initial trust we give to many kinds of experience, and not to write them off. Is it reasonable to believe that all "God-experients" are either deceiving themselves or others? Gutting, for one, does not think so:

> religion, throughout human history, has been an integral part of human life, attracting at all times the enthusiastic adherence of large numbers of good and intelligent people. To say that something that has such deep roots and that has been sustained for so long in such diverse contexts is nothing but credulity and hypocrisy is . . . extraordinary. (Gutting 1982, pp. 2–3)

So TE is not extraordinary. It is part and parcel of the human situation. Instead it is the overly skeptical attitude toward TE which is extraordinary. Suppose we come to know the life story of a person who has dramatic experiences of God *throughout his life*. We find that person honest, sane, and intelligent. We also find his story corroborated by many others' stories throughout history in many cultures. Is it not rash to say that *all of them are entirely and chronically deluded*? And for that person, he or she (e.g. Christiania Tsai, Jackie Pullinger) is not even entitled to trust his experiences at least initially? This does not seem to be reasonable.

The Structure of the CTA

The two basic components of CTA are the critical spirit and the attitude of trust. The CTA thinks that these two components are both essential elements in any viable epistemology, and they need to be kept in a kind of balance and healthy tension. It is similar to Thomas Kuhn's emphasis on a kind of *essential tension* between tradition and innovation in science (this phrase is the name of one of Kuhn's books).

Data gleaning – trust

The data for the CTA are *all* our experiences. The original incorporated epistemic seeming of a given experience is taken as the epistemological starting point and accorded PFJ. These *presumptive data* are defeasible. The basic principles are the weak Token PCT and moderate Type PCT discussed earlier.

Bonjour has provided a helpful classification of different kinds of foundationalism. While strong foundationalism requires basic beliefs to be infallible, moderate foundationalism allows basic beliefs to be fallible but insists that they are "sufficient by itself to satisfy the adequate-justification condition for knowledge" (if not defeated) (Bonjour 1985, p. 26). In contrast, weak foundationalism thinks that the "basic beliefs possess only a very low degree of epistemic justification on their own" (Bonjour 1985, p. 28). So my approach here is a kind of weak foundationalism. Gellman has moved from moderate foundationalism to weak foundationalism because of the kind of criticisms offered by Gutting.[12] In any case, the ARE can be mounted on the basis of either moderate foundationalism or weak foundationalism, but the latter is the one I adopt here (Kwan 2004).

Data sifting and epistemic ascent – critical trust

Ground-level sifting

Presumptive data can be defeated. Unfortunately, typically the defeater itself is also defeasible and there can be defeater-defeater as well as defeater-defeater-defeater, and so on. Suppose we have a defeater D of an originally *prima facie* justified belief B. Presumably, D also has PFJ. Why can we not use the original belief to defeat the defeater instead? Bonjour has summarized Rescher's suggestion in this way:

> the basic idea is to first segregate the total set of data or presumptions into maximal consistent subsets and then choose among these subsets. . . . one might then choose among the maximal consistent subsets on the basis of the plausibility of their members. (quoted in Bonjour 1985, pp. 224–5)

The idea is that we have to bring in coherence considerations to determine the weight of each presumptive datum. Once a presumptive datum coheres with many other presumptive data, its weight would be increased and it can serve to defeat another less weighty presumptive datum. A presumptive datum which conflicts with many other presumptive datum is then defeated. In general, we can formulate this methodological rule:

The rule of ground-level sifting
    Always choose the consistent subset of our presumptive data which has maximal weight.

---

12. I am not entirely sure that we have to do that. Perhaps moderate foundationalism is the better position (Van Cleve 2005, p. 173), but I do not need to settle the question here. I think that both are reasonable positions and the distinction between them may not be absolute.

Explanatory ascent and feedback sifting

We are not just happy to leave everything as it is. The data of experience (of various kinds) need to be ordered, explained, and made more intelligible. So the data of SE, when subjected to the search for order and intelligibility, yield the scientific framework. However, the framework itself can have feedback effect on the initial data. Some presumptive data of SE may be rejected due to theoretical reasons (e.g. the Principle of Simplicity). This can be captured by the following principle:

Principle of Epistemic Defeat
     We should not believe that things are as they seem to be in cases when such a belief is in conflict with the simplest theory compatible with a vast number of data obtained by supposing in a vast number of other cases that things are as they seem to be.

The CTA would regard this as the rational search for intellectual economy. In general, it is rational to believe in the theory which best explains our diverse presumptive data. It is the so-called *inference to the best explanation (IBE)*. When the presumptive data conflict and the best explanation cannot comprehend all the data, our best explanatory theory can serve as defeater of those "recalcitrant" data. That is also why a worldview can affect our feedback sifting because it is supposed to be an explanation of *all* our presumptive data.

Second-order critical principle

When we trust the majority of our presumptive data, those data may suggest to us that some types of presumptive data are not altogether reliable. For example, those presumptive data are found to be grossly inconsistent or they are contradicted by other well-established data. In such cases, we can formulate second-order critical principles. They are *second-order* principles because the justification of these principles depend on our basic trust of our presumptive data, by and large, which is prescribed by the first-order PCT. For example, our experiences may tell us that drunk people are prone to have hallucinations. So we can form this second-order critical principle: "Bizarre perceptual claims of drunk people are not to be trusted." Of course, without the first-order basic trust, we cannot establish the grounds for this principle, nor can we find out who are the drunk people! These principles are in fact crystallized out of repeated applications of our Principle of Epistemic Defeat.

Consensus and testimony

Our data consist of personal experiences as well as testimonies. The Principle of Testimony, which will be assumed here, dictates that others' testimonies are also presumptive data for one. We can formulate this:

Principle of Consensus
     When an epistemic seeming is consensually corroborated, it is justified to a much higher degree.

First, any consensus has to be *discovered* by each individual. Consensus is not, in any sense, given directly. Second, my principle does not entail that when an experience is not, or even cannot be, consensually corroborated, it should then be doubted. The latter position would amount to a reverse of PCT.

The need for both foundation and coherence

The pattern of reasoning given earlier is similar to Susan Haack's foundherentism, and her crossword puzzle metaphor is helpful (Haack 1994, p. 736). In short, an entry is much more likely to be correct if it not only corresponds to the clue given but also coheres with other entries which, in turn, correspond to their clues. We can formulate the following principle to capture this idea.

> Principle of Epistemic Enhancement
> When an epistemic seeming is coherent with other epistemic seemings, and its truth is coherent with or even suggested by the simplest theory which can explain many other epistemic seemings, then its degree of justification will considerably be enhanced.

The Principle of Consensus is just a special case of the Principle of Epistemic Enhancement. So the CTA needs to appeal to both a foundation and coherence. Without some foundation (albeit weak), the process of justification cannot take off the ground. Without coherence, we can hardly build a decent cognitive edifice on the foundation.

Comparison and conflict

We can evaluate a type of experience by its coherence with other types of experience: *intercoherence*:
> A type of experience E_1 is coherent with another type E_2 if

(a) the ontology of E_1 is consistent with E_2, and either
(b) one type helps to explain the nature, possibility, veridicality, and so on of the other type of experience, or
(c) the realization of the ontology of one type receives inferential support from the other type, or
(d) they are analogous in some respects (e.g. phenomenology, structure).

I would call a doxastic system a *worldview* if it is meant to incorporate all the phenomena into its scope and unify them by explaining the whole lot with reference to a few fundamental principles or ideas. The weight of a type of experience would also be affected by its *worldview coherence*: the degree of ease this type of experience can be accommodated within a coherent worldview with high explanatory power. This is just the application of the Principle of Epistemic Enhancement to a larger context. It is obvious that the possession of the above kinds of coherence to a higher degree would make a type of experience better established.

> Principle of Comparison
> A type of experience E_1 is better established than E_2 if either
> (a) *ceteris paribus*, E_1 has a higher degree of intracoherence than E_2, or

(b)   *ceteris paribus*, E_1 has a higher degree of intercoherence than E_2, or

(c)   *ceteris paribus*, E_1 has a higher degree of worldview coherence than E_2, or

This Principle of Comparison seems to imply the following principle:

Principle of Conflict Resolution
    If type E_1 conflicts with type E_2 and that E_1 is better established than E_2, then E_1 can serve as a defeater of E_2.

Cognitive adjustment

When a *prima facie* justified belief is defeated, what kind of cognitive adjustment should we make to our original cognitive structure? An experiential claim can be false in different ways and to different extent. Suppose I thought I seemed to see John on a street in London last Monday but this was defeated by many reliable witnesses. I ought to retract my claim. Consider these possibilities: (a) I may be hallucinating, or (b) I actually saw someone who looks very like John. The second is at a higher level of epistemic seeming than the first. *All other things being equal*, we should reinterpret the original experience so as to preserve as much truth in the original experience as possible. So (b) is rationally preferable. We can formulate the following:

Principle of Conservation
    When an experience is defeated, it is rational to salvage as much noetic content as possible from that epistemic seeming, that is, to retain the highest undefeated level of epistemic seeming embedded in that experience.

The Impartiality Argument for the PCT

Different ways to defend the PCT

Defenders have offered several main lines of argument for the PCT. Some say that the PCT is intuitively correct or even self-evident (Swinburne 1979, p. 254; Wall 1995, p. 19; Huemer 2001, p. 103). Others emphasize that the PCT is not a radically new invention. It is a principle which we do, in fact, employ in our actual epistemic practice (Mawson 2005, p. 166). While the former focus more on our epistemic practice, John Hick argues that the PCT is implicit in our whole life: "We could not live on any other basis . . . Critical trust, then, is part of our working definition of sanity" (Hick 2006, p. 130). Still others argue that the PCT is justifiable on the basis of pragmatic utility (Rescher 1995, pp. 96–7). Rescher's argument in fact has some similarity to Alston's argument from practical rationality and impartiality. Alston argues that we cannot provide any non-circular proof for any of our socially established doxastic practices. How should we proceed then? To *suspend* our acceptance of the doxastic practices is either impossible or extremely costly. To *replace* the current doxastic practices with some others is no wiser because the new ones will not do better. So it is "eminently *reasonable* for us to form beliefs in the ways we standardly do" (Alston 1993, p. 126).

Alston (1993) is aware of the possibility to "take our stand on one or more of these [doxastic practices], and hold the others subject to judgment on that basis," but this approach is "vulnerable to a charge of *undue partiality* in taking some of our firmly established doxastic practices for granted and requiring vindication of the others in the light of the former" (p. 126; italics added). Layman also presses this point about impartiality:

> Having seen that we cannot prove the reliability of sense experience-that we must give sense experience "the benefit of the doubt," how can we reasonably demand proofs for the reliability of other types of experience? To do so is to operate with an unjustified double standard. (Layman 2007, p. 45)

I will unpack this line of thinking in the following impartiality argument for PCT.

The impartiality argument

(T1)   *Impartiality Thesis*
       If we adopt a certain epistemological attitude toward a certain type of noetic experience, we should adopt the same attitude toward other types of noetic experience when we can find no epistemologically relevant distinction.

(T2)   *Applicability Thesis*
       The Type PCT should be applied as a *fundamental* principle to at least some types of our noetic experience. (Note that "Type PCT" here actually means a principle identical to my generalized Type PCT except that its scope is unspecified.)

(T3)   *Seamless Web Thesis*
       We can find no clear-cut distinctions within the whole web of our noetic experience which are epistemologically relevant *with respect to the applicability of the Type PCT*.

Therefore,

(T4)   The Type PCT should be applied as a fundamental principle to all types of noetic experience.

The argument seems valid. Let us look at the credibility of the premises.

Impartiality Thesis

(T1) is intuitively very plausible, and is also the implication of the general principle of impartiality: "treat similar cases similarly unless the relevant differences are shown." If we let go this principle, then effectively we are abandoning any rationality in various kinds of discourse, for example, legal reasoning, personal judgment of scientists, literary criticism, social sciences, and philosophy. These consequences seem too costly. If we reject the Principle of Impartiality in epistemology, then we can just choose to treat different token experiences in arbitrary ways. It would also be difficult to justify how we can treat a *type* of experience, say sense perception, as an epistemological unit because certainly there are differences between every two individual perceptions and it is hardly possible to *show* that each of this is not epistemologically relevant. If we have to discuss whether *each* perceptual claim is credible and which attitude we should adopt to *this* or *that*, epistemology would hardly be possible!

Applicability Thesis

One common response is that we should not accord PFJ to any kind of experience. The critics contend that we can justify claims of experience without appealing to the PCT. We will consider the cases of SE and memory.

Application of the Type PCT to SE

Alston (1991, 1993) has extensively and convincingly argued for the thesis that we cannot noncircularly show the reliability of SE. To avoid repeating his points all over again, I offer only brief discussions and put my focus more on memory. It may be argued that our belief in the general reliability of SE is justified by inductive evidence. But it is not hard to see that in gathering this inductive evidence, we cannot avoid the use of memory: "an induction from past experiences to future experiences is only reliable if we correctly recall our past experiences. And what grounds have we got for supposing that we do? Clearly not inductive grounds- an inductive justification of the reliability of memory-claims would obviously be circular. Here we must rely on the principle that things are the way they seem, as a basic principle not further justifiable" (Swinburne 1979, p. 256).

So in the end to "justify" ordinary perception inductively, we have to rely on the *prima facie* reliability of memory. But, of course, memory claims can be *prima facie* reliable as data concerning what the world is only if our past perceptions were *prima facie* reliable. We are trapped in a circle if we deny PCT's status as a fundamental principle.

Application of the Type PCT to memory

It is clear that our memory is fallible. How can we safeguard from mistakes and distinguish real memory from false ones or even imagination? Some philosophers have suggested that the reliable memory claims have intrinsic characteristics which are accessible to us, for example, vividness of the images associated or degree of conviction. However, after a long exploration in his book on memory, Von Leyden concludes, "since a false memory claim is as a rule qualitatively indistinguishable from a correct one, no memory experience alone can make it certain that what is alleged to be remembered really occurred" (1961, pp. 115–6).

Since reliance on memory is almost ubiquitous in formation of our beliefs, it is extremely difficult to see how there can be noncircular justification of memory. Consider the suggestion that the general reliability of one's memory is to be established by our perceptual experiences. However, unless we take the reliability of memory for granted to some extent, it is well-nigh impossible to gather sufficient empirical evidence for memory. It is because our experiences almost all happened in the past. Without our basic trust in memory, what we can get from an even infallible SE is only and always a vanishing point.

Some philosophers suggested we can check our memories with documents and archaeological evidence (e.g. Hamlyn). However, if we do not already trust our memory of the meaning of the words, how can we be sure that we have interpreted the documents correctly? Moreover, what is the basis of my belief that the documents are reliable? Their reliability cannot be read off directly. Here we again need some inductive evidence from the past, *which we can remember*, to support it. So this kind of check is also in the end circular.

In the case of our memory beliefs, the appeal to the PCT as a fundamental principle seems inescapable. I have surveyed quite a few authors, and found that almost all of them reach similar conclusions. For example, Russell claims that "the past occurrence is itself a premiss for my knowledge. It cannot be inferred from the present fact of my recollecting it except by assuming the general trustworthiness of memory" (1948, p. 205).

Other authors concur: "in the last analysis . . . we cannot justify or validate our memories further than by allowing a great number, possibly the majority, to be reliable and hence by assuming that the sufficient conditions of remembering are in fact very often fulfilled" (Von Leyden 1961, p. 119). Ginet also thinks we "should trust the direct deliverance of one's senses, or the direct perceptual deliverance of one's memory, when they belong to the part that is coherent relative to all that their deliverance imply about one's direct perceptions. *Why* should one do this? Why not?" (1975, p. 202). The last question is supposed to be a rhetorical one. To suspend our trust in them is simply "too intolerably frustrating to be borne and in practice impossible."

Explanatory foundationalism

The CTA also emphasizes explanatory considerations, and indeed some scholars are forced by their explanationism to accept PCT (e.g. Lycan 1988, pp. 165–6). However, explanatory foundationalism wants to deny that the PCT is a fundamental principle by suggesting that the hypothesis of the external world can be justified as the best explanation of our SEs (interpreted as appearance beliefs such as "it appears to me that a table is there"). Alston (1993) has already criticized many versions of explanatory foundationalism (e.g. Goldman, Slote). I want to discuss the more recent attempt by Jonathan Vogel (1998, 2005) here.

Vogel considers the isomorphic skeptical hypothesis (ISH), which is, in a way, parasitic upon the real-world hypothesis (RWH). "The relationships among causes and effects according to the ISH match those of the RWH. To that extent, it seems, the explanations provided by the one are no better or worse than the explanations provided by the other" (2005, p. 75). For example, if our experiences are produced by the computer of a mad neuroscientist, then different portions of the computer disk can be supposed to occupy the explanatory roles we normally assign to familiar objects. This is called the computer skeptical hypothesis (CSH).

This kind of improved skeptical hypothesis apparently can do as well or as bad a job as the RWH does. However, he contends that necessary truths such as "two distinct objects connot be in the same place at the same time" in the RWH has some explanatory power, but ISH has to guarantee that by invoking "an extra empirical regularity," say, one written down in the computer program of the superscientist. So the ISH is shown to be inferior by its "lack of simplicity" (2005, p. 77).

I doubt whether this really works. For argument's sake, let us concede his point about extra empirical regularities in the CSH. However, we can equally argue that the ISH just needs a computer and a brain, whereas RWH needs myriad of separate objects. Hence, the former scheme is much more economical. Vogel is aware of this point but then he goes on to assert that "it is far from clear that, all by itself, positing fewer entities is a theoretical virtue" (1998, p. 355). Well, it seems to me quite clear that when we consider our practice of IBE, a theory which posits fewer entities is indeed simpler than another theory which posits more. A detective will not posit 10 murderers to explain a dead body when one can do. Astronomers will not posit 10 more planets to explain the deviation of Uranus' orbit from Newton's theory if just one (Neptune) can do, and so on.

Moreover:

> we can compare our commonsense hypotheses about physical objects to, let us say, a Berkeleyean hypothesis about a very complex mind orchestrating the comings and goings of sensations. Which theory is simpler? Well Berkeley had just minds, mental states, and causation. The commonsense hypothesis has minds, mental states, causation, and physical objects. On any criteria of simplicity, Berkeley seems to win. (Fumerton 1992, p. 165)

So in terms of simplicity, it is, by no means, clear that the RWH will win over skeptical competitors. To make a successful epistemic *ascent* possible, the Principle of Simplicity alone is not enough because its basic inclination it to trim things *down*. It needs to work together with the PCT.

Fumerton has further pointed out serious problems about IBE. Concerning the status of IBE, Vogel just says: "If . . . you are skeptical about IBE . . . , you will also be a skeptic about induction of all kinds . . . skepticism about IBE is exotic and, consequently, may be ignored" (2005, p. 79). It seems to me this kind of dismissal of exotic skepticism is quite dogmatic. I agree that the "skeptic has every right to insist . . . that one can and ultimately *must* ask questions concerning the legitimacy of the reasoning . . . One philosopher's domestic species of skeptic . . . is another philosopher's exotic skeptic" (Fumerton 2005, p. 94).

In any case, there are some general problems with explanatory foundationalism which even Vogel's version cannot overcome. First, the basic trust in memory seems quite inescapable. The common data for the competing hypotheses such as RWH or CSH are the *continued coherence* of our experiences. But this datum we can only know through our memory. Indeed the presupposition of memory in almost all attempts to vindicate SE's reliability is not far from the surface. Or perhaps we can try to provide a coherentist justification for memory, or even an IBE for the reliability of memory? Bonjour clearly points out the problems:

> But then the issue arises of how, according to a coherence theory, the memory beliefs upon which any access to the fact of *continued* coherence must rely are themselves to be justified. Many philosophers have offered coherence theories of the justification of memory beliefs, but such an account seems clearly to be involved in vicious circularity if the only reason for thinking that coherentist justification is conducive to truth, and so that the memory beliefs in particular are true, relies on the existence of coherence over time and so on those very memory

beliefs themselves. The upshot is that there is no noncircular way for a coherentist to appeal to sustained or long-run coherence. (Bonjour 1999, p. 130)[13]

Second, memory is also vital in reasoning. Suppose we have a valid mathematical proof which needs 10 pages to write it out. When you come to the end and believe that the theorem is proved, what justifies this? Not directly by the steps because we cannot hold all of them together in our minds and see all at once their connections; but by the *memory* that you have checked all the connections and found them convincing. So any reasoning with more than a few premises, *including the explanatory argument for RWH*, has to depend on the memory belief that the argument has proceeded correctly.

Third, how do we justify the appearance beliefs themselves? Sometimes we claim that they are infallible or incorrigible. But then how do we know that? Well, the answer can only be "it seems self-evident or obvious to me." (The problem would be more serious if we believe that these beliefs are not incorrigible.) Some form of PCT(introspection) seems to be inescapable. The Applicability Thesis is also justified then.[14]

Seamless Web Thesis

Suppose the critic wants to reject (T3). The basic strategy is to acknowledge SE and memory as the only BSJs. All other kinds of experience are then non-BSJs which must be justified by the deliverances of the BSJ. However, how do we justify this kind of "discrimination," which apparently violates the Principle of Impartiality? Perhaps we may claim that the BSJs *alone* are infallible, incorrigible, or uncontaminated by theory. But then it is doubtful that any *type* of experiential claim can aspire to this status, not even SE and memory. We may claim the BSJs *alone* are public. But to know a type of experience is public, we need to first know that it is shared by many people, and they agree quite a lot. But we cannot know that unless we *presuppose* PCT(SE and memory).

Some may claim that the BSJs *alone* are the *most* reliable, and SE and memory are the only candidates here. However, once it is admitted that the difference between the various kinds of experience is only a matter of degree, is it still plausible to cling to the *qualitative* distinction between the BSJs and the non-BSJs? Admittedly, SE and memory are more reliable but this judgment is only possibly arrived at when we give initial trust to our various kinds of experience. Furthermore, given two kinds of experiences E_1 and E_2, is it plausible to demand that E_2 *has to be validated by* E_1 *before it has force* if E_1 is *only more*

---

13. Despite this criticism, Bonjour is ambivalent about the ultimate prospect of explanation foundationalism. On the one hand, he thinks that "some explanation is needed for the combination of involuntariness and coherence, and that the conclusion advocated by the philosopher in question is thereby justified as the best explanation of the facts in question. My own conviction is that such a inference, to Locke's conclusion . . . , is ultimately cogent and can be justified on a priori ground." This sounds like he is hopeful but then it is puzzling that he immediately goes on to say that it is "a very familiar and serious problem for which no developed solution is yet available" (Bonjour 1999, p. 139). So at most he is only issuing a promissory note. He seems to be struggling here. I admire his heroic struggle with skepticism, and in the process he has not evaded the hard problems. In fact he also has doubts about whether the argument he promised can in the end succeed: "it still seems to me that some forms of skepticism are unavoidable and will simply have to be lived with" (Bonjour 1999, p. 129).
14. My argument does not need to start with SE or memory.

reliable than E_2? Suppose a mutant species of human beings (X-men) start to emerge among us, and they possess a kind of super-perception which is much more reliable than our perception. They may insist *only their* super-perception is a BSJ, and that our perception needs to be validated by their superperception before it can be trusted. Would it be a reasonable requirement? No!

(T3) asserts that we can find no relevant distinction between the various kinds of experience with respect to the applicability of the PCT. Although this is hard to *prove conclusively*, the earlier discussions suggest it may be well-nigh impossible to defeat (T3) once we accept (T2). If we grant (T2), then we are conceding that the Type PCT should be applied as a *fundamental* principle to, say, our SE as epistemic seeming, and on this ground alone. That means we accept SE for no other reason than that it seems to us to be true. Then when we consider experiences in other areas, the only relevant point seems to be whether they are also epistemic seemings. The other factors are just irrelevant. So (T3) follows. Anyway, the burden is equally on the critic who rejects the (T3) to *show* what is the relevant distinction.

Now I have defended the Type PCT and this is sufficient for my ARE. However, the Type PCT also requires the weak Token PCT. If token experiences have no force at all, it is hard to understand why then tokens of a type can have PFJ.

Objections to the ARE

Disanalogy objection

Some critics argue that the serious disanalogy of RE or TE with SE undermines its veridicality. The logic is like this:

(A1)   A kind of experience is cognitive *only if* it is analogous with SE, especially in the aspect of (e.g. having analogous tests).
(A2)   RE (or TE) is not analogous with SE.
(A3)   Hence, RE (or TE) is not cognitive.

It is instructive to consider a parallel argument against induction:

(B1)   Induction is justifiable (or reliable) *only if* it is analogous with deduction.
(B2)   Induction is not analogous with deduction.
(B3)   Hence, induction is not justifiable (or reliable).

The second premise seems true. Deduction is truth-preserving while induction is not, and so on. The differences are quite obvious. However, there are problems for (B1). Why do we regard analogy with deduction as essential for a kind of inference to be reliable? Is it not implicitly assuming that there is and can only be one kind of reliable inference? Exactly because the two methods are concerned with different kinds of epistemological connection, is it not to be expected that the two methods should also show differences accordingly? The fact that induction is disanalogous with deduction only suggests that the two cannot be reliable *in the same way or to the same degree*. It is still a live possibility that induction can be as reliable as it can be in its own realm. So this parallel argument against induction is not sound.

Similarly, the earlier argument against TE should be rejected. Why should we expect that there is only one kind of reliable experience? Is it not possible that we can have *some* access to different kinds of contingent truths about different aspects of the world? If it is the case, is it not to be expected that there will be several kinds of experience accordingly? Each may be reliable in its own way and to different degrees. So (A1) seems to presuppose narrow empiricism whose employment of disanalogy objection is self-refuting. Typically, it is also claimed that the assumption that only SE and its like are reliable is also justified by the facts of the matter (Daniels 1989, p. 489). But this justification of SE is dependent upon the reliability of memory, which is also disanalogous with SE in many respects. If (A1) is upheld, would it not destroy justifiability of memory as well? This is to undermine the earlier justification of SE. The appeal to science to reinforce (A1) also suffers from similar problems. The actual success of science also depends on deductive reasoning and the capacity for making rational judgment, which are both very disanalogous from SE. So (A1) would damage justifiability of science as well! So (A1) is quite implausible. On the contrary, if TE is, in general, veridical, we should positively expect TEs to be somewhat different from sensory experiences.

The bracket in (A1) can be filled in with different content, emphasizing a different aspect of disanalogy. Let us further examine the objection (from A1 to A3) which has been put forward by Richard Gale: REs "are cognitive *only if* they are subject to similar tests to those that SEs are" (1991, p. 316) (his prominent target is also TE). The reason for Gale's negative assessment is that:

> A veridical sense perception must have an object that is able to exist when not actually perceived and be the common object of different sense perceptions. For this to be possible, the object must be housed in a space and time that includes both the object and perceiver. . . . there is no RE analogue to this concept of objective existence . . . Because of this big disanalogy, God is categoreally unsuited to serve as the object of a veridical perception, whether sensory or nonsensory. (1991, pp. 326–7)

Gale's discussions clearly display his epistemic chauvinism. Even if he is correct about the necessary conditions for a veridical *sense* perception, it is only *one* concept of an objective empirical particular. To argue that it is the only viable concept would have presupposed that physical object is the only possible kind of objective existent and that SE is the only viable kind of experience. It is just arguing in a circle. Gale admits that his argument would commit him to reject intellectual and moral intuition and the like as noncognitive. It also seems clear that introspection and some personal memories are not of spatiotemporal particulars. So on Gale's criteria, they should also be rejected as noncognitive. These debilitating consequences of his argument in fact count against his argument. That Gale's disanalogy argument has such sweeping consequences is a reason to suspect that his standard for cognitive experience is too stringent.[15] Whether TE is called a cognitive experience does not really matter. The crucial question is whether TE is a BSJ. It is quite clear that Gale's disanalogy objection offers an unreasonably restrictive criterion for BSJ in general. So his objection is not a sufficient reason for discounting TE as a BSJ.

---

15. We should note that he himself appeals to necessary truth, for example, "no two empirical individuals of the same kind spatiotemporally coincide" (1991, p. 328). I would like to see how he is going to justify the said claim apart from an appeal to intuitions. He has not even hinted at the answer.

In any case, Gale's objection does not undermine my argument for TE.[16] The general idea is that the determination of analogy or disanalogy must be subsequent to our basic trust in experiences. The PCT is prior to knowledge about details of analogy or disanalogy.[17]

The conflicting claims objection

Many critics claim that, since REs are so various and mutually contradictory, we should regard all of them with suspicion. Even if we grant some force to REs, different REs cancel one another's force in the end (Flew 1966, pp. 126–7; Martin 1986, pp. 87–8). So it seems that the challenge of RE to naturalism can be easily neutralized.

The application of the PCT to conflicting experiences

First, the existing contradictions between REs do not render the PCT inapplicable to them. To apply the PCT to some experiences is to have *initial* trust in them and, if they are defeated, to salvage as much as possible from them. It does not entail that they are all or mostly reliable. There is no contradiction in saying that we should have initial trust in conflicting experiences. Indeed, almost all sorts of experience or doxastic practices produce conflicting beliefs sooner or later. Empirically speaking, no experience in which we trust is completely free from this problem. (Just think of the empiricists' "argument from illusion.") So why do we think that the presence of contradictions in RE should debar us from having initial trust, at least to some degree, in RE?

Now the critics seem to suggest a skeptical rule (SR):
(SR) When experiences or claims conflict with one another, we should reject all of them.

Should we adopt the SR instead? I do not think so. Consider the conflict of witnesses in the courts. It would be indeed stupid to reject all their accounts just because they conflict! It seems to be a rational strategy to try to reconcile their reports as much as possible. For example, a common core[18] can be identified. Another example: suppose a phenomenon occurred very briefly, which led to conflicting reports – A reported seeing an airplane, B a spaceship, and C an air balloon. It is absurd to suggest that we should reject all their statements and think that nothing has ever happened! At the very least, we should accept the common content of their experiences: there is an *unidentified flying object*. Moreover,

---

16. For a more detailed reply to Gale, see Gellman (2001, chap. 3).

17. Everitt's critique of ARE also includes a form of the disanalogy objection. Initially, he directly attacks the tests of RE by applying the standards of SE (2004, p. 169). When he later considers the plausible suggestion that some kind of variability of tests across practices is to be expected, he just insists that these tests cannot be too different from the standards of SE (2004, p. 170). Besides being a mere assertion than an argument, it is unclear how different is "too different."

18. Indeed it is not the case that a "common core" has to be shared by all the eyewitness accounts. Sometimes it is sufficient that it is shared by the large majority of the accounts, provided that either the error of the deviant witness in that aspect can be explained or overwhelming explanatory power is attained by adopting the common core. Admittedly, there are borderline cases in which we have to rely on our judgments.

historical documents are also liable to massive contradictions. However, we do not deduce from this phenomenon that historical enquiry is entirely pointless. The job of the historian is to utilize all these materials to reconstruct the past by harmonizing them without producing too much strain in the overall interpretation. Many historical accounts of a momentous historical event (e.g. China's Cultural Revolution) are contradictory. It is difficult to determine the exact course or nature of this event but it would be preposterous to deny that the Cultural Revolution has happened. All the given examples count against the skeptical policy and show that conflict of presumptive data is not irremediable.

In line with the said suggestions, although there is a significant degree of conflict of the REs at the highest level of description, a certain common core can still be extracted from them at a lower level of description.[19] For example, Davis carefully sifts through the data and suggests the following as the common core:

(i)   the mundane world of physical bodies, physical processes, and narrow centres of consciousness is not the whole or ultimate reality.

(ii)   ... there is a far deeper 'true self' which in some way depends on and participates in the ultimate reality.

(iii)   Whatever *is* the ultimate reality is holy, eternal, and of supreme value; it can appear to be more truly real than all else, since everything else depends on it.

(iv)   This holy power can be experienced as an awesome, loving, pardoning, guiding (etc.) presence with whom individuals can have a personal relationship ...

(v)   ... at least some mystical experiences are experiences of a very intimate union with the holy power ...

(vi)   Some kind of union or harmonious relation with the ultimate reality is the human being's *summum bonum*, his final liberation or salvation, and the means by which he discovers his 'true self' or 'true home'. (1989, p. 191)

All the REs point to the fact that there is another realm *up there* or *beyond* the naturalistic world. So even if REs have internal conflicts, arguably they can still lend support to ARE insofar as they tilt the balance away from naturalism. However, it is a kind of general support for the religious worldview instead of a specific support for theism at this level.

Reclassification of RE

To evaluate the epistemic status of TE relative to other kinds of RE, the rule of ground-level sifting is helpful. What we need to do is to segregate the presumptive data into consistent subsets and then choose the one which has maximal weight. So let us reclassify REs in the following way:

(A)   *TE*

(B)   *Theism-compatible non-TE*
These REs, though not specifically theistic, are logically compatible with theism. It can be further divided into the following:

19. Davis (1989, chap. 7) provides detailed suggestions how the conflicts can be reconciled.

(1) *Theism-friendly non-TEs*: these experiences go quite well with theism and they can be readily interpreted theistically without distortion or implausible reinterpretation.

(2) *Theism-neutral non-TEs*: these experiences are compatible with theism and they can be interpreted theistically; however, they do not strongly suggest a theistic interpretation, and they can also be interpreted in a way that goes against theism.

(3) *Theism-unfriendly non-TEs*: these experiences are logically compatible with theism but seem to suggest an interpretation that is in tension with theism.

(C) *Theism-incompatible non-TEs*
These experiences, if veridical in their most ramified description, are incompatible with theism because the Ultimate disclosed in these experiences is not personal.

I just explained my classification scheme, and I will soon discuss what kinds of RE can be placed within it. I have defended the claim that TE is a well-established type, and so the Type PCT is applicable to it. As far as other non-TEs are concerned, they are also covered by the Token PCT, which means that they at least have some force. Now there seems to be a major conflict between TE and theism-incompatible non-TE. If we also take into consideration the theism-compatible non-TEs, then there are two competing groups of RE: the *pro-theistic group*, which consists of TE plus theism-friendly non-TEs, and the *anti-theistic group*, which consists of theism-incompatible plus theism-unfriendly non-TEs. (Since the theism-neutral non-TEs do not point in any specific direction, we can ignore them here.) The question is to decide which group has the greater weight. Before discussing this question, we need to clarify the nature of monistic mystical experience.

PCE and monistic mystical experience

How to accurately describe the monistic mystical experience is in fact a controversial question, and the mystics sometimes offer paradoxical descriptions. To clarify the problem, we need to distinguish these two experiences:

(1) Awareness *of* undifferentiated unity, the One, the Self, and so on.
(2) A pure state of awareness which *is* undifferentiated unity.

The first experience is more like an intuition, an insight into reality but the intentional structure of experience is intact. The second experience is the PCE and it does not have an intentional structure at all. They are logically incompatible: no person can have both experiences at the same time. I propose that the phrase "monistic mystical experience" should be used to refer to the first intuitive experience rather than the PCE because the PCE in itself is not specifically monistic. Indeed it *cannot* yield support to monism by virtue of its epistemic seeming because there is no conceptual element in the PCE. The PCE is not without its conceptual difficulties (see Katz) but we have empirical evidence for the PCE (Forman 1990, pt. I).

Consider this report:

I would settle down, . . . and there would just be a sort of complete silence void of content. The whole awareness would turn in, and there would be no thought, no activity, and no perception, yet it was somehow comforting. . . . I did not yet identify myself with this silent, content-free inner space. . . . Then . . . I began to recognize in it the essence of my own self as pure consciousness. Eventually, . . . "I" as a separate entity just started to have no meaning . . . There is no thought, there is no activity, there is no experiencer. (Forman 1990, pp. 27–8).

The description is littered with paradoxes. Certainly, there was some experience akin to a PCE but it was also "somehow comforting." Did this sense of comfort feature within the experience or not? If yes, the experience is no longer pure. If no, then the sense of comfort should be another experience *subsequent* to the PCE. This is probably the case. I also wonder how the person can report a PCE afterward. In the PCE, there is no thought and feeling and no awareness of any sort. How then can the subject later ascribe this experience to *himself?* This must be explained by the continuous operation of the memory, even if it is somehow hidden during the PCE. But whose memory and whose PCE? To give intelligible answers to this question, it is difficult to avoid positing a self who possesses this PCE even though the sense of self is not present *in* the PCE. Indeed it is the interpretation adopted by the subject originally. But later the subject comes to another interpretation: "there is no thought, activity and experiencer." But this *thought* cannot be *given* in that experience. So this must be an *interpretation* imposed on the PCE due to subsequent reflection. So the question as to why this interpretation is justified has to be raised.

Perhaps we can conceive of the experiences as a unity. First, the subject has a PCE without monistic mystical experiences. However, when he comes back from this contentless state, *he* immediately has some monistic illuminations. The two experiences seem to go together and the PCE *in this context* may then be legitimately interpreted as an experience *of* the Self. However, the same move is available to the theists. Pike argues that when the Christian mystics experience a "monistic" interval within the context of dualistic experiences of God, it is legitimate to think that this "moment of experience in which the soul detects no distinction between itself and God is a kind of experiential fiction" (Pike 1992, p. 156). The spirit is simply "deluded by love into not noticing the difference between itself and God." The upshot is that there is no simple way to connect PCEs with monistic mystical experiences, either conceptually or evidentially. So PCEs are theism-neutral.

Coherence and conflict of TE with other REs

I have just argued that PCEs are theism-neutral. The main reason is that a PCE has no propositional content, and hence it cannot contradict theism. In fact in the earlier cases, some people can have both PCEs and TEs, and they do not see any contradiction between them.

I think nature mysticism is also theism-neutral. It can be interpreted in either a monistic or theistic way. For example, Jonathan Edwards's experience of nature mysticism is explicitly integrated with a TE:

The appearance of everything was altered; there seemed to be, as it were, a calm, sweet cast, or appearance of divine glory, in almost everything. God's excellency, his wisdom, his purity and love, seemed to appear in everything; in the sun, moon and stars; in the clouds and blue sky; in the grass, flowers, and trees; in the water and all nature. (quoted in Hick 2006, p. 29)

The kind of unity sensed in nature mysticism can reflect either the unity of all things rooted in their common source – their Creator God, or the kind of metaphysical unity envisaged by monism.

Second, let us assess the weight of the pro-theistic group. I have contended that TE is a well-established type of experience, and it is plausible to think it has the highest degree of intracoherence among REs. So TE is weighty in itself. Furthermore, many kinds of REs are compatible with theism and can readily be interpreted theistically, and hence theism-friendly:

(a)   Ecstasy and peak experience
(b)   Encounter of the Light Being in a near-death experience
(c)   Experience of evil spirit, angels, or departed saints
(d)   Experience of contingency – a spontaneous feeling that the world is somehow dependent on something beyond
(e)   Experience of design – experience of being struck by the beauty and intricacy of the natural order and the feeling that this order is ultimately due to Intelligence

(a) suggests a kind of spiritual depth in human beings which is more consonant with theism than with naturalism. If (b) and (c) are veridical, then there exist immaterial beings outside the bounds of nature. This is compatible with theism but incompatible with naturalism. (d) and (e) point somewhat in the direction of a transcendent Creator-Designer. If these experiences are veridical, they are certainly friendly with theism, and can even offer significant support for theism. I think these experiences are not that uncommon but the empirical case cannot be made here. Anyway, as far as RE is concerned, the pro-theistic group has considerable weight.

Now let us assess the weight of the anti-theistic group. The prime examples of theism-incompatible non-TE are monistic mysticism and the experience of Nirvana. Since these experiences suggest the Ultimate is essentially impersonal, it conflicts with theism. I will examine this conflict later. Let us now discuss theism-unfriendly non-TEs. Perhaps the experience of minor deities (e.g. visions of Kali or Buddha or Apollo) belong to this group. Michael Martin argues that they are *indirectly* incompatible with theism because they are embedded in a worldview which is at odds with the theistic one. Martin has a point but I would like to emphasize that logically speaking, it is possible that both God and these minor deities exist at the same time. The tension only arises because we have a further assumption that if God exists, He would not have created these minor deities. Otherwise, we can just regard these beings as spiritual creatures in God's world. However, perhaps given some plausible assumptions, these experiences may be *theism-unfriendly*. Since the conflict is not directly given in the experiences, I think it is quite possible to remove the tension by appropriate adjustment of our underlying assumptions and reinterpretation of those experiences.

As I have argued, cognitive adjustment is frequently needed even in our SEs, memories, and scientific inquiry. Deliverances of SE and memory often directly and indirectly conflict with one another. Some experimental data are frequently "indirectly incompatible" with other experimental data because the former are incompatible with the simplest law which are suggested by the latter. We might decide to stick to each and every experimental datum *no matter what*, but no cognitive systematization is then possible. If we are not willing to forgo at least some presumptive data and take theoretical gain into considerations, no universal laws can be substantiated. For example, after performing an experiment, we have six data which fall roughly on a straight line but also an anomalous datum not even close to that line. I submit it is rational to discard the anomalous datum in favor of the six others. This is what the CTA advises, and is also what the scientists in fact are doing.

Martin objects that acceptance of the PCT would result in a bloated ontology. This reflects a lack of understanding of the CTA. He seems to think that the PCT automatically commits us to accept each and every experience of minor deity *in toto*. This kind of picture is not even true of our more mundane epistemic practices. So in accordance with the CTA, the following is the rational way to do:

- We search for the neatest ontology or worldview which can preserve the maximal weight of the presumptive data here.
- Some of these data can be rejected if they are more vulnerable to defeaters and it results in a sufficient gain in simplicity or coherence. However, even in this situation, we should try to preserve their cognitive force as much as possible.

These considerations are just corollaries of the principles of the CTA. The theist does not need to give detailed answers about each and every RE in human history. He can be contented to point out that the argument for TE would be defeated *only if* the process of cognitive adjustment described results in the truncation of the whole lot of TE. I do not think it is the case. To the contrary, it seems to me that those lesser divine beings are not as widely experienced as God is. So it seems to be justified, on all the evidence, to regard the existence of God as the defeater of the experiences of those lesser beings who are incompatible with existence of God, and not the other way round. Moreover, it is much simpler to accept theism, which is supported by the significant weight of the pro-theistic group.

We also need to investigate how common are these experiences (e.g. experience of Apollo). We can raise these questions: does it survive the test of age and culture? Is it widespread? Does anybody claim to have an experience of Apollo which can be described as a "life in Apollo"? As far as I know, there is no evidence to show at least one-third of people in contemporary Western societies have had an experience of Apollo, and that significant minorities in every culture have organized their life around the experiences of Apollo. I have never heard of a single Chinese having an experience of Apollo, but many of them have definitely experienced God.

A theist does not need to choose between blanket rejection or blanket acceptance. He can adopt a more nuanced, case-by-case approach toward these experiences of minor deities.

- For those minor deities who are not really experienced by a sizable number of people across eras and cultures, the related experiences can be treated as anomalous data- either rejected or shelved.
- There is no need to reduce all those REs to sheer self-deception or hallucination. For those minor deities who have a more substantial experiential basis, the related experiences can be explained as the work of spiritual beings, or treated as genuine phenomena in the spiritual world, of which we do not yet have a full understanding. In cases like an experience of Virgin Mary, it may readily be interpreted as a veridical vision that does not commit us to her literal existence in the manifested form.

- In any case, experiences of minor deities *apparently* point in a consistent direction beyond naturalism. If they can be readily defeated, say, by naturalistic explanations, then the problem of indirect conflict with TE is removed. If the naturalistic explanations available are not really adequate,[20] then the whole group of such experiences can be taken to support a less specific claim: there are some spiritual forces in the world. This would actually provide further support for the theistic interpretation of the world.
- These experiences may be reinterpreted by monism as part of the *maya*. For example, Kali can be regarded as just one aspect of the Ultimate (the One) rather than an independently existing deity. This is possible but it is hard to see how those experiences can provide positive support for monism.

The theistic interpretation is further reinforced by considerations of intercoherence and worldview coherence: we can also ask does anybody have an experience of Apollo or the like through experiences of nature, goodness, beauty, finitude, freedom, and so on? How does the veridicality of the experience of Apollo help to explain other experiences? Is there any worldview that revolves around the existence of Apollo which is coherent and having explanatory power, say, with regard to contemporary scientific findings like fine-tuning? Is there ever a natural theology for the existence of Apollo? I think the theistic worldview will fare much better in these aspects. The entire content of this book is a support for this claim.

To sum up, experiences of minor deities taken at their most ramified description may be somewhat theism-unfriendly. However, from the perspective of TE, there are plausible reinterpretations of experiences of minor deities (whereas the reverse does not seem to be true) that can salvage much of their epistemic force, which supports the claim that there are spiritual forces in this world. This is confirming theism as well.

Is the ultimate reality personal or impersonal?

As for the contradiction between the personal versus impersonal understanding of the *nature of the ultimate reality*, I believe it is not as stark as it is commonly made out. The Personal Ultimate can manifest himself in a nonpersonal way. The manifestation can still be veridical and revelatory. Consider Yahweh's epiphany to Elijah. God can be said to be manifested in the earthquake and the whirlwind but this is not yet a personal manifestation. However, the whole thing is transformed when the "still small voice" is added to the scene. The whole experience becomes an unambiguous personal manifestation. So nonpersonal manifestation need not mean that it is antipersonal. Indeed, the Old Testament scholar Rowley says, "we find *personal and impersonal factors* woven together in what the Hebrews believed to be God's manifestation of himself" (1956, p. 45).

Wall suggests that:

> experiences of God, some personal and some impersonal, may be analogous to viewing an object from different sides. Or perhaps it is like viewing an object from different distances: From a distance we do not see the needles of a pine, but up close we do; yet regardless of the

---

20. For example, those experiences of minor deities may be supported by paranormal experiences that are hard to discredit.

differences in the experiences, we do not begin to think that we have seen different trees." So "we might say that 'from a distance' we may see God as impersonal but 'up close' as personal. (1995, pp. 319–20)

So in the end, there is a conflict only if one claims that the Ultimate is *essentially personal*, and the other claims that the Ultimate is *essentially impersonal*. However, "we rarely, if ever, run across claims to the effect that someone was aware of experiencing God's essential nature or some aspect of God as essential. In all cases I collected or examined I found neither claim made" (Wall 1995, p. 320).

So in the end, we do need to resolve the conflict between the claim that the Ultimate is essentially personal and the contrary claim that the Ultimate is essentially impersonal. I now explore the conflict of theism and monism of the Advaita Vedanta school.

Conflict of theism and monism

The Advaita Vedanta school makes these claims:

(a) Brahman as the Impersonal Absolute is the Ultimate Reality in which there is no distinction and differentiation.
(b) Atman is Brahman, that is, every human self is metaphysically identical to Brahman; hence every self is metaphysically identical to another self.
(c) The world is ultimately *maya* (illusion).

Obviously, these claims conflict with theism which asserts that the Ultimate is a Personal God who creates the world and distinct selves. Theism also claims that although all the latter are contingent upon the continuous creative act of God, they are nonetheless real and distinct from one another. In my CTA, we have resources to resolve this conflict: Principle of Comparison and Principle of Conflict Resolution. The crucial point is whether TE is a better-established type than monistic experience (ME) or vice versa. Let us briefly discuss this question.

Intracoherence

(a) It seems to me the people who have MEs are confined to a relatively small group of mystics in various religious traditions, and mainly Eastern ones, whereas I have argued that TE is present in various traditions and shared by a substantial portion of humankind.
(b) I have argued that tokens of TE do form intricate coherence relationships, whereas MEs do not exhibit many modalities nor do their tokens exhibit a complex pattern of coherence.
(c) It seems to me the articulation of the ME suffers from many conceptual difficulties: how is an experience of Nirvana or the Absolute possible? A noetic experience has an intrinsic structure but the Absolute is structureless. If it is literally ineffable, how can it be communicated to form an intersubjective type of experience? Hick is also aware of this kind of problem:

> to lose one's individual identity completely, like a drop becoming part of the ocean – a familiar simile in mystic literature – would be to lose the individual continuity of

consciousness and memory in virtue of which the mystic would later be able to report the experience. How could someone remember being in a state in which he or she no longer existed as a distinct individual? There must, surely, have been a continuing strand of consciousness to enable them later to speak about it, while still enjoying something of its bliss. (Hick 2006, p. 22)

I have defended here the conceptual coherence of TE. TE seems to have a higher degree of intracoherence than ME.

Intercoherence

The degree of intercoherence of TE is high. It does not conflict with other basic types of human experience. It can even provide a framework for explaining them (e.g. moral experience and rational intuition). The following points concentrate on the intercoherence of ME with various kinds of noetic experience.

SE

It seems that SE discloses a world of multiplicity and change. Since SE is one of the best-established types of experience, then SE can serve as the defeater of almost all other types of experience. Now ME apparently comes in conflict with SE, and this seems to be a serious problem. For example, Gale thinks that concerning MEs, their "descriptions are often contradictory or in conflict with our best-established empirical beliefs, such as that there exists a multiplicity of distinct objects and events in space and time" (1991, p. 303). This criticism has been pressed by Madhva in the thirteenth century *within the Hindu tradition itself* (Copleston 1982, p. 80). The postulation of *maya* does not clearly help: is it not introducing multiplicity within Brahman itself? There is also the move of *qualification*: there are degrees of reality, and SE discloses something real at its level but not ultimately real. I, however, have the problem of understanding its exact meaning. If it means that the physical world, although real, is only contingent, it does not conflict with either SE or theism. If it means that the world is real only as an appearance, it again comes into conflict with SE.

Moral experience

Monism also seems to come in conflict with the basic assumption of moral experience, that is, there is an objective distinction between good and evil, right and wrong. It is questionable how this can be preserved in a system when All is One. Does it mean that in the end, we cannot distinguish Hitler from Mother Teresa, and Stalin from Gandhi? If so, it is a mockery of our ordinary consciousness, not to mention the morally dangerous doctrine that Brahman is beyond good and evil. Of course, many monistic mystics exhibit a high degree of moral consciousness and display virtues in their lives. What I am pressing is the *logical* problem: are the moral experiences of the monistic mystics compatible with their MEs? Furthermore, moral strife seems to presuppose a self distinct from Brahman:

> the teaching of the Advaita school about the need for moral purification, for detachment from selfish passions, and for the advance from ignorance to knowledge presupposes that it is in fact the human being who is being urged to turn to the One. It is the human being, not

Brahman, who is called upon to recognize his or her relationship with the One. If the Advaita really means that the human being must disappear altogether, he should say so in an unambiguous manner ... Further, if the human being is appearance, to whom the appearance appear? To Brahman? If so, the Absolute presumably misleads itself, though why and how remains obscure. (Copleston 1982, p. 84)

TE, on the other hand, provides an ontological explanation or basis for the basic distinction in morality and the categorical imperative, and there is experiential fusion between moral experience and TE. Conscience sometimes mediates the voice of God and experience of grace is often experienced in and with the experience of moral improvement and so on (see Kwan 2006c).

Interpersonal experience

Our interpersonal experience reveals the otherness of the *Thou*. Again this seems to be in conflict with the monistic doctrine that all these distinctions are just illusory. On the other hand, this type of experience is coherent with TE. For example, theism allows for the ecstatic union of souls, and the ecclesiological doctrine of the Body of Christ also suggests that although human persons are distinct, they are destined for intimate communion. So some insights of monism are preserved.

Experience of change

According to monism, change is an illusion. But "nothing seems plainer than that there are a multiplicity of things in the world around us and that these, and our experience of them, are constantly changing. To deny the reality of change, variety and multiplicity seems to be the most bizarre of all religious or metaphysical procedures" (Lewis 1969, p. 296).

So TE also seems to have a higher degree of intercoherence than ME.

Worldview coherence

I assume that the theistic worldview has substantial explanatory power (see other chapters in this book). If there is not a comparable rational case for monism, then TE will have an advantage over ME. This question cannot be fully settled here, of course.

As a summary, it seems possible to argue, with respect to clauses (a) and (b) (and possibly (c)) of the Principle of Comparison, that TE should be taken as the better established subtype of RE. Therefore, in accordance with the Principle of Conflict Resolution, it is plausible to claim that TE would serve as the defeater of ME rather than the other way round.

Cognitive adjustment

Of course, it is not plausible just to dismiss the whole type of ME. For my case to be more convincing, some plausible postexperiential reinterpretation of ME is needed. First, let us consider the case of extrovertive mysticism which:

takes its start from the facts of the world around us, and ... finds that all things run into one another in a unity in which all separate existence and variety is lost. There is nothing but the One, but the One is seen 'in or through the multiplicity of objects'. (Lewis 1969, p. 302)

It seems that the core experience is a kind of nature mysticism which, as I have argued, is compatible with theism. On the other hand, there are also plausible interpretations of introvertive mysticism. Maritain suggests that:

> The Hindu experience does appear therefore, to be a mystical experience in the natural order, a fruitive experience of the absolute, of that absolute which is the substantial *esse* of the soul and, in it and through it, of the divine absolute. (1966, pp. 97–8)

The PCE can be interpreted as an experience of the substance of one's soul which is indeed grounded in God. Because the PCE is a purely negative experience, it is not surprising that a monistic intuition can occur after that. Although it is defeated, it can be seen to be a plausible error. Furthermore, theistic mysticism shows that the mystical path can be accommodated within theism, that is, it is not at all surprising that God will bring about the experiences of emptiness. According to Louis Dupre, negative theology may be the first step to achieve spiritual poverty and humility. This enables us to see the emptiness of creaturely things and our inadequacies and liberates us from the attachment to things (Dupre 1981, p. 48).

Can it be done the other way round? Can the way of devotion be incorporated into the mystical path? Yes, but ultimately, it is more like a concession than an integration. The Advaitin would allow that the *bhakti* is a legitimate way to Brahman, but ultimately, a loving devotion to Brahman, if he is consistent, must be regarded as based on ignorance. It is because devotion presupposes some sort of dualism and it conflicts with Advaita's nondualism. So:

> theism can give us a profound and beautiful way of integrating the insights of prophets with those of contemplatives and combining the paths of devotional worship and mystical endeavour. But if you try to do it the other way round the main teachings of theism begin to disappear: devotion fades and the revelations wither. While theism can convincingly absorb and enrich the mystical path without detriment to the latter, the mystical path cannot absorb theistic belief without relegating it to second place. (Smart 1960, p. 72)

If this is the case, then the theistic way of cognitive adjustment preserves more PFJ than the monistic way. In accordance with the Principle of Conservation, the former is to be recommended.

Of course, the above is just the beginning of a critical dialogue between different religious traditions. I also have no time to discuss other theism-incompatible REs, for example, the experience of Nirvana (yet many things said earlier also count against these "mystical" theism-incompatible REs). Nevertheless, I suggest tentatively that the CTA may have significant resources to resolve the conflicts, and at least it is not obvious that TE *is defeated* by ME or other types.[21] Yandell (1999, chap. 13) has also offered a strong critique of monistic non-TEs.

---

21. Perhaps some may object that my interpretation of ME is uncharitable. For example, Hick agrees that accounts of ME, when taken literally, are indeed incoherent. His solution is that we should interpret the mystical literature metaphorically: "the unitive language of Advaita Vedanta is ... metaphorically ... expressing a ... vivid awareness of the limitless reality in which we are rooted" (Hick 2006, p. 23). I am not sure Hick's revisionism is really true to the monistic mystics' experience or traditions. In any case, a vivid awareness of the limitless reality in which we are rooted is compatible with theism because God is limitless, and we are indeed rooted in Him. So in any case, TE seems less problematic than ME. If taken literally, the ME is plagued by apparent incoherence. If taken metaphorically, it is not incompatible with theism, and it cannot be taken to offer support for monism over against theism.

Conclusion

The degree of conflicts among REs is usually grossly overestimated. Many REs are just different and far from being logically inconsistent. REs as a whole still support theism more than naturalism. Among the REs, TE is a relatively well-established type, and it is also widely corroborated by a diverse group of theism-friendly REs. It is, at least, compatible with many mystical experiences (e.g. nature mysticism). Moreover, in accordance with the principles of CTA, a plausible case can be made that the pro-theistic group has a greater weight than the anti-theistic group. So TEs are, by no means, defeated by conflicting REs. I have a fuller treatment elsewhere (Kwan 2003).

Brief discussions of several objections to TE

I have treated quite a few major objections: logical gap objection, theory-ladenness objection, privacy objection, conceptual incoherence of TE objection, and disanalogy objection. I have written at length responding to the conflicting claims objection because I think it is the most serious one. In my section on "Intracoherence of TE," I have also implicitly dealt with the oddness of TE objection. There are still a few objections which I have not explicitly dealt with. I give some brief comments on them further in the discussion.

Impossibility of individuation objection

James Harris has built on Gale's idea, and has made heavy weather of the problem of individuating God in TE. I think it is indeed impossible to *prove* that it is the same God all the time and not similar but different gods appearing in different occasions. However, I do not think the requirement of absolute or noncircular proof is realistic because even our SEs cannot satisfy this. Outside the critical trust framework, we cannot in fact prove that our experiences apparently of the same table are really caused by the same table, and not really the results of two qualitatively similar acts of deception by the Cartesian demon. I agree with Gellman's (2001, chap. 3) idea that reidentifying physical objects is also a holistic practice, which is inescapably circular in the end. If we also accept the reidentification of God as a holistic practice, then I think given the basic trust in TE (revelatory experiences of prophets and Jesus, the experience of maximal greatness-making properties in TE) and the Principle of Simplicity, the problem can be largely solved. Even if in the end we cannot do that, then at most we can say that the ARE does not uniquely support monotheism over against polytheism. But this would be small comfort for naturalists because polytheism is equally unacceptable to them.

The no criteria/uncheckability objection

Critics allege that there is no criterion to distinguish the veridical REs from the nonveridical ones. Of course, there are in fact criteria from within the religious framework, but the critics object that these are not objective, noncircular criteria. The first line of response is to point out that it is also the case that SEs can only be checked by other SEs, and that it is also circular (see Kwan 2006b). This point should be obvious after discussions in this chapter. Moreover, my lengthy section on the "Structure of CTA" is, in fact, meant to show that there is a universal method which governs how second-order critical principles or principles of epistemic enhancement arise from the experiences themselves. In fact, criteria of veridicality and unveridicality are just corollaries of these principles. I have also demonstrated how the rules of CTA can be used to settle the problem of conflicting REs. So the basic thrust of the no criteria objection has been neutralized.

The naturalistic explanation objection

The prior question that needs to be settled is when would a naturalistic explanation of TE really constitute a defeater. I think it needs to fulfill several conditions:

(a)   It can specify a set of causally sufficient conditions for TE.
(b)   We have reasons to believe that that set of conditions will render the veridicality of the TE unlikely.
(c)   We have reasons to believe that set of conditions really obtain in the majority of cases of TE.

I doubt that any available naturalistic explanation can satisfy these requirements, but I have not said much about this here. Fortunately, many authors have a good response to this problem: Davis (1989, chap. 8), Yandell (1993, chaps. 6 and 7), Gellman (1997, chap. 5; 2001, chap. 5), and Griffith-Dickson (2000, chap. 4). Wall's book is entirely devoted to this issue and he utilizes concrete examples of REs to point out the inadequacy of various naturalistic explanations. I have also offered a detailed critique of projectionism (Kwan 2006a).

Gullibilism objection

Many critics like to produce alleged counterexamples to the PCT such as experiences of UFO, apparitions, and so on. They contend that the PCT leads to the acceptance of all these strange claims, and hence the approach is too gullible. I have taken care of this objection in the very first stage of my argument. I only argue for a weak Token PCT, emphasize the need for critical sifting, and explain how the CTA can produce an orderly and coherent noetic structure.

The ARE in the Twenty-First Century

Although the ARE is hotly contended, I think Swinburne's route of taking RE as *prima facie* evidence for the transcendent realm is a promising one. Following this line, I have defended a version of ARE in this chapter.

I have argued that the Type PCT is a fundamental principle. Even if my impartiality argument is not conclusive, I hope I have made, or at least suggested, a plausible case for the CTA, which is clearly delineated here. I contend that, since TE does have impressive empirical grounding and intracoherence, it deserves to be accorded PFJ. I have also argued that many popular alleged defeaters of TE do not really succeed. Of course, I cannot deal with *all* the proposed defeaters here. However, the recurrent pattern of discussions shows that the objections often commit fallacies of double standard, epistemic chauvinism, or requirement of superreliability. So those alleged defeaters are more implicitly the rejection of the PCT and CTA. Otherwise, it seems rather difficult to show the entire corpus of TE to be unreliable. So it may not be unreasonable to believe that the critics are yet to produce a convincing defeater. It follows that belief in God can at least be tentatively justified.

I do not expect that the ARE will gain consensus, but in any case, philosophical arguments rarely achieve this. The ARE is worthy of further exploration together with the deep epistemological questions in the twenty-first century. It may well lead to fruitful developments in both philosophy of religion and epistemology.

References

Alston, W. (1991) *Perceiving God: The Epistemology of Religious Experience*. Ithaca, NY and London: Cornell University Press.

Alston, W. (1993) *The reliability of Sense Perception*. Ithaca, NY and London: Cornell University Press.

Alston, W. (1999) Perceptual knowledge. In J. Greco and E. Sosa (eds.), *The Blackwell Guide to Epistemology*, 223–42. Oxford: Blackwell.

Baergen, R. (1993) The influence of cognition upon perception: the empirical story. *Australian Journal of Philosophy* 71: 1, 13–23.

Bagger, M. C. (1999) *Religious Experience, Justification, and History*. Cambridge: Cambridge University Press.

Baillie, J. (1962) *The Sense of the Presence of God*. London: Oxford University Press.

Beardsworth, T. (1977) *Sense of Presence*. Oxford: The Religious Experience Research Unit, Manchester College.

Bonjour, L. (1985) *The Structure of Empirical Knowledge*. Cambridge, MA: Harvard University Press.

Bonjour, L. (1999) The dialectic of foundationalism and coherentism. In J. Greco and E. Sosa (eds.), *The Blackwell Guide to Epistemology*, 117–42. Oxford, Blackwell.

Broad, C. D. (1953) *Religion, Philosophy and Psychical Research*. London: Routledge and Kegan Paul.

Cartwright, N. (1994) How we relate theory to observation. In P. Horwich (ed.), *World Changes: Thomas Kuhn and the Nature of Science*, 259. Cambridge, MA: MIT Press.

Chisholm, R. M. (1973) *The Problem of the Criterion*. Milwaukee, WI: Marquette University Press.

Copleston, F. (1982) *Religion and the One*. London: Search Press.

Dancy, J. (ed.) (1988) *Perceptual Knowledge*. Oxford: Oxford University Press.

Daniels, C. (1989) Experiencing God. *Philosophy and Phenomenological Research* XLIX, 487–99.

Davies, B. (1985) *Thinking about God*. London: Geoffrey Chapman.

Davis, C. (1989) *The Evidential Force of Religious Experience*. Oxford: Clarendon Press.

Donovan, P. (1979) *Interpreting Religious Experience*. London: Sheldon Press.

Dorr, D. (1978) *Remove the Heart of Stone – Charismatic Renewal and the Experience of Grace*. Dublin: Gill and Macmillan.

Draper, P. (1992) God and perceptual evidence. *International Journal for Philosophy of Religion* 32, 149–65.

Dupre, L. (1981) *The Deeper Life*. New York: Crossroad.

Edwards, R. (1972) *Reason and Religion: An Introduction to the Philosophy of Religion*. New York: Harcourt Brace Jovanovich.

Elgin, C. Z. (1996) *Considered Judgment*. Princeton, NJ: Princeton University Press.

Elgin, C. Z. (2005) Non-foundationalist epistemology: holism, coherence, and tenability. In M. Steup and E. Sosa (eds.), *Contemporary Debates in Epistemology*, 156–67. Oxford: Blackwell.

Everitt, N. (2004) *The Non-Existence of God*. London: Routledge.

Ewing, A. C. (1973) *Value and Reality*. London: George Allen and Unwin Ltd.

Farmer, H. H. (1935) *The World and God.* London: Nisbet and Co. Ltd.

Flew, A. (1966) *God and Philosophy.* London: Hutchinson and Co. Ltd.

Flew, A. and MacIntyre, A. (eds.) *New Essays in Philosophical Theology.* London: SCM.

Flew, A. and Varghese, R. A. (2007) *There is a God: How the World's Most Notorious Atheist Changed His Mind.* New York: HarperCollins.

Forgie, J. W. (1998) The possibility of theistic experience. *Religious Studies* 34, 317–23.

Forman, R. K. C. (ed.) (1990) *The Problem of Pure Consciousness – Mysticism and Philosophy.* New York: Oxford University Press.

Frank, S. L. (1946) *God with Us.* London: Jonathan Cape Ltd.

Fumerton, R. (1992) Skepticism and reasoning to the best explanation. In E. Villanueva (ed.), *Rationality in Epistemology,* 149–70. Atascadero, CA: Ridgeview Publishing Co.

Fumerton, R. (2005) The challenge of refuting skepticism. In M. Steup and E. Sosa (eds.), *Contemporary Debates in Epistemology,* 85–97. Oxford: Blackwell.

Gale, R. (1991) *On the Nature and Existence of God.* Cambridge: Cambridge University Press.

Geivett, R. D. (2003) The evidential value of religious experience. In P. Copan and P. Moser (eds.), *The Rationality of Theism,* 175–203. London: Routledge.

Gellman, J. (1994) Experiencing God's infinity. *American Philosophical Quarterly* 31: 1, 53–61.

Gellman, J. (1997) *Experience of God and the Rationality of Theistic Belief.* Ithaca, NY: Cornell University Press.

Gellman, J. (2001) *Mystical Experience of God: A Philosophical Inquiry.* Aldershot: Ashgate.

Ginet, C. (1975) *Knowledge, Perception, and Memory.* Dordrecht: Reidel.

Grice, H. P. (1988). The causal theory of perception. In J. Dancy (ed.), *Perceptual Knowledge,* 66–78. Oxford: Oxford University Press.

Griffith-Dickson, G. (2000) *Human and Divine: An Introduction to the Philosophy of Religious Experience.* London: Duckworth.

Griffith-Dickson, G. (2005) *The Philosophy of Religion.* London: SCM Press.

Griffiths, B. (1989) *A New Vision of Reality – Western Science, Eastern Mysticism and Christian Faith.* London: Collins.

Gutting, G. (1982) *Religious Belief and Religious Skepticism.* Notre Dame, IN: University of Notre Dame Press.

Haack, S. (1994) Double-aspect foundherentism: a new theory of empirical justification. In E. Sosa (ed.), *Knowledge and Justification,* 729–44. Aldershot: Dartmouth.

Hallett, G. (2000) *A Middle Way to God.* Oxford: Oxford University Press.

Hamlyn, D. W. (1970) *The Theory of Knowledge.* London: Macmillan.

Harris, J. F. (2002) *Analytic Philosophy of Religion.* Dordrecht: Kluwer.

Harrison, J. (1999) *God, Freedom and Immortality.* Aldershot: Ashgate.

Hay, D. (1990) *Religious Experience Today.* London: Mowbray.

Hay, D. (1994) 'The biology of God': what is the current status of Hardy's hypothesis? *International Journal for the Psychology of Religion* 4: 1, 1–23.

He, Guanghu. (1995) The root and flower of Chinese culture. *Primordial Dao,* 2: 29–56. (何光滬,〈中國文化的根與花〉,《原道》第二輯, 1995年5月, 頁29–56。).

Hesse, M. (1981) Retrospect. In A. R. Peacocke (ed.), *The Sciences and Theology in the Twentieth Century* 281–96. Stocksfield: Oriel Press.

Hick, J. (2006) *The New Frontier of Religion and Science: Religious Experience, Neuroscience and the Transcendent.* Basingstoke, England and New York: Palgrave Macmillan.

Huemer, M. (2001) *Skepticism and the Veil of Perception.* Lanham, MD: Rowan and Littlefield.

Katz, S. T. (ed.) (1978) *Mysticism and Philosophical Analysis.* New York: Oxford University Press.

Kwan, K.-M. (2001) A critical appraisal of a non-realist philosophy of religion: an Asian perspective. *Philosophia Christi* 3: 1, 225–35.

Kwan, K.-M. (2003) Is the critical trust approach to religious experience incompatible with religious particularism? A reply to Michael Martin and John Hick. *Faith and Philosophy* 20: 2, 152–69.

Kwan, K.-M. (2004) Review of Jerome Gellman, *Mystical Experience of God: A philosophical Inquiry.* *Faith and Philosophy* 21: 4, 553–60.

Kwan, K.-M. (2006a) Are religious beliefs human projections? In R. Pelly and P. Stuart (eds.), *A Religious Atheist? Critical Essays on the Work of Lloyd Geering*, 41–66. Dunedin, New Zealand: Otago University Press.

Kwan, K.-M. (2006b) Can religious experience provide justification for belief in God? The debate in contemporary analytic philosophy. *Philosophy Compass* November.

Kwan, K.-M. (2006c) Moral arguments for the existence of God [addendum]. In D. Borchert (ed.), *Encyclopedia of Philosophy*, 2nd edn. Detroit, MI: Macmillan Reference USA.

Kwan, K.-M. and Han, S. (2007) The Quest for God in Chinese Culture and Contemporary China. Paper presented in the Trinity Newman Lecture, July 16, 2007, Victoria University, Wellington, New Zealand.

Layman, C. S. (2007) *Letters to Doubting Thomas: A Case for the Existence of God.* New York: Oxford University Press.

Lewis, H. D. (1969) *The Elusive Mind.* London: George Allen and Unwin Ltd.

Lycan, W. (1988) *Judgment and Justification.* Cambridge: Cambridge University Press.

Mackie, J. (1982) *The Miracle of Theism.* Oxford: Clarendon Press.

Maritain, J. (1966) *Challenges and Renewals.* Cleveland and New York: Meridian Books, The World Publishing Co.

Martin, C. B. (1959) *Religious Belief.* Ithaca: Cornell University Press.

Martin, M. (1986) The principle of credulity and religious experience. *Religious Studies* 22, 79–93.

Martin, M. (1990) *Atheism: A Philosophical Justification.* Philadelphia: Temple University Press.

Mawson, T. J. (2005) *Belief in God: An Introduction to the Philosophy of Religion.* Oxford: Clarendon.

Miles, G. (2007) *Science and Religious Experience: Are They Similar Forms of Knowledge?* Sussex: Academic Press.

Moody, R. (1975) *Life after life.* New York: Bantam Books.

Newberg, A, D'Aquili, E., and Rause, V. (2001) *Why God Won't Go Away: Brain Science and the Biology of Belief.* New York: Ballantine Books.

Oppy, G. (2006) *Arguing about Gods.* Cambridge: Cambridge University Press.

Otto, R. (1924) *The Idea of the Holy.* Oxford: Oxford University Press.

Owen, H. P. (1969) *The Christian Knowledge of God.* London: The Athleone Press.

Papineau, D. (1979) *Theory and Meaning.* Oxford: Clarendon Press.

Pike, N. (1992) *Mystic Union – An Essay in the Phenomenology of Mysticism.* Ithaca, NY: Cornell University Press.

Pullinger, J. (1980) *Chasing the Dragon.* London: Hodder and Stoughton.

Rescher, N. (1995) *Satisfying Reason: Studies in the Theory of Knowledge.* Dordrecht: Kluwer.

Rowe, W. (1982) Religious experience and the principle of credulity. *International Journal for Philosophy of Religion* 13, 85–92.

Rowley, H. H. (1956) *The Faith of Israel.* London: SCM Press.

Russell, B. (1948) *Human Knowledge: Its Scope and Limits.* London: George Allen and Unwin Ltd.

Schaefer, R. T. and Lamm, R. P. (1995) *Sociology*, 5th edn. New Yord: McGraw-Hill.

Schoen, E. L. (1990) The sensory presentation of divine infinity. *Faith and Philosophy* 7: 1, 3–18.

Slote, M. (1970) *Reason and Scepticism.* London: George Allen and Unwin Ltd.

Smart, N. (1960) *A Dialogue of Religions.* London: SCM Press.

Swinburne, R. (1979) *The Existence of God.* Oxford: Clarendon Press.

Swinburne, R. (1981) The evidential value of religious experience, and Comments. In A. R. Peacocke (ed.), *The Sciences and Theology in the Twentieth Century*, 182–96, 303–4. Stocksfield: Oriel Press.

Swinburne, R. (1986) *The Evolution of the Soul.* Oxford: Clarendon Press.

Trueblood, E. (1957) *Philosophy of Religion.* Grand Rapids, MI: Baker.

Tsai, C. (1953) *Queen of the Dark Chamber.* Chicago: Moody Press.

Tsai, C. (2000) *Queen of the Dark Chamber*. Hong Kong: The Bellman House. (This is a Chinese book: 蔡蘇娟,《暗室之后》, 香港: 晨星出版社,2000。).

Van Cleve, J. (2005) Why coherence is not enough. In M. Steup and E. Sosa (eds.), *Contemporary Debates in Epistemology*, 168–80. Oxford: Blackwell.

Vardy, P. (1990) *The Puzzle of God*. London: Collins, Flame.

Vogel, J. (1998) Cartesian skepticism and the inference to the best explanation. In L. Martin Alcoff (ed.), *Epistemology: The Big Questions*, 352–9. Oxford: Blackwell.

Vogel, J. (2005) The refutation of skepticism. In M. Steup and E. Sosa (eds.), *Contemporary Debates in Epistemology*, 73–84. Oxford: Blackwell.

Von Leyden, W. (1961) *Remembering: A Philosophical Problem*. New York: Philosophical Library.

Wainwright, W. (1981) *Mysticism*. Brighton: The Harvester Press.

Wall, G. (1995) *Religious Experience and Religious Belief*. Lanham, MD: University Press of America.

Waterhouse, E. S. (1923) *The Philosophy of Religious Experience*. London: The Epworth Press.

Wynn, M. R. (2005) *Emotional Experience and Religious Understanding: Integrating Perception, Conception and Feeling*. Cambridge: Cambridge University Press.

Xi, Y. (1990) *Song of the Valley*. Petaluma, CA: Chinese Christian Mission. (This is a Chinese book: 希雲,《幽谷之歌》, 中國信徒佈道會, 1990。).

Yandell, K. (1984) *Christianity and Philosophy*. Grand Rapids, MI: Eerdmans.

Yandell, K. (1993) *The Epistemology of Religious Experience*. Cambridge: Cambridge University Press.

Yandell, K. (1999) *Philosophy of Religion: A Contemporary Introduction*. Cambridge: Cambridge University Press; London: Routledge.

10

The Ontological Argument

ROBERT E. MAYDOLE

Ontological arguments are deductive arguments for the existence of God from general metaphysical principles and other assumptions about the nature or essence of God. There have been three very significant developments in the history of ontological arguments. The first is the ontological argument developed by St Anselm of Canterbury in the eleventh century. The second is the argument sketched by Descartes in the late seventeenth century and completed by Leibniz in the early eighteenth century. And the third development consists of the numerous ontological arguments of the twentieth century that explicitly utilize modal logic, particularly those of Malcolm, Hartshorne, Plantinga, and Gödel. My chief aim in this chapter is to logically evaluate logical reconstructions of each of these six arguments. I shall also present and logically discuss two of my own explicitly modal onto-logical arguments.[1]

The logical evaluation of a logical reconstruction of an argument often requires that we explicitly identify assumptions that are only implicit in the author's original presentation of the argument. And in some cases, it might involve the inclusion of "plausible" philo-sophical principles that are consistent with the author's worldview, principles that strengthen the argument if we include them among the premises of the reconstruction. My *modus operandi* will be to make each of the arguments as strong as possible before critically evalu-ating them. Even though I shall try to remain reasonably faithful to the intent of the original author of each argument, my main objective will be logical instead of historical.

A good deductive argument should be valid and have true premises. And if it is to be convincing it should not beg the question. Ontological arguments are frequently the target of parodies, perhaps more so than any other argument in philosophy. So in addition to checking the arguments we discuss for validity, truth, and question begging, I shall also test their vulnerability to being refuted by some of the well-known parodies in the philo-sophical literature. Like many other philosophical arguments of note, ontological argu-ments stand or fall on the acceptability of some very high-level and well-entrenched principles of metaphysics and logic. And, as we shall see, some ontological arguments are logically much stronger than what first meets the eye.

---

1. It would not be possible for me to discuss all or even most of the ontological arguments in the history of phi-losophy in this chapter. One of the most comprehensive and fairest discussions of many of these is by Graham Oppy (1995).

1a. The Validity of Anselm's Ontological Argument

Anselm expresses his ontological argument of *Proslogium,* Chapter ll as follows:

> Hence, even the fool is convinced that something exists in the understanding, at least, than which nothing greater can be conceived. For, when he hears of this, he understands it. And whatever is understood, exists in the understanding. And assuredly that, than which nothing greater can be conceived, cannot exist in the understanding alone. For, suppose it exists in the understanding alone: then it can be conceived to exist in reality; which is greater.
>
> Therefore, if that, than which nothing greater can be conceived, exists in the understanding alone, the very being, than which nothing greater can be conceived, is one, than which a greater can be conceived. But obviously this is impossible. Hence, there is no doubt that there exists a being than which nothing greater can be conceived, and it exists both in the understanding and in reality. (1962, p. 8)

There are a few key ideas in this passage that require our attention before we present the main argument. First, Anselm understands the predicate "is greater than" to mean the same as "objectively better or more worthy than." It was commonplace for philosophers of the Middle Ages to order things into a great chain of being according to the degree to which they possess great-making properties, such as wisdom, power, goodness, and completeness, and existence-in-reality. What Anselm argues here is that God is an upper bound to the great chain of being. He makes this point very explicitly in his *Monologion*:

> Furthermore, if one considers the nature of things, one cannot help realizing that they are not all of equal value, but differ by degrees. For the nature of a horse is better than that of a tree, and that of a human more excellent than that of a horse . . . It is undeniable that some natures can be better than others. None the less reason argues that there is some nature that so overtops the others that it is inferior to none. (1998, p. 14)

Second, the conclusion of Anselm's argument is that something than which nothing greater can be conceived has the property of existence-in-reality. Now if something has the property of existence-in-reality, then it exists, period. But the property of existence-in-reality is only one kind of existence. The property of existence-in-the-understanding is another. Notions, concepts, ideas, thoughts, beliefs, and so on are the kinds of things that do or might have existence-in-the-understanding. And tables, persons, angels, numbers, forces, and so on, and God, are the kinds of things that do or might have existence-in-reality. We can identify the realm of things that have existence-in-the-understanding with the totality of mental things that actually exist in minds; and we can identify the realm of things that have existence-in-reality with the totality of nonmental things that actually exist in the world.[2] It is crucial, however, not to conflate existence-in-reality with existence

---

2. Deane translates the phrase "*esse in intellectu*" as "exists in the understanding" (Anselm 1962), and Charlesworth translates it as "exists in the mind" (Anselm 1998). But McGill translates it as "stands in relation to the understanding" (Anselm 1967) because, he contends, "exists in the understanding" and "exists in the mind" both have a Cartesian connotation of existing *in* a substantial place of some sort with*in* which certain mental phenomena occur, which is not, he says, what Anselm intended. "For him the intellect is the *intentional* phase of human being [*sic*]. It is man's active openness towards reality, toward real entities through "understanding" and towards possible entities through "conceiving". "It is never a self-enclosed place within which certain phenomena

generally. For Anselm, mental things that have existence-in-the-understanding exist just as much as nonmental things that have existence-in-reality, but in a different way.

Third, it is inconceivable that one and the same thing could have both existence-in-reality and existence-in-the-understanding. Things that have existence-in-reality are very different kinds of things from things that have existence-in-the-understanding. A table, for example, is different from the concept or idea of a table. Likewise, it impossible to think of God, even *qua* pure spirit, as having existence-in-the-understanding, even if God fails to have existence-in-reality or even if "the fool is convinced that something exists in the understanding, at least, than which nothing greater can be conceived." Either Anselm has been mistranslated or he misspoke and should have said that even the fool is convinced that the *concept* of something than which nothing greater can be conceived has existence-in-the-understanding; and instead of saying "whatever is understood, exists in the understanding," he should have said "the concept of whatever is understood has existence-in-the-understanding" and so on. That said, a neo-Platonist such as Anselm might hold that things that have existence-in-reality and things that have existence-in-the-understanding *might* share many or most of the same properties, including the property of it being inconceivable for something to be greater.

Fourth, it is clear that for Anselm the phrase "that than which nothing greater can be conceived" should be understood as a definite description which refers to the one and only one thing than which nothing greater can be conceived, God, even if there is no such being. Similarly, the proposition "the concept of whatever is understood has existence-in-the-understanding" should be understood in the context of his argument as saying that the concept of whatever a definite description that is understood refers to has existence-in-the-understanding. This is consistent with Anselm's belief that even though we cannot fully and adequately understand God, we do at least have a partial concept of God as a being than which nothing greater can be conceived, and thereby we can understand our referential talk *about* God. The presupposition is that some referring singular terms and definite descriptions could be free of existential import, and quantifiers should be allowed to range over possibilia (Girle 2003, chap. 4). Otherwise, some referential terms that refer to nonmental things, such as "God" and "the being than which nothing greater can be conceived," would have to refer to mental things that have existence-in-the-understanding, which makes no sense; or those referential terms would have to have to refer to things that have existence-in-reality, which would make the Anselmian ontological argument beg the question.

Finally, in order to be able to test our Anselmian argument for validity, it will be useful to present it in standard form and to express it in the language of quantification theory. We shall use the following lexicon:

$Ux =_{df}$ x is understood
$Sy =_{df}$ the concept of y exists-in-the-understanding
$Ex =_{df}$ x exists-in-reality
$Gxy =_{df}$ x is greater than y
$Fxy =_{df}$ x refers to y

occur, such as ideas and inferences ..." (McGill 1967, p. 82). The first two translations are consistent with the assumptions and presuppositions of this chapter. McGill's is not. Anselm was both a Christian and a neo-Platonist, and he had to be committed as such to the existence of minds or souls *qua* substantial entities within which mental phenomena occur.

Dx $=_{df}$ x is a definite description
d $=_{df}$ the definite description "$(\imath x)$ ~©$(\exists y)Gyx$"
g $=_{df}$ $(\imath x)$~©$(\exists y)Gyx$
P(Y) $=_{df}$ Y is a great-making property
©... $=_{df}$ it is conceivable that ...[3]

Here then is our logical reconstruction of Anselm's ontological argument:

A1   The definite description "that than which it is not conceivable for something to be greater" is understood. (*Premise*)

$$(Dd \& Ud)$$

A2   "That than which it is not conceivable for something to be greater" refers to that than which it is not conceivable for something to be greater. (*Premise*)

$$Fdg$$

A3   The *concept* of whatever a definite description that is understood refers to has existence-in-the-understanding. (*Premise*)

$$(x)(y)((Dx \& Fxy \& Ux) \supset Sy)$$

A4   It is conceivable that something is greater than anything that lacks a great-making property that it conceivably has. (*Premise*)

$$(x_1)(Y)[(P(Y) \& {\sim}Yx_1 \& ©Yx_1) \supset ©(\exists x_2)Gx_2x_1]$$

A5   Existence-in-reality is a great making property. (*Premise*)

$$P(E)$$

A6   Anything the concept of which has existence-in-the-understanding conceivably has existence-in-reality. (*Premise*)

$$(x)(Sx \supset ©Ex)$$

A7   It is not conceivable that *something* is greater than that than which it is not conceivable for something to be greater. (*Premise*)

$$\sim©(\exists y)Gyg$$

Therefore,

A8   That than which it is not conceivable for something to be greater exists-in-reality.

$$Eg$$

The following deduction proves that this argument is valid:
Deduction[4]

1.   Dd & Ud   pr
2.   Fdg   pr

---

3. The conceivability operator need not be made explicit for this argument, since the deduction shows that the argument is valid in nonmodal first-order quantification theory. However, I include it because it will be needed later, and it also improves readability.
4. See Appendix 1 for the rules of inference and so on of the logic used in this chapter.

3.	$(x)(y)((Dx \& Fxy \& Ux) \supset Sy)$	pr
4.	$(x_1)(Y)[(P(Y) \& \sim Yx_1 \& \copyright Yx_1) \supset \copyright(\exists x_2)Gx_2x_1]$	pr
5.	$P(E)$	pr
6.	$(x)(Sx \supset \copyright Ex)$	pr
7.	$\sim\copyright(\exists y)Gyg$	pr
8.	$Fdg \& \sim\copyright(\exists y)Gyg$	2, 7 Conj
9.	$(\exists x)[\sim\copyright(\exists y)Gyx \& (z)(\sim\copyright(\exists y)Gyx \supset z{=}x)$	8, theory of descriptions
	$\& (Fdx \& \sim\copyright(\exists y)Gyx)]$	
10.	$\sim\copyright(\exists y)Gyv \& (z)(\sim\copyright(\exists y)Gyz \supset z{=}v)$	9, EI
	$\& (Fdv \& \sim\copyright(\exists y)Gyv)$	
11.	$\sim\copyright(\exists y)Gyv$	10, Simp
12.	Fdv	10, Simp
13.	$(P(E) \& \sim Ev \& \copyright Ev) \supset \copyright(\exists x_2)Gx_2v$	4 UI
14.	$(Dd \& Fdv \& Ud) \supset Sv$	3 UI
15.	$(Dd \& Fdv \& Ud)$	1, 12, Simp, Conj
16.	Sv	14, 15 MP
17.	$Sv \supset \copyright Ev$	6, UI
18.	$\copyright Ev$	16, 17 MP
19.	$\sim(P(E) \& \sim Ev \& \copyright Ev)$	13, 11 MT
20.	$\sim((P(E) \& \copyright Ev) \& \sim Ev)$	19 Com, Assoc
21.	$\sim(P(E) \& \copyright Ev) \lor \sim\sim Ev)$	20, DeM
22.	$P(E) \& \copyright Ev$	5, 18 Conj
23.	Ev	21, 22, DS, DN
24.	$\sim\copyright(\exists y)Gyv \& (z)(\sim\copyright(\exists y)Gyx) \supset z{=}v)$	10 Simp
25.	$\sim\copyright(\exists y)Gyv \& (z)(\sim\copyright(\exists y)Gyx) \supset z{=}v) \& Ev$	23, 24 Conj
26.	$(\exists x)[\sim\copyright(\exists y)Gyx \& (z)(\sim\copyright(\exists y)Gyx) \supset z{=}x) \& Ex]$	25 EG
27.	Eg	26, theory of descriptions

1b. The Truth of the Anselmian Premises

The first conjunct of A1 is true by definition. The second is introspectively true. For it does seem as though we understand the phrase "that than which it is not possible for something to be greater." As Anselm would say, "many people appear to understand it when they hear it – even the fool." This assumes, of course, that the relational predicate "is greater than" is meaningful and understood by those who claim that they understand it when they use it and hear it. Such an assumption could be challenged, although not lightly and not without good reason. Perhaps the absence of a plausible theory of great-making properties would constitute a challenge to the meaningfulness of "is greater than." However, the burden of proof of a claim that a word or phrase is meaningless must always fall on the challenger, especially when the word appears to be used with understanding by a great many people. And the predicate "is greater than" is just such a term. Indeed, many philosophers from Plato to the present, including most neo-Platonists, scholastics, and rationalists, believe that the things of the world can be ordered in terms of both ontological and/or normative greatness, the absence of a nearly complete and coherent theory of great-making properties notwithstanding.

A2 also is analytically true, given the presupposition that in order for the definite description "that than which it is not conceivable for something to be greater" to genuinely refer, that than which it is not conceivable for something to be greater must be a member of the domain of some possible world.

Anselm constructs an insightful, but somewhat muddled, argument for the bogus proposition "whatever is understood exists in the understanding" that we might be able to use in support of the more plausible A3.

> ... When the fool hears mentioned a being than which a greater is inconceivable, he understands what he hears ... Moreover ... if this being is understood, it is in the understanding ... For as what is conceived, is conceived by conception, and what is conceived by conception, as it is conceived, so is in conception; so what is understood, is understood by understanding, and what is understood by understanding, as it is understood, so is in the understanding. What can be clearer than this? (1962, p. 157)

This passage suggests either a deductive or an analogical argument for A3.
The deductive argument is:

1   Concepts are in that which conceives of concepts.
2   Whatever is in that which conceives of concepts has existence-in-the-understanding.
3   Therefore, the *concept* of whatever a definite description that is understood refers to has existence-in-the-understanding.

And the analogical argument is identical to the deductive argument, save for 2* in place of 2.

2*   Having the property of existence-the-understanding is like having the property of being *in* that which conceives of concepts.

The deductive argument is clearly valid, and the analogical argument certainly appears to be inductively strong, with a degree of inductive strength that is proportional to the degree of likeness between conceiving and understanding. The common first premise is analytic. Premise 2 is true if the degree of likeness between conceiving and understanding is 100 percent; and 2* is true if that degree of likeness is high, which it surely is, even if less than 100 percent.

A4 is only implicit in Anselm's *Proslogium*. Yet it is so intuitively obvious that I know of nothing more intuitive and general from which we might infer it. We might, of course, classify it as analytic and say that it is built into the very meaning of being a great-making property that it potentially increases greatness when instantiated. But such a move would presuppose a better idea of greatness than I have been able to give. This is not to say that we do not know what greatness is, or that we do not know that some principles of greatness are true. Rather, it is that a good theory of greatness has yet to be constructed, as far as I know. And were such a theory to be developed, it would be tempting to view A4 as an axiom or first principle.

Let us now turn to A5, arguably the centerpiece of Anselm's ontological argument, but a proposition for which he never appears to argue. Note first that A5 does not say that existence *per se* is a great-making property. It says rather that existence-in-reality is great-making. There is a big difference. If existence is a property, it applies, for Anselm, to *both* the contents of minds (existence-in-the-understanding) and the contents of worlds. Existence-in-reality is narrower than existence, for there are things that exist (in-the-understanding) that do not exist (in-reality).

One interesting characteristic seemingly possessed by things that have existence-in-reality but not by things that only have existence-in-the-understanding is ontological completeness.[5] Something is *ontologically complete* if and only if every property or its negation is a member of the set of all its properties. This computer on which I am writing is ontologically complete because it possesses every possible property or its negation, including the property or its negation of containing a hydrogen atom that was formed a split second after the Big Bang. The set of properties possessed by this computer is also infinite. But my rather limited idea of this computer, howsoever accurate and robust, is surely finite. Nor does that idea include either the property or its negation of containing a hydrogen atom that was formed a split second after the Big Bang. And even if I now were to amend my idea of this computer to include such a property or its negation, there would always some other property and its negation, neither of which I attribute to my idea of the computer.

We can now formulate a plausible argument sketch for A5 that might appeal to an Anselmian:

1　Things that have existence-in-reality are ontologically complete. (*Premise*)
2　The property of being ontologically complete has the property of being great-making. (*Premise*)
3　For every property X and Y, X has Y if and only if everything that has X has a property that has Y. (*Premise*)
4　The property of being ontologically complete has the property of being great-making if and only if everything that has the property of being ontologically complete has a property that has the property being great-making. (*3, UI*)
5　Everything that has the property of being ontologically complete has a property that has the property being great-making. (*2,4, Equiv, Simp, MP*)
6　Hence, everything that has the property of existence-in-reality has a property that has the property of being great-making. (*1, 5, UI, HS, UG*)
7　The property of existence-in-reality has the property of being great-making if and only if everything that has the property of existence-in-reality has a property that has the property of being great-making. (*3, UI*)
8　Hence, the property of existence-in-reality has the property of being great-making. (*6, 7, Equiv, Simp, MP*)

A6 is the Anselmian cognate of the proposition that it is possible for God to exist, a premise common to many ontological arguments. One way of showing that A6 is true would be via ultrarealism. As a neo-Platonist, Anselm would have thought of the ontology of the world as partitioned in three ways: particulars, Forms, and minds. The Forms are instantiated either as the properties of the particulars or as universal ideas in minds. While Plato himself believed at times that the Forms had a greater degree of reality than the

---

5. This is not true of things that exist in the mind of God, all of which are ontologically complete.

particulars, which he relegates in *The Republic* to the shadows, the Platonist must still think of particulars together with the Forms as real existents. Anselm could therefore comfortably think of the world as divided into things that have existence-in-reality and things that have existence-in-minds. Forms and particulars exist-in-reality, and universal ideas exist-in-minds. We can therefore say that for an Anselmian, if the concept of something has existence-in-the-understanding, then a universal idea of it exists-in-a-mind. Or we can say that if the concept of something has existence-in-the-understanding, then a *it is possible that* a universal idea of it exists-in-a-mind.

Some medieval neo-Platonists, the so-called ultrarealists, believed that the order of thought (the universals) and the order of extramental particulars correspond exactly.[6] To each particular real chair, for example, there corresponds a universal idea of that chair, a so-called mental chair. The real chair and the mental chair instantiate exactly the same Forms, but in different mediums. Real chairs instantiate the Forms in matter. Mental chairs instantiate the Forms in-mind. Otherwise, real chairs and mental chairs have *exactly* the same nonexistential properties.[7]

It strikes me as a bit far-fetched to think that particulars and their corresponding mental replicas share exactly the same nonexistential properties. There is more to reality than what meets the mind's eye, and vice versa. But because conceivability generally outruns actuality, it is less far-fetched to think that for each conceivable mental replica of something, it is conceivable that there exists another real particular that has each and every nonexistential property of the replica. Call this "weak ultrarealism."

We can formulate two similar neo-Platonic and ultrarealistic arguments for A6. Let "Mx" $=_{df}$ "a mental replica of x exists-in-a-mind."

Argument 1

1   $(x)(Mx \supset \copyright Ex)$
2   $(x)(Sx \supset Mx)$
∴ $(x)(Sx \supset \copyright Ex)$

Argument 2

1   $(x)(Mx \supset \copyright Ex)$
2   $(x)(Sx \supset \copyright Mx)$
∴ $(x)(Sx \supset \copyright Ex)$

Argument 1 is valid in first-order quantification theory. Argument 2 is valid in an S4 modal-like extension of first-order quantification theory that licenses inferences from conceivable conceivability to conceivability. The same first premise of both arguments is quite weak and difficult to challenge. The second premise of Argument 1 could easily be challenged by a non-Platonist and a nondualist. Yet it would be harder to challenge the second premise of Argument 2, since it too makes a very weak claim.

A7 appears to be self-evident. Yet we can show that it is true in a couple of ways. First, the following argument is valid and both premises are logical truths:

---

6. Some historians of philosophy believe that Anselm was an ultrarealist (Copleston 1961, p. 35).
7. A nonexistential property is a property other than existence-in-reality and other than existence-in-the-mind.

1   $(Y)(z)[z=(\imath x)Yx \supset Yz]$
2   $g=(\imath x) \sim\!\copyright(\exists y)Gyx$
∴ $\sim\!\copyright(\exists y)Gyg$

Second, if we use Russell's Theory of Descriptions to eliminate the definite description "$(\imath x) \sim\!\copyright(\exists y)Gyx$" from A7, we get:

A7a. $\sim\!\copyright(\exists x)[\sim\!\copyright(\exists y)Gyx \,\&\, (z)(\sim\!\copyright(\exists y)Gyz \supset z= x) \,\&\, (\exists y)Gyx].$[8]

If we then modestly assume that conceivability is equivalent to possibility, A7b becomes:

A7b. $\sim\!\Diamond(\exists x)[\sim\!\Diamond(\exists y)Gyx \,\&\, (z)(\sim\!\Diamond(\exists y)Gyz \supset z= x) \,\&\, (\exists y)Gyx].$[9]

But A7b is logically true in even the weakest of modal logics. Therefore, A7 is true.

1c. On Whether Anselm's Ontological Argument Begs the Question

An argument begs the question just in case belief in the truth of the conclusion is included among the reasons for asserting the truth of the premises.[10] Some sound arguments sometimes beg the question. Consider the following valid argument:

Either $1 + 1 = 3$ or God exists.
Not $1 + 1 = 3$.
Hence, God exists.

While it is true that theists will believe that it is sound and nontheists believe that it is not, neither belief makes it so. Assume that no one believes that $1 + 1 = 3$. If some theists believe that the argument is sound because they believe *qua* theists that the second disjunct of the first premise is true, then they beg the question. Likewise, if some nontheists believe that the argument is not sound because they believe *qua* nontheists that the second disjunct is false, then they too beg the question. Yet the argument would not beg the question if its proponent believed that the first premise is true for reasons that do not include the proposition that God exists. It would only be pointless.

William L. Rowe argues that Anselm's ontological argument begs the question by granting what it tries to prove (2001, pp. 39–41). According to Rowe, Anselm's ontological argument boils down to one that defines God as a greatest possible being, and also counts

8.   The description "$(\imath x)\sim\!\copyright(\exists y)Gyx$" occurs within the scope of "$\sim\!\copyright$" and, clearly, has a secondary occurrence in A7. If we were to construe it as having a primary occurrence, then A7 would expand to "$(\exists x)[\sim\!\copyright(\exists y)Gyx \,\&\, (z)(\sim\!\copyright(\exists y)Gyz \supset z=x) \,\&\, \sim\!\copyright(\exists y)Gyx]$," and Anselm's argument would thereby beg the question.
9.   I realize that equating conceivability with possibility is controversial. But it is an issue that is beyond the scope of this chapter.
10.   Strictly speaking, arguments do not beg the questions. Arguers do. Thus, an argument might beg the question for one person and not for another.

the property of existence-in-reality as great-making.[11] These two things, he correctly argues, imply that nothing that fails to exist-in-reality can be a greatest possible being; but they do not alone imply that a greatest possible being actually exists-in-reality. However, if we also assume that a greatest possible being possibly exists-in-reality, we can then infer that a greatest possible being actually exists-in-reality because no such possible being could fail to exist-in-reality and still be a greatest possible being, given that the property of existence-in-reality is great-making. This means, Rowe then concludes, that the assumption that a greatest possible being possibly exists-in-reality is "virtually equivalent" to the concluding proposition that it actually exists-in-reality. "In granting that Anselm's God is a possible thing, we are in fact granting that it actually exists . . . the argument begs the question: it assumes the point it is trying to prove" (Rowe 2001, p. 41).

Rowe is wrong on two counts. First, he equivocates on the word "grant." It can mean either "assume" or "implies." We assume (grant) the premises of an argument. And in granting these premises, we are in fact granting (implying) its conclusion if the argument is valid. Surely, the fact that the premises of an argument imply its conclusion does not mean that the argument begs the question. Second, the proposition that a greatest possible being possibly exists-in-reality is not at all equivalent to the proposition that it actually exists-in-reality, Rowe's use of the hedge word "virtually" notwithstanding. Indeed, the former does not even imply the latter, unless we assume that the other premises of Anselm's argument are logical truths. But one of the other premises is that the property of existence-in-reality is great-making, which is not a logical truth. Moreover, even if the proposition that a greatest possible being possibly exists-in-reality did imply the proposition that it actually exists-in-reality, the argument would beg the question only if the latter were given as a reason for believing the former.

The upshot is that Rowe's analysis does not show that his distilled version of Anselm's ontological argument begs the question. Nor is there any reason to think that the reasons I have given for believing the premises of the expanded version of the argument I have presented in sections 1a and 1b of this chapter include the proposition that the greatest conceivable being has the property of existence-in-reality. Therefore, we can confidently believe that it does not beg the question.

1d. On Parodies

A parody of an argument is a structurally similar argument with an absurd conclusion. There are two ways parodies can refute what they parody. First, if the parody has true premises and the same logical form as the argument parodied, then the argument parodied

---

11. Rowe's distilled version of Anselm's argument can be expressed schematically, thus:

1   Some possible object exemplifies the concept of God.
2   No object that fails to exist-in-reality could exemplify the concept of God. (Because God is defined as a being than which none greater is possible, and it assumed that the property of existence-in-reality is great-making.)
3   Every possible object either exists-in-reality or does not.
4   Therefore, God exemplifies the property of existence-in-reality.

must be invalid. Second, if both the parody and the argument parodied are valid, and the premises of the parody are at least as justifiable as the premises of the argument parodied, then the parody *refutes* the argument parodied because the argument parodied will also have to have at least one unjustifiable premise, and it will thereby fail to support its conclusion. In other words, if the premises of a valid parody are as justifiable as premises of the argument parodied, then it cannot be rational to believe that the premises of the argument parodied are true, for then it would be rational also to believe that the absurd conclusion of the parody is true. Conversely, if either the parody is invalid or some of its premises are arguably less justifiable than the respective corresponding premises of the argument parodied, then the parody *per se* fails to refute the argument parodied, and the argument parodied might well be sound.

Perhaps the most famous parody in the history of philosophy is the one formulated against Anselm's ontological argument by Gaunilo, a contemporary of Anselm, who reasoned that one could infer the absurd conclusion that a greatest conceivable island exists-in-reality from premises structurally similar to those of Anselm's argument. Let us add the following to our lexicon:

$Ix =_{df} x$ is an island
$i =_{df} (\imath x) \sim\copyright(\exists y)(Iy \& Gyx)$
$h =_{df}$ the definite description "$(\imath x)(Ix \& \sim\lozenge(\exists y)(Ix \& Gyx))$"

Then Gaunilo's parody is this:

G1	Dh & Uh	pr
G2	Fhi	pr
G3	$(x)(y)((Dx \& Fxy \& Ux) \supset Sy)$	pr
G4	$(x_1)(Y)[(P(Y) \& \sim Yx_1 \& \copyright Yx_1) \supset \copyright(\exists x_2)Gx_2x_1]$	pr
G5	$P(E)$	pr
G6	$(x)(Sx \supset \copyright Ex)$	pr
G7	$\sim\copyright(\exists y)Gyi$	pr

Therefore,

G8   Ei

This parody is valid but not sound because G7 is false. So it fails to refute Anselm's argument. Replace G7 with G7a.

$$G7a. \quad \sim\copyright(\exists x_2)(Ix_2 \& Gx_2i)$$

Then the premises of the new parody are true if Anselm's premises are true; but the parody is not valid. So it fails to refute Anselm's argument. Replace G7 with G7a, and replace G4 with G4a.

$$G4a. \quad (x_1)(Y)[(P(Y) \& \sim Yx_1 \& \copyright Yx_1) \supset \copyright(\exists x_2)(Ix_2 \& Gx_2x_1)]$$

This parody is valid but not sound because G4a is false.

Let "Lx_2x_1" be short for "x_2 is exactly like x_1 except for having Y in place of the negation of Y." Replace G4 with G4b, and replace G7 with G7a.

G4b. $(x_1)(Y)[(P(Y) \& \sim Yx_1 \& \copyright Yx_1) \supset \copyright(\exists x_2)(Lx_2x_1 \& Gx_2x_1)]$.

Since "$\copyright(\exists x_2)(Lx_2i \& Gx_2i)$" entails "$\copyright(\exists x_2)(Ix_2 \& Gx_2i)$," the resulting parody is valid.

Or let "Kx_2x_1" be short for "x_2 is the same *kind* of thing as x_1." Replace G4 with G4c, and replace G7 with G7a.

G4c. $(x_1)(Y)[(P(Y) \& \sim Yx_1 \& \copyright Yx_1) \supset \copyright(\exists x_2)(Kx_2x_1 \& Gx_2x_1)]$.

Since "$\copyright(\exists x_2)(Kx_2i \& Gx_2i)$" entails "$\copyright(\exists x_2)(Ix_2 \& Gx_2i)$," this resulting parody is also valid.

But do the last two parodies refute Anselm's ontological argument? While it is certainly true that the addition of a great-making property to anything that conceivably has that property would result in something which would conceivably be greater than the first thing would be without that property, there is no guarantee I can think of for believing that the thing that would result from the addition of a great-making property would be exactly like the first thing sans that property, or even the same kind of thing as the first thing is without that property. In other words, the addition of a great-making property might change the nature of the thing it is added to. Take the property of existence-in-reality as an example. Things that exist-in-reality are very different from corresponding things that exist-in-the-understanding. A real table is different than the concept of a table, and a real tree is from the concept of a tree, and so on. So it is far from obvious that either G4b or G4c is true. But A4 is true intuitively. Consequently, neither of these parodies refutes Anselm's argument.

Oppy suggests that Anselm's ontological argument can be successfully refuted by paro-dies that purport to establish the existence of different kinds of devils:

> . . . Consider the formula 'a being than which no worse can be conceived'. It seems that it would be worse if a very bad being existed both in the understanding and in reality than if it merely existed in the understanding. Consequently, it seems that if the Anselmian formula is under-stood as 'a being than which no better can be conceived' – then the Anselmian argument can be successfully parodied using this formula. (1995, p. 181)

Let us add the following notations to our growing lexicon:

$Vyx =_{df}$ y is more evil than x
$e =_{df} (\imath x) \sim \copyright(\exists y)Vyx$
$j =_{df}$ the definite description "$(\imath x)\sim\Diamond(\exists y)Vyx$"

Now replace "G" by "V," "g" by "e," and "d" by "j" in our reconstruction of Anselm's onto-logical argument. Assuming that proposition "Ee" is absurd, Oppy's putative *devils* parody is the result. Does it refute Anselm? Answer: only if premises O4 and O7 are arguably just as justifiable as A4 and A7, respectively.

O4. $(x_1)(Y)[(P(Y) \& \sim Yx_1 \& \copyright Yx_1) \supset \copyright(\exists x_2)Vx_2x_1]$
O7. $\sim\copyright(\exists y)Vye$

Oppy suggests that O4 is true because an evil that exists-in-reality is more evil than it would be if it only existed-in-the-understanding. If the property of existence-in-reality is great-making, as it is assumed to be in the antecedent of O4, then an evil that exists-in-reality cannot be worse than any evil that does not. The addition of great-making properties make things better, not worse. So it is questionable that O4 is true, at least for the reason given by Oppy. Suppose, however, that an evil that exists-in-reality could be worse than one that does not. Then proposition "©(∃y)Vye" would presumably be true, and O7 false. The conclusion is that this parody also fails to refute Anselm's ontological argument.

2a. The Validity of the Ontological Argument of Descartes and Leibniz

Descartes expresses his ontological argument in "Meditation V," thus:

> It is certain that I no less find the idea of God, that is to say, the idea of a supremely perfect Being, in me, than that of any figure or number whatever it is; and I do not know any less clearly and distinctly that an [actual and] eternal existence pertains to this nature . . .
>
>   I clearly see that existence can no more be separated from the essence of God than can the idea of its three angles equal to two right angles be separated from the idea of a [rectilinear] triangle.
>
>   . . . from the fact that I cannot conceive of God without existence, it follows that existence is inseparable from Him, and hence that He really exists; not that my thought can bring this to pass, or impose any necessity on things, but on the contrary, because the necessity which lies in the thing itself, i.e., the necessity of the existence of God determines me to think this way . . . (1952, pp. 93–4)

He expresses it more clearly and succinctly in his "Arguments . . . in Geometrical Fashion":

> To say that something is contained in the nature of a concept of anything is the same as to say that it is true of that thing. But necessary existence is contained in the concept of God. Hence it is true to affirm of God that necessary existence exists in Him, or that God Himself exists. (1952, p. 132)

There are two key ideas in these passages. First, while Descartes says in "Meditation V" that *existence* is contained in the concept or essence of a supremely perfect being, it is clear from the context, and from the "Arguments . . . in Geometrical Fashion" that he really meant to say (or should have said) that God is a *necessary being*, where a necessary being is one that exists only if it exists necessarily.[12] Moreover, it would (should) have been obvious to him that the categorical property of *existence* (or nonexistence) cannot be included in the concept of anything without ultimately begging the question of its very existence (or non-existence).[13] Thus, for Descartes, it is really the conditional property of *existing necessarily*

---

12. The property of *existence* for Descartes is not split into *existence-in-reality* and *existence-in-the understanding*, as it is for Anselm.

13. We might call this the *Principle of Existential Noninclusion*. This principle does not preclude *asserting* that a supremely perfect being exists, only that existence must not be included in its concept or essence.

if existing at all, not the categorical property of *existence per se* (and not even the categorical property of having the property of *existence* necessarily), that is included in the concept or essence of a supremely perfect being. In other words, whether God exists or does not exist, He is not the kind of being who can exist contingently. Relatedly, a supremely perfect being possesses *supremity* necessarily.

Second, we need to clearly understand what is implied by the proposition that a certain property is contained in the concept or essence of something.[14] When we say, to use Descartes' own example, that the property of having its three angles equal to two right angles is contained in the concept or essence of a triangle, we imply that every triangle has the property of having its three angles equal to two right angles. In general, if property Y is contained in the concept or essence of something of kind X, then everything that is an X is a Y.

We are now in a position to logically reconstruct Descartes' ontological argument. Suppose

$Rx =_{df} x$ is supremely perfect
$Nx =_{df} (Ex \supset \Box Ex)$
$C(Y, X) =_{df} Y$ is included in the concept or essence of an X.

It would appear from the said quotations that Descartes' argument might be as follows:

D1   For every X and Y, if the property of being a Y is contained in the concept or essence of being an X, then necessarily everything that is an X is a Y.

$$(X)(Y)(C(\hat{y}[Yy], \hat{y}[Xy]) \supset \Box(z)(Xz \supset Yz)$$

D2   The property of *necessarily existing if existing at all* is contained in the concept or essence of a supremely perfect being.

$$C(\hat{y}[Ny], \hat{y}[Ry])$$

Therefore,

DC   A supremely perfect being exists.

$$(\exists x)(Rx \& Ex)$$

It should at once be obvious, however, that this is an invalid argument. The only thing that relevantly follows from D1 and D2 is that everything that is supremely perfect necessarily exists if exists. But, if we add D3 and D4 as premises, then the argument is valid in S5 quantificational modal logic.[15]

D3   It is possible that a supremely perfect being exists.

$$\Diamond(\exists x)(Rx \& Ex)$$

---

14. Descartes vacillates between talking about the concept of things and talking about their essence. While concepts are generally thought of as subjective, and essences as objective, both will work in his ontological argument.

15. Although Descartes must have had sharp modal insights in order to be able to see that his enthymeme was valid, he could not have been aware of the exact modal principles used, since modal logic was not developed formally until the twentieth century.

D4   Necessarily, supremely perfect beings are necessarily supremely perfect.

$$\Box(x)(Rx \supset \Box Rx)$$

Then the following deduction proves that the argument D1, D2, D3, D4/∴DC is valid:

1	$(X)(Y)(C(\hat{y}[Yy], \hat{y}[Xy]) \supset \Box(z)(Xz \supset Yz)$	pr
2	$C(\hat{y}[Ny], \hat{y}[Ry])$	pr
3	$\Diamond(\exists x)(Rx \& Ex)$	pr
4	$\Box(x)(Rx \supset \Box Rx)$	pr
5	$C(\hat{y}[Ny], \hat{y}[Ry]) \supset \Box(x)(Rx \supset Nx)$	1 UI
6	$\Box(x)(Rx \supset Nx)$	2, 5 MP
7	$\Box(x)(Rx \supset (Ex \supset \Box Ex))$	6, df "N"
8	$(\Box(x)(Rx \supset (Ex \supset \Box Ex)) \& \Box(x)(Rx \supset \Box Rx)) \supset$	theorem[16]
	$\Box(x)((Rx \& Ex) \supset \Box(Rx \& Ex))$	
9	$\Box(x)(Rx \supset (Ex \supset \Box Ex)) \& \Box(x)(Rx \supset \Box Rx)$	4, 7 Conj
10	$\Box(x)((Rx \& Ex) \supset \Box(Rx \& Ex))$	8, 9 MP
11	$\Box(x)((Rx \& Ex) \supset \Box(Rx \& Ex)) \supset (\Diamond(\exists x)(Rx \& Ex) \supset \Diamond(\exists x)\Box(Rx \& Ex))$	theorem
12	$\Diamond(\exists x)(Rx \& Ex) \supset \Diamond(\exists x)\Box(Rx \& Ex)$	10, 11 MP
13	$\Diamond(\exists x)\Box(Rx \& Ex)$	3, 12 MP
14	$\Diamond(\exists x)\Box(Rx \& Ex) \supset \Diamond\Box(\exists x)(Rx \& Ex)$	theorem
15	$\Diamond\Box(\exists x)(Rx \& Ex)$	13, 14 MP
16	$\Diamond\Box(\exists x)(Rx \& Ex) \supset (\exists x)(Rx \& Ex)$	theorem
17	$(\exists x)(Rx \& Ex)$	15, 16 MP

2b. On the Truth of the Descartes–Leibniz Premises

D1 is analytically true. D2 and D4 are synthetic a priori metaphysical truths. D2 is true, according to Descartes, because the concept of *being supremely perfect* includes the having of all nonexistential perfections, and the property of *necessarily existing if at all* is a non-existential perfection. But why is the conditional property of *existing necessarily if at all* a perfection (great-making)? Descartes says in "Meditation V" that existence ($\hat{y}[Ey]$) is a perfection (1952, p. 94).[17] If it is, then it should also be true that the categorical property of existing necessarily ($\hat{y}[\Box Ey]$) is a perfection. But property $\hat{y}[\Box Ey]$ entails the *conditional* property of *existing necessarily if at all*, $\hat{y}[Ey \supset \Box Ey]$. If we then accept that perfections entail only perfections, as I think we should, it follows that property $\hat{y}[Ey \supset \Box Ey]$ is a nonexistential perfection. Schematically,

1   $P(\hat{y}[Ey])$
2   $P(\hat{y}[Ey]) \supset P(\hat{y}[\Box Ey])$
3   $\Box(x)(\hat{y}[\Box Ey]x \supset \hat{y}[Ey \supset \Box Ey]x)$

---

16. The word "theorem" in these annotated proofs and deductions refers to theorems of the logic Q2S5. See Appendix 1.

17. The proposition that existence is a perfection is consistent with not including the property of existence in the concept or essence of a supremely perfect being, per the Principle of Existential NonInclusion.

4   $(Y)(Z)(P(Y) \ \& \ \Box(x)(Yx \supset Zx)) \supset P(Z))$

∴ $P(\hat{y}[Ey \supset \Box Ey])$

Or, as John Findlay has argued, supremely perfect beings are beings that by nature are worthy of worship, and beings that by nature are worthy of worship cannot exist contingently – because to be worthy of worship is to be absolutely perfect in every possible respect (1998, pp. 95–6). So supremely perfect beings must exist necessarily if at all.

Findlay also notes that a supremely perfect being cannot "possess its various excellences in some adventitious or contingent manner"(1998, p. 95). But the property of being supremely perfect is surely one of the excellences (great-makers). Therefore, if a being is supremely perfect, it must be supremely perfect necessarily. So D4 is true.

Descartes was clearly aware of the need to show that it is possible for a supremely perfect being (God) to exist (D3), even though he does not explicitly include it among the premises of the ontological argument he formulates in "Meditation V." Father Mersenne pointed it out to him in "The Second Set of Objections" that Descartes had attached to his first publication of the *Meditations*, and he responded to Mersenne in his appended "Reply," thus:

> But though we conceive of God only inadequately . . . this does not prevent its being certain that His nature is possible, or not contradictory; nor does it prevent our affirming truly that we have examined it with sufficient precision in order to know that necessary existence appertains to this same Divine nature. For all contradictoriness or impossibility is constituted by our thought . . . it cannot reside in anything external to the mind, because by the very fact that it is outside the mind it is clear that it is not contradictory, but is possible. Moreover, contradictoriness in our concepts arises merely from their obscurity and confusion. Hence it suffices us to understand clearly and distinctly those few things that we perceive about God . . . to note that among the other constituents of this idea . . . necessary existence is found . . . [and] . . . to maintain that it contains no contradiction. (Descartes 1952, p. 127)

In short, God is possible, according to Descartes, because our concept of God is clear and distinct. Or formally,

1   I (Descartes) have a clear and distinct idea of a supremely perfect being (God).
2   Whatever someone has a clear and distinct idea of possibly exists.
3   Therefore, a supremely perfect being possibly exists.

This is a valid argument for D3. But even if we grant the somewhat controversial assumption that clarity and distinctness are sufficient for logical possibility, the first premise might well be challenged as being all too subjective. Consider the comments of Leibniz:

> The reasoning of Descartes concerning the existence of the most perfect being assumed that the most perfect being can be known, or is possible.
> For this being assumed . . . it immediately follows that that being exists. But the question is asked whether it is within our power to conceive such a being . . . and [whether it] can be clearly known without contradiction. For the opponents will say that such a notion of the most perfect being . . . is a chimera. Nor is it sufficient for Descartes to appeal to experience and to allege that he perceives the same in such a manner in himself clearly and distinctly, for this is to break off, not complete the demonstration, unless he shows the method through which others also can attain the same experience . . . [otherwise] we wish to convince them by our authority alone. (1964, pp. 38–9)

Leibniz agrees with Descartes' ontological argument except for the subjective and authoritative argument for D3. Instead, Leibniz sketches an argument for God's possibility that is objective and *a priori* (1964, p. 38). Here is a valid reconstruction:

L1   All perfections are compatible.
L2   Every essential property of a supremely perfect being (God) is a perfection.
L3   If something's essential properties are perfections and all perfections are compatible, then its essential properties are compatible.
L4   If the essential properties of something are compatible, then it is possible that it exists.

Therefore,

D3   It is possible that a supremely perfect being (God) exists.

L2, L3, and L4 are self-evident. L1 is not. So Leibniz constructs an argument for L1 based on his definition of a *perfection* as a "simple quality which is positive and absolute, or expresses whatever it expresses without any limits" (1964, p. 37), and his belief that true propositions that express incompatibility are necessary truths which must be "either demonstrable or known *per se*" (1964, p. 38). A valid and arguably sound logical reconstruction of his argument is this:

S1   If any two perfections are compatible, then all perfections are compatible.
S2   If any two perfections are incompatible, then they are necessarily incompatible.
S3   If any two perfections are necessarily incompatible, then it is either self-evident that they are incompatible or it can be demonstrated that they are incompatible. (Because necessary truths are *a priori*, and *a priori* truths are either self-evident or demonstrable.)
S4   It is not self-evident that any two perfections are incompatible.
S5   If it can be demonstrated that any two perfections are incompatible, then either one is the negation of the other or some part of the one is incompatible with the other.
S6   If one perfection is the negation of the other, then one of them is not positive.
S7   Perfections are simple, positive qualities.
S8   If some part a perfection is incompatible with another, then one of them is not simple.

Therefore,

L1   All perfections are compatible.

2c. Critiques of the Descartes–Leibniz Ontological Argument

There are three fairly well-known critiques of the Descartes–Leibniz ontological argument. The first is Kant's claim that Descartes and Leibniz illicitly include *existence* as a property in the concept or essence of a supremely perfect being. According to Kant, existence is not a property at all. Even our logical reconstruction of the argument fails to avoid this critique by merely including the putative conditional property of *necessarily existing if at all* in the concept or essence of a supremely perfect being, for if existence is not a property, then it is not a property to exist necessarily if at all. Moreover, we explicitly assume that existence is a perfection in our Cartesian justification of D2.

Kant's main worry, if I read him correctly, is less about whether existence is a property per se, and more about whether it makes sense to include existence in the concept or essence of something. "'*Being*' is obviously not a real predicate; that is, it is not a concept of something which could be added to the concept of a thing" (1933, p. 504). Kant argues for this on the grounds that nothing new is said about anything that is said to exist.

> By whatever and by however many predicates we may think a thing . . . we do not make the least addition to the thing when we further declare that it *is*. Otherwise, it would not be exactly the same thing that exists, but something more than we had thought in the concept . . . (1933, p. 505)

Kant is half right and half wrong. He is right that existence is not a property in the usual sense of being includable in the concept of a thing. His explanation is that existence is not a property at all. A better explanation would be that we beg the question of the thing's very existence if we include existence in its concept or essence. True, we do not add to the *concept* of a thing when we say that it exists. So existential propositions are indeed synthetic. But, contrary to Kant, I think that we do predicate something new of a thing when we say that it exists. Kant seems to acknowledge as much when he says, "My financial position is affected . . . very differently by a hundred real thalers than it is by the mere concept of them" (1933, p. 505). Real money, because it exists, adds financial value to things that exist. Merely possible money, because it does not exist, does not add financial value to things that exist. It would seem, then, that Kant could consistently hold that existence is not only a property but also that it is a perfection, so long as it is not included in a thing's concept.[18]

The second critique is that the argument begs the question. But there is no evidence that it does because neither the Cartesian nor Leibnizian reasons for asserting the premises of the argument include the assertion that the conclusion is true. Perhaps the argument would beg the question were *existence* really included (by definition) in the concept of a supremely perfect being. However, our reconstruction of the argument does not make that assumption.

The third critique is that the argument is easily parodied. In the "First Set of Objections" to the *Meditations*, Caterus attempts to parody Descartes' ontological argument by saying that the same kind of argument could be used to prove the existence (in-reality) of an existent Lion, a being whose essence includes both being a lion and existing.

> This complex existent Lion includes both *lion* and the mode *existence* . . . *essentially* . . . But now, has not God from all eternity had a clear and distinct knowledge of this complex? . . . Yet . . . the distinct cognition of it which God possesses . . . does not constrain either part of the complex to exist, unless you assume that the complex does exist . . . Therefore . . . even though *you* have a distinct knowledge of the highest being, and granted that a being of supreme

---

18. Kant can still object to ontological arguments by arguing that a supremely perfect being is not an object of possible experience, and the synthetic proposition "a supremely perfect being exists" is neither a posteriori justifiable nor an *a priori* condition for the possibility of experience, the only two avenues of real knowledge for him.

perfection includes *existence* in the concept of its essence, yet it does not follow that its existence is anything actual... (1952, p. 107)

Descartes parries this parody in "Reply to First Objections" by saying that:

> ... even though other things are conceived only as existing, yet it does not thence follow that they do exist, but only that they may exist, because we do not conceive that there is any necessity for actual existence being conjoined with their other properties; but, because we understand that actual existence is necessarily and at all times linked to God's other attributes, it follows that God actually exists. (1952, p. 113)

What I think Descartes is struggling to say here is that an existent Lion is a contingent being, one that exists only if it possibly exists and possibly does not exist. This is because an existent Lion is still a lion, and lions are, by nature, contingent. All that relevantly follows from saying that *contingency* is contained in the concept or essence of an existent Lion is that anything that is an existent Lion possibly exists and possibly does not exist, if it exists. So if we assume that existent Lions possibly exist, we can only relevantly infer that it is possible that they possibly exist, and possible that they possibly do not exist. A supremely perfect being, by contrast, is a *necessary being*; one that exists noncontingently by nature. And, as we saw earlier, what follows from saying that the property of being a necessary being is contained in the concept or essence of a supremely perfect being is that a supremely perfect being exists necessarily if it exists at all. If we assume that a supremely perfect being possibly exists, we can validly infer that it does in fact exist. It appears, then, that Caterus' putative parody fails to refute Descartes' ontological argument.

Suppose, however, that we define a W* as a nonsupreme *necessary* being. We then get the parody "D1, K2, K3, K4/∴ KC" of Descartes' ontological argument, where K2, K3, K4, and KC are the same as D2, D3, D4, and DC, respectively, except for "W*" in place of "supremely perfect." Call this parody "the necessary being parody." Unlike Caterus' invalid putative parody of Descartes' argument, the necessary being parody is valid. But is it refuting?

Since the conclusion of the necessary being parody is obviously absurd, at least one of its premises must be false. So if each premise of the necessary being parody is at least as justifiable as the corresponding premise of Descartes' ontological argument, then the necessary being parody refutes it.

But it is not at all clear that each premise of the necessary being parody is at least as justifiable as the corresponding premise of Descartes' argument. Consider K3. We gave two arguments earlier for why D3 is true: Descartes' *clear and distinct* ideas argument, and Leibniz's *compatibility of perfections* argument. Might similar arguments be mustered in support of K3? I doubt it. An analogue of the Cartesian argument will not work because, I would guess, no one really has a clear and distinct idea of a W*. And a Leibnizian analogue will not work, because it must be false that every essential property of a W* (a nonsupreme being) is a perfection: otherwise, W* beings would be supremely perfect.

It is also doubtful that K4 could be justified in the same way that we justified D4 because it is not at all clear that W* is a perfection. And even if we were disposed to say that K4 is true because it is analytically or conceptually true that every of kind of thing is a thing of that kind essentially, then some other premise of the necessary being parody would have to be false. (It would also thereby make D4 analytically or conceptually true.) But both D1 and K2 are analytically true. So K3 would then definitely have to be false. Yet D3 is arguably true. Hence, the necessary being parody is nonrefuting.

3. Ontological Arguments of the Twentieth Century

Even though we made use of modal logic in proving the validity of our logical reconstruction of the ontological argument of Descartes and Leibniz, philosophers do not explicitly use modal reasoning in ontological arguments until the twentieth century. In this section, I shall present and very briefly discuss logical reconstructions of three explicitly modal arguments that are modeled on Anselm's ontological argument but do not assume that existence-in-reality is great-making. In the next section, I shall give an exposition and analysis of the lesser-known modal ontological argument of Gödel, which looks to be fashioned, in part, after Leibniz's proof of the compatibility of all perfections. And in the last two sections I shall present and briefly discuss two of my own ontological arguments: the modal perfection argument (MPA), and the temporal-contingency argument (TCA).

Norman Malcolm thought that Anselm had actually presented a convincing modal argument in *Proslogion III*. Here is a logical reconstruction of his 1960 rendition of that argument:

C1   It is possible that the greatest conceivable being exists.
C2   The greatest conceivable being is unlimited.
C3   Everything that is unlimited is so if and only if it does not depend on anything else for its existence or nonexistence and it neither just happens to exist nor just happens not to exist.
C4   Everything that does not depend on anything else for its existence or nonexistence is such if and only if no other being causes it to begin to exist and no other being causes it to cease to exist.
C5   Anything that begins to exist is caused to begin to exist by some other being, or it just happens to begin to exist.
C6   Anything that ceases to exist is caused to cease to exist by some other being, or it just happens to cease to exist.
C7   Anything that neither begins nor ceases to exist exists necessarily if it exists at all, and fails to exist necessarily if it exists at all.

Therefore,

C8   The greatest conceivable being exists.

Charles Hartshorne, who was also inspired by Anselm's *Proslogion III*, formulated a very elegant modal argument "1962, pp. 47–57". Here is a reconstruction:

H1   It is possible that a perfect being exists.
H2   Necessarily, if a perfect being exists, then a perfect being necessarily exists. (Anselm's Principle)

Therefore,

H3   A perfect being exists.

Then in 1974, Alvin Plantinga developed what he calls "A Victorious Modal Version" of the Anselmian argument that he embeds in the extensional language of possible worlds. A reconstruction is this:

P1   The property of being maximally great is exemplified in some possible world.
P2   The property of being maximally great is equivalent, by definition, to the property of being maximally excellent in every possible world.
P3   The property of being maximally excellent entails the properties of omniscience, omnipotence, and moral perfection.
P4   A universal property is one that is exemplified in every possible world or none.
P5   Any property that is equivalent to some property that holds in every possible world is a universal property.

Therefore,

P6   There exists a being that is essentially omniscient, omnipotent, and morally perfect (God).

These three modal arguments are valid.[19] But are they sound? A pretty good case might be made for C2–C6, H2, and P2–P5. But C7 is clearly questionable, especially if the modalities are construed logically, because an eternal being that does not exist in all possible words certainly is possible. And what should we think about the first premise of each of these arguments, which effectively says in each case that it is possible for God to exist? None of the authors of these respective arguments is particularly sanguine about proving this. Hartshorne merely suggests that we might "employ one or more of the other theistic proofs ... to demonstrate that perfection must at least be conceivable" (1962, p. 52). Plantinga treats the possibility premise as a philosophical hypothesis, which he says it is rational to accept because otherwise "we should find ourselves with a pretty slim and pretty dull philosophy" (1974, p. 221). (Hardly the highest standard for what counts as rational!) And Malcolm says that he does "not know how to demonstrate the concept of God ... is not self-contradictory" (1967, p. 318). Yet he assumes that it is not self-contradictory because it has "a place in the thinking and lives of human beings" (1967, p. 318).

One consequence of not attempting to prove that it is possible for God to exist is that the arguments of Malcolm, Hartshorne, and Plantinga do not beg the question. On the other hand, they thereby become particularly vulnerable to being refuted by parodies. For example, one might easily validly argue contra Hartshorne that Anselm's Principle, and the premise that it is possible that a supremely perfect being does not exist, jointly entail that a supremely perfect being does not exist. If we were merely to *postulate* that, possibly, a supremely perfect being exists, then we could also rightfully *postulate* that, possibly, a

19. See Appendix 2 for the deductions that prove that these are valid arguments.

supremely perfect does not exist. But then the parody would refute Hartshorne's argument because we should not be able to rightfully claim that the premises of the parody are less justifiable than those of Hartshorne's argument.

4a. Gödel's Ontological Argument

Gödel's "Ontological Proof" consisted of two very cryptic and highly technical handwritten pages dated February 10, 1970, which he subsequently shared with Dana Scott. It was first published as an appendix to Sobel's "Gödel's Ontological Proof" and then posthumously in the *Collected Works of Gödel*. Yet Gödel's ontological "proof" is still not widely known in the philosophical and theological communities, with only a dozen or so discussions of it in print, mostly by logicians, and is quite technical.

Gödel develops his ontological argument as a formal axiomatic theory with a theorem that says that there exists a so-called *God-like* being, where a being is God-like just in case it has every *positive* property. Although the second-order predicate "positive" is left undefined, Gödel suggests that it should be understood in either a moral-aesthetic sense (independent of the accidental structure of the world) or in the sense of pure attribution (as opposed to privation).[20] He cautions, however, not to interpret "positive" in the moral-aesthetic sense to mean the same thing as "good" (in the ordinary utilitarian sense) because "good" (in the ordinary utilitarian sense) means "greatest advantage + smallest disadvantage [which] is negative" (1995b, p. 435). Rather, he says that "positive" could be interpreted as "perfective," meaning "purely good" and implying nothing negative (1995b, p. 435). It is thus tempting to view the property of being positive in the moral-aesthetic sense as coextensive with the property of being a Platonic form. In other words, each Platonic form is positive, and each positive property is a Platonic form.

But "positive" in the sense of pure attribution rings more Leibnizian. In a footnote to his "Ontological Proof" Gödel says that a property (or proposition) that is expressed in "disjunctive normal form in terms of elementary properties [that] contains a member without negation" illustrates pure attribution (1995a, p. 404). And in his "Text" he says, "the positive properties are precisely those that can be formed out of the elementary ones through application of the operations &, V, ⊃ " (1995b, p. 437). Adams interprets these cryptic remarks in Leibnizian fashion and suggests that "the purely positive properties will be those that involve no negation at all in their construction from elementary properties (provided the disjunction operation here too is inclusive)" (1995, p. 398).

Gödel's theory does not assume or presuppose that either existence or existence-in-reality is a property, and his logic has full existential import: the job of saying that something exists is performed by existential quantification. It has one primitive, three defined notions, five axioms, and three important theorems.[21]

Primitive

Property Y is *positive*.

$$P_1(Y) =_{df} \text{Property Y is positive}$$

20. Koons argues that the two conceptions of positivity "coincide perfectly" (2005, p. 3).
21. The formulation presented here is Scott's. But see Gödel's "Ontological Proof" (1995a, p. 403) or Sobel's "Gödel's Ontological Proof" (1987, pp. 256–7) for Gödel's own cryptic formulation.

Definitions

Df 1 A being has the property of being *God-like* (G_1) if and only if it has every positive property.

$$G_1x =_{df} (Y)(P_1(Y) \supset Yx)$$

Df 2 A property is an *essence* (E_1) of something if and only if it has the property, and the property entails each of its properties.

$$E_1(Y, x) =_{df} Yx \& (Z)(Zx \supset \Box(y)(Yz \supset Zy))$$

Df 3 Something has the property of being a *necessary being* (N_2) if and only if every essence it has is necessarily instantiated.

$$N_2x =_{df} (Y)(E_1(Y, x) \supset \Box(\exists z)Yz)$$

Axioms

Ax 1 A property is positive if and only if its negation is not positive.

$$(Z)(P_1(Z) \equiv {\sim}P_1(\hat{y}[{\sim}Zy]))$$

Ax 2 Positive properties entail only positive properties.

$$(Y)(Z)(P_1(Y) \& \Box(x)(Yx \supset Zx)) \supset P_1(Z))$$

Ax 3 God-likeness is positive.

$$P_1(G_1)$$

Ax 4 Positive properties are necessarily positive.

$$(Y)(P_1(Y) \supset \Box P_1(Y))$$

Ax 5 The property of being a necessary being is a positive.

$$P_1(N_2)$$

Theorems

Tm 1 It is possible that something is God-like.

$$\Diamond(\exists y)G_1y$$

Tm 2 God-likeness is an essence of whatever is God-like.

$$(x)(G_1x \supset E_1(G_1, x))$$

Tm 3 Something is God-like.

$$(\exists y)G_1y$$

Proof-sketch of Tm 1.[22] Assume that it is not possible for something God-like to exist. Then God-likeness is an impossible property. Since impossible properties entail all properties, God-likeness entails the negation of God-likeness. Now God-likeness is positive by Ax 3. So the negation of God-likeness must be positive by Ax 2. But the negation of God-likeness cannot be positive by Ax 1. Therefore, by *reductio ad absurdum*, it must be possible that something is God-like.

22. I construct formal proofs of these three theorems in Appendix 2.

Proof sketch of Tm 2. Suppose that anything x is God-like, and that x has property Θ. Then Θ is positive: otherwise the negation of Θ would be positive by Ax 1; and if x had the negation of Θ, it would not have Θ. But then, Θ necessarily is positive by Ax 4. Now every positive property is possessed by anything that is God-like. So necessarily every property that is necessarily positive must be possessed by anything that is God-like. Since Θ is necessarily positive, it follows that necessarily Θ must be possessed by x. In other words, God-likeness entails Θ. Therefore, God-likeness is an essence of anything that is God-like.

Proof-sketch of Tm 3. Assume that something x is God-like. Since the property of being a necessary being is positive, and things that are God-like have all positive properties, x must be a necessary being. But things are necessary beings only if, for each of their essences, there is something that necessarily has that essence. Since God-likeness is an essence of x, it follows that something necessarily is God-like. Therefore, if it is possible that something is God-like, then it is possible that it is necessary that something is God-like. Now it is possible that something is God-like by Tm 1. So it is possible that it is necessary that something is God-like. But whatever is possibly necessary is necessary. And whatever is necessary is actually the case. Therefore, something is God-like.

4b.   On Whether Gödel's Argument is Sound

Gödel's axioms imply that something is God-like.[23] While the argument is valid, Sobel shows that Gödel's axioms also imply the absurdity that every true proposition is necessarily true – the so-called modal collapse argument (1987, p. 253).[24] A modification of that argument shows that Gödel's argument cannot be sound:

> Assume that Gödel's argument is sound, and that it proves the existence of the God-like being g_1. By Tm 2 the property of being God-like is an essence of g_1. By the proof of Tm 3, God-likeness is necessarily instantiated. Let *p* be any contingent truth, and let Q be the property that a thing has if and only if *p*. It follows from the Principle of Abstraction that g_1 has Q if and only if *p*. This and the truth of *p* imply that g_1 has Q. Since the property of being God-like is an essence of g_1, the property of being God-like entails Q. But then property Q is necessarily instantiated, because the property of being God-like is necessarily instantiated. From Abstraction and Necessity Introduction, we have it that Q is necessarily instantiated if and only if it is necessarily the case that *p*. Therefore, *p* is necessarily true, which contradicts our assumption that *p* is contingent. So Gödel's argument cannot be sound.

At least one of Gödel's axioms must be false. Sobel objects to Ax 2, Ax 3, and Ax 5. His argument against Ax 2 is this:

---

23. Gödel's five axioms are the premises of his ontological argument, and Tm 3 is the conclusion.

24. Sobel also shows that Gödel's axioms imply that if everything has an essence, $(x)(\exists Y)E_1(Y, x))$, then everything is a necessary being, $(x)N_2x$. But that result does not prove that Gödel's argument is unsound. It makes perfect sense to think that free or contingent things do not have essences in Gödel's sense of essence. Ironically, Sobel notes that things with no essence are necessary beings: $(x)(\sim(\exists Y)(E_1(Y, x) \supset ((Y)(E_1(Y, x) \supset \Box(\exists z)Yz))$. That is true, vacuously; and there is no warrant thereby for claiming that everything is a necessary being, or that some essence of a free being is necessarily instantiated (1987, p. 252).

Gödel's generous interpretation of properties is at least awkward for an axiological interpretation of Axiom 2, since, according to it, if there is a positive property, then every necessarily universal property such as being self-identical, and being either red or not red, is a positive property. (2004, p. 120)

There are two quick challenges to this argument. First, Gödel's argument for a God-like being is valid even if tautological or necessarily universal properties are positive. Second, if Ax 2 were replaced by a modification which says that nontautological properties which are entailed by a positive property are positive, and Ax 3 were replaced by a modification which says that *God-likeness* is nontautological and positive, then the resulting ontological argument would still be valid, but its premises would not imply that tautological properties are positive.

Hàjek argues that there are difficulties with either Ax 2 or Ax 3. Let Devil-likeness (D_1) be the property of having all properties that are not positive. Now God-likeness entails the property of being either God-like or Devil-like. So by Ax 2 and Ax 3, the property of being either God-like or Devil-like ($G_1 \vee D_1$) must be positive. Hàjek believes that that result is "counterintuitive." Maybe it is and maybe it is not; but even if it is counterintuitive, that does not mean that either Ax 2 or Ax 3 is false.

Sobel says that the difficulty is worse than counterintuitive. "There is *prima facie* no more reason for saying that that [a] disjunctive property is positive than there is for saying that it is not positive; it is entailed by a property that is positive according to Axiom 3 ... and it is entailed by a property that is 'equally negative'" (2004, p. 122). True enough, it is reasonable to assume that D_1 is negative (not positive), and D_1 surely entails ($G_1 \vee D_1$). But Sobel is surely wrong to presuppose that these two things imply that ($G_1 \vee D_1$) is negative. Properties that are negative entail properties that are positive, but not vice versa. The property of being morally evil, for example, entails the property of having some intelligence.

Ax 5 is the axiom that Sobel objects to the most. He maintains that nothing worthy of worship can exist necessarily. And he argues that if the property of being a necessary being is positive, and if any being whose essence is to be worthy of worship can be assumed have to have all positive properties, which is plausible, then any being worthy of worship would have to have the property of being a necessary being and would, therefore, exist necessarily if all.[25] So if we abandon Ax 5, we not only block the proof of Tm 3, as well as the modal collapse argument for why Gödel's argument is not sound, we also mollify Sobel's angst about objects of worship being necessary beings. I shall return later to the issue of Ax 5.

---

25. Sobel holds that Gödel's god (or the *demonstrable* god of any ontological argument) cannot be the God of Theism (1987, pp. 254–5). When fully stated in standard logical form, his argument appears to be this:

1 Gödel's god is a necessary being.
2 Every necessary being is an abstract entity.
3 No abstract entity is worthy of being worshipped.
4 The God of Theism is worthy of being worshipped.
5 Therefore, Gödel's god is not the God of Theism

Although valid, the second premise of this argument is arguably false. I see no good reason for not thinking that something with causal powers could exist in every possible world. But it is hard to imagine an abstract entity with causal powers. So some necessary beings might not be abstract entities.

What about Ax 1? Anderson splits Ax 1 into Ax 1^a and Ax 1^b:

Ax 1^a If a property is positive, then its negation is not positive

$$(Z)(P_1(Z) \supset \sim P_1(\dot{y}[\sim Zy]))$$

Ax 1^b If the negation of a property is not positive, then the property is positive.

$$(Z)(\sim P_1(\sim \dot{y}[\sim Z] \supset P_1(Z)))$$

He then persuasively argues that Ax 1^a is true, and he correctly notes that Ax 1^b is false.[26] Many properties and their negations appear not to be positive, such as the property of being red and the property of not being red. But if we abandon Ax 1 in favor of Ax 1^a, and make no other changes, we also block the proof of Tm 3. Interestingly, Ax 1^b is also used in our version of the Sobel modal collapse argument, because an instance of Ax 1^b occurs in line 3 of the proof of Tm 2.

Anderson, Hazen, Koons, and Hàjek have all formulated different emendations of Gödel's theory that successfully dodge Sobel's modal collapse refutation of Gödel's ontological argument. Since space here will not permit a detailed analysis, comparison, and evaluation of all four emendations, I shall provide just a summary of the key ideas of Anderson's emendation. I shall then briefly discuss a class of ingenious parodies designed by Graham Oppy that he says inflict Anderson's theory, and quite possibly the others, too.

Anderson's emendation has three new definitions, Df 1^a, Df 2^a, and Df 3^a. Its axioms are Ax 1^a, Ax 2, Ax 3^a, Ax 4, and Ax 5^a.

Df 1^a A being has the property of being *God^a-like* (G^a_1) if and only if its essential properties are all and only those properties that are positive.[27]

Df 2^a A property Y is an *essence^a* (E^a_1) of being x if and only if, for every property Z, x has Z essentially if and only if Y entails Z.

Df 3^a Something has the property of being a *necessary^a being* (N^a_2) if and only if every essence^a it has is necessarily instantiated.

Ax 3^a God^a-likeness is positive.

Ax 5^a The property of being a necessary^a being is positive.

Anderson's axioms imply that something is God^a-like (Anderson's ontological argument). But Sobel's modal collapse argument is not valid in Anderson's theory.[28] One very interesting feature of Anderson's theory, unlike Gödel's, is that it allows for the possibility that God^a-like beings have some nonpositive properties contingently. Another is that the concept of *essence^a* closely resembles the common philosophical concept of *essence*, whereas an essence for Gödel is best understood as a complete characterization.

Oppy's theory (1996) is just like Anderson's except for Df 1^* in place of Df 1^a, Ax 3^* in place of Ax 3^a, and Ax 5^* in place of Ax 5^a.

---

26. Anderson deduces Ax 1^a from *plausible* principles about intrinsic preferability (1990, p. 295).

27. Although Anderson includes a "*" in the names of his key terms and axioms to distinguish them from those of Gödel, we instead include an "a" in the names of Anderson's key terms and axioms in order to distinguish them from names used by Oppy, who also includes a "*" in the names of still other Gödel-like terms and axioms.

28. Our modification of Sobel's argument shows why. The property Q that a thing has if and only if p (where p is some contingent truth) cannot be an essential property of a God^a-like being, and God^a-likeness does not entail Q.

Df 1*   A being has the property of being *God*-like* (G^*_1) if and only if its essential properties are those and only those which are positive, except for $\Phi_1, \ldots, \Phi_n$.

Ax 3*   God*-likeness is positive.

Ax 5*   Necessary existence is a positive property, and distinct from $\Phi_1, \ldots, \Phi_n$.

His axioms imply the absurdity that there are almost as many God*-like beings as there are positive properties (Oppy's ontological parody).[29]

Oppy misinterprets his ontological parody as showing that at least one of Anderson's axioms must be false, and he only conjectures that an "obvious candidate is [Ax 3ᵃ]" (2000, p. 2).[30] It is also certain that not all of Oppy's axioms can be true because the conclusion of his valid parody is absurd. Oppy's parody will, however, substantively refute Anderson's ontological argument if and only if Ax 3* and Ax 5* are at least as justifiable as Ax 3ᵃ and Ax 5ᵃ, respectively, assuming that Ax 1ᵃ, Ax 2, and Ax 4 are at least modestly justifiable (more so than not); and Oppy's parody will vacuously refute Anderson's ontological argument if either Ax 1ᵃ, Ax 2, or Ax 4 is not even modestly justifiable.

We could show that Oppy's parody does not substantively refute Anderson's ontological argument if we could assume that the property of not having Φ_i essentially is not positive, given that Φ_i is a positive property excluded by definition from being an essential property of anything that is God*-like. For we could then prove that Ax 3* is false with the following Gettings (1999)-style argument:

1   The property of being God*-like entails the property of not having Φ_i essentially. (Derived from the definiens of "God*-like.")[31]

2   If the property of being God*-like is positive, and the property of being God*-like entails the property of not having Φ_i essentially, then the property of not having Φ_i essentially is positive. (Ax 2)

3   The property of not having Φ_i essentially is not positive.

∴   The property of being God*-like is not positive.

It would be difficult to know, however, whether Oppy's parody substantively refutes Anderson's argument without knowing more about what a positive property is, and whether it is true that the property of not having Φ_i essentially is not positive.[32] In the next section,

---

29. Oppy constructs a slightly different parody of a slight modification of Anderson's argument that includes the new premise that if a property Z is positive then the property $\hat{y}[\Box Zy]$ is positive (2007, pp. 16–7).

30. Instead of arguing directly for the falsity of Ax 3ᵃ, Oppy merely says, "atheists and agnostics may (perhaps should) say that the property of being [Godᵃ-like] is positive only if it is exemplified," and then notes that if this new proposition were to replace Ax 3ᵃ of Anderson's argument, then the resulting argument would beg the question (2000, p. 2). This is a red herring, and it fails to show that Ax 3ᵃ itself is false.

31. Symbolically: $\Box(x)[(Y)((P_1(Y) \,\&\, Y \neq \Phi_i) \equiv \Box Yx) \supset \sim\Box\Phi_i x]$. Use a conditional proof and utilize the fact that "$\Phi_i = \Phi_i$" is a logical truth.

32. If the mere presence of the word "not" in a description of a property were a guarantor of nonpositivity, then the property of not having property Φ_i essentially would be nonpositive. But the presence of "not" does not guarantee nonpositivity. Otherwise, the property of not having the negation of a positive property would be nonpositive, which it is not.

We might attempt to prove that the property of not having Φ_i essentially is not positive with another Gettings (1999)-style argument:

a. $P_1(\Phi_i)$ given

b. $(Y)(P_1(Y) \supset P_1(\hat{y}[\Box Yy]))$ new axiom

c. $P_1(\Phi_i) \supset \sim P_1(\hat{y}[\sim\Box\Phi_i y])$ Ax 1ᵃ

∴ $\sim P_1(\hat{y}[\sim\Box\Phi_i y])$

The problem is that the "new axiom" is no more obvious than the conclusion.

I shall replace the predicate "is a positive property" with the predicate "is a perfection," and I shall replace "is God^a-like" with "is supreme." I shall then argue that the analogues of Ax 1^a, Ax 2, and Ax 3^a are true, but that the analogue of Ax 3* is false. Those three analogues will constitute the premises of the MPA. The analogues of Ax 4 and Ax 5^a will not be needed.

5. The Modal Perfection Argument

The Modal Perfection Argument (MPA) is an ontological argument that is rooted in the ontological arguments of Anselm, Descartes–Leibniz, and Gödel.[33] Think of a perfection (P_2) as a property that it is necessarily better to have than not; and define the property of being supreme (S_1) as the property that a thing has if and only if it is impossible for something to be greater and impossible for there to be something else than which it is not greater: $S_1x =_{df} (\sim\lozenge(\exists y)Gyx \,\&\, \sim\lozenge(\exists y)(x{\neq}y \,\&\, \sim Gxy))$. The conclusion of MPA is that exactly one supreme being exists,[34] and the premises are the following:

M1   A property is a perfection only if its negation is not a perfection.
M2   Perfections entail only perfections.
M3   The property of being supreme is a perfection.

We can show that MPA is valid by first showing that M1, M2, and M3 jointly imply that it is possible that a supreme being exists. The proof is the same as our proof of Gödel's Tm 1 in Appendix 2, save for "P_2" in place of "P_1" and "S_1" in place of "G_1." (The annotation also substitutes M1, M2, and M3 for A1, A2, and A3, respectively, and drops "Equiv" and "Simp" from line 10.) We can then prove that the possibility of a supreme being implies the existence of a supreme being as follows:

Deduction

1	$\lozenge(\exists x)S_1x$	pr
2	$\lozenge(\exists x)S_1x \supset (\exists x)\lozenge S_1x$	theorem[35]
3	$(\exists x)\lozenge S_1x$	1, 2 MP
4	$\lozenge S_1v$	3, EI
5	$\lozenge(\sim\lozenge(\exists y)Gyv \,\&\, \sim\lozenge(\exists y)(v{\neq}y \,\&\, \sim Gvy))$	4, df "S_1"
6	$\lozenge(\sim\lozenge(\exists y)Gyv \,\&\, \sim\lozenge(\exists y)(v{\neq}y \,\&\, \sim Gvy)) \supset$	theorem
	$(\lozenge\sim\lozenge(\exists y)Gyv \,\&\, \lozenge\sim\lozenge(\exists y)(v{\neq}y \,\&\, \sim Gvy))$	

---

33. I first formulated a version of MPA in November 2001, and I presented it at The Second Annual Saint Anselm Conference held in April 2002 at Saint Anselm College, Manchester, NH. *Philo* published an improved version of MPA by Maydole (2003), replies by Oppy (2004) and Metcalf (2005), and my counterreplies (2005a and 2005b). 34. MPA does not assume or presuppose that existence is a property, and its quantifiers have existential import.
35. "$\lozenge(\exists x)S_1x \supset (\exists x)\lozenge S_1x$" is an instance of the controversial Barcan Formula (BF). Plantinga argues against BF (1974, pp. 59–60). I refute his argument (Maydole 1980, pp. 140–2). And I argue for BF (Maydole 2003, pp. 303–7).

7	$(\Diamond\sim\Diamond(\exists y)Gyv \ \& \ \Diamond\sim\Diamond(\exists y)(v{\neq}y \ \& \ \sim Gvy))$	4, 5 MP
8	$\Diamond\sim\Diamond(\exists y)Gyv$	7 Simp
9	$\Diamond\sim\Diamond(\exists y)(v{\neq}y \ \& \ \sim Gvy)$	7 Com, Simp
10	$\Diamond\sim\Diamond(\exists y)Gyv \supset \sim\Diamond(\exists y)Gyv$	theorem
11	$\Diamond\sim\Diamond(\exists y)(v{\neq}y \ \& \ \sim Gvy) \supset \sim\Diamond(\exists y)(v{\neq}y \ \& \ \sim Gvy)$	theorem
12	$\sim\Diamond(\exists y)Gyv$	8, 10 MP
13	$\sim\Diamond(\exists y)(v{\neq}y \ \& \ \sim Gvy)$	9, 11 MP
14	$\sim\Diamond(\exists y)Gyv \ \& \ \sim\Diamond(\exists y)(v{\neq}y \ \& \ \sim Gvy)$	12, 13 Conj
15	$S_1 v$	14, df "S_1"
16	$(\exists x)S_1 x$	15 EG

It is also logically true that, *at most*, one thing is supreme. (Maydole 2003, p. 302). Therefore, exactly one supreme being exists.

I show that M1, M2, and M3 are true, and that MPA is resistant to sundry salient parodies (Maydole 2003). Here is a small snapshot of how I argue there for the premises: M1 is true because it is better to have a property than not only if it is not better to not have that property than not; M2 is true because it is always better to have that which is a necessary condition for whatever it is better to have than not; and M3 is true because it is reasonable to assume that a thing is supreme if and only if it is necessarily greater than everything else solely by virtue of having some set of perfections, making the extension of the property of being supreme identical with the intersection of the extensions of those perfections. Premises of a different argument for the truth of M3 might be as follows:

M31   For every Z, all of the nontautological essential properties entailed by Z are perfections if and only if the property of being a Z is a perfection.

M32   Every nontautological essential property entailed by the property of being supreme is a perfection.

Therefore,

M3   The property of being supreme is a perfection.

This argument is clearly valid, and the premises are plausible. M31 is arguably true because (1) it is necessarily better to have a property if and only if the property endows whatever has it with nontautological properties that are necessarily better to have than not, and (2) for any properties Y and Z, if Z endows something with Y, then Z entails Y, and (3) perfections are properties that are better to have than not. M32 is arguably true because (4) all the nontautological essential properties entailed by the essence of a supreme being are perfections, and (5) anything entailed by the essence of a thing of kind Z is entailed by the property of being a Z.

There is no evidence to indicate that MPA begs the question. And we can easily show that an Oppy-style parody based on the idea of being almost supreme does not refute MPA, where something is almost supreme just in case it is impossible for anything to be almost greater: from M31, and the fact that it is not the case that every nontautological essential property entailed by the property of being almost supreme is a perfection, it follows that the property of being almost supreme is not a perfection.

6. The Temporal-Contingency Argument

We have shown that the first three premises of MPA imply that it is possible that a supreme (greatest possible) being exists. But any valid argument for the existence of a supreme being that has copossible premises would show the same thing, even if one or more of its premises happens to be false. Consider the Third Way of St Thomas Aquinas.

> The third way is taken from possibility and necessity and runs thus. We find in nature things that are possible to be and not possible to be, since they are found to be generated and corrupted. But it is impossible for these always to exist, for that which can not-be at some time is not. Therefore, if everything can not-be, then at one time there was nothing in existence. Now if this were true then even now there would be nothing in existence, because that which does not exist begins to exist only through something already existing. Therefore if at one time nothing was in existence, it would have been impossible for anything to have begun to exist; and thus now nothing would be in existence – which is absurd. Therefore, not all beings are merely possible, but there must exist something the existence of which is necessary. But every necessary thing has its necessity caused by another, or not. Now it is impossible to go on to infinity in necessary things which have their necessity caused by another, as has already been proved in regard to efficient causes. Therefore, we cannot but admit the existence of some being having of itself its own necessity, and not receiving it from another, but rather causing in others their necessity. This all men speak of as God. (1998, pp. 4–5)

Aquinas' Third Way is invalid *per se* because the proposition that everything fails to exist at some time does not entail the proposition that there is a time when everything fails to exist. Temporally contingent things might be eternal in the actual world yet fail to exist at some time in some other possible world. But the Third Way is fertile, and it can easily be transformed into a valid argument for the existence of a supreme being that has copossible premises.

Think of something as *generated* just in case there is a time when it exists and an earlier time when it does not; and as *corrupted* just in case there is a time when it exists and a later time when it does not. Define something as *temporally necessary* if and only if it is necessarily not generated and necessarily not corrupted. And define something as *temporally contingent* if and only if it is possibly generated or possibly corrupted. Then our modified Third Way is this.

T1   Something presently exists.

T2   Only finitely many things have existed to date.

T3   Every temporally contingent being begins to exist at some time and ceases to exist at some time.

T4   Everything that begins to exist at some time and ceases to exist at some time exists for a finite period of time.

T5   If everything exists for only a finite period of time, and there have been only finitely many beings to date, then there was a time when nothing existed.

T6   If there was a time when nothing existed, then nothing presently exists.

T7   A being is temporally necessary if and only if it is not temporally contingent.

T8   Everything has a sufficient reason for its existence.

T9   Anything that has a sufficient reason for its existence also has a sufficient reason for its existence that is a sufficient reason for its own existence.

T10   No temporally contingent being is a sufficient reason for the existence of a temporally necessary being.

T11   Every temporally necessary being that is a sufficient reason for its own existence is
a being without any limitations.

T12   A being without any limitations is necessarily greater than any other being.

T13   It is not possible for anything to be greater than itself.

T14   It is necessarily the case that "greater than" is asymmetric.

Therefore,

T15   There exists a supreme being.

The Temporal-Contingency Argument (TCA) is the argument "$\lozenge$(T1 & T2 & ... & T14) /∴ ($\exists$x)S_1x." The later deduction for "(T1, T2, . . . , T14) /∴ ($\exists$x)S_1x" plus the deduction (in the previous section) for "$\lozenge$($\exists$x)S_1x /∴ ($\exists$x)S_1x" together prove that TCA is valid.[36] First, let us add to our lexicon, thus

B_2x $=_{df}$ x begins to exist at some time and ceases to exist at some time
T_2x $=_{df}$ x is temporally necessary
C_2x $=_{df}$ x is temporally-contingent
F_2x $=_{df}$ x exists for a finite period of time
M_2 $=_{df}$ Only finitely many things have existed to date
P_3 $=_{df}$ Something presently exists
N_2 $=_{df}$ There was a time when nothing existed
S_2xy $=_{df}$ x is a sufficient reason for y for the existence of y
W_2x $=_{df}$ x is without any limitations

Deduction[37]

1	P_3	pr 1
2	M_2	pr 2
3	$(x)(C_2x \supset B_2x)$	pr 3
4	$(x)(B_2x \supset F_2x)$	pr 4
5	$((x)F_2x \,\&\, M_2\,) \supset N_2$	pr 5
6	$N_2 \supset {\sim}P_3$	pr 6
7	$(x)(T_2x \equiv {\sim}C_2x)$	pr 7
8	$(x)C_2x$	AIP
9	$C_2\mu \supset B_2\mu$	3 UI
10	$C_2\mu$	8 UI
11	$B_2\mu$	9, 11 MP

36. The modified Third Way that I present here is a variation on a modification of Aquinas' Third Way that I discuss in "A Modal Model . . ." (1980, pp. 139–40). It is also different from the central argument (MTW) of my "The Modal Third Way" (2000, pp. 1–28). MTW is sound, but the supreme being it proves is not defined as a greatest possible being; and it is not necessarily the God of Anselm, unless we postulate that such a supreme being is a greatest possible being. By contrast, the supreme being of TCA is a greatest possible being by definition.

37. This deduction departs slightly from the norm of beginning with all premises.

12	$B_2u \supset F_2u$	4 UI
13	F_2u	11,12 MP
14	$(x)F_2x$	13 UG
15	$(x)F_2x$ & M_2	2, 14 Conj
16	N_2	5, 15 MP
17	$\sim P_3$	6, 16 MP
18	P_3 & $\sim P_3$	1, 17 Conj
19	$\sim(x)C_2x$	8–19 IP
20	$(\exists x)\sim C_2x$	19 QN
21	$\sim C_2v_1$	20 EI
22	$T_2v_1 \equiv \sim C_2v_1$	7 UI
23	$(T_2v_1 \supset \sim C_2v_1)$ & $(\sim C_2v_1 \supset T_2v_1)$	22 Equiv
24	$(\sim C_2v_1 \supset T_2v_1)$	23 Com, Simp
25	T_2v_1	21, 24 MP
26	$(\exists x)T_2x$	25 EG
27	$(x)(\exists y)S_2yx$	pr 8
28	$(x)[(\exists y)S_2yx \supset (\exists z)(S_2zx$ & $S_2zz)]$	pr 9
29	$(x)(y)[(T_2x$ & $S_2yx) \supset \sim C_2y]$	pr 10
30	$(y)[(T_2y$ & $S_2yy) \supset W_2y]$	pr 11
31	$(y)[W_2y \supset \Box(z)(z{\neq}y \supset Gyz)]$	pr 12
32	$\sim\Diamond(\exists y)Gyy$	pr 13
33	$\Box(x)(y)(Gxy \supset \sim Gyx)$	pr 14
34	$(\exists y)S_2yv_1$	27, UI
35	$(\exists y)S_2yv_1 \supset (\exists z)(S_2zv_1$ & $S_2zz)$	28, UI
36	$(\exists y)(S_2zv_1$ & $S_2zz)$	34, 35 MP
37	S_2vv_1 & S_2vv	36, EI
38	$(T_2v_1$ & $S_2vv_1) \supset \sim C_2v$	29, UI twice
39	S_2vv_1	37 Simp
40	T_2v_1 & S_2vv_1	25, 39 Conj
41	$\sim C_2v$	38, 40 MP
42	$T_2v \equiv \sim C_2v$	7, UI
43	$(T_2v \supset \sim C_2v)$ & $(\sim C_2v \supset T_2v)$	42 Equiv
44	$\sim C_2v \supset T_2v$	43 Com, Simp
45	T_2v	44, 41 MP
46	S_2vv	37 Com, Simp
47	T_2v & S_2vv	45, 46 Conj
48	$(T_2v$ & $S_2vv) \supset W_2v$	30 UI
49	$W_2v \supset \Box(z)(z{\neq}v \supset Gvz)$	31 UI
50	$\Box(z)(z{\neq}v \supset Gvz)$	47, 48, 49 MP
51	$\Box(z)(\sim z{\neq}v \vee Gvz)$	50 Impl
52	$\Box(z)(\sim z{\neq}v \vee \sim\sim Gvz)$	51 DN
53	$\Box(z)\sim(z{\neq}v$ & $\sim Gvz)$	52 DeM
54	$\Box\sim(\exists z)(z{\neq}v$ & $\sim Gvz)$	53 QN
55	$\sim\Diamond(\exists z)(z{\neq}v$ & $\sim Gvz)$	54 ME
56	$\Box\sim(\exists y)Gyy$	32 ME
57	$\Box(y)\sim Gyy$	56 QN
58	$(y)\sim Gyy$	ACP

59	$\sim$G$\mu\mu$	58 UI
60	$\sim$G$\mu\mu$ $\vee$ $\nu\neq\mu$	59 Add
61	$\nu\neq\mu$ $\vee$ $\sim$G$\mu\mu$	60 Com
62	$\nu=\mu$ $\supset$ $\sim$G$\mu\mu$	61 Impl
63	$\mu=\nu$ $\supset$ $\nu=\mu$	theorem
64	$\mu=\nu$ $\supset$ $\sim$G$\mu\nu$	62, 63 HS
65	(y)$\sim$Gyy $\supset$ ($\mu=\nu$ $\supset$ $\sim$G$\mu\nu$)	58–64 CP
66	$\Box$[(y)$\sim$Gyy $\supset$ ($\mu=\nu$ $\supset$ $\sim$G$\mu\nu$)]	65 (theorem) NI
67	$\Box$($\mu=\nu$ $\supset$ $\sim$G$\mu\nu$)	57, 66 MMP
68	$\Box$(x)(y)(Gxy $\supset$ $\sim$Gyx) & $\Box$(z)(z$\neq\nu$ $\supset$ Gvz)	33, 50 Conj
69	$\Box$ [(x)(y)(Gxy $\supset$ $\sim$Gyx) & $\Box$(z)(z$\neq\nu$ $\supset$ Gvz)] $\supset$ $\Box$[(x)(y)(Gxy $\supset$ $\sim$Gyx) & (z)(z$\neq\nu$ $\supset$ Gvz)]	theorem
70	$\Box$[(x)(y)(Gxy $\supset$ $\sim$Gyx) & (z)(z$\neq\nu$ $\supset$ Gvz)]	68, 69 MP
71	$\Box$ {[(x)(y)(Gxy $\supset$ $\sim$Gyx) & (z)(z$\neq\nu$ $\supset$ Gvz)] $\supset$ ($\mu\neq\nu$ $\supset$ $\sim$G$\mu\nu$)}	theorem
72	$\Box$($\mu\neq\nu$ $\supset$ $\sim$G$\mu\nu$)	70, 71 MMP
73	[$\Box$($\mu=\nu$ $\supset$ $\sim$G$\mu\nu$) & $\Box$($\mu\neq\nu$ $\supset$ $\sim$G$\mu\nu$)] $\supset$ [$\Box$($\mu=\nu$ $\vee$ $\mu\neq\nu$) $\supset$ $\Box$($\sim$G$\mu\nu$ $\vee$ $\sim$G$\mu\nu$)]	theorem
74	$\Box$($\mu=\nu$ $\supset$ $\sim$G$\mu\nu$) & $\Box$($\mu\neq\nu$ $\supset$ $\sim$G$\mu\nu$)	67, 72 Conj
75	$\Box$[($\mu=\nu$ $\vee$ $\mu\neq\nu$) $\supset$ ($\sim$G$\mu\nu$ $\vee$ $\sim$G$\mu\nu$)]	73, 74 MP
76	$\Box$($\mu=\nu$ $\vee$ $\mu\neq\nu$)	theorem
77	$\Box$($\sim$G$\mu\nu$ $\vee$ $\sim$G$\mu\nu$)	75, 76 MMP
78	$\Box$($\sim$G$\mu\nu$ $\vee$ $\sim$G$\mu\nu$) $\supset$ $\Box$$\sim$G$\mu\nu$	theorem
79	$\Box$$\sim$G$\mu\nu$	77, 78 MP
80	(z)$\Box$$\sim$Gzv	79, UG
81	(z)$\Box$$\sim$Gzv $\supset$ $\Box$(z)$\sim$Gzv	theorem[38]
82	$\Box$(z)$\sim$Gzv	80, 81 MP
83	$\Box$$\sim$($\exists$z)Gzv	82, QN
84	$\sim$$\Diamond$($\exists$z)Gzv	83, ME
85	$\sim$$\Diamond$($\exists$z)Gzv & $\sim$$\Diamond$($\exists$z)(z$\neq\nu$ & $\sim$Gvz)	84, 55 Conj
86	S₁v	85, def "S₁"
87	($\exists$x)S₁x	86 EG

The sole premise of TCA is true if and only if there is some possible world where the premises T1, T2 . . . and T14 are true. Now I know of no reason to believe that there could not be a possible world ω where the propositions T1, T2, T3, T6, T8, T9, T10, and T11 express logically contingent facts about ω. Propositions T4, T5, T7, T13, and T14 appear to be self-evident analytic truths which are true in every possible world, including ω. Only T12 requires special justification:

> Assume x is a being without limitations in ω. Then x possesses every great making property in ω. In particular, x possesses the property in ω of not being limited in world ω_1 by anything.

---

38. Line 81 is an instance of another version of the BF. The two versions are equivalent, by the rules, to Trans, DN, ME, and QN. It is also interesting to note, however, that the validity of our modified Third Way can be proven in the logic QS4, which is just like QS5, save for the rule ⌜$\Diamond p$ /∴ $\Diamond\Diamond p$⌝ in place of ⌜$\Diamond p$ /∴ $\Box\Diamond p$⌝. The BF is not a theorem of QS4.

In other words, if x is a being without any limitations in ω, then x possesses every great making property in ω. But the property of not being limited in ω_1 is a great making property of ω. So it is true in ω that it is true in ω_1 that x is unlimited. But for any statement p, if it is true in world α that p is true in world β, then p is true in world β. Hence, x is unlimited in world ω_1. Now if x is unlimited in ω_1, then in ω_1 x is greater than any other being in ω_1; otherwise x would be limited by not possessing a great making property possessed by something else. Hence it is true in ω_1 that x is greater than every other being. Since ω_1 is an arbitrarily selected possible world, it follows that it is true in every possible world that x is greater than every other being. Consequently, it is necessarily the case that x is greater than every other being. So T12 is true in ω. (Maydole 1980, p. 140)

TCA is a quasi-ontological argument that is arguably sound. There is also no evidence to indicate that it begs the question. And it seems that it would be particularly resistant to being parodied, given its dependence on sundry logically contingent facts about a possible world, and the historical absence of any parodies against Third Way arguments.

7. Conclusion

Ontological arguments are captivating. They convince some people but not others. Our purpose here was not to convince but simply to show that some ontological arguments are sound, do not beg the question, and are insulated from extant parodies. Yet good logic does convince sometimes. Other times, something else is needed.

References

Adams, R. M. (1994) *Leibniz: Determinist, Theist, Idealist*. New York: Oxford University Press.

Adams, R. M. (1995) Introductory note to *1970. In S. Feferman (ed.), *Kurt Gödel, Collected Works*, vol lll, 388–402. New York: Oxford University Press.

Anderson, C. A. (1990) Some emendations of Gödel's ontological proof. *Faith and Philosophy* 7, 291–303.

Anselm (1962) *Basic Writing*, 2nd edn. Trans. S. N. Deane. La Salle, IL: Open Court.

Anselm (1967) Proslogion (*Chapters II–IV*). Trans. A. C. McGill. In J. H. Hick and A. C. McGill (eds.), *The Many-Faced Argument*, 3–8. New York: Macmillan.

Anselm (1998) Proslogion. Trans. M. J. Charlesworth. In B. Davies and G. Evans (eds.), *Anselm of Canterbury: The Major Works*, 1–34. New York: Oxford University Press.

Thomas Aquinas (1998) *Summa Theologica*, First Part, Q. II, Art. 3. Trans. A. C. Pegis. Reprinted in *Philosophy of Religion*, 3rd edn. Ed. L. P. Pojman. Belmont, CA: Wadsworth.

Copleston, F. C. (1961) *Medieval Philosophy*. New York: Harper Torchbooks.

Descartes, R. (1952) *Meditations on First Philosophy* and *Objections Against the Meditations and Replies* (including "arguments demonstrating the existence of God . . . drawn up in geometrical fashion"). Trans. E. S. Haldane and G. R. T. Ross. In R. M. Hutchins (ed.), *The Great Books*, vol. 31, 69–293. Chicago: Encyclopedia Britannica.

Findlay, J. N. (1998) Can God's existence be disproved? In L. P. Pojman (ed.), *Philosophy of Religion*, 3rd edn, 93–7. Belmont, CA: Wadsworth.

Gettings, M. (1999) Gödel's ontological argument: a reply to Oppy. *Analysis* 59: 4, 309–13.

Girle, R. (2003) *Possible Worlds*. Montreal: McGill-Queens University Press.

Gödel, K. (1995a) Ontological proof (*1970). In S. Feferman (ed.), *Kurt Gödel, Collected Works*, vol. III, 403–4. New York: Oxford University Press.

Gödel, K. (1995b) Texts relating to the ontological proof. In S. Feferman (ed.), *Kurt Gödel, Collected Works*, vol. III, 429–37. New York: Oxford University Press.

Gustason, W. and Ulrich, D. E. (1989) *Elementary Symbolic Logic*. Prospect Heights, IL: Waveland Press.

Hàjek, P. (2002) A new small emendation of Gödel's ontological proof. *Studia Logica* 71, 149–64.

Hartshorne, C. (1962) *The Logic of Perfection and Other Essays in Neoclassical Metaphysics*. La Salle, IL: Open Court.

Hazen, A. P. (1998) On Gödel's ontological proof. *Australian Journal of Philosophy* 76, 361–77.

Kant, I. (1933) *Critique of Pure Reason*. Trans. N. K. Smith. New York: St. Martin's Press.

Konyndyk, K. (1986) *Introductory Modal Logic*. Notre Dame, IN: University of Notre Dame Press.

Koons, R. C. (2005) Sobel on Gödel's Ontological Proof, http://www.scar.utoronto.ca/~sobel/OnL_T/ (accessed October 12, 2007).

Kripke, S. (1959) A Completeness theorem in modal logic. *The Journal of Symbolic Logic* 24: 1, 1–14.

Leibniz, G. W. (1964) *The Existence of God*. Ed. J. Hick. New York: Macmillan. Reprinted from *New Essays Concerning Human Understanding* by G. W. Leibniz (1896). Trans. A. G Langley. New York: Macmillan, Appendix X.

Malcolm, N. (1967) Anselm's ontological arguments. In J. H. Hick and A. C. McGill (eds.), *The Many-Faced Argument*, 301–20. New York: Macmillan. Reprinted from *The Philosophical Review* LXIX: 1 (1960).

Maydole, R. (1980) A modal model for proving the existence of God. *American Philosophical Quarterly* 17, 135–42.

Maydole, R. (2000) "The Modal Third Way." *International Journal for Philosophy of Religion* 47: 1–28.

Maydole, R. (2003) The modal perfection argument for the existence of God. *Philo* 6, 299–313.

Maydole, R. (2005a) On Oppy's objections to the modal perfection argument. *Philo* 8: 2, 123–130.

Maydole, R. (2005b) On Metcalf's objections to the modal perfection argument. *Philo* 8: 2, 134–6.

McGill, A. C (1967) Recent discussions of Anselm's argument. In J. H. Hick and A. C. McGill (eds.), *The Many-Faced Argument*, 33–110. New York: Macmillan.

Metcalf, T. (2005) Entailment and ontological arguments: reply to Maydole, *Philo* 8: 2, 131–3.

Oppy, G. (1995) *Ontological Arguments and Belief in God*. Cambridge: Cambridge University Press.

Oppy, G. (1996) Gödelian ontological arguments. *Analysis* 56, 226–30.

Oppy, G. (2000) Response to Gettings. *Analysis* 60: 4, 363–7.

Oppy, G. (2004) Maydole's 2QS5 argument. *Philo* 77: 2, 203–11.

Oppy, G. (2007) Ontological Arguments. *Stanford Encyclopedia of Philosophy*, http://plato.stanford.edu/entries/ontological-arguments/ (accessed July 29, 2007).

Plantinga, A. (1974) *The Nature of Necessity*. Oxford: Oxford University Press.

Rowe W. L. (2001) *Philosophy of Religion*, 3rd edn. Belmont, CA: Wadsworth.

Sobel, J. H. (1987) Gödel's ontological proof. In J. J. Thomson (ed.), *On Being and Saying: Essays for Richard Cartwright*, 241–61. Cambridge, MA: MIT Press.

Sobel, J. H. (2004) *Logic and Theism*. Cambridge: Cambridge University Press.

Appendix 1. Logic Matters

The strongest logic used in this chapter is a standard natural deduction system of second-order quantificational modal logic with identity (2QS5). It is equivalent to a standard second-order extension of Kripke's 1959 system of first-order modal logic. A weaker subsystem of 2QS5 is frequently used. The language of 2QS5 includes first- (lowercase) and second-order (uppercase) variables, constants and pseudo-names, property abstracts, and the standard array of quantifiers, connectives, punctuation marks, and so on.

The nonmodal propositional and quantificational inference rules of 2QS5 are from Gustason and Ulrich: Conjunction (Conj), Addition (Add), Simplification (Simp), Disjunctive Syllogism (DS), Excluded Middle Introduction (E-M I), Modus Ponens (MP), Modus Tollens (MT), Hypothetical Syllogism (HS), Constructive Dilemma (CD), Commutation (Com), Distribution (Dist), Association (Assoc) Double Negation (DN), DeMorgan (DeM), Transposition (Trans), Exportation (Exp), Equivalence (Equiv), Existential Instantiation (EI), Existential Generalization (EG), Universal Instantiation (UI), Universal Generalization (UG), Quantifier Negation (QN), Identity Introduction (II), Identity Elimination (IE), Conditional Proof (CP) and Indirect Proof (IP).[39]

The five Modal Inference Rules of 2QS5 are as follows:

	For every substitution instance of $\ulcorner p \urcorner$ and $\ulcorner q \urcorner$
NE (necessity elimination)	$\Box p /\therefore p$
MMP (modal modus ponens)	$\Box(p \supset q), \Box p /\therefore \Box q$
NI (necessity introduction)	If $\ulcorner p \urcorner$ is a theorem then $\ulcorner \Box p \urcorner$ is a theorem
ME (modal equivalence)	$\ulcorner \Diamond p \urcorner$ for $\ulcorner \sim\Box\sim p \urcorner$ and $\ulcorner \Box p \urcorner$ for $\ulcorner \sim\Diamond\sim p \urcorner$
PN (possibility necessity)	$\Diamond p /\therefore \Box\Diamond p$

2QS5 also includes the Principle of Abstraction (Abs) as an axiom schema: $(x)(\hat{y}[\Psi y]x \equiv \Psi x)$, where $\ulcorner \hat{y}[\Psi y] \urcorner$ denotes the property of being a Ψ.[40]

Appendix 2. Formal Proofs of Some Modal Arguments

The validity of Malcolm's ontological argument

Let

$U_1 x =_{df}$ x is unlimited
$D_1 x =_{df}$ x depends on something else for its existence or nonexistence
$Hx =_{df}$ x happens to exist

---

39. The quantification rules apply to both first-order and second-order variables, and no pseudo-names are allowed in the last line of a deduction.

40. Theorems and theorem schemata of Q2S5 are sometimes used in the proofs and deductions in this chapter. It would make this chapter too long to include proofs of them. They are, however, fairly straightforward, and should be fairly common in the literature.

$Jx =_{df} x$ happens not to exist
$B_1x =_{df} x$ is caused to begin to exist by some other being
$C_1x =_{df} x$ is caused to cease to exist by some other being
$M_1x =_{df} x$ begins to exist
$N_1x =_{df} x$ ceases to exist

Deduction

1	$\Diamond Eg$	pr[41]
2	U_1g	pr
3	$(x)(U_1x \equiv (\sim D_1x\ \&\ \sim Hx\ \&\ \sim Jx))$	pr
4	$(x)(\sim D_1x \equiv (\sim B_1x\ \&\ \sim C_1x))$	pr
5	$(x)(M_1x \supset (B_1x \lor Hx))$	pr
6	$(x)(N_1x \supset (C_1x \lor Jx))$	pr
7	$(x)((\sim M_1x\ \&\ \sim N_1x) \supset ((Ex \supset \Box Ex)\ \&\ (\sim Ex \supset \Box \sim Ex)))$	pr
8	$U_1g \equiv (\sim D_1g\ \&\ \sim Hg\ \&\ \sim Jg)$	3, UI
9	$(\sim D_1g\ \&\ \sim Hg\ \&\ \sim Jg)$	2, 8 Equiv, Simp, MP
10	$\sim D_1g \equiv (\sim B_1g\ \&\ \sim C_1g)$	4 UI
11	$\sim D_1g$	9 Simp
12	$(\sim B_1g\ \&\ \sim C_1g)$	10, 11 Equiv, Simp, MP
13	$\sim Hg$	9 Assoc, Simp
14	$\sim B_1g$	12 Simp
15	$\sim (B_1g \lor Hg)$	13, 14 Conj, DeM
16	$\sim Jg$	9 Assoc, Simp
17	$\sim C_1g$	12 Simp
18	$\sim (C_1g \lor Jg)$	16, 17 Conj, DeM
19	$M_1g \supset (B_1g \lor Hg)$	5 UI
20	$\sim M_1g$	15, 19 MT
21	$N_1g \supset (C_1g \lor Jg)$	6 UI
22	$\sim N_1g$	18, 21 MT
23	$(\sim M_1g\ \&\ \sim N_1g) \supset ((Eg \supset \Box Eg)\ \&\ (\sim Eg \supset \Box \sim Eg))$	7 UI
24	$(\sim M_1g\ \&\ \sim N_1g)$	20, 22 Conj
25	$((Eg \supset \Box Eg)\ \&\ (\sim Eg \supset \Box \sim Eg))$	23, 24 MP
26	$(\sim Eg \supset \Box \sim Eg)$	25 Simp
27	$\sim \Box \sim Eg \supset Eg$	26 Trans
28	$\Diamond Eg \supset Eg$	27 ME
29	Eg	1, 28 MP

The validity of Hartshorne's ontological argument

Let

$q =_{df}$ There is a perfect being

Deduction

41. "Eg" could be replaced by "$(\exists x)x = g$." The existential quantifier would then have to have existential import, as it does for both Hartshorne and Plantinga.

1	$\Box(q \supset \Box q)$	pr
2	$\Diamond q$	pr
3	$\Box(q \supset \Box q) \supset (\Diamond q \supset \Diamond \Box q)$	theorem
4	$(\Diamond q \supset \Diamond \Box q)$	1, 3 MP
5	$\Diamond \Box q$	2, 4 MP
6	$\Diamond \Box q \supset \Box q$	theorem
7	$\Box q$	5,6 MP
8	q	7, NE

The validity of Plantinga's ontological argument

Let

$Ax =_{df}$ x is maximally great
$Bx =_{df}$ x is maximally excellent
$W(Y) =_{df}$ Y is a universal property
$Ox =_{df}$ x is omniscient, omnipotent, and morally perfect

Deduction

1	$\Diamond(\exists x)Ax$	pr
2	$\Box(x)(Ax \equiv \Box Bx)$	pr
3	$\Box(x)(Bx \supset Ox)$	pr
4	$(Y)[W(Y) \equiv (\Box(\exists x)Yx \vee (\Box\sim(\exists x)Yx)]$	pr
5	$(Y)[(\exists Z)\Box(x)(Yx \equiv \Box Zx) \supset W(Y)]$	pr
6	$(\exists Z)\Box(x)(Ax \equiv \Box Zx)$	2, EG
7	$[(\exists Z)\Box(x)(Ax \equiv \Box Zx) \supset W(A)]$	5, UI
8	$W(A) \equiv (\Box(\exists x)Ax \vee (\Box\sim(\exists x)Ax)$	4, UI
9	$W(A)$	6, 7 MP
10	$W(A) \supset (\Box(\exists x)Ax \vee (\Box\sim(\exists x)Ax)$	8, Equiv, Simp
11	$\Box(\exists x)Ax (\Box\sim(\exists x)Ax)$	9, 10 MP
12	$\sim\Diamond\sim\sim(\exists x)Ax \vee (\Box(\exists x)Ax)$	11, Com, ME
13	$\Diamond(\exists x)Ax \supset \Box(\exists x)Ax$	DN, Impl
14	$\Box(\exists x)Ax$	1, 13 MP
15	$\Box(x)(Ax \equiv \Box Bx) \supset (\Box(\exists x)Ax \supset \Box(\exists x)\Box Bx)$	theorem
16	$\Box(\exists x)\Box Bx$	14, 15 MP (twice)
17	$\Box(x)(Bx \supset Ox) \supset (\Box(\exists x)\Box Bx \supset \Box(\exists x)\Box Ox)$	theorem
18	$\Box(\exists x)\Box Ox$	16, 17 MP (twice)
19	$(\exists x)\Box Ox$	18, NE

Complete proofs of Gödel's ontological theorems

Proof of Tm 1

1	$\sim\Diamond(\exists y)G_1 y$	AIP
2	$\sim\Diamond(\exists y)G_1 y \supset \Box(x)(G_1 x \supset \sim G_1 x)$	theorem

3	$\Box(x)(G_1x \supset \sim G_1x)$	1, 2 MP
4	$\Box(x)(\hat{y}[\sim G_1y]x \equiv \sim G_1x)$	Abs, NI[42]
5	$(\Box(x)(G_1x \supset \sim G_1x) \& \Box(x)(\hat{y}[\sim G_1y]x \equiv \sim G_1x)) \supset$	theorem
	$\Box(x)(G_1x \supset \hat{y}[\sim G_1y]x)$	
6	$\Box(x)(G_1x \supset \hat{y}[\sim G_1y]x)$	3, 4, 5, Conj, MP
7	$P_1(G_1)$	Ax 3[43]
8	$(P_1(G_1) \& \Box(x)(G_1x \supset \hat{y}[\sim G_1y]x)) \supset P_1\hat{y}[\sim G_1y])$	Ax 2, UI
9	$P_1\hat{y}[\sim G_1y]$	6, 7, 8, Conj, MP
10	$P_1(G_1) \supset \sim P_1(\hat{y}[\sim G_1y])$	Ax 1, UI, Equiv, Simp
11	$\sim P_1(\hat{y}[\sim G_1y])$	9, 10 MP
12	$\Diamond(\exists y)G_1y$	1–11 IP

Proof of Tm 2

1	$G_1\mu \& \Theta\mu$	ACP
2	$\sim P_1(\Theta)$	AIP
3	$\sim P_1(\hat{y}[\sim\Theta y]) \supset P_1(\Theta)$	Ax 1, UI, Equiv, Simp
4	$P_1(\hat{y}[\sim\Theta y])$	2, 3, DN, MT
5	$P_1(\hat{y}[\sim\Theta y]) \supset \hat{y}[\sim\Theta y]\mu$	1, Simp, df "G_1", UI
6	$\hat{y}[\sim\Theta y]\mu$	4, 5 MP
7	$\hat{y}[\sim\Theta y]\mu \equiv \sim\Theta\mu$	Abs, UI
8	$\sim\Theta\mu$	6, 7 Equiv, Simp, MP
9	$\Theta\mu \& \sim\Theta\mu$	1, 8 Simp, Conj
10	$P_1(\Theta)$	2–7 IP
11	$\Box(x)(G_1x \supset (Y)(P_1(Y) \supset Yx))$	theorem, df "G_1"
12	$\Box(x)(G_1x \supset (Y)(P_1(Y) \supset Yx)) \supset (x)(Y)(\Box P_1(Y) \supset$	theorem
	$\Box(x)(G_1x \supset Yx))$	
13	$(x)(Y)(\Box P_1(Y) \supset \Box(x)(G_1x \supset Yx))$	11, 12 MP
14	$\Box P_1(\Theta) \supset \Box(x)(G_1x \supset \Theta x)$	13 UI
15	$P_1(\Theta) \supset \Box P_1(\Theta)$	Ax 4, UI
16	$\Box P_1(\Theta)$	10, 15 MP
17	$\Box(x)(G_1x \supset \Theta x)$	14, 16 MP
18	$(G_1\mu \& \Theta\mu) \supset \Box(x)(G_1x \supset \Theta x)$	1–17 CP
19	$(x)(Z)((G_1x \& Zx) \supset \Box(x)(G_1x \supset Zx))$	18, UG
20	$(x)(Z)((G_1x \& Zx) \supset \Box(x)(G_1x \supset Zx)) \supset$	theorem
	$(x)(G_1x \supset (G_1x \& (Z)(Zx \supset \Box(x)(G_1x \supset Zx))))$	
21	$(x)(G_1x \supset (G_1x \& (Z)(Zx \supset \Box(x)(G_1x \supset Zx))))$	19, 20, MP
22	$(x)(G_1x \supset E_1(G_1, x))$	21, df "E_1"

42. Scott and Sobel omit necessitated Abstraction in their proofs of Tm 1. (Anderson acknowledges that it is implicit.) Their proofs assume that it is necessarily true that self-difference is identical to the negation of self-identity. But howsoever obvious that identity might be, its proof requires necessitated Abstraction:

$$\Box(x)(\hat{y}[y{\neq}y]x \equiv \sim x{=}x)$$
$$\Box(x)(\hat{y}[\sim y{=}y]x \equiv \sim x{=}x)$$
$$\therefore \hat{y}[y{\neq}y] = \hat{y}[\sim y{=}y]$$

43. See section (4a) for a formal expression of Gödel's axioms.

Proof of Tm 3

1	$G_1\mu$	ACP
2	$P_1(N_2)$	Ax 5
3	$P_1(N_2) \supset N_2\mu$	1, UI, df "G_1"
4	$N_2\mu$	2, 3 MP
5	$E_1(G_1, \mu) \supset \Box(\exists z)G_1 z$	4, UI, df "N_2"
6	$G_1\mu \supset (G_1\mu \& (Z)(Zx \supset \Box(x)(G_1\mu \supset Z\mu)))$	Tm 2, df "E_1", UI
7	$(G_1\mu \supset (G_1\mu \& (Z)(Zx \supset \Box(x)(G_1\mu \supset Z\mu)))) \supset$ $(G_1\mu \& (Z)(Zx \supset \Box(x)(G_1\mu \supset Z\mu)))$	theorem
8	$E_1(G_1, \mu)$	6, 7 MP, df "E_1"
9	$\Box(\exists z)G_1 z$	5, 8 MP
10	$G_1\mu \supset \Box(\exists z)G_1 z$	1–9 CP
11	$\Box(x)(G_1 x \supset \Box(\exists z)G_1 z)$	10 UG, NI
12	$\Box(x)(G_1 x \supset \Box(\exists z)G_1 z) \supset (\Diamond(\exists y)G_1 y \supset \Diamond\Box(\exists z)G_1 z)$	theorem
13	$\Diamond(\exists y)G_1 y \supset \Diamond\Box(\exists z)G_1 z$	11, 12 MP
14	$\Diamond\Box(\exists z)G_1 z$	13 Tm 1, MP
15	$\Diamond\Box(\exists z)G_1 z \supset \Box(\exists z)G_1 z$	theorem
16	$\Box(\exists z)G_1 z$	14, 15 MP
17	$(\exists z)G_1 z$	16 NE

11

The Argument from Miracles: A Cumulative Case for the Resurrection of Jesus of Nazareth

TIMOTHY MCGREW AND LYDIA MCGREW

Introduction

It is a curiosity of the history of ideas that the argument from miracles is today better known as the object of a famous attack than as a piece of reasoning in its own right. It was not always so. From Paul's defense before Agrippa to the polemics of the orthodox against the deists at the heart of the Enlightenment, the argument from miracles was central to the discussion of the reasonableness of Christian belief, often supplemented by other considerations but rarely omitted by any responsible writer. But in the contemporary literature on the philosophy of religion it is not at all uncommon to find entire works that mention the positive argument from miracles only in passing or ignore it altogether.

Part of the explanation for this dramatic change in emphasis is a shift that has taken place in the conception of philosophy and, in consequence, in the conception of the project of natural theology. What makes an argument distinctively philosophical under the new rubric is that it is substantially *a priori*, relying at most on facts that are common knowledge. This is not to say that such arguments must be crude. The level of technical sophistication required to work through some contemporary versions of the cosmological and teleological arguments is daunting. But their factual premises are not numerous and are often commonplaces that an educated nonspecialist can readily grasp – that something exists, that the universe had a beginning in time, that life as we know it could flourish only in an environment very much like our own, that some things that are not human artifacts have an appearance of having been designed.

Measured by this standard, the argument from miracles is not purely philosophical. Its evaluation requires the patient sifting of a welter of details, the consideration of putatively analogous events, the assessment of the probability or improbability of fraud or muddle or the gradual growth of legend. And this specificity carries through to its conclusion. More than any other argument in the repertoire of natural theology, the argument from miracles confronts us with the scandal of particularity. For unlike any of the other traditional proofs, the argument from miracles purports to establish not merely theism, but Christianity.

The other and perhaps more significant part of the explanation for the relative neglect of the argument from miracles lies in Hume's famous essay, first published in 1748, which sets out with the ambitious goal of providing "the wise and the learned" with an "everlasting check to all kinds of superstitious delusions." In a historical accident as curious as it is unfortunate, Hume's brief, vigorous polemic is now generally included in anthologies as a set piece, isolated from the dialectical context in which it was originally embedded and presented almost as if it had simultaneously inaugurated and ended the discussion of miracles as a serious ground for religious belief. This may be explained partly by Hume's high reputation and partly by the rhetorical elegance of the piece. But the enduring popularity of Hume's essay is no doubt a function of the fact that he is saying what many philosophers want to hear.

It is not the primary purpose of this essay to refute the arguments of Hume; rather, we are concerned to set the principal argument for the truth of Christianity in its proper light. But at the end we shall return to Hume, both to put his argument in its historical context and to evaluate the significance of the considerations he and his modern progeny have raised against the argument from miracles.

Goal and Scope of the Argument

At the outset, we need to make it clear what argument we are making and how we propose to do it. The phrase "the argument from miracles" implies that this is an argument *to* some other conclusion, and that conclusion is most naturally understood to be theism (T), the existence of a God at least roughly similar to the one believed in by Jews and Christians.

It is, however, not our purpose to argue that the probability of T is high. Nor do we propose to argue that the probability of Christianity (C) is high. Nor, despite the plural "miracles," do we propose to discuss more than one putative miracle. We intend to focus on a single claim for a miraculous event – the bodily resurrection of Jesus of Nazareth ca. AD 33 (R). We shall argue that there is significant positive evidence for R, evidence that cannot be ignored and that must be taken into account in any evaluation of the total evidence for Christianity and for theism.

That the resurrection is positively relevant to theism on ordinary background evidence should be obvious. To state the matter modestly and slightly loosely, the probability that God exists is higher if there is significant independent evidence that Jesus rose from the dead than if there is no such evidence, and this is true because the probability that the resurrection took place is virtually nil if there is no God and higher if there is. On any plausible background assumptions, if Jesus of Nazareth died and then rose again bodily three days later, the probability of T is approximately equal to 1.

The resurrection is also positively relevant to Christianity. On any construal of Christianity worth the name, the assertion that Jesus rose bodily and miraculously from the dead is one of its core assertions. It is fairly easy to see that the probability that Christianity is true is greater given that the resurrection of Jesus occurred than it is otherwise on our present background evidence.

We are not, of course, simply "given" that the resurrection occurred. It is a contingent proposition, and any evidence we bring for it will be less than certain. Our contention is that this evidence, which raises the probability of R, also raises the probability of

Christianity and of theism. For most of the facts we shall bring forward – the testimony of the disciples to having seen Christ alive and their willingness to die for this testimony, and the testimony of the women to the empty tomb and to their sight of the resurrected Christ – the resurrection stands in a relation both to the evidence and to Christianity that we shall explain later as "acting as a conduit for" or "channeling" the force of that evidence both to theism and to Christianity. The resurrection can be thought of as standing epistemically between this evidence and these other propositions; the evidential force of the testimonial evidence flows through R to T and C. It is possible to give an interesting and probabilistically precise explanation of this notion of the channeling of evidence (McGrew & McGrew 2008). In the case of the conversion of Paul, on the other hand, the force of the evidence plausibly has impact upon Christianity even independent of the resurrection; even given that the resurrection occurred, Paul's conversion provides additional evidence for Christianity (for such propositions as that Jesus is in heaven and is God, for example), since Paul's conversion and the heavenly vision that occasioned it were not simply an attestation to the fact that Christ had risen bodily from the dead. This means that R does not act as a "conduit" of the force of Paul's conversion to C. However, on our ordinary background evidence it is correct to say that Christianity is such a conduit of the force of Paul's conversion to theism – roughly put, that the evidential relevance of Paul's conversion to theism is entirely a function of its impact on the truth of Christianity. In either event, all of the evidence we shall adduce is relevant to theism *by way of* its relevance to more specific or stronger claims – the resurrection and the truth of Christianity. Hence this evidence does indeed support theism, and the argument for the resurrection is indirectly an argument for theism. But it is an argument for theism that goes by way of its direct impact upon richer, more specific claims than the mere claim that God exists.

Even as we focus on the resurrection of Jesus, our aim is limited. To show that the probability of R given all evidence relevant to it is high would require us to examine other evidence bearing on the existence of God, since such other evidence – both positive and negative – is indirectly relevant to the occurrence of the resurrection. Examining every piece of data relevant to R more directly – including, for example, the many issues in textual scholarship and archeology which we shall discuss only briefly – would require many volumes. Our intent, rather, is to examine a small set of salient public facts that strongly support R. The historical facts in question are, we believe, those most pertinent to the argument. Our aim is to show that this evidence, taken cumulatively, provides a strong argument of the sort Richard Swinburne calls "C-inductive" – that is, whether or not $P(R)$ is greater than some specified value such as 0.5 or 0.9 given *all* evidence, this evidence itself heavily favors R over ~R.

At a first approximation, our argument is explanatory: the conjunction of the salient facts we shall adduce is well explained by R. But this is an incomplete description, since it does not bring out the contrastive sense of explanation we have in mind. At a second approximation, our argument is comparative: we contend that no alternative hypothesis that is not itself enormously improbable – even on the assumption that the resurrection did not occur – explains the conjunction of the facts in question anywhere nearly as well as R explains them. Finally, our argument gives a probabilistic analysis to the notion of explanation. We argue that, given our background knowledge, the ratio of the probability of all the facts in question given R over the probability of all of those facts given ~R is extremely top-heavy. This is to say that the disjunction of alternatives to R (all the possible hypotheses that fall under ~R) does not account for the facts in question nearly as well as does R. Formally,

$$\frac{P(F_1 \& \dots \& F_n | R)}{P(F_1 \& \dots \& F_n | \sim R)} \gg 1$$

It follows from this assertion that the set of facts in question is highly confirmatory of R.

The Concept of a Miracle

Philosophical discussions of miracles often involve a detailed examination of different notions of "miracle." Hume's own discussion features two definitions that are not equivalent: "A violation of a law of nature" and "a transgression of a law of nature by a particular volition of the Deity, or by the interposition of some invisible agent." These definitions suffer from various drawbacks, as many subsequent commentators have noted. Some conceptions of natural law would rule out miracles altogether (McKinnon 1967, pp. 308–14; Earman 2000, p. 8). On other conceptions, miracles are not violations of the real laws of the universe but merely of those local generalizations which we, in ignorance, are apt to call the laws of nature.[1] On still other conceptions, an event may be truly miraculous although its occurrence is in full accordance with the laws of nature.[2] In any event, the concept of a miracle makes sense even on an account of nature that predates the notion of natural laws, so long as there is a normal order of nature as a background against which the miraculous stands out (Swinburne 1989, pp. 2–10; Houston 1994, chaps. 1 and 2). Whether the working of miracles is the prerogative of God alone is itself a disputed point in the history of theology.[3]

Fortunately, we do not need to offer necessary and sufficient conditions for something's being a miracle in order to pursue the present line of argument, since our discussion is focused on the resurrection of Jesus, and all parties to the discussion are agreed that the resurrection of Jesus, if in fact it took place, would be a paradigm case of a miracle. For our purposes, it suffices to stipulate that *a miracle is a specific event that would not have happened if only the natural order had been operating*, where the natural order is understood to involve physical entities, their interactions, and the actions and interactions of animals, humans, and beings with powers much like ours. There is some vagueness in this definition, particularly with respect to what "powers much like ours" might amount to; but it has the merit of avoiding semantic questions about what constitutes a physical law and whether a physical law cannot, by definition, be violated.[4]

---

1. John Venn (1888, pp. 428f) seems inclined to endorse this sort of position. C. S. Lewis also appeals to it both in his philosophical work and in his fiction (see Lewis 1946, pp. 367–8; 1947, p. 61). For a critique, see Wardlaw (1852, pp. 31–41).
2. See Larmer (1988, pp. 3–30) and Larmer's contributions to Larmer (1996).
3. For a useful historical discussion, see Burns (1981).
4. We do not wish to imply that the definition of a miracle as a suspension of physical causation or a violation of physical law is *wrong*; McKinnon's argument in particular strikes us as mere semantic jugglery. But it is simpler to stipulate that a miracle is an event that would not have happened in the natural order and then to define the natural order as we have done.

Textual Assumptions

At the beginning of the first volume of *A Marginal Jew*, John Meier facetiously suggests that the problem of the historical Jesus might be resolved by resort to an "unpapal enclave" in which a Protestant, a Catholic, a Jew, and an agnostic are locked into the Harvard Divinity School library and fed on bread and water until they hammer out "a consensus document on who Jesus of Nazareth was and what he intended in his own time and place." (Meier 1991, p. 1) The jest underscores a difficulty we must face at this point. A historical argument of the sort we propose to lay out must proceed on some assumptions regarding the relevant texts, and at the point where philosophers most naturally enter the discussion, we might hope that the historians and scholars of those particular texts would have arrived already at some consensus regarding their subject matter. Unhappily, this is not the case: the field of New Testament scholarship is riven with disputes among acknowledged experts. We must, therefore, give at least a statement of what we are (and what we are not) taking for granted and a very brief sketch of our reasons.

Our argument will proceed on the assumption that we have a substantially accurate text of the four Gospels, Acts, and several of the undisputed Pauline epistles (most significantly Galatians and 1 Corinthians); that the Gospels were written, if not by the authors whose names they now bear, at least by disciples of Jesus or people who knew those disciples – people who knew at first hand the details of his life and teaching or people who spoke with those eyewitnesses – and that the narratives, at least where not explicitly asserting the occurrence of a miracle, deserve as much credence as similarly attested documents would be accorded if they reported strictly secular matters.[5] Where the texts do assert something miraculous – for example, Jesus' postresurrection appearances – we take it, given the basic assumption of authenticity, that the narrative represents what someone relatively close to the situation claimed. For the purposes of our argument, we make no assumption of inspiration, much less inerrancy, for these documents, and we accept that there are small textual variations and minor signs of editing, though we do not in any place rely on any passage where the textual evidence leaves serious doubt about the original meaning. Indeed, much of our argument could be made without even the general claim of reliability, since as we shall point out many of the salient facts are agreed upon by scholars across the spectrum. But we have chosen to frame the argument this way, since we think the general reliability claim is quite defensible and since this allows us to tackle the philosophically interesting questions regarding evidence for the miraculous on the same plane where Hume leveled his famous attack, prior to the rise of higher criticism of the New Testament texts.

A favorite tactic of the adversaries of Christianity in the eighteenth century, vigorously employed by Hermann Samuel Reimarus in the Wolfenbüttel Fragments, is to point to various discrepancies, real or imagined, in the telling of the same story and to conclude that the texts contradict each other and therefore are untrustworthy at best and worthless at worst. The accounts of Peter's denial of Christ in the four Gospels differ in various minor details; the resurrection narratives vary in the names of the women they place at the tomb and the details noted there; John reports that Mary Magdalene ran to find the disciples,

---

5. Lest anyone should be tempted to over-interpret this rather minimal statement, we note that it is not our intention to concede as unhistorical texts on which the present argument does not depend.

while Matthew makes no mention of this. Such minor discrepancies have afforded skeptics a pretext for discounting the narratives *tout court*, and some earnest defenders of the Gospels have played into their hands by insisting that every detail is reported with minute accuracy, even if this forces one to the conclusion that Peter denied Christ six or twelve times rather than three.

The number of alleged discrepancies in the Gospels is greatly exaggerated by a free use of the *argumentum ex silentio*: if an author does not mention some piece of information, it is too often assumed that he was unaware of it or even that he positively believed the contrary. Such arguments from silence are pervasive in New Testament scholarship, but they are tenuous at best. By such reasoning we can easily find "contradictions" even in the writings of one and the same historian, as when Josephus mentions facts in his *Antiquities* that we might have expected him to repeat in his *Jewish War* (Paley 1859, p. 337). When we extend it to the comparison of multiple authors who treat of the same subject, the results are ridiculous.[6] The moral to be drawn is that it is a risky business to speculate upon the motives of authors for including or omitting various facts. To create an appearance of inconsistency by this device, or by such means to justify elaborate hypotheses regarding editors and recensions of the Gospels, is methodologically unsound.[7]

Some of the alleged contradictions among the Gospel narratives arise from demonstrably uncharitable or uninformed readings of the texts. But with respect to the historical argument, the debate over the resolution of such issues is beside the point. Even a passing acquaintance with the documents that form the basis of secular history reveals that the reports of reliable historians, even of eyewitnesses, always display selection and emphasis and not infrequently contradict each other outright. Yet this fact does not destroy or even significantly undermine their credibility regarding the main events they report. Almost no two authors agree regarding how many troops Xerxes marshaled for his invasion of Greece; but the invasion and its disastrous outcome are not in doubt. Florus's account of the number of troops at the battle of Pharsalia differs from Caesar's own account by 150,000 men; but no one doubts that there was such a battle, or that Caesar won it. According to Josephus, the embassy of the Jews to the Emperor Claudius took place in seed time, while Philo places it in harvest time; but that there was such an embassy is uncontroversial. Examples of this kind can be multiplied almost endlessly.

In law, it has long been recognized that minor discrepancies among witnesses do not invalidate their testimony – indeed, that they provide an argument against collusion. The eminent legal scholar Thomas Starkie stresses this point in his discussion of testimonial evidence:

> It is here to be observed, that partial variances in the testimony of different witnesses, on minute and collateral points, although they frequently afford the adverse advocate a topic for copious observation, are of little importance, unless they be of too prominent and striking a nature to be ascribed to mere inadvertence, inattention, or defect of memory.

6. Our principal sources for the life of Tiberius Caesar, for example, are Suetonius, Tacitus, and Dio Cassius. These three authors actually do contradict each other in a number of places. But the number of "contradictions" would be vastly increased if we were to assume that each instance of events mentioned by one but omitted by another counts as a contradiction.

7. For a thoughtful critique of this device in New Testament scholarship, with special reference to Reginald Fuller's work on the gospels, see Alston (1997, pp. 148–83).

It has been well remarked by a great observer, that "the usual character of human testimony is substantial truth under circumstantial variety." It so rarely happens that witnesses of the same transaction perfectly and entirely agree in all points connected with it, that an entire and complete coincidence in every particular, so far from strengthening their credit, not unfrequently engenders a suspicion of practice and concert.

The real question must always be, whether the points of variance and of discrepancy be of so strong and decisive a nature as to render it impossible, or at least difficult, to attribute them to the ordinary sources of such varieties, inattention or want of memory. (Starkie 1833, pp. 488–9)[8]

The case is no different with respect to the Gospels. Granting the most that could be said on behalf of the critic – that a comparison of the Gospel accounts reveals real and unresolvable contradictions regarding some subsidiary details of setting or circumstance – it would not follow that they are less reliable than any other historical document regarding the principal facts they relate.

The assumption that the Gospels and Acts are basically historically reliable has knowledgeable contemporary advocates.[9] But it flies in the face of nearly a century of New Testament scholarship based on form criticism and its methodological offshoot, redaction criticism. In brief, these are versions of literary criticism whose adherents have proclaimed the Gospels in their present form to be late productions of the Christian community and have attempted to excavate the texts as they have come down to us in order to discover the hypothesized original layers beneath the postulated accretion of oral tradition and legend or to determine the intentions of the last redactor, or editor. The chief requirement for this theory of literary layers is time – time for originals to be gradually edited into a radically different form, time for the development of miracle legends, time for the evolution of John's high Christology that could be grafted onto a set of original simple parables and sayings of Jesus or for those sayings to be midrashically expanded without the fact's attracting notice or criticism. It is therefore no accident that the dominant position in New Testament studies since the pioneering *Formgeschichtliche* work of Martin Dibelius and Rudolf Bultmann has been that the Gospels are very late productions, preferably well into the second century but in all events after AD 70, since any earlier dating would require us to attribute to Jesus prophetic abilities with respect to the destruction of Jerusalem that would run afoul of the philosophical naturalism driving the project.

The role of such naturalism as a motivating factor in the work of the form critics is often explicit, but as an argument against a more traditional position it suffers from the obvious drawback of circularity. Consequently, form critics have typically supported their conclusion of late dating of the Gospels and Acts by pointing to ostensible anachronisms and errors of detail that show the authors to have been, not eyewitnesses, but creative and tendentious redactors writing at a substantial remove from the events they are purportedly recording.

Unquestionably, if we examine the Gospels with a literary lens of sufficient resolving power, we find that they contain material belonging to various literary types: *logia*, parables, pronouncement stories, speeches, and so forth. To recognize this fact is not to make any

---

8. The "great observer" quoted by Starkie is William Paley (1859, p. 336). For examples in cases at law, see Starkie's note (1833, p. 488) and also Simon Greenleaf (1874, pp. 32–6). Starkie is by no means alone among legal scholars in making this observation.

9. See in particular Craig Blomberg (1987, 2001).

concession on the point of interest to us here. And anyone who has read much biblical criticism knows that the form and redaction critics often command much real scholarship and sometimes display astonishing imagination. But there are good reasons for dismissing the sweeping negative conclusions of form criticism regarding the authenticity and reliability of the narratives. There are no independent textual traditions preserving the allegedly earliest forms; one must discern them in the existing text, and in many cases the layers are visible only when the text is viewed with eyes of form-critical faith. There is a substantial and growing body of evidence that the Gospels were indeed written by eyewitnesses or by those with access to eyewitnesses. And the conjectures of the form critics regarding the dating and accuracy of the New Testament writings have repeatedly been shown by scholars in other fields to be embarrassing blunders.

A few examples may help to illustrate the latter point. In the early twentieth century, the French critic Alfred Loisy dismissed the description in the fourth Gospel (John 5:2) of the pool of Bethesda as having five porches. This, Loisy said, was a literary alteration or addition designed to represent the five books of the law which Jesus had come to fulfill. On the basis of such reasoning, and in harmony with the late dating advocated in the previous century by the Tübingen scholar Ferdinand Christian Baur, Loisy set the date for the composition of the Gospel at some time after AD 150. Excavations of the pool of Bethesda in 1956 revealed that it was located where John said it was, bounded on the sides with four colonnades and spanned across the middle by a fifth (Jeremias 1966, pp. 36–8; Leon-Dufour 1967, p. 67). As E. M. Blaiklock says, "No further comment is necessary" (1983, p. 65).

Archaeology has not been kind to literary criticism of the Gospels and Acts. The discovery in Caesarea Maritima in 1961 of an inscription bearing Pilate's name and title, the discovery of a boundary stone of the emperor Claudius bearing the name of Sergius Paulus (cf. Acts 13:7), the very recent discovery of the Pool of Siloam (John 9) from the time of Jesus, and numerous other discoveries indicate a level of accuracy incompatible with the picture of the development of the Gospels as an accretion of legend over the course of two or more generations. Our point is not that these discoveries demonstrate the accuracy of all other portions of the Gospels; rather, it is the commonsense principle that authors who have been shown to be accurate in matters that we can check against existing independent evidence deserve, within reasonable bounds, the benefit of the doubt when they speak of matters of putative public fact that we cannot at present verify independently. Several such discoveries also indicate that the author of the Gospel of John was familiar with Jerusalem prior to its destruction, a point that directly addresses the attempt to place a very late date on the text (see Shanks 2005, p. 23).

The extreme late dating of John's Gospel advocated by Loisy had already been undermined by discoveries in another field. The papyrus fragment $\mathbf{p}^{52}$, which is independently dated by paleographers to the first half of the second century, contains a few sentences of John's Gospel (see Metzger 1978, pp. 38–9). Since there is a strong tradition that the fourth Gospel was written in Ephesus, and since this is undoubtedly a copy at several removes from the autograph, the discovery of this fragment in a provincial town on the banks of the Nile provides a serious argument for a first-century date of the Gospel of John.

Scholars of Roman history have also dismissed the late dating of the New Testament. Small details that were questioned by members of the Tübingen school, such as the use of *kyrios* as a designation for the emperor in Acts 25:26, have turned out instead to provide evidence for the accuracy of Acts, since numerous papyri subsequently discovered show that this term had been used in Egypt and the East for the reigning emperor since Ptolemaic times, though it became widespread under Nero and later. Adolf Deissmann sums up the matter incisively:

> The insignificant detail, questioned by various commentators, who, seated at their writing-tables in Tübingen or Berlin, vainly imagined that they knew the period better than St. Luke, now appears thoroughly credible. (Deissmann 1965, p. 354)

Such examples are not isolated. The critical assault on the book of Acts, in particular, has produced a sufficiently embarrassing track record that form criticism of it can no longer be taken seriously (see Hengel 1983 and especially Hemer 1989). "For Acts," as Roman historian A. N. Sherwin-White writes,

> the confirmation of historicity is overwhelming. . . . [A]ny attempt to reject its basic historicity even in matters of detail must now appear absurd. Roman historians have long taken it for granted. (Sherwin-White 1963, p. 189)

The confirmation of the historicity of Acts in turn reflects favorably on the authenticity of the Gospel of Luke, which is widely acknowledged to have been written earlier than Acts and by the same author.

The results of literary analysis and source criticism are hardly more compelling when applied to the synoptic Gospels as a whole. Consider the attempt to sort out, by literary means, the interrelations of the synoptic Gospels. A favorite theory of the past century is that Matthew and Luke, where they contain material not found in Mark, owe this material to a source called "Q." There is no doubt that at least two of the synoptic Gospels had sources; Luke explicitly says that he obtained material from earlier sources (Luke 1:2–3), and tradition identifies the source of Mark's Gospel as Peter. But insofar as it is conceived as a document, Q is entirely hypothetical. Notwithstanding the zeal with which some advocates have approached the matter – the world of biblical scholarship is now graced by commentaries on Q, literary analyses of Q, excavations of the literary strata of Q – there is not one scrap of textual evidence for any such document, not a whisper of it in any writing of the early church fathers. Yet Q is one of the pillars of the dominant two-source hypothesis for the development of the synoptics, and speculations regarding its strata provide the votaries of Q with an almost limitless source of new ideas. For example, in both the Gospel of Mark and the passages of Matthew and Luke attributed to Q, Jesus repeatedly refers to himself as the Son of Man. The New Testament scholar John Dominic Crossan is convinced, however, that the idea of the suffering and risen Son of Man is a Markan invention (Crossan 1991, p. 259). How, then, to account for its presence in Q? Crossan has a ready answer: the term did not appear in the original version of Q but was inserted by a later editor (Crossan 1991, pp. 244–9). "How," asks a trenchant critic of Crossan, "does one differentiate the older from the later versions of Q? By the fact that these features are absent from the earlier stage – a triumph of circular reasoning!" (Kee 1995, p. 22).

Alternative theories of the interrelationships of the synoptics and Q proliferate alarmingly: the two-source hypothesis (priority and independence of Mark + Q, then Matthew and Luke dependent on both but independent of each other), the Griesbach hypothesis (priority of Matthew, next Luke, then Mark), the Farrer hypothesis (priority of Mark, next Matthew, then Luke), the Augustinian hypothesis (priority of Matthew, next Mark, then

Luke), and even Lukan priority positions like the Jerusalem School hypothesis of Lindsey and Bivin. To make matters worse, most of these theories have several variants or near relations, like Riley's proto-Matthew variant on Griesbach and Koester's proto- and deutero-Mark variant on the two-source hypothesis.

Faced with such a Babel of conflicting voices, what should the interested layman do? Some would doubtless proclaim the whole thing inscrutable. But when we widen the view and see what light can be shed on this matter from outside the field of literary criticism, we encounter a striking and incontestable fact. Virtually every piece of external evidence we have from the first few centuries regarding the authorship and composition of the Gospels concurs that Matthew's Gospel was the first written, that it was written in the Hebrew language and later translated, and that Mark wrote what he heard from Peter but without regard to the order of events, making sure only that he did not leave anything out. In Papias's account (ca. 125) of the testimony of John (d. ca. 100), in Irenaeus's account (*Adversus Haereses* 3.1.1, ca. 185) which offers even more chronological detail, in the account of Clement of Alexandria (ca. 190) in his *Hypotyposeis* (this part preserved in Eusebius, though Clement's work itself is now lost), in the account of the tradition given by Clement's immediate successor Origen (with details not found in what Eusebius preserves of Clement), and even in the subscriptions to Arabic and Syriac manuscripts of Matthew, we find consistent corroboration of this account. Here, for example, is the translation of an Arabic subscription to one of the codices:

> Here ends the Gospel of the Apostle Matthew. He wrote it in the land of Palestine, by inspiration of the Holy Spirit, in the Hebrew language, eight years after the bodily ascension of Jesus the Messiah into heaven, and in the first year of the Roman Emperor Claudius Caesar. (Michaelis 1801, p. 133)

The point here is not that every one of these claims must be true; the question of whether Matthew first wrote his Gospel in Aramaic, for example, is notoriously problematic. But the widespread agreement of early sources on a number of points is remarkable and cannot be brushed aside, particularly since discrepancies among these sources regarding other points strongly suggest that they are not, for the most part, simply copying one another.

To those cynical of excavations of imaginary strata in an imaginary source document, the external evidence looks like a rock in a weary land. And indeed, if we go back to the door of that library at Harvard and listen closely, we can hear a few voices insisting that the breadth, consistency and unanimity of the external evidence ought to be taken seriously (notably Robinson 1976; Gundry 1982; Wenham 1992). Yet they are in a minority. This fact is partly due to a fashionable fixation on literary analysis and a downplaying, out of disciplinary insularity, of patristic claims. But there is a second and significant factor at work here. For if we take the account indicated by the external evidence at face value, we shall be essentially forced to concede two points: (1) the first two Gospels were written very early, well before AD 70, and (2) they came, either directly (Matthew) or at one remove (Mark, reporting what Peter had said) from independent eyewitnesses who had been Christ's own disciples. That would make it hard for people who want to argue that Mark is high-level mythmaking, the culmination of multiple recensions of Q. And it does not provide a sufficiently wide window of time for the stories of Jesus' miracles and the resurrection to develop and flower as a myth, not enough removal in time and space from eyewitnesses of the ministry of Jesus who could have contradicted such accounts. It would, moreover, leave those embarrassing predictions by Jesus of the destruction of Jerusalem in place, opening the door to the possibility of real prophecy. At this point, philosophical presuppositions are exerting a palpable pressure on synoptic studies.

The distorting effects of that pressure are often clear to those who look at the field from without. "A classical scholar," E. M. Blaiklock writes,

> finds it difficult to be patient with some of the exotic theories of literary criticism which have bedevilled New Testament studies. Classical historians have been a little ironical in recent decades over the calculated scepticism of New Testament scholars who refuse to see what the classicists so naturally see – a record of life in the first century, if no more than that, which must at least be accorded its unique value as historical material.... [W]hen critical theory seeks to persuade that liturgical and spiritual needs and aspirations, taking shape from nowhere, and within the lifetime of those who had known the first half of the first century, themselves created a supporting literature, the narratives and sayings which form the gospels, fantasy is propounded which would provoke ridicule in any less confined and introverted sphere of literary criticism. (Blaiklock 1983, pp. 34–5)

In a revealing autobiographical narrative, classics scholar John Rist describes his own growing realization of the extent to which form criticism had distorted the picture of the New Testament. In the wake of Vatican II, he writes, there seemed "no sense of the limitations of such methods, no grasp of how to distinguish between their use and their abuse."

> Examination of the early evidence and of the Gospels themselves convinced me that Matthew's Gospel could not depend on Mark's and was more or less equally early (certainly before A.D. 70)....
>
> Thus the full range of Christian claims must go back to the very earliest followers of Jesus, and in all probability to Jesus himself.... I could no longer delude myself that "real" scholarship told us that we have no evidence that Jesus himself, as well as the earliest generation of his followers, made claims for his divinity. The attempt of the biblical critics to show that such claims grew up (or were fabricated) within the Church seemed to be a tissue of bad argument, unhistorical treatment of the sources and wishful thinking: the wish being to make Christianity acceptable to the conventional "liberal" orthodoxy, with its characteristic bad faith, of the nineteenth and twentieth centuries. The resulting "scholarship" was defective to a degree that would not be acceptable in other philological disciplines. (Rist 1993, p. 100)

Indeed it would not. Outside the field of New Testament studies, form criticism has been tried and found wanting. Classics scholars quickly tired of the game, as H. J. Rose points out:

> ... [T]he chief weapon of the separatists has always been literary criticism, and of this it is not too much to say that such niggling word-baiting, such microscopic hunting of minute inconsistencies and flaws in logic, has hardly been seen, outside of the Homeric field, since Rymar and John Dennis died. (Rose 1950, pp. 42–3)

Examples of this sort in various other fields are not difficult to find.[10]

---

10. See, in particular, the tragicomic venture of the methods of biblical criticism into the legal field in the story of Florence Deeks's plagiarism lawsuit against H. G. Wells, summarized in Wenham (1992, pp. 253–5).

One of the most interesting developments in recent scholarship is the realization that the Gospels, notwithstanding their distinctive emphases, accord closely with the ideals of Greco-Roman history as exhibited in the work of Thucydides, Xenophon, Polybius, Josephus, and Tacitus, particularly in their preference for the testimony of involved eyewitnesses over written records.[11] Richard Bauckham argues that we find the literary device of *inclusio* – a standard means of identifying a principal eyewitness source by bracketing the narrative with references to the individual – in three of the Gospels, and he gives illustrations of similar use of the *inclusio* by Lucian and Porphyry (Bauckham 2006, pp. 124–47). "Thus," writes Bauckham,

> contrary to first impressions, with which most Gospels scholars have been content, the Gospels do have their own literary ways of indicating their eyewitness sources. If it be asked why these are not more obvious and explicit in our eyes, we should note that most ancient readers or hearers of these works, unlike scholars of the twentieth and twenty-first centuries, would have expected them to have eyewitness sources, and that those readers or hearers to whom the identity of the eyewitnesses was important would have been alert to the indications the Gospels actually provide. (Bauckham 2006, p. 147)

Finally, the most scandalous miracle story of all, the story of the death, burial, resurrection, and appearances of Jesus, is attested earlier than even the most conservative date for any of the Gospels in the early creed embedded in 1 Corinthians 15:3–7.[12] Virtually all contemporary New Testament scholars acknowledge that these verses contain a pre-Pauline formula that originated with the primitive church. But with this acknowledgment comes the dilemma of accounting for the origins of Christianity. If the earliest Christians, some of whom were eyewitnesses of the life and ministry of Christ, were firmly persuaded that he had indeed risen from the dead and appeared to known and named disciples who were active in the church, then the mythic option is ruled out. The Gospels give us fuller and more detailed accounts of the events following Jesus' death. But most of the core facts (at least) were already in wide circulation within a few years of those events.

A great deal more might be said here. We expect that some readers will find our brief sketch more compelling than others, but it would take a different sort of work to fill the argument out more completely. Those who are unpersuaded may note the extent to which their reservations affect the subsequent argument, but even for them it should be of interest to see what can be said for the historical argument from miracles under the assumptions that Hume and the deists shared with the defenders of orthodoxy when they clashed in the great theological battle of the eighteenth century.

Background Facts: Death and Burial

Before we proceed to the consideration of the salient facts, we need to mention briefly two pieces of information that we shall take for the purpose of this argument as unproblematic

11. The position is outlined by Samuel Byrskog (2002) and defended in considerable detail in Richard Bauckham (2006). See also Allison Trites (2004, pp. 128ff.).

12. For a survey of the state of the argument regarding this passage, see Craig (2002, pp. 3–37).

background facts. The first is that Jesus did indeed die, more or less as the existing narratives explain; the second is that he was buried in a tomb.

It is now almost universally acknowledged by New Testament scholars that Jesus died on the cross. The swoon theory, which attracted Schleiermacher, is intrinsically highly improbable. The only recorded instance we are aware of where someone survived a Roman crucifixion was the case recorded in Josephus (*Life of Flavius Josephus*, 75). On an errand for Titus Caesar, Josephus sees some of his old acquaintances being crucified; he tells Titus, who orders that they be taken down and have the greatest care taken of them. Two die under the physician's care; one recovers. One skeptic has tried to argue from this passage that there is a 33 percent probability that any given crucifixion victim, "after a mere beating," would survive more than a day, though in order to carry this optimism over to Jesus he must dismiss John's account of the spear wound as inauthentic (Carrier 2006, chap. 3).[13] Needless to say, the relevant reference class is the set of victims of Roman crucifixion who were *not* taken down and given the best available medical treatment. The number of known survivors in this class is precisely zero.

Besides its antecedent improbability, the swoon theory is wholly inadequate to explain the Easter faith of the disciples, which we shall discuss later. The remarks of Strauss – himself no friend to the traditional belief in the resurrection – are sufficiently trenchant to be worth quoting:

> It is impossible that a being who had stolen half-dead out of the sepulchre, who crept about weak and ill, wanting medical treatment, who required bandaging, strengthening, and indulgence, and who still at last yielded to his sufferings, could have given to the disciples the impression that he was a Conqueror over death and the grave, the Prince of Life, an impression which lay at the bottom of their future ministry. Such a resuscitation could only have weakened the impression he had made upon them in life and in death, at the most could only have given it an elegiac voice, but could by no possibility have changed their sorrow into enthusiasm, have elevated their reverence into worship. (Strauss 1879, p. 412)

Recently, John Dominic Crossan has maintained the radical position that Jesus was not buried in a tomb at all but was rather buried in a common grave or thrown in a pit along with some lime to speed decomposition of the body (Crossan 1994, pp. 152–8; 1998, pp. xxvii, 550–9). He offers no specific evidence in favor of this hypothesis; it is, he admits, a mere extrapolation from a guess as to what was most common.

> I keep thinking of all those other thousands of Jews crucified around Jerusalem in that terrible first century from among whom we have found only one skeleton and one nail. I think I know what happened to their bodies, and I have no reason to think Jesus' body did not join them. (Crossan 1996, p. 188)[14]

In order to maintain this position, Crossan must dismiss the burial narrative in Mark 15:42–7 as a fabrication; accordingly he does, stressing the incongruity in the description

---

13. Compare the assessments of Strauss (1879, pp. 410–1), Paul Maier (1997, pp. 194–6), and Martin Hengel (1977).
14. For further discussion of Crossan's creative approach to history, see Craig (1997, pp. 249–71).

of Joseph of Arimathea (a follower of Jesus versus a member of the Sanhedrin, who all condemned Jesus) and the absence of a motive for his burying just Jesus rather than all three of the crucifixion victims. Crossan argues that the motive cannot have been either piety or duty, for then he would have buried the thieves as well; he concludes that "Mark created that burial by Joseph of Arimathea in 15:42–47. It contains no pre-Markan tradition" (Crossan 1998, p. 555). For good measure, Crossan adds that Mark created the story of the women's discovery of the empty tomb.

In company with the majority of New Testament scholars, we find this argument wholly unpersuasive. The very tension Crossan sees in the description of Joseph of Arimathea would count as evidence against his being an invented character. Why, if Mark were embellishing the narrative, would he invent someone who appears nowhere else in his Gospel and give him such a pivotal role? If he did, why would he present a description of that character that generated questions? But in any event, it is not terribly hard to find plausible answers to Crossan's questions. Anyone who has ever been a member of a committee understands that sometimes decisions are made by the committee as a body in the absence of some of its members, and those decisions are recorded as unanimous. As for Joseph's motives for burying Jesus, Crossan employs too narrow a set of alternatives when he considers only piety and duty. There is also the reason implicitly given in the text itself: a disciple's love, which would not extend to the thieves. And we do not know in any event whether, had he been so inclined, he would have had either time or the opportunity to bury the others. This is a profoundly inadequate set of reasons to abandon an inconvenient section of a primary source – or, in this case, four primary sources.

It is also insufficient to get rid of the burial, which is a component not only of Mark 15 but also of the early creed embedded in 1 Corinthians 15. Here again, Crossan's approach is to ignore the obvious idea that this creed gives us information about the events at the heart of the birth of Christianity and to talk instead in terms of literary categories: narrative patterns, stories (but not as history), mythical hymns, parallelisms (Crossan 1998, pp. 546–50). Confronted with the undeniable fact that the first Christians grounded their faith on the resurrection, Crossan simply reinterprets the primal proclamation as an existential metaphor: "This *is* the resurrection, the continuing presence in a continuing community of the past Jesus in a radically new and transcendental mode of present and future existence" (Crossan 1991, p. 404). At no point does he engage directly with the possibility that this creed is a summary of an actual series of events. One gets the impression that this possibility simply does not occur to him.

These instances are characteristic of Crossan's entire approach, which involves picking and choosing passages to take seriously or to reject, relying almost exclusively on conjectures regarding literary forms and purposes. Such a methodology calls to mind Martin Hengel's blistering indictment of the pattern of so-called critical scholarship:

> We know too little to be able to reject in advance what sources say, in a hypercritical attitude which is at the same time hostile to history, without examining them carefully. Today, after more than 200 years of historical-critical work on the New Testament, such an attitude must be termed uncritical and unhistorical. The real danger in the interpretation of Acts (and the Gospels) is no longer an uncritical apologetic but the hypercritical ignorance and arrogance which – often combined with unbridled fantasy – has lost any understanding of living historical reality. (Hengel & Schwemer 1997, pp. 6–7)

The Salient Facts: W, D, and P

The first set of facts that constitutes evidence for the resurrection is the testimony of putative eyewitnesses to the empty tomb and of these same witnesses (the women who claimed to have found the tomb empty) to postresurrection appearances of Jesus. We shall consider the testimony of the (male) disciples to postresurrection appearances separately.

That some women testified that they found Jesus' tomb empty on the Sunday following his crucifixion is difficult to deny as a historical matter. A succinct account of the women's discovery of the empty tomb and of their vision of angels is found in Mark, the shortest and, some scholars believe, the earliest of the Gospels (Mark 16:1–8). Similar accounts are repeated in all the other Gospels. Mark names the women coming to the tomb and finding it empty as Mary Magdalene, Mary the mother of James, and Salome. Luke names Mary Magdalene, Mary the mother of James, and Joanna and says that there were "other women with them" (Luke 24:1–11). Matthew names Mary Magdalene and "the other Mary" (Matt. 28:1–7) while John mentions only Mary Magdalene (John 20:1–18).

In a survey of recent New Testament scholarship, Gary Habermas has documented the interesting fact that a notable majority (approximately 75 percent) of scholars writing on the subject during the 30 years from 1975 to 2005 agree that Jesus' tomb was in fact found empty (Habermas 2006a, p. 292). This includes scholars who are skeptical of Christianity itself. We shall argue that the testimony of the women to the empty tomb is evidence for R, and so we are obviously taking it that their testimony is evidence that the tomb was indeed empty. But here we are concerned only to note that this large scholarly acceptance of the empty tomb almost certainly represents a scholarly acceptance of the more modest claim that some female witnesses *said* that they found the tomb empty. The only other recorded witnesses to the empty tomb are Peter and John.[15] Two Gospels mention Peter's going to the tomb, and one mentions John (Luke 24:12; John 20:3–10). Moreover, in those accounts Peter and John go to the tomb only after and because they have heard from the women a report of the empty tomb. An important part of the evidence that the tomb was in fact empty comes from the report of the women.

That some women claimed to have seen Jesus risen is a slightly more controversial matter, but it is supported by the existing evidence. Mary Magdalene's meeting with Jesus is not mentioned in Mark except in the long ending which is probably spurious, but the account of Mary Magdalene and Jesus is found in John 20:1–8 in some detail, and it ends with her going to the disciples and telling them what has happened. In Matthew 28:9–10 a brief account is given of Jesus' meeting the women who had been to the tomb in a group.

Though some scholars have challenged these accounts as later additions, there are serious reasons to take them to be authentic reports of what the women said. First, the *prima facie* tensions in the narratives of the discovery of the tomb and the first appearances of Christ tell strongly against collusion, copying, and embellishment. One evangelist gives an account of one angel at the tomb, another of two; one has the women setting out "early, while it was yet dark," another sets the scene "when the sun was risen." The lists of the women who are named in the various Gospels overlap only partially. Some puzzling details

---

15. We accept the traditional identification of John the son of Zebedee as "the apostle Jesus loved" and the author of the fourth Gospel, largely for the sorts of reasons outlined by Craig Blomberg (2001, pp. 22–41).

are never worked out for the reader. If Mary Magdalene ran back to tell Peter and John, how did they fail to meet the other women as they returned? What did Jesus mean when he said "Touch me not" to Mary Magdalene? These are the sorts of loose ends and incongruities one would expect from independent eyewitness accounts of the same event, where substantial unity – agreement on the main facts – is accompanied by circumstantial variety.

Second, there is the remarkable fact that in the accounts in Matthew and John where the women are shown as seeing the risen Christ, they are the first witnesses. It is not controversial that in first-century Jewish society women were widely considered to be unreliable as witnesses to serious matters (see Wright 2003, pp. 607–8). A few quotations illustrate this point:

> But let not the testimony of women be admitted, on account of the levity and boldness of their sex; . . . (Josephus, *Antiquities*, 4.8.15).

> Any evidence which a woman [gives] is not valid (to offer) . . . (Talmud, *Rosh Hashana* 1.8c).

The point should not be overstated, for there are disagreements reported in the Talmud regarding the degree of credibility to be granted to the testimony of women.

> Wherever the Torah accepts the testimony of one witness, it follows the majority of persons, so that two women against one man is identical with two men against one man. But there are some who declare that wherever a competent witness came first, even a hundred women are regarded as equal to one witness . . . but when it is a woman who came first, then two women against one man is like half-and-half (Talmud, b. *Mas. Sotah* 31b).

Nevertheless, it would plainly be better from the standpoint of enhancing the credibility of a contrived story to put a group of respectable males at the tomb and as the first to see the risen Christ than a group of women.

The last important fact concerning the women's reports is that they were not believed. Luke says of the women's report of the empty tomb to the disciples, "And these words appeared to them as nonsense, and they would not believe them" (Luke 24:11). Peter and John did consider it worth going to the tomb to see for themselves, but Luke's account makes it clear that they thought the women unreliable. They continued to be unhappy and (as we shall note later) afraid even after hearing the women's reports. Obviously the story of the angels who said that Jesus was risen made little impression on them, and this not only because of its antecedent improbability. And this attitude to female testimony is scarcely surprising in light of the legal situation we have just described. It is highly plausible that the disciples would have thought the women's story of an empty tomb and angels nonsense, or as the King James Version has it, "idle tales."

Perhaps the most important of the salient facts that, we shall argue, constitutes evidence for the resurrection of Jesus of Nazareth is the testimony, and the circumstances surrounding that testimony, of a number of specific people whose names are known. The later history of the women is largely unknown, but now we turn to the accounts given by specific witnesses who later maintained their witness in the face of clear threat and danger of death, and in some cases to the point of death itself.

As in the case of the testimony of the women, the facts of the testimony and transformation of the disciples are not as controversial as one might expect, even among skeptical scholars. Though we are assuming the authenticity and general historical reliability of the Gospel texts and of Acts, the secularly describable facts we are emphasizing are not considered highly dubious among biblical scholars generally. On the contrary, even those unlikely to agree that the Gospels (for example) are authentic and generally reliable tend to agree that the disciples testified as they are traditionally taken to have done. In fact, Habermas has documented that a large majority of scholars, including scholars who are not in general theologically conservative, grant that the disciples believed that Jesus had risen from the dead and came to believe this soon after his execution (Habermas 2005, pp. 151–2, footnote 92; 2006a, p. 289; 2006b, pp. 79–82).

Eleven disciples – the original twelve minus Judas – said that they had seen Jesus after his resurrection. The names of these eleven are given in Acts 1:13 as Peter, John, James, Andrew, Philip, Thomas, Bartholomew, Matthew, James the son of Alphaeus, Simon the Zealot, and Judas the son of James.

To begin with, it appears that these eleven disciples' experiences – characterized by them as seeing and speaking with Jesus risen – occurred in an atmosphere not of expectation or emotional excitement but rather of fear and depression. The fear that the same thing that had happened to Jesus would happen to them is evident even before Jesus' death, in Peter's embarrassing but believable denial during Jesus' trial before the high priest (Mark 14:66–72); and their concern for their own safety continued, according to the account in John, even after Mary Magdalene told them that she had seen Jesus: ". . . [T]he doors were shut where the disciples were, for fear of the Jews" (John 20:19).[16]

But the attitude of some of the disciples, most notably Thomas, was not only one of fear but also of open skepticism about the accounts of others. John's account gives the fullest story of Thomas's doubt, including the justly famous demand, "Unless I shall see in His hands the imprint of the nails, and put my finger into the place of the nails, and put my hand into His side, I will not believe" (John 20:25). Matthew's account attributes doubt to some followers of Jesus even upon first seeing him (Matt. 28:17). All accounts agree in portraying the initial attitude of the disciples as anything but expectant of visions or receptive to the idea that Jesus was alive.

The accounts of the eleven's encounters with Jesus are striking in a number of respects, and while in the context of this argument we are not entitled, on pain of circularity, to assume that these accounts are true, we need to get clear in our minds what sort of claim is being made. When we consider the fact that at least thirteen men were willing to die for the claim that Jesus of Nazareth had risen again, it is important to consider what sort of account they gave of what had happened in order to know what it was that they were willing to die for. First, the accounts of Jesus' appearances to the disciples are neither vague nor "spiritualized" but rather circumstantial, empirical, and detailed. Not only do they purport to give a number of his statements, they also state expressly that he deliberately displayed empirical evidence that he was not a spirit but rather a physical being. It was therefore a physical resurrection claim that the disciples made: "See my hands and my feet, that it is I myself; touch me, and see; for a spirit does not have flesh and bones, as you see that I have." And when they still do not believe, he asks what food is available and eats a piece of fish

---

16. Wright (2003, chap. 4, especially pp. 200–6) also argues at some length that Jewish thought at the time would not have led the disciples to predict Jesus' resurrection from their belief that he was a great prophet or even that he was the Messiah. Bodily resurrection at the end of the world in the general resurrection was indeed a feature of Jewish thought, but it was not expected for individuals before that time.

and a honeycomb. Later he cooks fish for them and invites them to breakfast (Luke 24:39–43; cf. John 20:27; John 21:9–13).

That the disciples were attesting to a physical resurrection is further supported by Peter's allusion in his Pentecost sermon to the decay of David's body in contrast with Christ's body, which did not decay:

> Brethren, I may confidently say to you regarding the patriarch David that he both died and was buried, and his tomb is with us to this day. And so, because he was a prophet, . . . he looked ahead and spoke of the resurrection of the Christ, that he was neither abandoned to Hades, nor did His flesh suffer decay. This Jesus God raised up again, to which we are all witnesses. (Acts 2:29–32)

Second, the personality attributed to a postresurrection Jesus is not inspiring, kindly, and helpful. On the contrary, he is portrayed as being very much the sort of person he always was, and no more comfortable a companion than ever: Patient but sometimes caustic, commanding and compelling but unnerving and unpredictable, a superb teacher but one not inclined to answer questions he considers impertinent or unnecessary. He responds with an almost word-for-word allusion to Thomas's own demand: "Reach here your finger, and see my hands; and reach here your hand, and put it into my side, and be not unbelieving, but believing" (John 20:27). There is perhaps a touch of amusement in the tone, but the invitation is serious, too. He gives the disciples every opportunity to examine his bona fides but chides them for not believing the testimony of others. He says and does strange things that they are highly unlikely to have understood, such as breathing on them and telling them they now have power to remit sins. He shows himself, talks with them, then goes away again, only to show up again later with what must have been highly frustrating unpredictability (see, e.g., John 21:1–14). He brusquely dismisses their understandable queries about his Messianic plans now that he is risen (Acts 1:7). So far from soothing their fears and generally dispensing religious uplift, he gives Peter a hard time in the course of verifying his love and faithfulness and then very nearly tells him that he will suffer martyrdom (John 21:15–9). Not only do these accounts indicate that the disciples claimed extensive and direct personal interaction with the risen Jesus, they also manifest a level of realism and vividness of personality that is not consistent with their merely being inspired with a rush of enthusiasm or feeling that they had received vague spiritual "communications" from their master.

Whatever happened to the eleven during the 40-odd days following Jesus' crucifixion, we find a notable difference in their behavior thereafter and an even more striking difference at Pentecost (see Westcott 1906, pp. 102–3). Pursuant, so they apparently said, to the risen Jesus' commands, they waited and spent their time praying in Jerusalem from about 40 days after Passover until Pentecost. During that time we also find them electing an apostolic replacement for Judas, namely Matthias (Acts 1:15–26).[17]

In passing we should note that the election of Matthias supports Paul's contention (1 Corinthians 15:1–8) that Jesus after his resurrection appeared to a larger number of people than the eleven. The account in Acts shows that despite some fairly specific requirements, Peter has his pick among candidates for Judas's replacement:

---

17. We shall assume in what follows that when the writer of Acts thereafter refers to "the apostles" as a group he is including Matthias.

It is therefore necessary that of the men who have accompanied us all the time that the Lord Jesus went in and out among us – beginning with the baptism of John, until the day that He was taken up from us – one of these should become a witness with us of His resurrection. (Acts 1:21–2)

The disciples appoint Matthias and Joseph called Justus to be the finalists, and they draw lots for Judas's vacant position. Not only does this account give us the name of another putative witness (Joseph), it also can plausibly be taken to imply that there were more to choose from originally who met the requirements (cf. Trites 2004, p. 137).

Beginning on the day of Pentecost, the (now twelve) apostles engaged in behavior that virtually invited martyrdom, persisting in asserting that Jesus was risen in the face of known danger and explicit and escalating threats. The facts we now recount strongly support the contention that they knew in multiple ways that it was very likely that they would die for their testimony and that they were willing, if necessary, to do so.

First, the commotion they created on the day of Pentecost (Acts 2) was likely to draw them to the attention of the very religious leaders who had connived at and succeeded in bringing about Jesus' death. It had been less than two months since Jesus' crucifixion, and the apostles appeared before a large group of people, deliberately drawing attention to themselves, speaking in multiple languages to the crowds of people gathered in Jerusalem for Pentecost, saying some highly uncomplimentary things about the leaders who plotted Jesus' death, and asserting that he had risen again. Acts states that about 3,000 people joined the new movement on that very day, which makes for an eyebrow-raising conjecture as to how many people heard Peter's provocative sermon.

And while they were apparently popular for a while (Acts 2:47), before long they did get in exactly the sort of trouble anyone would have anticipated. After Peter and John were believed to have healed a lame man, and after more public sermons in the temple, they were roughly invited by the temple police to appear before the Jewish rulers – the high priest, the elders and scribes (Acts 4). There they reiterated their assertion that God raised Jesus from the dead. The leaders, used to being the learned elite among the people, were surprised at their boldness (v. 13), recognized them with displeasure as disciples of Jesus, and wanted very much to shut them up. As had happened before in the case of Jesus, they hesitated to do anything drastic immediately because of their popularity with the people. But they threatened them and told them, on pain of nonspecified but easily guessed penalties, not to "speak or teach at all in the name of Jesus." Peter and John's reply deserves to be highlighted: "Whether it is right in the sight of God to give heed to you rather than to God, you be the judge. For we cannot stop speaking what we have seen and heard" (Acts 4:18–20). The emphasis on testimony to events directly and empirically witnessed is unmistakable, as is the defiance of threats.

It might be argued that the failure of the leaders immediately to try to have Peter and John executed, and indeed their releasing them for fear of the people, would be taken by the apostles to mean that they could get away with preaching that Jesus was risen, that in fact they did not have to fear death. But exactly the opposite is the case. First, the events of the life of Jesus would have made it clear to them that such "fearing the people" would go only so far. Eventually Jesus' enemies had him arrested by night and, despite his popularity – even greater than the apostles' so far – and his putative miracles – far more numerous than theirs – got the people themselves to demand his death of Pontius Pilate. This was all fresh in the apostles' memories. Second, when Peter and John told the rest of their group what had happened, they immediately prayed at length in terms that showed that they took the threats very seriously indeed (Acts 4:23–30).

The encounters with the Jewish leadership did not stop at one warning. The apostles (it would appear, the whole group of them) were thrown into prison again shortly thereafter for their defiance by the order of an angered high priest (Acts 5:17–8). Released, ostensibly by supernatural aid, they return immediately to preaching in the temple. Arrested again, though with relative gentleness ("without violence") by the temple police, brought up before the leaders again, and ordered not to keep preaching as they have been, Peter and the other apostles answer, "We must obey God rather than men" (Acts 5:19) and proceed to reiterate their blame on the leaders for the death of Jesus and their assertion of his resurrection. At this point, the priests "were intending to slay them" (Acts 5:33). Dissuaded for the time being by Gamaliel, they instead beat the apostles and order them *again* to stop preaching, which of course they do not do.

At this point, again, we need to respond to the argument that the apostles may have believed that they would not die because they had been threatened and released several times and that their continued preaching therefore does not indicate a willingness to die for their testimony. Technically, the Jewish people were not permitted by the Romans to exact the death penalty. This was the reason for their bringing Jesus before Pilate and threatening a riot to get Pilate to crucify him. But every indication is that this rule was difficult for the Romans to enforce. More than once, for example, Jesus was very nearly killed by a mob (Luke 4:29; John 10:31). Moreover, the Jewish leaders did apparently have the power of force and a temple police to arrest, the authority to exact the punishment of beatings, and the power to imprison, which hardly would have inspired confidence in the Romans' ability to prevent their taking matters farther. The leaders obviously thought that they might well be able to kill the apostles, for they began conspiring to do so, and Gamaliel's dissuasion does not touch on their not having authority from the Romans to kill. It is fairly evident, then, even from the facts given thus far, that death by stoning, instigated by the Jewish leaders, was very much a live possibility and was met with utter defiance by the apostles.

And events proved that this possibility was not merely theoretical. Stephen was stoned after being denounced for blasphemy by witnesses before a religious tribunal and, in response to the charges, preaching a particularly fiery sermon along much the same lines as the preaching of the apostles (Acts 7). The stoning of Stephen appears to have occurred fairly soon after Gamaliel had tried to calm the Jewish leaders and stop the persecution of the apostles (Acts 5:34–9). Dating from the life of Paul, who was present and opposed to Christianity at the time of Stephen's death, places the event very likely within a year (three years at the most) of Jesus' crucifixion.

Moreover, there is no evidence that the Romans punished this particular abuse of power on the part of the Jewish leadership. Like all bureaucracies, the Roman government was not always consistent nor inclined to enforce all rules at all times. About a generation later the higher authorities did depose a high priest after the killing of James Jesus' brother by a Jewish mob, but on the occasion of Stephen's stoning they appear to have washed their hands of the matter. So far were the Christians from receiving protection from Rome that a widespread anti-Christian persecution, led by Saul of Tarsus, broke out just after the murder of Stephen, and Christians were hauled off to prison or brought before the religious authorities in large numbers (Acts 8).

The epicenter of this persecution was Jerusalem, and the Christians scattered from there carrying their new teachings with them – with the exception of the apostles, who remained at Jerusalem (Acts 8:1). Luke does not say exactly why. Perhaps they thought their refusal to flee the persecution was important for the strengthening of the new church. Whatever their reason, their willingness to suffer death is here especially clear.

Several of those who claimed to be eyewitnesses of the resurrected Christ undoubtedly did suffer death for their testimony. We shall discuss the three best attested of these martyrdoms later. Other martyrdom accounts come from traditions whose historical reliability is difficult to assess and from documents that include obvious oddities and embellishments. And by all accounts John the apostle was not martyred but died at an old age of natural causes. This is why we are focusing here on the *willingness* of multiple witnesses to suffer death, a fact of great evidential importance in itself. Nor is this simply to say that they changed their manner of life and that they suffered hardships for their beliefs. At this early date the majority of their hardships – the missionary work some of them undertook in distant lands, for example – remained ahead of them. The point rather is simply and starkly that they knew from the beginning that they were likely to die and did not change their story in the face of this probable outcome. For whether they were eventually killed or not, they had their moment of truth at Jerusalem very early on. One account of the death of Andrew's martyrdom as an old man reports that, threatened with crucifixion, he replied, "Had I feared the death of the cross, I should not have preached the majesty and gloriousness of the cross of Christ." Whether this quotation is authentic or not, it brings out the salient fact that Andrew, like the other witnesses, had long before his actual martyrdom faced and persevered in the face of the prospect of a gruesome death.

Two more events point to the same conclusion. Around the year AD 41, Herod Agrippa arrested and executed James bar Zebedee, an apostle and a major leader in the church. About the same time he arrested Peter (who was then supposedly released by miraculous intervention), presenting Peter with yet another clear warning of the probable outcome of his course of action (see Wenham 1992, pp. 146–7).

For those Christians who escaped these early Jewish persecutions, a different threat arose some years later. Nero may not have originally been opposed to Christianity. The Romans were inclined at first to regard Christianity as a Jewish sect and the Jews' anger and rioting about it as evidence of an internecine religious squabble (see, e.g., Acts 18:14–5). Paul, after his conversion, was indeed protected by the Romans from the Jews, though this may have been in no small measure because he was a Roman citizen and also because he had used his right as a citizen to appeal to Caesar (Acts 23). It is even possible that Nero is responsible for releasing Paul from his first Roman imprisonment, though this idea remains conjectural (Maier 1997, pp. 329–30). But in 64, all of that changed. In a well-known series of events, Nero chose to distract attention from rumors that he was responsible for the burning of Rome by instituting a fierce persecution of the Christians. After this point, any apostles who remained within the sphere of Roman government, including especially Peter and John, had to consider very seriously the possibility that they would be executed by the Romans.

It appears that what Nero instituted at this time was a local persecution. Nonetheless, anyone who was not a Roman citizen was liable thereafter to arrest and execution by the Romans on the charge of being a Christian. A formal law against Christianity was not required for this outcome, as magistrates had a great deal of latitude in their treatment of noncitizens. By this time, Christianity was regarded with suspicion by the Roman authorities – religious conservatives in their own way – as a "superstition," or, as we would now say, a cult. Now that it was known that it was not merely an offshoot of Judaism, it was considered a distraction from the traditional worship of the Roman gods and not covered by the exception made for Judaism. And for persistence in such a cult, one could indeed be sentenced to death, as many were. In the famous letter of Pliny the Younger to Trajan, ca. AD 113, Pliny says that he sentenced noncitizens to death merely for their stubbornness in continuing to assert that they were Christians in the face of his threats. They could, however, be pardoned if they renounced their Christianity, sacrificed to the Roman gods, and cursed Jesus. Trajan praises Pliny's procedure in his reply. While this exchange occurs later than both the Neronian persecution and the deaths of the apostles, such powers for magistrates were almost certainly available earlier; the procedure of pardon in return for apostasy may even have been previously used in the case of people who said that they were no longer Christians (Barnes 1968, pp. 36–7). We can say then with confidence that after AD 64 the remaining apostles had another source, the Roman government, from which they could expect death in some highly unpleasant form or another for their continued adherence to their story.

And some did die for their testimony, one way or another. One of the best attested of these is James bar Zebedee, whom we have already mentioned. His death was apparently the first martyrdom of an apostle. It is documented in Acts 12 and is not in any real historical doubt. The author of Acts gives few details, saying only that Herod "had James the brother of John put to death with a sword." Whether James expected specifically to be executed by Herod, who evidently did so in an attempt to please the Jewish leaders, it is hard to say, but the documentation already given shows that martyrdom at that point in history would not have come as a surprise to any of the apostles.

Chronologically, the next of the best-documented martyrdoms is that of the other James, not an apostle but one who evidently claimed to have seen the resurrected Jesus, James the Just, often listed as Jesus' brother. He is our thirteenth witness, and his conversion appears to have been individual and independent of the experiences of the twelve apostles. Evidence from the Gospels indicates that he was not a follower of Jesus during his lifetime and indeed deplored Jesus' embarrassing the family by going about preaching and healing (Mark 3:21, 31; cf. John 8:5). But by Acts 12:17 (ca. AD 41); and even more clearly in Acts 15 (the Jerusalem Council, probably ca. AD 49), James was an important leader in the new church. Paul provides an explanation in his listing of those who saw Jesus after his resurrection: "Then he appeared to James, then to all the apostles . . ." (1 Corinthians 15:5). This looks as though it is being listed as an individual appearance, and the accounts of Jesus' earliest appearances to those who were already his disciples seem to indicate that at least in several cases there were no "outsiders" present. James seems to have come forward as a convert to his brother's cause on the basis of an experience of his own.

An early account (ca. AD 93) of James's death is found in Josephus, who says that he was killed by stoning (*Antiquities* 20.9.1). Josephus agrees in large measure with the later church historian Hegisippus, who wrote in the mid-second century. Both date the event quite precisely by the death of Festus as governor of Judea, which puts it at AD 62. Both agree that it took place during a window of opportunity while the newly appointed governor, Albinus, had not yet arrived to take up control of the region. Hegisippus's account is more detailed and makes James's death not precisely one by stoning. According to Hegisippus, James retained enormous prestige among the non-Christian Jews, largely because of his ascetic practices and many hours in prayer. He was widely known as "the Just, " and his witness that Jesus was the Savior was resulting in the conversion of many of the Jewish rulers to Christianity. When the death of Festus left the province momentarily without a present Roman governor, the Jewish leaders decided to do something about it:

So they assembled and said to James: "We call on you to restrain the people, since they have gone astray after Jesus, believing him to be the Christ. We call on you to persuade all who come for the Passover concerning Jesus, since all of us trust you. We and the entire populace can vouch for the fact that you are righteous and take no one at face value. . . . So stand on the parapet of the temple, where you can be clearly seen . . ." So the scribes and Pharisees made James stand on the temple parapet, and they shouted to him, "O righteous one, whom we all ought to believe, since the people are going astray after Jesus who was crucified, tell us, what does 'the door of Jesus' mean?" He replied with a loud voice, "Why do you ask me about the Son of Man? He is sitting in heaven at the right hand of the Great Power, and he will come on the clouds of heaven." . . . Then the scribes and Pharisees said to each other, "We made a bad mistake in providing such testimony to Jesus, but let us go up and throw him down so that they will be afraid and not believe him." . . . So they went up and threw down the righteous one. Then they said to each other, "Let us stone James the Just," and they began to stone him, since the fall had not killed him. . . . Then one of them, a laundryman, took the club that he used to beat out clothes and hit the Just on the head. Such was his martyrdom . . . (quoted in Eusebius 2.23, Maier 1999, pp. 81–3)

The combination of flattery and threat here deserves special notice. It seems quite clear that, if this account is substantially correct, the Jewish leaders hoped to strike a blow against the entire Christian sect by getting so prestigious a leader to recant publicly. Placing him on a high point from which he could be thrown down was an obvious attempt at coercion, and James must have known what his fate would be if he did not give the desired answer. In Josephus's account, Ananus, the high priest, "delivered" James up to be stoned. The two accounts are compatible in outline, especially since a recantation from James would have been even more useful in squelching Christianity than his being stoned as an example. It may be that Ananus delivered him to his fellow Jewish leaders and that they made a last attempt to wring from him a public renunciation of Jesus in return for his life. While this theory would contradict what appears to be the implication in Hegisippus that the scribes and Pharisees were ad libbing the scene, Josephus is more likely to be correct about the involvement of Ananus the high priest. According to Josephus, Ananus was subsequently removed from his high priestly position for exceeding his authority by convening the Sanhedrin (which condemned James to death) without permission.

Peter's martyrdom, too, has reliable warrant, though its details – for example, the mode of execution – are not so well documented as those of the previous two witnesses. Clement of Rome, writing no later than ca. AD 96, refers to Peter's and Paul's "contending unto death" and making their "testimony" (μαρτυρήσας, sometimes translated "witness" or even "martyrdom") for the faith (I Clement chapters 5 and 6). He uses their examples in a discussion of heroes of the faith, rather like that in Hebrews 11, to encourage his hearers to be similarly patient and steadfast in the face of suffering and death. Further support for Peter's martyrdom comes from the mid-second-century writer Gaius, who says that the monuments or "trophies" of the apostles Peter and Paul are to be found at the Vatican and on the Ostian Way, respectively. These are the traditional sites of the martyrdoms of Peter and Paul, and Gaius's statement shows that monuments to their deaths were found in these locations from ancient times. Nero's gardens and hippodrome, where Christians were tortured and killed during the Neronian persecution, were indeed located in the Vatican Valley across the Tiber (Maier 1997, p. 335).

The last of the salient facts we shall touch on here is the conversion of Paul. Neither Paul's historicity nor the fact of his sudden conversion is in serious doubt by most historians, including those skeptical of Christianity itself (Habermas 2005, pp. 142–3, 151–2; 2006a, pp. 289–91). The details of Paul's conversion, combined with what he believed thereafter, provide evidence for Christianity and for the resurrection. Here, briefly, are the nonmiraculous facts to be explained: Saul of Tarsus, known later as a Christian as Paul, had studied under Gamaliel, who counseled that the apostles be left alone. Unlike his mentor, however, Saul was a fanatical persecutor of the new sect of Christianity. How long his persecution went on after the stoning of Stephen is not known exactly, though it was most probably less than a year. On a journey to Damascus to arrest followers of Jesus, Saul had some overwhelming experience that left him temporarily blind. He stayed for several days alone, fasting, in Damascus when he arrived there, after which he had a visitor named Ananias, a member of the very group he had been coming to persecute. Saul regained his sight, received baptism by which he identified himself with the followers of Jesus, and immediately began disputing in the Damascus synagogues in favor of the beliefs of the Christians (Acts 9).

Paul apparently gave as an explanation of his dramatic change of heart the well-known account of an auditory and visual experience on the Damascus road. He said that he saw a bright light, saw Jesus (1 Corinthians 15:8), and spoke with him. Jesus, Paul said, asked him why he was persecuting him and then told him to go to Damascus and await further instructions. The account in Acts also says that this vision had some intersubjective aspects in that Saul's companions heard a voice but saw no one, but we shall not place weight on the experience of the companions.

Paul's message after his conversion is also unmistakable, and we have many of his letters in which he gives an enormous amount of theological teaching. But the elementary creed of 1 Corinthians 15 summarizes his new beliefs:

> For I delivered to you as of first importance what I also received, that Christ died for our sins according to the Scriptures, and that he was buried, and that he was raised on the third day according to the Scriptures, and that he appeared to Cephas, then to the twelve ... and last of all, as it were to one untimely born, he appeared to me also. (1 Corinthians 15:3–8)[18]

Paul's new beliefs also had a strongly Judaic element. He was particularly concerned to argue that Jesus was the Messiah whose coming had been prophesied long ago, and he disputed this point with his fellow Jews at every opportunity (e.g. Acts 9:22, 13:16ff).

When, then, Paul said that he saw Jesus and spoke with him on the Damascus Road, he was saying that he saw the person who was the Messiah, who had died, and who was risen from the dead. According to the apostles' own account, by the time of Paul's conversion, Jesus had already ascended into heaven and was not physically present on earth. This would seem to indicate that in some sense Paul was saying that he saw Jesus "in heaven" rather than, as the other disciples did, on earth. Nonetheless, there is no question that Paul regarded himself as having seen *the one* who was risen from the dead. If his experiences were veridical, they were experiences in which he saw the Jesus preached by Peter and the other apostles – that is, Jesus who had died and risen from the dead.

---

18. Habermas (2005, pp. 142–3) documents the wide critical acceptance of the early date of this confession of Paul's and the historical significance of that fact.

Probabilistic Cumulative Case Arguments: Nature and Structure

"The evidence of any complex argument," George Campbell observes, "depends very much on the order into which the material circumstances are digested, and the manner in which they are displayed" (Campbell 1839, p. iii). Cumulative case arguments are indeed particularly difficult to evaluate, and before we proceed to show in probabilistic terms the force of the facts just adduced, we need to discuss such arguments in general and to show the form that ours will take.

In the nature of the case, such arguments draw on many details and often require, for their full appreciation, more than a passing acquaintance with multiple disciplines. Beyond this, there is the sheer cognitive difficulty of appreciating the evidential impact of multiple pieces of evidence on a single point; we are apt to focus on two or three considerations and discount the rest. Finally, the pieces of evidence must themselves be not only considered in isolation but coordinated, that is, considered in connection with each other. This coordination requires good judgment.

Though it does not resolve all of these problems, a Bayesian framework enables us to approach each of them in a principled way. It enables us to identify and incorporate as wide a set of relevant facts as possible. It provides a means for representing the significance of the facts taken singly and of viewing their coordinated force under the simplifying assumption of independence. And it gives us guidance regarding the evaluation of the argument when that simplifying assumption fails. The argument developed here illustrates each of these features.

To begin to understand how a cumulative case works, we need to find a convenient way to express the significance of a particular piece of evidence with respect to a particular hypothesis. In the present case, the hypothesis in question is

R: Jesus of Nazareth rose miraculously from the dead.

Considering any fact F that is pertinent (positively or negatively) to R, we want to ask two questions: how probable is F, on the hypothesis that R is true? And how probable is F, on the hypothesis that R is false? The answers to these two questions can be expressed as conditional probabilities, and it turns out to be most convenient for us to consider their ratio:

$$\frac{P(F|R)}{P(F|\sim R)}$$

Assuming that both the numerator and the denominator are defined and nonzero, this fraction, sometimes called a Bayes factor, can take any real value from zero upward without bound. If the conditional probabilities in question are interval-valued, we can take upper and lower bounds on the possible values of the fraction.

In a Bayesian analysis, the use of a Bayes factor provides a particularly convenient method for representing the significance of a particular fact F for R. It is a simple consequence of Bayes's Theorem that, where all of the relevant terms are defined and the denominators are nonzero,

$$\frac{P(R|F)}{P(\sim R|F)} = \frac{P(R)}{P(\sim R)} \times \frac{P(F|R)}{P(F|\sim R)}$$

Put in words, this says that the posterior odds on R (that is, the ratio of the posterior probability of R to the posterior probability of its negation) equal the product of the prior odds and the Bayes factor. A little more colloquially, R becomes more plausible when we take into account a fact F that is more to be expected if R is true than if R is false.

The foregoing representation accounts for a single fact. If we take the odds form of Bayes's Theorem for facts $F_1, F_2, \ldots, F_n$, under the assumption of independence, we obtain the following equation:

$$\frac{P(R|F_1 \& \ldots \& F_n)}{P(\sim R|F_1 \& \ldots \& F_n)} = \frac{P(R)}{P(\sim R)} \times \frac{P(F_1|R)}{P(F_1|\sim R)} \times \ldots \times \frac{P(F_n|R)}{P(F_n|\sim R)}$$

Verbally, this says that the ratio of the posterior probabilities is equal to the product of the ratio of their priors with the product of the Bayes factors for each of the independent pieces of evidence. It is in the product of those Bayes factors that the cumulative force of the evidence of the set of facts $F_1 \& \ldots \& F_n$ can be seen. If each factor is somewhat top-heavy, the cumulative force of a significant number of these factors will be enormous.

The foregoing equation holds only under the simplifying assumption that each fact, *modulo* both R and ~R, is probabilistically independent of all of the other facts. This assumption simplifies the math, and in some cases it is warranted. But where it is not, a more general formula is available.[19]

If R gains a high degree of confirmation from all of the facts in question under the independence assumption, and if we can show that the independence assumption does not exaggerate the impact of the cumulative case in favor of R, it may be most useful simply to calculate the effect of the facts under the assumption of independence and then to show that taking into account dependence among the facts in question can only make the case yet stronger. We shall return to this matter later when discussing a part of the argument where it is plausible that independence does fail.

The fact that mathematics is being employed here may give the impression that what is going on is rather arcane. In fact, the mathematics is simply a means of making explicit a common process of reasoning described well by Butler.

> [T]he truth of our religion, like the truth of common matters, is to be judged of by all the evidence taken together. And unless the whole series of things which may be alleged in this argument, and every particular thing in it, can reasonably be supposed to have been by accident (for here the stress of the argument for Christianity lies); then is the truth of it proved: in like manner as if in any common case numerous events acknowledged were to be alleged in proof of any other event disputed; the truth of the disputed event would be proved, not only if any one of the acknowledged ones did of itself clearly imply it, but though no one of them singly did so if the whole of the acknowledged events taken together could not in reason be supposed to have happened unless the disputed one were true. (Butler 1890, p. 261)

Butler's use of "proved" here is the old sense that pertains to probable proofs, but his reasoning is sound. If the facts can be readily accounted for on the supposition of R but not,

---

19. $\dfrac{P(R|F_1 \& \ldots \& F_n)}{P(\sim R|F_1 \& \ldots \& F_n)} = \dfrac{P(R)}{P(\sim R)} \times \dfrac{P(F_1|R)}{P(F_1|\sim R)} \times \dfrac{P(F_2|R \& F_1)}{P(F_2|\sim R \& F_1)} \times \ldots \times \dfrac{P(F_n|R \& F_1 \& \ldots \& F_{n-1})}{P(F_n|\sim R \& F_1 \& \ldots \& F_{n-1})}$

without great implausibility, on the assumption of ~R, then they provide significant evidence in favor of R.

In understanding Butler's comment, we must be on guard against a plausible error. It might seem that our analysis of cumulative case arguments in terms of Bayes factors puts the emphasis on likelihoods in such a way that finding any subhypothesis under ~R that gives a high probability to some piece of evidence always represents a significant gain for the proponent of ~R in answering the case for R. But when an auxiliary hypothesis H_a is very improbable given ~R, its contribution to the explanation of a fact F is negligible even when it has high likelihood. Suppose, for example, that H_a actually guarantees F, given ~R (so $P(F|\sim R \& H_a) = 1$) but H_a is itself very far-fetched assuming ~R (say, $P(H_a|\sim R) = 0.000001$). It is easy to show that H will make only a very small absolute difference to the average likelihood $P(F|\sim R)$, which is the likelihood of interest in the Bayes factor. All that these conditions tell us is that $P(F|\sim R) \geq 0.000001$. If $P(F|R)$ is on the order of $P(H_a|\sim R)$, that small effect may be evidentially significant. But if $P(F|R) \gg P(H_a|\sim R)$, then the mere fact that $P(F|\sim R \& H_a) = 1$ does not make a significant difference to the Bayes factor. Supplementing ~R with a wildly implausible auxiliary hypothesis H_a in order to account for F is a hopeless strategy when R gives even a moderately high probability to F.

It is easy, also, to slip into a different false assumption – that in making a probabilistic argument of the sort in question for R, we are obliged to restrict ourselves to those subhypotheses under ~R that make some attempt to explain the facts in question. We shall, for example, be discussing theories like hallucination, conspiracy, and the wrong tomb in seeing how skeptics might try to account for various bits of the evidence with which we are presented. Naturally, responding to theories of this sort will take up much of our time in defending R. But it does not follow that such would-be-explanatory subhypotheses represent most of the probability space under ~R. In point of fact, if we are talking about what would be expected given ~R, the largest part of the probability space on that assumption must be assigned to the expectation that nothing special would happen at all after Jesus' death – no hallucinations by his disciples, no visions, no conspiracies – but rather that things would just go on in some perfectly ordinary way. The skeptic will of course insist that ~R has a much higher prior probability than R, and we shall be discussing the question of prior probabilities later on. But by the same token, the negation of all of the facts in evidence has a much higher prior probability than those facts themselves. It is true that many people die and do not rise. And furthermore, many people die, and no one believes that they have risen or has any reason whatsoever to believe it. If we repeatedly say that various would-be-explanatory hypotheses under ~R have poor prior probabilities, the reader may wonder what hypothesis then is dominating the ~R probability space. The answer is that most of it is going to the generic hypothesis that Jesus died and that all went on as usual thereafter, which provides *no* explanation, not even an attempted explanation, of the evidential facts in question. This fact results in a very high cumulative Bayes factor favoring R.

When we move from general considerations regarding the epistemology of cumulative case arguments to the salient facts noted earlier, it is useful first to consider the significance of each piece of evidence independently and then model the cumulative argument under the assumption of independence. Let W, D, and P respectively stand for the reports of the women regarding the empty tomb and the risen Christ, the testimony of the disciples, and the conversion of Paul. Then as a first approximation we can combine the evidence in the following fashion:

$$\frac{P(R|F_1 \& \ldots \& F_n)}{P(\sim R|F_1 \& \ldots \& F_n)} = \frac{P(R)}{P(\sim R)} \times \frac{P(W|R)}{P(W|\sim R)} \times \frac{P(D|R)}{P(D|\sim R)} \times \frac{P(P|R)}{P(P|\sim R)}$$

The product of the last three terms – the respective Bayes factors for W, D, and P – will give the impact of these pieces of evidence on the odds under the assumption of independence.

The Testimony of the Women: Bayes Factor Analysis

There is no difficulty accounting for W if the resurrection had in fact occurred. The bewilderment of the women, Mary Magdalene's frantic rush to tell the disciples, and even the discrepancies of detail in their several accounts taken together with their agreement on the central fact all fall into place very neatly on the supposition of R.

We therefore need to ask what could plausibly have prompted such reports if Jesus had not been raised from the dead. At the outset we may dismiss the suggestion that the whole thing was due to mere bewilderment or confusion. An empty tomb and a beloved rabbi are objects readily accessible to the senses. We can also set aside the suggestion that the women invented the tale, since it has a prohibitively low prior probability. Because they were women, they could not plausibly have formulated a plan to spread something they knew was a falsehood, for they would have known that in Jewish society their word would be questioned or dismissed, as in fact it was even by other followers of Jesus (Luke 24:11, 22). Means and motive for a deliberate fabrication are both absent. This supposition is a nonstarter.

Hallucination hypotheses do not fare much better. Because the women had no expectation of a resurrection – their entire purpose in the early morning expedition was to anoint the dead body – there were no preconditions that would render a hallucination probable. Luke, who seems to have interviewed some of the women themselves, reports that they were perplexed to find the tomb empty (Luke 24:4). This is borne out by the striking fact that Mary Magdalene did not recognize Jesus at first (John 20:15). Finally, any hallucination would have had to affect the group, and there appear to have been at least five women involved. The prior probability for a group hallucination under these circumstances is prohibitively low, not in the sense that it is strictly zero but in the sense that it is nowhere near the magnitude of $P(W|R)$ and therefore cannot significantly affect the strength of the argument from W for R.

A century ago, Kirsopp Lake suggested that, in the semidarkness, the women simply went to the wrong tomb (Lake 1907, pp. 250–3). The prior probability that the whole group would go to the wrong tomb is low, since according to Luke they saw the place on the eve of the Sabbath (Luke 23:55–6). This hypothesis does account effortlessly for their report of the empty tomb, since on this hypothesis the tomb to which they actually went was empty. But beyond that narrow point the "wrong tomb" hypothesis breaks down sharply, since it offers no explanation for the other details in the women's reports, for their report of having seen the risen Jesus, for the failure of the apostles to set them straight on the actual location of the tomb, or for the failure of the Jewish authorities to clarify the matter.

A more creative attempt to explain part of the evidence in W is the conjecture that Joseph of Arimathea merely stored Jesus' body in his own tomb temporarily and then moved it on Saturday night after the Sabbath was over to burial in a graveyard of the condemned, unintentionally leaving the women to discover an empty tomb on Sunday morning. The problems with this hypothesis would be difficult to exaggerate. To begin with, it is very difficult to see why Joseph of Arimathea would care enough about what happened to Jesus' body to provide his own new tomb for it immediately after Jesus' death but would then want to move it out as quickly as possible after the Sabbath. Joseph Klausner, an early proponent of the theory, merely says, "We must assume that the owner of the tomb, Joseph of Arimathaea, thought it unfitting that one who had been crucified should remain in his own ancestral tomb" (Klausner 1925, p. 357).

Jeffrey Lowder, a more recent advocate of the theory, seems to imply (contrary to Matthew 27:57) that Joseph was not really a follower of Jesus at all, that he was in fact a devout member of the Sanhedrin and (evidently) consenting to Jesus' crucifixion, and that he merely put the body in his own tomb in the first place because it was near Calvary and he did not want the body to remain unburied over the Sabbath (Lowder 2005, pp. 267–9). The conjecture that Joseph would have been willing to use his own ancestral tomb for the interment of one he despised and opposed is particularly implausible.

The treatment of Joseph of Arimathea by this theory is strikingly *ad hoc*. The theory accepts his existence from the Gospel texts, so as to have a person to whom to attribute the moving of the body, but it alters his attitudes and motives and adds the otherwise unsubstantiated claim that he did in fact move Jesus' body after carefully burying it in his own tomb. Moreover, there is reason to believe that such moving of a body once buried as Jesus' body was would have been contrary to rabbinic tradition (Talmud, *Semahot* IV.7, XIII.6, XIII.7).[20]

Lowder gives only the feeblest account of why his "Joseph" did not speak out after the disciples began to declare that Jesus was risen, suggesting that he would have thought there was no point in bothering to tell what he knew by Pentecost, when the disciples were preaching Jesus' resurrection, as the body would have been unrecognizable by then (Lowder 2005, pp. 288–90). Whether this last forensic claim is true or not, it is absurd to say that there would have been no point in Joseph's speaking, as he could have testified, as a respected member of the Jewish community, to having moved Jesus' body and to knowing its present location, and he could have shown that in fact he was in possession of the body of a crucified man. If he were opposed to Jesus and his followers, he would certainly have made some such attempt to debunk the resurrection claims. If he were a follower of Jesus, he would have had no reason to keep his action secret and to leave his fellow disciples to promulgate and die for a falsehood.

Finally, this theory is entirely powerless to explain the women's claims actually to have seen Jesus.

These hypotheses, weak as they are, exhaust the remotely plausible means of explaining the testimony of the women as reported in the Gospels without appeal to the resurrection. If there was no resurrection, the body was not moved, they went to the right tomb, and their senses were operating correctly, they must have made up the story; therefore if there was no resurrection, either they made up the story (fabrication), their senses were not operating correctly (hallucination), the body had been moved, or they went to the wrong tomb. Yet none of these alternative hypotheses has both a high enough intrinsic credibility

---

20. These rabbinic citations, together with a great deal more discussion of the issues surrounding the theory in question, are collected in Miller (2002).

and great enough explanatory strength to come even close to rivaling R as an explanation for W.

On any reasonable account, then, W is much more strongly to be expected on the supposition that R than on the supposition that ~R. Given the textual assumptions we specified at the outset, a factor of 100 seems to us to be a conservative estimate for $P(W|R)/P(W|\sim R)$. As we pointed out earlier, there is no algorithm for this sort of thing; if someone wants to claim that the foregoing considerations provide only weak evidence for R, we can deplore his judgment but cannot treat the disagreement as if it were a simple computational error. But in view of the wild implausibility of the naturalistic accounts that have been offered, it will be incumbent on someone who does not think that W is strong evidence for R to explain in some detail why we should not judge $P(W|R)$ to be at least several orders of magnitude greater than $P(W|\sim R)$.

The Testimony of the Disciples: Bayes Factor Analysis

The second fact to be reckoned with is the testimony of the disciples to having seen Jesus risen and their willingness to die for it, a testimony that arose in the context of their demoralization following Jesus' crucifixion. The issue here is somewhat different from that of the women at the tomb. What draws our attention is not only the disciples' accounts of their encounters with the risen Christ but also the suddenness of the change in their outlook, the unexpected boldness of their actions, and their willingness to die in attestation of what they claimed to have witnessed.

One hypothesis that need not detain us for long is that the disciples themselves did not believe what they were proclaiming, that they were neither more nor less than frauds engaging in an elaborate conspiracy. Under this hypothesis falls the further claim that the disciples themselves – or some subset of them – stole the body, according to Matthew (28:13–5) a charge that arose very early. The conspiracy hypothesis had its heyday in the early 1700s but has had few adherents since. Nor is this a merely sociological point, for the theory never had much to be said in its favor. The prior probability of such a conspiracy in the specific context is not very high. It is hard to see what motive the disciples could have had for planning a conspiracy to convince others that Jesus had risen from the dead. Even before their own warnings from the Sanhedrin, after they began teaching that Jesus was risen and spreading the message of forgiveness through his name, they knew full well that such preaching was unlikely to gain them societal power (not counting the possibility of influence in a small and well-hated new sect), sexual gratification, wealth, or anything else of value to unscrupulous men, but rather persecution and death. This, in fact, is why they were in hiding after the horror of Jesus' crucifixion. Wisely enough, they wanted nothing better than to remain unnoticed by the Jewish religious leaders and by the Romans.

But the prior problems of the hypothesis are just the beginning. That the vast majority of scholars – skeptical as well as Christian – acknowledge the Easter faith of the disciples is plainly a result of the extremely low explanatory power of the conspiracy hypothesis *vis a vis* the evidence. Why should all of those witnesses die or be willing to die for an empirical claim which they themselves knew to be false, a claim they had fraudulently induced others to believe by way of an act of theft? Even if they had been foolish enough to think initially that they could get something out of such an elaborate scam (perhaps the skeptic would refer here to the fact that early Christians sold their property and brought the proceeds to the apostles for distribution (Acts 5), they would have had ample opportunity to recant when, as we have documented, they received incontrovertible evidence over a period of months and years that things were not working out according to plan.

Richard Carrier makes an unconvincing attempt to revive the theft hypothesis by conjecturing that one or two followers of Jesus stole his body in order to make it appear that God, despite having previously allowed him to be crucified, had vindicated his good teachings by taking his body up to heaven. Carrier's idea is that these pious thieves had no idea that the theory that Jesus was actually risen from the dead would arise and get so far "out of hand" and that they did not admit what they had done out of the fear of shame before their fellow disciples (Carrier 2005b, pp. 349–52). But Carrier is forced simply to brush off both the resurrection appearance accounts and the fact that his theory has no explanatory power for them whatsoever. And in his further claims that "the devout" – those for whom Jesus was a "beloved rabbi" – would prefer to believe in a conspiracy by the Jews (as in Matthew's account) rather than give up their belief in Jesus' resurrection, he conveniently elides the fact that the resurrection was accepted in the first place because specific, nameable witnesses said they had seen the risen Jesus. Instead, he simply talks about what devout Christians (who lived, he assures us, in a "superstitious" and "illiterate" society) would be likely to want to think "once inspired to believe in the resurrection of their beloved leader" (Carrier 2005b, pp. 354–6). This, of course, does nothing whatsoever to account for the actual evidence, which is not that the pious followers of Jesus were inexplicably and vaguely "inspired" to believe in his resurrection but that a significant number of them claimed actually to have seen and interacted with him repeatedly, over 40 days, in a physical body, after his resurrection, and that those very people persisted in this claim and were willing to die for it. The probability of the evidence given conspiracy is ridiculously low, which doubtless accounts for its relative lack of a following even among skeptical scholars.

What, then, gave rise to the enduring Easter faith of the disciples? Could their belief that Jesus had been raised again to life have been an honest error? The possible naturalistic explanations are limited in somewhat the same way as naturalistic explanations for the testimony of the women at the tomb. Purely naturalistic explanations must appeal either to some external factors or to internal experiences. The former fare very poorly as attempts to account for the facts. The wrong tomb theory, already discussed in our analysis of W, is intrinsically highly improbable, since it requires that no one in the entire group of Jesus' followers even have raised the question of whether the tomb had been properly identified; and in any event it gives no account of the belief of the disciples that they had seen their risen Lord.[21]

In probabilistic terms, where D_i is the testimony of one disciple and X is the disjunction of the external naturalistic theories on offer, $P(D_i|\sim R \ \& \ X)$ is many orders of magnitude lower than $P(D_i|R)$, and $P(X|\sim R)$ is itself exceedingly low. External theories contribute nothing worth mentioning to the overall likelihood $P(D|\sim R)$.

The would-be naturalist is forced, therefore, to search for an internal explanation, some private experience not caused by a public physical stimulus. Given both what the disciples claimed to have experienced and what they endured on behalf of it, vague gestures in the direction of enthusiasm will not do the job. If their belief that Christ was raised from the

---

21. Another external theory, so bizarre as scarcely to be worth mentioning, is that someone else pretended to be Jesus (hated by the local leaders and recently crucified by the Roman authorities), a role Robert Greg Cavin assigns to a hypothetical twin brother (Cavin 1993, pp. vii, 314–58).

dead was false, either they had good reasons to believe it or they did not. The analogy of their belief to the subjective enthusiasm of religious zealots assumes that they did not. But their actual actions would be highly improbable under this condition. It is easy to assume that attributing to an individual a very high subjective probability, or degree of belief, is always a good explanation for his actions. But surely it is not in general true that subjective enthusiasm and considered judgment are equally robust causes. A gambler in a fit of frenzy may offer hundred to one odds that the roulette wheel will come up red on the next spin; a trained surgeon might offer similar odds that a certain procedure will cure his patient. But the gambler is apt to sober up quickly and abandon his enthusiasm if his child's life is put on the line, whereas the surgeon may well proceed even if the patient is his daughter. The manner in which a strong belief is held, in particular the role of evidence in its formation and maintenance, often makes a difference to its value as an explanation for subsequent action. The theory that the apostles believed strongly that Christ rose from the dead but lacked good reasons for that belief has poor likelihood with respect to the evidence at hand.

It is sometimes urged that kamikaze pilots, suicide bombers, and Nazis were willing to give their lives for what they believed was true.[22] The objection may be put more broadly. Virtually every religion has its zealous adherents who have been willing to die for what they believe; why, then, should the willingness of the apostles to die as martyrs be of special epistemic interest? The answer is that this description blurs the distinction between the willingness to die for an ideology and the willingness to die in attestation of an empirical fact.[23] Robert Jenkin put the point with exceptional clarity three centuries ago when he stressed the original meaning of the term *martyrs*:

> An ignorant Zeal in a wrong Cause is no Argument against the Goodness of any Cause, which is maintained and promoted by such a Zeal as is reasonable, and proceeds upon sure Grounds. Indeed, it were very hard and very strange, if that which is true, should be ever the less certain, or the less to be regarded and esteemed, because there may be other things, that are false, of which some Men are as firmly persuaded, and are as much concerned for them, as any one can be for the Truth itself. And yet this is the wisest Thing that many have to pretend against the Certainty of the Religion, in which they were baptized, that there are many Impostures in the World, and none is without its Zealots to appear in Vindication of it. I am confident no Man ever parted with any thing, but his Religion, upon so weak a Pretence.
>
> ... It is commonly and truly said, that it is not the Suffering, but the Cause, which makes the Martyr; and if Men of false Religions have never so much Confidence of the Truth of them, and have no Ground for it, this can be no Argument against the Grounds and Proofs upon which the Evidence of the Christian Religion depends. Other Religions may have their Zealots, who offer themselves to die for them, but the Christian Religion properly has the only Martyrs. For Martyrs are *Witnesses*, and no other Religion is capable of being attested in such a Manner as the Christian Religion; no other Religion was ever propagated by Witnesses, who had seen, and heard, and been every way conversant in what they witnessed concerning the Principles of their Religion; no Religion besides was ever preach'd by Men, who, after an unalterable Constancy under all Kinds of Sufferings, at last died for asserting it, when they must of necessity have known, whether it were true or false, and therefore certainly knew it to be true, or else they would never have suffer'd and died in that Manner for it ... (Jenkin 1734, pp. 529, 531)

22. Regrettably, this sort of argument is sometimes employed by authors who should know better (see Plantinga 2006, pp. 15–6).
23. This is a point Gary Habermas stresses (Habermas 2006b, pp. 79–80).

It is clear that neither kamikazes, Nazis, nor suicide bombers died to affirm the reality of something that they had seen with their eyes and their hands had handled. Thus, their deaths and the falsehood of some of their beliefs tell us nothing about the probability that a man will die to make an affirmation *like that of the apostles* when it is in fact false. The educational resources of an entire nation, applied over the course of a decade or more to minds at their most impressionable stage, may be sufficient to induce in the young the general belief that their country or their religion is worth dying for. But what would induce grown men to break with the religious community in which they had been raised and to confess with their blood that they had seen with their own eyes and handled with their own hands their dead rabbi raised again to life?

Suppose, on the other hand, that the witnesses did have good reasons for their belief in the resurrection but were nevertheless mistaken. How is this supposed to have come about? The hallucination theory has at least this advantage over both external naturalistic explanations and the appeal to enthusiasm: the supposition that the disciples suffered from sufficiently vivid and persistent hallucinations provides the resources to explain why they firmly believed they had seen Jesus risen.[24] But this gain in explanatory power comes at a prohibitive cost in prior probability, for four reasons. First, the disciples were not in a psychological state that rendered them susceptible to a hallucination. Unlike the eager pilgrims who flock to holy sites hoping to see visions and prodigies, the disciples were not anticipating a miracle of any sort, let alone a resurrection; the Gospels make it plain that the disciples, to their embarrassment, did not understand Jesus' somewhat enigmatic predictions of his own death and return to life to indicate an imminent bodily resurrection until after the fact. Their primary emotion was not exalted expectation but a combination of grief and simple fear (Matthew 26:56; John 19:38, 20:19). Messianic expectations in Judaism at the time did not include the resurrection of the messiah except in the general resurrection at the final judgment.[25] As we have pointed out, they – collectively at first and individually in the case of Thomas – were understandably skeptical of others' accounts of the empty tomb or of encounters with Jesus. When Jesus did appear to them, they sometimes failed to recognize him (John 21:4–7). These were not men who were likely to suffer a hallucination of any sort, much less one of their risen master.

Second, to explain the facts the hallucination theory would have to be invoked for more than a dozen people simultaneously (Luke 24:36–43).[26] The plausibility of a collective hallucination is, for obvious reasons, inversely related to the amount of detail it involves.[27]

---

24. In the most natural and common meaning of the word, a hallucination is a private experience (see Slade & Bentall 1988, p. 16). Some examples given in popular authors (e.g. Rawcliffe 1959, pp. 114–5) are of misidentification rather than a hallucination properly speaking. See, for example, the tale of the walking cook in John Brand (1842, p. 44). In cases of collective hallucination, expectation, emotional excitement, and suggestion are the primary factors. In particular, "all participants in the hallucination must be informed beforehand, at least concerning the broad outlines of the phenomenon that will constitute the collective hallucination" (Zusne & Jones 1982, p. 135).

25. For an extensive scholarly discussion of messianic expectations and resurrection in Judaism, see Wright (2003, pp. 85–206).

26. "More than a dozen" here does not refer to precisely the thirteen witnesses we have listed, because we do not know whether Matthias was with the eleven in the passage cited here, and it seems plausible that James Jesus' brother was not. The phrase rather refers to the fact that, on the account in Luke, several "others" were present on this particular occasion with the eleven.

27. Rawcliffe (1959, p. 111) points out that the comparatively dissimilar hallucinatory experiences of different people "often attain a spurious similarity by a process of harmonisation" as they recollect and discuss them. But detailed experiences full of verbal and tactile interactions both with the one seen and with other witnesses cannot be brushed aside like this.

Given the level of polymodal interactive detail reported in cases like the one in Luke 24, the probability of coincidence is vanishing. A third factor exacerbates this problem: the hallucinations would have to be not only parallel but also integrated. According to the Gospels, the risen Jesus interacted with his disciples in numerous ways, including eating food they gave him (Luke 24:41–3) and cooking fish for them (John 21:1–14). In such contexts, the disciples were interacting not only with Jesus but with one another, physically and verbally. The suggestion that their parallel polymodal hallucinations were seamlessly integrated is simply a nonstarter, an event so improbable in natural terms that it would itself very nearly demand a supernatural explanation. Finally, these detailed, parallel, integrated hallucinations must be invoked repeatedly across a period of more than a month during which the disciples were persuaded that they repeatedly interacted with their Lord and master here on earth.

And then, abruptly, they stopped. Christ no longer appeared on earth. Whatever their causes, the visions of Peter and Cornelius in Acts and even of Paul on the road to Damascus are qualitatively distinct from these appearances. Paul never claimed that Jesus broke bread with him or ate a meal with him. Theodore Keim's argument on this point is inexorable:

> Not one of the five hundred repeats the ecstasy, and all the cases of ecstasy irrevocably end with the fifth vision. What a contradiction of high-swollen enthusiasm and of sudden ebb even to the point of disappearance! Just when fervid minds are beginning to grow fanatical, the fanaticism absolutely and entirely ceases. It might be possible that a few less ardent natures, though perhaps not Peter, rather James, would quickly recover their mental equilibrium; but in the greater number of the twelve and of the five hundred a movement which had burst the dams would certainly not be stayed in an instant; and yet the narrative says nothing of a third vision to the twelve and nothing of a second to the five hundred. (Keim 1883, p. 356)[28]

From the standpoint of calculating a Bayes factor, the problem with the hallucination theory is that it has a vanishingly small probability conditional on ~R. The sort of complex, repeated, integrated hallucination that would be required to explain even one disciple's testimony and willingness to die for it would represent a serious mental illness. But the advocate of this theory must suppose that it simultaneously struck all of the disciples and left them with a lasting conviction that carried them through their lives and to defiant witness in the face of death. We shall return to this point regarding the cumulative force of their testimony when we come to assess the overall impact of the testimony of the disciples on the argument for the resurrection.

Naturalistic theories are, therefore, severely wanting. But not all who hold theistic theories agree that Jesus was physically raised from the dead. One popular position has been what Gary Habermas calls the "objective vision" theory, developed by Theodore Keim in the nineteenth century and favored by Hans Grass in the middle of the twentieth, according to which the disciples had, by direct divine dispensation, experiences of the noncorporeal appearance of Jesus that assured them that he was alive and well. Terminology here is somewhat confusing, since in one sense these visions were subjective, instances of "graced seeing" rather than physical events. But advocates of this position have insisted from the beginning that they are not simply collapsing into the naturalistic subjective position. Keim argues that the visions must have been miraculous, and he couples his argument on behalf

---

28. See also Keim's (1883, p. 355) contrast of these appearances with the Montanist visions of the second century.

of the objective vision theory with a vigorous attack on Strauss's naturalistic vision hypothesis (Keim 1883, pp. 334ff, particularly pp. 351–60; cf. Fuller 1993, p. 648).

The objective vision theory thus defined is a theistic theory; anyone who invokes it cannot, for obvious reasons, be using it as part of an argument against the existence of God. Nontheists are apt to think of it as pettifogging on the part of the theists, and in the dialectic of theism and atheism they have a point. Any Christian who explains the testimony of the disciples by appeal to private experiences that cannot be historically demonstrated will find that he is unable to gain much in the way of argumentative traction against a skeptic, who will simply shrug off the suggestion as an attempt to put a theistic spin on simple delusion.[29]

From the standpoint of a historical apologetic, however, the objective vision theory still poses a challenge, since it is clearly intended to be incompatible with any sort of physical resurrection and must therefore be considered as an alternative attempt to explain the Easter faith of the disciples. But for several reasons it is an unimpressive alternative explanation. First, the idea that the disciples had a vision of a Jesus who was physically dead but was speaking to them from heaven has on its face a low likelihood with respect to the evidence of what the disciples said. For Jesus, they said, offered to let them touch him, said expressly that he had "flesh and bones" as a spirit does not have, and, when they were still incredulous, ate fish and honeycomb with them (Luke 24:39ff). On John's account, they saw him "standing on the beach." This in itself is hardly the language of a heavenly vision. (Contrast, for example, what Stephen says in Acts 7:56: "I see the heavens opened up and the Son of Man standing at the right hand of God.") John's Gospel also relates that Jesus cooked fish for them and shared a meal with them by the Sea of Tiberias (John 21:12–4). Whatever else may be the case, it is beyond reasonable doubt that the first Christians believed that Jesus had been physically raised.[30] This is clear not only from the early creed embedded in 1 Corinthians 15:3–8 but also, as we noted earlier, from the teaching of Peter on the day of Pentecost (Acts 2:29–32).

Suppose that we assume, though, that the disciples' visions were experientially exactly as if Jesus had been raised bodily from the dead, making the objective vision theory phenomenologically indistinguishable from a vivid hallucination theory. It makes no sense to attribute such visions to the power of any being other than the Judeo-Christian God. Zeus, were he to exist, would have no motive for persuading the disciples of the Christ's victory over death. But equally it makes no sense for the Judeo-Christian God to give them such visions. A God who is capable of working miracles – which the God of Abraham and Isaac was certainly conceived to be, and which God would have to be in any event in order to give the witnesses these sorts of visions – and whose followers are strictly enjoined to be truthful would have no conceivable reason for skipping the physical miracle of a resurrection and befuddling His earnest followers into the bargain.

How much weight, then, should we put on the testimony of the disciples? The question is complex in part because of the multiplicity of alternative theories and the varied difficulties they face. But also, as we have argued at length, we know by name at least thirteen who professed to be eyewitnesses of the risen Christ and were willing to die for this profession,

---

29. Keith Parsons (2005, p. 436) makes this point forcefully.
30. Richard Carrier (2005a) has attempted to argue to the contrary. For a critique see Davis (2006, pp. 56–9). Habermas (2006b, pp. 88–9) points out that even scholars such as Gerd Lüdemann who are skeptical of the resurrection acknowledge that the disciples believed that Jesus was physically resurrected.

some of them being eventually put to death. So we need to consider not just the implausibility of the testimony of one witness but the compounded implausibility of such testimony from multiple witnesses.

As a first step, let us consider a single disciple. The best of the available naturalistic explanations, the hallucination theory, requires (if it is to match R in likelihood) an extraordinary level of detailed delusion, seamlessly integrated (so far as he can tell) with his experience of those around him. Such delusions do occur in waking life in those who suffer from severe mental illness, but such illness is mercifully rare and is accompanied by other noticeable conditions that were absent in the case of the disciples. The other naturalistic hypotheses have higher prior probabilities, perhaps as high as 0.001, but they do not come close to matching the explanatory power of R; their contribution to the likelihood $P(D_i|\sim R)$ is negligible even by comparison to the hallucination theory. The objective vision theory on a plausible construal has very low likelihood; we would not expect a heavenly vision to behave the way the disciples said Jesus behaved and to interact with them in the way that they said he did. We would not expect them to come away from a heavenly vision of Jesus firmly convinced that his body had not decayed and that they had talked and eaten with him physically on earth. A suitably modified vision theory (which we may call O^*) does not have this defect, since $P(D_i|\sim R \& O^*) = P(D_i|R)$ more or less by definition. But it suffers from the fact that $P(O^*|\sim R)$ is itself very low (say, <0.001) even if (as few skeptics will grant) $P(T|\sim R) \gg 0$. The simple fact is that if the resurrection did not occur, we would not expect to have anything remotely like the testimony of even a single witness as recorded in Acts and the Gospels, his defiance in the face of death, and such a witness's sudden and permanent transformation reported in Acts and confirmed by the evidence of the early church. In the individual case, it would seem that $P(D_i|R)$ is at least three orders of magnitude greater than $P(D_i|\sim R)$.

But having assigned a single factor, we must ask what happens when we take into account the fact that there were thirteen such disciples. We can get a first approximation to the result by assuming independence. Recall, first, that where the pieces of evidence are all independent given R and given $\sim R$, the assumption of independence entails that

$$\frac{P(D_1 \& \ldots \& D_{13}|R)}{P(D_1 \& \ldots \& D_{13}|\sim R)} = \frac{P(D_1|R)}{P(D_1|\sim R)} \times \ldots \times \frac{P(D_{13}|R)}{P(D_{13}|\sim R)}$$

So under the assumption of independence, the Bayes factors for each of the thirteen D_i must be multiplied, which yields a staggering combined factor $P(D|R)/P(D|\sim R) = 10^{39}$.[31]

The Conversion of Paul: Bayes Factor Analysis

The fourth of our salient facts is the conversion of Paul. It is a striking event, difficult to explain. Saul of Tarsus, fanatical and implacable foe of the Christians and rising star in the Jewish community in Jerusalem, on his way to Damascus with letters of authorization from

---

31. Michael Martin (2005, pp. 465–6) estimates – very much off the cuff – a probability of the evidence for the resurrection given that Jesus did not rise of 1/500, saying that this estimate is still "absurdly low," and he uses this number to replace what he considers an unrealistic estimate of the same probability by Richard Swinburne as 1/1,000. But a detailed consideration of the evidence, taking it apart piece by piece and then recombining its force by multiplication, indicates that *both* estimates are far too high. And our estimate here has not yet included the Bayes factors for the other salient facts but only for D.

the high priest in Jerusalem for the explicit purpose of stamping out this upstart sect, was suddenly transformed into an utterly convinced believer in the risen Christ and became Paul the apostle, tireless missionary and ultimately martyr for the religion he had so vigorously persecuted.

From the accounts of Paul's experience given in Acts we know that he took the experience to be an encounter, albeit not an earthly one like that of the disciples, with Jesus – the very Jesus whose followers he was bent on persecuting. And those followers were from the earliest days proclaiming that Jesus had risen *physically* from the dead, a theme on which Paul elaborates in several places. The connection, then, to the resurrection is more direct than it might appear; Paul considered himself commissioned directly by God to preach the resurrection and messiahship of Jesus, and his teaching corresponded to that of the apostles in Jerusalem (Galatians 2:2). His unwavering conviction of that commission permeates both the record of his teaching in Acts and his own epistles (see, e.g., Acts 22:10–6; Acts 26; 2 Corinthians 1:1; Galatians 1:1, 11–6; Philippians 3:4–8; Colossians 1:1; 1 Timothy 1:1, 12–3).

The suggestion that Paul was deliberately promulgating something he knew to be false is too absurd to detain us; his ardor for Judaism, his rising status among the Jews, and the opprobrium that attached to Christianity leave no room for any human motive for deceit. He had everything to lose and nothing earthly to gain. Nor need we take seriously the suggestion that he was the victim of an audacious prank, fooled somehow into thinking that Jesus was speaking to him out of heaven while his dumbfounded companions looked on. The fearful Christians were wary of approaching him even after receiving word of his conversion; and even if they wanted to deceive him, there are no means by which they could have contrived, on the open road and in the presence of his companions, any deception that they might hope would convert so determined and powerful an adversary.[32]

Perhaps aware of just how feeble these explanations would be, Strauss suggests delicately that Paul might have been overcome by feelings of doubt and guilt during a thunderstorm (Strauss 1879, pp. 420–5).[33] This remarkable conjecture might be worth discussing were it not for the fact that the doubt, the guilt, and the thunderstorm are all invented out of whole cloth. Having made the insinuation, Strauss wisely drops this hypothesis and takes refuge behind the claim that the book of Acts cannot possibly be historical.

The field of possible explanations for Paul's conversion is therefore reduced to this: either he was subject to an extraordinary – and extraordinarily effective – delusion, or else what he declared to be the cause of his conversion really happened, in which latter case we have as strong an argument as one could wish both for the resurrection and for the truth of the Christian religion. The strength of the evidence for the resurrection from the conversion of Paul is therefore for all practical purposes inversely proportional to the probability that on the road to Damascus he suffered from a hallucination. But as with the hallucination theories invoked to explain the testimony of the disciples, this theory requires layer upon layer of improbability. Delusions that change the minds of vicious persecutors and transform them into faithful martyrs are unfortunately quite rare; one looks in vain for comparable conversions among the notorious murdering zealots of the ages. And it is not just any hallucination we need here, but a complex waking one of the despised Jesus in

---

32. For a vigorous and extended discussion of these points, still valuable today, see Lyttleton (1800, pp. 1–60).

33. Other contemporaries of Strauss similarly pass over Paul's transformation with nothing worth calling an explanation at all; see, for example, Geiger (1865, pp. 238–9).

glory, remonstrating with him. It is, moreover, an odd sort of hallucination that is followed by several days of blindness.

The layers of improbability involved in this hypothesis cannot be evaded without abandoning the text itself and striking off into creative fiction in the manner of Strauss. Taking the secularly described component of the relevant texts at face value, we would suggest that $P(P|\sim R)$ is at best on the order of 10^{-4} and plausibly a good deal lower, whereas on the assumption of R there is no difficulty whatsoever accounting for P. As a consequence, we conservatively take the Bayes factor for the conversion of Paul in favor of the resurrection to be at least 10^3.

The Collective Force of the Salient Facts

Each of the salient facts surveyed makes a significant contribution to the case for the resurrection. Taken in conjunction, they provide an overwhelming argument for the conclusion that the resurrection did indeed occur.

The first approximation for the strength of the argument should be under the assumption of independence. In that case, we have to multiply the factors in accordance with the formula exhibited earlier:

$$\text{Strength of the combined evidence} = \frac{P(W|R)}{P(W|\sim R)} \times \frac{P(D|R)}{P(D|\sim R)} \times \frac{P(P|R)}{P(P|\sim R)}$$

But our estimated Bayes factors for these pieces of evidence were, respectively, 10^2, 10^{39}, and 10^3. Sheer multiplication through gives a Bayes factor of 10^{44}, a weight of evidence that would be sufficient to overcome a prior probability (or rather improbability) of 10^{-40} for R and leave us with a posterior probability in excess of 0.9999.

It is true that this conclusion is predicated on the assumption that in matters other than the explicit claims of miracles, the Gospels and the book of Acts are generally reliable – that they may be trusted as much as any ordinary document of secular history with respect to the secularly describable facts they affirm. And where they do recount miraculous events, such as Jesus' postresurrection appearances, we assume that they are authentic – that is, that they tell us what the disciples claimed. This calculation tells us little about the evidence for the resurrection if those assumptions are false. We have provided reasons to accept them, but of course there is much more to be said on the issue.

This limitation, however, is not as severe as might be thought. "General reliability" admits of degrees, and we have deliberately kept our salient facts minimally stated with the intention that they should not require reliance at every point on the smallest details of the biblical texts. The weight placed on our textual assumptions varies from one fact to another and even from one aspect of a given fact to another. The facts we have designated as W are perhaps the most vulnerable to a challenge based on textual skepticism. Some aspects of D – for example, that the disciples made specific claims regarding the physical details of Jesus' postresurrection appearances – depend more heavily on the authenticity of the sources than others – for example, the witnesses' willingness to die for their belief in the resurrection, which is supported by extrabiblical sources. Finally, as we have repeatedly emphasized, crucial aspects of each of these facts are accepted even by scholars who would deny that the texts are early or highly reliable, with the disciples' belief that they had seen the risen Christ and the conversion of Paul being probably the most widely accepted by otherwise skeptical scholars. All that being said, it is only to be expected that the case for the salient facts is largely dependent on the reliability and authenticity of the most relevant and detailed textual sources available.

Second, the invocation of independence assumptions at several points is contestable; in fact, we believe that in the case of the calculation for D the independence assumption almost certainly breaks down. Surprisingly, however, this fact does not necessarily lessen the strength of the argument. Everything depends on the balance of considerations regarding the direction and extent of the breakdown of independence under R and under ~R. We explore this issue in detail in the next section.

Third, the values we have supplied will certainly be contested. We have provided *prima facie* reasons for the values we give, but it is only to be expected that anyone who denies R will find them unacceptable. On this score, our claim is simply that the arguments we have presented are sufficient to shift the burden of proof for the time being.

One point, however, is largely independent of the values put into the calculation. The use of the Bayesian structure illustrates dramatically how the compounding of independent pieces of positive evidence can rapidly create a powerful cumulative case even for a highly controversial claim. Historical arguments provide an excellent field for the illustration of this fact. In the felicitous words of Thomas Chalmers, history

> is a peculiar subject, and the men who stand at a distance from it may multiply their suspicions and their scepticism at pleasure; but no intelligent man ever entered into the details, without feeling the most familiar and satisfying conviction of that credit and confidence which it is in the power of historical evidence to bestow. (Chalmers 1817, p. 56)

Independence

We have argued that the combined impact of the three lines of argument sketched in favor of R over ~R is extremely strong. That argument, however, was based on the simplifying assumption that the lines of argument are independent. When it came to the willingness of the thirteen witnesses to die for their beliefs, we also assumed independence and thereby came up with a very high Bayes factor for the cumulative force of their testimony.

Critics of our argument are likely to balk at this assumption. John Venn puts the objection pointedly:

> [W]hen two, and of course still more when many, witnesses agree in a statement in a matter about which they might make many and various errors, the combination of their favourable testimony adds enormously to the likelihood of the event; provided always that there is no chance of collusion. . . . But then this condition, viz. absence of collusion, very seldom can be secured. Practically our main source of error and suspicion is in the possible existence of some kind of collusion. Since we can seldom entirely get rid of this danger, and when it exists it can never be submitted to numerical calculation, it appears to me that combination of testimony, in regard to detailed accounts, is yet more unfitted for consideration in Probability than even that of single testimony. (Venn 1888, p. 428)

Just as the force of a cumulative case is greatly enhanced by the assumption that the different lines of evidence are independent in their impact on the proposition in question, it is seriously jeopardized by evidence of collusion. If three men accused of committing a crime all give, in essentially the same words, the same innocent explanation of their actions, the plausibility of the claim that they are conspiring to give themselves an alibi undermines the force of their combined testimony. Even when there is no definite intent to deceive, witnesses may influence one another's testimony causally in a way that would obtain even if the event had not happened, or had not happened in the way that they are saying it did. This possibility is relevant to epistemic probabilities when we have reason to suspect this sort of mutual influence. William Kruskal sums up his detailed discussion of independence in the combination of testimony with a succinct cautionary moral: "Do not multiply lightly" (Kruskal 1988, p. 929). The question of independence is therefore critical.

First, let us consider the independence of the strands of argument which we have labeled W, D, and P. The testimony of the women to the empty tomb and to the appearances of Christ are independent, obviously, of Paul's conversion, which was not occasioned or rendered more probable by their testimony – which he rejected and after which he was a persecutor of Christians – but rather was caused by what he described as a direct revelation available to him alone. And the other testimonies to the risen Christ, including those of the male witnesses, were of course independent of Paul's conversion, having been given prior to it.[34] The women's testimony is essentially independent of that of the thirteen male witnesses. The women were the first witnesses, uninfluenced by the disciples; they came and told the disciples what they had seen before the disciples were making any claim that Jesus had risen. And since the disciples dismissed the women's report, there is no ground for taking the disciples' testimony and willingness to die for it to have any significant probabilistic dependence on the women's testimony.

But the assumption of independence *among* the thirteen male witnesses raises greater difficulties. For even if it is granted that the testimony of the thirteen (D) taken in aggregate is independent of W and of P, it might be argued that the twelve apostles and James the brother of Jesus were not testifying independently of each other and hence that our estimate of the cumulative Bayes factor for their testimony, expressly calculated under independence, is too high. And because there are so many witnesses, D is carrying a large amount of the weight of the case we are making, so the independence assumption there is crucial.

Here is the challenge to the legitimacy of our independence assumption among those thirteen witnesses: Would they not have been more likely to testify as they did and to be willing to die for their claims as a result of the willingness of each other? Were they not encouraging each other by their steadfastness?

The surprising answer is that the force of the case is arguably *underestimated* as a result of the independence assumption. To see why this is so, we must note that the independence of the witnesses' testimony and willingness to die for it holds only if

$$\frac{P(D_1 \& \ldots \& D_{13}|R)}{P(D_1|R) \times \ldots \times P(D_{13}|R)} = \frac{P(D_1 \& \ldots \& D_{13}|\sim R)}{P(D_1|\sim R) \times \ldots \times P(D_{13}|\sim R)}$$

34. Chronological priority does not in general guarantee independence, but for purposes of calculating the independent force of evidence on R, the question is not independence *tout court* but rather independence *modulo* R and *modulo* ~R, respectively, which does appear to obtain here and for which chronological priority is a relevant consideration.

This is true because, on the assumption of independence, the numerator of each ratio is the same as the denominator. Given independence, $P(D_1 \& \ldots \& D_{13}|R) = P(D_1|R) \times \ldots \times P(D_{13}|R)$, and *mutatis mutandis* for ~R. So under the assumption of independence for both R and ~R, each of the ratios above is simply equal to 1, making them trivially equal to each other.

The objection we are considering is that we should not be allowed to multiply the Bayes factors for the thirteen witnesses and that, if we did not do so, we would end up with a factor significantly *lower* than the 10^{39} we have calculated for their cumulative testimony. It is true that, absent independence, it may happen that this equality does not hold. If the pieces of evidence are positively or negatively relevant to each other, it *might* be the case that the calculation under independence exaggerates their force for R. But this will be the case *only if* the equality changes to an inequality favoring ~R, like this:

$$\frac{P(D_1 \& \ldots \& D_{13}|R)}{P(D_1|R) \times \ldots \times P(D_{13}|R)} < \frac{P(D_1 \& \ldots \& D_{13}|\sim R)}{P(D_1|\sim R) \times \ldots \times P(D_{13}|\sim R)}$$

To illustrate this case, suppose that two witnesses say that H, and each has a Bayes factor of 10 in favor of H, that is, $P(W_1|H)/P(W_1|\sim H) = P(W_2|H)/P(W_2|\sim H) = 10$. If we treat their testimonies as independent, these Bayes factors should be multiplied, yielding a compound Bayes factor of 100 in favor of H. But suppose that we have some reason to suspect that, if H is false, they have colluded in their story, making their testimonies somewhat positively relevant to one another *modulo* ~H. In that epistemic situation we should not multiply $P(W_1|\sim H)$ and $P(W_2|\sim H)$ when calculating $P(W_1 \& W_2|\sim H)$, because $P(W_1 \& W_2|\sim H)$ would be underestimated by multiplication. How much it would be underestimated would depend on the specifics of the situation and in particular on how probable collusion was given ~H. But in that case, an inequality like the one above would hold; for the witnesses' testimonies would be independent under the assumption of H (since there is no reason to suspect collusion if H is true) but positively relevant to each other given ~H.

The thirteen witnesses for the resurrection did certainly know one another and had ample opportunity to talk with one another. The testimony for the resurrection did not take the form of an experiment in which they were all in isolated rooms, unaware of each others' statements. The worry, then, is that we should take seriously the possibility of ~R plus some form of collusion or positive mutual relevance, which would raise the probability of the conjunction of all their testimonies under the assumption of ~R over the probability of their testimonies taken independently and would make the calculation under independence inapplicable.

But when probabilistic independence of testimonial evidence fails, it need not fail in the way sketched above. Probabilistic relevance can be either positive or negative, and in this case we have both sides of the inequality to evaluate. If the inequality breaks the other way, so that

$$\frac{P(D_1 \& \ldots \& D_{13}|R)}{P(D_1|R) \times \ldots \times P(D_{13}|R)} > \frac{P(D_1 \& \ldots \& D_{13}|\sim R)}{P(D_1|\sim R) \times \ldots \times P(D_{13}|\sim R)}$$

then abandoning the independence assumption will actually favor R over ~R and make the case for R from the conjunction of the testimonies stronger than the already huge factor calculated under independence. The critical question, then, is whether R unifies the disciples' testimonies more than does ~R. If independence fails in this particular case, will collusion concerns make the inequality favor ~R, or will we find that the conjunction of the witnesses' testimony is actually better predicted by the assumption of R?

Some of the witnesses in question actually did die for their testimony. For them, we may take the fact in question to be not simply that they were willing to die for their testimony but also that they *did* die. If A dies (especially in some unpleasant way) for his testimony to the risen Christ and B hears about it – and there is no serious doubt that the apostles knew when one of their number was put to death – does this make B *more* likely to stand firm until death in his own testimony? It seems to us that the opposite is true, that knowing of such a death is plausibly and under ordinary circumstances negatively relevant to B's willingness to remain steadfast. B may well be frightened by the fate of A and drop his claims. In this case, treating A's and B's deaths for their testimony – their martyrdoms in the original sense of the term *martyr* as *witness* – as probabilistically independent actually understates the case for R. Since human beings naturally fear death and are horrified by even the account of torture, the martyrdoms may indeed be somewhat negatively relevant under the assumption that their testimony was true. Even men speaking the truth may be frightened out of doing so by hearing that someone else saying the same thing has died for his witness.[35] But they are far more negatively relevant to each other under the assumption that their testimony is false. If their deaths are normally expected to be negatively relevant to each other, yet they do in fact go to their deaths, this is well explained by their knowing that what they are saying is the truth and feeling bound by that consideration to persist despite the fears occasioned by news of each others' deaths.[36] It is not to be expected at all if this is not the case. In other words, when we consider the deaths of, say, three of the witnesses, R makes better sense not merely of their deaths considered separately but also of the conjunction of their deaths than does ~R. This means that the Bayes factor calculated under independence for these witnesses is lower than the real impact of their martyrdoms warrants.

Short of death itself, suppose we consider the *willingness* of the thirteen witnesses to die. Probably they encouraged each other by their steadfastness in the face of the threat of death; and in that case, the willingness of A to die for his testimony is not independent of but positively relevant to the willingness of B, and vice versa. Does this mean that our case is weaker than the independence assumption would indicate and that it is illegitimate for us to multiply the Bayes factors for each of the thirteen witnesses to obtain a cumulative Bayes factor for all of them of 10^{39}? Does this make their case like one where we must be concerned about collusion in a falsehood?

Here, too, any dependence among the testimony of the witnesses actually favors our case; the independence assumption, if it has any prejudicial effect, underestimates the force of the evidence for R. When people are claiming to be eyewitnesses to some event (in this

---

35. This is one of the mechanisms operative in witness intimidation.
36. Laplace (1840, pp. 11, 121–2) makes much of the fact that, if a witness has an interest in lying in some particular direction, the value of his testimony in that direction is weakened. This is obviously correct, since the probability of his saying what he does say is in such a case greater than it would otherwise be on the hypothesis that what he says is false. In other words, he might be lying in his testimony because he has a known special interest in making this particular false statement. But Laplace fails to consider that interest can cut both ways. If lying in that particular way is highly likely to get you killed in a most unpleasant way, you have a special interest in *not* lying in that particular way. Anything that increased the apostles' expectation that persisting in their testimony would lead to unpleasant death decreased their interest in persisting.

case, the appearance of the risen Jesus), and when they are in danger of an unpleasant fate for making the claim in question, their believing and having better evidence for this claim is a better explanation of positive dependence among their accounts – their being able to encourage one another to continue making their testimony – than their not believing the claim or having worse evidence for it.

Consider, for example, the subhypothesis under ~R of fraudulent collusion. Not only does it have a low prior probability and low likelihood relative to the behavior of the disciples taken individually, it is also unable to explain any influence the witnesses were able have upon one another to encourage each other to continue their witness in the face of danger of death. Would rogues and liars have any such effect upon one another? On the contrary, if two men both face unpleasant deaths for a lie which they have concocted, the intransigence of one is most unlikely to influence the other to remain steadfast in the fraud. The evidence included in D is not simply that the witnesses in question made a single statement that Jesus was risen from the dead but that they persisted in their witness under threat of death. Under the assumption of ~R, then, the extreme conditions of duress upon multiple witnesses to drop their story makes collusion a poor explanation of their collective persistence. On the assumption of ~R such persistence would be at best independent rather than a result of mutual influence. So if multiple witnesses are able to influence one another to remain steadfast in some story in the face of unpleasant consequences for telling that story, this is itself evidence that they believe that the story is true rather than that they are colluding in a lie. Hence, acknowledging the plausibility of mutual influence among the disciples, that influence does not occur under the subhypothesis of initial collusion under ~R but rather under the assumption of R.

So far, it appears that the crucial inequality favors R rather than ~R if we abandon independence. But a critic might respond that what really matters, where the failure of independence is concerned, is neither conspiracy nor courage but rather something more like irrational religious enthusiasm or perhaps some nonspecific version of the objective vision hypothesis. People can and do work one another up to behave irrationally and to stick to an ideology or to a bizarre religion in the face of opposition. We have already considered and rejected the religious enthusiasm hypothesis as an explanation of the evidence of the disciples' testimony. One of the points we made there is that this is not a case of commitment to an ideology or set of religious propositions but to an empirical claim which the people in question were in a position to know to be true or false. And we have already rejected the generic vision hypothesis on the grounds that it does not account for the testimony each of the witnesses actually gave. But how do these hypotheses affect the issue of independence?

If two witnesses did not both have excellent evidence for such an empirical claim – if one or both of them merely felt religiously enthusiastic or had a fuzzy vision or vague experience – how likely is it that they would be able to influence one another to remain steadfast in their empirical testimony in the face of the likelihood of death? They are claiming not simply that Christianity is true but rather, concretely, to have seen the risen Jesus. They are the originators of this new religious movement, and others believe the distinctive claims of that movement such as "Jesus is Lord" on the basis of *their* testimony to an empirical fact, their physical encounters with the risen Jesus. This is emphatically not a case of their being committed to Christianity to the point of being willing to suffer martyrdom because they have taken someone else's word for its creedal claims, been raised in it as part of their religious or cultural identity, felt themselves part of a community, or anything of the sort. If any one of the witnesses in question had not actually had clear and realistic sensory experiences just as if Jesus were physically present, talking with them, eating before them, offering to let them inspect his hands and side and the like, it is not credible that he would listen to the urging of his fellows to remain steadfast in testifying to such experiences. To paraphrase Samuel Johnson, the credible threat of death concentrates the mind wonderfully; it tends to winnow the wheat from the chaff when it comes to good and bad evidence.

We must conclude that if the thirteen witnesses did influence one another to continue in their testimony, this positive influence itself is best explained by their really having seen and heard what they said they had seen and heard. Dependence among the thirteen's willingness to die arises in this context on the hypothesis that they all had excellent firsthand evidence that they were telling the truth and that they were encouraging one another not to give in to the fear of death and deny the truth to save themselves. In this case, as in the others, if we take a close look at the way that independence breaks down we find that R unifies the witnesses' persistence in the testimony they actually gave better than do the subhypotheses under ~R of religious enthusiasm or some sort of generic heavenly vision, though these factors might under *other* circumstances be expected to account for the willingness of a whole group of religious believers to die and for their influence over one another. Here again, the independence assumption underestimates the force of the argument for R.

It might be replied that we are assuming that under ~R the evidence is worse than under R. For the most part that is true, but there are two subhypotheses under ~R that have equal likelihood to R with respect to positive dependence among the witness of the thirteen: (1) the hypothesis that all thirteen of them just happened to have similar and absolutely convincing hallucinations as if of the risen Jesus – experiences *exactly like* those they would have had if he were really risen and appeared to them, spoke with them, offered to eat with them, and so forth – while R was in fact false, and (2) the specific version of the vision hypothesis (which we have called O*) that is just like hallucination in its phenomenological effects but with the added claim that these experiences were sent to the disciples by God or by Jesus in heaven.

We have already considered the hallucination hypothesis and rejected it as an enormously improbable subhypothesis under ~R. We have made a similar argument for O*; its ability to account for the evidence, like that of naturalistic hallucination, is purchased at the expense of its having only a negligible slice of the probability space under ~R. But the improbability of these theories is particularly manifest when we are asking them to provide an explanation not just of the fact of the witnesses' testimony as individuals but of their ability to encourage one another to maintain that testimony in the face of danger of death. For to explain that, such theories need to be the cousins of a Cartesian Evil Deceiver hypothesis where everything is "just as if" Jesus were really there and is just like that for all thirteen of the witnesses in question, sometimes when they are together and interacting with each other, and so forth. If such a hypothesis does not make everything evidentially just as if Jesus had really appeared physically, alive, after his resurrection as the disciples believed to be true, the problem already considered for religious enthusiasm and vaguer visions arises: witnesses who had unclear experiences are likely to ignore the urgings of their fellows and apostasize. If the urgings of A move B to hold firm regarding an explicit empirical claim, this is best explained by the assumption that B himself has had so clear and unequivocal an experience that he knows A is urging him to do what he ought to do anyway. And the same is true if A falters through fear and is encouraged by B.[37] The prohibitively low prior probability of these two hypotheses becomes especially clear if we assume and seek to explain an effect of mutual encouragement among that many witnesses.

In considering matters of explanatory power, it is important to keep in mind that if a subhypothesis H has a negligible prior probability under ~R, then even if H predicts the evidence with a high probability it will add little to the average probability of the evidence given ~R, which is what is relevant to the Bayes factor. An extreme hallucination theory or hallucination-like objective vision theory can unify the disciples' steadfastness and testimony as well as does R; but this gives little help to ~R as a whole in terms of unifying that testimony, because these theories are so improbable under ~R. Taking ~R as a whole, then, we conclude that the crucial inequality favors R: if we take into account the influence of the disciples on one another, the influence is of the sort more to be expected on the assumption of R than on the assumption of ~R. Hence, the independence assumption, which has already given us so overwhelming a Bayes factor for the testimony and steadfastness of the thirteen witnesses, has the effect of underestimating the force of their combined evidence.

Hume's Maxim and Worldview Worries

Historically, critics of the historical case for the resurrection have adopted two major strategies. The first is to engage with the evidence in detail – to dispute the facts on which a given version of the historical case is based, to offer an alternative, nonmiraculous explanation of the facts, or both. The second is to take an oblique approach – to stay out of the details and to look instead for very general considerations or abstract arguments that will undermine the historical case without requiring a direct engagement with the evidence. In the preceding pages we have addressed some of the primary moves associated with the first strategy. We now turn to the second.

The most famous instance of this strategy is Hume's essay "Of Miracles," first published in 1748. In part one, Hume lays out an argument that would undermine the rationality of belief in miracles on the basis of any testimony whatsoever. "A miracle," he explains,

> is a violation of the laws of nature; and as a firm and unalterable experience has established these laws, the proof against a miracle, from the very nature of the fact, is as entire as any argument from experience can possibly be imagined. . . . [I]t is a miracle, that a dead man should come to life; because that has never been observed in any age or country. There must, therefore, be a uniform experience against every miraculous event, otherwise the event would not merit that appellation. And as a uniform experience amounts to a proof, there is here a direct and full *proof*, from the nature of the fact, against the existence of any miracle; nor can such a proof be destroyed, or the miracle rendered credible, but by an opposite proof, which is superior. (Hume 1748, pp. 86–7)

---

37. The implausibility of such hallucinations or visions for all the witnesses is notable in a special way in the case of James Jesus' brother, who was not even with the other disciples at the time of the putative post-resurrection appearances. While the problem with their simultaneous experiences lies in part in the need for them all to be interacting with each other and with Jesus as if he were physically present when in fact he was not, the problem with James's conversion is that it would have had to happen, coincidentally, in virtue of a similar experience at about the same time.

The point here appears to be that a report of a miracle is, by definition, at an epistemic disadvantage; it is defined in terms that guarantee that there is a powerful, perhaps insuperable, case against it. In what Hume calls a "contest of two opposite experiences" (Hume 1748, p. 86), the testimony for a miracle and the testimony for the unbroken uniformity of natural law, the one that is "as entire as any argument from experience can possibly be imagined" can scarcely come off second best.

But the language of "contest of experiences" is misleading. There is direct testimony for the resurrection of Christ. The observation that dead men generally remain dead has a bearing on the probability of a resurrection in a particular case, but that bearing is indirect and inductive; it is by no means as strong as if all or even a few of these witnesses had directly observed the cold, lifeless, unmoving body of Jesus and opposed their testimony to that of the women and the disciples that he was *at that very moment* alive and well and talking to his disciples in Galilee. To be sure, the inductive evidence creates some presumption against the particular miracle report, but as the protagonist in Thomas Sherlock's *Tryal of the Witnesses of the Resurrection* points out, that presumption is not insuperable.

> Suppose you saw a Man publickly executed, his Body afterwards wounded by the Executioner, and carry'd and laid in the Grave; that after this you should be told, that the Man was come to Life again; what would you suspect in this Case? Not that the Man had never been dead, for that you saw yourself: But you would suspect whether he was now alive: But would you say this Case excluded all human Testimony, and that Men could not possibly discern whether one with whom they convers'd familiarly was alive or no? Upon what Ground could you say this? A Man rising from the Grave is an Object of Sense, and can give the same Evidence of his being alive, as any other Man in the World can give. So that a Resurrection considered only as a Fact to be prov'd by Evidence, is a plain Case; it requires no greater Ability in the Witnesses, than that they be able to distinguish between a Man dead and a Man alive; a Point, in which I believe every Man living thinks himself a Judge.
>
> I do allow that this Case, and others of like Nature, require more Evidence to give them Credit than ordinary Cases do; you may therefore require more Evidence in these, than in other Cases; but it is absurd to say, that such Cases admit no Evidence, when the Things in Question are manifestly Objects of Sense. (Sherlock 1765, pp. 63–4)

Hume concludes the first part of his essay with a "general maxim":

> [N]o testimony is sufficient to establish a miracle, unless the testimony be of such a kind, that its falsehood would be more miraculous, than the fact, which it endeavours to establish. (Hume 1748, p. 87)

This has a ring of profundity, but it is hardly a deep insight. The maxim turns out, on examination, to say nothing more than that for the event to believable, the testimony must render it more probable than not. As John Earman observes:

> All of the parties on the opposite side from Hume in the eighteenth-century debate on miracles knew that miracle claims could not be established without the help of very strong evidence. In some cases they thought they had produced the required evidence. Perhaps they were wrong. But to show that they were wrong takes more than solemnly uttered platitudes. (Earman 2000, p. 42)

Earman concludes that Hume, if he wished to undermine rationally the argument for the resurrection, was bound to do what he was most determined not to do – to "leave the high ground and descend into the trenches" and there to engage with the specific historical evidence for Christianity (Earman 2000, p. 70).

Earman argues persuasively that Hume's maxim, viewed probabilistically, is an innocuous truism (Earman 2000, pp. 38–43). But perhaps it is possible either to interpret Hume in some different way or, at least, to say something in the spirit of Hume that makes it unnecessary for the skeptic to descend into the trenches.

In a letter to Hugh Blair, Hume lets fall a comment that sheds some light on why he felt that there must be a sweeping dismissal of all miracle claims. "Does a man of sense," he asks, "run after every silly tale of witches or hobgoblins or fairies, and canvass particularly the evidence?" (Campbell 1839, p. 7; see Earman 2000, p. 59). The question appears to provide the handle the skeptic needs to turn Hume's maxim into something more than the statement that the evidence for a miracle needs to be enough to support belief in a miracle. If the tabloid in the supermarket checkout lane proclaims that little green men have descended on a Midwest corn field, captured several people, and declared their intention to take over planet Earth, most of us would understandably not waste our valuable time reading the testimony of the "witnesses"; even if they expressed their willingness to die in the attempt to save the world from the aliens, we would probably conclude that they were insane, running a scam of some sort, or had been taking hallucinogenic drugs at the time of the alleged incident.

Skeptics confronted with claims for the miraculous are likely to take a similar attitude, to think that they need not bother thinking too much about the specific evidence in specific instances, because the prior probability that a miracle would take place is so low that, as in the case of the alleged alien kidnapings, it is not worth their time to investigate any specific miracle claim. And even Christian apologists have been concerned to varying degrees by the possibility that the prior probability for a miracle might be "too low," making their attempts to argue for a particular revelation from God pointless.

One of the most moderate and philosophically careful statements of a concern of this sort comes from Richard Swinburne.

> Reports of observations are rightly viewed very sceptically when the phenomena purportedly observed are ruled out by a well-established scientific theory, but believed when they are to be expected in the light of such a theory. If you have a well-established theory which says that change does not occur in the heavenly regions . . . , you will rightly discount reports of observers on a particular occasion who claim to have observed a new star appear where there was no star before. (Swinburne 1992, p. 69)

There is no question here of Swinburne's saying that *no* evidence in favor of a revelation can overcome a prior probability that is "too low." Swinburne is too knowledgeable about probability theory to say anything of the sort; he confines himself merely to pointing out that revelation claims will require less in the way of specific evidence than they otherwise would require if there is evidence from natural theology that renders the prior probability of a miracle something better than abysmal.

Others, less knowledgeable about the probabilistic issues than Swinburne, have said in so many words that a successful natural theology *must* precede historical apologetics, because otherwise it would be impossible to argue for specific miracle claims.

> Natural theology shows that there is a God. If there is a God, miracles are possible. If a God exists who created the world and operates it, there can be no doubting that He can modify His *modus operandi*. On the other hand, if we did not know that there is a God, we would have to step into an irrational view of the operation of nature by chance.... [M]iracles cannot prove God. God, as a matter of fact, alone can prove miracles. That is, only on the prior evidence that God exists is a miracle even possible. (Sproul, Lindsley, & Gerstner 1984, p. 146)

Even allowing for the imprecision of the use of "prove" here, Sproul et al. appear to be making a simple scope error, confusing "not knowing that there is a God" with "knowing that there is not a God." Their claims about the necessity for a preliminary natural theology fall into place once that error is made but are simply unargued assertions without it. Yet the nagging worry may remain, even without the simple error – is it possible to argue for a specific miracle unless one has first, on the basis of prior evidence, shown to a tolerably high probability that God exists?

It is not only contemporary apologists like Sproul who have espoused strong views about the importance of one's prior stance towards the miraculous. In fact, those on the other side of the debate have made some of the strongest statements. Hume himself is no friend to natural theology; his maxim hardly amounts to an encouragement to apologists to prepare the ground for their arguments by doing natural theology. The Marquis de Laplace, implicitly echoing Hume, says of reported miracles, "There are things so extraordinary that nothing can balance their improbability" (Laplace 1840, p. 119). And J. L. Mackie, with explicit reference to Hume, says this:

> Here one party to the debate is initially at least agnostic, and does not yet concede that there is a supernatural power at all. From this point of view the intrinsic improbability of a genuine miracle . . . is very great, and one or other of the alternative explanations in our fork will always be much more likely – that is, either that the alleged event is not miraculous, or that it did not occur....
>
>   This entails that it is pretty well impossible that reported miracles should provide a worthwhile argument for theism addressed to those who are initially inclined to atheism or even to agnosticism.... Not only are such reports unable to carry any rational conviction on their own, but also they are unable even to contribute independently to the kind of accumulation or battery of arguments referred to in the Introduction. To this extent Hume is right . . . (Mackie 1982, p. 27)

Laplace and Mackie are not making merely descriptive statements about what the skeptic will think, about what is likely or unlikely to persuade. They are making claims about how the epistemic situation must be: If you do not believe in God, no argument can ever convince you otherwise.[38]

But what reason is there to think this to be true? Laplace and Mackie seem to be making something like Sproul's claim that one should consider miracles possible only if one already believes in God. The idea, if we translate it into probabilistic terms, seems to be that there is some cutoff point in the prior probability of a miracle that is "too low" for evidence – any evidence – to overcome, as though the slope the evidence has to climb becomes impossibly slippery once it is very steep. And the notion of a prior improbability that is too great to be overcome is, of course, very much in the spirit of Hume.

---

38. Similarly, Dale Allison insists that historical arguments for the resurrection are irrelevant when it comes to establishing a worldview (Allison 2005, p. 342).

Thus far, this is simply a vague intuition and one that, on its face, is probabilistically incorrect. For any real, nonzero prior improbability can be overcome by sufficient evidence. Virtually all of Hume's critics, and quite a number of the orthodox writers before Hume, stressed that there can be no insuperable presumption of this sort. There is, as Gladstone remarks, "no limit to the strength of working, as distinguished from abstract, certainty, to which probable evidence may not lead us along its gently ascending paths" (Gladstone 1896, p. 349; cf. Earman 2000, pp. 53ff).

To give the claim a better run for its money, we might turn instead to a probabilistic point made by Jordan Howard Sobel: When we are considering the question of whether a miracle has taken place, and when we are presented with what purports to be evidence for it, it is a necessary condition for the miracle's posterior probability, conditioned on that evidence, to be greater than 0.5 that

$$P(M|K) > P(\sim M \,\&\, E|K) \text{(Sobel 2004, p. 317)}.$$

In other words, the prior probability of the miracle must be greater than the prior probability that the miracle does not happen and that we also have the evidence in question. This inequality seems, at first glance, to place an enormous amount of epistemic pressure on the prior probability of a miracle and to cause worries for the apologist if that prior probability is "too low." After all, if we admit up front (as we should) that on ordinary background evidence M is less probable than $\sim$M for any given miracle, it might seem that the question then becomes, "How much less probable?" What if it is a great deal less probable? Does this not mean that it might be "too hard" for the only sort of evidence we can get to overcome so great a prior disparity?

Consider one version of Sobel's inequality, discussed by Earman, in which for simplicity's sake it has been taken that a witness's being deceived is the only way in which the witness could testify to a miraculous event if the event had not taken place (Earman 2000, pp. 47–8). "Deception" here apparently includes mistake, self-deception, or deliberate deception by others. Then, $P(D|\sim M \,\&\, K)$ is simply the same thing as $P(t(M)|\sim M \,\&\, K)$, where $t(M)$ means the testimony to a miracle. The upshot is a special case of Sobel's inequality such that, for the posterior probability of a miracle, conditioned on $t(M)$, to be greater than 0.5, it is a necessary condition that

$$P(M|K) > P(\sim M|K)P(D|\sim M \,\&\, K).$$

The term on the right is equal to $P(\sim M \,\&\, D|K)$, which is just the same as the right-hand term in the simpler version of Sobel's inequality, since the only way to have the evidence in the absence of the miracle under the given assumptions is for the witness to have been deceived. If the apologist acknowledges that the prior probability of $\sim$M is very high, the only way for this inequality to hold is if the probability that the witness mistakenly believes a miracle to have occurred is extremely low. Once we have acknowledged that the prior probability of a miracle is low, does it not seem irrational to consider it to be higher than the probability that a witness will be deceived?

But a skeptic who wishes to make that claim cannot remain "above the fray." We have argued above that, given the Bayes factors of the various pieces of evidence, their cumulative impact would overcome a prior probability of R of 10^{-40} while leaving us with a posterior probability of approximately 0.9999. Even an exceptionally low prior may be overcome by extremely strong evidence. That argument deserves to be answered on its own terms, and it illustrates quite handily the fact that there is no such thing as a finite prior probability that is so low as to be "slippery" and hence impossible to overcome by evidence.

Certainly, a major point in the defense of the Bayes factors we have assigned is the extremely low probability of the specific evidence in question given ~R, and this includes the very poor showing for explaining the evidence in question of hypotheses in which the witnesses were "deceived" – that is, mistaken or self-deceived – in thinking that they saw the risen Christ over the course of 40 days. But this question can be decided only by considering the *specific* testimonial evidence in question under the *specific* circumstances. We are not considering in the abstract the probability that some miracle or other will fail to occur and that some witness or other under unspecified circumstances will mistakenly think that a miracle has happened. We must always be concerned with the specific evidence and the specific circumstances. The mere fact that we are, as it were, looking ahead and imagining the probability that the resurrection does not occur and that we have the testimonial evidence in question does not mean that we are considering the matter in an abstract fashion.

Moreover, the Sobel inequality does not really give us very much epistemic insight, if only because it is a necessary but not a sufficient condition for the posterior probability of a miracle to be greater than 0.5, a fact also noted by Earman (2000, p. 40) in rejecting it as an interpretation of Hume. If, for example, P(E|M) were equal to or even lower than P(E|~M), conditioning on E would not raise M to a posterior probability greater than 0.5.

Recall the odds form of Bayes's Theorem, as applied to a miracle and some putative evidence for it:

$$\frac{P(M|E)}{P(\sim M|E)} = \frac{P(M)}{P(\sim M)} \times \frac{P(E|M)}{P(E|\sim M)}$$

What must do the work in raising the probability of M from a poor prior to a respectable or even imposing posterior is the ratio of the likelihoods – the second ratio on the right. It is true that, if the posterior probability of M is greater than 0.5, this entails the satisfaction of Sobel's inequality. But the force of the argument comes from the ratio of the likelihoods, and if that ratio is sufficient to make the posterior of M greater than 0.5, this merely means that the Bayes factor has brought about the satisfaction of that inequality *ambulando*, because the evidence makes a strong argument for M.

We shall learn very little from staring at the Sobel inequality and asking ourselves whether the prior probability of M is greater or less than the prior probability that some witness will be mistaken or even will commit fraud. For one thing, such a procedure, by considering only an inequality and not either the force of the evidence (via a Bayes factor analysis) or any specific prior probability for R, caters to our biases either for or against a miracle. The theist or Christian may think the argument stronger than it is if he simply has to consider whether it is more probable that the witness gave his testimony falsely or that a miracle occurred. Similarly, the skeptic may casually say that he will *always* consider the inequality to fail to be satisfied for any testimonial evidence. If we focus instead, as our argument here has done, on the force of the evidence itself, the skeptic is forced to ask himself whether he really considers the prior probability of the resurrection of Jesus Christ to be lower than something like 10^{-43} – and if so, why.

Moreover, anyone who contemplates this inequality without considering exactly what the testimonial evidence is and exactly what sort of circumstances are supposed to attend it is almost certain to misevaluate the resultant probability. According to Mackie, even a skeptic who seemed to see a miracle with his own eyes would have to leave open the possibility that his senses were deceived, "as anyone knows who has ever been fooled by a conjurer" (Mackie 1982, p. 28). But no one is foolish enough actually to claim that someone was working a David Copperfield-style magic trick to deceive the disciples into thinking that Jesus was risen. The allusion to magic is irrelevant to the resurrection; and to ask in general terms whether it is likely that a miracle will not occur but someone will be deceived, perhaps by a conjurer's trick, is a piece of misdirection. The question, rather, must be this: What is the probability that Jesus will not rise from the dead and that, nonetheless, women will testify that his tomb is empty and that they have seen him, thirteen men will all be willing to die for the claim that they have seen him, spoken with him, and received enormous amounts of direct empirical evidence for his physical resurrection over a period of 40 days, and a persecutor of his followers will suddenly, upon what he claims to have been a vision of the resurrected Jesus, become an ardent preacher of the Christian message? And what is the probability that all of this will happen in a first-century Jewish context, with all that that means in terms of lack of resources for a convincing fraud, probable death for such claims, low opinion of the testimony of women, and all the rest of the details? In other words, the skeptic must examine, in detail, the relative explanatory power of R and ~R for the *specific* evidence in its *actual* context.

Here Earman's self-deprecating reference to his own cynicism is also relevant. Though he has argued at length and with care and accuracy that there is no in-principle argument against the establishment of a miracle by testimony, Earman comments that his one agreement with Hume is that he, like Hume, is personally disinclined to examine in detail evidence for specific miracle claims, even evidence given by multiple witnesses. Rather charmingly, he acknowledges that this disinclination cannot be given any *a priori* philosophical underpinning and does not yield any lofty principle to guide inquiry. But it is interesting nonetheless to see the form his skepticism takes. He analogizes UFO abduction stories, religious miracle claims, and the subset of the latter involving witnesses at faith healing services, and says that he is personally inclined to think of all of these as involving "a palpable atmosphere of collective hysteria that renders the participants unable to achieve the minimal reliability condition" (Earman 2000, pp. 59–61).

The minimal reliability condition as Earman defines it is the requirement that the Bayes factor for the evidence of a witness's testimony favors M (the occurrence of the miracle) over ~M (Earman 2000, p. 55). Earman's own reference to the atmosphere – the surrounding circumstances – of a faith healing service is itself the key to the apologist's answer to his brand of cynicism. For, as we have pointed out repeatedly, the witnesses who claimed to have seen the risen Jesus were *not* in a state of palpable excitement or enthusiastic hysteria at the time; they were not attending a meeting where they expected to see wonders. On the contrary, the women were going to anoint a dead body, and the disciples were hiding in fear and showed themselves notably skeptical of claims that Jesus was risen. If we accept at all the evidence that these people claimed to have seen the risen Jesus, we must do so on the basis of textual sources that give us strong evidence against the hypothesis that they worked themselves into a frenzy of expectation and, as a result, suffered detailed and sustained hallucinations. In other words, the "reliability" of witnesses is perhaps a slightly confusing term. We should speak rather of the explanatory power of the hypothesis that the event took place. This will be in part a function of what else we may happen to know about the probity of the given witness, but it will also be in no small degree a function of the various alternative subhypotheses available to explain what, specifically, the witnesses said in the specific circumstances in question. The Bayes factor involves an evaluation of all of these, and it is for this reason that Earman says, quite rightly,

> I acknowledge that the opinion is of the kind whose substantiation requires not philosophical argumentation and pompous solemnities about extraordinary claims requiring extraordinary proofs, but rather difficult and delicate empirical investigations . . . into the details of particular cases. (Earman 2000, p. 61)

All of which brings us back to the attempt to back off from these details by reference to other claims of wonders. The modern version of Hume's comment to Hugh Blair is the skeptic's scornful challenge to the apologist, "So, are you going to examine the specific evidence for every UFO abduction claim?" And the answer is that even a cursory understanding of what is involved in such stories shows them to have no such claim on our investigative time as does the evidence for the resurrection of Jesus Christ. Is anyone stoned, crucified, or killed with the sword for claiming that he has been given a tour of a space ship? The explanatory power of fraud is, on the face of it, enormously higher for the sort of evidence we have in those cases than for the evidence for the resurrection of Christ.

The Christian need never claim that testimony as such, testimony to any event under any circumstances and in any context, has a claim on our attention and belief. He should always draw attention to the striking and powerful nature of the specific testimony for the central miracle of his own faith. As Jacques Saurin (1843, vol. 1, p. 193) said, after canvassing particularly the evidence for the resurrection, "Was ever joy so rational?"

Plantinga's Principle of Dwindling Probabilities

One of the few novel probabilistic objections to the historical argument for Christianity has come in recent years from renowned Christian philosopher Alvin Plantinga in the form of a probabilistic strategy based on what he calls the Principle of Dwindling Probabilities (PDP) (Plantinga 2000, pp. 268–80).

Plantinga attempts to show roughly the probabilistic form that, in his view, the historical argument for Christianity takes, with the intention of arguing that it cannot bear the weight apologists have given it. His version of the historical argument chains together a series of propositions, assigning each one some probability which he considers generous, and treating the calculation of the conditional probability of one proposition on another or a set of others as an argumentative step. In this attempted reconstruction, Plantinga starts with our background knowledge K, which he defines as "what we all or nearly all know or take for granted or firmly believe, or what at any rate those conducting the inquiry know or take for granted or believe." He next considers the bare theistic claim that

T: God exists

and for the sake of the argument assigns it a probability of at least 0.9, conditional on K. Then he considers the probability (always relative to our background) that, given T,

A: God would want to make some sort of revelation of Himself to mankind.

Granting this as well, Plantinga moves on to

B: Jesus' teachings were such that they could be sensibly interpreted and extrapolated to G, the great claims of the gospel,

where G includes central Christian teachings about sin, the incarnation, the atonement, and the general availability of salvation. Supposing K, T, A, and B, he next considers the probability that

C: Jesus rose from the dead.

Now taking K, T, A, B, and C together, he assesses

D: In raising Jesus from the dead, God endorsed his teachings.

Finally, conditional on K, T, A, B, C, and D, Plantinga considers the probability of the conclusion

E: The extension and extrapolation of Jesus' teachings to G is true.

Plantinga's contention is that, since the connections between and among these propositions are nondeductive, we must consider the possibility of a breakdown in the chain at every point. Hence he multiplies the probabilities he has estimated using the Theorem on Total Probability and obtains a value just a bit over 0.21. He therefore concludes that the most we are entitled to say is that $P(E|K) \geq 0.21$. And since he considers his probability assignments for individual propositions to have erred on the side of generosity, he thinks that this is if anything an overestimate of the value of the historical argument for the truth of Christianity. "Our background knowledge, historical and otherwise," Plantinga concludes, "isn't anywhere nearly sufficient to support serious belief in G" (Plantinga 2000, p. 280).

But Plantinga's version of the historical argument has some peculiar features that make the case appear weaker than it really is. In understanding what is wrong with Plantinga's approach both to portraying and to critiquing the historical argument, we shall come to see better the relationship of the historical argument to natural theology and to theism.

The attempt to apply the PDP to the historical argument depends crucially on the issue of inference. How and why does Plantinga treat theism as a premise for Christianity? And how is this picture of the inference incomplete and, hence, confusing regarding the ultimate strength of the case?

To understand why it seems to Plantinga that the PDP is relevant to the historical case, consider the general procedure by which one views a set of evidence and a conclusion through the lens of the PDP. Begin with some proposition A that is positively relevant to some other proposition B but that is strictly weaker than B – that is, B entails A but not *vice versa*. Pick propositions A and B such that one could plausibly consider the weaker proposition A as a premise in an argument for the stronger proposition B. Note that, on ordinary background evidence, A will be more probable than B and hence P(A) will set an upper bound on P(B). Estimate, off the cuff, a probability for A on total evidence, trying in some vague fashion to be generous in this estimate. Treating A as a premise for B, construct an argument consisting of a chain of propositions leading from A to B. Apply the Theorem on Total Probability to show that the lower bound of an inequality representing P(B) on total evidence can end up much, much lower than the original probability estimated for A. Point out triumphantly that, once one has made such a "generous" guess at A's probability on all evidence, it is all downhill from there (see McGrew & McGrew 2006, p. 30).

In Plantinga's example concerning the historical argument, the simpler proposition with which he starts is the assertion of mere theism (T), and the conclusion (E) is the truth of G, which we might call mere Christianity. As in the strategy just sketched, Christianity does entail theism but not *vice versa*, so that in a single consistent probability distribution, the probability of theism puts an upper bound on the probability of Christianity. And the 0.21 lower bound of the inequality Plantinga eventually obtains is indeed a good deal lower than the 0.9 he has originally estimated for theism on total probability. Since Plantinga gives us only an inequality, one might initially think that this means very little; a mere inequality is compatible with there being a much higher actual probability for Christianity, supported by the public evidence. But since Christianity entails several of the propositions in Plantinga's chain (T, A, and C), the inequality seems to have something more than a merely formal significance.[39]

Plantinga treats not only theism but also the other propositions he concatenates as premises for Christianity, and in response to the suggestion that the independent evidence for the resurrection itself supports theism and that therefore inferential support of the resurrection for theism must be taken into account, he insists that the inference must go from theism to the resurrection (Plantinga 2006, pp. 13–4).

Since this matter of premises is so central to an understanding of what is wrong with the use of the PDP in this context, we need to see clearly what it means to say that theism is a premise for the resurrection (or for Christianity) and that the resurrection is a premise for theism. And to understand those relations, we need to understand more about the use of uncertain intermediate premises – intermediate, that is, between foundational beliefs and conclusions – in nondeductive arguments.

When an uncertain premise comes between foundational beliefs and some conclusion to which it is relevant, either positively or negatively, we ought to regard that premise as a conduit to the conclusion of independent evidence from elsewhere in the probability distribution. The notion of a conduit here is a delicate one in its technical details. But roughly, and speaking only of simple cases, a conduit is a proposition that is epistemically relevant to the conclusion and that, with its negation, "screens off" the probabilistic effect of some other relevant evidence on the conclusion in question. Screening off is a relation of probabilistic independence between two propositions *modulo* some other proposition or its negation. Formally, B screens off E from A just in case

---

39. For a more detailed discussion of the structure of Plantinga's attempted reconstruction, see McGrew (2004). It was noted there that his D is not entailed by Christianity (p. 13). We note here that his B is also not entailed by Christianity and that even without the record we have in the Gospels of Jesus' own teachings while on earth, to which B presumably refers, we would still have other evidence in the other parts of the New Testament, especially Acts and the epistles (combined with the evidence for Jesus' resurrection) for the propositions in G. Hence there would plausibly be a non-negligible probability for the propositions in G even if B were false.

$$P(A|\pm B \& E) = P(A|\pm B).$$

Take, for example, the proposition that Jesus rose from the dead. Plausibly and on the background evidence we are assuming here, this proposition is a conduit to the proposition that God exists of the evidential force of (say) Peter's assertion that Jesus rose from the dead. If we were given at probability 1 that Jesus rose from the dead, then being given in addition the proposition that Peter said that Jesus rose from the dead would not change the probability of theism. It would add nothing further. Similarly, if we were given with probability 1 that Jesus did not rise from the dead, adding to our evidential corpus the proposition that Peter said Jesus rose from the dead would make no difference to theism. Its evidential impact on theism is exhausted by its support for the proposition that Jesus really did rise from the dead. Moreover, the proposition that Jesus rose from the dead is probabilistically relevant to theism, as is the proposition that Peter said that Jesus rose from the dead. So the proposition that Jesus rose from the dead is a conduit to theism of the evidence of the testimony of the apostles. It is a premise for theism, then, in the sense that it conveys to theism the relevant evidential force of other information.[40]

But we have no stake in denying that theism is also, as a conduit of *other* evidence, a premise for the resurrection and also for Christianity. Theism can be a premise for Christianity both because it is probabilistically relevant to Christianity and because there is independent evidence, relevant to mere theism and also to Christianity, that theism screens off from Christianity. Consider, for example, the specific design argument made by advocates of intelligent design from the origin of life – the argument, say, that the first living cell was probably designed. The existence of God exhausts the relevance to Christianity of the argument from the design of the cell, and in this way the existence of God is a conduit to Christianity of whatever evidential force that argument has. And we can say the same for any evidence provided by the existence of a physical universe as used in, for example, the *Kalam* cosmological argument. These propositions are evidence for Christianity *by way of* their being evidence for theism. It is correct to say that, in this sense, theism is a premise for the resurrection. The advocate of Christianity should be pleased if there is at least some independent reason to believe theism, as this will raise the prior probability for the resurrection.

There are, then, different lines of evidence both for theism and for the resurrection, and we cannot get a good fix on the probability of either proposition on total evidence unless we consider all of the relevant lines of argument. There is evidence channeled to theism by the resurrection and evidence channeled to the resurrection by theism.

This point is related to the strategy Richard Swinburne follows when he argues for Christianity in stages, discussing, when he comes to miraculous revelations by God, the question of whether there is "other evidence" that would make theism probable (Swinburne 1992, pp. 69–70). "Other evidence" here means evidence for theism *other than* that which is directly pertinent to some specific revelation and pertinent to theism only by way of its pertinence to the occurrence of that revelatory event. Swinburne's diachronic or staged argument is one clean way of separating out lines of evidence and avoiding confusion,

---

40. The strong foundationalist will hold that all uncertain propositions involved in arguments are either conduits or, in more complicated cases, part of a set of propositions that make up a complex conduit "node," and that the evidential force conveyed by conduit premises to conclusions comes ultimately from certain foundations (see McGrew & McGrew 2008).

because each line is brought in by itself and all probabilities are updated each time using Bayes's Theorem.[41]

All of this helps us to see Plantinga's blunder in trying to bring his PDP to bear on Christianity. Plantinga's focus on the Theorem on Total Probability is central to the whole strategy of the PDP, which can be applied only when the probabilities of all propositions are fixed. Once one allows for updating on new evidence, all bets are off, as a new set of coherent probabilities will be generated every time one updates, and the initial estimate of the probability of theism on some minimal background evidence will constitute no upper bound on the probability of either theism or Christianity after all updates have taken place and all pertinent evidence is taken into account.

There would be nothing wrong with Plantinga's pointing out that the prior probability of theism is relevant to the prior probability of the resurrection. Yet Plantinga is not content to assert this. He resolutely and repeatedly insists that the probability of theism *on total evidence* must be found *first*, before considering the resurrection (Plantinga 2006, p. 13). He is thus saying that we must find, or at least estimate, the probability of theism on total evidence while deliberately setting aside the pertinent – and possibly very strong – evidence that bears on theism by way of its impact on the resurrection, a procedure nearly guaranteed to give us a probability different from the real probability of theism on total evidence. The only clear-eyed way to proceed when contemplating two mutually relevant propositions is to examine in as much detail as possible the various lines of evidence pertinent, directly or indirectly, to each of them.

Plantinga's most recent argument for such a strategy is unpersuasive:

According to the theorem on total probability

$$P(C|K) = [P(C|K \& T) \times P(T|K)] + [P(C|K \& {\sim}T) \times P({\sim}T|K)].$$

If $P(C|K\&{\sim}T)$ is very low, the second term on the right side will contribute very little, in which case $P(C|K)$ will be very close to $P(C|K\&T) \times P(T|K)$; and that means that $P(T|K)$ will be close to an upper bound on $P(C|K)$. So suppose you're agnostic about theism; you assign both T and ${\sim}T$ a probability of .5; and suppose furthermore you think theism and naturalism are the only real options. Then, even if you think the probability of the resurrection on K&T is very high – .9999, for example – you'll have to assign it a probability close to .5 on K. Under those conditions, once more, we might say that belief in C presupposes belief in T. If so, one couldn't sensibly believe C without believing or at any rate assigning a high probability to T – but not because there is a natural inference from C to T. (Plantinga 2006, p. 14)

This argument has a familiar sound; it is Plantinga's version of the "worldview" objection we considered in the previous section, with the difference that Plantinga's probabilistic formulation attempts to do without any distinction between prior and posterior probabilities and to use only the Theorem on Total Probability. But the only cash value of the argument lies in the formal truism that the probability of theism on total evidence sets something

---

41. But we need to stress that there is no sense in which the different lines of evidence become indistinguishable when all evidence is taken into account and considered synchronically. Even then, different lines of argument are distinct, because both the screening and relevance relations still hold. This point means, as we shall see, that the PDP is not relevant to the historical argument for Christianity, whether we think of it in diachronic or synchronic terms.

close to an upper bound on the probability of the resurrection on total evidence. This means nothing as to whether belief in the resurrection "presupposes" belief in theism or whether, as Plantinga says, "[O]ne must first determine the value of $P(T|K)$, or at least determine that it equals or exceeds some reasonably high probability" (Plantinga 2006, p. 13).[42]

Consider how Plantinga's argument would apply to two other propositions.

A: Alvin Plantinga exists.
B: Alvin Plantinga sent me an email on March 3, 2007.

Here we can go Plantinga one better, for B entails A, and so the probability of A in a coherent probability distribution sets an absolute upper bound on the probability of B. Let us suppose that, on the morning of March 3, 2007, you have never heard of Alvin Plantinga as a real person, never read any of his books or articles, and have no other specific evidence regarding his existence. Suppose that we attach to the name "Alvin Plantinga" a Russellian definite description like "A philosopher of religion, presently teaching at Notre Dame, who is known for his development of a school of thought known as Reformed Epistemology." You might be able, with effort, to come up with a probability for A based on extremely general considerations such as whether the first and last names are common or uncommon, how many philosophers there are in the world and at Notre Dame, and the like, but this is all. And the probability you would come up with would plausibly be well below 0.5, given the specificity of the description.

But on the evening of March 3, you sit down at your computer, access your email, and up comes a note from someone introducing himself as Alvin Plantinga, describing himself more or less as in the definite description, and asking you a question about something or other.

It would be folly to argue for B by first, and without considering B itself, guessing at the final probability of A on total evidence. Why estimate this first, without considering the highly pertinent evidence that you now have that bears on B directly and bears on A by way of B? Who would ever argue for B in this manner under these circumstances? While your vague independent evidence concerning A has bearing on B – on the prior probability of B – the far more powerful argument is the experience of reading the email note itself, and you would naturally and immediately argue for B by considering this direct evidence. Certainly, if Alvin Plantinga does not exist, he cannot be sending you email; but here, apparently, is the note itself.

Beyond the sheer oddity of guessing at the probability of A on total evidence before considering B, it would be a terrible blunder if you actually took as $P(A)$ on total evidence the probability it had in the morning and treated that as an upper bound on the probability for B. This would be flatly wrong, for both A and B must now be reevaluated on the strong evidence supporting B directly and A indirectly.

So despite the fact that A sets an upper bound on the probability of B and that the prior probability of A influences the prior probability of B, it simply is not true that belief in B

---

42. Nor, though Plantinga attempts once more to attribute this reasoning to Swinburne, is it Swinburne's reasoning, since what Swinburne considers "first" – as he has made clear repeatedly – is the probability of theism on independent evidence, not on total evidence (see Swinburne 2003, pp. 30–1; 2004, pp. 541–2). Swinburne has also emphasized this point repeatedly, in public at the SCP Pacific Division meeting (Biola University, February, 2004) and in personal communication with us and with Plantinga.

"presupposes" belief in A in the sense that the prior probability of A – its probability on the morning of March 3 – must be higher than some particular cutoff for one to believe B on the evening of March 3. Nor does it follow from the fact that B entails A but not *vice versa* that one must find the probability of A on total evidence before one can consider B.

In most of our interactions with ordinary people, our strongest evidence for their existence is the direct evidence for the things they have done and said – for what we might call their revelations of themselves. A really scrupulous Bayesian might insist on calculating first the prior probability for someone's existence based on general considerations and then updating it on the more interesting evidence for the person's actions, but so reflective and careful a Bayesian would never claim that the prior probability was, except by chance, at all like the probability for the person's existence on *total* evidence. Nor would it be a plausible strategy simply to guess at the final probability of a person's existence before considering available evidence for some act of his in the world.

In the case of the existence of God, a lot of argumentative action has taken place, both for and against, before we come to consider the resurrection or any other putative miracles or revelations. The logical problem of evil is brought up against God's existence; the apologist counters with the free will defense. The probabilistic problem of evil is brought up next; the apologist asks for a rigorous formulation and criticizes those given. The apologist brings forward the teleological or the moral or the ontological argument for God's existence; the skeptic counters. If one has studied this literature at all, or even engaged in late-night dorm-room arguments, one is bound to have some sort of probability for theism independent of the direct evidence for the resurrection. And this probability, whether high, low, or somewhere in the middle, will at least be more definite than is the imagined prior probability for Plantinga's existence on the morning of March 3.

But none of this argumentative back-and-forth should obscure the fact that all of these arguments concern the evidence about God's existence *independent of* the direct, historical evidence for the resurrection. Suppose that that evidence is extremely strong, as we have argued. By formal and semantic considerations we can see that it is pertinent to theism. But in that case we shall be far wide of the mark if we try to make a just approximation of the final probability of theism *before* considering the resurrection. And it would be irrational to assume at the outset and before considering the evidence for the resurrection – as Plantinga's hypothetical agnostic does – that in the final analysis theism will have a probability of 0.5. Even Plantinga's supposedly "generous" 0.9 estimate for the probability of theism on all evidence (Plantinga 2000, p. 274) is the merest guess and was quite deliberately made without consideration of the actual strength of the independent historical evidence. Who knows, under those conditions, whether it was generous or not? How could one possibly know?

So it becomes evident that there is no "Principle of Dwindling Probabilities" that shows the historical argument for Christianity or for the resurrection to be weak. There is nothing for it but to consider the empirical arguments on their merits.

Knavery, Folly, and the Love of Wonder

In the previous two sections, we have examined two manifestations of what we have called the oblique approach to critiquing the historical argument – the claim that the prior probability for the resurrection is so low that the specific evidence need not be examined and

Alvin Plantinga's attempt to undermine the historical argument by means of the Principle of Dwindling Probabilities. Now we turn to a slightly less abstract approach, one that at least makes reference to some historical matters, in the second part of Hume's essay.

Though Hume's treatment in part two is not on quite so abstract a level as the argument of part one, it is still quite general; it consists of little more than an assortment of general considerations and a few examples of alleged miracles designed to cast the evidence for the Gospel miracles in an unfavorable light. Most of his objections are not very fully developed, and several of them are derivative, having been exhaustively discussed in the deist controversy over the preceding decades (Burns 1981). But since the first part of the essay provides no cogent independent line of argument, the success of Hume's critique rests entirely on the considerations he advances here.

"[I]t is easy to shew," he writes, ". . . that there never was a miraculous event established on so full an evidence" as to "amount to an entire proof." Here he makes four claims that might serve as the premises of arguments:

1. that the witnesses to a miracle (it is clear that he has the apostles in mind) have never been sufficiently credible or numerous and the event has never been done in a prominent enough part of the world;
2. that the passion of surprise and wonder moves people to accept a miracle report in contradiction to their common sense;
3. that reports of miracles "are observed chiefly to abound among ignorant and barbarous nations" but live on in civilized society only because they were handed down from "ignorant and barbarous ancestors"; and
4. that reports of miracles in various opposing religions, if accepted as of equal credit, would cross-cancel each other, leaving all of the competing religious claims equally unsupported.

Neither singly nor taken together do these four considerations do the work Hume claims that they will.

In articulating the first consideration, Hume assures us that

> there is not to be found, in all history, any miracle attested by a sufficient number of men, of such unquestioned good sense, education, and learning, as to secure us against all delusion in themselves; of such undoubted integrity, as to place them beyond all suspicion of any design to deceive others; of such credit and reputation in the eyes of mankind, as to have a great deal to lose in case of their being detected in any falsehood; and at the same time, attesting facts, performed in such a public manner, and in so celebrated a part of the world, as to render the detection unavoidable: All which circumstances are requisite to give us a full assurance in the testimony of men. (Hume 1748, p. 88)

This is a bald assertion, question begging if taken at face value. The orthodox opponents of the deists were quite familiar with such objections and had argued at length and with force that the testimony of the apostles met every reasonable standard of evidence one could require. Responding to Annet's skeptical attack on Sherlock's *Tryal*, Samuel Chandler writes:

> [A]ll the Characters of Integrity appear in these Writers, that can possibly be demanded or desired. The very Inconsistencies that at first View they seem to be chargeable with, shew at

least there was no Contrivance amongst them, to deceive others. They make no Scruple to tell us, that the first Appearances of Christ were to a few Women, with whose single Testimony they well knew the World would be far from being satisfied. They seem to have concealed no Circumstances of Christ's Appearances, however exceptionable they might possibly be in some Mens Opinion and Judgment. They plainly assure us, that the Disciples imagin'd the first Accounts of the Resurrection, to be mere Dreams and Tales, and unsupported imaginations, and were not in the least disposed to receive or credit them. It doth not appear that they could have any present Interests to answer, by the Accounts they gave, if they had not known them to be true; or that they were set on to write them by Persons, who either could reward them, or receive themselves any worldly Advantages from the Publication of those Accounts to others. . . .

Now though 'tis scarce possible to conceive how any one Person could be deceived in the Proof that was given of the Resurrection, yet were they all deceived? What, was there not one of the Apostles, not one of those who were with them, not one of the Hundred and Twenty, or Five Hundred, that had Eyes to see, or Ears to hear, or Hands to feel, or Judgment to discern? Were they all deluded with a fantastick Appearance, and the Senses of such a Variety of Persons all absolutely imposed on, and deceived? What Credibility is there in such a Supposition? Or did they all agree to support a Lye, a known Lye, an incredible, obnoxious, and dangerous Lye? A few might have kept the important Secret, had the whole Affair been a Fraud. But could such a Secret ever be preserved where so large a Number was privy to it? Were they so steady and true to a Falsehood, as that neither Interest nor Persecution could move them to discover it? (Chandler 1744, pp. 133, 141–2)

Notably, Chandler makes these remarks only in summary after he has spent more than a hundred pages surveying and addressing the objections of adversaries to the credibility of the Gospel account of the resurrection and the character of the witnesses in particular. And this is only one of the works in which Chandler develops the historical argument. Measured against this standard, Hume's bare assertion counts for nothing.

The second and third *a posteriori* considerations are similarly derivative and ineffective. Hume sketches the second in these words:

[W]hen anything is affirmed utterly absurd and miraculous, [the mind] rather the more readily admits of such a fact, upon account of that very circumstance, which ought to destroy all its authority. The passion of surprise and wonder, arising from miracles, being an agreeable emotion, gives a sensible tendency towards the belief of those events, from which it is derived. And this goes so far, that even those who cannot enjoy this pleasure immediately, nor can believe those miraculous events, of which they are informed, yet love to partake of the satisfaction at second-hand or by rebound, and place a pride and delight in exciting the admiration of others. (Hume 1748, pp. 88–9)

In this bit of armchair psychologizing, Hume had been anticipated by Thomas Morgan:

Men are the more easily imposed on in such Matters, as they love to gratify the Passion of *Admiration*, and take a great deal of Pleasure in hearing or telling of Wonders. (Morgan 1738, p. 31)

But as a criticism of the resurrection, this banal observation is too blunt an instrument to do any damage. The love of wonder may cause people to listen eagerly to the wild tales of travelers, but as John Gorham Palfrey notes in his Lowell Lectures, there is a limit to what may be explained by this principle; everyone knows for himself that it would not be sufficient to make him accept such a story as the resurrection

> without inquiry and full proof, when the consequence would be, as unquestionably it was with the early Christians, that he must devote himself to a new course of life, relinquish old friendships and associations, undertake unaccustomed labors, and face a host of appalling dangers. (Palfrey 1843, pp. 293–4)

As for Hume's third consideration, the claim that miracles are readily received among the barbarous had been made by the deist John Toland in his work *Christianity not Mysterious*, and in the very words that Hume was to borrow:

> [i]t is very observable, that the more ignorant and barbarous any People remain, you shall find 'em most abound with Tales of this nature . . . (Toland 1702, p. 148)

But to call first-century Judaism "ignorant and barbarous" would be itself historically ignorant, and to suggest that this absolves us of taking the testimony of the eyewitnesses seriously is a classic example of trying to dismiss evidence without doing any actual argumentative work. Nor was first-century Judea, which had been a Greek possession for three centuries before the Romans took charge of it, such a backwater as Hume would have his readers suppose.

In order to overcome the arguments advanced in detail by writers like Chandler, Jacob Vernet, Thomas Stackhouse, Thomas Sherlock, John Leland, and Nathaniel Lardner, Hume would have had to descend into the fray and sort through the evidence. This was a trial that he was by no means fitted to endure. Instead, as John Earman writes,

> Hume pretends to stand on philosophical high ground, hurling down thunderbolts against miracle stories. . . . When Hume leaves the philosophical high ground to evaluate particular miracle stories, his discussion is superficial and certainly does not do justice to the extensive and vigorous debate about miracles that had been raging for several decades in Britain. (Earman 2000, p. 70)

Earman's judgment is proved correct when we look at Hume's fourth consideration, where he discusses actual miracle stories in an attempt to show that all miracle claims are on a par and are alike unsupported. Setting believers in miracles by the ears was a favorite tactic of many of the deists (Burns 1981, pp. 72–5). At the beginning of the deist controversy Charles Leslie had already proposed four marks by which genuine miracles might be distinguished from spurious ones; and throughout the whole of the deist controversy both before and after Hume there was, among the Protestants, a vigorous industry elaborating the means for separating out the apostolic wheat from the Papistical chaff.

Hume uses the trope of setting religious believers against one another to force an implicit dilemma upon the Christian apologist: Either accept all of these miracle stories as true or abandon belief in the resurrection of Jesus Christ. The first option will be unpalatable to the English Protestant apologists because the miracle story in question arises from some pagan religion, because it arises in Roman Catholicism, or because the story appears manifestly fraudulent.

But in pressing this line of argument, Hume refrains from responding to the actual evidence put forward in favor of the miracles of the Gospels, and the resurrection in particular, and instead focuses attention on an entirely different set of miracles which he expects his reader to find implausible. His critics were not slow in pointing out the evasion, but none put the point more vigorously than Peter Bayne:

> "When any one," proceeds Hume, "tells me that he saw a dead man restored to life, I immediately consider with myself whether it be more probable that this person should either deceive or be deceived, or that the fact which he relates should really have happened. I weigh the one miracle against the other; and according to the superiority which I discover, I pronounce my decision, and always reject the greater miracle. If the falsehood of his testimony would be more miraculous than the event which he relates, then, and not till then, can he pretend to demand my belief or opinion."
>
> Exactly; no statement could be more reasonable. Let us proceed, then, to the comparison. The Christian has to produce testimony to miracle whose falsehood would be a mightier wonder than the miracle attested, and Hume has to weigh miracle against miracle.
>
> What was the next step to be taken in Hume's argument? What did his own statement require him to do? Clearly, to take up the miracles which Christians allege to be true; to set their evidence fully and distinctly forth; and to point out that, however plausible that evidence might be, its fallaciousness would be no miracle compared with the miracle it affirmed. This, I say, is what the law on the case, as laid down by Hume, required; this is what, in his own court of evidence, Hume prescribed.
>
> But every reader of Hume's Essay knows that he has done nothing of the sort. The nature of the evidence required for the Christian miracles once fairly stated, those miracles are quietly put by him out of court. The trial proceeds by proxy. Hume does not ask what proof is offered that the Christian miracles took place; he calls to the bar certain "miracles" with which Christianity has nothing to do, enters upon their evidence, condemns them as falsities, and then calmly informs the court that the Christian miracles are disproven. Vespasian, according to Tacitus, performed two miraculous cures; the Cardinal de Retz mentions a "miracle" of the reality of which he was assured; and sundry prodigies are said to have taken place at the grave of the Abbe Paris. These last, Hume informs us, "might, with some appearance of reason, be said to surpass in evidence and authority" the miracles of the Saviour. But it is really too much to ask us to take his judgment in such a case. Our folly would be unexampled and inconceivable if we did not insist on putting aside his instances of miracle, and claiming what he has himself accorded us, the right to select a crucial instance of our own. (Bayne 1862, pp. 26–7)

What can be said on behalf of Hume's strategy of trial by proxy – substituting these other miracle stories for the resurrection? Formally speaking, the cross-cancellation argument requires too many dubious assumptions to be cogent (Earman 2000, pp. 67–70). But setting aside Hume's rather confused remarks about cross-cancellation, an examination of pagan and ecclesiastical miracle reports would have bearing on the credibility of the resurrection provided that two unspoken premises could be established: 1) that the evidence for these alternative miracles is in every way equal or superior to that for the resurrection, and 2) that the events thus reported are not worthy of credit.

Hume's rhetoric does, indirectly, suggest that he wants to endorse both claims, though he never supports either with a direct argument, and it would be impossible to support the first without considering the evidence for the resurrection directly. And Hume's presentation of the pagan and recent Catholic miracles suggests that he wanted to claim that they met criteria that Christians must endorse for genuine miracles. But William Adams, John Douglas, and George Campbell were more than willing to descend to particulars and to enquire more closely than Hume had into the very examples he had put forward. They had no difficulty showing that the first suppressed premise of Hume's inexplicit argument was undermined by his own one-sided scholarship, selective reporting, and the occasional outright bluff.

Hume's first purported parallel concerns the cures of Vespasian.

> One of the best attested miracles in all profane history, is that which Tacitus reports of Vespasian, who cured a blind man in Alexandria, by means of his spittle, and a lame man by the mere touch of his foot; in obedience to a vision of the god Serapis, who had enjoined them to have recourse to the Emperor, for these miraculous cures. The story may be seen in that fine historian; where every circumstance seems to add weight to the testimony, and might be displayed at large with all the force of argument and eloquence, if any one were now concerned to enforce the evidence of that exploded and idolatrous superstition. The gravity, solidity, age, and probity of so great an emperor, who, through the whole course of his life, conversed in a familiar manner with his friends and courtiers, and never affected those extraordinary airs of divinity assumed by Alexander and Demetrius. The historian, a cotemporary writer, noted for candour and veracity, and withal, the greatest and most penetrating genius, perhaps, of all antiquity; and so free from any tendency to credulity, that he even lies under the contrary imputation, of atheism and profaneness: The persons, from whose authority he related the miracle, of established character for judgement and veracity, as we may well presume; eye-witnesses of the fact, and confirming their testimony, after the Flavian family was despoiled of the empire, and could no longer give any reward, as the price of a lie. *Utrumque, qui interfuere, nunc quoque memorant, postquam nullum mendacio pretium.* To which if we add the public nature of the facts, as related, it will appear, that no evidence can well be supposed stronger for so gross and so palpable a falsehood. (Hume 1748, p. 92)

Hume's presentation here is so careless that it struck his opponents as disingenuous. The "candour and veracity" of the historian are beside the point, since the manner in which Tacitus introduces the story indicates plainly that he disbelieved it. Hume's characterization of the persons on whose authority Tacitus relied in relating the miracle as "of established character for judgement and veracity, as we may presume" drew special scorn from Campbell, for Tacitus says nothing of the sort (Campbell 1839, p. 98).

The entire affair bears on its face the marks of obvious imposture. It was conducted in Alexandria, the first major city to declare in favor of Vespasian's imperial aspirations, and it was done in honor both of the emperor, for whom a divine sign would be most convenient, and of the local deity. At Vespasian's request, physicians examined the two men who claimed to have received visions in the night telling them to appeal to Vespasian to be cured; the physicians reported that the blind man was not totally blind, nor the lame man totally lame, and added that any glory for a successful cure would redound to Vespasian himself, while any blame for a failure would fall back upon the two supplicants for having fraudulently represented the oracle of Serapis. The Egyptian populace, whom Tacitus describes in this context as "a people addicted to superstition," were hardly apt to be critical. "Where, then," asks Adams,

> is the wonder that two men should be instructed to act the part of lame and blind, when they were sure of succeeding in the fraud, and of being well rewarded (*as we may well suppose*) for their pains? (Adams 1767, p. 78)

As for Tacitus's reference to living witnesses, there is no mystery here. If the fraud was perpetrated publicly as described, there were doubtless many people who saw the two men leap up and claim to have been healed. There is no need to suggest that the witnesses were liars; it suffices that they were at most somewhat credulous. There was no need for them to inquire too closely since – unlike the apostles – they had absolutely nothing to lose in maintaining their account of what they had seen. "No evidence," Douglas concludes drily, inverting Hume's claim, "can well be supposed weaker" (Douglas 1757, p. 99).

At every point, the case of Vespasian differs critically from that of the resurrection. Indeed, from a Bayesian point of view, the wonder would be if, under the circumstances, some story of a miraculous demonstration in favor of Vespasian were *not* forthcoming. Given our background knowledge, the Bayes factor for the testimony is so close to 1 as to give us virtually no epistemic traction: the report was almost as strongly to be expected if the two men had been parties to the deceit as if they had genuinely been healed. It is absurd to suggest that the evidence for these miracles bears comparison with the evidence for the resurrection.

We might well leave the story of Vespasian here, were it not for one more curious point. For the two cures mentioned seem to have been suggested by two reported in the Gospel of Mark; in particular, the use of spittle to anoint the eyes of a blind man bears a striking resemblance to the cure at Bethsaida recounted in Mark 8:23. If so, the whole affair supports the ancient tradition, found in Eusebius, Epiphanius, and Jerome, that Mark published copies of his Gospel at Alexandria. The publication would have had to be at least a few years prior to Vespasian's arrival there ca. AD 69. Thus Hume's example turns under his hand in a way that he could not have anticipated. The very similarity between the cures attributed to Vespasian and those of Christ lends additional support to the claim that the Gospel accounts were published much earlier than skeptical biblical scholarship would like to allow.

Hume's second example is another account of a cure worked among the faithful, but for his third he takes a case where the reported miracles were unwelcome to a powerful and influential party. Hume tacitly suggests that these reported miracles meet a standard of evidence similar to that of the resurrection – namely, that the reports could not be refuted by contemporaries with a motive for challenging them. His attempt to force the Christian apologist to take all or leave all is particularly evident here:

> There surely never was a greater number of miracles ascribed to one person, than those, which were lately said to have been wrought in FRANCE upon the tomb of Abbé PARIS, the famous Jansenist, with whose sanctity the people were so long deluded. The curing of the sick, giving hearing to the deaf, and sight to the blind, were every where talked of as the usual effects of that holy sepulchre. But what is more extraordinary; many of the miracles were immediately proved upon the spot, before judges of unquestioned integrity, attested by witnesses of credit and distinction, in a learned age, and on the most eminent theatre that is now in the world. Nor is this all: A relation of them was published and dispersed every where; nor were the JESUITS, though a learned body, supported by the civil magistrate, and determined enemies to those opinions, in whose favour the miracles were said to have been wrought, ever able distinctly to refute or detect them. Where shall we find such a number of circumstances, agreeing to the corroboration of one fact? And what have we to oppose to such a cloud of witnesses, but the absolute impossibility or miraculous nature of the events, which they relate? And this surely, in the eyes of all reasonable people, will alone be regarded as a sufficient refutation. (Hume 1748, pp. 93–4)

Part of what Hume says here is true. The Jansenists, a large Catholic splinter group who had fallen sharply out of favor with Rome in the decades leading up to the death of the

Abbé Paris in 1727, were in desperate need of a sign from heaven of the rightness of their cause against the Jesuits; accordingly, numerous cures – and even more numerous convulsions – were reported to have taken place at the tomb of the Abbé. But the claim that the reports were not refuted is demonstrably false, and its presence in the first edition is excusable only on the assumption that Hume, who was working chiefly from a book by Louis Basile Carré de Montgeron, was unaware of the fact that many of Montgeron's claims had been refuted in the pastoral letter of the Archbishop of Sens.

If ignorance was the cause of Hume's error, he soon had the means to put it right, for his antagonists took the trouble to consult the literature on the controversy and provided a full account of multiple frauds perpetrated in the name of the Abbé. The "miraculous" cure of the Sieur le Doulx, for example, was detected by the recovered patient himself, who in a letter to the Bishop of Laon explained that the Jansenist convent of St. Hilaire had pressed a confessor and the sacraments upon him when he was in bed with the fever, which gave an unwarranted air of gravity to his condition. The widow de Lorme, who was ostensibly smitten with palsy for having gone to the tomb of the Abbé with intent to ridicule, confessed herself that it was a contrivance (Douglas 1757, p. 129). Anne le Franc, who was said to have been cured, *inter alia*, of a disorder in her eyes, turned out never to have had anything wrong with them; five notarized certificates to her cure were testified, by the signatories themselves, to have been tampered with after the signing (Adams 1767, pp. 85–6). Montgeron celebrates the recovery of Don Alphonso, whose eye had been inflamed. But the certificates collected by Montgeron himself show that, just prior to his trip to the tomb of the Abbé, the young man had begun using a medicine prescribed by the eminent oculist Dr. St. Yves (Douglas 1757, pp. 141–3). Examples of this sort, all detected by the Archbishop of Sens, can be multiplied *ad nauseam*.

Had the love of truth overpowered Hume's love of literary fame, he might have withdrawn the example in subsequent editions of his work or at least mentioned the contrary evidence provided by the Archbishop of Sens. But he did neither. Instead, he inserted a lengthy footnote into the second edition claiming that many of the miracles were "proved immediately by witnesses before the officiality or bishop's court at PARIS, under the eye of Cardinal NOAILLES, whose character for integrity and capacity was never challenged, even by his enemies" (Hume 1748, p. 94). This reference to the character and capacity of the Cardinal is another piece of misdirection. The only signatories to the petition were the 22 curés who presented it to Cardinal Noailles, and the Cardinal rejected the petition on the grounds of palpable falsehoods proved upon the witnesses *par des informations juridiques* (Adams 1767, p. 89). In the same footnote Hume claims that the successor to Cardinal Noailles, though pressed by 22 curés of Paris to examine the miracles, "wisely forbore" (Hume 1748, p. 94). This was yet another blunder: Charles-Gaspard de Ventimille, who succeeded Cardinal Noailles as Archbishop of Paris, ordered a public judicial inquest into the miracles and published the results on November 8, 1735, in what Adams describes as "an ordonnance" containing "convincing proofs, that the miracles, so strongly warranted by these curés, were forged and counterfeited" (Adams 1767, pp. 88–9).

From the fact that many of the cures were shown upon examination to be frauds, it does not follow that no one recovered from an illness after a visit to the Abbé's tomb. But as Adams points out, some recoveries are not particularly surprising:

> [T]he same, I dare pronounce, would happen, if a thousand people, taken at a venture, were at any time removed from their sick chambers in *London* to *St. Paul's Churchyard* or the *Park*,

especially if they went with any strong hope of a cure: in such a number, some are always upon the point of recovery – many only want to fancy themselves well – others may be flattered for a time into this belief, while they are ill – and many more, by fresh air and motion, and especially by forbearing the use of other means, will find a change for the better: but, that the blind received their sight, or the deaf were restored to hearing, by these visits, I deny that we have any competent or tolerable evidence. (Adams 1767, pp. 83–4)

Had the cures reported at the tomb of the Abbé Paris lived up to the characterization Hume gives of them, there would indeed be reason to believe that they had taken place. But they do not; and Hume never acknowledged, in any of the successive editions of his essay published in his lifetime, the numerous factual errors that critics like Adams, Douglas, and Campbell had pointed out in his presentation.

Throughout part two of his essay, Hume unintentionally illustrates the truth of his own observation:

[E]loquence, when at its highest pitch, leaves little room for reason or reflection; but addressing itself entirely to the fancy or the affections, captivates the willing hearers, and subdues their understanding. (Hume 1748, p. 89)

Certainly Hume's own eloquence has had that effect on many of his readers who, perhaps because they find his conclusions congenial, have accepted and recounted his accounts of the cures of Vespasian and the transactions at the tomb of the Abbe Paris without making even a modest attempt to verify his claims. What is worse, Hume seems to have forgotten his own sensible observation from the end of the *Enquiry* that "there is a degree of doubt, and caution, and modesty, which, in all kinds of scrutiny and decision, ought for ever to accompany a just reasoner" (Hume 1748, p. 120).

The trouble with the arguments in the second part of Hume's essay is not merely that they are unoriginal, nor is it simply that part two is, soberly considered, a very superficial treatment of issues that had already been addressed in vastly greater detail by the defenders of Christianity. It is above all that Hume resolutely refuses to come to grips with the historical evidence for the resurrection, despite the fact that this is the one miracle claim he absolutely must undermine if his essay is to be a significant contribution to the discussion. To substitute an examination of reports of other miracles, and to insinuate without argument that these others are as well attested as the central miracle of Christianity, is mere clever misdirection; to misrepresent the facts in the attempt to improve the parallel is irresponsible – or worse. Such substitutes for argument do not constitute a serious challenge to the credibility either of the resurrection or of Christianity itself.

Conclusion

Although we have offered a cumulative case for the resurrection, we make no pretense to have offered the whole of the case, much less the whole of the case for Christianity. We have focused on those facts we consider most salient, but the argument can be elaborated in numerous ways: buttressing assumptions, deflating or deflecting criticisms, and taking additional facts into account. Ultimately, it can be embedded in a comprehensive argument that marshals all the resources of natural theology.

Yet as Butler points out in the *Analogy of Religion*, the argument from miracles is one of the direct and fundamental proofs; no competent presentation of the evidence for theism can afford to omit it or to treat Hume's essay as the final word on the subject. Hume could not himself be bothered to descend into the fray and discuss the argument in detail. But philosophers who wish to evaluate the evidence provided by testimony to the miraculous must move beyond this shallow treatment and come to terms with the argument in its most plausible and persuasive form, following Bacon's wise advice "to examine things to the bottom; and not to receive upon credit, or reject upon improbabilities, until there hath passed a due examination" (Bacon 1862, p. 124).[43]

References

Adams, W. (1767) *An Essay in Answer to Mr. Hume's Essay on Miracles*, 3rd edn. London: B. White.

Allison, D. C. (2005) *Resurrecting Jesus: The Earliest Christian Tradition and Its Interpreters*. New York: T & T Clark.

Alston, W. (1997) Biblical criticism and the resurrection. In S. Davis, D. Kendall, and G. O'Collins (eds.), *The Resurrection*, 148–83. Oxford: Oxford University Press.

Bacon, F. (1862) *The Works of Francis Bacon*. Eds. J. Spedding, R. Ellis, and D. Heath. Boston: Brown and Taggard.

Barnes, T. D. (1968) Legislation against the Christians. *The Journal of Roman Studies* 58, 32–50.

Bauckham, R. (2006) *Jesus and the Eyewitnesses: The Gospels as Eyewitness Testimony*. Grand Rapids, MI: Eerdmans.

Bayne, P. (1862) *The Testimony of Christ to Christianity*. Boston: Gould and Lincoln.

Blaiklock, E. M. (1983) *Man or Myth*. Singapore: Anzea Books.

Blomberg, C. (1987) *The Historical Reliability of the Gospels*. Downer's Grove, IL: InterVarsity.

Blomberg, C. (2001) *The Historical Reliability of John's Gospel*. Downer's Grove, IL: InterVarsity.

Brand, J. (1842) *Observations on Popular Antiquities*, vol. 3. London: Charles Knight & Co.

Burns, R. M. (1981) *The Great Debate on Miracles from Joseph Glanvill to David Hume*. London: Associated University Presses.

Butler, J. (1890) *The Analogy of Religion*, 4th edn. Ed. H. Morley. London: George Routledge and Sons.

Byrskog, S. (2002) *Story as History – History as Story*. Leiden: Brill.

Campbell, G. (1839) *A Dissertation on Miracles*. London: Thomas Tegg.

Carrier, R. (2005a) The spiritual body of Christ and the legend of the empty tomb. In J. J. Lowder and R. M. Price (eds.), *The Empty Tomb*, 105–231. Amherst, NY: Prometheus.

Carrier, R. (2005b) The plausibility of theft. In J. J. Lowder and R. M. Price (eds.), *The Empty Tomb*, 349–68. Amherst, NY: Prometheus.

Carrier, R. (2006) *Why I Don't Buy the Resurrection Story*, 6th edn, http://www.infidels.org/library/modern/richard_carrier/resurrection/2.html (accessed 10/30/2008).

Cavin, R. G. (1993) *Miracles, Probability, and the Resurrection of Jesus: A Philosophical, Mathematical, and Historical Study*. PhD Dissertation, University of California Irvine.

Chalmers, T. (1817) *The Evidence and Authority of the Christian Revelation*. Edinburgh: Walker and Greig.

43. We wish to thank Paul Maier for his generous historical help, Gary Habermas and Clyde Billington for help with references, Vlastimil Vohanka for a careful reading that caught an important typographical slip, William Lane Craig for comments on the penultimate draft, and Ryan Pflum for his work on the bibliography. We are also grateful to *Philosophia Christi* for permission to incorporate some material originally published in that journal.

Chandler, S. (1744) *Witnesses of the Resurrection of Jesus Christ Re-examined*. London: J. Noon.

Craig, W. L. (1997) John Dominic Crossan on the resurrection of Jesus. In S. T. Davis, D. Kendall, and G. O'Collins (eds.), *The Resurrection: An Interdisciplinary Symposium on the Resurrection of Jesus*, 249–71. Oxford: Oxford University Press.

Craig, W. L. (2002) *Assessing the New Testament Evidence for the Historicity of the Resurrection of Jesus*. Lewiston, NY: Edwin Mellen Press.

Crossan, J. D. (1991) *The Historical Jesus: The Life of a Mediterranean Jewish Peasant*. San Francisco: HarperSanFrancisco.

Crossan, J. D. (1994) *Jesus: A Revolutionary Biography*. San Francisco: HarperSanFrancisco.

Crossan, J. D. (1996) *Who Killed Jesus?* San Francisco: HarperSanFrancisco.

Crossan, J. D. (1998) *The Birth of Christianity*. San Francisco: HarperSanFrancisco.

Davis, S. T. (2006) The counterattack of the resurrection skeptics: a review article. *Philosophia Christi* 8: 1, 39–64.

Deissmann, A. (1965) *Light from the Ancient East*. Grand Rapids, MI: Baker.

Douglas, J. (1757) *The Criterion*. London: A. Millar.

Earman, J. (2000) *Hume's Abject Failure*. Oxford: Oxford University Press.

Fuller, R. H. (1993) The resurrection. In B. M. Metzger and D. Coogan (eds.), *The Oxford Companion to the Bible*, 647–9. Oxford: Oxford University Press.

Geiger, A. (1865) *Judaism and Its History*. Trans. M. Meyer. London: Trübner and Co.

Gladstone, W. E. (1896) *Studies Subsidiary to the Works of Joseph Butler*. Oxford: Clarendon Press.

Greenleaf, S. (1874) *The Testimony of the Evangelists*. New York: J. Cockcroft and Co.

Gundry, R. H. (1982) *Matthew: A Commentary on His Literary and Theological Art*. Grand Rapids, MI: Eerdmans.

Habermas, G. (2005) Resurrection research from 1975 to the present: what are critical scholars saying? *Journal for the Study of the Historical Jesus* 3: 2, 135–53.

Habermas, G. (2006a) Experiences of the risen Jesus. *Dialog: A Journal of Theology* 45, 288–97.

Habermas, G. (2006b) Mapping the recent trend toward the bodily resurrection appearances of Jesus in light of other prominent critical positions. In R. B. Stewart (ed.), *The Resurrection of Jesus: John Dominic Crossan and N. T. Wright in Dialogue*, 78–92. Minneapolis: Fortress Press.

Hemer, C. J. (1989) *The Book of Acts in the Setting of Hellenistic History*. Tübingen: Mohr.

Hengel, M. (1977) *Crucifixion*. Minneapolis: Fortress Press.

Hengel, M. (1983) *Between Jesus and Paul*. London: Fortress Press.

Hengel, M. and Schwemer, A. M. (1997) *Paul between Damascus and Antioch: The Unknown Years*. Westminster: John Knox Press.

Houston, J. (1994) *Reported Miracles: A Critique of Hume*. Cambridge: Cambridge University Press.

Hume, D. (1748) *An Enquiry concerning Human Understanding: A Critical Edition*. Ed. T. Beauchamp. Oxford: Oxford University Press. (Cited from Oxford edition, 2000)

Jenkin, R. (1734) *Reasonableness and Certainty of the Christian Religion*, vol. 2, 6th edn. London: T. W.

Jeremias, J. (1966) *The Rediscovery of Bethesda*. Louisville, KY: New Testament Archeology.

Kee, H. C. (1995) A century of quests for the culturally compatible Jesus. *Theology Today* 52, 17–28.

Keim, T. (1883) *The History of Jesus of Nazar*, vol. 6. Trans. A. Ransom. London: Williams and Norgate.

Klausner, J. (1925) *Jesus of Nazareth: His Life, Times, and Teaching*. Trans. H. Danby. New York: MacMillan.

Kruskal, W. (1988) Miracles and statistics: the casual assumption of independence. *Journal of the American Statistical Association* 83, 929–40.

Lake, K. (1907) *The Historical Evidence for the Resurrection of Jesus Christ*. London: Williams and Norgate.

Laplace, P. S. (1840) *A Philosophical Essay on Probabilities*. Trans. F. W. Truscott and F. L. Emory. New York: Dover. (Cited from Dover edition, 1951)

Larmer, R. (1988) *Water Into Wine?: An Investigation of the Concept of Miracle*. Montreal: McGill-Queen's University Press.

Larmer, R. (ed.) (1996) *Questions of Miracle*. Montreal: McGill-Queen's University Press.

Leon-Dufour, X. (1967) *The Gospels and the Jesus of History*. London: Collins.

Lewis, C. S. (1946) *That Hideous Strength*. New York: MacMillan.

Lewis, C. S. (1947) *Miracles*. New York: MacMillan.

Lowder, J. J. (2005) Historical evidence and the empty tomb. In J. J. Lowder and R. M. Price (eds.), *The Empty Tomb*, 261–306. Amherst, NY: Prometheus.

Lyttleton, G. (1800) *Observations on the Conversion and Apostleship of St. Paul*. Boston: Manning and Loring.

Mackie, J. L. (1982) *The Miracle of Theism: Arguments for and against the Existence of God*. Oxford: Clarendon Press.

Maier, P. L. (1997) *In the Fullness of Time*. Grand Rapids, MI: Kregel.

Maier, P. L. (ed. and trans.) (1999) *Eusebius: The Church History*. Grand Rapids, MI: Kregel.

Martin, M. M. (2005) Swinburne on the resurrection. In J. J. Lowder and R. M. Price (eds.), *The Empty Tomb*, 453–68. Amherst, NY: Prometheus.

McGrew, T. (2004) Has Plantinga refuted the historical argument? *Philosophia Christi* 6, 7–26.

McGrew, T. and McGrew, L. (2006) On the historical argument: a rejoinder to Plantinga. *Philosophia Christi* 8, 23–38.

McGrew, T. and McGrew, L. (2008) Foundationalism, probability, and mutual support. *Erkenntnis* 68, 55–77.

McKinnon, A. (1967) "Miracle" and "paradox". *American Philosophical Quarterly* 4, 308–14.

Meier, J. P. (1991) *The Roots of the Problem and the Person (Vol. 1): A Marginal Jew: Rethinking the Historical Jesus*. New York: Doubleday.

Metzger, B. (1978) *The Text of the New Testament: Its Transmission, Corruption, and Restoration*, 2nd edn. Oxford: Oxford University Press.

Michaelis, J. D. (1801) *Introduction to the New Testament*, vol. 3. Trans. Herbert Marsh. Cambridge: Cambridge University Press.

Miller, G. (2002) Good question: was the burial of Jesus a temporary one, because of time constraints?, http://www.christian-thinktank.com/shellgame.html (accessed 10/30/2008).

Morgan, T. (1738) *The Moral Philosopher*, vol. 2. London: Printed for the Author.

Paley, W. (1859) *A View of the Evidences of Christianity*. London: John W. Parker and Son.

Palfrey, J. G. (1843) *Lowell Lectures on the Evidences of Christianity*, vol. 2. Boston: James Munroe and Co.

Parsons, K. (2005) Peter Kreeft and Ronald Tacelli on the hallucination theory. In J. J. Lowder and R. M. Price (eds.), *The Empty Tomb*, 433–51. Amherst, NY: Prometheus.

Plantinga, A. (2000) *Warranted Christian Belief*. Oxford: Oxford University Press.

Plantinga, A. (2006) Historical arguments and dwindling probabilities. *Philosophia Christi* 8, 7–22.

Rawcliffe, D. H. (1959) *Illusions and Delusions of the Supernatural and the Occult*. New York: Dover.

Rist, J. (1993) Where else? In K. J. Clark (ed.), *Philosophers Who Believe*, 83–104. Downer's Grove, IL: InterVarsity.

Robinson, J. A. T. (1976) *Redating the New Testament*. London: SCM.

Rose, H. J. (1950) *A Handbook of Greek Literature from Homer to the Age of Lucian*. London: Methuen.

Saurin, J. (1843) *The Sermons of the Rev. James Saurin*, vol. 1. Trans. R. Robinson, H. Hunter, and J. Sutcliffe. New York: Harper & Brothers.

Shanks, H. (2005) The Siloam pool. *Biblical Archeology Review* 31, 17–23.

Sherlock, T. (1765) *The Trial of the Witnesses of the Resurrection*, 14th edn. London: John Whiston and Benjamin White.

Sherwin-White, A. N. (1963) *Roman Society and Roman Law in the New Testament*. Oxford: Oxford University Press.

Slade, P. D. and Bentall, R. P. (1988) *Sensory Deception: A Scientific Analysis of Hallucination.* Baltimore, MD: Johns Hopkins University Press.

Sobel, J. H. (2004) *Logic and Theism: Arguments for and against Beliefs in God.* Cambridge: Cambridge University Press.

Sproul, R. C., Lindsley, A., and Gerstner, J. (1984) *Classical Apologetics: A Rational Defense of the Christian Faith and a Critique of Presuppositional Apologetics.* Grand Rapids, MI: Zondervan.

Starkie, T. (1833) *A Practical Treatise of the Law of evidence*, vol. 1. London: J. & W. T. Clarke.

Strauss, D. (1879) *A New Life of Jesus*, vol. 1, 2nd edn. London: Williams and Norgate.

Swinburne, R. (ed.) (1989) *Miracles.* New York: MacMillan.

Swinburne, R. (1992) *Revelation: From Metaphor to Analogy.* Oxford: Clarendon Press.

Swinburne, R. (2003) *The Resurrection of God Incarnate.* Oxford: Oxford University Press.

Swinburne, R. (2004) Natural theology, its 'dwindling probabilities' and 'lack of rapport'. *Faith and Philosophy* 4, 533–46.

Toland, J. (1702) *Christianity Not Mysterious.* London: No Publisher.

Trites, A. (2004) *The New Testament Concept of Witness.* Cambridge: Cambridge University Press.

Venn, J. (1888) *The Logic of Chance*, 3rd edn. New York: Chelsea Publishing Co.

Wardlaw, R. (1852) *On Miracles.* Edinburgh: A. Fullerton & Co.

Wenham, J. (1992) *Redating Matthew, Mark & Luke.* Downer's Grove, IL: InterVarsity.

Westcott, B. F. (1906) *The Gospel of the Resurrection*, 4th edn. London: MacMillan and Co.

Wright, N. T. (2003) *The Resurrection of the Son of God.* Minneapolis: Fortress Press.

Zusne, L. and Jones, W. H. (1982) *Anomalistic Psychology: A Study of Extraordinary Phenomena of Behavior and Experience.* Hillsdale, NJ: Lawrence Erlbaum Associates.

Index